EPIC COLL

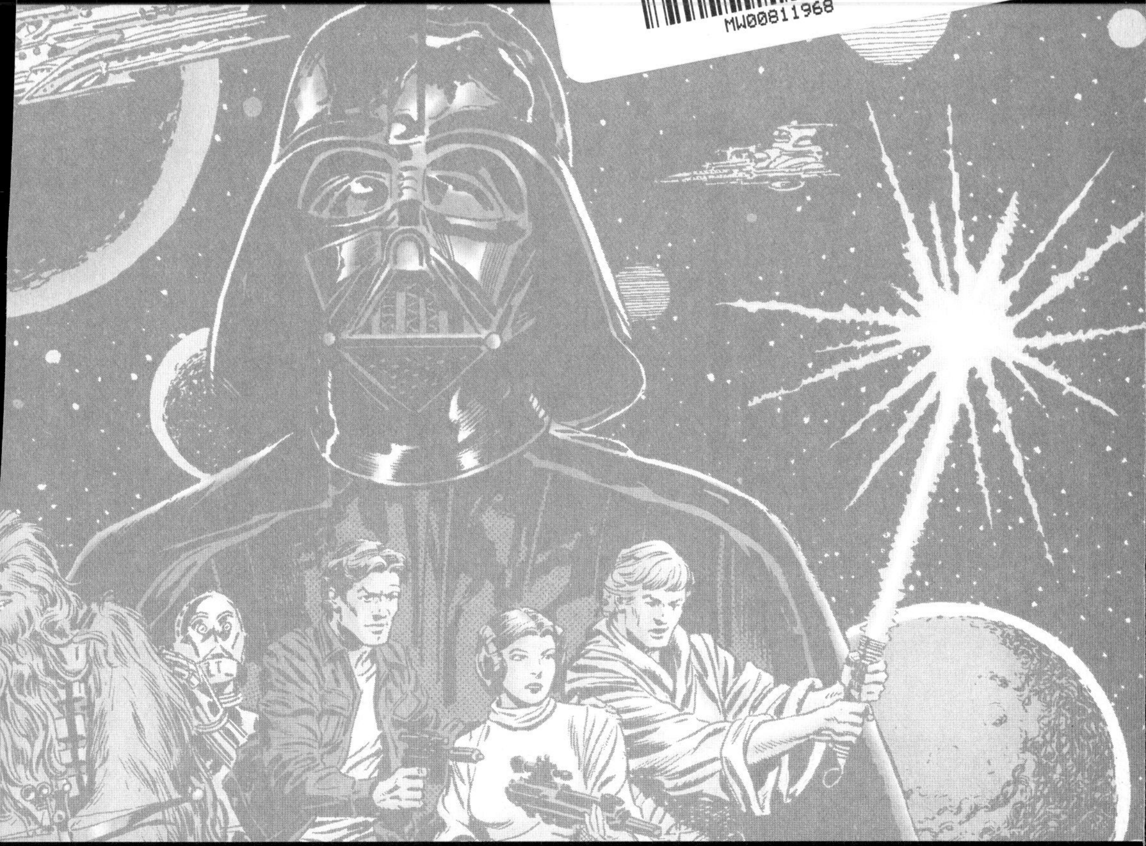

STAR WARS®

THE NEWSPAPER STRIPS

VOLUME 1

CLASSIC STAR WARS: THE EARLY ADVENTURES #1-9, *CLASSIC STAR WARS: HAN SOLO AT STARS' END #1-3*, *CLASSIC STAR WARS #1-3*, MATERIAL FROM *CLASSIC STAR WARS #4*, THE SUNDAY NEWSPAPER STRIPS ORIGINALLY PUBLISHED FROM MARCH 11 TO SEPT. 9, 1979, AND THE DAILY & SUNDAY STRIPS ORIGINALLY PUBLISHED FROM AUG. 11 TO OCT. 5, 1980

STAR WARS

LEGENDS

THE NEWSPAPER STRIPS

VOLUME 1

WRITERS:
RUSS MANNING, RUSS HELM, DON CHRISTENSEN & ARCHIE GOODWIN
WITH **STEVE GERBER, RICK HOBERG & BRIAN DALEY**

PENCILERS:
RUSS MANNING, ALFREDO ALCALA & AL WILLIAMSON WITH **RICK HOBERG**

INKERS:
**MIKE ROYER,
RUSS MANNING,
ALFREDO ALCALA &
AL WILLIAMSON** WITH
DAVE STEVENS

ART RETOUCHING:
**RICK HOBERG,
BRIAN SNODDY &
AL WILLIAMSON**

COLORISTS:
**RUSS MANNING,
RAY MURTAUGH,
PERRY MCNAMEE &
STEVE BUCCELLATO** WITH
**BRIAN NEUBAUER &
MICHELLE MADSEN**

LETTERERS:
**MIKE ROYER, RUSS MANNING,
ALFREDO ALCALA &
AL WILLIAMSON** WITH
DAVE STEVENS

ASSISTANT EDITOR:
IAN STUDE

EDITORS:
**BOB COOPER, PEET JANES &
ANINA BENNETT**

FRONT COVER ARTISTS:
**AL WILLIAMSON
& TOM ROBERTS**

BACK COVER ARTISTS:
**AL WILLIAMSON, ALLEN
NUNIS & GREGORY WRIGHT**

COLLECTION EDITOR: MARK D. BEAZLEY
ASSOCIATE MANAGING EDITOR: KATERI WOODY
ASSOCIATE EDITOR: SARAH BRUNSTAD
ASSOCIATE MANAGER, DIGITAL ASSETS: JOE HOCHSTEIN
SENIOR EDITOR, SPECIAL PROJECTS: JENNIFER GRÜNWALD
VP, PRODUCTION & SPECIAL PROJECTS: JEFF YOUNGQUIST
RESEARCH: MIKE HANSEN
LAYOUT: JEPH YORK
SVP PRINT, SALES & MARKETING: DAVID GABRIEL

EDITOR IN CHIEF: AXEL ALONSO
CHIEF CREATIVE OFFICER: JOE QUESADA
PUBLISHER: DAN BUCKLEY
EXECUTIVE PRODUCER: ALAN FINE

SPECIAL THANKS TO FRANK PARISI & LUCASFILM AND DE
MULLANEY, SCOTT DUNBIER, BARRY SHORT, DEIDRE HAN:
GARY HENDERSON & DOUG SHARK OF MYCOMICSHOP.CC

STAR WARS LEGENDS EPIC COLLECTION: THE NEWSPAPER STRIPS VOL. 1. Contains material originally published in magazine form as CLASSIC STAR WARS: THE EARLY ADVENTURES #1-9, CLASSIC STAR W
HAN SOLO AT STARS' END #1-3 and CLASSIC STAR WARS #1-4. First printing 2017. ISBN# 978-1-302-90464-7. Published by MARVEL WORLDWIDE, INC., a subsidiary of MARVEL ENTERTAINMENT, LLC. OFFI
PUBLICATION: 135 West 50th Street, New York, NY 10020. STAR WARS and related text and illustrations are trademarks and/or copyrights, in the United States and other countries, of Lucasfilm Ltd. and/or its affi
© & TM Lucasfilm Ltd. No similarity between any of the names, characters, persons, and/or institutions in this magazine with those of any living or dead person or institution is intended, and any such similarity w
may exist is purely coincidental. Marvel and its logos are TM Marvel Characters, Inc. Printed in the U.S.A. ALAN FINE, President, Marvel Entertainment; DAN BUCKLEY, President, TV, Publishing & Brand Manager
JOE QUESADA, Chief Creative Officer; TOM BREVOORT, SVP of Publishing; DAVID BOGART, SVP of Business Affairs & Operations, Publishing & Partnership; C.B. CEBULSKI, VP of Brand Management & Developn
Asia; DAVID GABRIEL, SVP of Sales & Marketing, Publishing; JEFF YOUNGQUIST, VP of Production & Special Projects; DAN CARR, Executive Director of Publishing Technology; ALEX MORALES, Director of Publi
Operations; SUSAN CRESPI, Production Manager; STAN LEE, Chairman Emeritus. For information regarding advertising in Marvel Comics or on Marvel.com, please contact Vit DeBellis, Integrated Sales Manag
vdebellis@marvel.com. For Marvel subscription inquiries, please call 888-511-5480. Manufactured between 12/2/2016 and 1/9/2017 by LSC COMMUNICATIONS INC., SALEM, VA, USA.

10 9 8 7 6 5 4 3 2 1

THE NEWSPAPER STRIPS — VOLUME 1

THE NEWSPAPER STRIPS
VOL. 1

The Rebel Alliance has won its first victory against the evil Empire, destroying its greatest super weapon, the Death Star, in the Battle of Yavin.

Imperial forces still hold an iron grip over much of the galaxy, but word is spreading quickly of its first defeat. The Rebellion has brought new hope to the many star systems under Imperial control.

Now, the rebel heroes have a new mission: to save the worlds in the greatest danger, to take resources and power from the Empire, and to gain new allies in their war to save the galaxy.

But the Emperor's reach is vast, and he will stop at nothing to crush the tiny Rebellion....

FROM 1979-1984, A STAR WARS COMIC STRIP RAN IN NEWSPAPERS ACROSS THE UNITED STATES. DECADES LATER, MOST OF THE NEWSPAPER-STRIP STORYLINES WERE REFORMATTED INTO A TRADITIONAL COLOR COMIC-BOOK FORMAT, WITH ARTWORK RETOUCHED AND EXPANDED BY THE ORIGINAL STRIP ARTISTS AND THEIR STUDIO PARTNERS, AND REPUBLISHED UNDER THE "CLASSIC STAR WARS" BANNER. THIS EPIC COLLECTION LINE COLLECTS THOSE REMASTERED STORIES ALONGSIDE THE PREVIOUSLY UNCOLLECTED NEWSPAPER STRIPS FOR THE FIRST TIME.

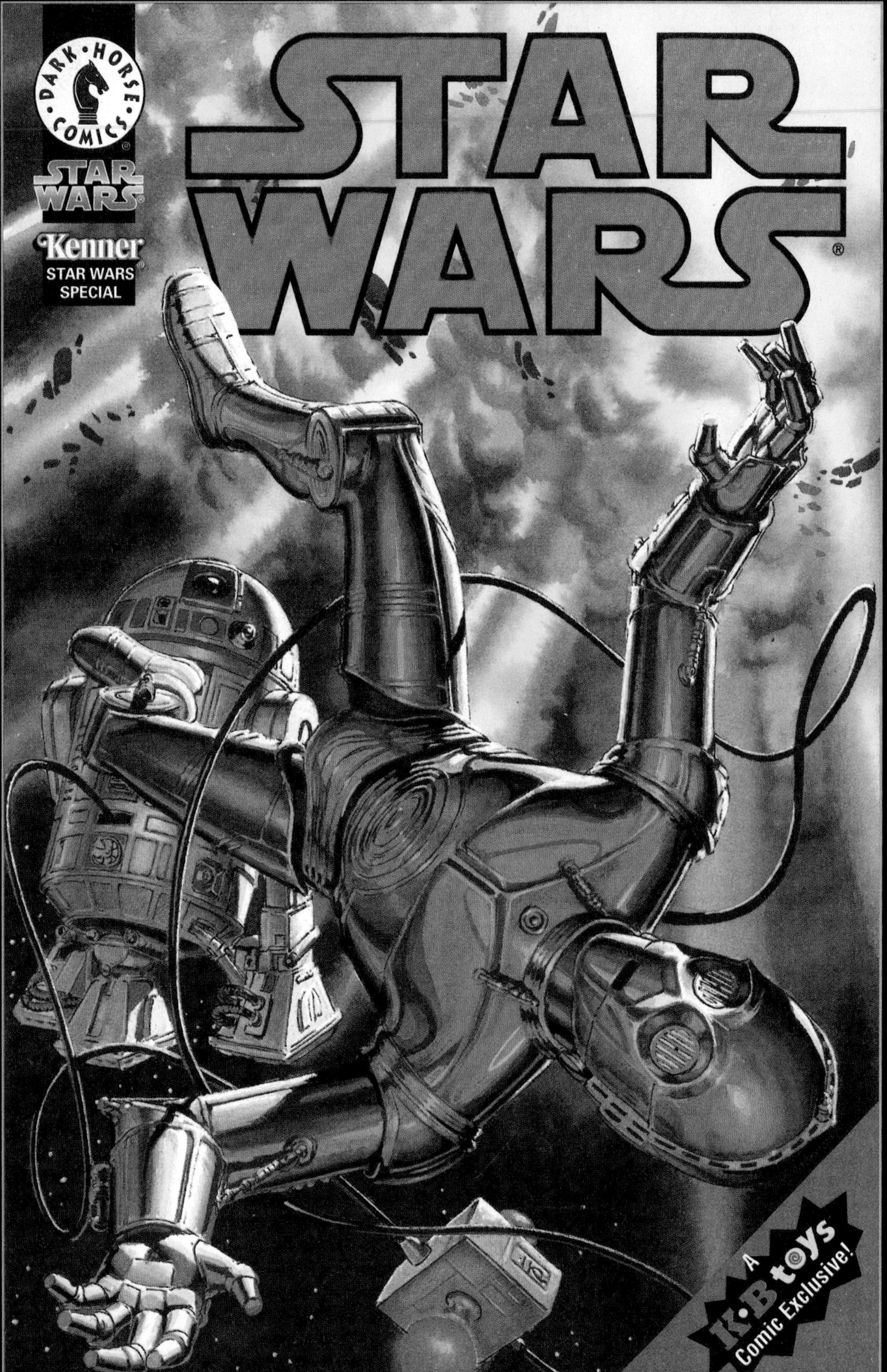
DARK HORSE COMICS
STAR WARS
Kenner
STAR WARS
SPECIAL
STAR WARS
A K•B toys Comic Exclusive!

STAR WARS NEWSPAPER STRIPS
ORIGINALLY PUBLISHED SUNDAYS FROM MARCH 11 TO SEPTEMBER 9, 1979

WRITER, PENCILER & COLORIST: RUSS MANNING • INKERS & LETTERERS: MIKE ROYER & RUSS MANNING

ORIGINALLY, THE *STAR WARS* NEWSPAPER STRIP RAN SEPARATE STORYLINES IN THE SUNDAY STRIPS AND THE WEEKDAY/SATURDAY STRIPS. THE FIRST TWO SUNDAY-ONLY STORYLINES (BOTH UNTITLED) WERE NEVER COLLECTED AND REMASTERED IN THE *CLASSIC STAR WARS* SERIES — THOUGH THE FIRST WAS REPRINTED IN HIGHLY TRUNCATED FORM IN THE 1998 GIVEAWAY ONE-SHOT *"STAR WARS: THE CONSTANCIA AFFAIR"* (COVER ART BY IGOR KORDEY, SEEN HERE).

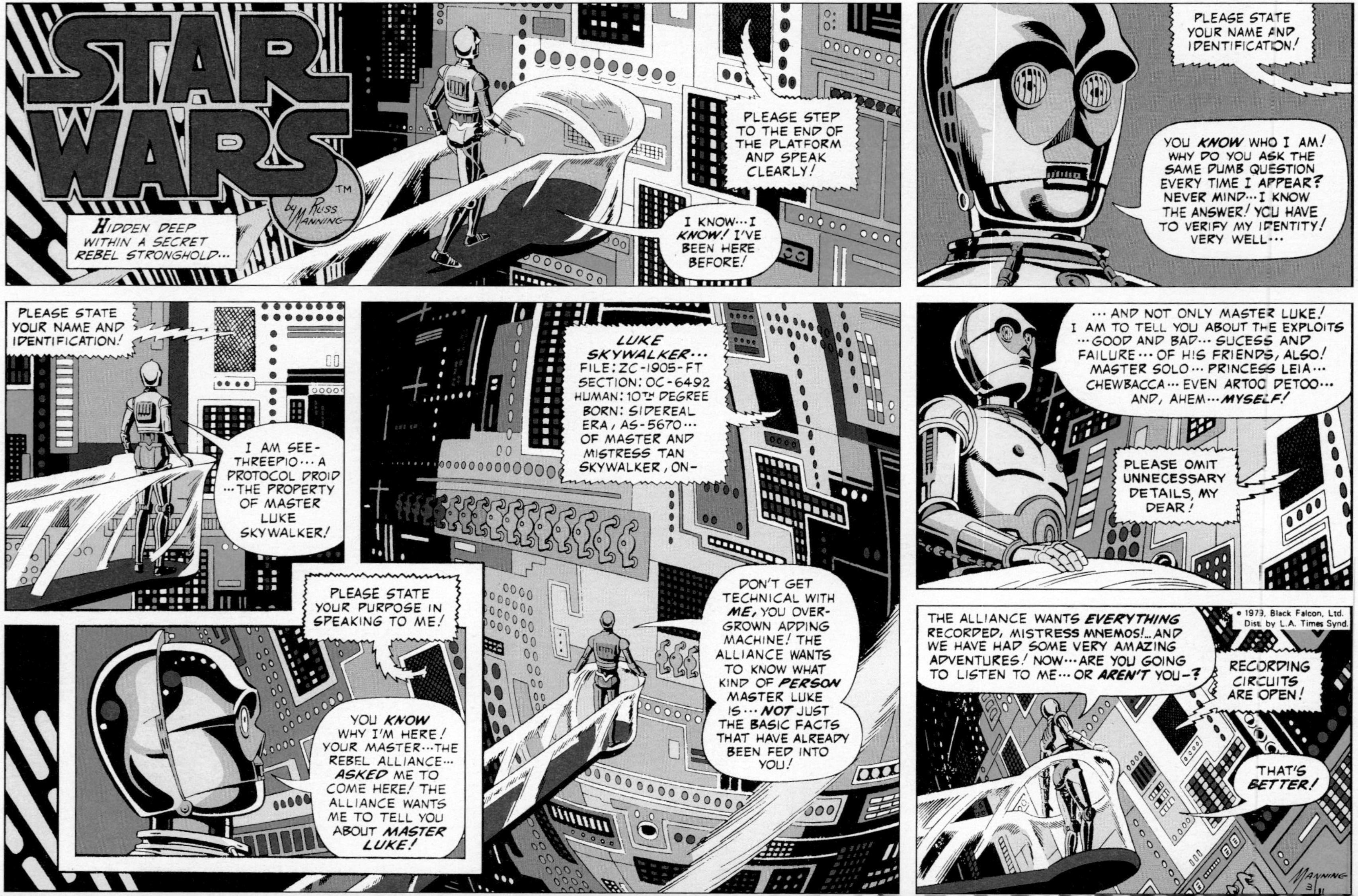
STAR WARS
TM
by Russ Manning
HIDDEN DEEP WITHIN A SECRET REBEL STRONGHOLD...
PLEASE STEP TO THE END OF THE PLATFORM AND SPEAK CLEARLY!
I KNOW... I KNOW! I'VE BEEN HERE BEFORE!
PLEASE STATE YOUR NAME AND IDENTIFICATION!
YOU KNOW WHO I AM! WHY DO YOU ASK THE SAME DUMB QUESTION EVERY TIME I APPEAR? NEVER MIND... I KNOW THE ANSWER! YOU HAVE TO VERIFY MY IDENTITY! VERY WELL...
PLEASE STATE YOUR NAME AND IDENTIFICATION!
I AM SEE-THREEPIO... A PROTOCOL DROID ...THE PROPERTY OF MASTER LUKE SKYWALKER!
PLEASE STATE YOUR PURPOSE IN SPEAKING TO ME!
YOU KNOW WHY I'M HERE! YOUR MASTER... THE REBEL ALLIANCE... ASKED ME TO COME HERE! THE ALLIANCE WANTS ME TO TELL YOU ABOUT MASTER LUKE!
LUKE SKYWALKER... FILE: ZC-1905-FT SECTION: OC-6492 HUMAN: 10TH DEGREE BORN: SIDEREAL ERA, AS-5670... OF MASTER AND MISTRESS TAN SKYWALKER, ON-
DON'T GET TECHNICAL WITH ME, YOU OVER-GROWN ADDING MACHINE! THE ALLIANCE WANTS TO KNOW WHAT KIND OF PERSON MASTER LUKE IS... NOT JUST THE BASIC FACTS THAT HAVE ALREADY BEEN FED INTO YOU!
... AND NOT ONLY MASTER LUKE! I AM TO TELL YOU ABOUT THE EXPLOITS ...GOOD AND BAD... SUCESS AND FAILURE... OF HIS FRIENDS, ALSO! MASTER SOLO... PRINCESS LEIA... CHEWBACCA... EVEN ARTOO DETOO... AND, AHEM... MYSELF!
PLEASE OMIT UNNECESSARY DETAILS, MY DEAR!
© 1979, Black Falcon, Ltd. Dist. by L.A. Times Synd.
THE ALLIANCE WANTS EVERYTHING RECORDED, MISTRESS MNEMOS!... AND WE HAVE HAD SOME VERY AMAZING ADVENTURES! NOW... ARE YOU GOING TO LISTEN TO ME... OR AREN'T YOU-?
RECORDING CIRCUITS ARE OPEN!
THAT'S BETTER!
MANNING 3/11

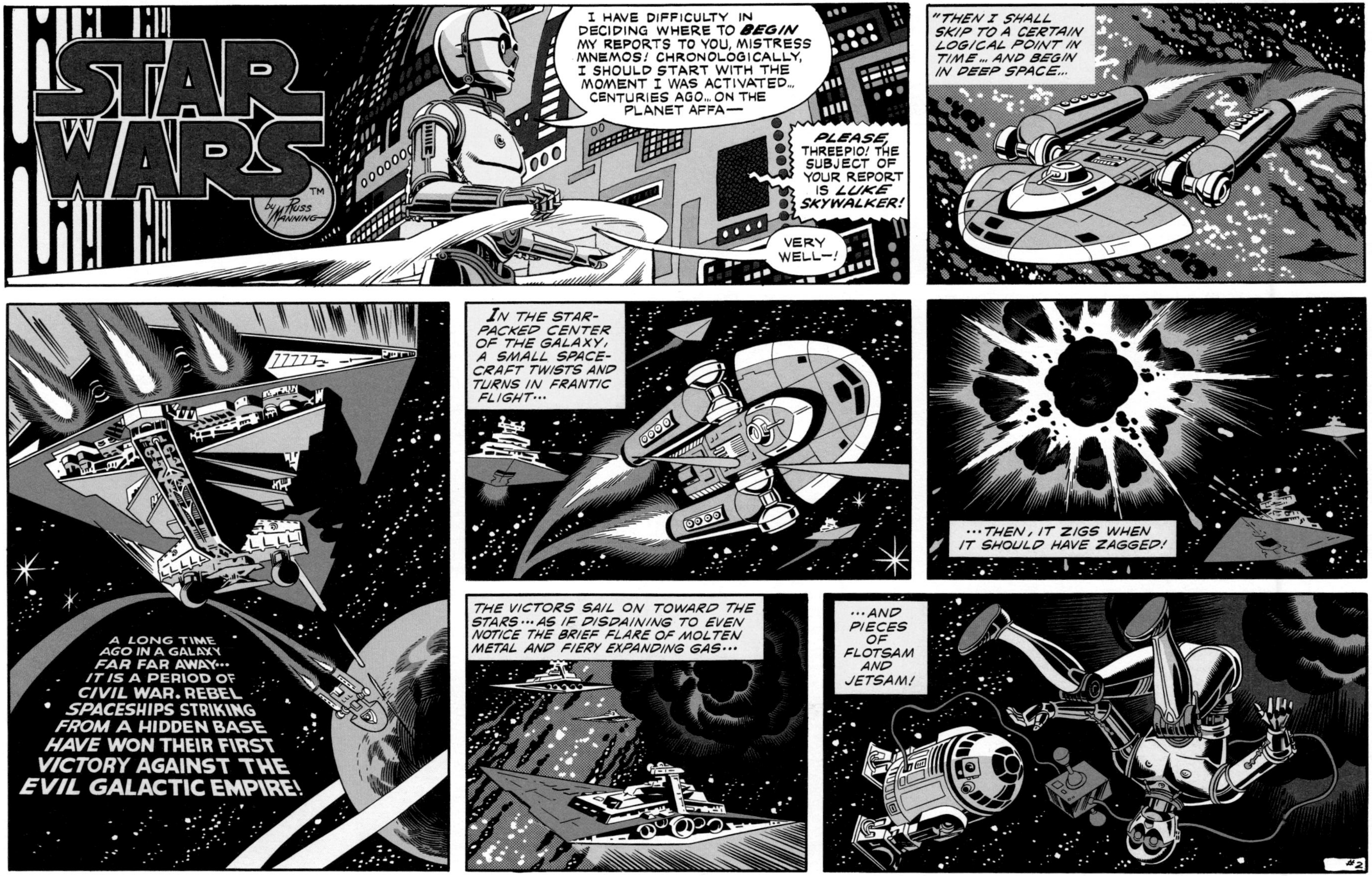
STAR WARS
TM
by Russ Manning
I HAVE DIFFICULTY IN DECIDING WHERE TO BEGIN MY REPORTS TO YOU, MISTRESS MNEMOS! CHRONOLOGICALLY, I SHOULD START WITH THE MOMENT I WAS ACTIVATED... CENTURIES AGO... ON THE PLANET AFFA—
PLEASE, THREEPIO! THE SUBJECT OF YOUR REPORT IS LUKE SKYWALKER!
VERY WELL—!
"THEN I SHALL SKIP TO A CERTAIN LOGICAL POINT IN TIME... AND BEGIN IN DEEP SPACE...
A LONG TIME AGO IN A GALAXY FAR FAR AWAY... IT IS A PERIOD OF CIVIL WAR. REBEL SPACESHIPS STRIKING FROM A HIDDEN BASE HAVE WON THEIR FIRST VICTORY AGAINST THE EVIL GALACTIC EMPIRE!
IN THE STAR-PACKED CENTER OF THE GALAXY, A SMALL SPACE-CRAFT TWISTS AND TURNS IN FRANTIC FLIGHT...
...THEN, IT ZIGS WHEN IT SHOULD HAVE ZAGGED!
THE VICTORS SAIL ON TOWARD THE STARS... AS IF DISDAINING TO EVEN NOTICE THE BRIEF FLARE OF MOLTEN METAL AND FIERY EXPANDING GAS...
...AND PIECES OF FLOTSAM AND JETSAM!
#2

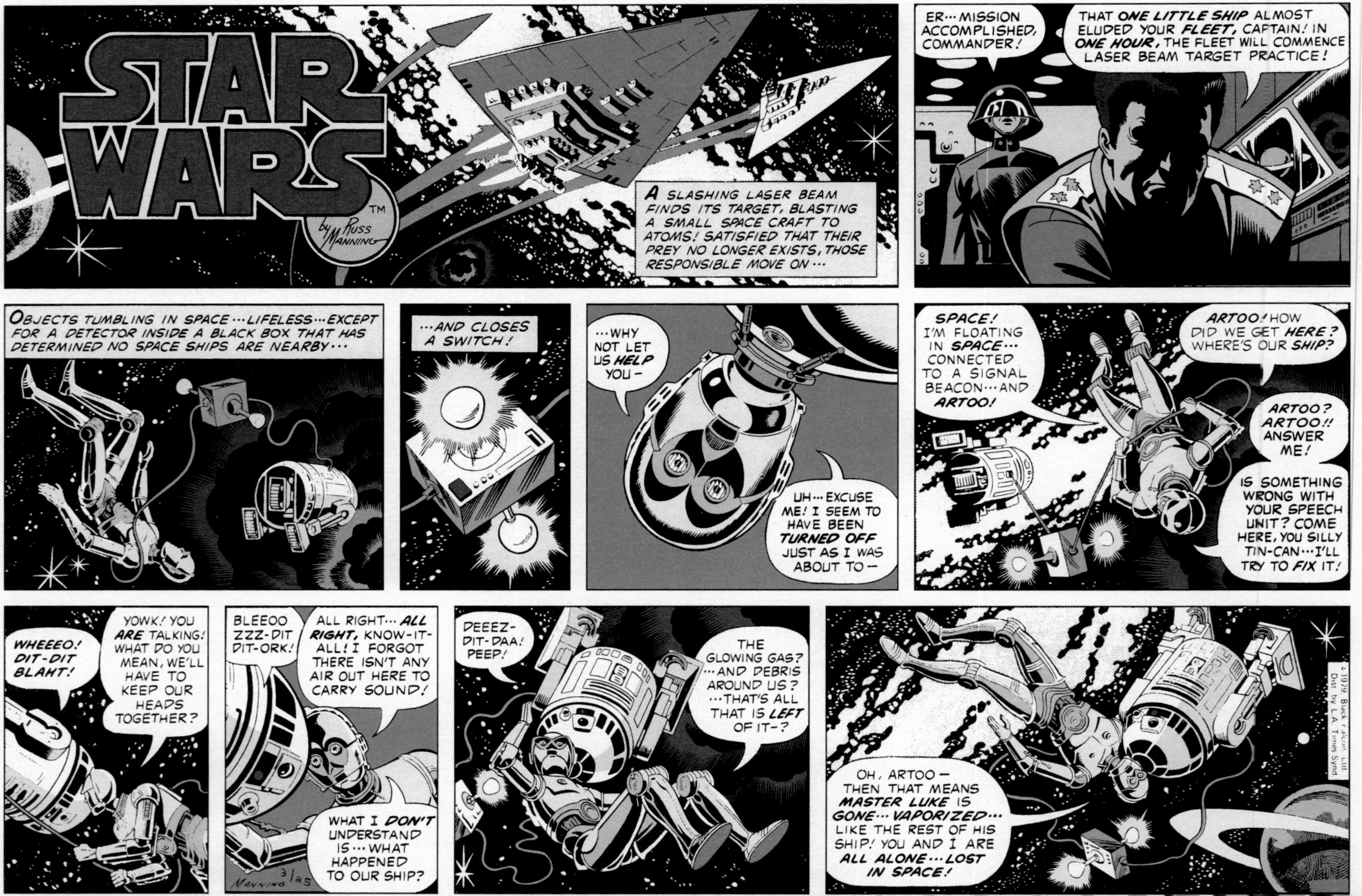
STAR WARS™
by Russ Manning
A SLASHING LASER BEAM FINDS ITS TARGET, BLASTING A SMALL SPACE CRAFT TO ATOMS! SATISFIED THAT THEIR PREY NO LONGER EXISTS, THOSE RESPONSIBLE MOVE ON ···
ER··· MISSION ACCOMPLISHED, COMMANDER!
THAT ONE LITTLE SHIP ALMOST ELUDED YOUR FLEET, CAPTAIN! IN ONE HOUR, THE FLEET WILL COMMENCE LASER BEAM TARGET PRACTICE!
OBJECTS TUMBLING IN SPACE ··· LIFELESS ··· EXCEPT FOR A DETECTOR INSIDE A BLACK BOX THAT HAS DETERMINED NO SPACE SHIPS ARE NEARBY ···
··· AND CLOSES A SWITCH!
··· WHY NOT LET US HELP YOU –
UH ··· EXCUSE ME! I SEEM TO HAVE BEEN TURNED OFF JUST AS I WAS ABOUT TO –
SPACE! I'M FLOATING IN SPACE ··· CONNECTED TO A SIGNAL BEACON ··· AND ARTOO!
ARTOO! HOW DID WE GET HERE? WHERE'S OUR SHIP?
ARTOO? ARTOO!! ANSWER ME!
IS SOMETHING WRONG WITH YOUR SPEECH UNIT? COME HERE, YOU SILLY TIN-CAN ··· I'LL TRY TO FIX IT!
WHEEEO! DIT-DIT BLAHT!
YOWK! YOU ARE TALKING! WHAT DO YOU MEAN, WE'LL HAVE TO KEEP OUR HEADS TOGETHER?
BLEEOO ZZZ-DIT DIT-ORK!
ALL RIGHT ··· ALL RIGHT, KNOW-IT-ALL! I FORGOT THERE ISN'T ANY AIR OUT HERE TO CARRY SOUND!
WHAT I DON'T UNDERSTAND IS ··· WHAT HAPPENED TO OUR SHIP?
MANNING 3/25
DEEEZ-DIT-DAA! PEEP!
THE GLOWING GAS? ··· AND DEBRIS AROUND US? ··· THAT'S ALL THAT IS LEFT OF IT–?
OH, ARTOO – THEN THAT MEANS MASTER LUKE IS GONE ··· VAPORIZED ··· LIKE THE REST OF HIS SHIP! YOU AND I ARE ALL ALONE ··· LOST IN SPACE!
© 1979, Black Falcon, Ltd.
Dist. by L.A. Times Synd.

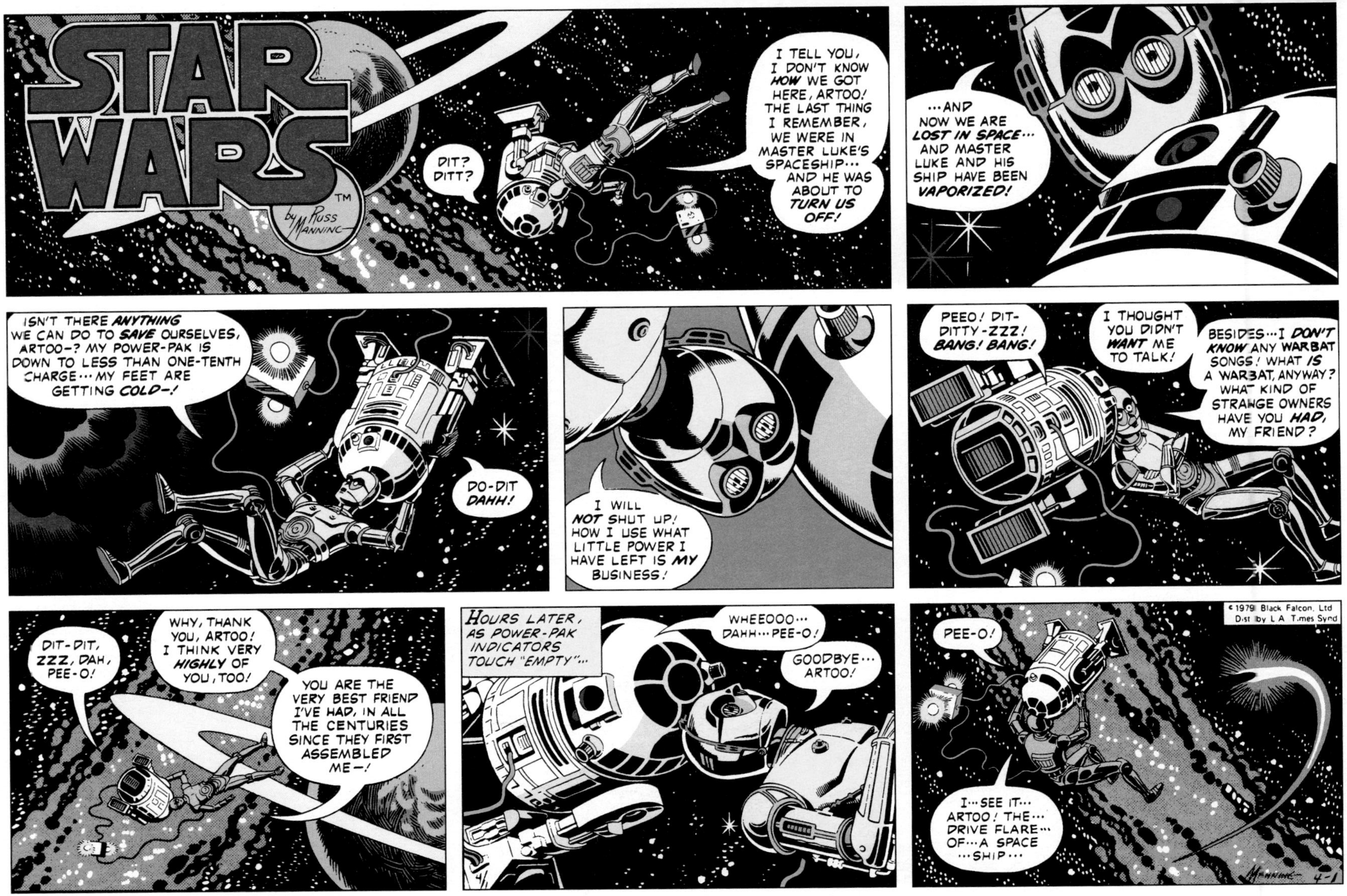
STAR WARS™
by Russ Manning
DIT? DITT?
I TELL YOU, I DON'T KNOW **HOW** WE GOT HERE, ARTOO! THE LAST THING I REMEMBER, WE WERE IN MASTER LUKE'S SPACESHIP... AND HE WAS ABOUT TO **TURN US OFF!**
...AND NOW WE ARE **LOST IN SPACE**... AND MASTER LUKE AND HIS SHIP HAVE BEEN **VAPORIZED!**
ISN'T THERE **ANYTHING** WE CAN DO TO **SAVE** OURSELVES, ARTOO-? MY POWER-PAK IS DOWN TO LESS THAN ONE-TENTH CHARGE... MY FEET ARE GETTING **COLD**-!
DO-DIT **DAHH!**
I WILL **NOT** SHUT UP! HOW I USE WHAT LITTLE POWER I HAVE LEFT IS **MY** BUSINESS!
PEEO! DIT-DITTY-ZZZ! **BANG! BANG!**
I THOUGHT YOU DIDN'T **WANT** ME TO TALK!
BESIDES... I **DON'T KNOW** ANY WARBAT SONGS! WHAT **IS** A WARBAT, ANYWAY? WHAT KIND OF STRANGE OWNERS HAVE YOU **HAD**, MY FRIEND?
DIT-DIT, **ZZZ**, DAH, PEE-O!
WHY, THANK YOU, ARTOO! I THINK VERY **HIGHLY** OF YOU, TOO!
YOU ARE THE VERY BEST FRIEND I'VE HAD, IN ALL THE CENTURIES SINCE THEY FIRST ASSEMBLED ME-!
HOURS LATER, AS POWER-PAK INDICATORS TOUCH "EMPTY"...
WHEEOOO... DAHH... PEE-O!
GOODBYE... ARTOO!
©1979 Black Falcon, Ltd
Dist by L A Times Synd
PEE-O!
I... SEE IT... ARTOO! THE... DRIVE FLARE... OF... A SPACE ...SHIP...
4-1

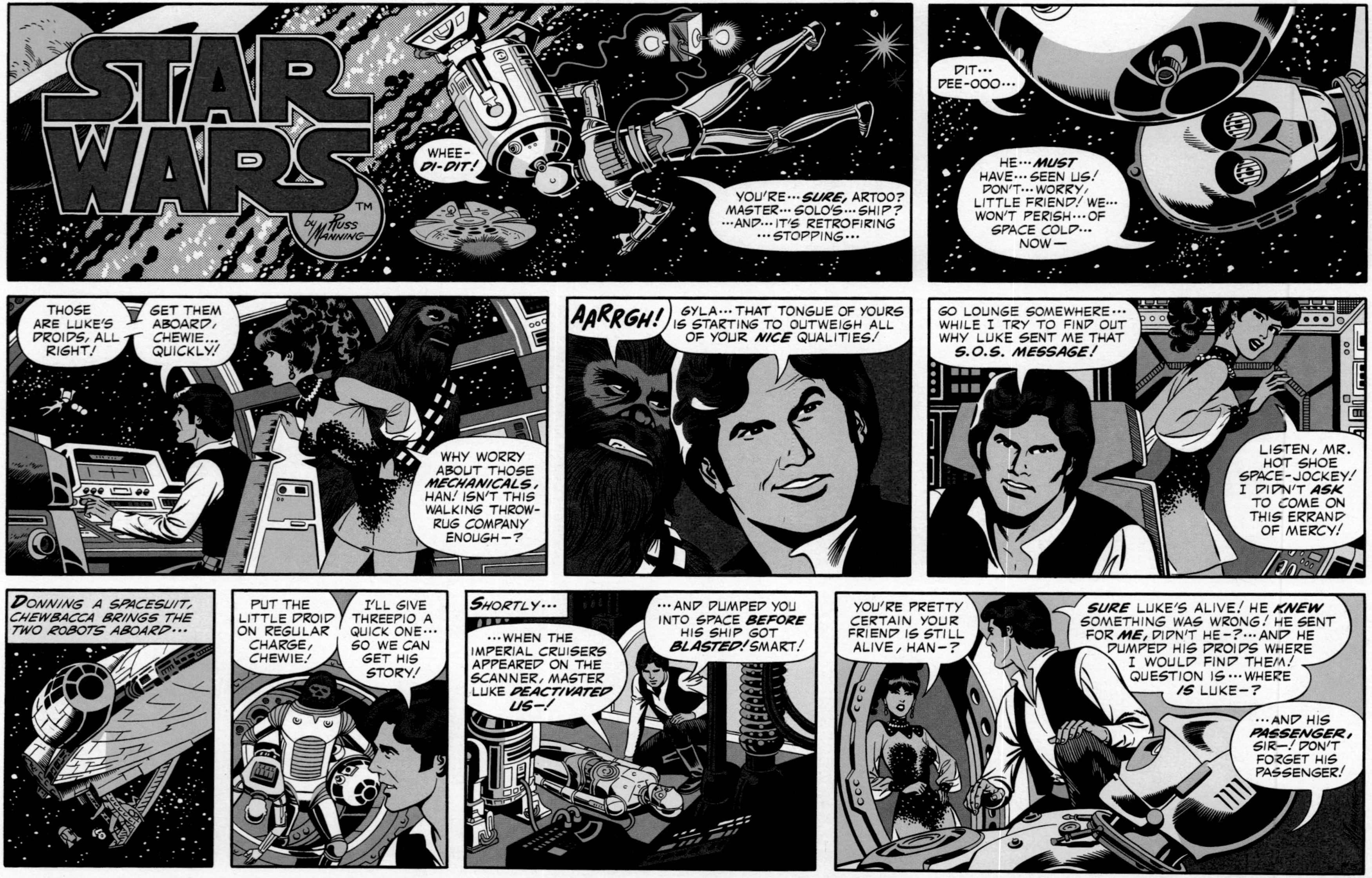
STAR WARS™
by Russ Manning
WHEE-DI-DIT!
YOU'RE... SURE, ARTOO? MASTER... SOLO'S... SHIP? ...AND... IT'S RETROFIRING ...STOPPING...
DIT... DEE-OOO...
HE... MUST HAVE... SEEN US! DON'T... WORRY, LITTLE FRIEND! WE... WON'T PERISH... OF SPACE COLD... NOW—
THOSE ARE LUKE'S DROIDS, ALL RIGHT!
GET THEM ABOARD, CHEWIE... QUICKLY!
WHY WORRY ABOUT THOSE MECHANICALS, HAN! ISN'T THIS WALKING THROW-RUG COMPANY ENOUGH—?
AARRGH!
GYLA... THAT TONGUE OF YOURS IS STARTING TO OUTWEIGH ALL OF YOUR NICE QUALITIES!
GO LOUNGE SOMEWHERE... WHILE I TRY TO FIND OUT WHY LUKE SENT ME THAT S.O.S. MESSAGE!
LISTEN, MR. HOT SHOE SPACE-JOCKEY! I DIDN'T ASK TO COME ON THIS ERRAND OF MERCY!
DONNING A SPACESUIT, CHEWBACCA BRINGS THE TWO ROBOTS ABOARD...
PUT THE LITTLE DROID ON REGULAR CHARGE, CHEWIE!
I'LL GIVE THREEPIO A QUICK ONE... SO WE CAN GET HIS STORY!
SHORTLY...
...WHEN THE IMPERIAL CRUISERS APPEARED ON THE SCANNER, MASTER LUKE DEACTIVATED US—!
...AND DUMPED YOU INTO SPACE BEFORE HIS SHIP GOT BLASTED! SMART!
YOU'RE PRETTY CERTAIN YOUR FRIEND IS STILL ALIVE, HAN—?
SURE LUKE'S ALIVE! HE KNEW SOMETHING WAS WRONG! HE SENT FOR ME, DIDN'T HE—?... AND HE DUMPED HIS DROIDS WHERE I WOULD FIND THEM! QUESTION IS... WHERE IS LUKE—?
...AND HIS PASSENGER, SIR—! DON'T FORGET HIS PASSENGER!

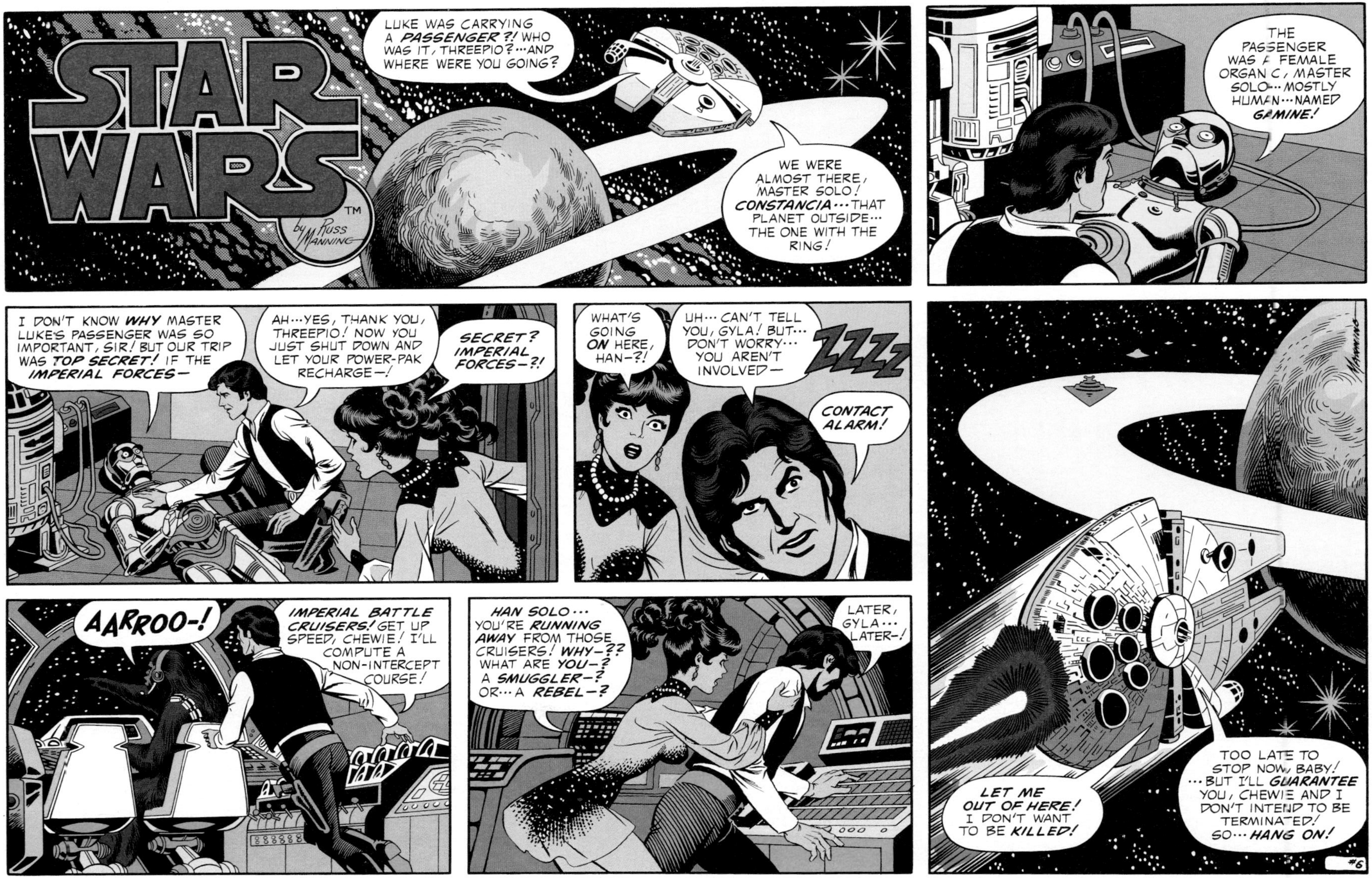
STAR WARS™
by Russ Manning
LUKE WAS CARRYING A PASSENGER?! WHO WAS IT, THREEPIO?...AND WHERE WERE YOU GOING?
WE WERE ALMOST THERE, MASTER SOLO! CONSTANCIA... THAT PLANET OUTSIDE... THE ONE WITH THE RING!
THE PASSENGER WAS A FEMALE ORGANIC, MASTER SOLO... MOSTLY HUMAN... NAMED GAMINE!
I DON'T KNOW WHY MASTER LUKE'S PASSENGER WAS SO IMPORTANT, SIR! BUT OUR TRIP WAS TOP SECRET! IF THE IMPERIAL FORCES—
AH...YES, THANK YOU, THREEPIO! NOW YOU JUST SHUT DOWN AND LET YOUR POWER-PAK RECHARGE—!
SECRET? IMPERIAL FORCES—?!
WHAT'S GOING ON HERE, HAN—?!
UH... CAN'T TELL YOU, GYLA! BUT... DON'T WORRY... YOU AREN'T INVOLVED—
ZZZZ
CONTACT ALARM!
AARROO—!
IMPERIAL BATTLE CRUISERS! GET UP SPEED, CHEWIE! I'LL COMPUTE A NON-INTERCEPT COURSE!
HAN SOLO... YOU'RE RUNNING AWAY FROM THOSE CRUISERS! WHY—?? WHAT ARE YOU—? A SMUGGLER—? OR... A REBEL—?
LATER, GYLA... LATER—!
LET ME OUT OF HERE! I DON'T WANT TO BE KILLED!
TOO LATE TO STOP NOW, BABY! ...BUT I'LL GUARANTEE YOU, CHEWIE AND I DON'T INTEND TO BE TERMINATED! SO... HANG ON!
#6

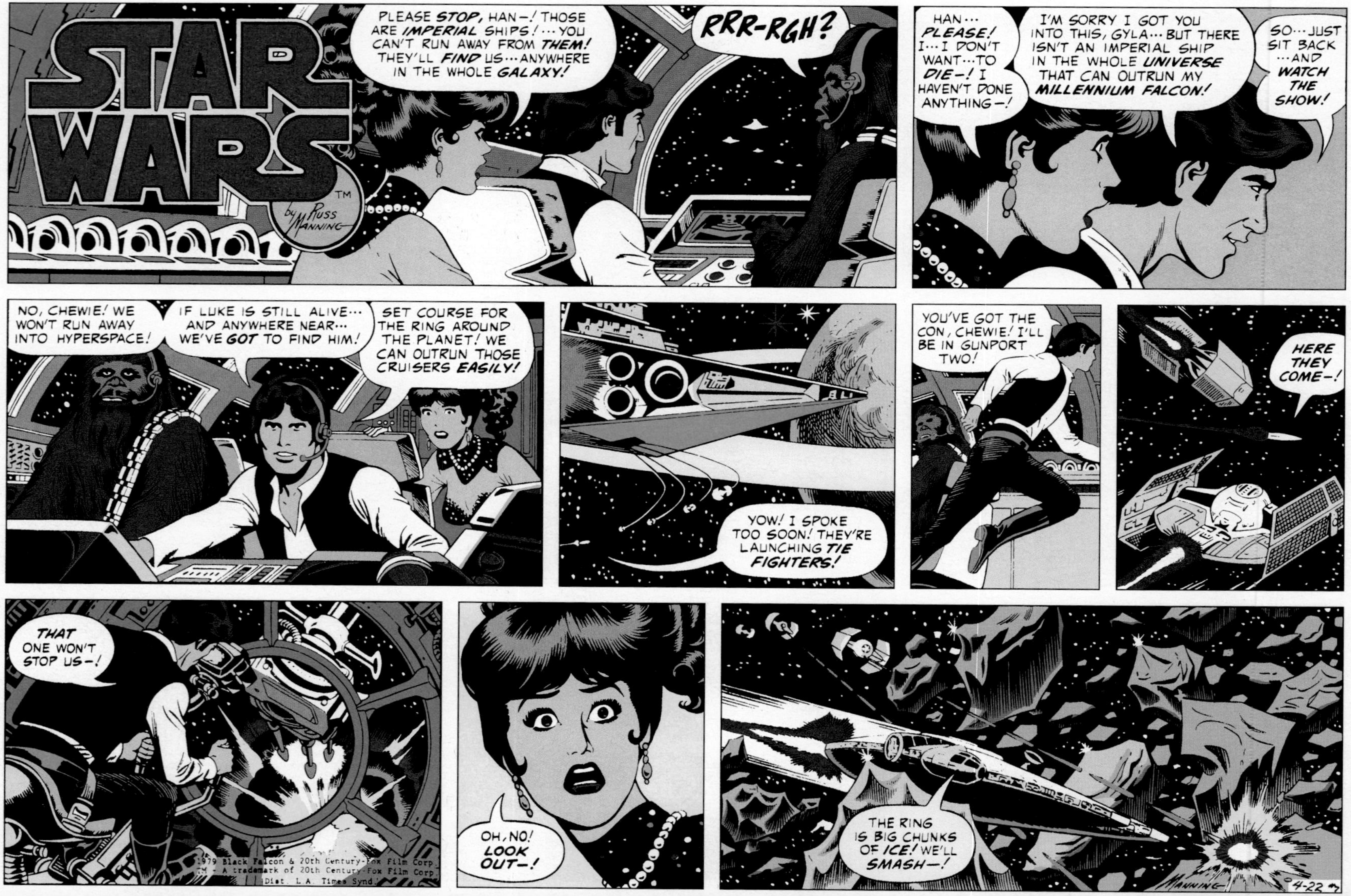
STAR WARS
TM
by Russ Manning
PLEASE STOP, HAN–! THOSE ARE IMPERIAL SHIPS! ... YOU CAN'T RUN AWAY FROM THEM! THEY'LL FIND US ... ANYWHERE IN THE WHOLE GALAXY!
RRR-RGH?
HAN... PLEASE! I...I DON'T WANT...TO DIE–! I HAVEN'T DONE ANYTHING–!
I'M SORRY I GOT YOU INTO THIS, GYLA... BUT THERE ISN'T AN IMPERIAL SHIP IN THE WHOLE UNIVERSE THAT CAN OUTRUN MY MILLENNIUM FALCON!
SO... JUST SIT BACK ...AND WATCH THE SHOW!
NO, CHEWIE! WE WON'T RUN AWAY INTO HYPERSPACE!
IF LUKE IS STILL ALIVE... AND ANYWHERE NEAR... WE'VE GOT TO FIND HIM!
SET COURSE FOR THE RING AROUND THE PLANET! WE CAN OUTRUN THOSE CRUISERS EASILY!
YOW! I SPOKE TOO SOON! THEY'RE LAUNCHING TIE FIGHTERS!
YOU'VE GOT THE CON, CHEWIE! I'LL BE IN GUNPORT TWO!
HERE THEY COME–!
THAT ONE WON'T STOP US–!
1979 Black Falcon & 20th Century-Fox Film Corp.
TM - A trademark of 20th Century-Fox Film Corp.
Dist. L.A. Times Synd.
OH, NO! LOOK OUT–!
THE RING IS BIG CHUNKS OF ICE! WE'LL SMASH–!
MANNING
4-22

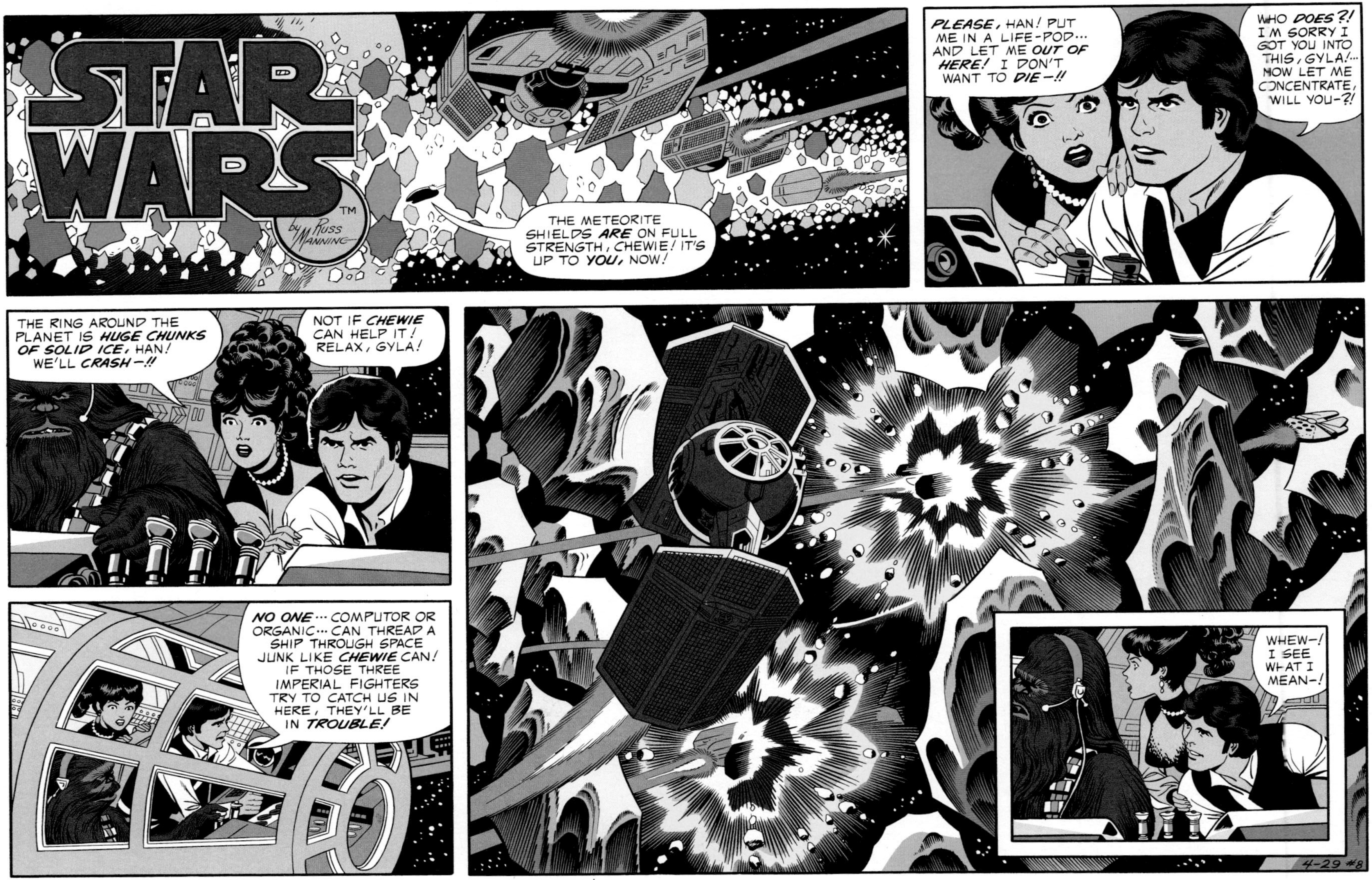
STAR WARS™
by Russ Manning
THE METEORITE SHIELDS *ARE* ON FULL STRENGTH, CHEWIE! IT'S UP TO *YOU,* NOW!
PLEASE, HAN! PUT ME IN A LIFE-POD... AND LET ME *OUT OF HERE!* I DON'T WANT TO *DIE*—!!
WHO *DOES*?! I'M SORRY I GOT YOU INTO THIS, GYLA!... NOW LET ME CONCENTRATE, WILL YOU—?!
THE RING AROUND THE PLANET IS *HUGE CHUNKS OF SOLID ICE*, HAN! WE'LL *CRASH*—!!
NOT IF *CHEWIE* CAN HELP IT! RELAX, GYLA!
NO ONE... COMPUTOR OR ORGANIC... CAN THREAD A SHIP THROUGH SPACE JUNK LIKE *CHEWIE* CAN! IF THOSE THREE IMPERIAL FIGHTERS TRY TO CATCH US IN HERE, THEY'LL BE IN *TROUBLE!*
WHEW—! I SEE WHAT I MEAN—!
4-29 #8

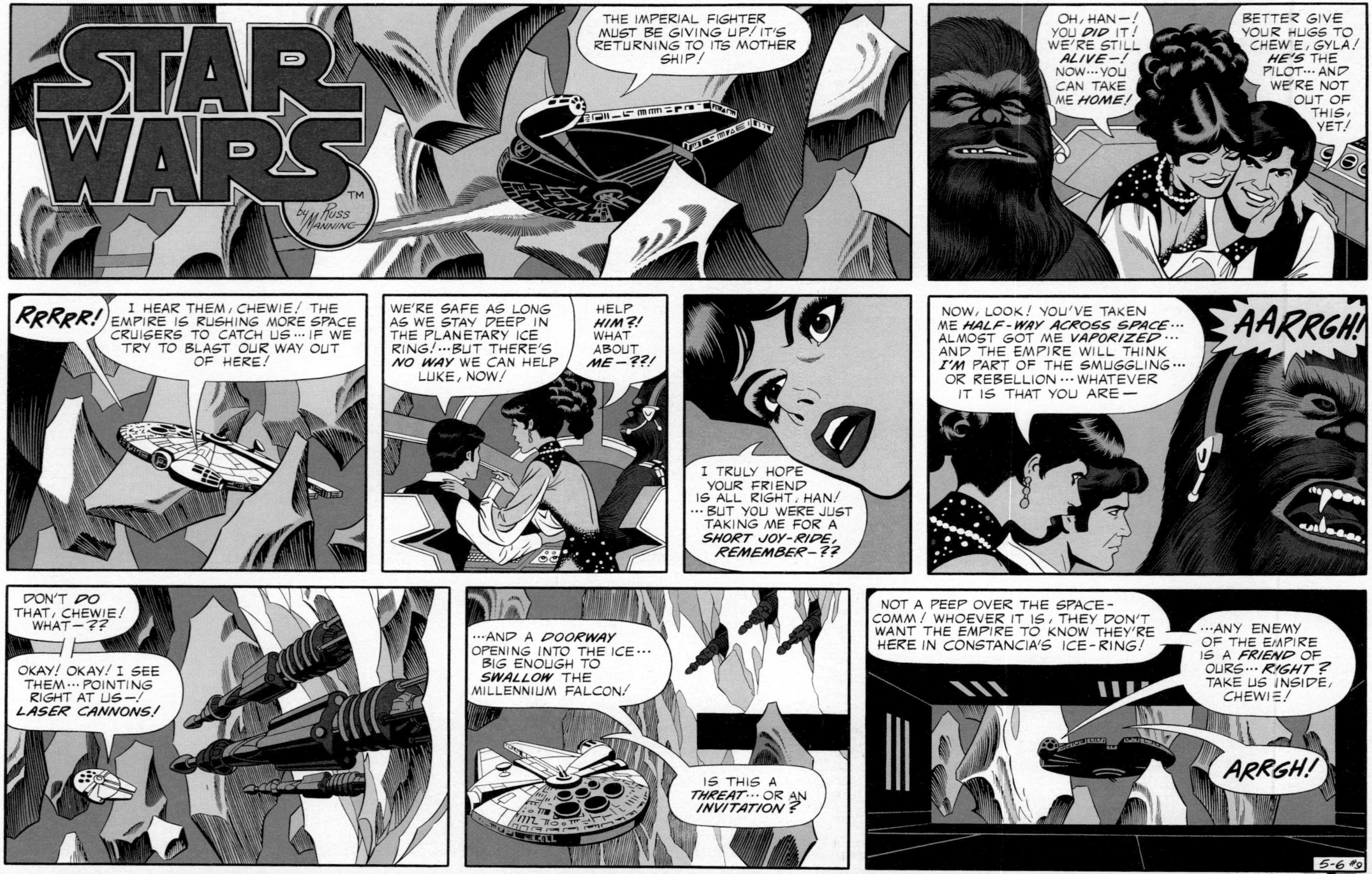
STAR WARS™
by Russ Manning
THE IMPERIAL FIGHTER MUST BE GIVING UP! IT'S RETURNING TO ITS MOTHER SHIP!
OH, HAN—! YOU DID IT! WE'RE STILL ALIVE—! NOW... YOU CAN TAKE ME HOME!
BETTER GIVE YOUR HUGS TO CHEWIE, GYLA! HE'S THE PILOT... AND WE'RE NOT OUT OF THIS, YET!
RRRRR!
I HEAR THEM, CHEWIE! THE EMPIRE IS RUSHING MORE SPACE CRUISERS TO CATCH US... IF WE TRY TO BLAST OUR WAY OUT OF HERE!
WE'RE SAFE AS LONG AS WE STAY DEEP IN THE PLANETARY ICE RING! ...BUT THERE'S NO WAY WE CAN HELP LUKE, NOW!
HELP HIM?! WHAT ABOUT ME—??!
I TRULY HOPE YOUR FRIEND IS ALL RIGHT, HAN! ...BUT YOU WERE JUST TAKING ME FOR A SHORT JOY-RIDE, REMEMBER—??
NOW, LOOK! YOU'VE TAKEN ME HALF-WAY ACROSS SPACE... ALMOST GOT ME VAPORIZED... AND THE EMPIRE WILL THINK I'M PART OF THE SMUGGLING... OR REBELLION... WHATEVER IT IS THAT YOU ARE—
AARRGH!
DON'T DO THAT, CHEWIE! WHAT—??
OKAY! OKAY! I SEE THEM... POINTING RIGHT AT US—! LASER CANNONS!
...AND A DOORWAY OPENING INTO THE ICE... BIG ENOUGH TO SWALLOW THE MILLENNIUM FALCON!
IS THIS A THREAT... OR AN INVITATION?
NOT A PEEP OVER THE SPACE-COMM! WHOEVER IT IS, THEY DON'T WANT THE EMPIRE TO KNOW THEY'RE HERE IN CONSTANCIA'S ICE-RING!
...ANY ENEMY OF THE EMPIRE IS A FRIEND OF OURS... RIGHT? TAKE US INSIDE, CHEWIE!
ARRGH!
5-6 #9

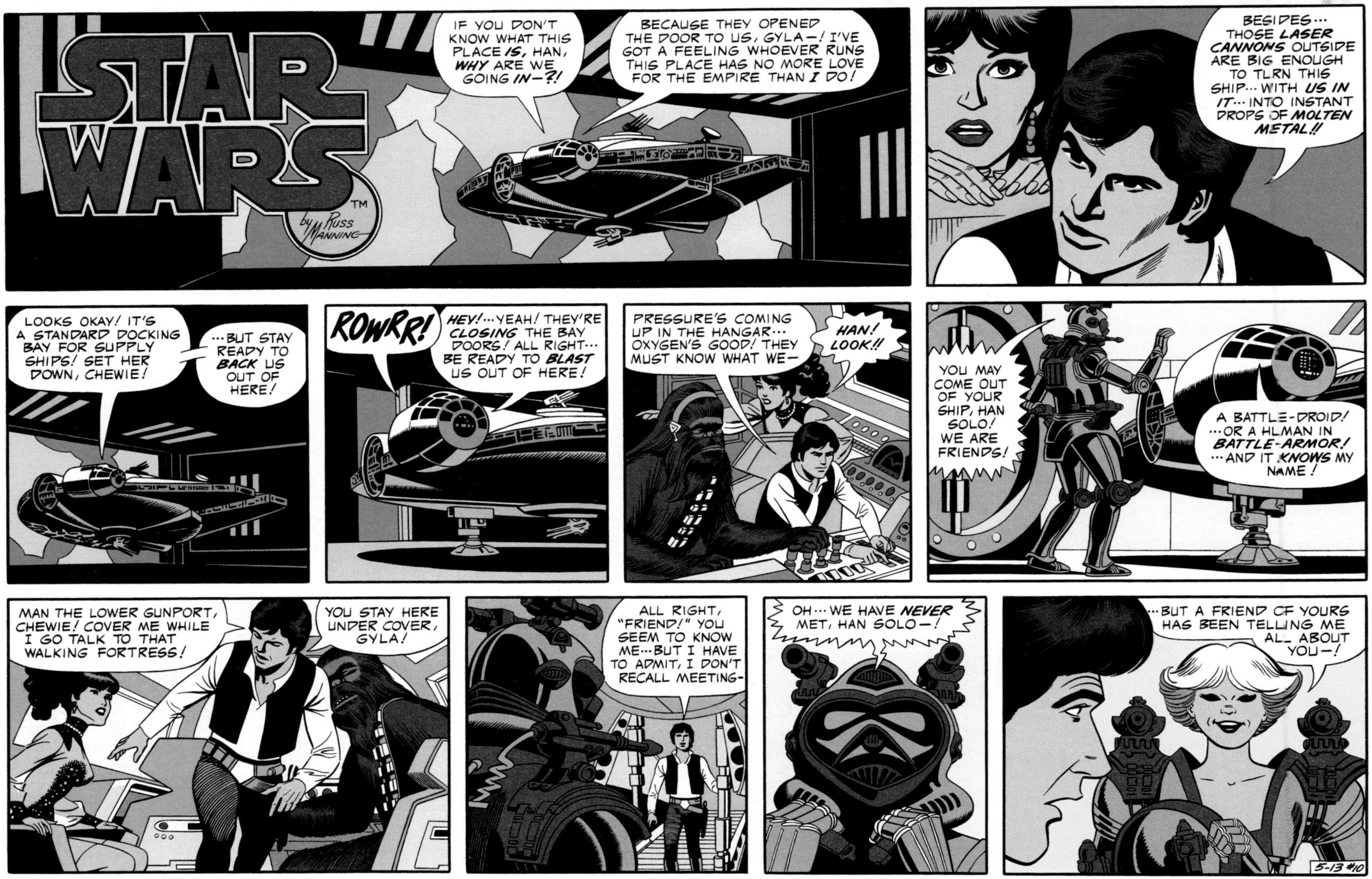
STAR WARS™
by Russ Manning
IF YOU DON'T KNOW WHAT THIS PLACE IS, HAN, WHY ARE WE GOING IN—?!
BECAUSE THEY OPENED THE DOOR TO US, GYLA—! I'VE GOT A FEELING WHOEVER RUNS THIS PLACE HAS NO MORE LOVE FOR THE EMPIRE THAN I DO!
BESIDES... THOSE LASER CANNONS OUTSIDE ARE BIG ENOUGH TO TURN THIS SHIP... WITH US IN IT... INTO INSTANT DROPS OF MOLTEN METAL!!
LOOKS OKAY! IT'S A STANDARD DOCKING BAY FOR SUPPLY SHIPS! SET HER DOWN, CHEWIE!
...BUT STAY READY TO BACK US OUT OF HERE!
ROWRR!
HEY!...YEAH! THEY'RE CLOSING THE BAY DOORS! ALL RIGHT... BE READY TO BLAST US OUT OF HERE!
PRESSURE'S COMING UP IN THE HANGAR... OXYGEN'S GOOD! THEY MUST KNOW WHAT WE—
HAN! LOOK!!
YOU MAY COME OUT OF YOUR SHIP, HAN SOLO! WE ARE FRIENDS!
A BATTLE-DROID! ...OR A HUMAN IN BATTLE-ARMOR! ...AND IT KNOWS MY NAME!
MAN THE LOWER GUNPORT, CHEWIE! COVER ME WHILE I GO TALK TO THAT WALKING FORTRESS!
YOU STAY HERE UNDER COVER, GYLA!
ALL RIGHT, "FRIEND!" YOU SEEM TO KNOW ME...BUT I HAVE TO ADMIT, I DON'T RECALL MEETING-
OH... WE HAVE NEVER MET, HAN SOLO—!
...BUT A FRIEND OF YOURS HAS BEEN TELLING ME ALL ABOUT YOU—!
5-13 #10

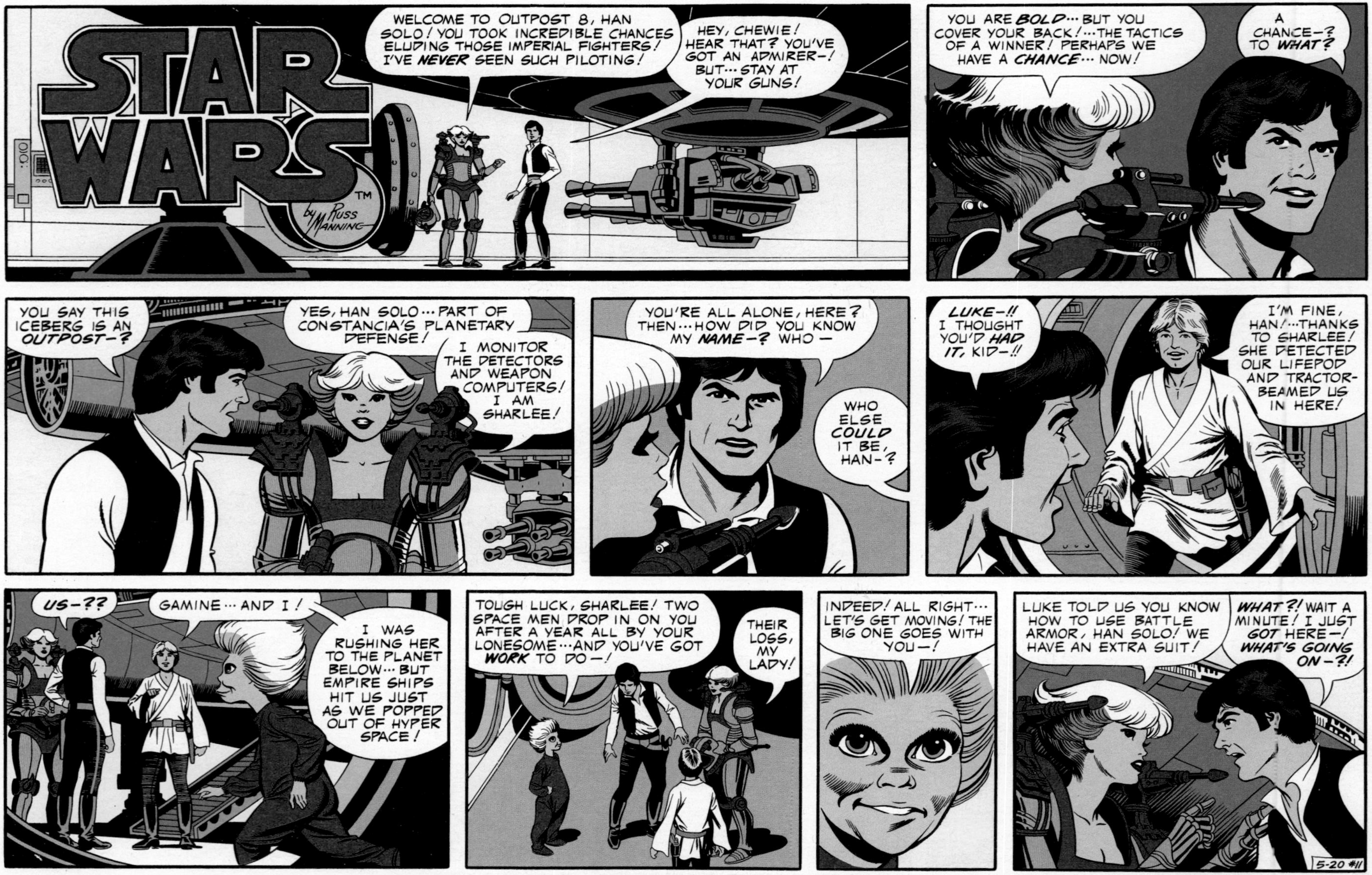
STAR WARS™
by Russ Manning
WELCOME TO OUTPOST 8, HAN SOLO! YOU TOOK INCREDIBLE CHANCES ELUDING THOSE IMPERIAL FIGHTERS! I'VE NEVER SEEN SUCH PILOTING!
HEY, CHEWIE! HEAR THAT? YOU'VE GOT AN ADMIRER—! BUT... STAY AT YOUR GUNS!
YOU ARE BOLD... BUT YOU COVER YOUR BACK!... THE TACTICS OF A WINNER! PERHAPS WE HAVE A CHANCE... NOW!
A CHANCE—? TO WHAT?
YOU SAY THIS ICEBERG IS AN OUTPOST—?
YES, HAN SOLO... PART OF CONSTANCIA'S PLANETARY DEFENSE!
I MONITOR THE DETECTORS AND WEAPON COMPUTERS! I AM SHARLEE!
YOU'RE ALL ALONE, HERE? THEN... HOW DID YOU KNOW MY NAME—? WHO—
WHO ELSE COULD IT BE, HAN—?
LUKE—!! I THOUGHT YOU'D HAD IT, KID—!!
I'M FINE, HAN!... THANKS TO SHARLEE! SHE DETECTED OUR LIFEPOD AND TRACTOR-BEAMED US IN HERE!
US—??
GAMINE... AND I!
I WAS RUSHING HER TO THE PLANET BELOW... BUT EMPIRE SHIPS HIT US JUST AS WE POPPED OUT OF HYPER SPACE!
TOUGH LUCK, SHARLEE! TWO SPACE MEN DROP IN ON YOU AFTER A YEAR ALL BY YOUR LONESOME... AND YOU'VE GOT WORK TO DO—!
THEIR LOSS, MY LADY!
INDEED! ALL RIGHT... LET'S GET MOVING! THE BIG ONE GOES WITH YOU—!
LUKE TOLD US YOU KNOW HOW TO USE BATTLE ARMOR, HAN SOLO! WE HAVE AN EXTRA SUIT!
WHAT?! WAIT A MINUTE! I JUST GOT HERE—! WHAT'S GOING ON—?!
5-20 #11

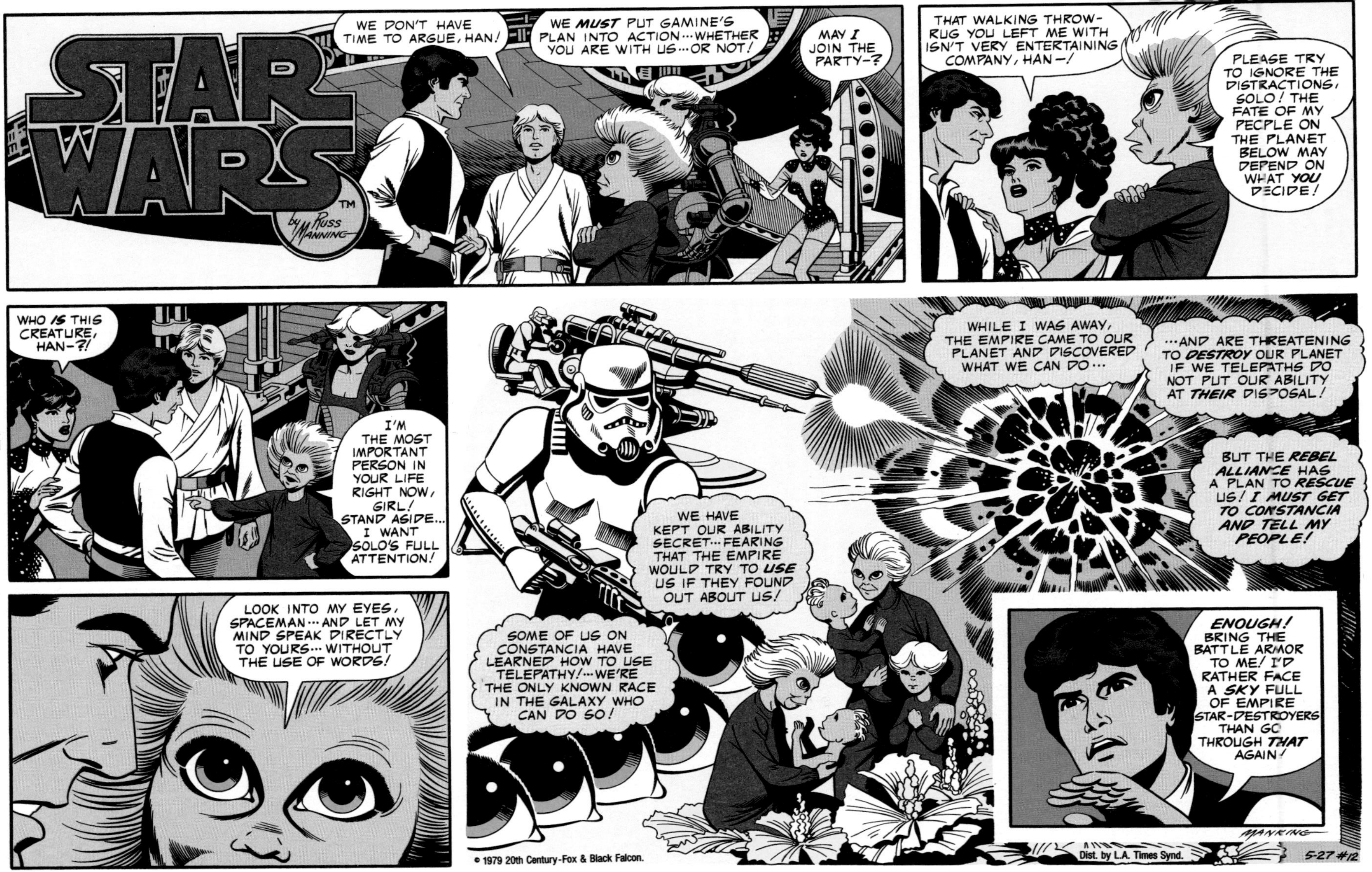
STAR WARS™
by Russ Manning
WE DON'T HAVE TIME TO ARGUE, HAN!
WE **MUST** PUT GAMINE'S PLAN INTO ACTION... WHETHER YOU ARE WITH US... OR NOT!
MAY **I** JOIN THE PARTY–?
THAT WALKING THROW-RUG YOU LEFT ME WITH ISN'T VERY ENTERTAINING COMPANY, HAN–!
PLEASE TRY TO IGNORE THE DISTRACTIONS, SOLO! THE FATE OF MY PEOPLE ON THE PLANET BELOW MAY DEPEND ON WHAT **YOU** DECIDE!
WHO **IS** THIS CREATURE, HAN–?!
I'M THE MOST IMPORTANT PERSON IN YOUR LIFE RIGHT NOW, GIRL! STAND ASIDE... I WANT SOLO'S FULL ATTENTION!
LOOK INTO MY EYES, SPACEMAN... AND LET MY MIND SPEAK DIRECTLY TO YOURS... WITHOUT THE USE OF WORDS!
SOME OF US ON CONSTANCIA HAVE LEARNED HOW TO USE TELEPATHY!... WE'RE THE ONLY KNOWN RACE IN THE GALAXY WHO CAN DO SO!
WE HAVE KEPT OUR ABILITY SECRET... FEARING THAT THE EMPIRE WOULD TRY TO **USE** US IF THEY FOUND OUT ABOUT US!
WHILE I WAS AWAY, THE EMPIRE CAME TO OUR PLANET AND DISCOVERED WHAT WE CAN DO...
...AND ARE THREATENING TO **DESTROY** OUR PLANET IF WE TELEPATHS DO NOT PUT OUR ABILITY AT **THEIR** DISPOSAL!
BUT THE **REBEL ALLIANCE** HAS A PLAN TO **RESCUE** US! **I MUST GET TO CONSTANCIA AND TELL MY PEOPLE!**
ENOUGH! BRING THE BATTLE ARMOR TO ME! I'D RATHER FACE A **SKY** FULL OF EMPIRE STAR-DESTROYERS THAN GO THROUGH **THAT** AGAIN!
MANNING
© 1979 20th Century-Fox & Black Falcon.
Dist. by L.A. Times Synd.
5-27 #12

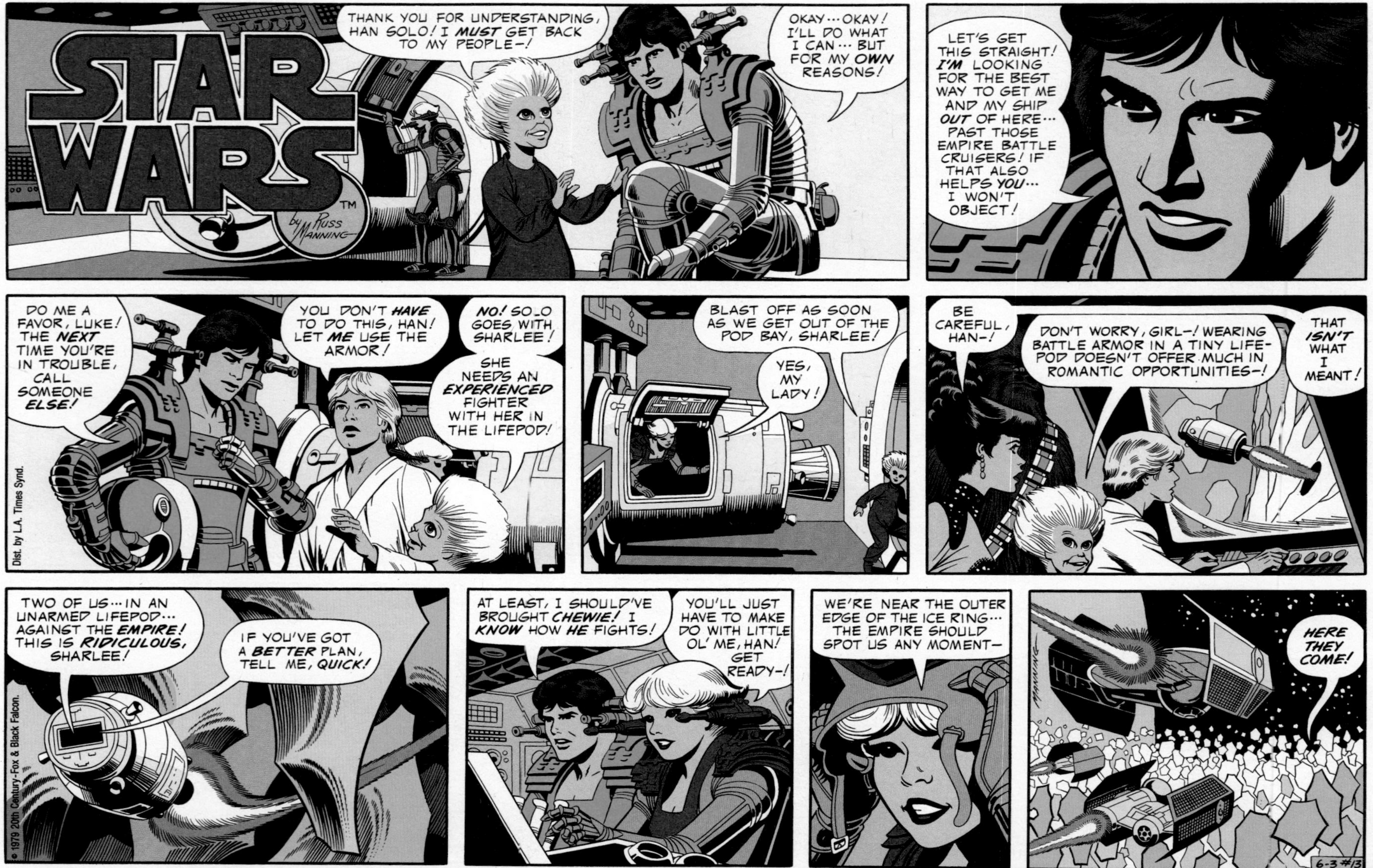
STAR WARS™
by Russ Manning
THANK YOU FOR UNDERSTANDING, HAN SOLO! I **MUST** GET BACK TO MY PEOPLE–!
OKAY... OKAY! I'LL DO WHAT I CAN... BUT FOR MY **OWN** REASONS!
LET'S GET THIS STRAIGHT! **I'M** LOOKING FOR THE BEST WAY TO GET ME AND MY SHIP **OUT** OF HERE... PAST THOSE EMPIRE BATTLE CRUISERS! IF THAT ALSO HELPS **YOU**... I WON'T OBJECT!
DO ME A FAVOR, LUKE! THE **NEXT** TIME YOU'RE IN TROUBLE, CALL SOMEONE **ELSE!**
YOU DON'T **HAVE** TO DO THIS, HAN! LET **ME** USE THE ARMOR!
NO! SOLO GOES WITH SHARLEE!
SHE NEEDS AN **EXPERIENCED** FIGHTER WITH HER IN THE LIFEPOD!
BLAST OFF AS SOON AS WE GET OUT OF THE POD BAY, SHARLEE!
YES, MY LADY!
BE CAREFUL, HAN–!
DON'T WORRY, GIRL–! WEARING BATTLE ARMOR IN A TINY LIFE-POD DOESN'T OFFER MUCH IN ROMANTIC OPPORTUNITIES–!
THAT **ISN'T** WHAT I MEANT!
TWO OF US... IN AN UNARMED LIFEPOD... AGAINST THE **EMPIRE!** THIS IS **RIDICULOUS,** SHARLEE!
IF YOU'VE GOT A **BETTER** PLAN, TELL ME, **QUICK!**
AT LEAST, I SHOULD'VE BROUGHT **CHEWIE!** I **KNOW** HOW **HE** FIGHTS!
YOU'LL JUST HAVE TO MAKE DO WITH LITTLE OL' ME, HAN! GET READY–!
WE'RE NEAR THE OUTER EDGE OF THE ICE RING... THE EMPIRE SHOULD SPOT US ANY MOMENT—
HERE THEY COME!
MANNING
6-3 #13
Dist. by L.A. Times Synd.
© 1979 20th Century-Fox & Black Falcon.

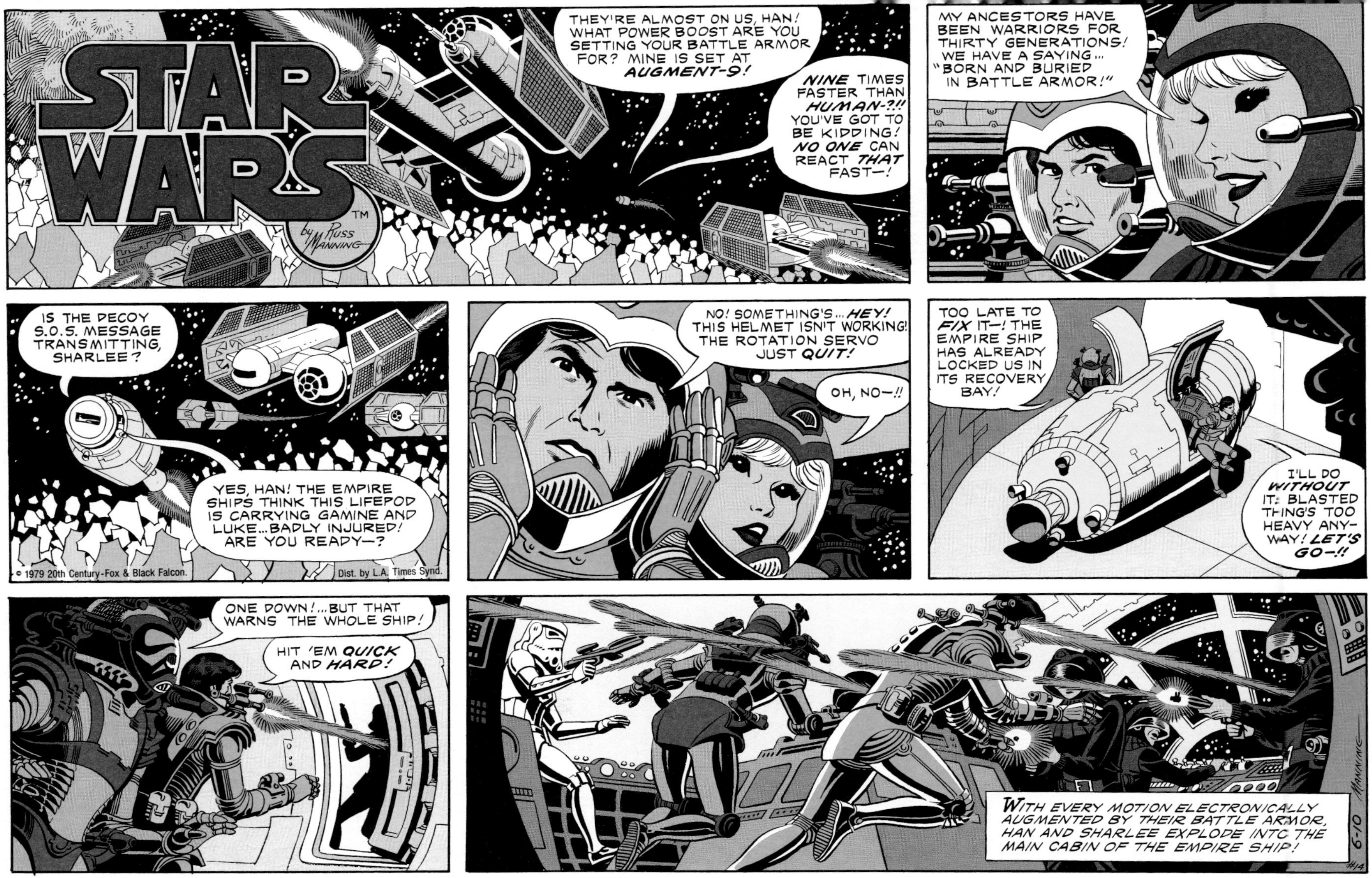
STAR WARS™
by Russ Manning
THEY'RE ALMOST ON US, HAN! WHAT POWER BOOST ARE YOU SETTING YOUR BATTLE ARMOR FOR? MINE IS SET AT AUGMENT-9!
NINE TIMES FASTER THAN HUMAN-?!! YOU'VE GOT TO BE KIDDING! NO ONE CAN REACT THAT FAST—!
MY ANCESTORS HAVE BEEN WARRIORS FOR THIRTY GENERATIONS! WE HAVE A SAYING... "BORN AND BURIED IN BATTLE ARMOR!"
IS THE DECOY S.O.S. MESSAGE TRANSMITTING, SHARLEE?
YES, HAN! THE EMPIRE SHIPS THINK THIS LIFEPOD IS CARRYING GAMINE AND LUKE...BADLY INJURED! ARE YOU READY—?
© 1979 20th Century-Fox & Black Falcon.
Dist. by L.A. Times Synd.
NO! SOMETHING'S...HEY! THIS HELMET ISN'T WORKING! THE ROTATION SERVO JUST QUIT!
OH, NO—!!
TOO LATE TO FIX IT—! THE EMPIRE SHIP HAS ALREADY LOCKED US IN ITS RECOVERY BAY!
I'LL DO WITHOUT IT! BLASTED THING'S TOO HEAVY ANYWAY! LET'S GO—!!
ONE DOWN!...BUT THAT WARNS THE WHOLE SHIP!
HIT 'EM QUICK AND HARD!
WITH EVERY MOTION ELECTRONICALLY AUGMENTED BY THEIR BATTLE ARMOR, HAN AND SHARLEE EXPLODE INTO THE MAIN CABIN OF THE EMPIRE SHIP!
6-10
MANNING
#14

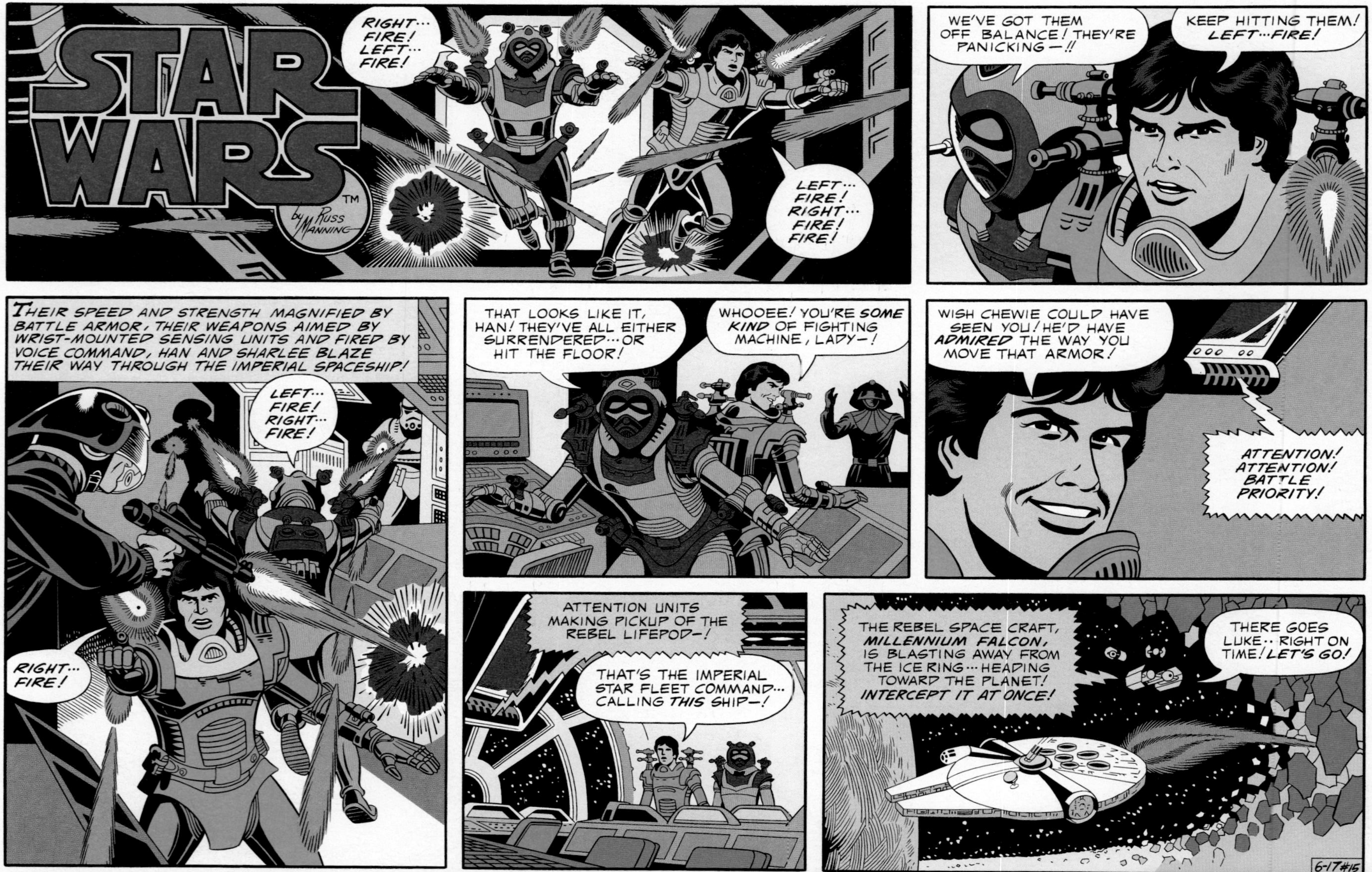
STAR WARS™
by Russ Manning
RIGHT… FIRE! LEFT… FIRE!
LEFT… FIRE! RIGHT… FIRE! FIRE!
WE'VE GOT THEM OFF BALANCE! THEY'RE PANICKING—!!
KEEP HITTING THEM! LEFT…FIRE!
THEIR SPEED AND STRENGTH MAGNIFIED BY BATTLE ARMOR, THEIR WEAPONS AIMED BY WRIST-MOUNTED SENSING UNITS AND FIRED BY VOICE COMMAND, HAN AND SHARLEE BLAZE THEIR WAY THROUGH THE IMPERIAL SPACESHIP!
LEFT… FIRE! RIGHT… FIRE!
RIGHT… FIRE!
THAT LOOKS LIKE IT, HAN! THEY'VE ALL EITHER SURRENDERED…OR HIT THE FLOOR!
WHOOEE! YOU'RE SOME KIND OF FIGHTING MACHINE, LADY—!
WISH CHEWIE COULD HAVE SEEN YOU! HE'D HAVE ADMIRED THE WAY YOU MOVE THAT ARMOR!
ATTENTION! ATTENTION! BATTLE PRIORITY!
ATTENTION UNITS MAKING PICKUP OF THE REBEL LIFEPOD—!
THAT'S THE IMPERIAL STAR FLEET COMMAND… CALLING THIS SHIP—!
THE REBEL SPACE CRAFT, MILLENNIUM FALCON, IS BLASTING AWAY FROM THE ICE RING…HEADING TOWARD THE PLANET! INTERCEPT IT AT ONCE!
THERE GOES LUKE… RIGHT ON TIME! LET'S GO!
6-17 #15

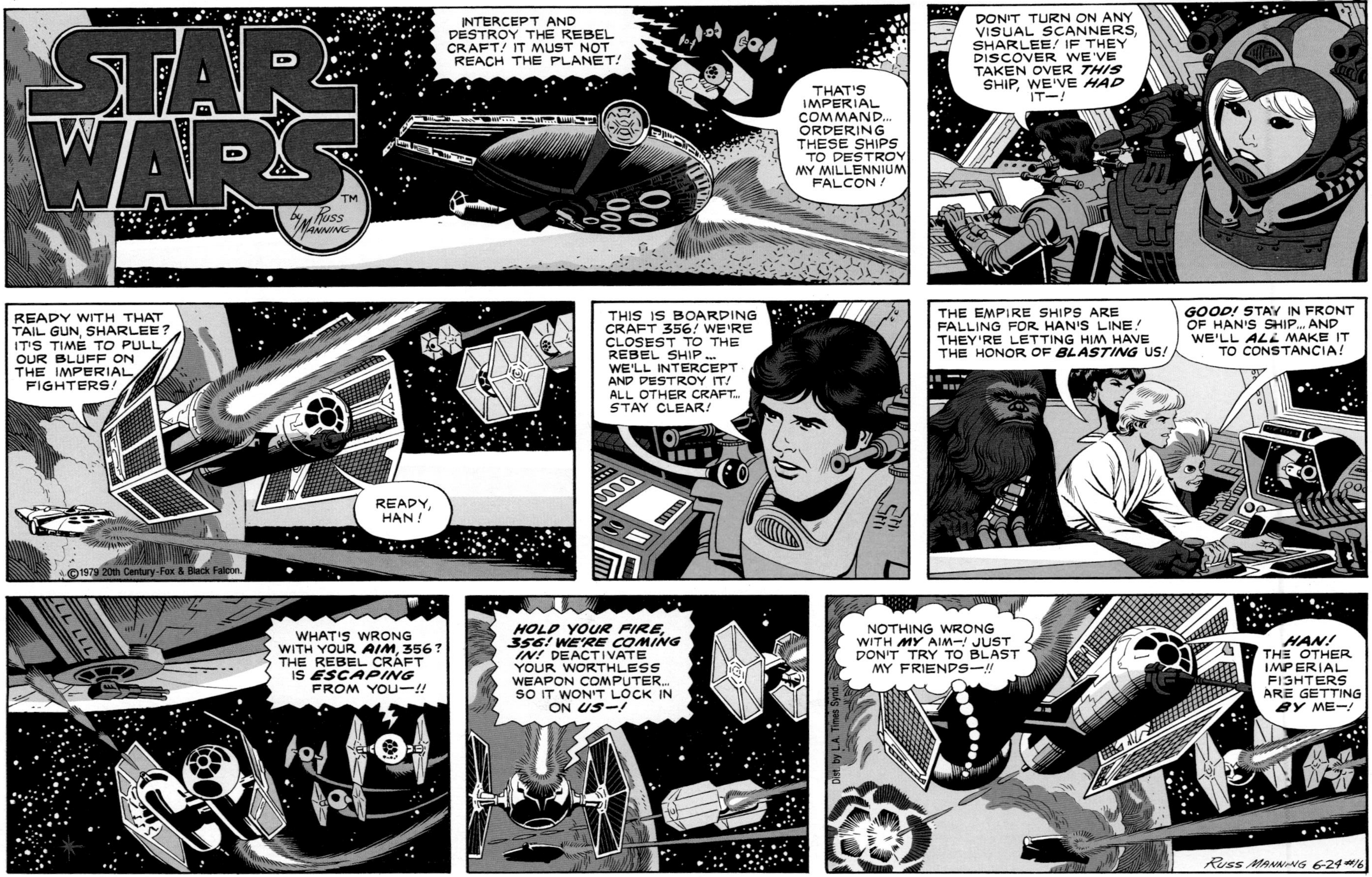
STAR WARS™
by Russ Manning
INTERCEPT AND DESTROY THE REBEL CRAFT! IT MUST NOT REACH THE PLANET!
THAT'S IMPERIAL COMMAND... ORDERING THESE SHIPS TO DESTROY MY MILLENNIUM FALCON!
DON'T TURN ON ANY VISUAL SCANNERS, SHARLEE! IF THEY DISCOVER WE'VE TAKEN OVER ***THIS*** SHIP, WE'VE ***HAD*** IT—!
READY WITH THAT TAIL GUN, SHARLEE? IT'S TIME TO PULL OUR BLUFF ON THE IMPERIAL FIGHTERS!
READY, HAN!
©1979 20th Century-Fox & Black Falcon.
THIS IS BOARDING CRAFT 356! WE'RE CLOSEST TO THE REBEL SHIP ... WE'LL INTERCEPT AND DESTROY IT! ALL OTHER CRAFT... STAY CLEAR!
THE EMPIRE SHIPS ARE FALLING FOR HAN'S LINE! THEY'RE LETTING HIM HAVE THE HONOR OF ***BLASTING*** US!
GOOD! STAY IN FRONT OF HAN'S SHIP... AND WE'LL ***ALL*** MAKE IT TO CONSTANCIA!
WHAT'S WRONG WITH YOUR ***AIM***, 356? THE REBEL CRAFT IS ***ESCAPING*** FROM YOU—!!
HOLD YOUR FIRE, 356! WE'RE COMING IN! DEACTIVATE YOUR WORTHLESS WEAPON COMPUTER... SO IT WON'T LOCK IN ON ***US***—!
Dist. by L.A. Times Synd.
NOTHING WRONG WITH ***MY*** AIM—! JUST DON'T TRY TO BLAST MY FRIENDS—!!
HAN! THE OTHER IMPERIAL FIGHTERS ARE GETTING ***BY*** ME—!
RUSS MANNING 6-24 #16

STAR WARS™
by Russ Manning
AT THE CONTROLS OF THE IMPERIAL BOARDING CRAFT, HAN SOLO WATCHES HELPLESSLY...
THE TIE-FIGHTERS ARE IGNORING ME... GOING AFTER LUKE! IT'S UP TO HIM AND CHEWIE, NOW!
THE IMPERIAL FIGHTERS HAVE GOTTEN PAST HAN... COMING AT US! I'LL BE IN GUNPORT TWO, CHEWIE—!
ARRGH!
GAMINE CALLING CONSTANCIA GROUND DEFENSE! BLAST ONLY THE TWO TIE-FIGHTERS! BLAST ONLY THE TWO TIE—
HERE THEY COME!!
GOT ONE! ...AND PLANETARY DEFENSE GOT THE OTHER!!
...AND THAT FINISHES THE EASY PART! ...NOW COMES THE HARD PART... LIVING THROUGH A HERO'S WELCOME ON MY PLANET!
MANNING
7-1 #7
©1979 20th Century-Fox & Black Falcon.
Dist. by L.A. Times Synd.

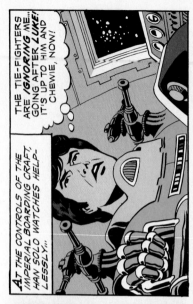

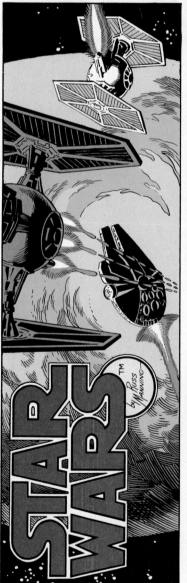

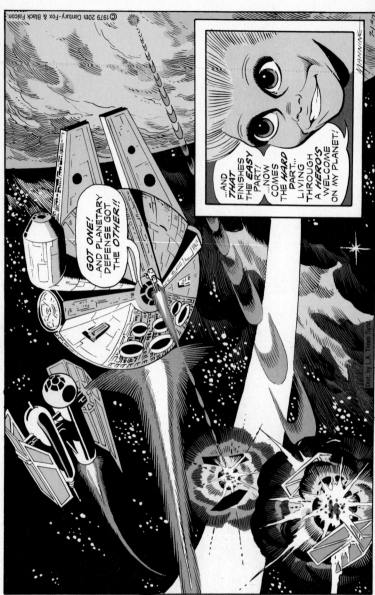

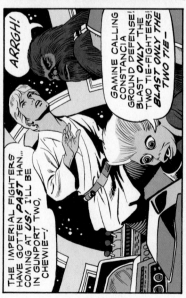

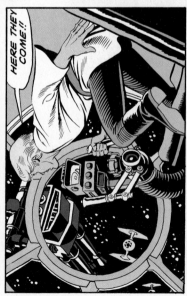

WHEW—! LISTEN TO THAT CROWD—!

YOU HAVEN'T SEEN A JOYOUS MOB....UNTIL YOU'VE BEEN WITH TELEPATHS PUMPING UP ON EACH OTHER'S GOOD THOUGHTS!

THE PEOPLE OF CONSTANCIA EVEN ERECTED A MONUMENT TO JS, LATER, MASTER LUKE, MASTER SOLO, CHEWIE...

...AND WE DELIVERED HER TO CONSTANCIA JUST IN TIME FOR HER TO SAVE THE PLANET!

BUT I WAS WITH MASTER SOLO ON CHEWIE'S PLANET WHEN THEY FIRST MET GYLA PETRO! IT ALMOST COST US OUR LIVES!!

CONTINUED NEXT WEEK 7-8-8

STAR WARS

™

by Russ Manning

YES, HAN! ...AND GET READY, EVERYBODY! I CAN SENSE THE WELCOMING COMMITTEE FROM HERE!

STRAIGHT IN TO THE LANDING PAD... AND STAY BELOW THE TURBO LASER TOWERS...RIGHT, GAMINE—?

THEY HAD GREAT FAITH IN GAMINE, MISTRESS MNEMOS!

CELEBRATING—!!? WHY WERE THEY CELEBRATING....WHEN THEIR WORLD WAS THREATENED WITH DESTRUCTION BY THE IMPERIAL FORCES—??

HOW DID HAN SOLO MEET CHEWBACCA?

I DON'T KNOW! I WASN'T THERE—.

GIVE ME A STRONG MENTAL IMAGE OF HIM! AH.....YES!

CHEWBACCA... FILE: WOOKIEE SECTION: OC-356 BORN: SIPEREAL ERA AF-5076 ON HAZHYYYK.

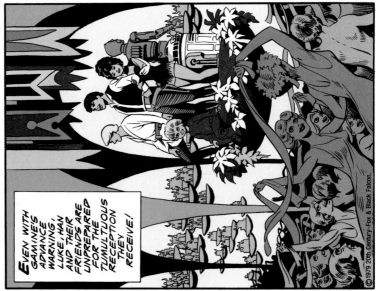

EVEN WITH GAMINE'S ADVANCE WARNING, LUKE, HAN AND THEIR FRIENDS ARE UNPREPARED FOR THE TUMULTUOUS RECEPTION THEY RECEIVE!

23

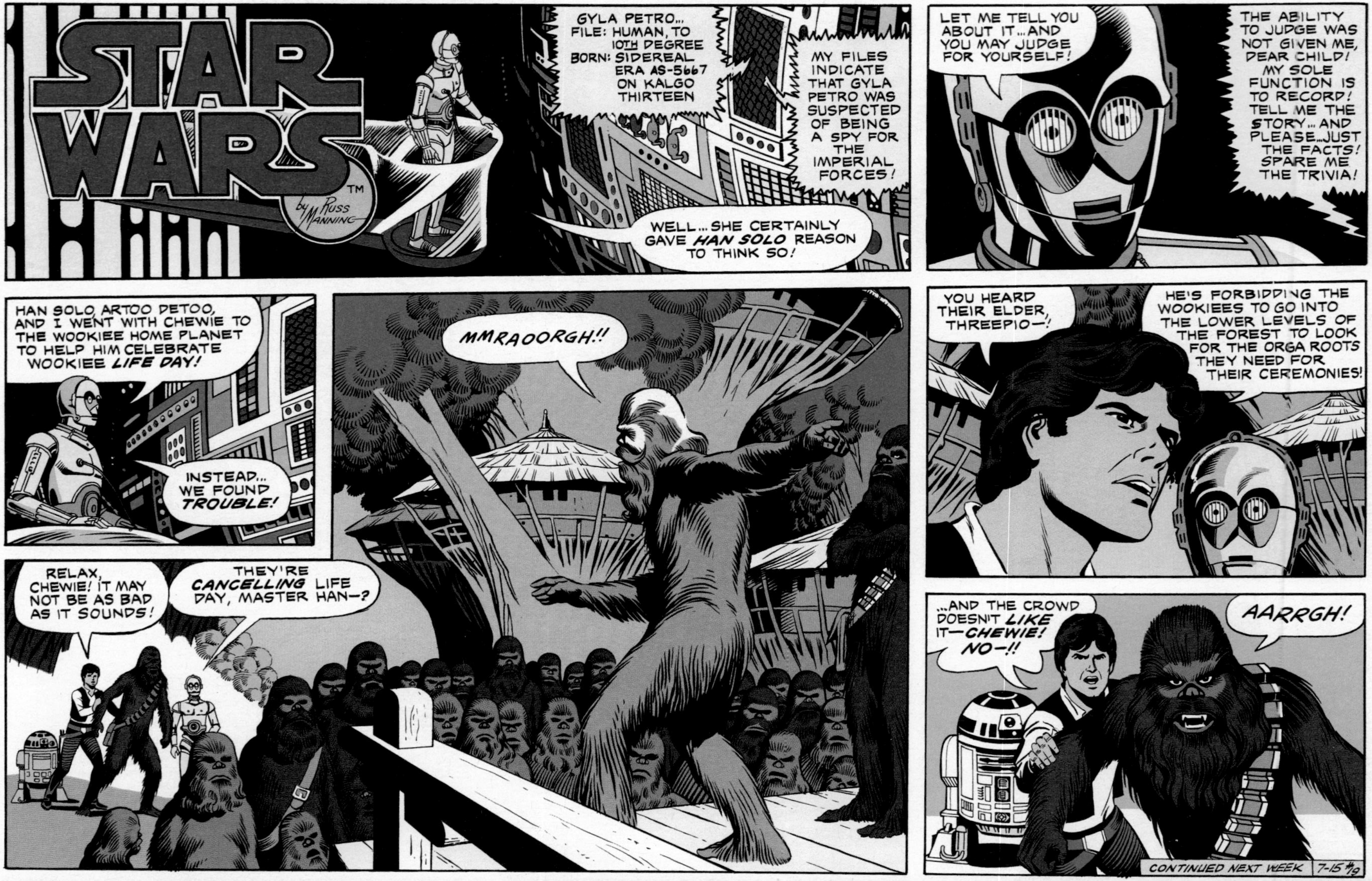
STAR WARS™
by Russ Manning
GYLA PETRO... FILE: HUMAN, TO 10TH DEGREE BORN: SIDEREAL ERA AS-5667 ON KALGO THIRTEEN
MY FILES INDICATE THAT GYLA PETRO WAS SUSPECTED OF BEING A SPY FOR THE IMPERIAL FORCES!
WELL... SHE CERTAINLY GAVE HAN SOLO REASON TO THINK SO!
LET ME TELL YOU ABOUT IT... AND YOU MAY JUDGE FOR YOURSELF!
THE ABILITY TO JUDGE WAS NOT GIVEN ME, DEAR CHILD! MY SOLE FUNCTION IS TO RECORD! TELL ME THE STORY... AND PLEASE... JUST THE FACTS! SPARE ME THE TRIVIA!
HAN SOLO, ARTOO DETOO, AND I WENT WITH CHEWIE TO THE WOOKIEE HOME PLANET TO HELP HIM CELEBRATE WOOKIEE LIFE DAY!
INSTEAD... WE FOUND TROUBLE!
MMRAOORGH!!
RELAX, CHEWIE! IT MAY NOT BE AS BAD AS IT SOUNDS!
THEY'RE CANCELLING LIFE DAY, MASTER HAN—?
YOU HEARD THEIR ELDER, THREEPIO—!
HE'S FORBIDDING THE WOOKIEES TO GO INTO THE LOWER LEVELS OF THE FOREST TO LOOK FOR THE ORGA ROOTS THEY NEED FOR THEIR CEREMONIES!
...AND THE CROWD DOESN'T LIKE IT—CHEWIE! NO—!!
AARRGH!
CONTINUED NEXT WEEK
7-15-79

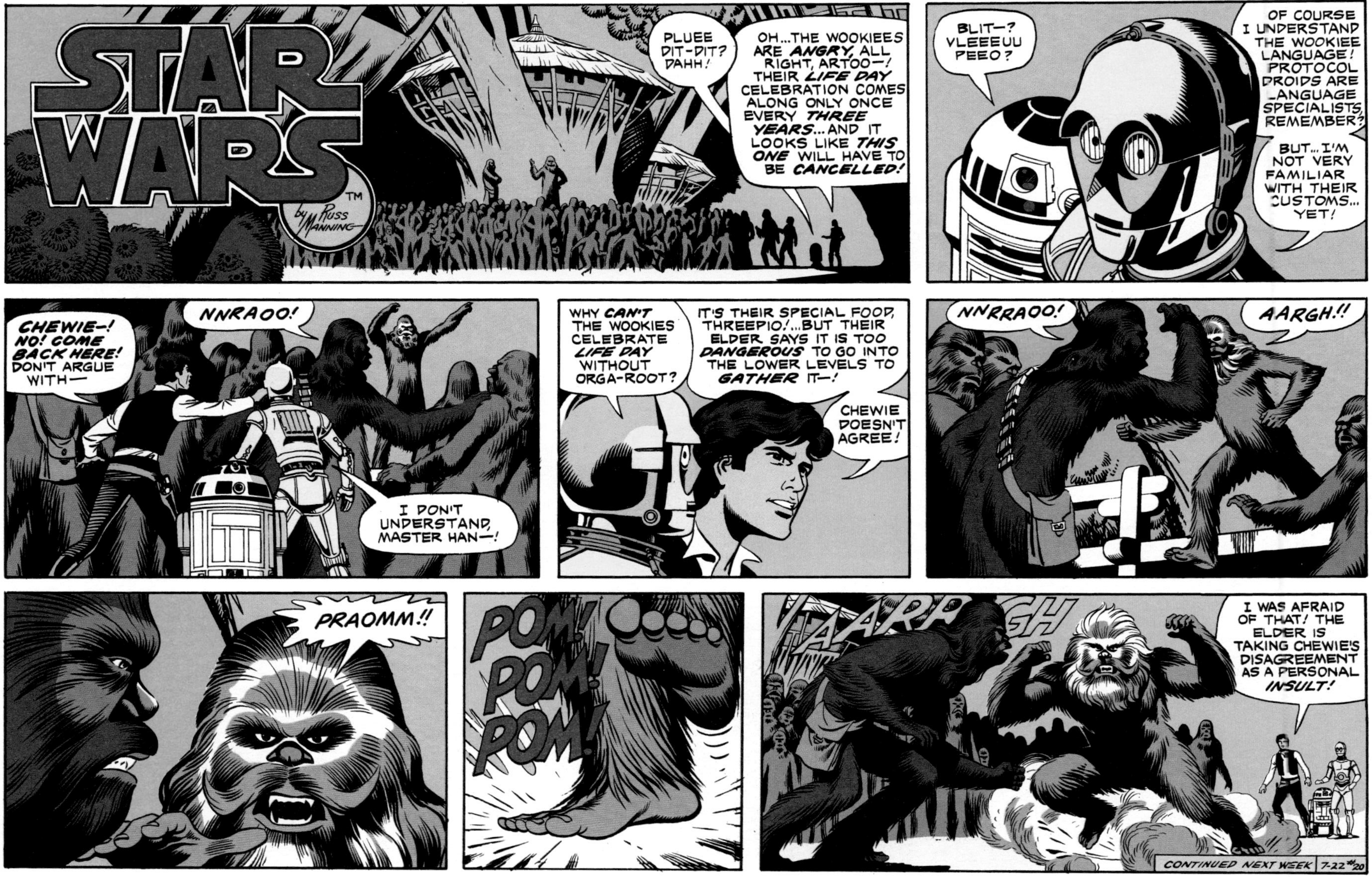
STAR WARS™
by Russ Manning
PLUEE DIT-DIT? DAHH!
OH...THE WOOKIEES ARE *ANGRY*, ALL RIGHT, ARTOO—! THEIR *LIFE DAY* CELEBRATION COMES ALONG ONLY ONCE EVERY *THREE YEARS*...AND IT LOOKS LIKE *THIS ONE* WILL HAVE TO BE *CANCELLED!*
BLIT—? VLEEEUU PEEO?
OF COURSE I UNDERSTAND THE WOOKIEE LANGUAGE! PROTOCOL DROIDS ARE LANGUAGE SPECIALISTS, REMEMBER?
BUT...I'M NOT VERY FAMILIAR WITH THEIR CUSTOMS...YET!
CHEWIE—! NO! COME BACK HERE! DON'T ARGUE WITH—
NNRAOO!
I DON'T UNDERSTAND, MASTER HAN—!
WHY *CAN'T* THE WOOKIES CELEBRATE *LIFE DAY* WITHOUT ORGA-ROOT?
IT'S THEIR SPECIAL FOOD, THREEPIO!...BUT THEIR ELDER SAYS IT IS TOO *DANGEROUS* TO GO INTO THE LOWER LEVELS TO *GATHER* IT—!
CHEWIE DOESN'T AGREE!
NNRRAOO!
AARGH!!
PRAOMM!!
POM! POM! POM!
AARRGH
I WAS AFRAID OF THAT! THE ELDER IS TAKING CHEWIE'S DISAGREEMENT AS A PERSONAL *INSULT!*
CONTINUED NEXT WEEK 7-22 #20

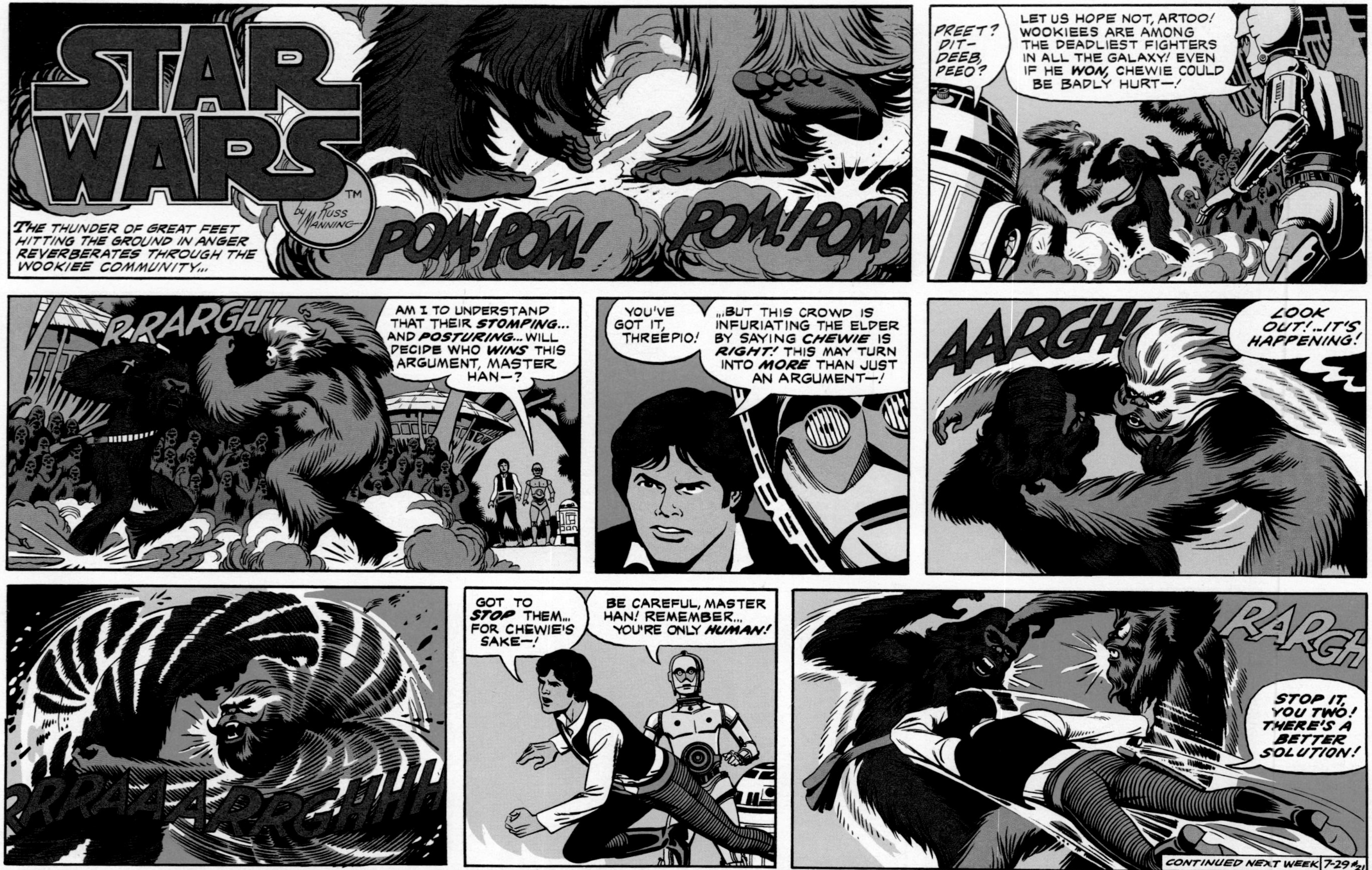
STAR WARS
by Russ Manning
THE THUNDER OF GREAT FEET HITTING THE GROUND IN ANGER REVERBERATES THROUGH THE WOOKIEE COMMUNITY...
POM! POM! POM! POM!
PREET? DIT-DEEB, PEEO?
LET US HOPE NOT, ARTOO! WOOKIEES ARE AMONG THE DEADLIEST FIGHTERS IN ALL THE GALAXY! EVEN IF HE WON, CHEWIE COULD BE BADLY HURT—!
RRARGH!
AM I TO UNDERSTAND THAT THEIR STOMPING... AND POSTURING... WILL DECIDE WHO WINS THIS ARGUMENT, MASTER HAN—?
YOU'VE GOT IT, THREEPIO!
...BUT THIS CROWD IS INFURIATING THE ELDER BY SAYING CHEWIE IS RIGHT! THIS MAY TURN INTO MORE THAN JUST AN ARGUMENT—!
AARGH!
LOOK OUT!...IT'S HAPPENING!
RRRAAAARRGHHH
GOT TO STOP THEM... FOR CHEWIE'S SAKE—!
BE CAREFUL, MASTER HAN! REMEMBER... YOU'RE ONLY HUMAN!
RARGH
STOP IT, YOU TWO! THERE'S A BETTER SOLUTION!
CONTINUED NEXT WEEK
7-29 #21

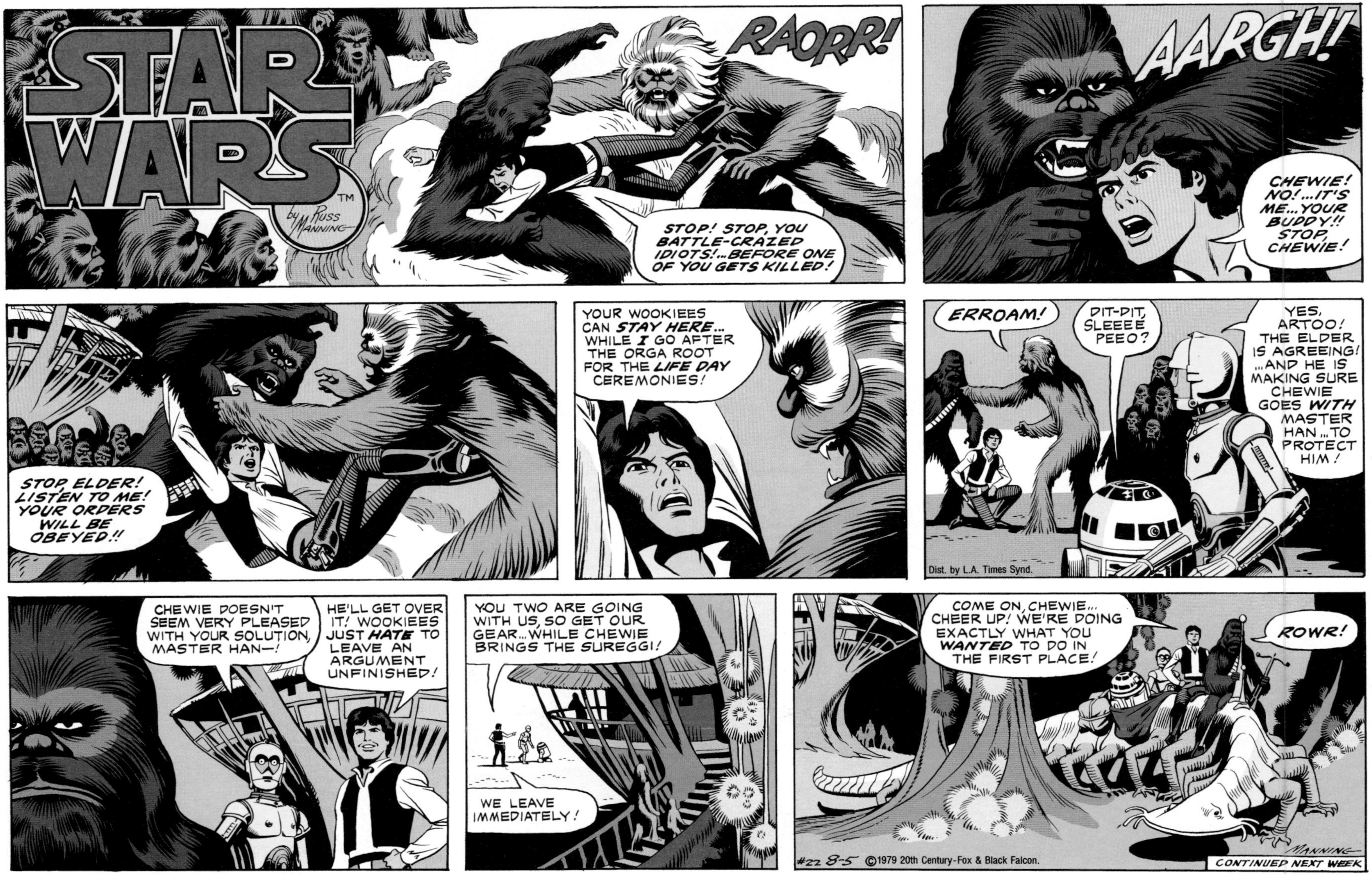
STAR WARS
TM
by Russ Manning
RAORR!
STOP! STOP, YOU BATTLE-CRAZED IDIOTS!...BEFORE ONE OF YOU GETS KILLED!
AARGH!
CHEWIE! NO!...IT'S ME...YOUR BUDDY!! STOP, CHEWIE!
STOP, ELDER! LISTEN TO ME! YOUR ORDERS WILL BE OBEYED!!
YOUR WOOKIEES CAN STAY HERE... WHILE I GO AFTER THE ORGA ROOT FOR THE LIFE DAY CEREMONIES!
ERROAM!
DIT-DIT, SLEEEE PEEO?
YES, ARTOO! THE ELDER IS AGREEING! ...AND HE IS MAKING SURE CHEWIE GOES WITH MASTER HAN...TO PROTECT HIM!
Dist. by L.A. Times Synd.
CHEWIE DOESN'T SEEM VERY PLEASED WITH YOUR SOLUTION, MASTER HAN—!
HE'LL GET OVER IT! WOOKIEES JUST HATE TO LEAVE AN ARGUMENT UNFINISHED!
YOU TWO ARE GOING WITH US, SO GET OUR GEAR...WHILE CHEWIE BRINGS THE SUREGGI!
WE LEAVE IMMEDIATELY!
COME ON, CHEWIE... CHEER UP! WE'RE DOING EXACTLY WHAT YOU WANTED TO DO IN THE FIRST PLACE!
ROWR!
MANNING
#22 8-5 ©1979 20th Century-Fox & Black Falcon.
CONTINUED NEXT WEEK

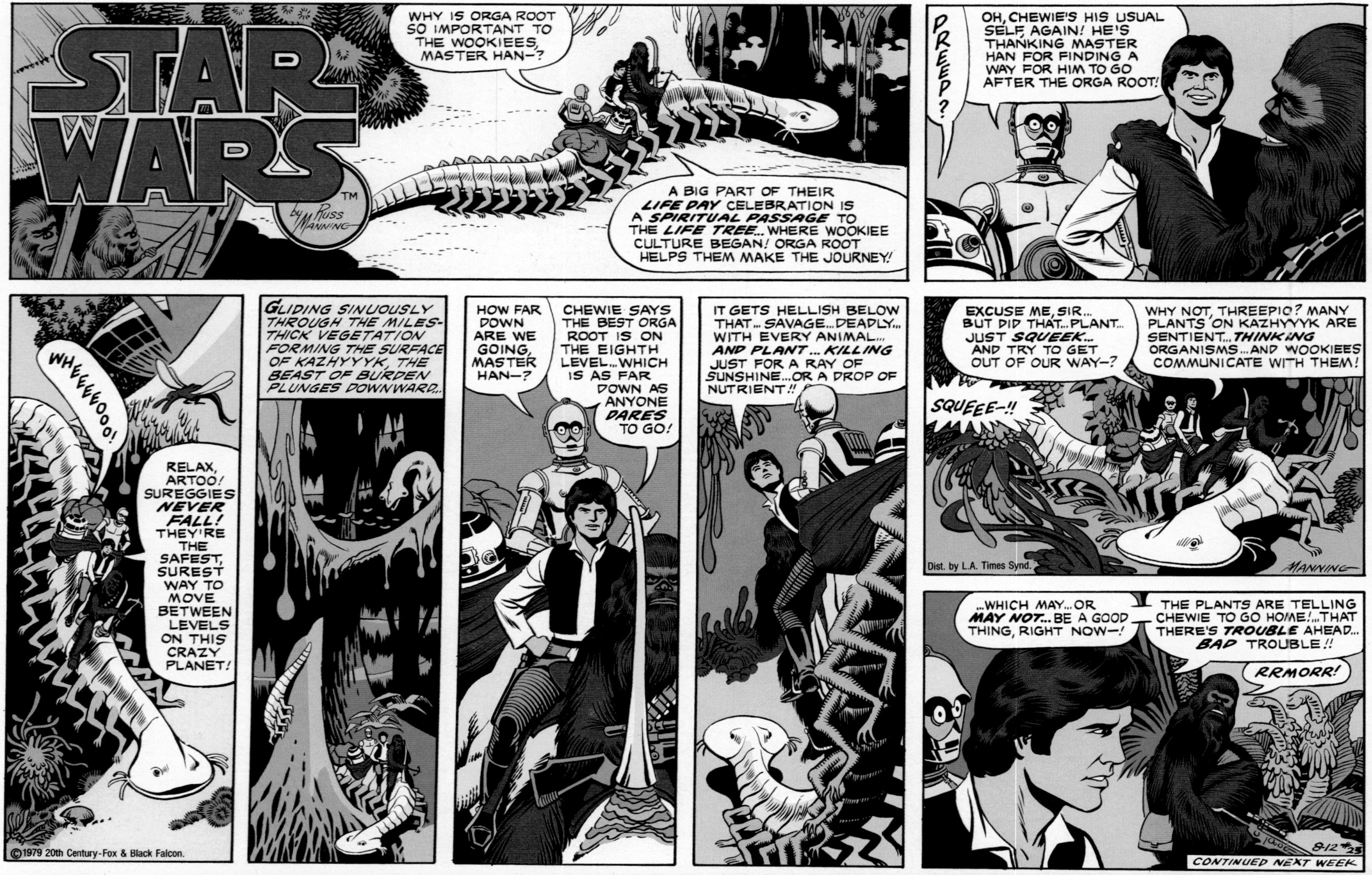
STAR WARS
by Russ Manning
WHY IS ORGA ROOT SO IMPORTANT TO THE WOOKIEES, MASTER HAN—?
A BIG PART OF THEIR LIFE DAY CELEBRATION IS A SPIRITUAL PASSAGE TO THE LIFE TREE... WHERE WOOKIEE CULTURE BEGAN! ORGA ROOT HELPS THEM MAKE THE JOURNEY!
PREEP?
OH, CHEWIE'S HIS USUAL SELF AGAIN! HE'S THANKING MASTER HAN FOR FINDING A WAY FOR HIM TO GO AFTER THE ORGA ROOT!
WHEEEEOOO!
RELAX, ARTOO! SUREGGIES NEVER FALL! THEY'RE THE SAFEST, SUREST WAY TO MOVE BETWEEN LEVELS ON THIS CRAZY PLANET!
©1979 20th Century-Fox & Black Falcon.
GLIDING SINUOUSLY THROUGH THE MILES-THICK VEGETATION FORMING THE SURFACE OF KAZHYYYK, THE BEAST OF BURDEN PLUNGES DOWNWARD...
HOW FAR DOWN ARE WE GOING, MASTER HAN—?
CHEWIE SAYS THE BEST ORGA ROOT IS ON THE EIGHTH LEVEL... WHICH IS AS FAR DOWN AS ANYONE DARES TO GO!
IT GETS HELLISH BELOW THAT... SAVAGE... DEADLY... WITH EVERY ANIMAL... AND PLANT... KILLING JUST FOR A RAY OF SUNSHINE... OR A DROP OF NUTRIENT!!
EXCUSE ME, SIR... BUT DID THAT... PLANT... JUST SQUEEK... AND TRY TO GET OUT OF OUR WAY—?
WHY NOT, THREEPIO? MANY PLANTS ON KAZHYYYK ARE SENTIENT... THINKING ORGANISMS... AND WOOKIEES COMMUNICATE WITH THEM!
SQUEEE—!!
Dist. by L.A. Times Synd.
MANNING
...WHICH MAY... OR MAY NOT... BE A GOOD THING, RIGHT NOW—!
THE PLANTS ARE TELLING CHEWIE TO GO HOME!... THAT THERE'S TROUBLE AHEAD... BAD TROUBLE!!
RRMORR!
8-12 #23
CONTINUED NEXT WEEK

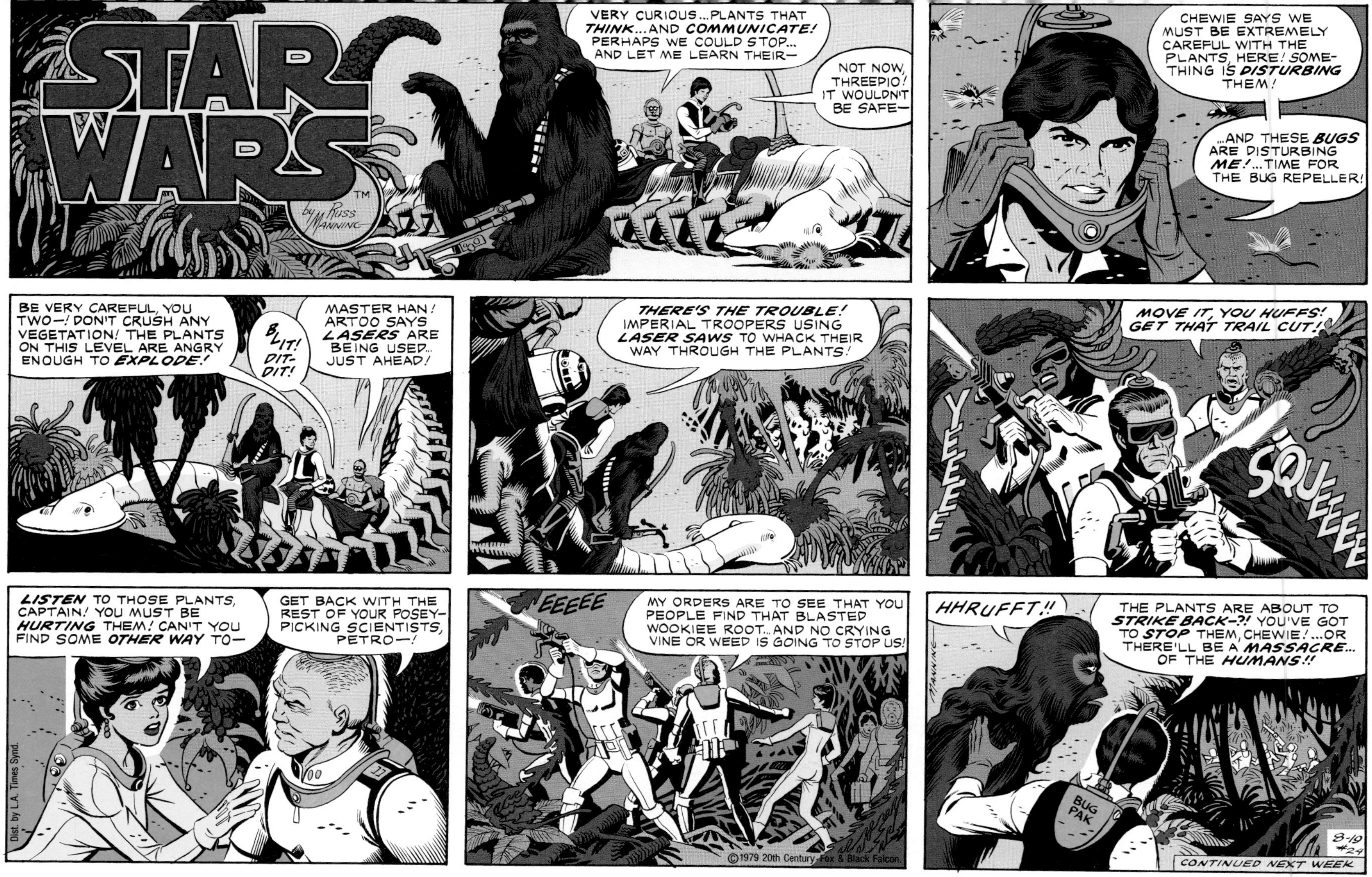
STAR WARS™
by Russ Manning
VERY CURIOUS...PLANTS THAT THINK...AND COMMUNICATE! PERHAPS WE COULD STOP... AND LET ME LEARN THEIR—
NOT NOW, THREEPIO! IT WOULDN'T BE SAFE—
CHEWIE SAYS WE MUST BE EXTREMELY CAREFUL WITH THE PLANTS, HERE! SOMETHING IS DISTURBING THEM!
...AND THESE BUGS ARE DISTURBING ME!...TIME FOR THE BUG REPELLER!
BE VERY CAREFUL, YOU TWO—! DON'T CRUSH ANY VEGETATION! THE PLANTS ON THIS LEVEL ARE ANGRY ENOUGH TO EXPLODE!
B'LIT! DIT-DIT!
MASTER HAN! ARTOO SAYS LASERS ARE BEING USED... JUST AHEAD!
THERE'S THE TROUBLE! IMPERIAL TROOPERS USING LASER SAWS TO WHACK THEIR WAY THROUGH THE PLANTS!
MOVE IT, YOU HUFFS! GET THAT TRAIL CUT!
YEEEE
SQUEEEEE
LISTEN TO THOSE PLANTS, CAPTAIN! YOU MUST BE HURTING THEM! CAN'T YOU FIND SOME OTHER WAY TO—
GET BACK WITH THE REST OF YOUR POSEY-PICKING SCIENTISTS, PETRO—!
Dist. by L.A. Times Synd.
EEEEE
MY ORDERS ARE TO SEE THAT YOU PEOPLE FIND THAT BLASTED WOOKIEE ROOT...AND NO CRYING VINE OR WEED IS GOING TO STOP US!
©1979 20th Century-Fox & Black Falcon.
HHRUFFT!!
THE PLANTS ARE ABOUT TO STRIKE BACK—?! YOU'VE GOT TO STOP THEM, CHEWIE! ...OR THERE'LL BE A MASSACRE... OF THE HUMANS!!
BUG PAK
MANNING
8-19 #24
CONTINUED NEXT WEEK

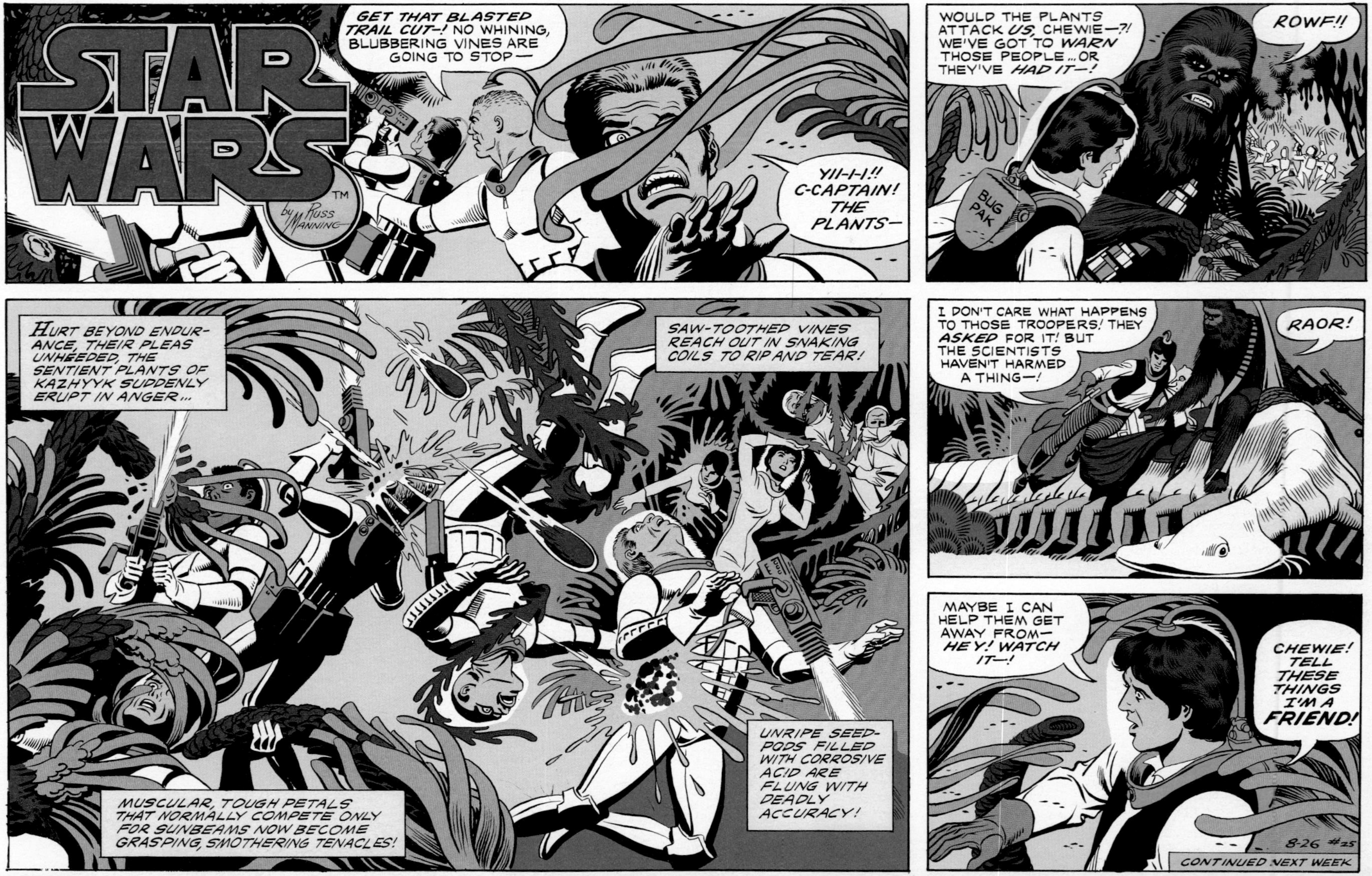
STAR WARS™
by Russ Manning
GET THAT BLASTED TRAIL CUT–! NO WHINING, BLUBBERING VINES ARE GOING TO STOP—
YII-I-I!! C-CAPTAIN! THE PLANTS—
WOULD THE PLANTS ATTACK US, CHEWIE—?! WE'VE GOT TO WARN THOSE PEOPLE…OR THEY'VE HAD IT—!
BUG PAK
ROWF!!
HURT BEYOND ENDURANCE, THEIR PLEAS UNHEEDED, THE SENTIENT PLANTS OF KAZHYYK SUDDENLY ERUPT IN ANGER…
SAW-TOOTHED VINES REACH OUT IN SNAKING COILS TO RIP AND TEAR!
MUSCULAR, TOUGH PETALS THAT NORMALLY COMPETE ONLY FOR SUNBEAMS NOW BECOME GRASPING, SMOTHERING TENACLES!
UNRIPE SEED-PODS FILLED WITH CORROSIVE ACID ARE FLUNG WITH DEADLY ACCURACY!
I DON'T CARE WHAT HAPPENS TO THOSE TROOPERS! THEY ASKED FOR IT! BUT THE SCIENTISTS HAVEN'T HARMED A THING—!
RAOR!
MAYBE I CAN HELP THEM GET AWAY FROM—HEY! WATCH IT—!
CHEWIE! TELL THESE THINGS I'M A FRIEND!
8-26 #25
CONTINUED NEXT WEEK

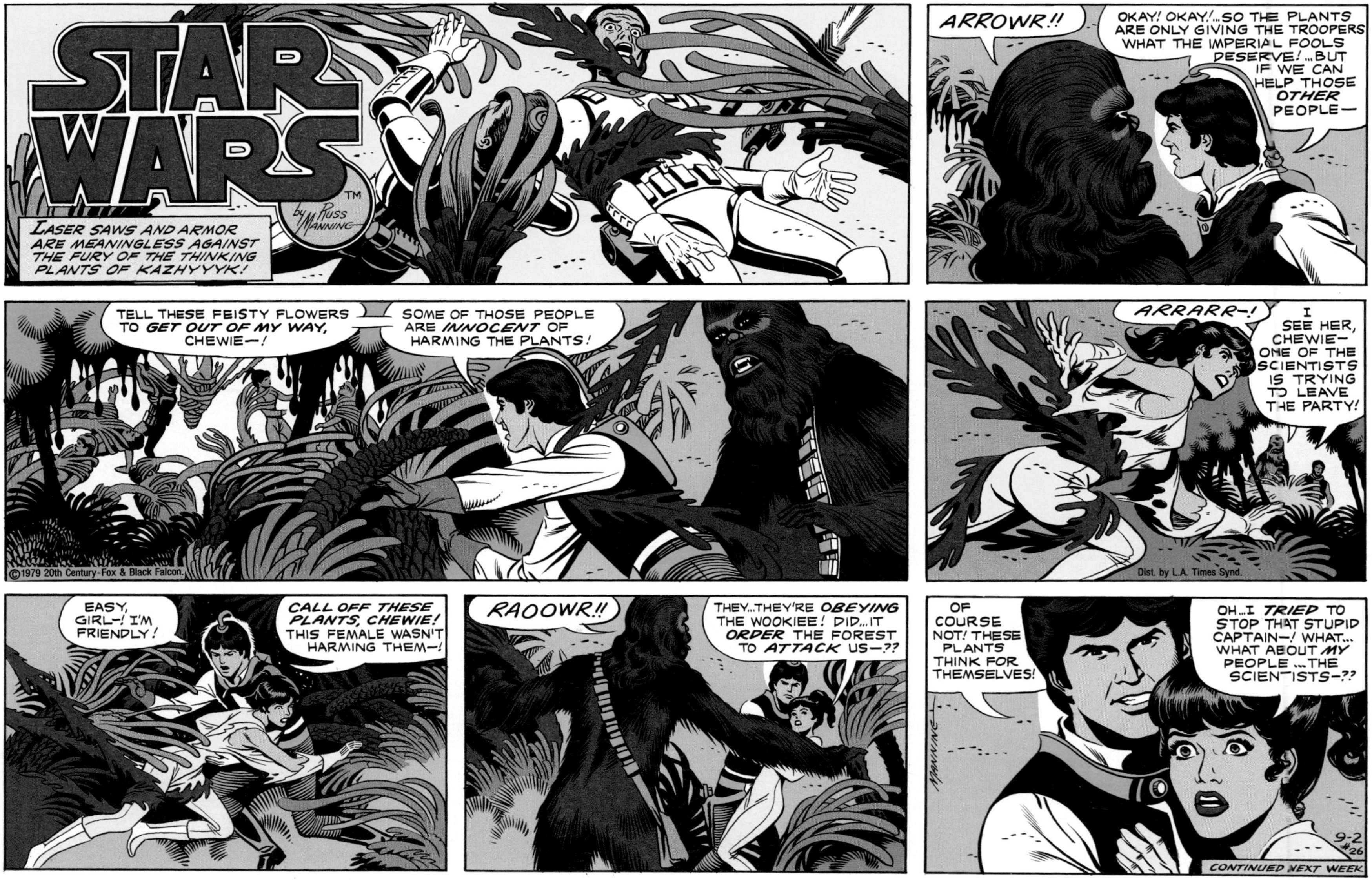
STAR WARS
TM
by Russ Manning
LASER SAWS AND ARMOR ARE MEANINGLESS AGAINST THE FURY OF THE THINKING PLANTS OF KAZHYYYK!
ARROWR!!
OKAY! OKAY!...SO THE PLANTS ARE ONLY GIVING THE TROOPERS WHAT THE IMPERIAL FOOLS DESERVE!...BUT IF WE CAN HELP THOSE OTHER PEOPLE—
TELL THESE FEISTY FLOWERS TO GET OUT OF MY WAY, CHEWIE—!
SOME OF THOSE PEOPLE ARE INNOCENT OF HARMING THE PLANTS!
©1979 20th Century-Fox & Black Falcon.
ARRARR—!
I SEE HER, CHEWIE— ONE OF THE SCIENTISTS IS TRYING TO LEAVE THE PARTY!
Dist. by L.A. Times Synd.
EASY, GIRL—! I'M FRIENDLY!
CALL OFF THESE PLANTS, CHEWIE! THIS FEMALE WASN'T HARMING THEM—!
RAOOWR!!
THEY...THEY'RE OBEYING THE WOOKIEE! DID...IT ORDER THE FOREST TO ATTACK US—??
OF COURSE NOT! THESE PLANTS THINK FOR THEMSELVES!
OH...I TRIED TO STOP THAT STUPID CAPTAIN—! WHAT... WHAT ABOUT MY PEOPLE ...THE SCIENTISTS—??
MANNING
9-2 #26
CONTINUED NEXT WEEK

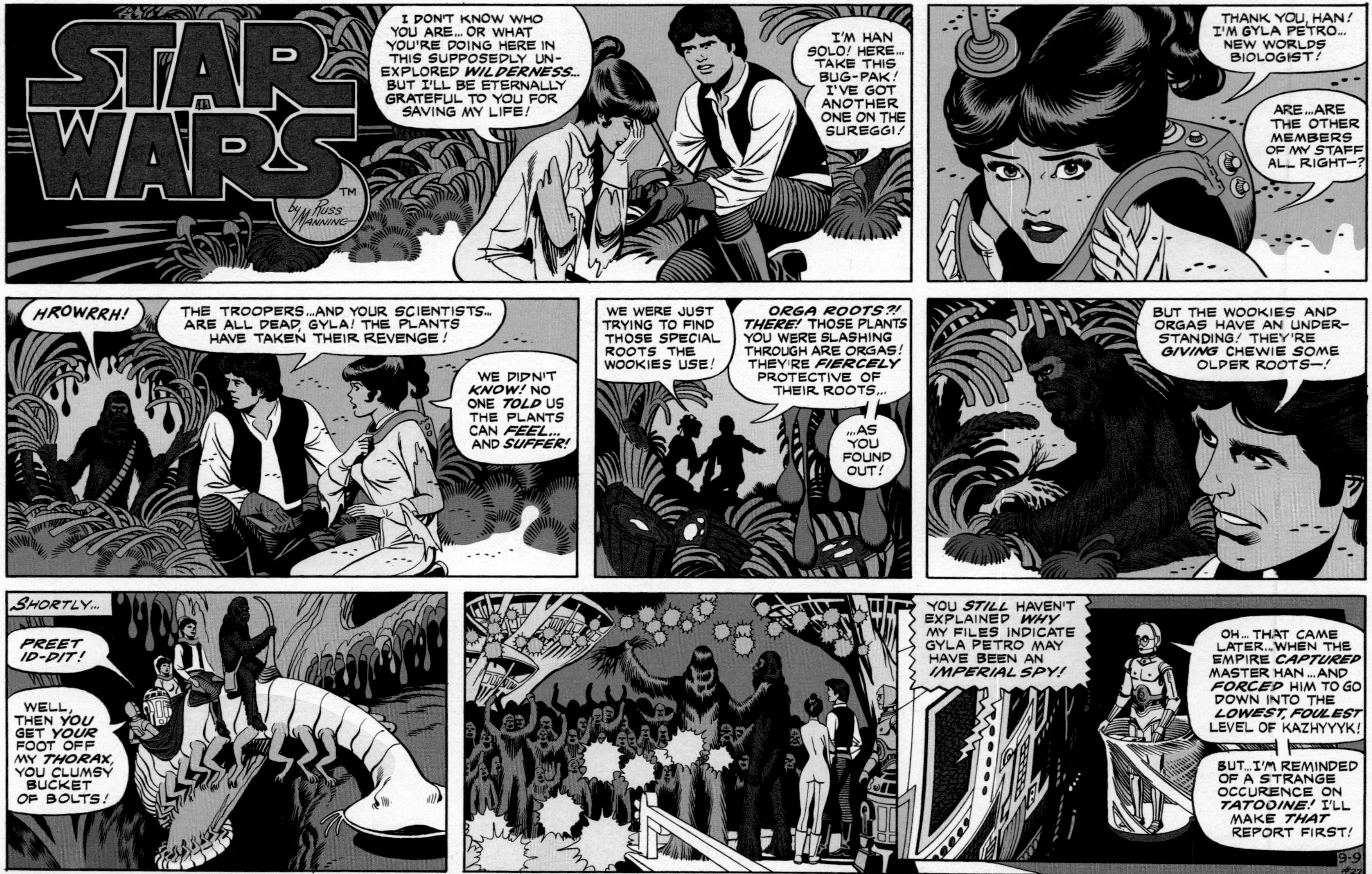
STAR WARS™
by Russ Manning
I DON'T KNOW WHO YOU ARE... OR WHAT YOU'RE DOING HERE IN THIS SUPPOSEDLY UN-EXPLORED WILDERNESS... BUT I'LL BE ETERNALLY GRATEFUL TO YOU FOR SAVING MY LIFE!
I'M HAN SOLO! HERE... TAKE THIS BUG-PAK! I'VE GOT ANOTHER ONE ON THE SUREGGI!
THANK YOU, HAN! I'M GYLA PETRO... NEW WORLDS BIOLOGIST!
ARE...ARE THE OTHER MEMBERS OF MY STAFF ALL RIGHT—?
HROWRRH!
THE TROOPERS...AND YOUR SCIENTISTS... ARE ALL DEAD, GYLA! THE PLANTS HAVE TAKEN THEIR REVENGE!
WE DIDN'T KNOW! NO ONE TOLD US THE PLANTS CAN FEEL... AND SUFFER!
WE WERE JUST TRYING TO FIND THOSE SPECIAL ROOTS THE WOOKIES USE!
ORGA ROOTS?! THERE! THOSE PLANTS YOU WERE SLASHING THROUGH ARE ORGAS! THEY'RE FIERCELY PROTECTIVE OF THEIR ROOTS...
...AS YOU FOUND OUT!
BUT THE WOOKIES AND ORGAS HAVE AN UNDER-STANDING! THEY'RE GIVING CHEWIE SOME OLDER ROOTS—!
SHORTLY...
PREET ID-DIT!
WELL, THEN YOU GET YOUR FOOT OFF MY THORAX, YOU CLUMSY BUCKET OF BOLTS!
YOU STILL HAVEN'T EXPLAINED WHY MY FILES INDICATE GYLA PETRO MAY HAVE BEEN AN IMPERIAL SPY!
OH... THAT CAME LATER...WHEN THE EMPIRE CAPTURED MASTER HAN...AND FORCED HIM TO GO DOWN INTO THE LOWEST, FOULEST LEVEL OF KAZHYYYK!
BUT...I'M REMINDED OF A STRANGE OCCURENCE ON TATOOINE! I'LL MAKE THAT REPORT FIRST!
9-9
#27

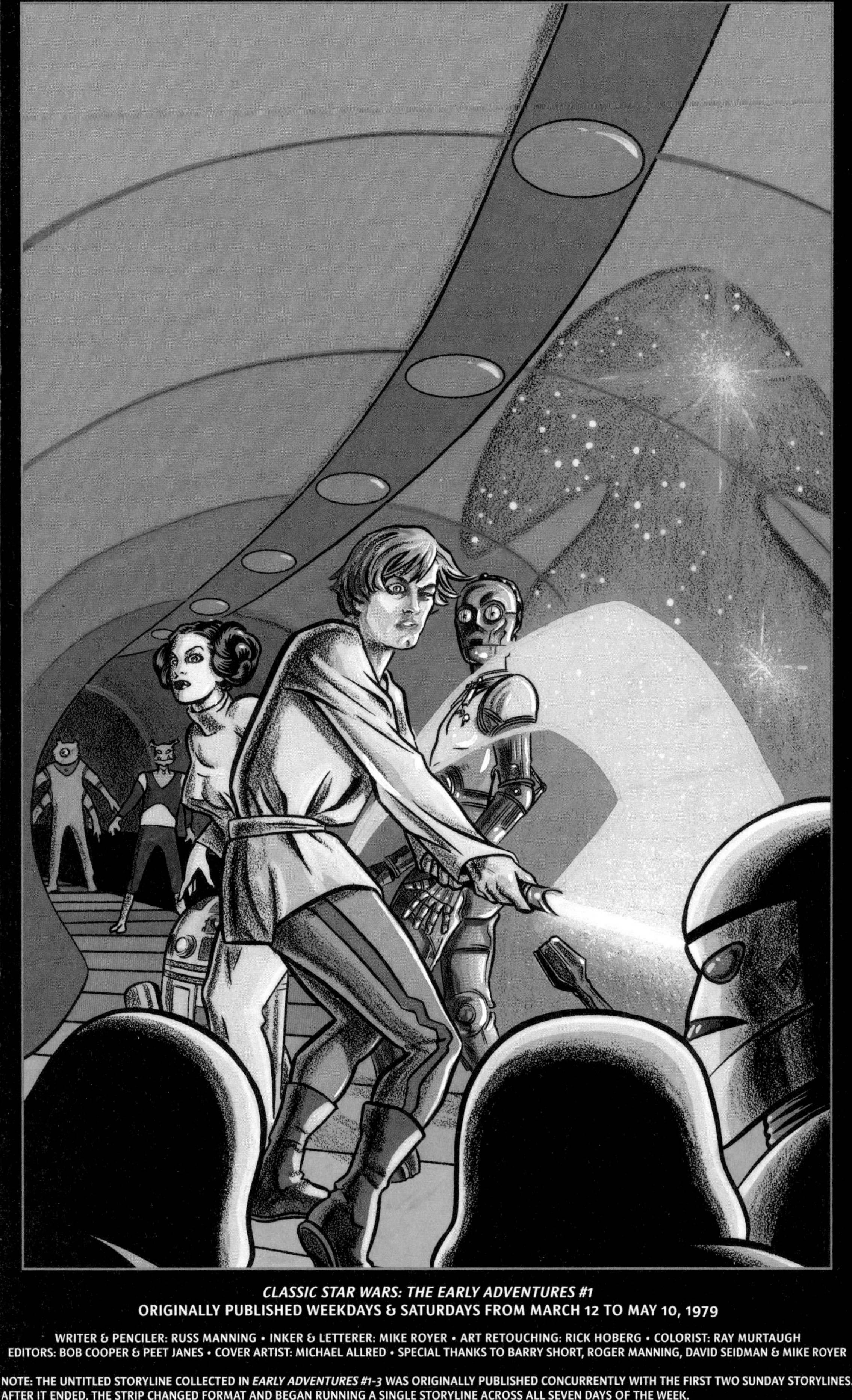

CLASSIC STAR WARS: THE EARLY ADVENTURES #1

ORIGINALLY PUBLISHED WEEKDAYS & SATURDAYS FROM MARCH 12 TO MAY 10, 1979

WRITER & PENCILER: RUSS MANNING • INKER & LETTERER: MIKE ROYER • ART RETOUCHING: RICK HOBERG • COLORIST: RAY MURTAUGH
EDITORS: BOB COOPER & PEET JANES • COVER ARTIST: MICHAEL ALLRED • SPECIAL THANKS TO BARRY SHORT, ROGER MANNING, DAVID SEIDMAN & MIKE ROYER

NOTE: THE UNTITLED STORYLINE COLLECTED IN *EARLY ADVENTURES #1–3* WAS ORIGINALLY PUBLISHED CONCURRENTLY WITH THE FIRST TWO SUNDAY STORYLINES. AFTER IT ENDED, THE STRIP CHANGED FORMAT AND BEGAN RUNNING A SINGLE STORYLINE ACROSS ALL SEVEN DAYS OF THE WEEK.

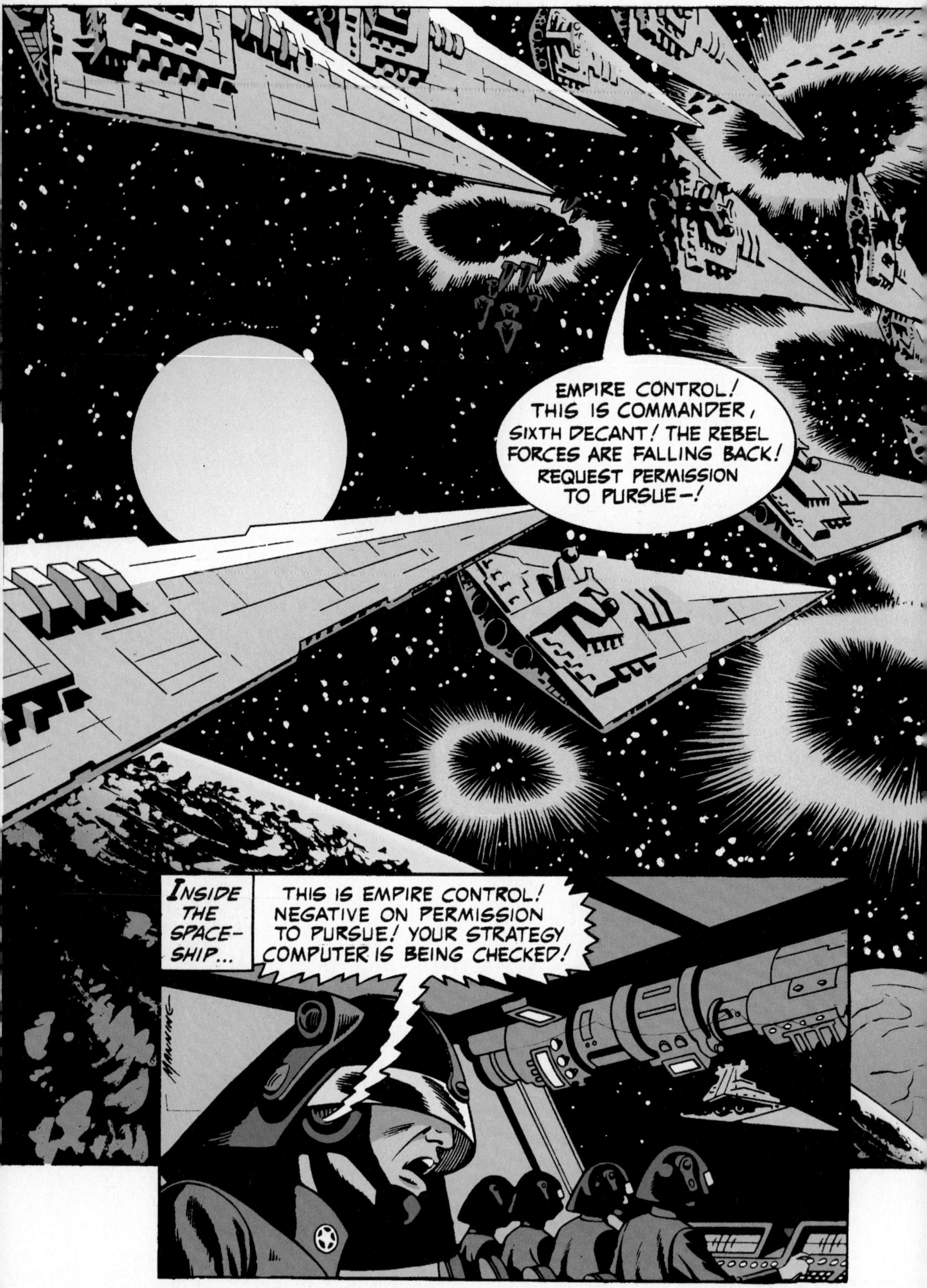
EMPIRE CONTROL! THIS IS COMMANDER, SIXTH DECANT! THE REBEL FORCES ARE FALLING BACK! REQUEST PERMISSION TO PURSUE—!
INSIDE THE SPACE-SHIP...
THIS IS EMPIRE CONTROL! NEGATIVE ON PERMISSION TO PURSUE! YOUR STRATEGY COMPUTER IS BEING CHECKED!
MANNING

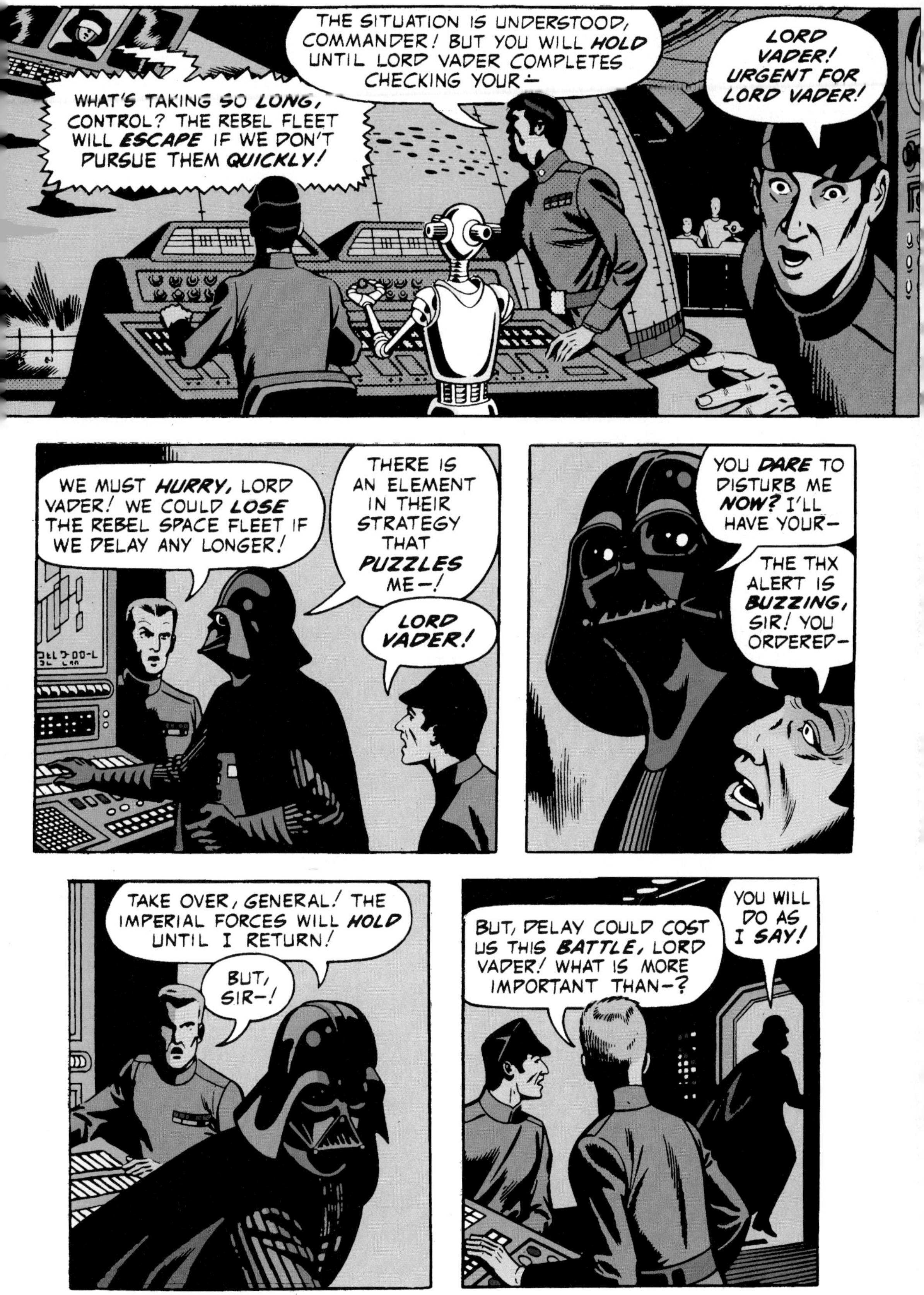
WHAT'S TAKING SO LONG, CONTROL? THE REBEL FLEET WILL ESCAPE IF WE DON'T PURSUE THEM QUICKLY!
THE SITUATION IS UNDERSTOOD, COMMANDER! BUT YOU WILL HOLD UNTIL LORD VADER COMPLETES CHECKING YOUR--
LORD VADER! URGENT FOR LORD VADER!
WE MUST HURRY, LORD VADER! WE COULD LOSE THE REBEL SPACE FLEET IF WE DELAY ANY LONGER!
THERE IS AN ELEMENT IN THEIR STRATEGY THAT PUZZLES ME--!
LORD VADER!
YOU DARE TO DISTURB ME NOW? I'LL HAVE YOUR--
THE THX ALERT IS BUZZING, SIR! YOU ORDERED--
TAKE OVER, GENERAL! THE IMPERIAL FORCES WILL HOLD UNTIL I RETURN!
BUT, SIR--!
BUT, DELAY COULD COST US THIS BATTLE, LORD VADER! WHAT IS MORE IMPORTANT THAN--?
YOU WILL DO AS I SAY!

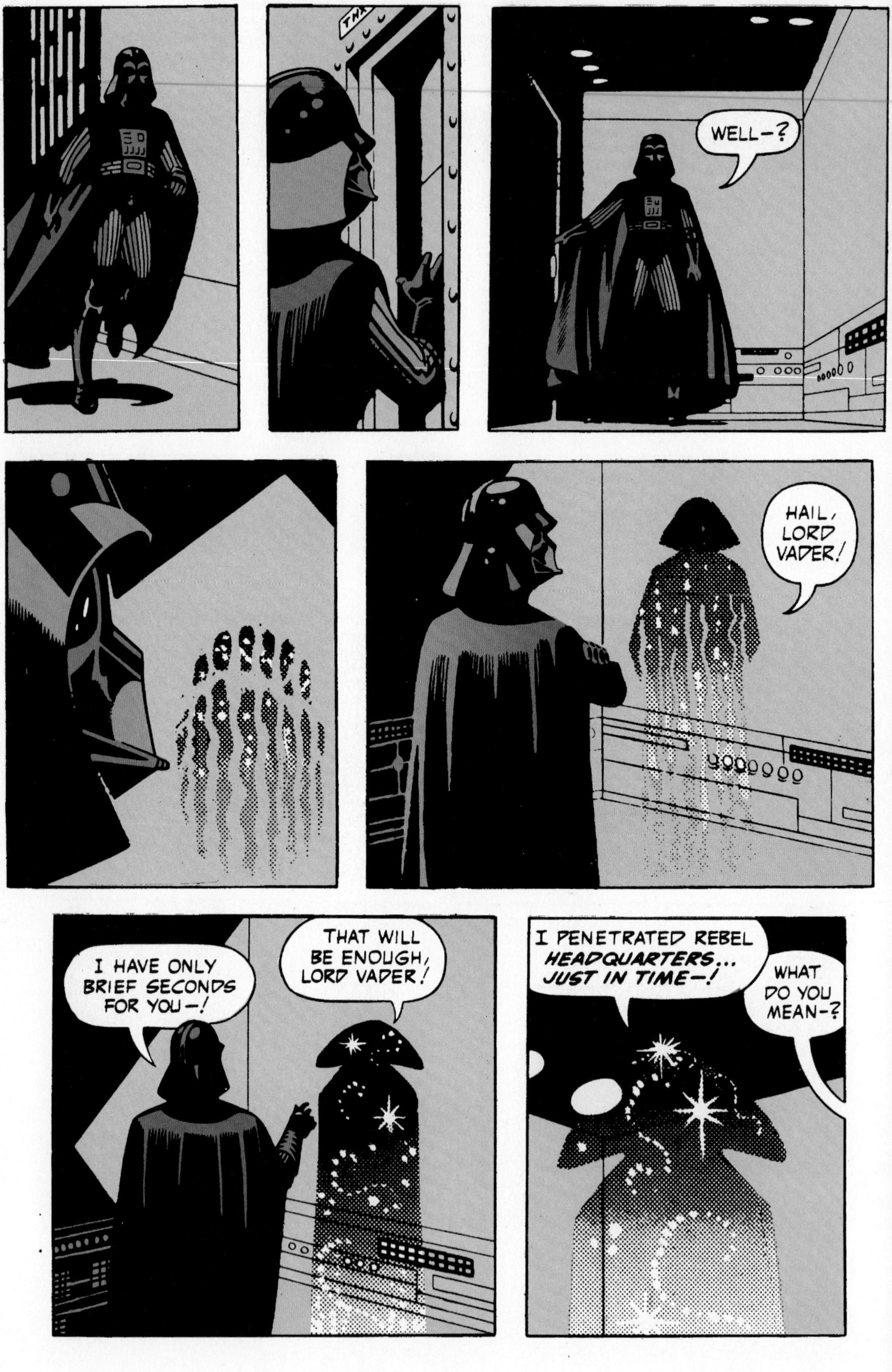
WELL—?
HAIL, LORD VADER!
I HAVE ONLY BRIEF SECONDS FOR YOU—!
THAT WILL BE ENOUGH, LORD VADER!
I PENETRATED REBEL HEADQUARTERS... JUST IN TIME—!
WHAT DO YOU MEAN—?

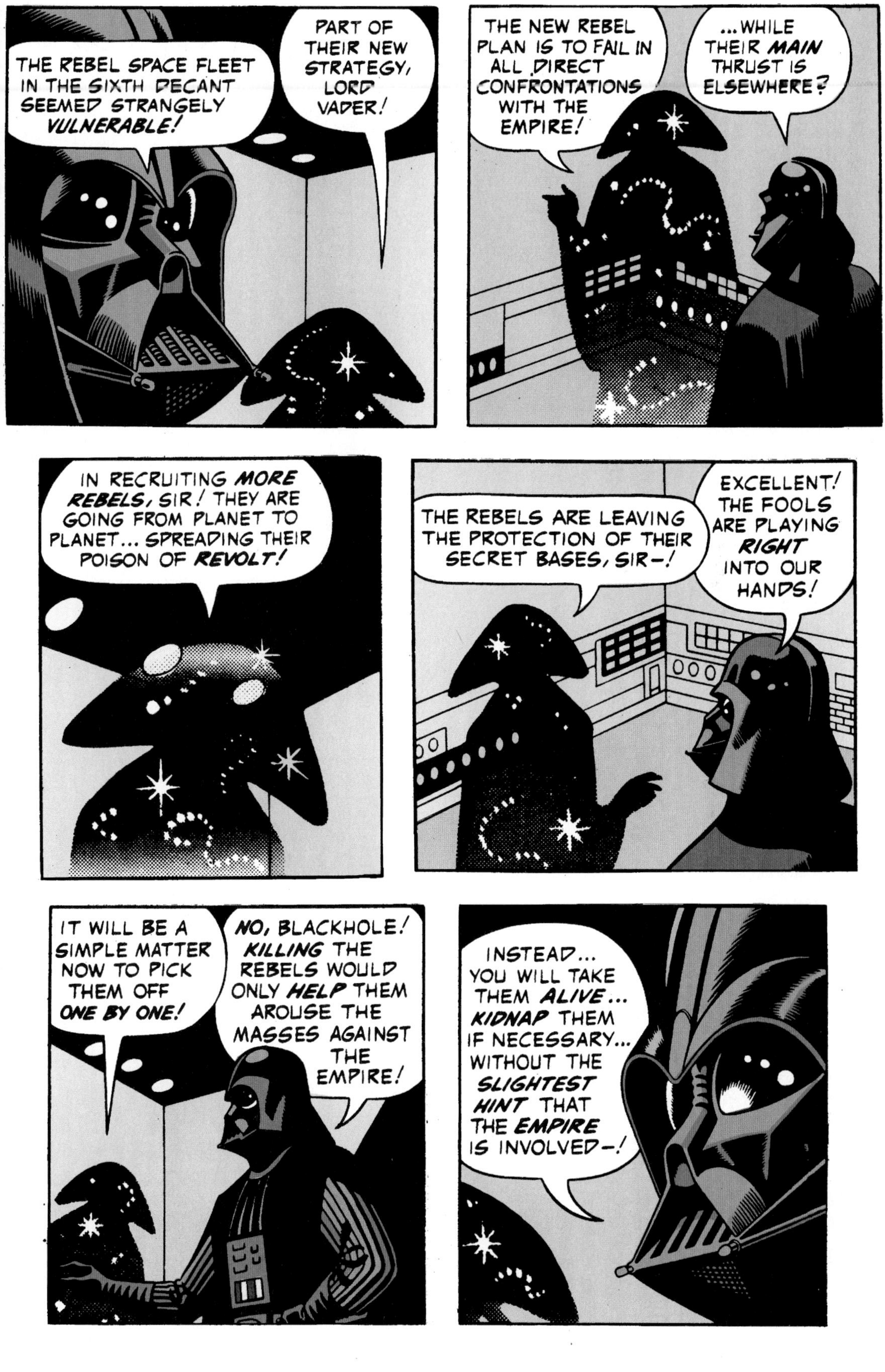
THE REBEL SPACE FLEET IN THE SIXTH DECANT SEEMED STRANGELY VULNERABLE!
PART OF THEIR NEW STRATEGY, LORD VADER!
THE NEW REBEL PLAN IS TO FAIL IN ALL DIRECT CONFRONTATIONS WITH THE EMPIRE!
...WHILE THEIR MAIN THRUST IS ELSEWHERE?
IN RECRUITING MORE REBELS, SIR! THEY ARE GOING FROM PLANET TO PLANET... SPREADING THEIR POISON OF REVOLT!
THE REBELS ARE LEAVING THE PROTECTION OF THEIR SECRET BASES, SIR-!
EXCELLENT! THE FOOLS ARE PLAYING RIGHT INTO OUR HANDS!
IT WILL BE A SIMPLE MATTER NOW TO PICK THEM OFF ONE BY ONE!
NO, BLACKHOLE! KILLING THE REBELS WOULD ONLY HELP THEM AROUSE THE MASSES AGAINST THE EMPIRE!
INSTEAD... YOU WILL TAKE THEM ALIVE... KIDNAP THEM IF NECESSARY... WITHOUT THE SLIGHTEST HINT THAT THE EMPIRE IS INVOLVED-!

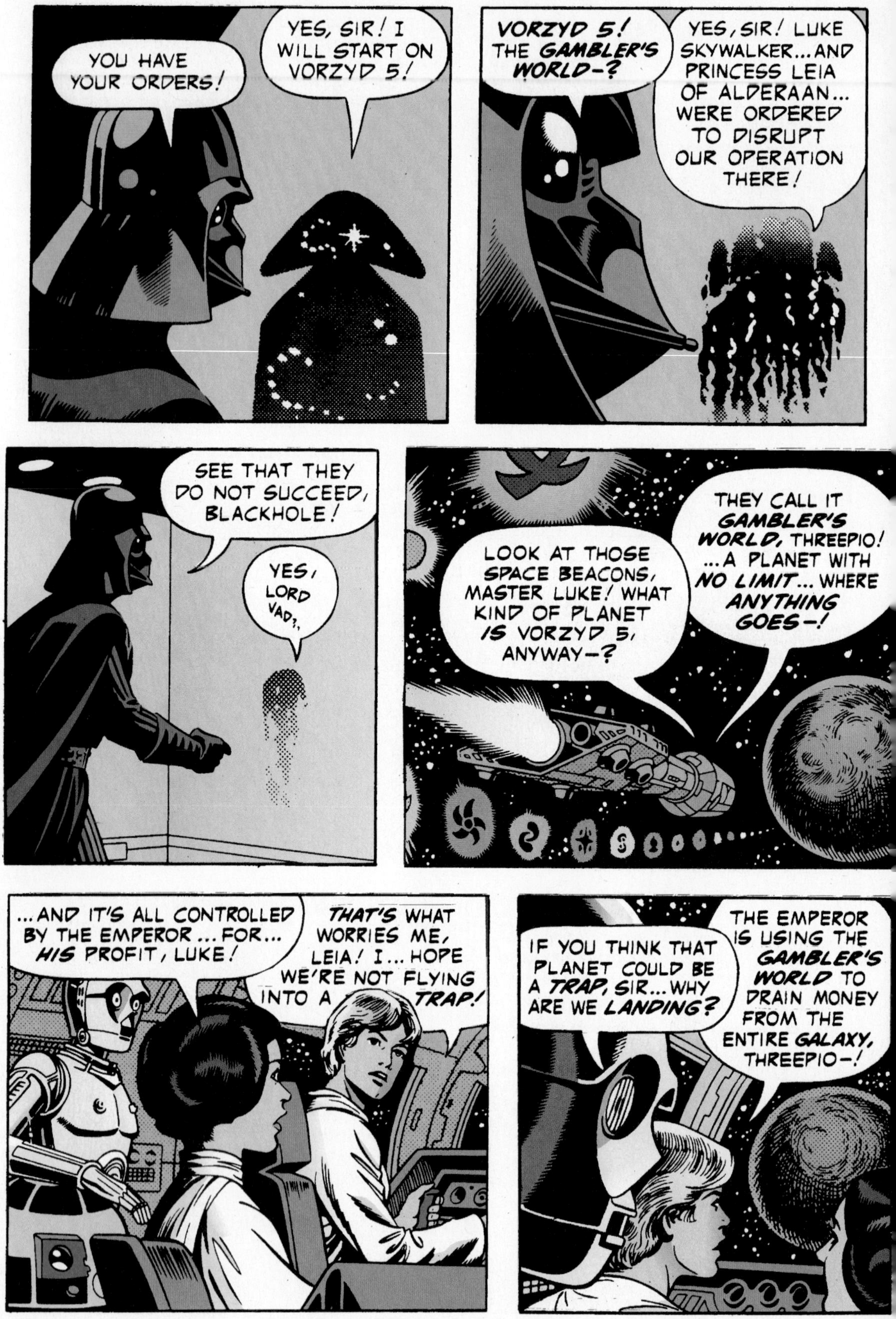
YOU HAVE YOUR ORDERS!
YES, SIR! I WILL START ON VORZYD 5!
VORZYD 5! THE GAMBLER'S WORLD-?
YES, SIR! LUKE SKYWALKER...AND PRINCESS LEIA OF ALDERAAN... WERE ORDERED TO DISRUPT OUR OPERATION THERE!
SEE THAT THEY DO NOT SUCCEED, BLACKHOLE!
YES, LORD VAD..
LOOK AT THOSE SPACE BEACONS, MASTER LUKE! WHAT KIND OF PLANET IS VORZYD 5, ANYWAY-?
THEY CALL IT GAMBLER'S WORLD, THREEPIO! ...A PLANET WITH NO LIMIT... WHERE ANYTHING GOES-!
...AND IT'S ALL CONTROLLED BY THE EMPEROR... FOR... HIS PROFIT, LUKE!
THAT'S WHAT WORRIES ME, LEIA! I... HOPE WE'RE NOT FLYING INTO A TRAP!
IF YOU THINK THAT PLANET COULD BE A TRAP, SIR...WHY ARE WE LANDING?
THE EMPEROR IS USING THE GAMBLER'S WORLD TO DRAIN MONEY FROM THE ENTIRE GALAXY, THREEPIO-!

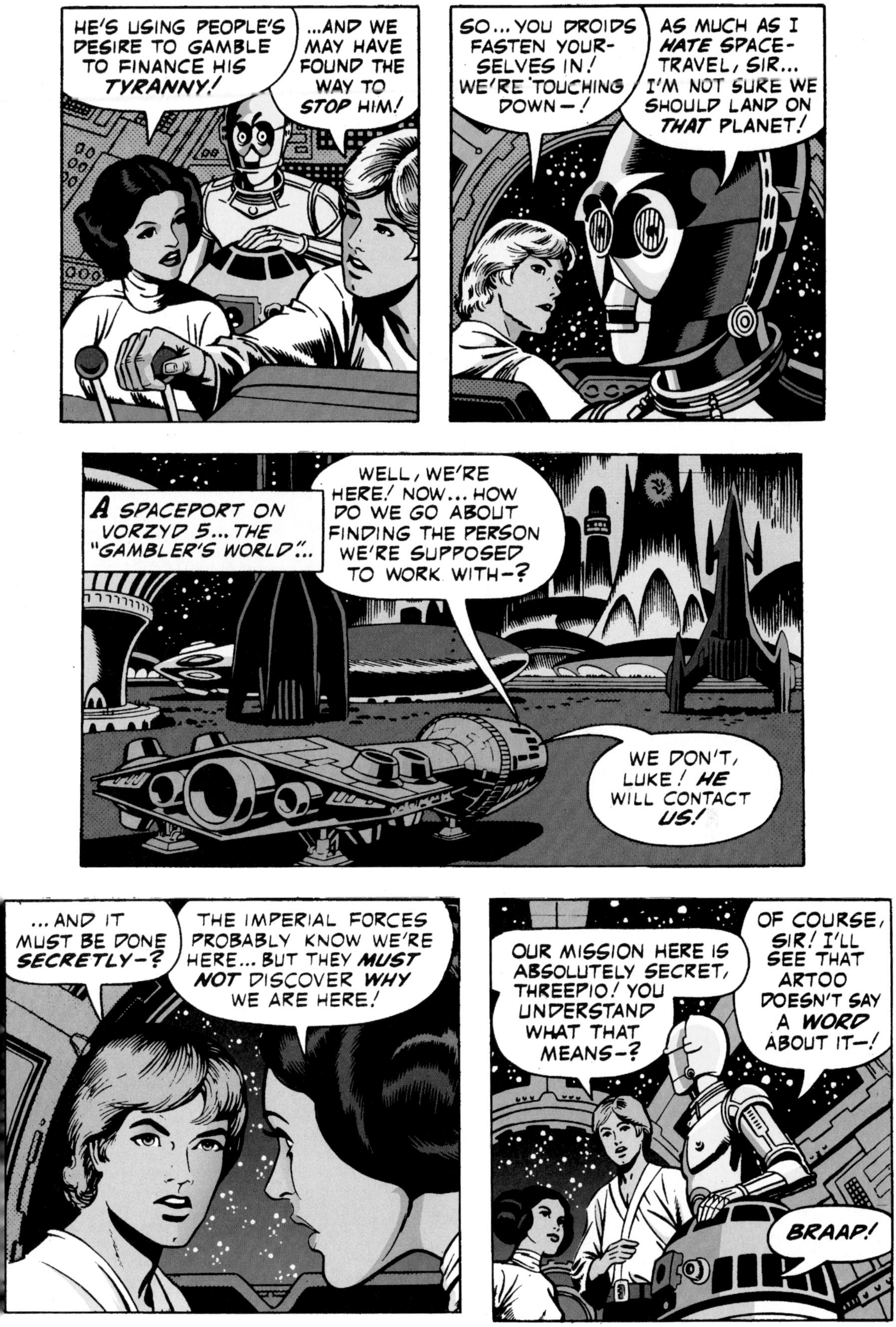
HE'S USING PEOPLE'S DESIRE TO GAMBLE TO FINANCE HIS TYRANNY!
...AND WE MAY HAVE FOUND THE WAY TO STOP HIM!
SO... YOU DROIDS FASTEN YOUR-SELVES IN! WE'RE TOUCHING DOWN—!
AS MUCH AS I HATE SPACE-TRAVEL, SIR... I'M NOT SURE WE SHOULD LAND ON THAT PLANET!
A SPACEPORT ON VORZYD 5... THE "GAMBLER'S WORLD"...
WELL, WE'RE HERE! NOW... HOW DO WE GO ABOUT FINDING THE PERSON WE'RE SUPPOSED TO WORK WITH—?
WE DON'T, LUKE! HE WILL CONTACT US!
...AND IT MUST BE DONE SECRETLY—?
THE IMPERIAL FORCES PROBABLY KNOW WE'RE HERE... BUT THEY MUST NOT DISCOVER WHY WE ARE HERE!
OUR MISSION HERE IS ABSOLUTELY SECRET, THREEPIO! YOU UNDERSTAND WHAT THAT MEANS—?
OF COURSE, SIR! I'LL SEE THAT ARTOO DOESN'T SAY A WORD ABOUT IT—!
BRAAP!

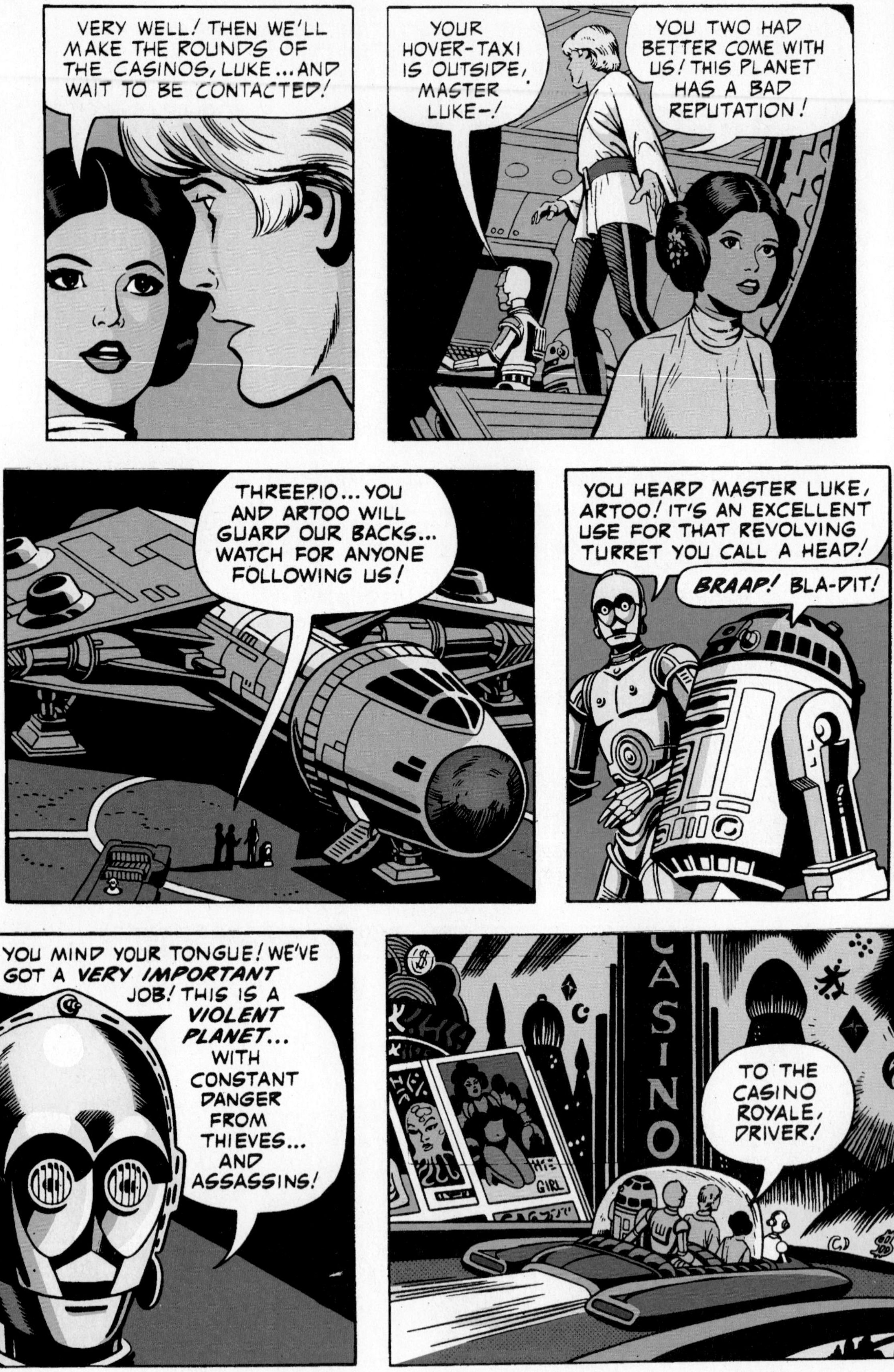
VERY WELL! THEN WE'LL MAKE THE ROUNDS OF THE CASINOS, LUKE...AND WAIT TO BE CONTACTED!
YOUR HOVER-TAXI IS OUTSIDE, MASTER LUKE-!
YOU TWO HAD BETTER COME WITH US! THIS PLANET HAS A BAD REPUTATION!
THREEPIO...YOU AND ARTOO WILL GUARD OUR BACKS... WATCH FOR ANYONE FOLLOWING US!
YOU HEARD MASTER LUKE, ARTOO! IT'S AN EXCELLENT USE FOR THAT REVOLVING TURRET YOU CALL A HEAD!
BRAAP! BLA-DIT!
YOU MIND YOUR TONGUE! WE'VE GOT A VERY IMPORTANT JOB! THIS IS A VIOLENT PLANET... WITH CONSTANT DANGER FROM THIEVES... AND ASSASSINS!
CASINO
GIRL
TO THE CASINO ROYALE, DRIVER!

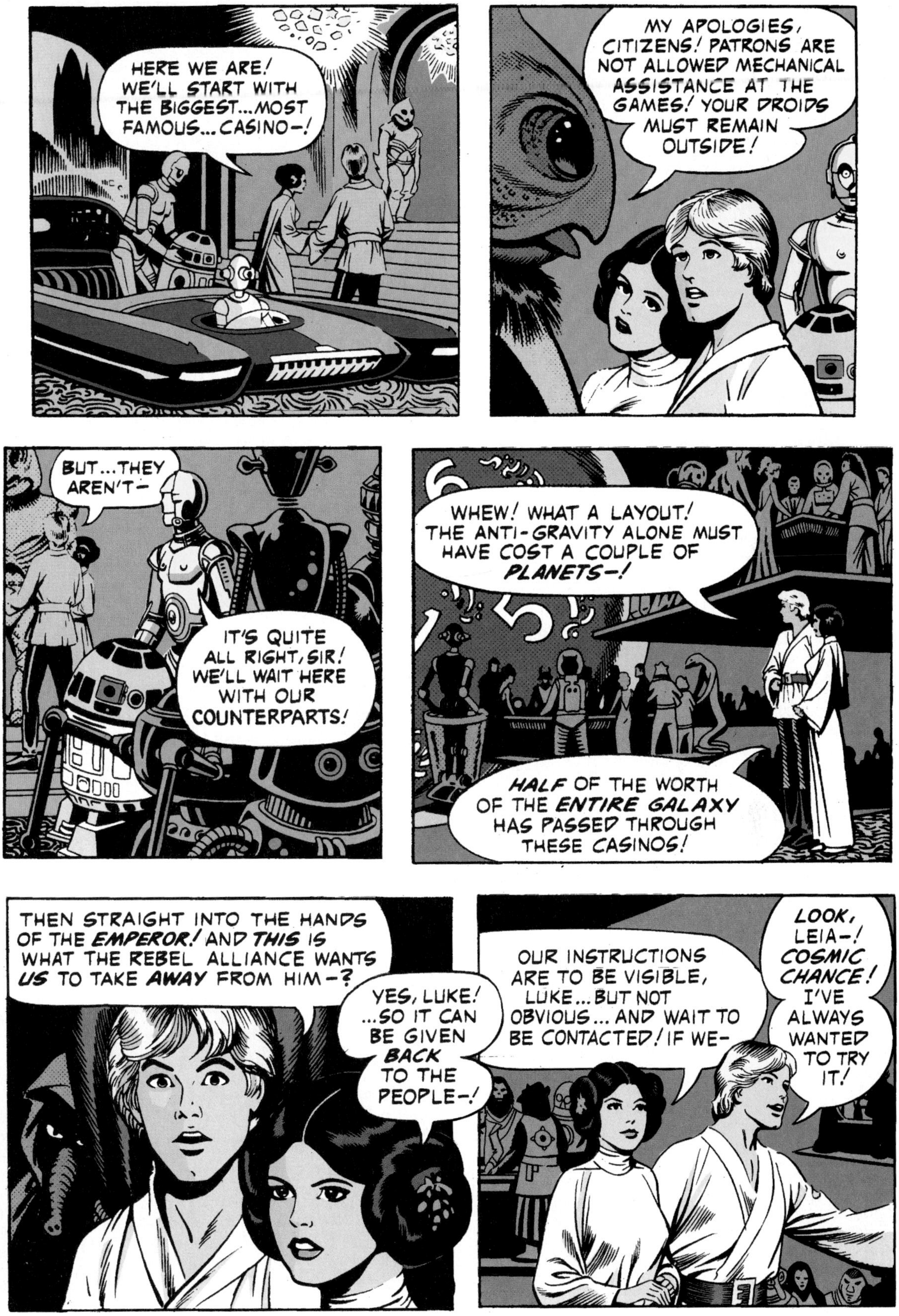
HERE WE ARE! WE'LL START WITH THE BIGGEST...MOST FAMOUS... CASINO-!
MY APOLOGIES, CITIZENS! PATRONS ARE NOT ALLOWED MECHANICAL ASSISTANCE AT THE GAMES! YOUR DROIDS MUST REMAIN OUTSIDE!
BUT...THEY AREN'T-
IT'S QUITE ALL RIGHT, SIR! WE'LL WAIT HERE WITH OUR COUNTERPARTS!
WHEW! WHAT A LAYOUT! THE ANTI-GRAVITY ALONE MUST HAVE COST A COUPLE OF PLANETS-!
HALF OF THE WORTH OF THE ENTIRE GALAXY HAS PASSED THROUGH THESE CASINOS!
THEN STRAIGHT INTO THE HANDS OF THE EMPEROR! AND THIS IS WHAT THE REBEL ALLIANCE WANTS US TO TAKE AWAY FROM HIM-?
YES, LUKE! ...SO IT CAN BE GIVEN BACK TO THE PEOPLE-!
OUR INSTRUCTIONS ARE TO BE VISIBLE, LUKE...BUT NOT OBVIOUS... AND WAIT TO BE CONTACTED! IF WE-
LOOK, LEIA-! COSMIC CHANCE! I'VE ALWAYS WANTED TO TRY IT!

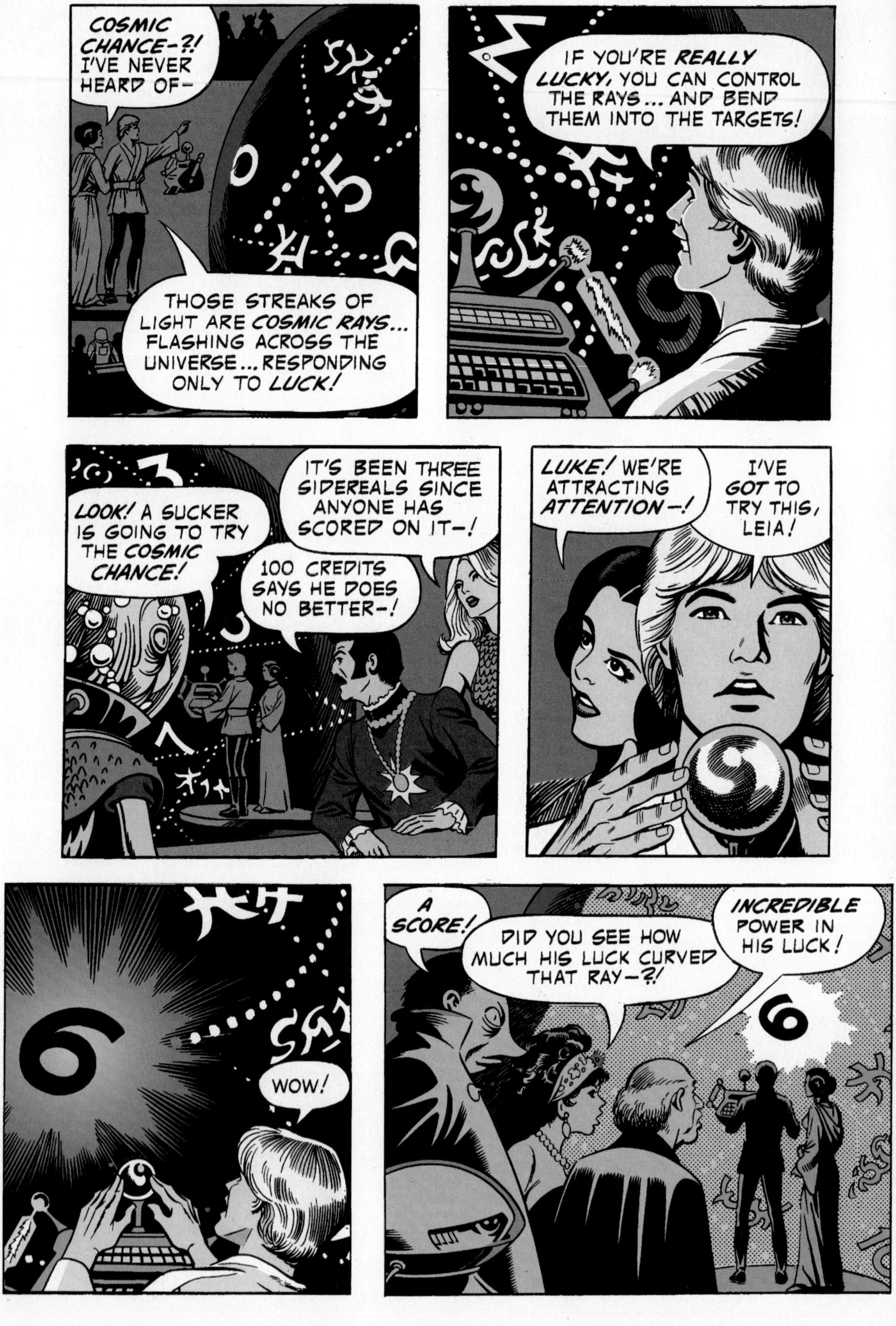

COSMIC CHANCE-?! I'VE NEVER HEARD OF-
THOSE STREAKS OF LIGHT ARE COSMIC RAYS... FLASHING ACROSS THE UNIVERSE... RESPONDING ONLY TO LUCK!
IF YOU'RE REALLY LUCKY, YOU CAN CONTROL THE RAYS... AND BEND THEM INTO THE TARGETS!
LOOK! A SUCKER IS GOING TO TRY THE COSMIC CHANCE!
IT'S BEEN THREE SIDEREALS SINCE ANYONE HAS SCORED ON IT-!
100 CREDITS SAYS HE DOES NO BETTER-!
LUKE! WE'RE ATTRACTING ATTENTION-!
I'VE GOT TO TRY THIS, LEIA!
WOW!
A SCORE!
DID YOU SEE HOW MUCH HIS LUCK CURVED THAT RAY-?!
INCREDIBLE POWER IN HIS LUCK!

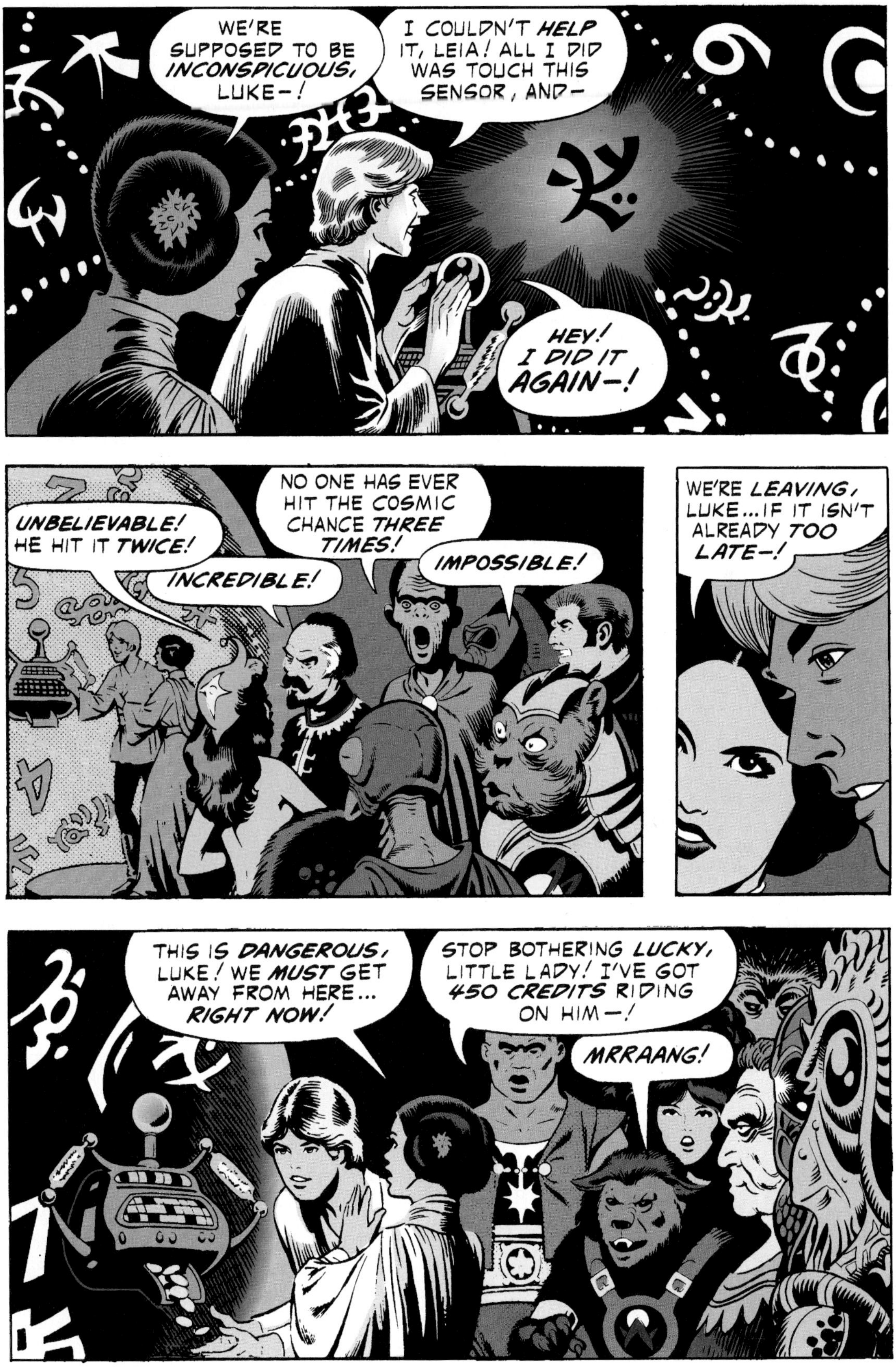
WE'RE SUPPOSED TO BE INCONSPICUOUS, LUKE-!
I COULDN'T HELP IT, LEIA! ALL I DID WAS TOUCH THIS SENSOR, AND-
HEY! I DID IT AGAIN-!
UNBELIEVABLE! HE HIT IT TWICE!
NO ONE HAS EVER HIT THE COSMIC CHANCE THREE TIMES!
INCREDIBLE!
IMPOSSIBLE!
WE'RE LEAVING, LUKE...IF IT ISN'T ALREADY TOO LATE-!
THIS IS DANGEROUS, LUKE! WE MUST GET AWAY FROM HERE... RIGHT NOW!
STOP BOTHERING LUCKY, LITTLE LADY! I'VE GOT 450 CREDITS RIDING ON HIM-!
MRRAANG!

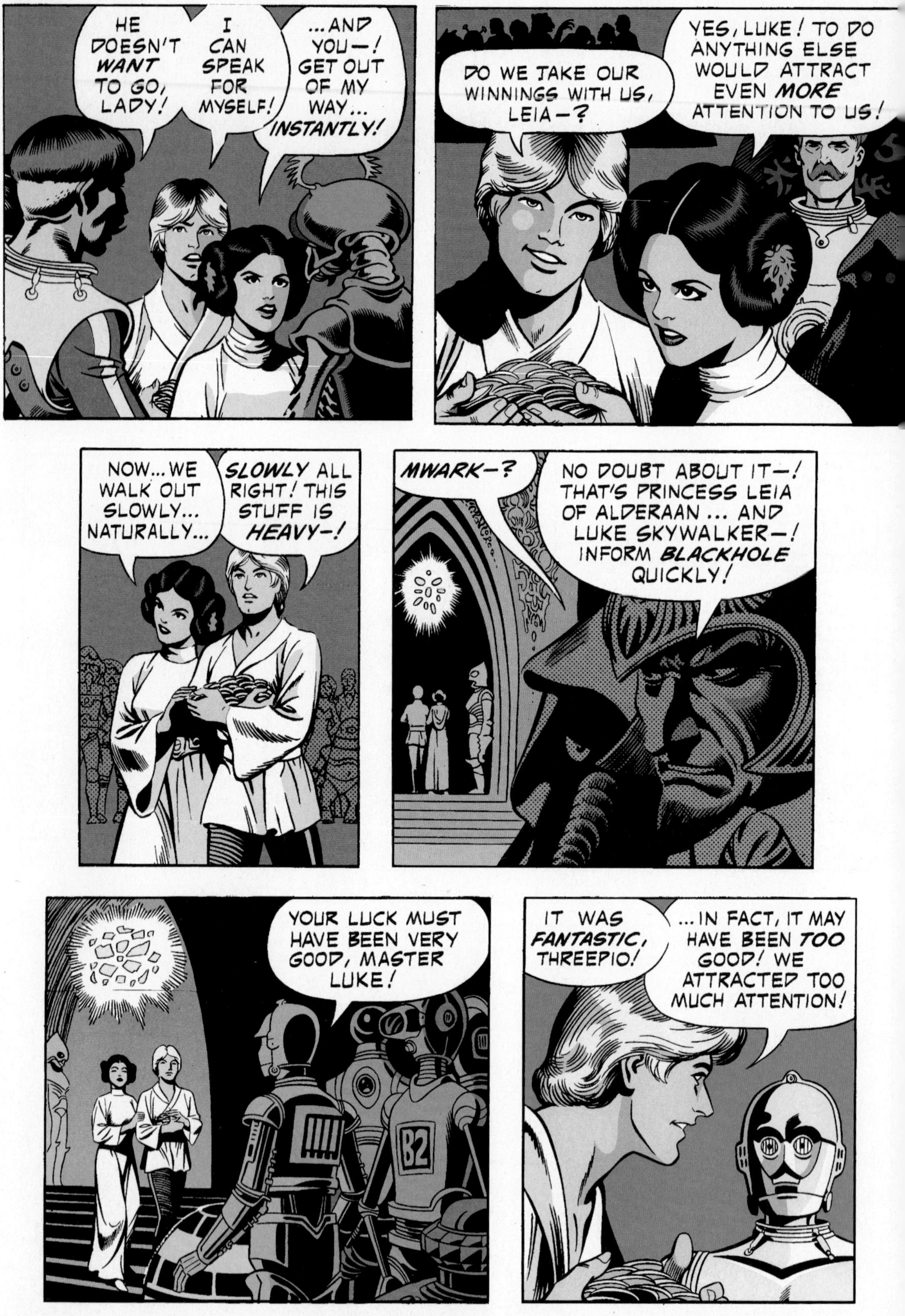
HE DOESN'T WANT TO GO, LADY!
I CAN SPEAK FOR MYSELF!
...AND YOU—! GET OUT OF MY WAY... INSTANTLY!
DO WE TAKE OUR WINNINGS WITH US, LEIA—?
YES, LUKE! TO DO ANYTHING ELSE WOULD ATTRACT EVEN MORE ATTENTION TO US!
NOW... WE WALK OUT SLOWLY... NATURALLY...
SLOWLY ALL RIGHT! THIS STUFF IS HEAVY—!
MWARK—?
NO DOUBT ABOUT IT—! THAT'S PRINCESS LEIA OF ALDERAAN ... AND LUKE SKYWALKER—! INFORM BLACKHOLE QUICKLY!
YOUR LUCK MUST HAVE BEEN VERY GOOD, MASTER LUKE!
IT WAS FANTASTIC, THREEPIO!
...IN FACT, IT MAY HAVE BEEN TOO GOOD! WE ATTRACTED TOO MUCH ATTENTION!

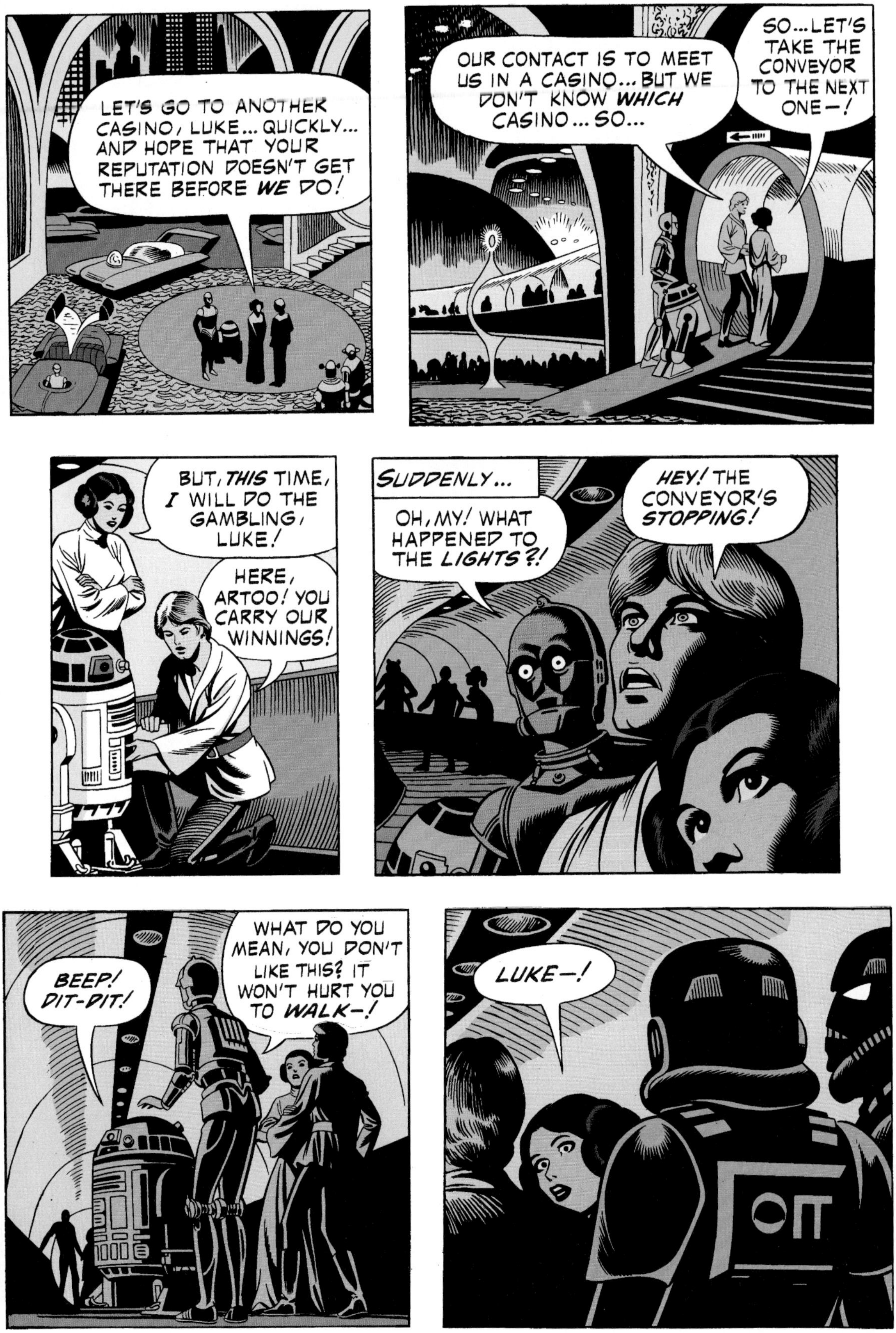
LET'S GO TO ANOTHER CASINO, LUKE... QUICKLY... AND HOPE THAT YOUR REPUTATION DOESN'T GET THERE BEFORE *WE* DO!
OUR CONTACT IS TO MEET US IN A CASINO... BUT WE DON'T KNOW *WHICH* CASINO... SO...
SO... LET'S TAKE THE CONVEYOR TO THE NEXT ONE—!
BUT, *THIS* TIME, *I* WILL DO THE GAMBLING, LUKE!
HERE, ARTOO! YOU CARRY OUR WINNINGS!
SUDDENLY...
OH, MY! WHAT HAPPENED TO THE *LIGHTS*?!
HEY! THE CONVEYOR'S *STOPPING!*
BEEP! DIT-DIT!
WHAT DO YOU MEAN, YOU DON'T LIKE THIS? IT WON'T HURT YOU TO *WALK*—!
LUKE—!

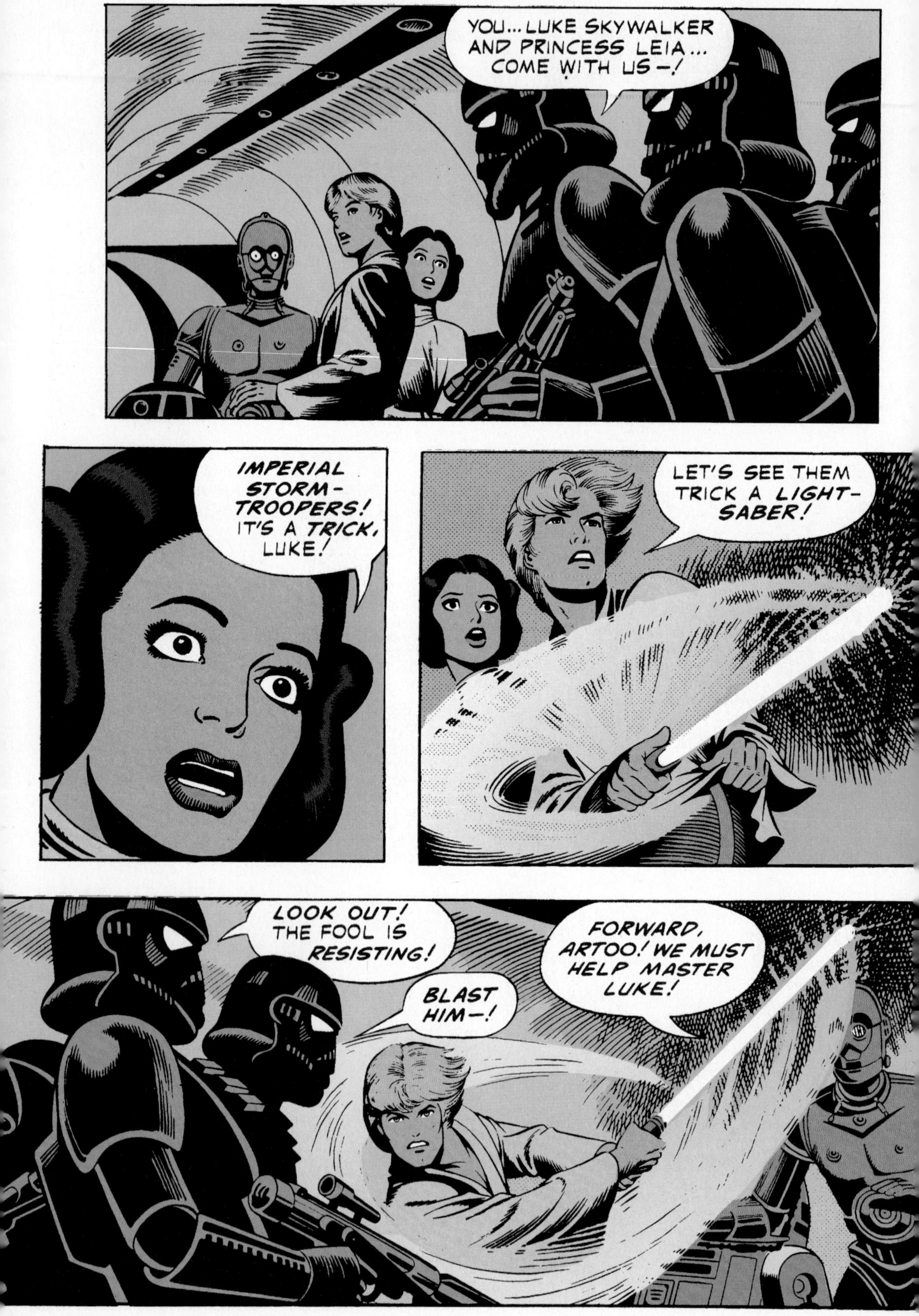
YOU...LUKE SKYWALKER AND PRINCESS LEIA... COME WITH US-!
IMPERIAL STORM-TROOPERS! IT'S A TRICK, LUKE!
LET'S SEE THEM TRICK A LIGHT-SABER!
LOOK OUT! THE FOOL IS RESISTING!
BLAST HIM-!
FORWARD, ARTOO! WE MUST HELP MASTER LUKE!

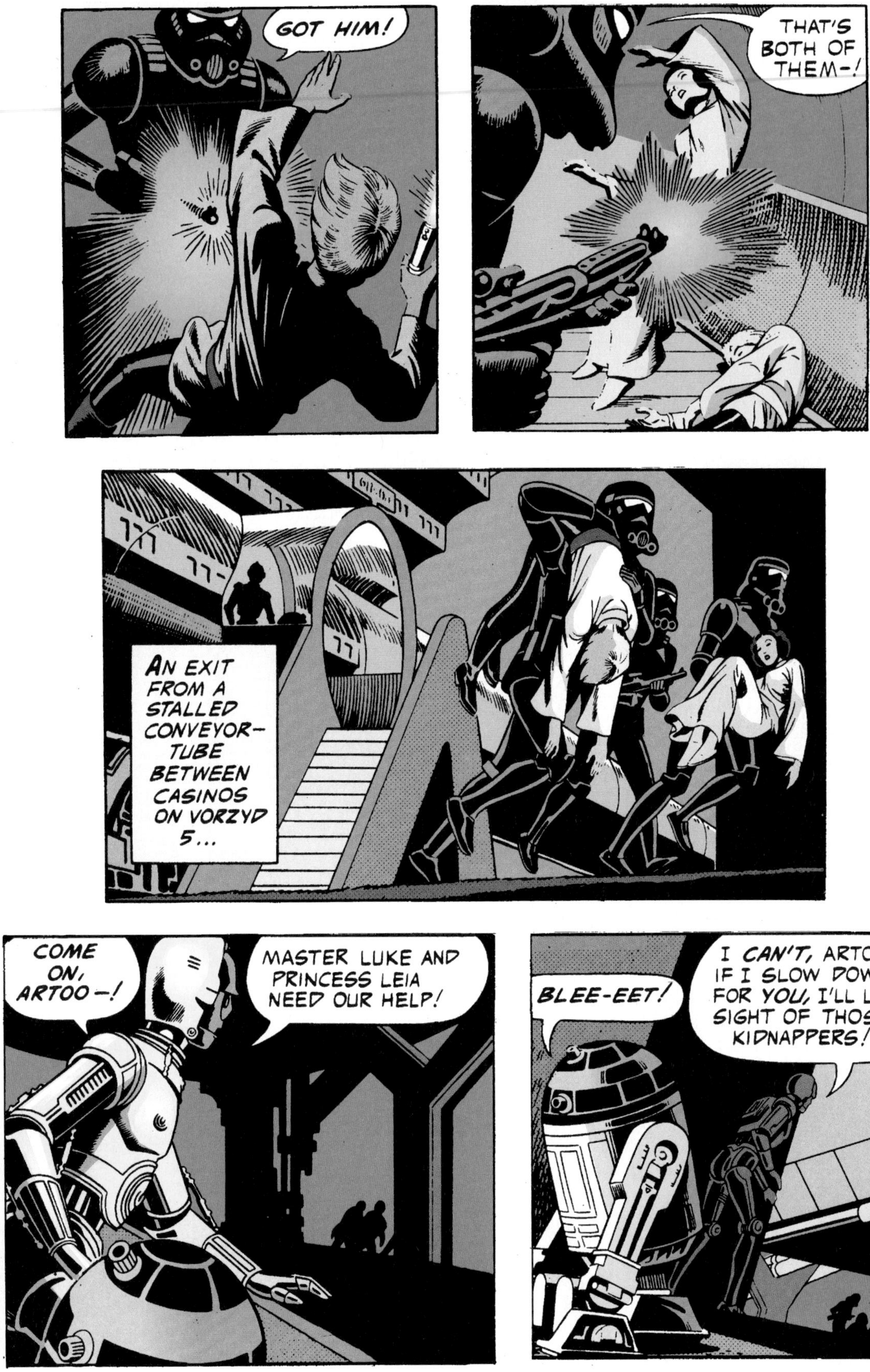
GOT HIM!
THAT'S BOTH OF THEM-!
AN EXIT FROM A STALLED CONVEYOR-TUBE BETWEEN CASINOS ON VORZYD 5...
COME ON, ARTOO-!
MASTER LUKE AND PRINCESS LEIA NEED OUR HELP!
BLEE-EET!
I CAN'T, ARTOO! IF I SLOW DOWN FOR YOU, I'LL LOSE SIGHT OF THOSE KIDNAPPERS!

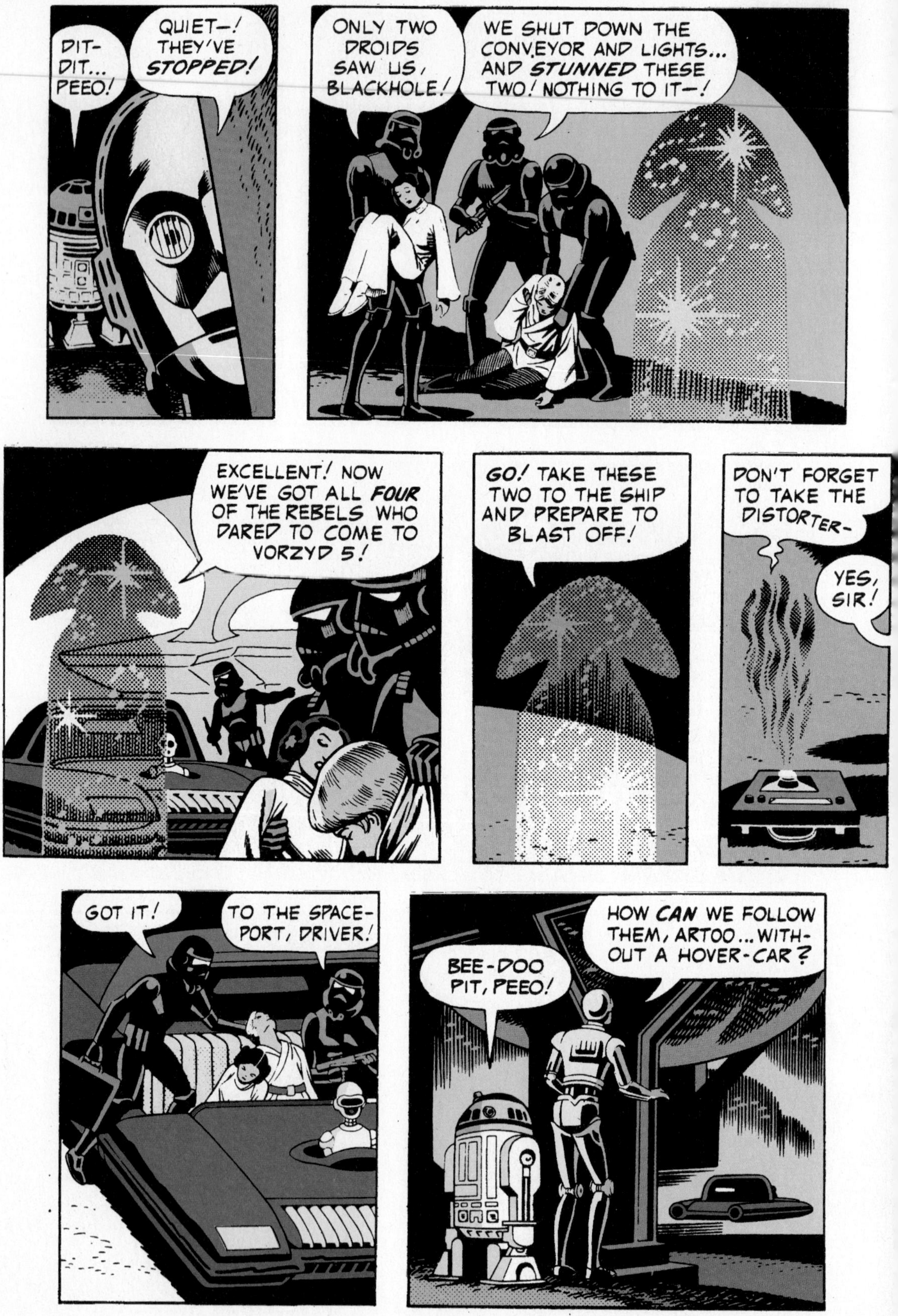
DIT-DIT... PEEO!
QUIET—! THEY'VE STOPPED!
ONLY TWO DROIDS SAW US, BLACKHOLE!
WE SHUT DOWN THE CONVEYOR AND LIGHTS... AND STUNNED THESE TWO! NOTHING TO IT—!
EXCELLENT! NOW WE'VE GOT ALL FOUR OF THE REBELS WHO DARED TO COME TO VORZYD 5!
GO! TAKE THESE TWO TO THE SHIP AND PREPARE TO BLAST OFF!
DON'T FORGET TO TAKE THE DISTORTER-
YES, SIR!
GOT IT!
TO THE SPACE-PORT, DRIVER!
HOW CAN WE FOLLOW THEM, ARTOO... WITH-OUT A HOVER-CAR?
BEE-DOO PIT, PEEO!

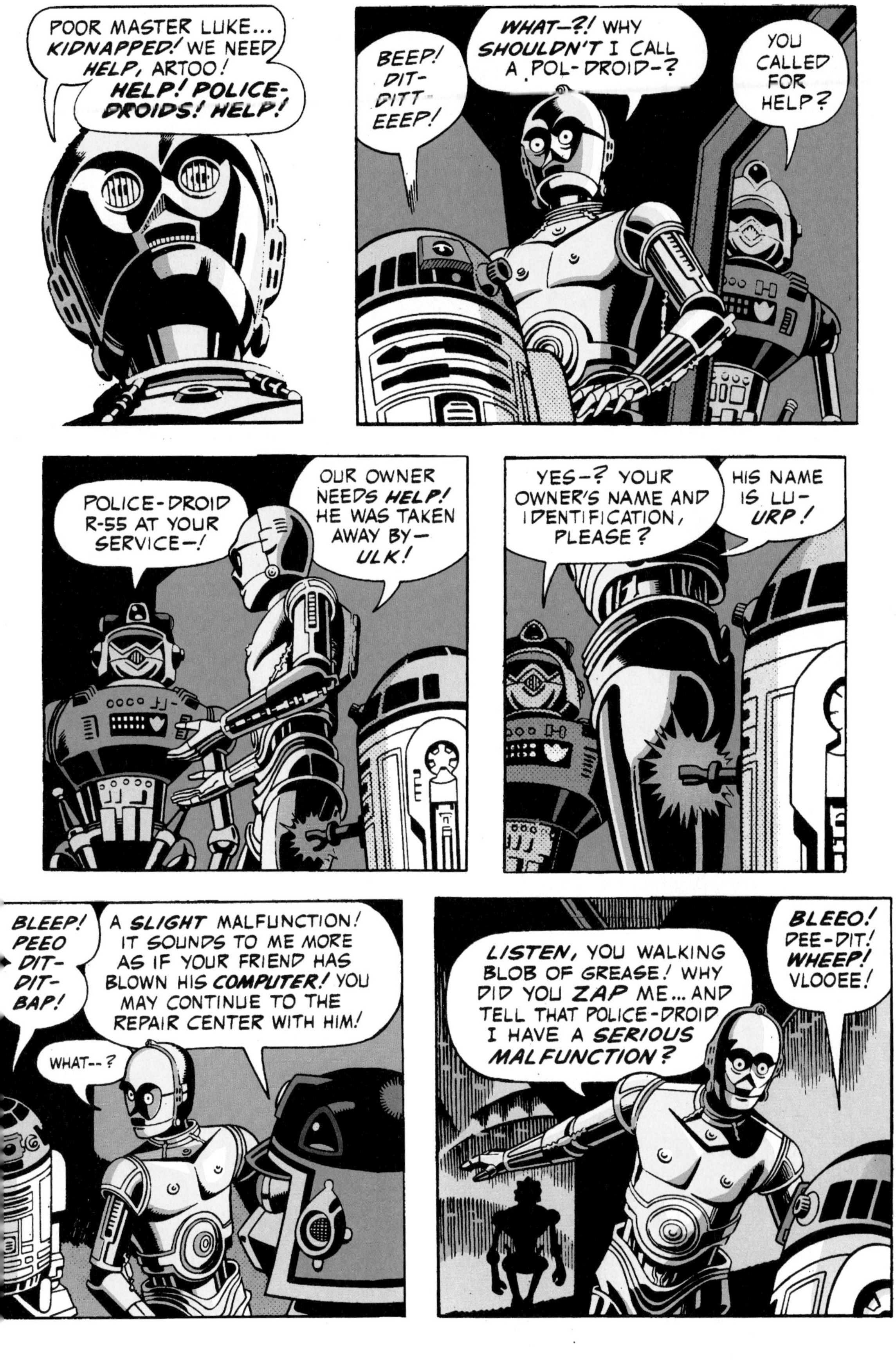
POOR MASTER LUKE... KIDNAPPED! WE NEED HELP, ARTOO!
HELP! POLICE-DROIDS! HELP!
BEEP! DIT-DITT EEEP!
WHAT--?! WHY SHOULDN'T I CALL A POL-DROID--?
YOU CALLED FOR HELP?
POLICE-DROID R-55 AT YOUR SERVICE--!
OUR OWNER NEEDS HELP! HE WAS TAKEN AWAY BY--ULK!
YES--? YOUR OWNER'S NAME AND IDENTIFICATION, PLEASE?
HIS NAME IS LU-URP!
BLEEP! PEEO DIT-DIT-BAP!
A SLIGHT MALFUNCTION! IT SOUNDS TO ME MORE AS IF YOUR FRIEND HAS BLOWN HIS COMPUTER! YOU MAY CONTINUE TO THE REPAIR CENTER WITH HIM!
WHAT--?
LISTEN, YOU WALKING BLOB OF GREASE! WHY DID YOU ZAP ME... AND TELL THAT POLICE-DROID I HAVE A SERIOUS MALFUNCTION?
BLEEO! DEE-DIT! WHEEP! VLOOEE!

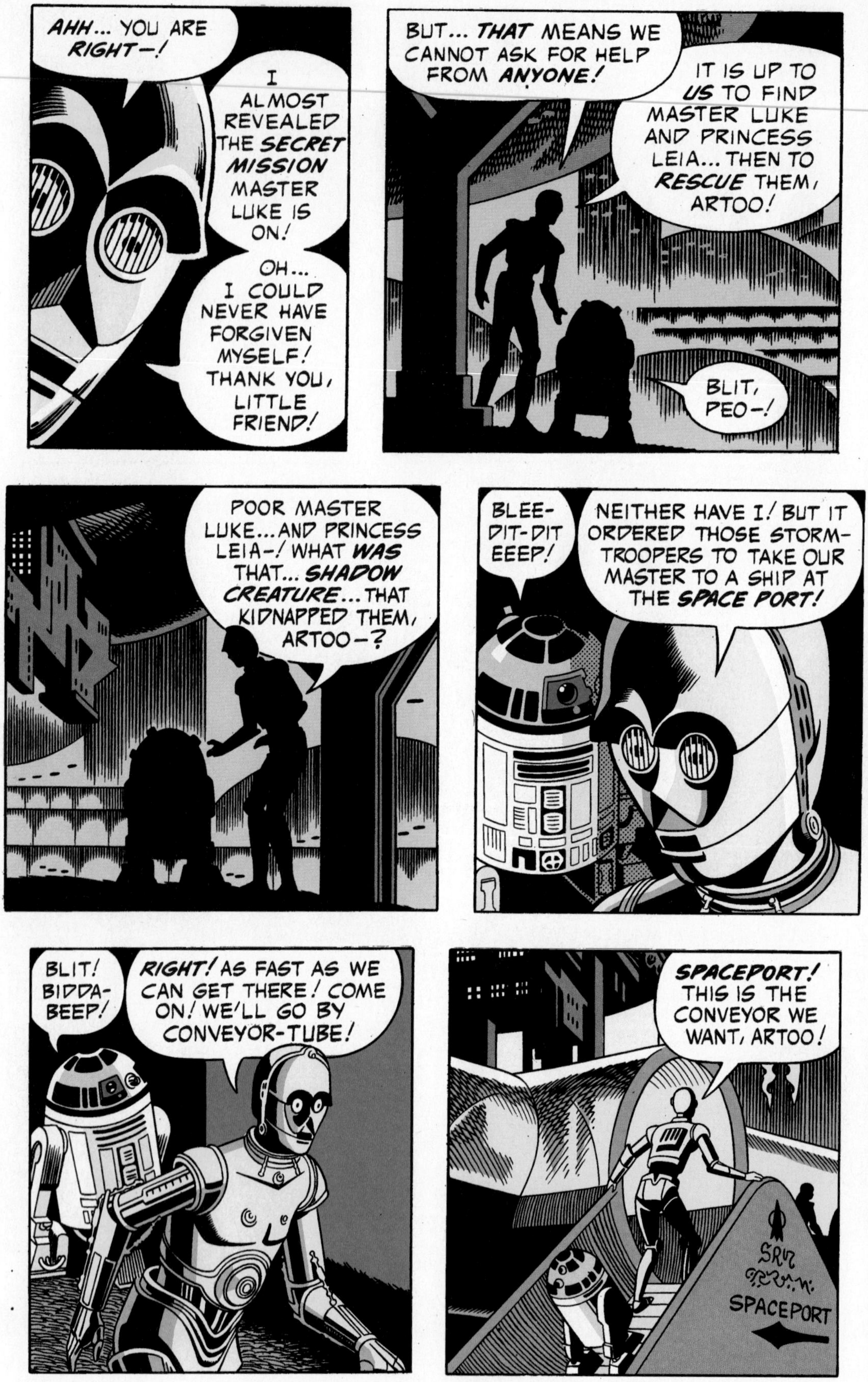
AHH... YOU ARE RIGHT-!
I ALMOST REVEALED THE SECRET MISSION MASTER LUKE IS ON!
OH... I COULD NEVER HAVE FORGIVEN MYSELF! THANK YOU, LITTLE FRIEND!
BUT... THAT MEANS WE CANNOT ASK FOR HELP FROM ANYONE!
IT IS UP TO US TO FIND MASTER LUKE AND PRINCESS LEIA... THEN TO RESCUE THEM, ARTOO!
BLIT, PEO-!
POOR MASTER LUKE...AND PRINCESS LEIA-! WHAT WAS THAT... SHADOW CREATURE...THAT KIDNAPPED THEM, ARTOO-?
BLEE-DIT-DIT EEEP!
NEITHER HAVE I! BUT IT ORDERED THOSE STORM-TROOPERS TO TAKE OUR MASTER TO A SHIP AT THE SPACE PORT!
BLIT! BIDDA-BEEP!
RIGHT! AS FAST AS WE CAN GET THERE! COME ON! WE'LL GO BY CONVEYOR-TUBE!
SPACEPORT! THIS IS THE CONVEYOR WE WANT, ARTOO!
SPACEPORT

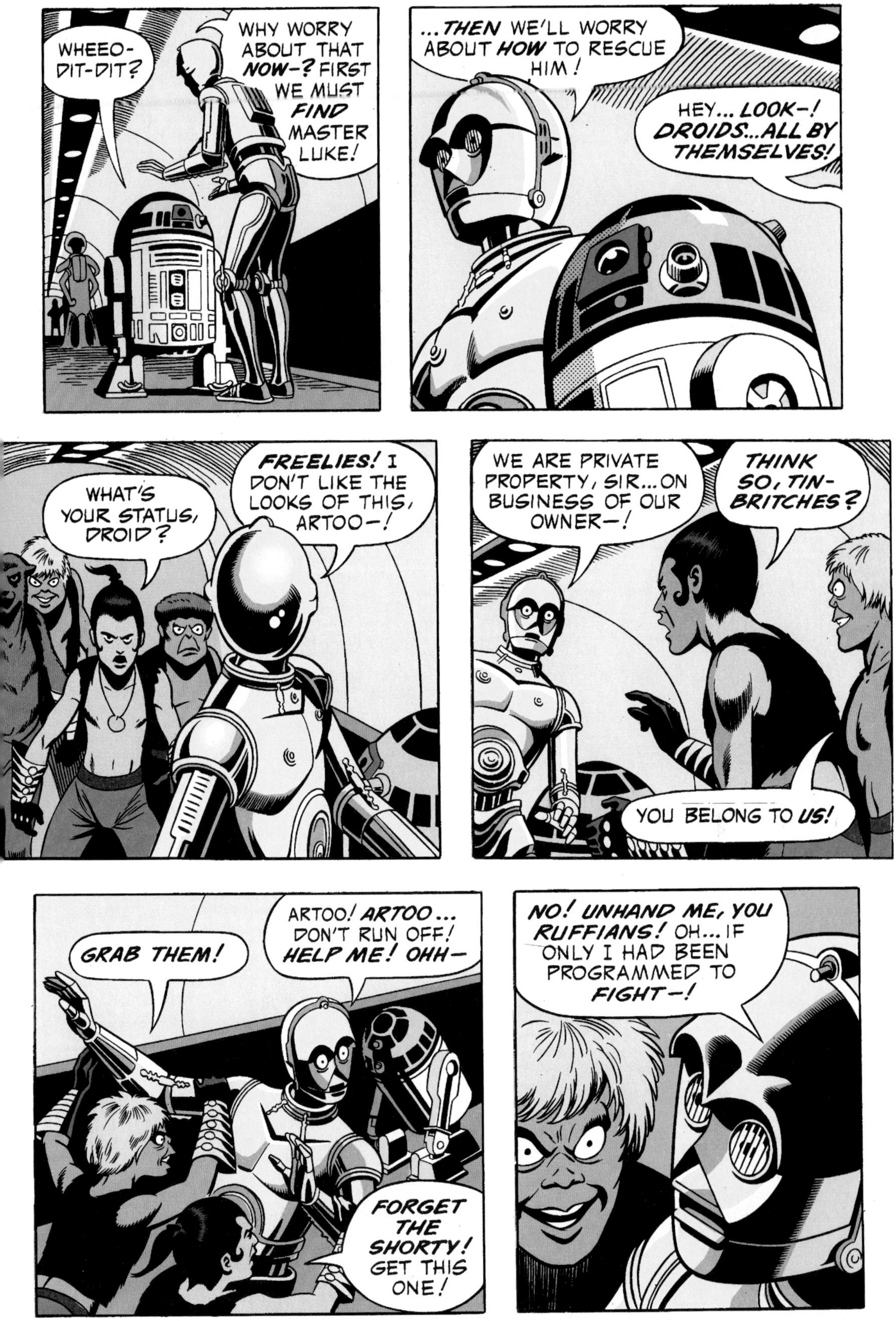
WHEEO-DIT-DIT?
WHY WORRY ABOUT THAT NOW-? FIRST WE MUST FIND MASTER LUKE!
...THEN WE'LL WORRY ABOUT HOW TO RESCUE HIM!
HEY... LOOK-! DROIDS...ALL BY THEMSELVES!
WHAT'S YOUR STATUS, DROID?
FREELIES! I DON'T LIKE THE LOOKS OF THIS, ARTOO-!
WE ARE PRIVATE PROPERTY, SIR...ON BUSINESS OF OUR OWNER-!
THINK SO, TIN-BRITCHES?
YOU BELONG TO US!
GRAB THEM!
ARTOO! ARTOO... DON'T RUN OFF! HELP ME! OHH-
FORGET THE SHORTY! GET THIS ONE!
NO! UNHAND ME, YOU RUFFIANS! OH... IF ONLY I HAD BEEN PROGRAMMED TO FIGHT-!

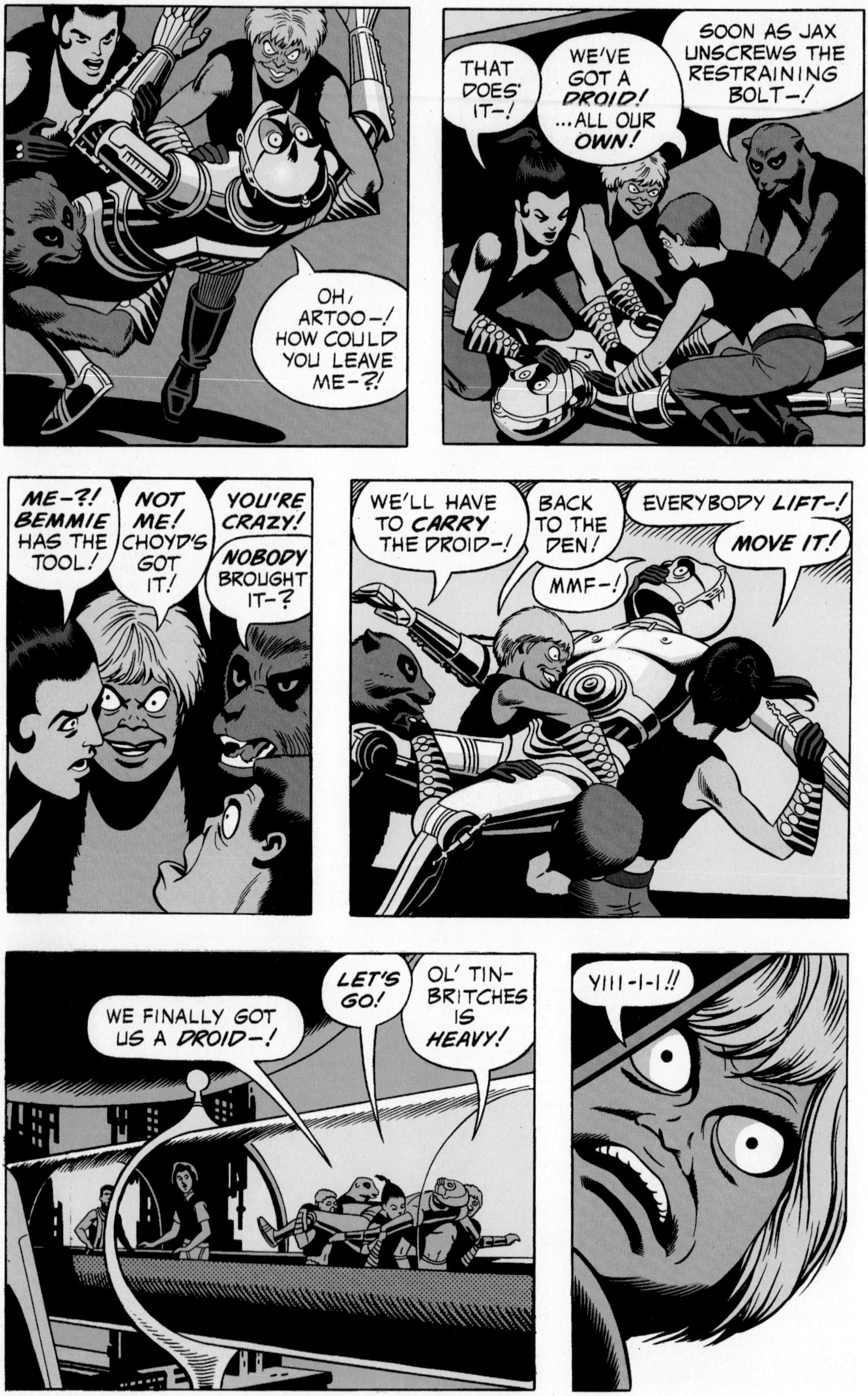
OH, ARTOO–! HOW COULD YOU LEAVE ME–?!
THAT DOES' IT–!
WE'VE GOT A DROID! ...ALL OUR OWN!
SOON AS JAX UNSCREWS THE RESTRAINING BOLT–!
ME–?! BEMMIE HAS THE TOOL!
NOT ME! CHOYD'S GOT IT!
YOU'RE CRAZY!
NOBODY BROUGHT IT–?
WE'LL HAVE TO CARRY THE DROID–!
BACK TO THE DEN!
EVERYBODY LIFT–!
MOVE IT!
MMF–!
WE FINALLY GOT US A DROID–!
LET'S GO!
OL' TIN-BRITCHES IS HEAVY!
YIII-I-I!!

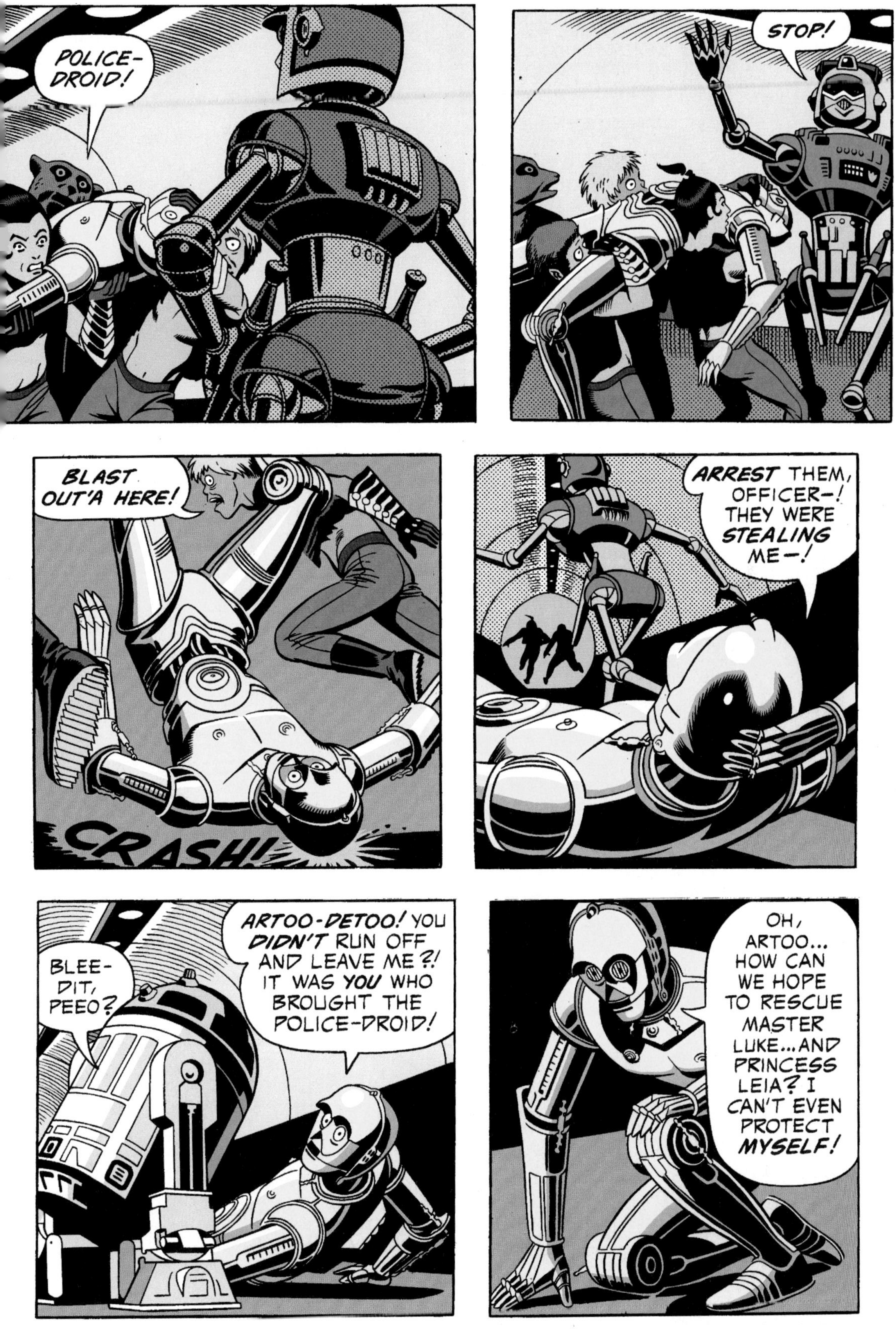
POLICE-DROID!
STOP!
BLAST OUT'A HERE!
CRASH!
ARREST THEM, OFFICER-! THEY WERE STEALING ME-!
BLEE-DIT, PEEO?
ARTOO-DETOO! YOU DIDN'T RUN OFF AND LEAVE ME?! IT WAS YOU WHO BROUGHT THE POLICE-DROID!
OH, ARTOO... HOW CAN WE HOPE TO RESCUE MASTER LUKE...AND PRINCESS LEIA? I CAN'T EVEN PROTECT MYSELF!

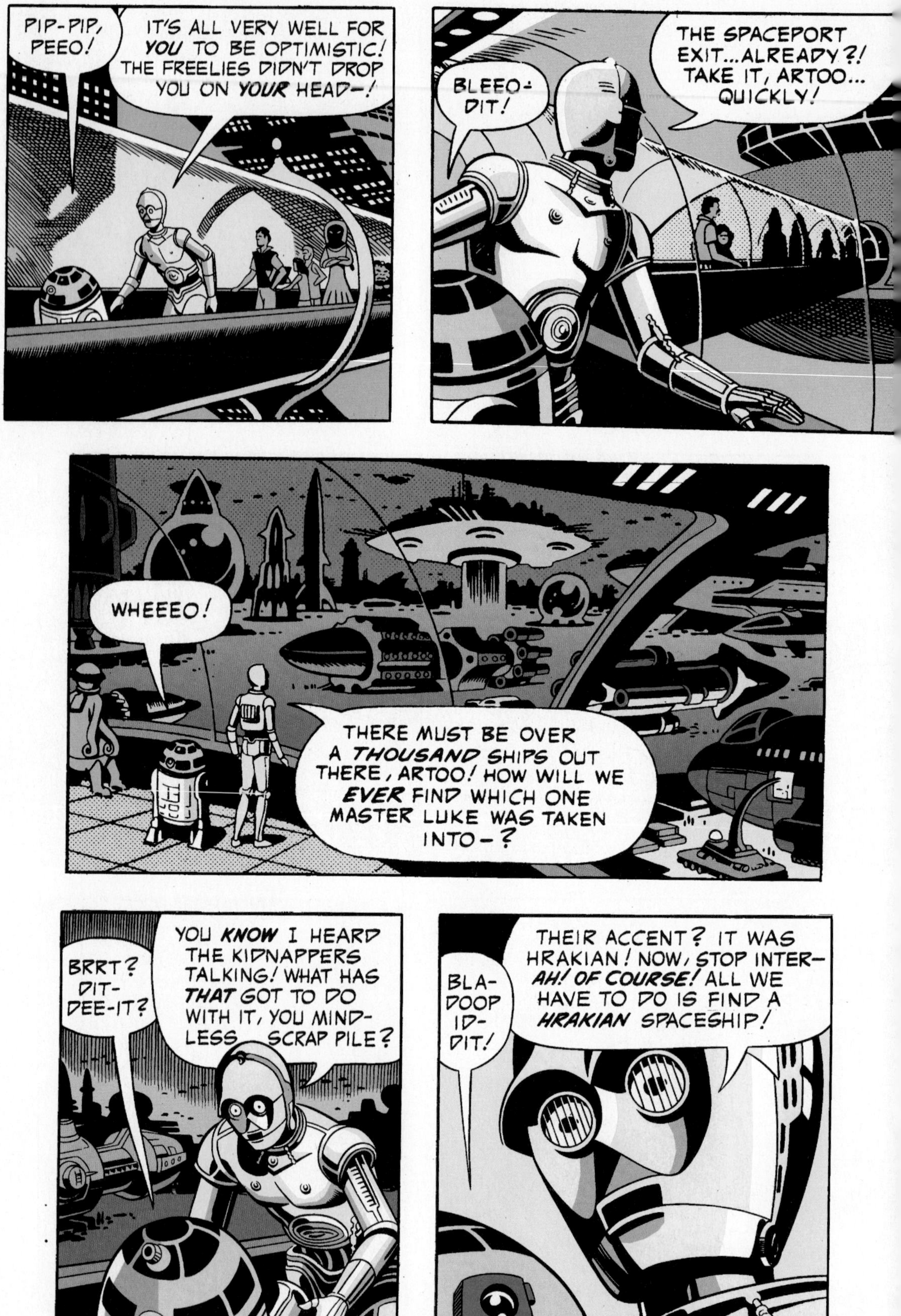
PIP-PIP, PEEO!
IT'S ALL VERY WELL FOR YOU TO BE OPTIMISTIC! THE FREELIES DIDN'T DROP YOU ON YOUR HEAD-!
BLEEO-DIT!
THE SPACEPORT EXIT...ALREADY?! TAKE IT, ARTOO... QUICKLY!
WHEEEO!
THERE MUST BE OVER A THOUSAND SHIPS OUT THERE, ARTOO! HOW WILL WE EVER FIND WHICH ONE MASTER LUKE WAS TAKEN INTO-?
BRRT? DIT-DEE-IT?
YOU KNOW I HEARD THE KIDNAPPERS TALKING! WHAT HAS THAT GOT TO DO WITH IT, YOU MINDLESS SCRAP PILE?
BLA-DOOP ID-DIT!
THEIR ACCENT? IT WAS HRAKIAN! NOW, STOP INTER- AH! OF COURSE! ALL WE HAVE TO DO IS FIND A HRAKIAN SPACESHIP!

THERE'S A HRAKIAN SHIP ON PAD 391!
...AND ANOTHER ON PAD 393! JUST TWO OF THEM! COME ON, ARTOO!
PAD DISPLAY
MINUTES LATER...
THIS ONE FIRST! NOW, REMEMBER... LET ME DO THE TALKING!
391
BLATT!
HALT, DROIDS! IDENTIFY! AND STATE YOUR BUSINESS!
SEE-THREEPIO... AND ARTOO-DETOO, SIR! WE ARE TRYING TO LOCATE OUR OWNER!
C-3PO... AND R2-D2? YOU ARE NOT LISTED ON EITHER SHIP'S COMPANY... OR ON PORT COMPLEMENT!
UNAUTHORIZED DROIDS ARE NOT ALLOWED ON BOARD... OR IN THE AREA! BLAST OFF!
OH, ARTOO!... WE'VE FAILED, AGAIN! HOW WILL WE EVER FIND MASTER LUKE—?

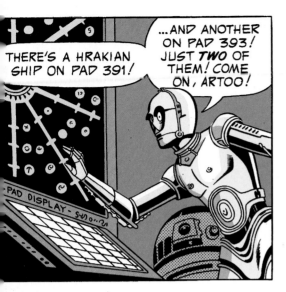

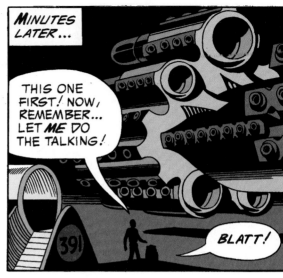

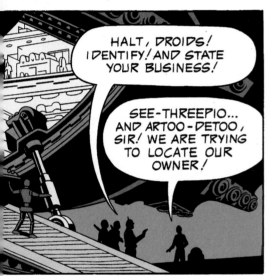

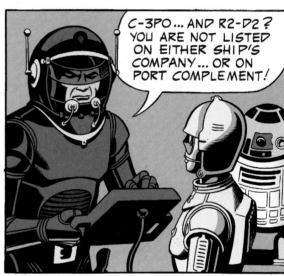

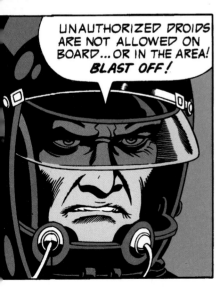

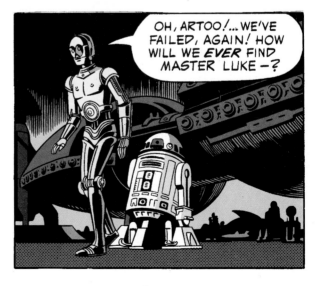

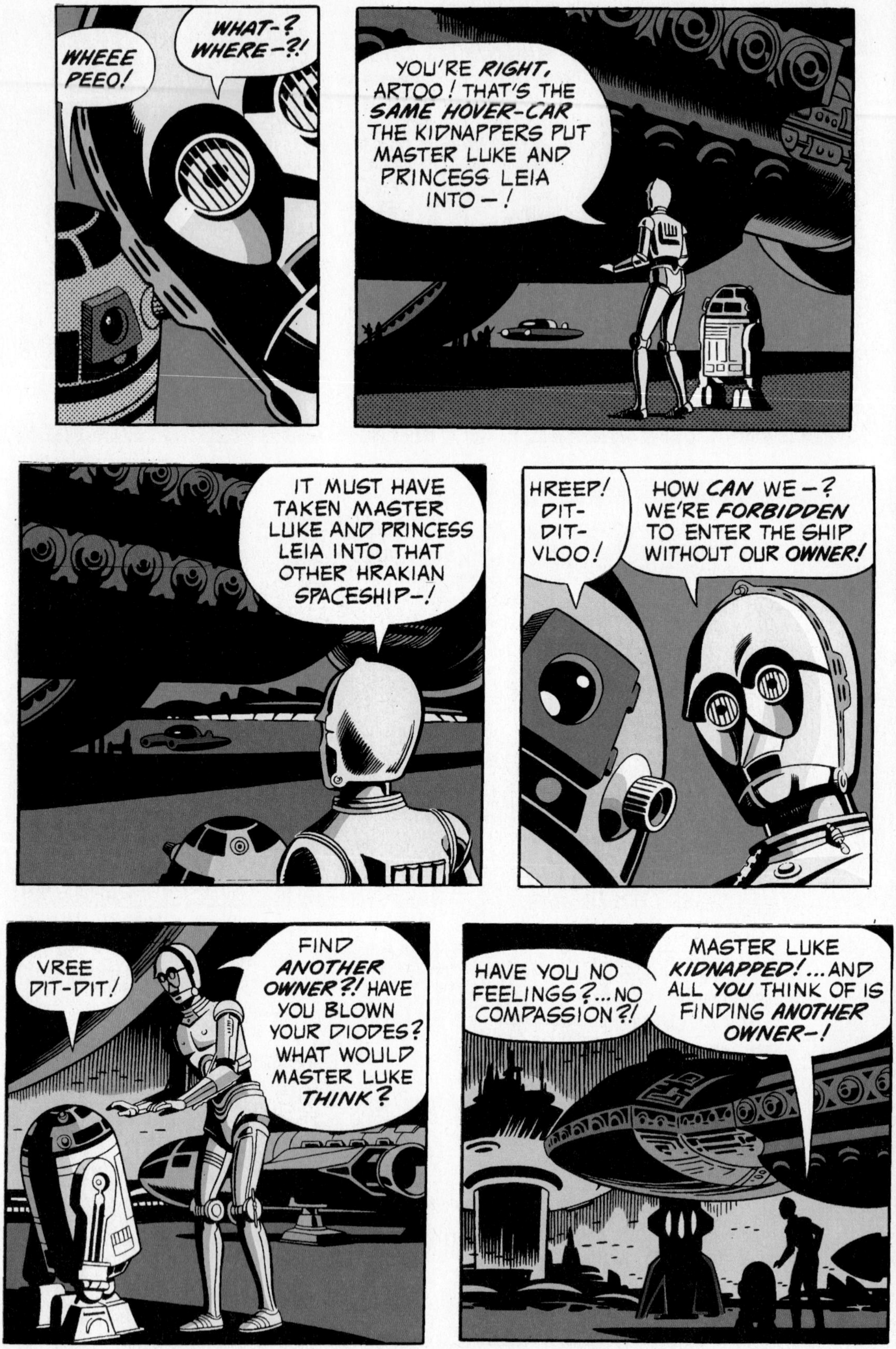
WHEEE PEEO!
WHAT-? WHERE-?!
YOU'RE RIGHT, ARTOO! THAT'S THE SAME HOVER-CAR THE KIDNAPPERS PUT MASTER LUKE AND PRINCESS LEIA INTO—!
IT MUST HAVE TAKEN MASTER LUKE AND PRINCESS LEIA INTO THAT OTHER HRAKIAN SPACESHIP–!
HREEP! DIT-DIT-VLOO!
HOW CAN WE—? WE'RE FORBIDDEN TO ENTER THE SHIP WITHOUT OUR OWNER!
VREE DIT-DIT!
FIND ANOTHER OWNER?! HAVE YOU BLOWN YOUR DIODES? WHAT WOULD MASTER LUKE THINK?
HAVE YOU NO FEELINGS?...NO COMPASSION?!
MASTER LUKE KIDNAPPED!...AND ALL YOU THINK OF IS FINDING ANOTHER OWNER–!

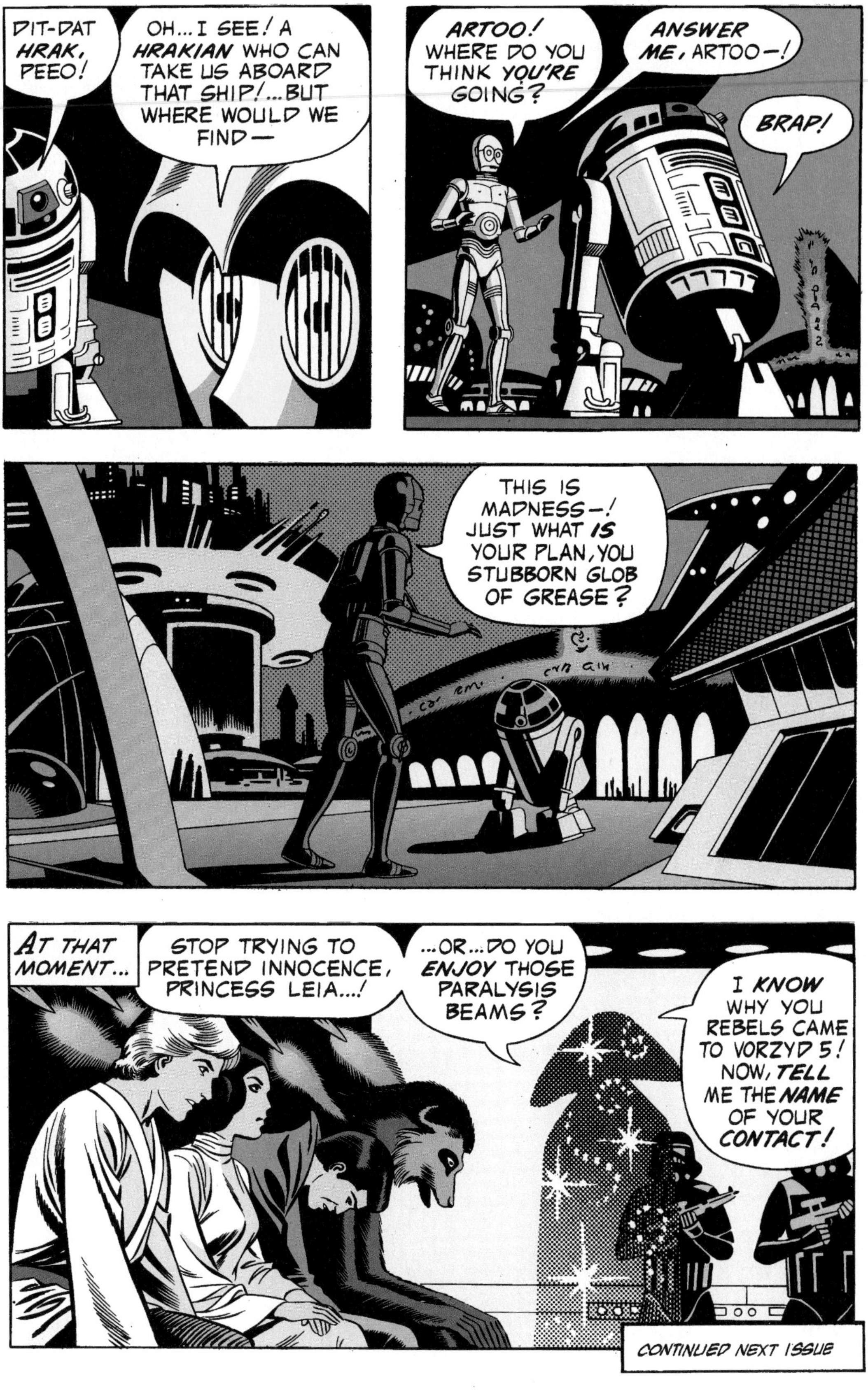
DIT-DAT HRAK, PEEO!
OH... I SEE! A HRAKIAN WHO CAN TAKE US ABOARD THAT SHIP!... BUT WHERE WOULD WE FIND—
ARTOO! WHERE DO YOU THINK YOU'RE GOING?
ANSWER ME, ARTOO—!
BRAP!
THIS IS MADNESS—! JUST WHAT IS YOUR PLAN, YOU STUBBORN GLOB OF GREASE?
AT THAT MOMENT...
STOP TRYING TO PRETEND INNOCENCE, PRINCESS LEIA...!
...OR...DO YOU ENJOY THOSE PARALYSIS BEAMS?
I KNOW WHY YOU REBELS CAME TO VORZYD 5! NOW, TELL ME THE NAME OF YOUR CONTACT!
CONTINUED NEXT ISSUE

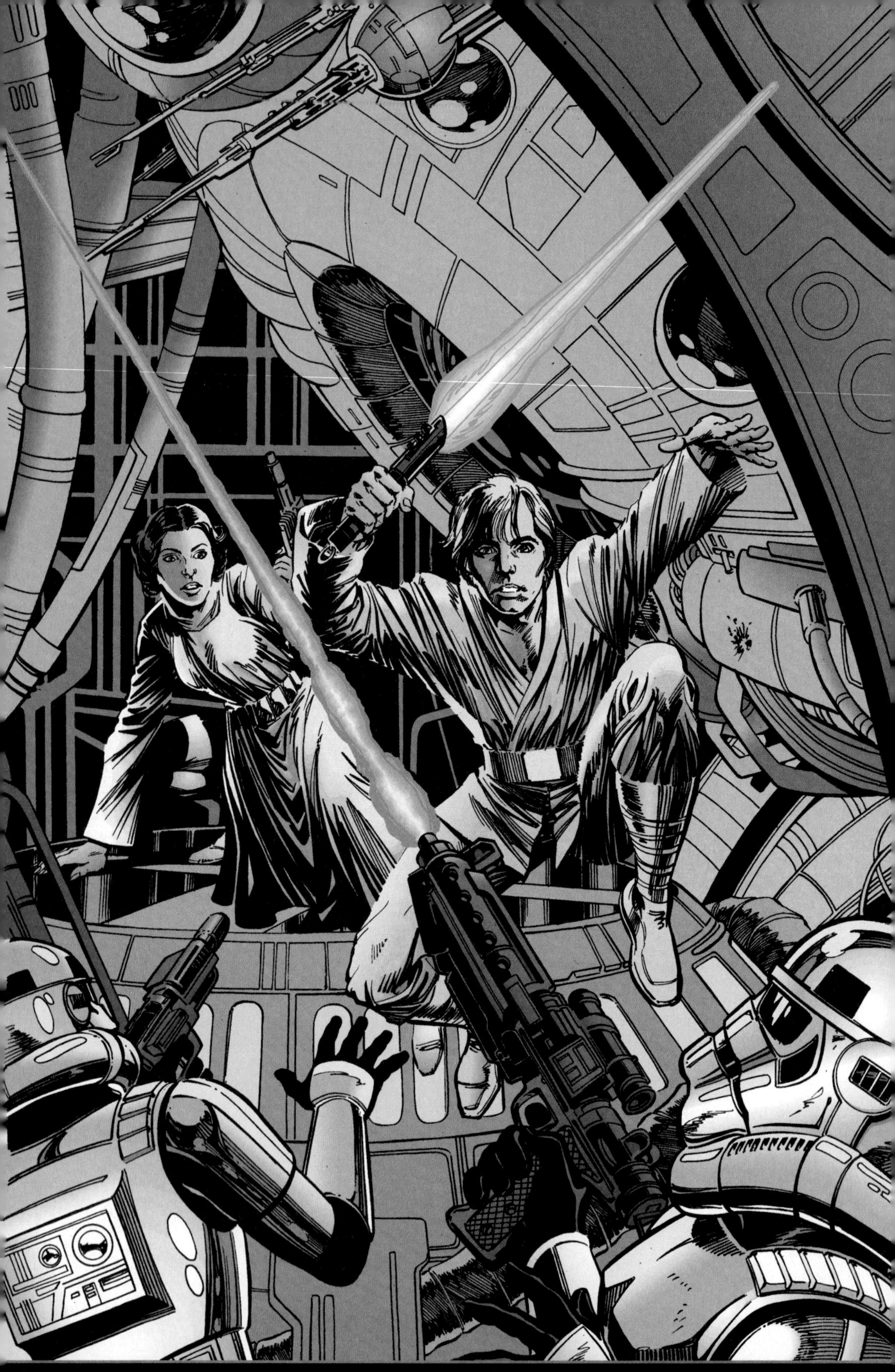

CLASSIC STAR WARS: THE EARLY ADVENTURES #2

ORIGINALLY PUBLISHED WEEKDAYS & SATURDAYS FROM MAY 11 TO JULY 10, 1979

WRITER & PENCILER: RUSS MANNING • INKER & LETTERER: MIKE ROYER • ART RETOUCHING: RICK HOBERG • COLORIST: RAY MURTAUGH
EDITORS: BOB COOPER & PEET JANES • COVER ARTISTS: RICK HOBERG, MIKE GRELL & MATTHEW HOLLINGSWORTH

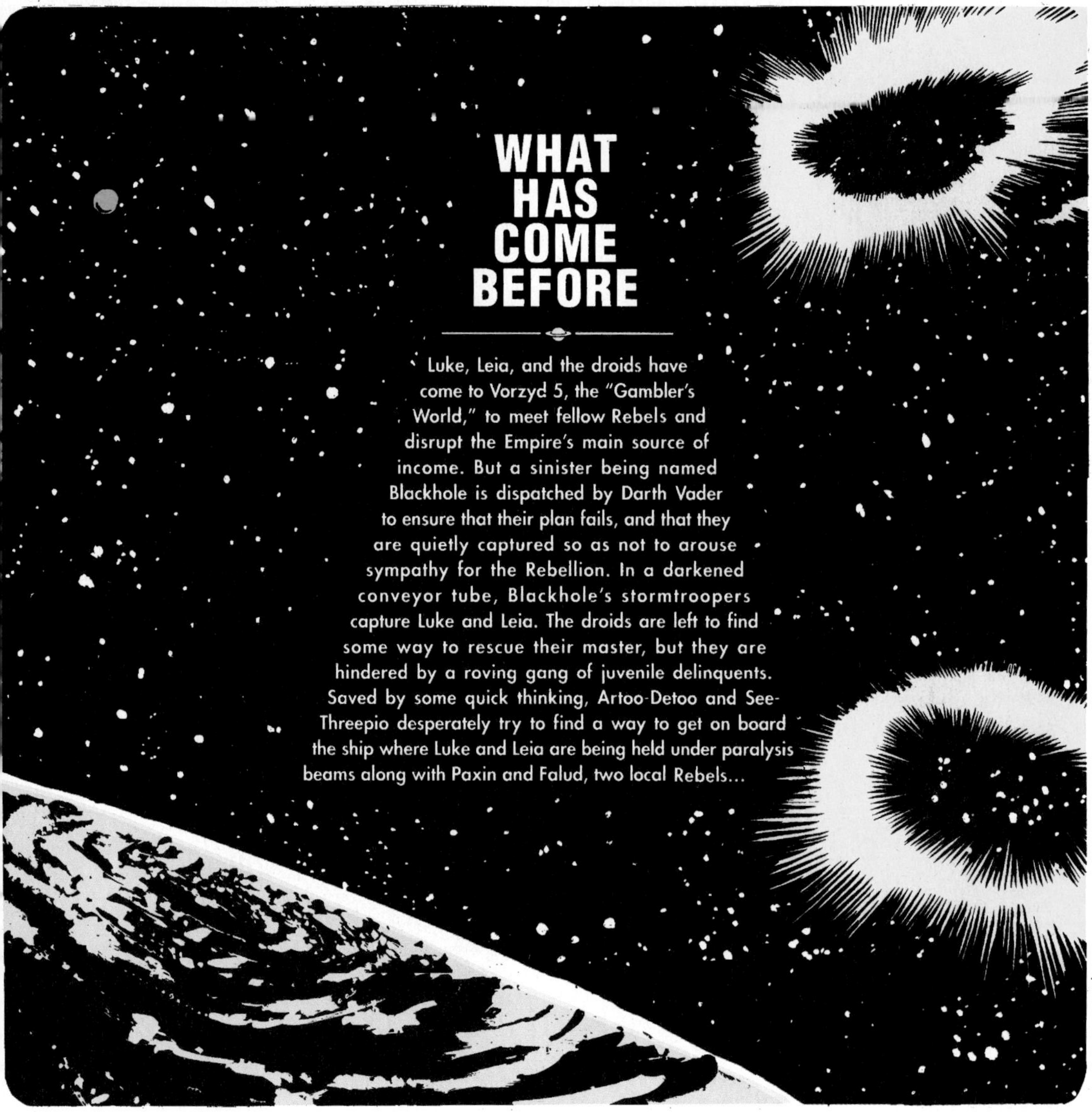

WHAT HAS COME BEFORE

Luke, Leia, and the droids have come to Vorzyd 5, the "Gambler's World," to meet fellow Rebels and disrupt the Empire's main source of income. But a sinister being named Blackhole is dispatched by Darth Vader to ensure that their plan fails, and that they are quietly captured so as not to arouse sympathy for the Rebellion. In a darkened conveyor tube, Blackhole's stormtroopers capture Luke and Leia. The droids are left to find some way to rescue their master, but they are hindered by a roving gang of juvenile delinquents. Saved by some quick thinking, Artoo-Detoo and See-Threepio desperately try to find a way to get on board the ship where Luke and Leia are being held under paralysis beams along with Paxin and Falud, two local Rebels...

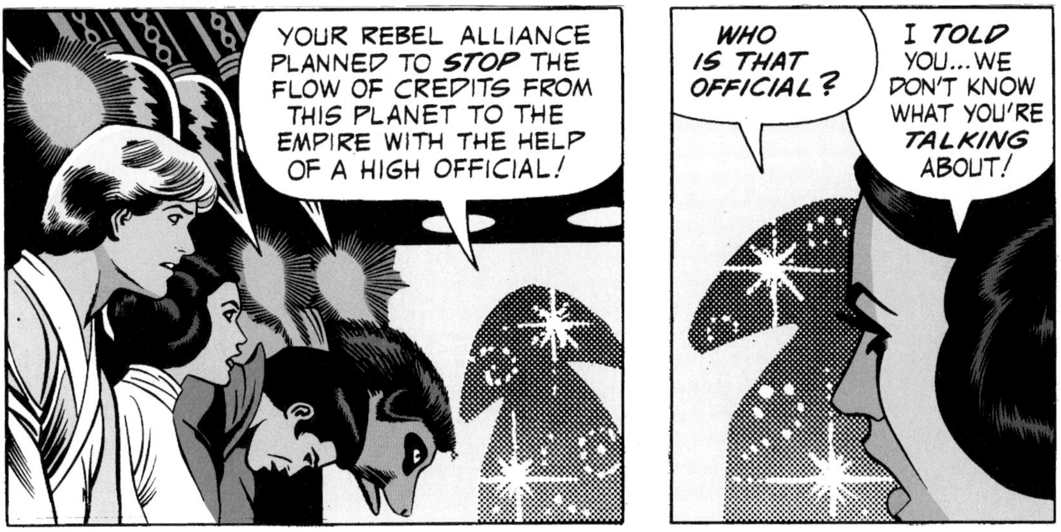
YOUR REBEL ALLIANCE PLANNED TO *STOP* THE FLOW OF CREDITS FROM THIS PLANET TO THE EMPIRE WITH THE HELP OF A HIGH OFFICIAL!
WHO IS THAT OFFICIAL?
I *TOLD* YOU...WE DON'T KNOW WHAT YOU'RE *TALKING* ABOUT!

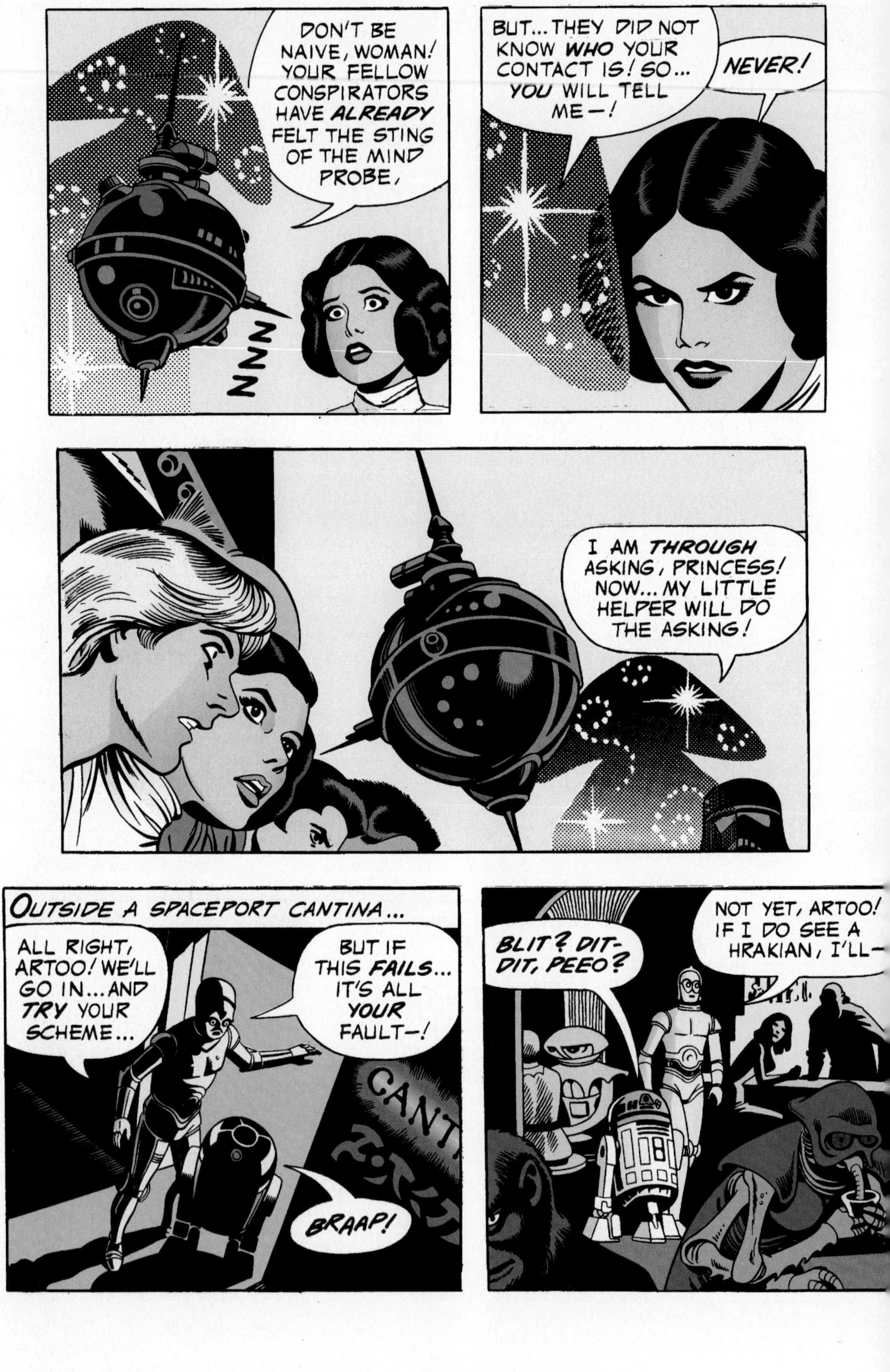
DON'T BE NAIVE, WOMAN! YOUR FELLOW CONSPIRATORS HAVE ALREADY FELT THE STING OF THE MIND PROBE,
NNN
BUT... THEY DID NOT KNOW WHO YOUR CONTACT IS! SO... YOU WILL TELL ME—!
NEVER!
I AM THROUGH ASKING, PRINCESS! NOW... MY LITTLE HELPER WILL DO THE ASKING!
OUTSIDE A SPACEPORT CANTINA...
ALL RIGHT, ARTOO! WE'LL GO IN... AND TRY YOUR SCHEME...
BUT IF THIS FAILS... IT'S ALL YOUR FAULT—!
BRAAP!
BLIT? DIT-DIT, PEEO?
NOT YET, ARTOO! IF I DO SEE A HRAKIAN, I'LL—

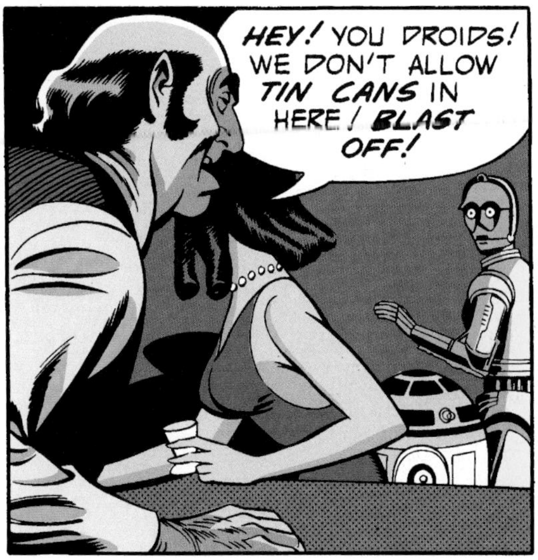
HEY! YOU DROIDS! WE DON'T ALLOW TIN CANS IN HERE! BLAST OFF!

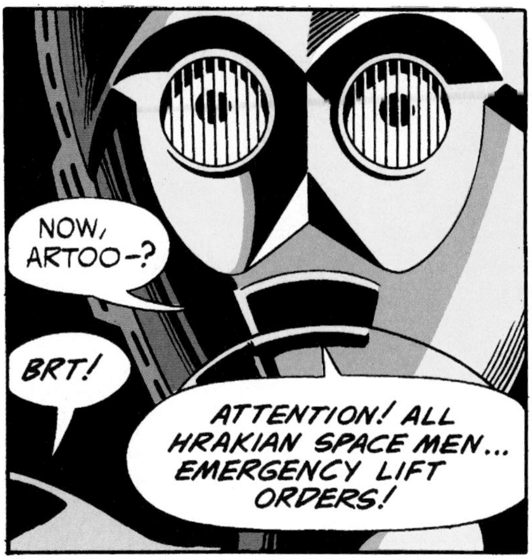
NOW, ARTOO-?
BRT!
ATTENTION! ALL HRAKIAN SPACE MEN... EMERGENCY LIFT ORDERS!

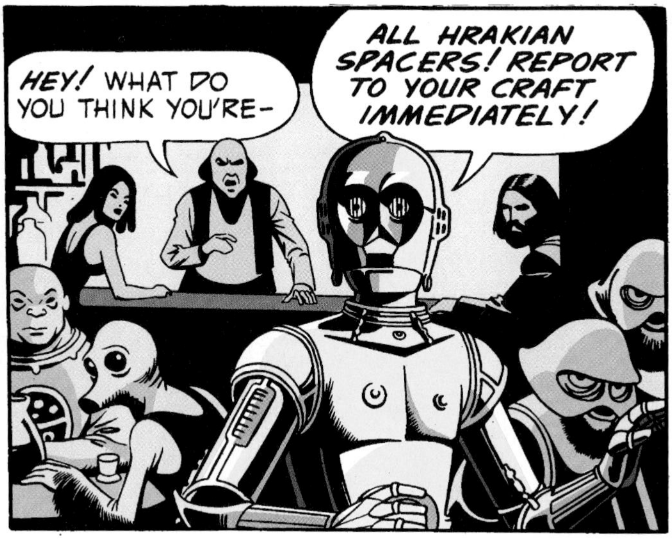
HEY! WHAT DO YOU THINK YOU'RE-
ALL HRAKIAN SPACERS! REPORT TO YOUR CRAFT IMMEDIATELY!

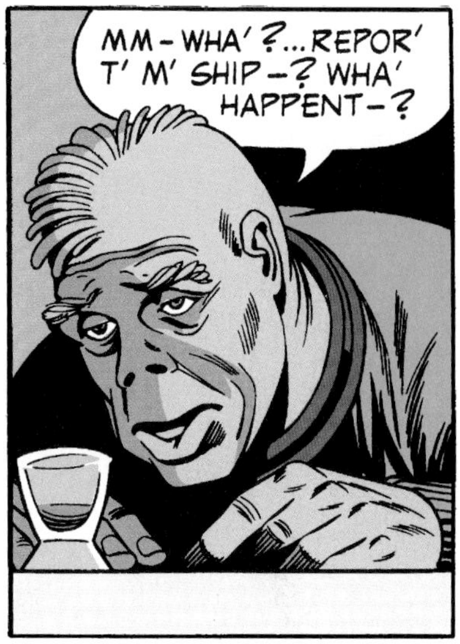
MM-WHA'?...REPOR' T' M' SHIP-? WHA' HAPPENT-?

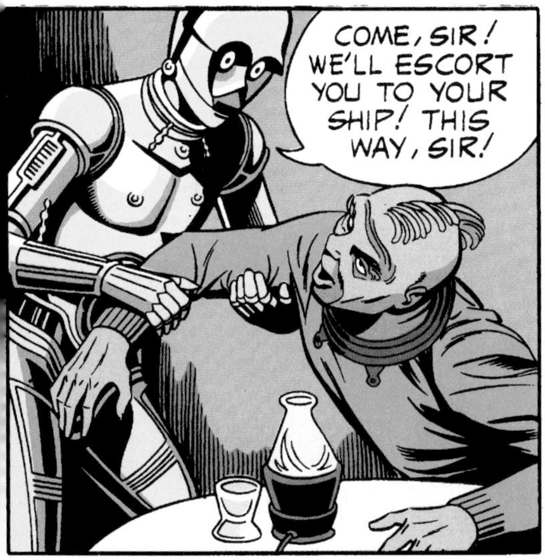
COME, SIR! WE'LL ESCORT YOU TO YOUR SHIP! THIS WAY, SIR!

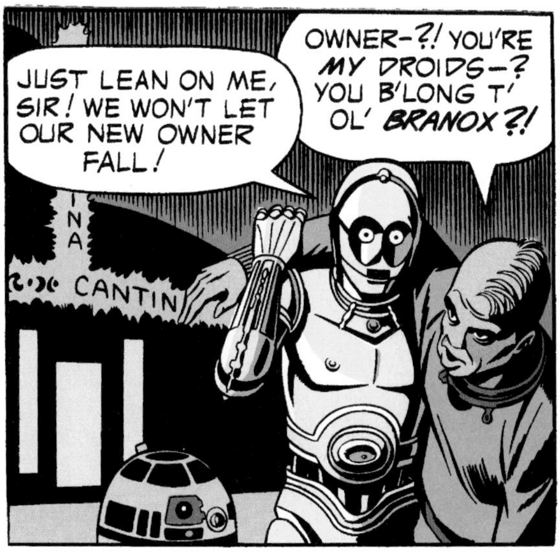
OWNER-?! YOU'RE MY DROIDS-? YOU B'LONG T' OL' BRANOX?!
JUST LEAN ON ME, SIR! WE WON'T LET OUR NEW OWNER FALL!
CANTIN

IN A MANNER OF SPEAKING, SIR...WHILE WE HELP EACH OTHER GET ON BOARD YOUR SHIP!

THIS WAY, SIR!

BACK *EARLY* TONIGHT, EH, BRANOX?

'MERGENCY—

OUR OWNER'S NOT FEELING WELL, SIR! WE'LL SEE THAT HE GETS TO HIS QUARTERS!

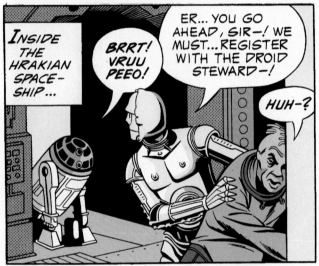

INSIDE THE HRAKIAN SPACE-SHIP...

BRRT! VRUU PEEO!

ER...YOU GO AHEAD, SIR—! WE MUST...REGISTER WITH THE DROID STEWARD—!

HUH—?

WHAT MAKES YOU THINK WE CAN FIND MASTER LUKE BY GOING INTO SHIP'S DROID CONTROL!

BLAP!

THIS IS NO TIME TO GET FLIPPANT, YOU— UH-OH! SOMEONE'S *HERE*, ARTOO!

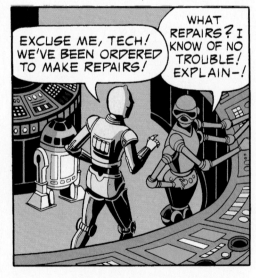

EXCUSE ME, TECH! WE'VE BEEN ORDERED TO MAKE REPAIRS!

WHAT REPAIRS? I KNOW OF NO TROUBLE! EXPLAIN—!

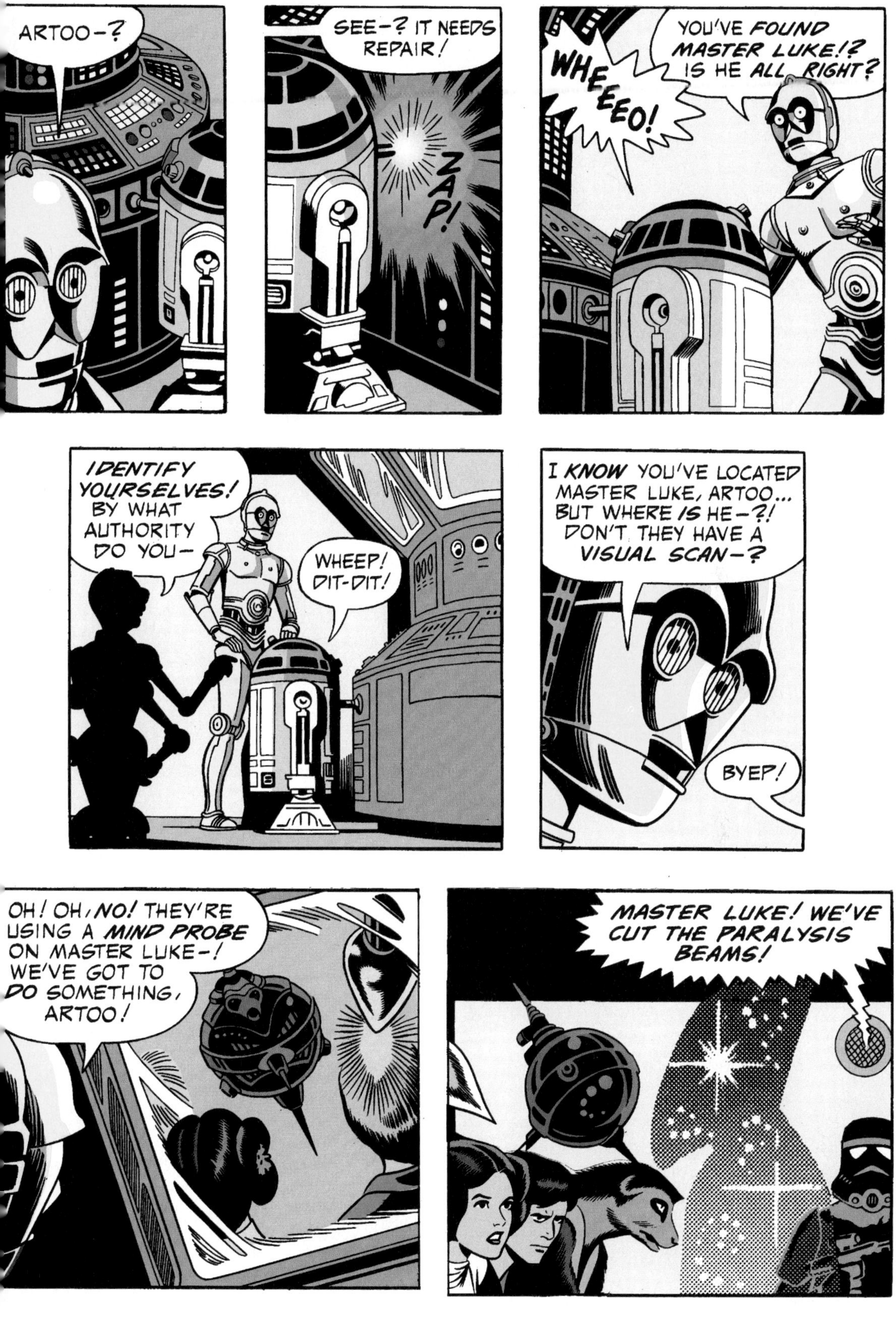
ARTOO–?
SEE–? IT NEEDS REPAIR!
ZAP!
WHEEEEO!
YOU'VE FOUND MASTER LUKE!? IS HE ALL RIGHT?
IDENTIFY YOURSELVES! BY WHAT AUTHORITY DO YOU–
WHEEP! DIT-DIT!
I KNOW YOU'VE LOCATED MASTER LUKE, ARTOO... BUT WHERE IS HE–?! DON'T THEY HAVE A VISUAL SCAN–?
BYEP!
OH! OH, NO! THEY'RE USING A MIND PROBE ON MASTER LUKE–! WE'VE GOT TO DO SOMETHING, ARTOO!
MASTER LUKE! WE'VE CUT THE PARALYSIS BEAMS!

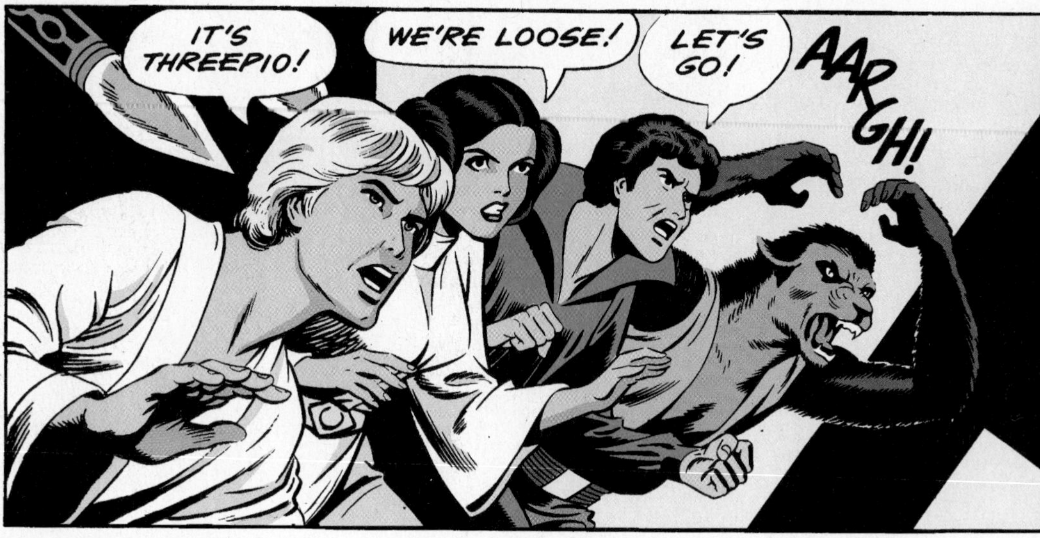
IT'S THREEPIO!
WE'RE LOOSE!
LET'S GO!
AARGH!

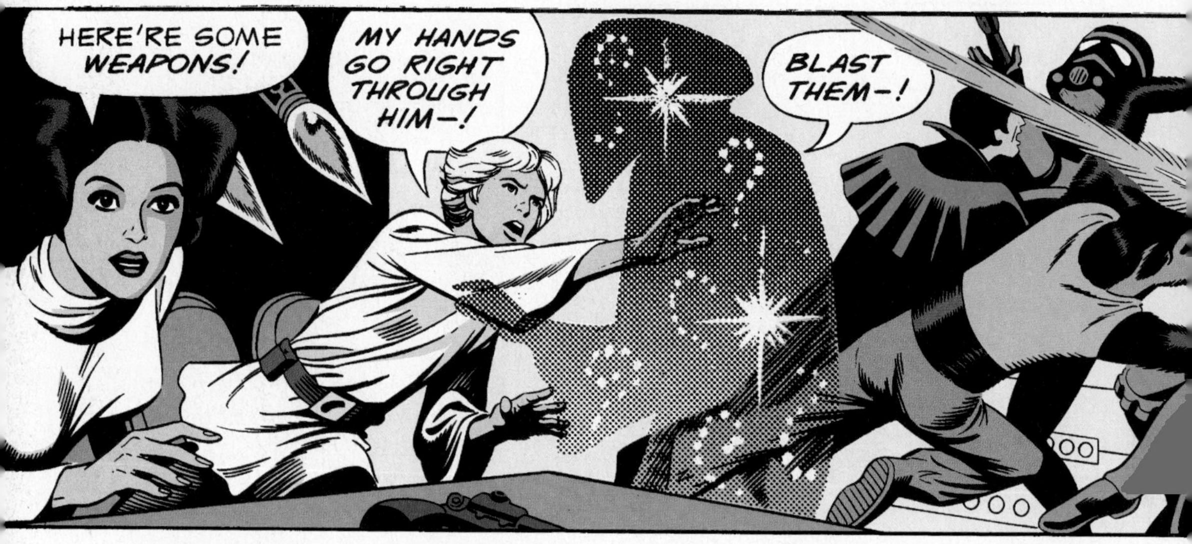
HERE'RE SOME WEAPONS!
MY HANDS GO RIGHT THROUGH HIM—!
BLAST THEM—!

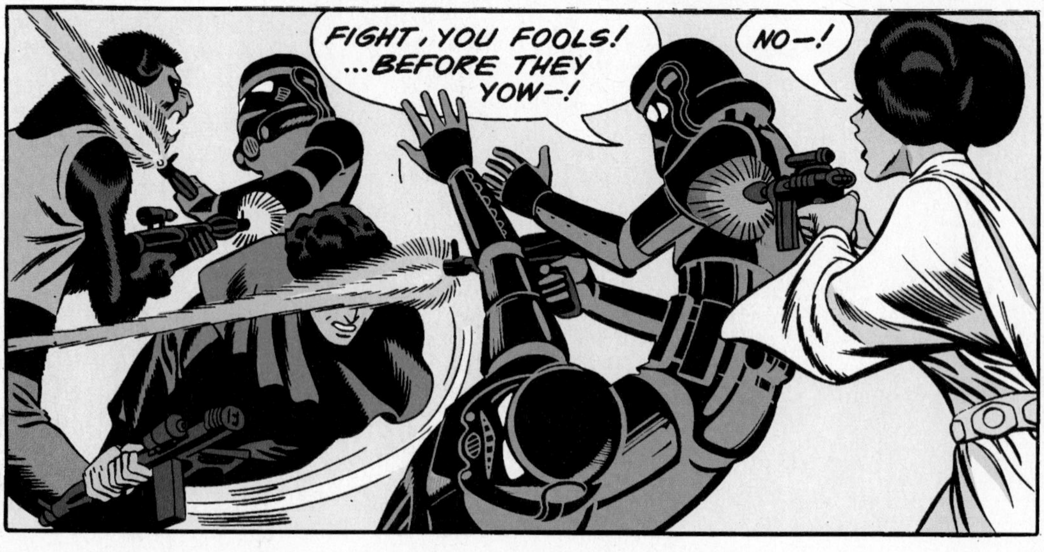
FIGHT, YOU FOOLS! ...BEFORE THEY YOW—!
NO—!

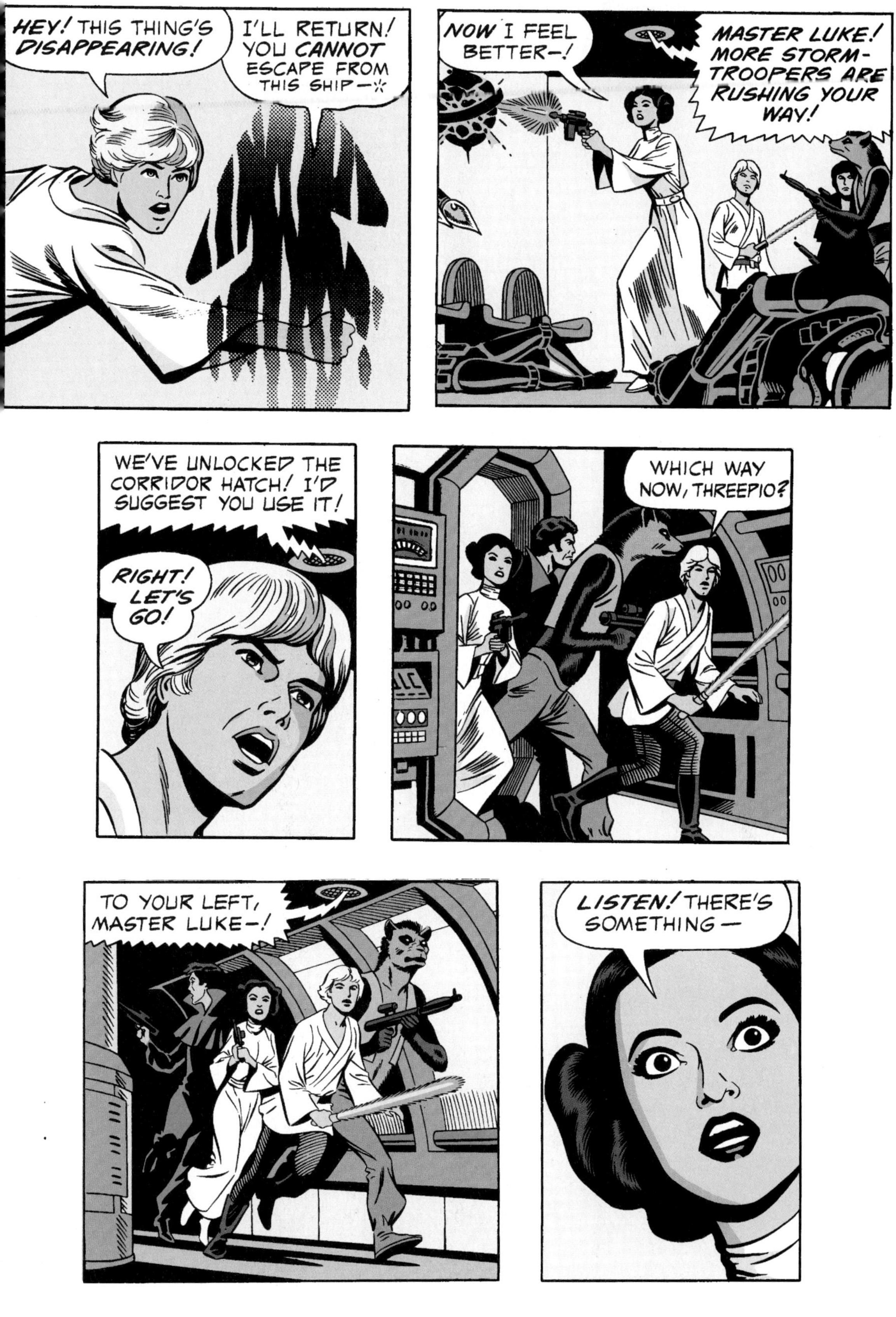
HEY! THIS THING'S DISAPPEARING!
I'LL RETURN! YOU CANNOT ESCAPE FROM THIS SHIP—!
NOW I FEEL BETTER—!
MASTER LUKE! MORE STORM-TROOPERS ARE RUSHING YOUR WAY!
WE'VE UNLOCKED THE CORRIDOR HATCH! I'D SUGGEST YOU USE IT!
RIGHT! LET'S GO!
WHICH WAY NOW, THREEPIO?
TO YOUR LEFT, MASTER LUKE—!
LISTEN! THERE'S SOMETHING—

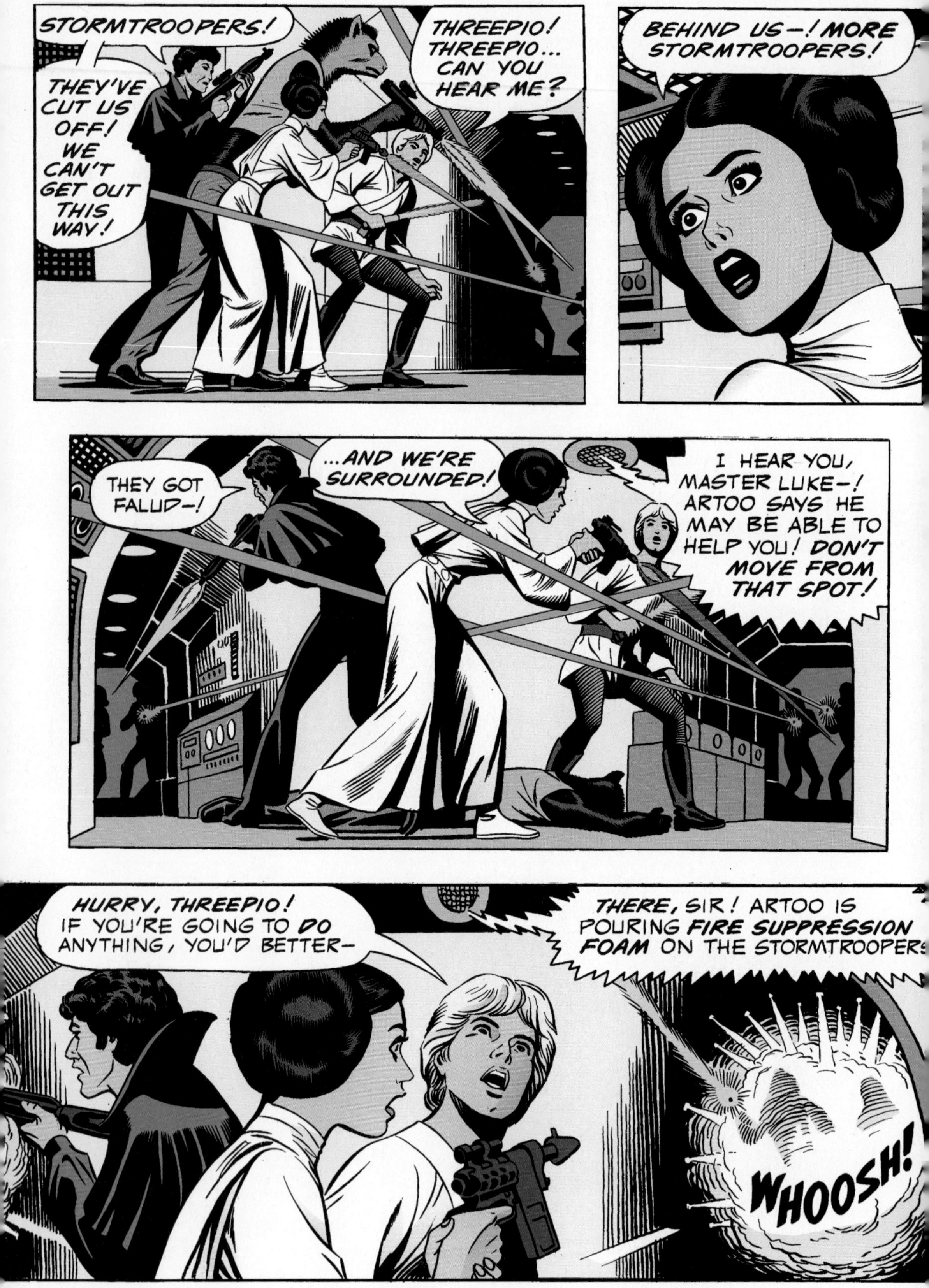
STORMTROOPERS!
THEY'VE CUT US OFF! WE CAN'T GET OUT THIS WAY!
THREEPIO! THREEPIO... CAN YOU HEAR ME?
BEHIND US—! MORE STORMTROOPERS!
THEY GOT FALUD—!
...AND WE'RE SURROUNDED!
I HEAR YOU, MASTER LUKE—! ARTOO SAYS HE MAY BE ABLE TO HELP YOU! DON'T MOVE FROM THAT SPOT!
HURRY, THREEPIO! IF YOU'RE GOING TO DO ANYTHING, YOU'D BETTER—
THERE, SIR! ARTOO IS POURING FIRE SUPPRESSION FOAM ON THE STORMTROOPERS
WHOOSH!

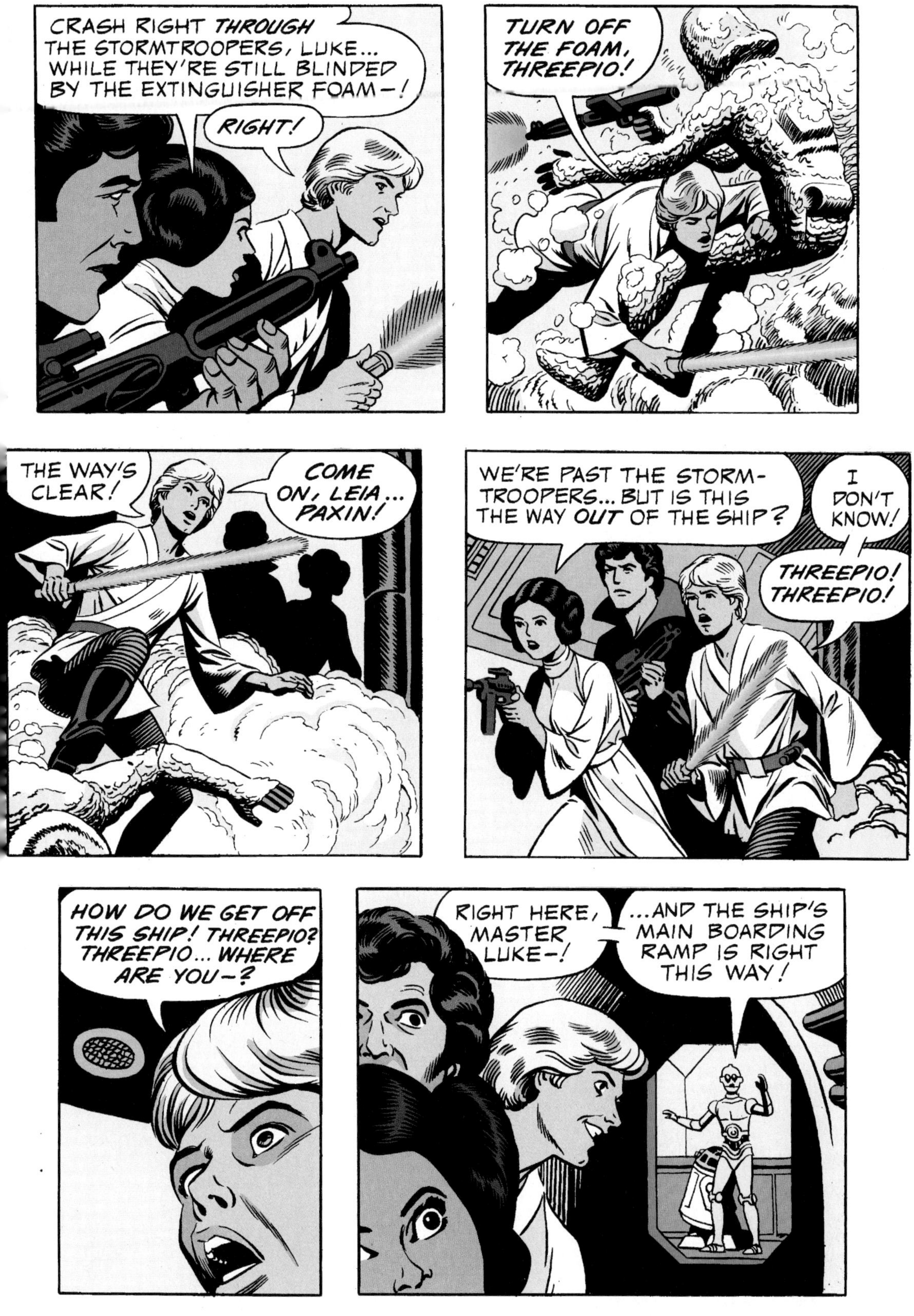
CRASH RIGHT THROUGH THE STORMTROOPERS, LUKE... WHILE THEY'RE STILL BLINDED BY THE EXTINGUISHER FOAM—!
RIGHT!
TURN OFF THE FOAM, THREEPIO!
THE WAY'S CLEAR!
COME ON, LEIA... PAXIN!
WE'RE PAST THE STORM-TROOPERS... BUT IS THIS THE WAY OUT OF THE SHIP?
I DON'T KNOW!
THREEPIO! THREEPIO!
HOW DO WE GET OFF THIS SHIP! THREEPIO? THREEPIO... WHERE ARE YOU—?
RIGHT HERE, MASTER LUKE—!
...AND THE SHIP'S MAIN BOARDING RAMP IS RIGHT THIS WAY!

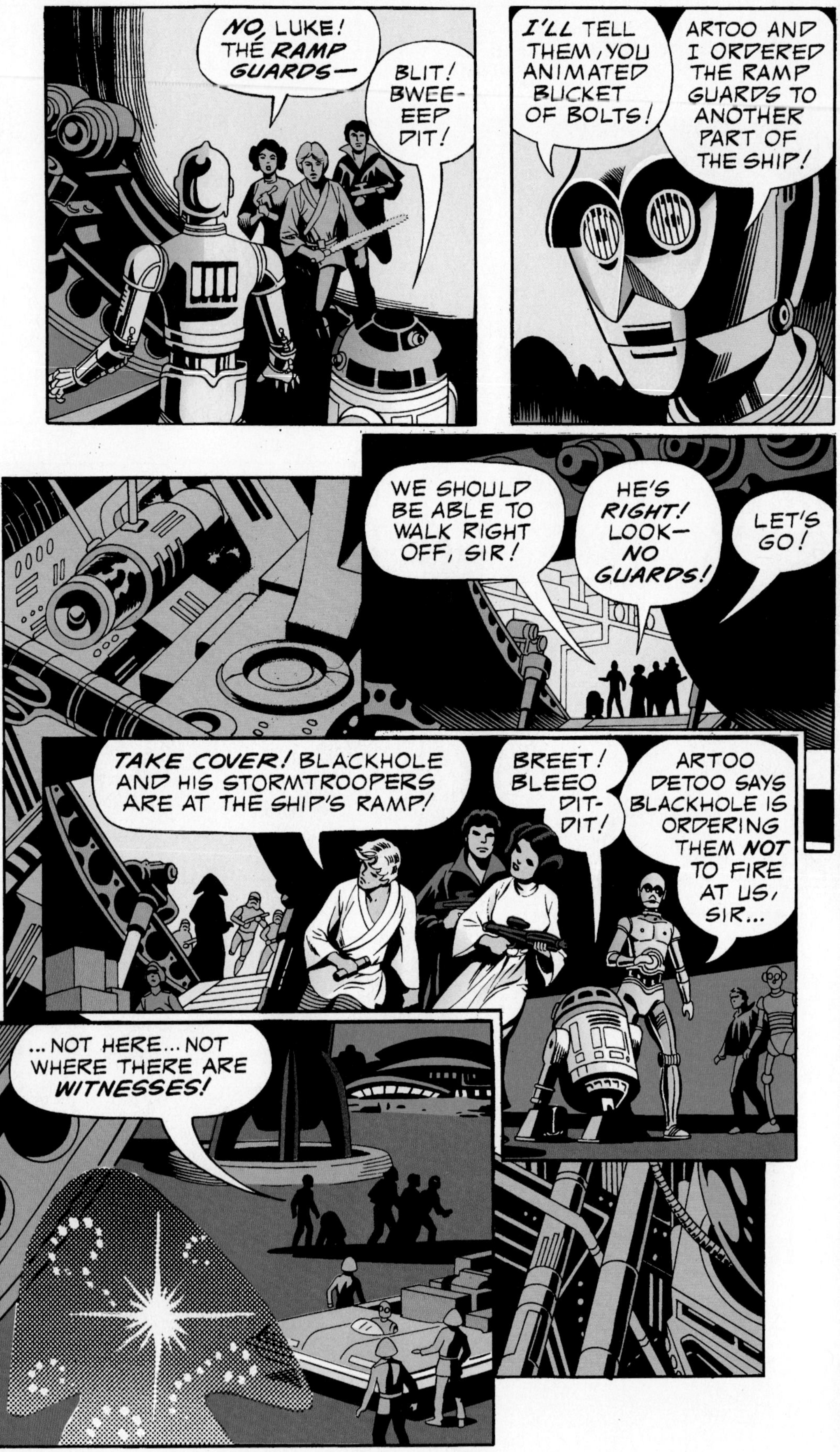
NO, LUKE! THE RAMP GUARDS—
BLIT! BWEE-EEP DIT!
I'LL TELL THEM, YOU ANIMATED BUCKET OF BOLTS!
ARTOO AND I ORDERED THE RAMP GUARDS TO ANOTHER PART OF THE SHIP!
WE SHOULD BE ABLE TO WALK RIGHT OFF, SIR!
HE'S RIGHT! LOOK— NO GUARDS!
LET'S GO!
TAKE COVER! BLACKHOLE AND HIS STORMTROOPERS ARE AT THE SHIP'S RAMP!
BREET! BLEEO DIT-DIT!
ARTOO DETOO SAYS BLACKHOLE IS ORDERING THEM NOT TO FIRE AT US, SIR...
... NOT HERE... NOT WHERE THERE ARE WITNESSES!

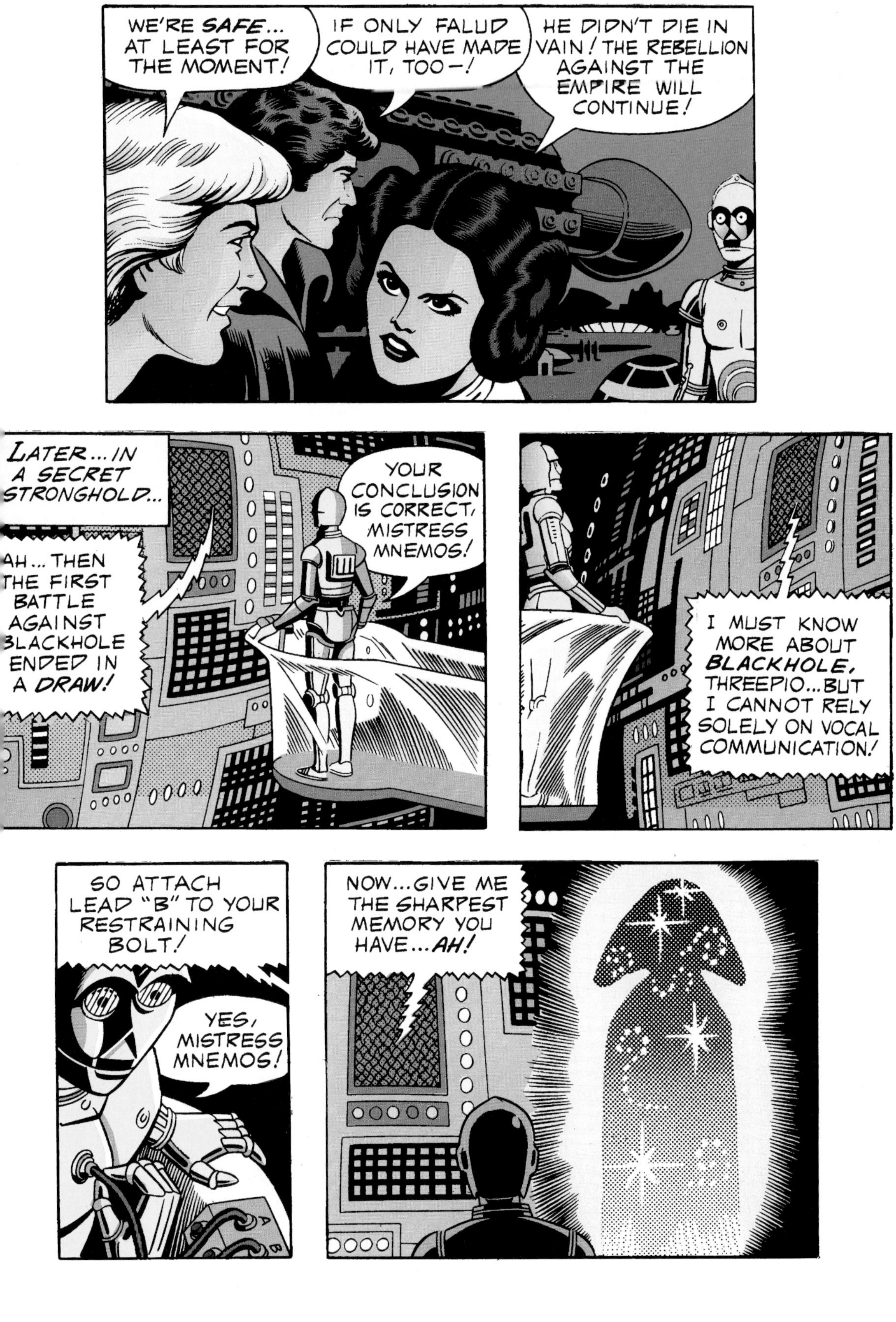
WE'RE SAFE... AT LEAST FOR THE MOMENT!
IF ONLY FALUD COULD HAVE MADE IT, TOO—!
HE DIDN'T DIE IN VAIN! THE REBELLION AGAINST THE EMPIRE WILL CONTINUE!
LATER... IN A SECRET STRONGHOLD...
AH... THEN THE FIRST BATTLE AGAINST BLACKHOLE ENDED IN A DRAW!
YOUR CONCLUSION IS CORRECT, MISTRESS MNEMOS!
I MUST KNOW MORE ABOUT BLACKHOLE, THREEPIO... BUT I CANNOT RELY SOLELY ON VOCAL COMMUNICATION!
SO ATTACH LEAD "B" TO YOUR RESTRAINING BOLT!
YES, MISTRESS MNEMOS!
NOW... GIVE ME THE SHARPEST MEMORY YOU HAVE... AH!

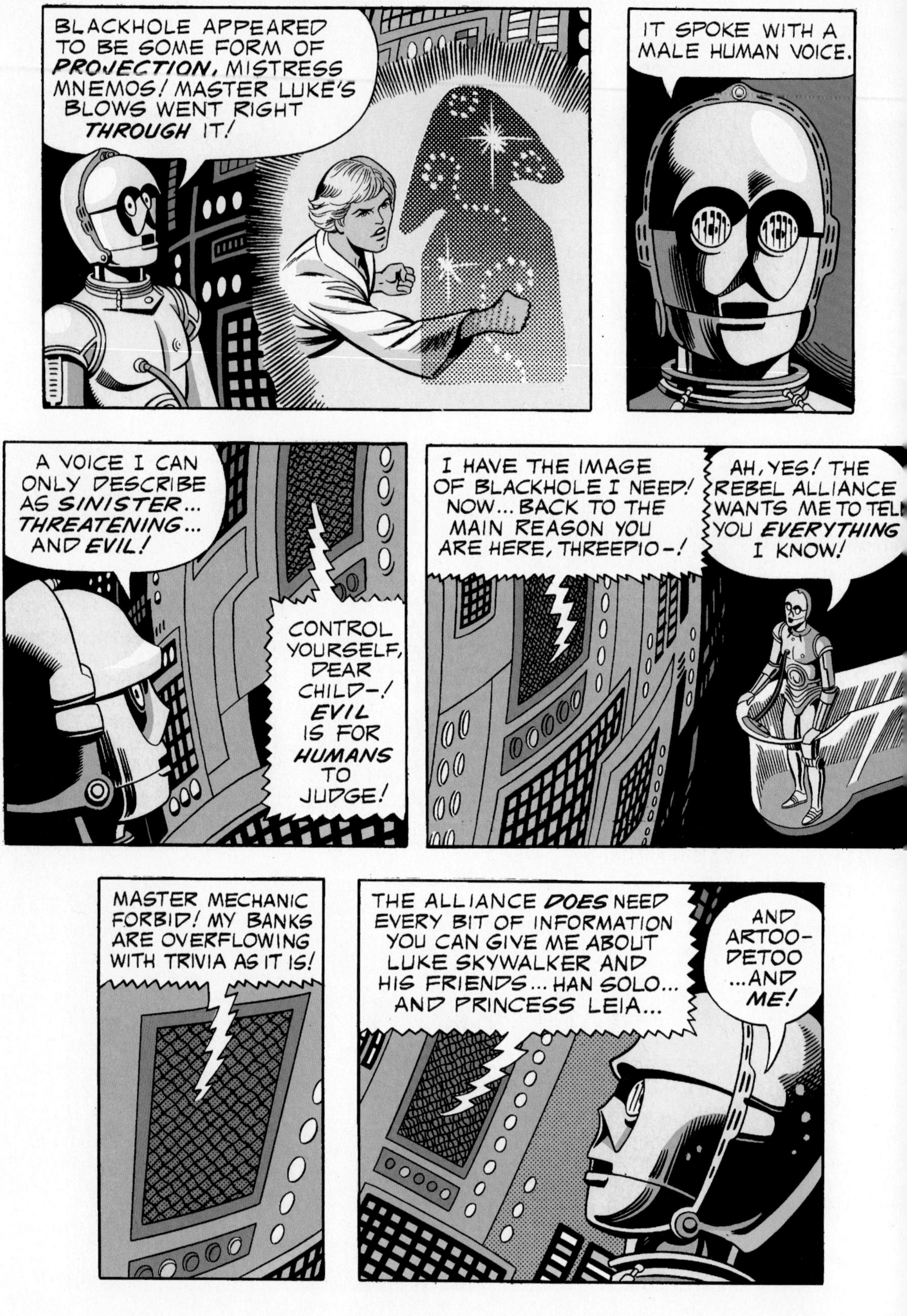
BLACKHOLE APPEARED TO BE SOME FORM OF PROJECTION, MISTRESS MNEMOS! MASTER LUKE'S BLOWS WENT RIGHT THROUGH IT!
IT SPOKE WITH A MALE HUMAN VOICE.
A VOICE I CAN ONLY DESCRIBE AS SINISTER... THREATENING... AND EVIL!
CONTROL YOURSELF, DEAR CHILD--! EVIL IS FOR HUMANS TO JUDGE!
I HAVE THE IMAGE OF BLACKHOLE I NEED! NOW... BACK TO THE MAIN REASON YOU ARE HERE, THREEPIO--!
AH, YES! THE REBEL ALLIANCE WANTS ME TO TELL YOU EVERYTHING I KNOW!
MASTER MECHANIC FORBID! MY BANKS ARE OVERFLOWING WITH TRIVIA AS IT IS!
THE ALLIANCE DOES NEED EVERY BIT OF INFORMATION YOU CAN GIVE ME ABOUT LUKE SKYWALKER AND HIS FRIENDS... HAN SOLO... AND PRINCESS LEIA...
AND ARTOO-DETOO ...AND ME!

WHAT HAPPENED NEXT IN THE BATTLE AGAINST BLACKHOLE?
OH... IT WAS TERRIBLE... TERRIBLE!
IT WAS ALL ARTOO-DETOO'S FAULT! IF THAT WALKING CATASTROPHE HADN'T CAUSED ME TO—
STOP, THREEPIO! I WANT TO HEAR ABOUT LUKE SKYWALKER... NOT JUST ABOUT YOU! NOW START WHERE YOUR LAST STORY ENDED!
AFTER WE ESCAPED FROM BLACKHOLE THE FIRST TIME—
STOP! I'VE JUST SCANNED A CROSS REFERENCE IN MY ESPIONAGE BANK...
...A SCRAP OF TAPE OBTAINED BY A REBEL SPY ABOARD THE IMPERIAL SPACE FLEET COMMAND SHIP...
I TELL YOU, IT COULDN'T BE HELPED, LORD VADER—!

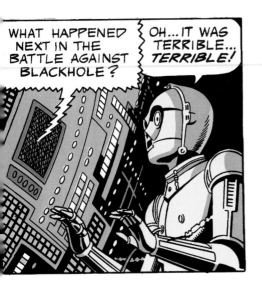

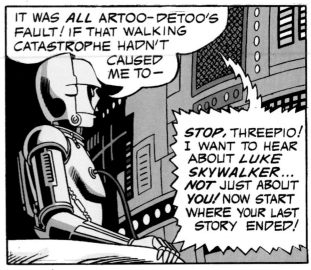

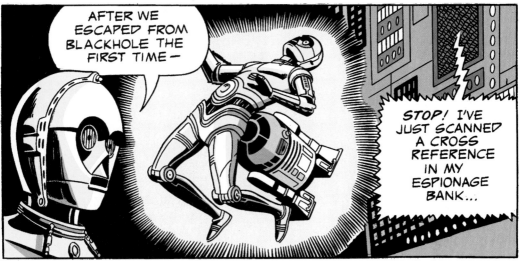

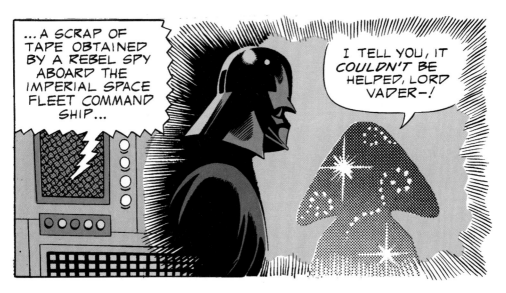

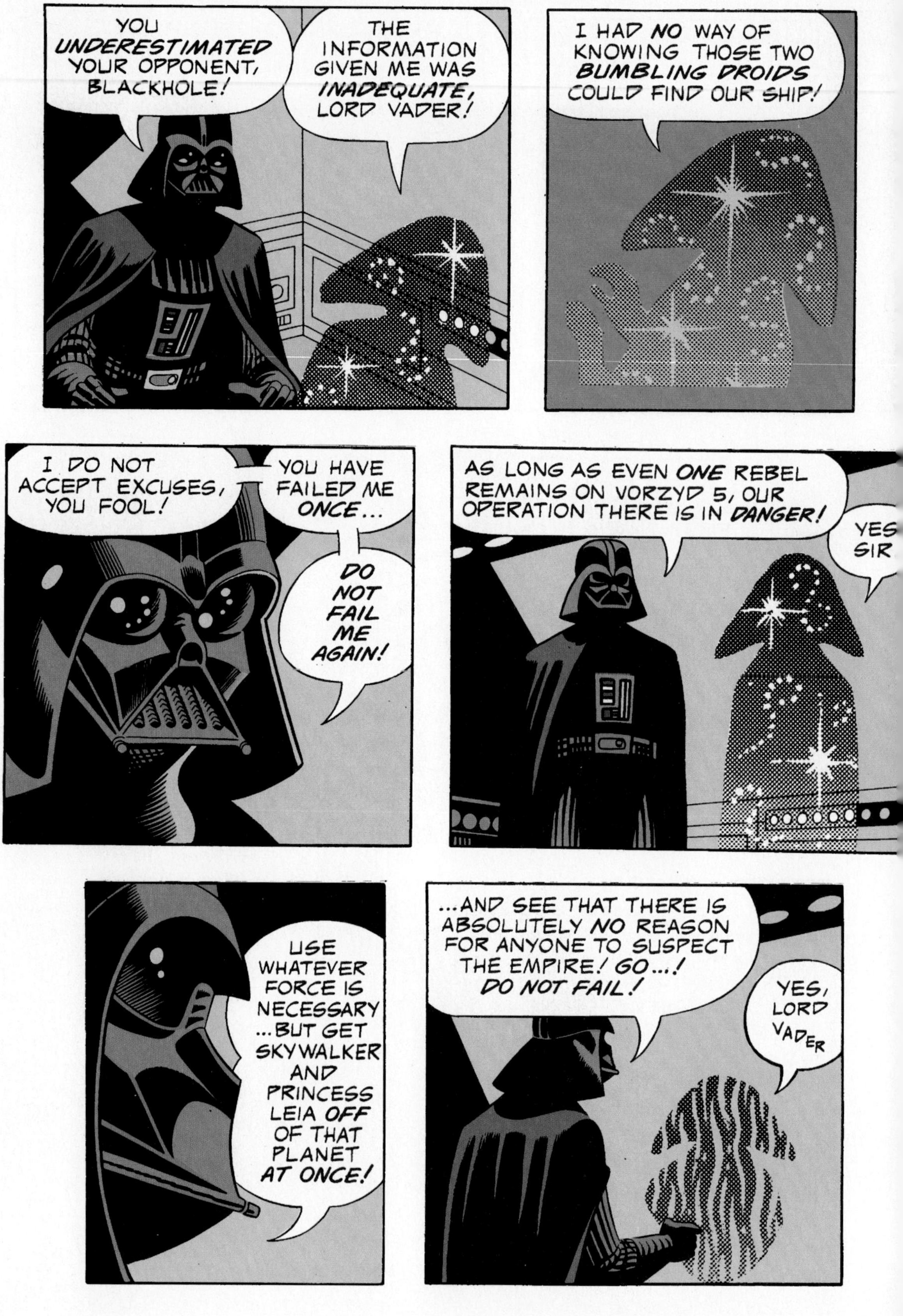
YOU UNDERESTIMATED YOUR OPPONENT, BLACKHOLE!
THE INFORMATION GIVEN ME WAS INADEQUATE, LORD VADER!
I HAD NO WAY OF KNOWING THOSE TWO BUMBLING DROIDS COULD FIND OUR SHIP!
I DO NOT ACCEPT EXCUSES, YOU FOOL!
YOU HAVE FAILED ME ONCE...
DO NOT FAIL ME AGAIN!
AS LONG AS EVEN ONE REBEL REMAINS ON VORZYD 5, OUR OPERATION THERE IS IN DANGER!
YES SIR
USE WHATEVER FORCE IS NECESSARY ...BUT GET SKYWALKER AND PRINCESS LEIA OFF OF THAT PLANET AT ONCE!
...AND SEE THAT THERE IS ABSOLUTELY NO REASON FOR ANYONE TO SUSPECT THE EMPIRE! GO...! DO NOT FAIL!
YES, LORD VADER

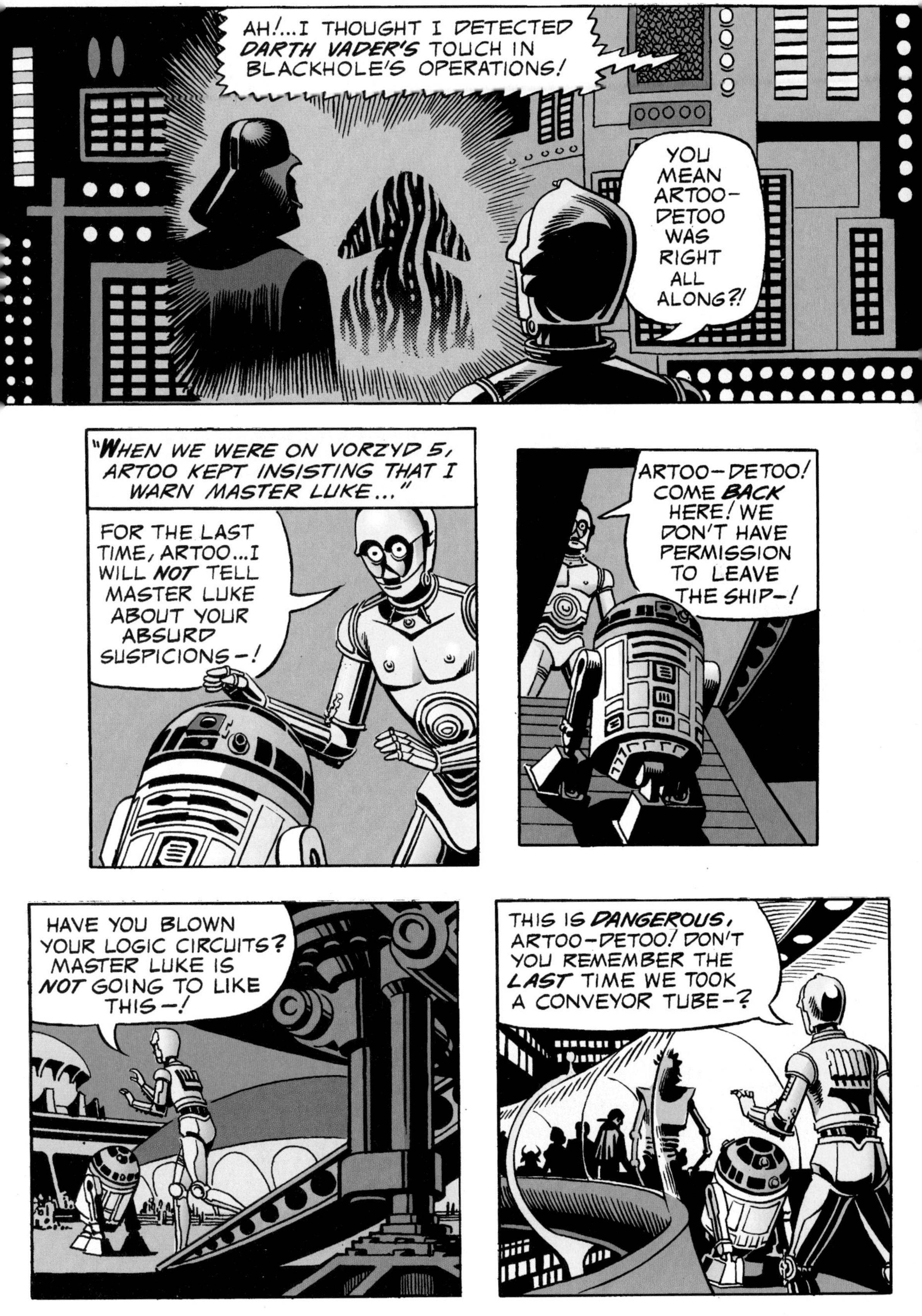
AH!...I THOUGHT I DETECTED DARTH VADER'S TOUCH IN BLACKHOLE'S OPERATIONS!
YOU MEAN ARTOO-DETOO WAS RIGHT ALL ALONG?!
"WHEN WE WERE ON VORZYD 5, ARTOO KEPT INSISTING THAT I WARN MASTER LUKE..."
FOR THE LAST TIME, ARTOO...I WILL NOT TELL MASTER LUKE ABOUT YOUR ABSURD SUSPICIONS-!
ARTOO-DETOO! COME BACK HERE! WE DON'T HAVE PERMISSION TO LEAVE THE SHIP-!
HAVE YOU BLOWN YOUR LOGIC CIRCUITS? MASTER LUKE IS NOT GOING TO LIKE THIS-!
THIS IS DANGEROUS, ARTOO-DETOO! DON'T YOU REMEMBER THE LAST TIME WE TOOK A CONVEYOR TUBE-?

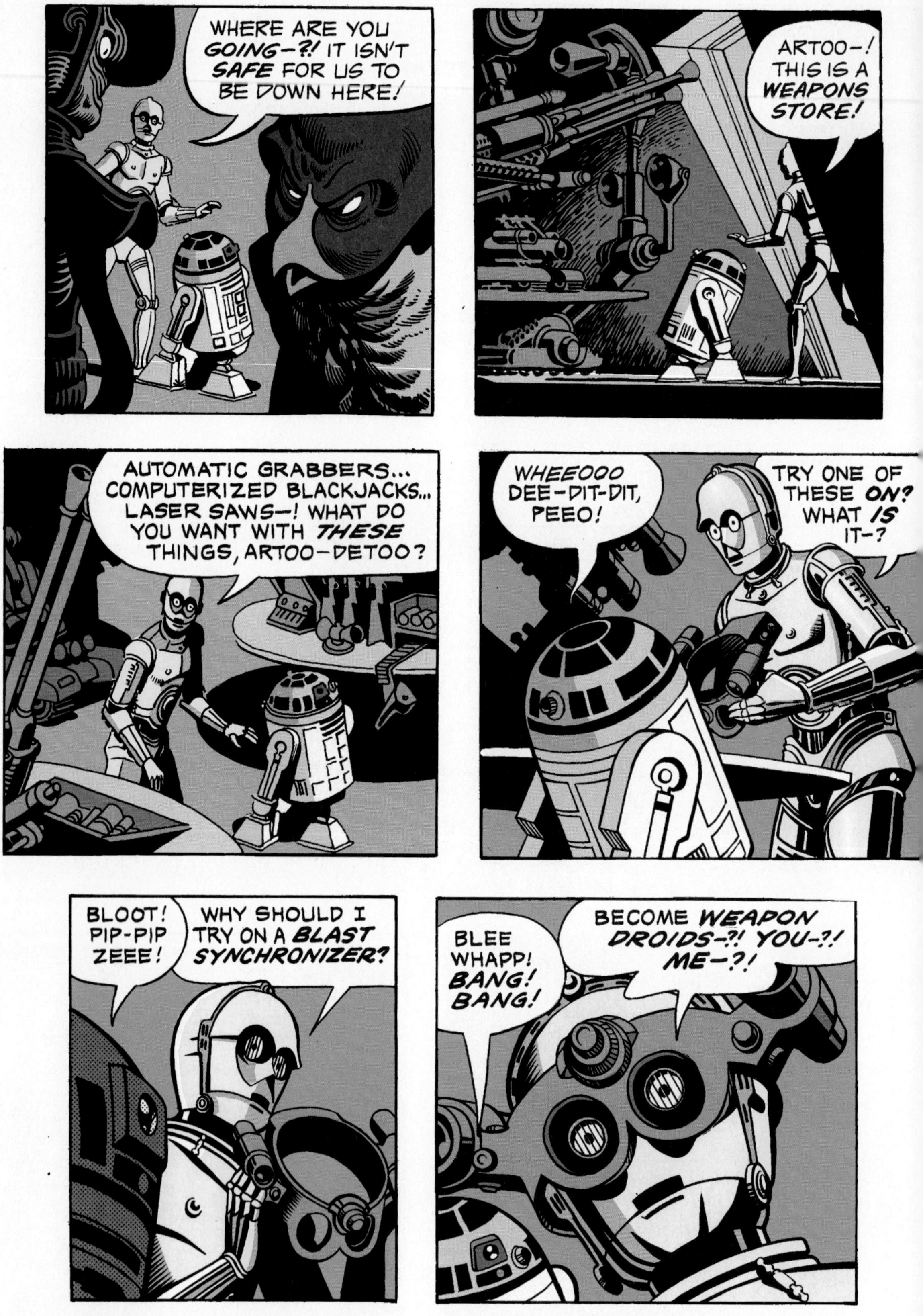
WHERE ARE YOU GOING--?! IT ISN'T SAFE FOR US TO BE DOWN HERE!
ARTOO--! THIS IS A WEAPONS STORE!
AUTOMATIC GRABBERS... COMPUTERIZED BLACKJACKS... LASER SAWS--! WHAT DO YOU WANT WITH THESE THINGS, ARTOO-DETOO?
WHEEOOO DEE-DIT-DIT, PEEO!
TRY ONE OF THESE ON? WHAT IS IT--?
BLOOT! PIP-PIP ZEEE!
WHY SHOULD I TRY ON A BLAST SYNCHRONIZER?
BLEE WHAPP! BANG! BANG!
BECOME WEAPON DROIDS--?! YOU--?! ME--?!

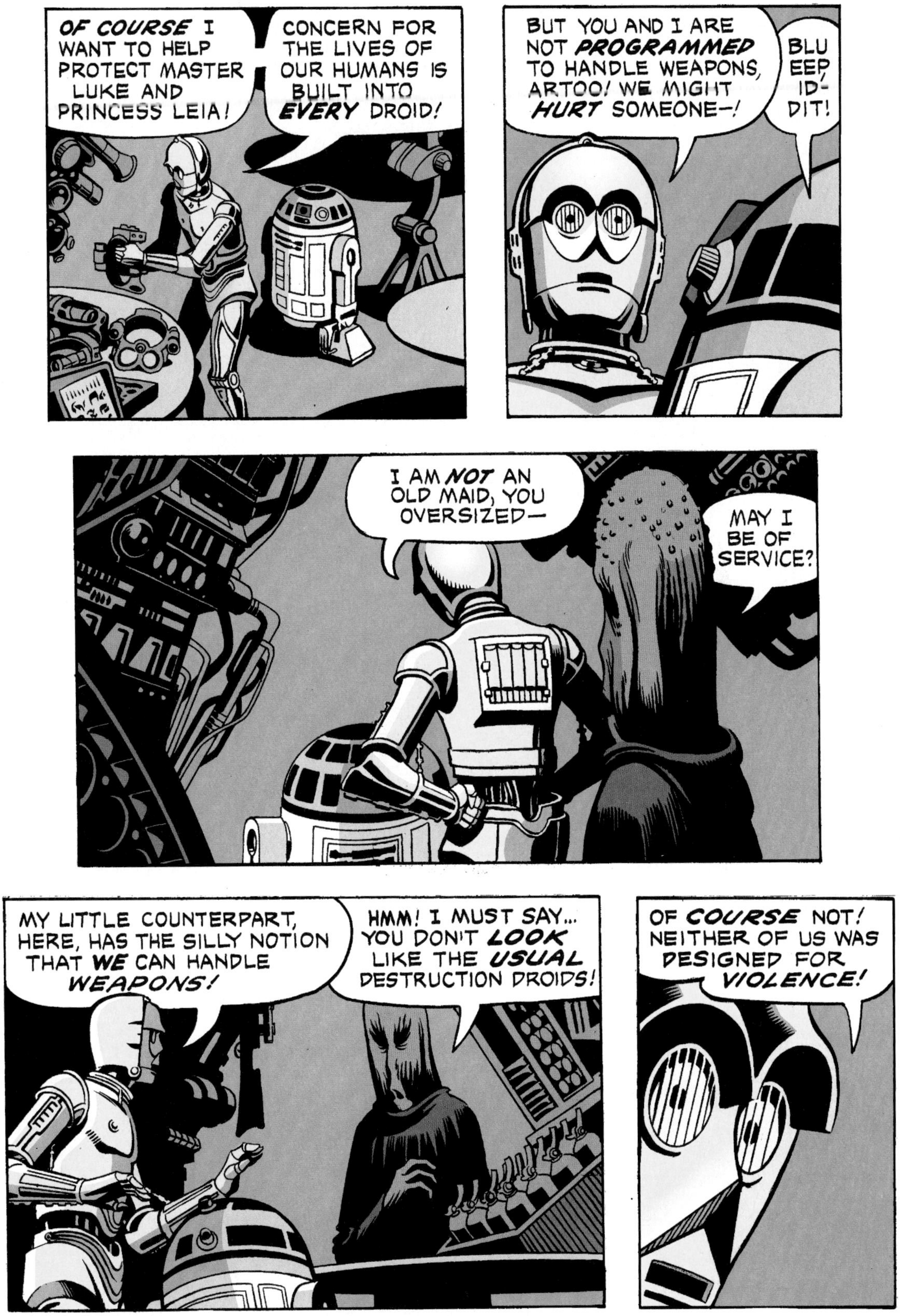
OF COURSE I WANT TO HELP PROTECT MASTER LUKE AND PRINCESS LEIA!
CONCERN FOR THE LIVES OF OUR HUMANS IS BUILT INTO EVERY DROID!
BUT YOU AND I ARE NOT PROGRAMMED TO HANDLE WEAPONS, ARTOO! WE MIGHT HURT SOMEONE--!
BLU EEP ID-DIT!
I AM NOT AN OLD MAID, YOU OVERSIZED--
MAY I BE OF SERVICE?
MY LITTLE COUNTERPART, HERE, HAS THE SILLY NOTION THAT WE CAN HANDLE WEAPONS!
HMM! I MUST SAY... YOU DON'T LOOK LIKE THE USUAL DESTRUCTION DROIDS!
OF COURSE NOT! NEITHER OF US WAS DESIGNED FOR VIOLENCE!

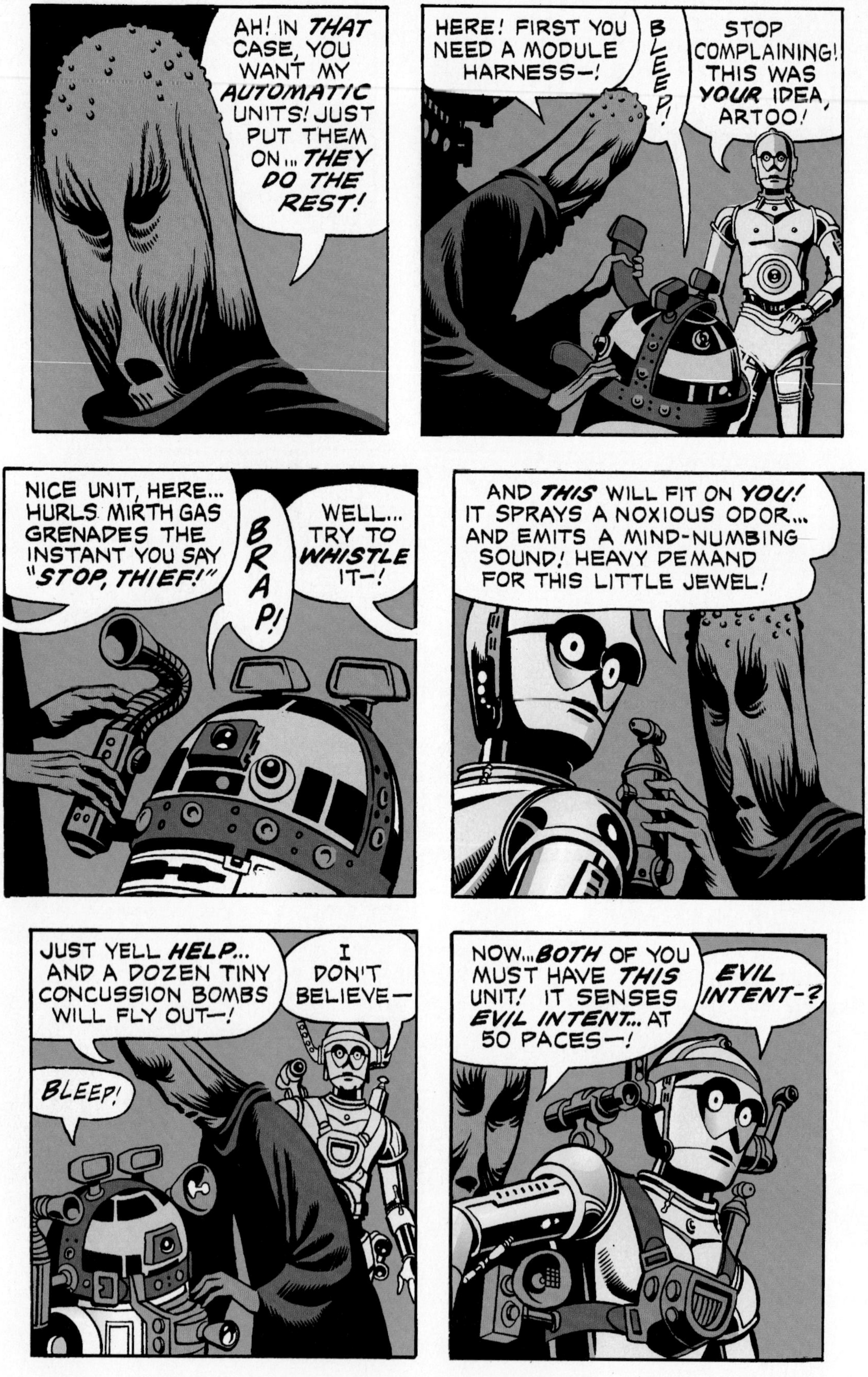
AH! IN THAT CASE, YOU WANT MY AUTOMATIC UNITS! JUST PUT THEM ON... THEY DO THE REST!
HERE! FIRST YOU NEED A MODULE HARNESS—!
BLEEP!
STOP COMPLAINING! THIS WAS YOUR IDEA, ARTOO!
NICE UNIT, HERE... HURLS MIRTH GAS GRENADES THE INSTANT YOU SAY "STOP, THIEF!"
BRAP!
WELL... TRY TO WHISTLE IT—!
AND THIS WILL FIT ON YOU! IT SPRAYS A NOXIOUS ODOR... AND EMITS A MIND-NUMBING SOUND! HEAVY DEMAND FOR THIS LITTLE JEWEL!
JUST YELL HELP... AND A DOZEN TINY CONCUSSION BOMBS WILL FLY OUT—!
I DON'T BELIEVE—
BLEEP!
NOW... BOTH OF YOU MUST HAVE THIS UNIT! IT SENSES EVIL INTENT... AT 50 PACES—!
EVIL INTENT—?

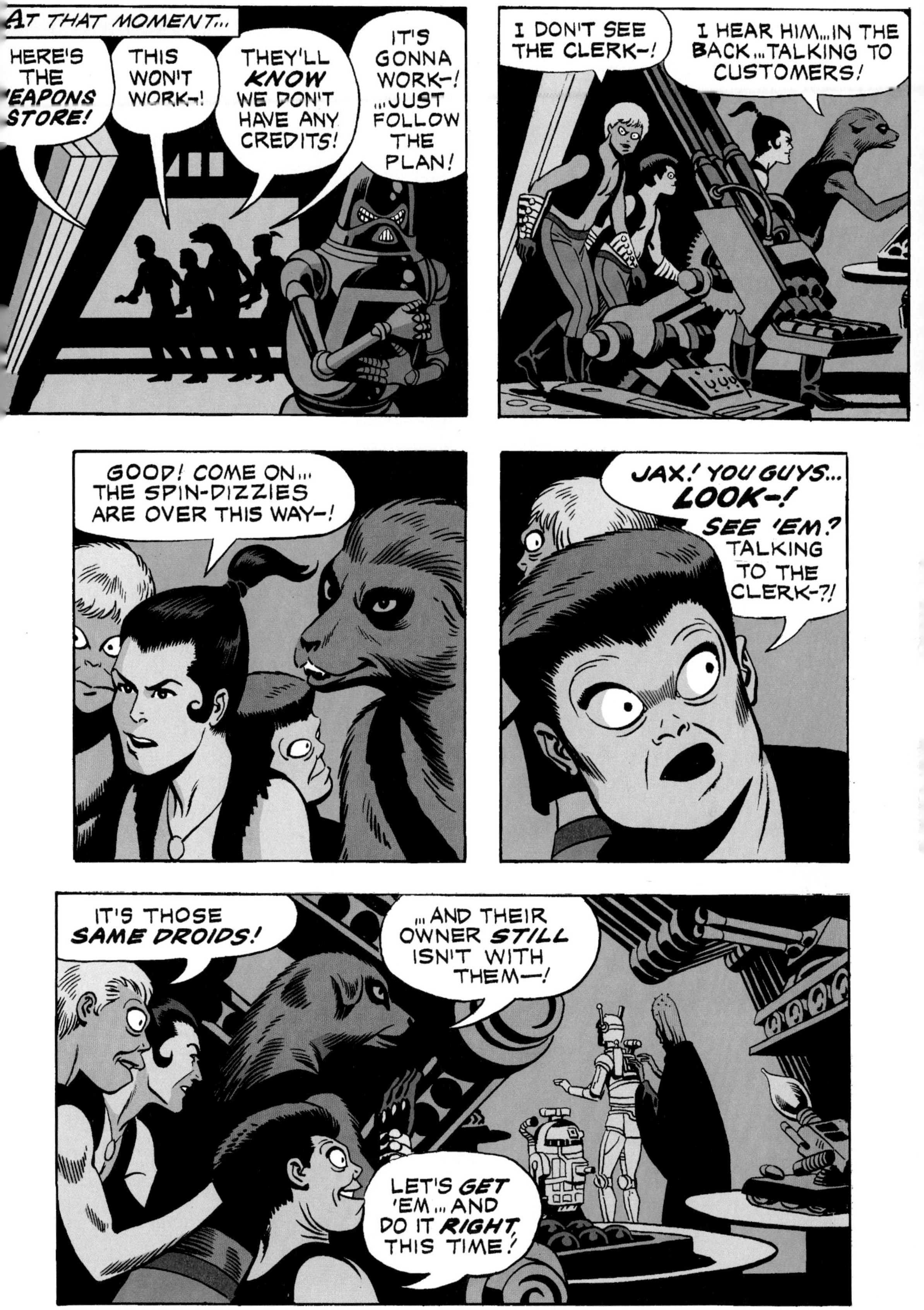
AT THAT MOMENT...
HERE'S THE 'EAPONS STORE!
THIS WON'T WORK--!
THEY'LL KNOW WE DON'T HAVE ANY CREDITS!
IT'S GONNA WORK--! ...JUST FOLLOW THE PLAN!
I DON'T SEE THE CLERK--!
I HEAR HIM...IN THE BACK...TALKING TO CUSTOMERS!
GOOD! COME ON... THE SPIN-DIZZIES ARE OVER THIS WAY--!
JAX! YOU GUYS... LOOK--!
SEE 'EM? TALKING TO THE CLERK--?!
IT'S THOSE SAME DROIDS!
...AND THEIR OWNER STILL ISN'T WITH THEM--!
LET'S GET 'EM...AND DO IT RIGHT THIS TIME!

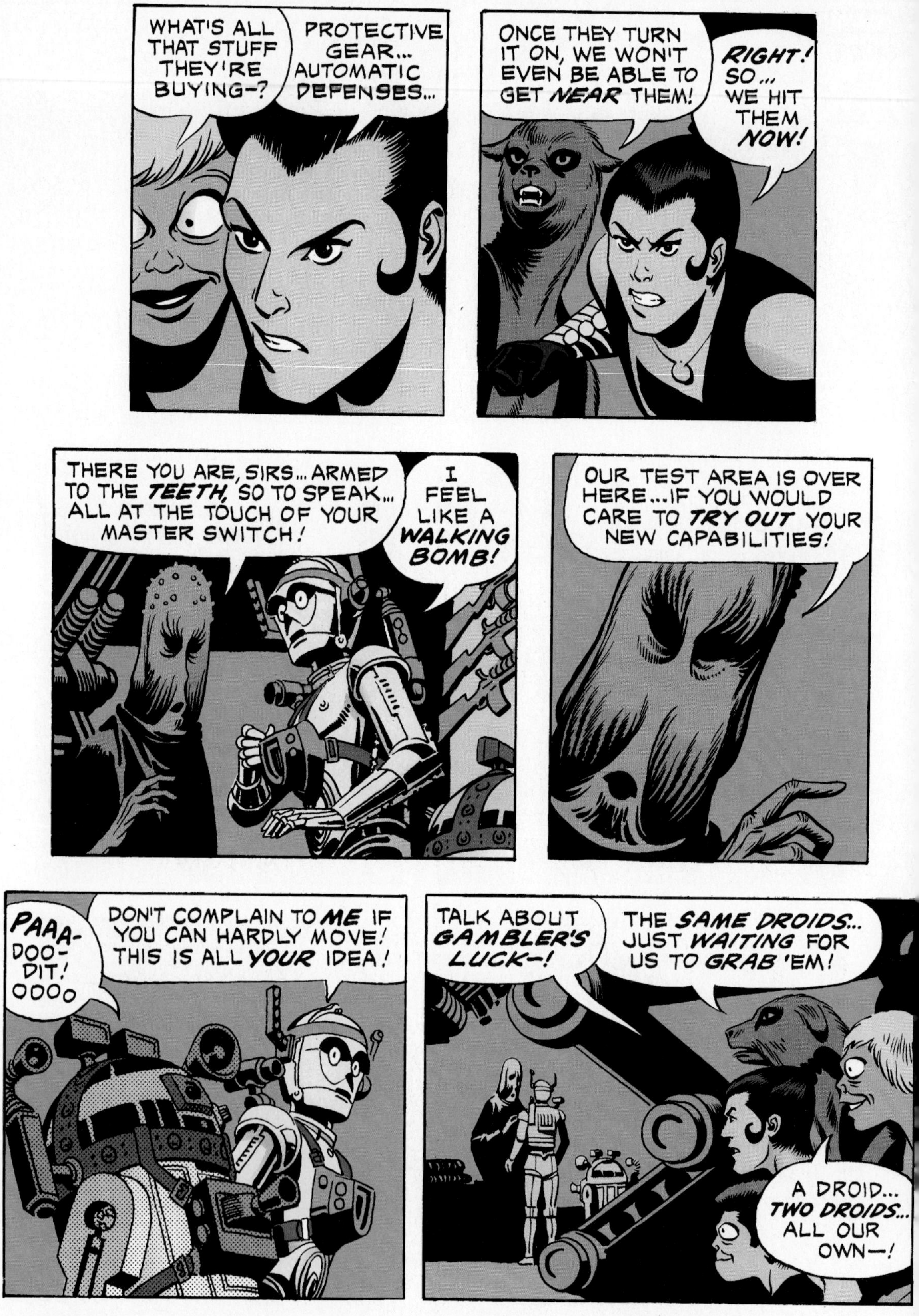
WHAT'S ALL THAT STUFF THEY'RE BUYING-?
PROTECTIVE GEAR... AUTOMATIC DEFENSES...
ONCE THEY TURN IT ON, WE WON'T EVEN BE ABLE TO GET NEAR THEM!
RIGHT! SO... WE HIT THEM NOW!
THERE YOU ARE, SIRS... ARMED TO THE TEETH, SO TO SPEAK... ALL AT THE TOUCH OF YOUR MASTER SWITCH!
I FEEL LIKE A WALKING BOMB!
OUR TEST AREA IS OVER HERE... IF YOU WOULD CARE TO TRY OUT YOUR NEW CAPABILITIES!
PAAA-DOO-DIT! OOOo
DON'T COMPLAIN TO ME IF YOU CAN HARDLY MOVE! THIS IS ALL YOUR IDEA!
TALK ABOUT GAMBLER'S LUCK-!
THE SAME DROIDS... JUST WAITING FOR US TO GRAB 'EM!
A DROID... TWO DROIDS... ALL OUR OWN-!

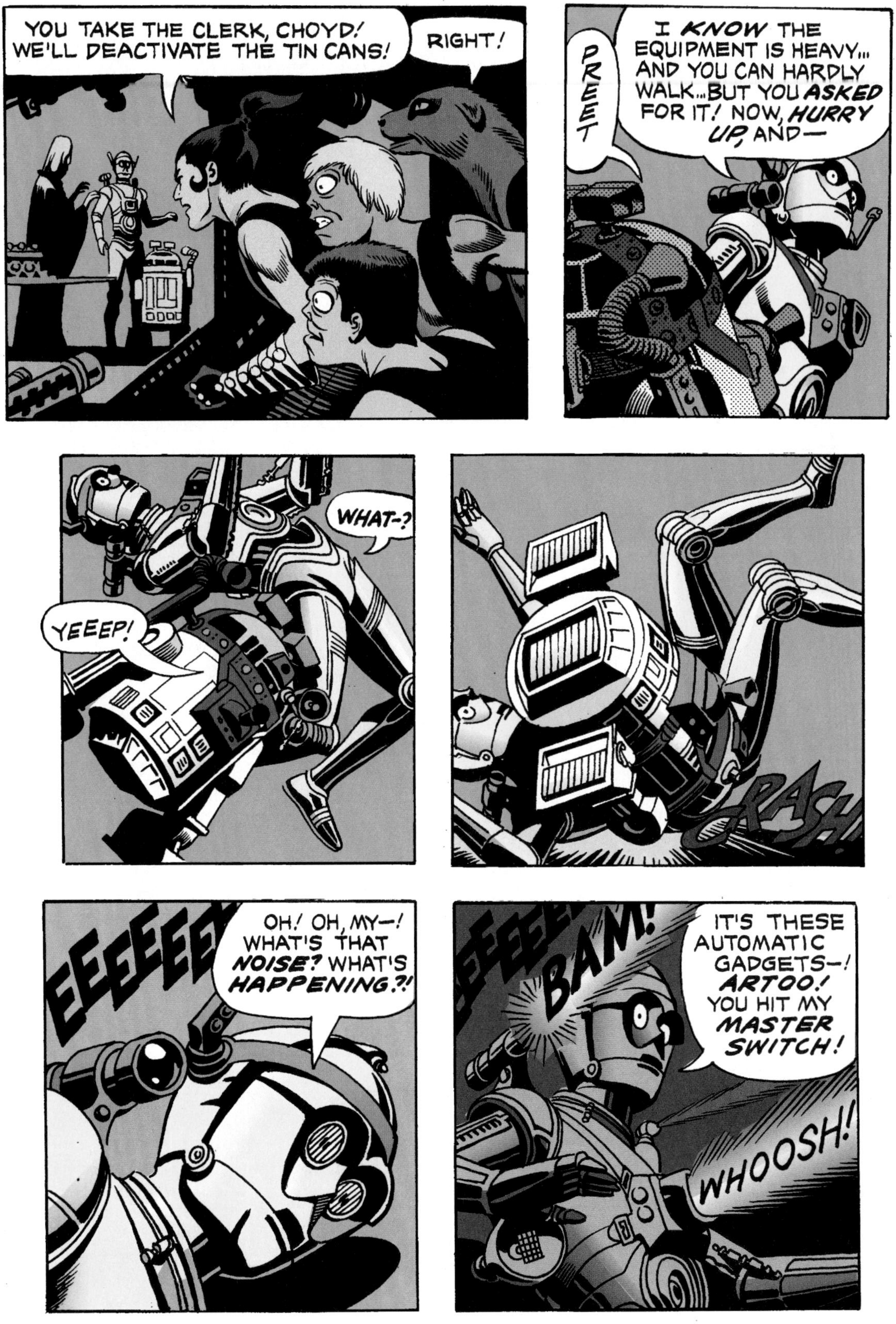
YOU TAKE THE CLERK, CHOYD! WE'LL DEACTIVATE THE TIN CANS!
RIGHT!
PREET
I KNOW THE EQUIPMENT IS HEAVY... AND YOU CAN HARDLY WALK... BUT YOU ASKED FOR IT! NOW, HURRY UP, AND—
WHAT-?
YEEEP!
CRASH!
EEEEEEE
OH! OH, MY—! WHAT'S THAT NOISE? WHAT'S HAPPENING?!
BAM!
IT'S THESE AUTOMATIC GADGETS—! ARTOO! YOU HIT MY MASTER SWITCH!
WHOOSH!

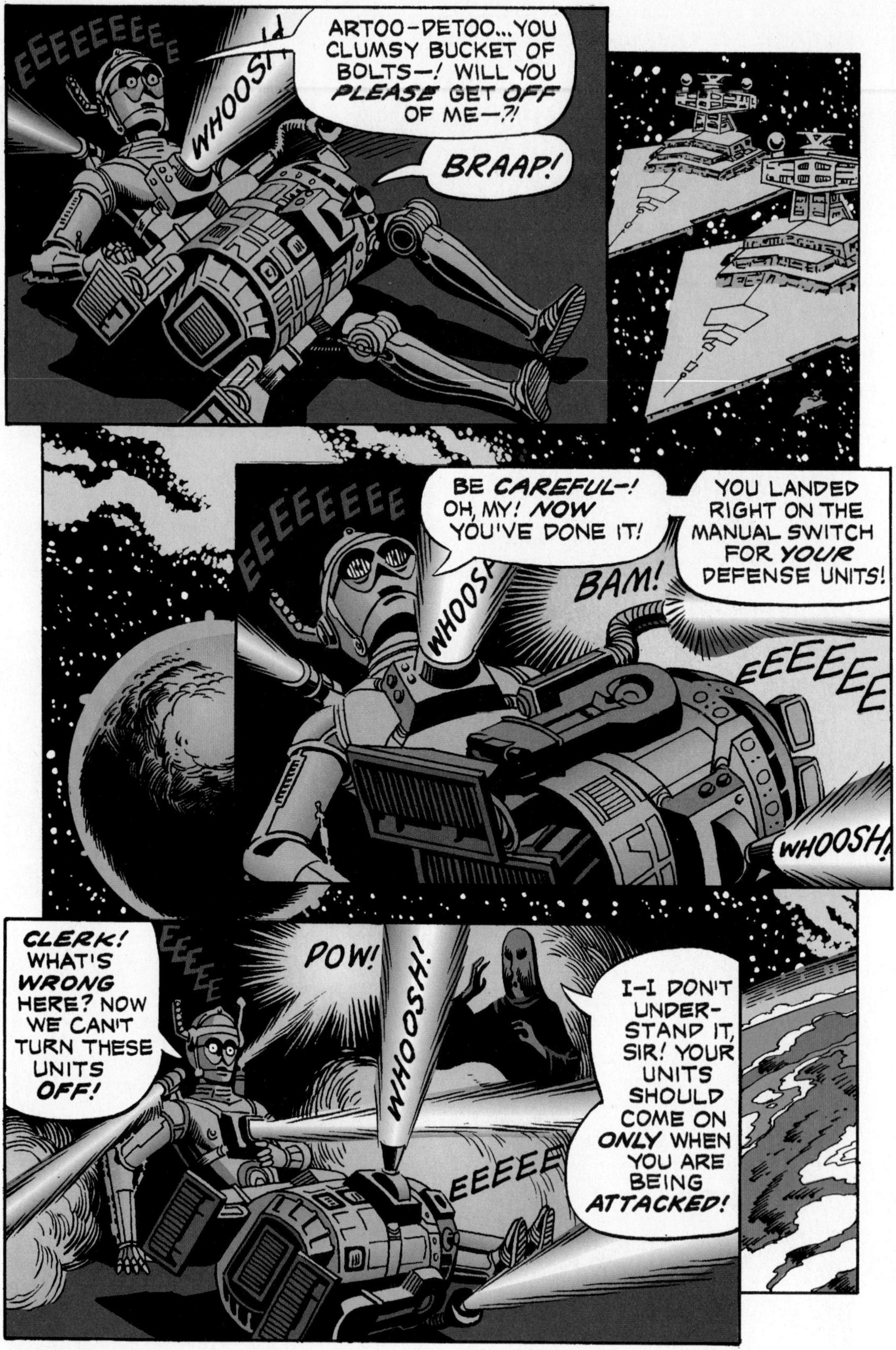

EEEEEEEEEE
WHOOSH!
ARTOO-DETOO...YOU CLUMSY BUCKET OF BOLTS—! WILL YOU PLEASE GET OFF OF ME—?!
BRAAP!
EEEEEEEEE
BE CAREFUL—! OH, MY! NOW YOU'VE DONE IT!
WHOOSH
BAM!
YOU LANDED RIGHT ON THE MANUAL SWITCH FOR YOUR DEFENSE UNITS!
EEEEEEE
WHOOSH!
CLERK! WHAT'S WRONG HERE? NOW WE CAN'T TURN THESE UNITS OFF!
EEEEE
POW!
WHOOSH!
I—I DON'T UNDER-STAND IT, SIR! YOUR UNITS SHOULD COME ON ONLY WHEN YOU ARE BEING ATTACKED!
EEEEE

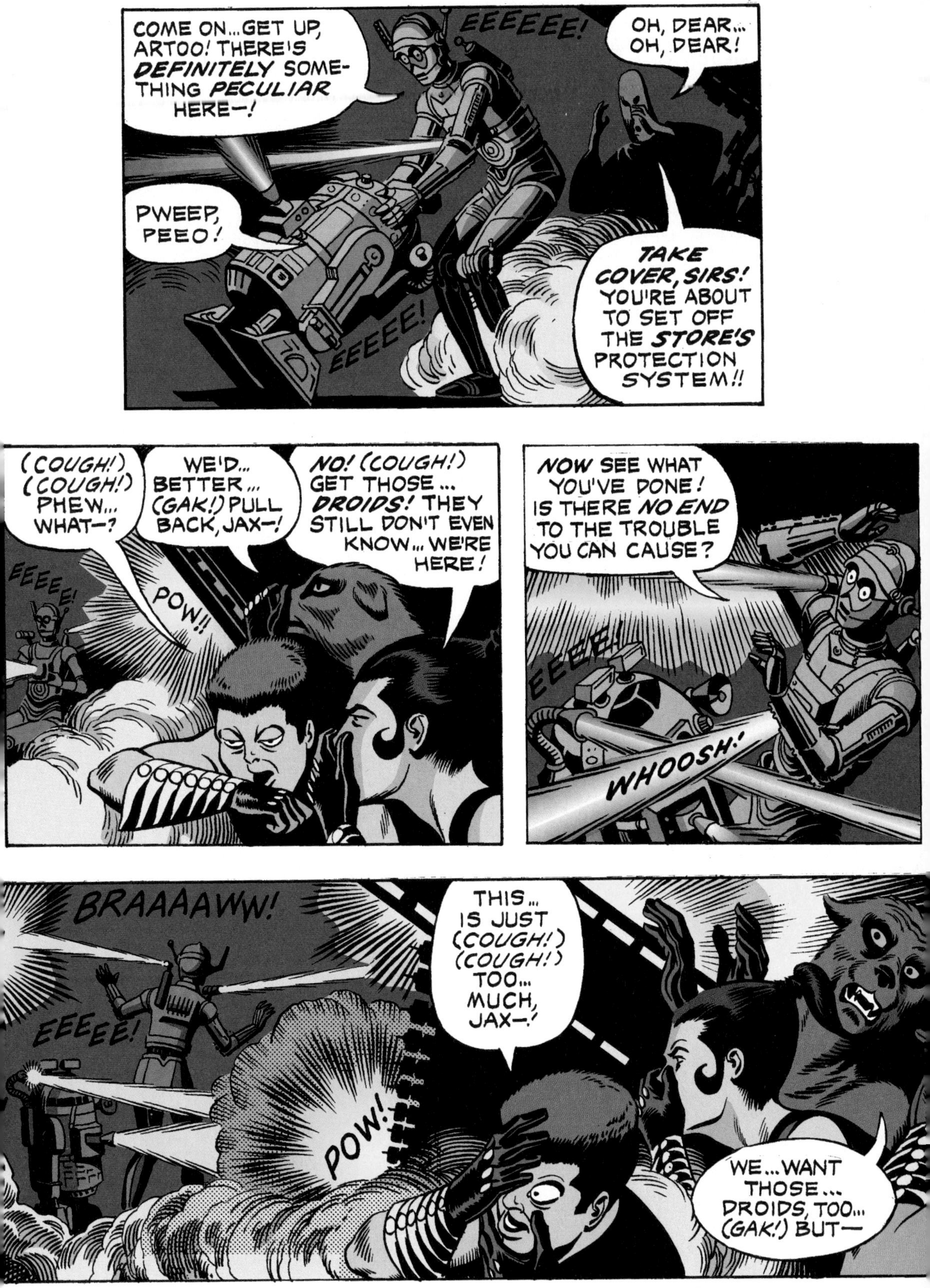
COME ON...GET UP, ARTOO! THERE'S DEFINITELY SOMETHING PECULIAR HERE—!
EEEEEEE!
OH, DEAR... OH, DEAR!
PWEEP, PEEO!
EEEEEE!
TAKE COVER, SIRS! YOU'RE ABOUT TO SET OFF THE STORE'S PROTECTION SYSTEM!!
(COUGH!) (COUGH!) PHEW... WHAT—?
WE'D... BETTER... (GAK!) PULL BACK, JAX—!
NO! (COUGH!) GET THOSE... DROIDS! THEY STILL DON'T EVEN KNOW... WE'RE HERE!
EEEEE!
POW!!
NOW SEE WHAT YOU'VE DONE! IS THERE NO END TO THE TROUBLE YOU CAN CAUSE?
WHOOSH!
BRAAAAWW!
EEEEEE!
THIS... IS JUST (COUGH!) (COUGH!) TOO... MUCH, JAX—!
POW!
WE...WANT THOSE... DROIDS, TOO... (GAK!) BUT—

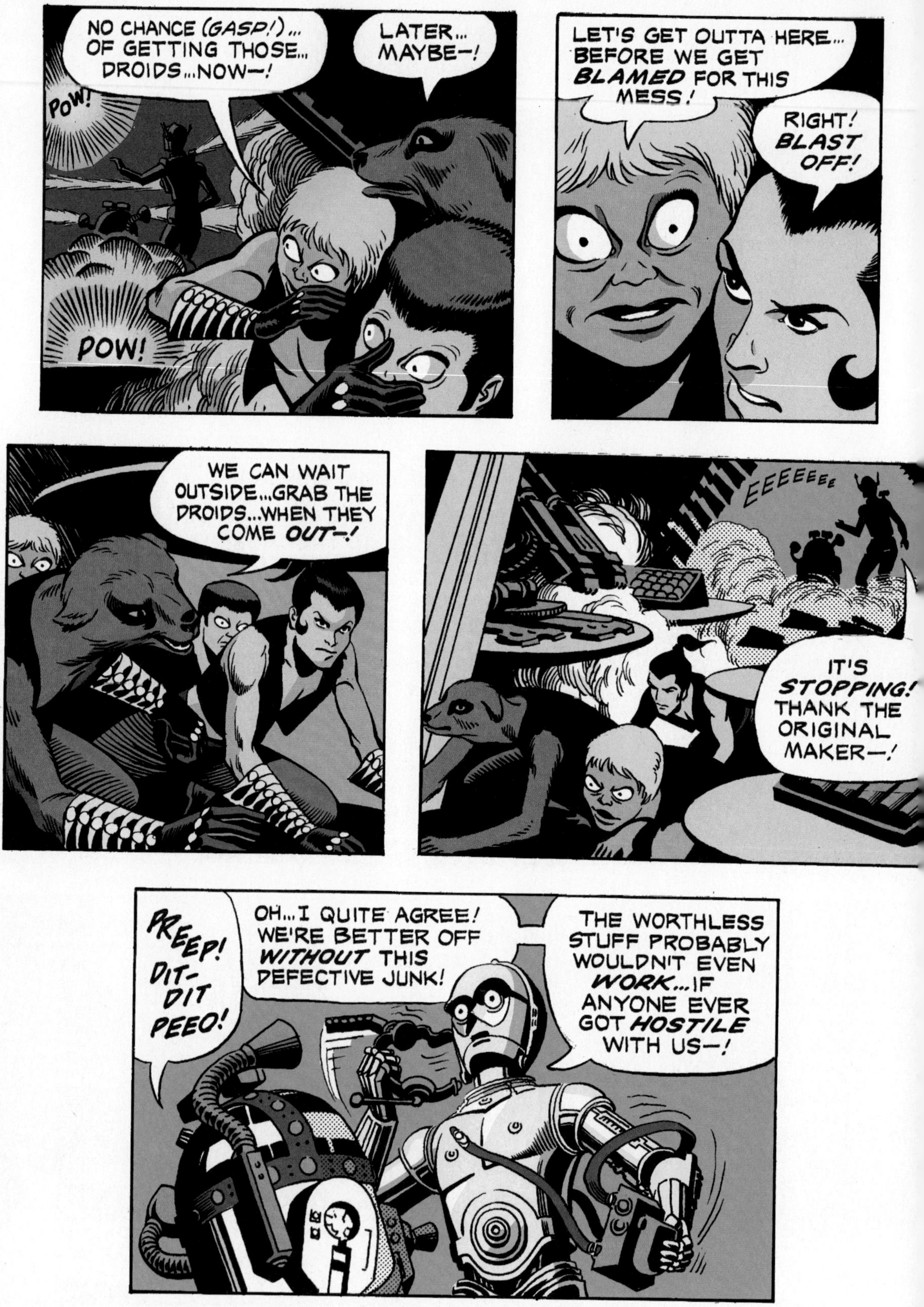
NO CHANCE (GASP!)... OF GETTING THOSE... DROIDS...NOW—!
LATER... MAYBE—!
POW!
POW!
LET'S GET OUTTA HERE... BEFORE WE GET BLAMED FOR THIS MESS!
RIGHT! BLAST OFF!
WE CAN WAIT OUTSIDE...GRAB THE DROIDS...WHEN THEY COME OUT—!
EEEEEEee
IT'S STOPPING! THANK THE ORIGINAL MAKER—!
PREEP! DIT-DIT PEEO!
OH... I QUITE AGREE! WE'RE BETTER OFF WITHOUT THIS DEFECTIVE JUNK!
THE WORTHLESS STUFF PROBABLY WOULDN'T EVEN WORK... IF ANYONE EVER GOT HOSTILE WITH US—!

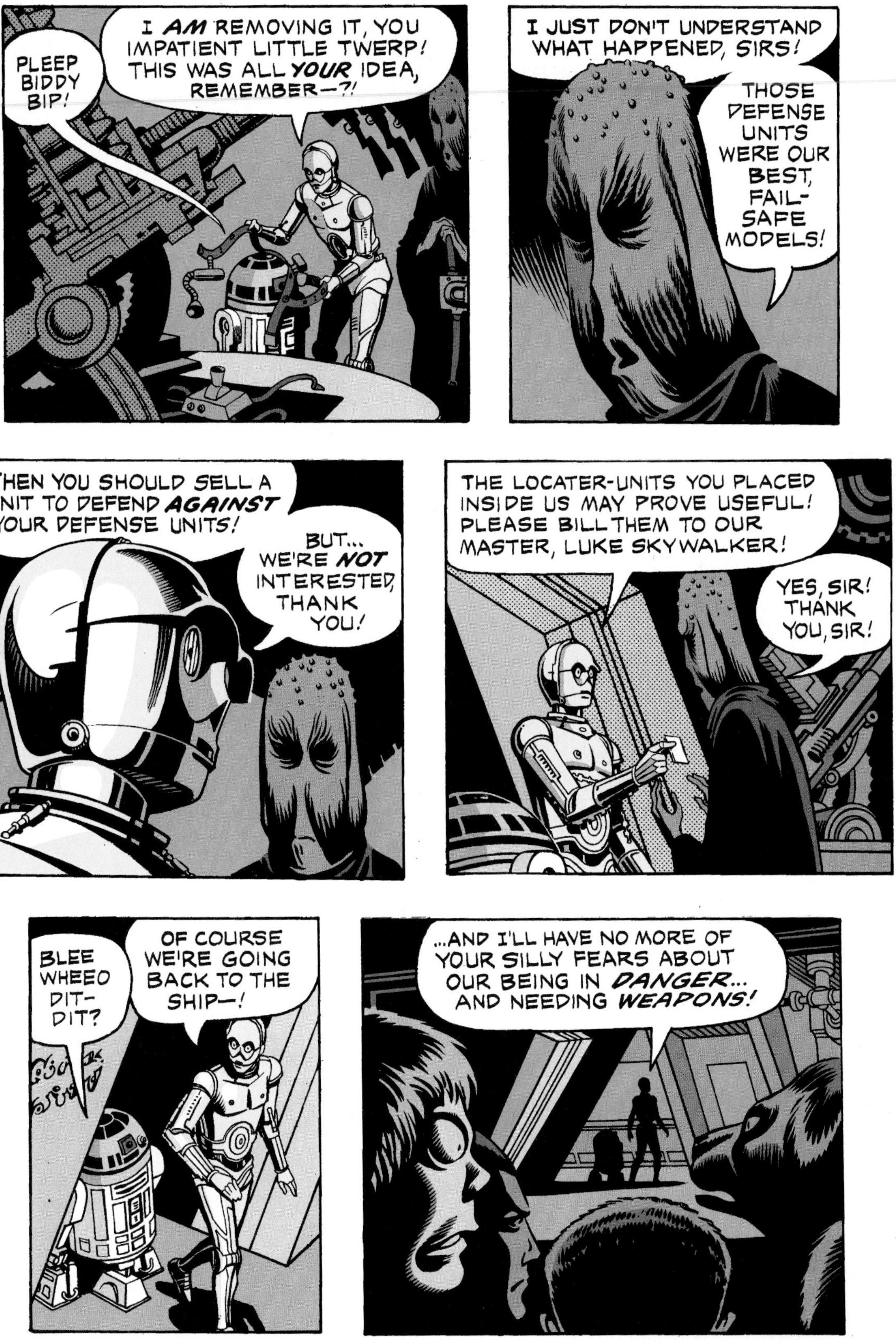
PLEEP BIDDY BIP!
I AM REMOVING IT, YOU IMPATIENT LITTLE TWERP! THIS WAS ALL YOUR IDEA, REMEMBER—?!
I JUST DON'T UNDERSTAND WHAT HAPPENED, SIRS!
THOSE DEFENSE UNITS WERE OUR BEST, FAIL-SAFE MODELS!
THEN YOU SHOULD SELL A UNIT TO DEFEND AGAINST YOUR DEFENSE UNITS!
BUT... WE'RE NOT INTERESTED, THANK YOU!
THE LOCATER-UNITS YOU PLACED INSIDE US MAY PROVE USEFUL! PLEASE BILL THEM TO OUR MASTER, LUKE SKYWALKER!
YES, SIR! THANK YOU, SIR!
BLEE WHEEO DIT-DIT?
OF COURSE WE'RE GOING BACK TO THE SHIP—!
...AND I'LL HAVE NO MORE OF YOUR SILLY FEARS ABOUT OUR BEING IN DANGER... AND NEEDING WEAPONS!

CONTINUED NEXT ISSUE

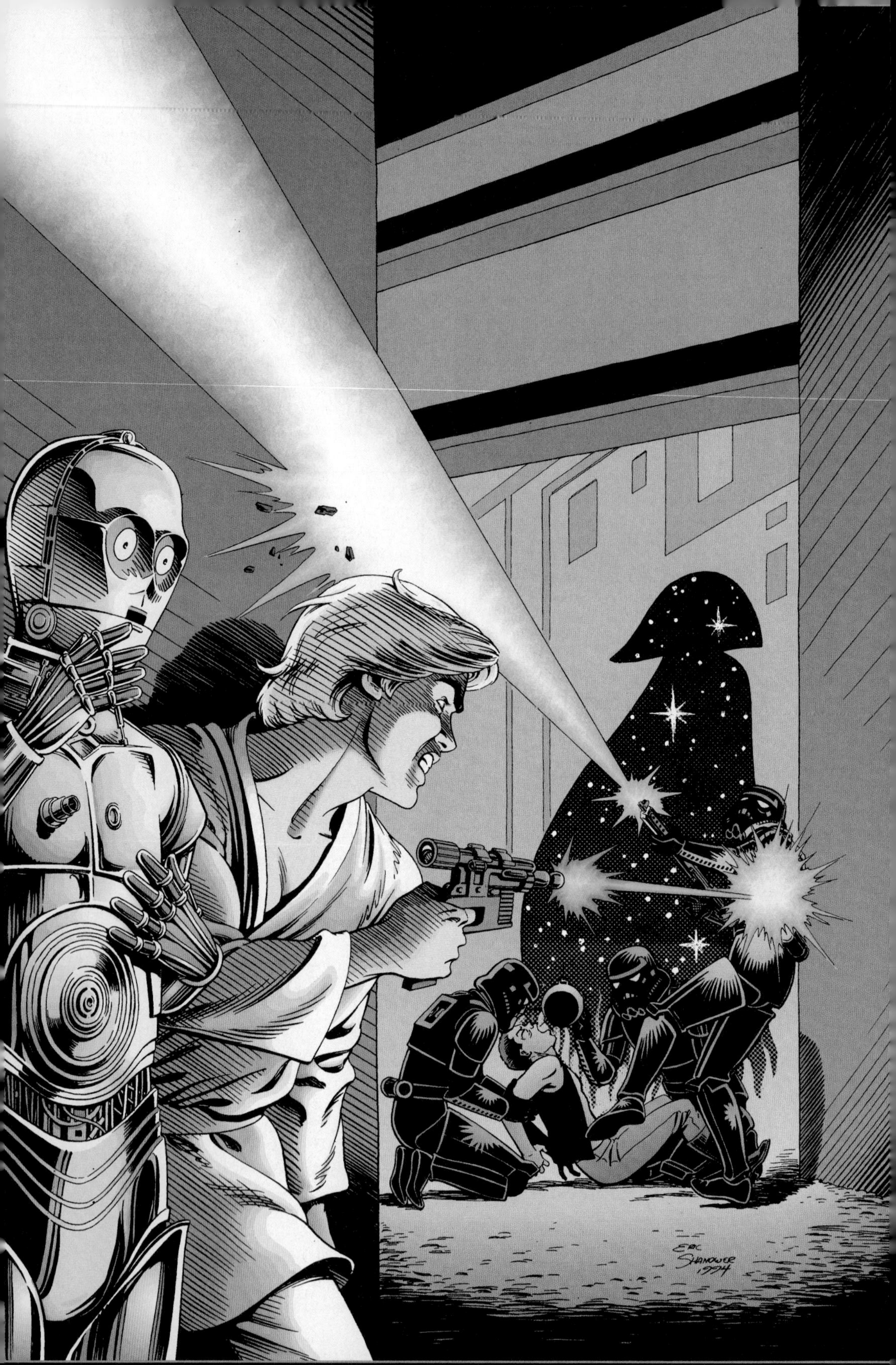
ERIC SHANOWER 1994

CLASSIC STAR WARS: THE EARLY ADVENTURES #3
ORIGINALLY PUBLISHED WEEKDAYS & SATURDAYS FROM JULY 11 TO SEPTEMBER 8, 1979

WRITER & PENCILER: RUSS MANNING • INKERS & LETTERERS: MIKE ROYER & RUSS MANNING • ART RETOUCHING: RICK HOBERG • COLORIST: RAY MURTAUGH
EDITORS: BOB COOPER & PEET JANES • COVER ARTISTS: ERIC SHANOWER & MATTHEW HOLLINGSWORTH

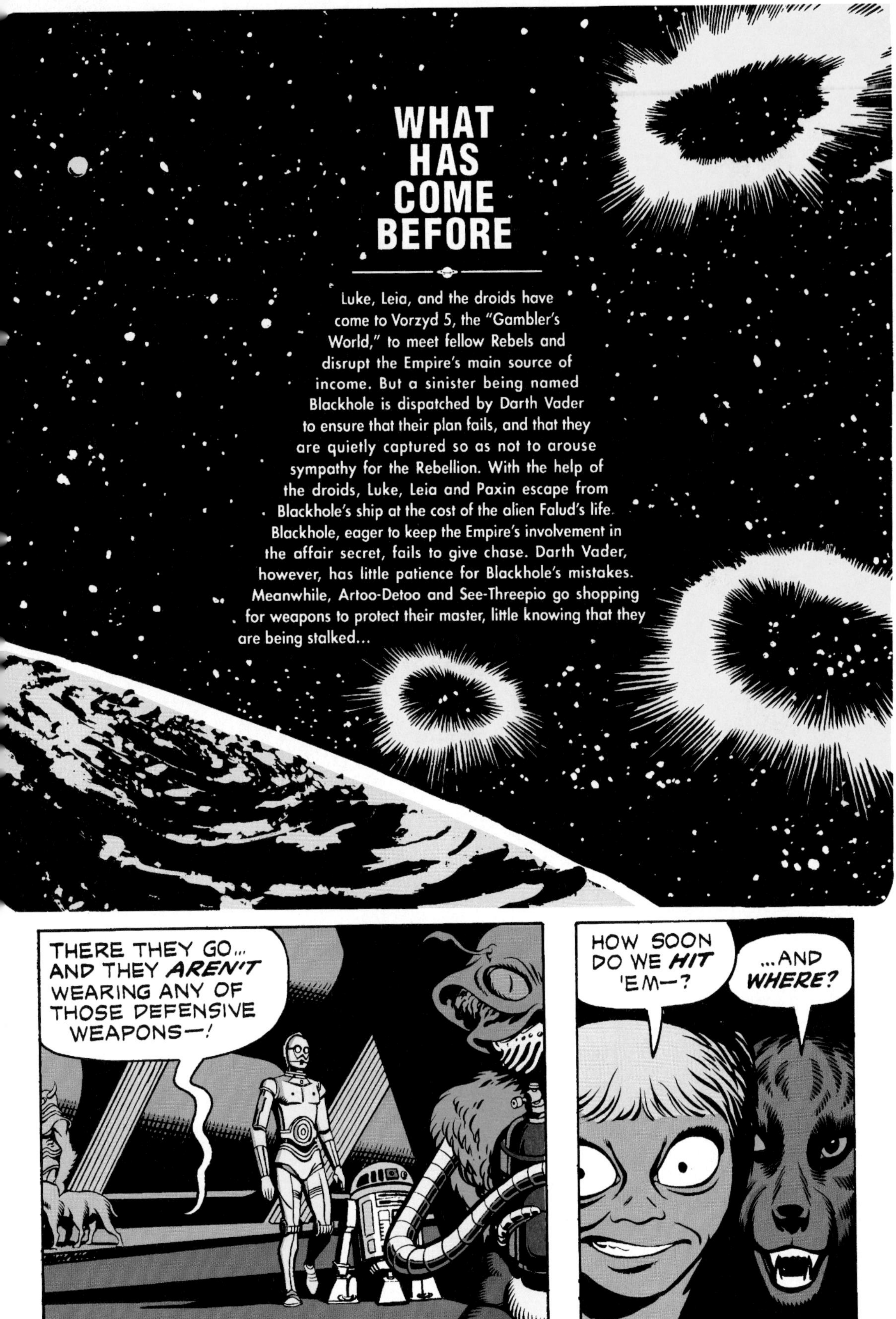
WHAT HAS COME BEFORE
Luke, Leia, and the droids have come to Vorzyd 5, the "Gambler's World," to meet fellow Rebels and disrupt the Empire's main source of income. But a sinister being named Blackhole is dispatched by Darth Vader to ensure that their plan fails, and that they are quietly captured so as not to arouse sympathy for the Rebellion. With the help of the droids, Luke, Leia and Paxin escape from Blackhole's ship at the cost of the alien Falud's life. Blackhole, eager to keep the Empire's involvement in the affair secret, fails to give chase. Darth Vader, however, has little patience for Blackhole's mistakes. Meanwhile, Artoo-Detoo and See-Threepio go shopping for weapons to protect their master, little knowing that they are being stalked...
THERE THEY GO... AND THEY *AREN'T* WEARING ANY OF THOSE DEFENSIVE WEAPONS—!
HOW SOON DO WE *HIT* 'EM—?
...AND *WHERE?*

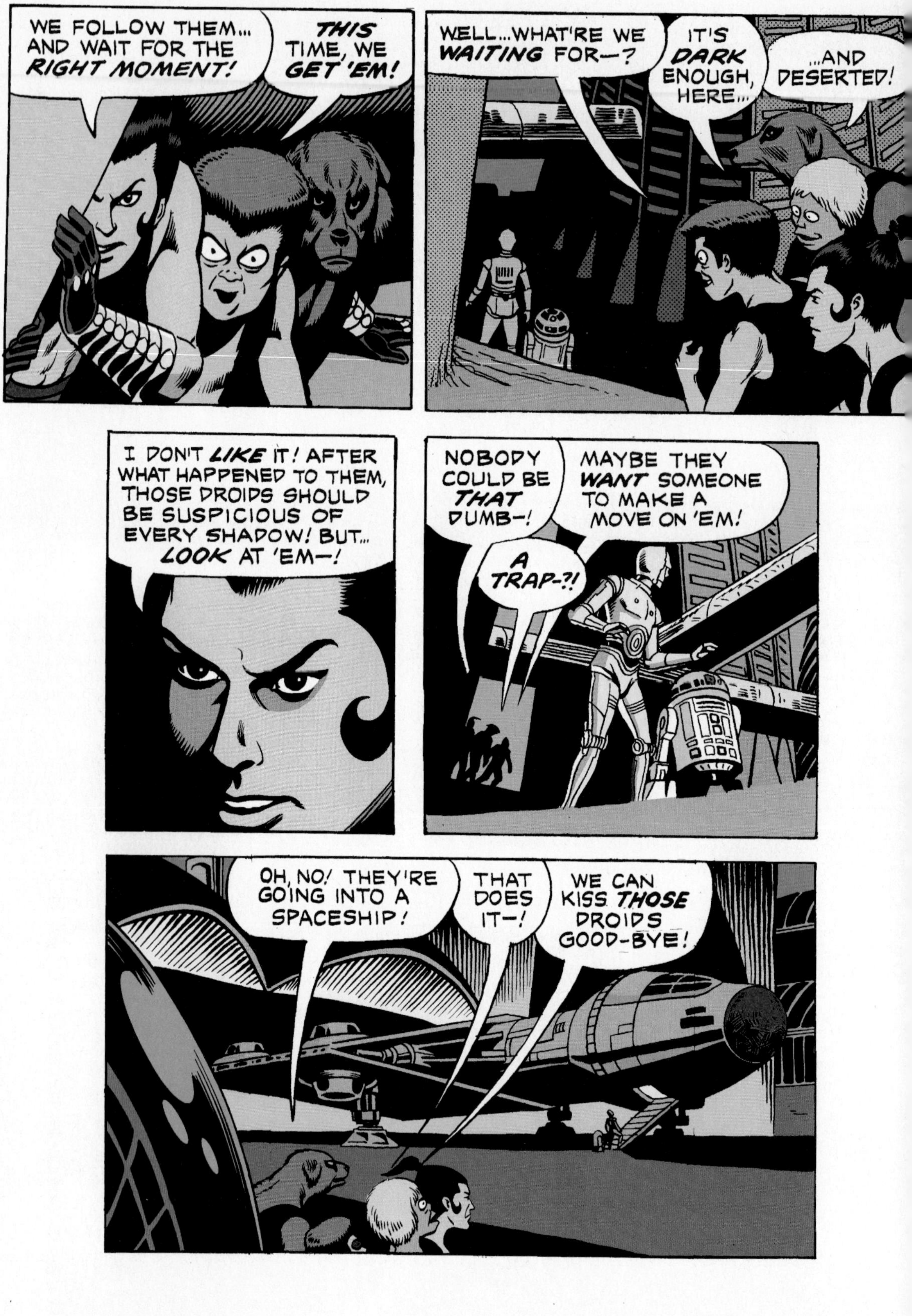
WE FOLLOW THEM... AND WAIT FOR THE RIGHT MOMENT!
THIS TIME, WE GET 'EM!
WELL...WHAT'RE WE WAITING FOR—?
IT'S DARK ENOUGH, HERE...
...AND DESERTED!
I DON'T LIKE IT! AFTER WHAT HAPPENED TO THEM, THOSE DROIDS SHOULD BE SUSPICIOUS OF EVERY SHADOW! BUT... LOOK AT 'EM—!
NOBODY COULD BE THAT DUMB—!
MAYBE THEY WANT SOMEONE TO MAKE A MOVE ON 'EM!
A TRAP-?!
OH, NO! THEY'RE GOING INTO A SPACESHIP!
THAT DOES IT—!
WE CAN KISS THOSE DROIDS GOOD-BYE!

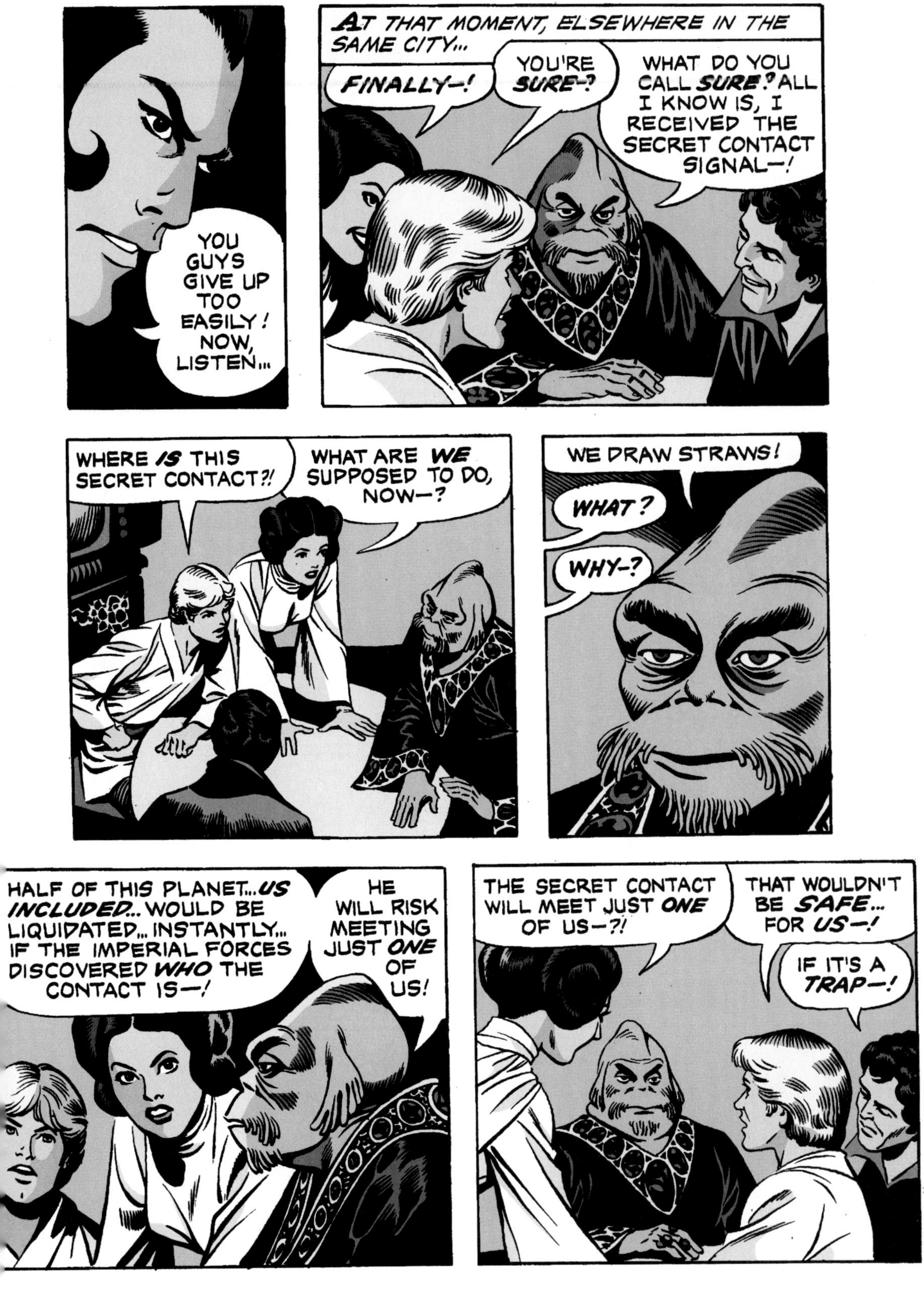
YOU GUYS GIVE UP TOO EASILY! NOW, LISTEN...
AT THAT MOMENT, ELSEWHERE IN THE SAME CITY...
FINALLY-!
YOU'RE SURE-?
WHAT DO YOU CALL SURE? ALL I KNOW IS, I RECEIVED THE SECRET CONTACT SIGNAL-!
WHERE IS THIS SECRET CONTACT?!
WHAT ARE WE SUPPOSED TO DO, NOW-?
WE DRAW STRAWS!
WHAT?
WHY-?
HALF OF THIS PLANET...US INCLUDED... WOULD BE LIQUIDATED... INSTANTLY... IF THE IMPERIAL FORCES DISCOVERED WHO THE CONTACT IS-!
HE WILL RISK MEETING JUST ONE OF US!
THE SECRET CONTACT WILL MEET JUST ONE OF US-?!
THAT WOULDN'T BE SAFE... FOR US-!
IF IT'S A TRAP-!

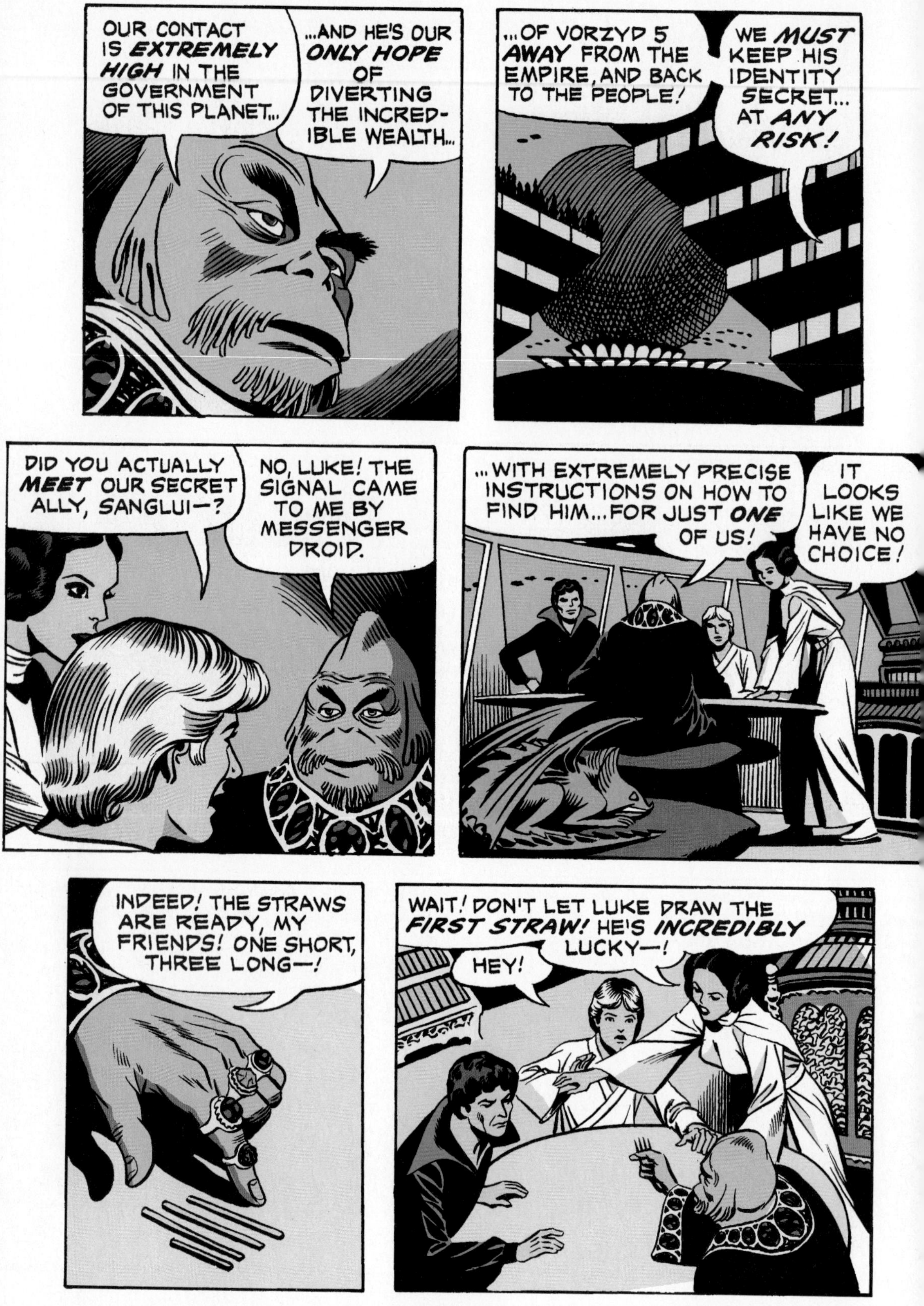
OUR CONTACT IS EXTREMELY HIGH IN THE GOVERNMENT OF THIS PLANET...
...AND HE'S OUR ONLY HOPE OF DIVERTING THE INCREDIBLE WEALTH...
...OF VORZYD 5 AWAY FROM THE EMPIRE, AND BACK TO THE PEOPLE!
WE MUST KEEP HIS IDENTITY SECRET... AT ANY RISK!
DID YOU ACTUALLY MEET OUR SECRET ALLY, SANGLUI—?
NO, LUKE! THE SIGNAL CAME TO ME BY MESSENGER DROID.
...WITH EXTREMELY PRECISE INSTRUCTIONS ON HOW TO FIND HIM... FOR JUST ONE OF US!
IT LOOKS LIKE WE HAVE NO CHOICE!
INDEED! THE STRAWS ARE READY, MY FRIENDS! ONE SHORT, THREE LONG—!
WAIT! DON'T LET LUKE DRAW THE FIRST STRAW! HE'S INCREDIBLY LUCKY—!
HEY!

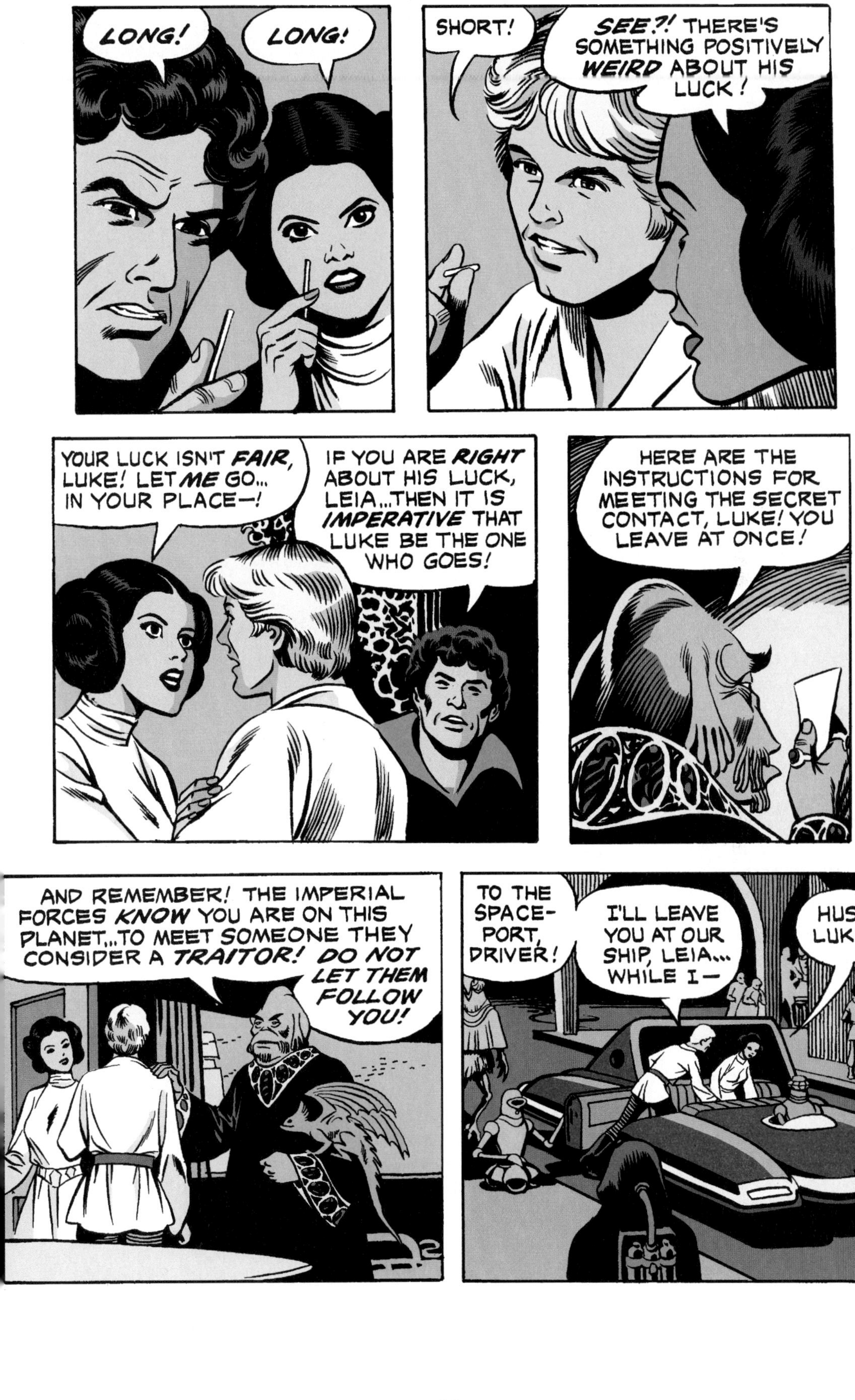
LONG!
LONG!
SHORT!
SEE?! THERE'S SOMETHING POSITIVELY WEIRD ABOUT HIS LUCK!
YOUR LUCK ISN'T FAIR, LUKE! LET ME GO... IN YOUR PLACE—!
IF YOU ARE RIGHT ABOUT HIS LUCK, LEIA...THEN IT IS IMPERATIVE THAT LUKE BE THE ONE WHO GOES!
HERE ARE THE INSTRUCTIONS FOR MEETING THE SECRET CONTACT, LUKE! YOU LEAVE AT ONCE!
AND REMEMBER! THE IMPERIAL FORCES KNOW YOU ARE ON THIS PLANET...TO MEET SOMEONE THEY CONSIDER A TRAITOR! DO NOT LET THEM FOLLOW YOU!
TO THE SPACE-PORT, DRIVER!
I'LL LEAVE YOU AT OUR SHIP, LEIA... WHILE I—
HUSH, LUKE!

DON'T FORGET...EVEN FOR AN INSTANT...THAT THE EMPIRE HAS SPIES...AND SURVEILLANCE METHODS... WE CAN'T EVEN *GUESS* AT!

THE UTTERLY UNSPEAKABLES MAY ALREADY BE TRACKING US—!

UWU! UWUTUWU!

PAD 583, DRIVER!

I SHOULD BE GOING *WITH* YOU, LUKE ...TO BACK YOU UP, IN CASE...

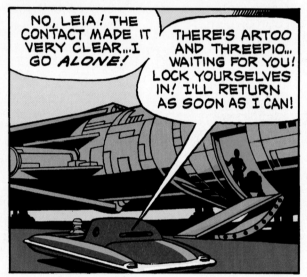

NO, LEIA! THE CONTACT MADE IT VERY CLEAR...I GO *ALONE!*

THERE'S ARTOO AND THREEPIO... WAITING FOR YOU! LOCK YOURSELVES IN! I'LL RETURN AS SOON AS I CAN!

ALL RIGHT, LUKE! BE CAREFUL... AND MAY THE FORCE BE WITH YOU—!

DON'T LET ANYONE ABOARD UNTIL I COME BACK, LEIA—!

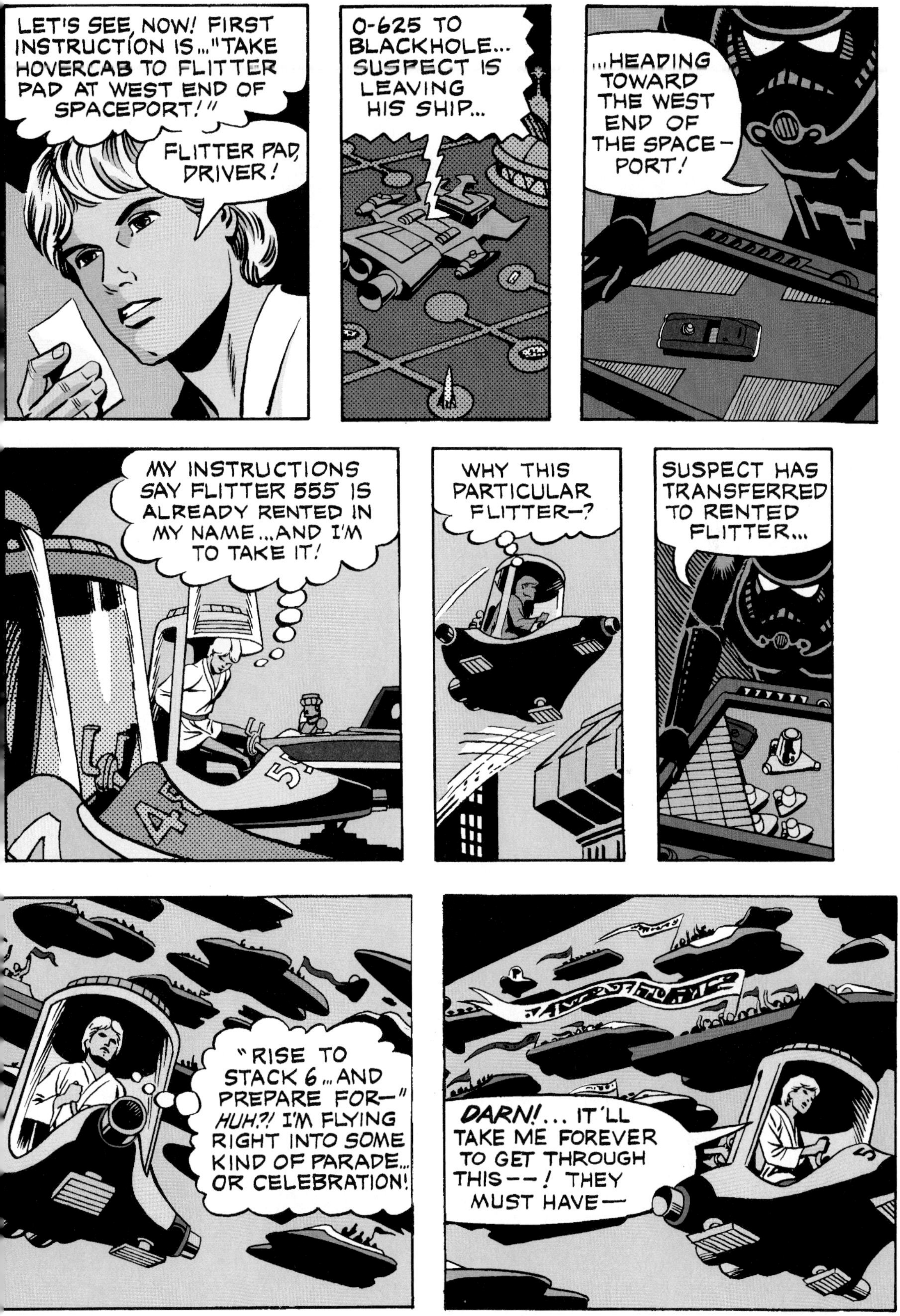
LET'S SEE, NOW! FIRST INSTRUCTION IS..."TAKE HOVERCAB TO FLITTER PAD AT WEST END OF SPACEPORT!"
FLITTER PAD, DRIVER!
0-625 TO BLACKHOLE... SUSPECT IS LEAVING HIS SHIP...
...HEADING TOWARD THE WEST END OF THE SPACE-PORT!
MY INSTRUCTIONS SAY FLITTER 555 IS ALREADY RENTED IN MY NAME...AND I'M TO TAKE IT!
WHY THIS PARTICULAR FLITTER—?
SUSPECT HAS TRANSFERRED TO RENTED FLITTER...
"RISE TO STACK 6...AND PREPARE FOR—" HUH?! I'M FLYING RIGHT INTO SOME KIND OF PARADE... OR CELEBRATION!
DARN!... IT'LL TAKE ME FOREVER TO GET THROUGH THIS--! THEY MUST HAVE—

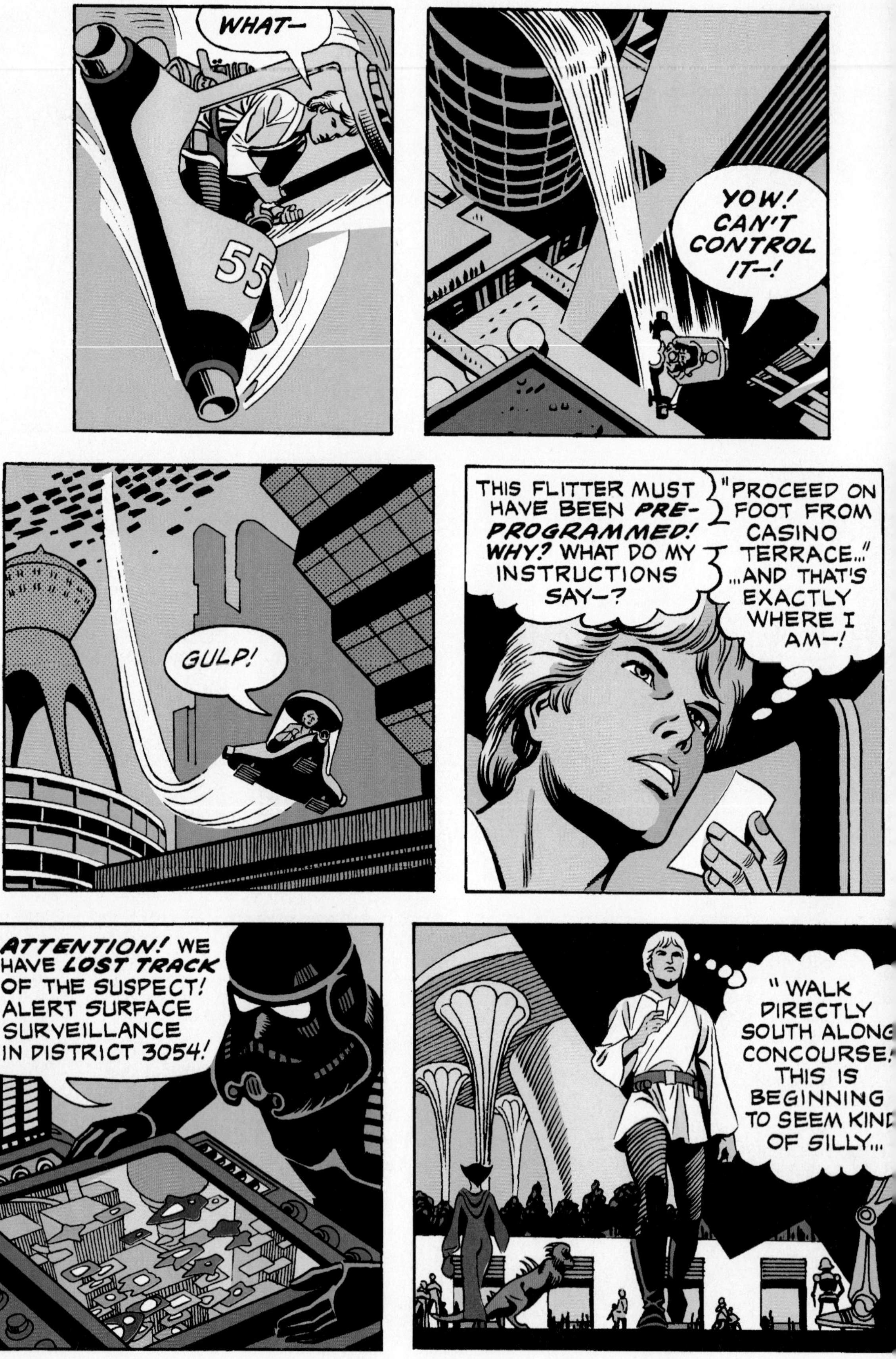
WHAT–
YOW! CAN'T CONTROL IT–!
GULP!
THIS FLITTER MUST HAVE BEEN PRE-PROGRAMMED! WHY? WHAT DO MY INSTRUCTIONS SAY–?
"PROCEED ON FOOT FROM CASINO TERRACE..." ...AND THAT'S EXACTLY WHERE I AM–!
ATTENTION! WE HAVE LOST TRACK OF THE SUSPECT! ALERT SURFACE SURVEILLANCE IN DISTRICT 3054!
"WALK DIRECTLY SOUTH ALONG CONCOURSE." THIS IS BEGINNING TO SEEM KIND OF SILLY...

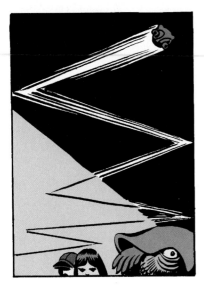

THERE HASN'T BEEN EVEN THE SLIGHTEST HINT OF ANYONE TRYING TO FOLLOW ME!

MOVING TOO SWIFTLY TO BE SEEN, AN ILLEGAL SPY-EYE HOVERS OVER LUKE...

THAT'S SKYWALKER! GET MORE EYES ON HIM BEFORE WE LOSE HIM AGAIN—!

WALK TO GRAV-TUBE OWN 53B!" GOOD... ALMOST THROUGH ITH THESE NSTRUCTIONS ...AND NO TROUBLE, YET!

I'VE GOT FIVE SPY-EYES ON SKYWALKER, BLACKHOLE—!

...AND TROOPERS CLOSING IN... HIDDEN FROM HIM AND FROM THE PUBLIC!

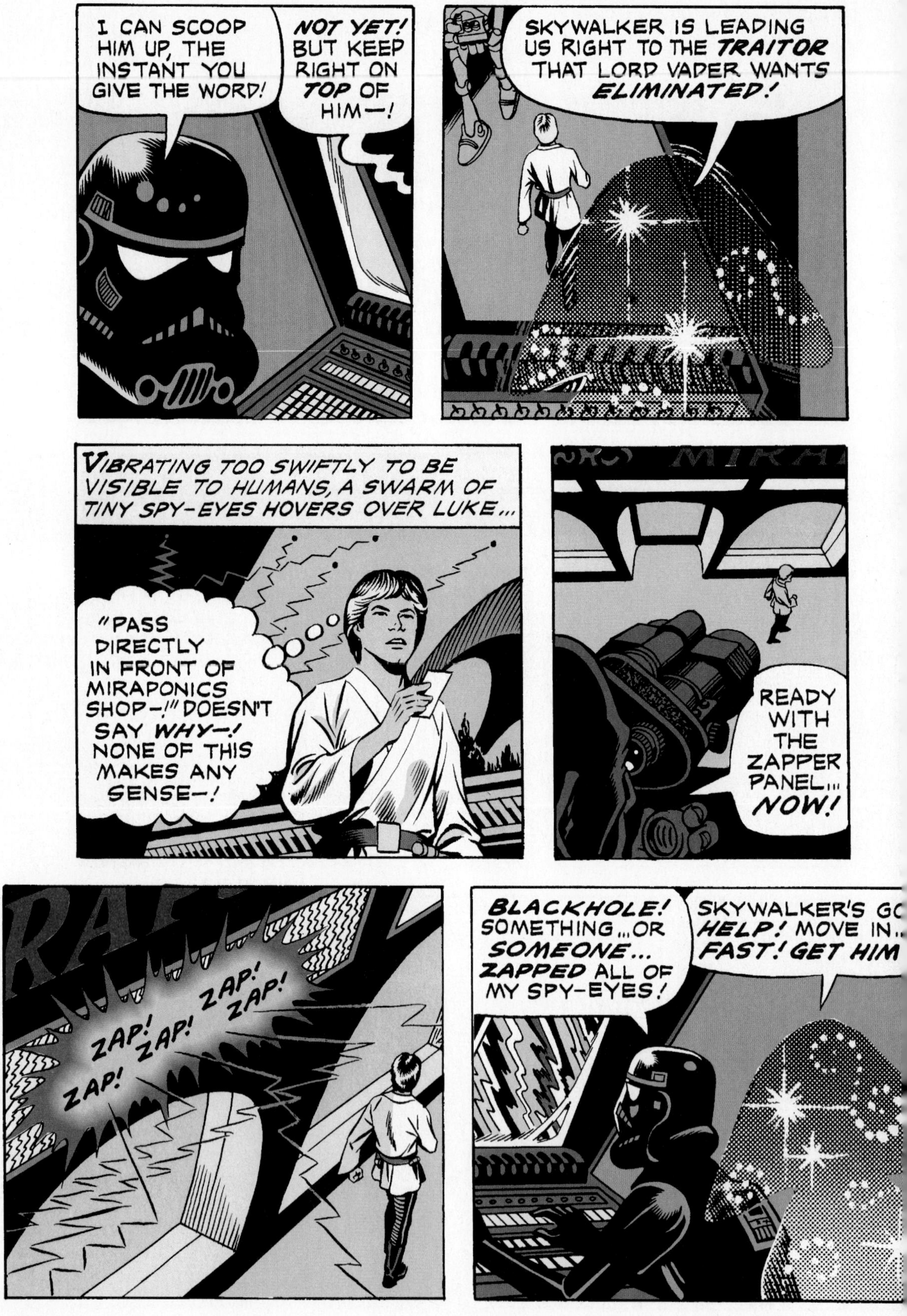

I CAN SCOOP HIM UP, THE INSTANT YOU GIVE THE WORD!
NOT YET! BUT KEEP RIGHT ON TOP OF HIM—!
SKYWALKER IS LEADING US RIGHT TO THE TRAITOR THAT LORD VADER WANTS ELIMINATED!
VIBRATING TOO SWIFTLY TO BE VISIBLE TO HUMANS, A SWARM OF TINY SPY-EYES HOVERS OVER LUKE...
"PASS DIRECTLY IN FRONT OF MIRAPONICS SHOP—!" DOESN'T SAY WHY—! NONE OF THIS MAKES ANY SENSE—!
READY WITH THE ZAPPER PANEL... NOW!
ZAP! ZAP! ZAP! ZAP! ZAP!
BLACKHOLE! SOMETHING... OR SOMEONE... ZAPPED ALL OF MY SPY-EYES!
SKYWALKER'S GO HELP! MOVE IN.. FAST! GET HIM

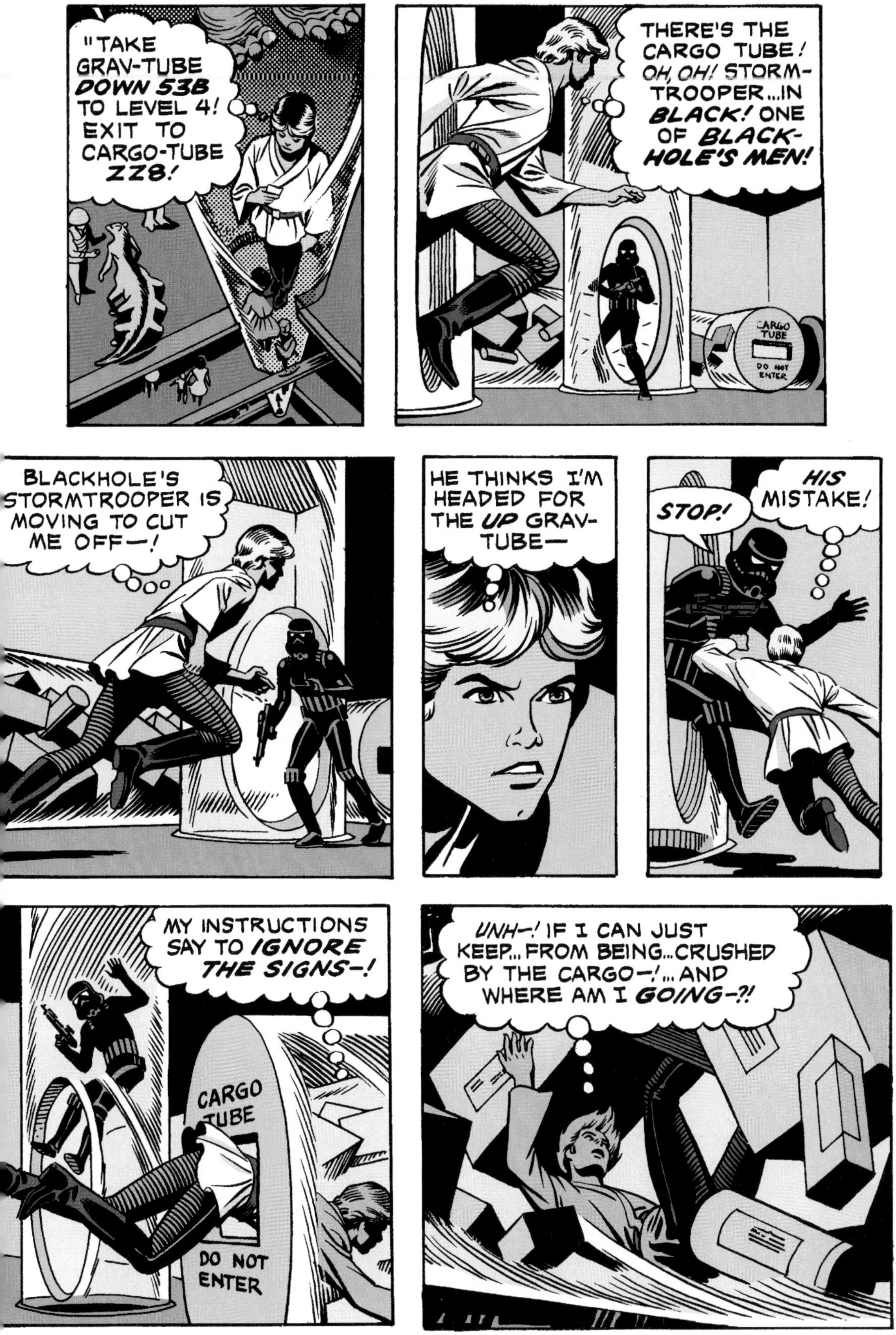
"TAKE GRAV-TUBE DOWN 53B TO LEVEL 4! EXIT TO CARGO-TUBE ZZ8!
THERE'S THE CARGO TUBE! OH, OH! STORM-TROOPER...IN BLACK! ONE OF BLACK-HOLE'S MEN!
CARGO TUBE
DO NOT ENTER
BLACKHOLE'S STORMTROOPER IS MOVING TO CUT ME OFF—!
HE THINKS I'M HEADED FOR THE UP GRAV-TUBE—
STOP!
HIS MISTAKE!
MY INSTRUCTIONS SAY TO IGNORE THE SIGNS—!
CARGO TUBE
DO NOT ENTER
UNH—! IF I CAN JUST KEEP... FROM BEING...CRUSHED BY THE CARGO—!... AND WHERE AM I GOING—?!

"PREPARE TO BE EJECTED!" WHAT? HOW? BUT...THAT'S THE LAST OF THE INSTRUCTIONS!

THE CARGO-TUBE IS SLANTING DOWNWARD... DEEP BENEATH THE CITY—HEY! DARK! NO LIGHTS AHEAD!

THE CARGO-TUBE CARRYING LUKE PLUNGES INTO DARKNESS...

...DON'T LIKE THIS—! BUT... THERE'S NO WAY TO GET OUT—!

CAN'T SEE A THING—! IF THESE PACKAGES JAM ON ME—

UNMEASURED TIME AND DISTANCE PASS... SUDDENLY...

HEY! SOMETHING'S GRABBING... PULLING ME OUT OF THE TUBE—

HUH—?!

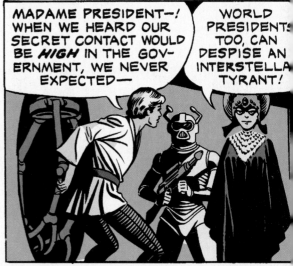

MADAME PRESIDENT—! WHEN WE HEARD OUR SECRET CONTACT WOULD BE HIGH IN THE GOVERNMENT, WE NEVER EXPECTED—

WORLD PRESIDENTS TOO, CAN DESPISE AN INTERSTELLAR TYRANT!

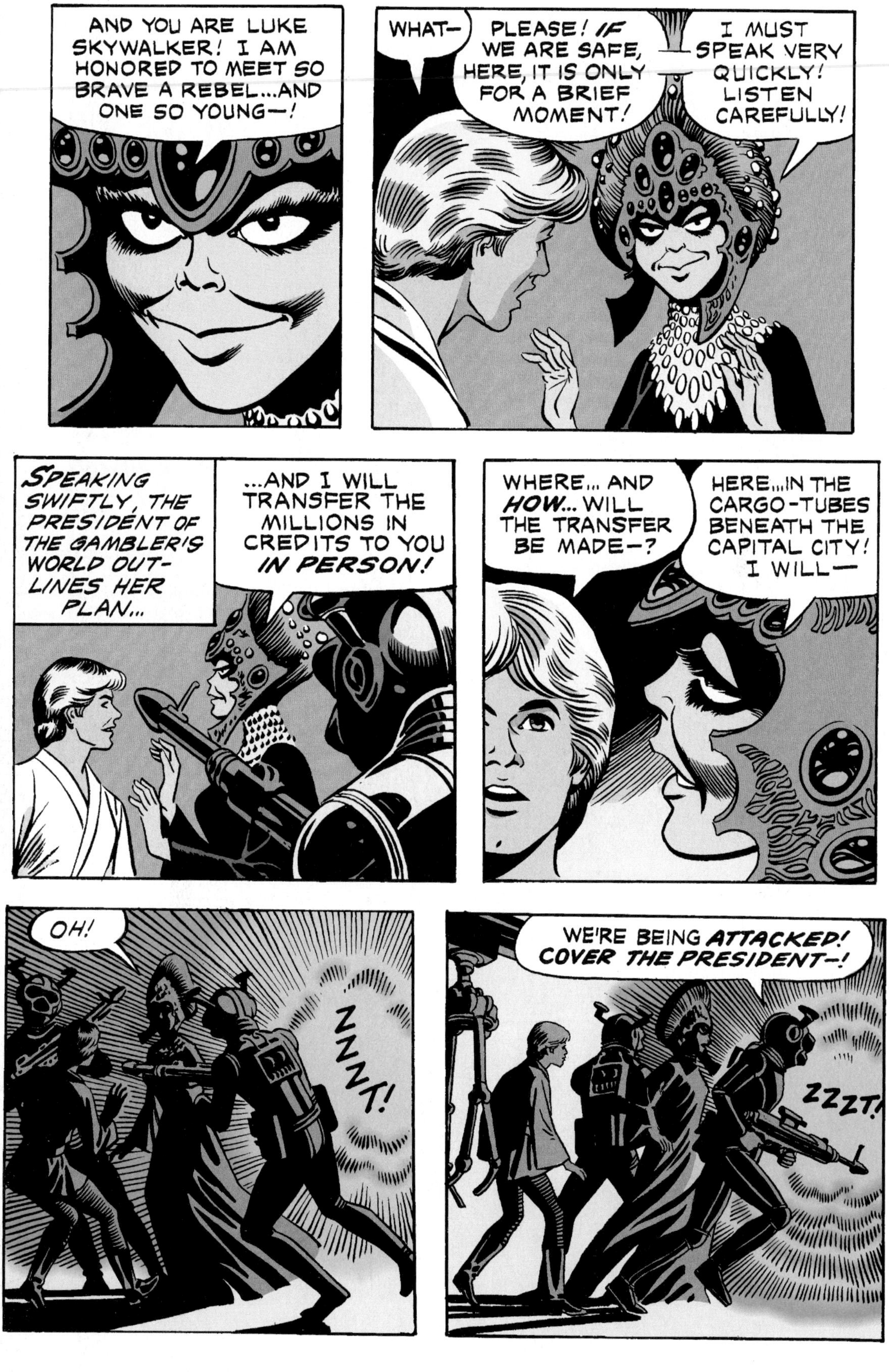
AND YOU ARE LUKE SKYWALKER! I AM HONORED TO MEET SO BRAVE A REBEL...AND ONE SO YOUNG—!
WHAT—
PLEASE! IF WE ARE SAFE, HERE, IT IS ONLY FOR A BRIEF MOMENT!
I MUST SPEAK VERY QUICKLY! LISTEN CAREFULLY!
SPEAKING SWIFTLY, THE PRESIDENT OF THE GAMBLER'S WORLD OUTLINES HER PLAN...
...AND I WILL TRANSFER THE MILLIONS IN CREDITS TO YOU IN PERSON!
WHERE... AND HOW... WILL THE TRANSFER BE MADE—?
HERE...IN THE CARGO-TUBES BENEATH THE CAPITAL CITY! I WILL—
OH!
NNNT!
WE'RE BEING ATTACKED! COVER THE PRESIDENT—!
ZZZT!

GET SKYWALKER OUT OF THIS!

HEY!

WAIT! DON'T TAKE ME AWAY! MAYBE I CAN HELP!

HEY! THIS ISN'T THE SAME TUBE I CAME IN—!

WHEW! MOVING FAST—!

MADAME PRESIDENT ...DID SHE... AND HER GUARDS... GET AWAY—?

...UP INTO THE CITY AGAIN—! NO SIGN OF WHOEVER THAT WAS WHO HIT US—!

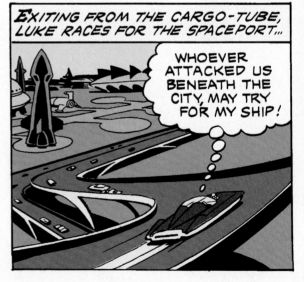

EXITING FROM THE CARGO-TUBE, LUKE RACES FOR THE SPACEPORT...

WHOEVER ATTACKED US BENEATH THE CITY, MAY TRY FOR MY SHIP!

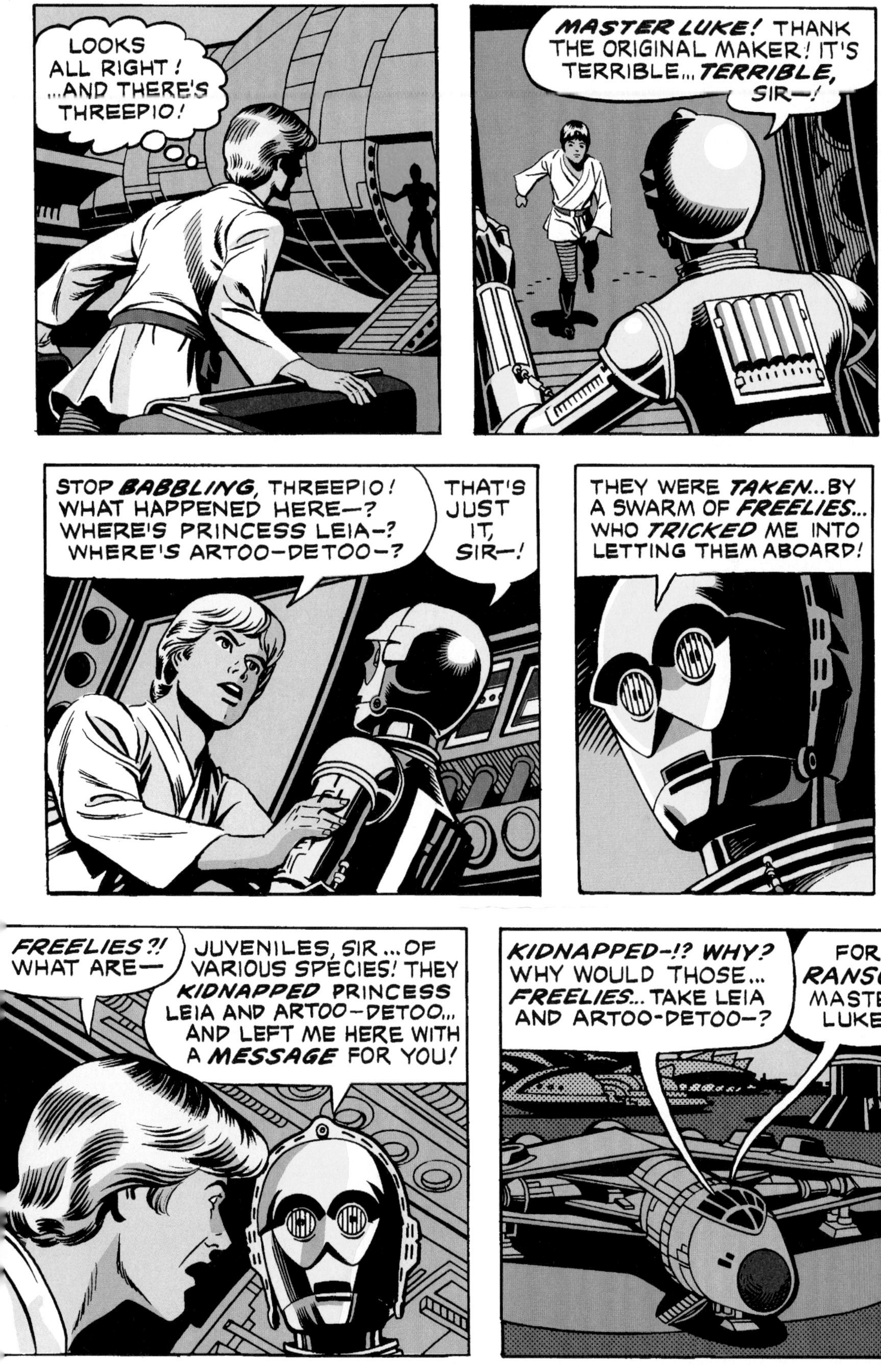

LOOKS ALL RIGHT! ...AND THERE'S THREEPIO!
MASTER LUKE! THANK THE ORIGINAL MAKER! IT'S TERRIBLE... TERRIBLE, SIR—!
STOP BABBLING, THREEPIO! WHAT HAPPENED HERE—? WHERE'S PRINCESS LEIA—? WHERE'S ARTOO-DETOO—?
THAT'S JUST IT, SIR—!
THEY WERE TAKEN...BY A SWARM OF FREELIES... WHO TRICKED ME INTO LETTING THEM ABOARD!
FREELIES?! WHAT ARE—
JUVENILES, SIR... OF VARIOUS SPECIES! THEY KIDNAPPED PRINCESS LEIA AND ARTOO-DETOO... AND LEFT ME HERE WITH A MESSAGE FOR YOU!
KIDNAPPED—!? WHY? WHY WOULD THOSE... FREELIES... TAKE LEIA AND ARTOO-DETOO—?
FOR RANSOM, MASTER LUKE—!

RANSOM!? HOW DID THEY *KNOW*—?

ONE OF THE FREELIES IS THE OFFSPRING OF *FALUD*... THE REBEL WHO WAS KILLED WHEN WE ESCAPED FROM BLACKHOLE'S SPACE-SHIP—!

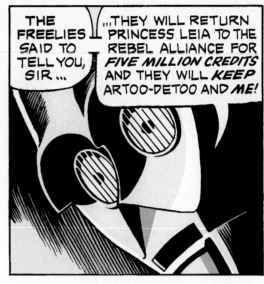

THE FREELIES SAID TO TELL YOU, SIR ...

...THEY WILL RETURN PRINCESS LEIA TO THE REBEL ALLIANCE FOR *FIVE MILLION CREDITS* AND THEY WILL *KEEP* ARTOO-DETOO AND *ME*!

FIVE MILLION CREDITS RANSOM FOR *PRINCESS LEIA*! THE REBEL ALLIANCE WOULD PAY IT, OF COURSE...

...BUT HOW DO I KNOW SHE'S SAFE *NOW*?! ...OR THAT THE FREELIES WOULD *RELEASE* HER—?

IF ONLY I KNEW WHERE THEY HAVE *TAKEN* HER ...

...I'D TRY FOR A *RESCUE*!

I KNOW WHERE SHE IS, MASTER LUKE!...THAT IS... I CAN LEAD YOU TO WHERE THE FREELIES HAVE TAKEN *ARTOO-DETOO*!

ARTOO HAD THE SILLY NOTION THAT HE AND I COULD WEAR WEAPONS AND *PROTECT* YOU, MASTER LUKE!

IT WAS A *DISASTROUS FAILURE*!

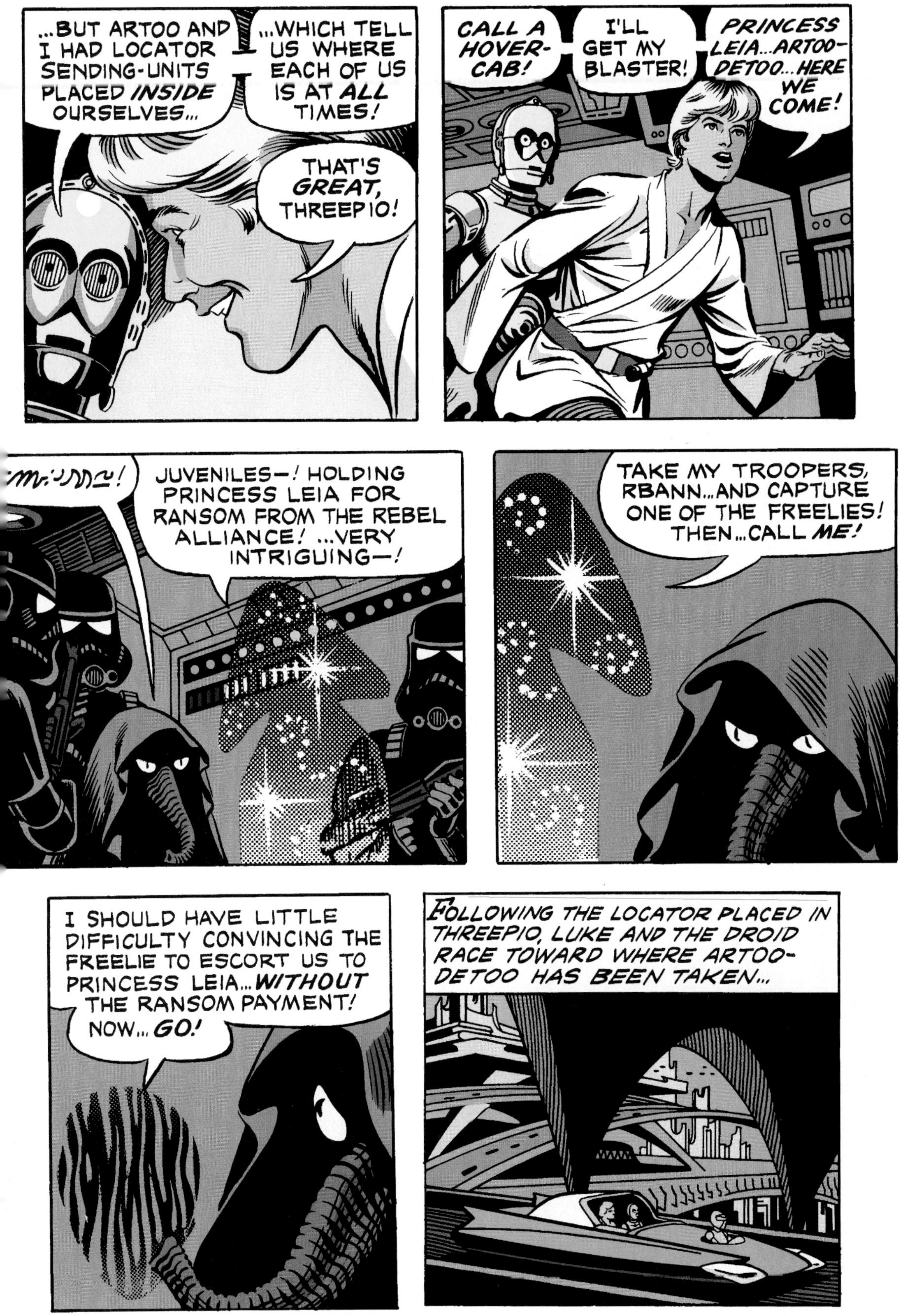
...BUT ARTOO AND I HAD LOCATOR SENDING-UNITS PLACED *INSIDE* OURSELVES...
...WHICH TELL US WHERE EACH OF US IS AT *ALL* TIMES!
THAT'S *GREAT*, THREEPIO!
CALL A HOVER-CAB!
I'LL GET MY BLASTER!
PRINCESS LEIA...ARTOO-DETOO...HERE WE COME!
JUVENILES—! HOLDING PRINCESS LEIA FOR RANSOM FROM THE REBEL ALLIANCE! ...VERY INTRIGUING—!
TAKE MY TROOPERS, RBANN...AND CAPTURE ONE OF THE FREELIES! THEN...CALL *ME!*
I SHOULD HAVE LITTLE DIFFICULTY CONVINCING THE FREELIE TO ESCORT US TO PRINCESS LEIA... *WITHOUT* THE RANSOM PAYMENT! NOW... *GO!*
FOLLOWING THE LOCATOR PLACED IN THREEPIO, LUKE AND THE DROID RACE TOWARD WHERE ARTOO-DETOO HAS BEEN TAKEN...

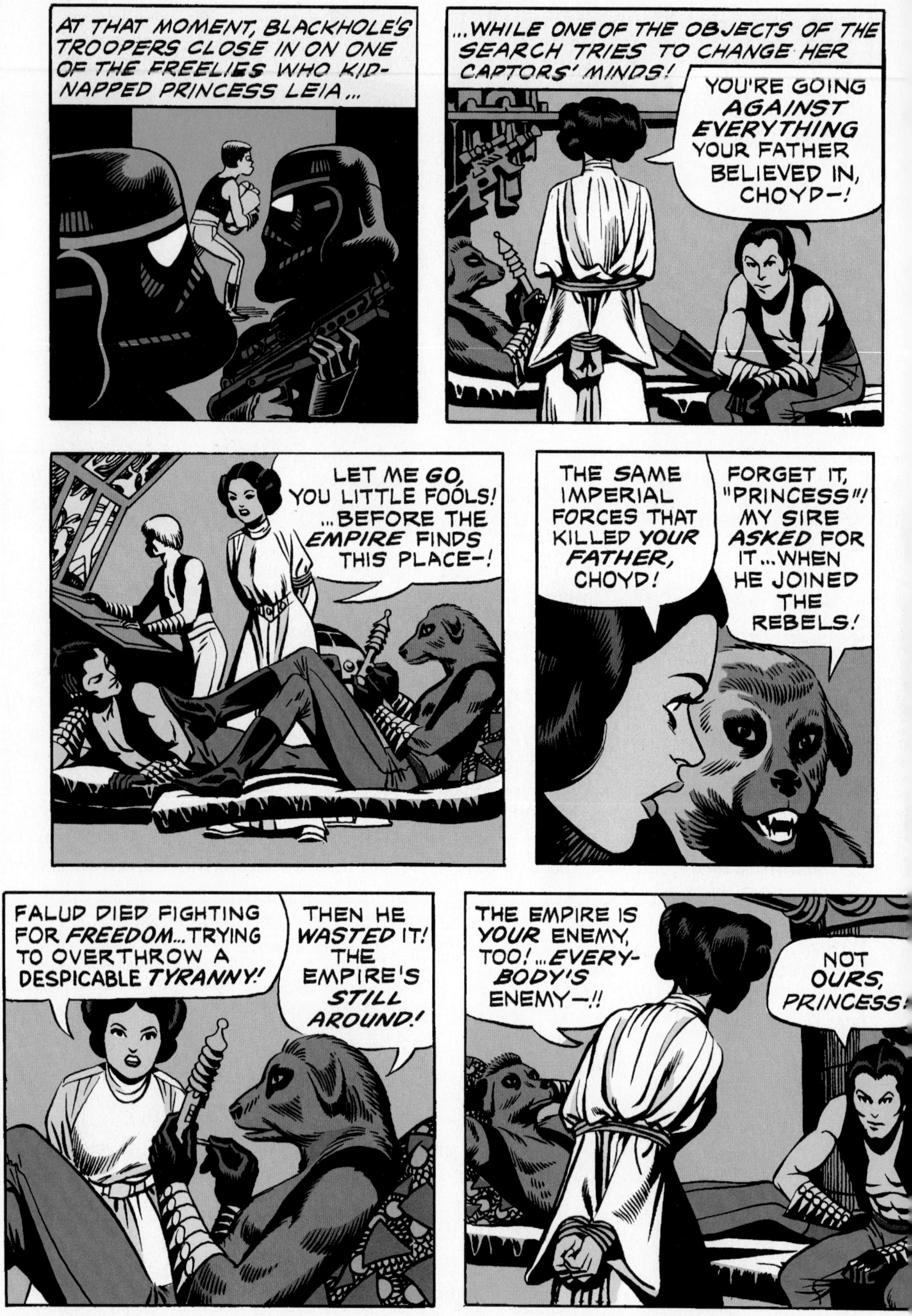
AT THAT MOMENT, BLACKHOLE'S TROOPERS CLOSE IN ON ONE OF THE FREELIES WHO KID-NAPPED PRINCESS LEIA...
...WHILE ONE OF THE OBJECTS OF THE SEARCH TRIES TO CHANGE HER CAPTORS' MINDS!
YOU'RE GOING AGAINST EVERYTHING YOUR FATHER BELIEVED IN, CHOYD-!
LET ME GO, YOU LITTLE FOOLS! ...BEFORE THE EMPIRE FINDS THIS PLACE-!
THE SAME IMPERIAL FORCES THAT KILLED YOUR FATHER, CHOYD!
FORGET IT, "PRINCESS"! MY SIRE ASKED FOR IT...WHEN HE JOINED THE REBELS!
FALUD DIED FIGHTING FOR FREEDOM...TRYING TO OVERTHROW A DESPICABLE TYRANNY!
THEN HE WASTED IT! THE EMPIRE'S STILL AROUND!
THE EMPIRE IS YOUR ENEMY, TOO! ...EVERY-BODY'S ENEMY-!!
NOT OURS, PRINCESS!

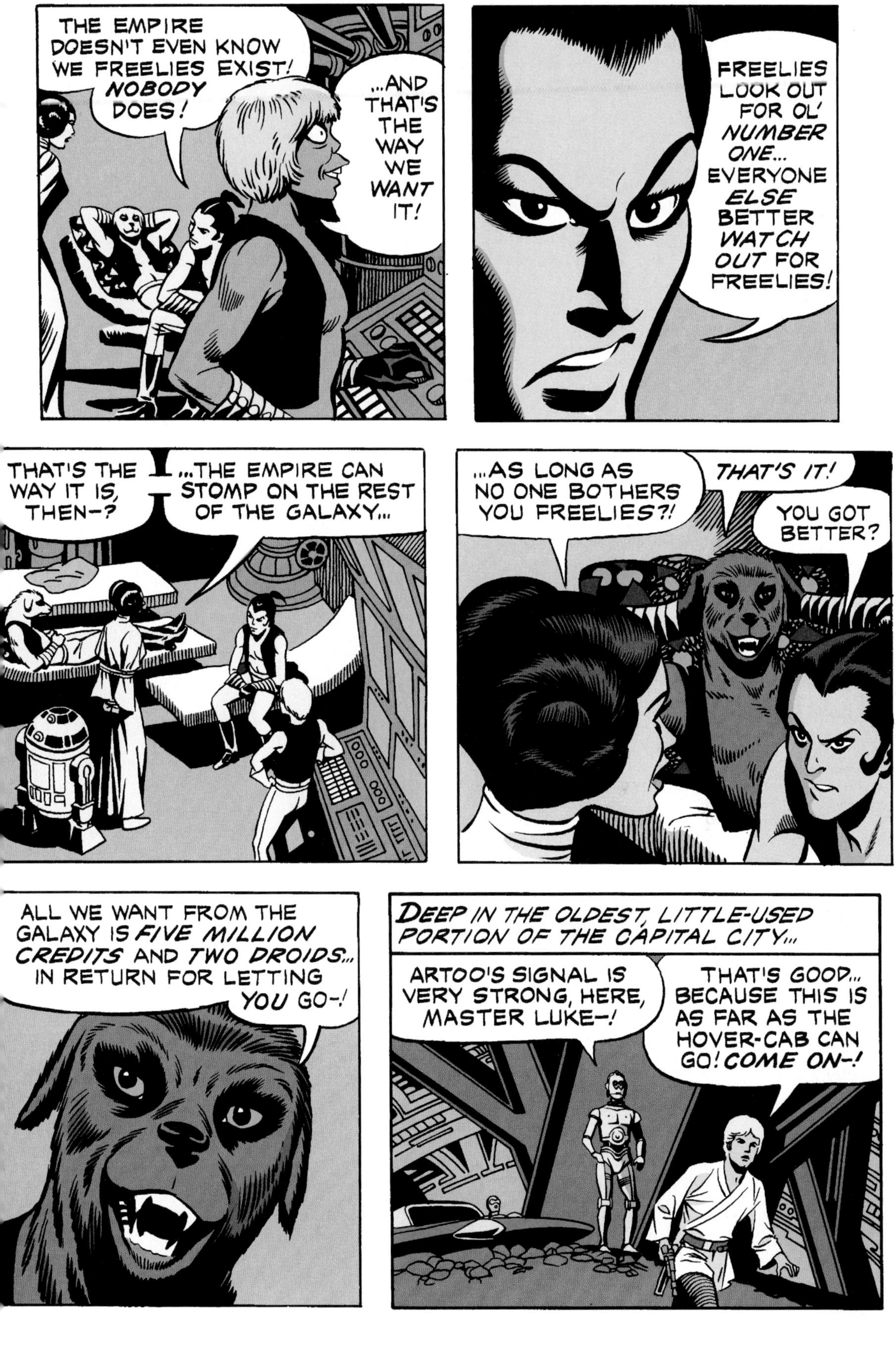
THE EMPIRE DOESN'T EVEN KNOW WE FREELIES EXIST! NOBODY DOES!
...AND THAT'S THE WAY WE WANT IT!
FREELIES LOOK OUT FOR OL' NUMBER ONE... EVERYONE ELSE BETTER WATCH OUT FOR FREELIES!
THAT'S THE WAY IT IS, THEN-?
...THE EMPIRE CAN STOMP ON THE REST OF THE GALAXY...
...AS LONG AS NO ONE BOTHERS YOU FREELIES?!
THAT'S IT!
YOU GOT BETTER?
ALL WE WANT FROM THE GALAXY IS FIVE MILLION CREDITS AND TWO DROIDS... IN RETURN FOR LETTING YOU GO-!
DEEP IN THE OLDEST, LITTLE-USED PORTION OF THE CAPITAL CITY...
ARTOO'S SIGNAL IS VERY STRONG, HERE, MASTER LUKE-!
THAT'S GOOD... BECAUSE THIS IS AS FAR AS THE HOVER-CAB CAN GO! COME ON-!

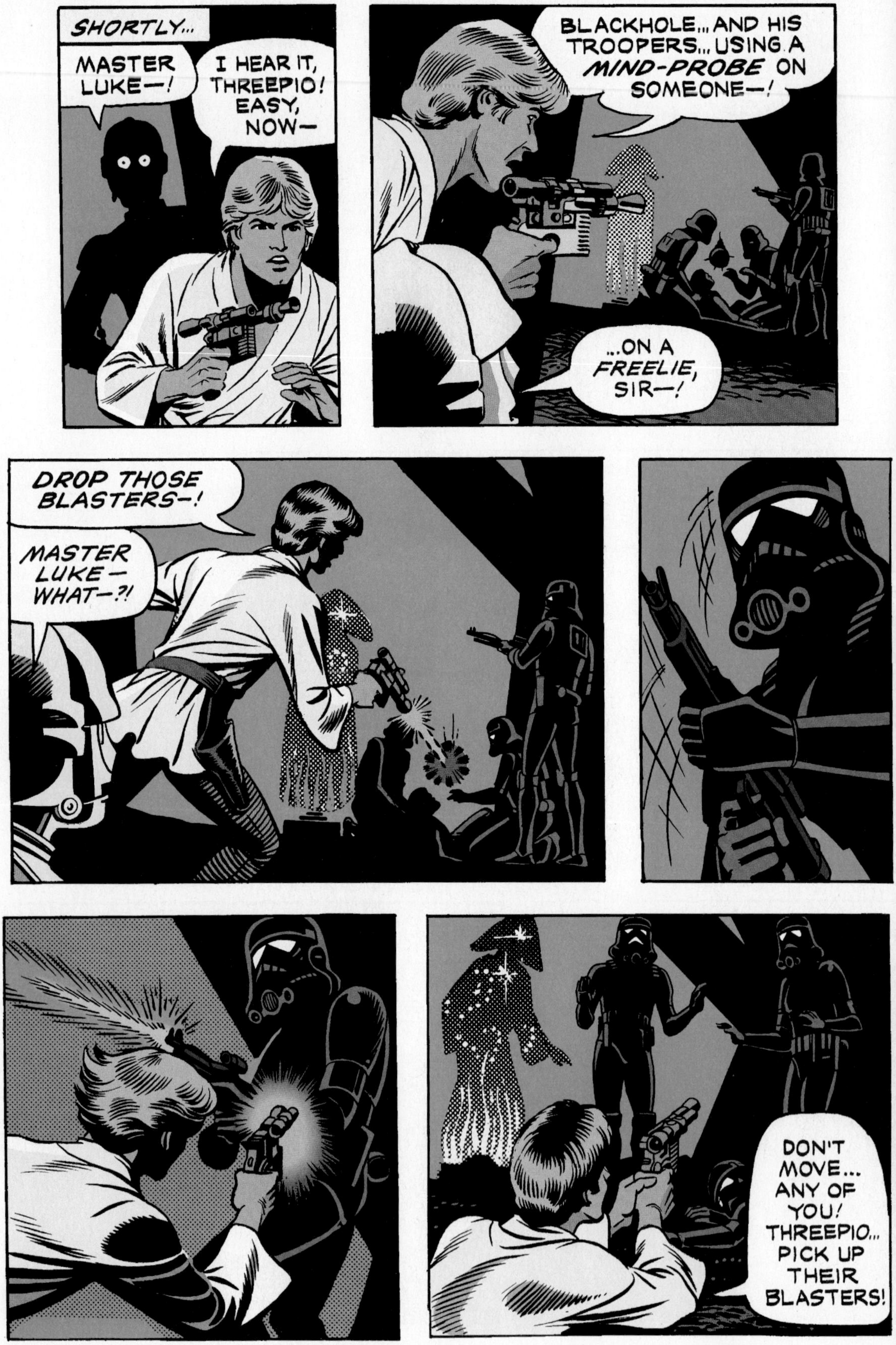
SHORTLY...
MASTER LUKE—!
I HEAR IT, THREEPIO! EASY, NOW—
BLACKHOLE... AND HIS TROOPERS... USING A MIND-PROBE ON SOMEONE—!
...ON A FREELIE, SIR—!
DROP THOSE BLASTERS—!
MASTER LUKE— WHAT—?!
DON'T MOVE... ANY OF YOU! THREEPIO... PICK UP THEIR BLASTERS!

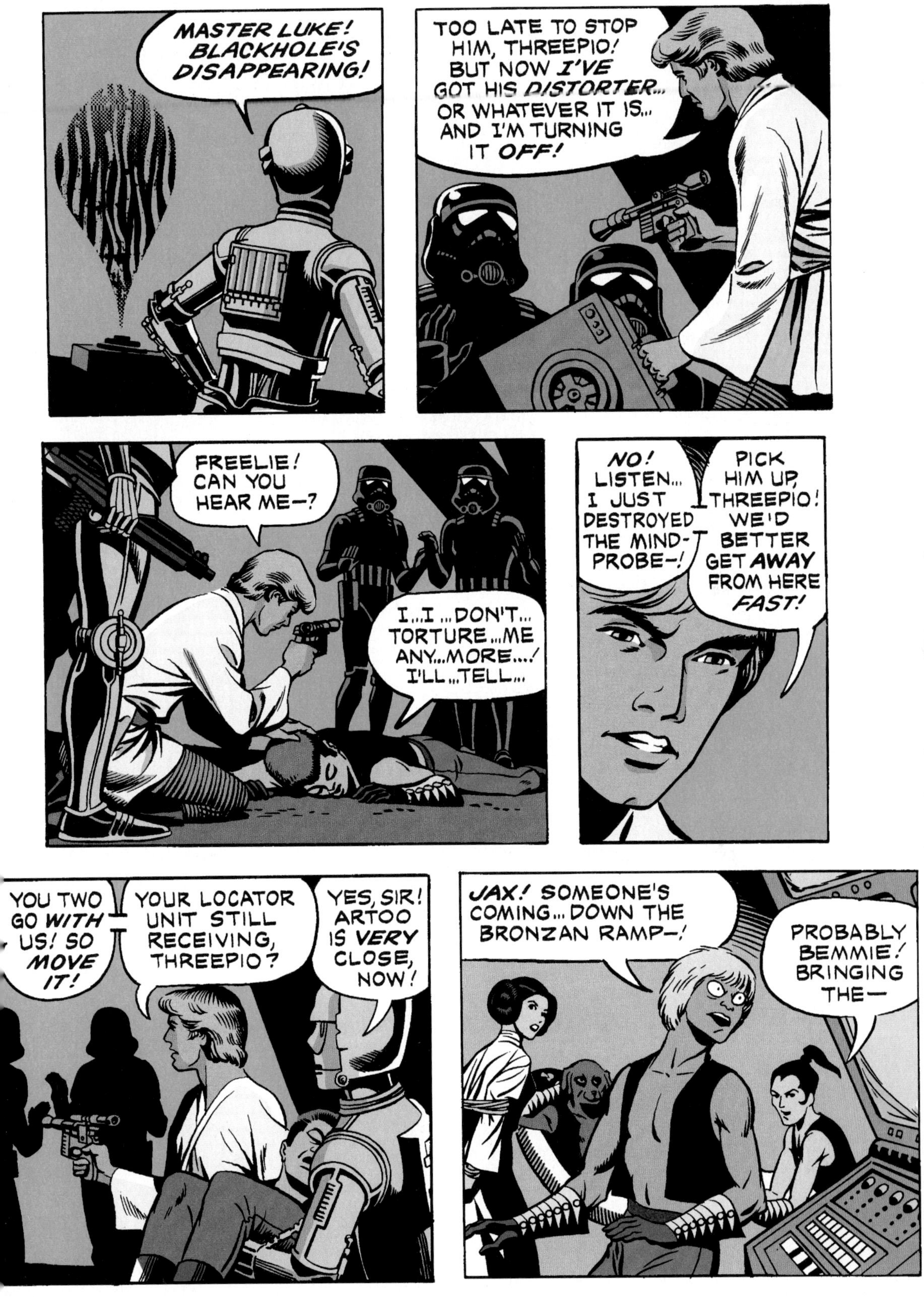
MASTER LUKE! BLACKHOLE'S DISAPPEARING!
TOO LATE TO STOP HIM, THREEPIO! BUT NOW I'VE GOT HIS DISTORTER... OR WHATEVER IT IS... AND I'M TURNING IT OFF!
FREELIE! CAN YOU HEAR ME—?
I...I ...DON'T... TORTURE...ME ANY...MORE....! I'LL...TELL...
NO! LISTEN... I JUST DESTROYED THE MIND-PROBE—!
PICK HIM UP, THREEPIO! WE'D BETTER GET AWAY FROM HERE FAST!
YOU TWO GO WITH US! SO MOVE IT!
YOUR LOCATOR UNIT STILL RECEIVING, THREEPIO?
YES, SIR! ARTOO IS VERY CLOSE, NOW!
JAX! SOMEONE'S COMING... DOWN THE BRONZAN RAMP—!
PROBABLY BEMMIE! BRINGING THE—

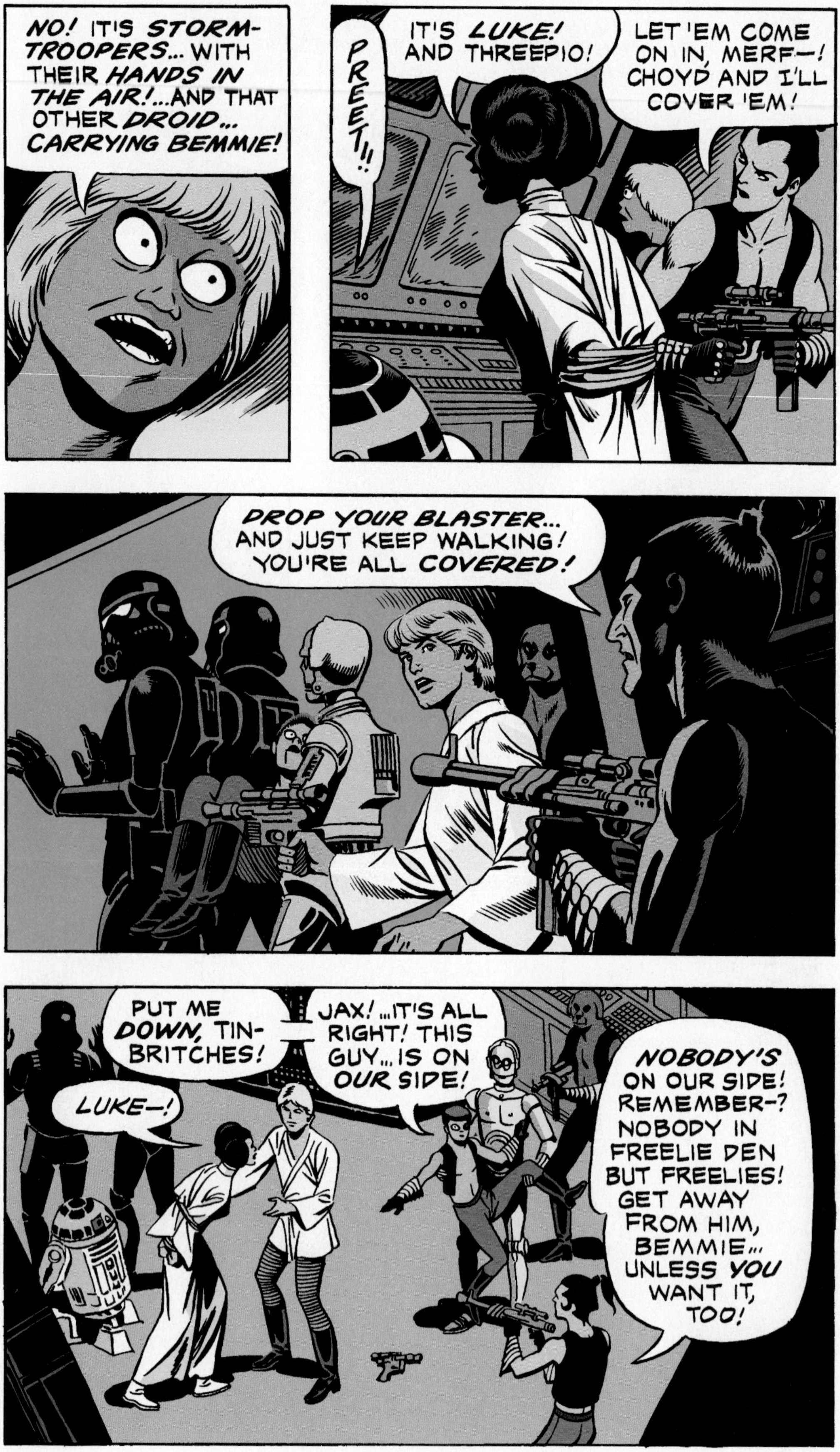
NO! IT'S STORM-TROOPERS... WITH THEIR HANDS IN THE AIR!...AND THAT OTHER DROID... CARRYING BEMMIE!
PREET!!
IT'S LUKE! AND THREEPIO!
LET 'EM COME ON IN, MERF—! CHOYD AND I'LL COVER 'EM!
DROP YOUR BLASTER... AND JUST KEEP WALKING! YOU'RE ALL COVERED!
PUT ME DOWN, TIN-BRITCHES!
JAX! ...IT'S ALL RIGHT! THIS GUY... IS ON OUR SIDE!
LUKE—!
NOBODY'S ON OUR SIDE! REMEMBER—? NOBODY IN FREELIE DEN BUT FREELIES! GET AWAY FROM HIM, BEMMIE... UNLESS YOU WANT IT, TOO!

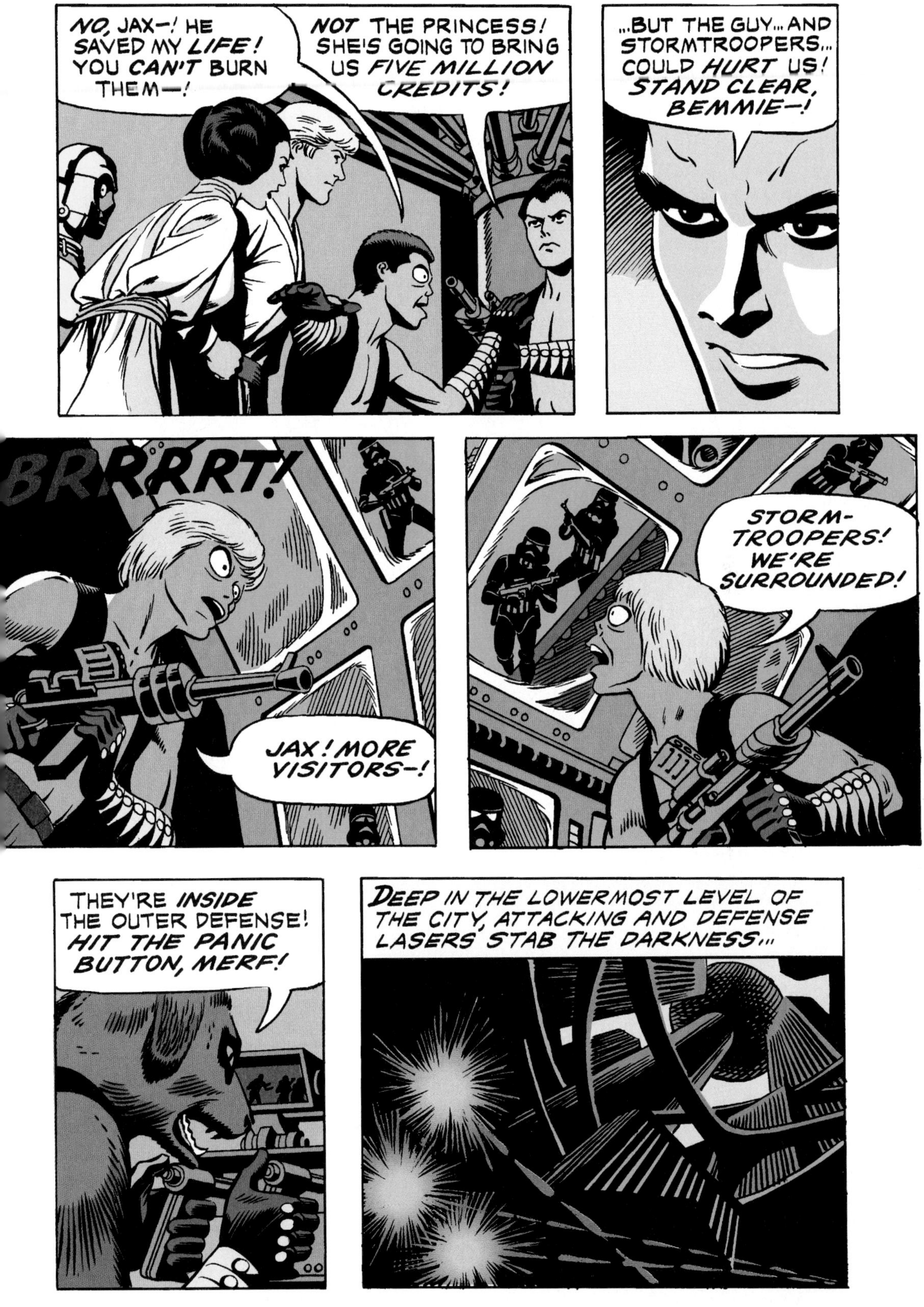
NO, JAX—! HE SAVED MY LIFE! YOU CAN'T BURN THEM—!
NOT THE PRINCESS! SHE'S GOING TO BRING US FIVE MILLION CREDITS!
...BUT THE GUY... AND STORMTROOPERS... COULD HURT US! STAND CLEAR, BEMMIE—!
BRRRRT!
JAX! MORE VISITORS—!
STORM-TROOPERS! WE'RE SURROUNDED!
THEY'RE INSIDE THE OUTER DEFENSE! HIT THE PANIC BUTTON, MERF!
DEEP IN THE LOWERMOST LEVEL OF THE CITY, ATTACKING AND DEFENSE LASERS STAB THE DARKNESS...

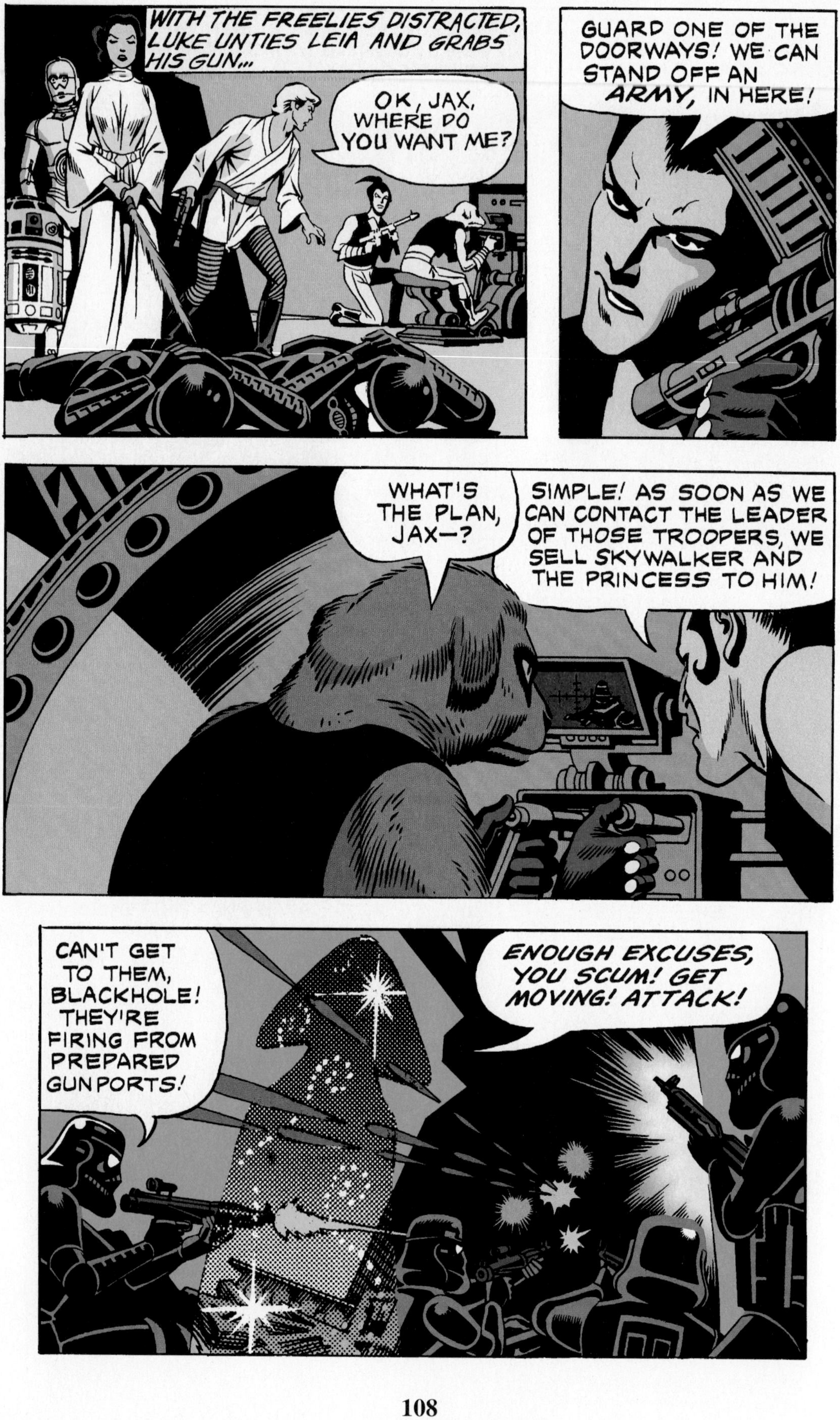
WITH THE FREELIES DISTRACTED, LUKE UNTIES LEIA AND GRABS HIS GUN...
OK, JAX, WHERE DO YOU WANT ME?
GUARD ONE OF THE DOORWAYS! WE CAN STAND OFF AN ARMY, IN HERE!
WHAT'S THE PLAN, JAX—?
SIMPLE! AS SOON AS WE CAN CONTACT THE LEADER OF THOSE TROOPERS, WE SELL SKYWALKER AND THE PRINCESS TO HIM!
CAN'T GET TO THEM, BLACKHOLE! THEY'RE FIRING FROM PREPARED GUNPORTS!
ENOUGH EXCUSES, YOU SCUM! GET MOVING! ATTACK!

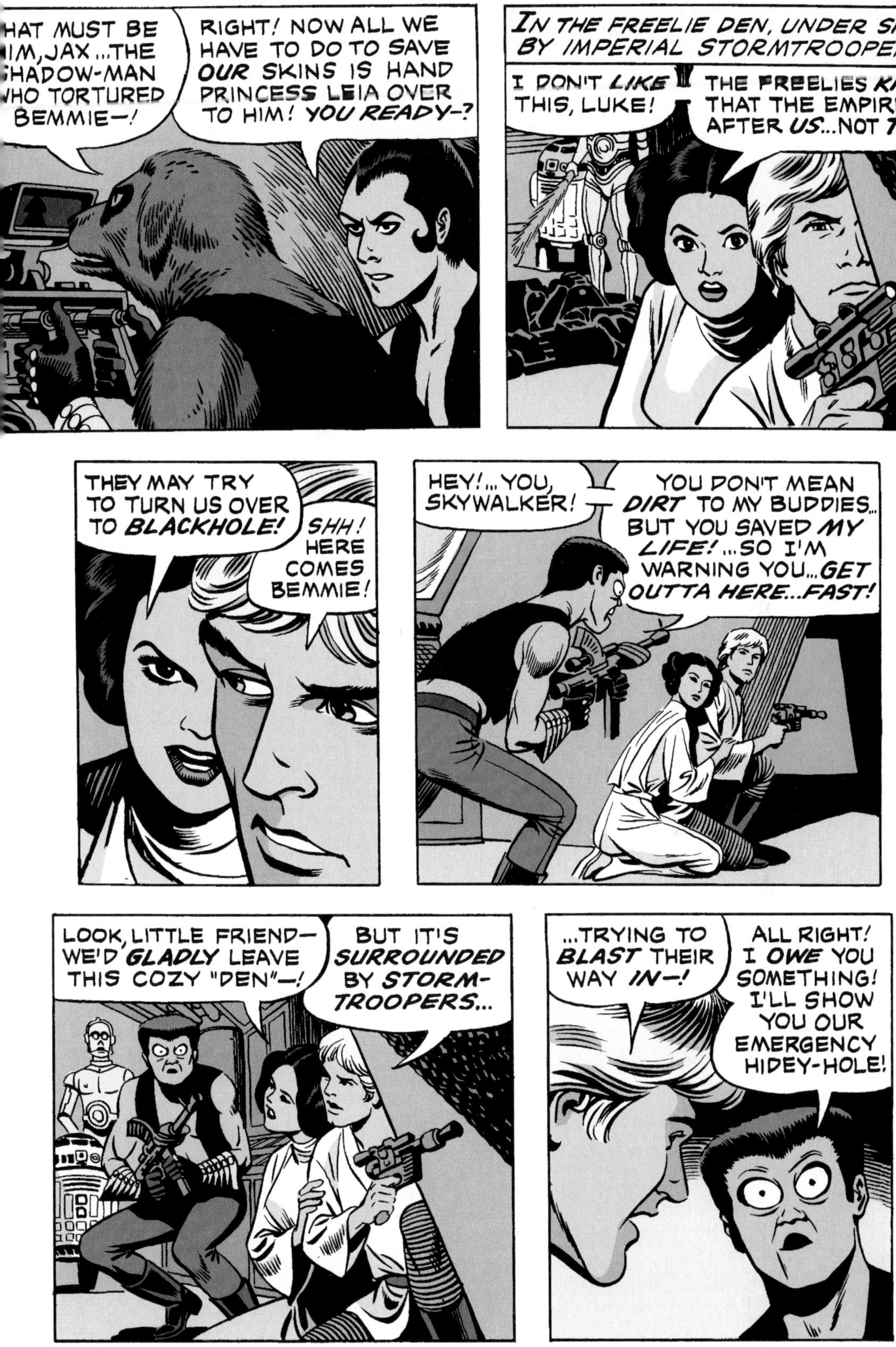
HAT MUST BE IM, JAX ...THE HADOW-MAN HO TORTURED BEMMIE—!
RIGHT! NOW ALL WE HAVE TO DO TO SAVE *OUR* SKINS IS HAND PRINCESS LEIA OVER TO HIM! *YOU READY—?*
IN THE FREELIE DEN, UNDER SIEGE BY IMPERIAL STORMTROOPERS...
I DON'T *LIKE* THIS, LUKE!
THE FREELIES *KNOW* THAT THE EMPIRE IS AFTER *US*...NOT *THEM!*
THEY MAY TRY TO TURN US OVER TO *BLACKHOLE!*
SHH! HERE COMES BEMMIE!
HEY! ...YOU, SKYWALKER!
YOU DON'T MEAN *DIRT* TO MY BUDDIES... BUT YOU SAVED *MY LIFE!* ...SO I'M WARNING YOU... *GET OUTTA HERE...FAST!*
LOOK, LITTLE FRIEND— WE'D *GLADLY* LEAVE THIS COZY "DEN"—!
BUT IT'S *SURROUNDED* BY *STORM-TROOPERS...*
...TRYING TO *BLAST* THEIR WAY *IN*—!
ALL RIGHT! I *OWE* YOU SOMETHING! I'LL SHOW YOU OUR EMERGENCY HIDEY-HOLE!

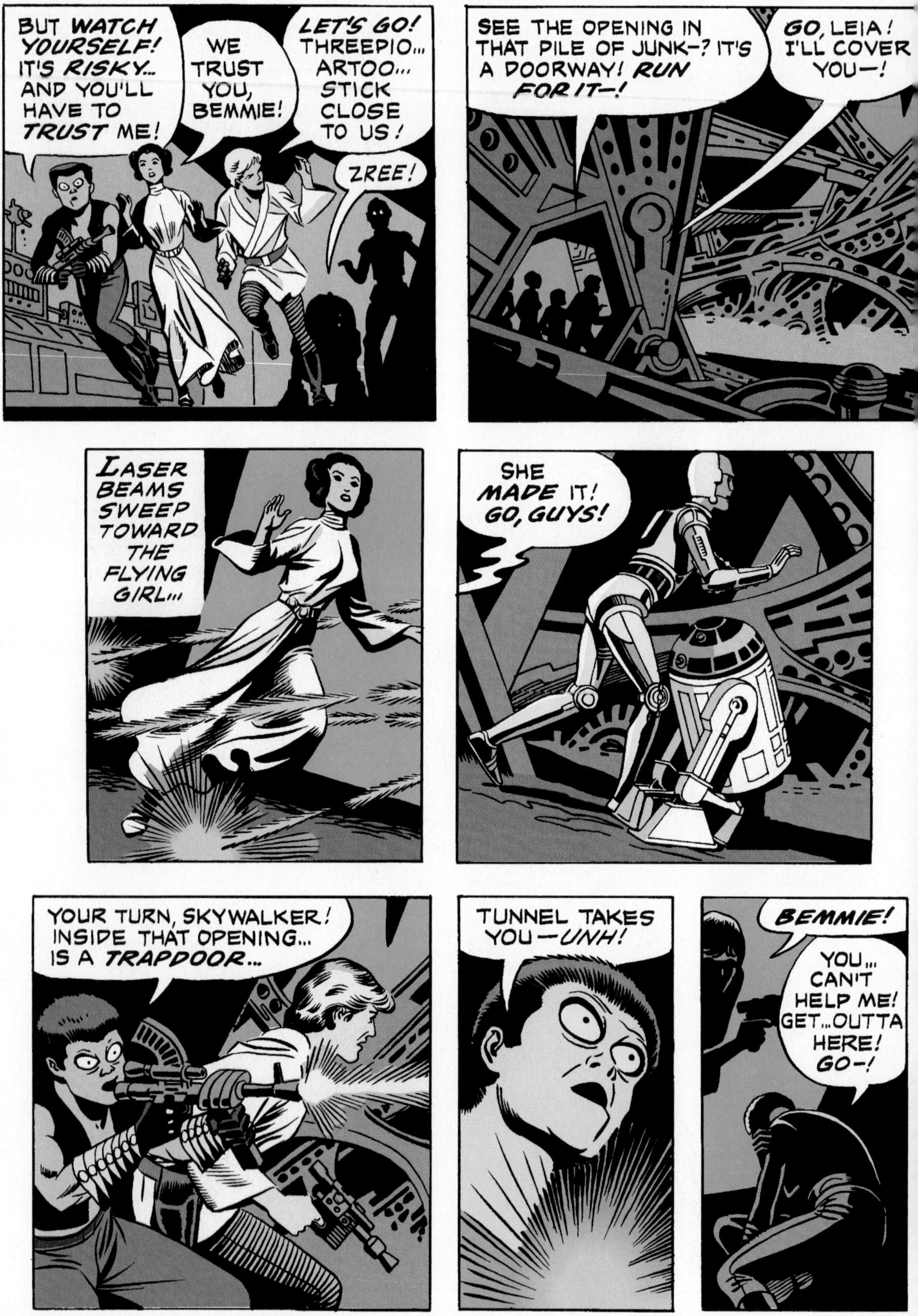
BUT WATCH YOURSELF! IT'S RISKY... AND YOU'LL HAVE TO TRUST ME!
WE TRUST YOU, BEMMIE!
LET'S GO! THREEPIO... ARTOO... STICK CLOSE TO US!
ZREE!
SEE THE OPENING IN THAT PILE OF JUNK-? IT'S A DOORWAY! RUN FOR IT-!
GO, LEIA! I'LL COVER YOU-!
LASER BEAMS SWEEP TOWARD THE FLYING GIRL...
SHE MADE IT! GO, GUYS!
YOUR TURN, SKYWALKER! INSIDE THAT OPENING... IS A TRAPDOOR...
TUNNEL TAKES YOU—UNH!
BEMMIE!
YOU... CAN'T HELP ME! GET...OUTTA HERE! GO-!

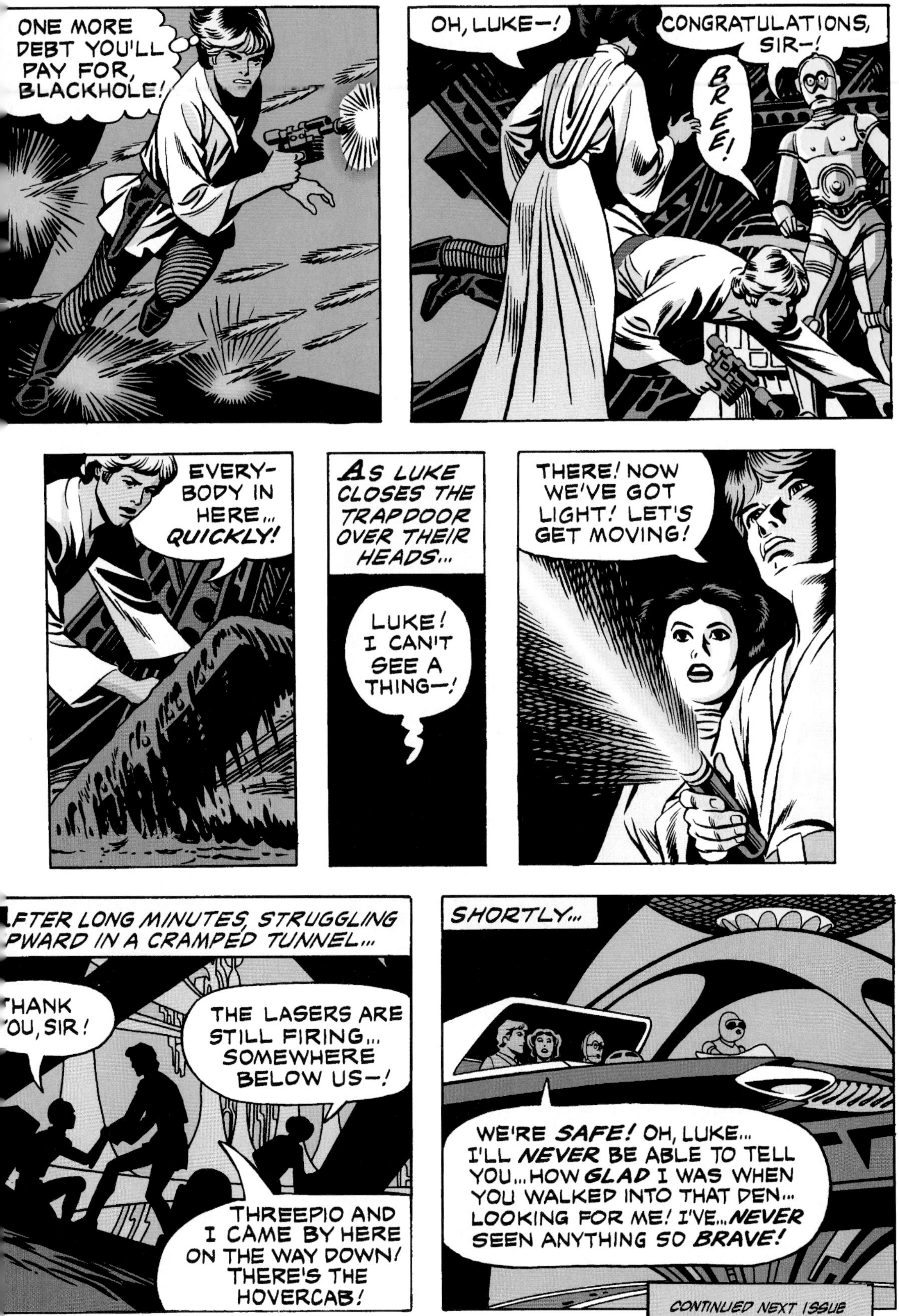
ONE MORE DEBT YOU'LL PAY FOR, BLACKHOLE!
OH, LUKE--!
CONGRATULATIONS, SIR--!
BREE!
EVERY-BODY IN HERE... QUICKLY!
AS LUKE CLOSES THE TRAPDOOR OVER THEIR HEADS...
LUKE! I CAN'T SEE A THING--!
THERE! NOW WE'VE GOT LIGHT! LET'S GET MOVING!
FTER LONG MINUTES, STRUGGLING PWARD IN A CRAMPED TUNNEL...
HANK OU, SIR!
THE LASERS ARE STILL FIRING... SOMEWHERE BELOW US--!
THREEPIO AND I CAME BY HERE ON THE WAY DOWN! THERE'S THE HOVERCAB!
SHORTLY...
WE'RE SAFE! OH, LUKE... I'LL NEVER BE ABLE TO TELL YOU... HOW GLAD I WAS WHEN YOU WALKED INTO THAT DEN... LOOKING FOR ME! I'VE... NEVER SEEN ANYTHING SO BRAVE!
CONTINUED NEXT ISSUE

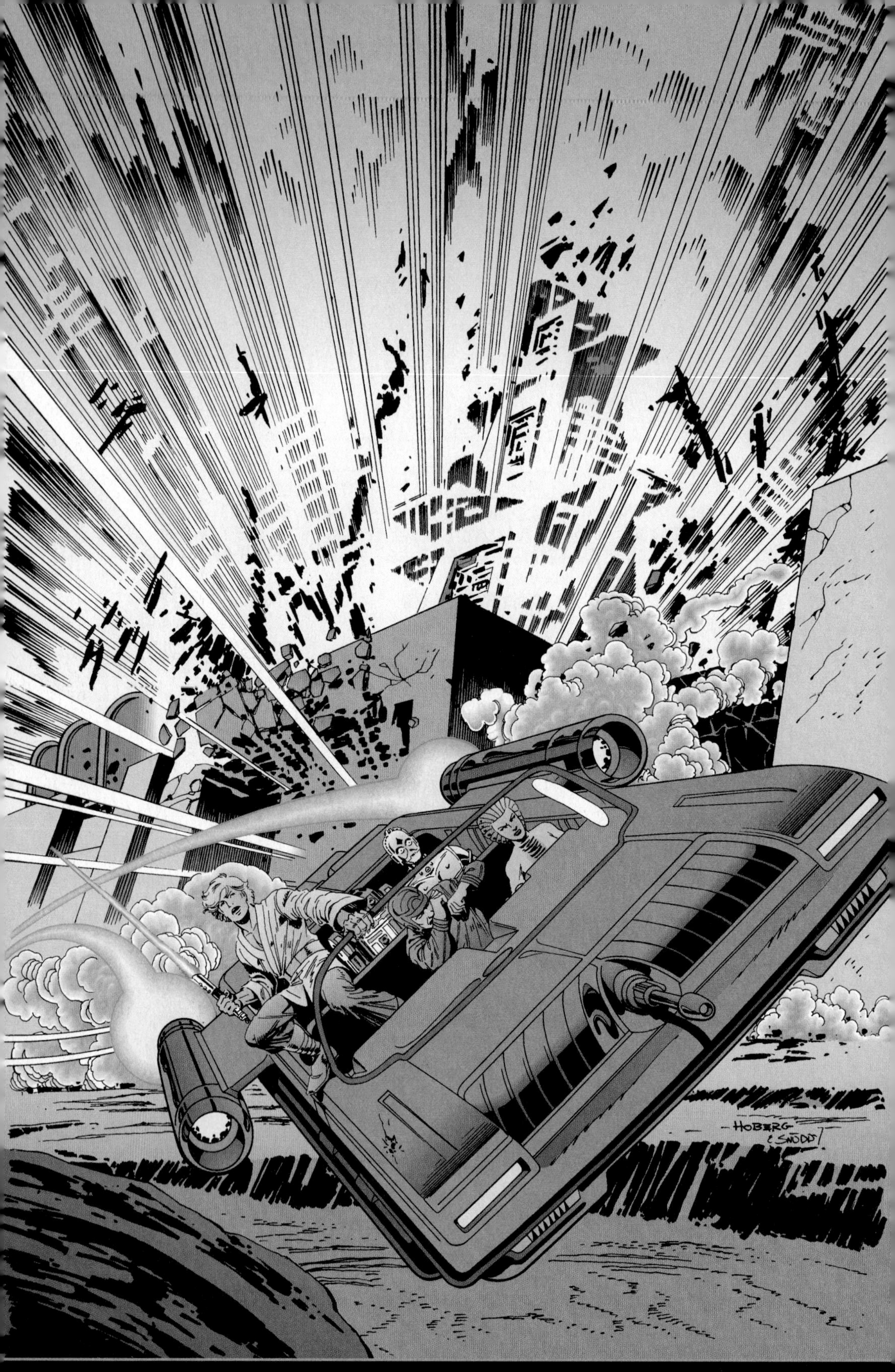
HOBERG & SNODDY

CLASSIC STAR WARS: THE EARLY ADVENTURES #4— "TATOOINE SOJOURN"
ORIGINALLY PUBLISHED FROM SEPTEMBER 10 TO NOVEMBER 5, 1979

WRITERS: RUSS MANNING & STEVE GERBER • ARTIST & LETTERER: RUSS MANNING • ART RETOUCHING: RICK HOBERG • COLORIST: RAY MURTAUGH
EDITOR: PEET JANES • COVER ARTISTS: RICK HOBERG, BRIAN SNODDY & MATTHEW HOLLINGSWORTH

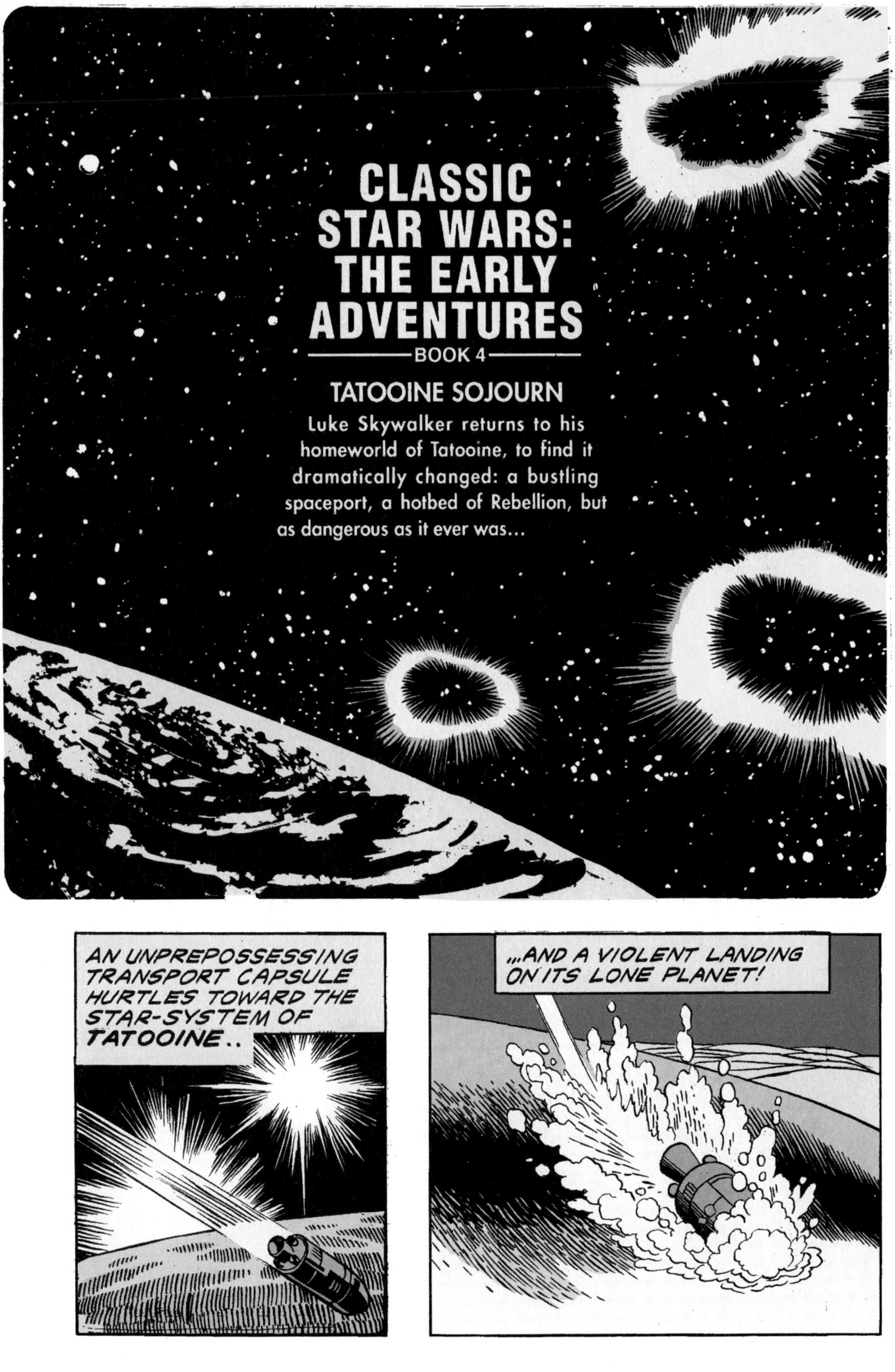
CLASSIC STAR WARS: THE EARLY ADVENTURES
BOOK 4
TATOOINE SOJOURN
Luke Skywalker returns to his homeworld of Tatooine, to find it dramatically changed: a bustling spaceport, a hotbed of Rebellion, but as dangerous as it ever was...
AN UNPREPOSSESSING TRANSPORT CAPSULE HURTLES TOWARD THE STAR-SYSTEM OF TATOOINE..
...AND A VIOLENT LANDING ON ITS LONE PLANET!

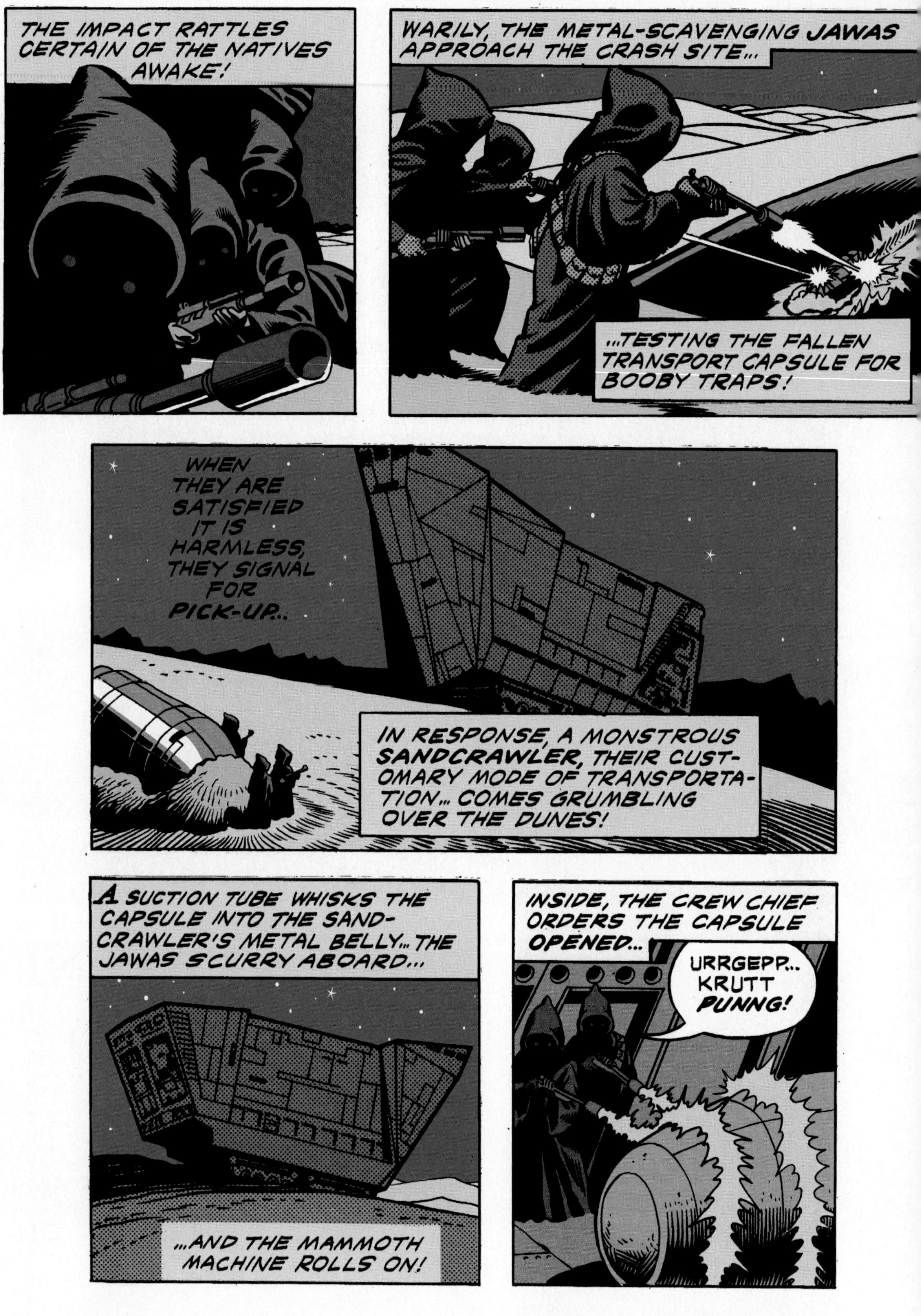
THE IMPACT RATTLES CERTAIN OF THE NATIVES AWAKE!
WARILY, THE METAL-SCAVENGING JAWAS APPROACH THE CRASH SITE...
...TESTING THE FALLEN TRANSPORT CAPSULE FOR BOOBY TRAPS!
WHEN THEY ARE SATISFIED IT IS HARMLESS, THEY SIGNAL FOR PICK-UP...
IN RESPONSE, A MONSTROUS SANDCRAWLER, THEIR CUSTOMARY MODE OF TRANSPORTATION... COMES GRUMBLING OVER THE DUNES!
A SUCTION TUBE WHISKS THE CAPSULE INTO THE SANDCRAWLER'S METAL BELLY... THE JAWAS SCURRY ABOARD...
...AND THE MAMMOTH MACHINE ROLLS ON!
INSIDE, THE CREW CHIEF ORDERS THE CAPSULE OPENED...
URRGEPP... KRUTT PUNNG!

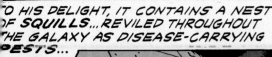

TO HIS DELIGHT, IT CONTAINS A NEST OF **SQUILLS**...REVILED THROUGHOUT THE GALAXY AS DISEASE-CARRYING PESTS...

IT HAS BEEN A PROFITABLE AFTERNOON FOR THE JAWAS... THEY'VE NOT ONLY ACQUIRED A TON OF SALABLE SCRAP...

...AND **PRIZED** BY JAWAS FOR THEIR TOUGH, PUNGENT MEAT!

...BUT A **FREE DINNER** CAME INSIDE!

WHILE, BACK AT THE CRASH SITE...

SEARCH DETAIL TO BASE...REPORT **NO VISUAL CONTACT** WITH TRANSPORT CAPSULE!

...AND THERE'S NOT GOING TO **BE** ANY!

CRAWLER TRACKS... **JAWAS!?**

THEY'LL SELL THE METAL...AND **EAT** THE SQUILLS!

...AND THEIR DEAD LITTLE **EYES** WILL BE **IMPOSSIBLE TO READ!**

MASSASSI-ONE TO SKYWALKER... DO YOU COPY—?

SKYWALKER... GO AHEAD, MASSASSI!

ALLIANCE **CODE GRAVE**, LUKE... ABANDON RECONNAISSANCE MISSION!

GLADLY! WE HAVEN'T SEEN ANYTHING BUT **SPACE DUST** FOR—

SET COURSE IMMEDIATELY FOR *TATOOINE!*

OBSERVERS ON *TATOOINE* REPORT THE LANDING OF AN UNSCHEDULED *TRANSPORT CAPSULE!* THE ALLIANCE IS *CONCERNED!*

SEND SOMEBODY ELSE!

BLEE-DIT-DAH!

I SHOULD SAY! AND FAR *MORE* SERIOUS FOR MASTER LUKE *PERSONALLY!*

TATOOINE IS HIS *HOME-WORLD,* YOU KNOW!

YOUR *FAMILIARITY* WITH THE PLANET MAKES YOU IDEAL FOR—

I AM *NOT* GOING BACK THERE!

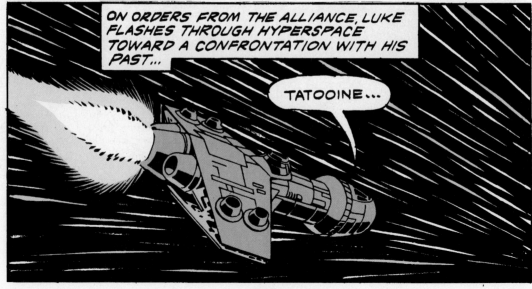

ON ORDERS FROM THE ALLIANCE, LUKE FLASHES THROUGH HYPERSPACE TOWARD A CONFRONTATION WITH HIS PAST...

TATOOINE...

116

JUST SAYING THE *NAME* MAKES ME *QUEASY*, THREEPIO! ...TOO MANY MEMORIES—!

I'M *ENTIRELY* SYMPATHETIC, MASTER LUKE!

MY OWN CIRCUITRY *BRISTLES* AT THE THOUGHT OF A CERTAIN *WELDER'S BENCH* ON *ALDERAAN!*

LUKE'S SHIP EMERGES FROM HYPERSPACE TO BE GREETED BY THE TWIN SUNS OF *TATOOINE* ...AND A CURIOUS MESSAGE...

IF YOU READ ME...DO NOT REPLY!

GO DIRECTLY TO MOS EISLEY CANTINA! ASK FOR *ANDUVIL* OF OGEM!

A FEMALE *ORGANIC* VOICE, WAS IT NOT?

A *FEMININE* VOICE...THAT HAD TO TALK *FAST*... OR *SEEM* LIKE IT!

I WONDER IF SHE'S WORKING WITH THE ALLIANCE... OR LAYING A *TRAP!*

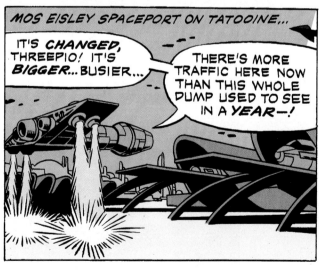

MOS EISLEY SPACEPORT ON TATOOINE...

IT'S *CHANGED*, THREEPIO! IT'S *BIGGER*...BUSIER...

THERE'S MORE TRAFFIC HERE NOW THAN THIS WHOLE DUMP USED TO SEE IN A *YEAR—!*

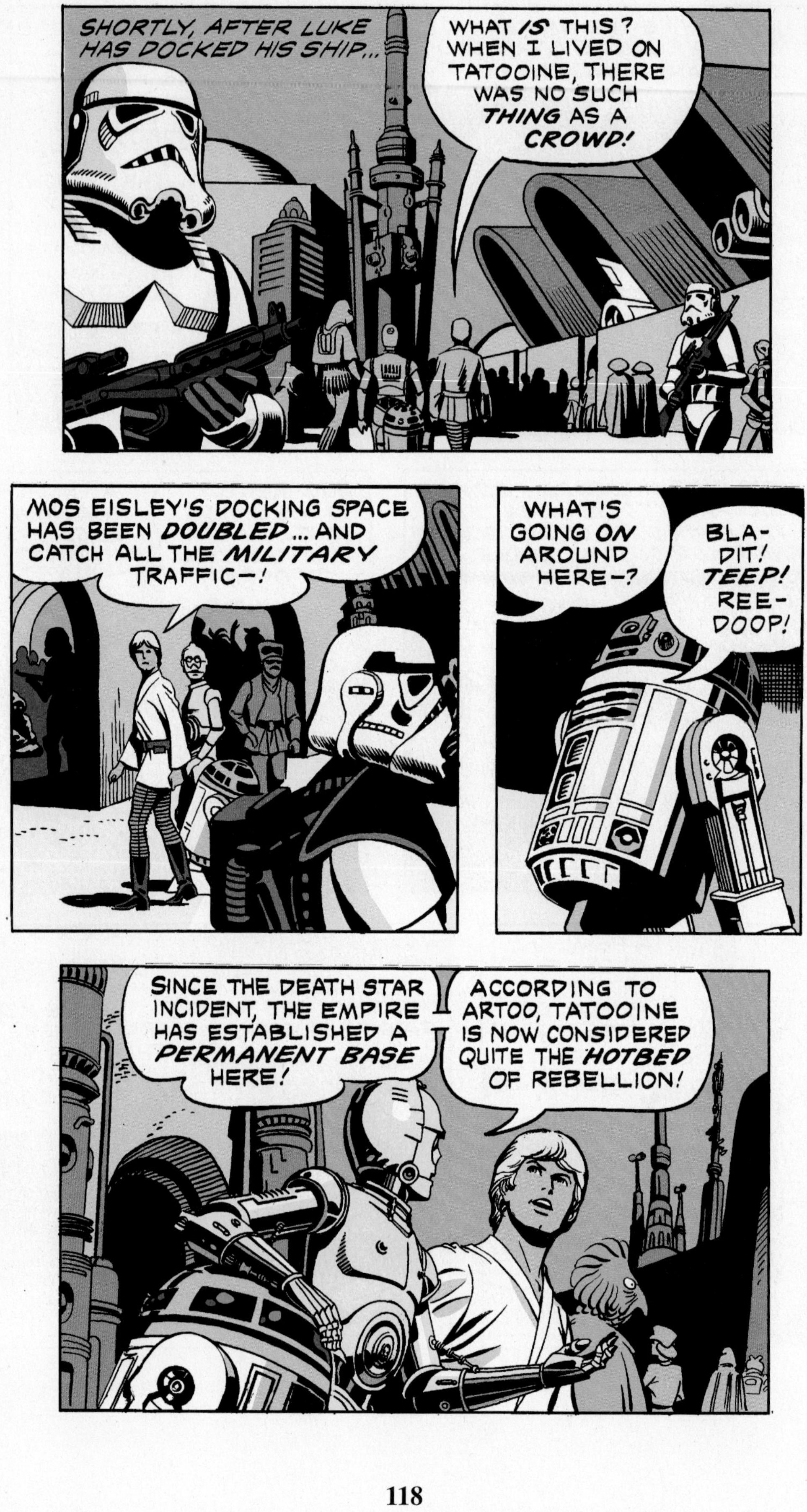
SHORTLY, AFTER LUKE HAS DOCKED HIS SHIP...
WHAT *IS* THIS? WHEN I LIVED ON TATOOINE, THERE WAS NO SUCH *THING* AS A *CROWD!*
MOS EISLEY'S DOCKING SPACE HAS BEEN *DOUBLED*... AND CATCH ALL THE *MILITARY* TRAFFIC–!
WHAT'S GOING *ON* AROUND HERE–?
BLA-DIT! *TEEP!* REE-DOOP!
SINCE THE DEATH STAR INCIDENT, THE EMPIRE HAS ESTABLISHED A *PERMANENT BASE* HERE!
ACCORDING TO ARTOO, TATOOINE IS NOW CONSIDERED QUITE THE *HOTBED* OF REBELLION!

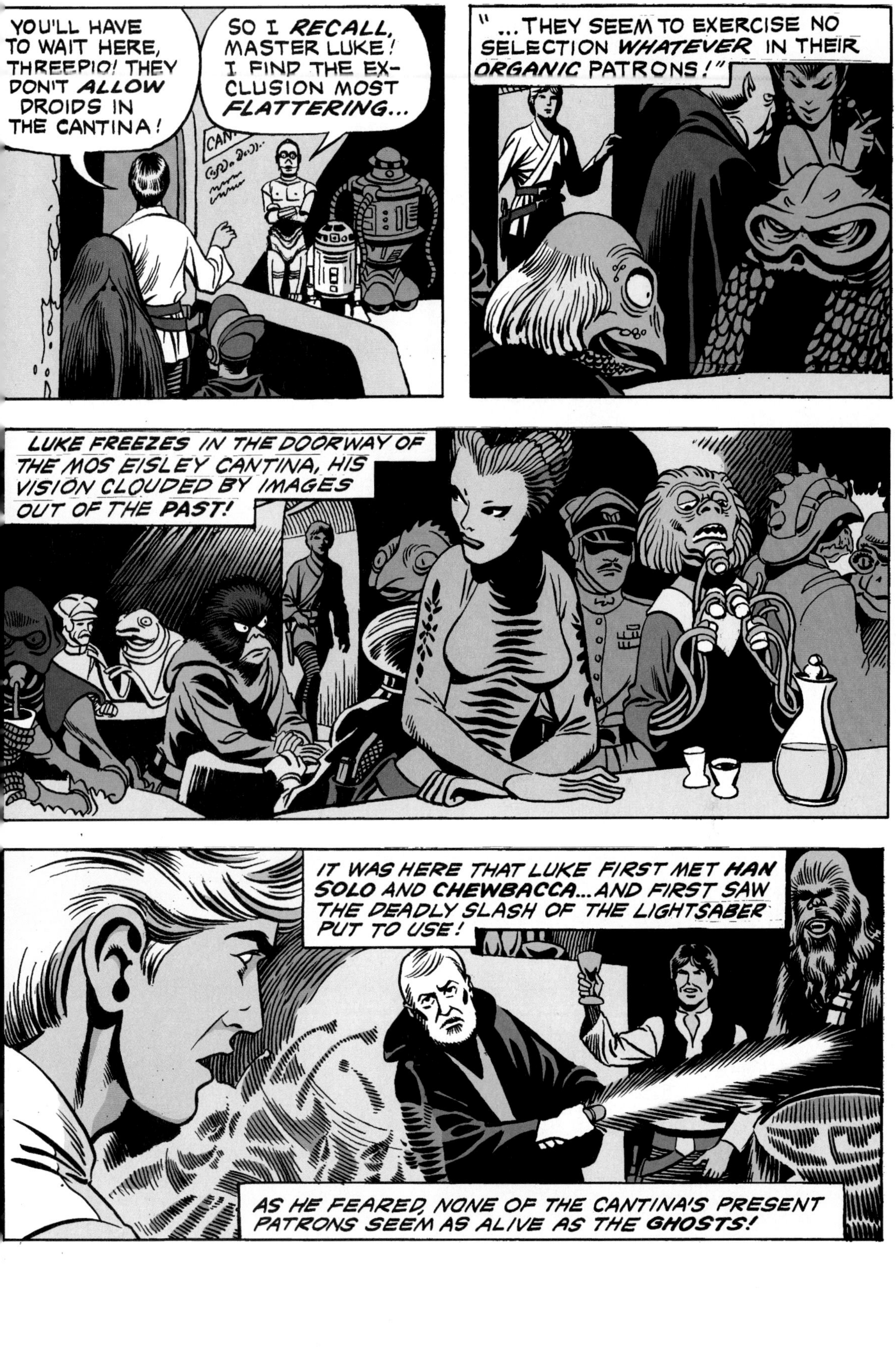
YOU'LL HAVE TO WAIT HERE, THREEPIO! THEY DON'T ALLOW DROIDS IN THE CANTINA!
SO I RECALL, MASTER LUKE! I FIND THE EXCLUSION MOST FLATTERING...
"...THEY SEEM TO EXERCISE NO SELECTION WHATEVER IN THEIR ORGANIC PATRONS!"
LUKE FREEZES IN THE DOORWAY OF THE MOS EISLEY CANTINA, HIS VISION CLOUDED BY IMAGES OUT OF THE PAST!
IT WAS HERE THAT LUKE FIRST MET HAN SOLO AND CHEWBACCA...AND FIRST SAW THE DEADLY SLASH OF THE LIGHTSABER PUT TO USE!
AS HE FEARED, NONE OF THE CANTINA'S PRESENT PATRONS SEEM AS ALIVE AS THE GHOSTS!

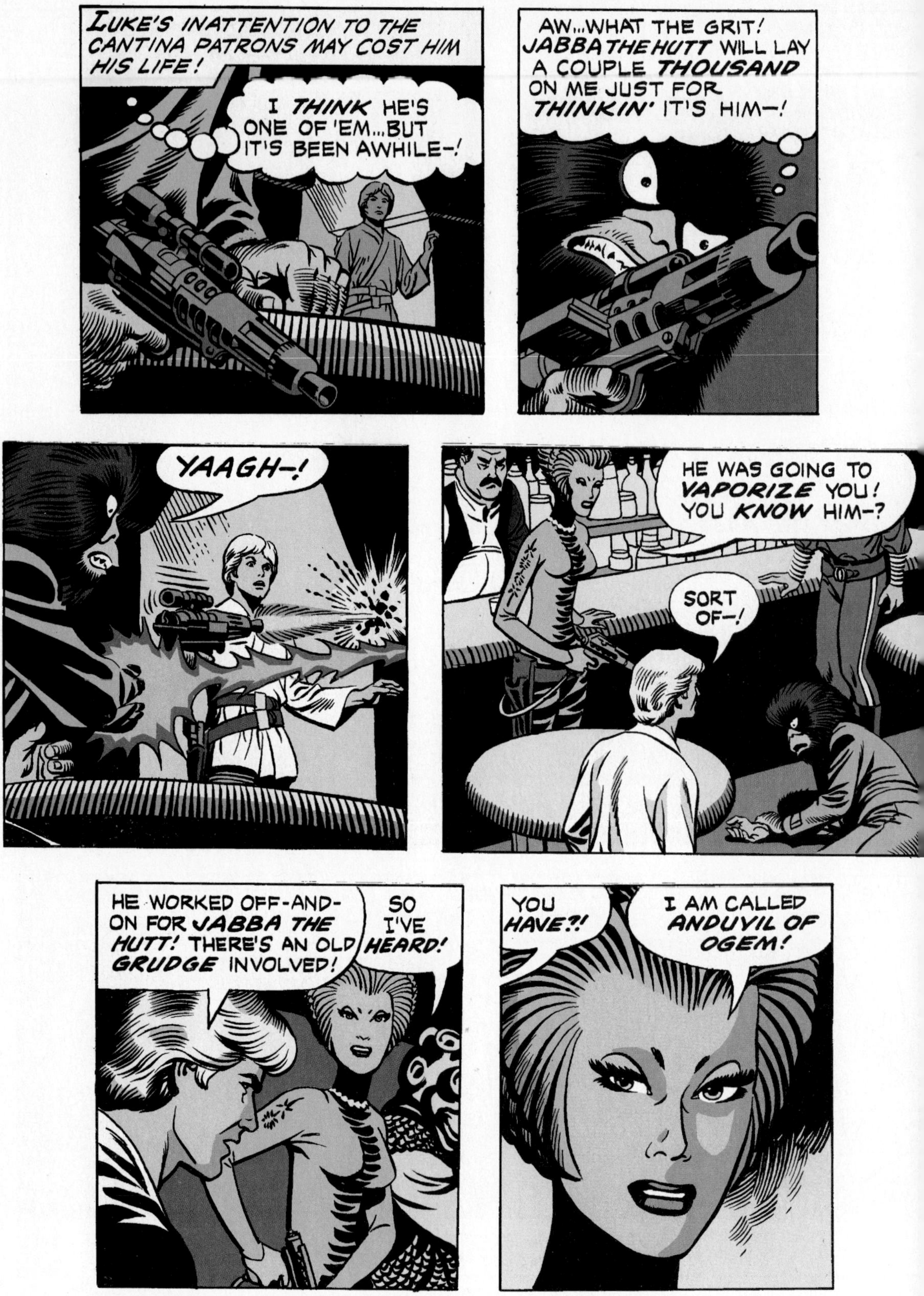
LUKE'S INATTENTION TO THE CANTINA PATRONS MAY COST HIM HIS LIFE!
I THINK HE'S ONE OF 'EM...BUT IT'S BEEN AWHILE-!
AW...WHAT THE GRIT! JABBA THE HUTT WILL LAY A COUPLE THOUSAND ON ME JUST FOR THINKIN' IT'S HIM-!
YAAGH-!
HE WAS GOING TO VAPORIZE YOU! YOU KNOW HIM-?
SORT OF-!
HE WORKED OFF-AND-ON FOR JABBA THE HUTT! THERE'S AN OLD GRUDGE INVOLVED!
SO I'VE HEARD!
YOU HAVE?!
I AM CALLED ANDUVIL OF OGEM!

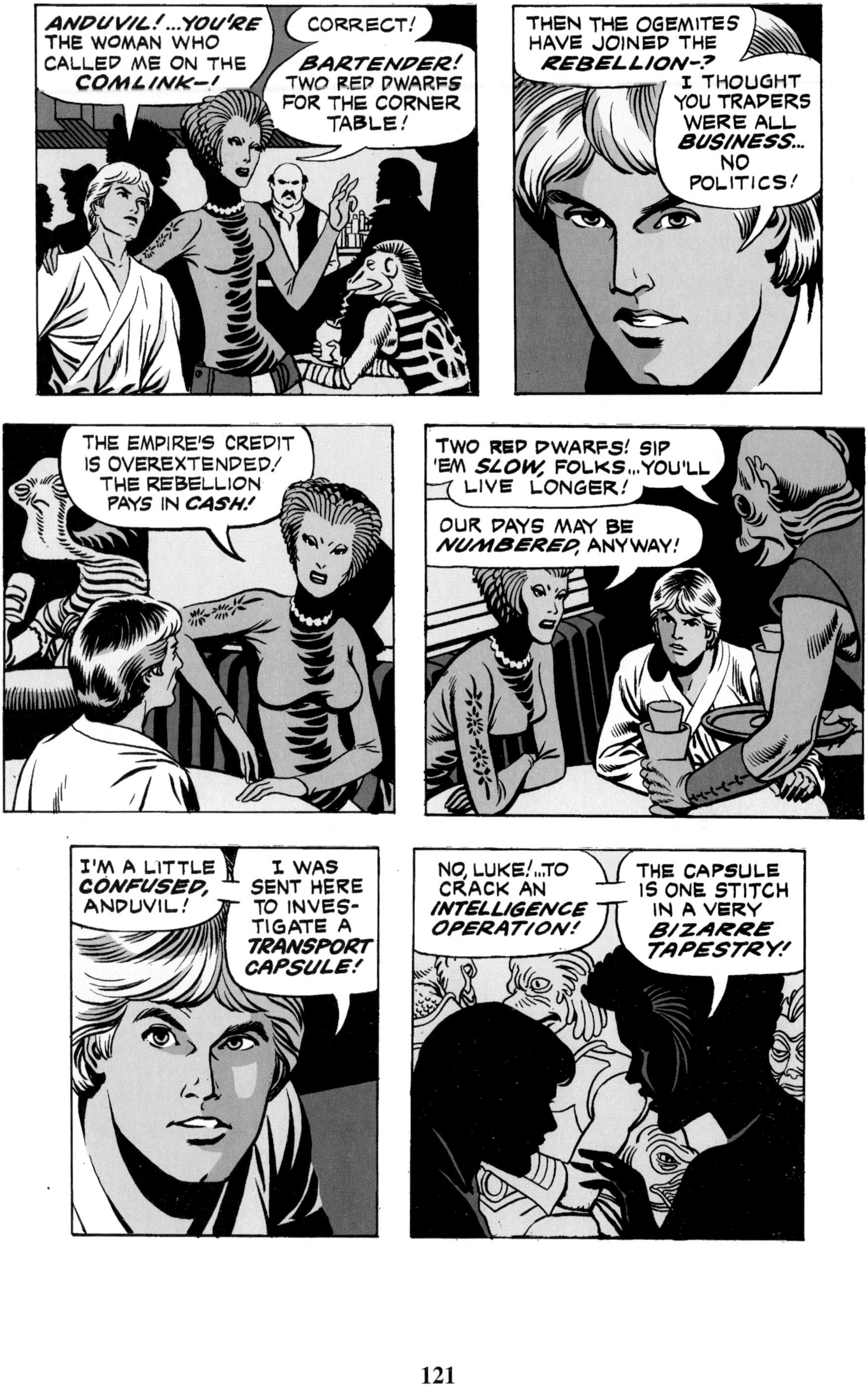
ANDUVIL! ...YOU'RE THE WOMAN WHO CALLED ME ON THE COMLINK-!
CORRECT!
BARTENDER! TWO RED DWARFS FOR THE CORNER TABLE!
THEN THE OGEMITES HAVE JOINED THE REBELLION-?
I THOUGHT YOU TRADERS WERE ALL BUSINESS... NO POLITICS!
THE EMPIRE'S CREDIT IS OVEREXTENDED! THE REBELLION PAYS IN CASH!
TWO RED DWARFS! SIP 'EM SLOW, FOLKS... YOU'LL LIVE LONGER!
OUR DAYS MAY BE NUMBERED, ANYWAY!
I'M A LITTLE CONFUSED, ANDUVIL!
I WAS SENT HERE TO INVESTIGATE A TRANSPORT CAPSULE!
NO, LUKE! ...TO CRACK AN INTELLIGENCE OPERATION!
THE CAPSULE IS ONE STITCH IN A VERY BIZARRE TAPESTRY!

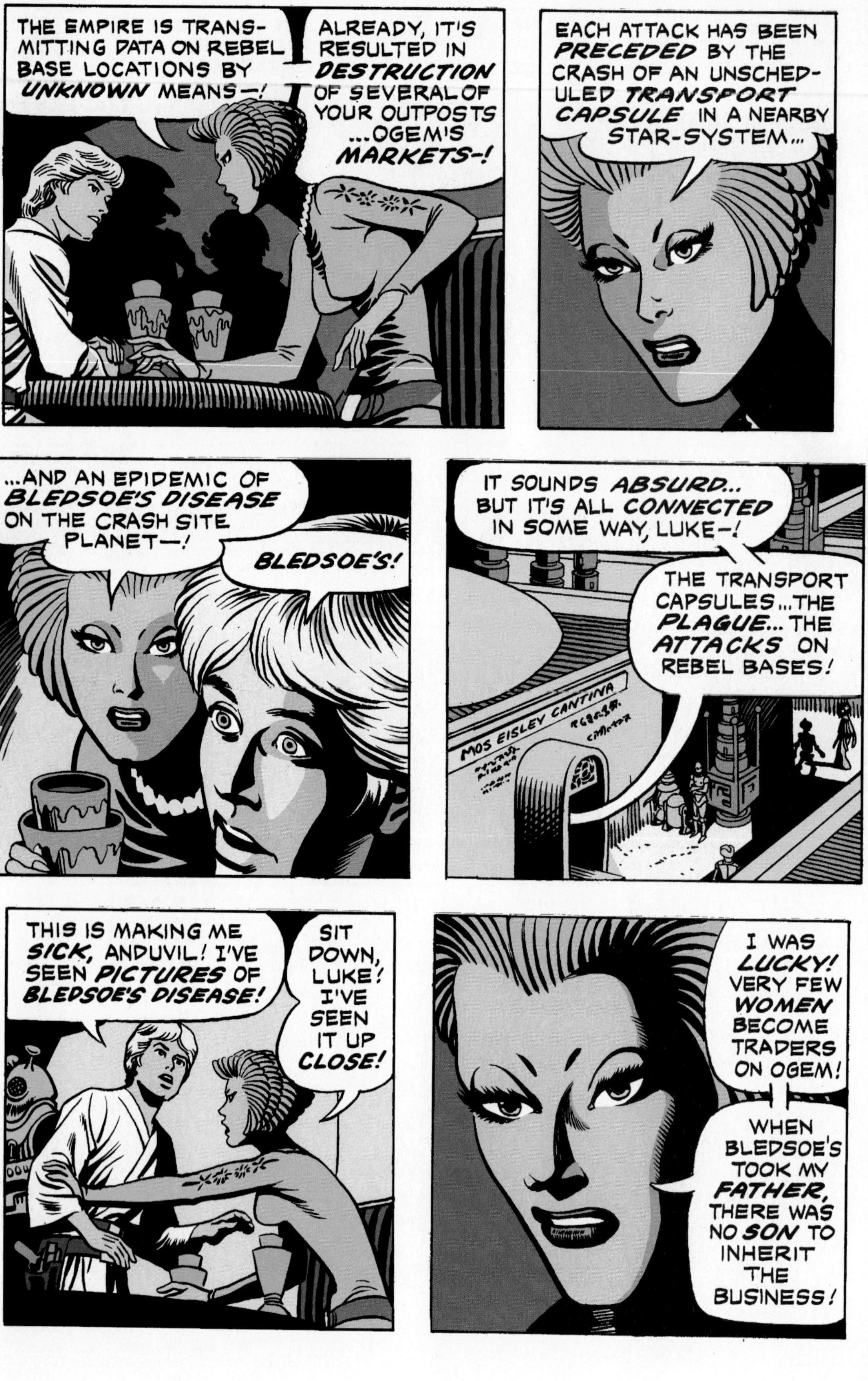
THE EMPIRE IS TRANSMITTING DATA ON REBEL BASE LOCATIONS BY UNKNOWN MEANS—!
ALREADY, IT'S RESULTED IN DESTRUCTION OF SEVERAL OF YOUR OUTPOSTS ...OGEM'S MARKETS—!
EACH ATTACK HAS BEEN PRECEDED BY THE CRASH OF AN UNSCHEDULED TRANSPORT CAPSULE IN A NEARBY STAR-SYSTEM...
...AND AN EPIDEMIC OF BLEDSOE'S DISEASE ON THE CRASH SITE PLANET—!
BLEDSOE'S!
IT SOUNDS ABSURD... BUT IT'S ALL CONNECTED IN SOME WAY, LUKE—!
THE TRANSPORT CAPSULES...THE PLAGUE...THE ATTACKS ON REBEL BASES!
MOS EISLEY CANTINA
THIS IS MAKING ME SICK, ANDUVIL! I'VE SEEN PICTURES OF BLEDSOE'S DISEASE!
SIT DOWN, LUKE! I'VE SEEN IT UP CLOSE!
I WAS LUCKY! VERY FEW WOMEN BECOME TRADERS ON OGEM!
WHEN BLEDSOE'S TOOK MY FATHER, THERE WAS NO SON TO INHERIT THE BUSINESS!

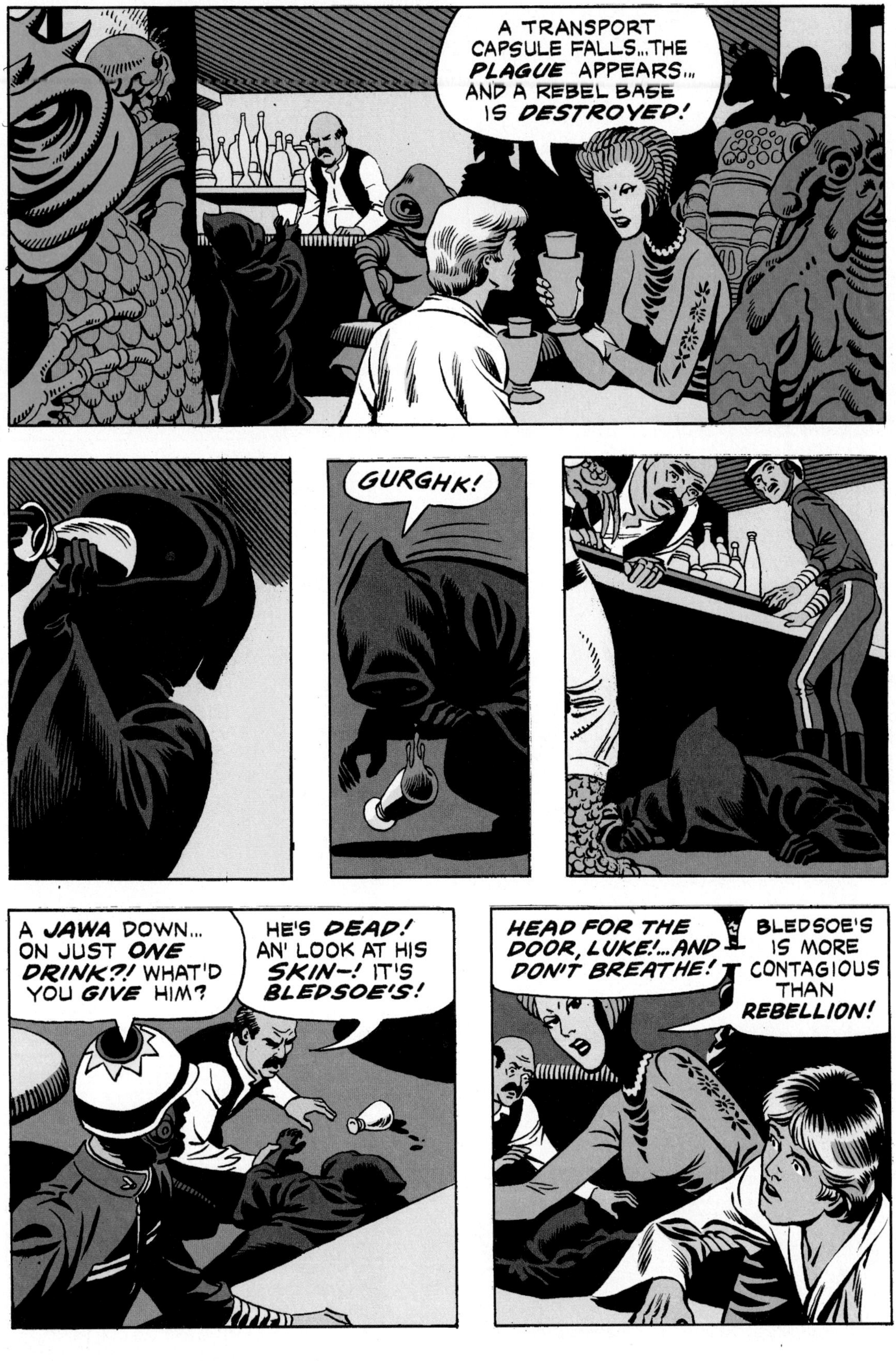
A TRANSPORT CAPSULE FALLS... THE PLAGUE APPEARS... AND A REBEL BASE IS DESTROYED!
GURGHK!
A JAWA DOWN... ON JUST ONE DRINK?! WHAT'D YOU GIVE HIM?
HE'S DEAD! AN' LOOK AT HIS SKIN-! IT'S BLEDSOE'S!
HEAD FOR THE DOOR, LUKE!... AND DON'T BREATHE!
BLEDSOE'S IS MORE CONTAGIOUS THAN REBELLION!

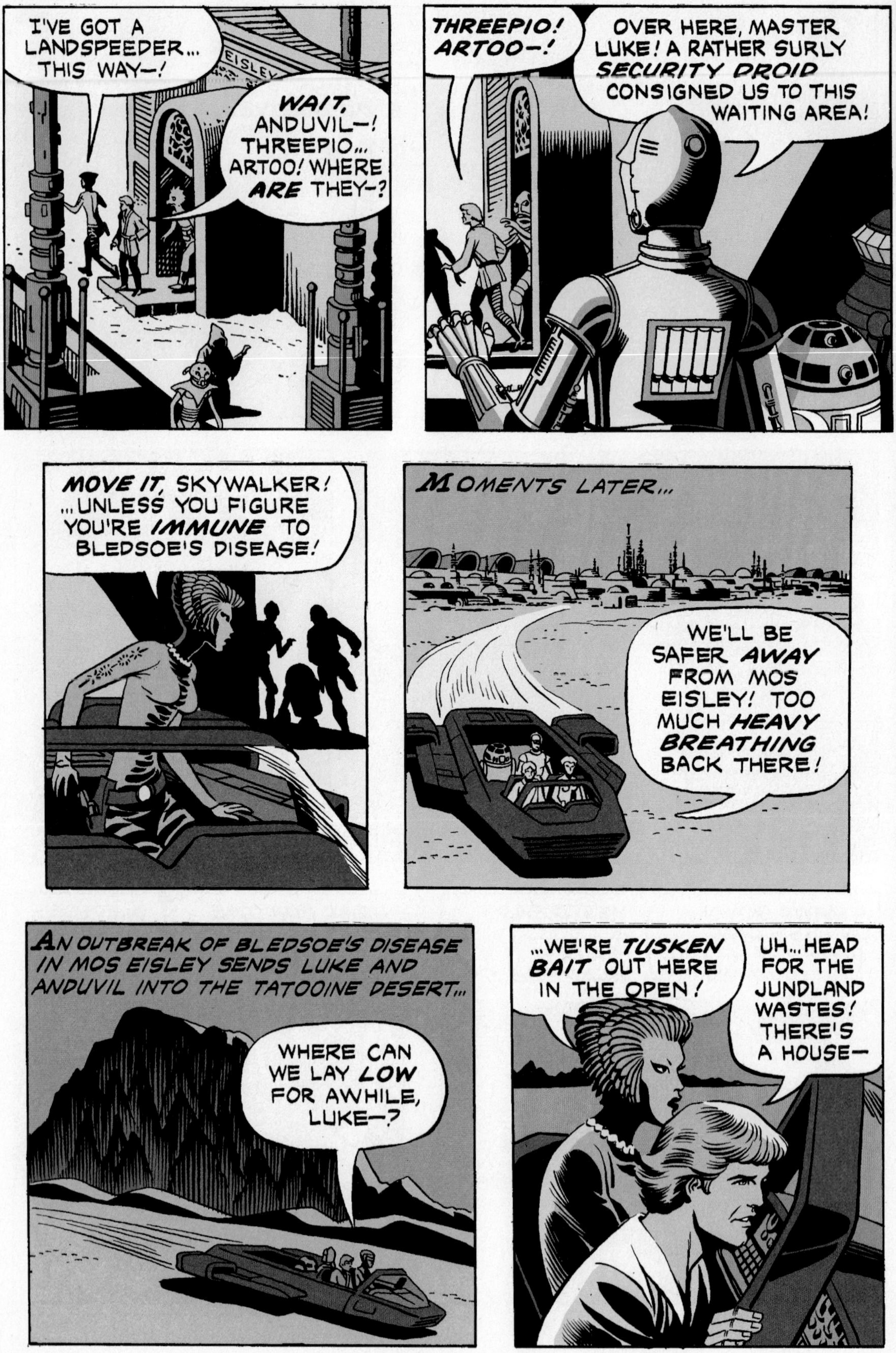
I'VE GOT A LANDSPEEDER... THIS WAY—!
WAIT, ANDUVIL—! THREEPIO... ARTOO! WHERE ARE THEY—?
EISLEY
THREEPIO! ARTOO—!
OVER HERE, MASTER LUKE! A RATHER SURLY SECURITY DROID CONSIGNED US TO THIS WAITING AREA!
MOVE IT, SKYWALKER! ...UNLESS YOU FIGURE YOU'RE IMMUNE TO BLEDSOE'S DISEASE!
MOMENTS LATER...
WE'LL BE SAFER AWAY FROM MOS EISLEY! TOO MUCH HEAVY BREATHING BACK THERE!
AN OUTBREAK OF BLEDSOE'S DISEASE IN MOS EISLEY SENDS LUKE AND ANDUVIL INTO THE TATOOINE DESERT...
WHERE CAN WE LAY LOW FOR AWHILE, LUKE—?
...WE'RE TUSKEN BAIT OUT HERE IN THE OPEN!
UH...HEAD FOR THE JUNDLAND WASTES! THERE'S A HOUSE—

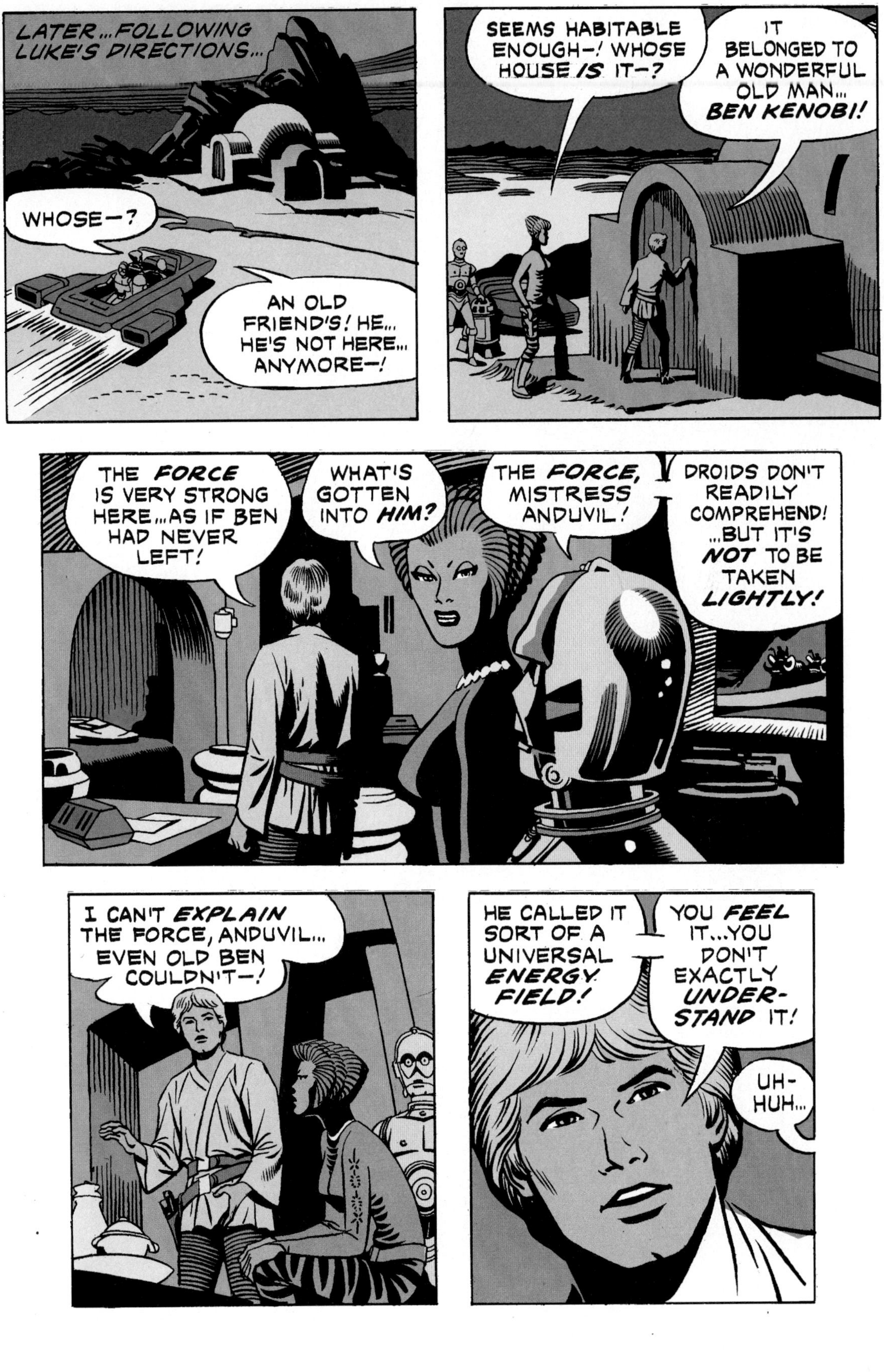
LATER...FOLLOWING LUKE'S DIRECTIONS...
WHOSE—?
AN OLD FRIEND'S! HE... HE'S NOT HERE... ANYMORE—!
SEEMS HABITABLE ENOUGH—! WHOSE HOUSE IS IT—?
IT BELONGED TO A WONDERFUL OLD MAN... BEN KENOBI!
THE FORCE IS VERY STRONG HERE...AS IF BEN HAD NEVER LEFT!
WHAT'S GOTTEN INTO HIM?
THE FORCE, MISTRESS ANDUVIL!
DROIDS DON'T READILY COMPREHEND! ...BUT IT'S NOT TO BE TAKEN LIGHTLY!
I CAN'T EXPLAIN THE FORCE, ANDUVIL... EVEN OLD BEN COULDN'T—!
HE CALLED IT SORT OF A UNIVERSAL ENERGY FIELD!
YOU FEEL IT...YOU DON'T EXACTLY UNDER-STAND IT!
UH-HUH...

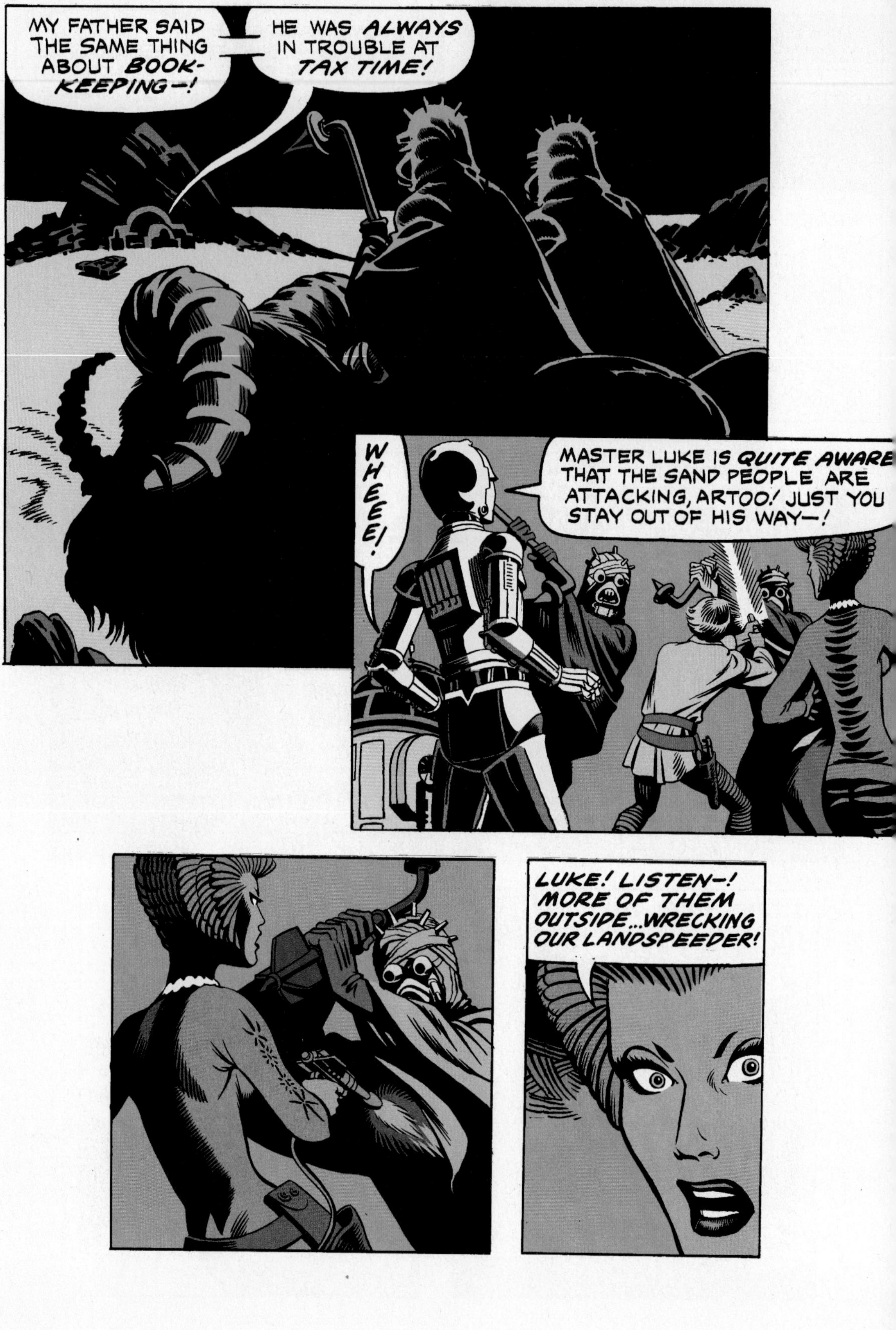
MY FATHER SAID THE SAME THING ABOUT BOOK-KEEPING—!
HE WAS ALWAYS IN TROUBLE AT TAX TIME!
WHEEE!
MASTER LUKE IS QUITE AWARE THAT THE SAND PEOPLE ARE ATTACKING, ARTOO! JUST YOU STAY OUT OF HIS WAY—!
LUKE! LISTEN—! MORE OF THEM OUTSIDE...WRECKING OUR LANDSPEEDER!

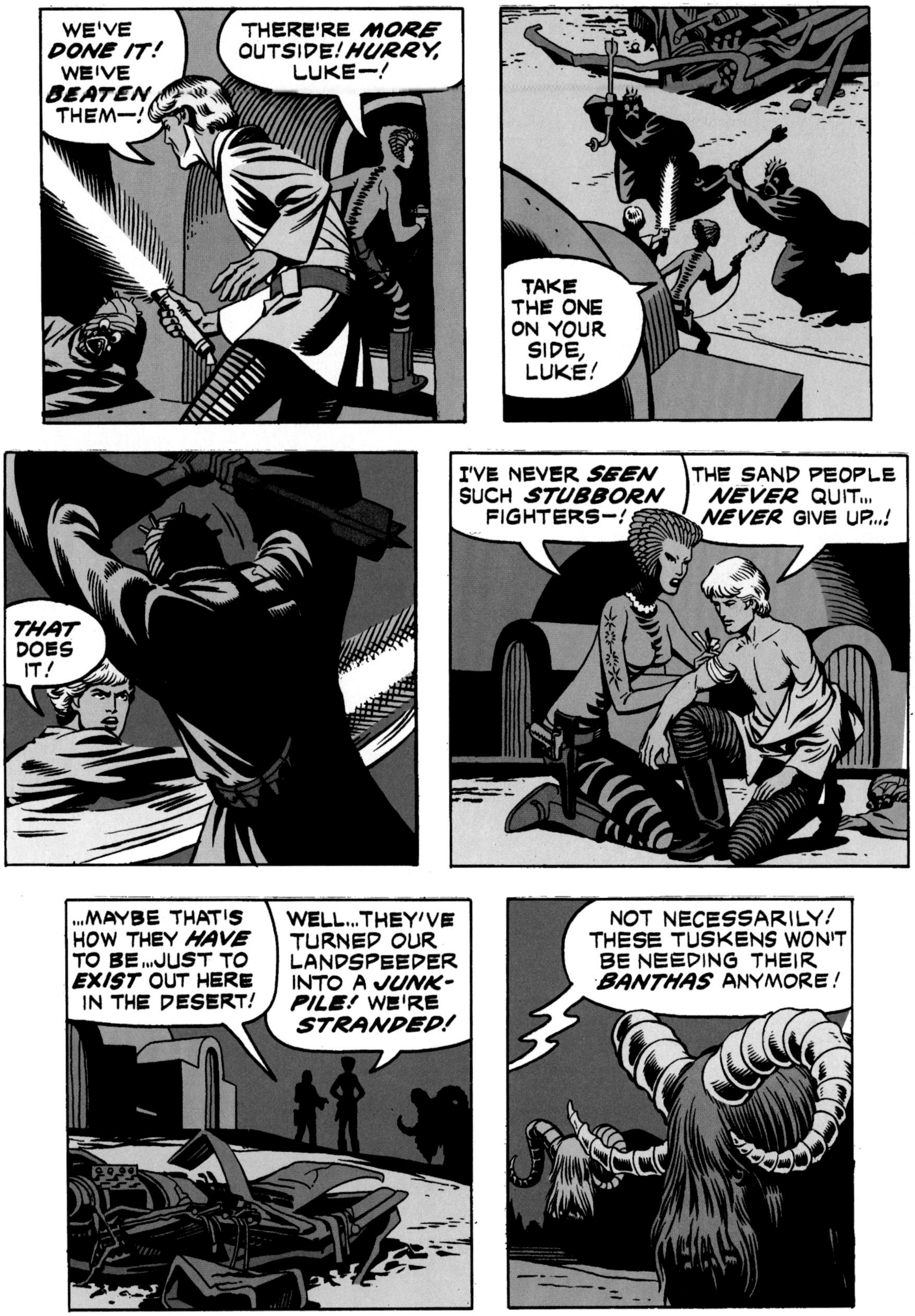
WE'VE DONE IT! WE'VE BEATEN THEM—!
THERE'RE MORE OUTSIDE! HURRY, LUKE—!
TAKE THE ONE ON YOUR SIDE, LUKE!
THAT DOES IT!
I'VE NEVER SEEN SUCH STUBBORN FIGHTERS—!
THE SAND PEOPLE NEVER QUIT... NEVER GIVE UP...!
...MAYBE THAT'S HOW THEY HAVE TO BE...JUST TO EXIST OUT HERE IN THE DESERT!
WELL...THEY'VE TURNED OUR LANDSPEEDER INTO A JUNK-PILE! WE'RE STRANDED!
NOT NECESSARILY! THESE TUSKENS WON'T BE NEEDING THEIR BANTHAS ANYMORE!

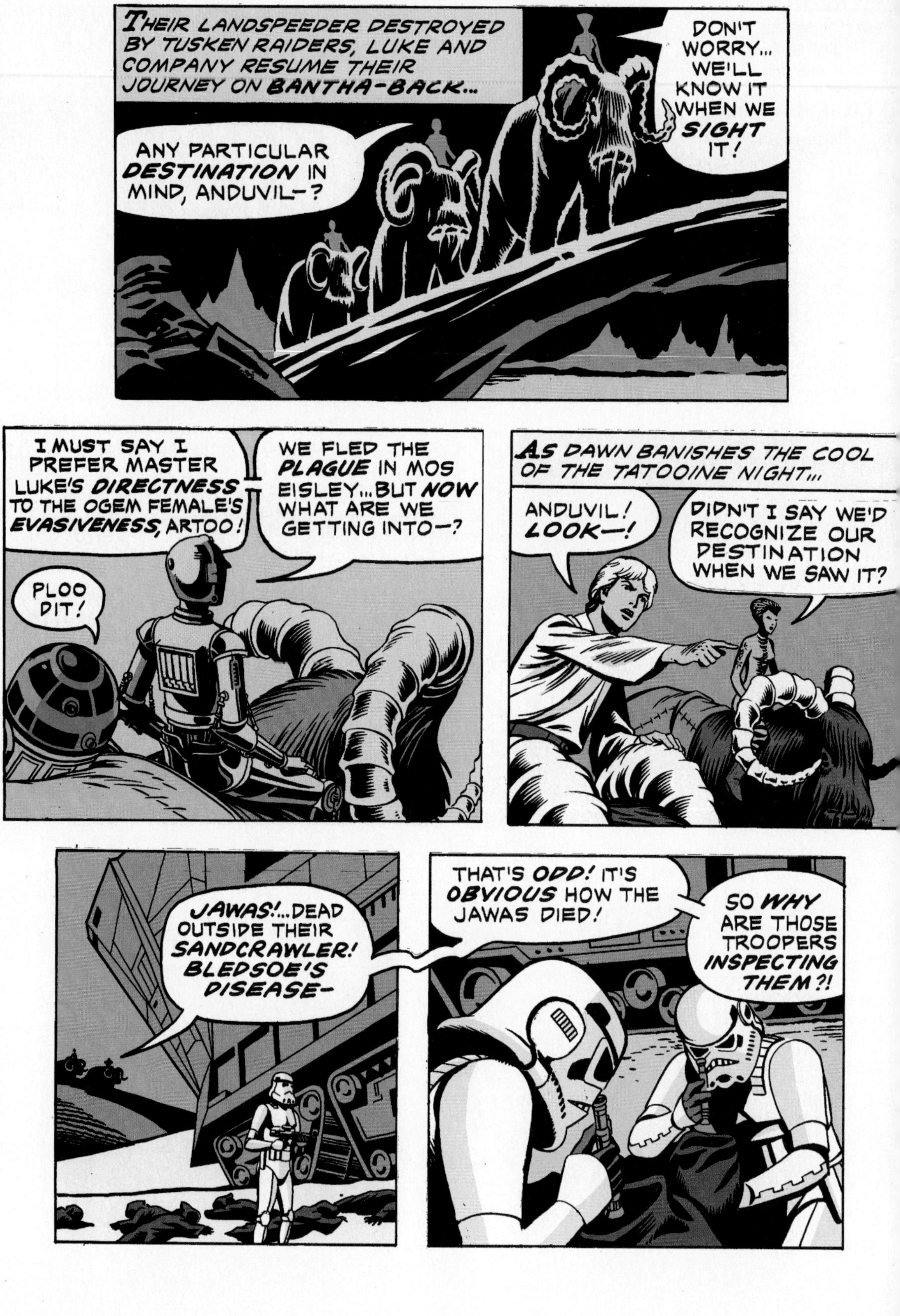
THEIR LANDSPEEDER DESTROYED BY TUSKEN RAIDERS, LUKE AND COMPANY RESUME THEIR JOURNEY ON BANTHA-BACK...
ANY PARTICULAR DESTINATION IN MIND, ANDUVIL--?
DON'T WORRY... WE'LL KNOW IT WHEN WE SIGHT IT!
I MUST SAY I PREFER MASTER LUKE'S DIRECTNESS TO THE OGEM FEMALE'S EVASIVENESS, ARTOO!
WE FLED THE PLAGUE IN MOS EISLEY...BUT NOW WHAT ARE WE GETTING INTO--?
PLOO DIT!
AS DAWN BANISHES THE COOL OF THE TATOOINE NIGHT...
ANDUVIL! LOOK--!
DIDN'T I SAY WE'D RECOGNIZE OUR DESTINATION WHEN WE SAW IT?
JAWAS!...DEAD OUTSIDE THEIR SANDCRAWLER! BLEDSOE'S DISEASE-
THAT'S ODD! IT'S OBVIOUS HOW THE JAWAS DIED!
SO WHY ARE THOSE TROOPERS INSPECTING THEM?!

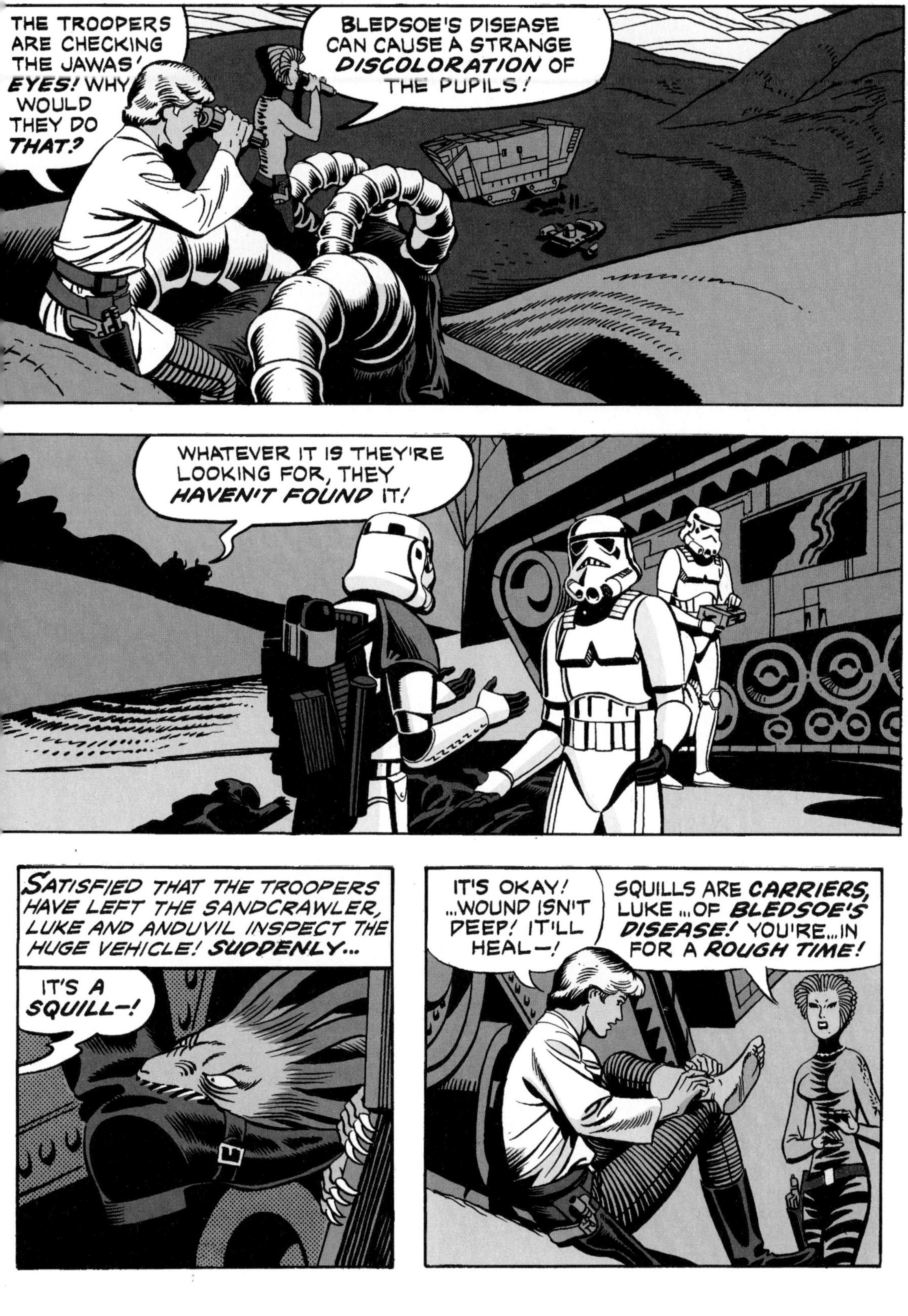
THE TROOPERS ARE CHECKING THE JAWAS' EYES! WHY WOULD THEY DO THAT?
BLEDSOE'S DISEASE CAN CAUSE A STRANGE DISCOLORATION OF THE PUPILS!
WHATEVER IT IS THEY'RE LOOKING FOR, THEY HAVEN'T FOUND IT!
SATISFIED THAT THE TROOPERS HAVE LEFT THE SANDCRAWLER, LUKE AND ANDUVIL INSPECT THE HUGE VEHICLE! SUDDENLY...
IT'S A SQUILL—!
IT'S OKAY! ...WOUND ISN'T DEEP! IT'LL HEAL—!
SQUILLS ARE CARRIERS, LUKE ... OF BLEDSOE'S DISEASE! YOU'RE...IN FOR A ROUGH TIME!

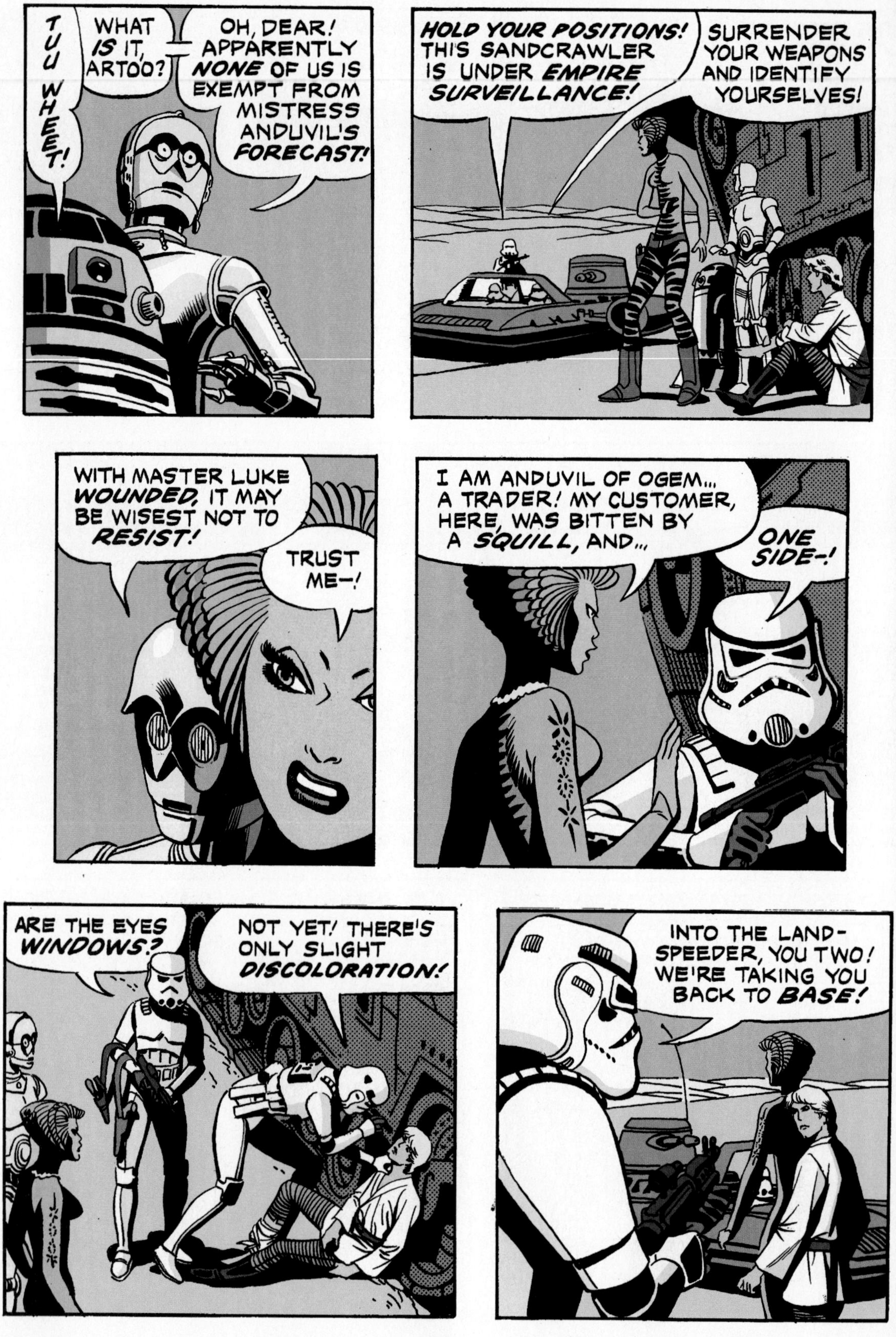
TUU WHEET!
WHAT IS IT, ARTOO?
OH, DEAR! APPARENTLY NONE OF US IS EXEMPT FROM MISTRESS ANDUVIL'S FORECAST!
HOLD YOUR POSITIONS! THIS SANDCRAWLER IS UNDER EMPIRE SURVEILLANCE!
SURRENDER YOUR WEAPONS AND IDENTIFY YOURSELVES!
WITH MASTER LUKE WOUNDED, IT MAY BE WISEST NOT TO RESIST!
TRUST ME—!
I AM ANDUVIL OF OGEM... A TRADER! MY CUSTOMER, HERE, WAS BITTEN BY A SQUILL, AND...
ONE SIDE—!
ARE THE EYES WINDOWS?
NOT YET! THERE'S ONLY SLIGHT DISCOLORATION!
INTO THE LAND-SPEEDER, YOU TWO! WE'RE TAKING YOU BACK TO BASE!

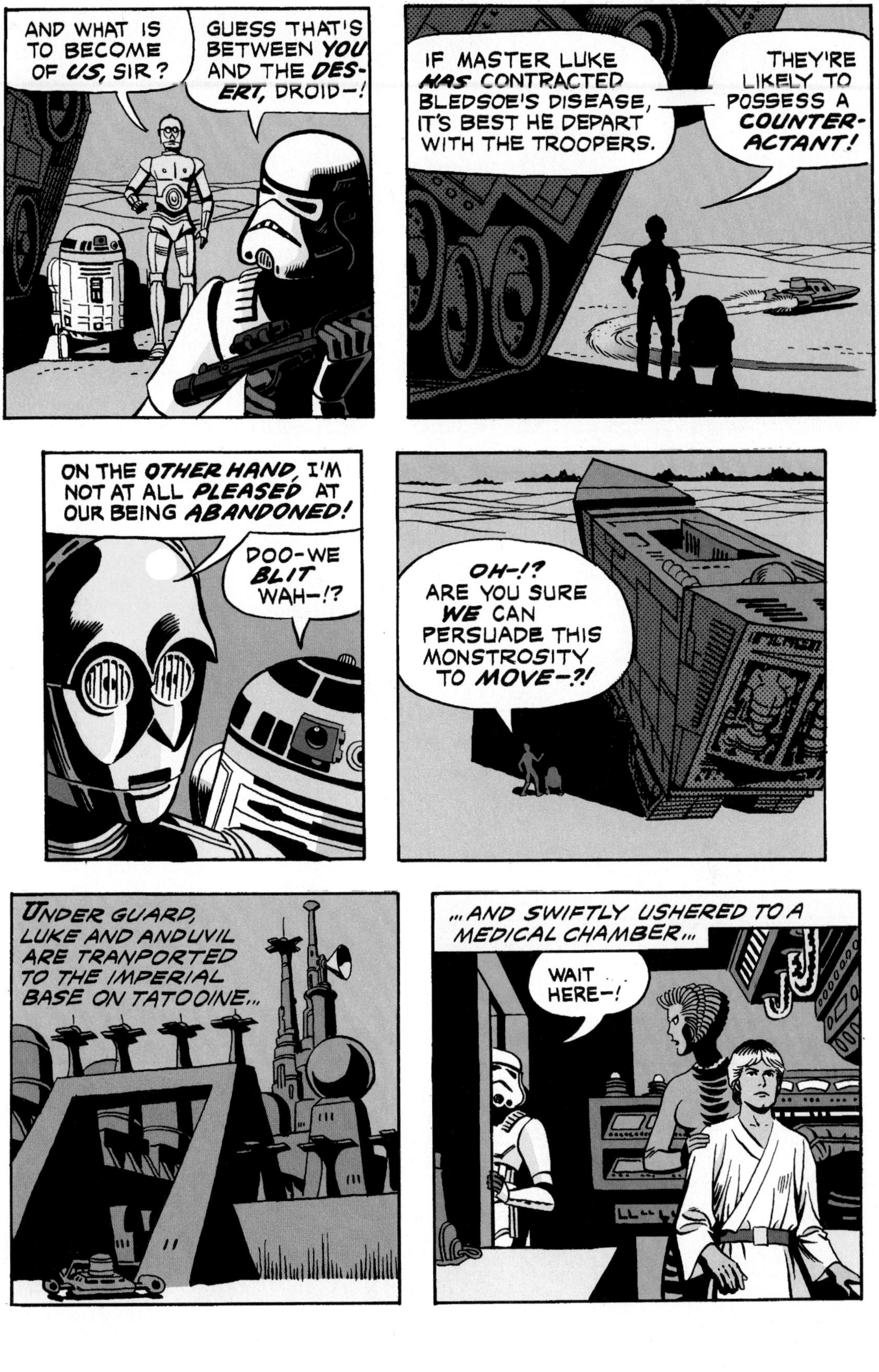

AND WHAT IS TO BECOME OF US, SIR?
GUESS THAT'S BETWEEN YOU AND THE DESERT, DROID—!
IF MASTER LUKE HAS CONTRACTED BLEDSOE'S DISEASE, IT'S BEST HE DEPART WITH THE TROOPERS.
THEY'RE LIKELY TO POSSESS A COUNTER-ACTANT!
ON THE OTHER HAND, I'M NOT AT ALL PLEASED AT OUR BEING ABANDONED!
DOO-WE BLIT WAH—!?
OH—!? ARE YOU SURE WE CAN PERSUADE THIS MONSTROSITY TO MOVE—?!
UNDER GUARD, LUKE AND ANDUVIL ARE TRANPORTED TO THE IMPERIAL BASE ON TATOOINE...
...AND SWIFTLY USHERED TO A MEDICAL CHAMBER...
WAIT HERE—!

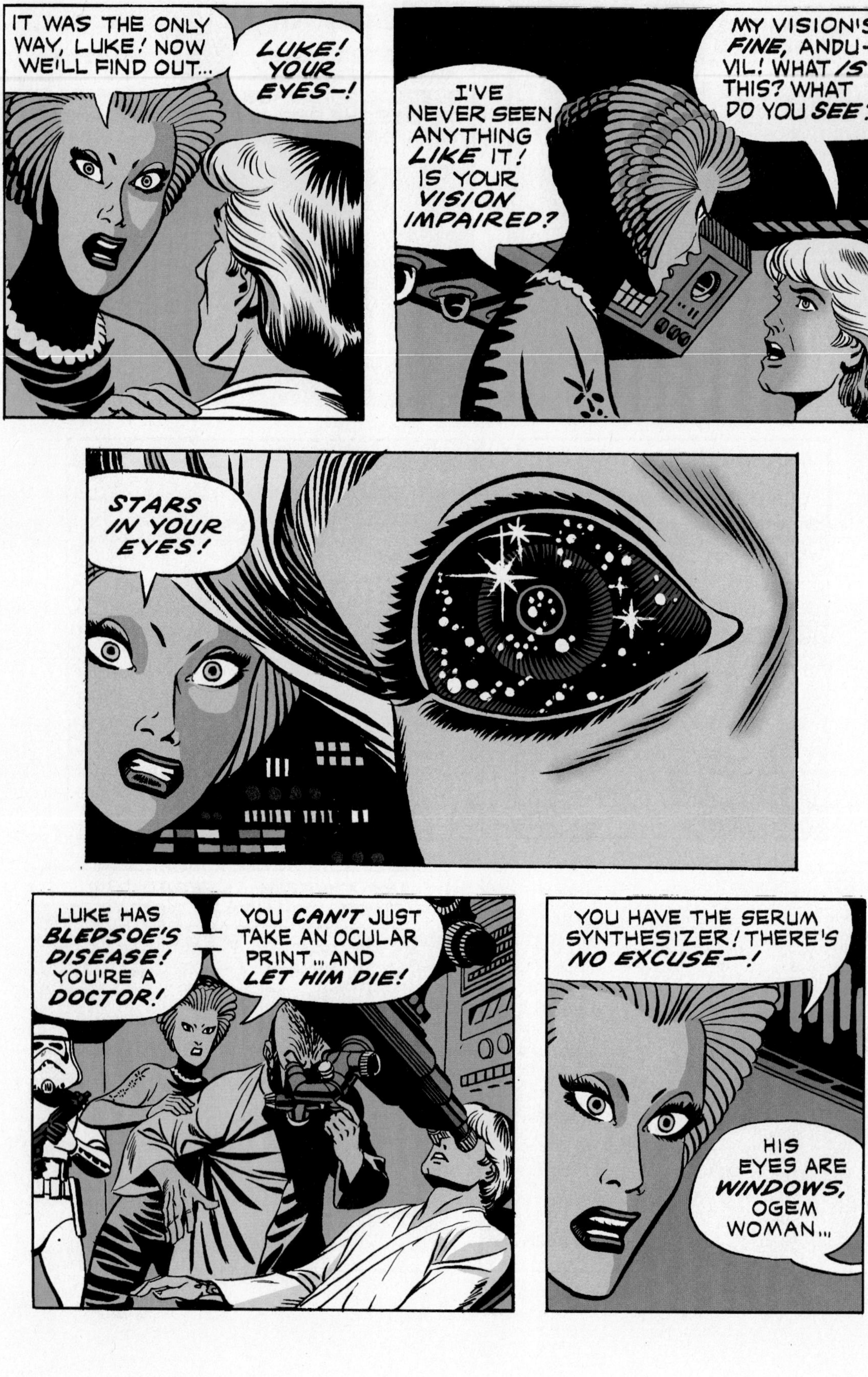
IT WAS THE ONLY WAY, LUKE! NOW WE'LL FIND OUT...
LUKE! YOUR EYES—!
I'VE NEVER SEEN ANYTHING LIKE IT! IS YOUR VISION IMPAIRED?
MY VISION'S FINE, ANDU-VIL! WHAT IS THIS? WHAT DO YOU SEE?
STARS IN YOUR EYES!
LUKE HAS BLEDSOE'S DISEASE! YOU'RE A DOCTOR!
YOU CAN'T JUST TAKE AN OCULAR PRINT... AND LET HIM DIE!
YOU HAVE THE SERUM SYNTHESIZER! THERE'S NO EXCUSE—!
HIS EYES ARE WINDOWS, OGEM WOMAN...

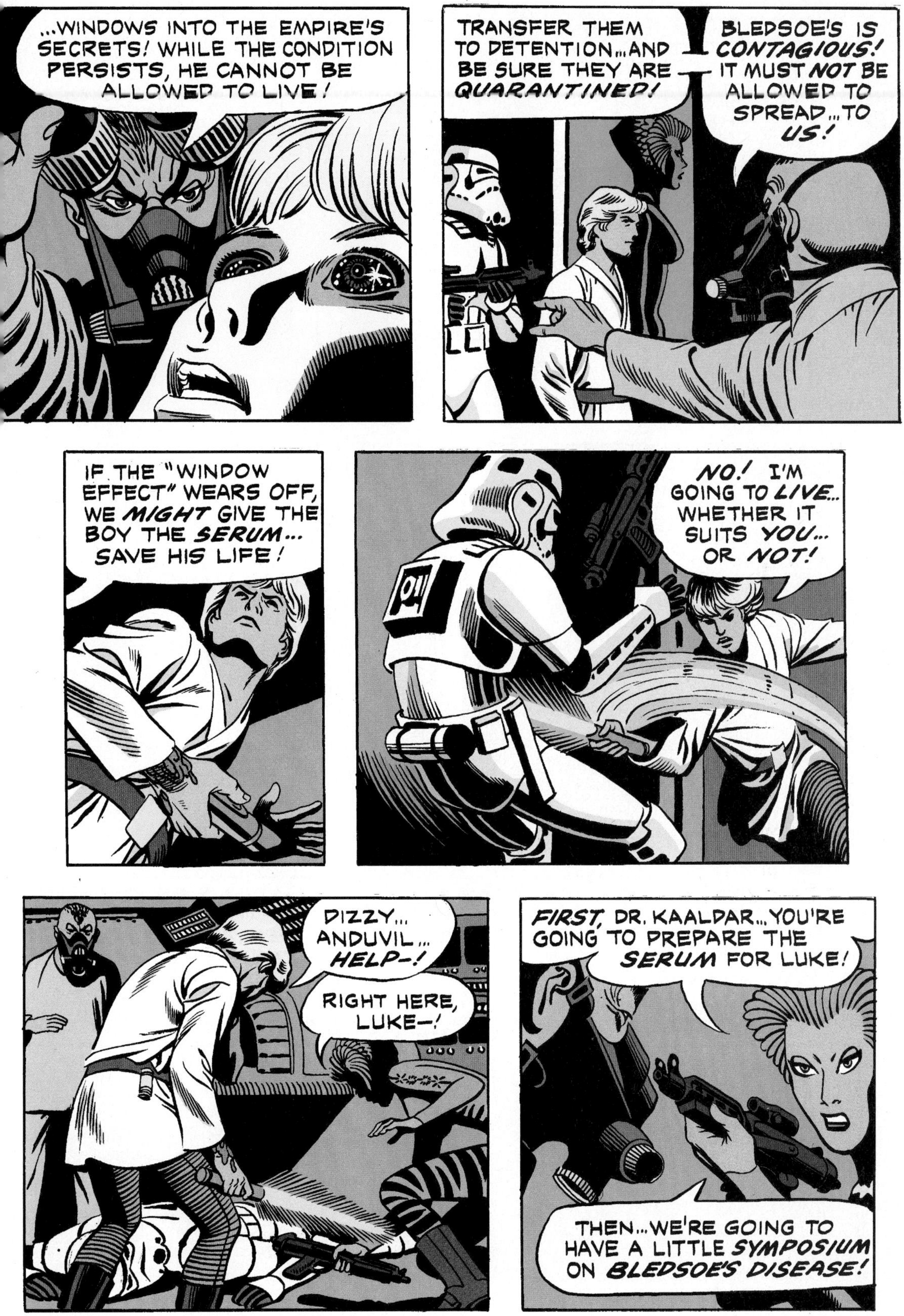

...WINDOWS INTO THE EMPIRE'S SECRETS! WHILE THE CONDITION PERSISTS, HE CANNOT BE ALLOWED TO LIVE!
TRANSFER THEM TO DETENTION... AND BE SURE THEY ARE QUARANTINED!
BLEDSOE'S IS CONTAGIOUS! IT MUST NOT BE ALLOWED TO SPREAD... TO US!
IF THE "WINDOW EFFECT" WEARS OFF, WE MIGHT GIVE THE BOY THE SERUM... SAVE HIS LIFE!
NO! I'M GOING TO LIVE... WHETHER IT SUITS YOU... OR NOT!
DIZZY... ANDUVIL... HELP-!
RIGHT HERE, LUKE-!
FIRST, DR. KAALDAR... YOU'RE GOING TO PREPARE THE SERUM FOR LUKE!
THEN... WE'RE GOING TO HAVE A LITTLE SYMPOSIUM ON BLEDSOE'S DISEASE!

THERE... IT'S *DONE!* THE SERUM REQUIRES A BRIEF PERIOD TO TAKE EFFECT—!

GOOD! THAT GIVES *YOU* TIME TO SAVE *YOUR* LIFE!

IT'S TRUE...THE OUTBREAKS OF BLEDSOE'S WERE CAUSED BY THE *EMPIRE*...FOR A TWOFOLD PURPOSE!

FIRST...TO UNDERMINE THE *SOCIAL ORDER* OF WORLDS LEANING TOWARD *REBELLION*...

...AND ALSO TO TRANSMIT THE *LOCATIONS* OF THE SECRET REBEL BASES!

I DON'T GET IT! HOW?

IN THE *EYES* OF THE VICTIMS! IT'S WHAT WE CALL THE *WINDOW EFFECT!*

THE EYES OF THE AFFLICTED SERVE AS *STAR MAPS!*

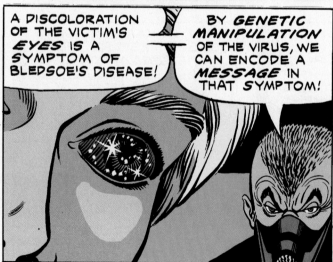

A DISCOLORATION OF THE VICTIM'S *EYES* IS A SYMPTOM OF BLEDSOE'S DISEASE!

BY *GENETIC MANIPULATION* OF THE VIRUS, WE CAN ENCODE A *MESSAGE* IN THAT SYMPTOM!

THE VIRUS BECOMES AN UNDETECTABLE COURIER OF *STAR CHARTS*...REVEALING REBEL BASES FOR THE IMPERIAL SPACE FLEET TO *DESTROY!*

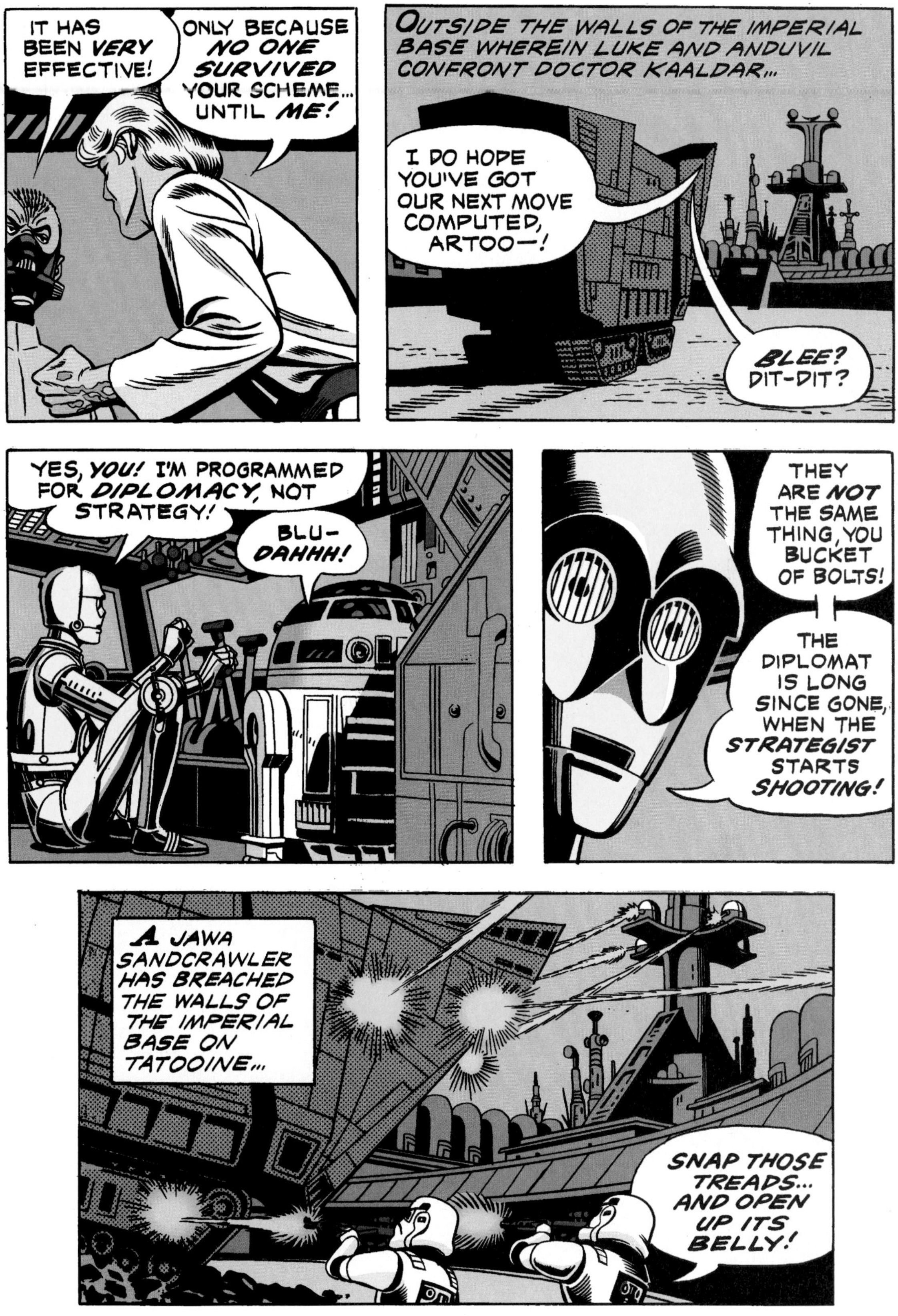

IT HAS BEEN VERY EFFECTIVE!
ONLY BECAUSE NO ONE SURVIVED YOUR SCHEME... UNTIL ME!
OUTSIDE THE WALLS OF THE IMPERIAL BASE WHEREIN LUKE AND ANDUVIL CONFRONT DOCTOR KAALDAR...
I DO HOPE YOU'VE GOT OUR NEXT MOVE COMPUTED, ARTOO—!
BLEE? DIT-DIT?
YES, YOU! I'M PROGRAMMED FOR DIPLOMACY, NOT STRATEGY!
BLU-DAHHH!
THEY ARE NOT THE SAME THING, YOU BUCKET OF BOLTS!
THE DIPLOMAT IS LONG SINCE GONE, WHEN THE STRATEGIST STARTS SHOOTING!
A JAWA SANDCRAWLER HAS BREACHED THE WALLS OF THE IMPERIAL BASE ON TATOOINE...
SNAP THOSE TREADS... AND OPEN UP ITS BELLY!

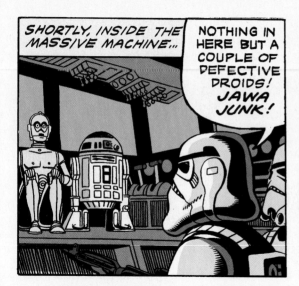

SHORTLY, INSIDE THE MASSIVE MACHINE...

NOTHING IN HERE BUT A COUPLE OF DEFECTIVE DROIDS! JAWA JUNK!

ONE 3PO, ONE R2 UNIT, COMMANDER! THERE'S NOTHING ALIVE IN THAT CRAWLER!

VERY WELL...DISPOSE OF THE DROIDS! AND TOW THAT HEAP BACK OUT INTO THE DESERT!

IT'S THREEPIO AND ARTOO! I CAN'T LET THEM BE SMELTED!

YOU CAN'T LET YOURSELF BE DISINTEGRATED, EITHER—!

MAY THE FORCE BE WITH YOU, SKYWALKER!

UNLESS I FIND SOMETHING MORE PRACTICAL, YOU'RE GOING TO NEED IT!

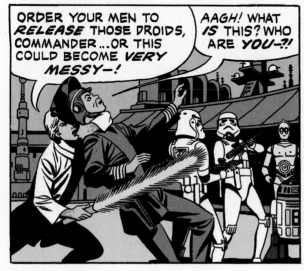

ORDER YOUR MEN TO RELEASE THOSE DROIDS, COMMANDER...OR THIS COULD BECOME VERY MESSY—!

AAGH! WHAT IS THIS? WHO ARE YOU—?!

JUST A RUN OF THE MILL REBEL...WITH BLEDSOE'S DISEASE!

PUT A RUSH ON THAT ORDER, COMMANDER! I AM STILL CONTAGIOUS!

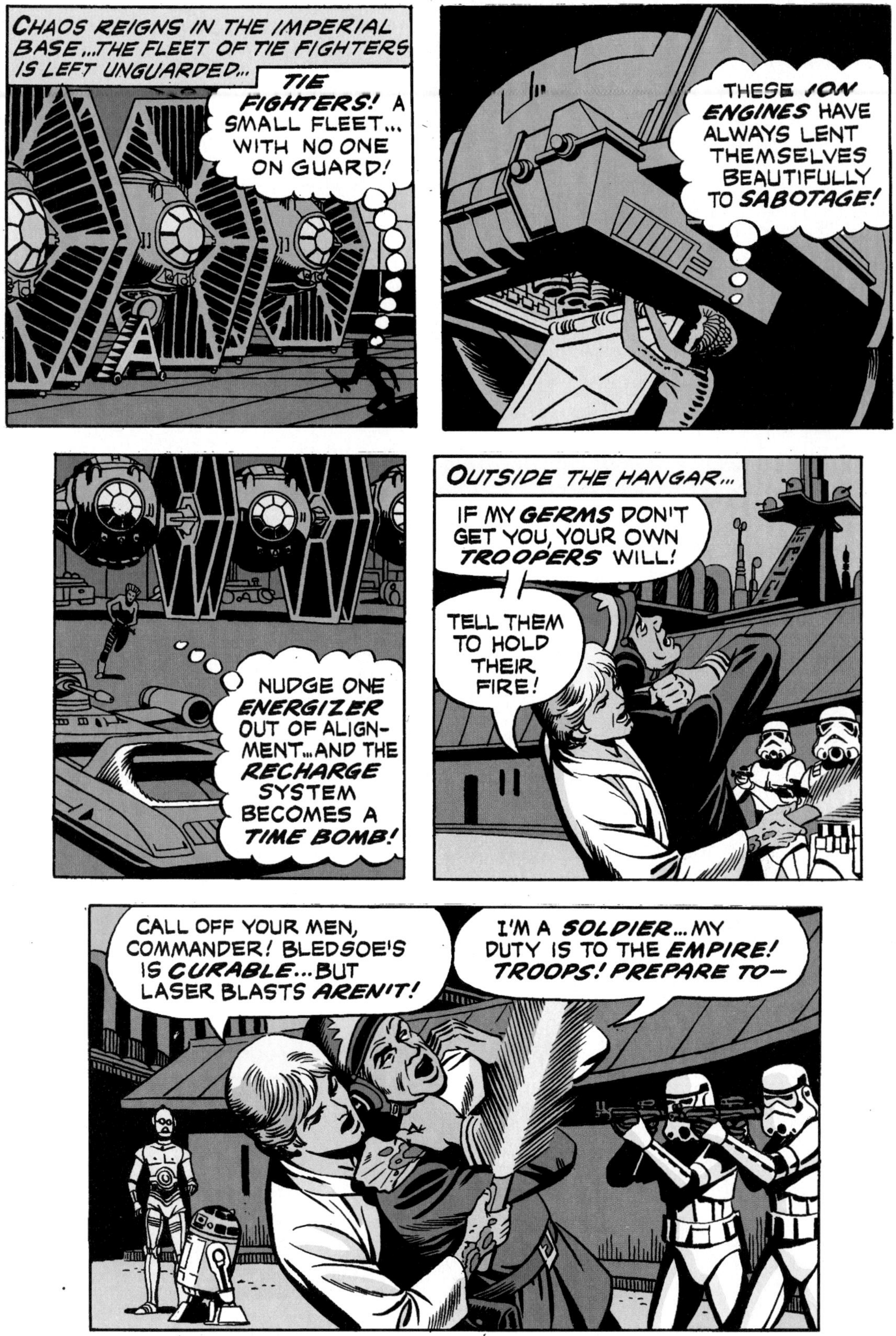
CHAOS REIGNS IN THE IMPERIAL BASE...THE FLEET OF TIE FIGHTERS IS LEFT UNGUARDED...
TIE FIGHTERS! A SMALL FLEET... WITH NO ONE ON GUARD!
THESE ION ENGINES HAVE ALWAYS LENT THEMSELVES BEAUTIFULLY TO SABOTAGE!
NUDGE ONE ENERGIZER OUT OF ALIGNMENT...AND THE RECHARGE SYSTEM BECOMES A TIME BOMB!
OUTSIDE THE HANGAR...
IF MY GERMS DON'T GET YOU, YOUR OWN TROOPERS WILL!
TELL THEM TO HOLD THEIR FIRE!
CALL OFF YOUR MEN, COMMANDER! BLEDSOE'S IS CURABLE...BUT LASER BLASTS AREN'T!
I'M A SOLDIER...MY DUTY IS TO THE EMPIRE! TROOPS! PREPARE TO—

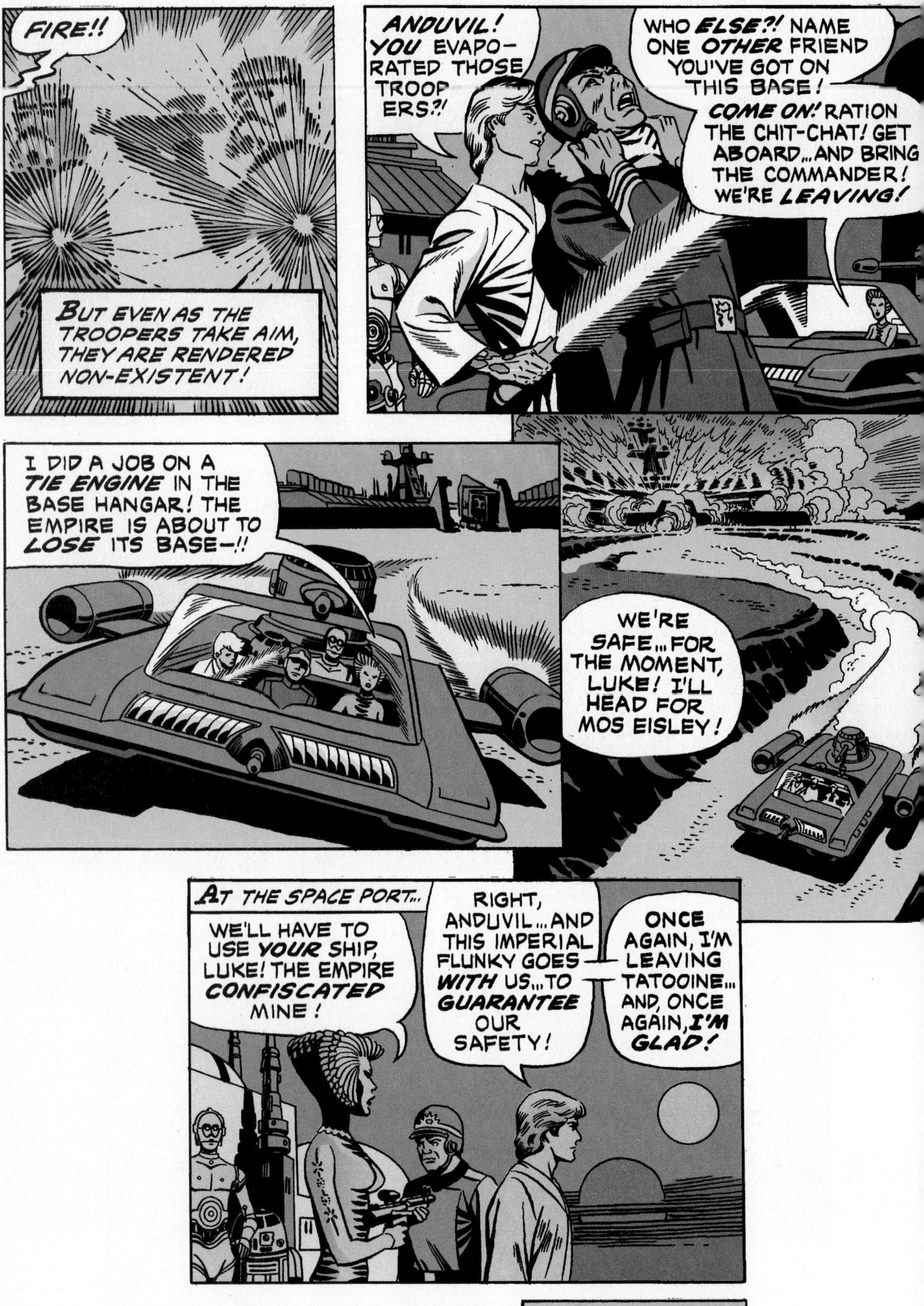
FIRE!!
BUT EVEN AS THE TROOPERS TAKE AIM, THEY ARE RENDERED NON-EXISTENT!
ANDUVIL! YOU EVAPO-RATED THOSE TROOP ERS?!
WHO ELSE?! NAME ONE OTHER FRIEND YOU'VE GOT ON THIS BASE!
COME ON! RATION THE CHIT-CHAT! GET ABOARD... AND BRING THE COMMANDER! WE'RE LEAVING!
I DID A JOB ON A TIE ENGINE IN THE BASE HANGAR! THE EMPIRE IS ABOUT TO LOSE ITS BASE--!!
WE'RE SAFE... FOR THE MOMENT, LUKE! I'LL HEAD FOR MOS EISLEY!
AT THE SPACE PORT...
WE'LL HAVE TO USE YOUR SHIP, LUKE! THE EMPIRE CONFISCATED MINE!
RIGHT, ANDUVIL... AND THIS IMPERIAL FLUNKY GOES WITH US... TO GUARANTEE OUR SAFETY!
ONCE AGAIN, I'M LEAVING TATOOINE... AND, ONCE AGAIN, I'M GLAD!

CONTINUED NEXT ISSUE

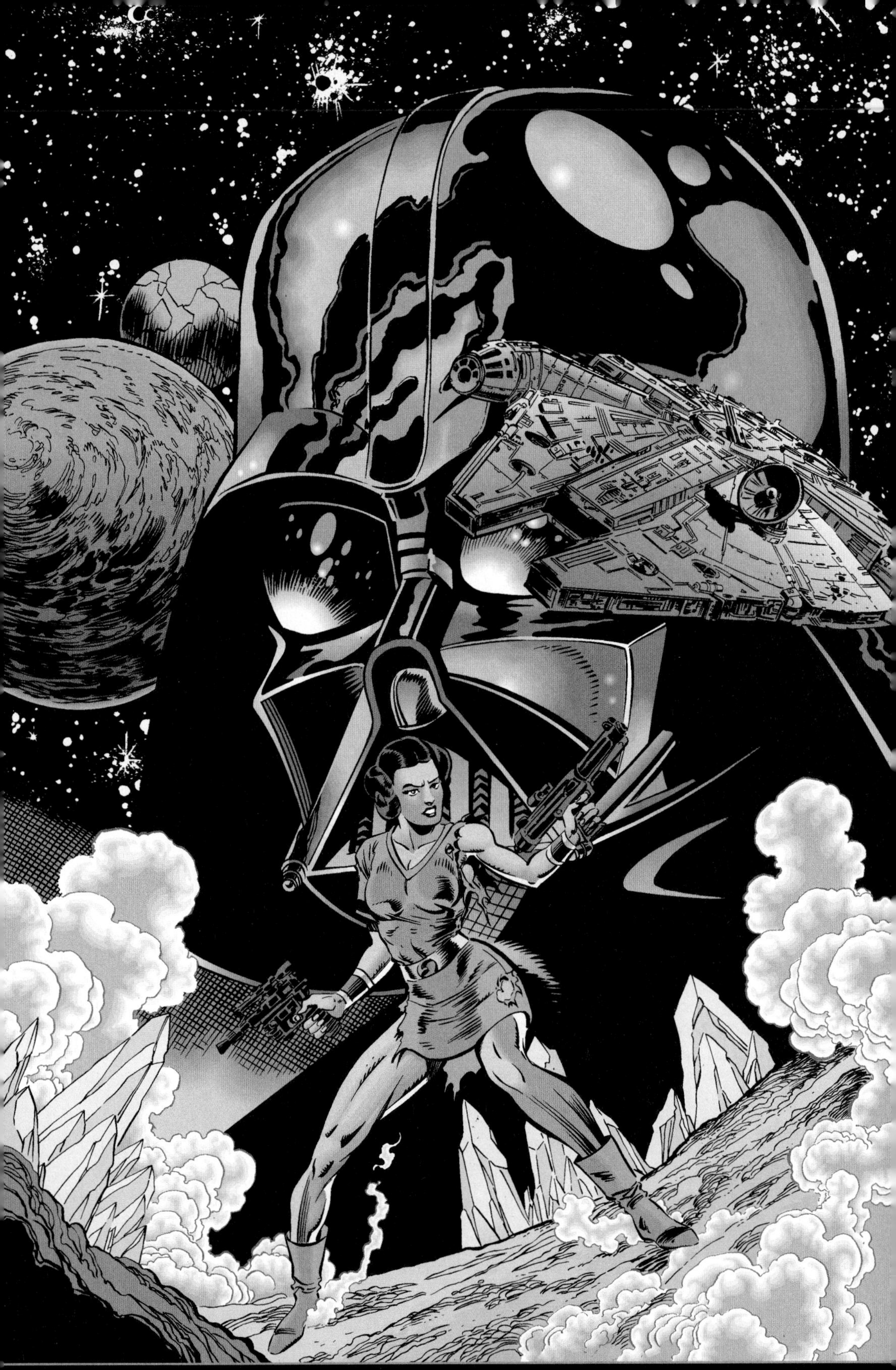

CLASSIC STAR WARS: THE EARLY ADVENTURES #5 — "PRINCESS LEIA, IMPERIAL SERVANT"
ORIGINALLY PUBLISHED FROM NOVEMBER 6 TO DECEMBER 31, 1979

WRITERS: RUSS MANNING & RUSS HELM • ARTIST & LETTERER: RUSS MANNING • ART RETOUCHING: RICK HOBERG & BRIAN SNODDY • COLORIST: RAY MURTAUGH
EDITOR: PEET JANES • COVER ARTISTS: RICK HOBERG, JIMMY PALMIOTTI & MATTHEW HOLLINGSWORTH

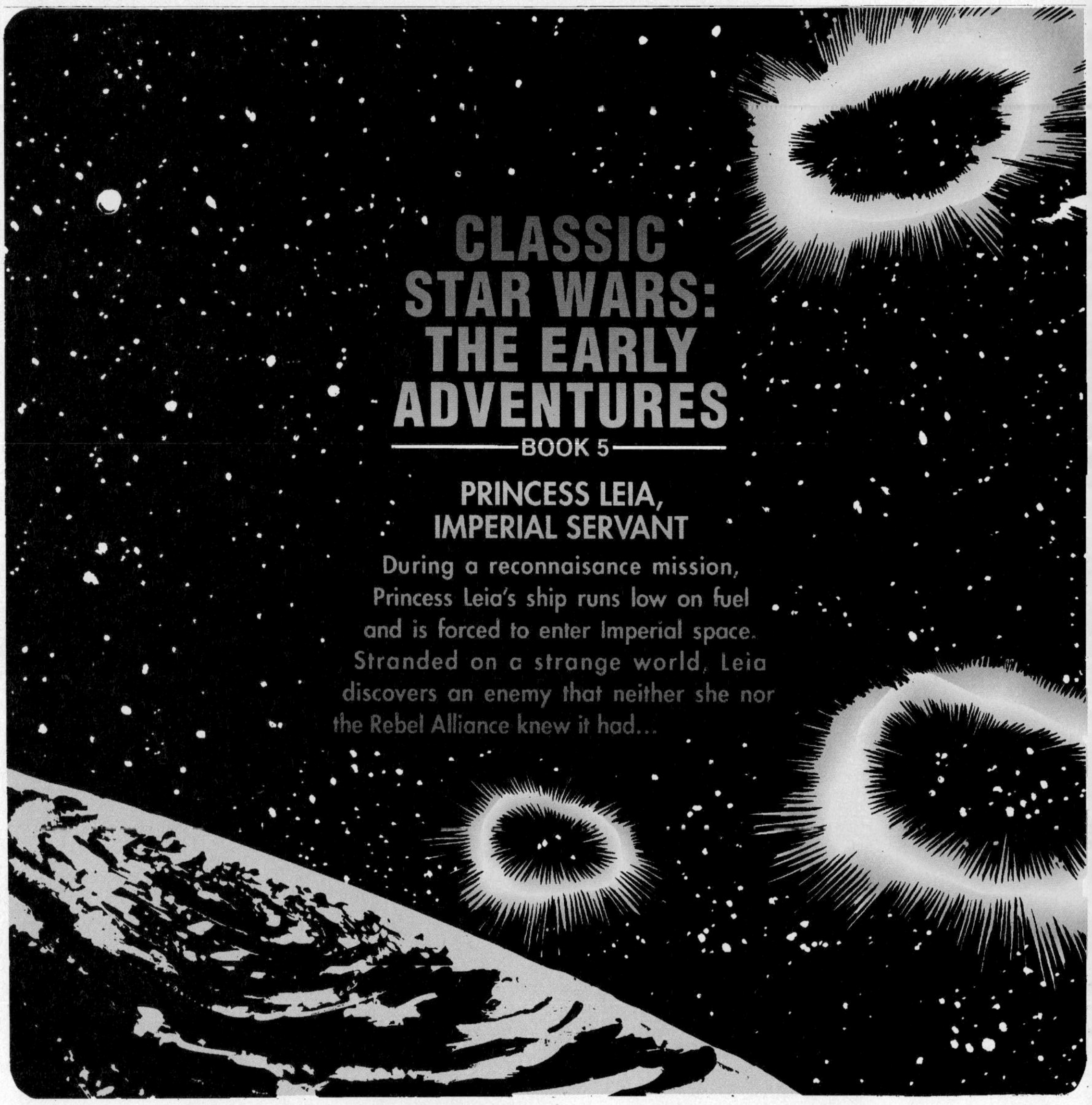
CLASSIC STAR WARS: THE EARLY ADVENTURES
BOOK 5
PRINCESS LEIA, IMPERIAL SERVANT
During a reconnaisance mission, Princess Leia's ship runs low on fuel and is forced to enter Imperial space. Stranded on a strange world, Leia discovers an enemy that neither she nor the Rebel Alliance knew it had...

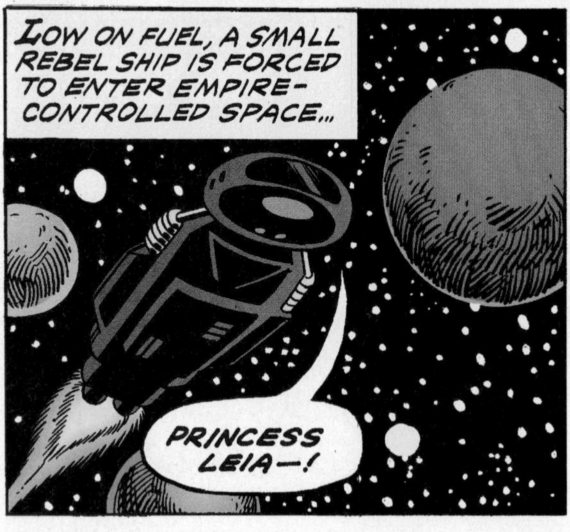
LOW ON FUEL, A SMALL REBEL SHIP IS FORCED TO ENTER EMPIRE-CONTROLLED SPACE...
PRINCESS LEIA—!

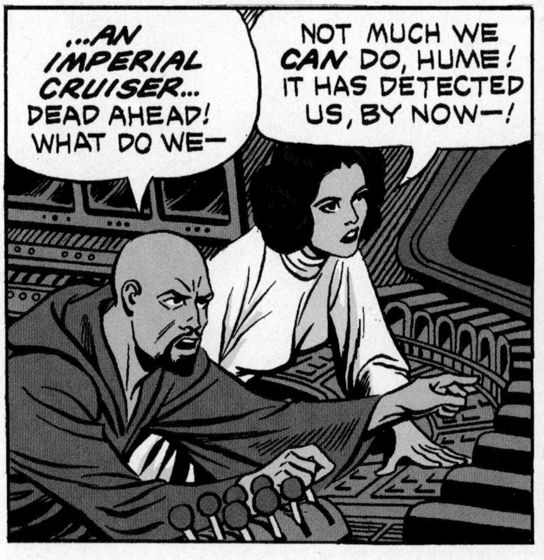
...AN IMPERIAL CRUISER... DEAD AHEAD! WHAT DO WE—
NOT MUCH WE CAN DO, HUME! IT HAS DETECTED US, BY NOW—!

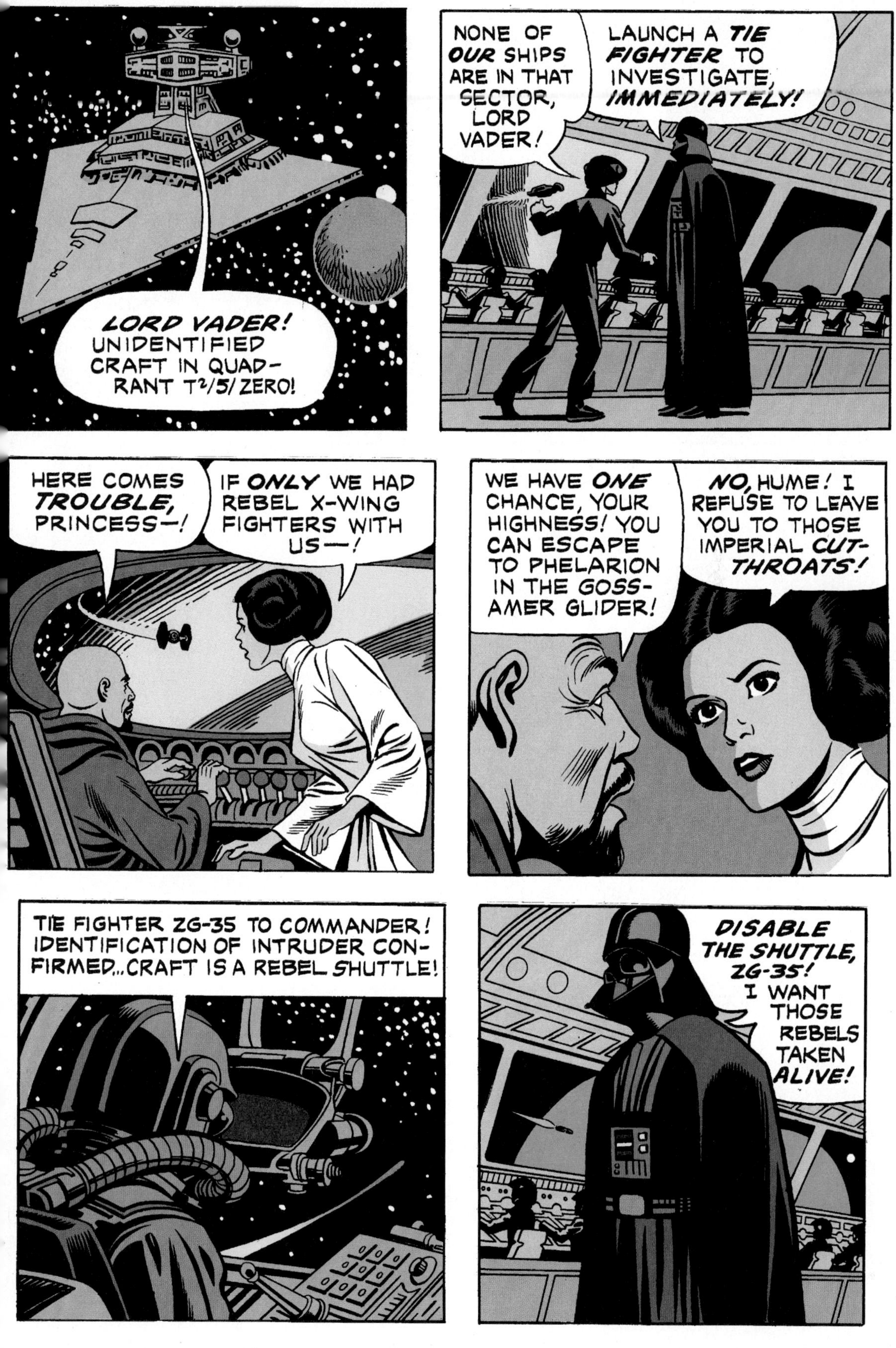
LORD VADER! UNIDENTIFIED CRAFT IN QUAD-RANT T2/5/ZERO!
NONE OF OUR SHIPS ARE IN THAT SECTOR, LORD VADER!
LAUNCH A TIE FIGHTER TO INVESTIGATE, IMMEDIATELY!
HERE COMES TROUBLE, PRINCESS—!
IF ONLY WE HAD REBEL X-WING FIGHTERS WITH US—!
WE HAVE ONE CHANCE, YOUR HIGHNESS! YOU CAN ESCAPE TO PHELARION IN THE GOSS-AMER GLIDER!
NO, HUME! I REFUSE TO LEAVE YOU TO THOSE IMPERIAL CUT-THROATS!
TIE FIGHTER ZG-35 TO COMMANDER! IDENTIFICATION OF INTRUDER CON-FIRMED...CRAFT IS A REBEL SHUTTLE!
DISABLE THE SHUTTLE, ZG-35! I WANT THOSE REBELS TAKEN ALIVE!

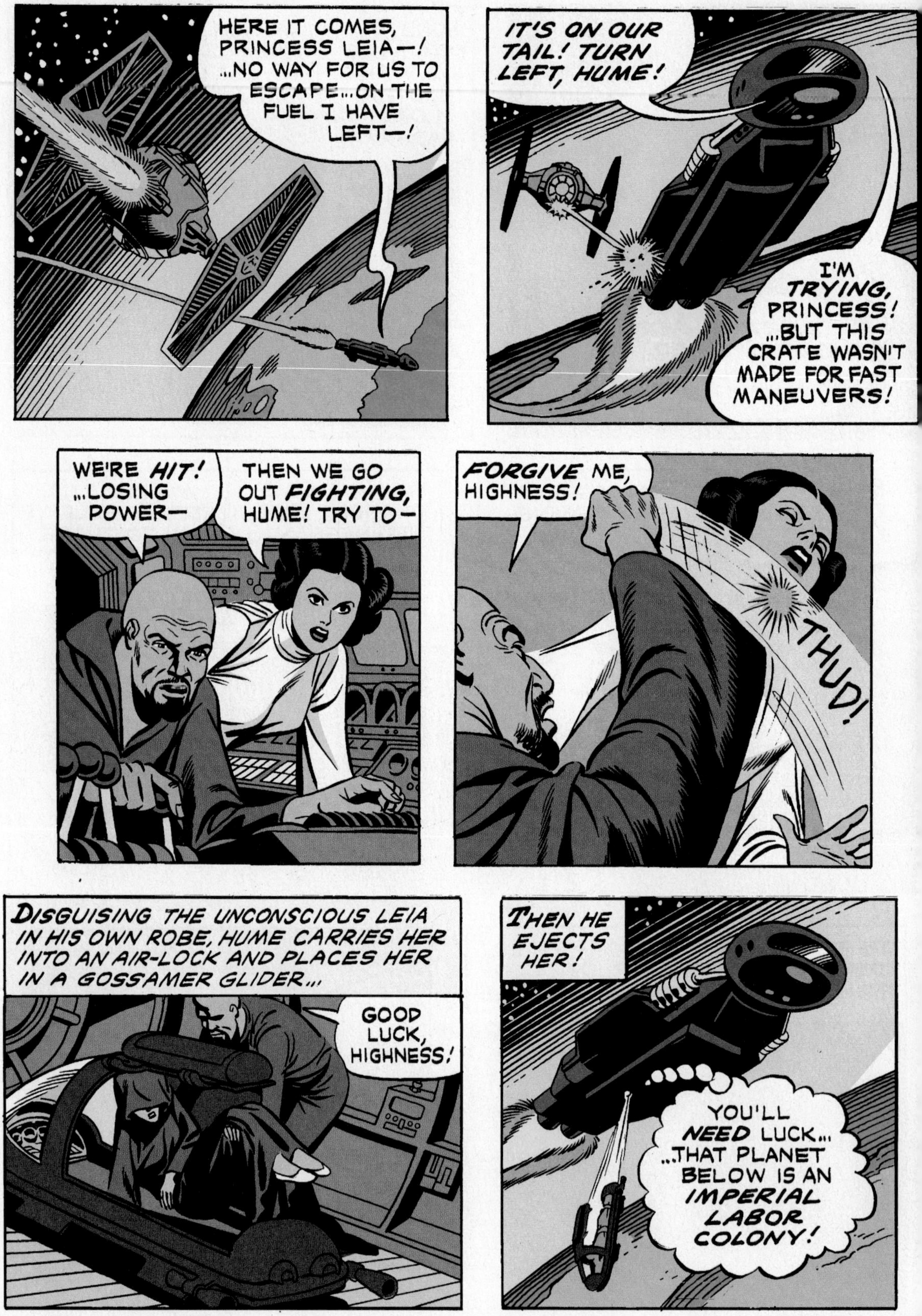
HERE IT COMES, PRINCESS LEIA—! ...NO WAY FOR US TO ESCAPE...ON THE FUEL I HAVE LEFT—!
IT'S ON OUR TAIL! TURN LEFT, HUME!
I'M TRYING, PRINCESS! ...BUT THIS CRATE WASN'T MADE FOR FAST MANEUVERS!
WE'RE HIT! ...LOSING POWER—
THEN WE GO OUT FIGHTING, HUME! TRY TO—
FORGIVE ME, HIGHNESS!
THUD!
DISGUISING THE UNCONSCIOUS LEIA IN HIS OWN ROBE, HUME CARRIES HER INTO AN AIR-LOCK AND PLACES HER IN A GOSSAMER GLIDER...
GOOD LUCK, HIGHNESS!
THEN HE EJECTS HER!
YOU'LL NEED LUCK... ...THAT PLANET BELOW IS AN IMPERIAL LABOR COLONY!

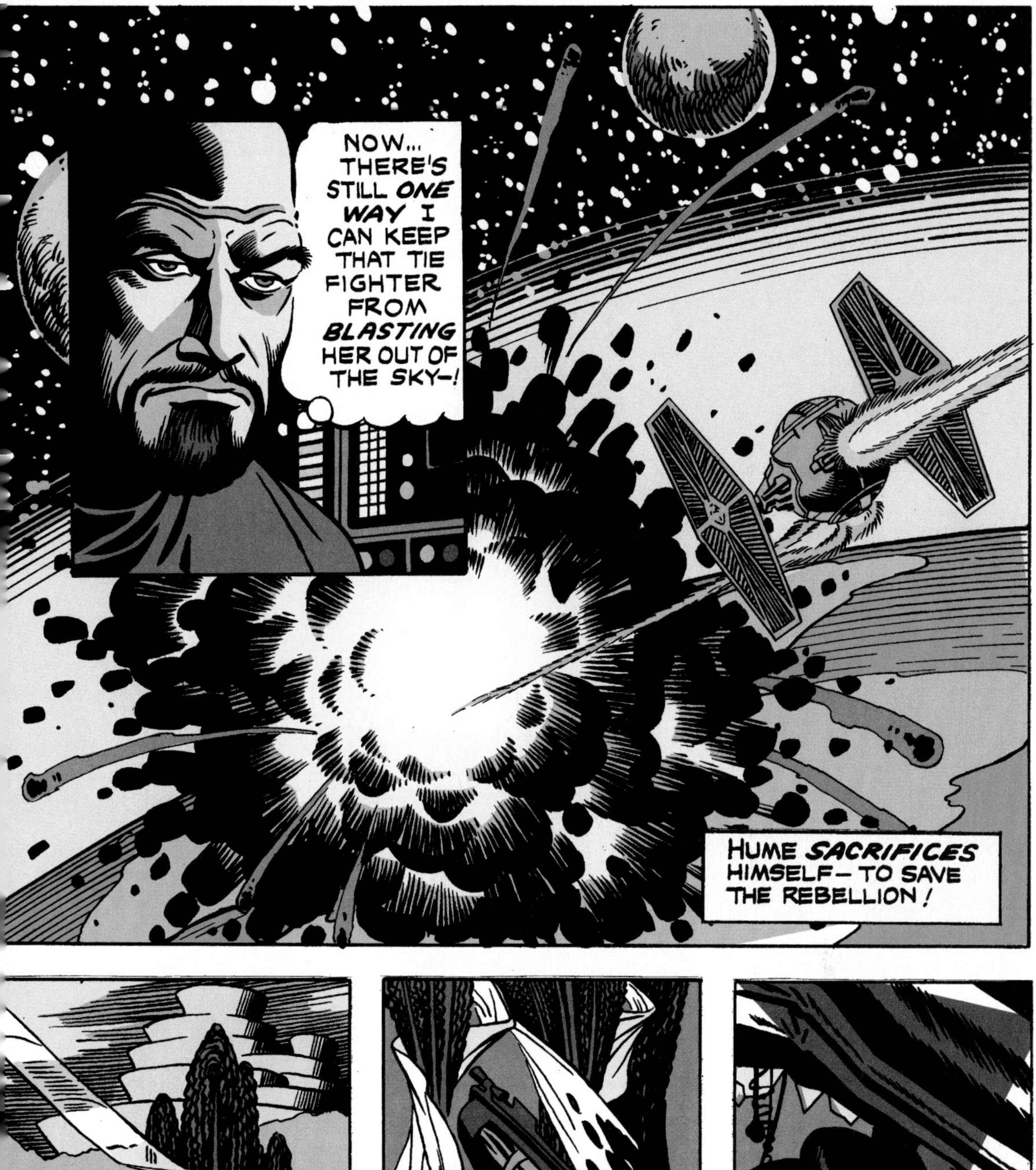
NOW... THERE'S STILL ONE WAY I CAN KEEP THAT TIE FIGHTER FROM BLASTING HER OUT OF THE SKY-!
HUME SACRIFICES HIMSELF- TO SAVE THE REBELLION!

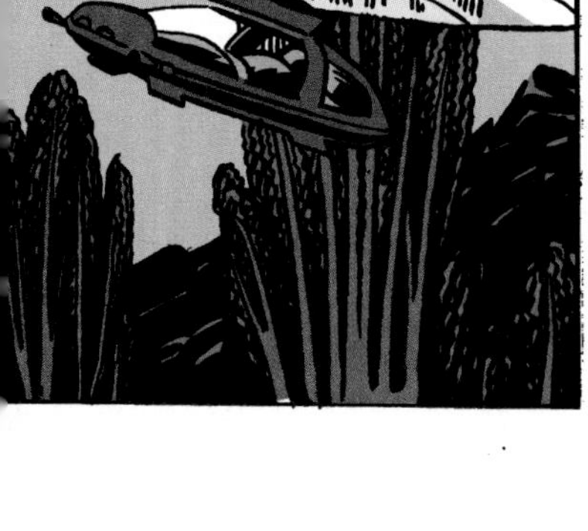

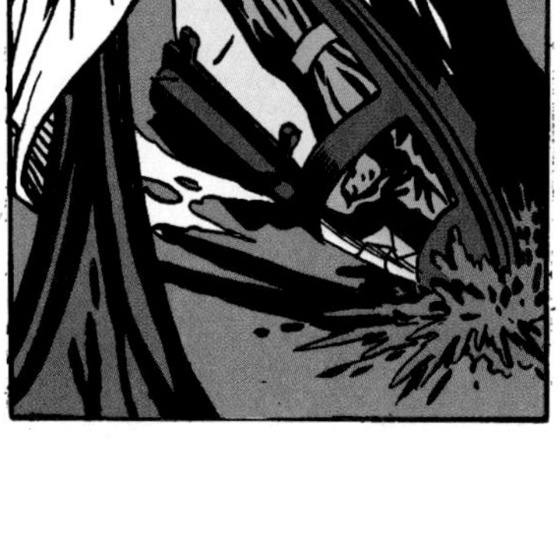

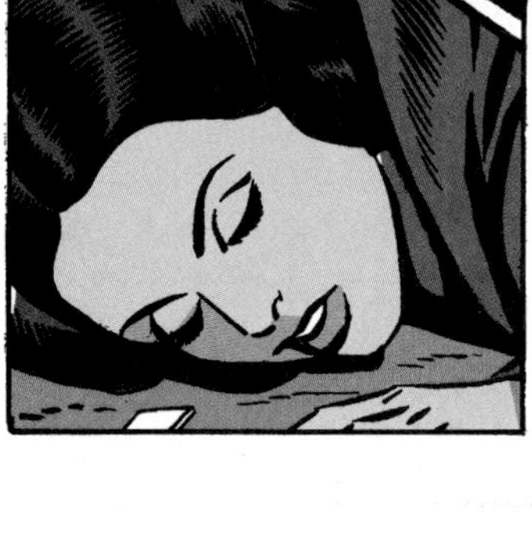

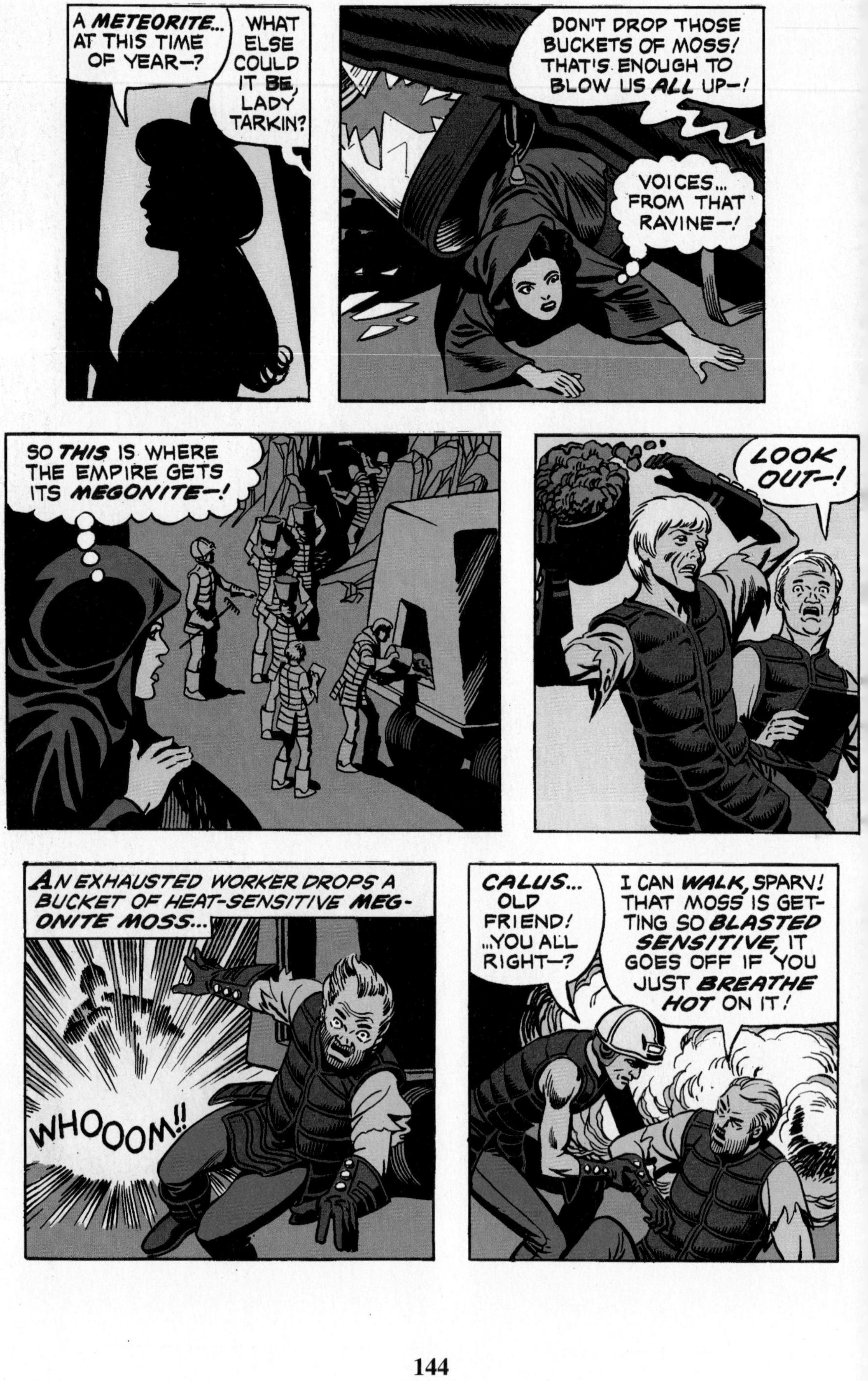
A METEORITE... AT THIS TIME OF YEAR—?
WHAT ELSE COULD IT BE, LADY TARKIN?
DON'T DROP THOSE BUCKETS OF MOSS! THAT'S ENOUGH TO BLOW US ALL UP—!
VOICES... FROM THAT RAVINE—!
SO THIS IS WHERE THE EMPIRE GETS ITS MEGONITE—!
LOOK OUT—!
AN EXHAUSTED WORKER DROPS A BUCKET OF HEAT-SENSITIVE MEG-ONITE MOSS...
WHOOOM!!
CALUS... OLD FRIEND! ...YOU ALL RIGHT—?
I CAN WALK, SPARV! THAT MOSS IS GETTING SO BLASTED SENSITIVE, IT GOES OFF IF YOU JUST BREATHE HOT ON IT!

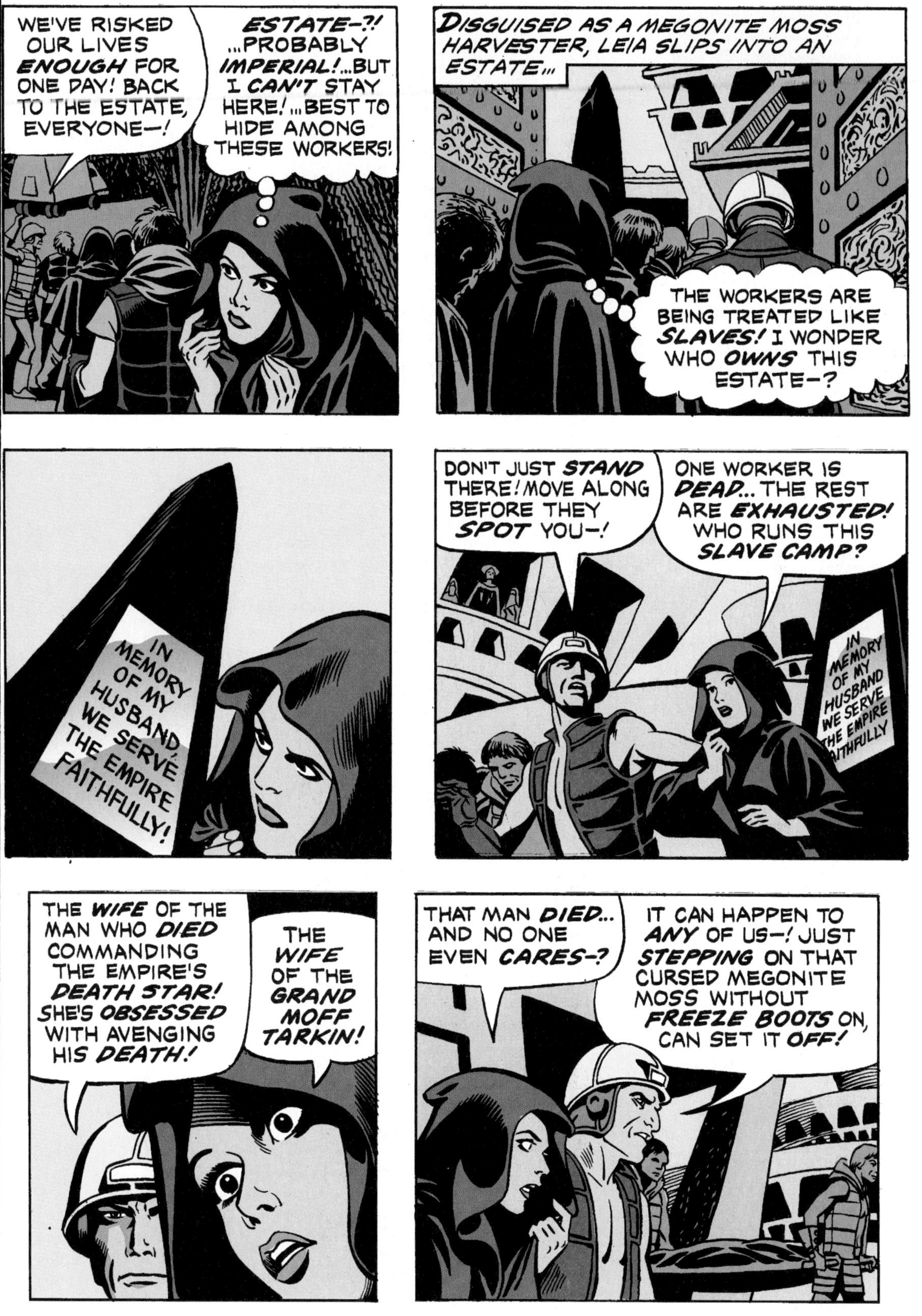
WE'VE RISKED OUR LIVES ENOUGH FOR ONE DAY! BACK TO THE ESTATE, EVERYONE--!
ESTATE--?! ...PROBABLY IMPERIAL!...BUT I CAN'T STAY HERE!...BEST TO HIDE AMONG THESE WORKERS!
DISGUISED AS A MEGONITE MOSS HARVESTER, LEIA SLIPS INTO AN ESTATE...
THE WORKERS ARE BEING TREATED LIKE SLAVES! I WONDER WHO OWNS THIS ESTATE--?
IN MEMORY OF MY HUSBAND, WE SERVE THE EMPIRE FAITHFULLY!
DON'T JUST STAND THERE! MOVE ALONG BEFORE THEY SPOT YOU--!
ONE WORKER IS DEAD... THE REST ARE EXHAUSTED! WHO RUNS THIS SLAVE CAMP?
IN MEMORY OF MY HUSBAND WE SERVE THE EMPIRE FAITHFULLY
THE WIFE OF THE MAN WHO DIED COMMANDING THE EMPIRE'S DEATH STAR! SHE'S OBSESSED WITH AVENGING HIS DEATH!
THE WIFE OF THE GRAND MOFF TARKIN!
THAT MAN DIED... AND NO ONE EVEN CARES--?
IT CAN HAPPEN TO ANY OF US--! JUST STEPPING ON THAT CURSED MEGONITE MOSS WITHOUT FREEZE BOOTS ON, CAN SET IT OFF!

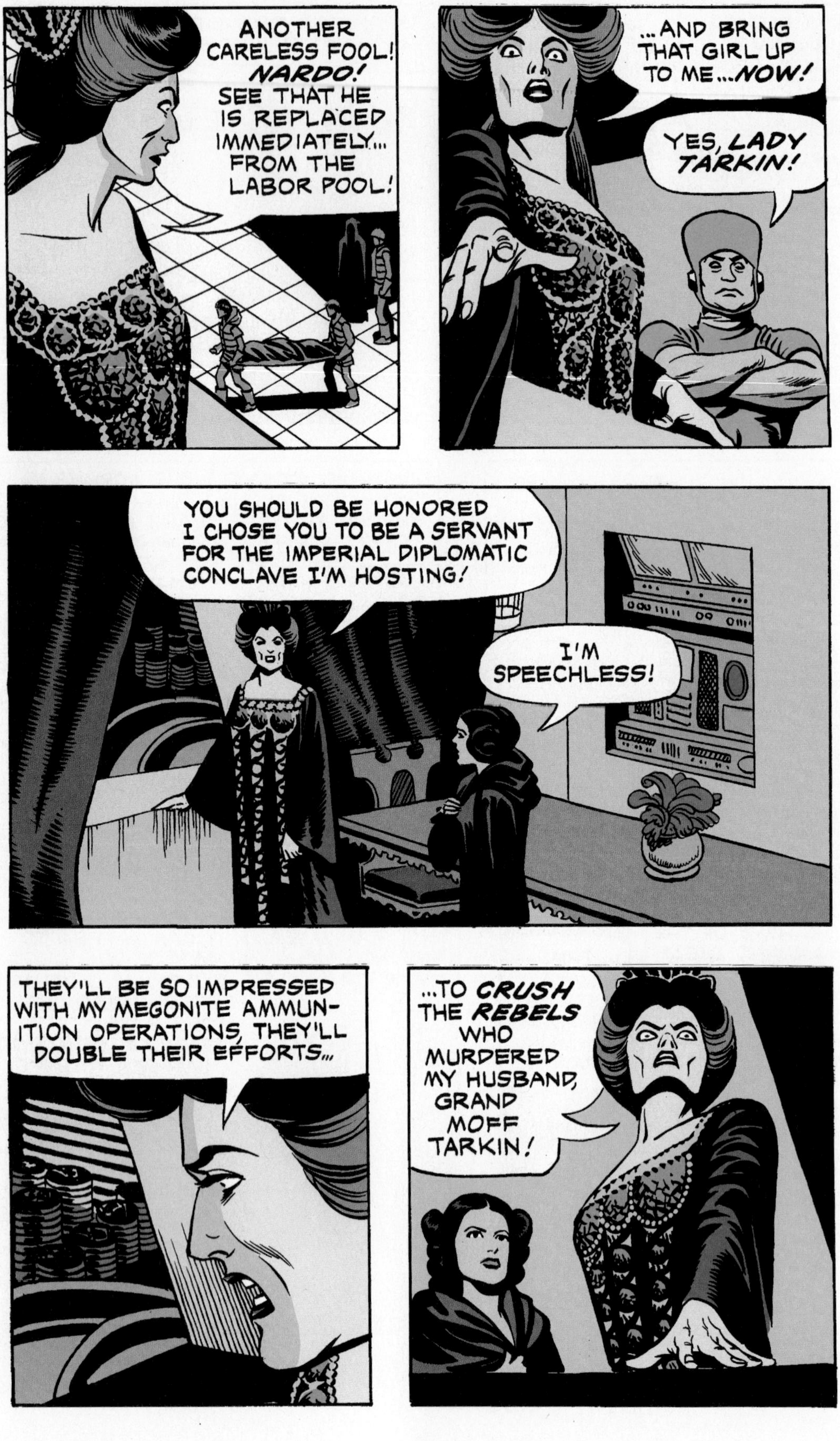
ANOTHER CARELESS FOOL! NARDO! SEE THAT HE IS REPLACED IMMEDIATELY... FROM THE LABOR POOL!
...AND BRING THAT GIRL UP TO ME...NOW!
YES, LADY TARKIN!
YOU SHOULD BE HONORED I CHOSE YOU TO BE A SERVANT FOR THE IMPERIAL DIPLOMATIC CONCLAVE I'M HOSTING!
I'M SPEECHLESS!
THEY'LL BE SO IMPRESSED WITH MY MEGONITE AMMUNITION OPERATIONS, THEY'LL DOUBLE THEIR EFFORTS...
...TO CRUSH THE REBELS WHO MURDERED MY HUSBAND, GRAND MOFF TARKIN!

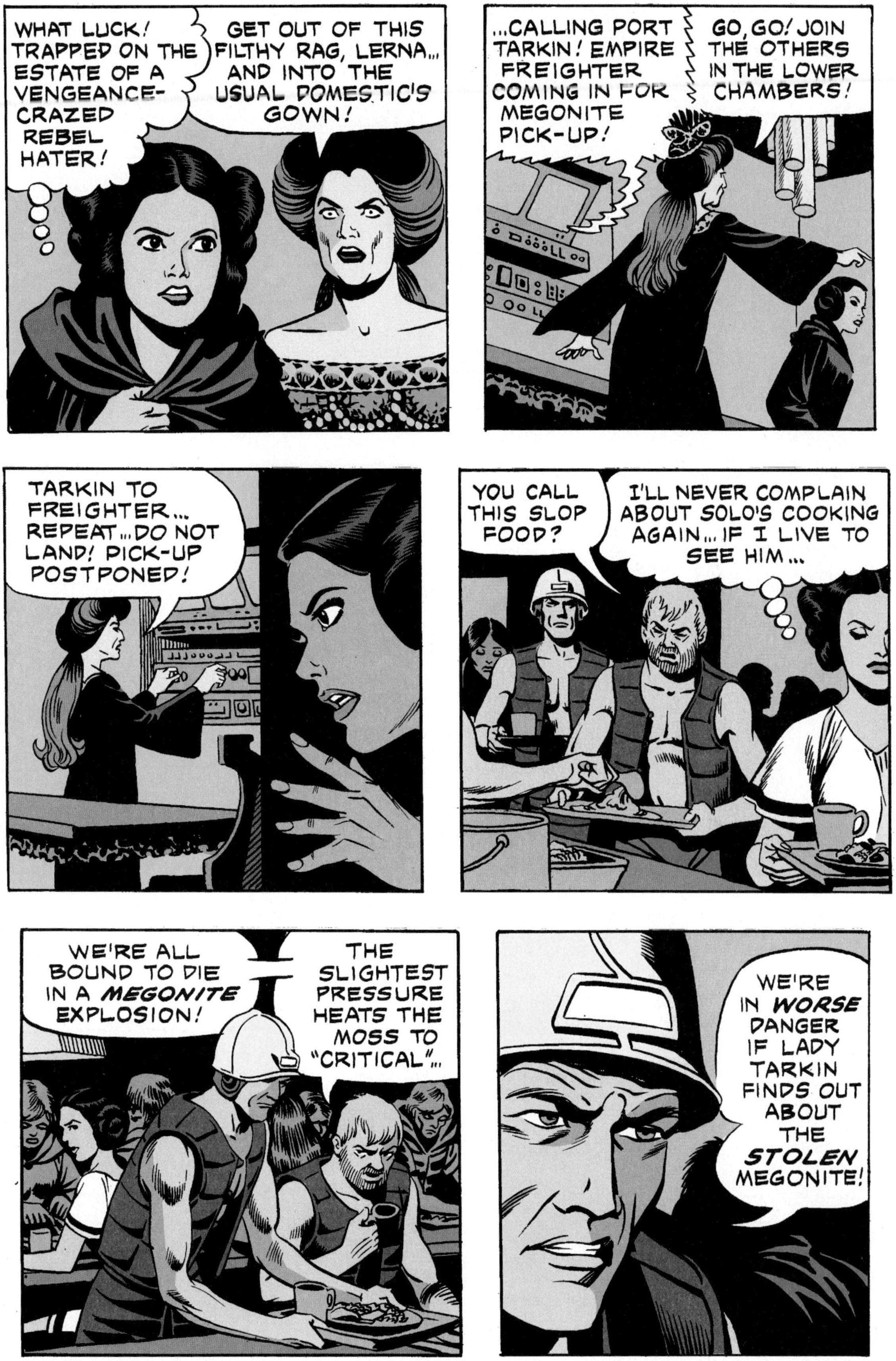
WHAT LUCK! TRAPPED ON THE ESTATE OF A VENGEANCE-CRAZED REBEL HATER!
GET OUT OF THIS FILTHY RAG, LERNA... AND INTO THE USUAL DOMESTIC'S GOWN!
...CALLING PORT TARKIN! EMPIRE FREIGHTER COMING IN FOR MEGONITE PICK-UP!
GO, GO! JOIN THE OTHERS IN THE LOWER CHAMBERS!
TARKIN TO FREIGHTER... REPEAT...DO NOT LAND! PICK-UP POSTPONED!
YOU CALL THIS SLOP FOOD?
I'LL NEVER COMPLAIN ABOUT SOLO'S COOKING AGAIN... IF I LIVE TO SEE HIM...
WE'RE ALL BOUND TO DIE IN A MEGONITE EXPLOSION!
THE SLIGHTEST PRESSURE HEATS THE MOSS TO "CRITICAL"...
WE'RE IN WORSE DANGER IF LADY TARKIN FINDS OUT ABOUT THE STOLEN MEGONITE!

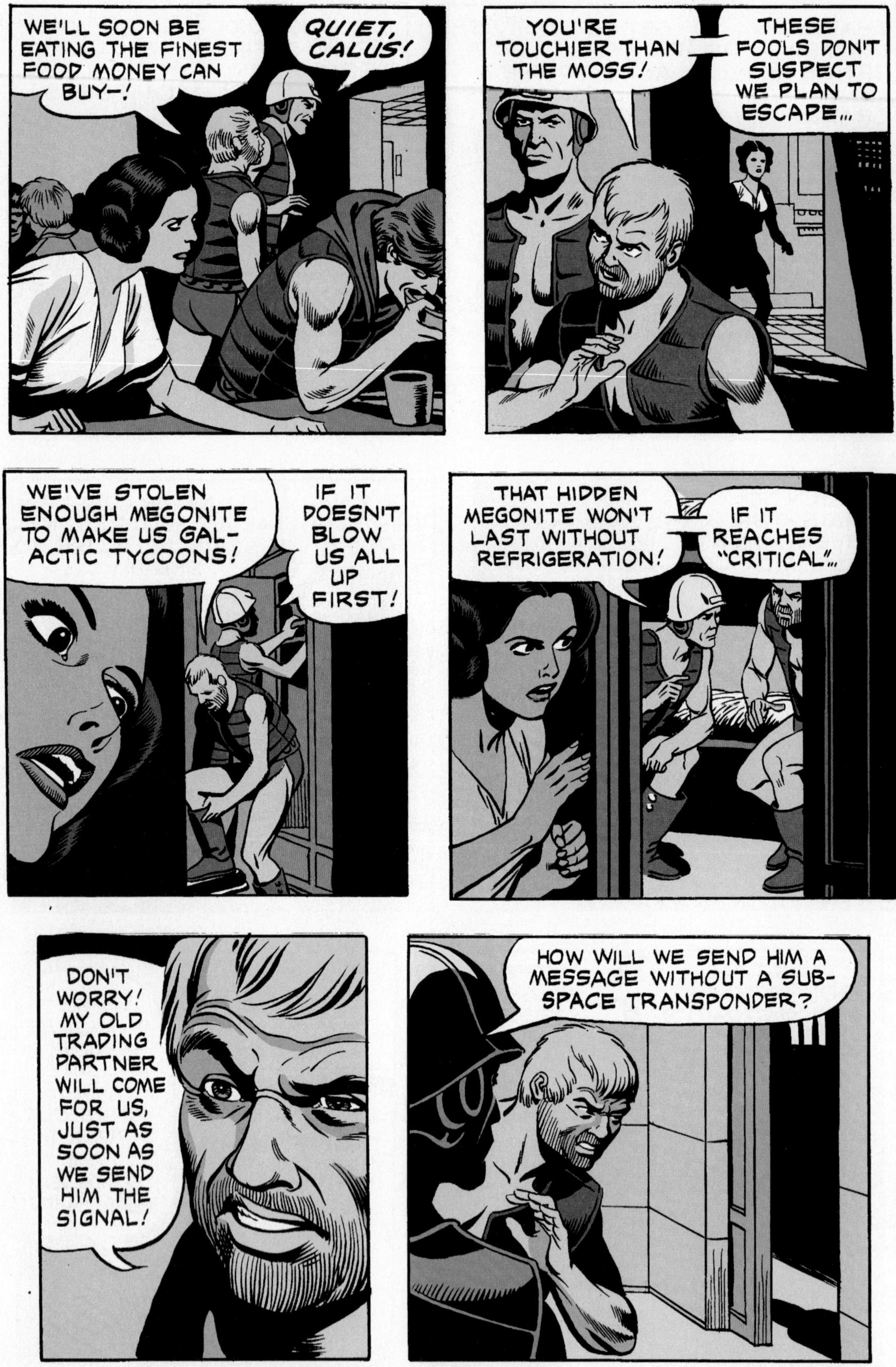

WE'LL SOON BE EATING THE FINEST FOOD MONEY CAN BUY-!
QUIET, CALUS!
YOU'RE TOUCHIER THAN THE MOSS!
THESE FOOLS DON'T SUSPECT WE PLAN TO ESCAPE...
WE'VE STOLEN ENOUGH MEGONITE TO MAKE US GAL-ACTIC TYCOONS!
IF IT DOESN'T BLOW US ALL UP FIRST!
THAT HIDDEN MEGONITE WON'T LAST WITHOUT REFRIGERATION!
IF IT REACHES "CRITICAL"...
DON'T WORRY! MY OLD TRADING PARTNER WILL COME FOR US, JUST AS SOON AS WE SEND HIM THE SIGNAL!
HOW WILL WE SEND HIM A MESSAGE WITHOUT A SUB-SPACE TRANSPONDER?

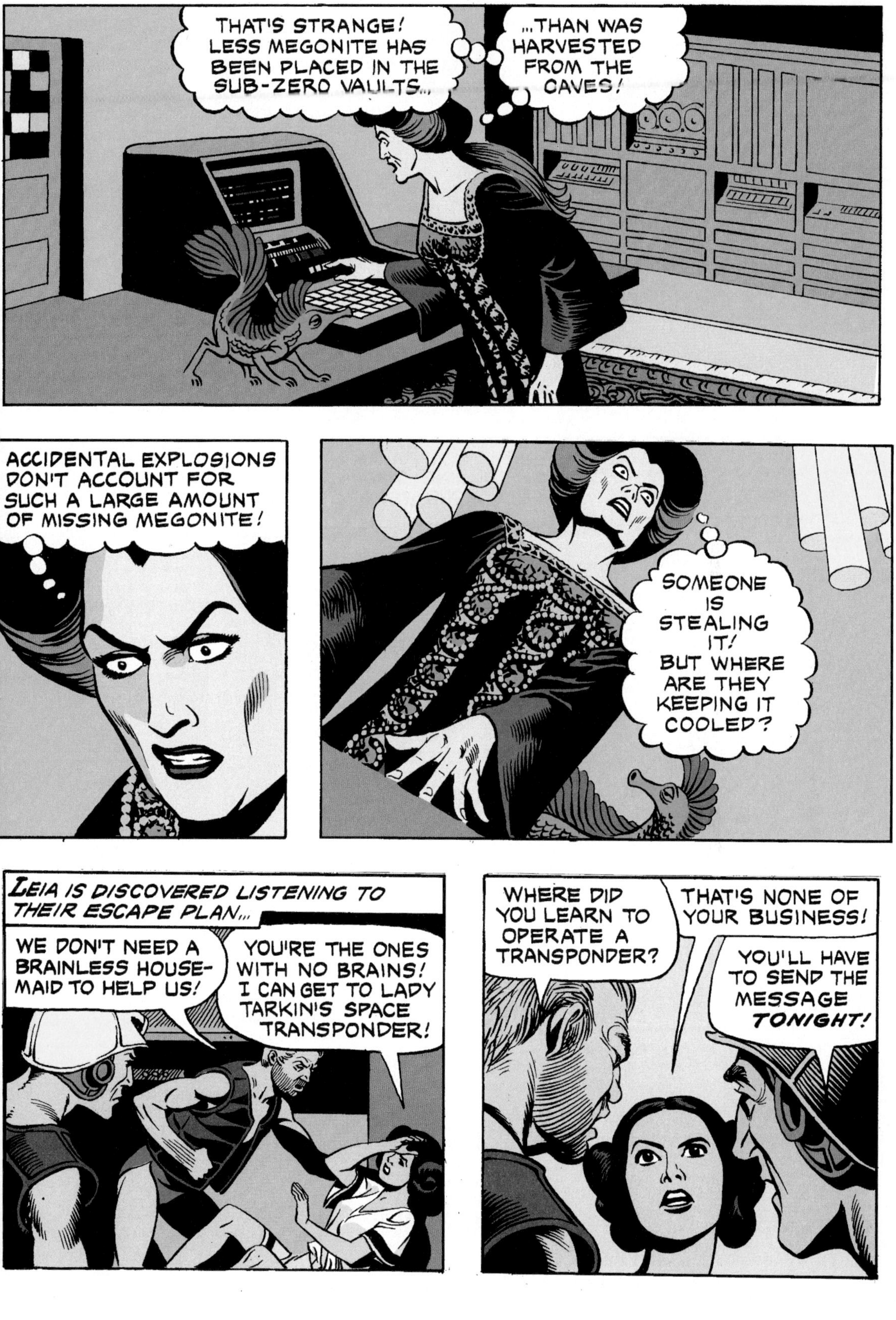
THAT'S STRANGE! LESS MEGONITE HAS BEEN PLACED IN THE SUB-ZERO VAULTS...
...THAN WAS HARVESTED FROM THE CAVES!
ACCIDENTAL EXPLOSIONS DON'T ACCOUNT FOR SUCH A LARGE AMOUNT OF MISSING MEGONITE!
SOMEONE IS STEALING IT! BUT WHERE ARE THEY KEEPING IT COOLED?
LEIA IS DISCOVERED LISTENING TO THEIR ESCAPE PLAN...
WE DON'T NEED A BRAINLESS HOUSE-MAID TO HELP US!
YOU'RE THE ONES WITH NO BRAINS! I CAN GET TO LADY TARKIN'S SPACE TRANSPONDER!
WHERE DID YOU LEARN TO OPERATE A TRANSPONDER?
THAT'S NONE OF YOUR BUSINESS!
YOU'LL HAVE TO SEND THE MESSAGE TONIGHT!

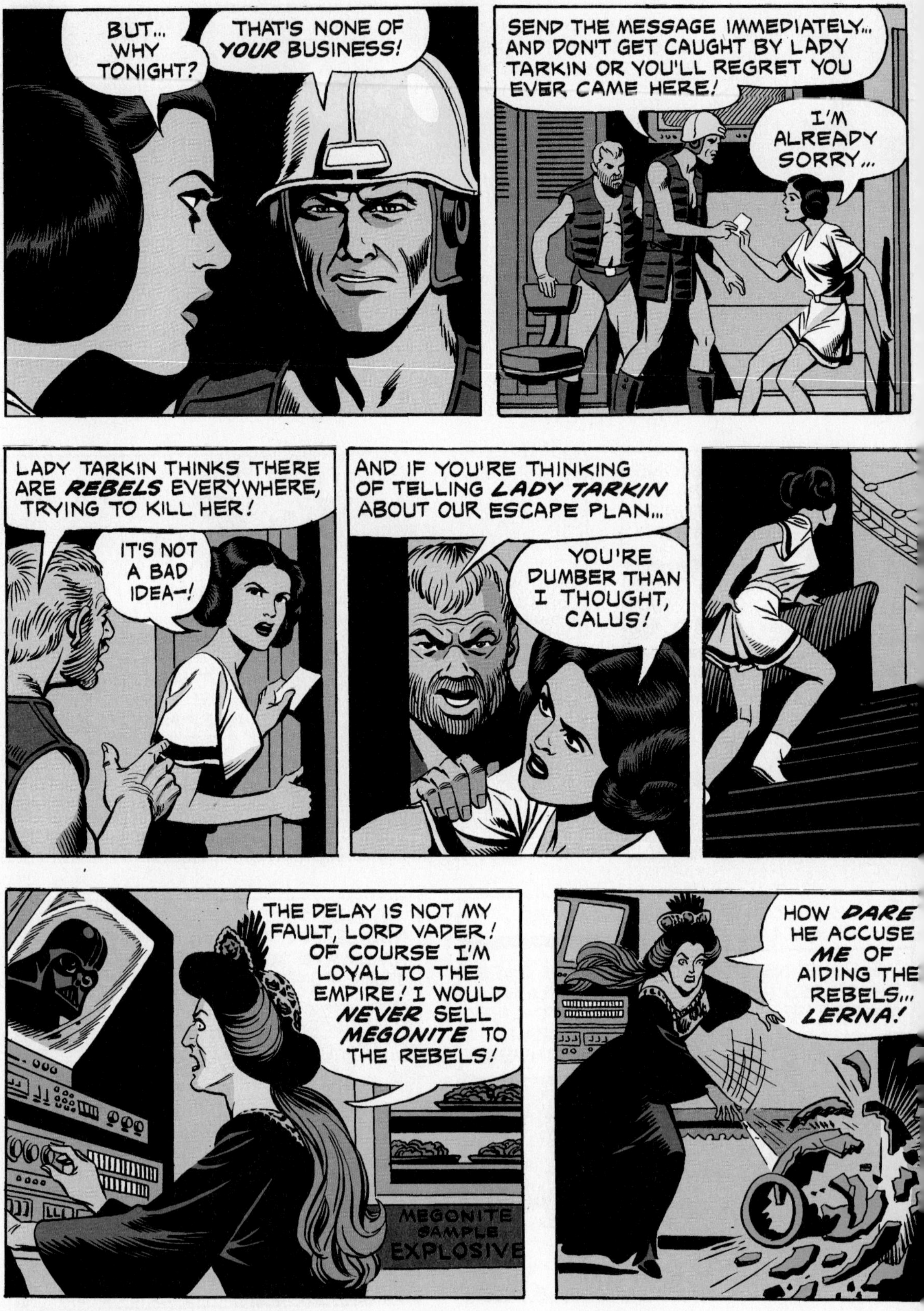
BUT... WHY TONIGHT?
THAT'S NONE OF YOUR BUSINESS!
SEND THE MESSAGE IMMEDIATELY... AND DON'T GET CAUGHT BY LADY TARKIN OR YOU'LL REGRET YOU EVER CAME HERE!
I'M ALREADY SORRY...
LADY TARKIN THINKS THERE ARE REBELS EVERYWHERE, TRYING TO KILL HER!
IT'S NOT A BAD IDEA—!
AND IF YOU'RE THINKING OF TELLING LADY TARKIN ABOUT OUR ESCAPE PLAN...
YOU'RE DUMBER THAN I THOUGHT, CALUS!
THE DELAY IS NOT MY FAULT, LORD VADER! OF COURSE I'M LOYAL TO THE EMPIRE! I WOULD NEVER SELL MEGONITE TO THE REBELS!
MEGONITE SAMPLE EXPLOSIVE
HOW DARE HE ACCUSE ME OF AIDING THE REBELS... LERNA!

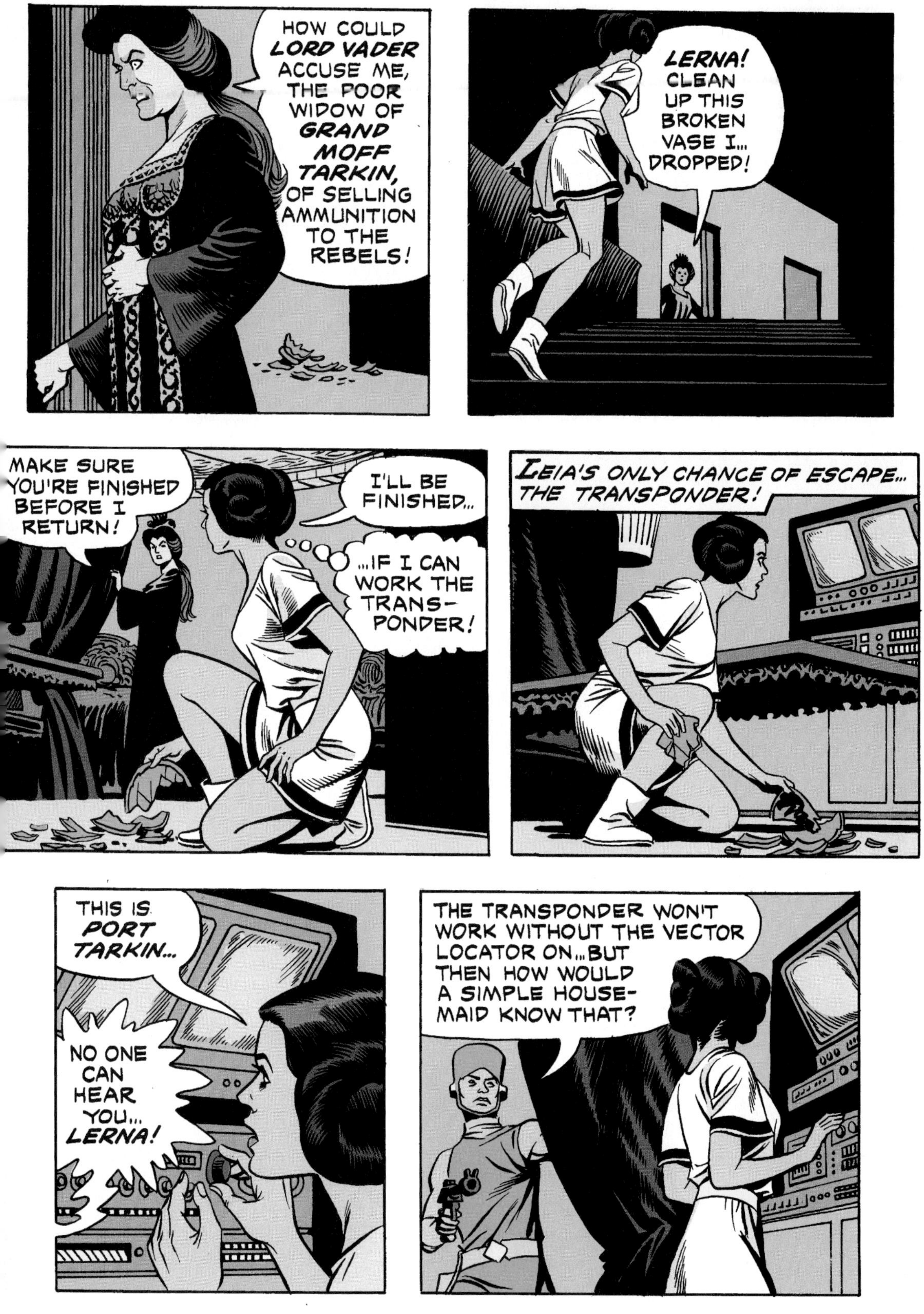
HOW COULD LORD VADER ACCUSE ME, THE POOR WIDOW OF GRAND MOFF TARKIN, OF SELLING AMMUNITION TO THE REBELS!
LERNA! CLEAN UP THIS BROKEN VASE I... DROPPED!
MAKE SURE YOU'RE FINISHED BEFORE I RETURN!
I'LL BE FINISHED...
...IF I CAN WORK THE TRANS-PONDER!
LEIA'S ONLY CHANCE OF ESCAPE... THE TRANSPONDER!
THIS IS PORT TARKIN...
NO ONE CAN HEAR YOU... LERNA!
THE TRANSPONDER WON'T WORK WITHOUT THE VECTOR LOCATOR ON... BUT THEN HOW WOULD A SIMPLE HOUSE-MAID KNOW THAT?

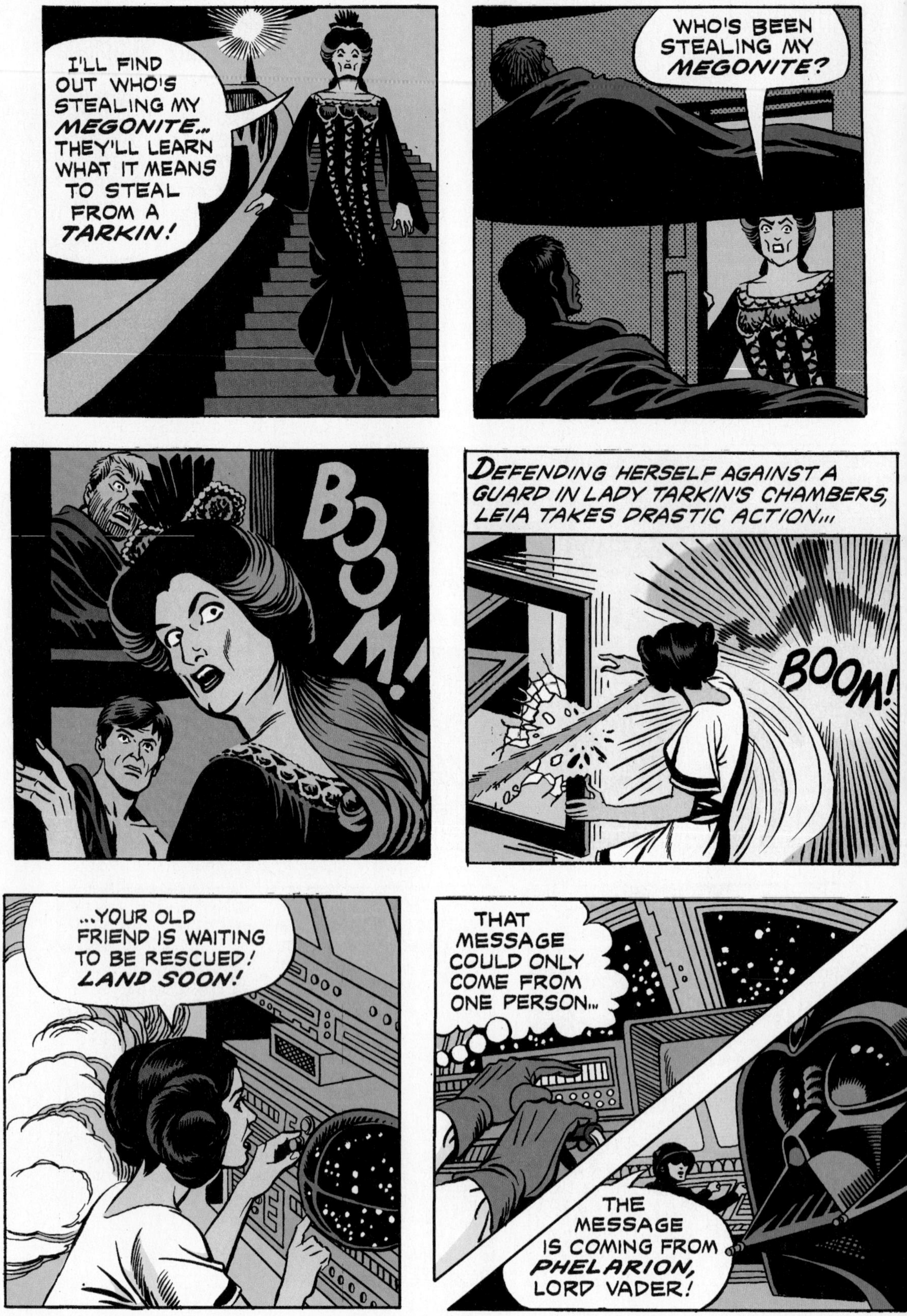
I'LL FIND OUT WHO'S STEALING MY MEGONITE... THEY'LL LEARN WHAT IT MEANS TO STEAL FROM A TARKIN!
WHO'S BEEN STEALING MY MEGONITE?
BOOM!
DEFENDING HERSELF AGAINST A GUARD IN LADY TARKIN'S CHAMBERS, LEIA TAKES DRASTIC ACTION...
BOOM!
...YOUR OLD FRIEND IS WAITING TO BE RESCUED! LAND SOON!
THAT MESSAGE COULD ONLY COME FROM ONE PERSON...
THE MESSAGE IS COMING FROM PHELARION, LORD VADER!

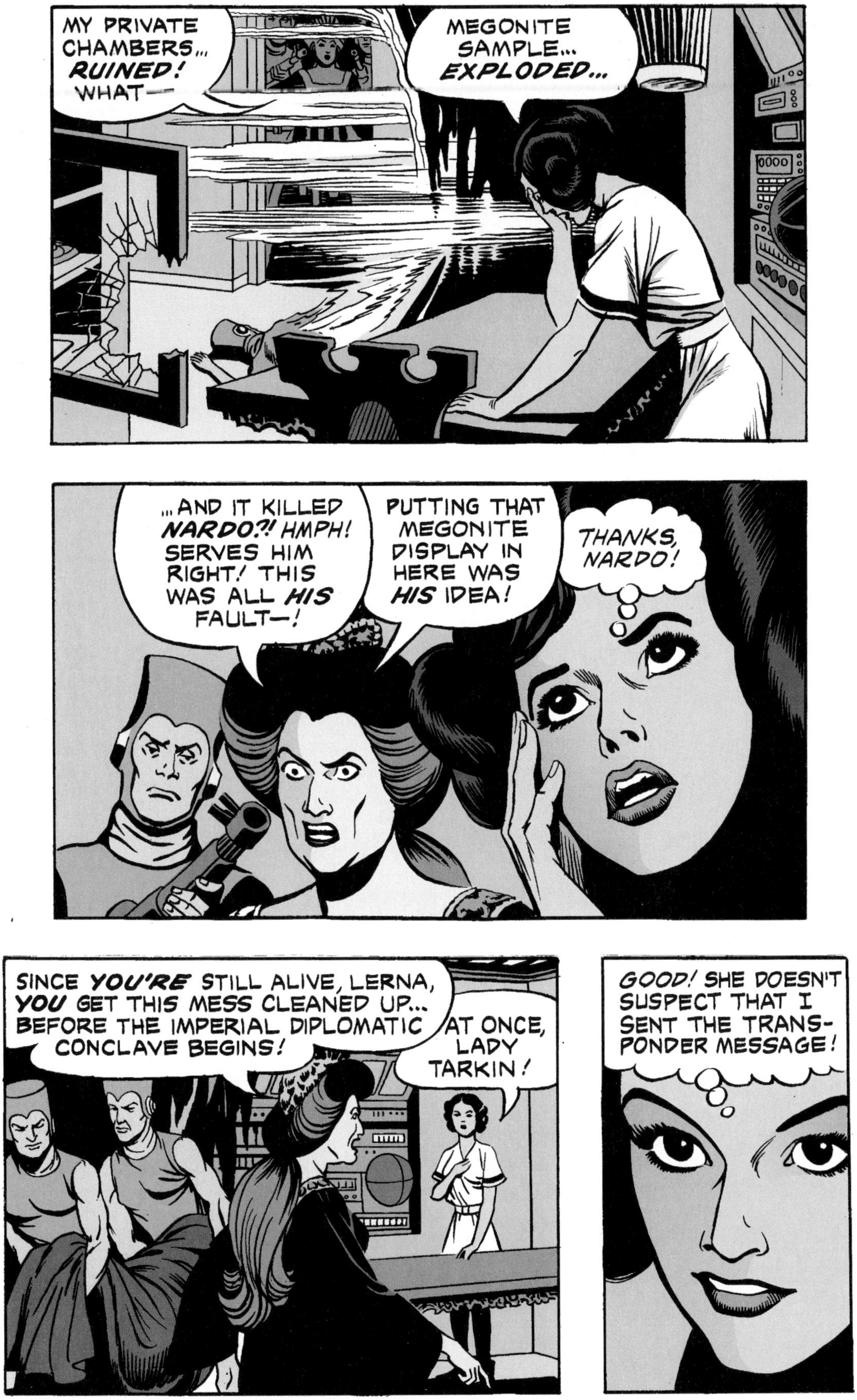
MY PRIVATE CHAMBERS... RUINED! WHAT—
MEGONITE SAMPLE... EXPLODED...
...AND IT KILLED NARDO?! HMPH! SERVES HIM RIGHT! THIS WAS ALL HIS FAULT—!
PUTTING THAT MEGONITE DISPLAY IN HERE WAS HIS IDEA!
THANKS, NARDO!
SINCE YOU'RE STILL ALIVE, LERNA, YOU GET THIS MESS CLEANED UP... BEFORE THE IMPERIAL DIPLOMATIC CONCLAVE BEGINS!
AT ONCE, LADY TARKIN!
GOOD! SHE DOESN'T SUSPECT THAT I SENT THE TRANS-PONDER MESSAGE!

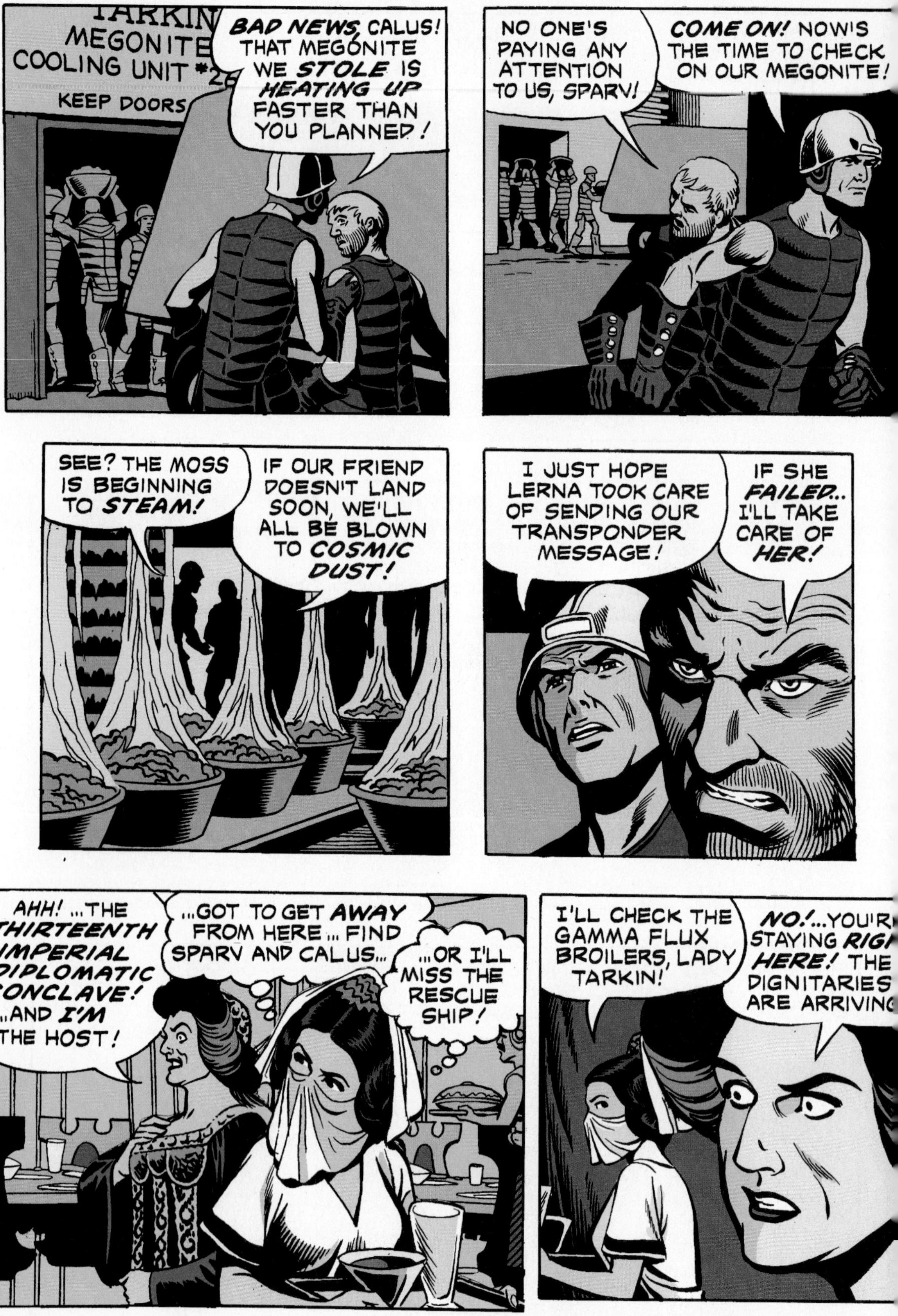
TARKIN
MEGONITE
COOLING UNIT #26
KEEP DOORS
BAD NEWS, CALUS! THAT MEGONITE WE STOLE IS HEATING UP FASTER THAN YOU PLANNED!
NO ONE'S PAYING ANY ATTENTION TO US, SPARV!
COME ON! NOW'S THE TIME TO CHECK ON OUR MEGONITE!
SEE? THE MOSS IS BEGINNING TO STEAM!
IF OUR FRIEND DOESN'T LAND SOON, WE'LL ALL BE BLOWN TO COSMIC DUST!
I JUST HOPE LERNA TOOK CARE OF SENDING OUR TRANSPONDER MESSAGE!
IF SHE FAILED.. I'LL TAKE CARE OF HER!
AHH! ...THE THIRTEENTH IMPERIAL DIPLOMATIC CONCLAVE! ...AND I'M THE HOST!
...GOT TO GET AWAY FROM HERE... FIND SPARV AND CALUS...
...OR I'LL MISS THE RESCUE SHIP!
I'LL CHECK THE GAMMA FLUX BROILERS, LADY TARKIN!
NO!...YOU'R STAYING RIG HERE! THE DIGNITARIES ARE ARRIVING

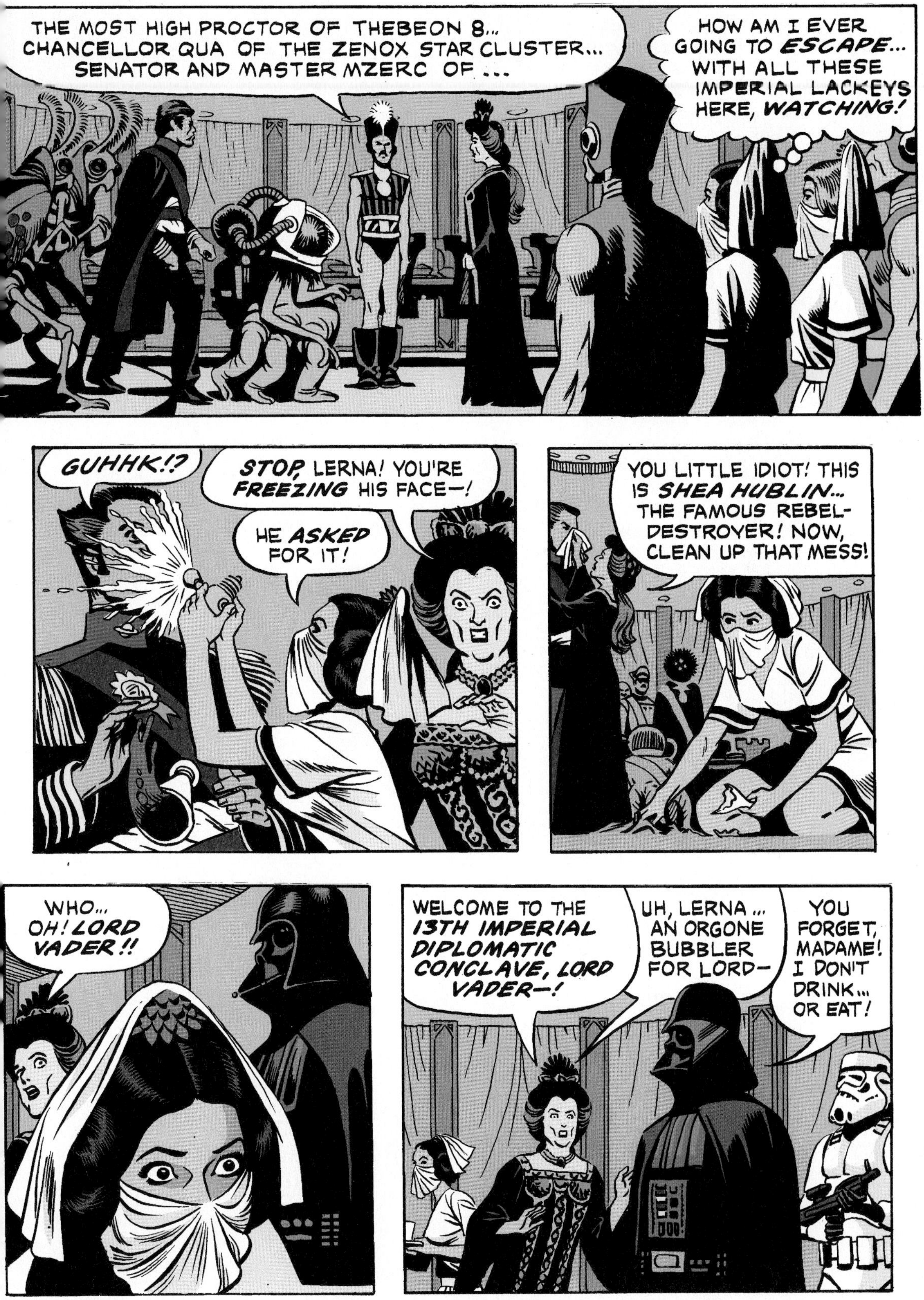
THE MOST HIGH PROCTOR OF THEBEON 8... CHANCELLOR QUA OF THE ZENOX STAR CLUSTER... SENATOR AND MASTER MZERC OF ...
HOW AM I EVER GOING TO *ESCAPE*... WITH ALL THESE IMPERIAL LACKEYS HERE, *WATCHING!*
GUHHK!?
STOP, LERNA! YOU'RE *FREEZING* HIS FACE--!
HE *ASKED* FOR IT!
YOU LITTLE IDIOT! THIS IS *SHEA HUBLIN*... THE FAMOUS REBEL-DESTROYER! NOW, CLEAN UP THAT MESS!
WHO... OH! *LORD VADER!!*
WELCOME TO THE *13TH IMPERIAL DIPLOMATIC CONCLAVE, LORD VADER--!*
UH, LERNA ... AN ORGONE BUBBLER FOR LORD--
YOU FORGET, MADAME! I DON'T DRINK... OR EAT!

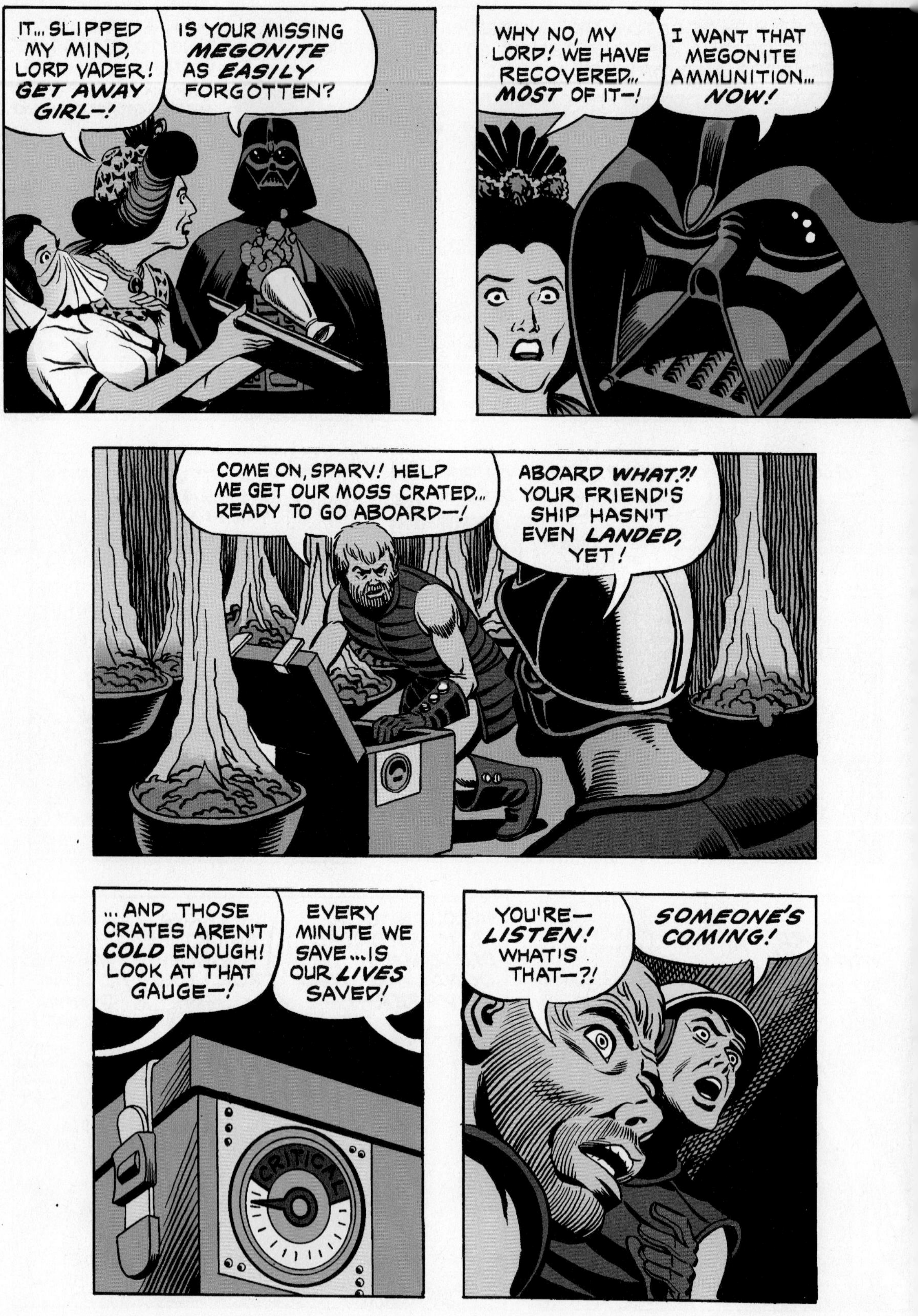
IT... SLIPPED MY MIND, LORD VADER! GET AWAY GIRL-!
IS YOUR MISSING MEGONITE AS EASILY FORGOTTEN?
WHY NO, MY LORD! WE HAVE RECOVERED... MOST OF IT-!
I WANT THAT MEGONITE AMMUNITION... NOW!
COME ON, SPARV! HELP ME GET OUR MOSS CRATED... READY TO GO ABOARD-!
ABOARD WHAT?! YOUR FRIEND'S SHIP HASN'T EVEN LANDED, YET!
...AND THOSE CRATES AREN'T COLD ENOUGH! LOOK AT THAT GAUGE-!
EVERY MINUTE WE SAVE...IS OUR LIVES SAVED!
CRITICAL
YOU'RE- LISTEN! WHAT'S THAT-?!
SOMEONE'S COMING!

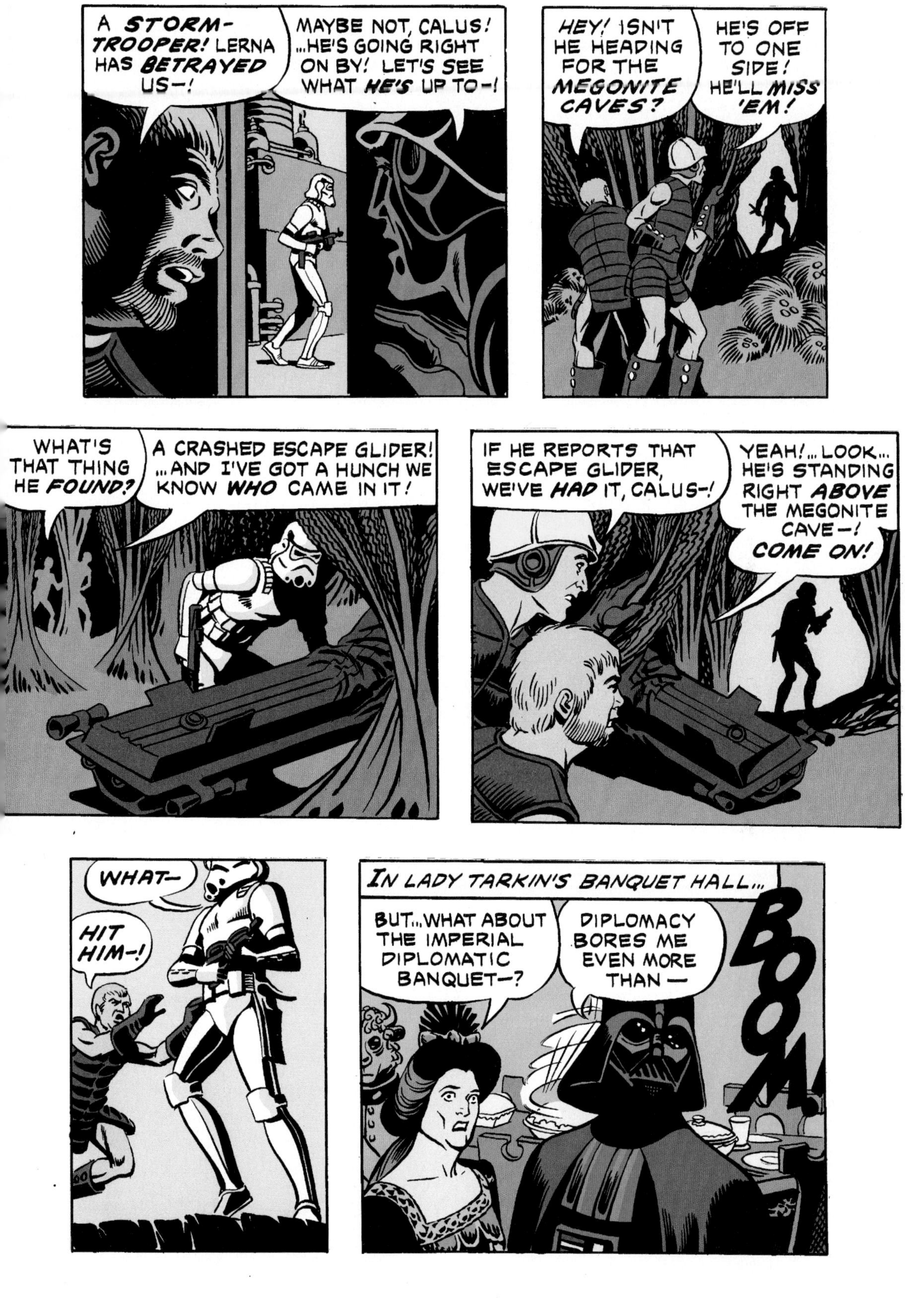
A STORM-TROOPER! LERNA HAS BETRAYED US—!
MAYBE NOT, CALUS! ...HE'S GOING RIGHT ON BY! LET'S SEE WHAT HE'S UP TO—!
HEY! ISN'T HE HEADING FOR THE MEGONITE CAVES?
HE'S OFF TO ONE SIDE! HE'LL MISS 'EM!
WHAT'S THAT THING HE FOUND?
A CRASHED ESCAPE GLIDER! ...AND I'VE GOT A HUNCH WE KNOW WHO CAME IN IT!
IF HE REPORTS THAT ESCAPE GLIDER, WE'VE HAD IT, CALUS—!
YEAH!... LOOK... HE'S STANDING RIGHT ABOVE THE MEGONITE CAVE—! COME ON!
WHAT—
HIT HIM—!
IN LADY TARKIN'S BANQUET HALL...
BUT...WHAT ABOUT THE IMPERIAL DIPLOMATIC BANQUET—?
DIPLOMACY BORES ME EVEN MORE THAN —
BOOM

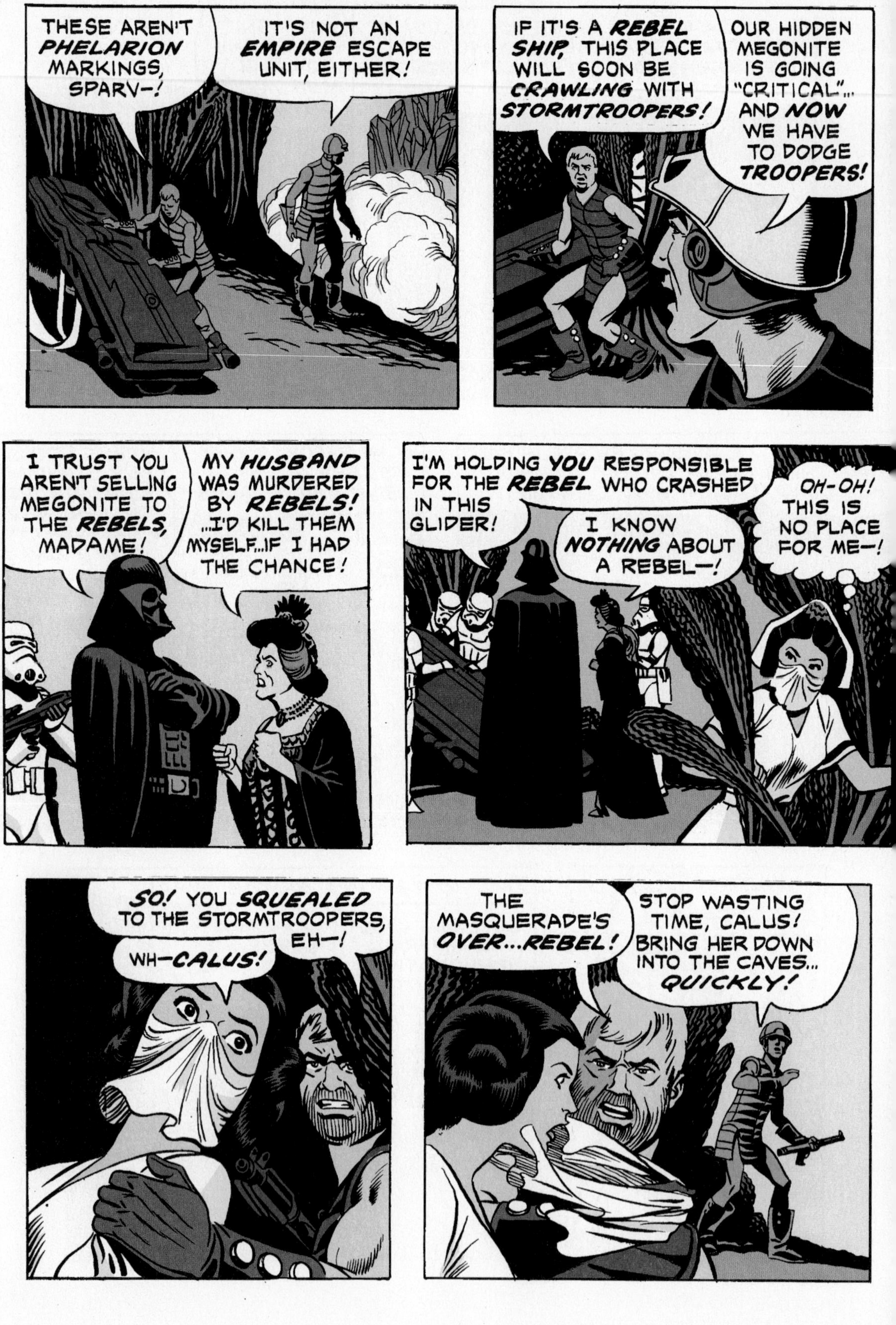
THESE AREN'T PHELARION MARKINGS, SPARV—!
IT'S NOT AN EMPIRE ESCAPE UNIT, EITHER!
IF IT'S A REBEL SHIP, THIS PLACE WILL SOON BE CRAWLING WITH STORMTROOPERS!
OUR HIDDEN MEGONITE IS GOING "CRITICAL"... AND NOW WE HAVE TO DODGE TROOPERS!
I TRUST YOU AREN'T SELLING MEGONITE TO THE REBELS, MADAME!
MY HUSBAND WAS MURDERED BY REBELS! ...I'D KILL THEM MYSELF...IF I HAD THE CHANCE!
I'M HOLDING YOU RESPONSIBLE FOR THE REBEL WHO CRASHED IN THIS GLIDER!
I KNOW NOTHING ABOUT A REBEL—!
OH-OH! THIS IS NO PLACE FOR ME—!
SO! YOU SQUEALED TO THE STORMTROOPERS, EH—!
WH—CALUS!
THE MASQUERADE'S OVER...REBEL!
STOP WASTING TIME, CALUS! BRING HER DOWN INTO THE CAVES... QUICKLY!

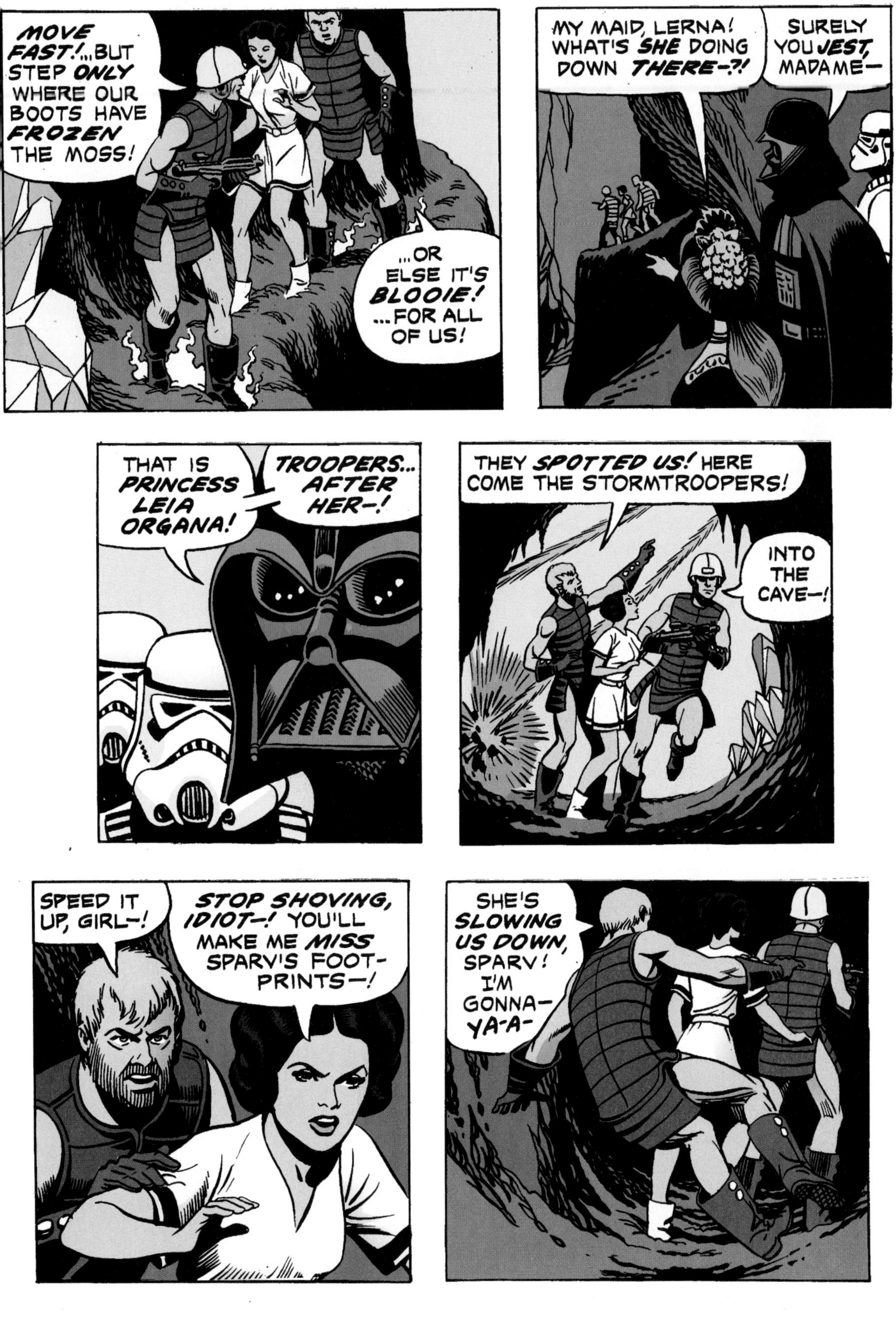
MOVE FAST!...BUT STEP ONLY WHERE OUR BOOTS HAVE FROZEN THE MOSS!
...OR ELSE IT'S BLOOIE! ...FOR ALL OF US!
MY MAID, LERNA! WHAT'S SHE DOING DOWN THERE-?!
SURELY YOU JEST, MADAME—
THAT IS PRINCESS LEIA ORGANA!
TROOPERS... AFTER HER—!
THEY SPOTTED US! HERE COME THE STORMTROOPERS!
INTO THE CAVE—!
SPEED IT UP, GIRL—!
STOP SHOVING, IDIOT—! YOU'LL MAKE ME MISS SPARV'S FOOT-PRINTS—!
SHE'S SLOWING US DOWN, SPARV! I'M GONNA- YA-A-

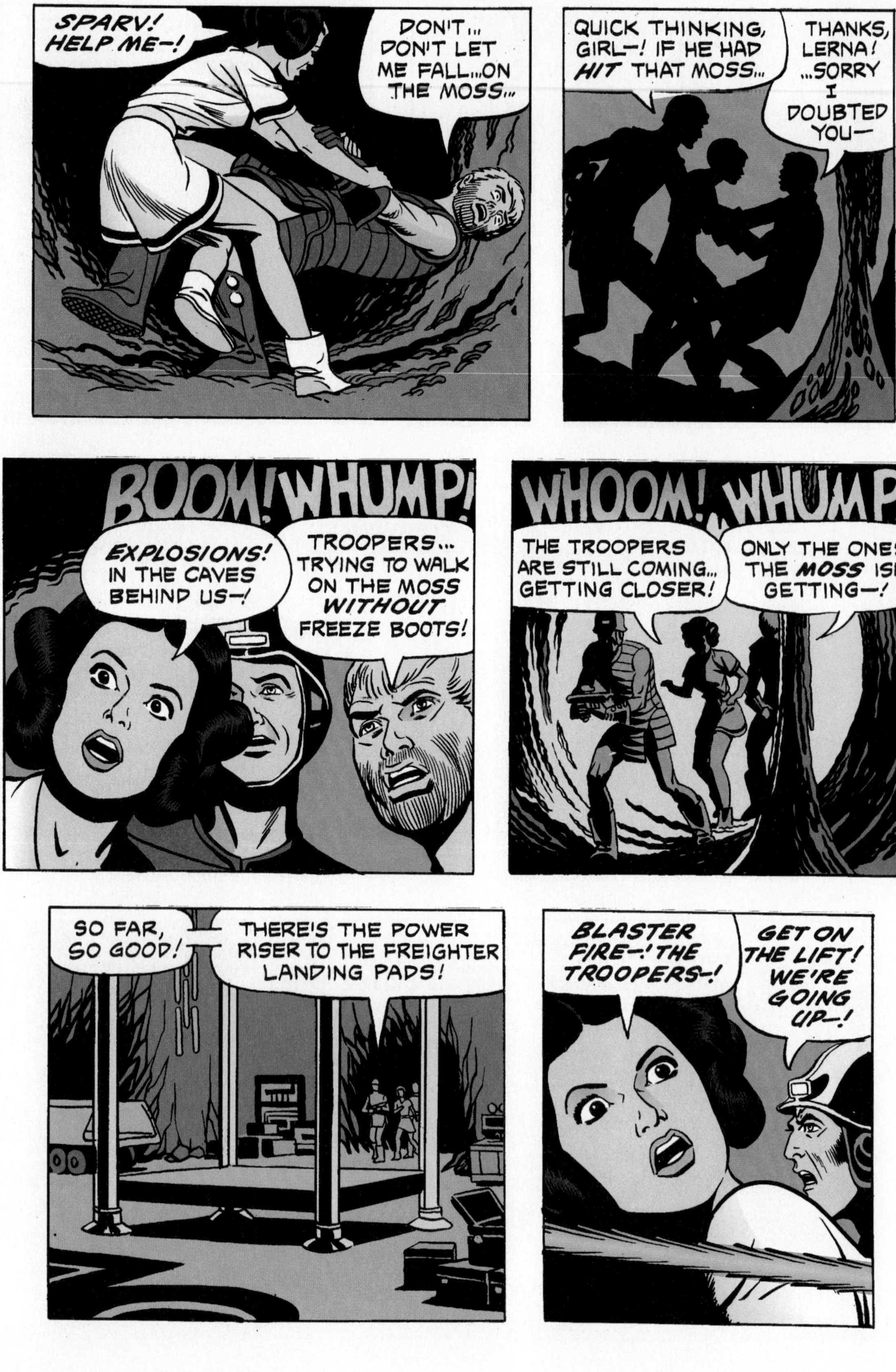
SPARV! HELP ME-!
DON'T... DON'T LET ME FALL...ON THE MOSS...
QUICK THINKING, GIRL-! IF HE HAD HIT THAT MOSS...
THANKS, LERNA! ...SORRY I DOUBTED YOU—
BOOM! WHUMP!
EXPLOSIONS! IN THE CAVES BEHIND US-!
TROOPERS... TRYING TO WALK ON THE MOSS WITHOUT FREEZE BOOTS!
WHOOM! WHUMP!
THE TROOPERS ARE STILL COMING... GETTING CLOSER!
ONLY THE ONES THE MOSS ISN'T GETTING-!
SO FAR, SO GOOD!
THERE'S THE POWER RISER TO THE FREIGHTER LANDING PADS!
BLASTER FIRE-! THE TROOPERS-!
GET ON THE LIFT! WE'RE GOING UP-!

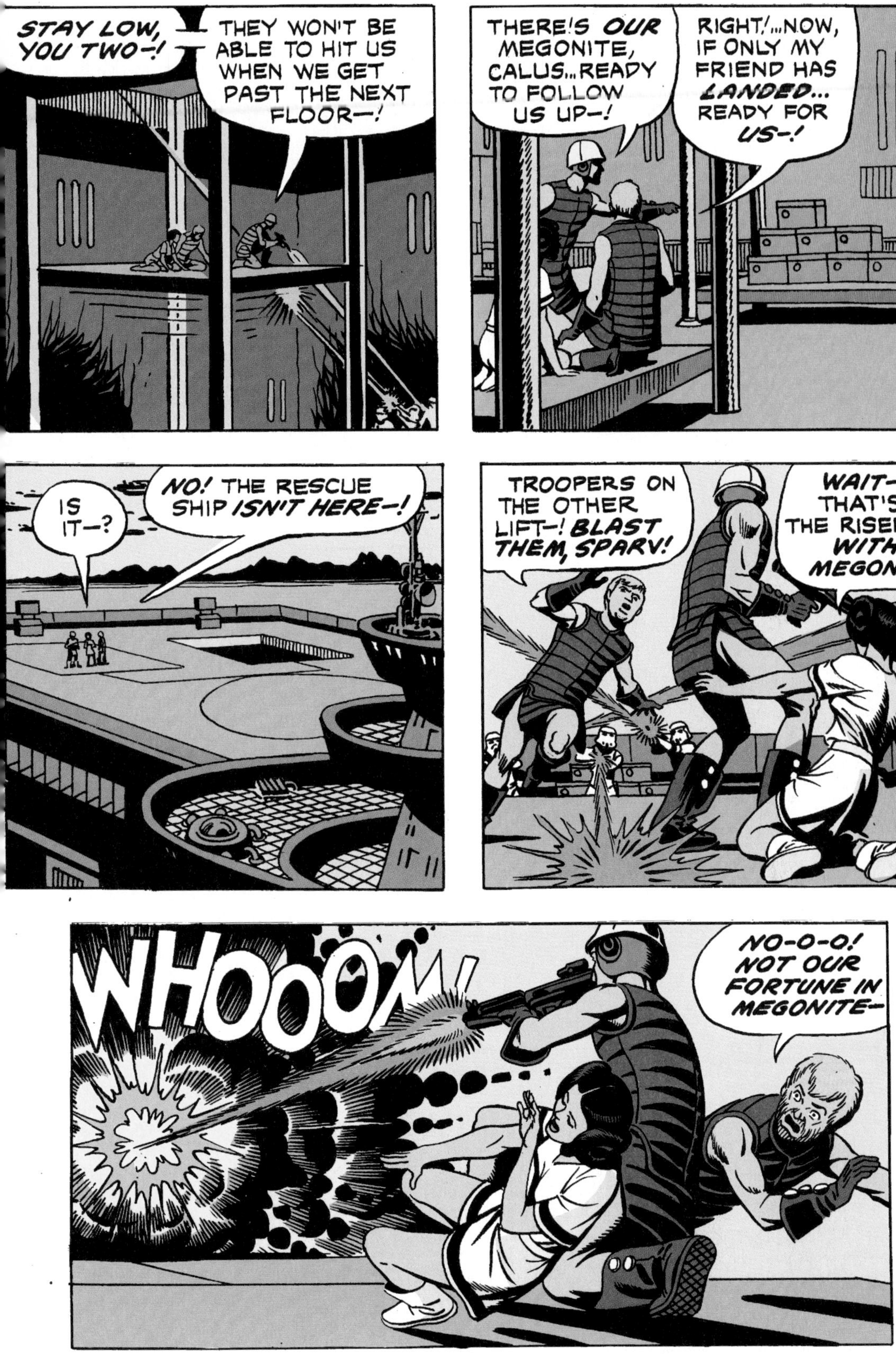
STAY LOW, YOU TWO-!
THEY WON'T BE ABLE TO HIT US WHEN WE GET PAST THE NEXT FLOOR--!
THERE'S OUR MEGONITE, CALUS...READY TO FOLLOW US UP-!
RIGHT!...NOW, IF ONLY MY FRIEND HAS LANDED... READY FOR US-!
IS IT-?
NO! THE RESCUE SHIP ISN'T HERE-!
TROOPERS ON THE OTHER LIFT-! BLAST THEM, SPARV!
WAIT-! THAT'S THE RISER WITH MEGONI-
WHOOOM!
NO-O-O! NOT OUR FORTUNE IN MEGONITE-

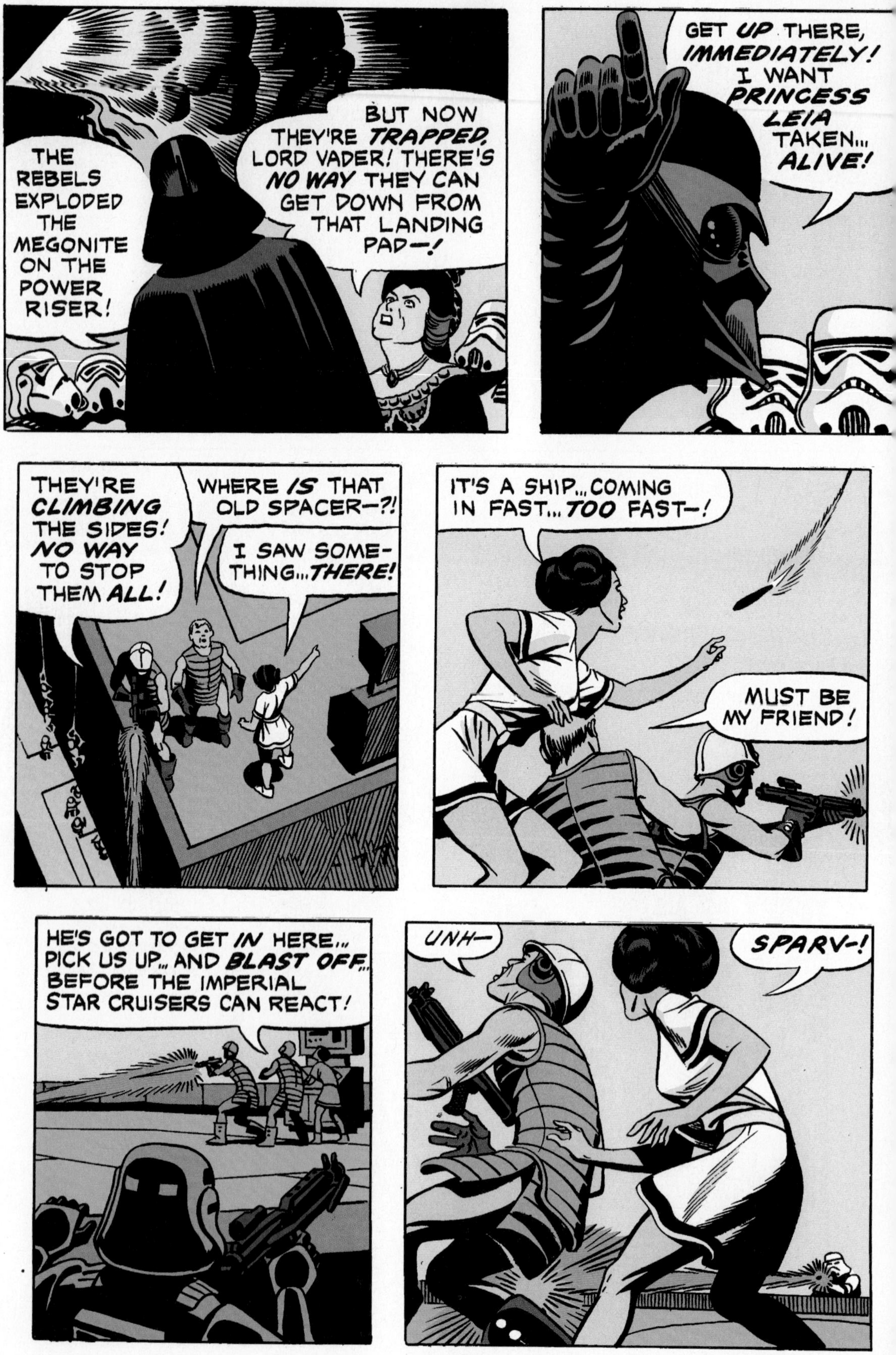
THE REBELS EXPLODED THE MEGONITE ON THE POWER RISER!
BUT NOW THEY'RE TRAPPED, LORD VADER! THERE'S NO WAY THEY CAN GET DOWN FROM THAT LANDING PAD--!
GET UP THERE, IMMEDIATELY! I WANT PRINCESS LEIA TAKEN... ALIVE!
THEY'RE CLIMBING THE SIDES! NO WAY TO STOP THEM ALL!
WHERE IS THAT OLD SPACER--?!
I SAW SOMETHING... THERE!
IT'S A SHIP... COMING IN FAST... TOO FAST--!
MUST BE MY FRIEND!
HE'S GOT TO GET IN HERE... PICK US UP... AND BLAST OFF... BEFORE THE IMPERIAL STAR CRUISERS CAN REACT!
UNH--
SPARV--!

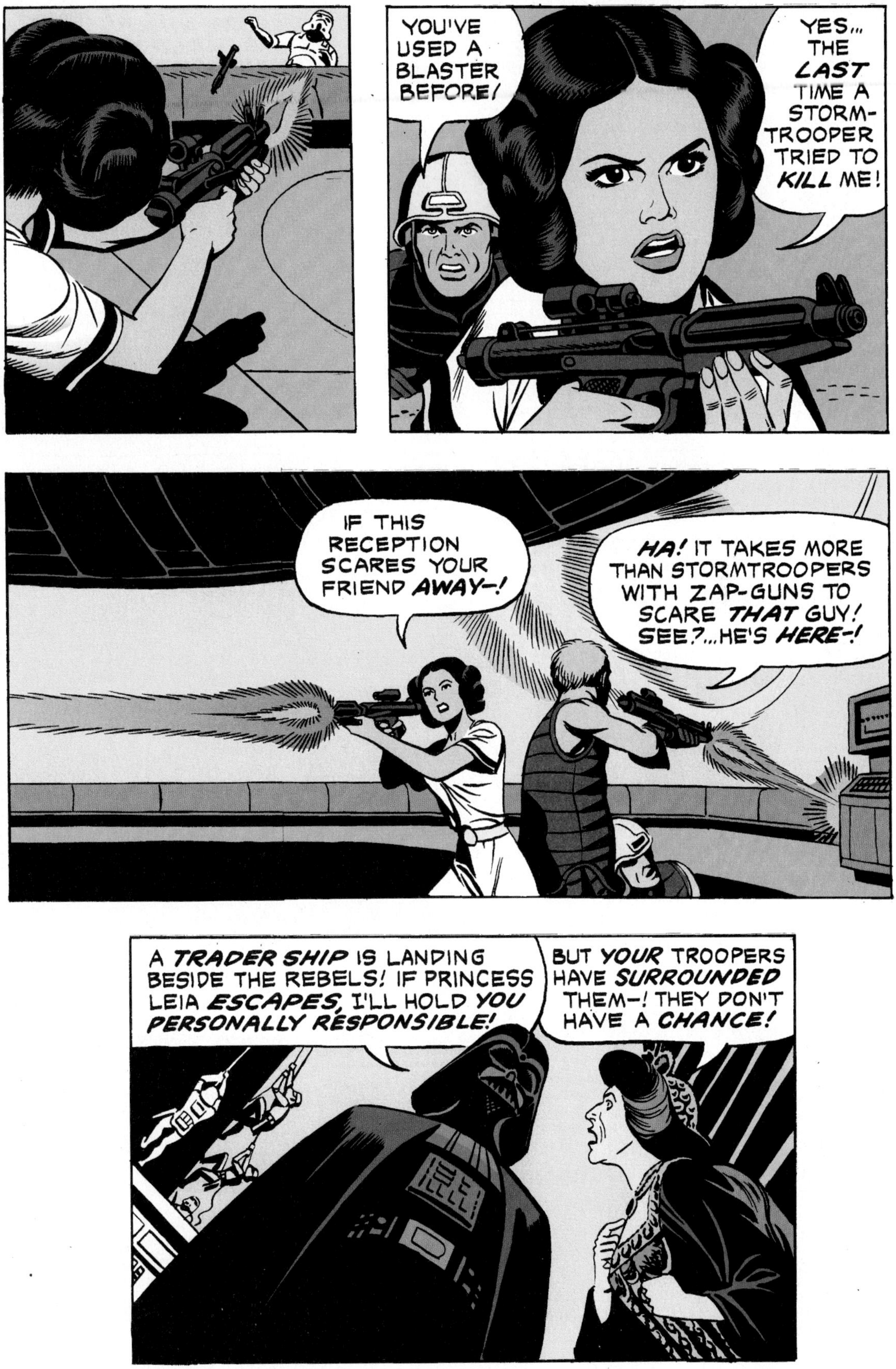
YOU'VE USED A BLASTER BEFORE!
YES... THE LAST TIME A STORM-TROOPER TRIED TO KILL ME!
IF THIS RECEPTION SCARES YOUR FRIEND AWAY-!
HA! IT TAKES MORE THAN STORMTROOPERS WITH ZAP-GUNS TO SCARE THAT GUY! SEE?...HE'S HERE-!
A TRADER SHIP IS LANDING BESIDE THE REBELS! IF PRINCESS LEIA ESCAPES, I'LL HOLD YOU PERSONALLY RESPONSIBLE!
BUT YOUR TROOPERS HAVE SURROUNDED THEM-! THEY DON'T HAVE A CHANCE!

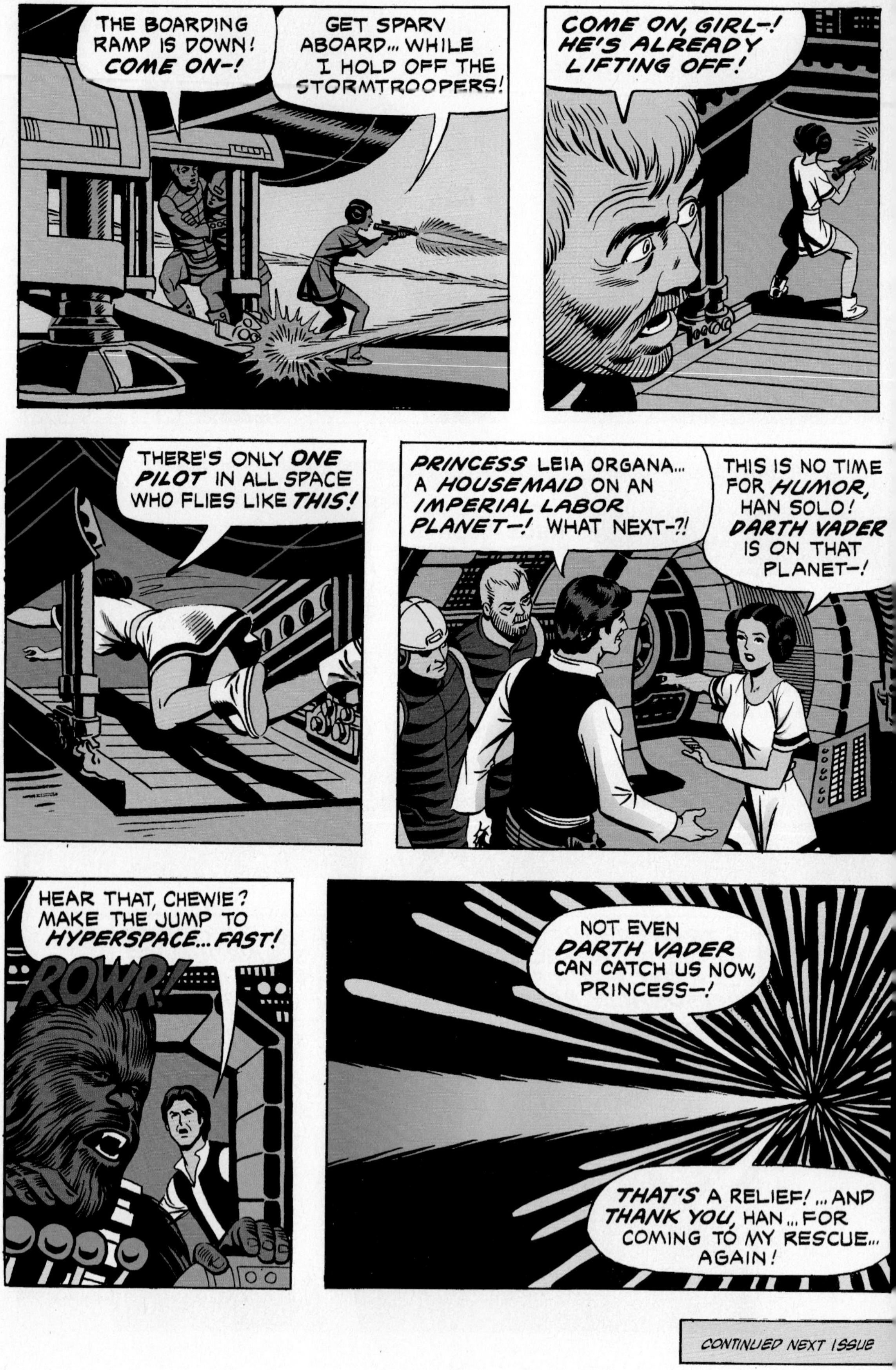
THE BOARDING RAMP IS DOWN! COME ON-!
GET SPARV ABOARD... WHILE I HOLD OFF THE STORMTROOPERS!
COME ON, GIRL-! HE'S ALREADY LIFTING OFF!
THERE'S ONLY ONE PILOT IN ALL SPACE WHO FLIES LIKE THIS!
PRINCESS LEIA ORGANA... A HOUSEMAID ON AN IMPERIAL LABOR PLANET-! WHAT NEXT-?!
THIS IS NO TIME FOR HUMOR, HAN SOLO! DARTH VADER IS ON THAT PLANET-!
HEAR THAT, CHEWIE? MAKE THE JUMP TO HYPERSPACE... FAST!
ROWR!
NOT EVEN DARTH VADER CAN CATCH US NOW, PRINCESS-!
THAT'S A RELIEF! ... AND THANK YOU, HAN ... FOR COMING TO MY RESCUE... AGAIN!
CONTINUED NEXT ISSUE

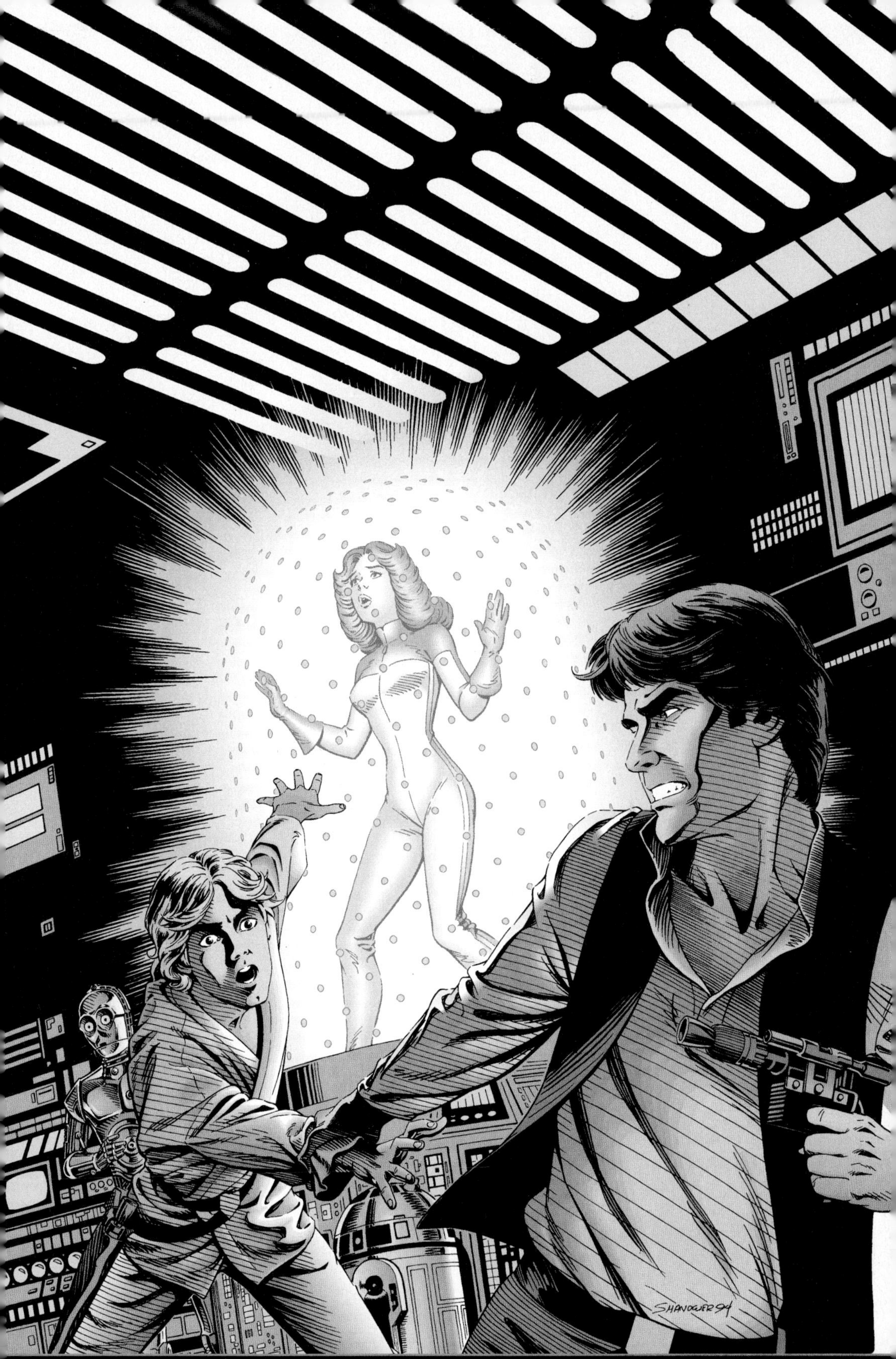
SHANOWER 94

CLASSIC STAR WARS: THE EARLY ADVENTURES #6 — "THE SECOND KESSEL RUN"
ORIGINALLY PUBLISHED FROM JANUARY 1 TO FEBRUARY 25, 1980

WRITERS: RUSS MANNING & RUSS HELM • ARTIST & LETTERER: RUSS MANNING • ART RETOUCHING: RICK HOBERG & BRIAN SNODDY • COLORIST: RAY MURTAUGH

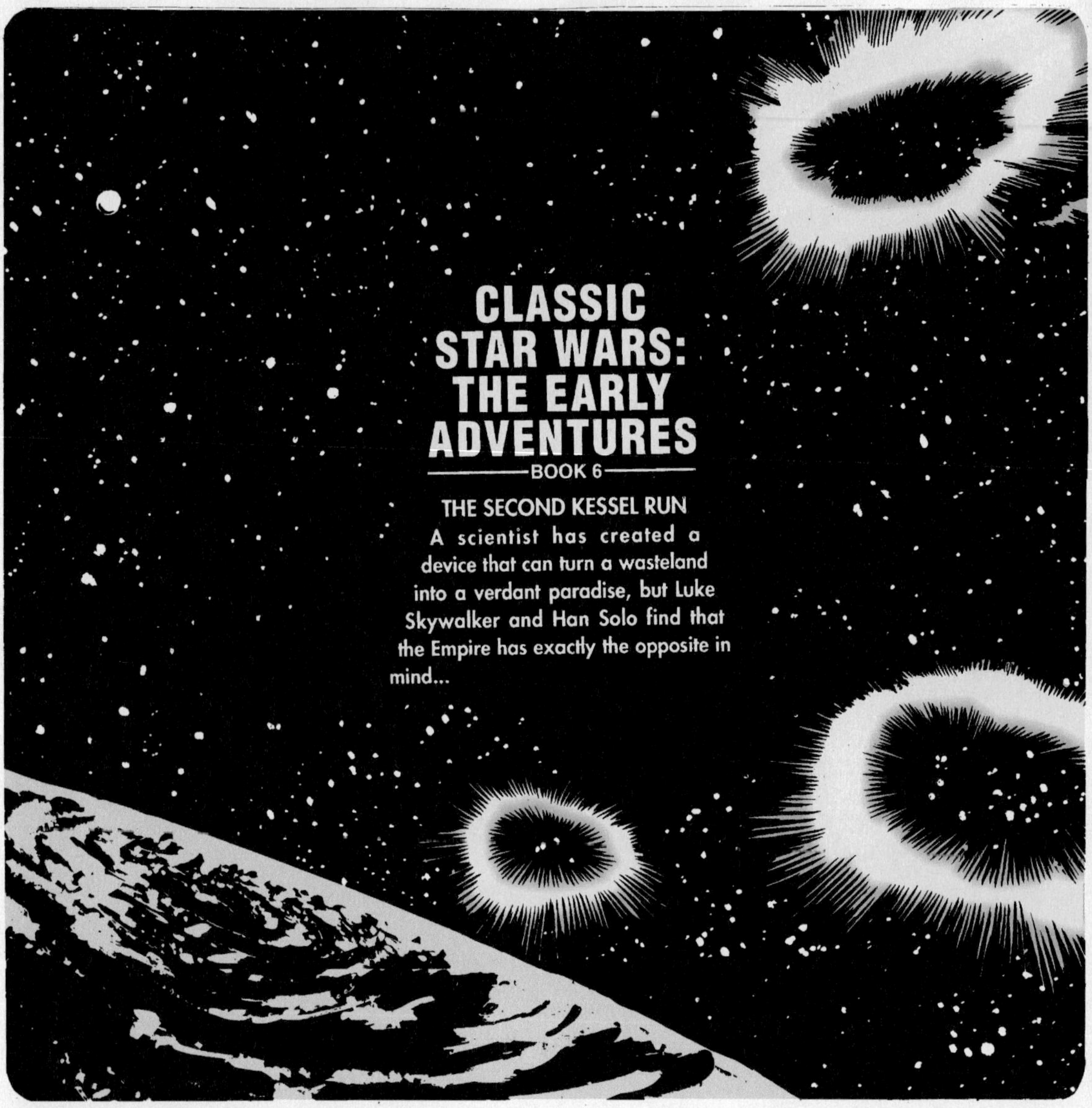
CLASSIC
STAR WARS:
THE EARLY
ADVENTURES
BOOK 6
THE SECOND KESSEL RUN
A scientist has created a device that can turn a wasteland into a verdant paradise, but Luke Skywalker and Han Solo find that the Empire has exactly the opposite in mind...

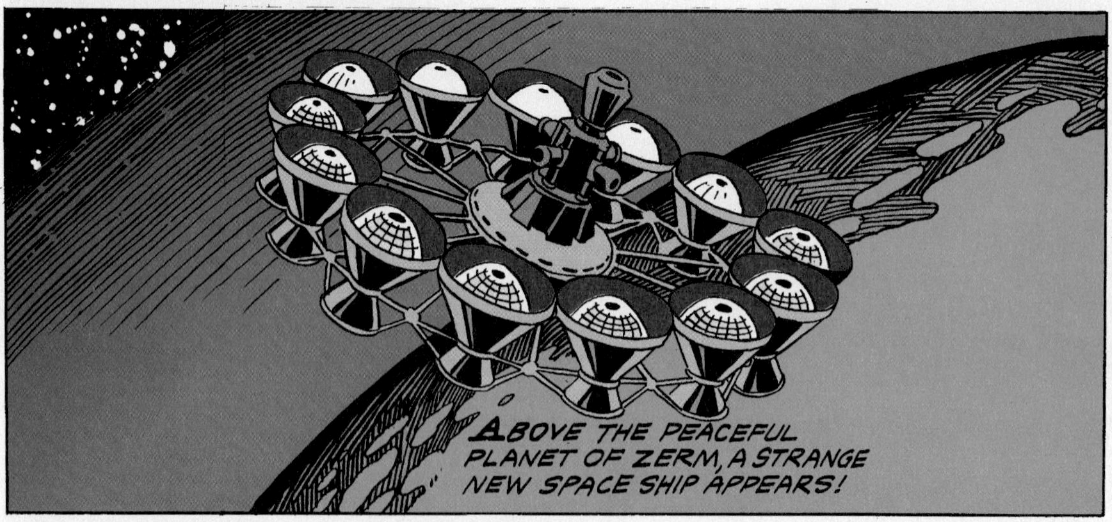
ABOVE THE PEACEFUL PLANET OF ZERM, A STRANGE NEW SPACE SHIP APPEARS!

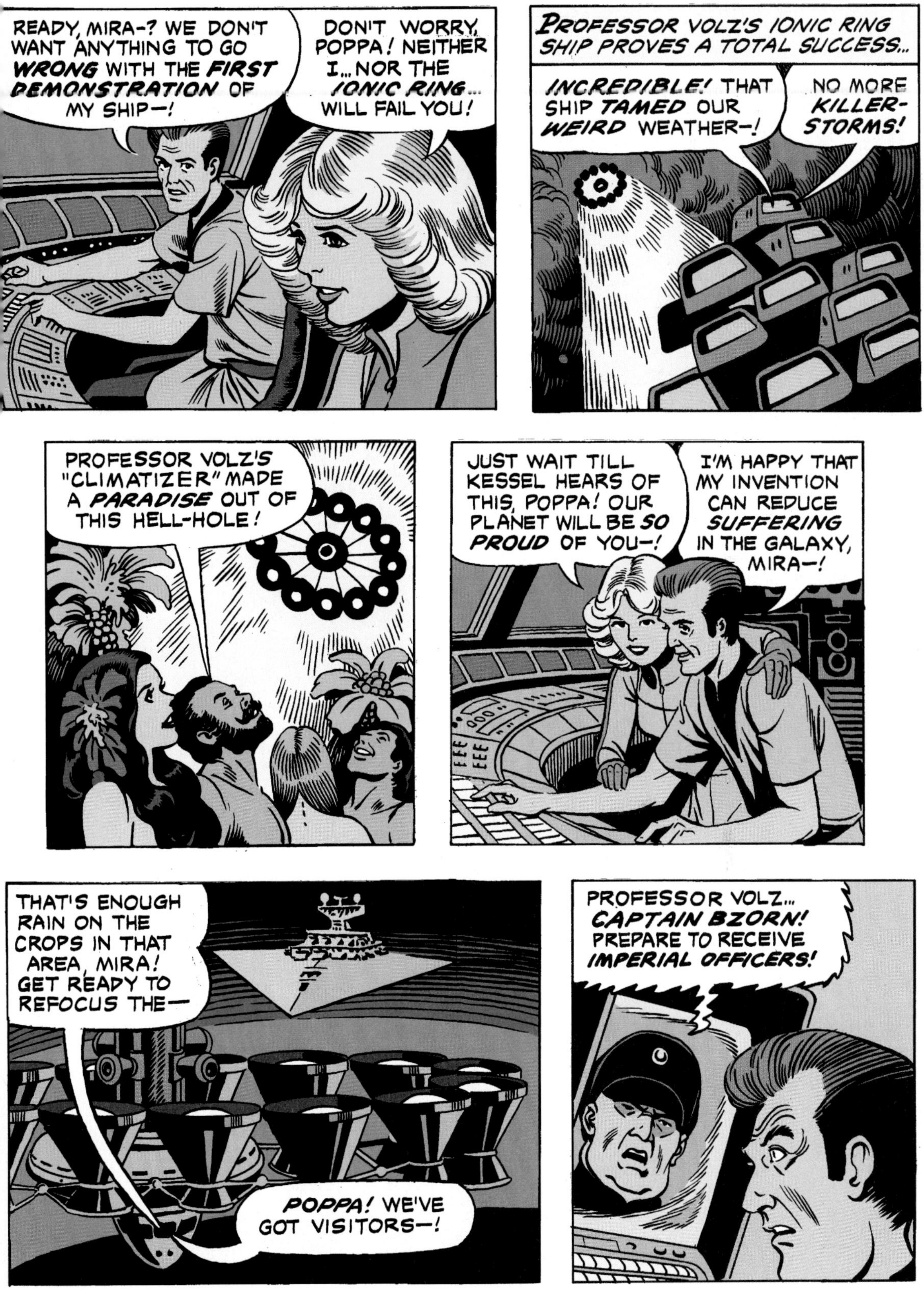
READY, MIRA-? WE DON'T WANT ANYTHING TO GO WRONG WITH THE FIRST DEMONSTRATION OF MY SHIP—!
DON'T WORRY, POPPA! NEITHER I... NOR THE IONIC RING... WILL FAIL YOU!
PROFESSOR VOLZ'S IONIC RING SHIP PROVES A TOTAL SUCCESS...
INCREDIBLE! THAT SHIP TAMED OUR WEIRD WEATHER—!
NO MORE KILLER-STORMS!
PROFESSOR VOLZ'S "CLIMATIZER" MADE A PARADISE OUT OF THIS HELL-HOLE!
JUST WAIT TILL KESSEL HEARS OF THIS, POPPA! OUR PLANET WILL BE SO PROUD OF YOU—!
I'M HAPPY THAT MY INVENTION CAN REDUCE SUFFERING IN THE GALAXY, MIRA—!
THAT'S ENOUGH RAIN ON THE CROPS IN THAT AREA, MIRA! GET READY TO REFOCUS THE—
POPPA! WE'VE GOT VISITORS—!
PROFESSOR VOLZ... CAPTAIN BZORN! PREPARE TO RECEIVE IMPERIAL OFFICERS!

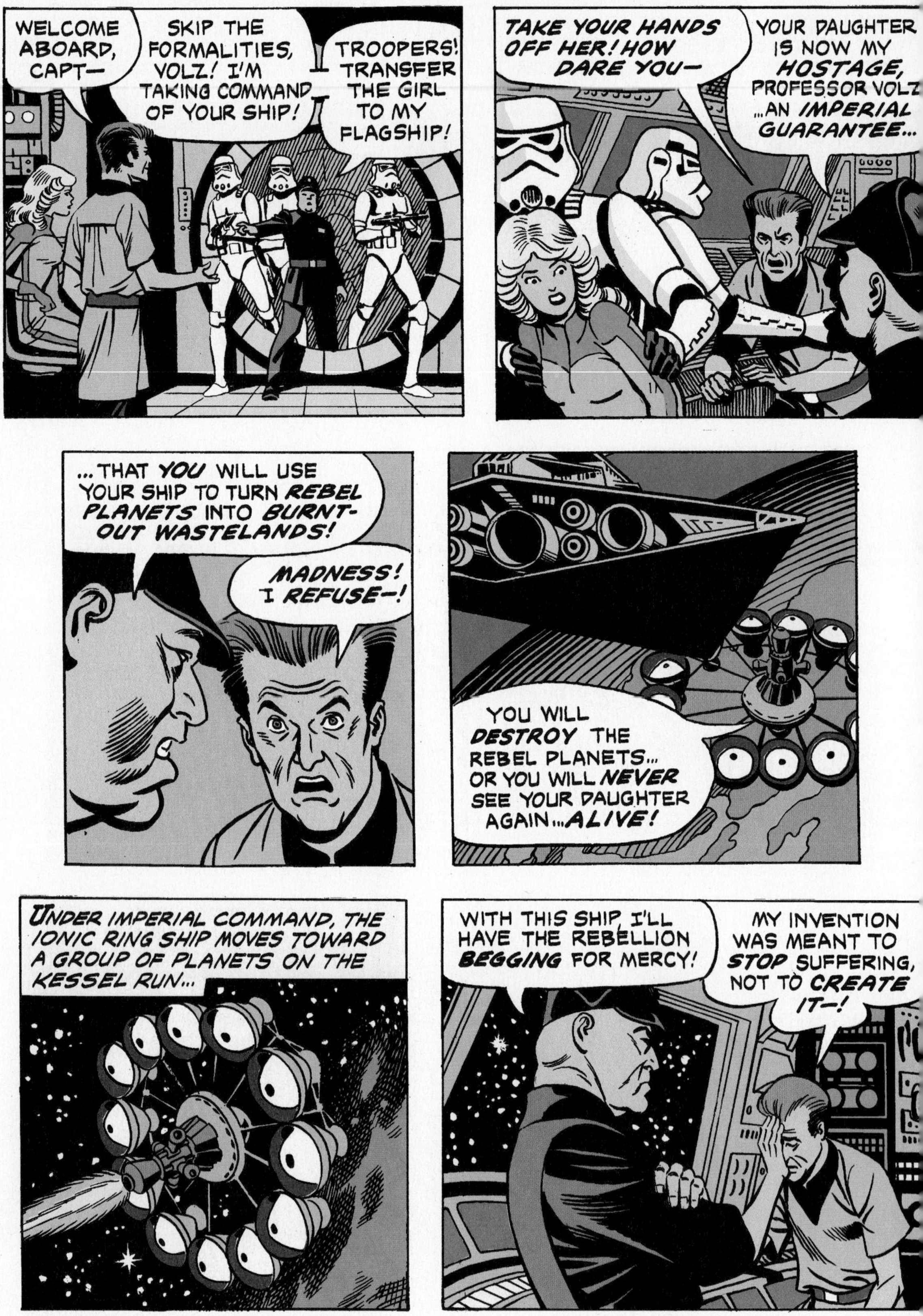
WELCOME ABOARD, CAPT—
SKIP THE FORMALITIES, VOLZ! I'M TAKING COMMAND OF YOUR SHIP!
TROOPERS! TRANSFER THE GIRL TO MY FLAGSHIP!
TAKE YOUR HANDS OFF HER! HOW DARE YOU—
YOUR DAUGHTER IS NOW MY HOSTAGE, PROFESSOR VOLZ ...AN IMPERIAL GUARANTEE...
...THAT YOU WILL USE YOUR SHIP TO TURN REBEL PLANETS INTO BURNT-OUT WASTELANDS!
MADNESS! I REFUSE—!
YOU WILL DESTROY THE REBEL PLANETS... OR YOU WILL NEVER SEE YOUR DAUGHTER AGAIN...ALIVE!
UNDER IMPERIAL COMMAND, THE IONIC RING SHIP MOVES TOWARD A GROUP OF PLANETS ON THE KESSEL RUN...
WITH THIS SHIP, I'LL HAVE THE REBELLION BEGGING FOR MERCY!
MY INVENTION WAS MEANT TO STOP SUFFERING, NOT TO CREATE IT—!

YOU'LL PREVENT YOUR *DAUGHTER'S* SUFFERING, VOLZ...AS LONG AS YOU OBEY *ME!*

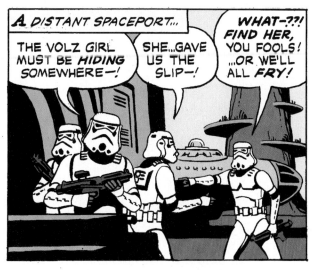

A DISTANT SPACEPORT...

THE VOLZ GIRL MUST BE *HIDING* SOMEWHERE—!

SHE...GAVE US THE *SLIP*—!

WHAT—??! FIND HER, YOU FOOLS! ...OR WE'LL ALL *FRY!*

ARE THE TROOPERS SEARCHING FOR OUR SPICE, MALO—?

OF COURSE NOT! OUR SPICE IS ON THE WAY TO *KESSEL* ABOARD *HAN SOLO'S* SHIP!

STOP *WORRYING,* CHEWIE—! WE'LL GET TO KESSEL ON TIME—!

...AFTER WE CHECK ON SKYWALKER!

A SMALL SECRET REBEL BASE ON THE PLANET RANDA...

GOOD TO SEE YOU, HAN—! LOOKS LIKE THE *FALCON'S* REALLY *LOADED!* WHAT—?

SPICE...ON ITS WAY TO *KESSEL*..JABBA PLANS TO *PROFIT* FROM AN IMPENDING FAMINE ...

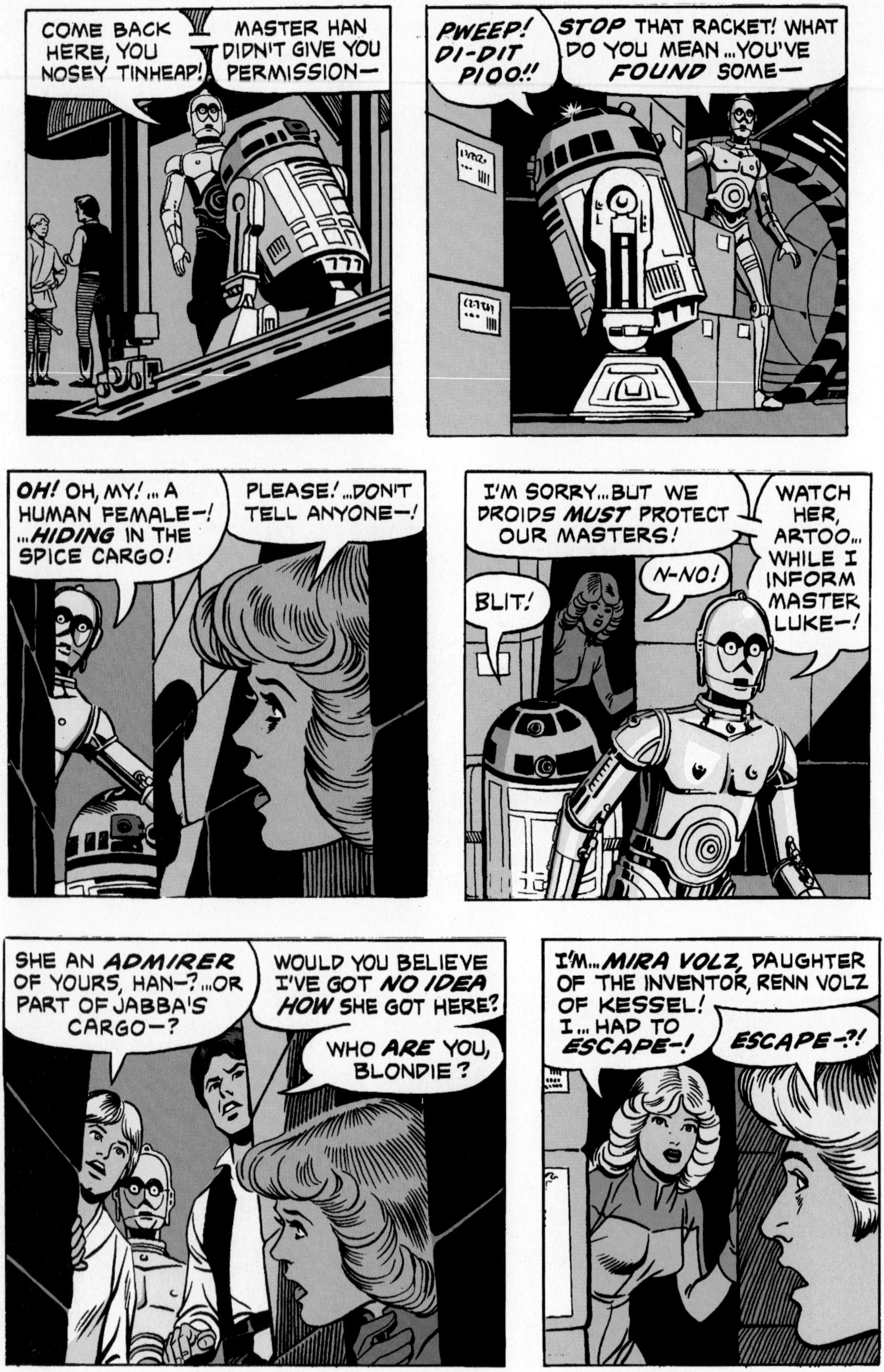
COME BACK HERE, YOU NOSEY TINHEAP!
MASTER HAN DIDN'T GIVE YOU PERMISSION—
PWEEP! DI-DIT PIOO!!
STOP THAT RACKET! WHAT DO YOU MEAN...YOU'VE FOUND SOME—
OH! OH, MY! ... A HUMAN FEMALE—! ...HIDING IN THE SPICE CARGO!
PLEASE! ...DON'T TELL ANYONE—!
I'M SORRY...BUT WE DROIDS MUST PROTECT OUR MASTERS!
WATCH HER, ARTOO... WHILE I INFORM MASTER LUKE—!
BLIT!
N-NO!
SHE AN ADMIRER OF YOURS, HAN—? ...OR PART OF JABBA'S CARGO—?
WOULD YOU BELIEVE I'VE GOT NO IDEA HOW SHE GOT HERE?
WHO ARE YOU, BLONDIE?
I'M...MIRA VOLZ, DAUGHTER OF THE INVENTOR, RENN VOLZ OF KESSEL! I... HAD TO ESCAPE—!
ESCAPE—?!

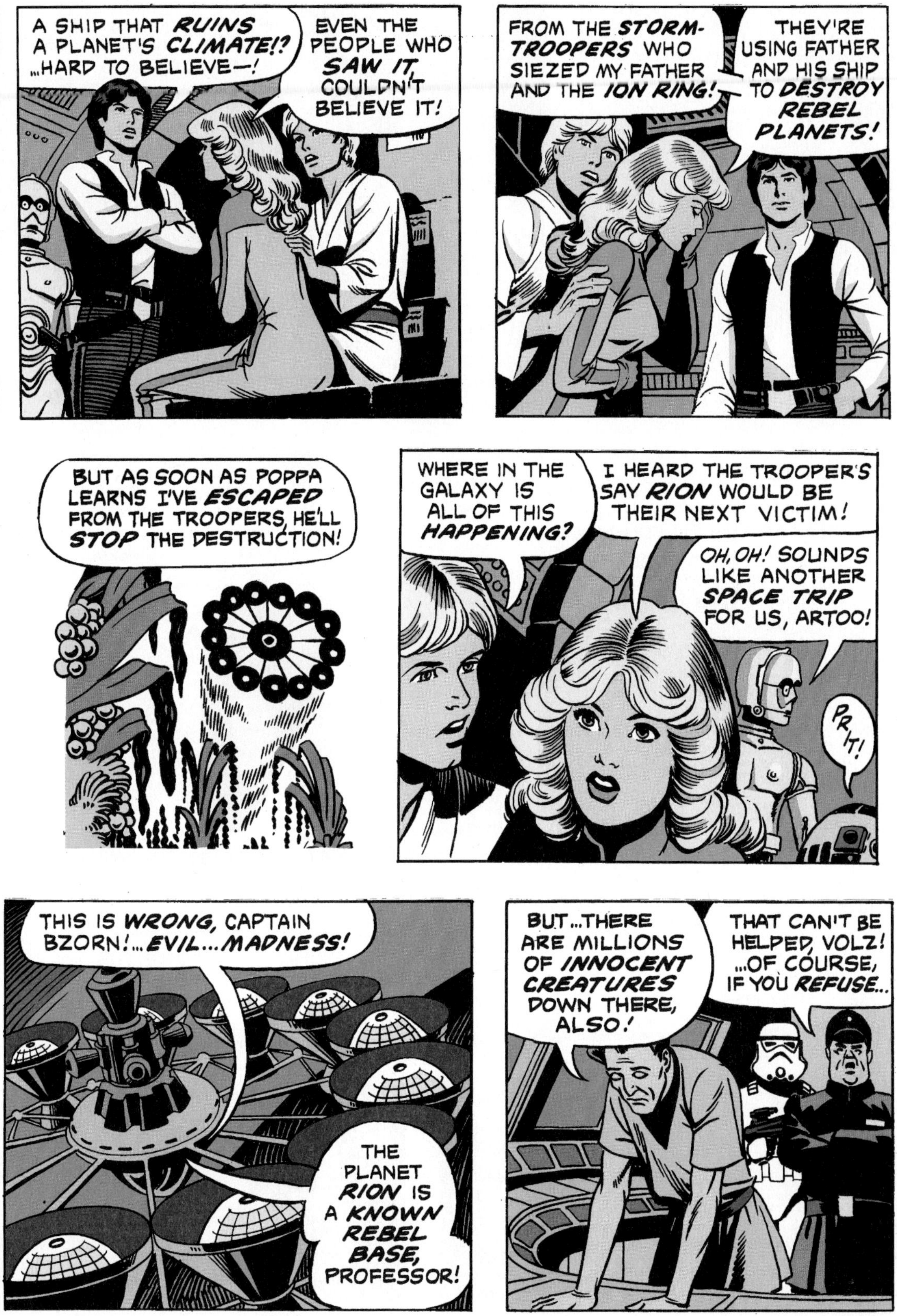

A SHIP THAT RUINS A PLANET'S CLIMATE!? ...HARD TO BELIEVE—!
EVEN THE PEOPLE WHO SAW IT, COULDN'T BELIEVE IT!
FROM THE STORM-TROOPERS WHO SIEZED MY FATHER AND THE ION RING!
THEY'RE USING FATHER AND HIS SHIP TO DESTROY REBEL PLANETS!
BUT AS SOON AS POPPA LEARNS I'VE ESCAPED FROM THE TROOPERS, HE'LL STOP THE DESTRUCTION!
WHERE IN THE GALAXY IS ALL OF THIS HAPPENING?
I HEARD THE TROOPER'S SAY RION WOULD BE THEIR NEXT VICTIM!
OH, OH! SOUNDS LIKE ANOTHER SPACE TRIP FOR US, ARTOO!
PRIT!
THIS IS WRONG, CAPTAIN BZORN!...EVIL...MADNESS!
THE PLANET RION IS A KNOWN REBEL BASE, PROFESSOR!
BUT...THERE ARE MILLIONS OF INNOCENT CREATURES DOWN THERE, ALSO!
THAT CAN'T BE HELPED, VOLZ! ...OF COURSE, IF YOU REFUSE...

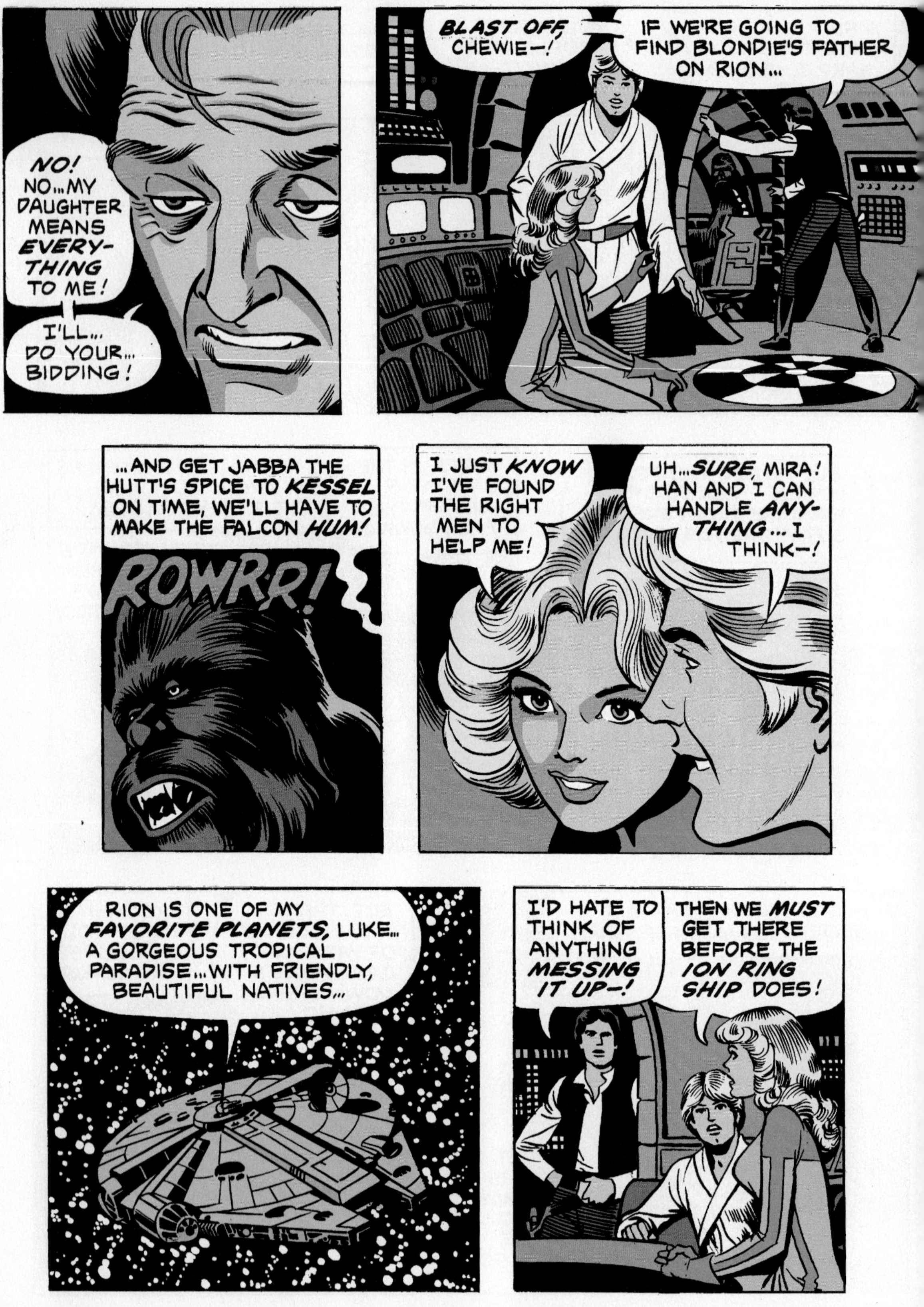
NO! NO...MY DAUGHTER MEANS EVERY-THING TO ME!
I'LL... DO YOUR... BIDDING!
BLAST OFF, CHEWIE--!
IF WE'RE GOING TO FIND BLONDIE'S FATHER ON RION...
...AND GET JABBA THE HUTT'S SPICE TO KESSEL ON TIME, WE'LL HAVE TO MAKE THE FALCON HUM!
ROWRR!
I JUST KNOW I'VE FOUND THE RIGHT MEN TO HELP ME!
UH...SURE, MIRA! HAN AND I CAN HANDLE ANY-THING... I THINK--!
RION IS ONE OF MY FAVORITE PLANETS, LUKE... A GORGEOUS TROPICAL PARADISE...WITH FRIENDLY, BEAUTIFUL NATIVES...
I'D HATE TO THINK OF ANYTHING MESSING IT UP--!
THEN WE MUST GET THERE BEFORE THE ION RING SHIP DOES!

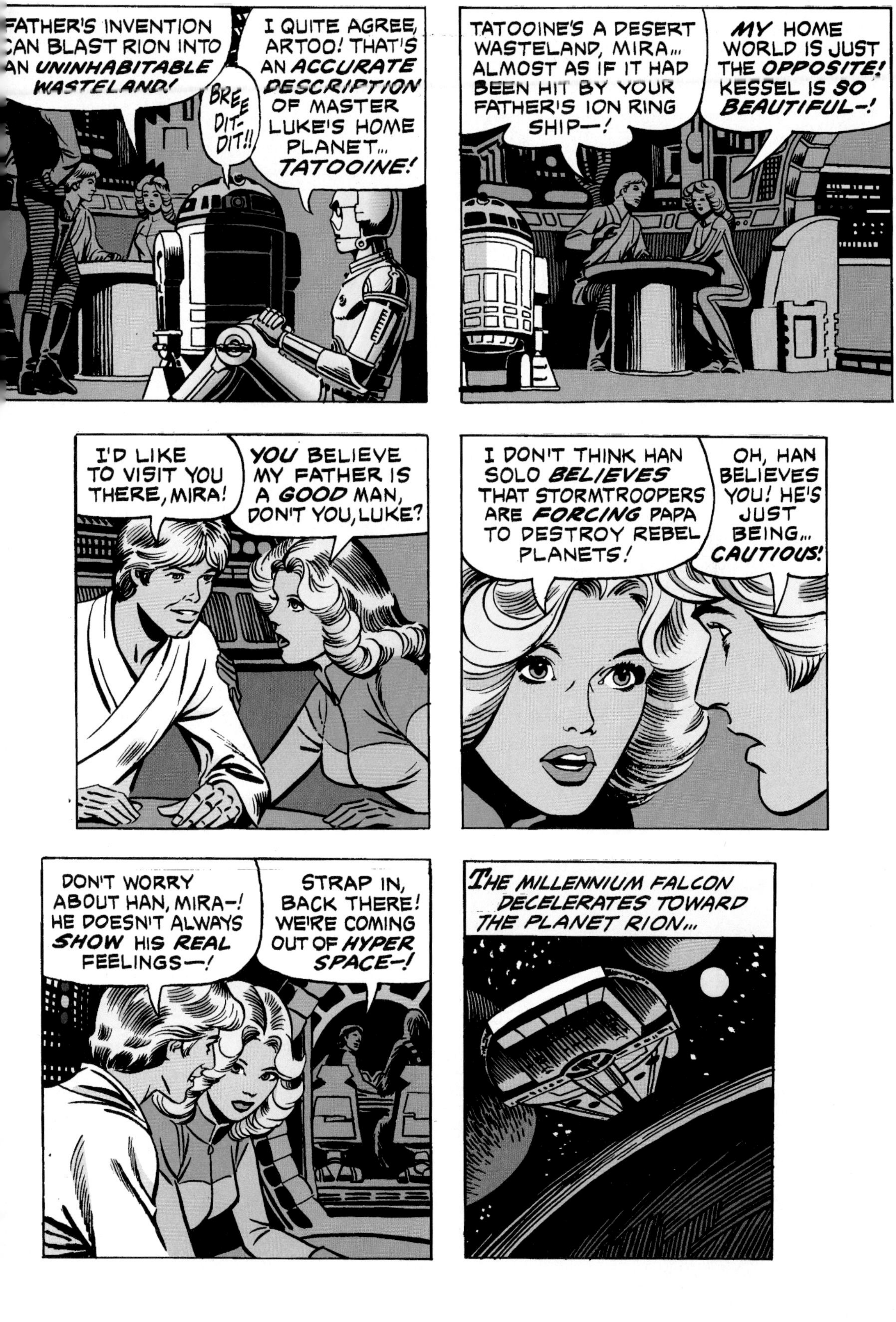
FATHER'S INVENTION CAN BLAST RION INTO AN UNINHABITABLE WASTELAND!
BREE DIT-DIT!!
I QUITE AGREE, ARTOO! THAT'S AN ACCURATE DESCRIPTION OF MASTER LUKE'S HOME PLANET... TATOOINE!
TATOOINE'S A DESERT WASTELAND, MIRA... ALMOST AS IF IT HAD BEEN HIT BY YOUR FATHER'S ION RING SHIP—!
MY HOME WORLD IS JUST THE OPPOSITE! KESSEL IS SO BEAUTIFUL—!
I'D LIKE TO VISIT YOU THERE, MIRA!
YOU BELIEVE MY FATHER IS A GOOD MAN, DON'T YOU, LUKE?
I DON'T THINK HAN SOLO BELIEVES THAT STORMTROOPERS ARE FORCING PAPA TO DESTROY REBEL PLANETS!
OH, HAN BELIEVES YOU! HE'S JUST BEING... CAUTIOUS!
DON'T WORRY ABOUT HAN, MIRA—! HE DOESN'T ALWAYS SHOW HIS REAL FEELINGS—!
STRAP IN, BACK THERE! WE'RE COMING OUT OF HYPER SPACE—!
THE MILLENNIUM FALCON DECELERATES TOWARD THE PLANET RION...

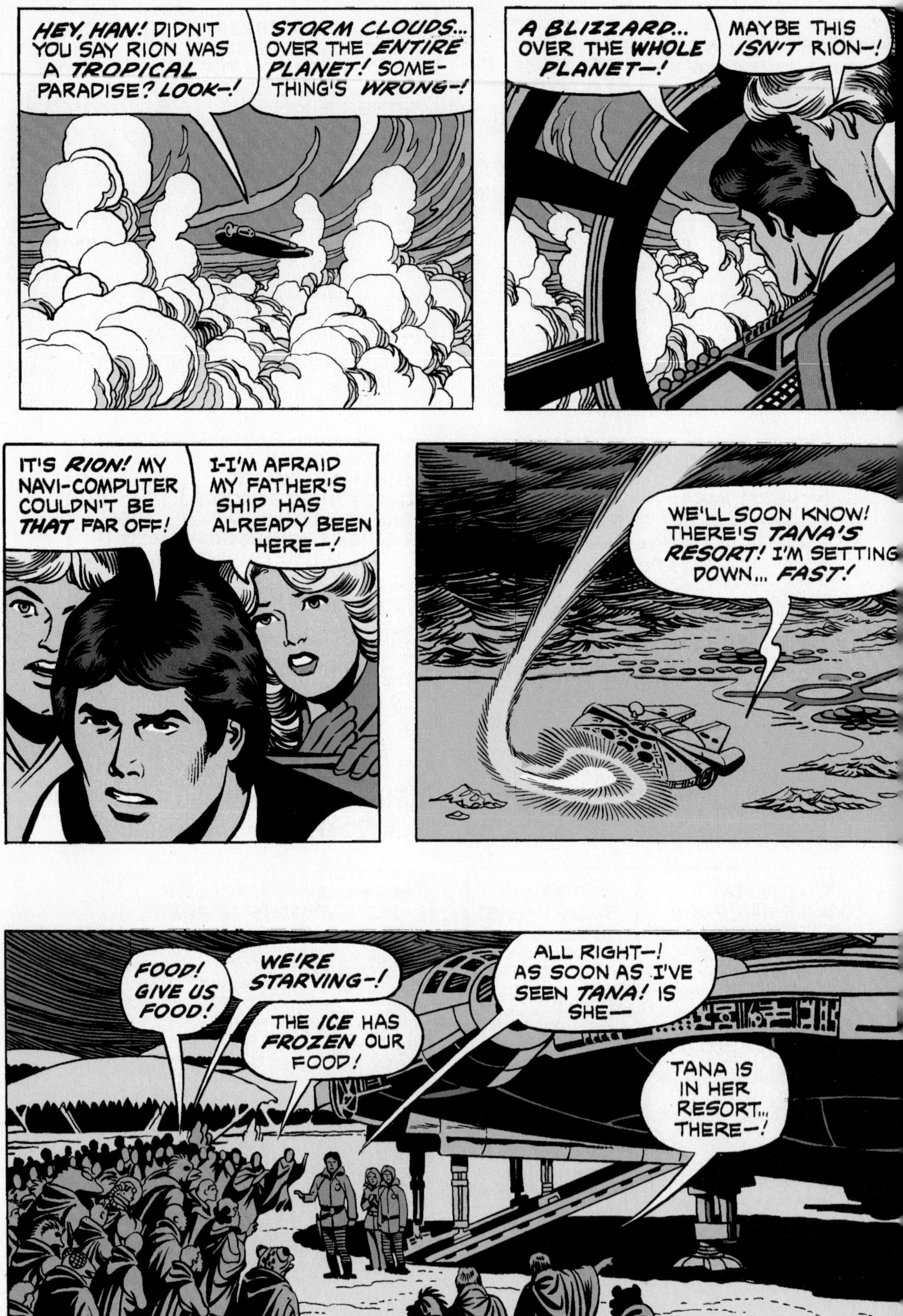
HEY, HAN! DIDN'T YOU SAY RION WAS A TROPICAL PARADISE? LOOK-!
STORM CLOUDS... OVER THE ENTIRE PLANET! SOME-THING'S WRONG-!
A BLIZZARD... OVER THE WHOLE PLANET-!
MAYBE THIS ISN'T RION-!
IT'S RION! MY NAVI-COMPUTER COULDN'T BE THAT FAR OFF!
I-I'M AFRAID MY FATHER'S SHIP HAS ALREADY BEEN HERE-!
WE'LL SOON KNOW! THERE'S TANA'S RESORT! I'M SETTING DOWN... FAST!
FOOD! GIVE US FOOD!
WE'RE STARVING-!
THE ICE HAS FROZEN OUR FOOD!
ALL RIGHT-! AS SOON AS I'VE SEEN TANA! IS SHE-
TANA IS IN HER RESORT... THERE-!

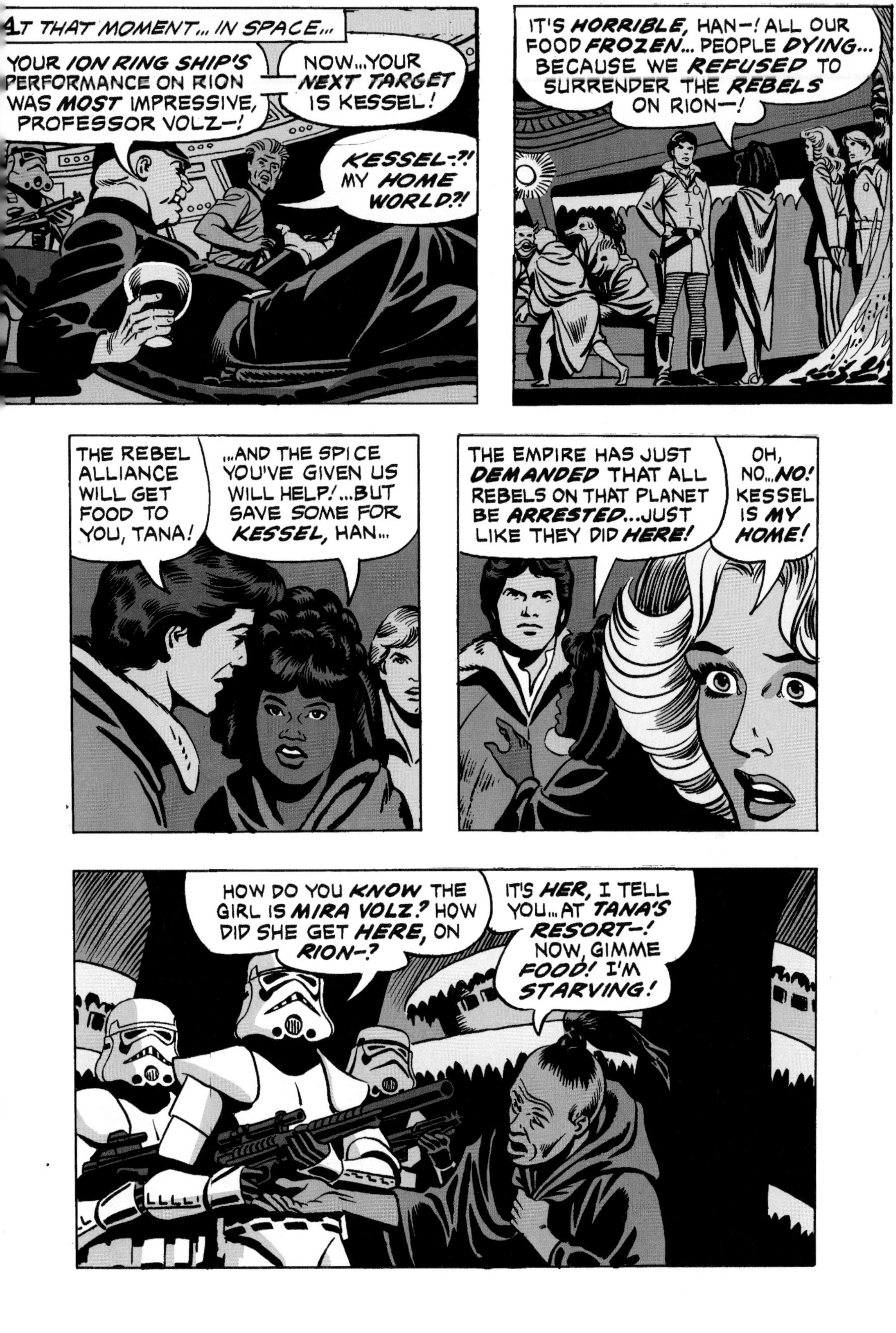
AT THAT MOMENT... IN SPACE...
YOUR ION RING SHIP'S PERFORMANCE ON RION WAS MOST IMPRESSIVE, PROFESSOR VOLZ--!
NOW...YOUR NEXT TARGET IS KESSEL!
KESSEL-?! MY HOME WORLD?!
IT'S HORRIBLE, HAN--! ALL OUR FOOD FROZEN... PEOPLE DYING... BECAUSE WE REFUSED TO SURRENDER THE REBELS ON RION--!
THE REBEL ALLIANCE WILL GET FOOD TO YOU, TANA!
...AND THE SPICE YOU'VE GIVEN US WILL HELP! ...BUT SAVE SOME FOR KESSEL, HAN...
THE EMPIRE HAS JUST DEMANDED THAT ALL REBELS ON THAT PLANET BE ARRESTED...JUST LIKE THEY DID HERE!
OH, NO...NO! KESSEL IS MY HOME!
HOW DO YOU KNOW THE GIRL IS MIRA VOLZ? HOW DID SHE GET HERE, ON RION-?
IT'S HER, I TELL YOU...AT TANA'S RESORT--! NOW, GIMME FOOD! I'M STARVING!

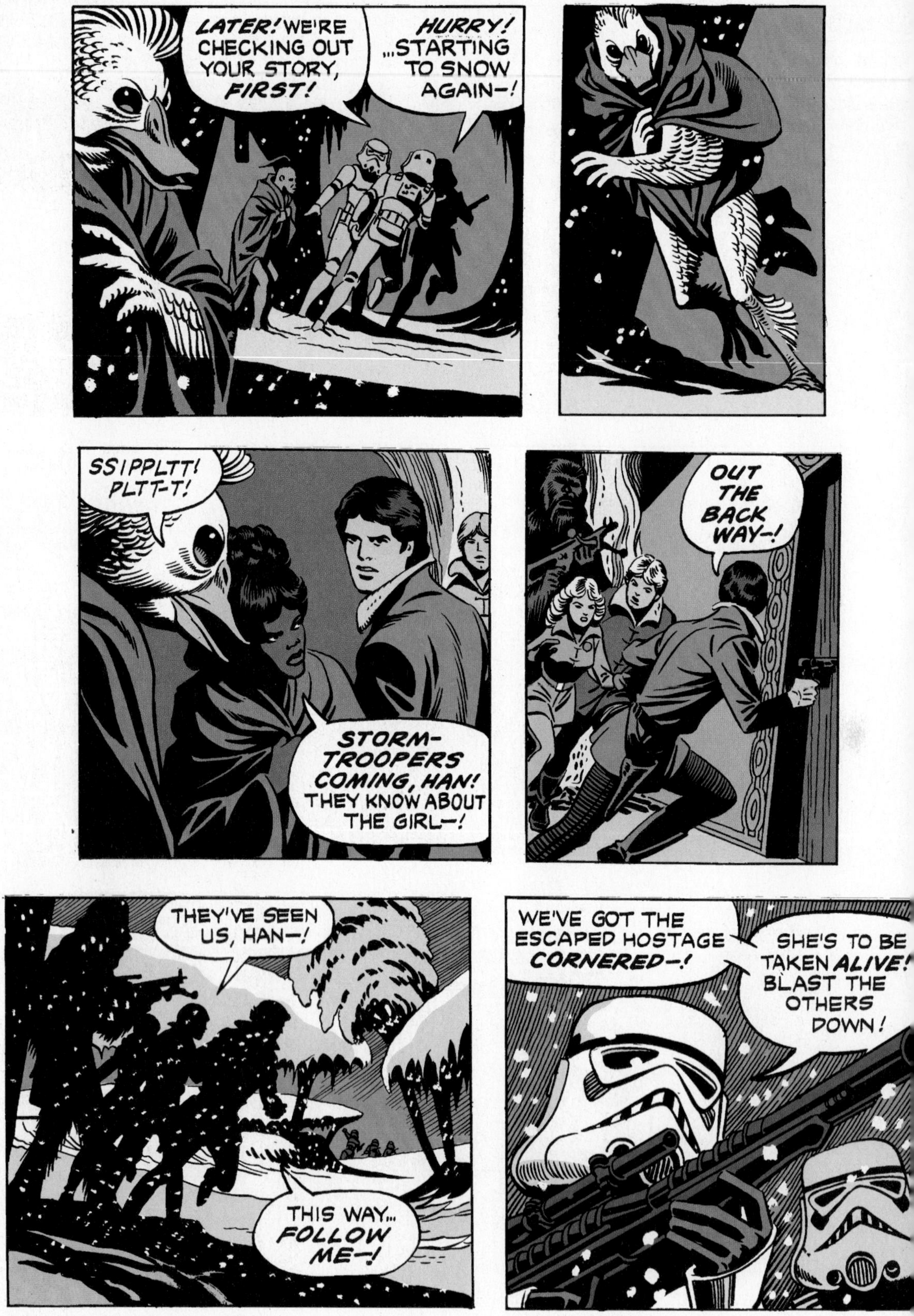
LATER! WE'RE CHECKING OUT YOUR STORY, FIRST!
HURRY! ...STARTING TO SNOW AGAIN-!
SSIPPLTT! PLTT-T!
STORM-TROOPERS COMING, HAN! THEY KNOW ABOUT THE GIRL-!
OUT THE BACK WAY-!
THEY'VE SEEN US, HAN-!
THIS WAY... FOLLOW ME-!
WE'VE GOT THE ESCAPED HOSTAGE CORNERED-!
SHE'S TO BE TAKEN ALIVE! BLAST THE OTHERS DOWN!

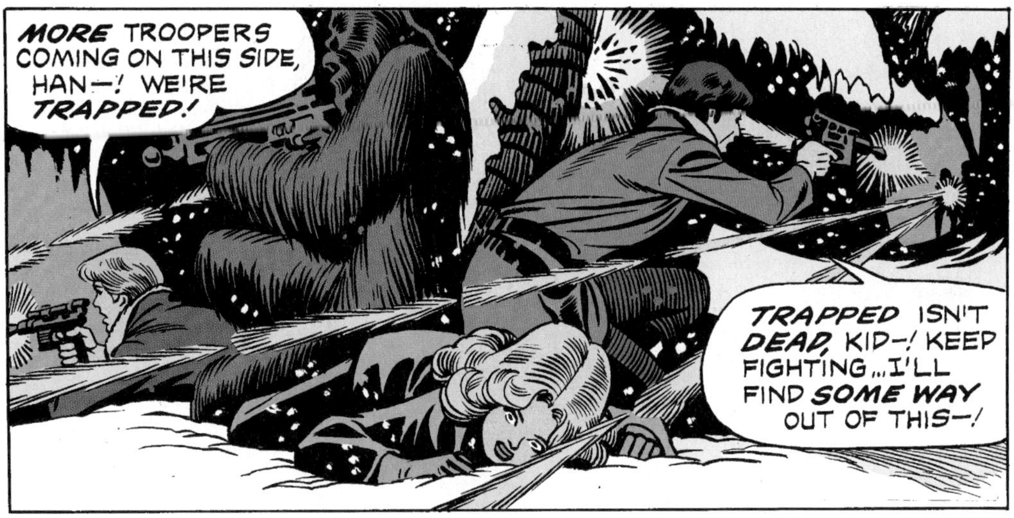
MORE TROOPERS COMING ON THIS SIDE, HAN—! WE'RE TRAPPED!
TRAPPED ISN'T DEAD, KID—! KEEP FIGHTING...I'LL FIND SOME WAY OUT OF THIS—!

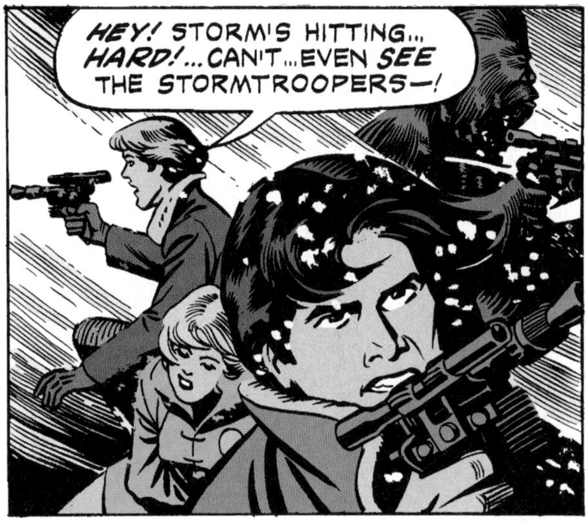
HEY! STORM'S HITTING... HARD!...CAN'T...EVEN SEE THE STORMTROOPERS—!

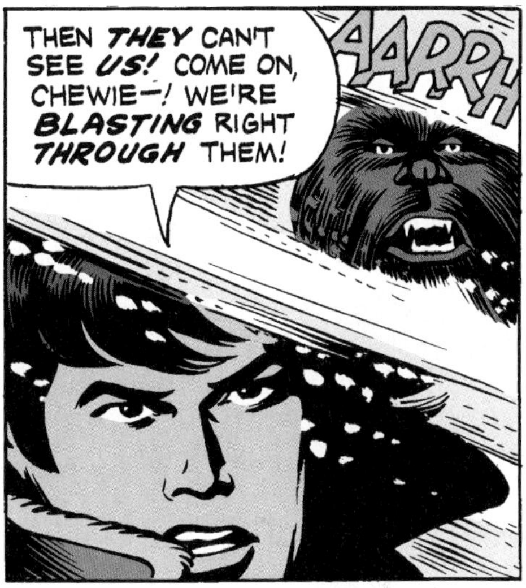
THEN THEY CAN'T SEE US! COME ON, CHEWIE—! WE'RE BLASTING RIGHT THROUGH THEM!
AARRH

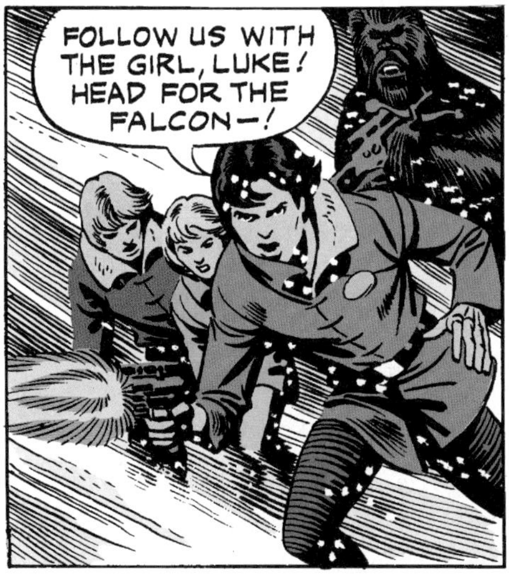
FOLLOW US WITH THE GIRL, LUKE! HEAD FOR THE FALCON—!

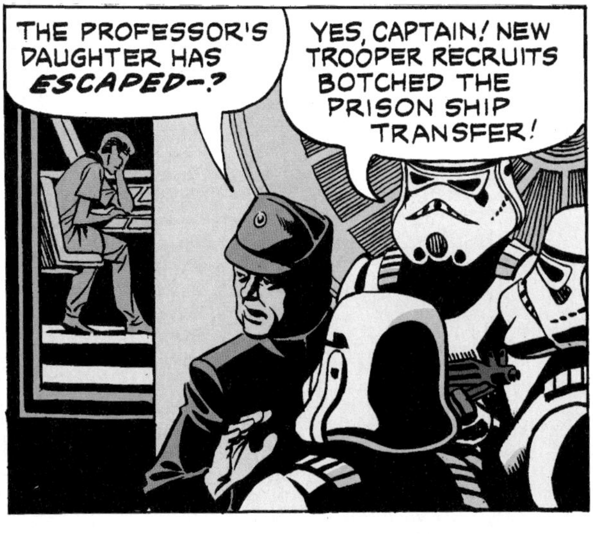
THE PROFESSOR'S DAUGHTER HAS ESCAPED—?
YES, CAPTAIN! NEW TROOPER RECRUITS BOTCHED THE PRISON SHIP TRANSFER!

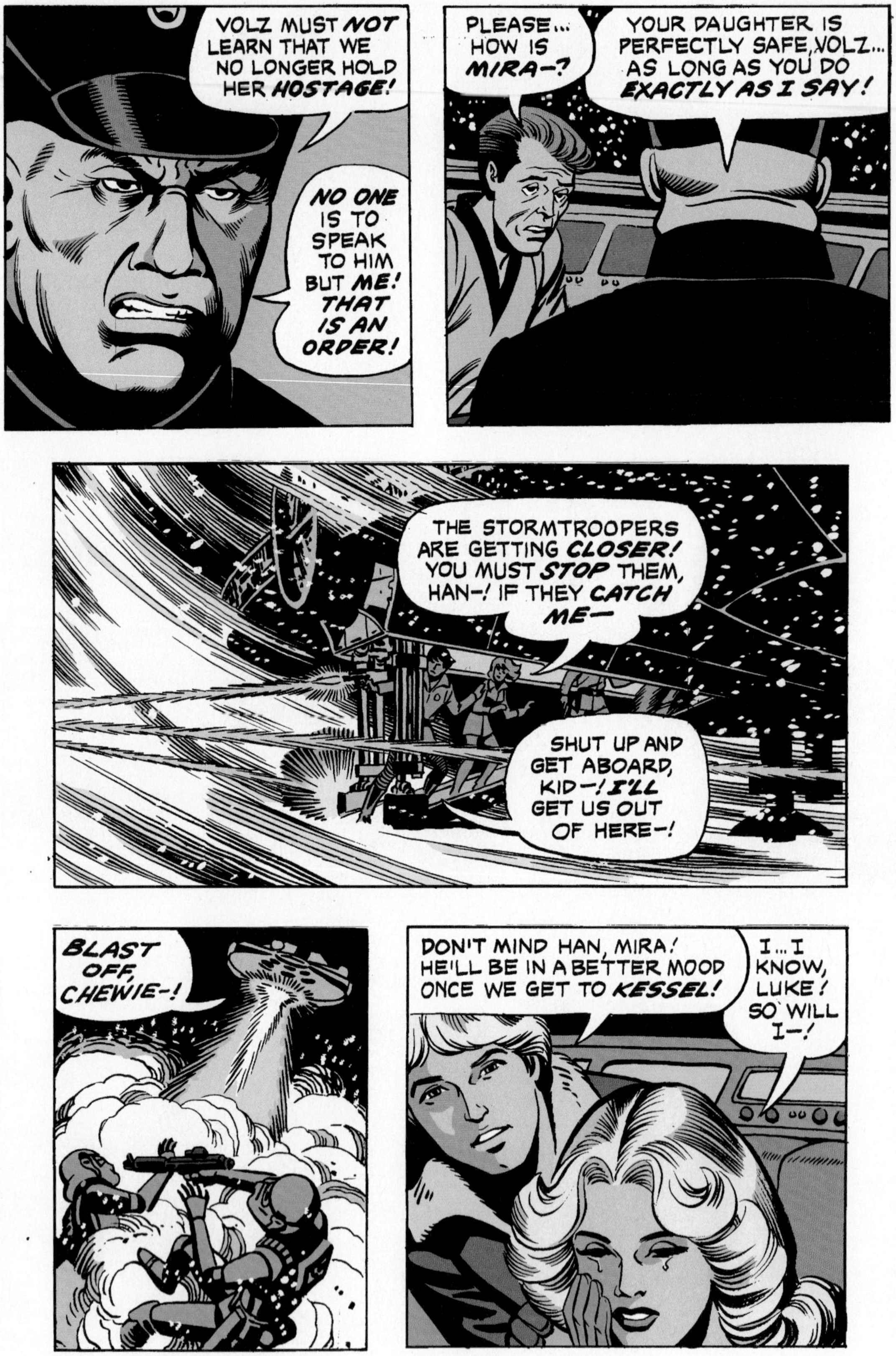
VOLZ MUST NOT LEARN THAT WE NO LONGER HOLD HER HOSTAGE!
NO ONE IS TO SPEAK TO HIM BUT ME! THAT IS AN ORDER!
PLEASE... HOW IS MIRA-?
YOUR DAUGHTER IS PERFECTLY SAFE, VOLZ... AS LONG AS YOU DO EXACTLY AS I SAY!
THE STORMTROOPERS ARE GETTING CLOSER! YOU MUST STOP THEM, HAN-! IF THEY CATCH ME—
SHUT UP AND GET ABOARD, KID-! I'LL GET US OUT OF HERE-!
BLAST OFF, CHEWIE-!
DON'T MIND HAN, MIRA! HE'LL BE IN A BETTER MOOD ONCE WE GET TO KESSEL!
I... I KNOW, LUKE! SO WILL I-!

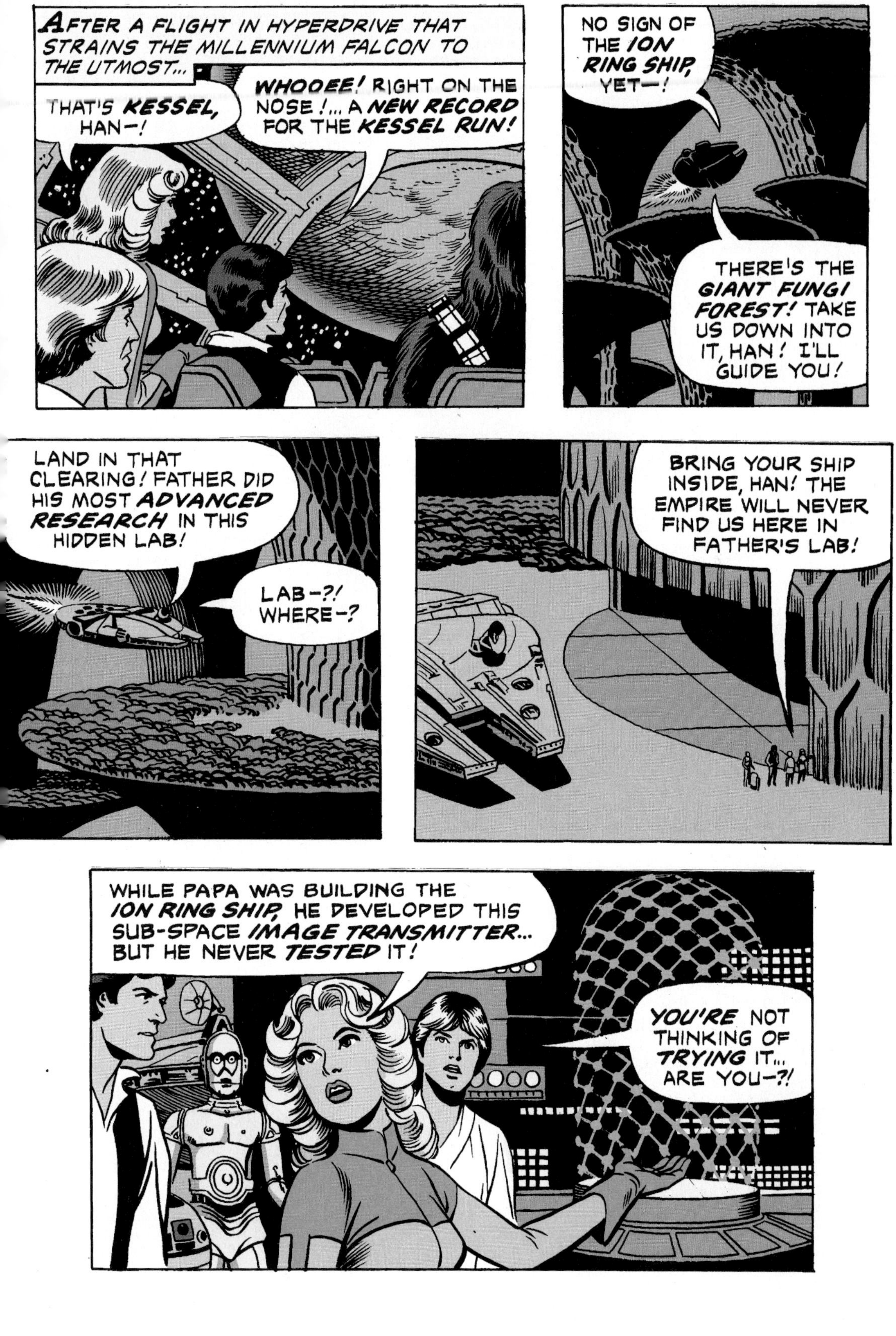
AFTER A FLIGHT IN HYPERDRIVE THAT STRAINS THE MILLENNIUM FALCON TO THE UTMOST...
THAT'S KESSEL, HAN--!
WHOOEE! RIGHT ON THE NOSE!... A NEW RECORD FOR THE KESSEL RUN!
NO SIGN OF THE ION RING SHIP, YET--!
THERE'S THE GIANT FUNGI FOREST! TAKE US DOWN INTO IT, HAN! I'LL GUIDE YOU!
LAND IN THAT CLEARING! FATHER DID HIS MOST ADVANCED RESEARCH IN THIS HIDDEN LAB!
LAB--?! WHERE--?
BRING YOUR SHIP INSIDE, HAN! THE EMPIRE WILL NEVER FIND US HERE IN FATHER'S LAB!
WHILE PAPA WAS BUILDING THE ION RING SHIP, HE DEVELOPED THIS SUB-SPACE IMAGE TRANSMITTER... BUT HE NEVER TESTED IT!
YOU'RE NOT THINKING OF TRYING IT... ARE YOU--?!

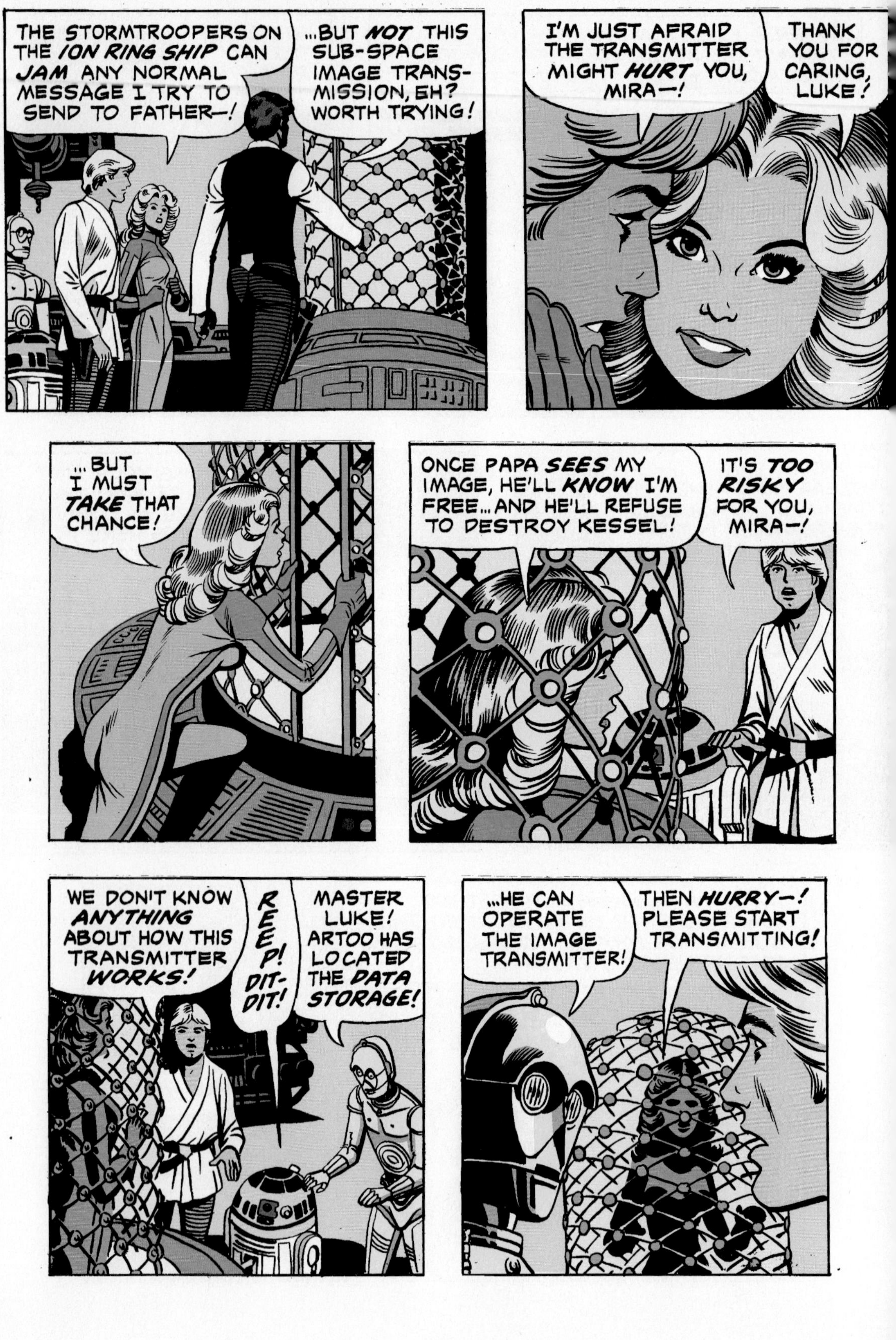
THE STORMTROOPERS ON THE ION RING SHIP CAN JAM ANY NORMAL MESSAGE I TRY TO SEND TO FATHER—!
...BUT NOT THIS SUB-SPACE IMAGE TRANSMISSION, EH? WORTH TRYING!
I'M JUST AFRAID THE TRANSMITTER MIGHT HURT YOU, MIRA—!
THANK YOU FOR CARING, LUKE!
...BUT I MUST TAKE THAT CHANCE!
ONCE PAPA SEES MY IMAGE, HE'LL KNOW I'M FREE... AND HE'LL REFUSE TO DESTROY KESSEL!
IT'S TOO RISKY FOR YOU, MIRA—!
WE DON'T KNOW ANYTHING ABOUT HOW THIS TRANSMITTER WORKS!
REEP! DIT-DIT!
MASTER LUKE! ARTOO HAS LOCATED THE DATA STORAGE!
...HE CAN OPERATE THE IMAGE TRANSMITTER!
THEN HURRY—! PLEASE START TRANSMITTING!

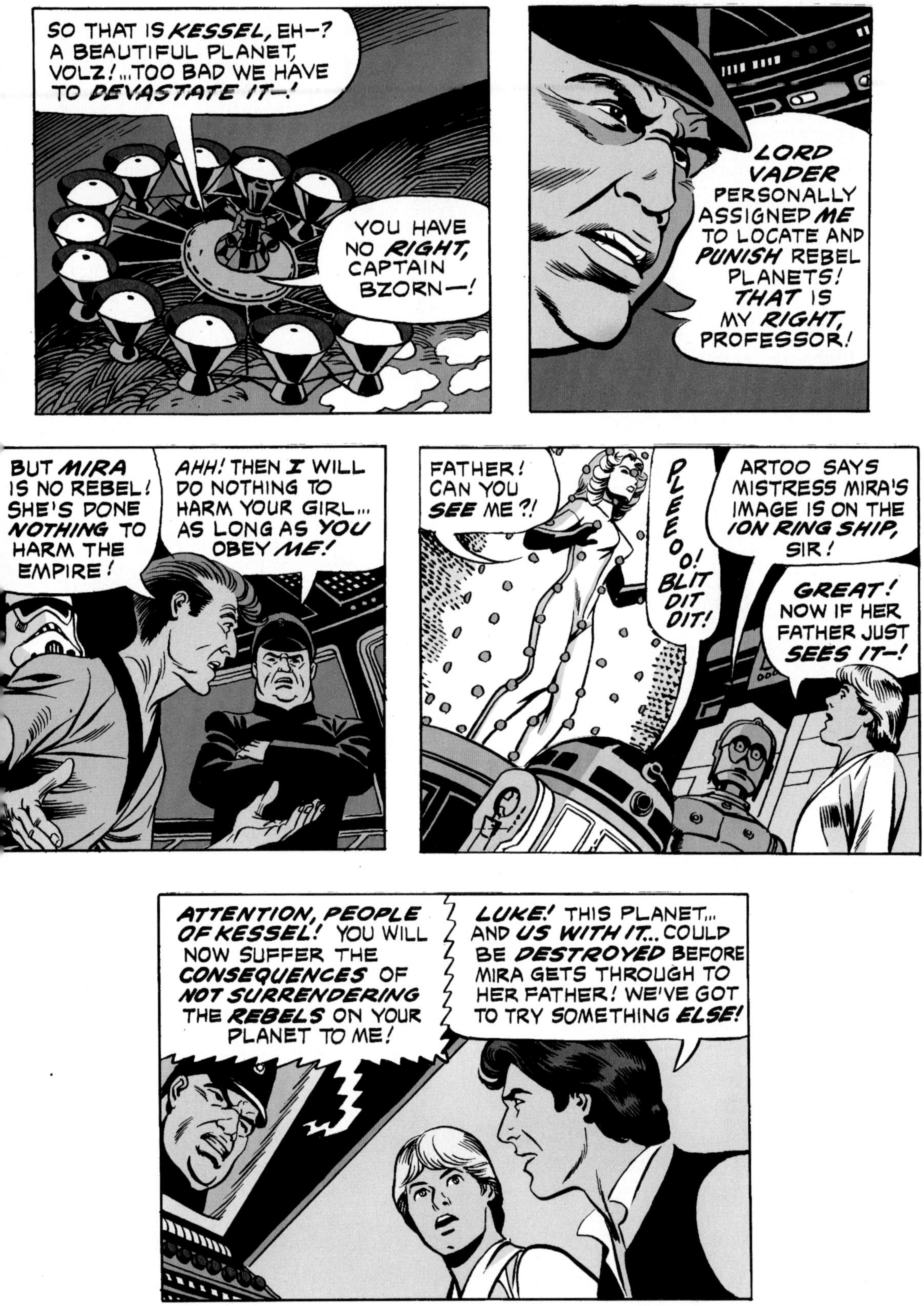

SO THAT IS KESSEL, EH-? A BEAUTIFUL PLANET, VOLZ!...TOO BAD WE HAVE TO DEVASTATE IT-!
YOU HAVE NO RIGHT, CAPTAIN BZORN-!
LORD VADER PERSONALLY ASSIGNED ME TO LOCATE AND PUNISH REBEL PLANETS! THAT IS MY RIGHT, PROFESSOR!
BUT MIRA IS NO REBEL! SHE'S DONE NOTHING TO HARM THE EMPIRE!
AHH! THEN I WILL DO NOTHING TO HARM YOUR GIRL... AS LONG AS YOU OBEY ME!
FATHER! CAN YOU SEE ME?!
PLEEEOO! BLIT DIT DIT!
ARTOO SAYS MISTRESS MIRA'S IMAGE IS ON THE ION RING SHIP, SIR!
GREAT! NOW IF HER FATHER JUST SEES IT-!
ATTENTION, PEOPLE OF KESSEL! YOU WILL NOW SUFFER THE CONSEQUENCES OF NOT SURRENDERING THE REBELS ON YOUR PLANET TO ME!
LUKE! THIS PLANET... AND US WITH IT... COULD BE DESTROYED BEFORE MIRA GETS THROUGH TO HER FATHER! WE'VE GOT TO TRY SOMETHING ELSE!

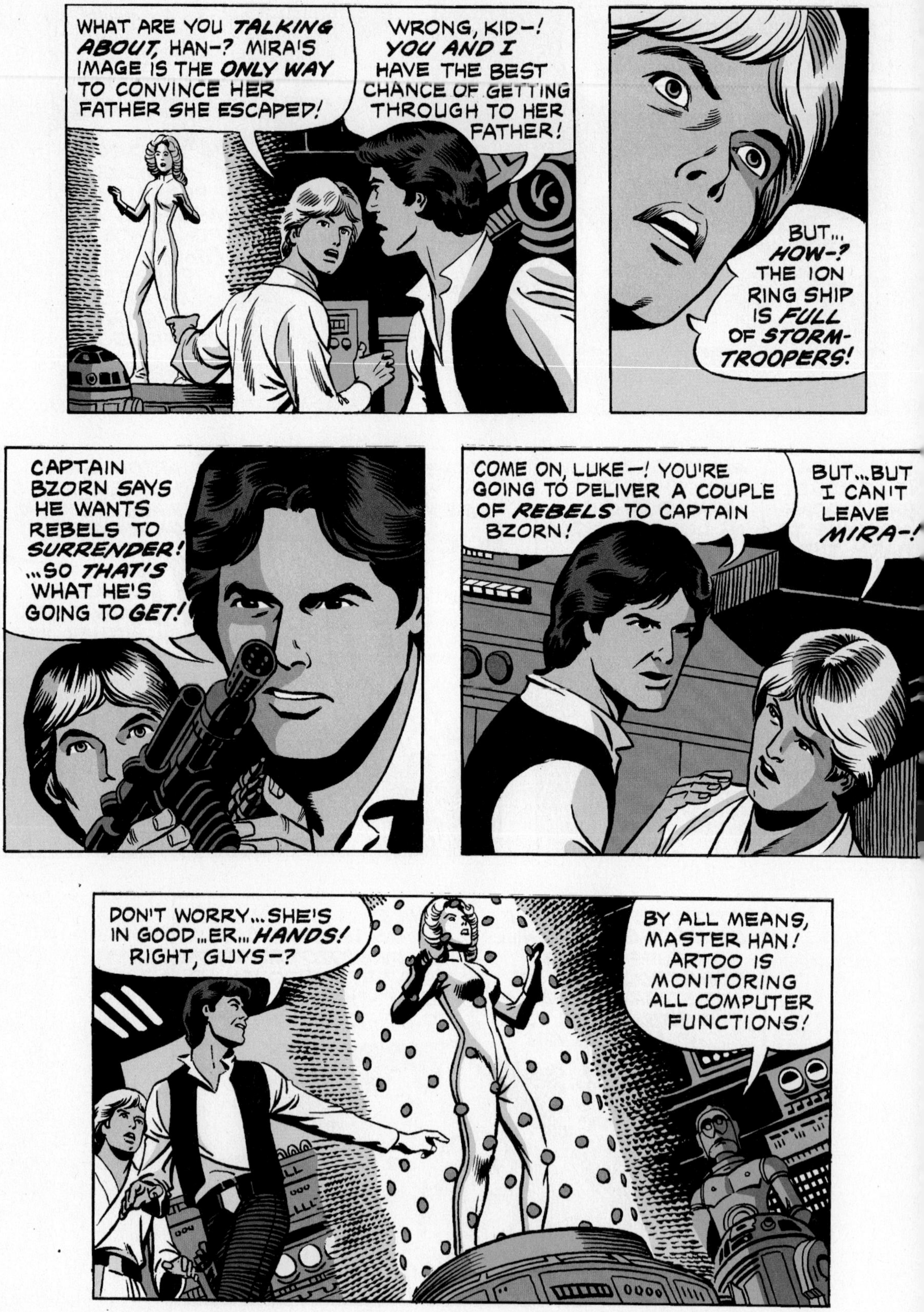
WHAT ARE YOU TALKING ABOUT, HAN-? MIRA'S IMAGE IS THE ONLY WAY TO CONVINCE HER FATHER SHE ESCAPED!
WRONG, KID-! YOU AND I HAVE THE BEST CHANCE OF GETTING THROUGH TO HER FATHER!
BUT... HOW-? THE ION RING SHIP IS FULL OF STORM-TROOPERS!
CAPTAIN BZORN SAYS HE WANTS REBELS TO SURRENDER! ...SO THAT'S WHAT HE'S GOING TO GET!
COME ON, LUKE-! YOU'RE GOING TO DELIVER A COUPLE OF REBELS TO CAPTAIN BZORN!
BUT...BUT I CAN'T LEAVE MIRA-!
DON'T WORRY...SHE'S IN GOOD...ER... HANDS! RIGHT, GUYS-?
BY ALL MEANS, MASTER HAN! ARTOO IS MONITORING ALL COMPUTER FUNCTIONS!

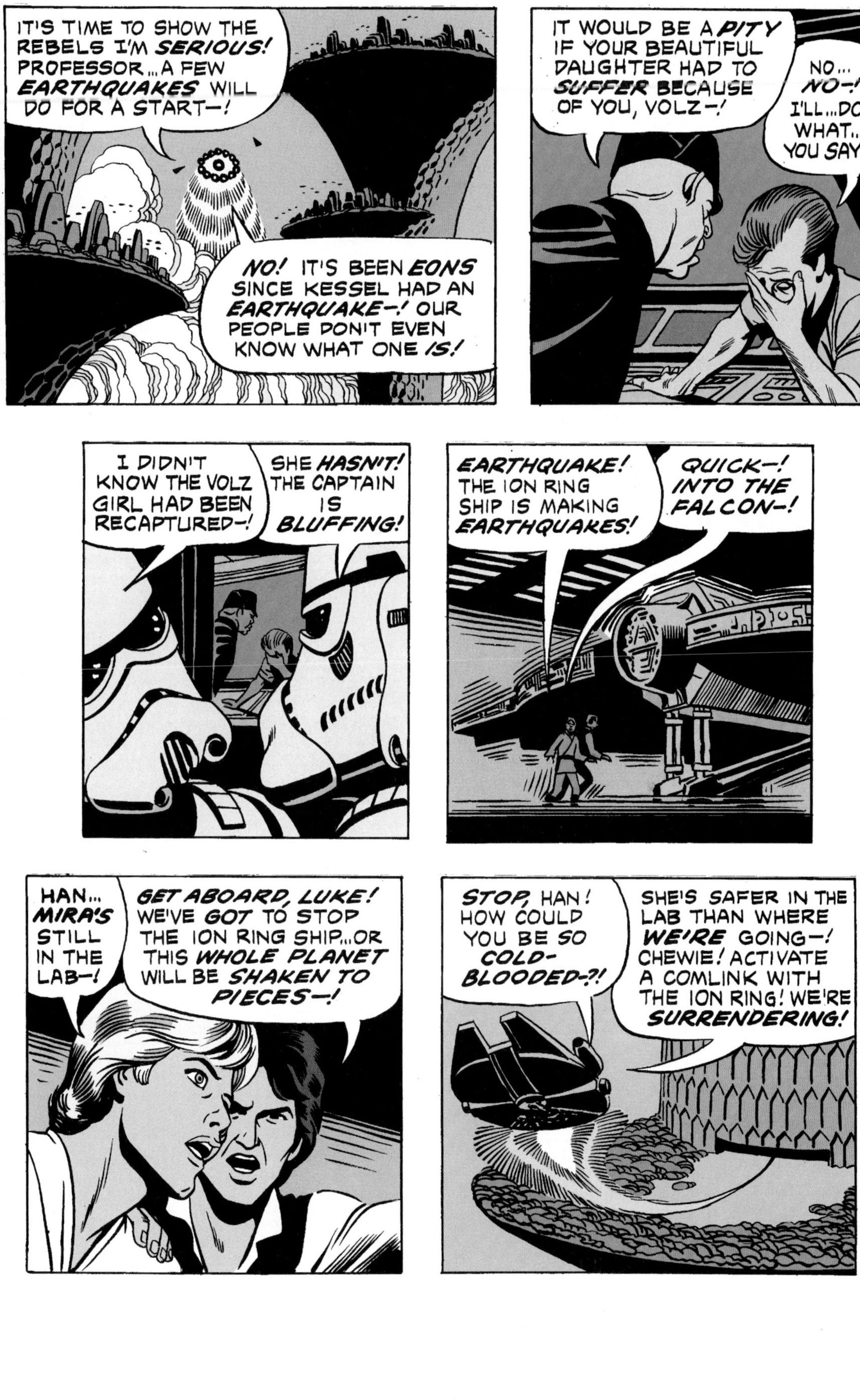
IT'S TIME TO SHOW THE REBELS I'M SERIOUS! PROFESSOR... A FEW EARTHQUAKES WILL DO FOR A START--!
NO! IT'S BEEN EONS SINCE KESSEL HAD AN EARTHQUAKE--! OUR PEOPLE DON'T EVEN KNOW WHAT ONE IS!
IT WOULD BE A PITY IF YOUR BEAUTIFUL DAUGHTER HAD TO SUFFER BECAUSE OF YOU, VOLZ--!
NO... NO--! I'LL... DO WHAT... YOU SAY!
I DIDN'T KNOW THE VOLZ GIRL HAD BEEN RECAPTURED--!
SHE HASN'T! THE CAPTAIN IS BLUFFING!
EARTHQUAKE! THE ION RING SHIP IS MAKING EARTHQUAKES!
QUICK--! INTO THE FALCON--!
HAN... MIRA'S STILL IN THE LAB--!
GET ABOARD, LUKE! WE'VE GOT TO STOP THE ION RING SHIP... OR THIS WHOLE PLANET WILL BE SHAKEN TO PIECES--!
STOP, HAN! HOW COULD YOU BE SO COLD-BLOODED--?!
SHE'S SAFER IN THE LAB THAN WHERE WE'RE GOING--! CHEWIE! ACTIVATE A COMLINK WITH THE ION RING! WE'RE SURRENDERING!

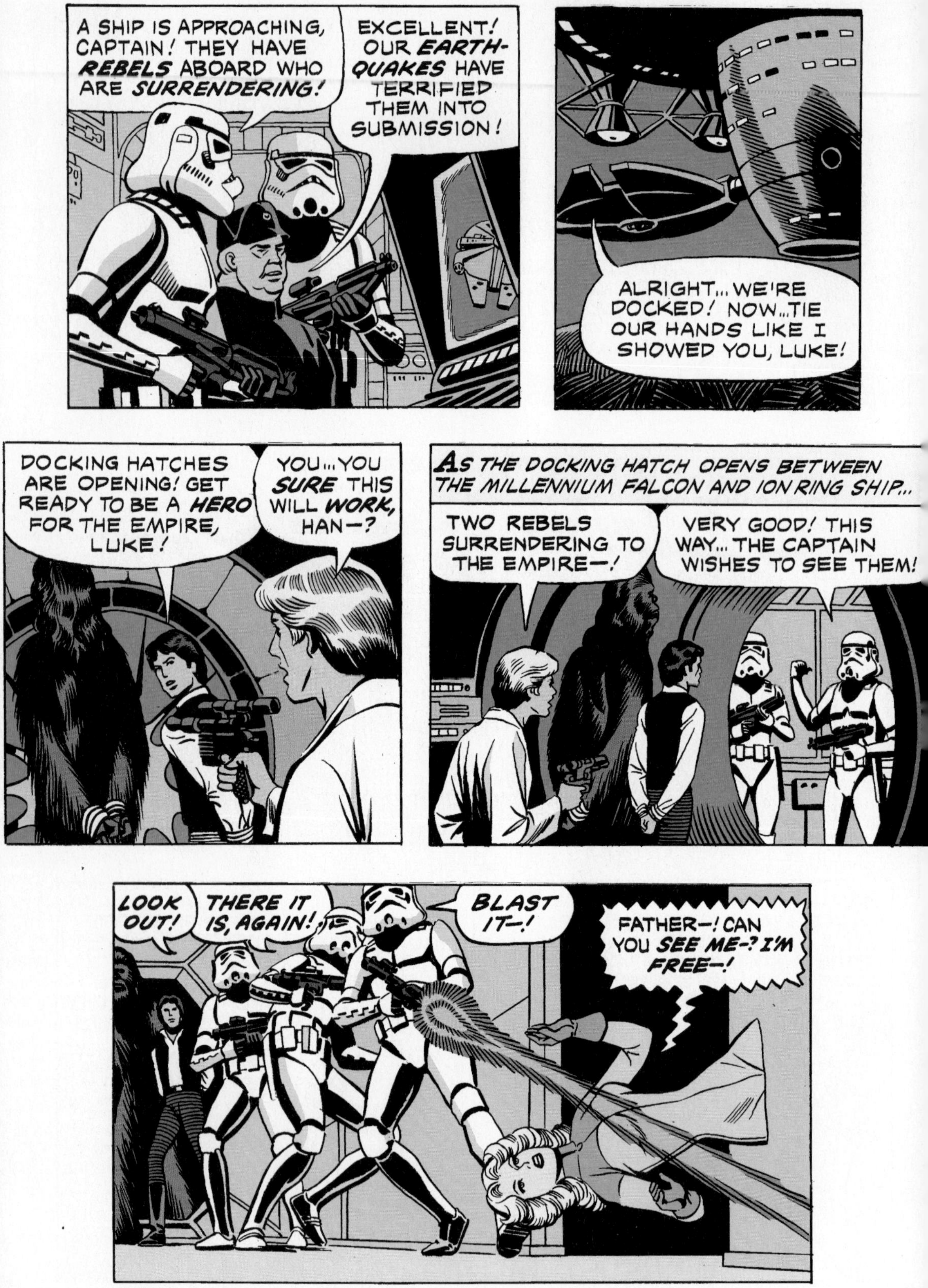
A SHIP IS APPROACHING, CAPTAIN! THEY HAVE REBELS ABOARD WHO ARE SURRENDERING!
EXCELLENT! OUR EARTH-QUAKES HAVE TERRIFIED THEM INTO SUBMISSION!
ALRIGHT... WE'RE DOCKED! NOW... TIE OUR HANDS LIKE I SHOWED YOU, LUKE!
DOCKING HATCHES ARE OPENING! GET READY TO BE A HERO FOR THE EMPIRE, LUKE!
YOU... YOU SURE THIS WILL WORK, HAN—?
AS THE DOCKING HATCH OPENS BETWEEN THE MILLENNIUM FALCON AND ION RING SHIP...
TWO REBELS SURRENDERING TO THE EMPIRE—!
VERY GOOD! THIS WAY... THE CAPTAIN WISHES TO SEE THEM!
LOOK OUT!
THERE IT IS, AGAIN!
BLAST IT—!
FATHER—! CAN YOU SEE ME—? I'M FREE—!

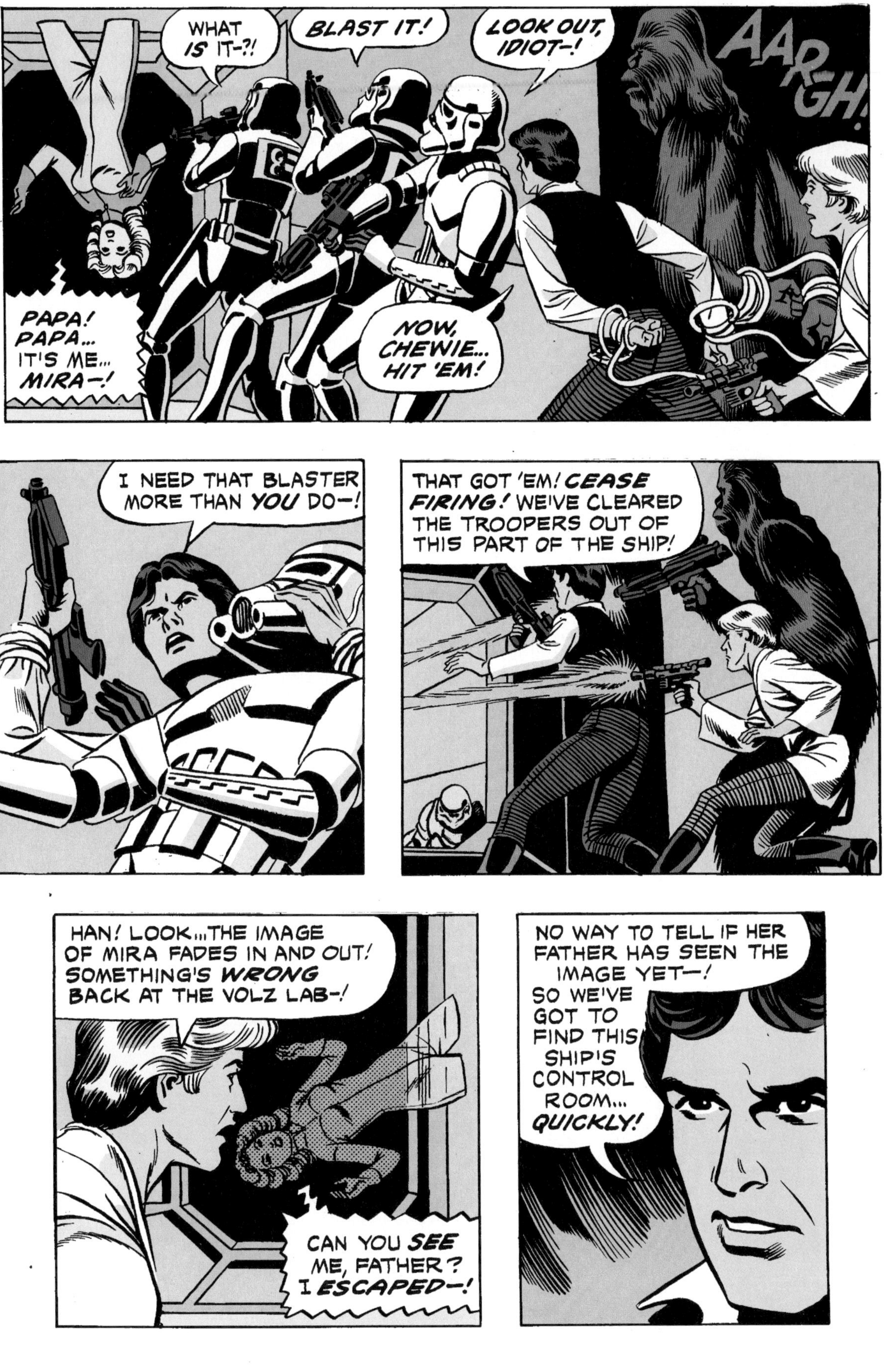
WHAT IS IT-?!
BLAST IT!
LOOK OUT, IDIOT-!
AARGH!
PAPA! PAPA... IT'S ME... MIRA-!
NOW, CHEWIE... HIT 'EM!
I NEED THAT BLASTER MORE THAN YOU DO-!
THAT GOT 'EM! CEASE FIRING! WE'VE CLEARED THE TROOPERS OUT OF THIS PART OF THE SHIP!
HAN! LOOK...THE IMAGE OF MIRA FADES IN AND OUT! SOMETHING'S WRONG BACK AT THE VOLZ LAB-!
CAN YOU SEE ME, FATHER? I ESCAPED-!
NO WAY TO TELL IF HER FATHER HAS SEEN THE IMAGE YET-! SO WE'VE GOT TO FIND THIS SHIP'S CONTROL ROOM... QUICKLY!

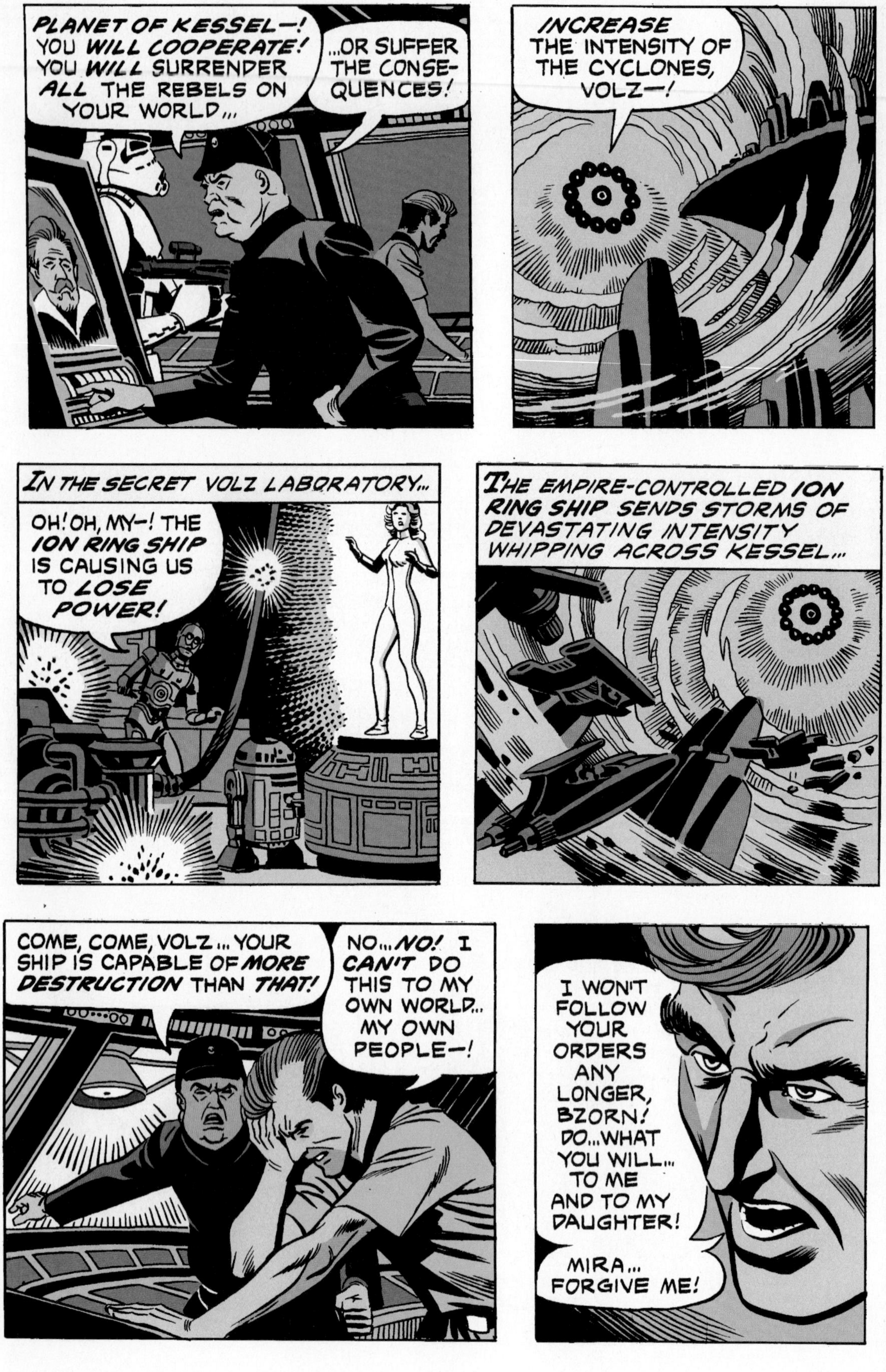
PLANET OF KESSEL—! YOU WILL COOPERATE! YOU WILL SURRENDER ALL THE REBELS ON YOUR WORLD...
...OR SUFFER THE CONSE-QUENCES!
INCREASE THE INTENSITY OF THE CYCLONES, VOLZ—!
IN THE SECRET VOLZ LABORATORY...
OH! OH, MY—! THE ION RING SHIP IS CAUSING US TO LOSE POWER!
THE EMPIRE-CONTROLLED ION RING SHIP SENDS STORMS OF DEVASTATING INTENSITY WHIPPING ACROSS KESSEL...
COME, COME, VOLZ... YOUR SHIP IS CAPABLE OF MORE DESTRUCTION THAN THAT!
NO... NO! I CAN'T DO THIS TO MY OWN WORLD... MY OWN PEOPLE—!
I WON'T FOLLOW YOUR ORDERS ANY LONGER, BZORN! DO...WHAT YOU WILL... TO ME AND TO MY DAUGHTER!
MIRA... FORGIVE ME!

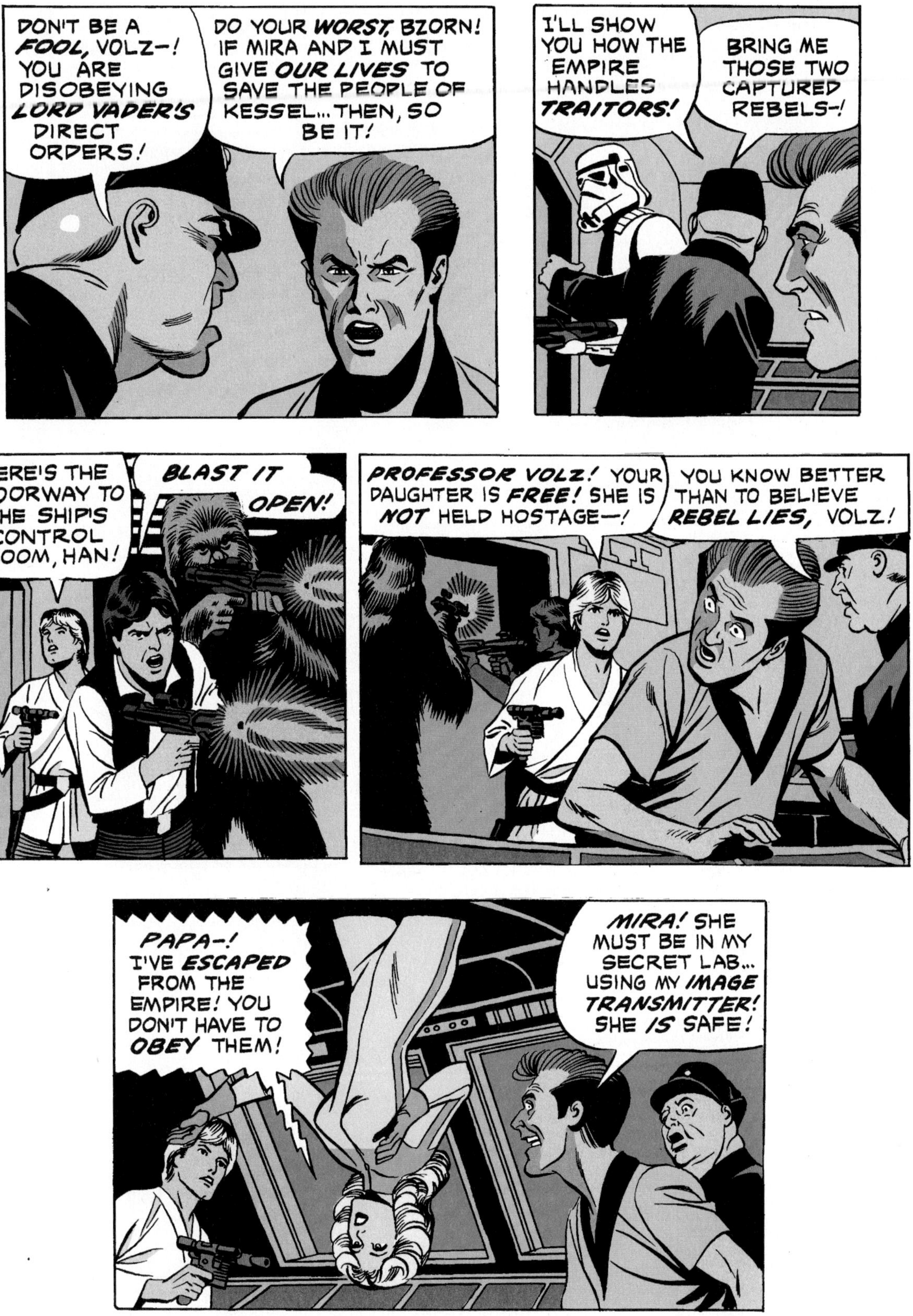
DON'T BE A FOOL, VOLZ-! YOU ARE DISOBEYING LORD VADER'S DIRECT ORDERS!
DO YOUR WORST, BZORN! IF MIRA AND I MUST GIVE OUR LIVES TO SAVE THE PEOPLE OF KESSEL... THEN, SO BE IT!
I'LL SHOW YOU HOW THE EMPIRE HANDLES TRAITORS!
BRING ME THOSE TWO CAPTURED REBELS-!
HERE'S THE DOORWAY TO THE SHIP'S CONTROL ROOM, HAN!
BLAST IT OPEN!
PROFESSOR VOLZ! YOUR DAUGHTER IS FREE! SHE IS NOT HELD HOSTAGE—!
YOU KNOW BETTER THAN TO BELIEVE REBEL LIES, VOLZ!
PAPA-! I'VE ESCAPED FROM THE EMPIRE! YOU DON'T HAVE TO OBEY THEM!
MIRA! SHE MUST BE IN MY SECRET LAB... USING MY IMAGE TRANSMITTER! SHE IS SAFE!

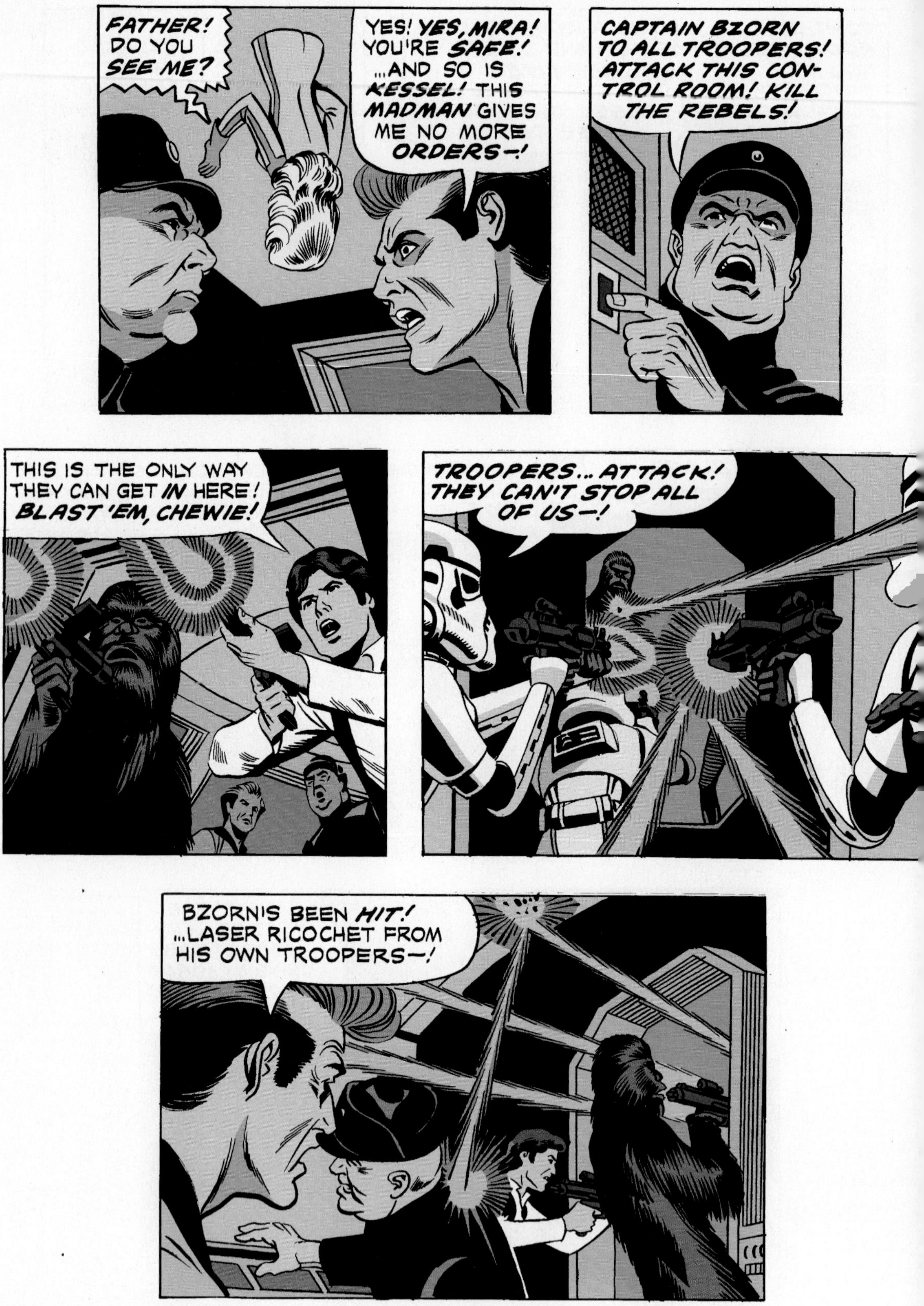
FATHER! DO YOU SEE ME?
YES! YES, MIRA! YOU'RE SAFE! ...AND SO IS KESSEL! THIS MADMAN GIVES ME NO MORE ORDERS—!
CAPTAIN BZORN TO ALL TROOPERS! ATTACK THIS CONTROL ROOM! KILL THE REBELS!
THIS IS THE ONLY WAY THEY CAN GET IN HERE! BLAST 'EM, CHEWIE!
TROOPERS... ATTACK! THEY CAN'T STOP ALL OF US—!
BZORN'S BEEN HIT! ...LASER RICOCHET FROM HIS OWN TROOPERS—!

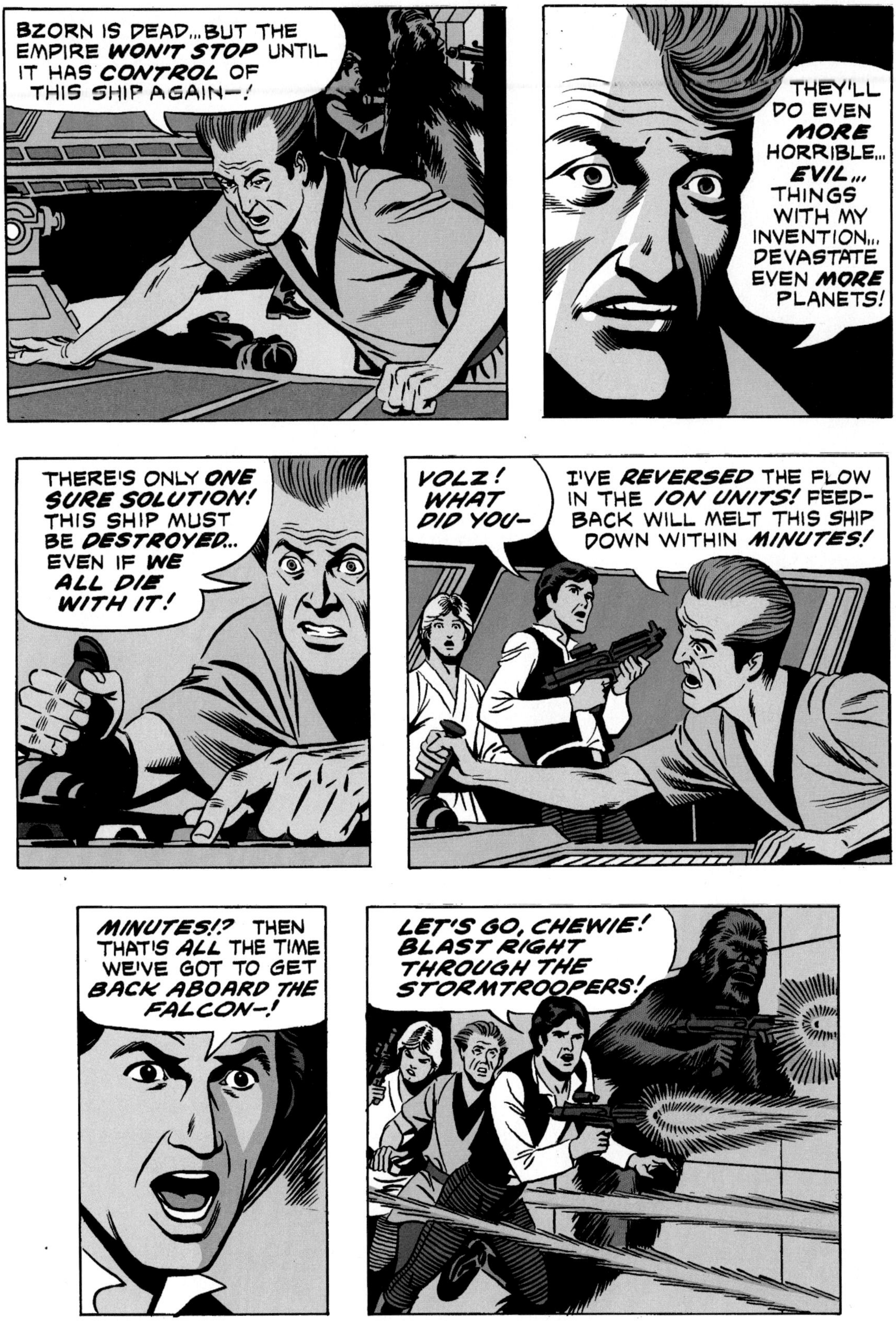
BZORN IS DEAD... BUT THE EMPIRE WON'T STOP UNTIL IT HAS CONTROL OF THIS SHIP AGAIN—!
THEY'LL DO EVEN MORE HORRIBLE... EVIL... THINGS WITH MY INVENTION... DEVASTATE EVEN MORE PLANETS!
THERE'S ONLY ONE SURE SOLUTION! THIS SHIP MUST BE DESTROYED... EVEN IF WE ALL DIE WITH IT!
VOLZ! WHAT DID YOU—
I'VE REVERSED THE FLOW IN THE ION UNITS! FEED-BACK WILL MELT THIS SHIP DOWN WITHIN MINUTES!
MINUTES!? THEN THAT'S ALL THE TIME WE'VE GOT TO GET BACK ABOARD THE FALCON—!
LET'S GO, CHEWIE! BLAST RIGHT THROUGH THE STORMTROOPERS!

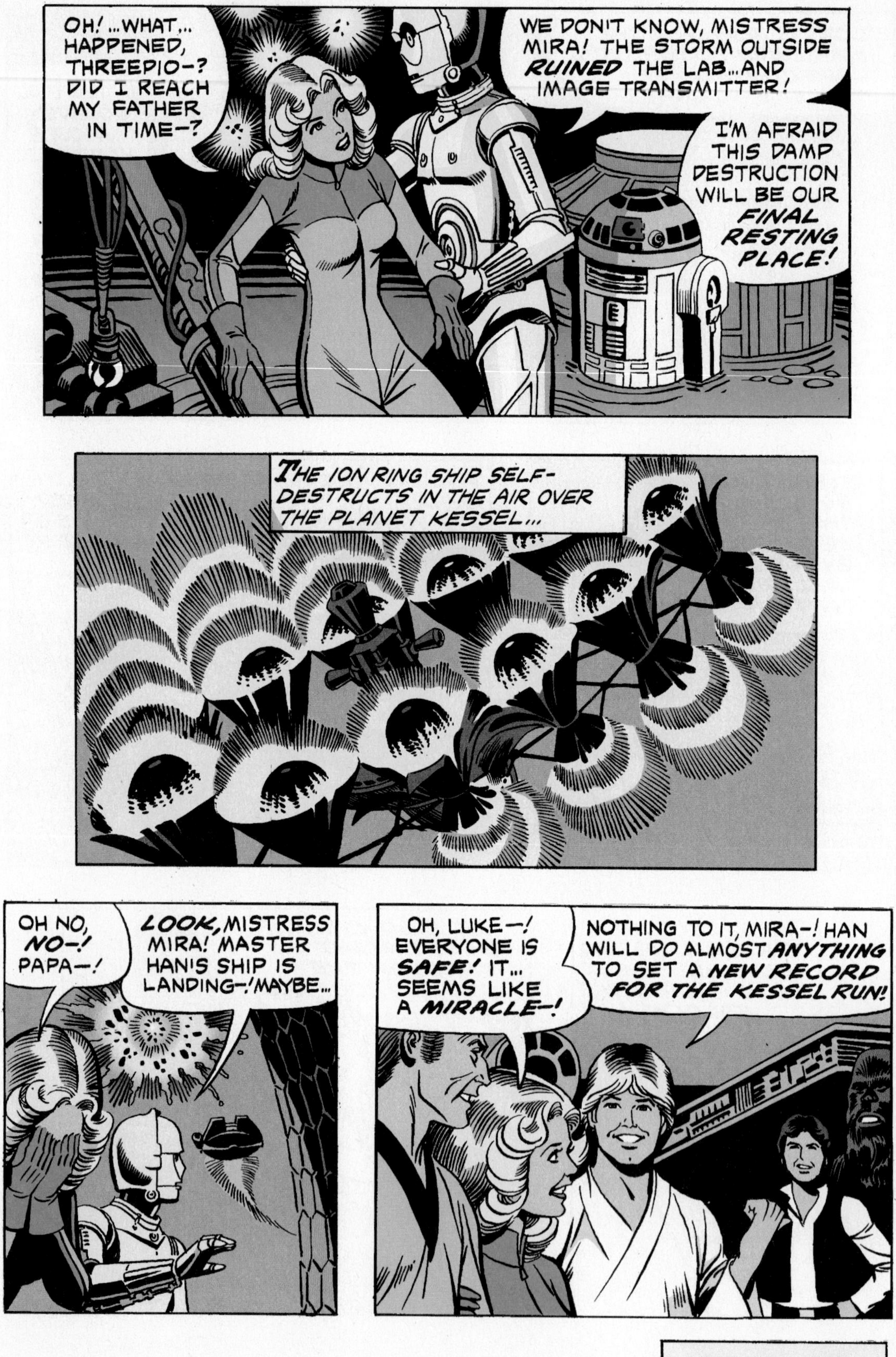
OH! ...WHAT,... HAPPENED, THREEPIO-? DID I REACH MY FATHER IN TIME-?
WE DON'T KNOW, MISTRESS MIRA! THE STORM OUTSIDE *RUINED* THE LAB...AND IMAGE TRANSMITTER!
I'M AFRAID THIS DAMP DESTRUCTION WILL BE OUR *FINAL RESTING PLACE!*
THE ION RING SHIP SELF-DESTRUCTS IN THE AIR OVER THE PLANET KESSEL...
OH NO, *NO-!* PAPA-!
LOOK, MISTRESS MIRA! MASTER HAN'S SHIP IS LANDING-! MAYBE...
OH, LUKE-! EVERYONE IS *SAFE!* IT... SEEMS LIKE A *MIRACLE-!*
NOTHING TO IT, MIRA-! HAN WILL DO ALMOST *ANYTHING* TO SET A *NEW RECORD FOR THE KESSEL RUN!*
CONTINUED NEXT ISSUE!

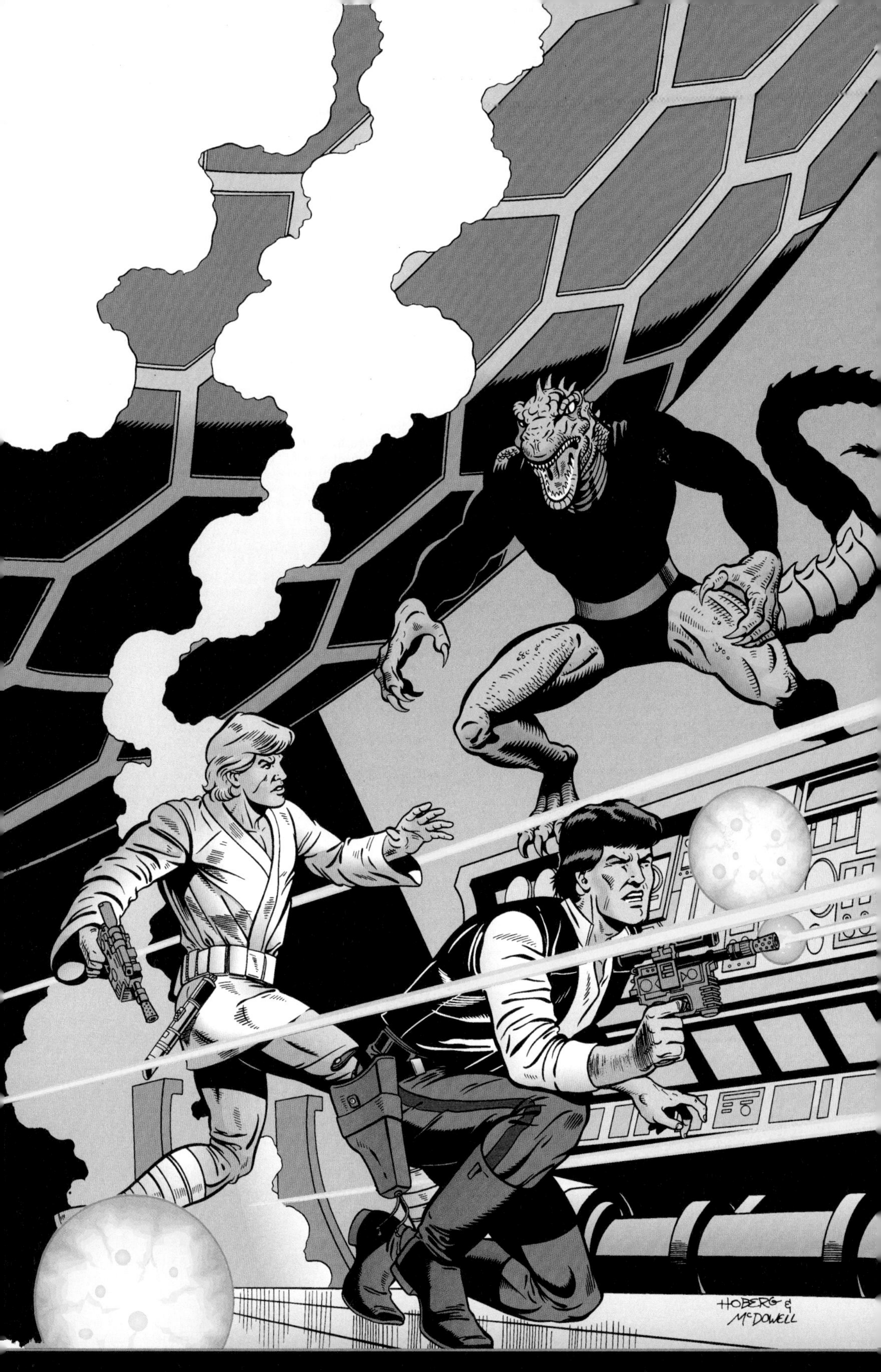
HOBERG &
McDOWELL

CLASSIC STAR WARS: THE EARLY ADVENTURES #7 **— "BRING ME THE CHILDREN"**
ORIGINALLY PUBLISHED FROM FEBRUARY 26 TO APRIL 21, 1980

WRITERS: RUSS MANNING & DON CHRISTENSEN • ARTIST & LETTERER: RUSS MANNING • ART RETOUCHING: RICK HOBERG & BRIAN SNODDY
COLORIST: RAY MURTAUGH • EDITOR: PEET JANES • COVER ARTISTS: RICK HOBERG, MISCHA MCDOWELL & MATTHEW HOLLINGSWORTH

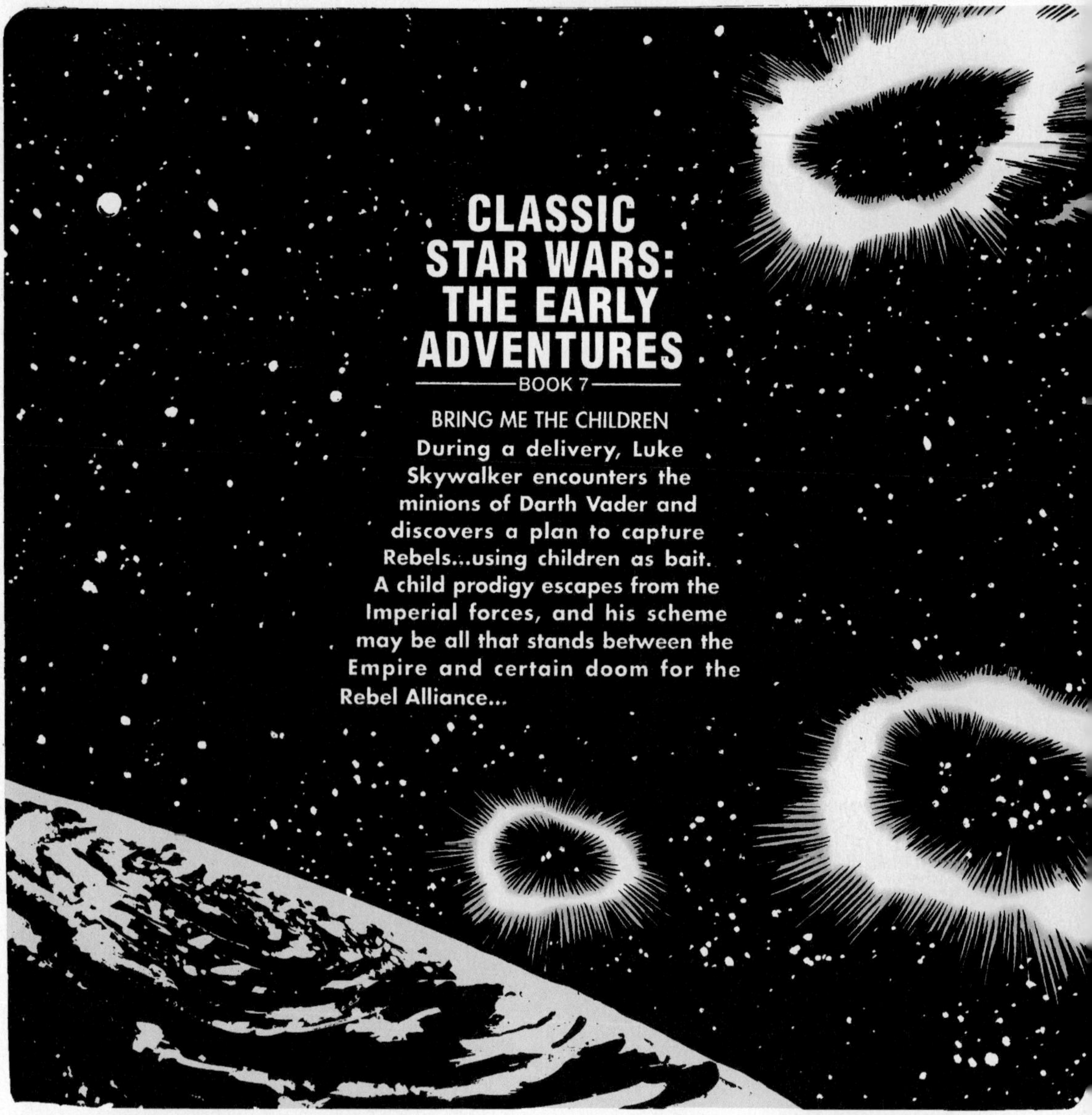
CLASSIC STAR WARS: THE EARLY ADVENTURES
BOOK 7
BRING ME THE CHILDREN
During a delivery, Luke Skywalker encounters the minions of Darth Vader and discovers a plan to capture Rebels...using children as bait. A child prodigy escapes from the Imperial forces, and his scheme may be all that stands between the Empire and certain doom for the Rebel Alliance...

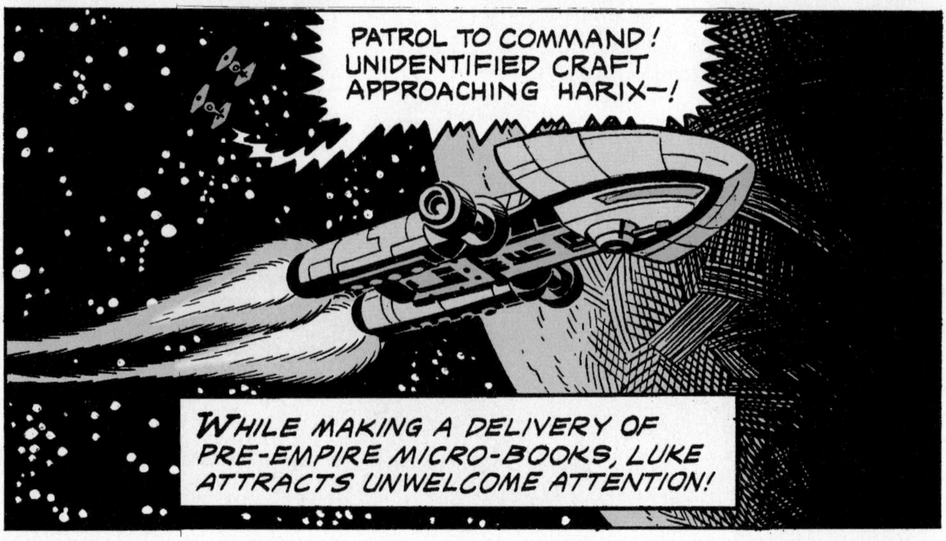
PATROL TO COMMAND! UNIDENTIFIED CRAFT APPROACHING HARIX—!
WHILE MAKING A DELIVERY OF PRE-EMPIRE MICRO-BOOKS, LUKE ATTRACTS UNWELCOME ATTENTION!

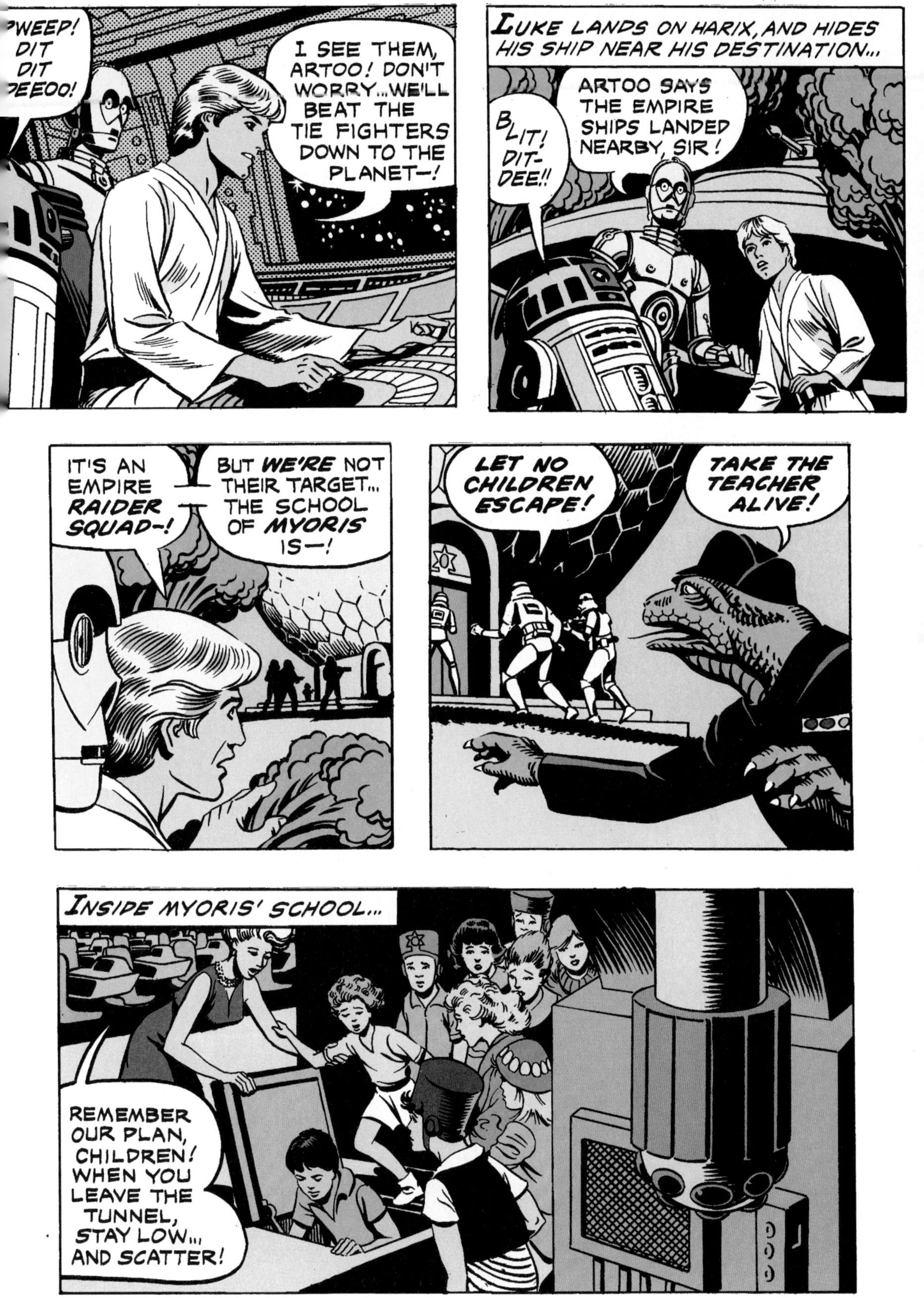
PWEEP! DIT DIT DEEOO!
I SEE THEM, ARTOO! DON'T WORRY...WE'LL BEAT THE TIE FIGHTERS DOWN TO THE PLANET--!
LUKE LANDS ON HARIX, AND HIDES HIS SHIP NEAR HIS DESTINATION...
BLIT! DIT-DEE!!
ARTOO SAYS THE EMPIRE SHIPS LANDED NEARBY, SIR!
IT'S AN EMPIRE RAIDER SQUAD--!
BUT WE'RE NOT THEIR TARGET... THE SCHOOL OF MYORIS IS--!
LET NO CHILDREN ESCAPE!
TAKE THE TEACHER ALIVE!
INSIDE MYORIS' SCHOOL...
REMEMBER OUR PLAN, CHILDREN! WHEN YOU LEAVE THE TUNNEL, STAY LOW... AND SCATTER!

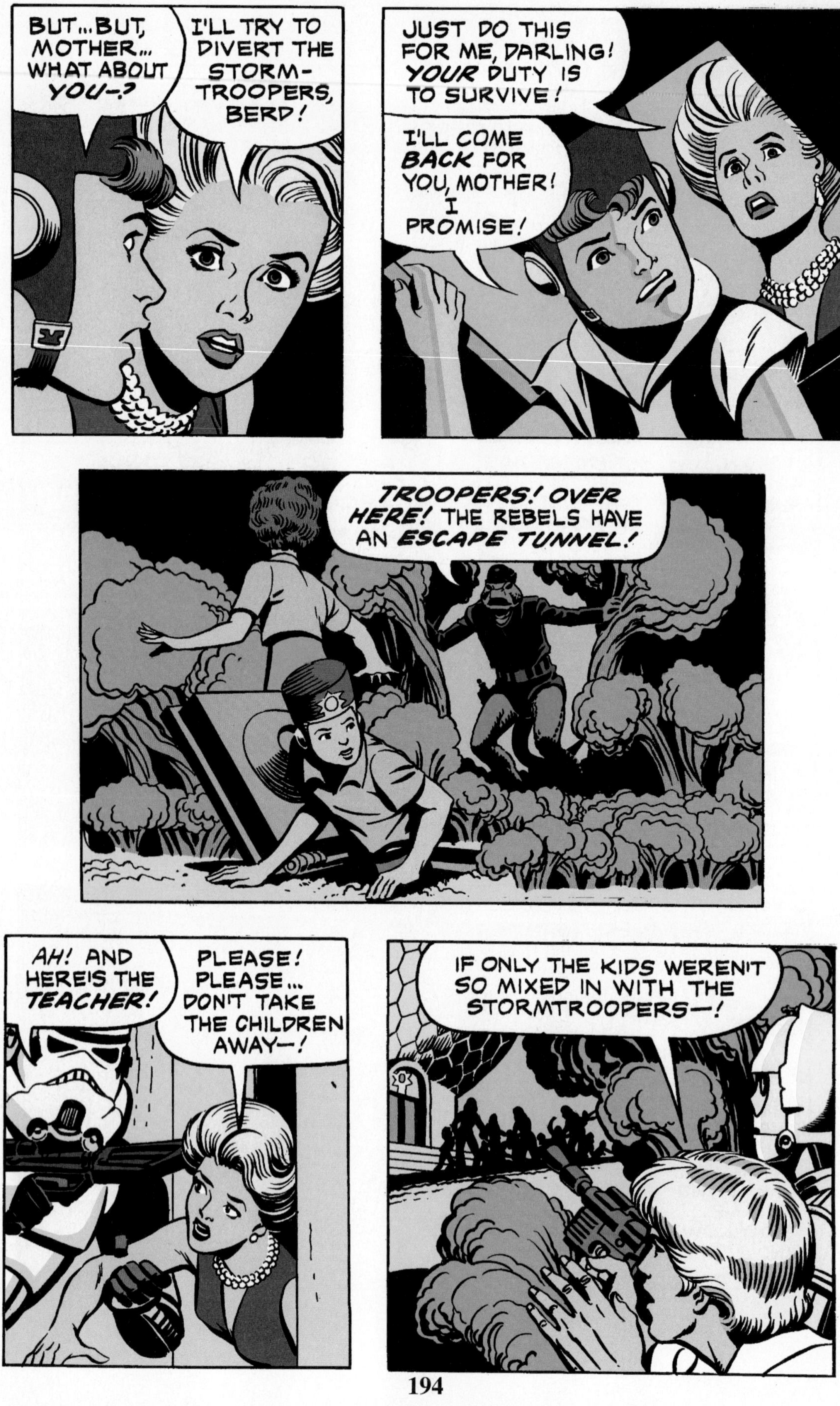
BUT... BUT, MOTHER... WHAT ABOUT YOU-?
I'LL TRY TO DIVERT THE STORM-TROOPERS, BERD!
JUST DO THIS FOR ME, DARLING! YOUR DUTY IS TO SURVIVE!
I'LL COME BACK FOR YOU, MOTHER! I PROMISE!
TROOPERS! OVER HERE! THE REBELS HAVE AN ESCAPE TUNNEL!
AH! AND HERE'S THE TEACHER!
PLEASE! PLEASE... DON'T TAKE THE CHILDREN AWAY-!
IF ONLY THE KIDS WEREN'T SO MIXED IN WITH THE STORMTROOPERS-!

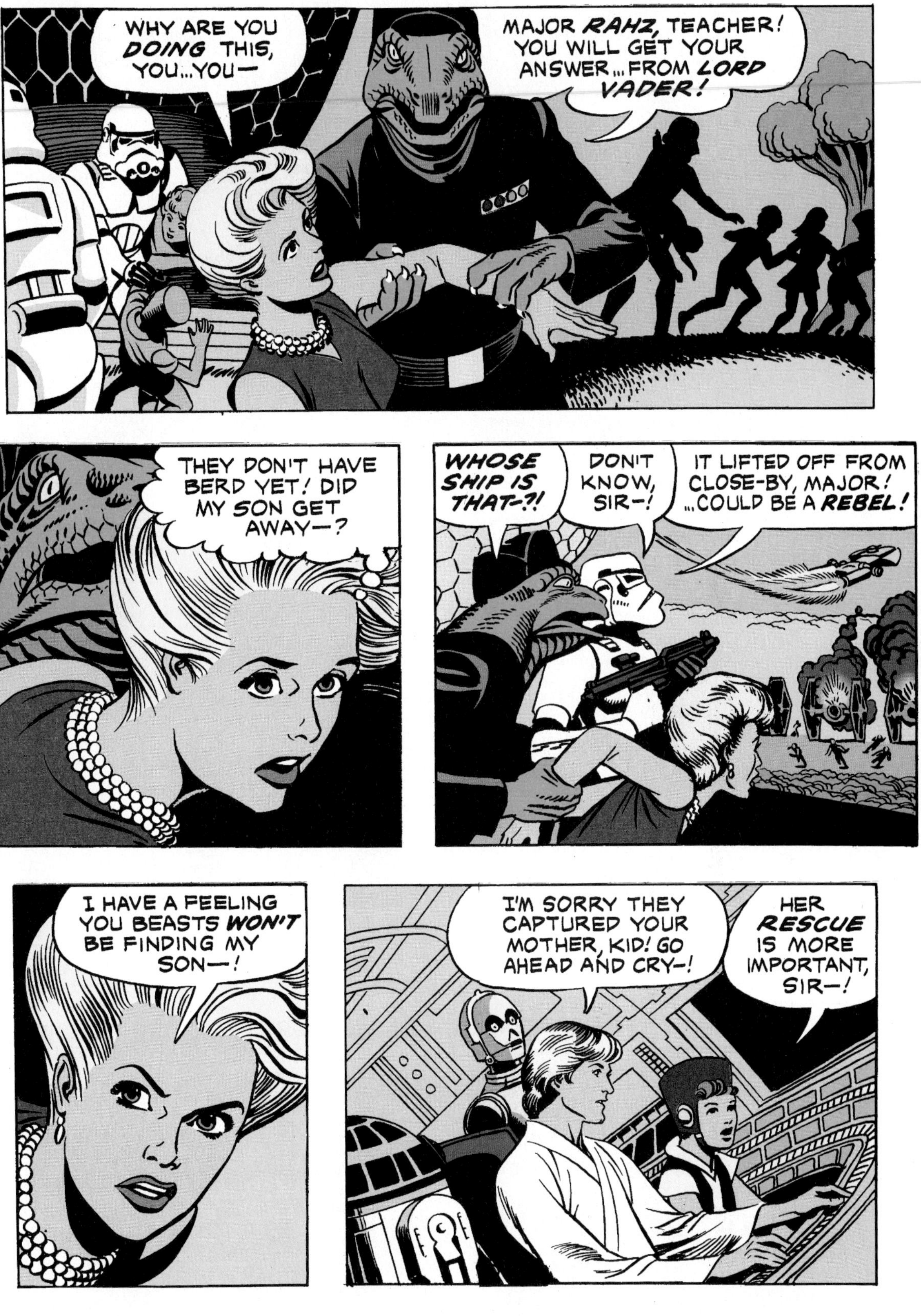

WHY ARE YOU DOING THIS, YOU...YOU—
MAJOR RAHZ, TEACHER! YOU WILL GET YOUR ANSWER... FROM LORD VADER!
THEY DON'T HAVE BERD YET! DID MY SON GET AWAY—?
WHOSE SHIP IS THAT-?!
DON'T KNOW, SIR-!
IT LIFTED OFF FROM CLOSE-BY, MAJOR! ...COULD BE A REBEL!
I HAVE A FEELING YOU BEASTS WON'T BE FINDING MY SON—!
I'M SORRY THEY CAPTURED YOUR MOTHER, KID! GO AHEAD AND CRY-!
HER RESCUE IS MORE IMPORTANT, SIR-!

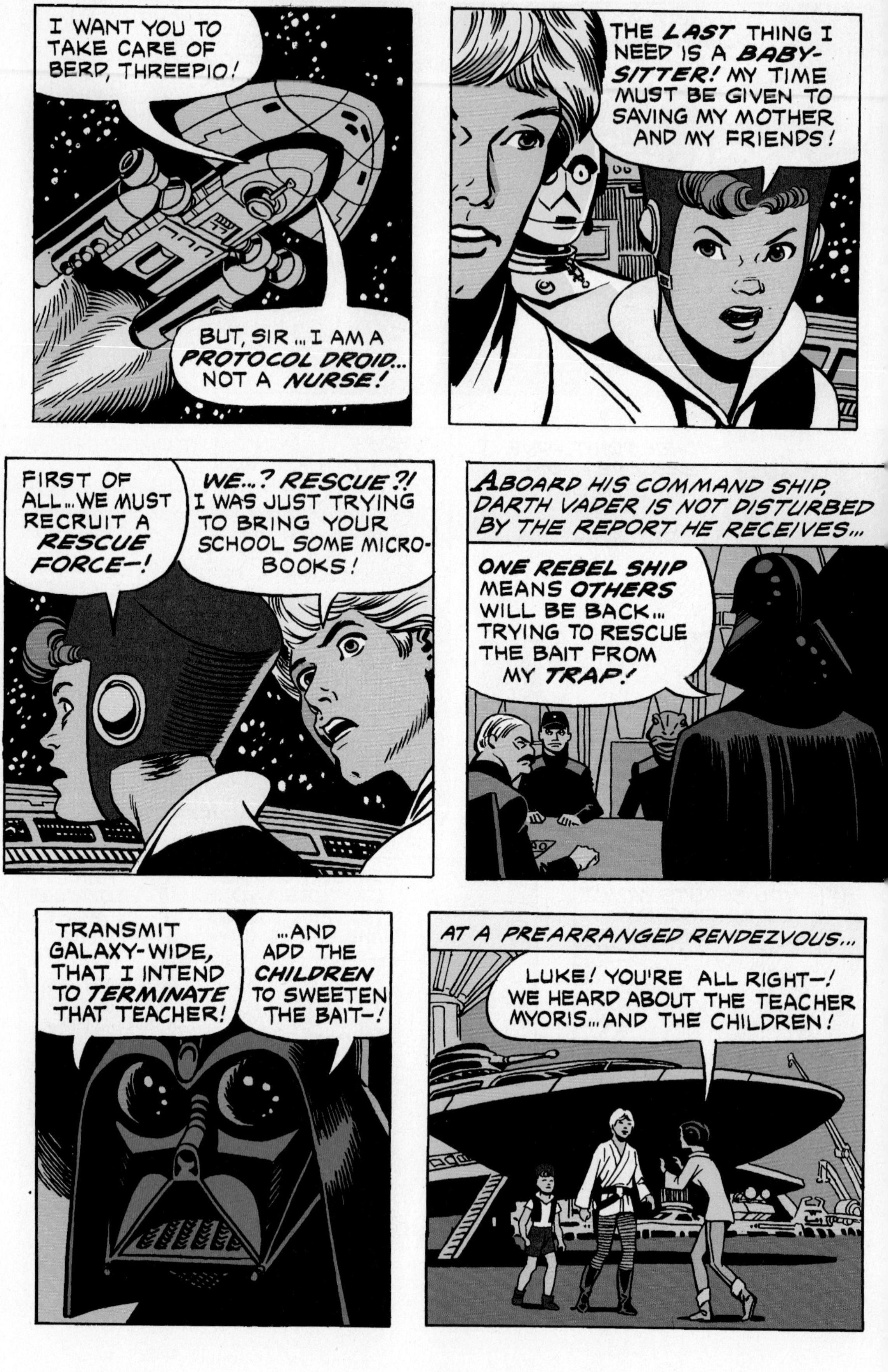
I WANT YOU TO TAKE CARE OF BERD, THREEPIO!
BUT, SIR ... I AM A PROTOCOL DROID... NOT A NURSE!
THE LAST THING I NEED IS A BABY-SITTER! MY TIME MUST BE GIVEN TO SAVING MY MOTHER AND MY FRIENDS!
FIRST OF ALL... WE MUST RECRUIT A RESCUE FORCE—!
WE...? RESCUE?! I WAS JUST TRYING TO BRING YOUR SCHOOL SOME MICRO-BOOKS!
ABOARD HIS COMMAND SHIP, DARTH VADER IS NOT DISTURBED BY THE REPORT HE RECEIVES...
ONE REBEL SHIP MEANS OTHERS WILL BE BACK... TRYING TO RESCUE THE BAIT FROM MY TRAP!
TRANSMIT GALAXY-WIDE, THAT I INTEND TO TERMINATE THAT TEACHER!
...AND ADD THE CHILDREN TO SWEETEN THE BAIT—!
AT A PREARRANGED RENDEZVOUS...
LUKE! YOU'RE ALL RIGHT—! WE HEARD ABOUT THE TEACHER MYORIS... AND THE CHILDREN!

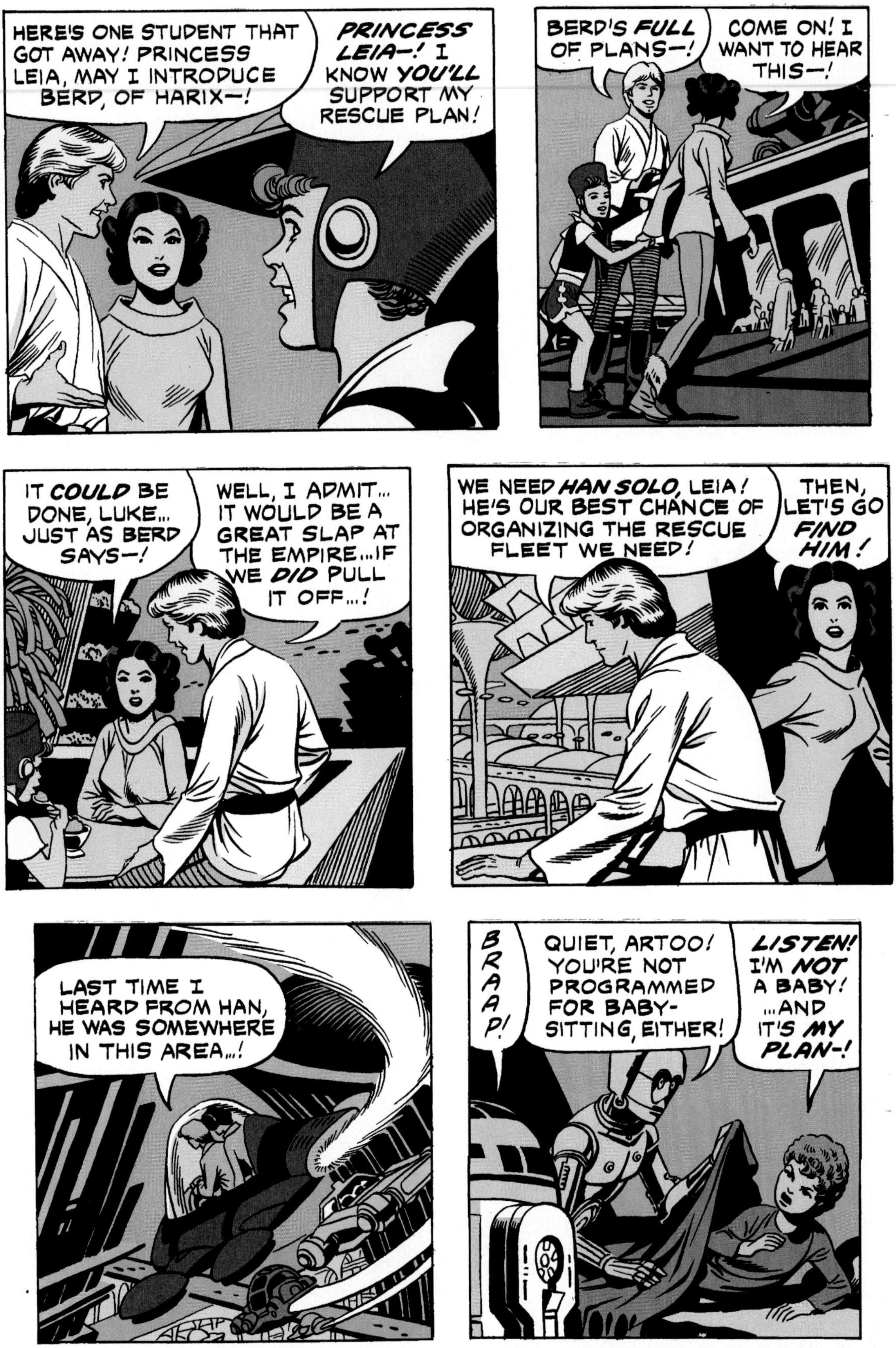
HERE'S ONE STUDENT THAT GOT AWAY! PRINCESS LEIA, MAY I INTRODUCE BERD, OF HARIX—!
PRINCESS LEIA—! I KNOW YOU'LL SUPPORT MY RESCUE PLAN!
BERD'S FULL OF PLANS—!
COME ON! I WANT TO HEAR THIS—!
IT COULD BE DONE, LUKE... JUST AS BERD SAYS—!
WELL, I ADMIT... IT WOULD BE A GREAT SLAP AT THE EMPIRE...IF WE DID PULL IT OFF...!
WE NEED HAN SOLO, LEIA! HE'S OUR BEST CHANCE OF ORGANIZING THE RESCUE FLEET WE NEED!
THEN, LET'S GO FIND HIM!
LAST TIME I HEARD FROM HAN, HE WAS SOMEWHERE IN THIS AREA...!
BRAAP!
QUIET, ARTOO! YOU'RE NOT PROGRAMMED FOR BABY-SITTING, EITHER!
LISTEN! I'M NOT A BABY! ...AND IT'S MY PLAN-!

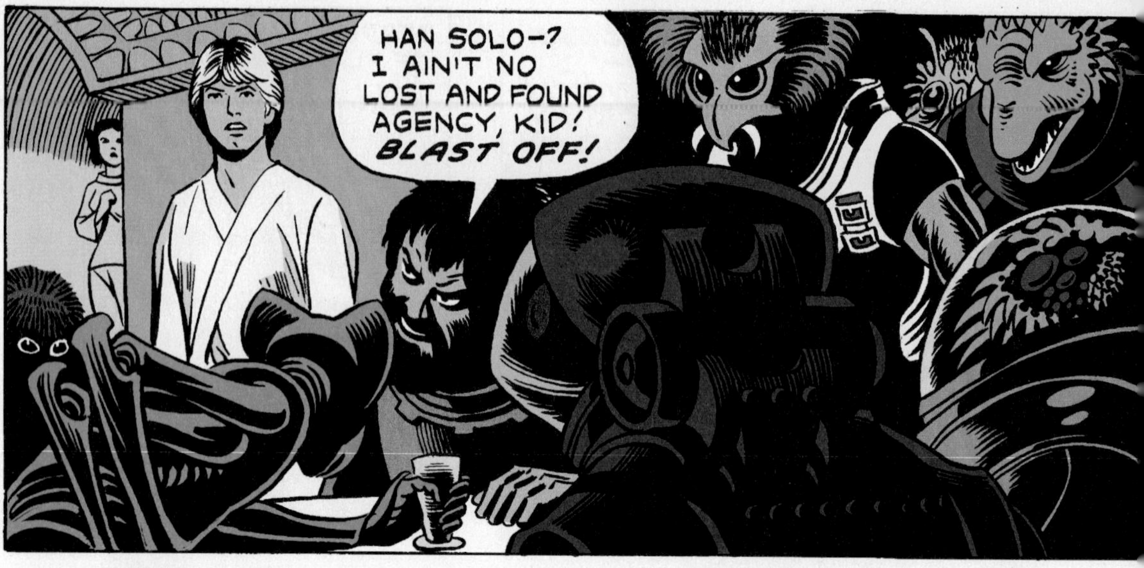
HAN SOLO-? I AIN'T NO LOST AND FOUND AGENCY, KID! BLAST OFF!

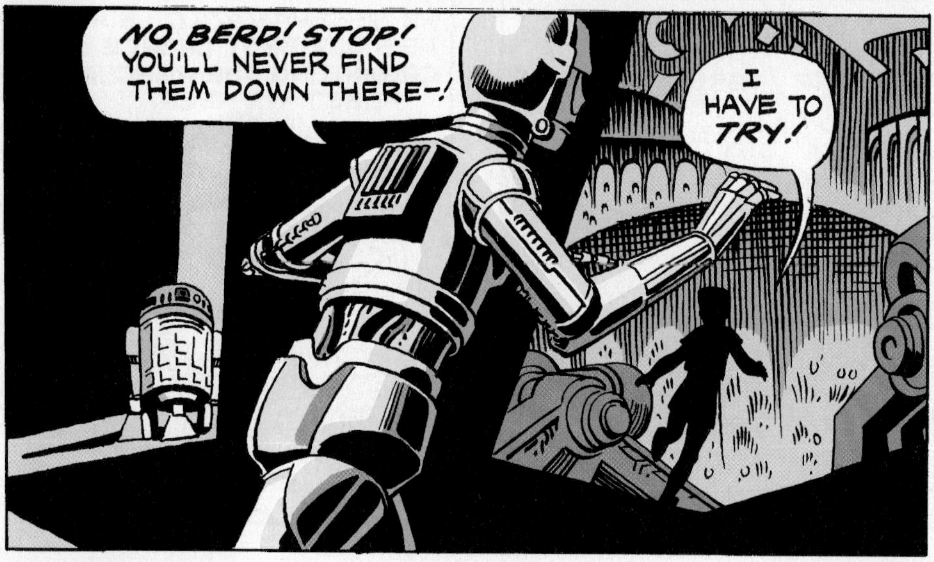
NO, BERD! STOP! YOU'LL NEVER FIND THEM DOWN THERE-!
I HAVE TO TRY!

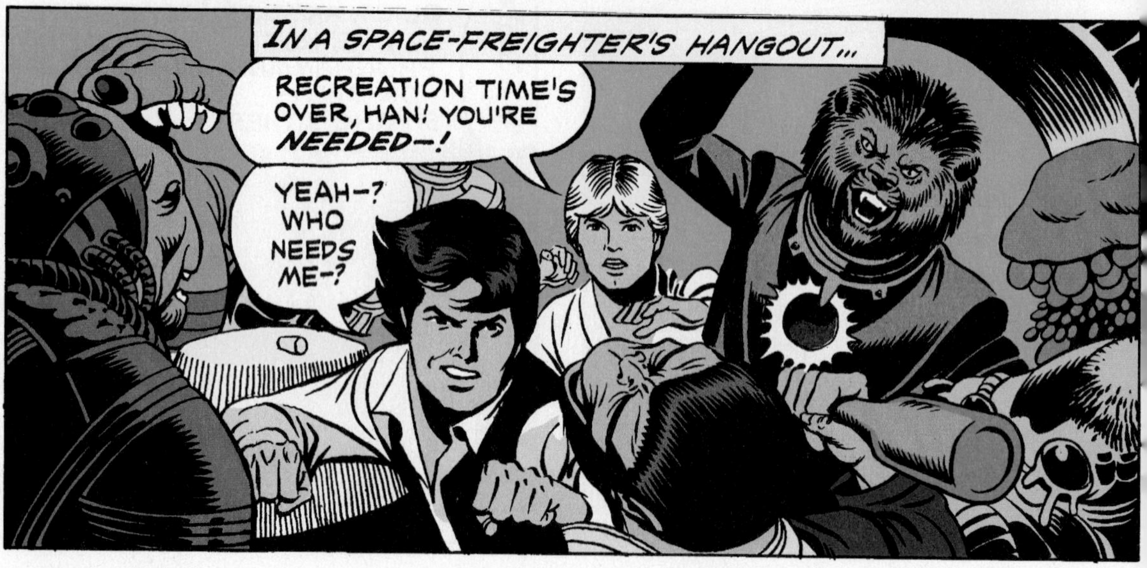
IN A SPACE-FREIGHTER'S HANGOUT...
RECREATION TIME'S OVER, HAN! YOU'RE NEEDED-!
YEAH-? WHO NEEDS ME-?

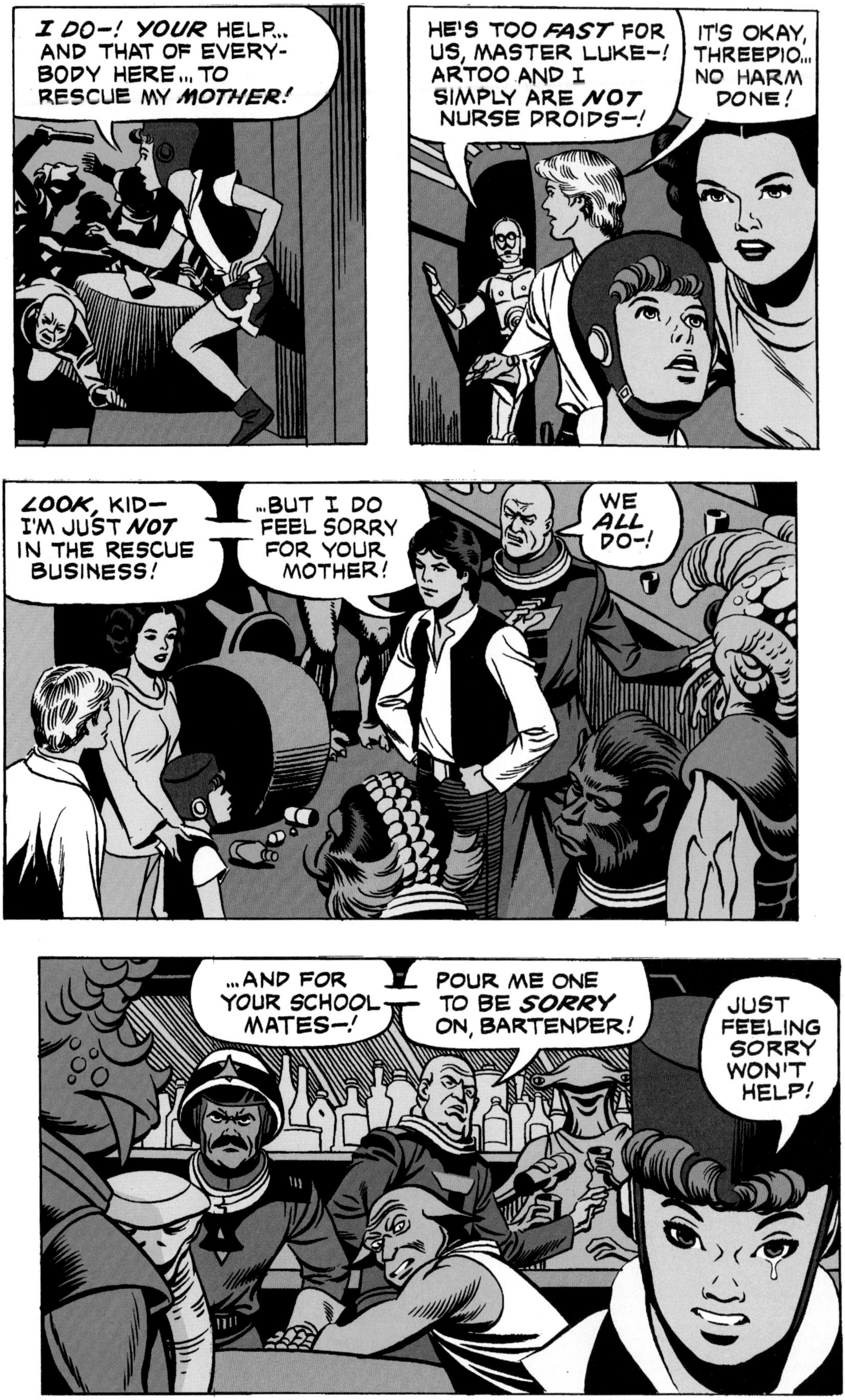
I DO-! YOUR HELP... AND THAT OF EVERYBODY HERE... TO RESCUE MY MOTHER!
HE'S TOO FAST FOR US, MASTER LUKE-! ARTOO AND I SIMPLY ARE NOT NURSE DROIDS-!
IT'S OKAY, THREEPIO... NO HARM DONE!
LOOK, KID— I'M JUST NOT IN THE RESCUE BUSINESS!
...BUT I DO FEEL SORRY FOR YOUR MOTHER!
WE ALL DO-!
...AND FOR YOUR SCHOOL MATES-!
POUR ME ONE TO BE SORRY ON, BARTENDER!
JUST FEELING SORRY WON'T HELP!

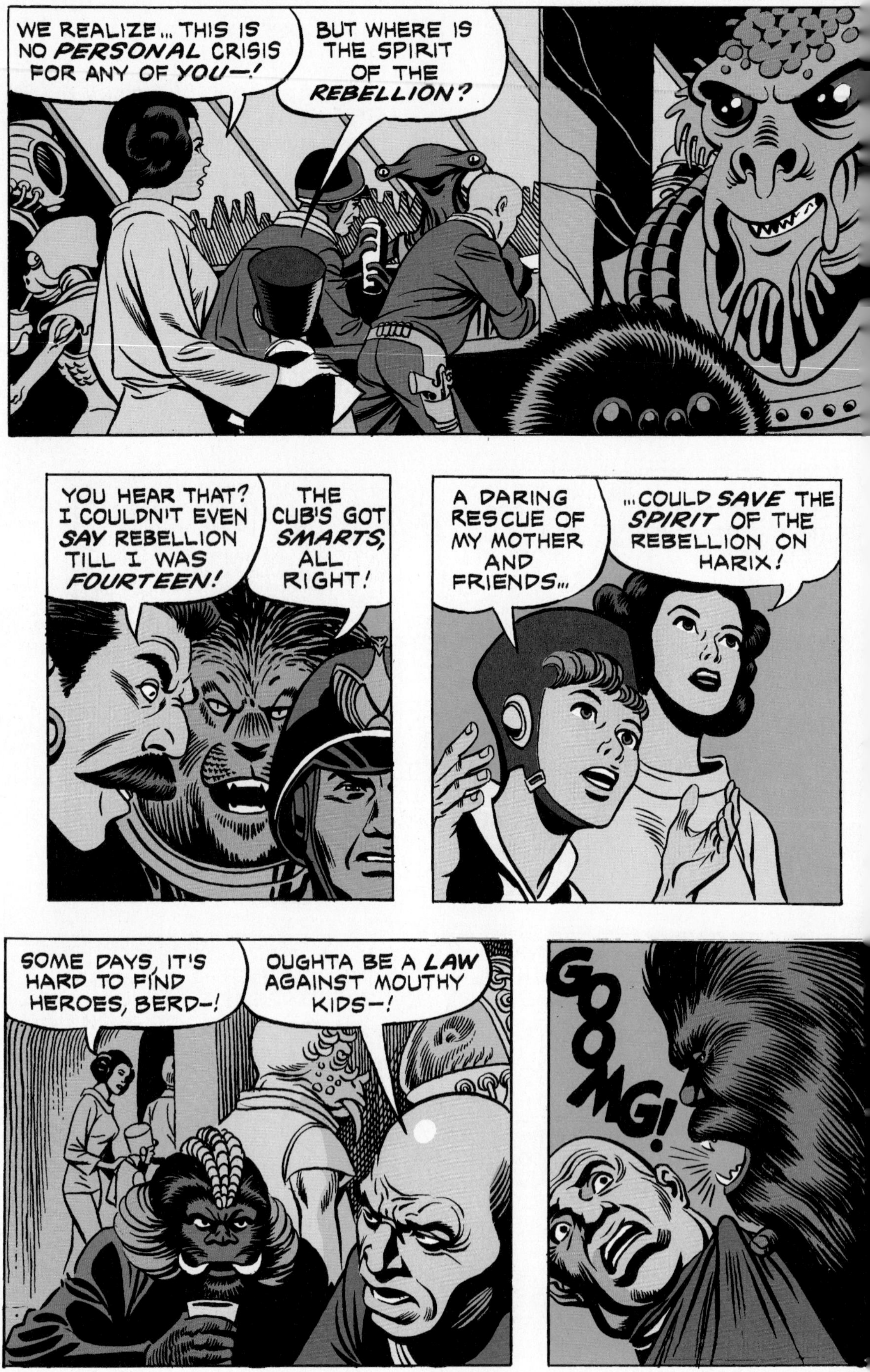
WE REALIZE... THIS IS NO PERSONAL CRISIS FOR ANY OF YOU—!
BUT WHERE IS THE SPIRIT OF THE REBELLION?
YOU HEAR THAT? I COULDN'T EVEN SAY REBELLION TILL I WAS FOURTEEN!
THE CUB'S GOT SMARTS, ALL RIGHT!
A DARING RESCUE OF MY MOTHER AND FRIENDS...
...COULD SAVE THE SPIRIT OF THE REBELLION ON HARIX!
SOME DAYS, IT'S HARD TO FIND HEROES, BERD—!
OUGHTA BE A LAW AGAINST MOUTHY KIDS—!
GOOMG!

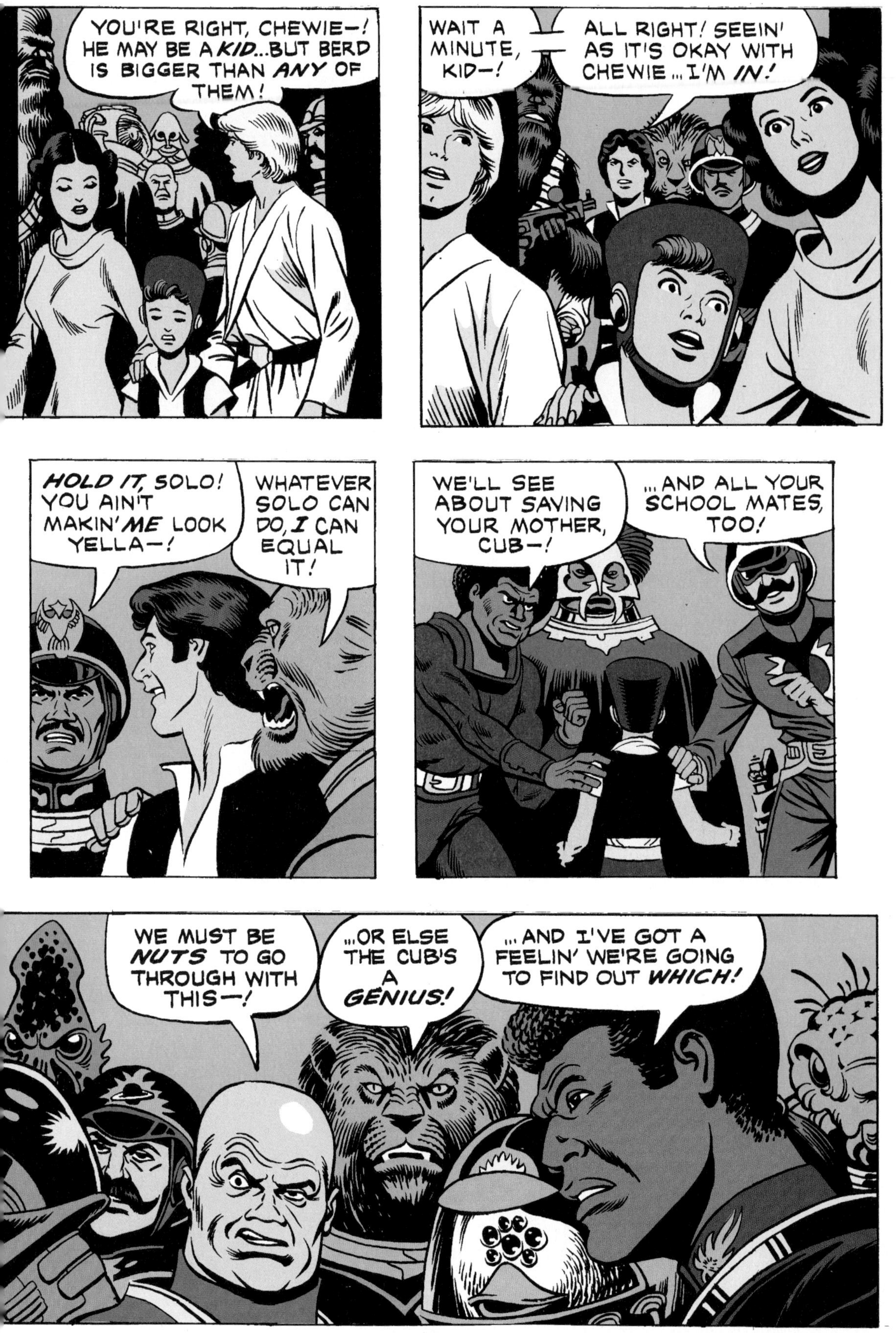
YOU'RE RIGHT, CHEWIE—! HE MAY BE A KID...BUT BERD IS BIGGER THAN ANY OF THEM!
WAIT A MINUTE, KID—!
ALL RIGHT! SEEIN' AS IT'S OKAY WITH CHEWIE... I'M IN!
HOLD IT, SOLO! YOU AIN'T MAKIN' ME LOOK YELLA—!
WHATEVER SOLO CAN DO, I CAN EQUAL IT!
WE'LL SEE ABOUT SAVING YOUR MOTHER, CUB—!
...AND ALL YOUR SCHOOL MATES, TOO!
WE MUST BE NUTS TO GO THROUGH WITH THIS—!
...OR ELSE THE CUB'S A GENIUS!
...AND I'VE GOT A FEELIN' WE'RE GOING TO FIND OUT WHICH!

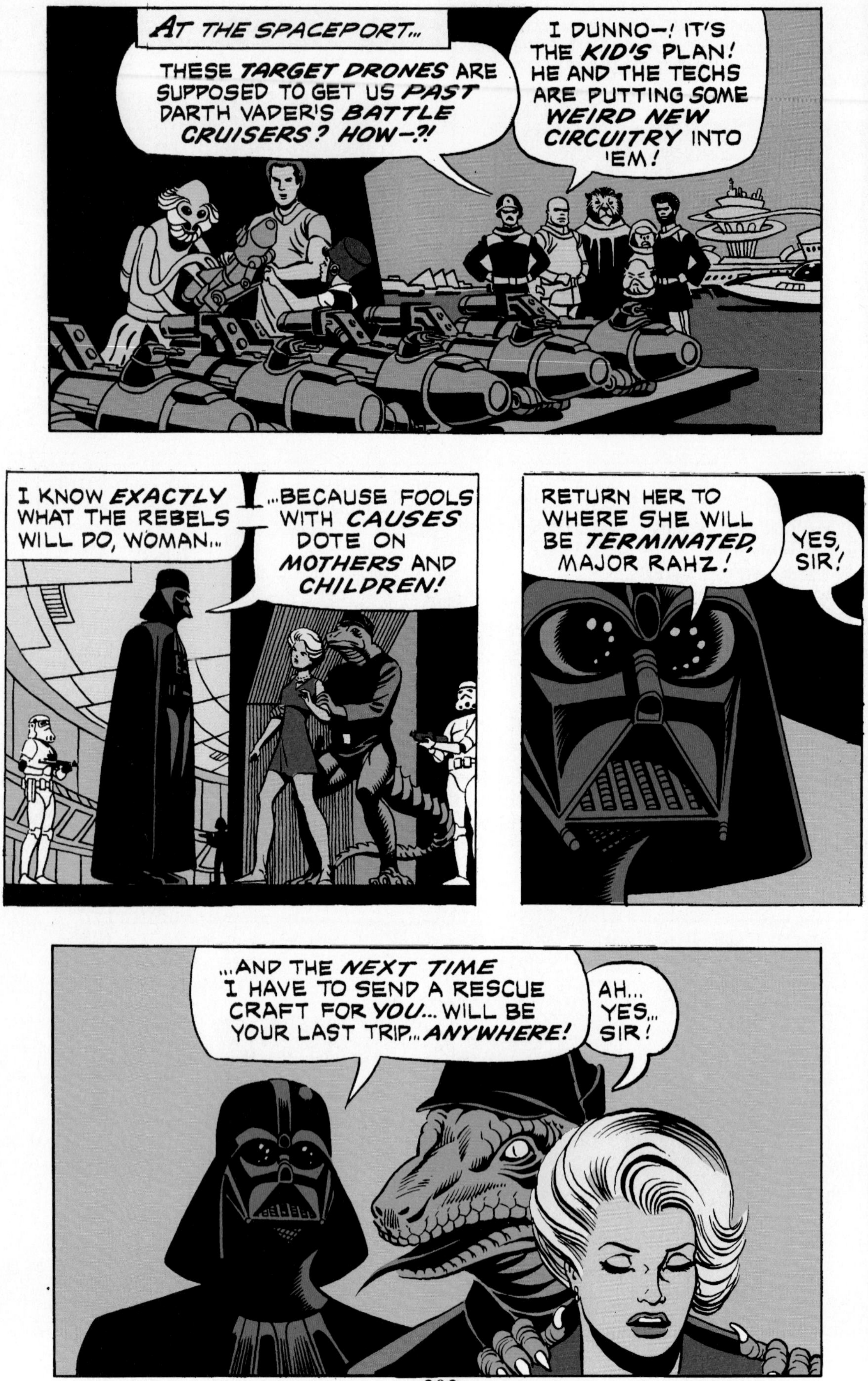
AT THE SPACEPORT...
THESE TARGET DRONES ARE SUPPOSED TO GET US PAST DARTH VADER'S BATTLE CRUISERS? HOW-?!
I DUNNO-! IT'S THE KID'S PLAN! HE AND THE TECHS ARE PUTTING SOME WEIRD NEW CIRCUITRY INTO 'EM!
I KNOW EXACTLY WHAT THE REBELS WILL DO, WOMAN...
...BECAUSE FOOLS WITH CAUSES DOTE ON MOTHERS AND CHILDREN!
RETURN HER TO WHERE SHE WILL BE TERMINATED, MAJOR RAHZ!
YES, SIR!
...AND THE NEXT TIME I HAVE TO SEND A RESCUE CRAFT FOR YOU... WILL BE YOUR LAST TRIP... ANYWHERE!
AH... YES... SIR!

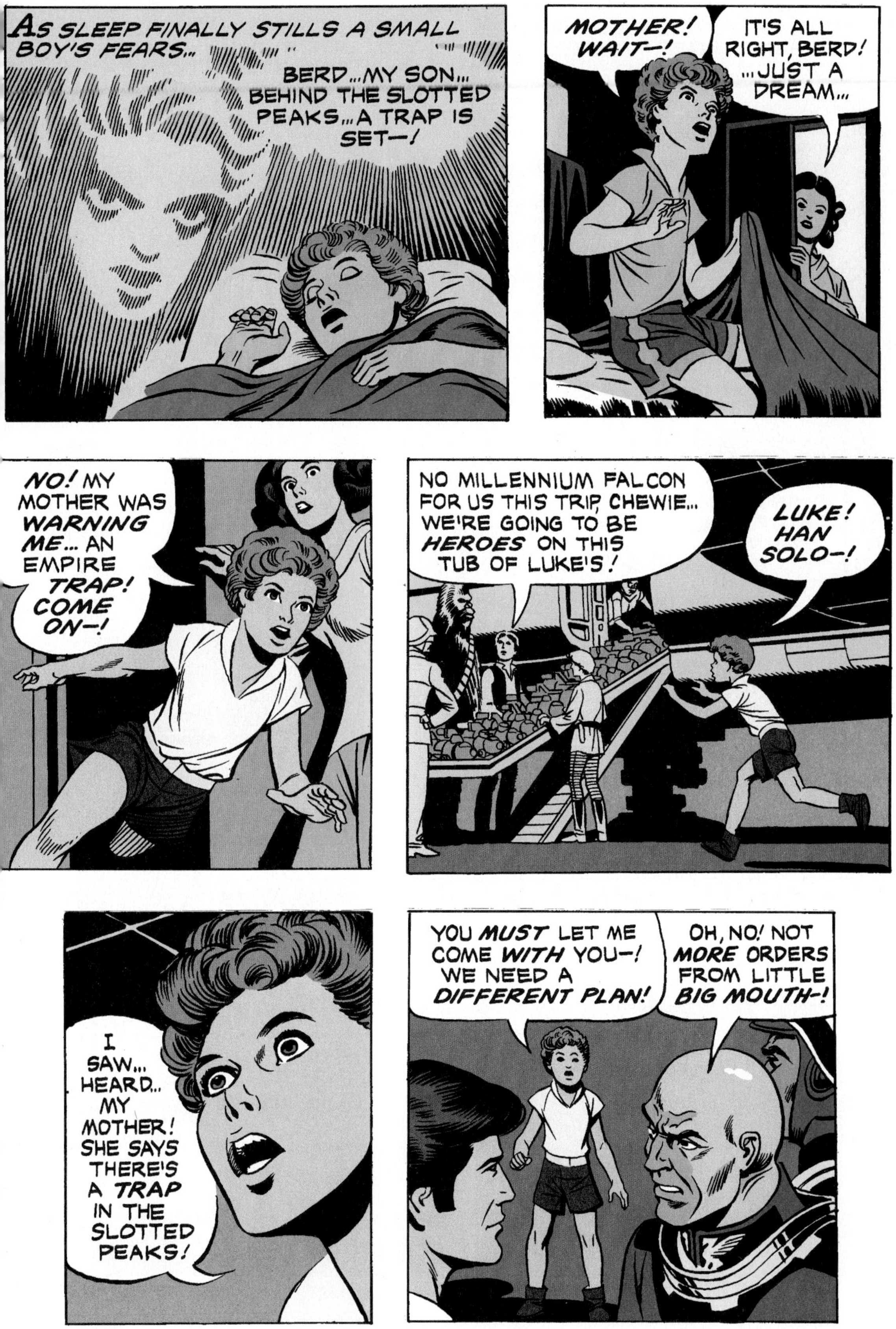
AS SLEEP FINALLY STILLS A SMALL BOY'S FEARS...
BERD...MY SON... BEHIND THE SLOTTED PEAKS...A TRAP IS SET—!
MOTHER! WAIT—!
IT'S ALL RIGHT, BERD! ...JUST A DREAM...
NO! MY MOTHER WAS WARNING ME... AN EMPIRE TRAP! COME ON—!
NO MILLENNIUM FALCON FOR US THIS TRIP, CHEWIE... WE'RE GOING TO BE HEROES ON THIS TUB OF LUKE'S!
LUKE! HAN SOLO—!
I SAW... HEARD... MY MOTHER! SHE SAYS THERE'S A TRAP IN THE SLOTTED PEAKS!
YOU MUST LET ME COME WITH YOU—! WE NEED A DIFFERENT PLAN!
OH, NO! NOT MORE ORDERS FROM LITTLE BIG MOUTH—!

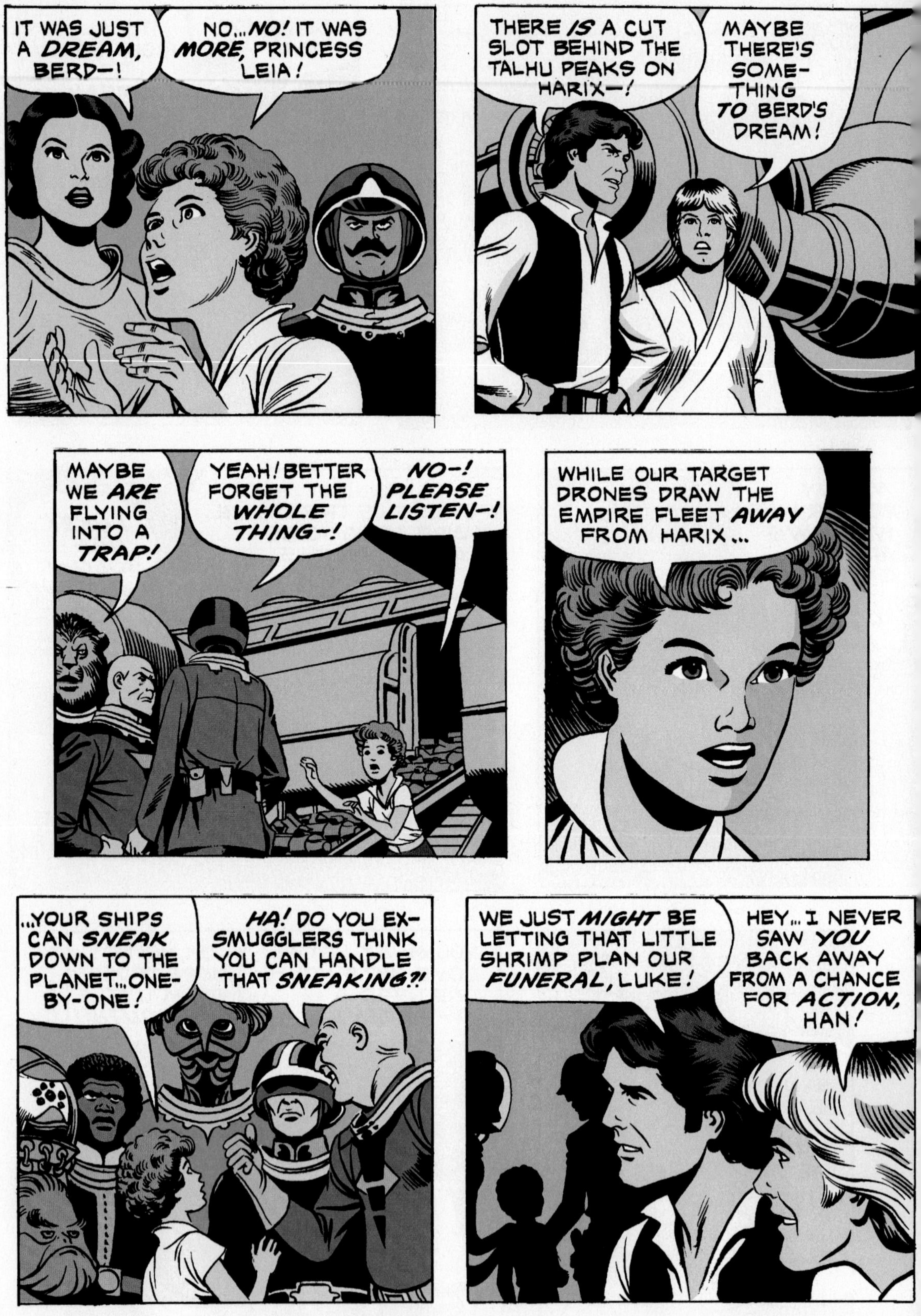
IT WAS JUST A DREAM, BERD—!
NO... NO! IT WAS MORE, PRINCESS LEIA!
THERE IS A CUT SLOT BEHIND THE TALHU PEAKS ON HARIX—!
MAYBE THERE'S SOME-THING TO BERD'S DREAM!
MAYBE WE ARE FLYING INTO A TRAP!
YEAH! BETTER FORGET THE WHOLE THING—!
NO—! PLEASE LISTEN—!
WHILE OUR TARGET DRONES DRAW THE EMPIRE FLEET AWAY FROM HARIX...
...YOUR SHIPS CAN SNEAK DOWN TO THE PLANET...ONE-BY-ONE!
HA! DO YOU EX-SMUGGLERS THINK YOU CAN HANDLE THAT SNEAKING?!
WE JUST MIGHT BE LETTING THAT LITTLE SHRIMP PLAN OUR FUNERAL, LUKE!
HEY... I NEVER SAW YOU BACK AWAY FROM A CHANCE FOR ACTION, HAN!

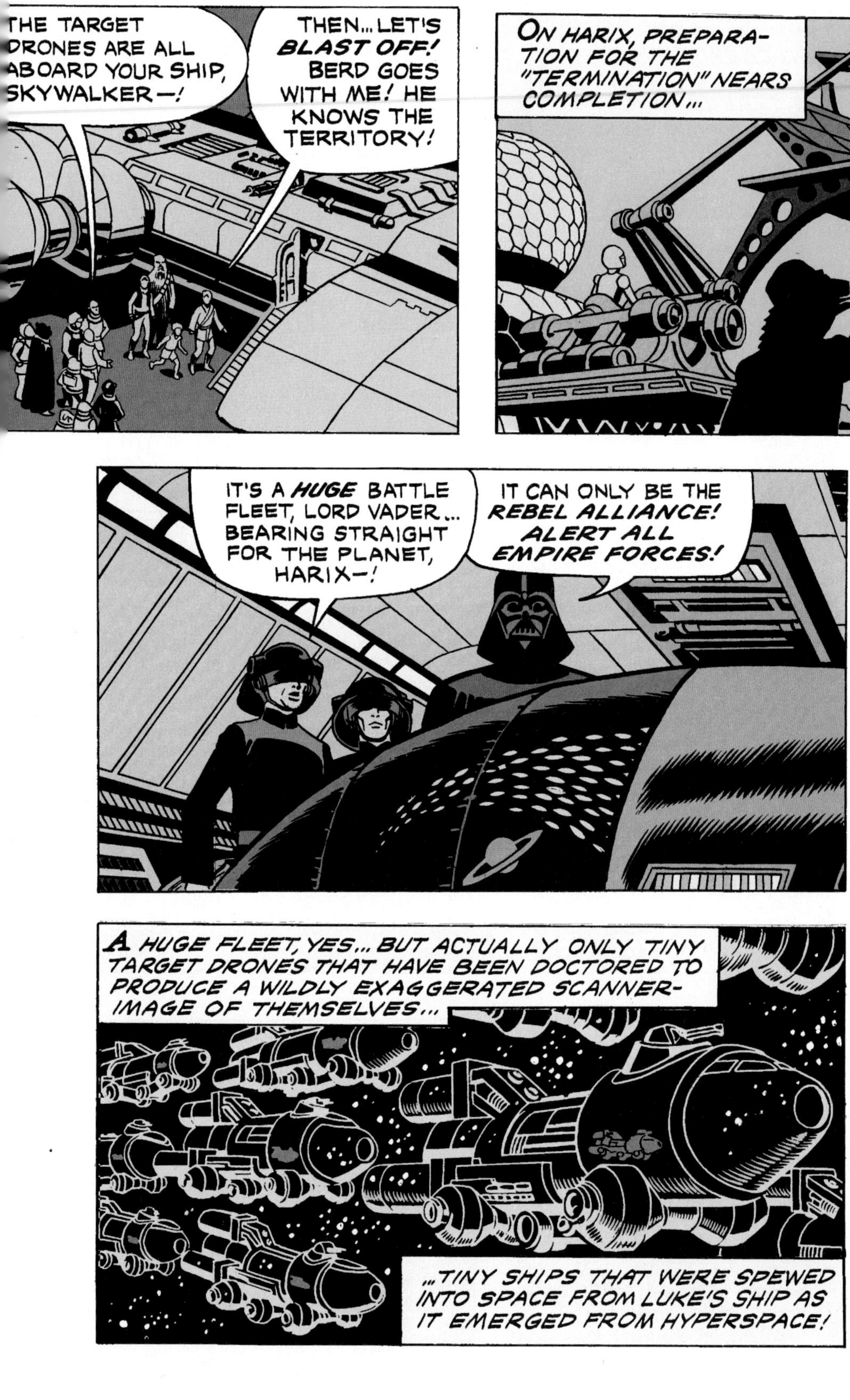
THE TARGET DRONES ARE ALL ABOARD YOUR SHIP, SKYWALKER—!
THEN... LET'S BLAST OFF! BERD GOES WITH ME! HE KNOWS THE TERRITORY!
ON HARIX, PREPARATION FOR THE "TERMINATION" NEARS COMPLETION...
IT'S A HUGE BATTLE FLEET, LORD VADER... BEARING STRAIGHT FOR THE PLANET, HARIX—!
IT CAN ONLY BE THE REBEL ALLIANCE! ALERT ALL EMPIRE FORCES!
A HUGE FLEET, YES... BUT ACTUALLY ONLY TINY TARGET DRONES THAT HAVE BEEN DOCTORED TO PRODUCE A WILDLY EXAGGERATED SCANNER-IMAGE OF THEMSELVES...
...TINY SHIPS THAT WERE SPEWED INTO SPACE FROM LUKE'S SHIP AS IT EMERGED FROM HYPERSPACE!

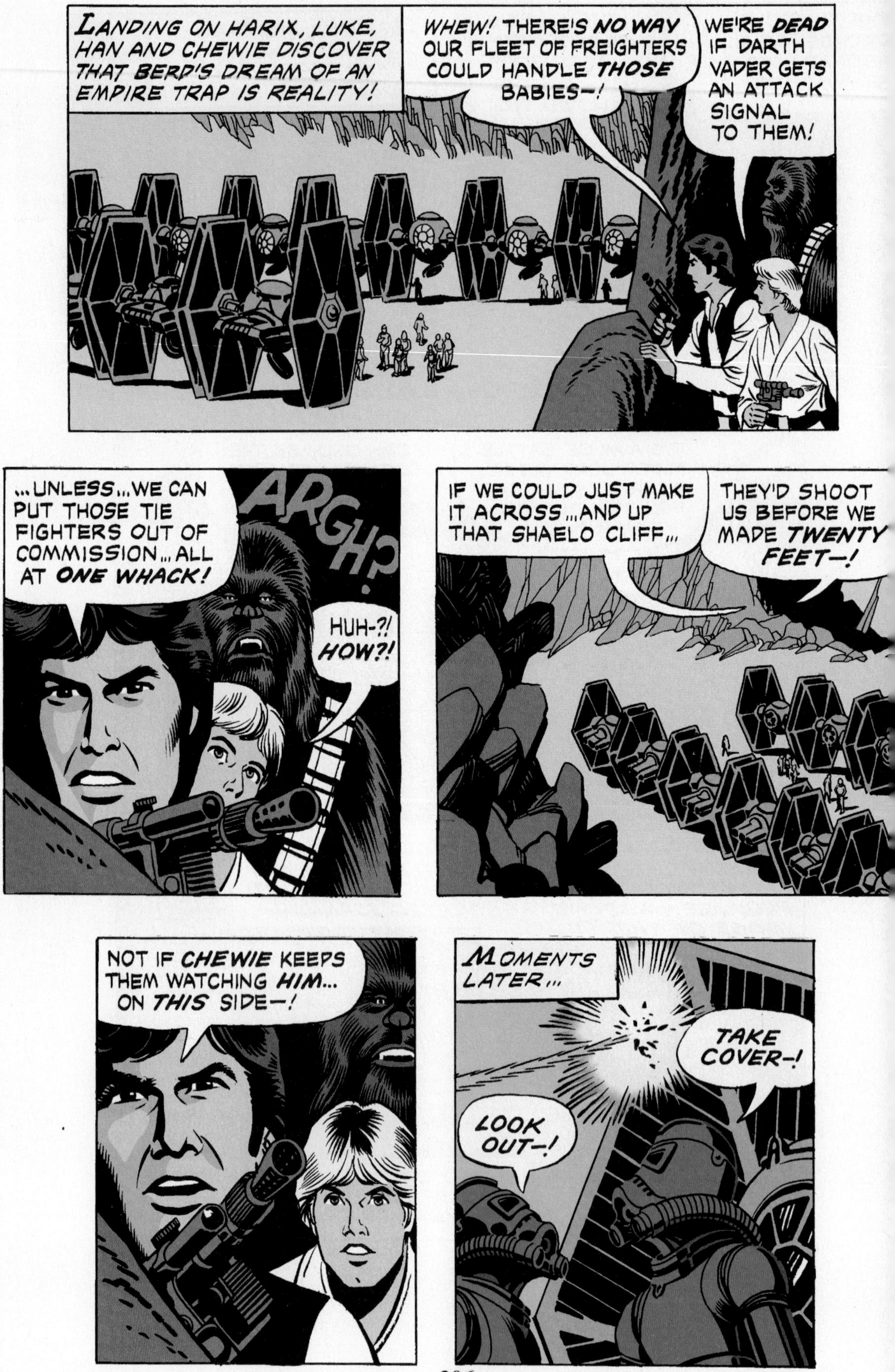
LANDING ON HARIX, LUKE, HAN AND CHEWIE DISCOVER THAT BERD'S DREAM OF AN EMPIRE TRAP IS REALITY!
WHEW! THERE'S NO WAY OUR FLEET OF FREIGHTERS COULD HANDLE THOSE BABIES--!
WE'RE DEAD IF DARTH VADER GETS AN ATTACK SIGNAL TO THEM!
...UNLESS...WE CAN PUT THOSE TIE FIGHTERS OUT OF COMMISSION...ALL AT ONE WHACK!
ARGH?
HUH-?! HOW?!
IF WE COULD JUST MAKE IT ACROSS...AND UP THAT SHAELO CLIFF...
THEY'D SHOOT US BEFORE WE MADE TWENTY FEET--!
NOT IF CHEWIE KEEPS THEM WATCHING HIM... ON THIS SIDE--!
MOMENTS LATER...
TAKE COVER--!
LOOK OUT--!

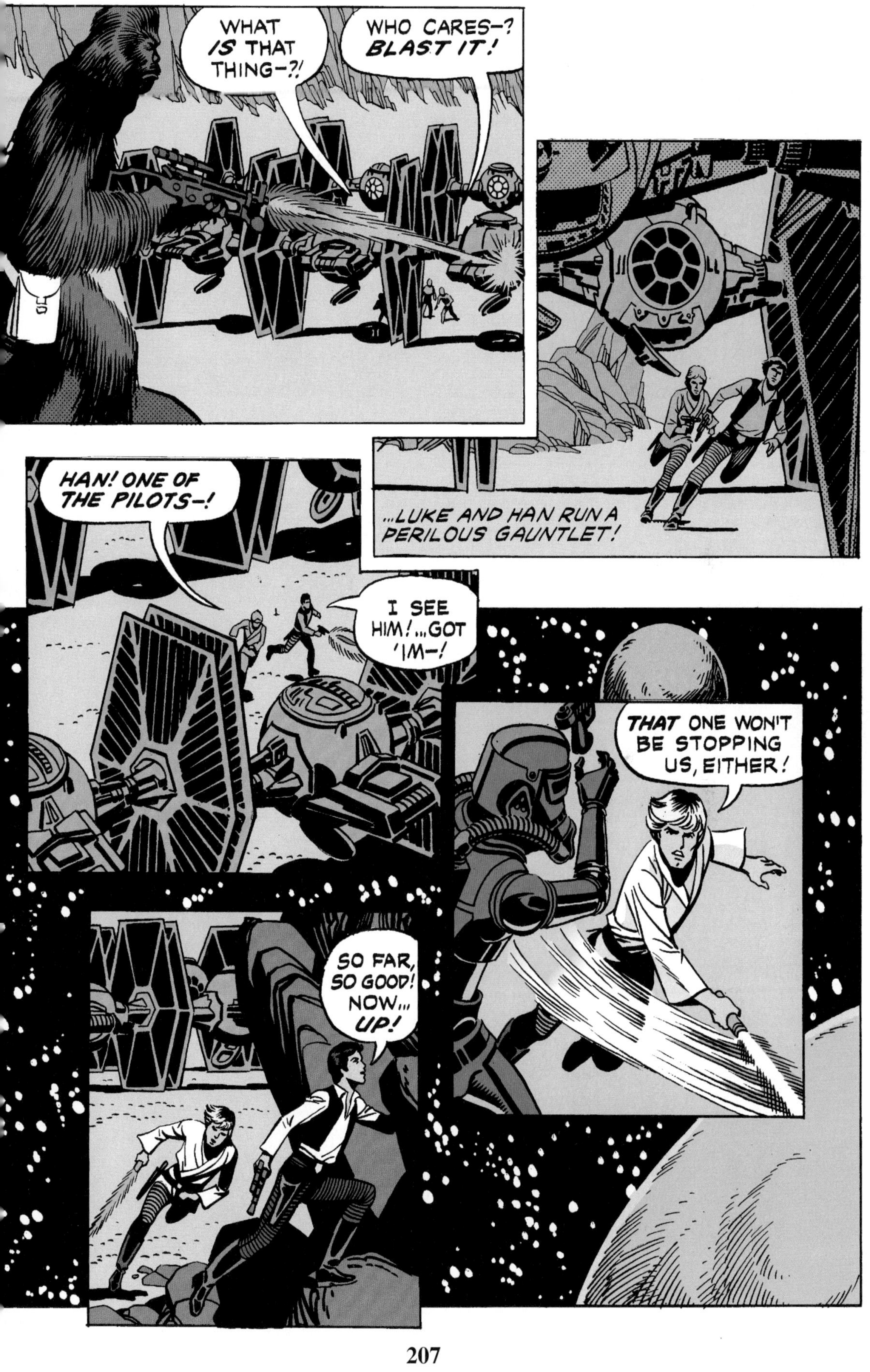
WHAT *IS* THAT THING–?!
WHO CARES–? *BLAST IT!*
...LUKE AND HAN RUN A PERILOUS GAUNTLET!
HAN! ONE OF THE PILOTS–!
I SEE HIM! ...GOT 'IM–!
THAT ONE WON'T BE STOPPING US, EITHER!
SO FAR, SO GOOD! NOW... *UP!*

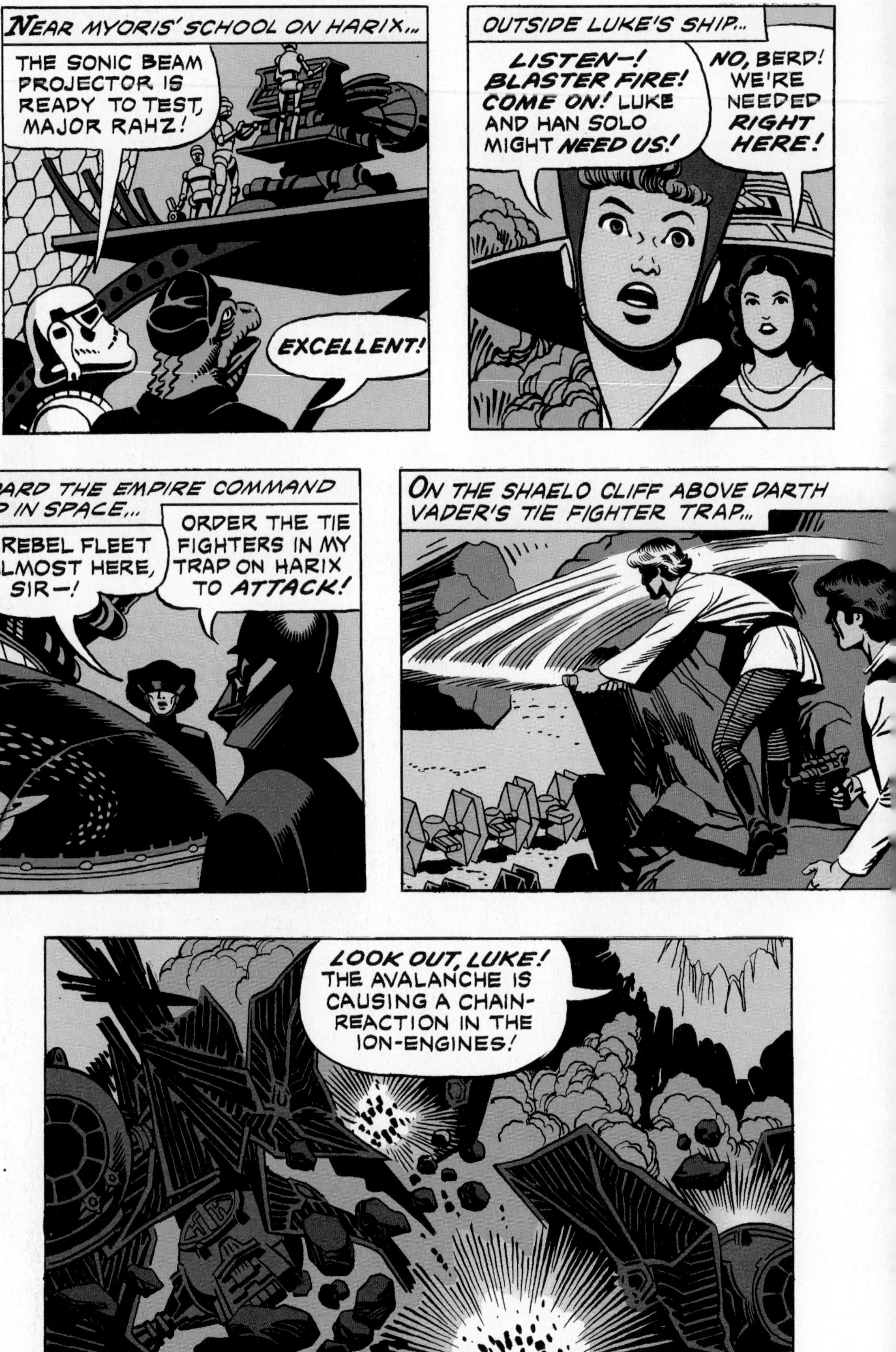
NEAR MYORIS' SCHOOL ON HARIX...
THE SONIC BEAM PROJECTOR IS READY TO TEST, MAJOR RAHZ!
EXCELLENT!
OUTSIDE LUKE'S SHIP...
LISTEN-! BLASTER FIRE! COME ON! LUKE AND HAN SOLO MIGHT NEED US!
NO, BERD! WE'RE NEEDED RIGHT HERE!
ABOARD THE EMPIRE COMMAND SHIP IN SPACE...
THE REBEL FLEET IS ALMOST HERE, SIR-!
ORDER THE TIE FIGHTERS IN MY TRAP ON HARIX TO ATTACK!
ON THE SHAELO CLIFF ABOVE DARTH VADER'S TIE FIGHTER TRAP...
LOOK OUT, LUKE! THE AVALANCHE IS CAUSING A CHAIN-REACTION IN THE ION-ENGINES!

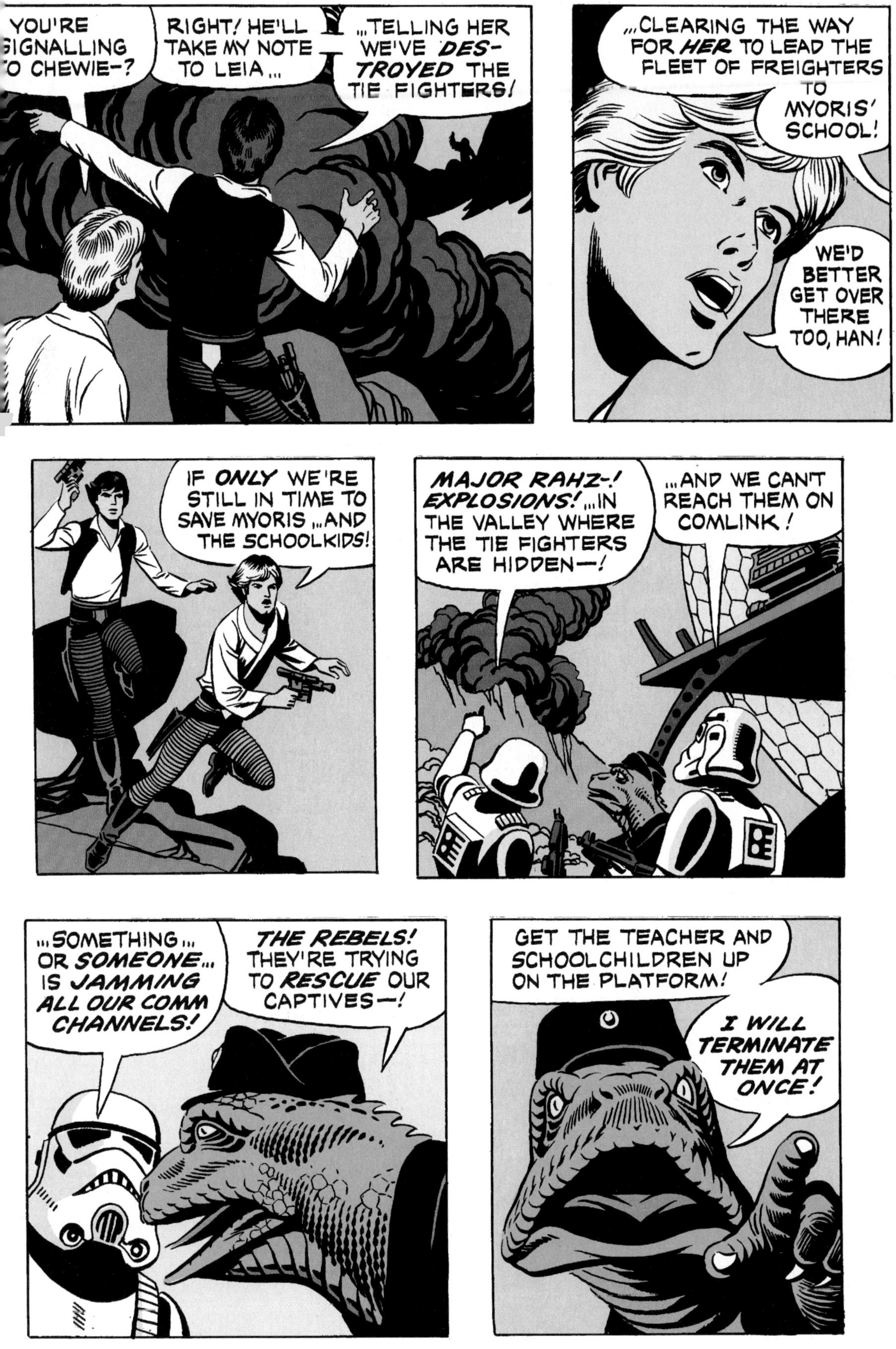
YOU'RE SIGNALLING TO CHEWIE–?
RIGHT! HE'LL TAKE MY NOTE TO LEIA...
...TELLING HER WE'VE DESTROYED THE TIE FIGHTERS!
...CLEARING THE WAY FOR HER TO LEAD THE FLEET OF FREIGHTERS TO MYORIS' SCHOOL!
WE'D BETTER GET OVER THERE TOO, HAN!
IF ONLY WE'RE STILL IN TIME TO SAVE MYORIS ...AND THE SCHOOLKIDS!
MAJOR RAHZ–! EXPLOSIONS! ...IN THE VALLEY WHERE THE TIE FIGHTERS ARE HIDDEN–!
...AND WE CAN'T REACH THEM ON COMLINK!
...SOMETHING... OR SOMEONE... IS JAMMING ALL OUR COMM CHANNELS!
THE REBELS! THEY'RE TRYING TO RESCUE OUR CAPTIVES–!
GET THE TEACHER AND SCHOOLCHILDREN UP ON THE PLATFORM!
I WILL TERMINATE THEM AT ONCE!

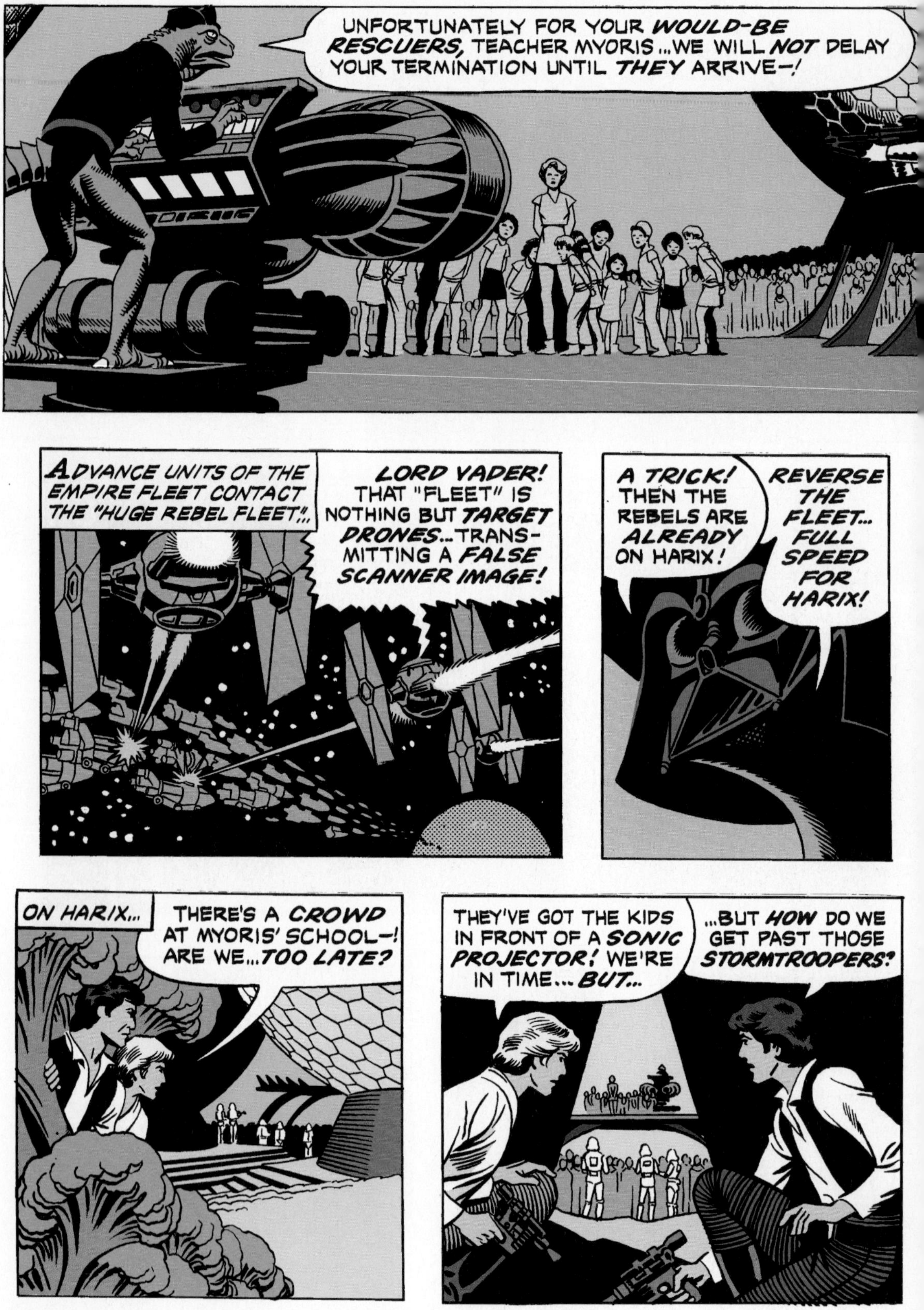
UNFORTUNATELY FOR YOUR WOULD-BE RESCUERS, TEACHER MYORIS ...WE WILL NOT DELAY YOUR TERMINATION UNTIL THEY ARRIVE-!
ADVANCE UNITS OF THE EMPIRE FLEET CONTACT THE "HUGE REBEL FLEET"...
LORD VADER! THAT "FLEET" IS NOTHING BUT TARGET DRONES...TRANS-MITTING A FALSE SCANNER IMAGE!
A TRICK! THEN THE REBELS ARE ALREADY ON HARIX!
REVERSE THE FLEET... FULL SPEED FOR HARIX!
ON HARIX...
THERE'S A CROWD AT MYORIS' SCHOOL-! ARE WE...TOO LATE?
THEY'VE GOT THE KIDS IN FRONT OF A SONIC PROJECTOR! WE'RE IN TIME... BUT...
...BUT HOW DO WE GET PAST THOSE STORMTROOPERS?

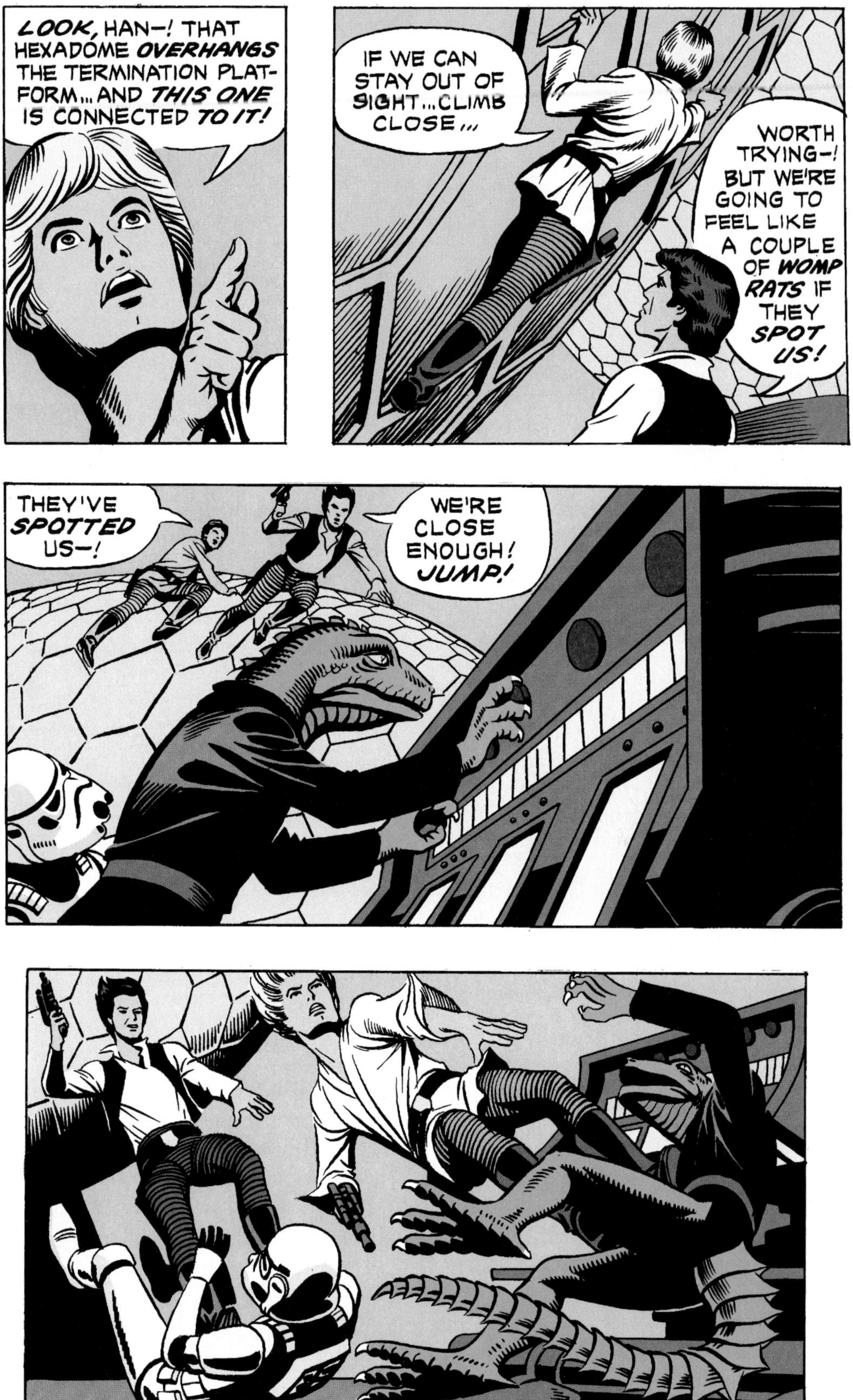
LOOK, HAN—! THAT HEXADOME OVERHANGS THE TERMINATION PLATFORM... AND THIS ONE IS CONNECTED TO IT!
IF WE CAN STAY OUT OF SIGHT... CLIMB CLOSE...
WORTH TRYING—! BUT WE'RE GOING TO FEEL LIKE A COUPLE OF WOMP RATS IF THEY SPOT US!
THEY'VE SPOTTED US—!
WE'RE CLOSE ENOUGH! JUMP!

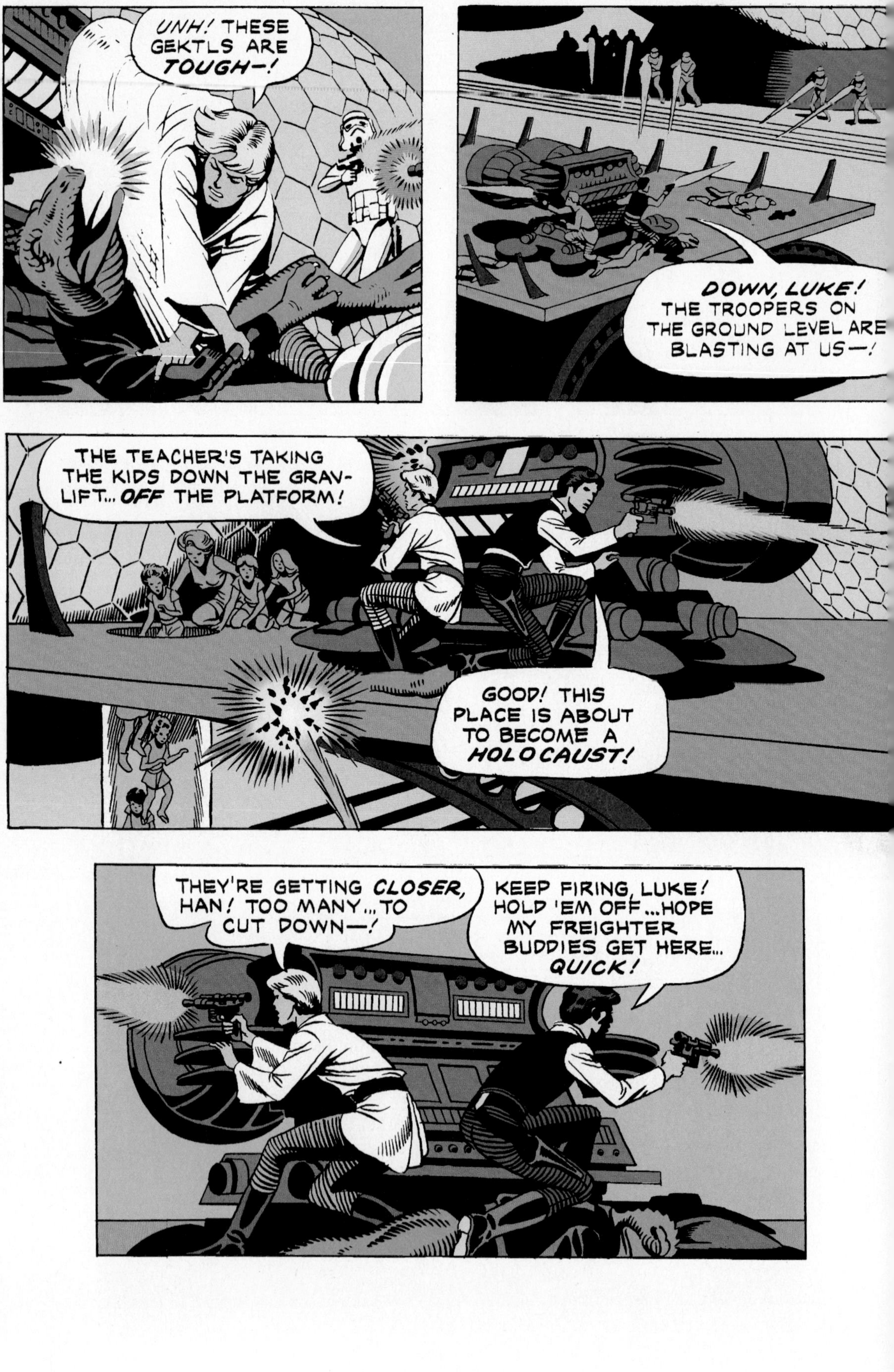
UNH! THESE GEKTLS ARE TOUGH—!
DOWN, LUKE! THE TROOPERS ON THE GROUND LEVEL ARE BLASTING AT US—!
THE TEACHER'S TAKING THE KIDS DOWN THE GRAV-LIFT... OFF THE PLATFORM!
GOOD! THIS PLACE IS ABOUT TO BECOME A HOLOCAUST!
THEY'RE GETTING CLOSER, HAN! TOO MANY... TO CUT DOWN—!
KEEP FIRING, LUKE! HOLD 'EM OFF... HOPE MY FREIGHTER BUDDIES GET HERE... QUICK!

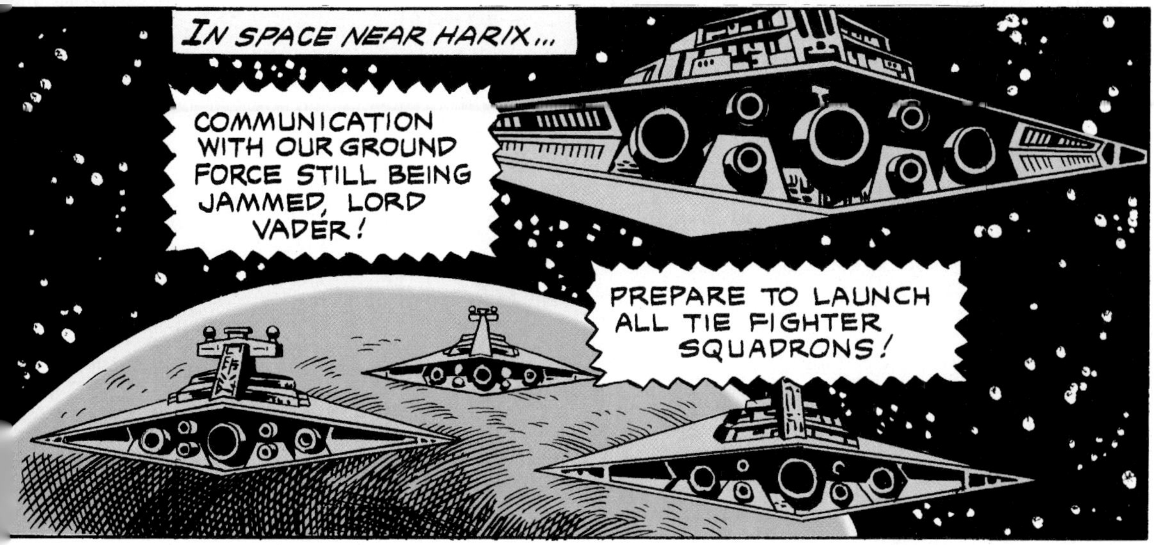
IN SPACE NEAR HARIX...
COMMUNICATION WITH OUR GROUND FORCE STILL BEING JAMMED, LORD VADER!
PREPARE TO LAUNCH ALL TIE FIGHTER SQUADRONS!

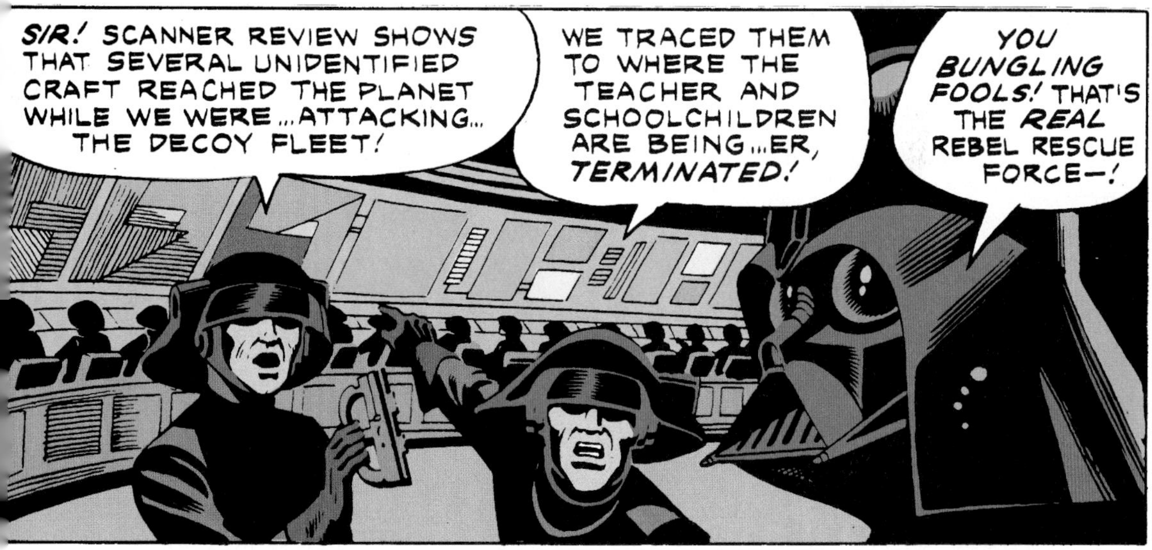
SIR! SCANNER REVIEW SHOWS THAT SEVERAL UNIDENTIFIED CRAFT REACHED THE PLANET WHILE WE WERE...ATTACKING... THE DECOY FLEET!
WE TRACED THEM TO WHERE THE TEACHER AND SCHOOLCHILDREN ARE BEING...ER, TERMINATED!
YOU BUNGLING FOOLS! THAT'S THE REAL REBEL RESCUE FORCE--!

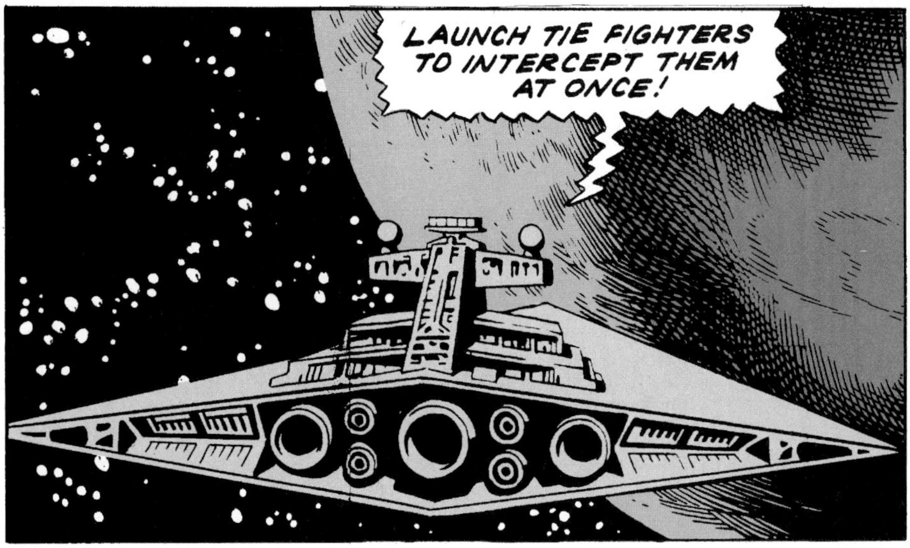
LAUNCH TIE FIGHTERS TO INTERCEPT THEM AT ONCE!

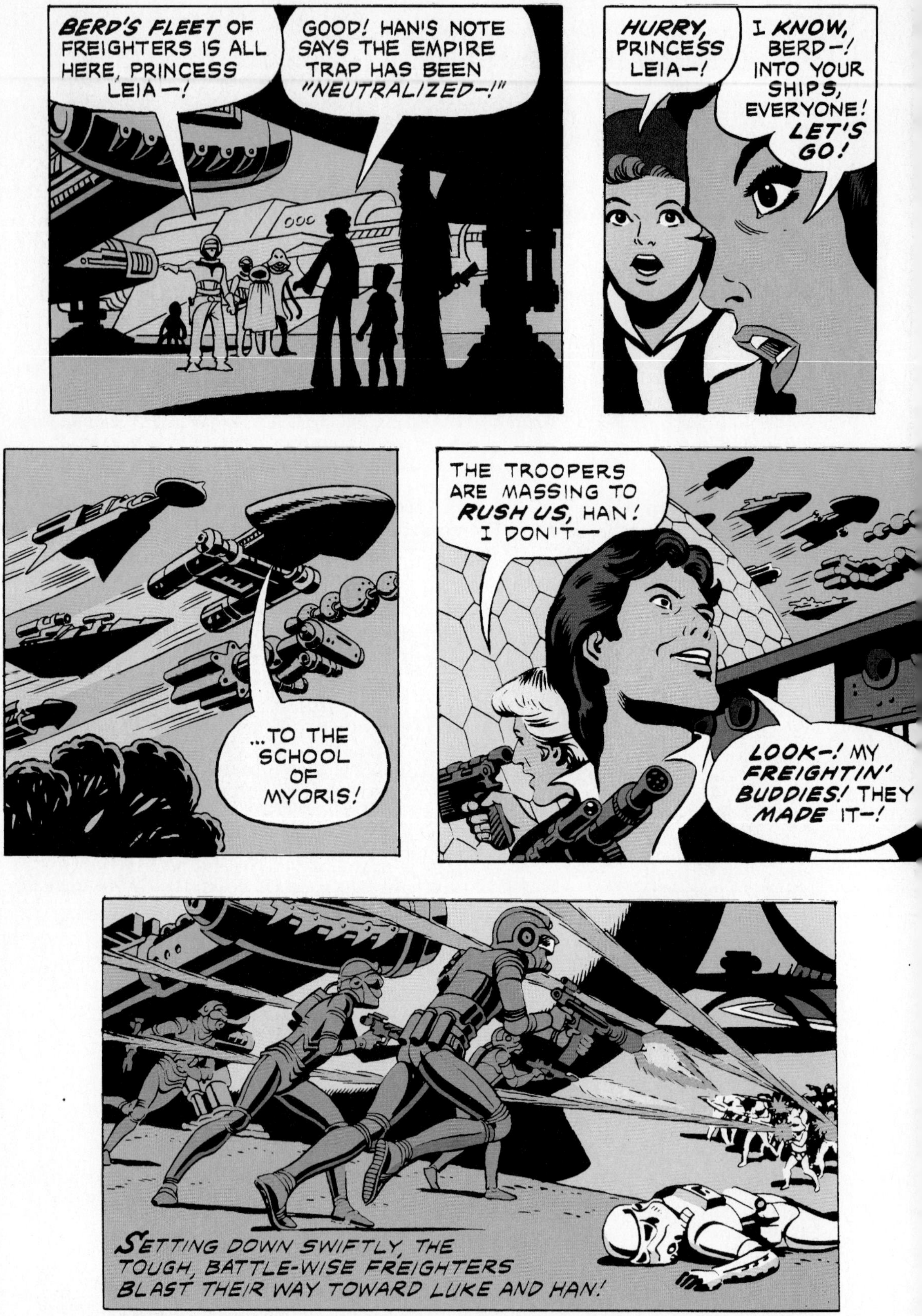
BERD'S FLEET OF FREIGHTERS IS ALL HERE, PRINCESS LEIA—!
GOOD! HAN'S NOTE SAYS THE EMPIRE TRAP HAS BEEN "NEUTRALIZED—!"
HURRY, PRINCESS LEIA—!
I KNOW, BERD—! INTO YOUR SHIPS, EVERYONE! LET'S GO!
...TO THE SCHOOL OF MYORIS!
THE TROOPERS ARE MASSING TO RUSH US, HAN! I DON'T—
LOOK—! MY FREIGHTIN' BUDDIES! THEY MADE IT—!
SETTING DOWN SWIFTLY, THE TOUGH, BATTLE-WISE FREIGHTERS BLAST THEIR WAY TOWARD LUKE AND HAN!

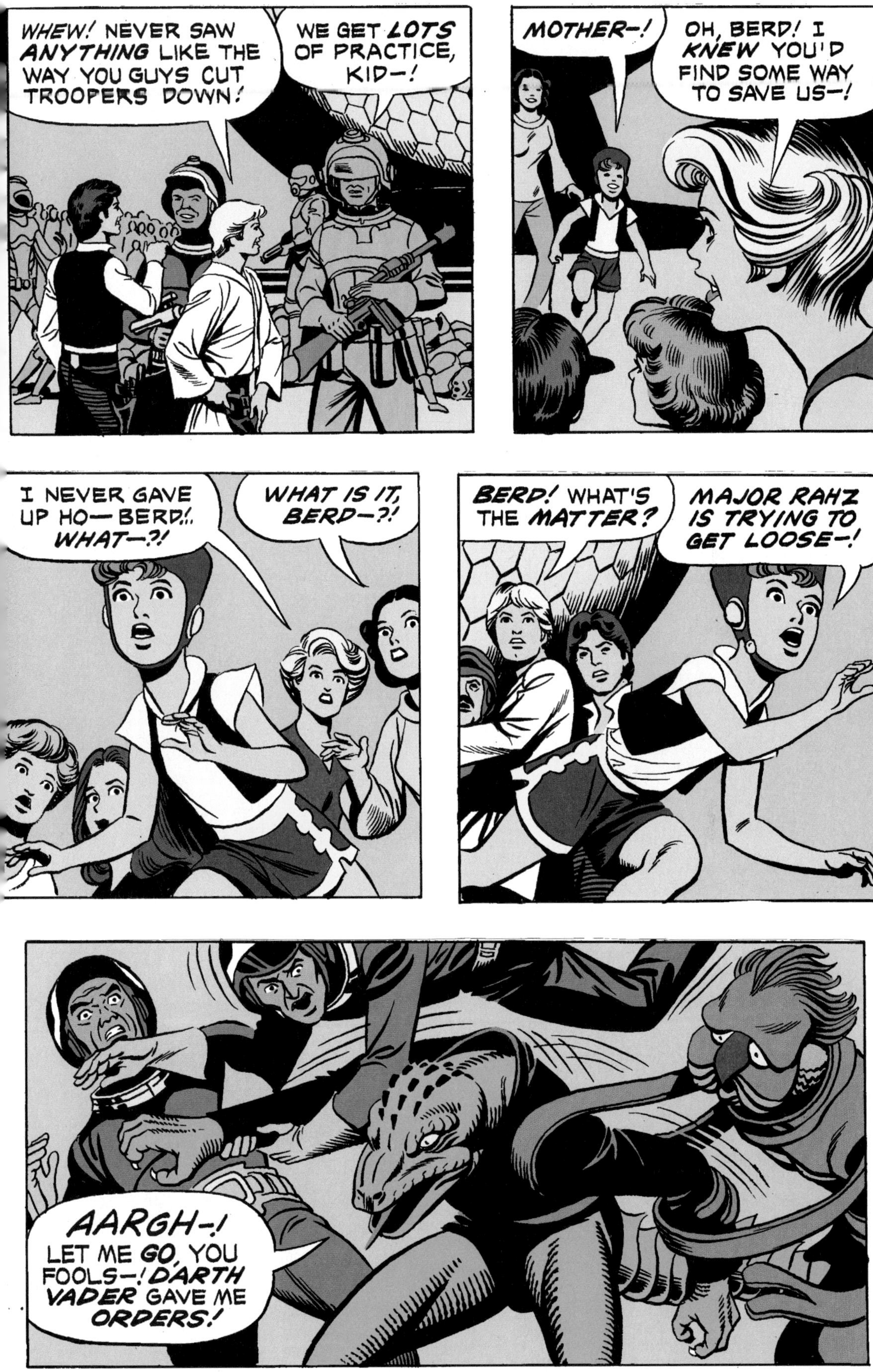
WHEW! NEVER SAW ANYTHING LIKE THE WAY YOU GUYS CUT TROOPERS DOWN!
WE GET LOTS OF PRACTICE, KID-!
MOTHER-!
OH, BERD! I KNEW YOU'D FIND SOME WAY TO SAVE US-!
I NEVER GAVE UP HO— BERD!! WHAT-?!
WHAT IS IT, BERD-?!
BERD! WHAT'S THE MATTER?
MAJOR RAHZ IS TRYING TO GET LOOSE-!
AARGH-! LET ME GO, YOU FOOLS-! DARTH VADER GAVE ME ORDERS!

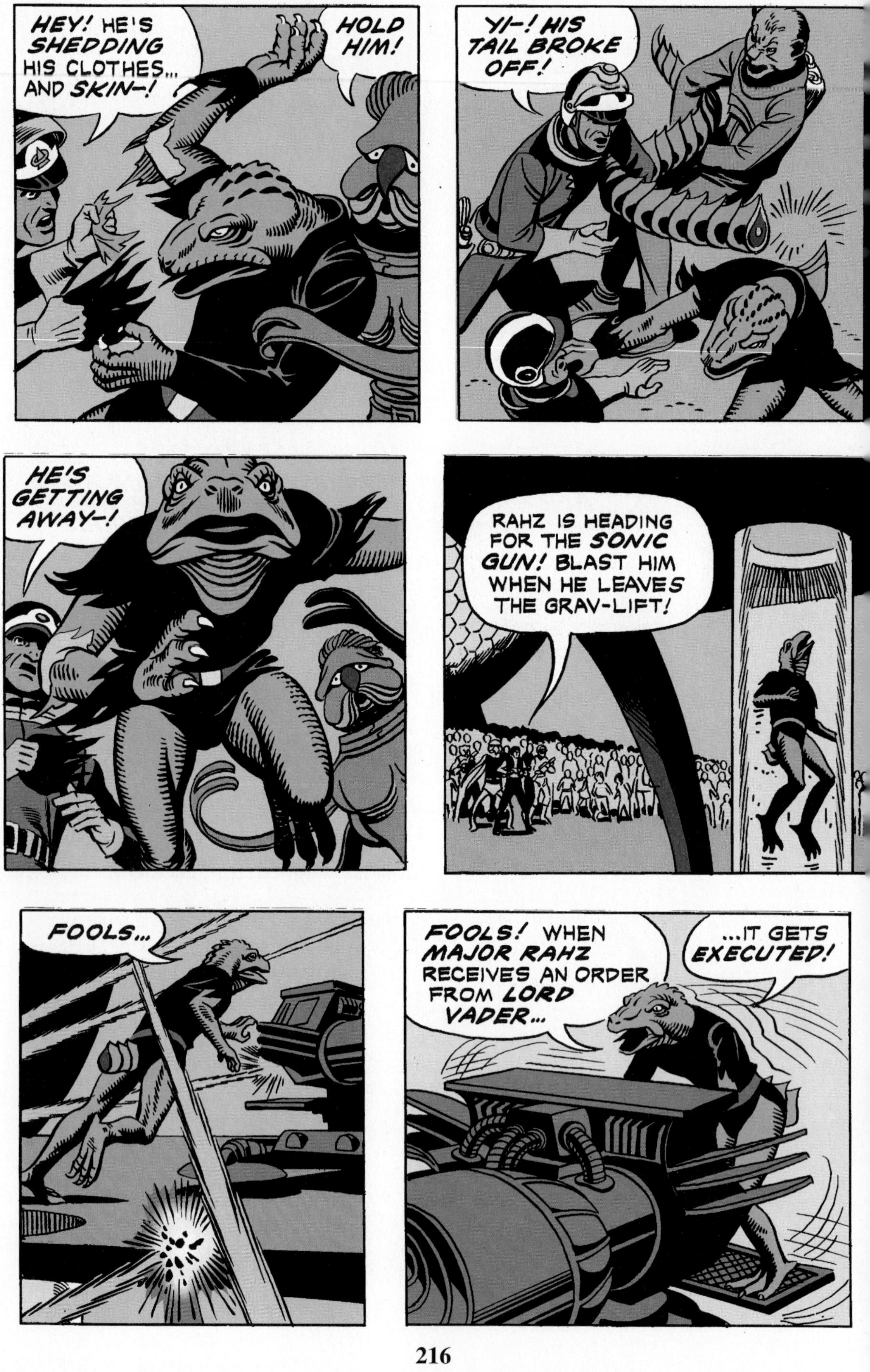
HEY! HE'S SHEDDING HIS CLOTHES... AND SKIN--!
HOLD HIM!
YI--! HIS TAIL BROKE OFF!
HE'S GETTING AWAY--!
RAHZ IS HEADING FOR THE SONIC GUN! BLAST HIM WHEN HE LEAVES THE GRAV-LIFT!
FOOLS...
FOOLS! WHEN MAJOR RAHZ RECEIVES AN ORDER FROM LORD VADER...
...IT GETS EXECUTED!

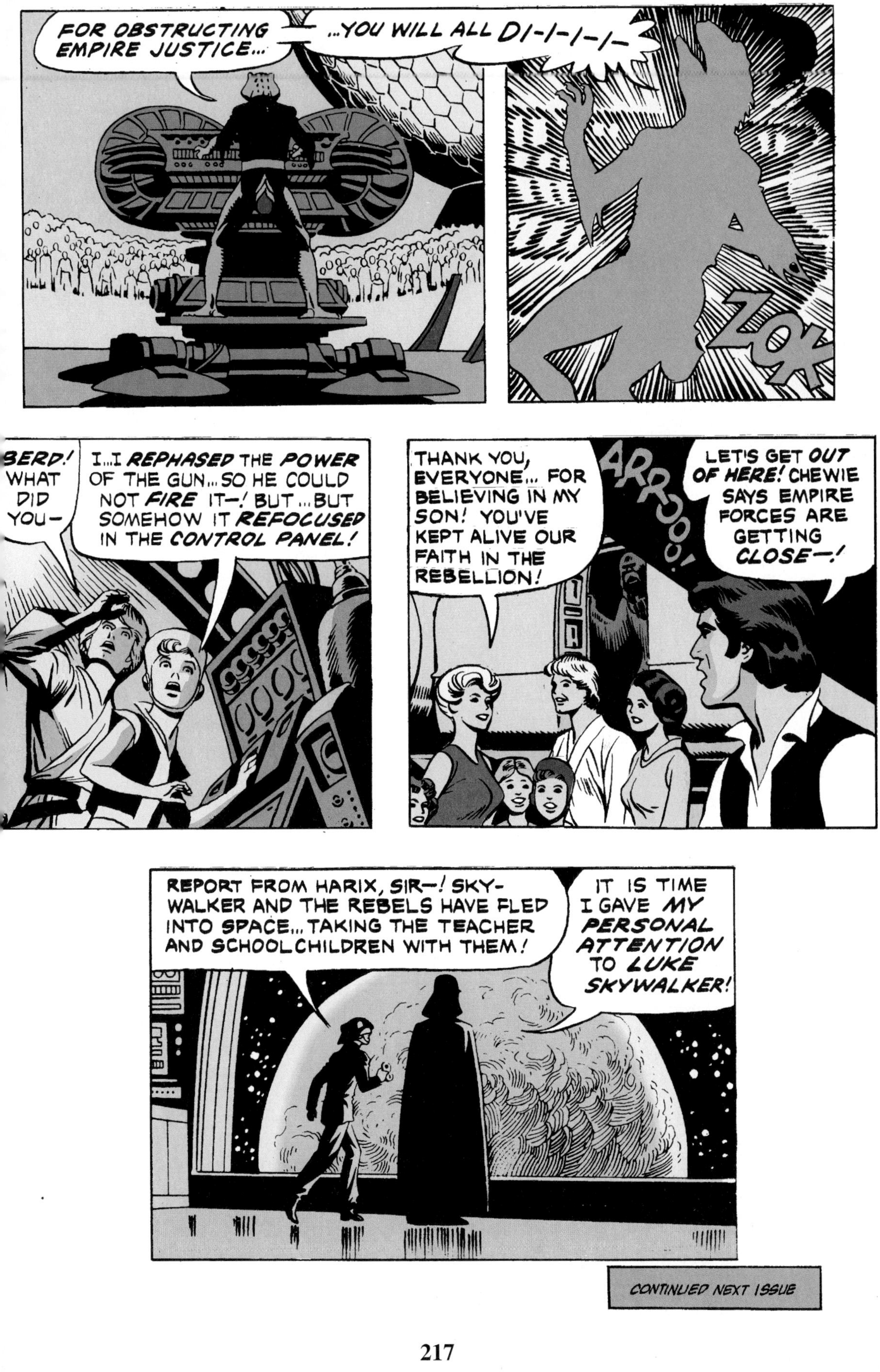
FOR OBSTRUCTING EMPIRE JUSTICE...
...YOU WILL ALL DI-I-I-I-I-
ZOK
BERD! WHAT DID YOU-
I...I REPHASED THE POWER OF THE GUN...SO HE COULD NOT FIRE IT-! BUT...BUT SOMEHOW IT REFOCUSED IN THE CONTROL PANEL!
THANK YOU, EVERYONE... FOR BELIEVING IN MY SON! YOU'VE KEPT ALIVE OUR FAITH IN THE REBELLION!
ARROOO!
LET'S GET OUT OF HERE! CHEWIE SAYS EMPIRE FORCES ARE GETTING CLOSE-!
REPORT FROM HARIX, SIR-! SKY-WALKER AND THE REBELS HAVE FLED INTO SPACE...TAKING THE TEACHER AND SCHOOLCHILDREN WITH THEM!
IT IS TIME I GAVE MY PERSONAL ATTENTION TO LUKE SKYWALKER!
CONTINUED NEXT ISSUE

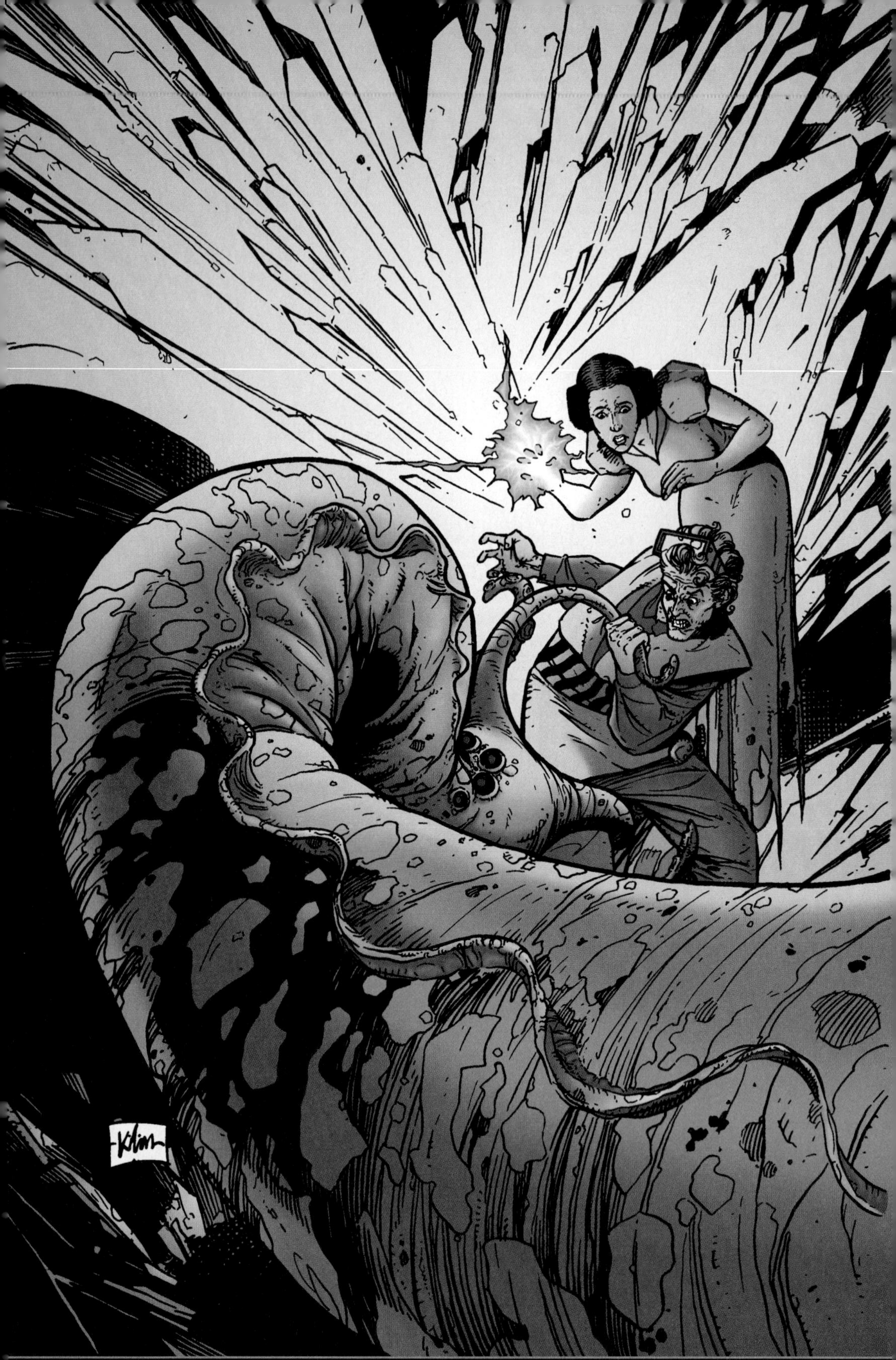

CLASSIC STAR WARS: THE EARLY ADVENTURES #8 — "AS LONG AS WE LIVE..."
ORIGINALLY PUBLISHED FROM APRIL 22 TO JUNE 16, 1980

WRITERS: RUSS MANNING & DON CHRISTENSEN • ARTIST & LETTERER: RUSS MANNING • ART RETOUCHING: RICK HOBERG & BRIAN SNODDY
COLORIST: RAY MURTAUGH • EDITOR: PEET JANES • COVER ARTISTS: KILIAN PLUNKETT & MATTHEW HOLLINGSWORTH

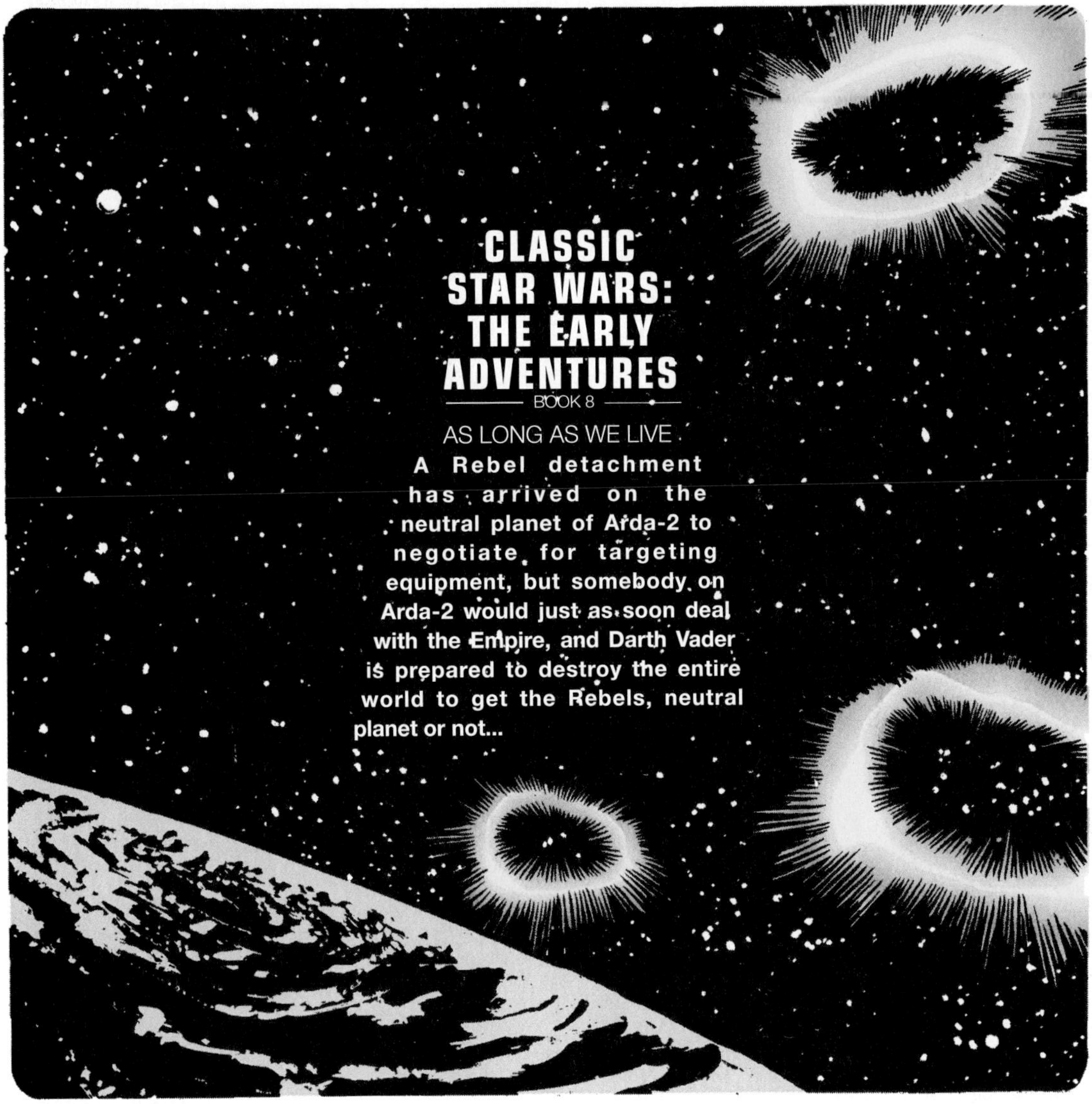
CLASSIC STAR WARS: THE EARLY ADVENTURES
BOOK 8
AS LONG AS WE LIVE
A Rebel detachment has arrived on the neutral planet of Arda-2 to negotiate for targeting equipment, but somebody on Arda-2 would just as soon deal with the Empire, and Darth Vader is prepared to destroy the entire world to get the Rebels, neutral planet or not...

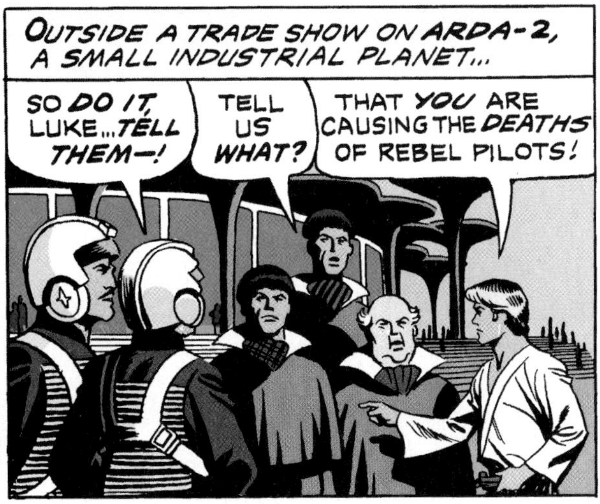
OUTSIDE A TRADE SHOW ON ARDA-2, A SMALL INDUSTRIAL PLANET...
SO DO IT, LUKE... TELL THEM--!
TELL US WHAT?
THAT YOU ARE CAUSING THE DEATHS OF REBEL PILOTS!

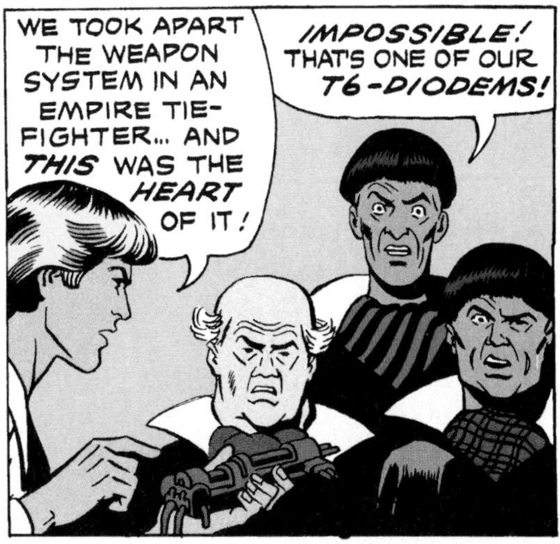
WE TOOK APART THE WEAPON SYSTEM IN AN EMPIRE TIE-FIGHTER... AND THIS WAS THE HEART OF IT!
IMPOSSIBLE! THAT'S ONE OF OUR T6-DIODEMS!

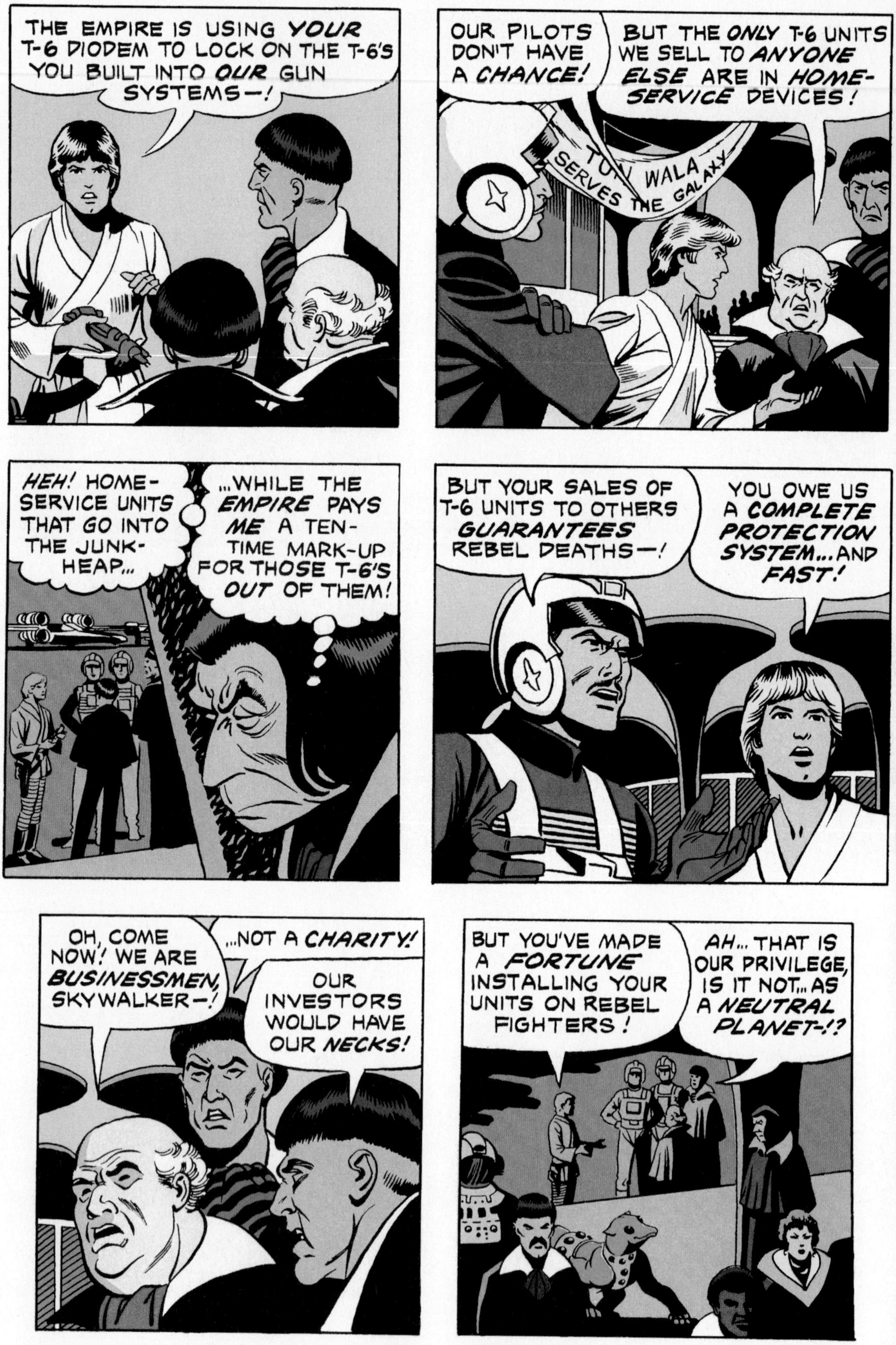
THE EMPIRE IS USING YOUR T-6 DIODEM TO LOCK ON THE T-6'S YOU BUILT INTO OUR GUN SYSTEMS—!
OUR PILOTS DON'T HAVE A CHANCE!
BUT THE ONLY T-6 UNITS WE SELL TO ANYONE ELSE ARE IN HOME-SERVICE DEVICES!
TON WALA SERVES THE GALAXY
HEH! HOME-SERVICE UNITS THAT GO INTO THE JUNK-HEAP...
...WHILE THE EMPIRE PAYS ME A TEN-TIME MARK-UP FOR THOSE T-6'S OUT OF THEM!
BUT YOUR SALES OF T-6 UNITS TO OTHERS GUARANTEES REBEL DEATHS—!
YOU OWE US A COMPLETE PROTECTION SYSTEM... AND FAST!
OH, COME NOW! WE ARE BUSINESSMEN, SKYWALKER—!
...NOT A CHARITY!
OUR INVESTORS WOULD HAVE OUR NECKS!
BUT YOU'VE MADE A FORTUNE INSTALLING YOUR UNITS ON REBEL FIGHTERS!
AH... THAT IS OUR PRIVILEGE, IS IT NOT... AS A NEUTRAL PLANET-!?

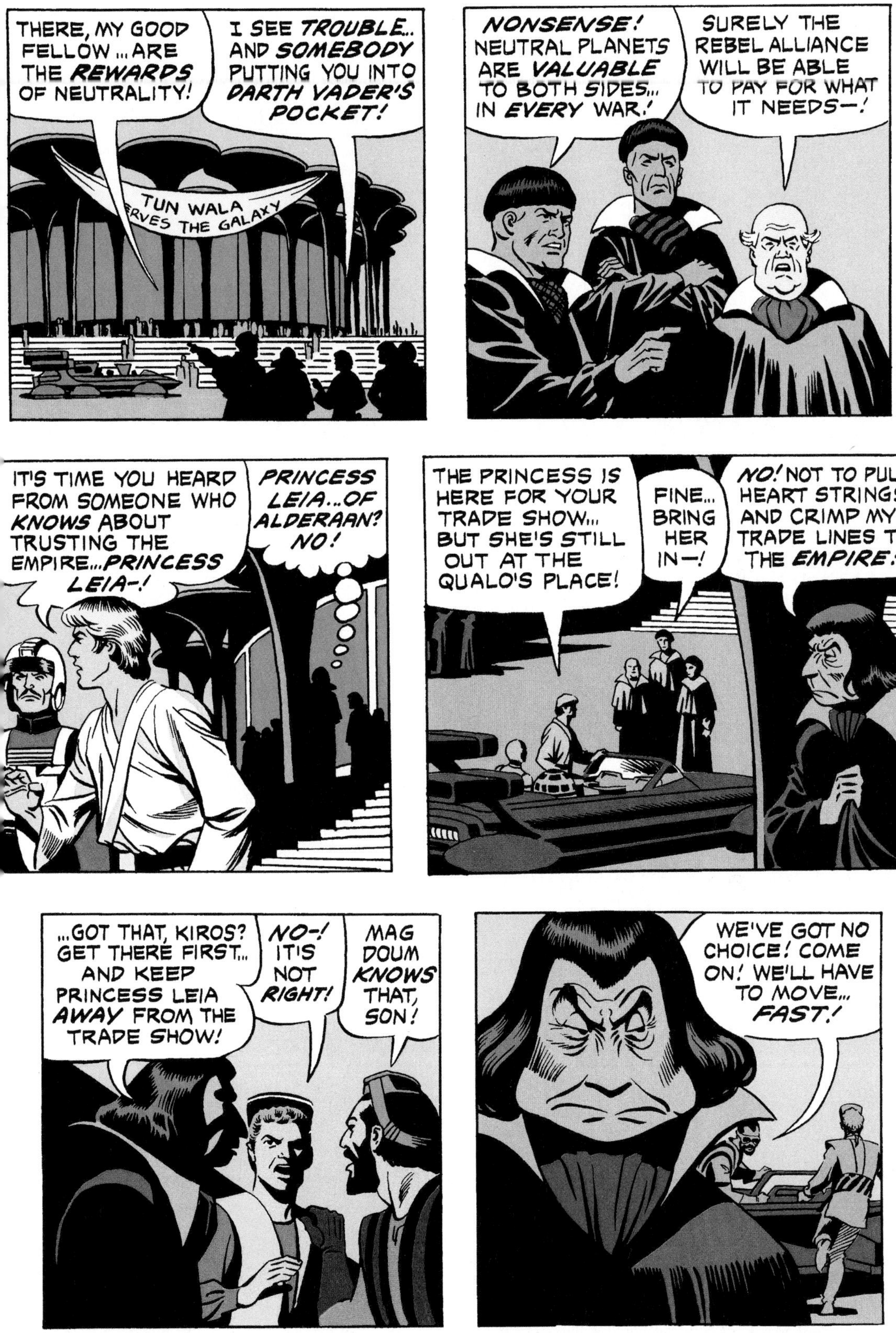
THERE, MY GOOD FELLOW ...ARE THE REWARDS OF NEUTRALITY!
I SEE TROUBLE... AND SOMEBODY PUTTING YOU INTO DARTH VADER'S POCKET!
TUN WALA SERVES THE GALAXY
NONSENSE! NEUTRAL PLANETS ARE VALUABLE TO BOTH SIDES... IN EVERY WAR!
SURELY THE REBEL ALLIANCE WILL BE ABLE TO PAY FOR WHAT IT NEEDS—!
IT'S TIME YOU HEARD FROM SOMEONE WHO KNOWS ABOUT TRUSTING THE EMPIRE...PRINCESS LEIA—!
PRINCESS LEIA...OF ALDERAAN? NO!
THE PRINCESS IS HERE FOR YOUR TRADE SHOW... BUT SHE'S STILL OUT AT THE QUALO'S PLACE!
FINE... BRING HER IN—!
NO! NOT TO PULL HEART STRINGS... AND CRIMP MY TRADE LINES TO THE EMPIRE!
...GOT THAT, KIROS? GET THERE FIRST... AND KEEP PRINCESS LEIA AWAY FROM THE TRADE SHOW!
NO—! IT'S NOT RIGHT!
MAG DOUM KNOWS THAT, SON!
WE'VE GOT NO CHOICE! COME ON! WE'LL HAVE TO MOVE... FAST!

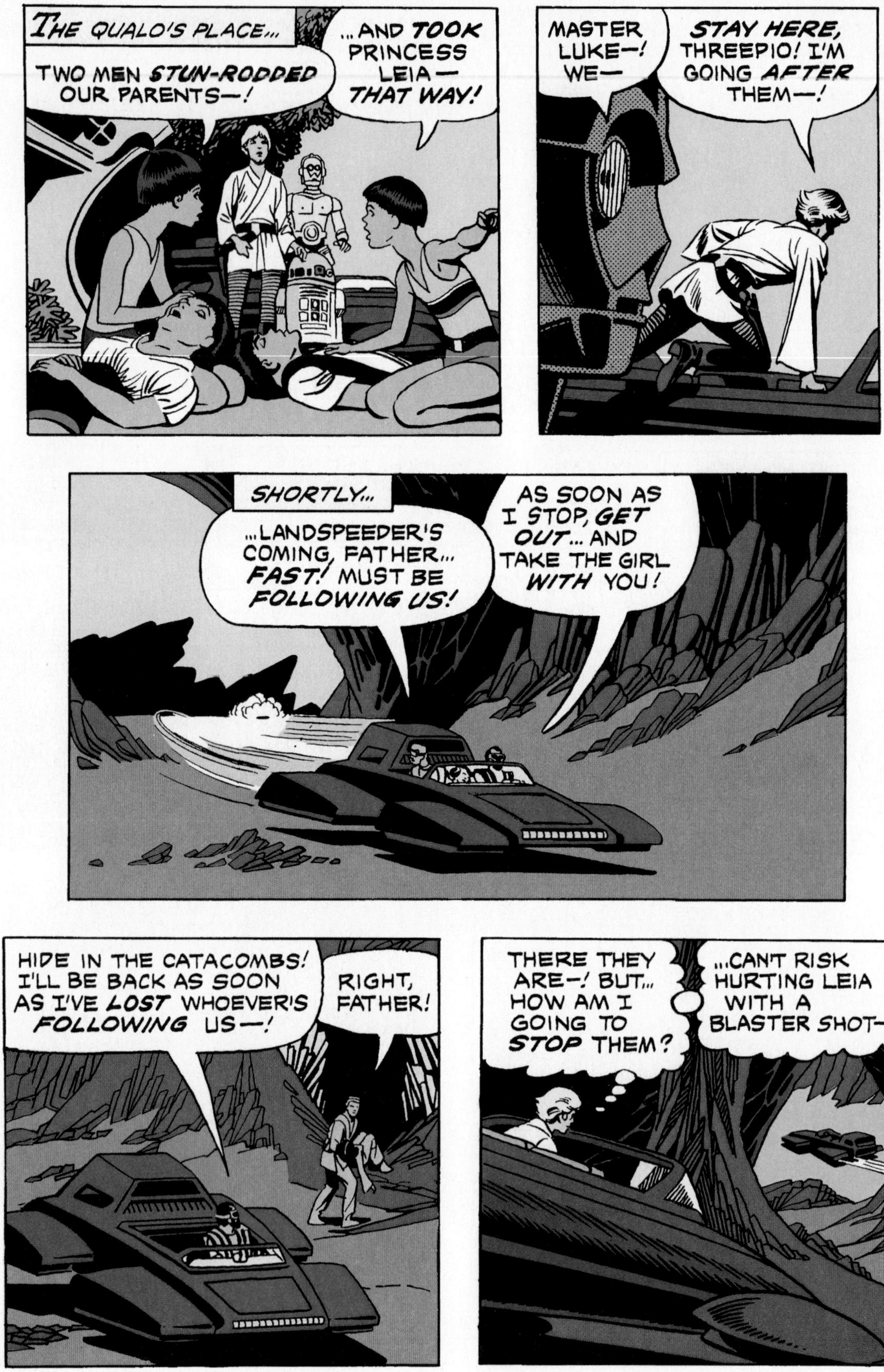
THE QUALO'S PLACE...
TWO MEN STUN-RODDED OUR PARENTS—!
...AND TOOK PRINCESS LEIA—THAT WAY!
MASTER LUKE—! WE—
STAY HERE, THREEPIO! I'M GOING AFTER THEM—!
SHORTLY...
...LANDSPEEDER'S COMING, FATHER... FAST! MUST BE FOLLOWING US!
AS SOON AS I STOP, GET OUT... AND TAKE THE GIRL WITH YOU!
HIDE IN THE CATACOMBS! I'LL BE BACK AS SOON AS I'VE LOST WHOEVER'S FOLLOWING US—!
RIGHT, FATHER!
THERE THEY ARE—! BUT... HOW AM I GOING TO STOP THEM?
...CAN'T RISK HURTING LEIA WITH A BLASTER SHOT—!

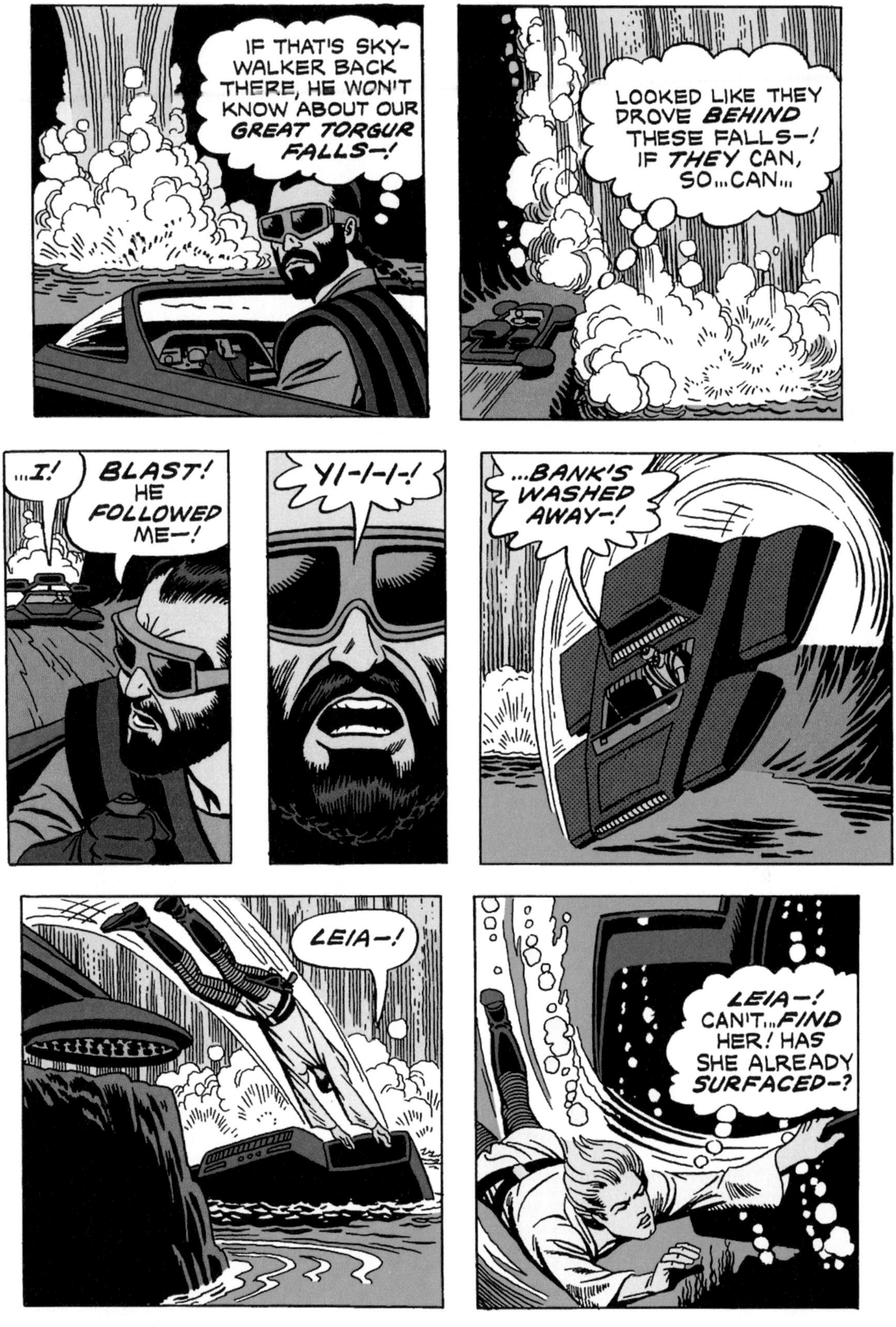
IF THAT'S SKY-WALKER BACK THERE, HE WON'T KNOW ABOUT OUR GREAT TORGUR FALLS—!
LOOKED LIKE THEY DROVE BEHIND THESE FALLS—! IF THEY CAN, SO...CAN...
...I!
BLAST! HE FOLLOWED ME—!
YI-I-I-I-!
...BANK'S WASHED AWAY—!
LEIA—!
LEIA—! CAN'T...FIND HER! HAS SHE ALREADY SURFACED—?

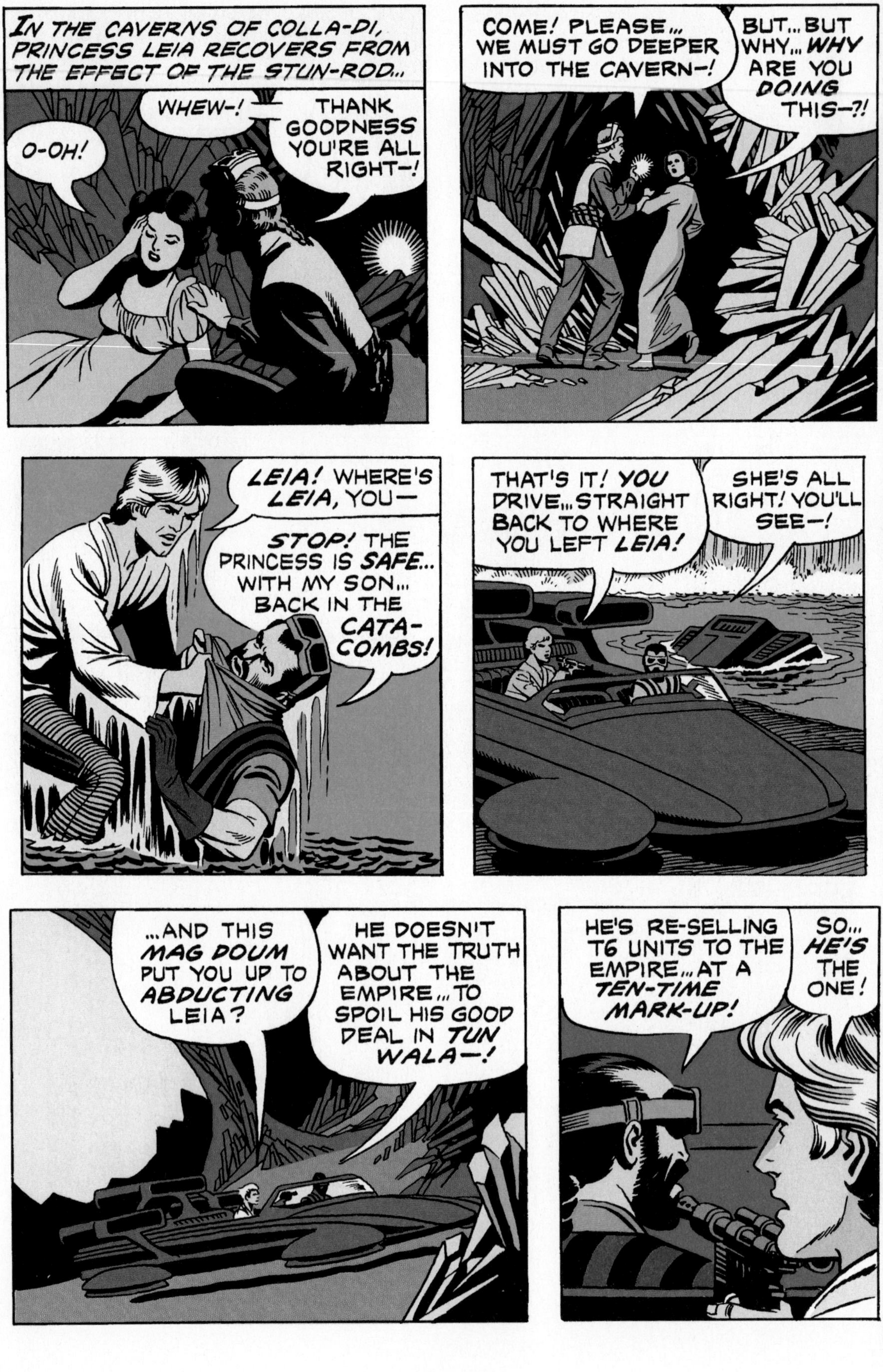

IN THE CAVERNS OF COLLA-DI, PRINCESS LEIA RECOVERS FROM THE EFFECT OF THE STUN-ROD...
O-OH!
WHEW-!
THANK GOODNESS YOU'RE ALL RIGHT-!
COME! PLEASE... WE MUST GO DEEPER INTO THE CAVERN-!
BUT... BUT WHY... WHY ARE YOU DOING THIS-?!
LEIA! WHERE'S LEIA, YOU—
STOP! THE PRINCESS IS SAFE... WITH MY SON... BACK IN THE CATA-COMBS!
THAT'S IT! YOU DRIVE... STRAIGHT BACK TO WHERE YOU LEFT LEIA!
SHE'S ALL RIGHT! YOU'LL SEE-!
...AND THIS MAG DOUM PUT YOU UP TO ABDUCTING LEIA?
HE DOESN'T WANT THE TRUTH ABOUT THE EMPIRE... TO SPOIL HIS GOOD DEAL IN TUN WALA-!
HE'S RE-SELLING T6 UNITS TO THE EMPIRE... AT A TEN-TIME MARK-UP!
SO... HE'S THE ONE!

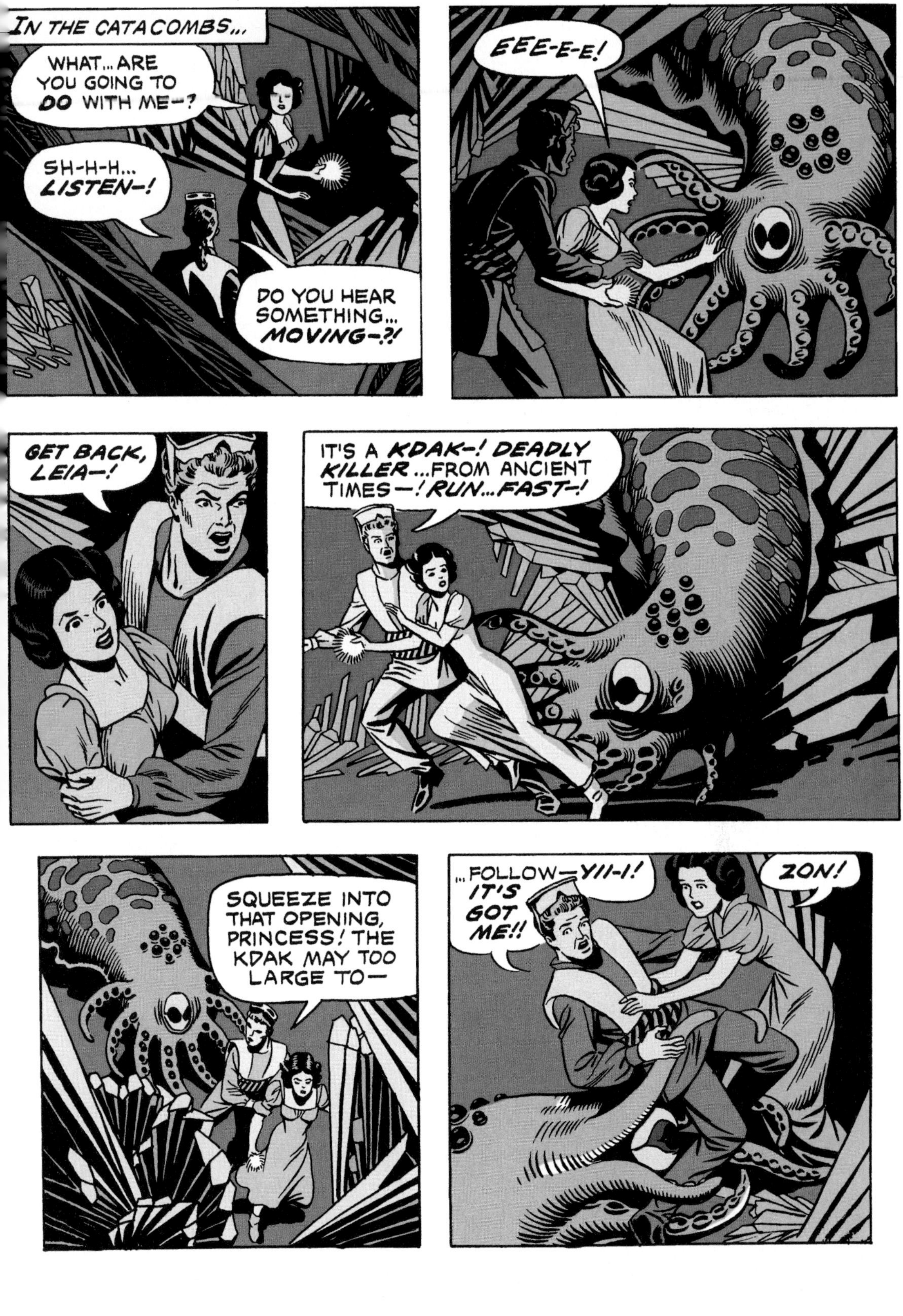
IN THE CATACOMBS...
WHAT... ARE YOU GOING TO DO WITH ME-?
SH-H-H... LISTEN-!
DO YOU HEAR SOMETHING... MOVING-?!
EEE-E-E!
GET BACK, LEIA-!
IT'S A KDAK-! DEADLY KILLER...FROM ANCIENT TIMES-! RUN...FAST-!
SQUEEZE INTO THAT OPENING, PRINCESS! THE KDAK MAY TOO LARGE TO—
...FOLLOW—YII-I! IT'S GOT ME!!
ZON!

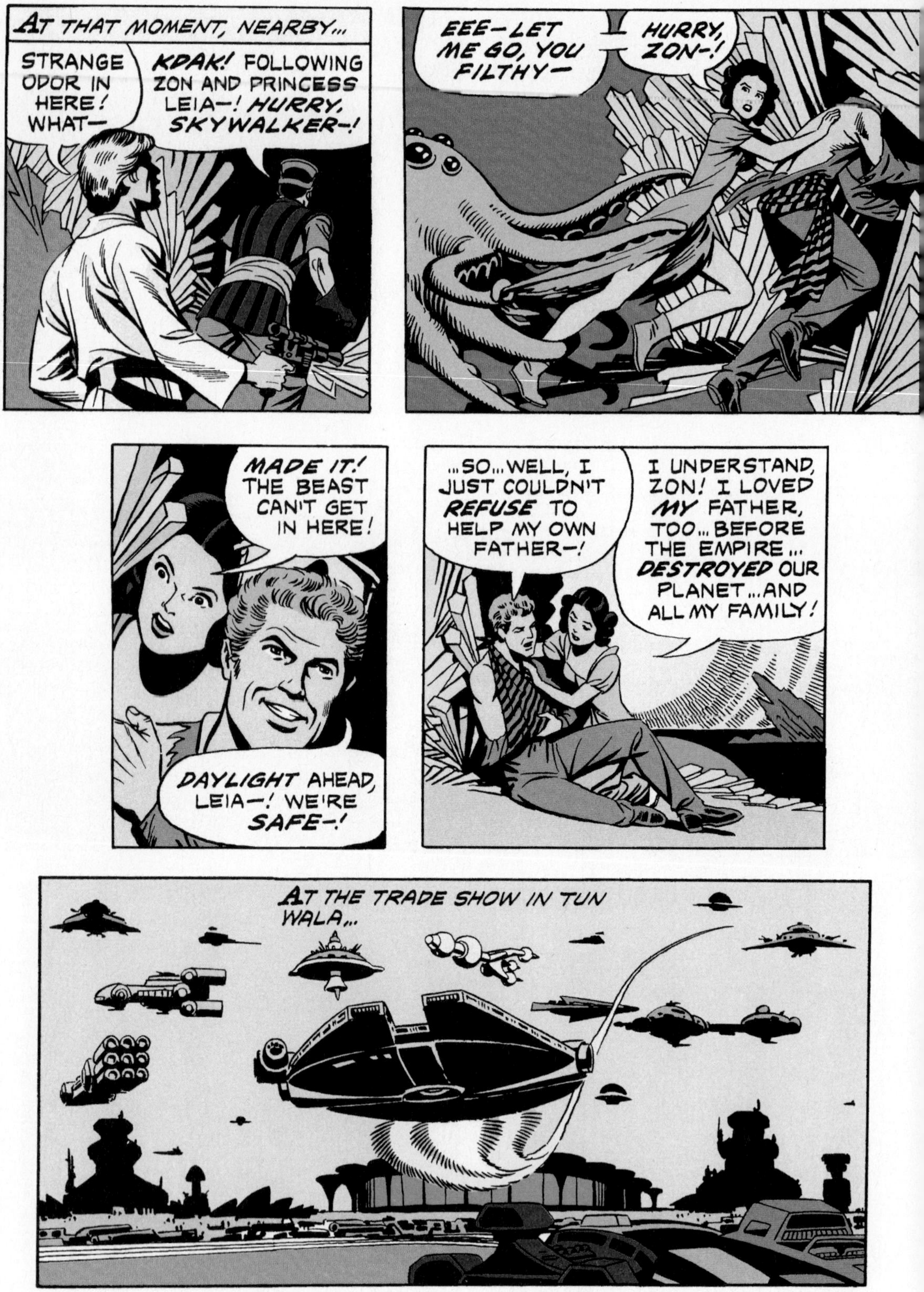
AT THAT MOMENT, NEARBY...
STRANGE ODOR IN HERE! WHAT—
KPAK! FOLLOWING ZON AND PRINCESS LEIA—! HURRY, SKYWALKER—!
EEE—LET ME GO, YOU FILTHY—
HURRY, ZON—!
MADE IT! THE BEAST CAN'T GET IN HERE!
DAYLIGHT AHEAD, LEIA—! WE'RE SAFE—!
...SO...WELL, I JUST COULDN'T REFUSE TO HELP MY OWN FATHER—!
I UNDERSTAND, ZON! I LOVED MY FATHER, TOO...BEFORE THE EMPIRE... DESTROYED OUR PLANET...AND ALL MY FAMILY!
AT THE TRADE SHOW IN TUN WALA...

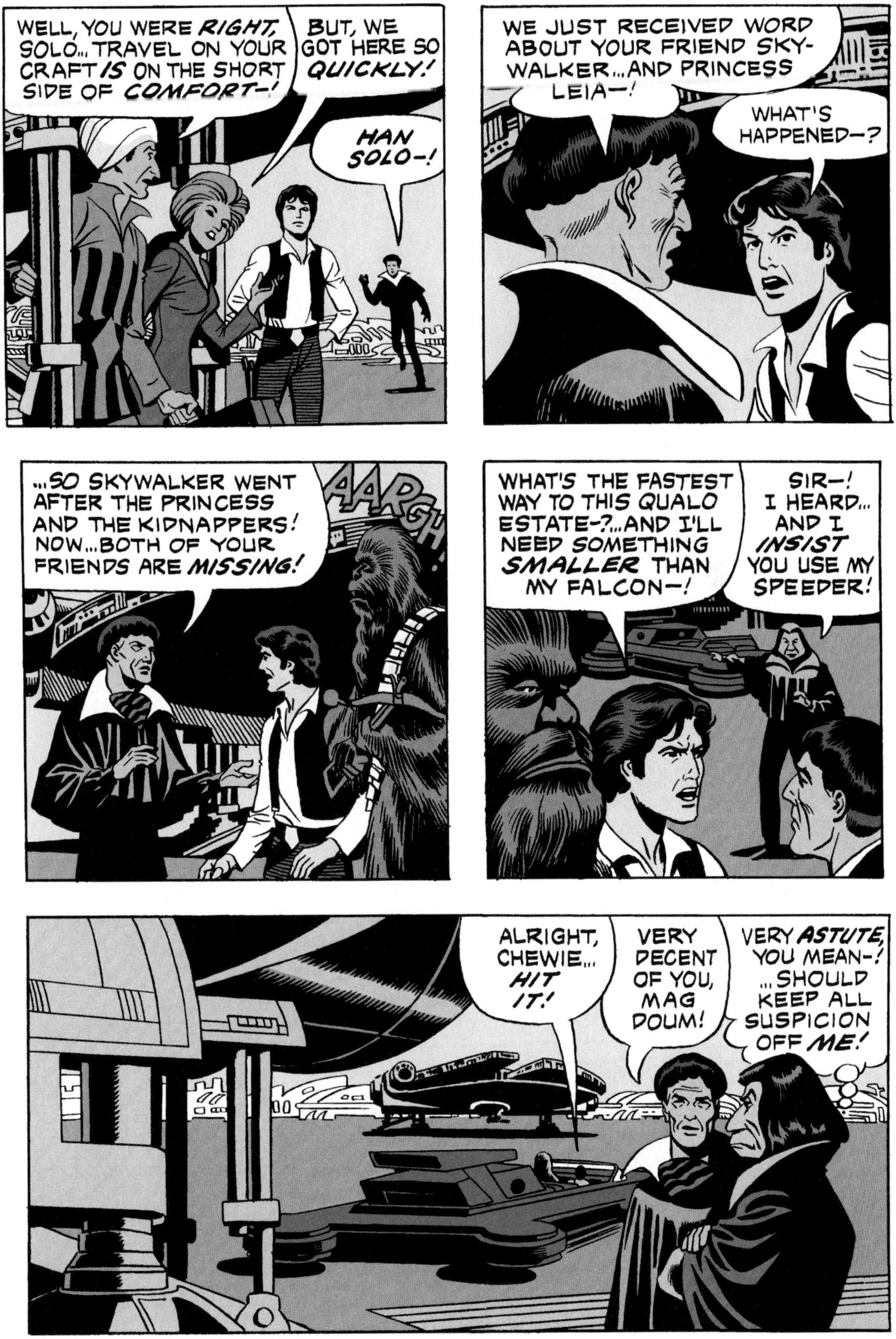
WELL, YOU WERE RIGHT, SOLO... TRAVEL ON YOUR CRAFT IS ON THE SHORT SIDE OF COMFORT-!
BUT, WE GOT HERE SO QUICKLY!
HAN SOLO-!
WE JUST RECEIVED WORD ABOUT YOUR FRIEND SKY-WALKER...AND PRINCESS LEIA-!
WHAT'S HAPPENED-?
...SO SKYWALKER WENT AFTER THE PRINCESS AND THE KIDNAPPERS! NOW...BOTH OF YOUR FRIENDS ARE MISSING!
AARGH
WHAT'S THE FASTEST WAY TO THIS QUALO ESTATE-?...AND I'LL NEED SOMETHING SMALLER THAN MY FALCON-!
SIR-! I HEARD... AND I INSIST YOU USE MY SPEEDER!
ALRIGHT, CHEWIE... HIT IT!
VERY DECENT OF YOU, MAG DOUM!
VERY ASTUTE, YOU MEAN-! ...SHOULD KEEP ALL SUSPICION OFF ME!

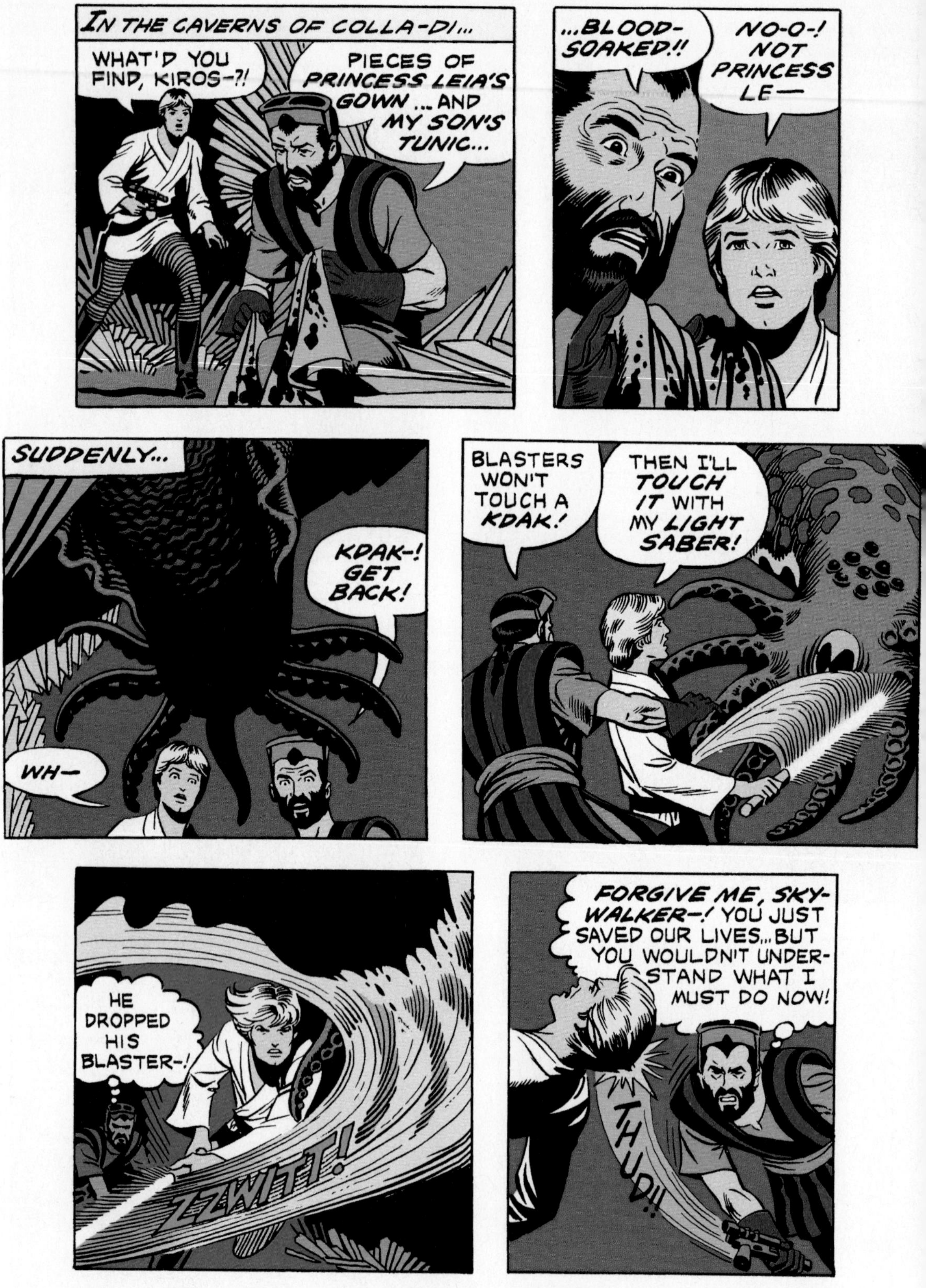

IN THE CAVERNS OF COLLA-DI...
WHAT'D YOU FIND, KIROS-?!
PIECES OF PRINCESS LEIA'S GOWN ... AND MY SON'S TUNIC...
...BLOOD-SOAKED!!
NO-O-! NOT PRINCESS LE—
SUDDENLY...
KDAK-! GET BACK!
WH—
BLASTERS WON'T TOUCH A KDAK!
THEN I'LL TOUCH IT WITH MY LIGHT SABER!
HE DROPPED HIS BLASTER-!
ZZWITT!
FORGIVE ME, SKY-WALKER-! YOU JUST SAVED OUR LIVES...BUT YOU WOULDN'T UNDER-STAND WHAT I MUST DO NOW!
THUD!!

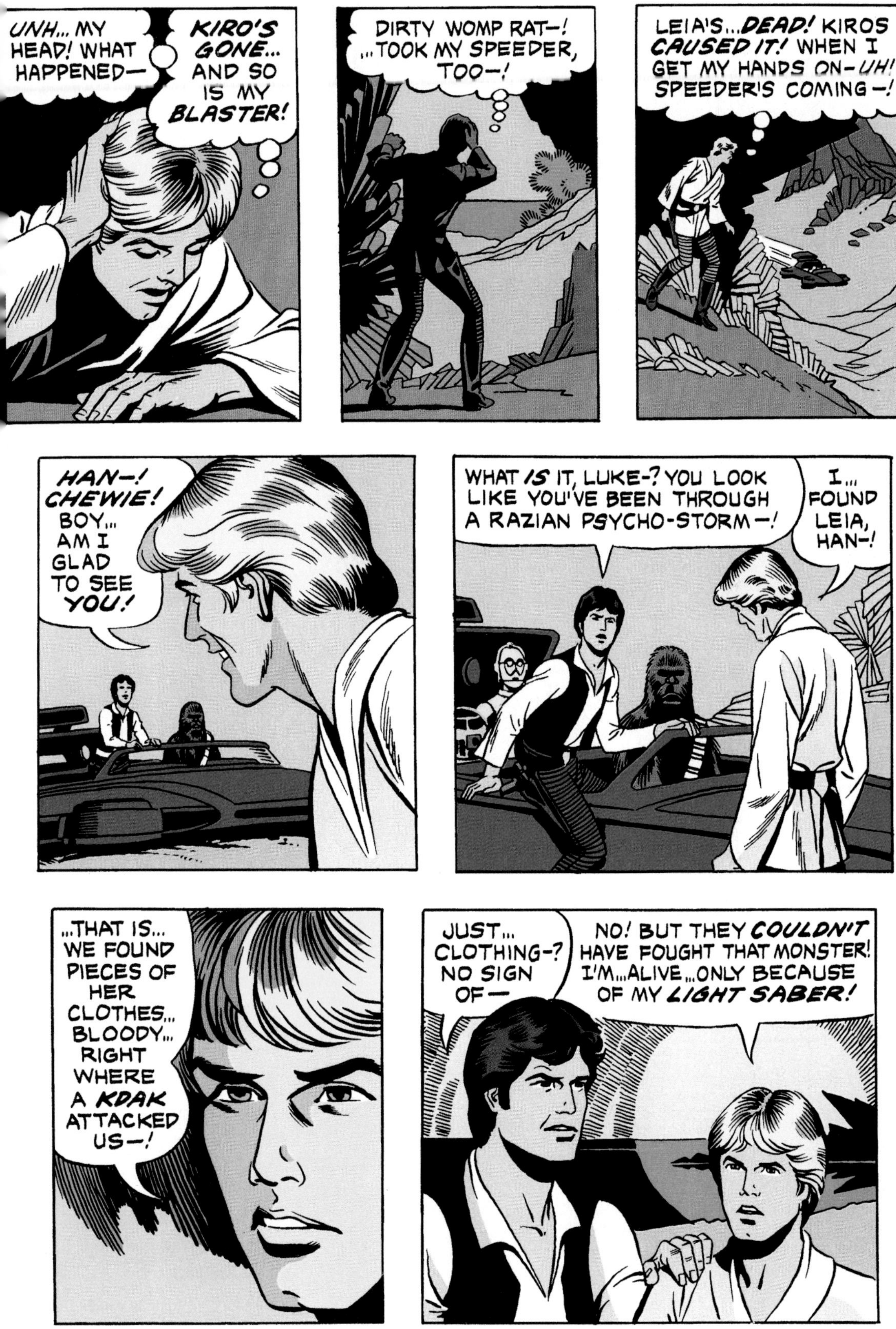

UNH... MY HEAD! WHAT HAPPENED—
KIRO'S GONE... AND SO IS MY BLASTER!
DIRTY WOMP RAT—! ...TOOK MY SPEEDER, TOO—!
LEIA'S...DEAD! KIROS CAUSED IT! WHEN I GET MY HANDS ON—UH! SPEEDER'S COMING—!
HAN—! CHEWIE! BOY... AM I GLAD TO SEE YOU!
WHAT IS IT, LUKE—? YOU LOOK LIKE YOU'VE BEEN THROUGH A RAZIAN PSYCHO-STORM—!
I... FOUND LEIA, HAN—!
...THAT IS... WE FOUND PIECES OF HER CLOTHES... BLOODY... RIGHT WHERE A KDAK ATTACKED US—!
JUST... CLOTHING—? NO SIGN OF—
NO! BUT THEY COULDN'T HAVE FOUGHT THAT MONSTER! I'M...ALIVE...ONLY BECAUSE OF MY LIGHT SABER!

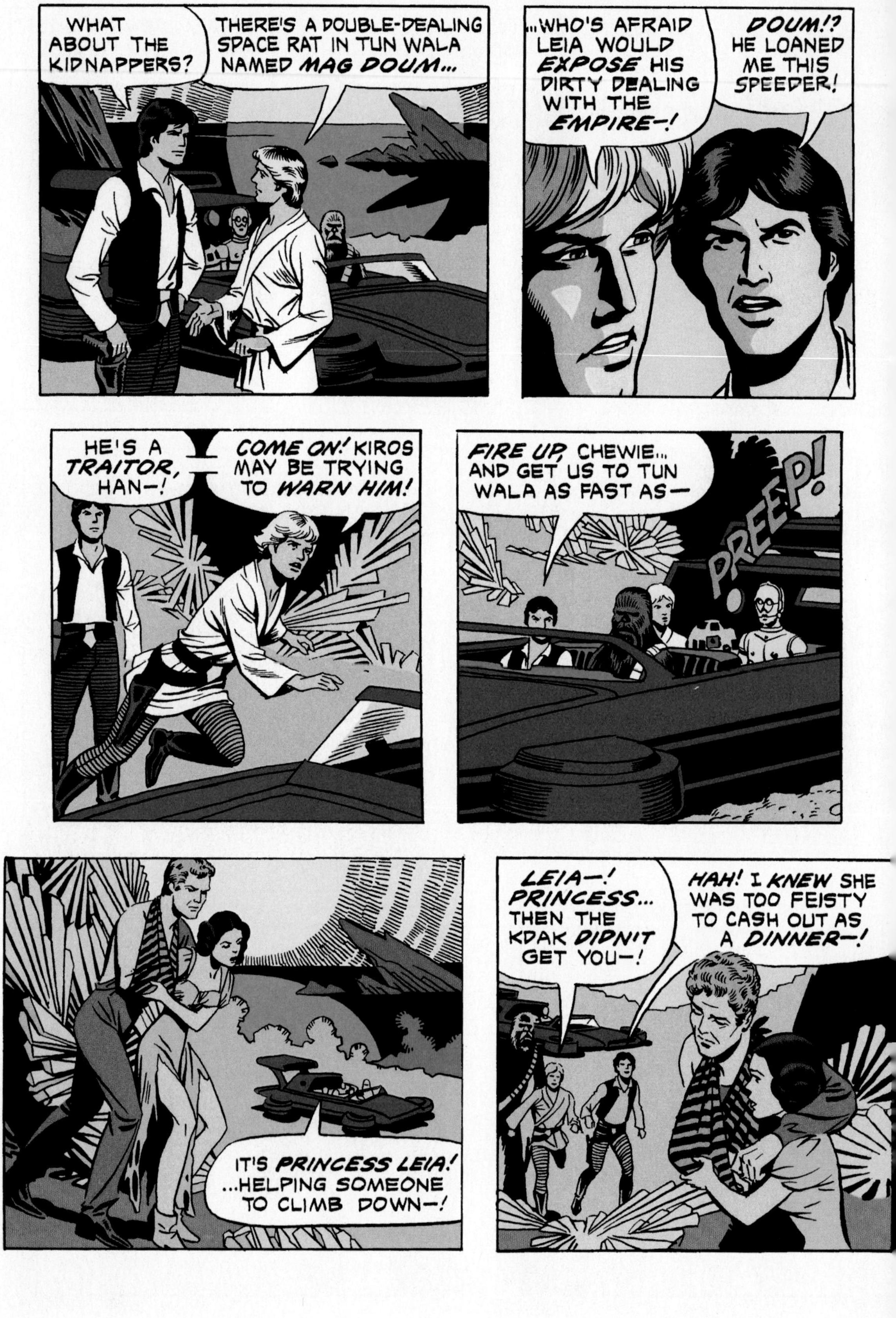
WHAT ABOUT THE KIDNAPPERS?
THERE'S A DOUBLE-DEALING SPACE RAT IN TUN WALA NAMED MAG DOUM...
...WHO'S AFRAID LEIA WOULD EXPOSE HIS DIRTY DEALING WITH THE EMPIRE--!
DOUM!? HE LOANED ME THIS SPEEDER!
HE'S A TRAITOR, HAN--!
COME ON! KIROS MAY BE TRYING TO WARN HIM!
FIRE UP, CHEWIE... AND GET US TO TUN WALA AS FAST AS—
PREEP!
IT'S PRINCESS LEIA! ...HELPING SOMEONE TO CLIMB DOWN--!
LEIA--! PRINCESS... THEN THE KDAK DIDN'T GET YOU--!
HAH! I KNEW SHE WAS TOO FEISTY TO CASH OUT AS A DINNER--!

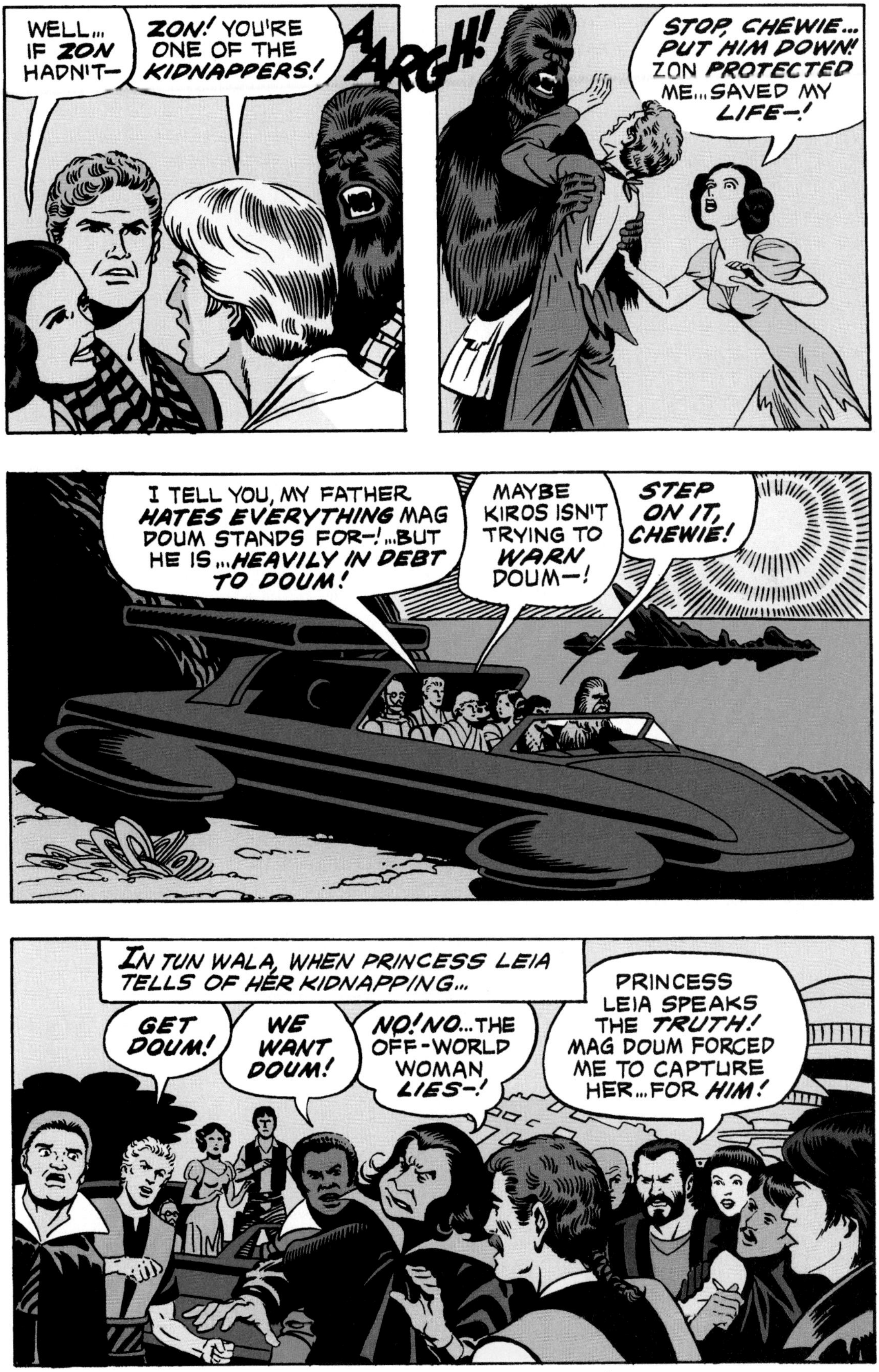
WELL... IF ZON HADN'T—
ZON! YOU'RE ONE OF THE KIDNAPPERS!
AARGH!
STOP, CHEWIE... PUT HIM DOWN! ZON PROTECTED ME... SAVED MY LIFE—!
I TELL YOU, MY FATHER HATES EVERYTHING MAG DOUM STANDS FOR—!...BUT HE IS... HEAVILY IN DEBT TO DOUM!
MAYBE KIROS ISN'T TRYING TO WARN DOUM—!
STEP ON IT, CHEWIE!
IN TUN WALA, WHEN PRINCESS LEIA TELLS OF HER KIDNAPPING...
GET DOUM!
WE WANT DOUM!
NO! NO... THE OFF-WORLD WOMAN LIES—!
PRINCESS LEIA SPEAKS THE TRUTH! MAG DOUM FORCED ME TO CAPTURE HER... FOR HIM!

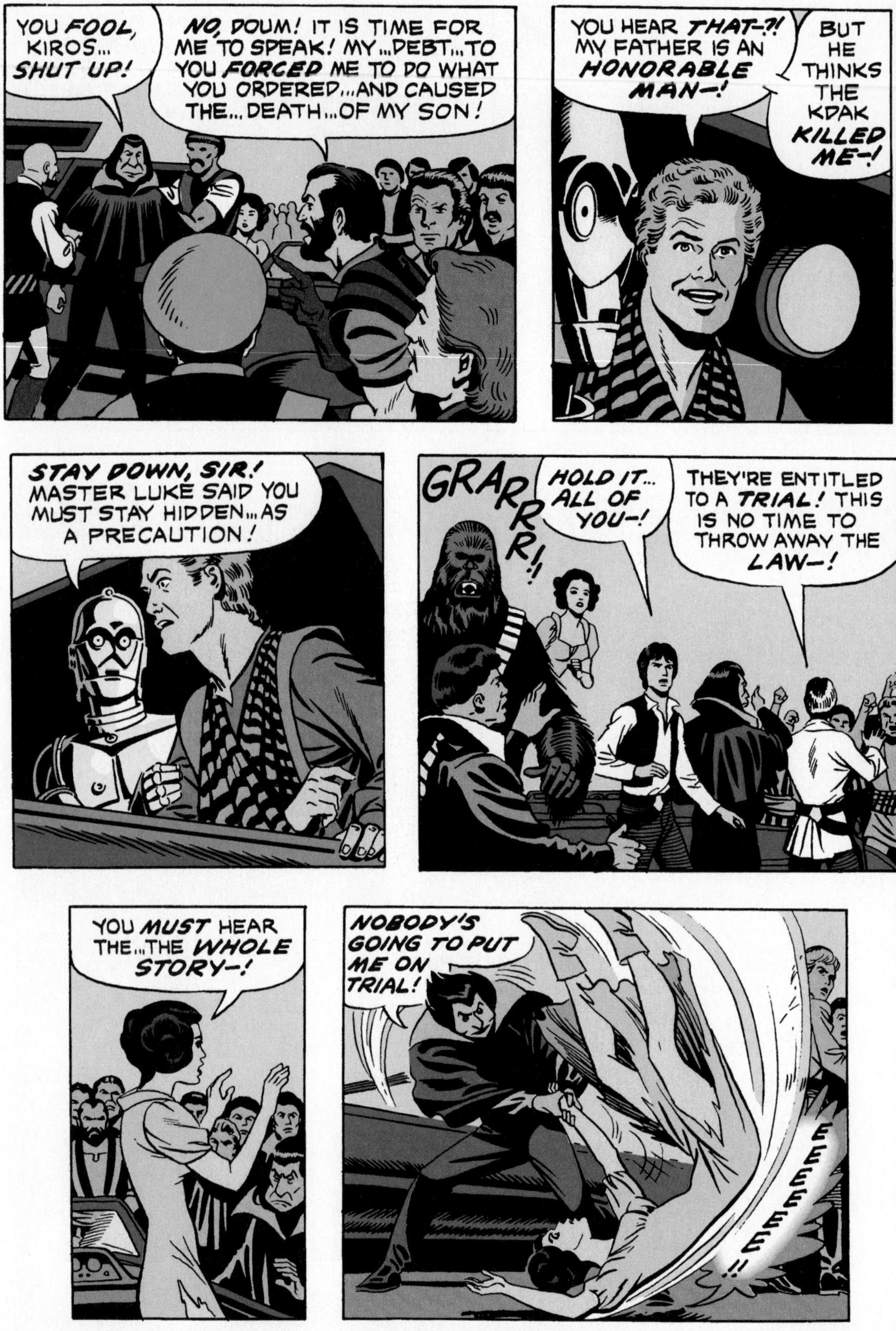
YOU FOOL, KIROS... SHUT UP!
NO, DOUM! IT IS TIME FOR ME TO SPEAK! MY...DEBT...TO YOU FORCED ME TO DO WHAT YOU ORDERED...AND CAUSED THE...DEATH...OF MY SON!
YOU HEAR THAT-?! MY FATHER IS AN HONORABLE MAN-!
BUT HE THINKS THE KDAK KILLED ME-!
STAY DOWN, SIR! MASTER LUKE SAID YOU MUST STAY HIDDEN...AS A PRECAUTION!
GRARRR!!
HOLD IT... ALL OF YOU-!
THEY'RE ENTITLED TO A TRIAL! THIS IS NO TIME TO THROW AWAY THE LAW-!
YOU MUST HEAR THE...THE WHOLE STORY-!
NOBODY'S GOING TO PUT ME ON TRIAL!
EEEEEEE!!

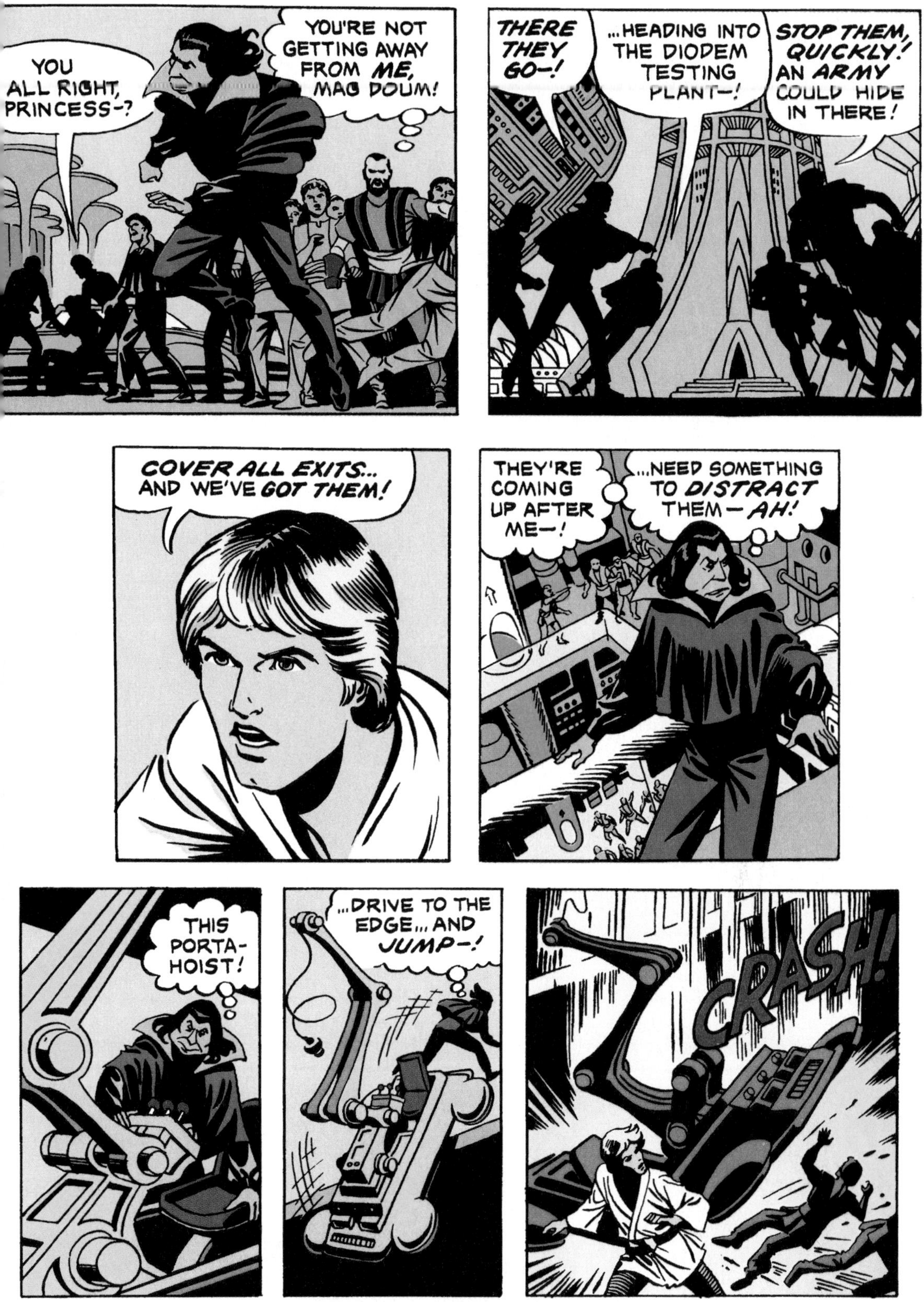
YOU ALL RIGHT, PRINCESS-?
YOU'RE NOT GETTING AWAY FROM ME, MAG DOUM!
THERE THEY GO-!
...HEADING INTO THE DIODEM TESTING PLANT-!
STOP THEM, QUICKLY! AN ARMY COULD HIDE IN THERE!
COVER ALL EXITS... AND WE'VE GOT THEM!
THEY'RE COMING UP AFTER ME-!
...NEED SOMETHING TO DISTRACT THEM-AH!
THIS PORTA-HOIST!
...DRIVE TO THE EDGE... AND JUMP-!
CRASH!

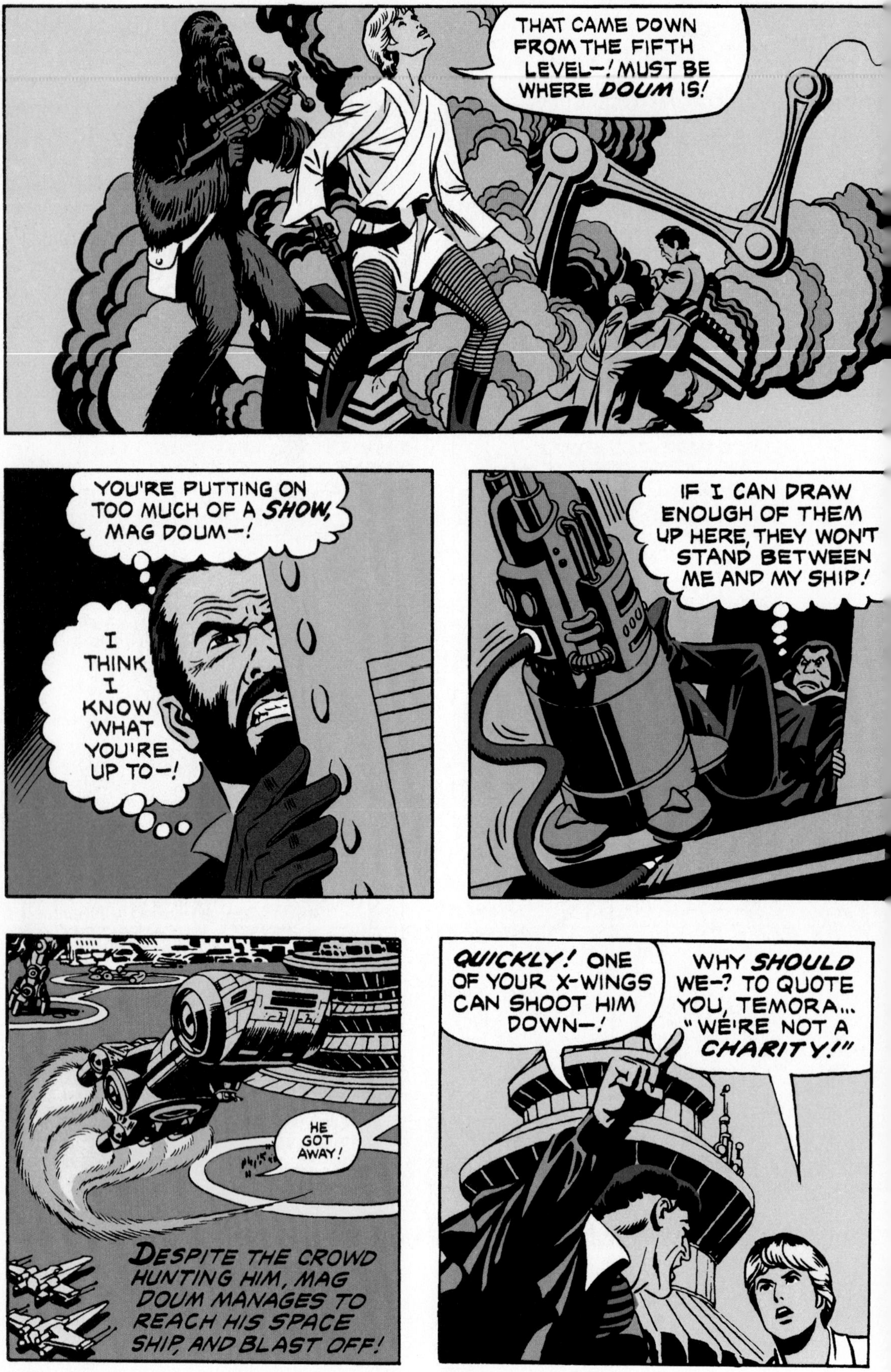
THAT CAME DOWN FROM THE FIFTH LEVEL--! MUST BE WHERE DOUM IS!
YOU'RE PUTTING ON TOO MUCH OF A SHOW, MAG DOUM--!
I THINK I KNOW WHAT YOU'RE UP TO--!
IF I CAN DRAW ENOUGH OF THEM UP HERE, THEY WON'T STAND BETWEEN ME AND MY SHIP!
HE GOT AWAY!
DESPITE THE CROWD HUNTING HIM, MAG DOUM MANAGES TO REACH HIS SPACE SHIP, AND BLAST OFF!
QUICKLY! ONE OF YOUR X-WINGS CAN SHOOT HIM DOWN--!
WHY SHOULD WE--? TO QUOTE YOU, TEMORA... "WE'RE NOT A CHARITY!"

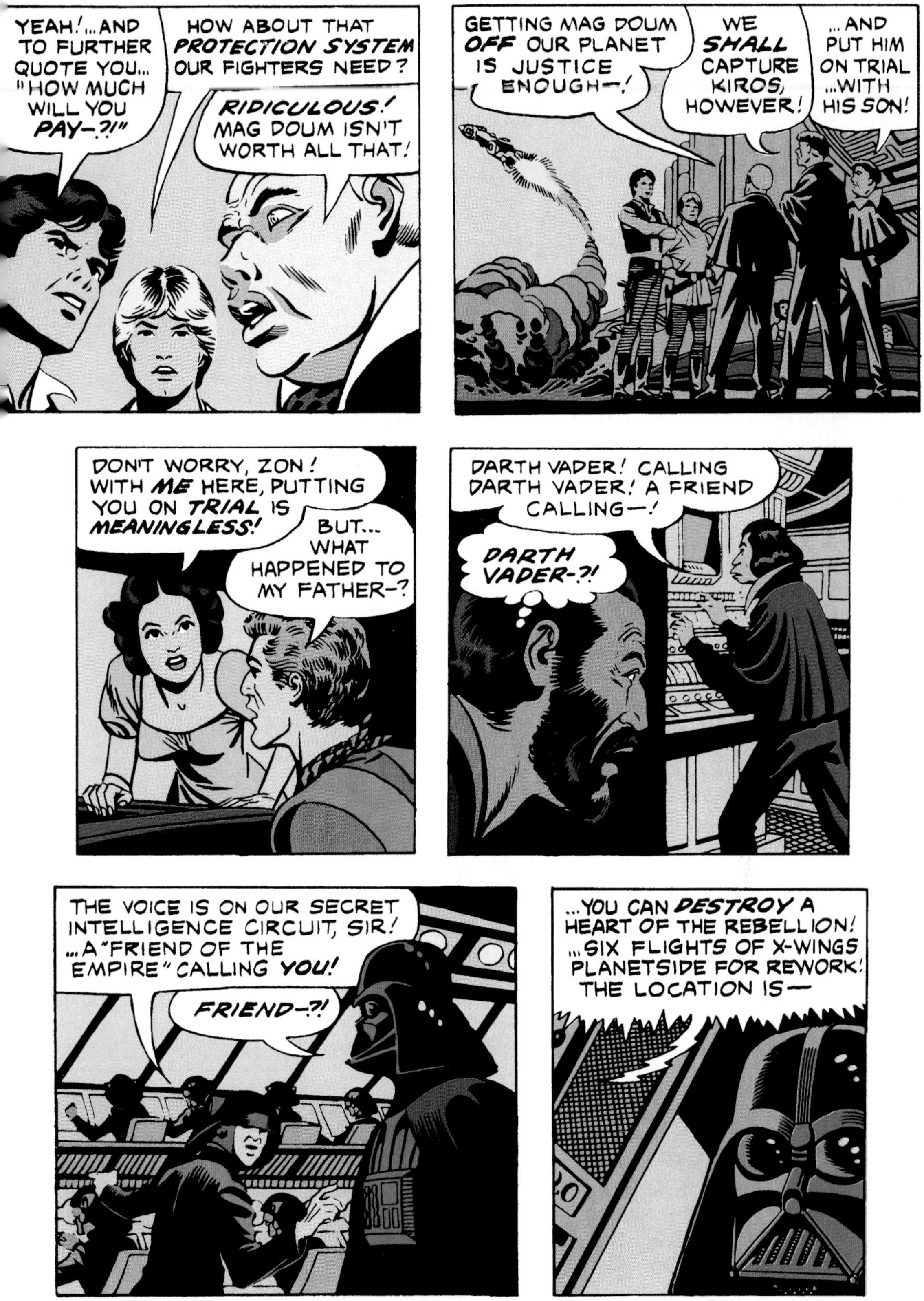
YEAH! ...AND TO FURTHER QUOTE YOU... "HOW MUCH WILL YOU PAY-?!"
HOW ABOUT THAT PROTECTION SYSTEM OUR FIGHTERS NEED?
RIDICULOUS! MAG DOUM ISN'T WORTH ALL THAT!
GETTING MAG DOUM OFF OUR PLANET IS JUSTICE ENOUGH-!
WE SHALL CAPTURE KIROS, HOWEVER!
...AND PUT HIM ON TRIAL ...WITH HIS SON!
DON'T WORRY, ZON! WITH ME HERE, PUTTING YOU ON TRIAL IS MEANINGLESS!
BUT... WHAT HAPPENED TO MY FATHER-?
DARTH VADER! CALLING DARTH VADER! A FRIEND CALLING-!
DARTH VADER-?!
THE VOICE IS ON OUR SECRET INTELLIGENCE CIRCUIT, SIR! ...A "FRIEND OF THE EMPIRE" CALLING YOU!
FRIEND-?!
...YOU CAN DESTROY A HEART OF THE REBELLION! ...SIX FLIGHTS OF X-WINGS PLANETSIDE FOR REWORK! THE LOCATION IS—

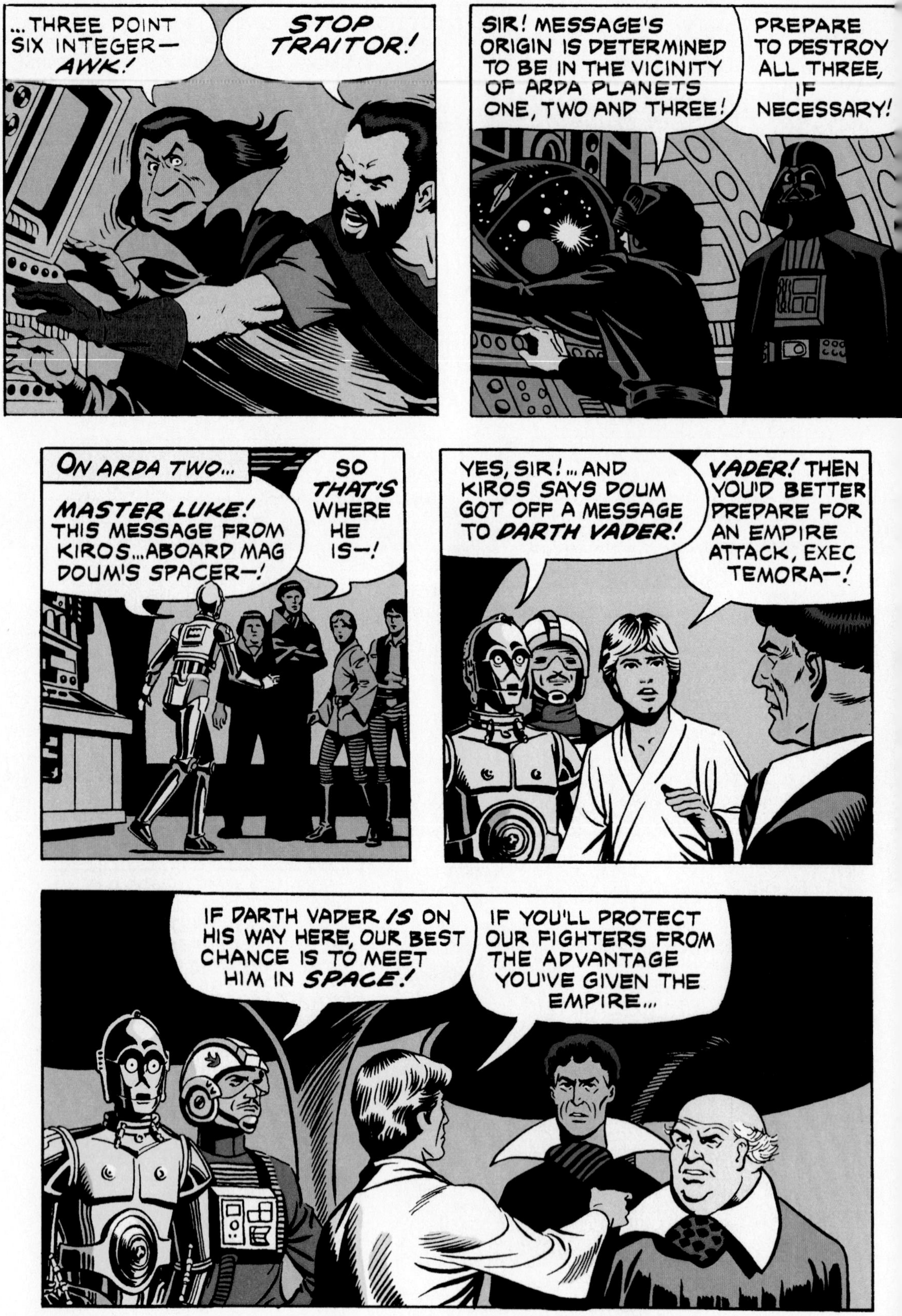
...THREE POINT SIX INTEGER— AWK!
STOP TRAITOR!
SIR! MESSAGE'S ORIGIN IS DETERMINED TO BE IN THE VICINITY OF ARDA PLANETS ONE, TWO AND THREE!
PREPARE TO DESTROY ALL THREE, IF NECESSARY!
ON ARDA TWO...
MASTER LUKE! THIS MESSAGE FROM KIROS...ABOARD MAG DOUM'S SPACER—!
SO THAT'S WHERE HE IS—!
YES, SIR!...AND KIROS SAYS DOUM GOT OFF A MESSAGE TO DARTH VADER!
VADER! THEN YOU'D BETTER PREPARE FOR AN EMPIRE ATTACK, EXEC TEMORA—!
IF DARTH VADER IS ON HIS WAY HERE, OUR BEST CHANCE IS TO MEET HIM IN SPACE!
IF YOU'LL PROTECT OUR FIGHTERS FROM THE ADVANTAGE YOU'VE GIVEN THE EMPIRE...

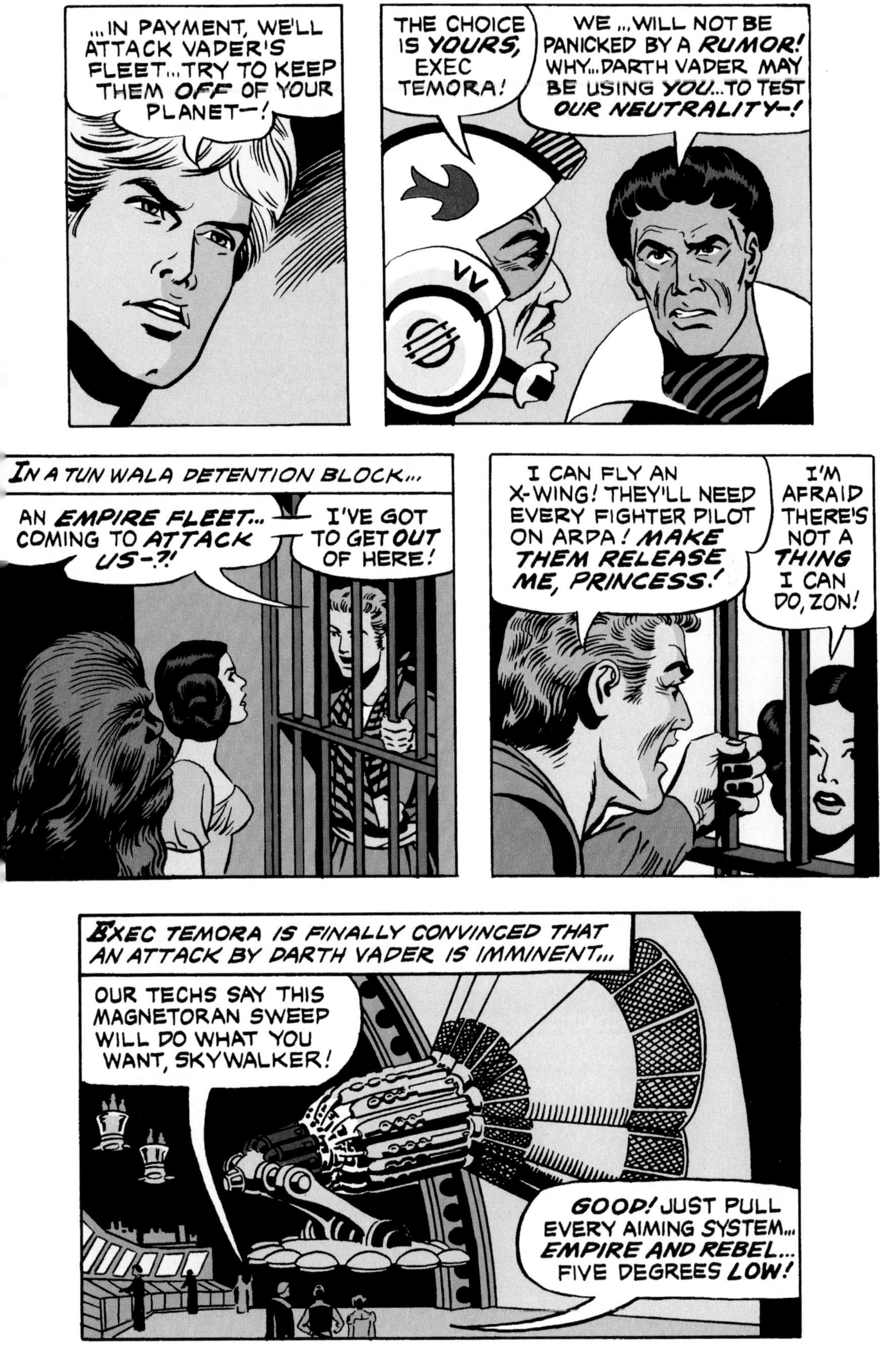
...IN PAYMENT, WE'LL ATTACK VADER'S FLEET...TRY TO KEEP THEM OFF OF YOUR PLANET--!
THE CHOICE IS YOURS, EXEC TEMORA!
WE ...WILL NOT BE PANICKED BY A RUMOR! WHY...DARTH VADER MAY BE USING YOU...TO TEST OUR NEUTRALITY--!
IN A TUN WALA DETENTION BLOCK...
AN EMPIRE FLEET... COMING TO ATTACK US-?!
I'VE GOT TO GET OUT OF HERE!
I CAN FLY AN X-WING! THEY'LL NEED EVERY FIGHTER PILOT ON ARDA! MAKE THEM RELEASE ME, PRINCESS!
I'M AFRAID THERE'S NOT A THING I CAN DO, ZON!
EXEC TEMORA IS FINALLY CONVINCED THAT AN ATTACK BY DARTH VADER IS IMMINENT...
OUR TECHS SAY THIS MAGNETORAN SWEEP WILL DO WHAT YOU WANT, SKYWALKER!
GOOD! JUST PULL EVERY AIMING SYSTEM... EMPIRE AND REBEL... FIVE DEGREES LOW!

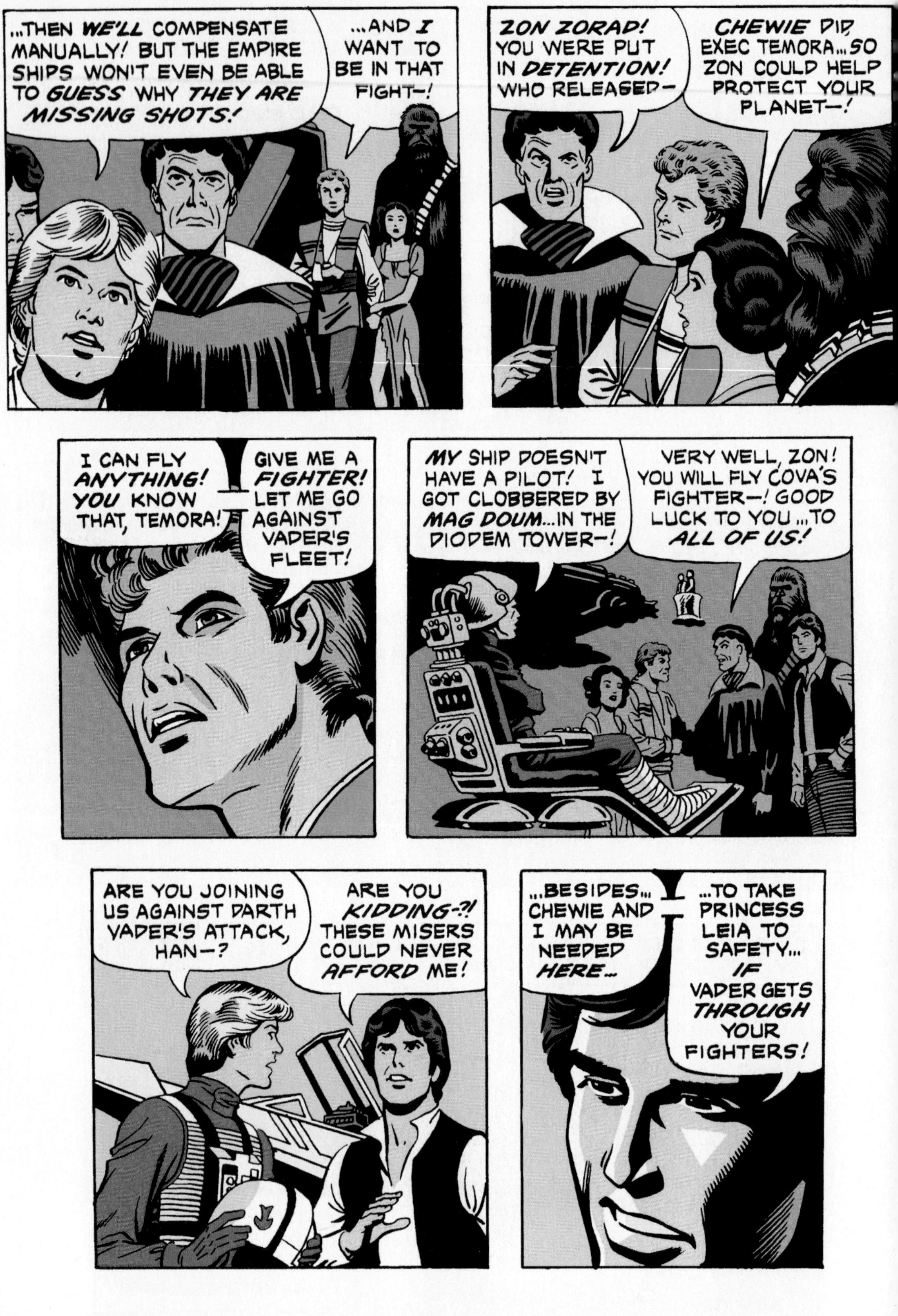

...THEN *WE'LL* COMPENSATE MANUALLY! BUT THE EMPIRE SHIPS WON'T EVEN BE ABLE TO *GUESS* WHY *THEY ARE MISSING SHOTS!*
...AND *I* WANT TO BE IN THAT FIGHT--!
ZON ZORAD! YOU WERE PUT IN *DETENTION!* WHO RELEASED--
CHEWIE DID, EXEC TEMORA...SO ZON COULD HELP PROTECT YOUR PLANET--!
I CAN FLY *ANYTHING! YOU* KNOW THAT, TEMORA!
GIVE ME A *FIGHTER!* LET ME GO AGAINST VADER'S FLEET!
MY SHIP DOESN'T HAVE A PILOT! I GOT CLOBBERED BY *MAG DOUM*...IN THE DIODEM TOWER--!
VERY WELL, ZON! YOU WILL FLY COVA'S FIGHTER--! GOOD LUCK TO YOU ...TO *ALL OF US!*
ARE YOU JOINING US AGAINST DARTH VADER'S ATTACK, HAN--?
ARE YOU *KIDDING--?!* THESE MISERS COULD NEVER *AFFORD* ME!
...BESIDES... CHEWIE AND I MAY BE NEEDED *HERE...*
...TO TAKE PRINCESS LEIA TO SAFETY... *IF* VADER GETS *THROUGH* YOUR FIGHTERS!

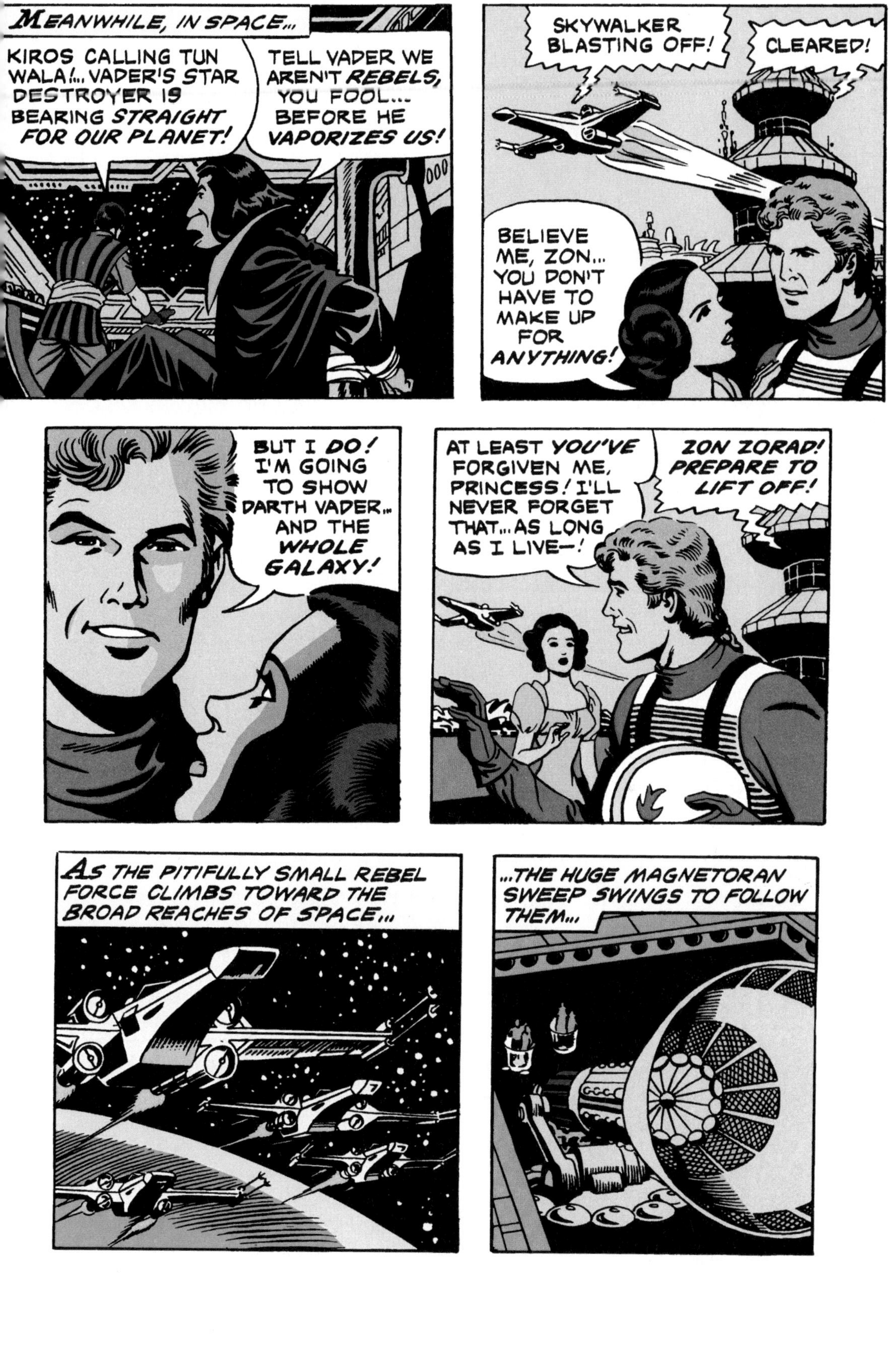
MEANWHILE, IN SPACE...
KIROS CALLING TUN WALA!... VADER'S STAR DESTROYER IS BEARING STRAIGHT FOR OUR PLANET!
TELL VADER WE AREN'T REBELS, YOU FOOL... BEFORE HE VAPORIZES US!
SKYWALKER BLASTING OFF!
CLEARED!
BELIEVE ME, ZON... YOU DON'T HAVE TO MAKE UP FOR ANYTHING!
BUT I DO! I'M GOING TO SHOW DARTH VADER... AND THE WHOLE GALAXY!
AT LEAST YOU'VE FORGIVEN ME, PRINCESS! I'LL NEVER FORGET THAT... AS LONG AS I LIVE--!
ZON ZORAD! PREPARE TO LIFT OFF!
AS THE PITIFULLY SMALL REBEL FORCE CLIMBS TOWARD THE BROAD REACHES OF SPACE...
...THE HUGE MAGNETORAN SWEEP SWINGS TO FOLLOW THEM...

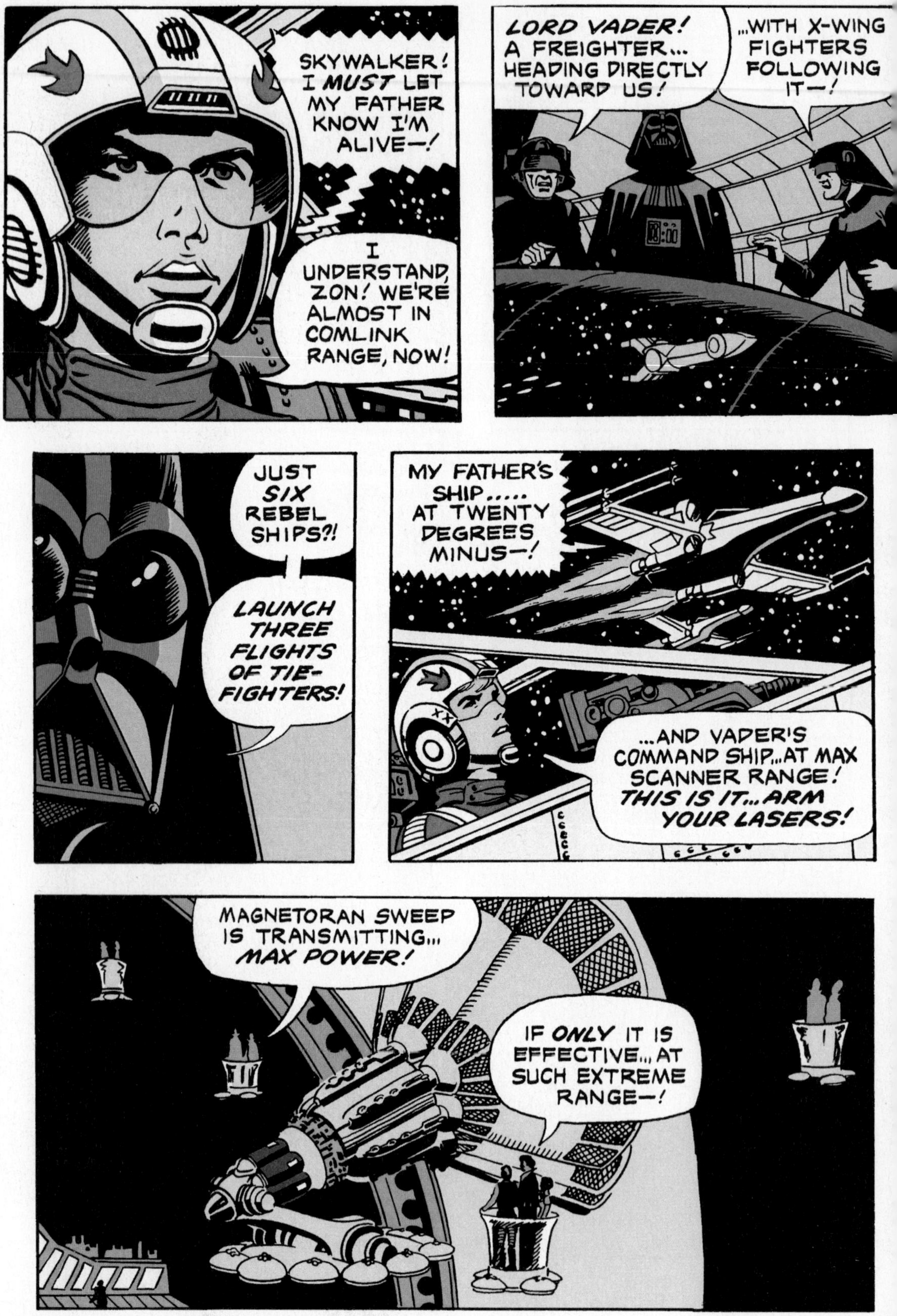
SKYWALKER! I MUST LET MY FATHER KNOW I'M ALIVE—!
I UNDERSTAND, ZON! WE'RE ALMOST IN COMLINK RANGE, NOW!
LORD VADER! A FREIGHTER... HEADING DIRECTLY TOWARD US!
...WITH X-WING FIGHTERS FOLLOWING IT—!
JUST SIX REBEL SHIPS?!
LAUNCH THREE FLIGHTS OF TIE-FIGHTERS!
MY FATHER'S SHIP..... AT TWENTY DEGREES MINUS—!
...AND VADER'S COMMAND SHIP...AT MAX SCANNER RANGE! THIS IS IT...ARM YOUR LASERS!
MAGNETORAN SWEEP IS TRANSMITTING... MAX POWER!
IF ONLY IT IS EFFECTIVE... AT SUCH EXTREME RANGE—!

YIPEE! ALL OF THEIR SHOTS ARE TOO LOW! THE DEFLECTOR IS WORKING!
YAHOO! AS LONG AS THOSE TIE-FIGHTERS KEEP MISSING, WE'VE GOT A CHANCE--!
LET'S GET 'EM GUYS!
ZON!? IS THAT YOUR VOICE I HEAR--?! YOU'RE NOT--
DEAD-?! NOT ME, SIR--! I'M RIGHT HERE...READY TO FIGHT! YOU CAN TURN BACK TO ARDA, NOW--!
NO, SON! I...LET EVERYONE ON OUR PLANET DOWN!...NOW I'M GOING TO MAKE UP FOR IT!
FATHER! WHAT ARE YOU--
STAY CLEAR OF VADER'S SHIP...ALL OF YOU! I'M TAKING IT OUT!

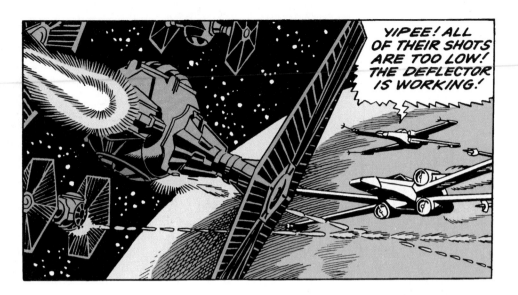

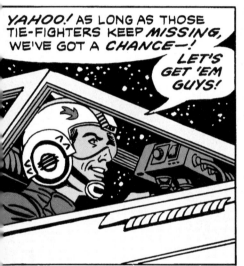

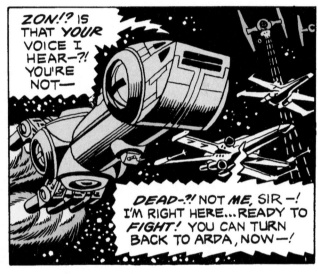

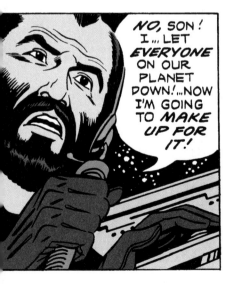

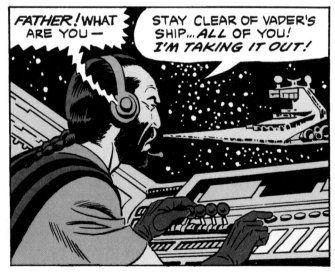

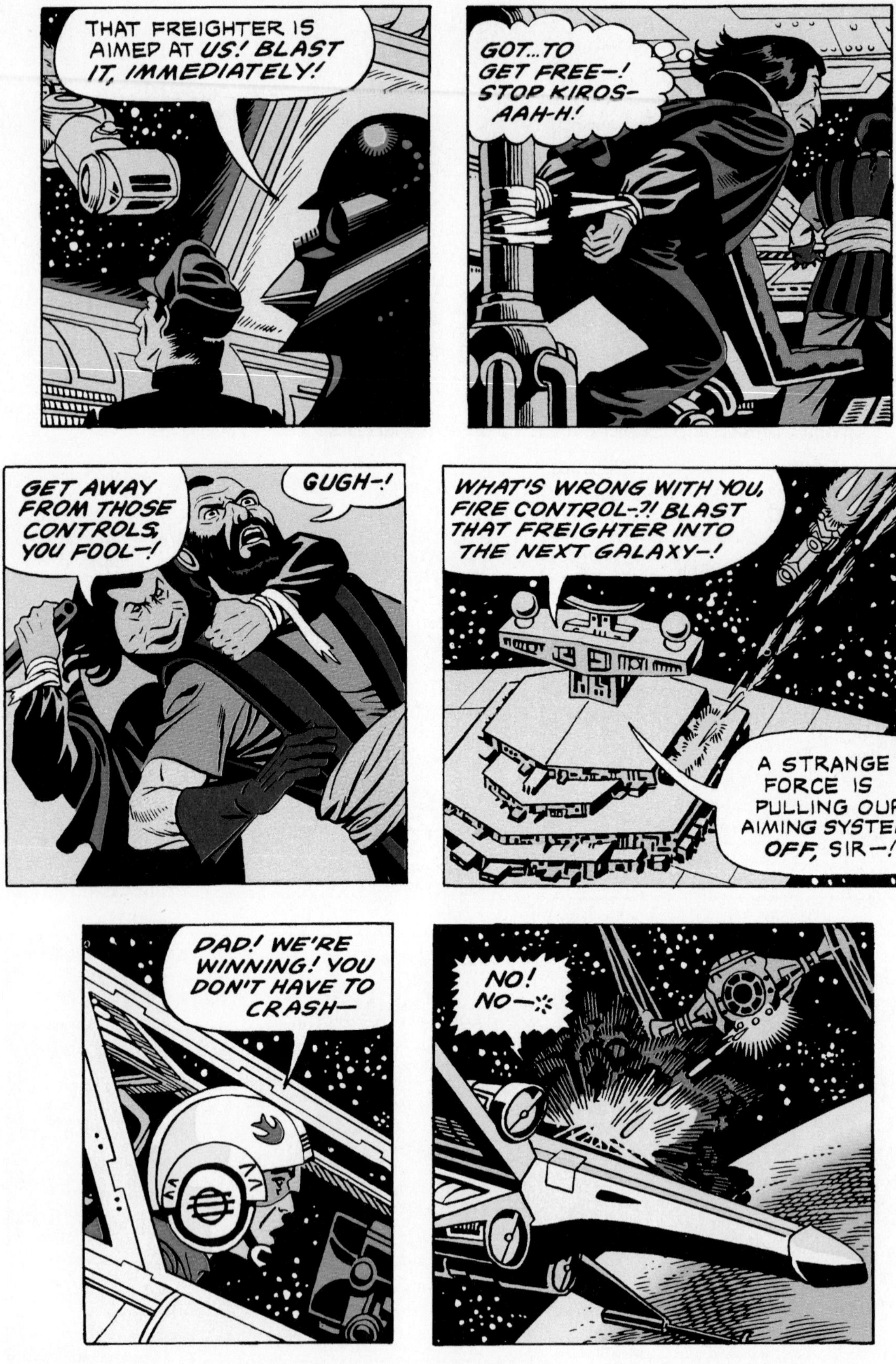
THAT FREIGHTER IS AIMED AT US! BLAST IT, IMMEDIATELY!
GOT...TO GET FREE–! STOP KIROS– AAH-H!
GET AWAY FROM THOSE CONTROLS, YOU FOOL–!
GUGH–!
WHAT'S WRONG WITH YOU, FIRE CONTROL–?! BLAST THAT FREIGHTER INTO THE NEXT GALAXY–!
A STRANGE FORCE IS PULLING OUR AIMING SYSTEM OFF, SIR–!
DAD! WE'RE WINNING! YOU DON'T HAVE TO CRASH—
NO! NO–

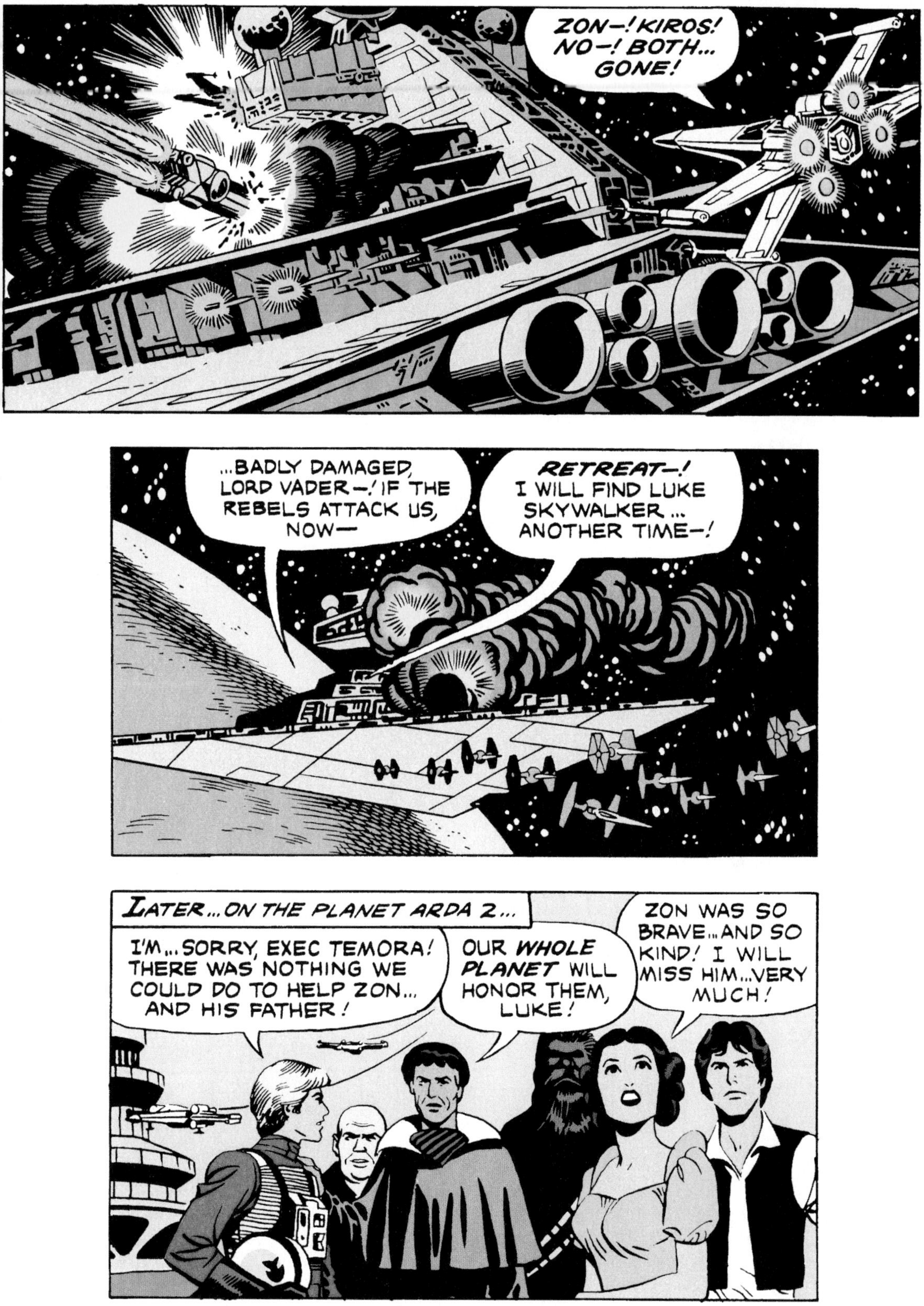
ZON—! KIROS! NO—! BOTH... GONE!
...BADLY DAMAGED, LORD VADER—! IF THE REBELS ATTACK US, NOW—
RETREAT—! I WILL FIND LUKE SKYWALKER... ANOTHER TIME—!
LATER... ON THE PLANET ARDA 2...
I'M... SORRY, EXEC TEMORA! THERE WAS NOTHING WE COULD DO TO HELP ZON... AND HIS FATHER!
OUR WHOLE PLANET WILL HONOR THEM, LUKE!
ZON WAS SO BRAVE... AND SO KIND! I WILL MISS HIM... VERY MUCH!

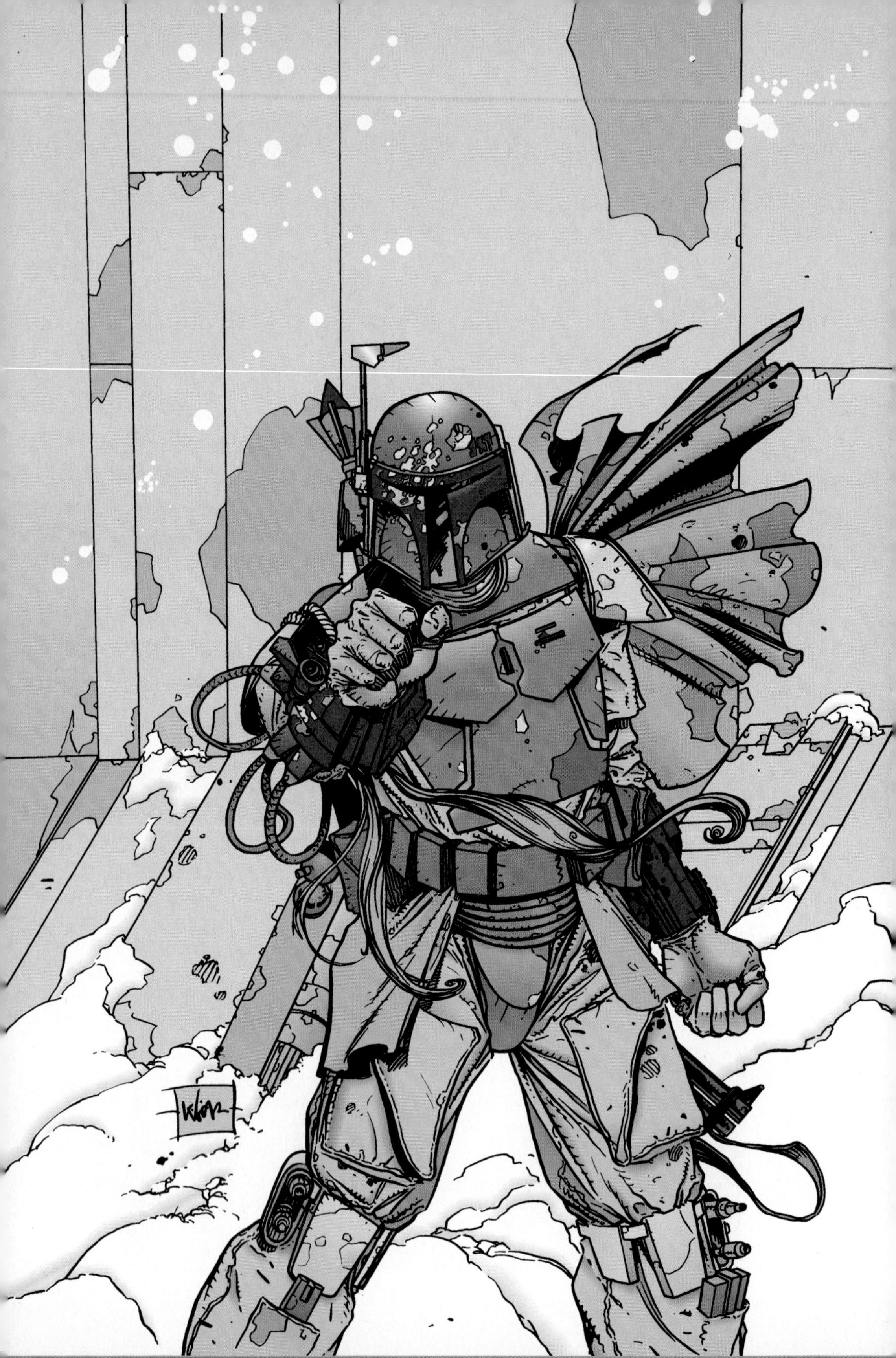

CLASSIC STAR WARS: THE EARLY ADVENTURES #9 — "THE FROZEN WORLD OF OTA"
ORIGINALLY PUBLISHED FROM JUNE 17 TO AUGUST 10, 1980

WRITERS: RUSS MANNING (PP.1-17) & RICK HOBERG (PP.18-23) WITH DON CHRISTENSEN • PENCILERS: RUSS MANNING (PP.1-11 & 23) & RICK HOBERG (PP.12-22)
INKERS & LETTERES: RUSS MANNING (PP.1-11 & 23), DAVE STEVENS (PP.12-17) & ALFREDO ALCALA (PP.18-22) • ART RETOUCHING: RICK HOBERG & BRIAN SNODDY
COLORIST: RAY MURTAUGH • EDITOR: PEET JANES • COVER ARTISTS: KILIAN PLUNKETT & MATTHEW HOLLINGSWORTH

CLASSIC STAR WARS: THE EARLY ADVENTURES

BOOK 9

THE FROZEN WORLD OF OTA

While on patrol near the frozen world of Ota, Luke Skywalker encounters a lone Imperial TIE fighter. After a brief exchange of fire, Luke follows the damaged Imperial ship down to the planet's surface, but Luke is about to find out that this is no ordinary Imperial fighter pilot...

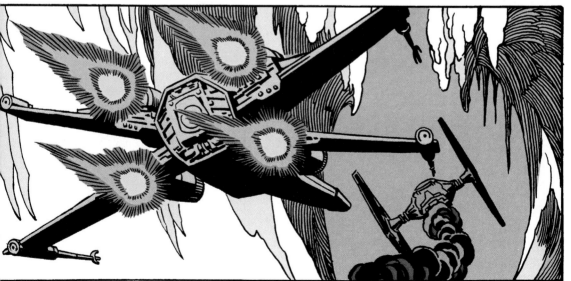

245

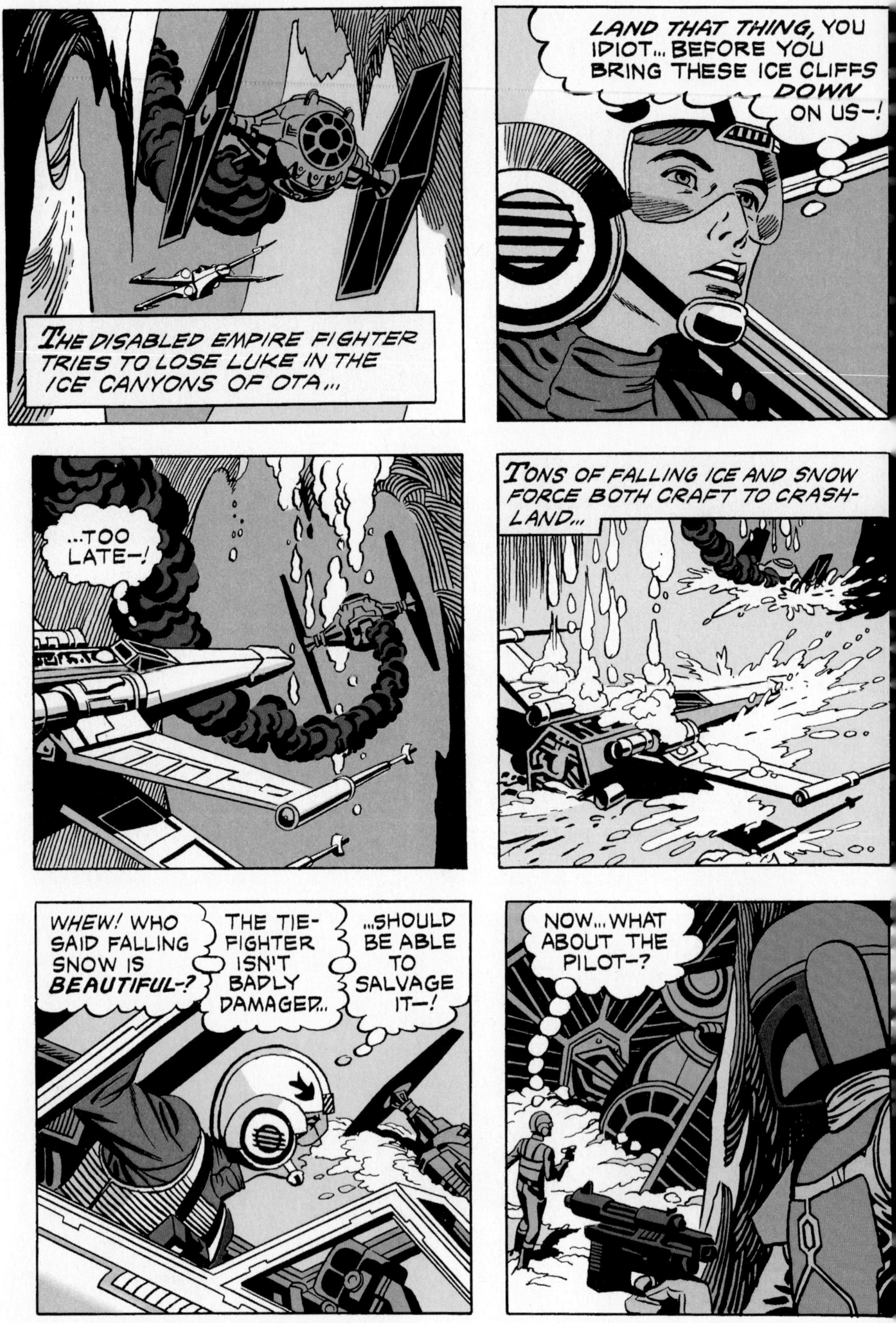
THE DISABLED EMPIRE FIGHTER TRIES TO LOSE LUKE IN THE ICE CANYONS OF OTA...
LAND THAT THING, YOU IDIOT... BEFORE YOU BRING THESE ICE CLIFFS DOWN ON US-!
...TOO LATE-!
TONS OF FALLING ICE AND SNOW FORCE BOTH CRAFT TO CRASH-LAND...
WHEW! WHO SAID FALLING SNOW IS BEAUTIFUL-?
THE TIE-FIGHTER ISN'T BADLY DAMAGED...
...SHOULD BE ABLE TO SALVAGE IT-!
NOW... WHAT ABOUT THE PILOT-?

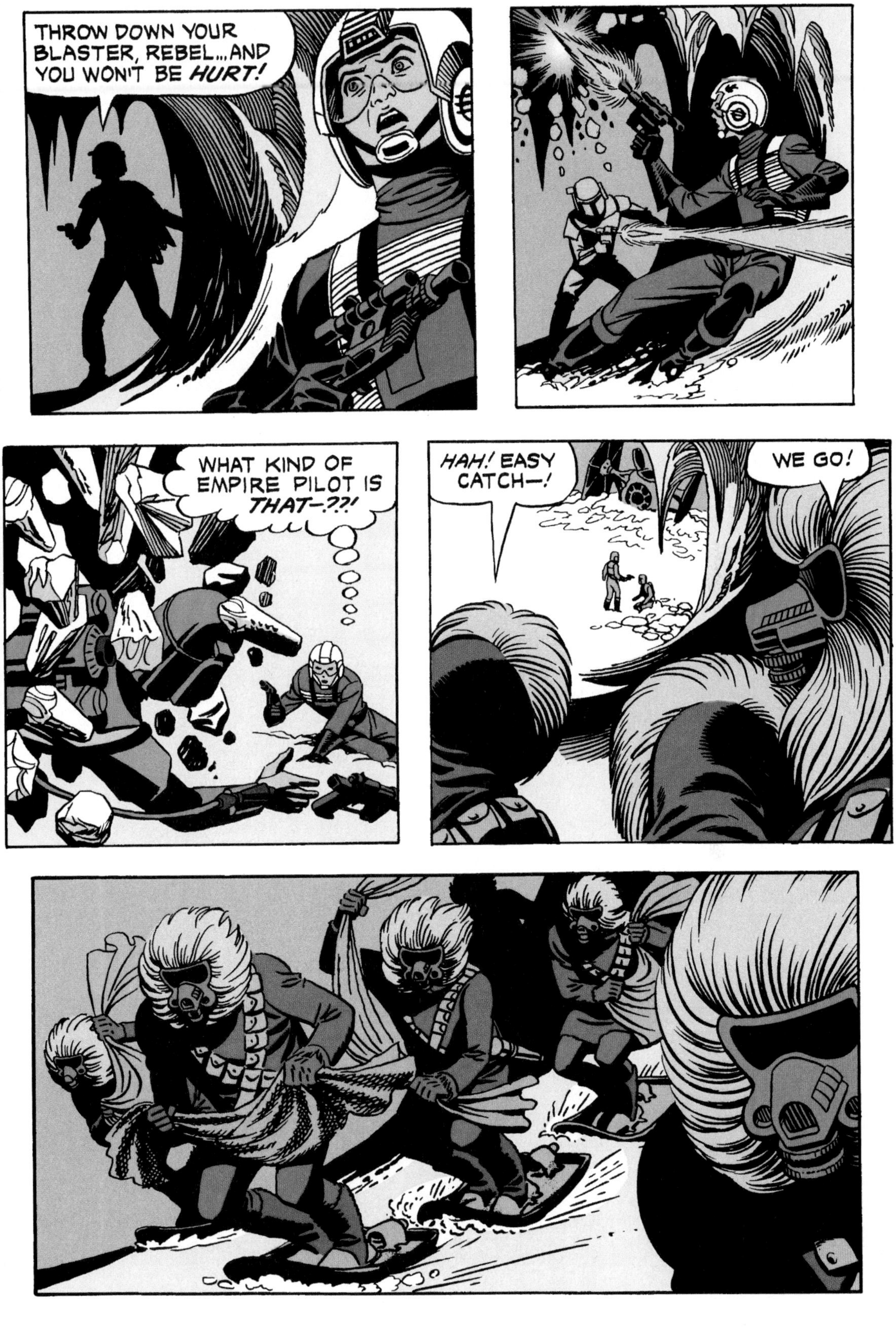
THROW DOWN YOUR BLASTER, REBEL...AND YOU WON'T BE HURT!
WHAT KIND OF EMPIRE PILOT IS THAT-??!
HAH! EASY CATCH-!
WE GO!

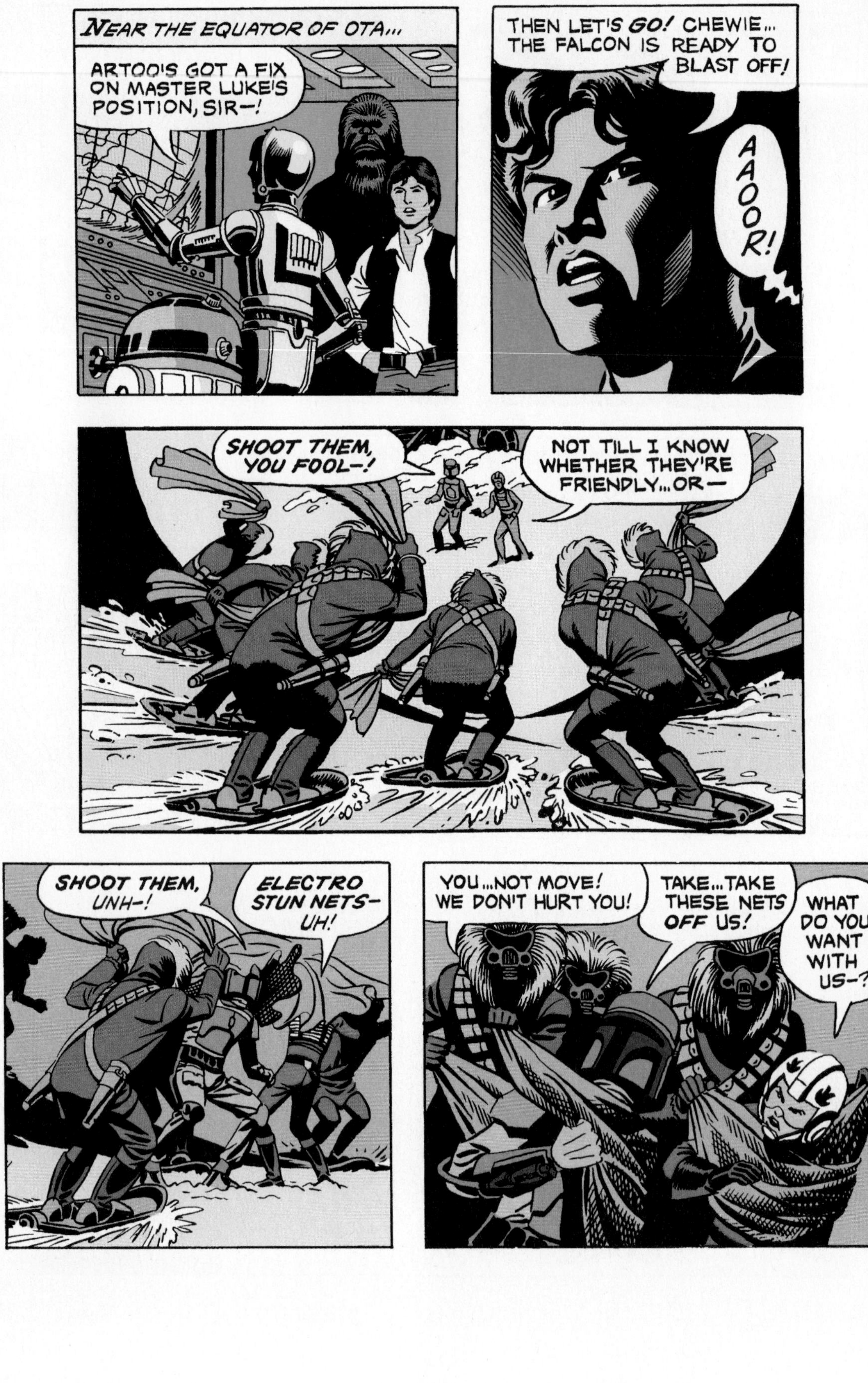
NEAR THE EQUATOR OF OTA...
ARTOO'S GOT A FIX ON MASTER LUKE'S POSITION, SIR-!
THEN LET'S GO! CHEWIE... THE FALCON IS READY TO BLAST OFF!
AAOOR!
SHOOT THEM, YOU FOOL-!
NOT TILL I KNOW WHETHER THEY'RE FRIENDLY...OR—
SHOOT THEM, UNH-!
ELECTRO STUN NETS- UH!
YOU...NOT MOVE! WE DON'T HURT YOU!
TAKE...TAKE THESE NETS OFF US!
WHAT DO YOU WANT WITH US-?

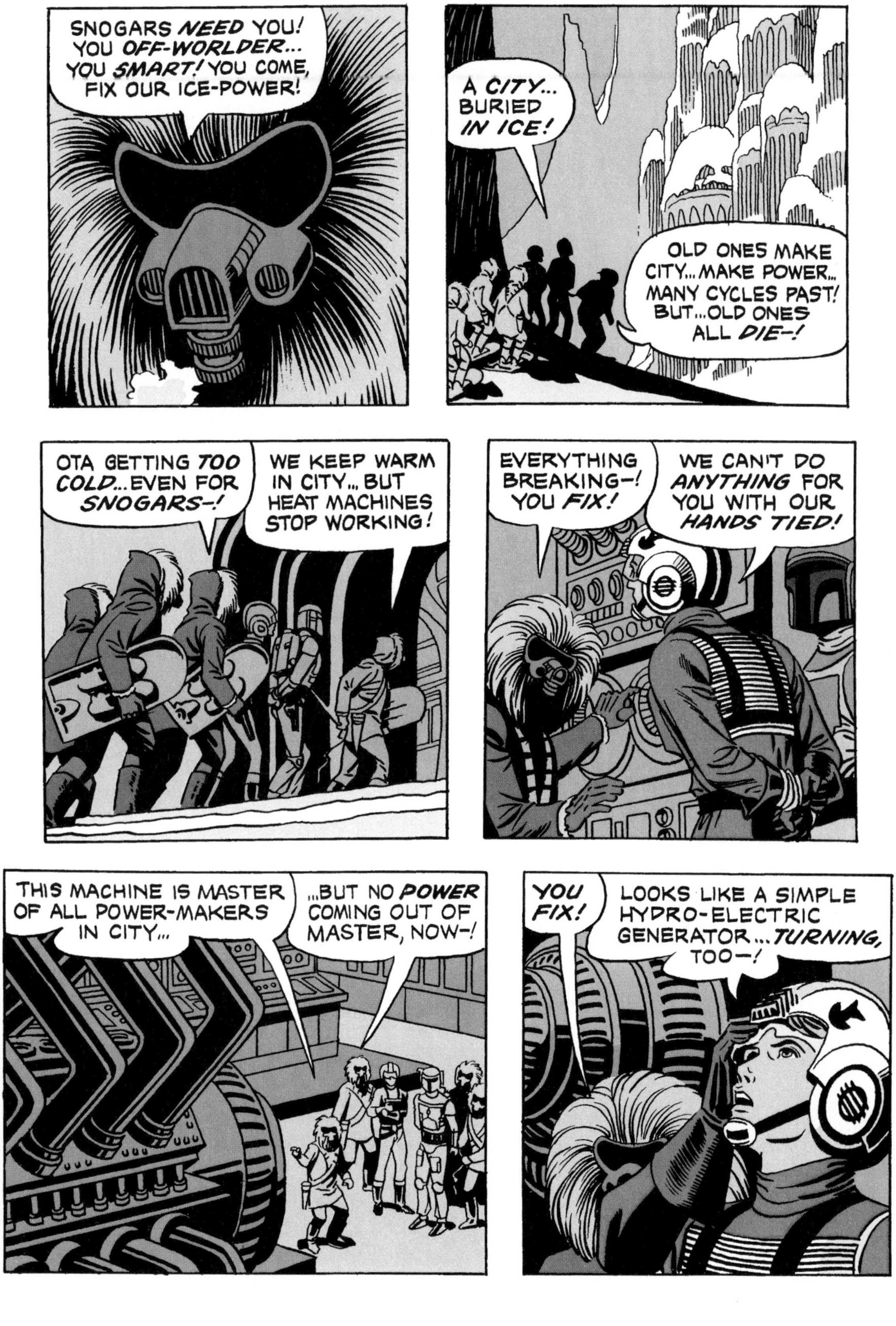
SNOGARS NEED YOU! YOU OFF-WORLDER... YOU SMART! YOU COME, FIX OUR ICE-POWER!
A CITY... BURIED IN ICE!
OLD ONES MAKE CITY... MAKE POWER... MANY CYCLES PAST! BUT...OLD ONES ALL DIE-!
OTA GETTING TOO COLD...EVEN FOR SNOGARS-!
WE KEEP WARM IN CITY... BUT HEAT MACHINES STOP WORKING!
EVERYTHING BREAKING-! YOU FIX!
WE CAN'T DO ANYTHING FOR YOU WITH OUR HANDS TIED!
THIS MACHINE IS MASTER OF ALL POWER-MAKERS IN CITY...
...BUT NO POWER COMING OUT OF MASTER, NOW-!
YOU FIX!
LOOKS LIKE A SIMPLE HYDRO-ELECTRIC GENERATOR...TURNING, TOO-!

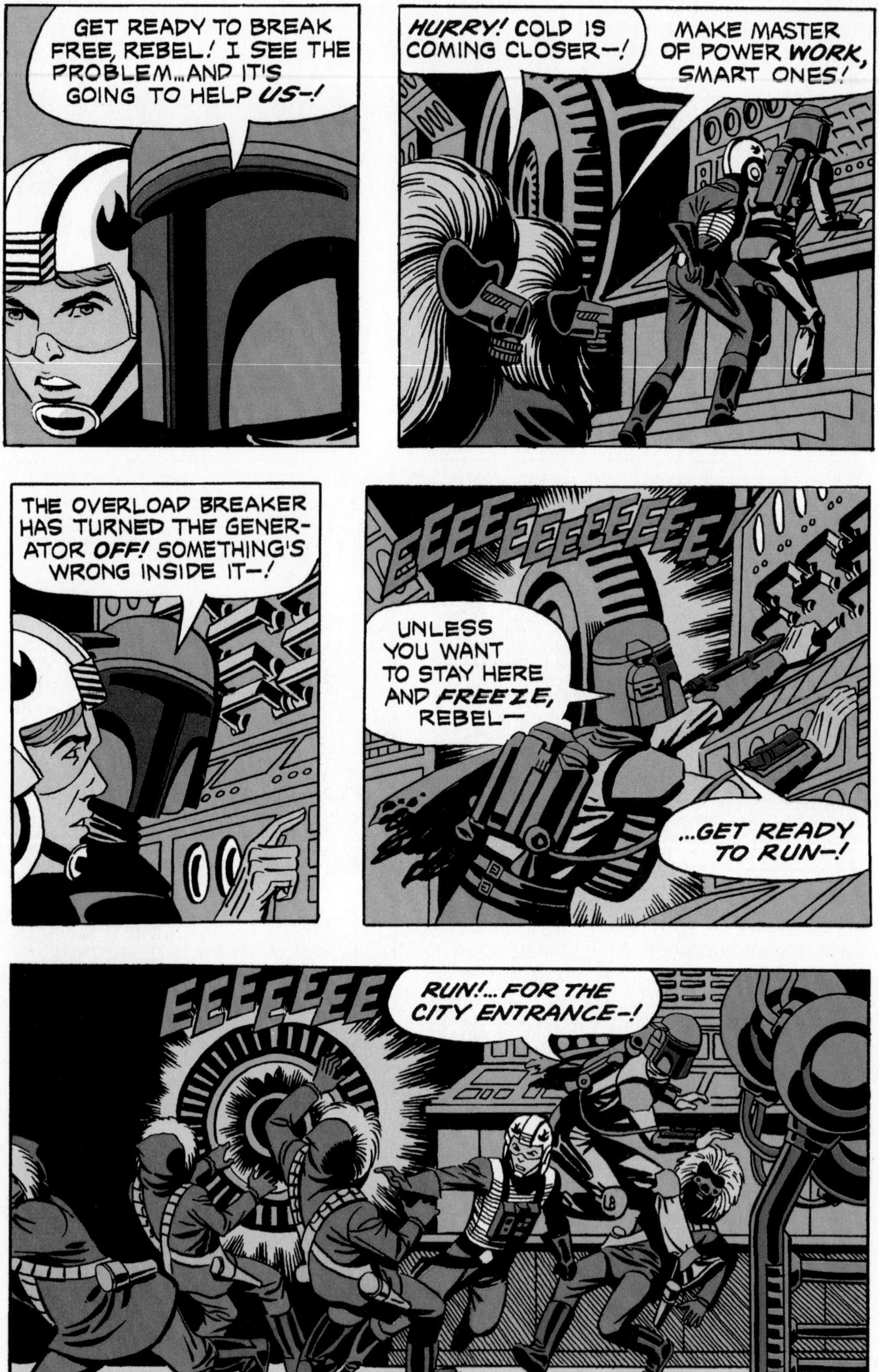
GET READY TO BREAK FREE, REBEL! I SEE THE PROBLEM...AND IT'S GOING TO HELP US-!
HURRY! COLD IS COMING CLOSER-!
MAKE MASTER OF POWER WORK, SMART ONES!
THE OVERLOAD BREAKER HAS TURNED THE GENERATOR OFF! SOMETHING'S WRONG INSIDE IT-!
EEEEEEEEEEEEE!
UNLESS YOU WANT TO STAY HERE AND FREEZE, REBEL—
...GET READY TO RUN-!
EEEEEEE
RUN!... FOR THE CITY ENTRANCE-!

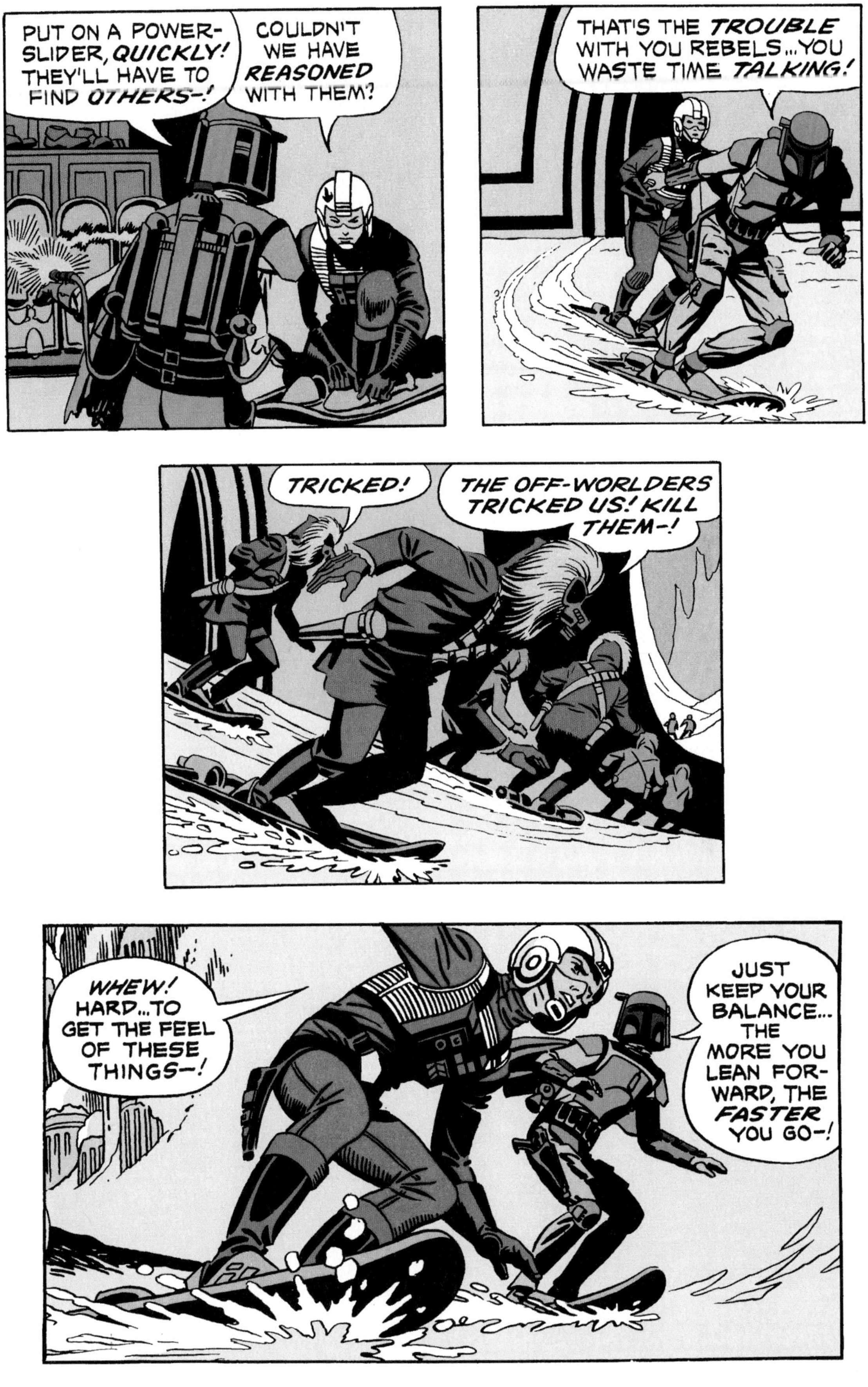

PUT ON A POWER-SLIDER, QUICKLY! THEY'LL HAVE TO FIND OTHERS-!
COULDN'T WE HAVE REASONED WITH THEM?
THAT'S THE TROUBLE WITH YOU REBELS...YOU WASTE TIME TALKING!
TRICKED!
THE OFF-WORLDERS TRICKED US! KILL THEM-!
WHEW! HARD...TO GET THE FEEL OF THESE THINGS-!
JUST KEEP YOUR BALANCE... THE MORE YOU LEAN FOR-WARD, THE FASTER YOU GO-!

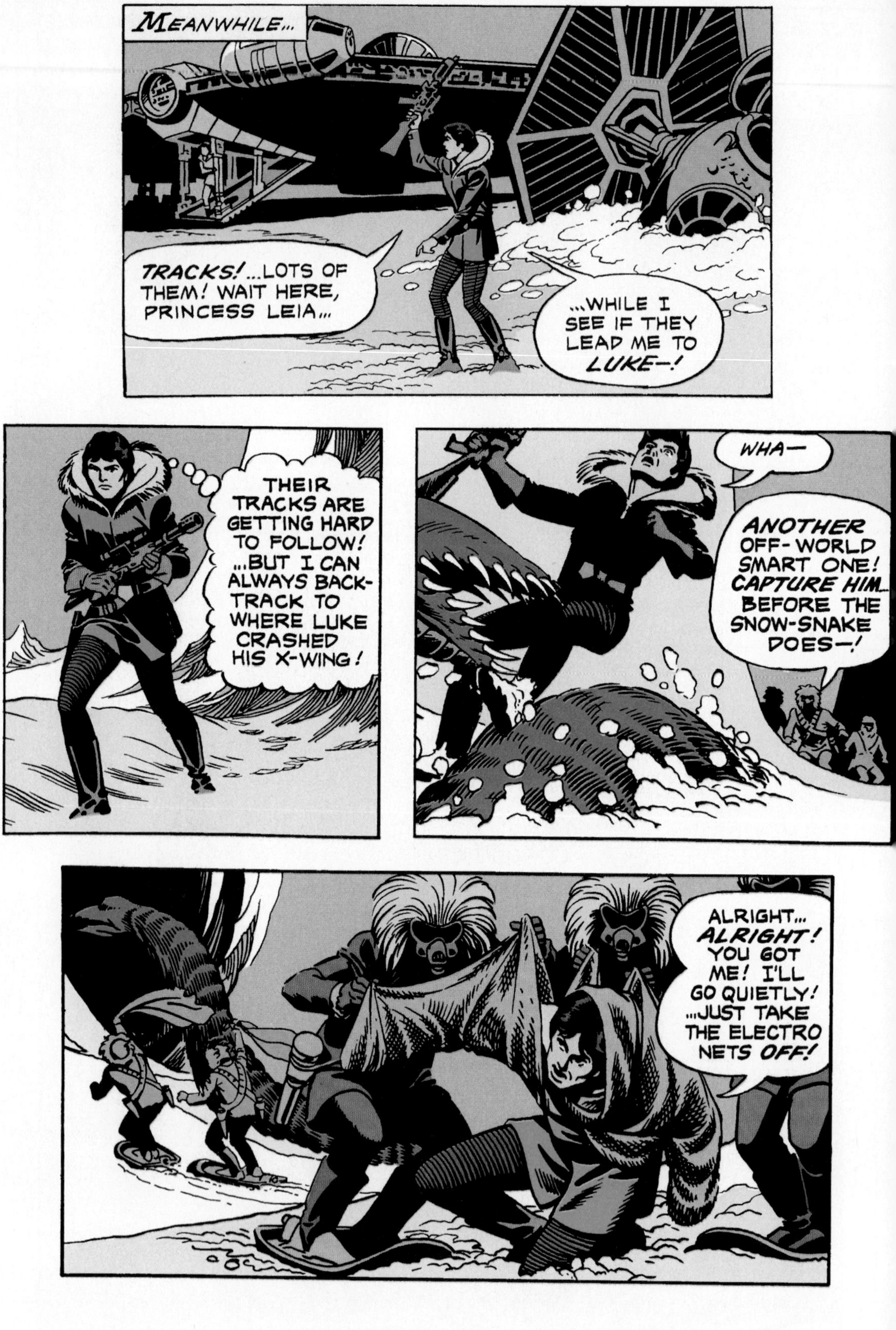
MEANWHILE...
TRACKS! ...LOTS OF THEM! WAIT HERE, PRINCESS LEIA...
...WHILE I SEE IF THEY LEAD ME TO LUKE—!
THEIR TRACKS ARE GETTING HARD TO FOLLOW! ...BUT I CAN ALWAYS BACK-TRACK TO WHERE LUKE CRASHED HIS X-WING!
WHA—
ANOTHER OFF-WORLD SMART ONE! CAPTURE HIM BEFORE THE SNOW-SNAKE DOES—!
ALRIGHT... ALRIGHT! YOU GOT ME! I'LL GO QUIETLY! ...JUST TAKE THE ELECTRO NETS OFF!

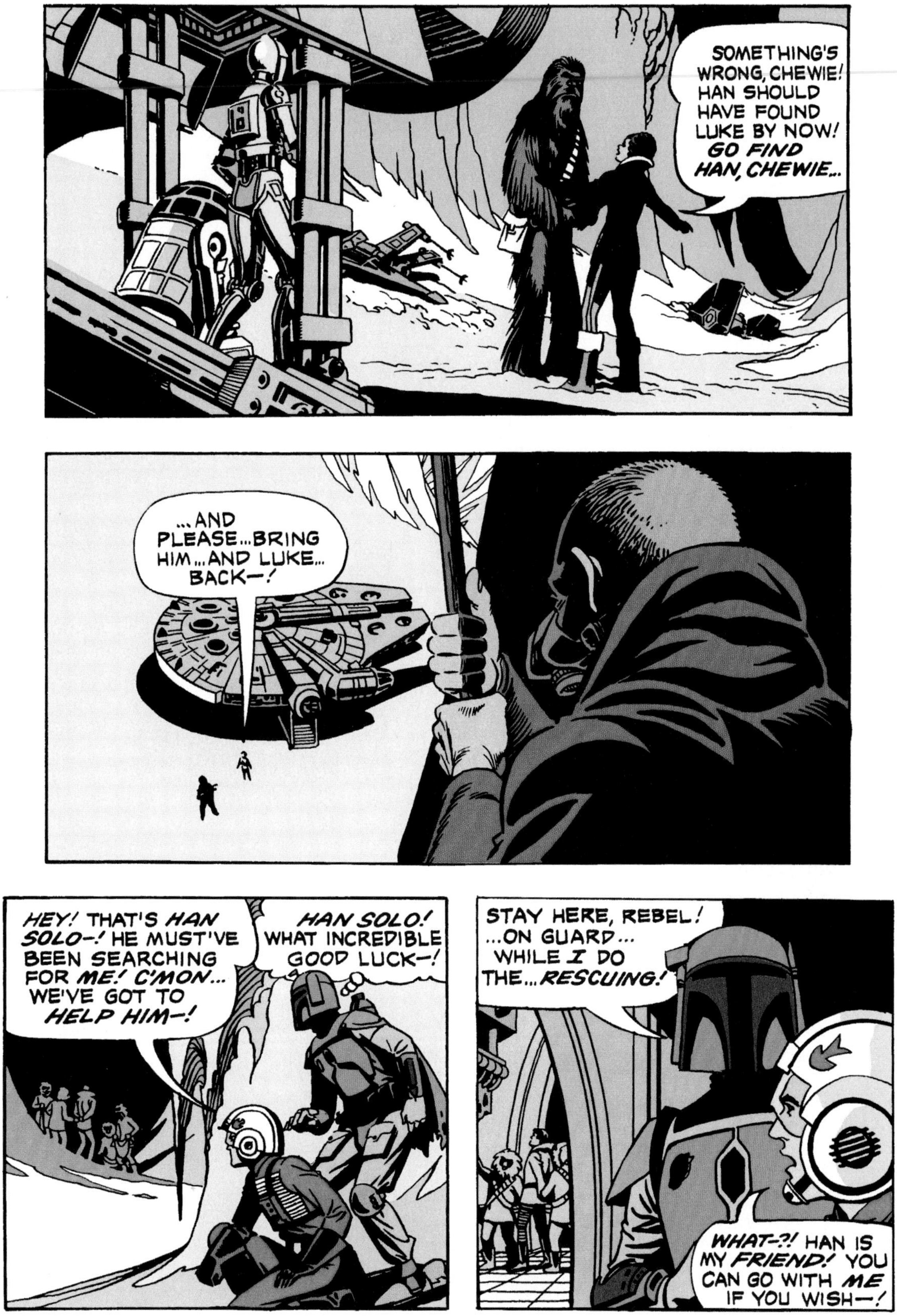
SOMETHING'S WRONG, CHEWIE! HAN SHOULD HAVE FOUND LUKE BY NOW! GO FIND HAN, CHEWIE...
...AND PLEASE...BRING HIM...AND LUKE... BACK--!
HEY! THAT'S HAN SOLO--! HE MUST'VE BEEN SEARCHING FOR ME! C'MON... WE'VE GOT TO HELP HIM--!
HAN SOLO! WHAT INCREDIBLE GOOD LUCK--!
STAY HERE, REBEL! ...ON GUARD... WHILE I DO THE...RESCUING!
WHAT--?! HAN IS MY FRIEND! YOU CAN GO WITH ME IF YOU WISH--!

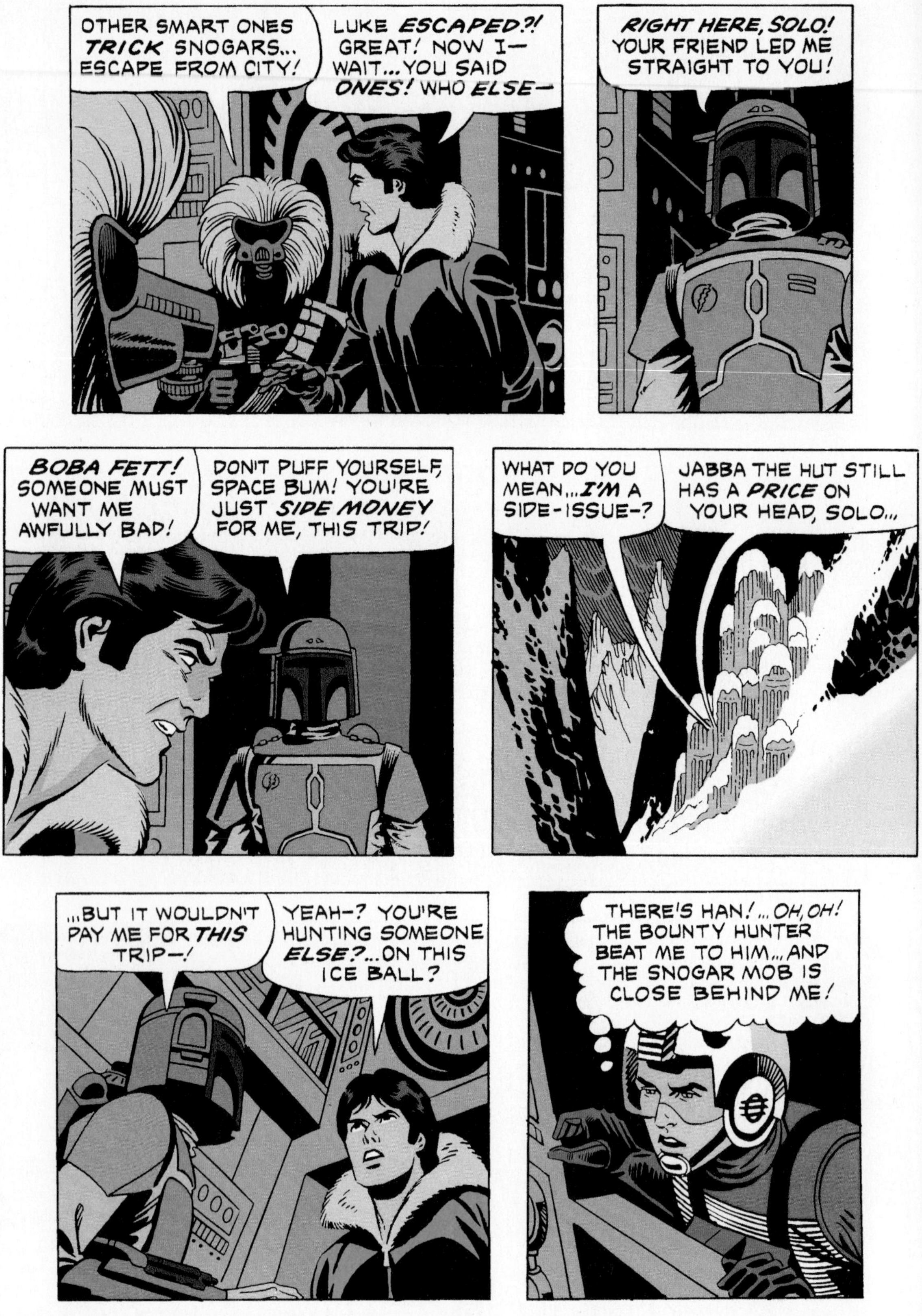
OTHER SMART ONES TRICK SNOGARS... ESCAPE FROM CITY!
LUKE ESCAPED?! GREAT! NOW I— WAIT... YOU SAID ONES! WHO ELSE—
RIGHT HERE, SOLO! YOUR FRIEND LED ME STRAIGHT TO YOU!
BOBA FETT! SOMEONE MUST WANT ME AWFULLY BAD!
DON'T PUFF YOURSELF, SPACE BUM! YOU'RE JUST SIDE MONEY FOR ME, THIS TRIP!
WHAT DO YOU MEAN... I'M A SIDE-ISSUE-?
JABBA THE HUT STILL HAS A PRICE ON YOUR HEAD, SOLO...
...BUT IT WOULDN'T PAY ME FOR THIS TRIP—!
YEAH—? YOU'RE HUNTING SOMEONE ELSE?... ON THIS ICE BALL?
THERE'S HAN! ... OH, OH! THE BOUNTY HUNTER BEAT ME TO HIM... AND THE SNOGAR MOB IS CLOSE BEHIND ME!

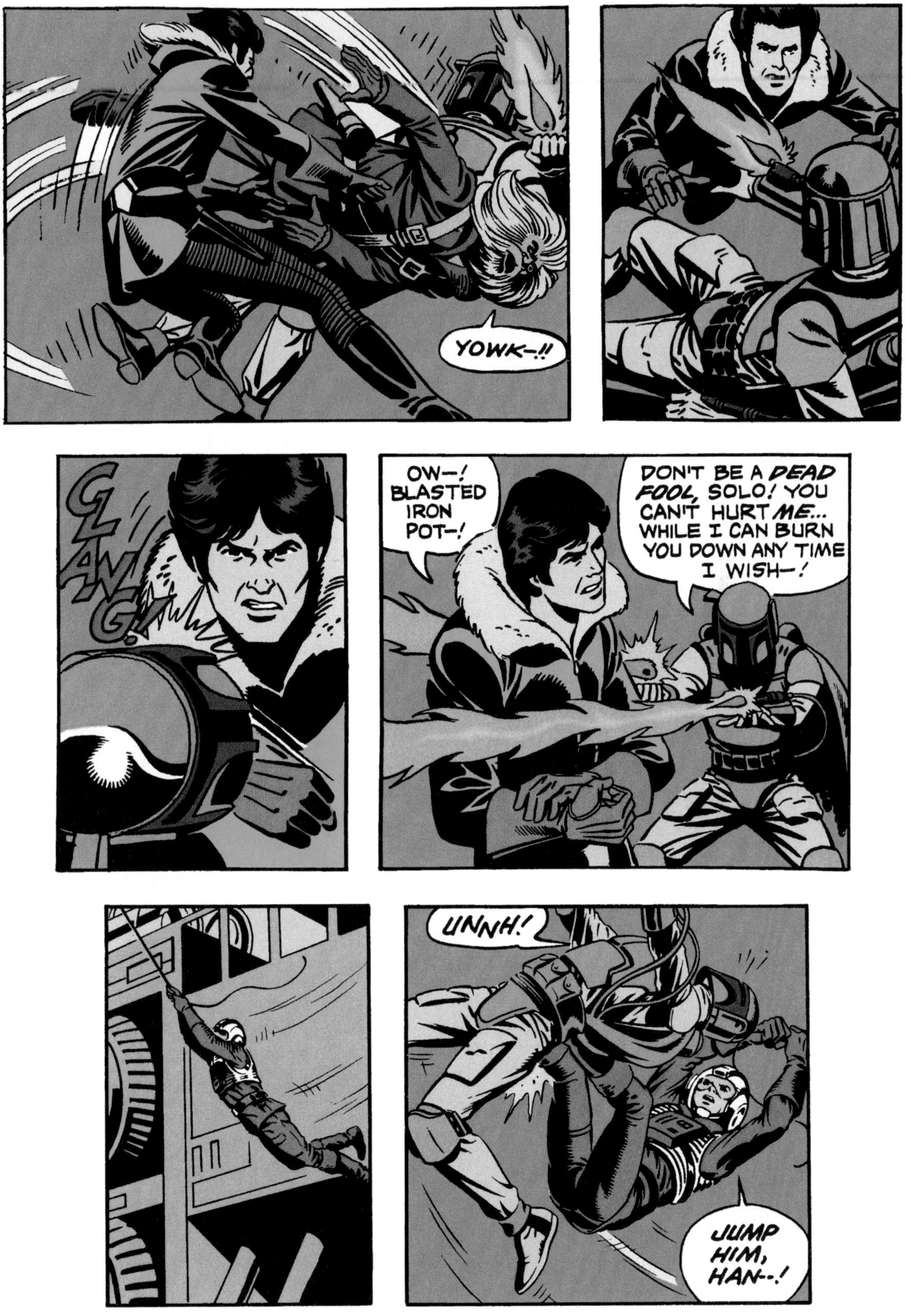
YOWK--!!
CLANG!
OW--! BLASTED IRON POT--!
DON'T BE A DEAD FOOL, SOLO! YOU CAN'T HURT ME... WHILE I CAN BURN YOU DOWN ANY TIME I WISH--!
UNNH!
JUMP HIM, HAN--!

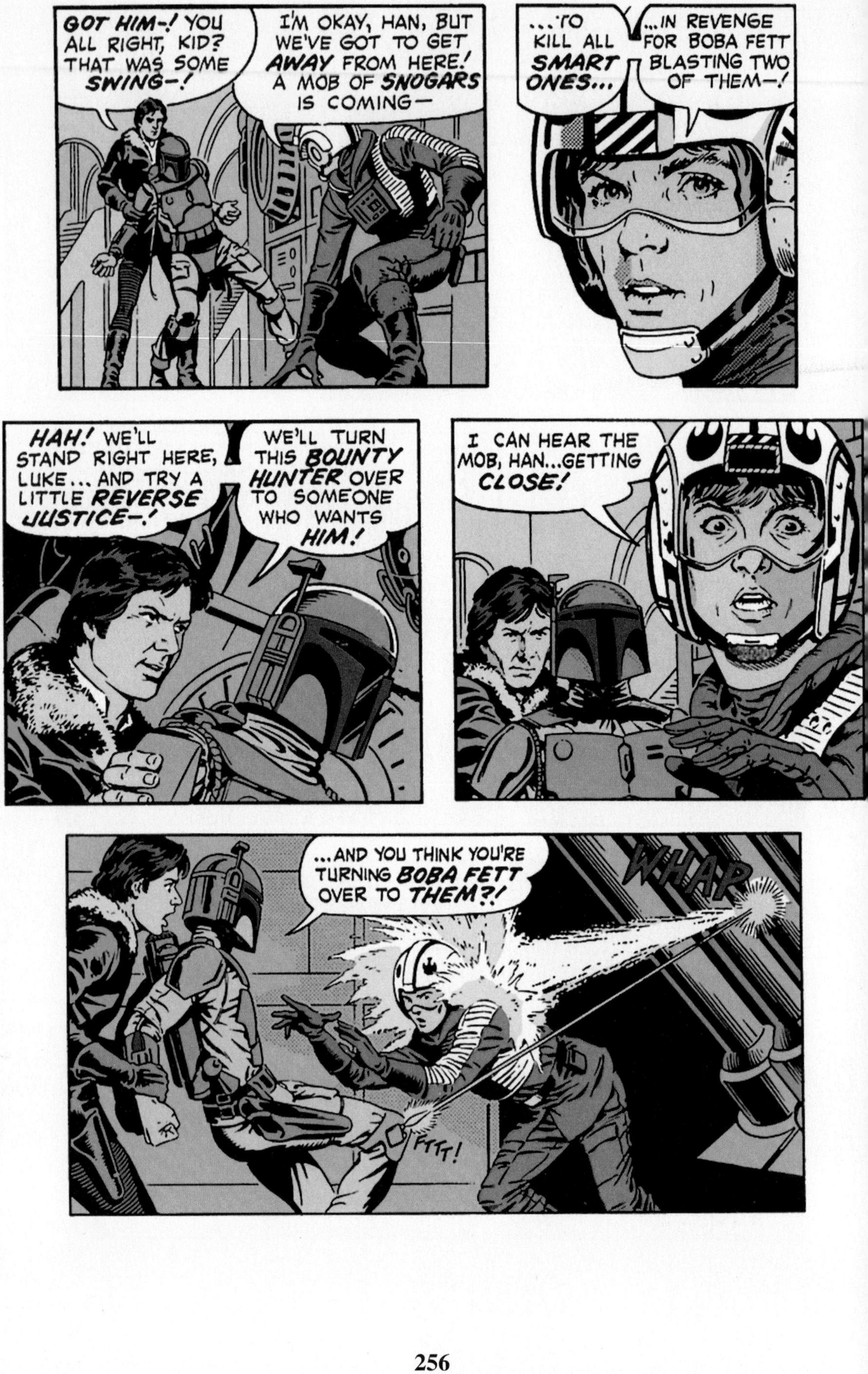
GOT HIM-! YOU ALL RIGHT, KID? THAT WAS SOME SWING-!
I'M OKAY, HAN, BUT WE'VE GOT TO GET AWAY FROM HERE! A MOB OF SNOGARS IS COMING—
...TO KILL ALL SMART ONES...
...IN REVENGE FOR BOBA FETT BLASTING TWO OF THEM-!
HAH! WE'LL STAND RIGHT HERE, LUKE... AND TRY A LITTLE REVERSE JUSTICE-!
WE'LL TURN THIS BOUNTY HUNTER OVER TO SOMEONE WHO WANTS HIM!
I CAN HEAR THE MOB, HAN...GETTING CLOSE!
...AND YOU THINK YOU'RE TURNING BOBA FETT OVER TO THEM?!
WHAP
FTTT!

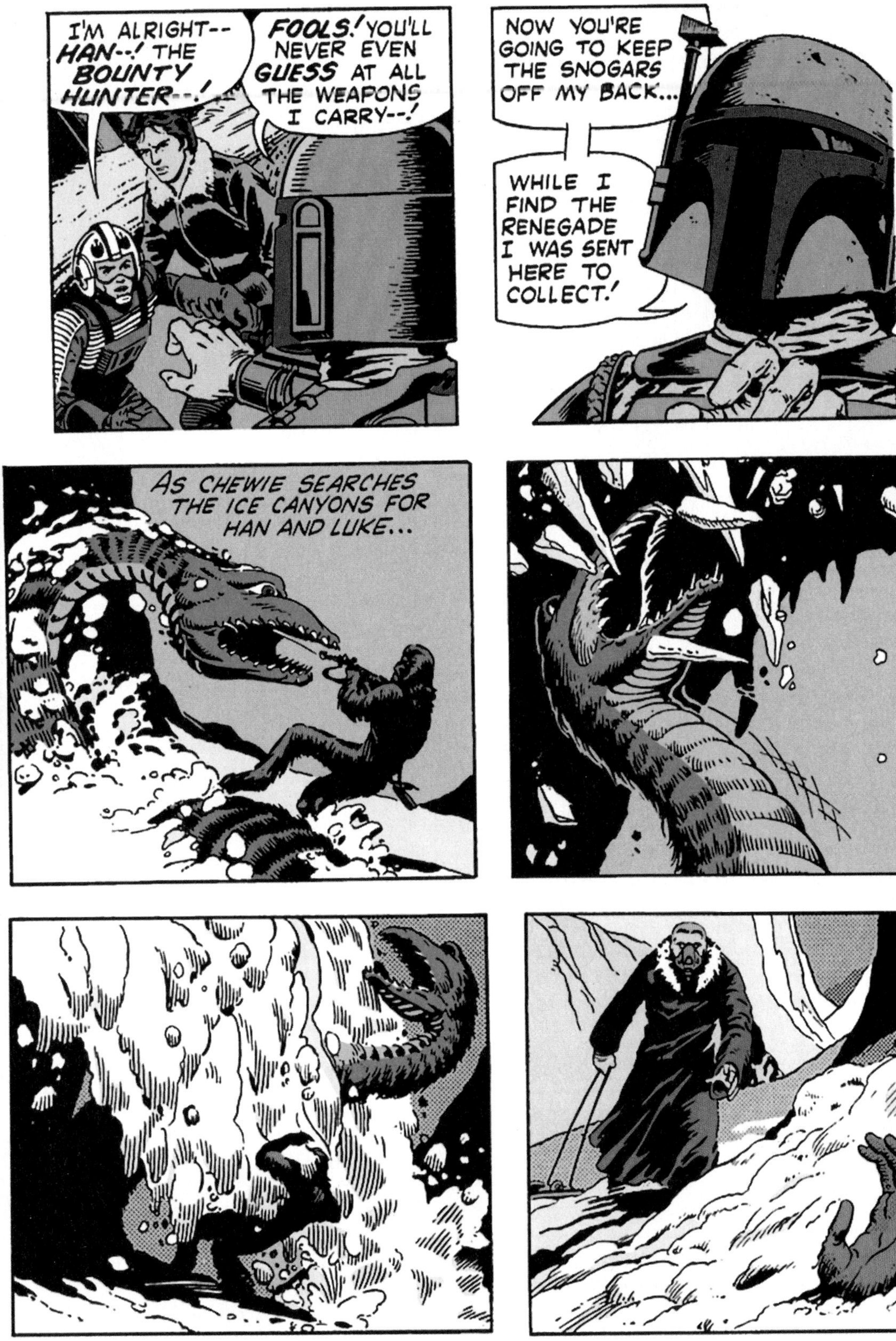
I'M ALRIGHT--
HAN--! THE BOUNTY HUNTER--!
FOOLS! YOU'LL NEVER EVEN GUESS AT ALL THE WEAPONS I CARRY--!
NOW YOU'RE GOING TO KEEP THE SNOGARS OFF MY BACK...
WHILE I FIND THE RENEGADE I WAS SENT HERE TO COLLECT!
AS CHEWIE SEARCHES THE ICE CANYONS FOR HAN AND LUKE...

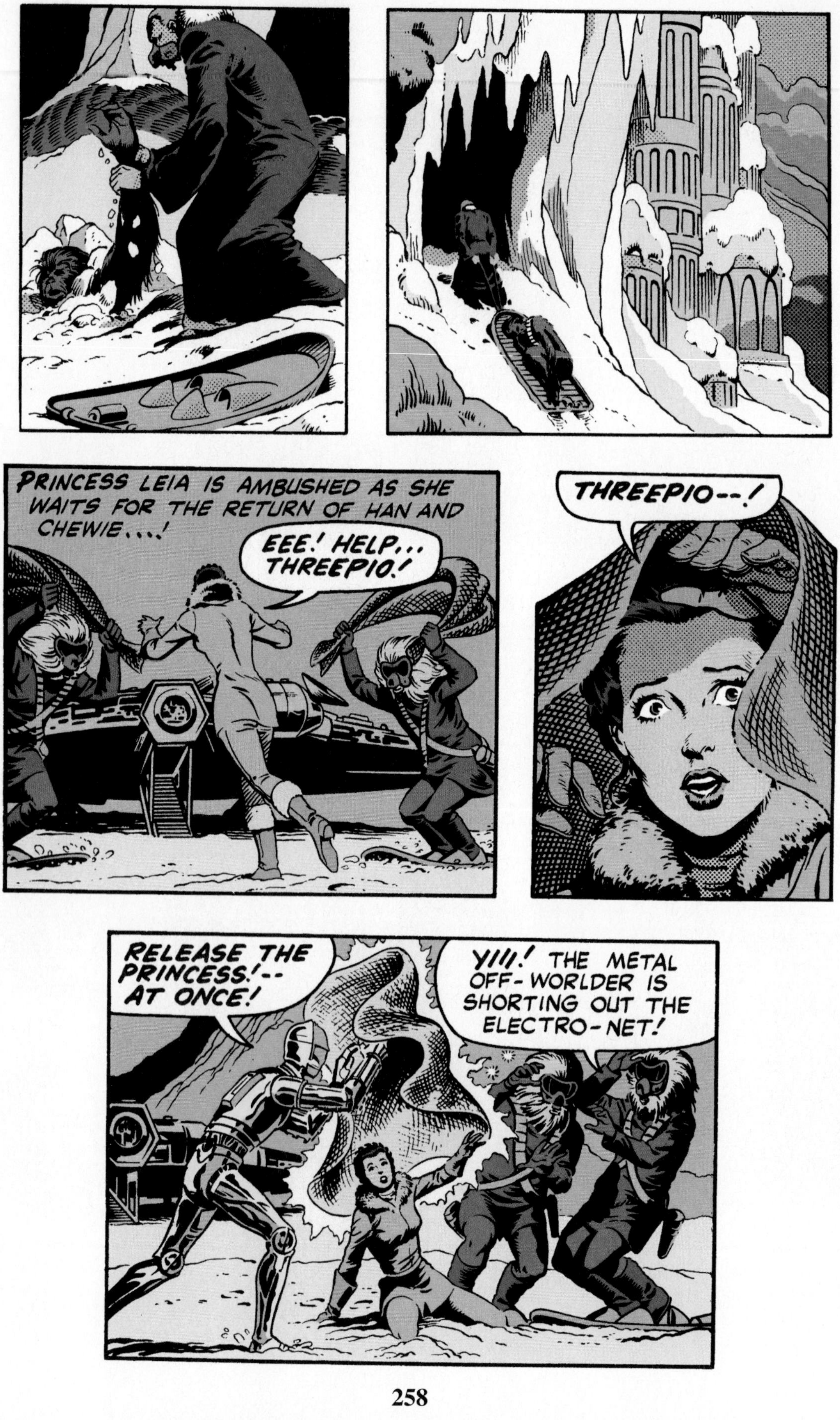
PRINCESS LEIA IS AMBUSHED AS SHE WAITS FOR THE RETURN OF HAN AND CHEWIE...!
EEE! HELP... THREEPIO!
THREEPIO--!
RELEASE THE PRINCESS!-- AT ONCE!
YIII! THE METAL OFF-WORLDER IS SHORTING OUT THE ELECTRO-NET!

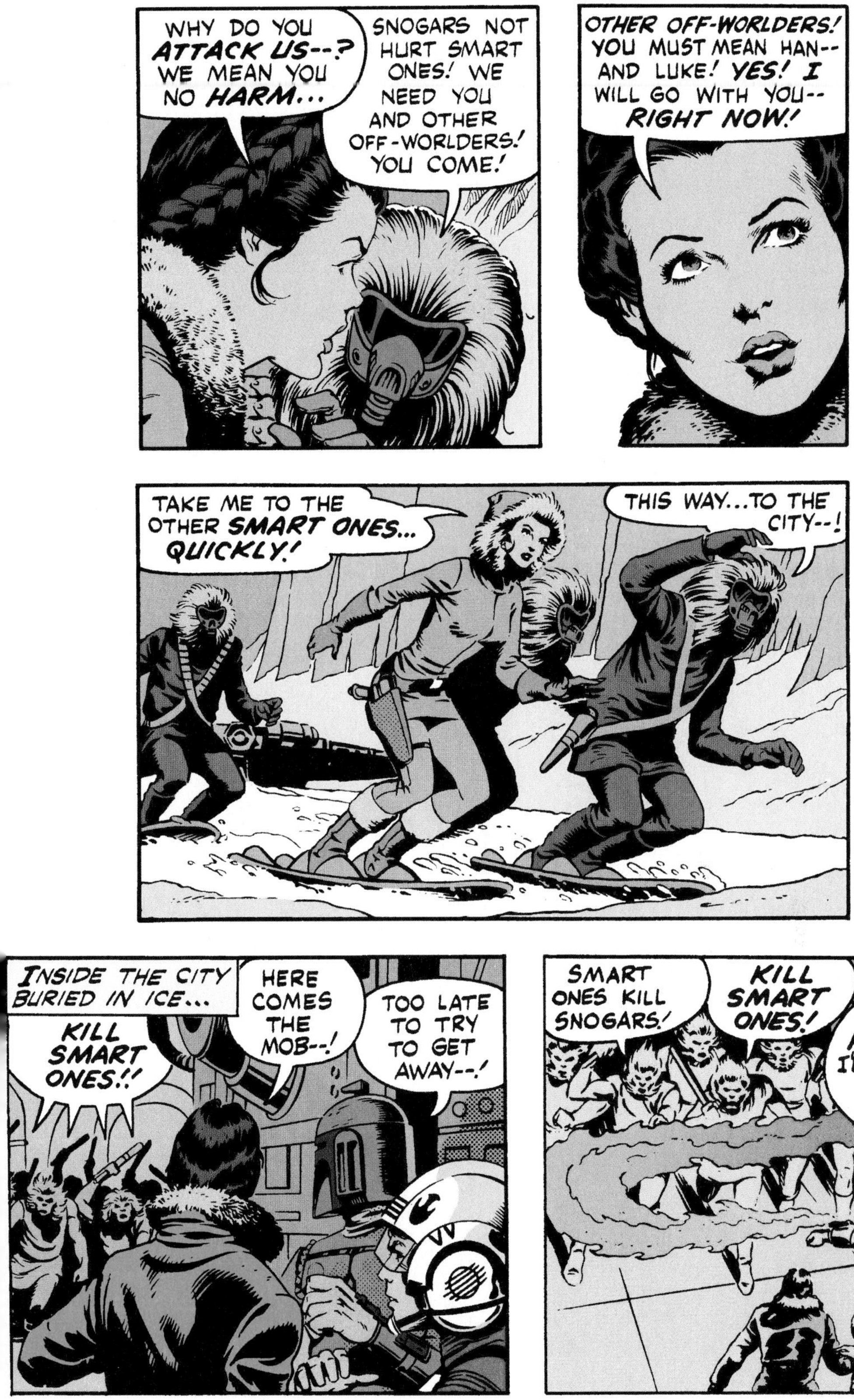
WHY DO YOU ATTACK US--? WE MEAN YOU NO HARM...
SNOGARS NOT HURT SMART ONES! WE NEED YOU AND OTHER OFF-WORLDERS! YOU COME!
OTHER OFF-WORLDERS! YOU MUST MEAN HAN-- AND LUKE! YES! I WILL GO WITH YOU-- RIGHT NOW!
TAKE ME TO THE OTHER SMART ONES... QUICKLY!
THIS WAY...TO THE CITY--!
INSIDE THE CITY BURIED IN ICE...
KILL SMART ONES!!
HERE COMES THE MOB--!
TOO LATE TO TRY TO GET AWAY--!
SMART ONES KILL SNOGARS!
KILL SMART ONES!
STOP, FOOLS!-OR I'LL BURN YOU IN YOUR TRACKS!

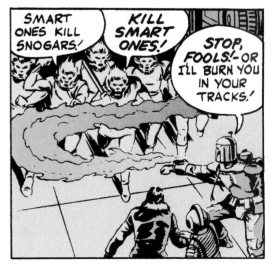

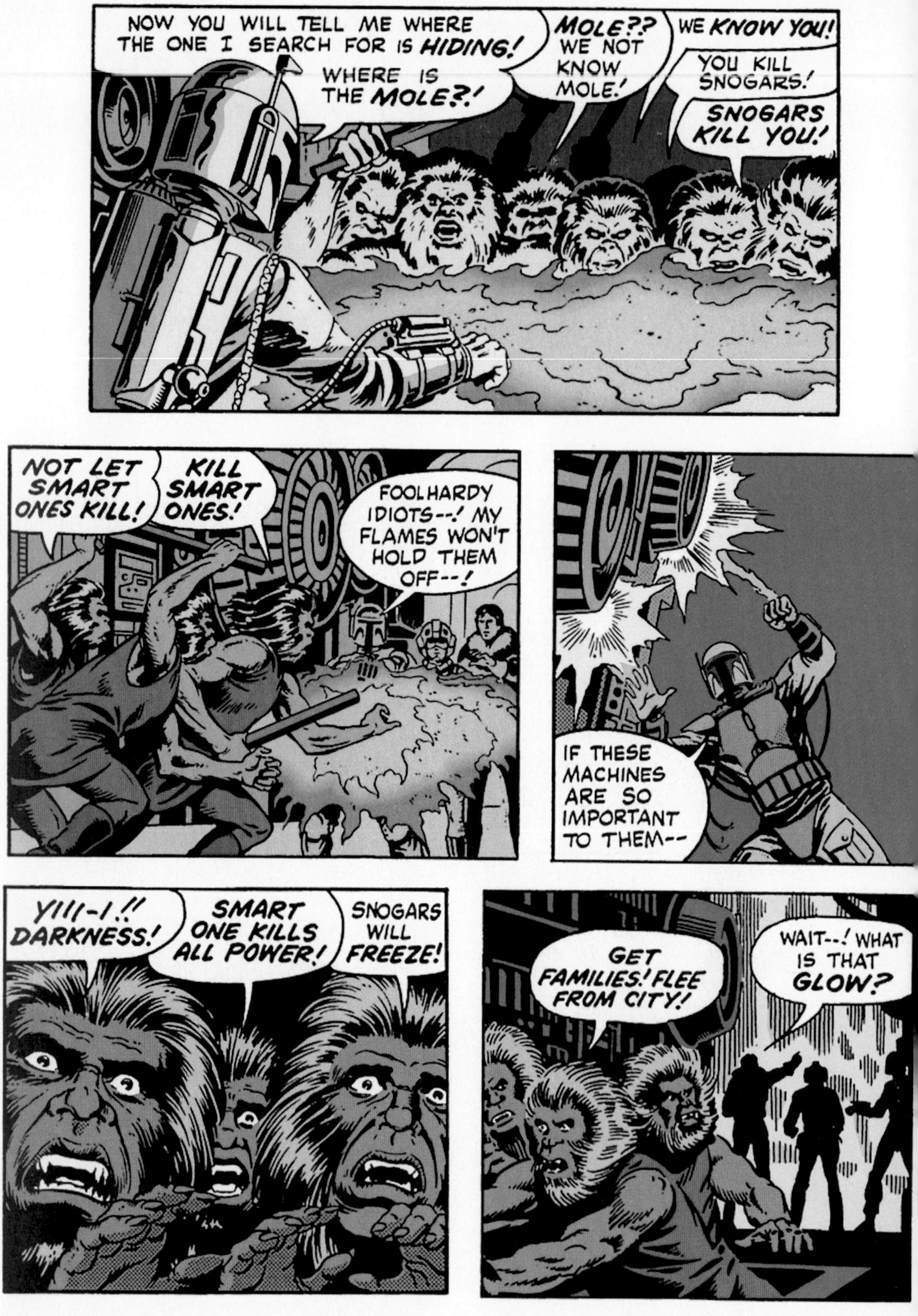
NOW YOU WILL TELL ME WHERE THE ONE I SEARCH FOR IS HIDING!
WHERE IS THE MOLE?!
MOLE?? WE NOT KNOW MOLE!
WE KNOW YOU!
YOU KILL SNOGARS!
SNOGARS KILL YOU!
NOT LET SMART ONES KILL!
KILL SMART ONES!
FOOLHARDY IDIOTS--! MY FLAMES WON'T HOLD THEM OFF--!
IF THESE MACHINES ARE SO IMPORTANT TO THEM--
YIII-I!! DARKNESS!
SMART ONE KILLS ALL POWER!
SNOGARS WILL FREEZE!
GET FAMILIES! FLEE FROM CITY!
WAIT--! WHAT IS THAT GLOW?

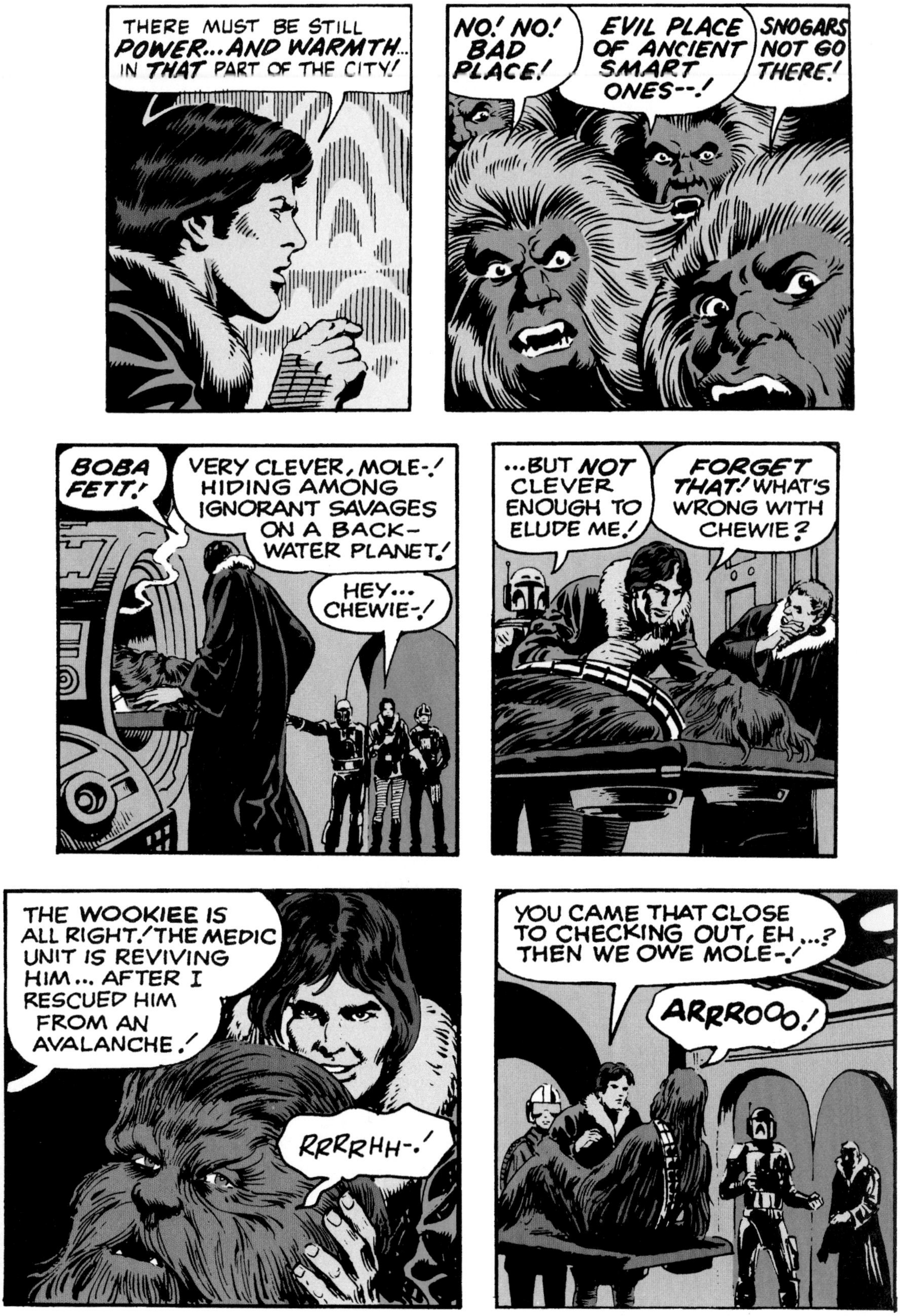
THERE MUST BE STILL POWER...AND WARMTH... IN THAT PART OF THE CITY!
NO! NO! BAD PLACE!
EVIL PLACE OF ANCIENT SMART ONES--!
SNOGARS NOT GO THERE!
BOBA FETT!
VERY CLEVER, MOLE-! HIDING AMONG IGNORANT SAVAGES ON A BACK-WATER PLANET!
HEY... CHEWIE-!
...BUT NOT CLEVER ENOUGH TO ELUDE ME!
FORGET THAT! WHAT'S WRONG WITH CHEWIE?
THE WOOKIEE IS ALL RIGHT! THE MEDIC UNIT IS REVIVING HIM... AFTER I RESCUED HIM FROM AN AVALANCHE!
RRRRHH-!
YOU CAME THAT CLOSE TO CHECKING OUT, EH ...? THEN WE OWE MOLE-!
ARRROOO!

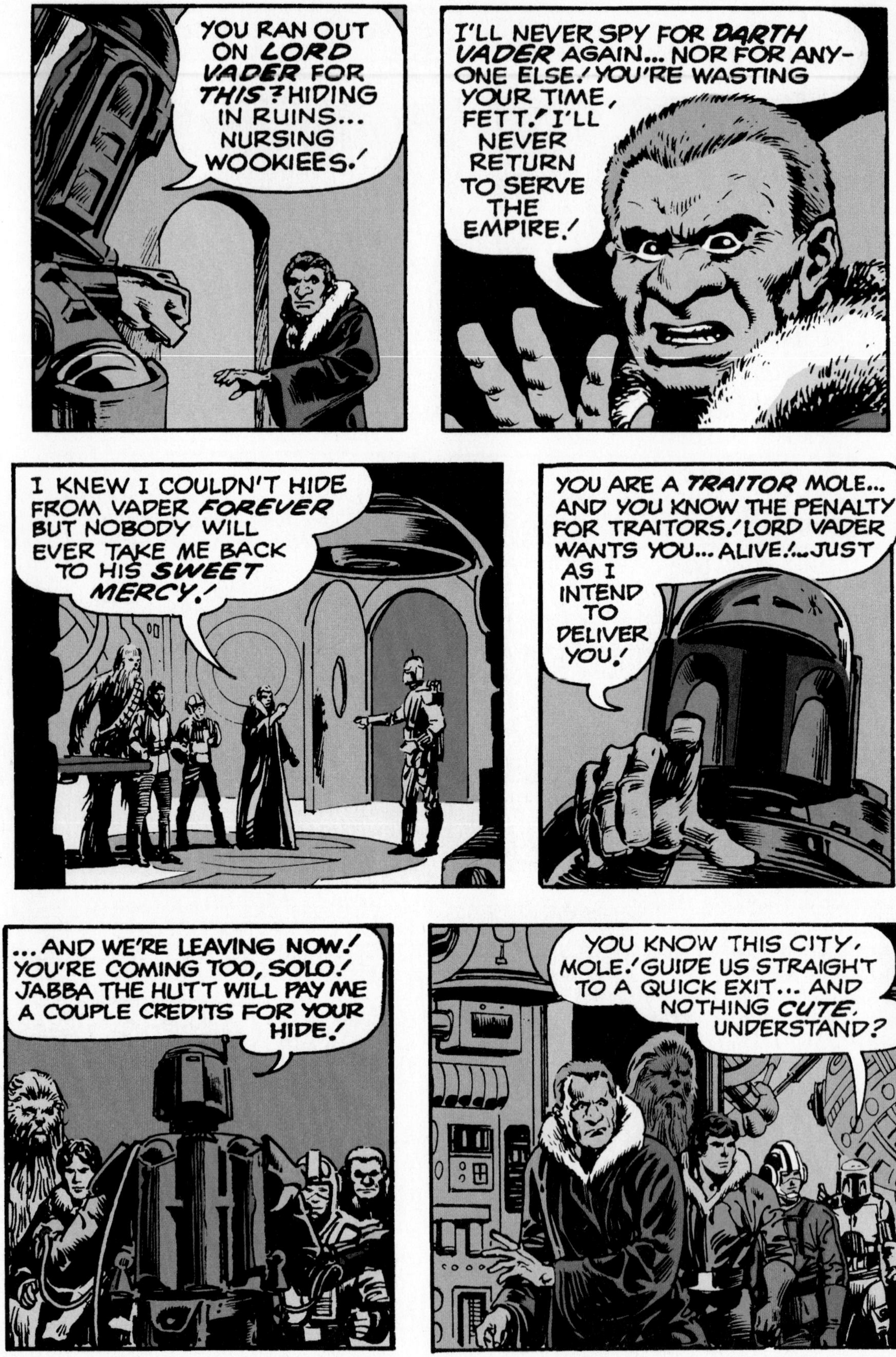
YOU RAN OUT ON LORD VADER FOR THIS? HIDING IN RUINS... NURSING WOOKIEES!
I'LL NEVER SPY FOR DARTH VADER AGAIN... NOR FOR ANY-ONE ELSE! YOU'RE WASTING YOUR TIME, FETT! I'LL NEVER RETURN TO SERVE THE EMPIRE!
I KNEW I COULDN'T HIDE FROM VADER FOREVER BUT NOBODY WILL EVER TAKE ME BACK TO HIS SWEET MERCY!
YOU ARE A TRAITOR MOLE... AND YOU KNOW THE PENALTY FOR TRAITORS! LORD VADER WANTS YOU... ALIVE!...JUST AS I INTEND TO DELIVER YOU!
...AND WE'RE LEAVING NOW! YOU'RE COMING TOO, SOLO! JABBA THE HUTT WILL PAY ME A COUPLE CREDITS FOR YOUR HIDE!
YOU KNOW THIS CITY, MOLE! GUIDE US STRAIGHT TO A QUICK EXIT... AND NOTHING CUTE, UNDERSTAND?

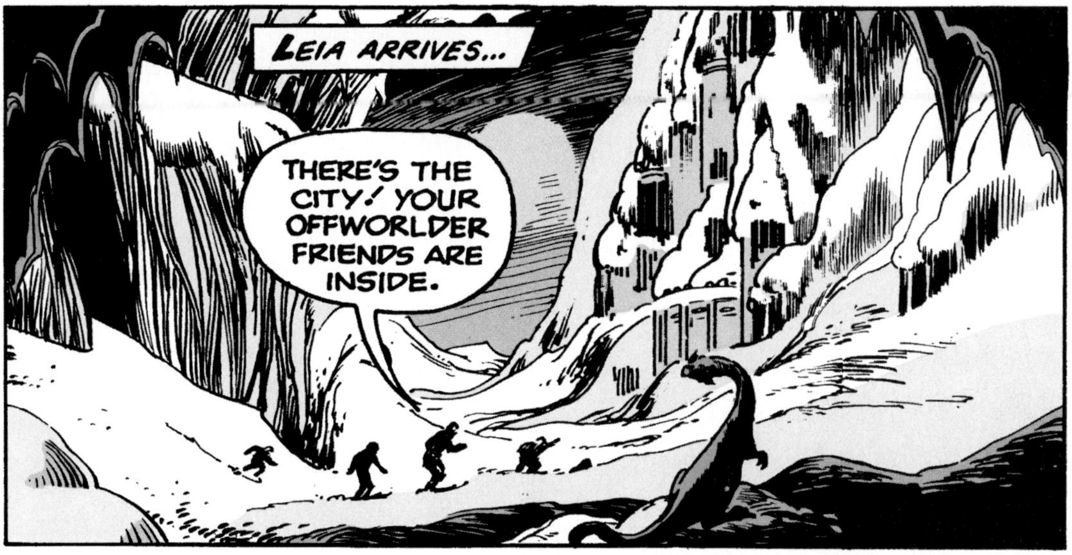
LEIA ARRIVES...
THERE'S THE CITY! YOUR OFFWORLDER FRIENDS ARE INSIDE.

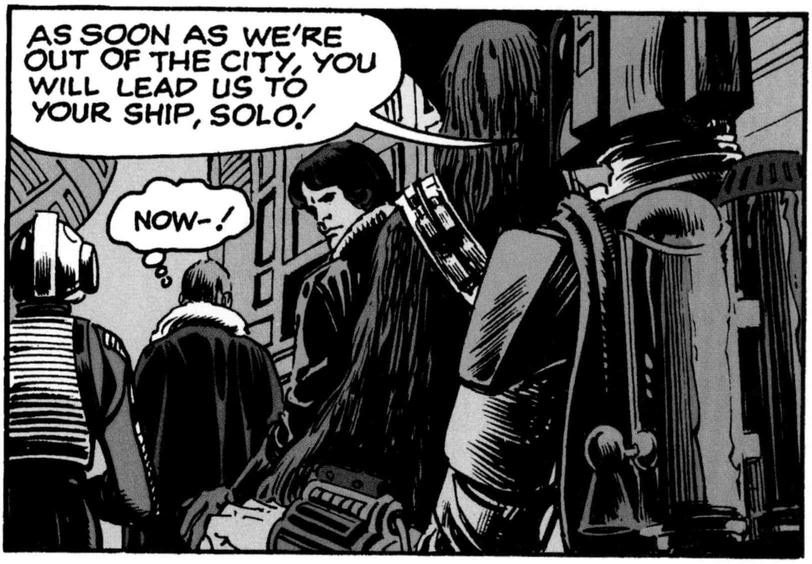
AS SOON AS WE'RE OUT OF THE CITY, YOU WILL LEAD US TO YOUR SHIP, SOLO!
NOW-!

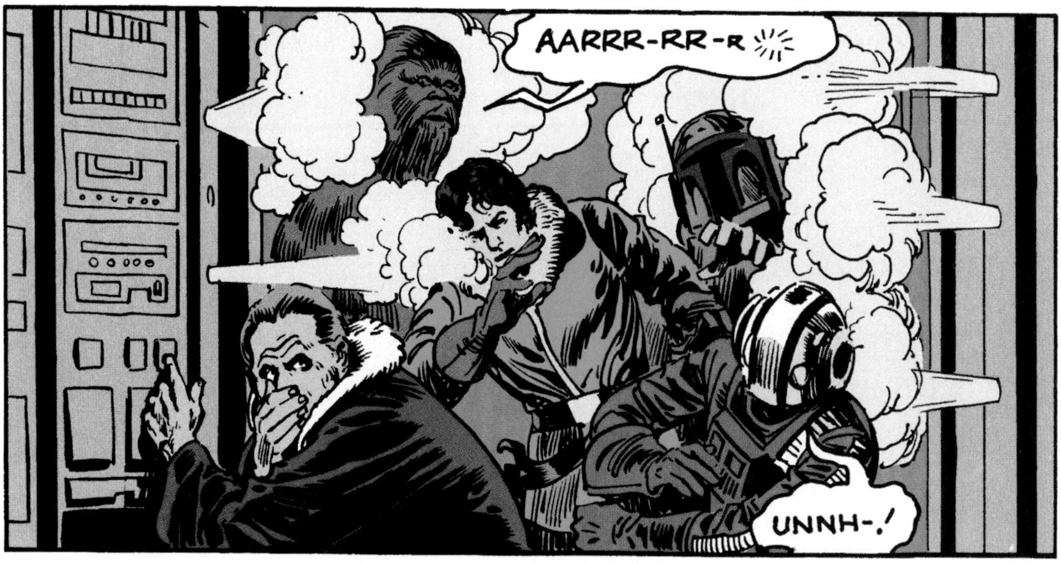
AARRR-RR-R
UNNH-!

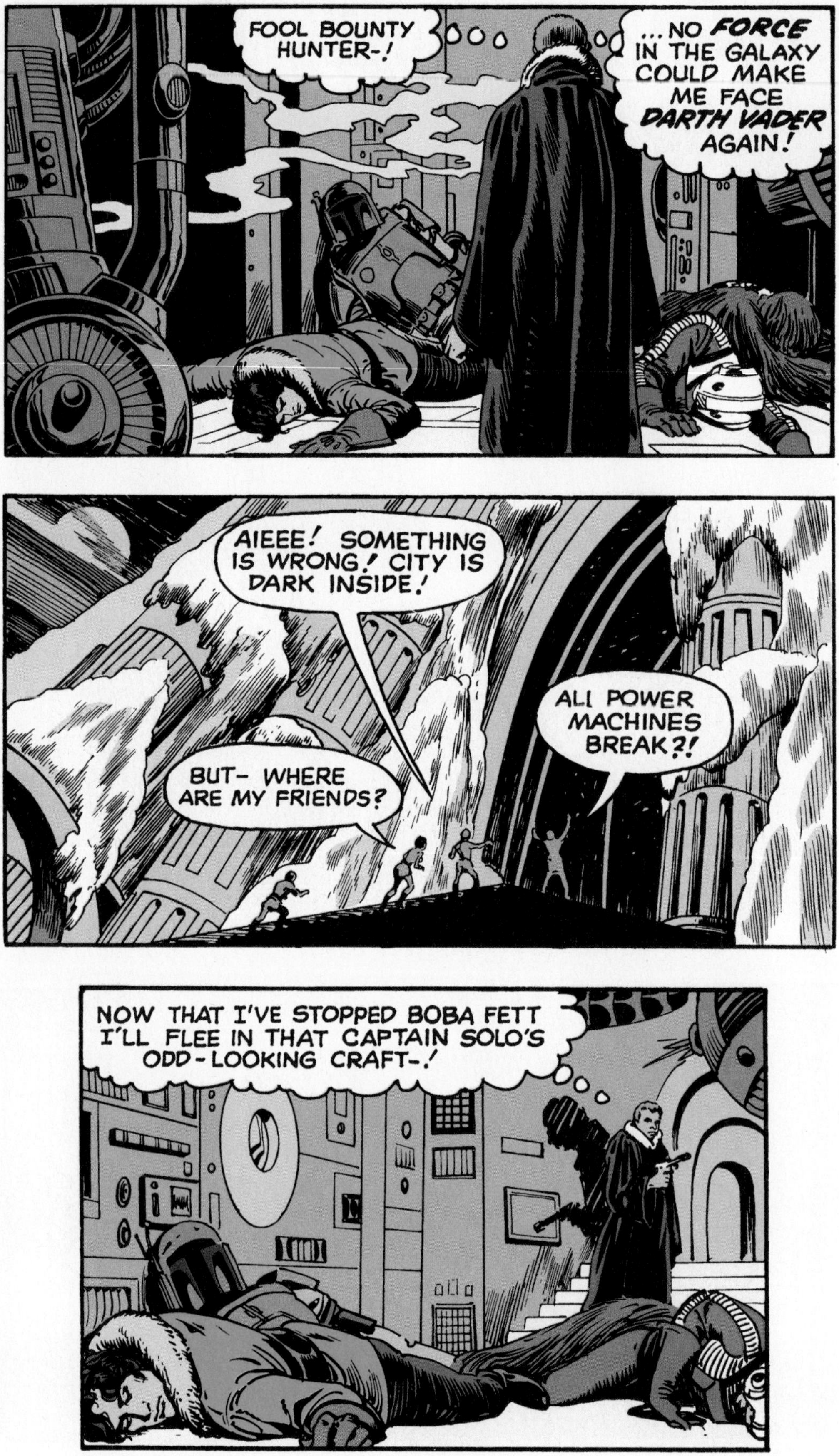
FOOL BOUNTY HUNTER-!
...NO FORCE IN THE GALAXY COULD MAKE ME FACE DARTH VADER AGAIN!
AIEEE! SOMETHING IS WRONG! CITY IS DARK INSIDE!
BUT- WHERE ARE MY FRIENDS?
ALl POWER MACHINES BREAK?!
NOW THAT I'VE STOPPED BOBA FETT I'LL FLEE IN THAT CAPTAIN SOLO'S ODD-LOOKING CRAFT-!

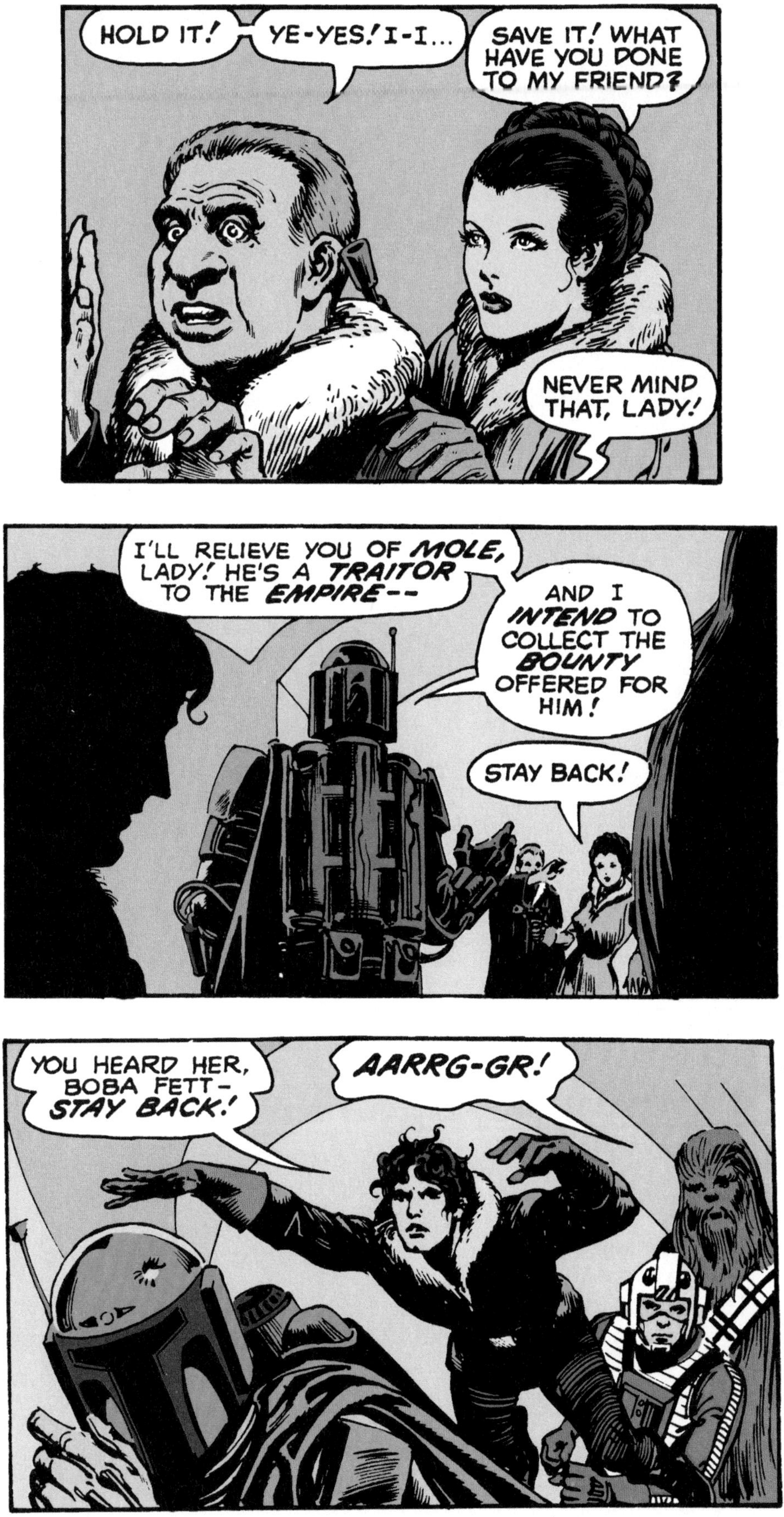
HOLD IT!
YE-YES! I-I...
SAVE IT! WHAT HAVE YOU DONE TO MY FRIEND?
NEVER MIND THAT, LADY!
I'LL RELIEVE YOU OF MOLE, LADY! HE'S A TRAITOR TO THE EMPIRE--
AND I INTEND TO COLLECT THE BOUNTY OFFERED FOR HIM!
STAY BACK!
YOU HEARD HER, BOBA FETT- STAY BACK!
AARRG-GR!

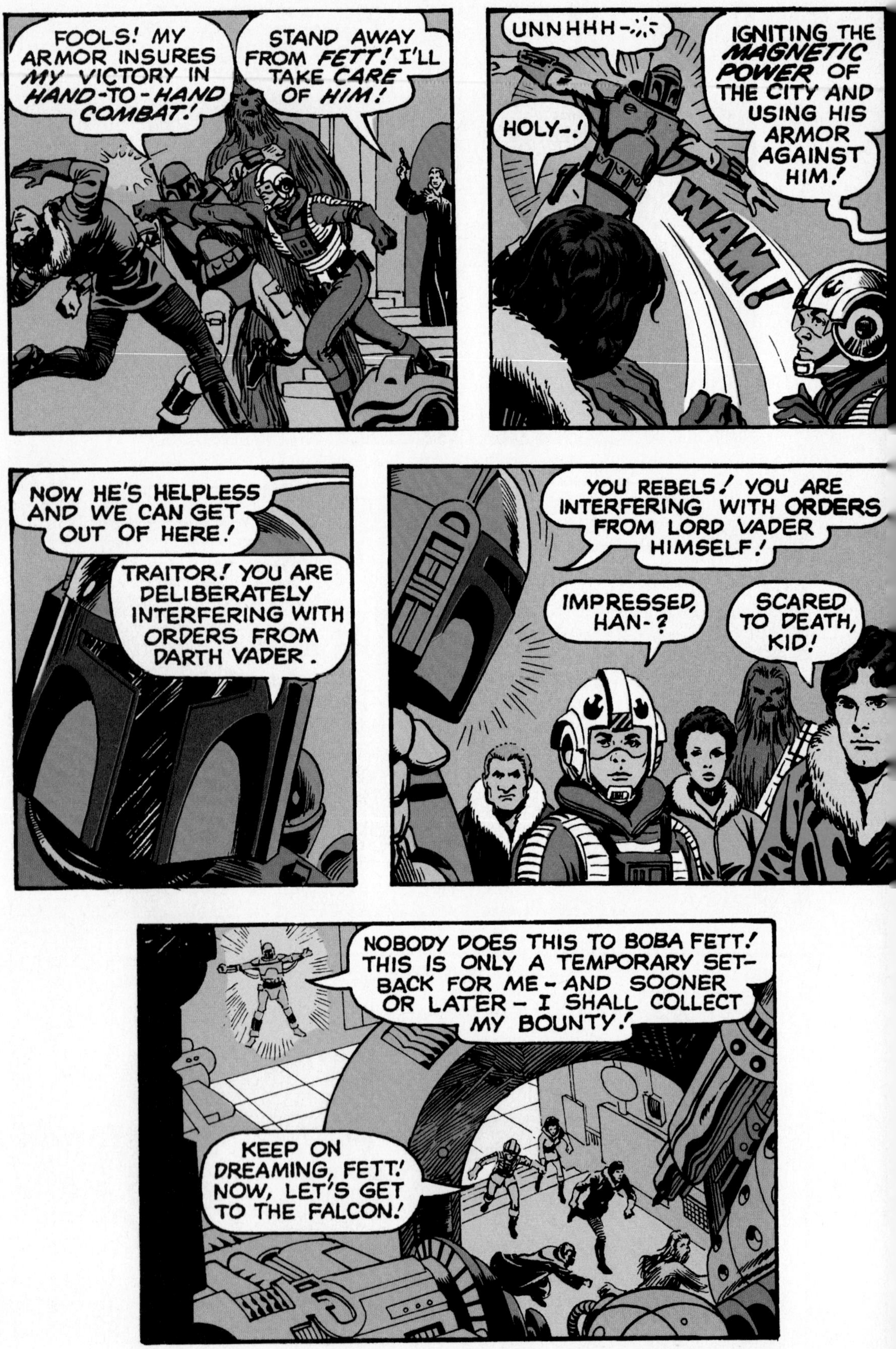
FOOLS! MY ARMOR INSURES MY VICTORY IN HAND-TO-HAND COMBAT!
STAND AWAY FROM FETT! I'LL TAKE CARE OF HIM!
UNNHHH-
HOLY-!
IGNITING THE MAGNETIC POWER OF THE CITY AND USING HIS ARMOR AGAINST HIM!
WAM!
NOW HE'S HELPLESS AND WE CAN GET OUT OF HERE!
TRAITOR! YOU ARE DELIBERATELY INTERFERING WITH ORDERS FROM DARTH VADER.
YOU REBELS! YOU ARE INTERFERING WITH ORDERS FROM LORD VADER HIMSELF!
IMPRESSED, HAN-?
SCARED TO DEATH, KID!
NOBODY DOES THIS TO BOBA FETT! THIS IS ONLY A TEMPORARY SET-BACK FOR ME - AND SOONER OR LATER - I SHALL COLLECT MY BOUNTY!
KEEP ON DREAMING, FETT! NOW, LET'S GET TO THE FALCON!

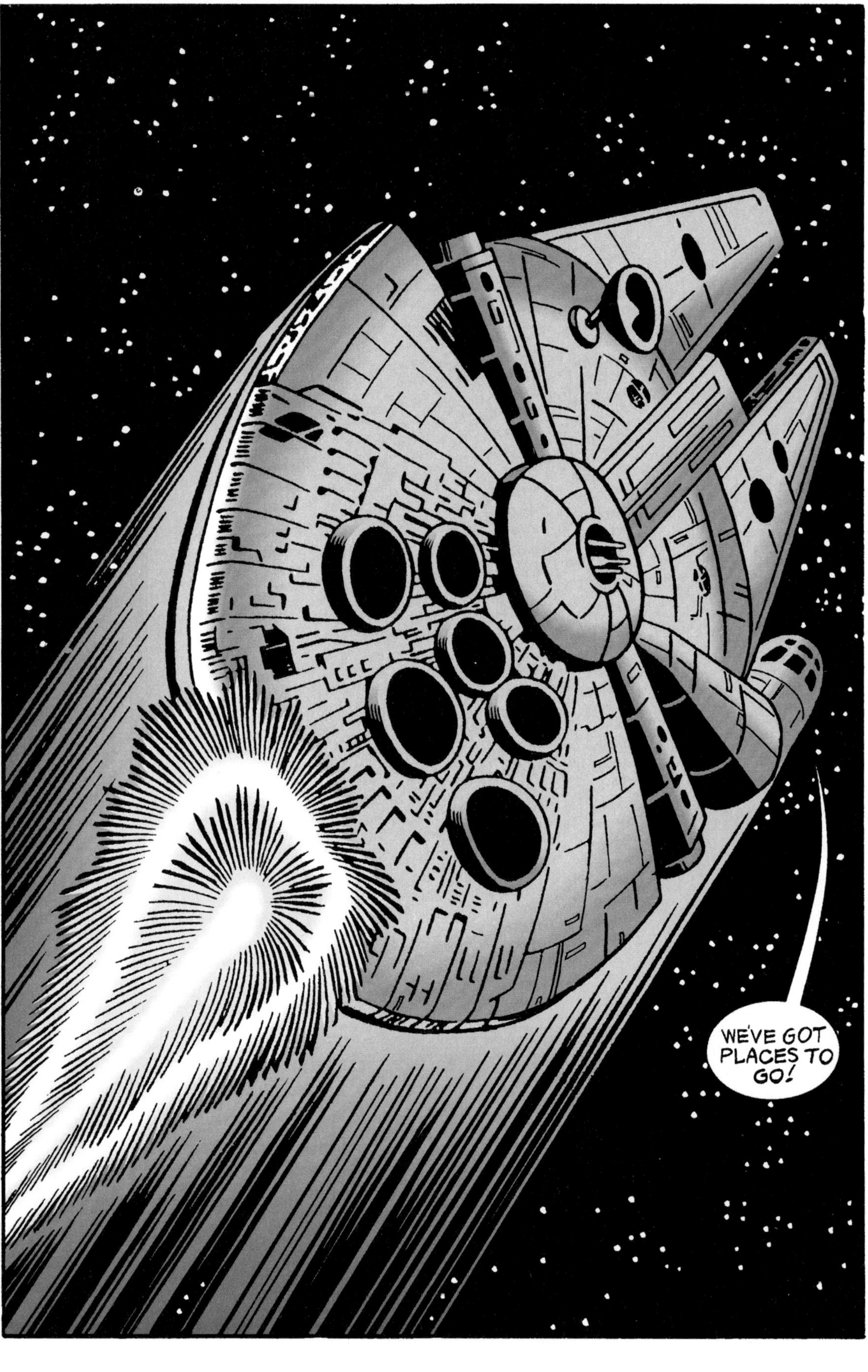
WE'VE GOT PLACES TO GO!

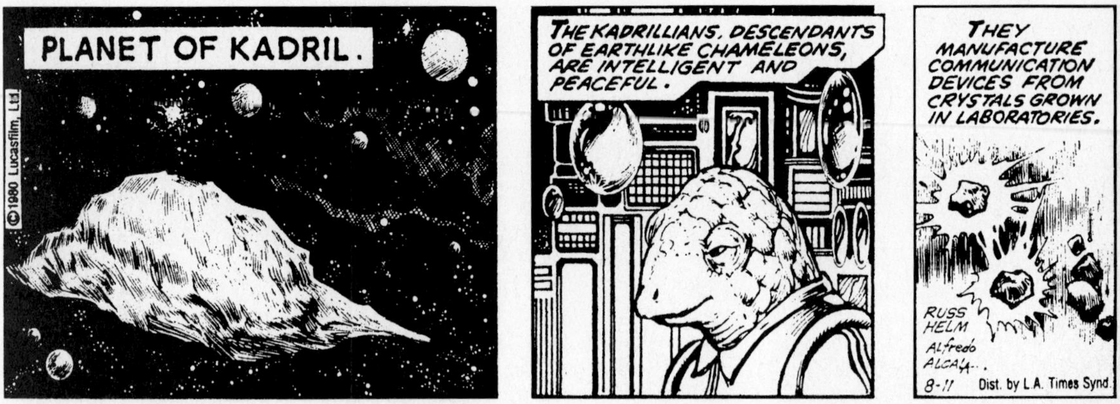
PLANET OF KADRIL.
THE KADRILLIANS, DESCENDANTS OF EARTHLIKE CHAMELEONS, ARE INTELLIGENT AND PEACEFUL.
THEY MANUFACTURE COMMUNICATION DEVICES FROM CRYSTALS GROWN IN LABORATORIES.
RUSS HELM
Alfredo ALCALA
8-11
Dist. by L.A. Times Synd.
© 1980 Lucasfilm, Ltd.

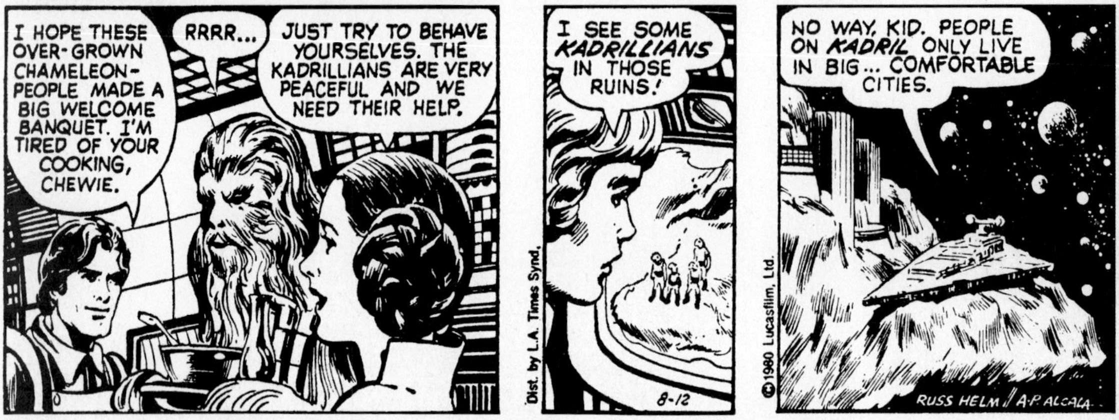
I HOPE THESE OVER-GROWN CHAMELEON-PEOPLE MADE A BIG WELCOME BANQUET. I'M TIRED OF YOUR COOKING, CHEWIE.
RRRR...
JUST TRY TO BEHAVE YOURSELVES. THE KADRILLIANS ARE VERY PEACEFUL AND WE NEED THEIR HELP.
I SEE SOME KADRILLIANS IN THOSE RUINS!
NO WAY, KID. PEOPLE ON KADRIL ONLY LIVE IN BIG... COMFORTABLE CITIES.
Dist. by L.A. Times Synd.
8-12
© 1980 Lucasfilm, Ltd.
RUSS HELM // A.P. ALCALA

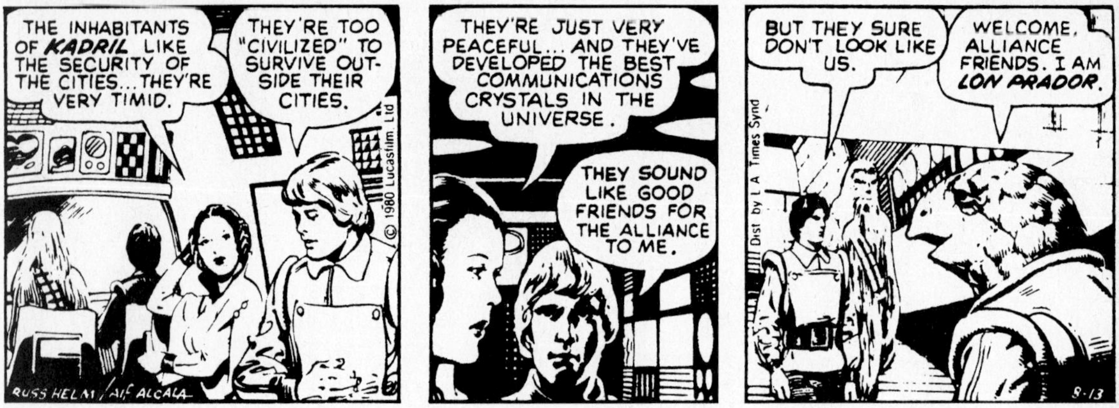
THE INHABITANTS OF KADRIL LIKE THE SECURITY OF THE CITIES...THEY'RE VERY TIMID.
THEY'RE TOO "CIVILIZED" TO SURVIVE OUT-SIDE THEIR CITIES.
© 1980 Lucasfilm, Ltd
RUSS HELM / ALF ALCALA
THEY'RE JUST VERY PEACEFUL... AND THEY'VE DEVELOPED THE BEST COMMUNICATIONS CRYSTALS IN THE UNIVERSE.
THEY SOUND LIKE GOOD FRIENDS FOR THE ALLIANCE TO ME.
BUT THEY SURE DON'T LOOK LIKE US.
WELCOME, ALLIANCE FRIENDS. I AM LON PRADOR.
Dist by L A Times Synd
8-13

"PLANET OF KADRIL"

ORIGINALLY PUBLISHED FROM AUGUST 11 TO OCTOBER 5, 1980

WRITER: RUSS HELM • ARTIST & LETTERER: ALFREDO ALCALA

NOTE: THE "PLANET OF KADRIL" STORYLINE WAS NEVER COLLECTED AND REMASTERED IN THE *CLASSIC STAR WARS* SERIES. IT IS PRESENTED HERE IN ITS ORIGINAL NEWSPAPER-STRIP FORMAT.

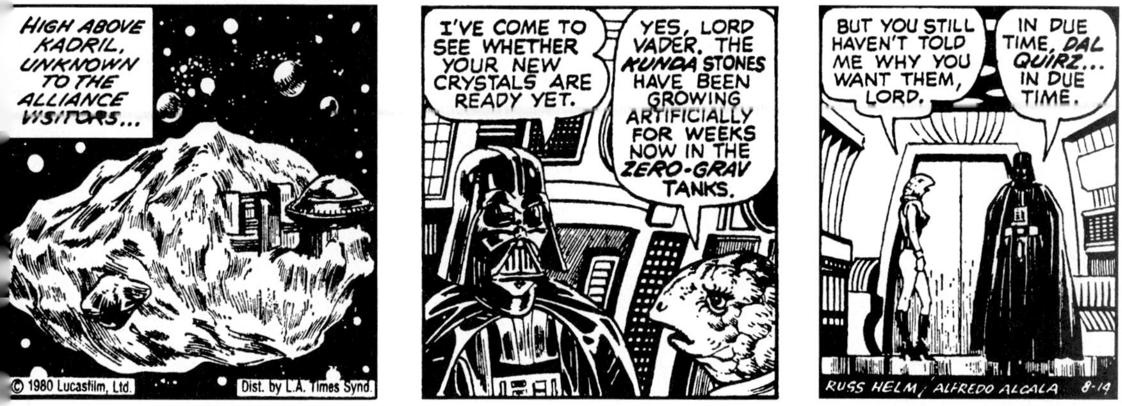
HIGH ABOVE KADRIL, UNKNOWN TO THE ALLIANCE VISITORS...
© 1980 Lucasfilm, Ltd.
Dist. by L.A. Times Synd.
I'VE COME TO SEE WHETHER YOUR NEW CRYSTALS ARE READY YET.
YES, LORD VADER. THE KUNDA STONES HAVE BEEN GROWING ARTIFICIALLY FOR WEEKS NOW IN THE ZERO-GRAV TANKS.
BUT YOU STILL HAVEN'T TOLD ME WHY YOU WANT THEM, LORD.
IN DUE TIME, DAL QUIRZ... IN DUE TIME.
RUSS HELM / ALFREDO ALCALA 8-14

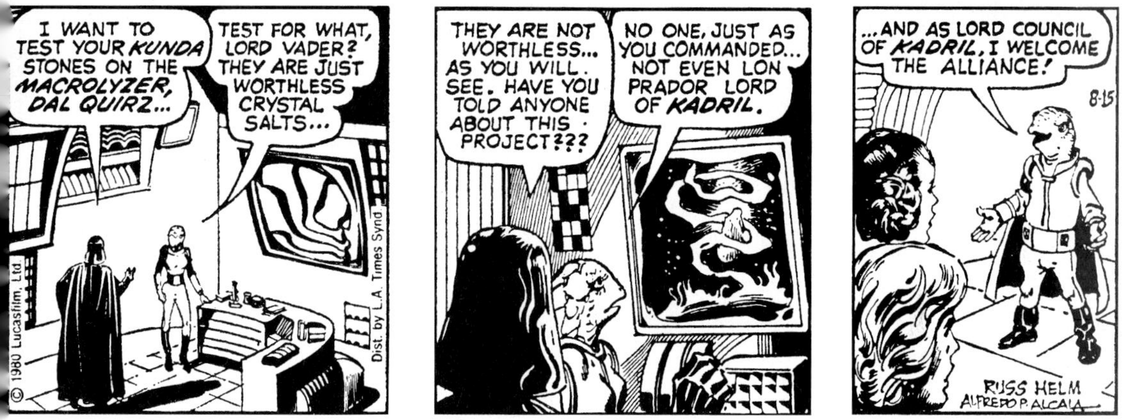
I WANT TO TEST YOUR KUNDA STONES ON THE MACROLYZER, DAL QUIRZ...
TEST FOR WHAT, LORD VADER? THEY ARE JUST WORTHLESS CRYSTAL SALTS...
© 1980 Lucasfilm, Ltd.
Dist. by L.A. Times Synd.
THEY ARE NOT WORTHLESS... AS YOU WILL SEE. HAVE YOU TOLD ANYONE ABOUT THIS PROJECT???
NO ONE, JUST AS YOU COMMANDED... NOT EVEN LON PRADOR LORD OF KADRIL.
...AND AS LORD COUNCIL OF KADRIL, I WELCOME THE ALLIANCE!
8-15
RUSS HELM
ALFREDO P. ALCALA

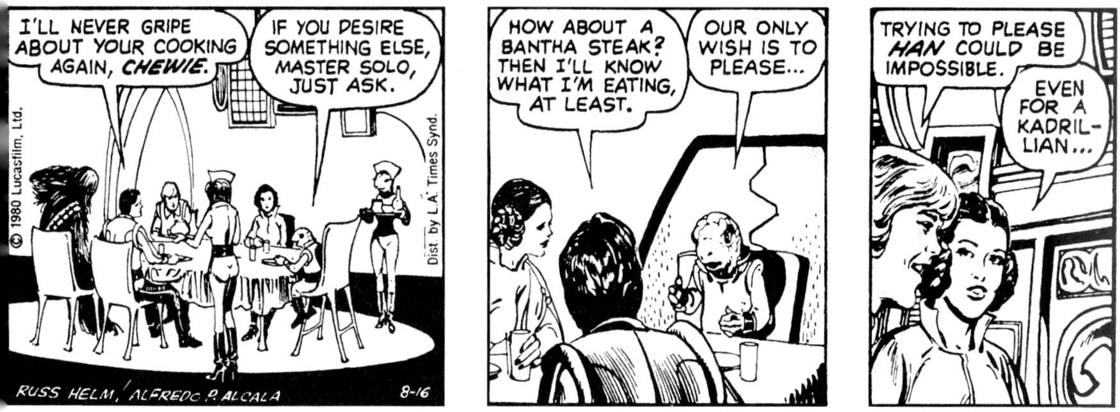
I'LL NEVER GRIPE ABOUT YOUR COOKING AGAIN, CHEWIE.
IF YOU DESIRE SOMETHING ELSE, MASTER SOLO, JUST ASK.
© 1980 Lucasfilm, Ltd.
Dist. by L.A. Times Synd.
RUSS HELM / ALFREDO P. ALCALA 8-16
HOW ABOUT A BANTHA STEAK? THEN I'LL KNOW WHAT I'M EATING, AT LEAST.
OUR ONLY WISH IS TO PLEASE...
TRYING TO PLEASE HAN COULD BE IMPOSSIBLE.
EVEN FOR A KADRIL-LIAN...

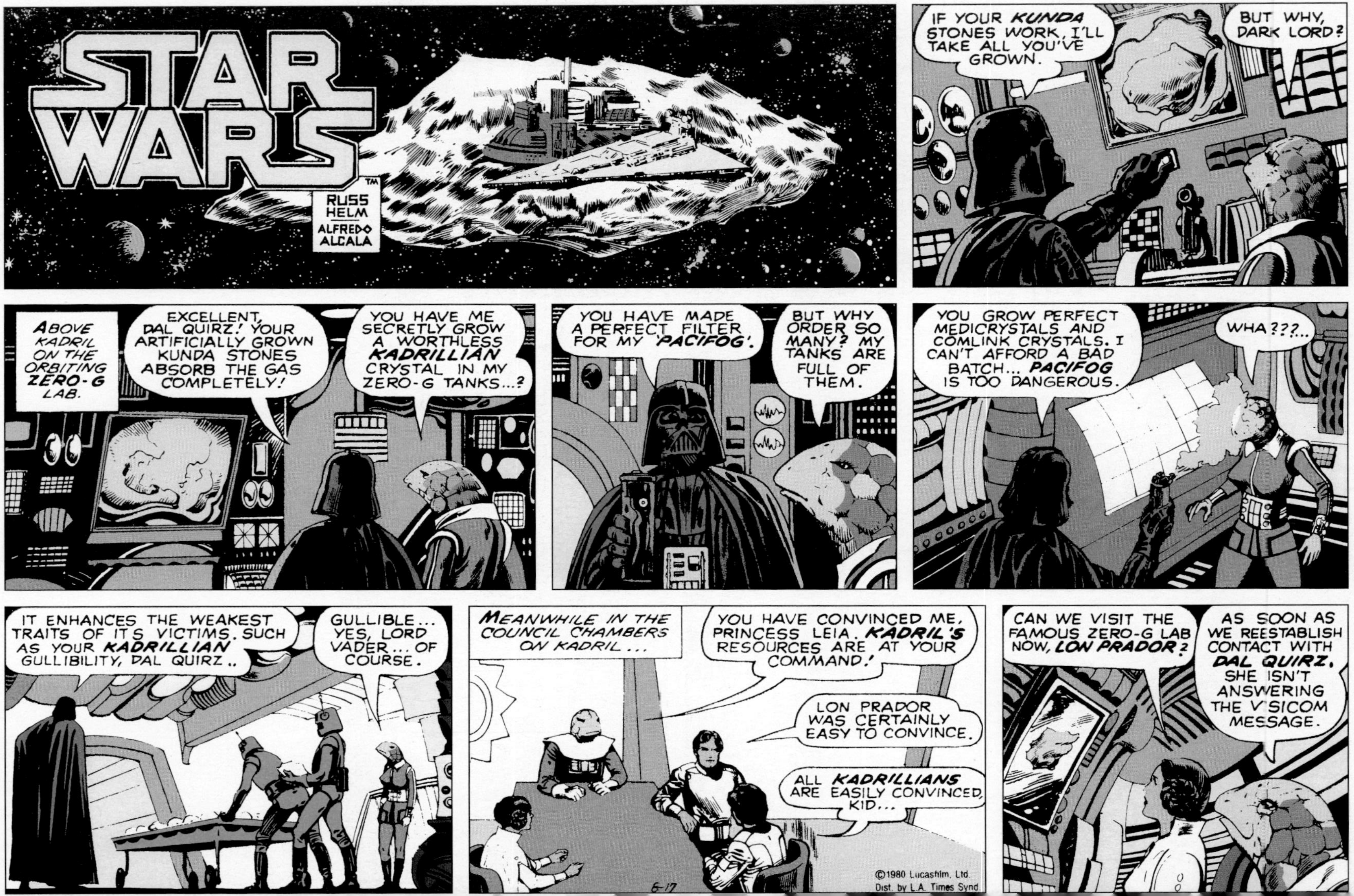
STAR WARS
RUSS HELM
ALFREDO ALCALA
IF YOUR KUNDA STONES WORK, I'LL TAKE ALL YOU'VE GROWN.
BUT WHY, DARK LORD?
ABOVE KADRIL ON THE ORBITING ZERO-G LAB.
EXCELLENT, DAL QUIRZ! YOUR ARTIFICIALLY GROWN KUNDA STONES ABSORB THE GAS COMPLETELY!
YOU HAVE ME SECRETLY GROW A WORTHLESS KADRILLIAN CRYSTAL IN MY ZERO-G TANKS...?
YOU HAVE MADE A PERFECT FILTER FOR MY 'PACIFOG'.
BUT WHY ORDER SO MANY? MY TANKS ARE FULL OF THEM.
YOU GROW PERFECT MEDICRYSTALS AND COMLINK CRYSTALS. I CAN'T AFFORD A BAD BATCH... PACIFOG IS TOO DANGEROUS.
WHA???...
IT ENHANCES THE WEAKEST TRAITS OF IT'S VICTIMS. SUCH AS YOUR KADRILLIAN GULLIBILITY, DAL QUIRZ..
GULLIBLE... YES, LORD VADER... OF COURSE.
MEANWHILE IN THE COUNCIL CHAMBERS ON KADRIL...
YOU HAVE CONVINCED ME, PRINCESS LEIA. KADRIL'S RESOURCES ARE AT YOUR COMMAND!
LON PRADOR WAS CERTAINLY EASY TO CONVINCE.
ALL KADRILLIANS ARE EASILY CONVINCED, KID...
6-17
©1980 Lucasfilm, Ltd.
Dist. by L.A. Times Synd.
CAN WE VISIT THE FAMOUS ZERO-G LAB NOW, LON PRADOR?
AS SOON AS WE REESTABLISH CONTACT WITH DAL QUIRZ. SHE ISN'T ANSWERING THE VISICOM MESSAGE.

MY TROOPERS WILL BE PROTECTED FROM THE PACIFOG. THANKS TO YOUR KUNDA FILTERS, QUIRZ!
...PACIFOG... PROTECTED... WEAKEST TRAIT.
NOW, PREPARE FOR THE FIRST FULL-SCALE TEST... ON... KADRIL.
WHY ISN'T DAL QUIRZ ANSWERING YOUR VISICOM CALL?
I DON'T KNOW... WE'RE ALWAYS IN TOTAL COMMUNICATION.
LON PRADOR... AN EMPIRE CRUISER HAS BEEN SPOTTED LEAVING THE ZERO-G LAB!
8-18
RUSS HELM / ALFREDO ALCALA
Dist by L A Times Synd

DAL QUIRZ! I WAS WORRIED THAT YOU DIDN'T RECEIVE OUR TRANSMISSION... ARE YOU ALRIGHT?
YES... I... AM... FINE... LON PRADOR.
© 1980 Lucasfilm, Ltd
DID YOU SEE AN EMPIRE CRUISER NEAR YOUR ZERO-G COMPLEX?
EMPIRE CRUISER?... NO... I SAW NO CRUISER OR TROOPERS.
Dist by L A Times Synd
SHE SOUNDS AS IF SHE'S BEEN BRAINWASHED, HAN.
I WONDER WHAT AN EMPIRE SHIP IS DOING IN THIS VECTOR ANYWAY?
8-19
RUSS HELM / ALFREDO ALCALA

THIS IS RODNO, DAL QUIRZ'S ASSISTANT. HE CAN BE YOUR GUIDE.
WHY ISN'T YOUR SKIN MARKED WITH I.Q. WHIRLS? ARE YOU NOT SMART ENOUGH?
Dist. by L A Times Synd
WE CAN'T SHOW OUR INTELLIGENCE ON OUR SKIN LIKE YOU DO, RODNO.
TOO BAD. I'M VERY PROUD OF MY PATTERNS.
RUSS HELM / ALFREDO ALCALA
© 1980 Lucasfilm, Ltd.
WOULD DAL QUIRZ KEEP A SECRET FROM LON PRADOR?
WE CANNOT KEEP SECRETS... IT IS AGAINST OUR NATURE...
HANG ON!... WE'RE LIFTING OFF!
8-20

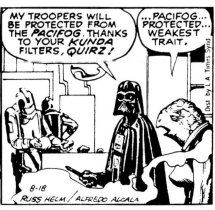

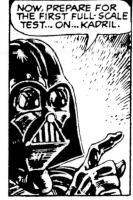

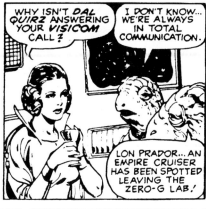

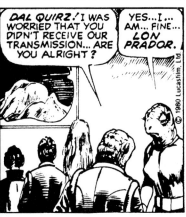

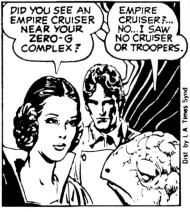

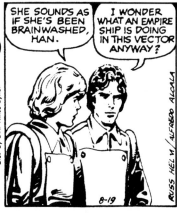

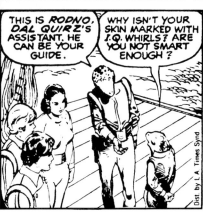

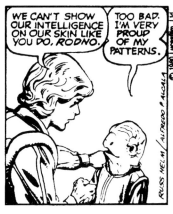

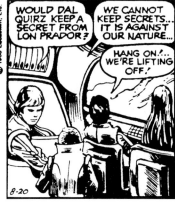

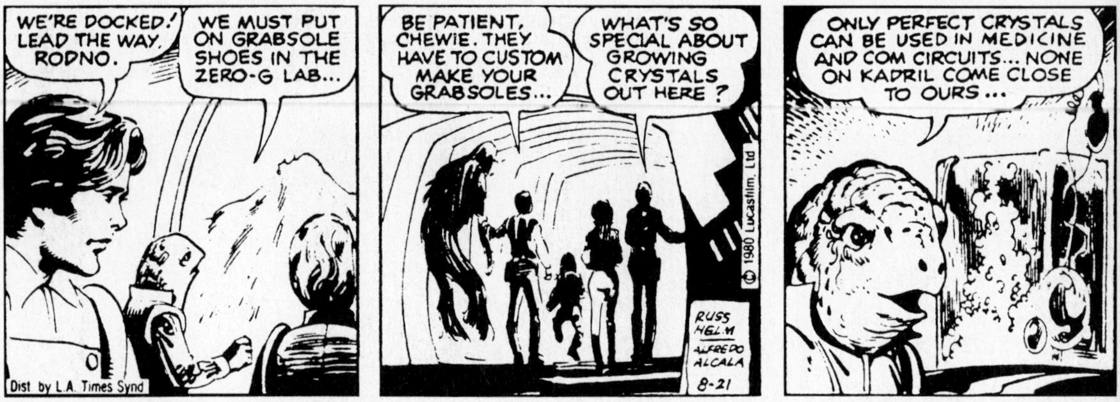

WE'RE DOCKED! LEAD THE WAY, RODNO.
WE MUST PUT ON GRABSOLE SHOES IN THE ZERO-G LAB...
Dist. by L.A. Times Synd
BE PATIENT, CHEWIE. THEY HAVE TO CUSTOM MAKE YOUR GRABSOLES...
WHAT'S SO SPECIAL ABOUT GROWING CRYSTALS OUT HERE?
© 1980 Lucasfilm, Ltd
RUSS HELM
ALFREDO ALCALA
8-21
ONLY PERFECT CRYSTALS CAN BE USED IN MEDICINE AND COM CIRCUITS... NONE ON KADRIL COME CLOSE TO OURS...

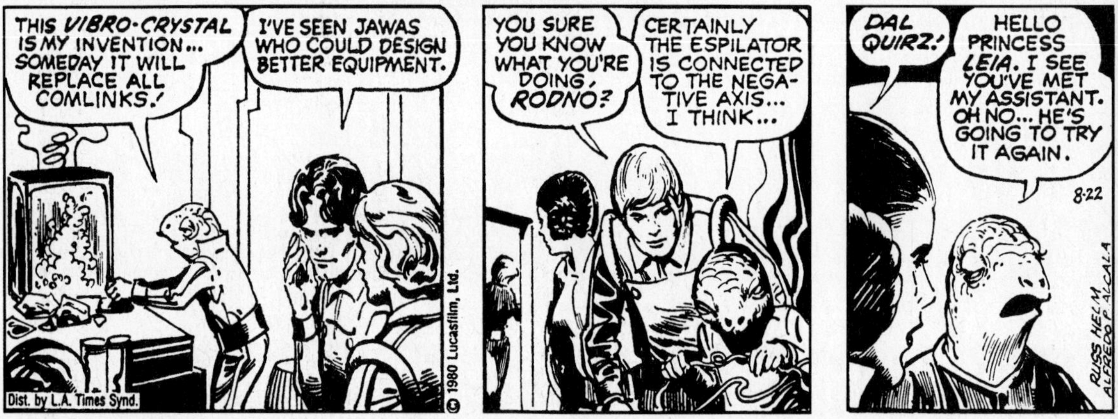

THIS VIBRO-CRYSTAL IS MY INVENTION... SOMEDAY IT WILL REPLACE ALL COMLINKS!
I'VE SEEN JAWAS WHO COULD DESIGN BETTER EQUIPMENT.
Dist. by L.A. Times Synd.
© 1980 Lucasfilm, Ltd.
YOU SURE YOU KNOW WHAT YOU'RE DOING, RODNO?
CERTAINLY THE ESPILATOR IS CONNECTED TO THE NEGATIVE AXIS... I THINK...
DAL QUIRZ!
HELLO PRINCESS LEIA. I SEE YOU'VE MET MY ASSISTANT. OH NO... HE'S GOING TO TRY IT AGAIN.
8-22
RUSS HELM
ALFREDO P. ALCALA

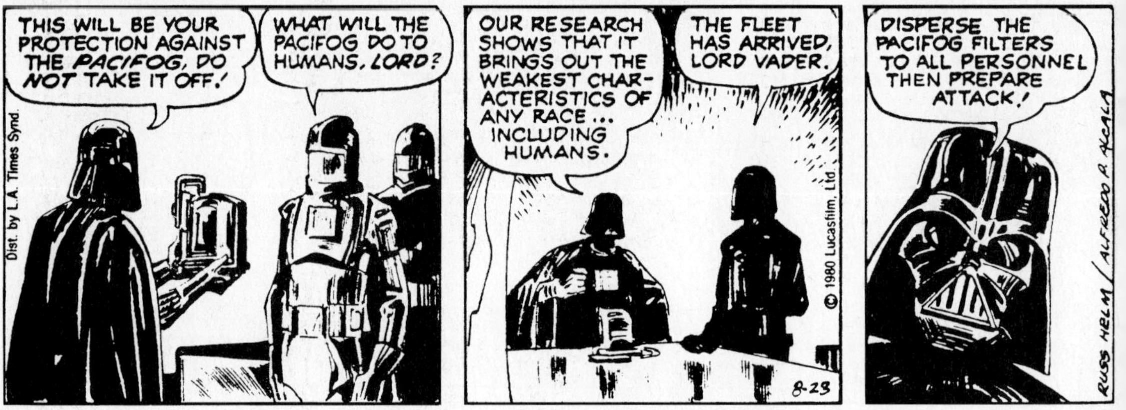

THIS WILL BE YOUR PROTECTION AGAINST THE PACIFOG, DO NOT TAKE IT OFF!
WHAT WILL THE PACIFOG DO TO HUMANS, LORD?
Dist. by L.A. Times Synd.
OUR RESEARCH SHOWS THAT IT BRINGS OUT THE WEAKEST CHARACTERISTICS OF ANY RACE... INCLUDING HUMANS.
THE FLEET HAS ARRIVED, LORD VADER.
© 1980 Lucasfilm, Ltd.
8-23
DISPERSE THE PACIFOG FILTERS TO ALL PERSONNEL THEN PREPARE ATTACK!
RUSS HELM / ALFREDO P. ALCALA

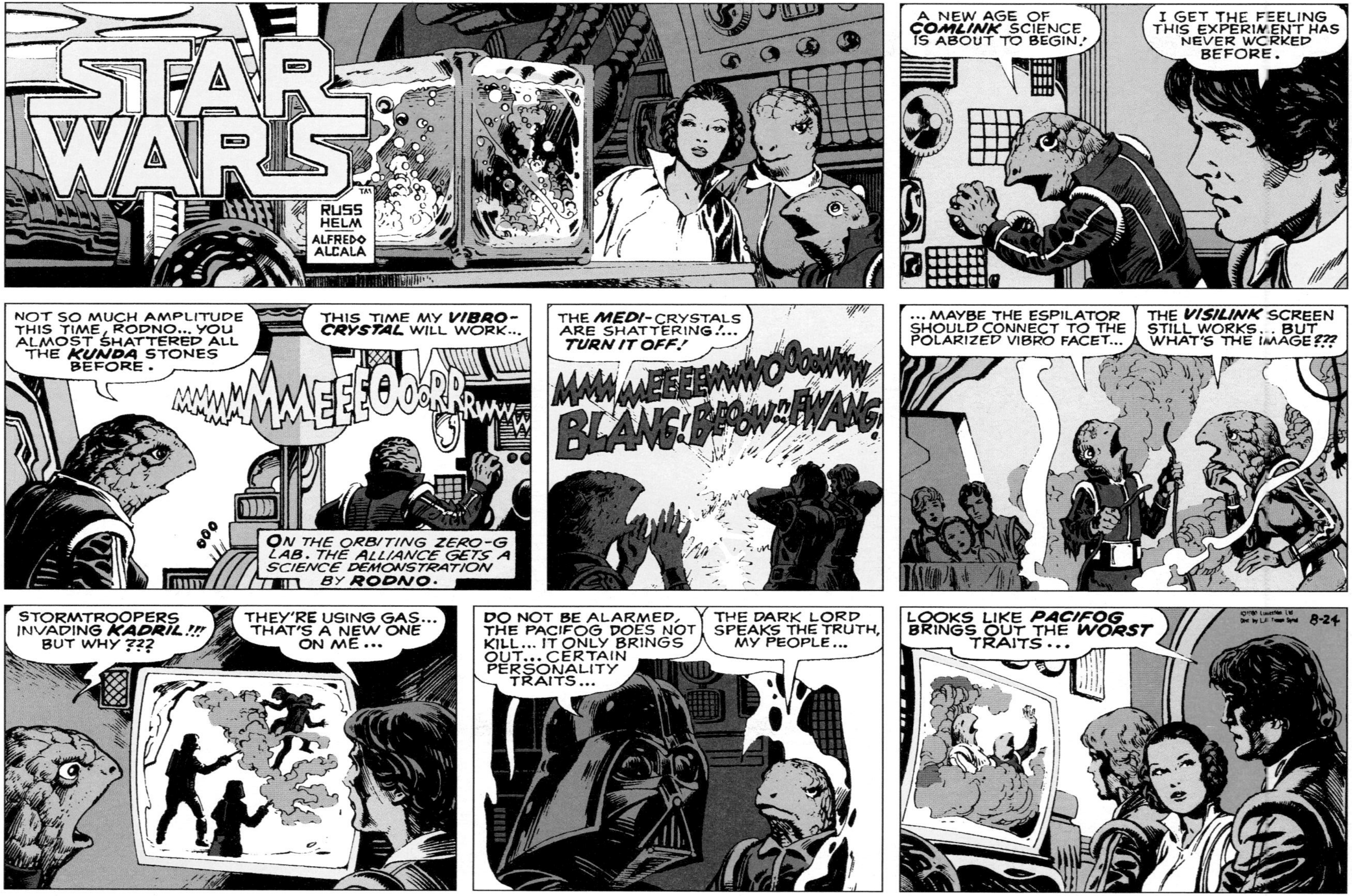
STAR WARS
RUSS HELM
ALFREDO ALCALA
A NEW AGE OF COMLINK SCIENCE IS ABOUT TO BEGIN!
I GET THE FEELING THIS EXPERIMENT HAS NEVER WORKED BEFORE.
NOT SO MUCH AMPLITUDE THIS TIME, RODNO... YOU ALMOST SHATTERED ALL THE KUNDA STONES BEFORE.
THIS TIME MY VIBRO-CRYSTAL WILL WORK...
MMMMMMMEEEOOoRRrwww
ON THE ORBITING ZERO-G LAB. THE ALLIANCE GETS A SCIENCE DEMONSTRATION BY RODNO.
THE MEDI-CRYSTALS ARE SHATTERING!... TURN IT OFF!
MMMMEEEEWWWOOOoWWW
BLANG! BEOW!! FWANG!
... MAYBE THE ESPILATOR SHOULD CONNECT TO THE POLARIZED VIBRO FACET...
THE VISILINK SCREEN STILL WORKS... BUT WHAT'S THE IMAGE???
STORMTROOPERS INVADING KADRIL!!! BUT WHY???
THEY'RE USING GAS... THAT'S A NEW ONE ON ME...
DO NOT BE ALARMED, THE PACIFOG DOES NOT KILL... IT ONLY BRINGS OUT... CERTAIN PERSONALITY TRAITS...
THE DARK LORD SPEAKS THE TRUTH, MY PEOPLE...
LOOKS LIKE PACIFOG BRINGS OUT THE WORST TRAITS...
©1980 Lucasfilm Ltd Dist by L.A. Times Synd
8-24

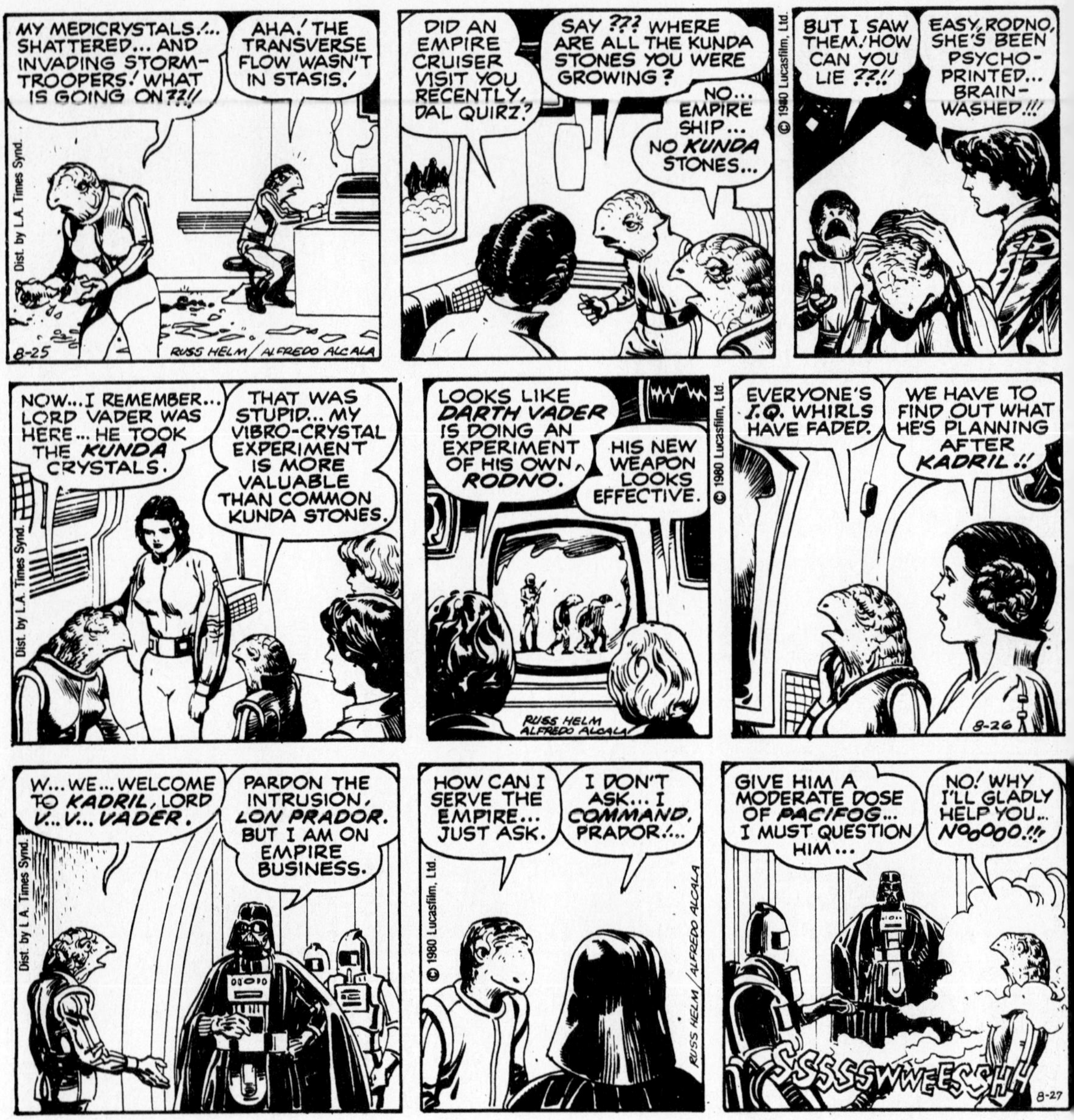
MY MEDICRYSTALS!... SHATTERED... AND INVADING STORM-TROOPERS! WHAT IS GOING ON??!!
AHA! THE TRANSVERSE FLOW WASN'T IN STASIS!
Dist. by L.A. Times Synd.
8-25
RUSS HELM / ALFREDO ALCALA
DID AN EMPIRE CRUISER VISIT YOU RECENTLY, DAL QUIRZ?
SAY ??? WHERE ARE ALL THE KUNDA STONES YOU WERE GROWING?
NO... EMPIRE SHIP... NO KUNDA STONES...
© 1980 Lucasfilm, Ltd.
BUT I SAW THEM! HOW CAN YOU LIE ??!!
EASY, RODNO, SHE'S BEEN PSYCHO-PRINTED... BRAIN-WASHED!!!
NOW... I REMEMBER... LORD VADER WAS HERE... HE TOOK THE KUNDA CRYSTALS.
THAT WAS STUPID... MY VIBRO-CRYSTAL EXPERIMENT IS MORE VALUABLE THAN COMMON KUNDA STONES.
Dist. by L.A. Times Synd.
LOOKS LIKE DARTH VADER IS DOING AN EXPERIMENT OF HIS OWN, RODNO.
HIS NEW WEAPON LOOKS EFFECTIVE.
RUSS HELM ALFREDO ALCALA
© 1980 Lucasfilm, Ltd.
EVERYONE'S I.Q. WHIRLS HAVE FADED.
WE HAVE TO FIND OUT WHAT HE'S PLANNING AFTER KADRIL!!
8-26
W... WE... WELCOME TO KADRIL, LORD V... V... VADER.
PARDON THE INTRUSION, LON PRADOR. BUT I AM ON EMPIRE BUSINESS.
Dist. by L.A. Times Synd.
HOW CAN I SERVE THE EMPIRE... JUST ASK.
I DON'T ASK... I COMMAND, PRADOR!...
© 1980 Lucasfilm, Ltd.
RUSS HELM / ALFREDO ALCALA
GIVE HIM A MODERATE DOSE OF PACIFOG... I MUST QUESTION HIM...
NO! WHY I'LL GLADLY HELP YOU... NOooOO!!!
SSSSSWWEESSHH
8-27

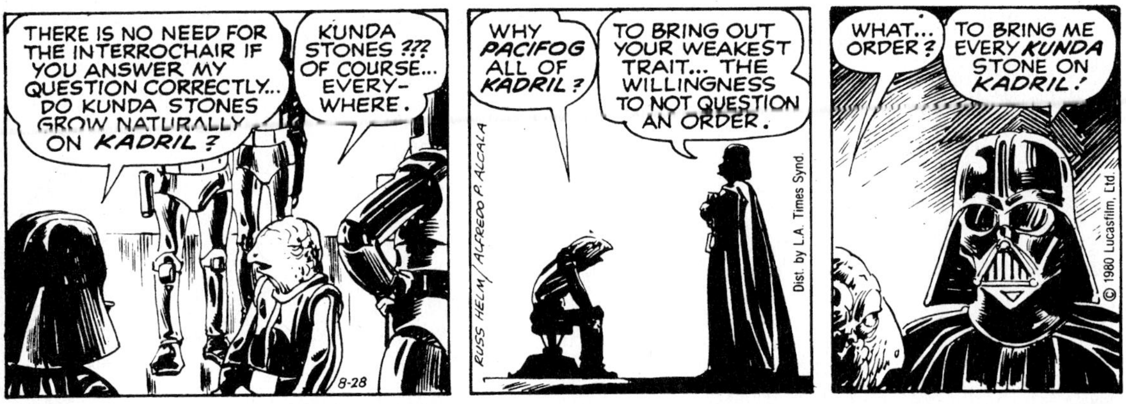
THERE IS NO NEED FOR THE INTERROCHAIR IF YOU ANSWER MY QUESTION CORRECTLY... DO KUNDA STONES GROW NATURALLY ON KADRIL?
KUNDA STONES ??? OF COURSE... EVERY-WHERE.
8-28
WHY PACIFOG ALL OF KADRIL?
TO BRING OUT YOUR WEAKEST TRAIT... THE WILLINGNESS TO NOT QUESTION AN ORDER.
RUSS HELM / ALFREDO P. ALCALA
Dist. by L.A. Times Synd.
WHAT... ORDER?
TO BRING ME EVERY KUNDA STONE ON KADRIL!
© 1980 Lucasfilm, Ltd.

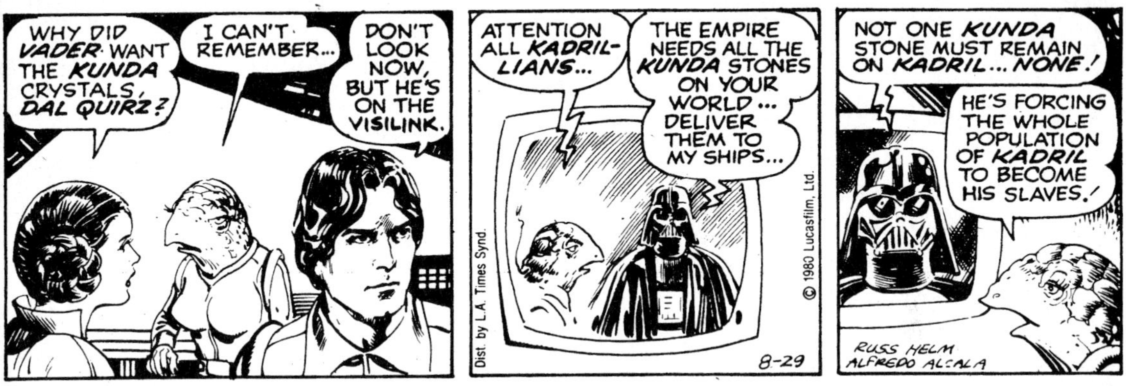
WHY DID VADER WANT THE KUNDA CRYSTALS, DAL QUIRZ?
I CAN'T REMEMBER...
DON'T LOOK NOW, BUT HE'S ON THE VISILINK.
ATTENTION ALL KADRIL-LIANS...
THE EMPIRE NEEDS ALL THE KUNDA STONES ON YOUR WORLD... DELIVER THEM TO MY SHIPS...
Dist. by L.A. Times Synd.
© 1980 Lucasfilm, Ltd.
8-29
NOT ONE KUNDA STONE MUST REMAIN ON KADRIL... NONE!
HE'S FORCING THE WHOLE POPULATION OF KADRIL TO BECOME HIS SLAVES.!
RUSS HELM
ALFREDO ALCALA

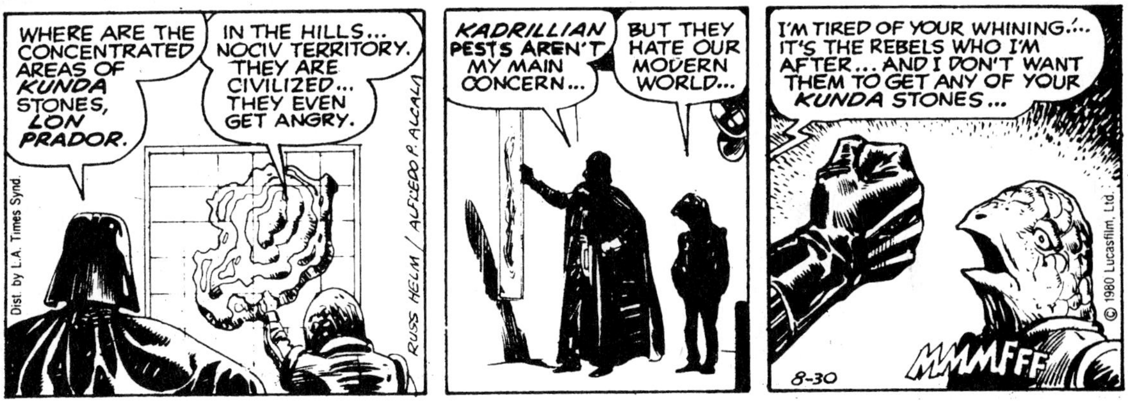
WHERE ARE THE CONCENTRATED AREAS OF KUNDA STONES, LON PRADOR.
IN THE HILLS... NOCIV TERRITORY. THEY ARE CIVILIZED... THEY EVEN GET ANGRY.
Dist. by L.A. Times Synd.
RUSS HELM / ALFREDO P. ALCALA
KADRILLIAN PESTS AREN'T MY MAIN CONCERN...
BUT THEY HATE OUR MODERN WORLD...
I'M TIRED OF YOUR WHINING!... IT'S THE REBELS WHO I'M AFTER... AND I DON'T WANT THEM TO GET ANY OF YOUR KUNDA STONES...
MMMFFF
8-30
© 1980 Lucasfilm, Ltd.

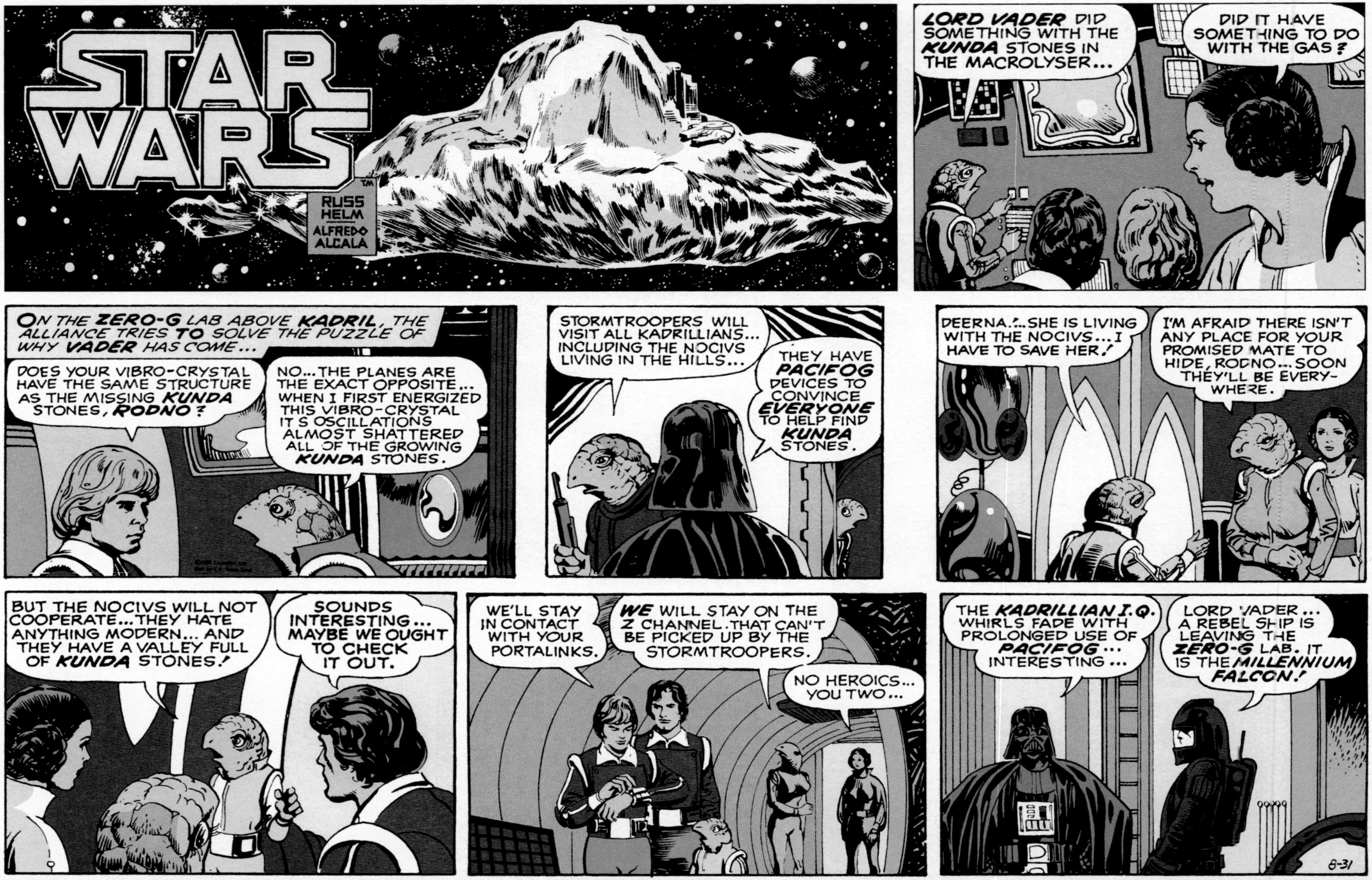
STAR WARS
RUSS HELM
ALFREDO ALCALA
LORD VADER DID SOMETHING WITH THE KUNDA STONES IN THE MACROLYSER...
DID IT HAVE SOMETHING TO DO WITH THE GAS?
ON THE ZERO-G LAB ABOVE KADRIL, THE ALLIANCE TRIES TO SOLVE THE PUZZLE OF WHY VADER HAS COME...
DOES YOUR VIBRO-CRYSTAL HAVE THE SAME STRUCTURE AS THE MISSING KUNDA STONES, RODNO?
NO... THE PLANES ARE THE EXACT OPPOSITE... WHEN I FIRST ENERGIZED THIS VIBRO-CRYSTAL IT S OSCILLATIONS ALMOST SHATTERED ALL OF THE GROWING KUNDA STONES.
STORMTROOPERS WILL VISIT ALL KADRILLIANS... INCLUDING THE NOCIVS LIVING IN THE HILLS...
THEY HAVE PACIFOG DEVICES TO CONVINCE EVERYONE TO HELP FIND KUNDA STONES.
DEERNA.!..SHE IS LIVING WITH THE NOCIVS... I HAVE TO SAVE HER!
I'M AFRAID THERE ISN'T ANY PLACE FOR YOUR PROMISED MATE TO HIDE, RODNO... SOON THEY'LL BE EVERYWHERE.
BUT THE NOCIVS WILL NOT COOPERATE... THEY HATE ANYTHING MODERN... AND THEY HAVE A VALLEY FULL OF KUNDA STONES!
SOUNDS INTERESTING... MAYBE WE OUGHT TO CHECK IT OUT.
WE'LL STAY IN CONTACT WITH YOUR PORTALINKS.
WE WILL STAY ON THE Z CHANNEL. THAT CAN'T BE PICKED UP BY THE STORMTROOPERS.
NO HEROICS... YOU TWO...
THE KADRILLIAN I.Q. WHIRLS FADE WITH PROLONGED USE OF PACIFOG... INTERESTING...
LORD VADER... A REBEL SHIP IS LEAVING THE ZERO-G LAB. IT IS THE MILLENNIUM FALCON!
8-31

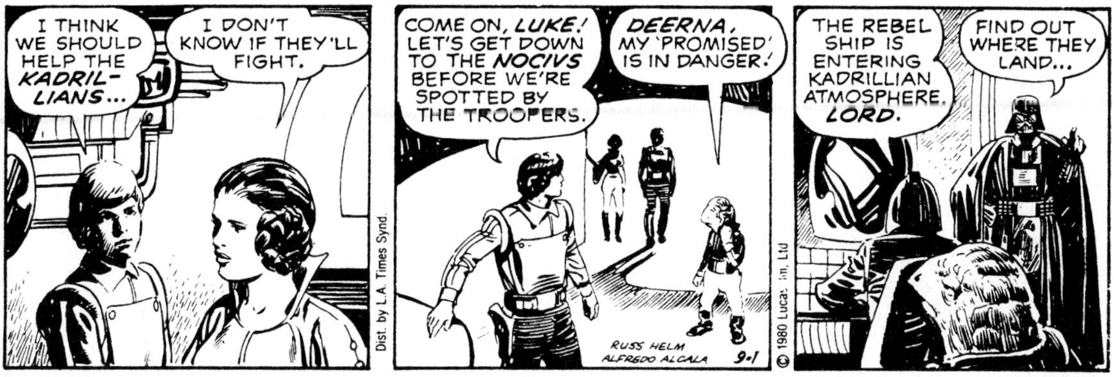
I THINK WE SHOULD HELP THE KADRILLIANS...
I DON'T KNOW IF THEY'LL FIGHT.
Dist. by L.A. Times Synd.
COME ON, LUKE! LET'S GET DOWN TO THE NOCIVS BEFORE WE'RE SPOTTED BY THE TROOPERS.
DEERNA, MY 'PROMISED' IS IN DANGER!
RUSS HELM
ALFREDO ALCALA
9-1
THE REBEL SHIP IS ENTERING KADRILLIAN ATMOSPHERE, LORD.
FIND OUT WHERE THEY LAND...

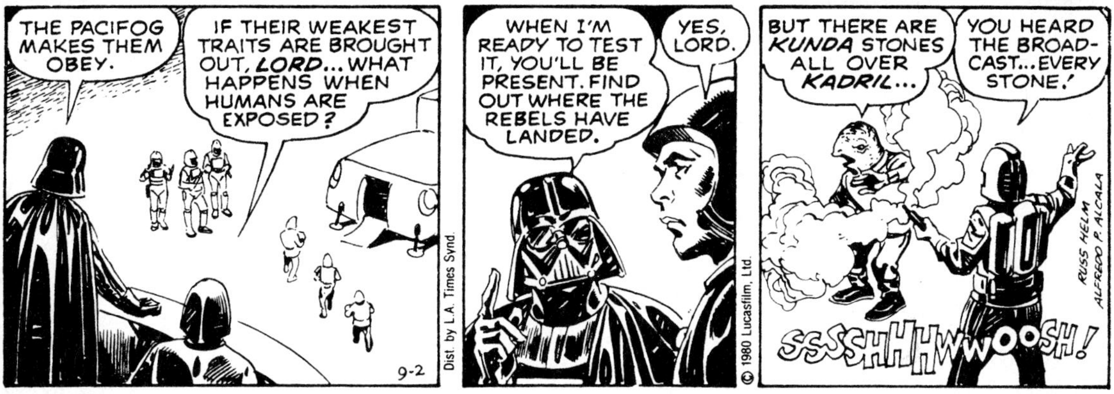
THE PACIFOG MAKES THEM OBEY.
IF THEIR WEAKEST TRAITS ARE BROUGHT OUT, LORD... WHAT HAPPENS WHEN HUMANS ARE EXPOSED?
9-2
Dist. by L.A. Times Synd.
WHEN I'M READY TO TEST IT, YOU'LL BE PRESENT. FIND OUT WHERE THE REBELS HAVE LANDED.
YES, LORD.
© 1980 Lucasfilm, Ltd.
BUT THERE ARE KUNDA STONES ALL OVER KADRIL...
YOU HEARD THE BROADCAST... EVERY STONE!
RUSS HELM
ALFREDO P. ALCALA
SSSSHHHWWOOSH!

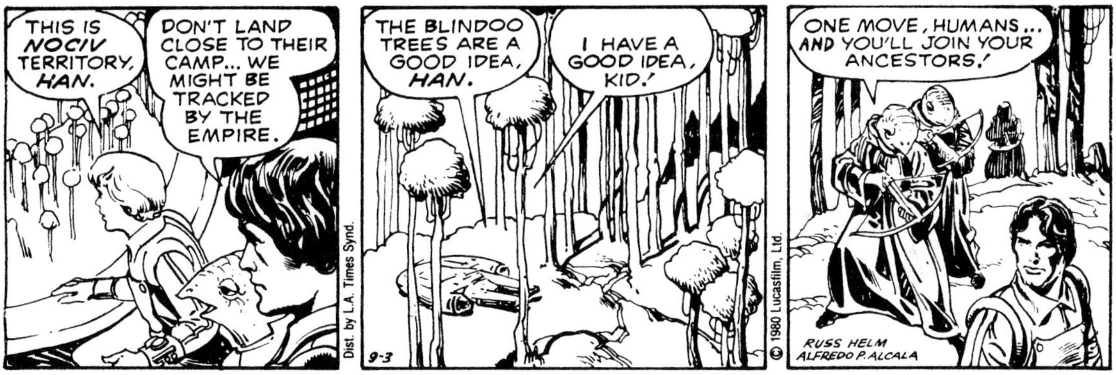
THIS IS NOCIV TERRITORY, HAN.
DON'T LAND CLOSE TO THEIR CAMP... WE MIGHT BE TRACKED BY THE EMPIRE.
Dist. by L.A. Times Synd.
THE BLINDOO TREES ARE A GOOD IDEA, HAN.
I HAVE A GOOD IDEA, KID!
9-3
© 1980 Lucasfilm, Ltd.
ONE MOVE, HUMANS... AND YOU'LL JOIN YOUR ANCESTORS!
RUSS HELM
ALFREDO P. ALCALA

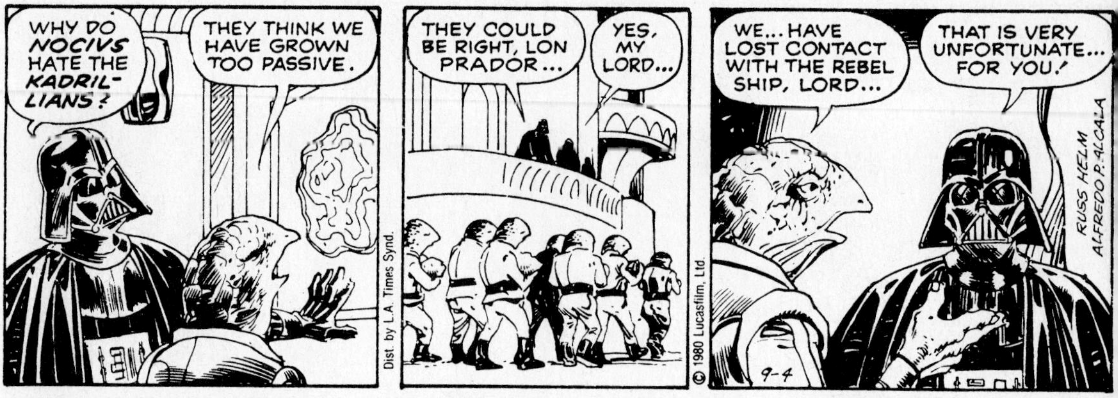
WHY DO NOCIVS HATE THE KADRIL-LIANS?
THEY THINK WE HAVE GROWN TOO PASSIVE.
Dist. by L.A. Times Synd.
THEY COULD BE RIGHT, LON PRADOR...
YES, MY LORD...
© 1980 Lucasfilm, Ltd.
WE... HAVE LOST CONTACT WITH THE REBEL SHIP, LORD...
THAT IS VERY UNFORTUNATE... FOR YOU.!
RUSS HELM
ALFREDO P. ALCALA
9-4

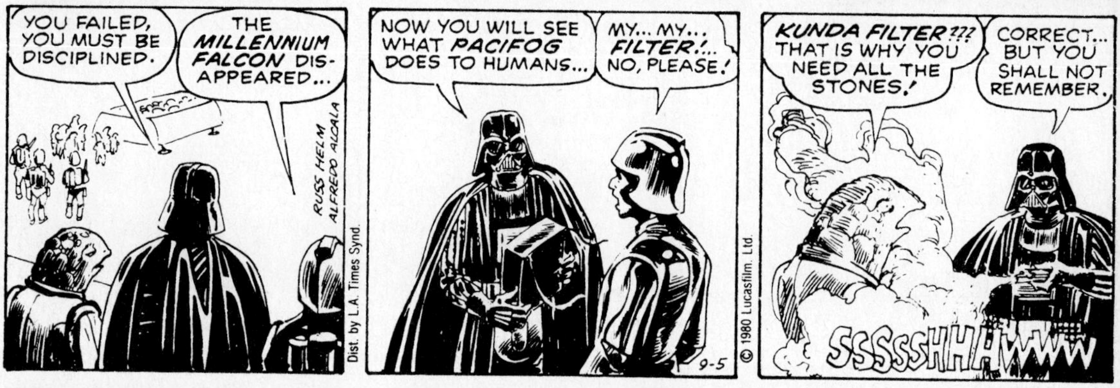
YOU FAILED, YOU MUST BE DISCIPLINED.
THE MILLENNIUM FALCON DIS-APPEARED...
RUSS HELM
ALFREDO ALCALA
Dist. by L.A. Times Synd.
NOW YOU WILL SEE WHAT PACIFOG DOES TO HUMANS...
MY... MY... FILTER!... NO, PLEASE!
9-5
© 1980 Lucasfilm, Ltd.
KUNDA FILTER??? THAT IS WHY YOU NEED ALL THE STONES!
CORRECT... BUT YOU SHALL NOT REMEMBER.
SSSSSHHHAWWWW

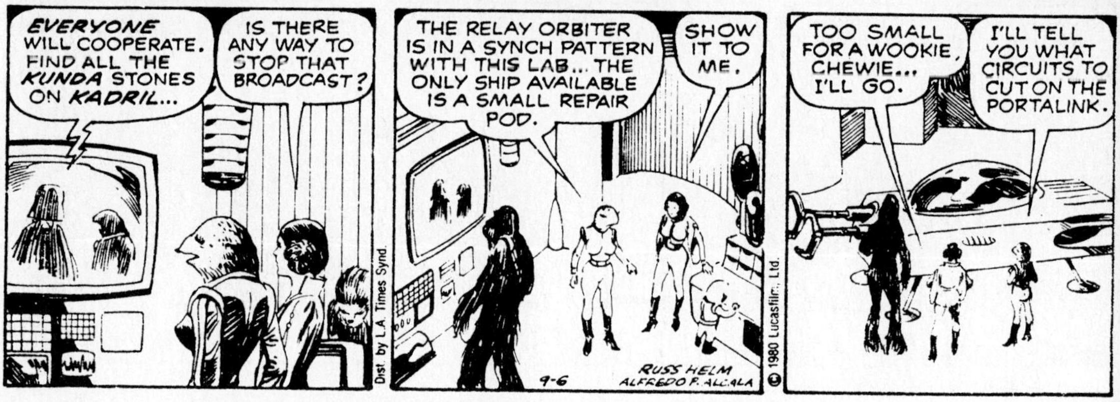
EVERYONE WILL COOPERATE. FIND ALL THE KUNDA STONES ON KADRIL...
IS THERE ANY WAY TO STOP THAT BROADCAST?
Dist. by L.A. Times Synd.
THE RELAY ORBITER IS IN A SYNCH PATTERN WITH THIS LAB... THE ONLY SHIP AVAILABLE IS A SMALL REPAIR POD.
SHOW IT TO ME.
9-6
RUSS HELM
ALFREDO P. ALCALA
© 1980 Lucasfilm, Ltd.
TOO SMALL FOR A WOOKIE, CHEWIE... I'LL GO.
I'LL TELL YOU WHAT CIRCUITS TO CUT ON THE PORTALINK.

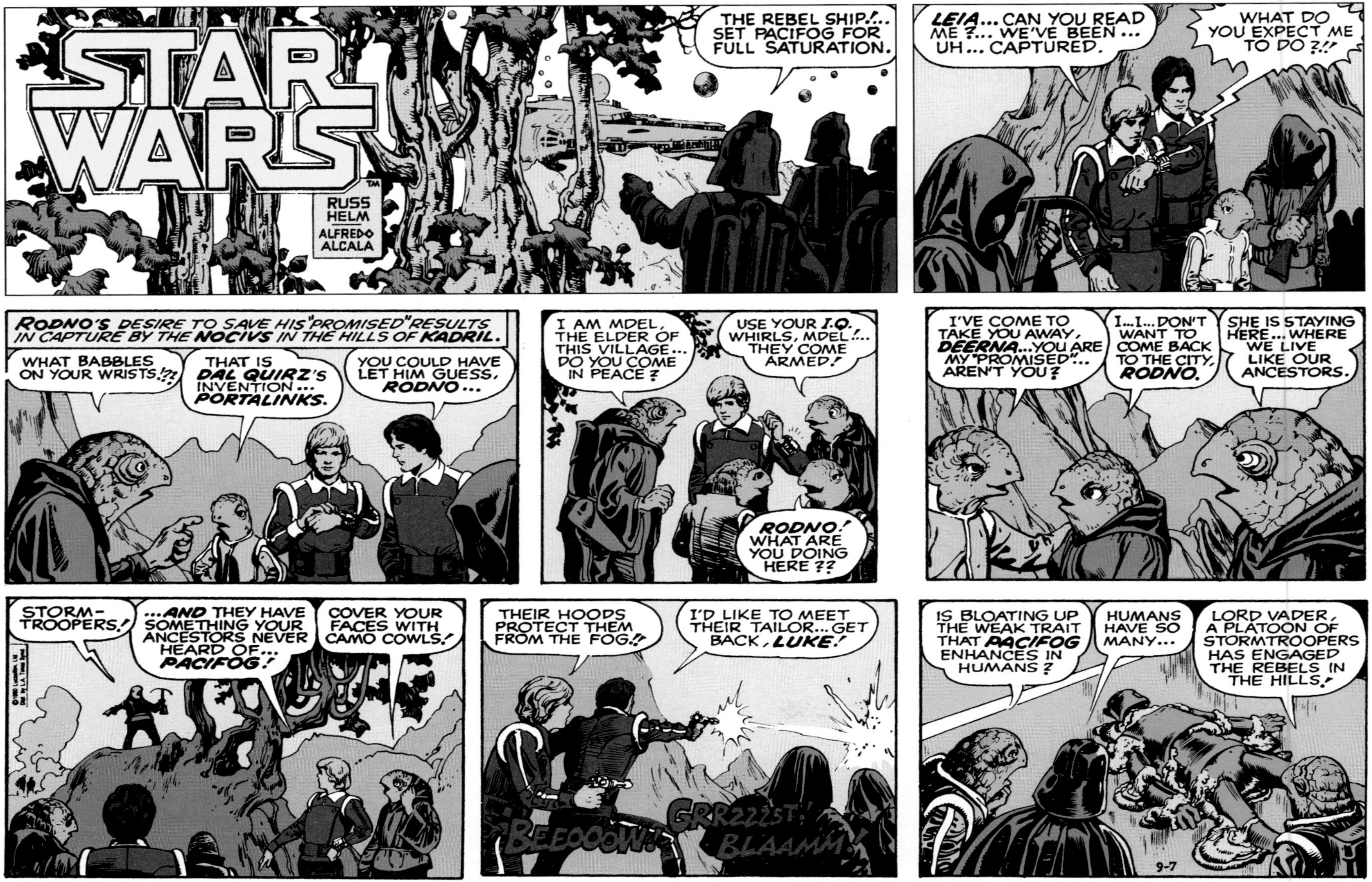
STAR WARS
RUSS HELM
ALFREDO ALCALA
THE REBEL SHIP!... SET PACIFOG FOR FULL SATURATION.
LEIA... CAN YOU READ ME ?... WE'VE BEEN ... UH... CAPTURED.
WHAT DO YOU EXPECT ME TO DO ?!!
RODNO'S DESIRE TO SAVE HIS "PROMISED" RESULTS IN CAPTURE BY THE NOCIVS IN THE HILLS OF KADRIL.
WHAT BABBLES ON YOUR WRISTS !??
THAT IS DAL QUIRZ'S INVENTION... PORTALINKS.
YOU COULD HAVE LET HIM GUESS, RODNO...
I AM MDEL, THE ELDER OF THIS VILLAGE... DO YOU COME IN PEACE ?
USE YOUR I.Q. WHIRLS, MDEL!... THEY COME ARMED!
RODNO! WHAT ARE YOU DOING HERE ??
I'VE COME TO TAKE YOU AWAY, DEERNA...YOU ARE MY "PROMISED"... AREN'T YOU ?
I...I...DON'T WANT TO COME BACK TO THE CITY, RODNO.
SHE IS STAYING HERE... WHERE WE LIVE LIKE OUR ANCESTORS.
STORM-TROOPERS!
...AND THEY HAVE SOMETHING YOUR ANCESTORS NEVER HEARD OF... PACIFOG!
COVER YOUR FACES WITH CAMO COWLS!
THEIR HOODS PROTECT THEM FROM THE FOG!!
I'D LIKE TO MEET THEIR TAILOR...GET BACK, LUKE!
BEEOOOW!
GRRZZZST!
BLAAMM!
IS BLOATING UP THE WEAK TRAIT THAT PACIFOG ENHANCES IN HUMANS ?
HUMANS HAVE SO MANY...
LORD VADER, A PLATOON OF STORMTROOPERS HAS ENGAGED THE REBELS IN THE HILLS!
9-7

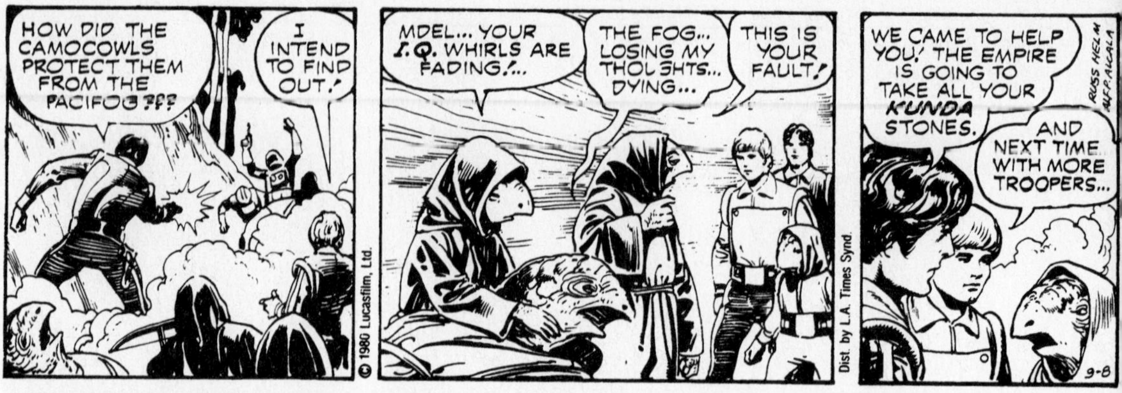
HOW DID THE CAMOCOWLS PROTECT THEM FROM THE PACIFOG ???
I INTEND TO FIND OUT.!
© 1980 Lucasfilm, Ltd.
MDEL... YOUR I.Q. WHIRLS ARE FADING!...
THE FOG... LOSING MY THOUGHTS... DYING...
THIS IS YOUR FAULT!
Dist. by L.A. Times Synd.
WE CAME TO HELP YOU! THE EMPIRE IS GOING TO TAKE ALL YOUR KUNDA STONES.
AND NEXT TIME WITH MORE TROOPERS...
RUSS HELM ALF.P. ALCALA
9-8

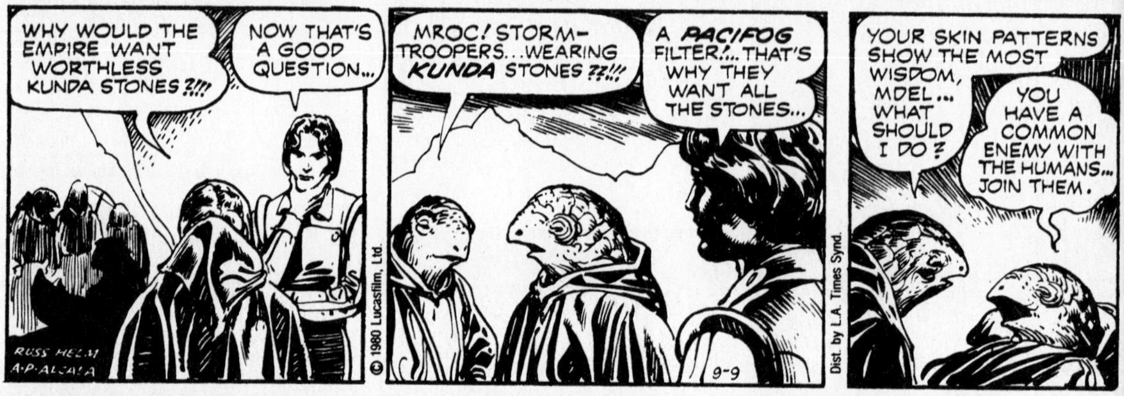
WHY WOULD THE EMPIRE WANT WORTHLESS KUNDA STONES ?!!!
NOW THAT'S A GOOD QUESTION...
RUSS HELM A·P·ALCALA
© 1980 Lucasfilm, Ltd.
MROC! STORM-TROOPERS...WEARING KUNDA STONES ??!!!
A PACIFOG FILTER!... THAT'S WHY THEY WANT ALL THE STONES...
9-9
Dist. by L.A. Times Synd.
YOUR SKIN PATTERNS SHOW THE MOST WISDOM, MDEL... WHAT SHOULD I DO ?
YOU HAVE A COMMON ENEMY WITH THE HUMANS... JOIN THEM.

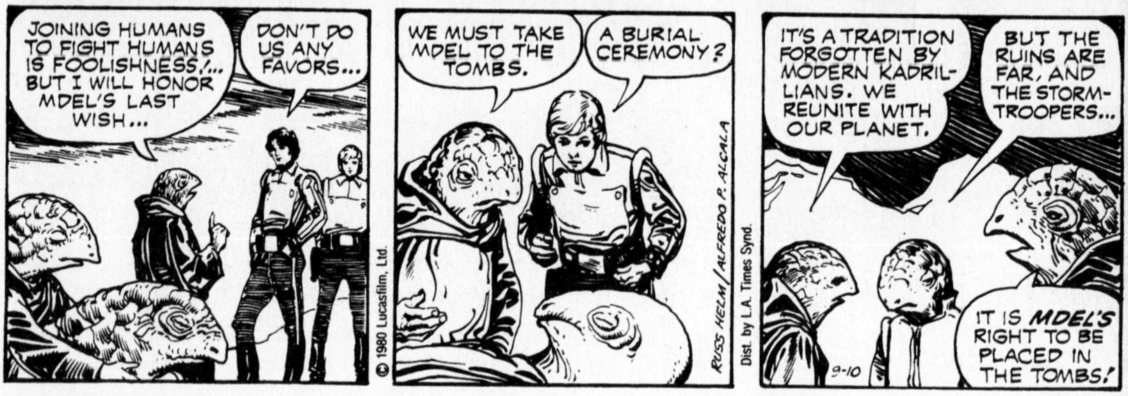
JOINING HUMANS TO FIGHT HUMANS IS FOOLISHNESS!... BUT I WILL HONOR MDEL'S LAST WISH...
DON'T DO US ANY FAVORS...
© 1980 Lucasfilm, Ltd.
WE MUST TAKE MDEL TO THE TOMBS.
A BURIAL CEREMONY ?
RUSS HELM / ALFREDO P. ALCALA
Dist. by L.A. Times Synd.
IT'S A TRADITION FORGOTTEN BY MODERN KADRIL-LIANS. WE REUNITE WITH OUR PLANET.
BUT THE RUINS ARE FAR, AND THE STORM-TROOPERS...
IT IS MDEL'S RIGHT TO BE PLACED IN THE TOMBS!
9-10

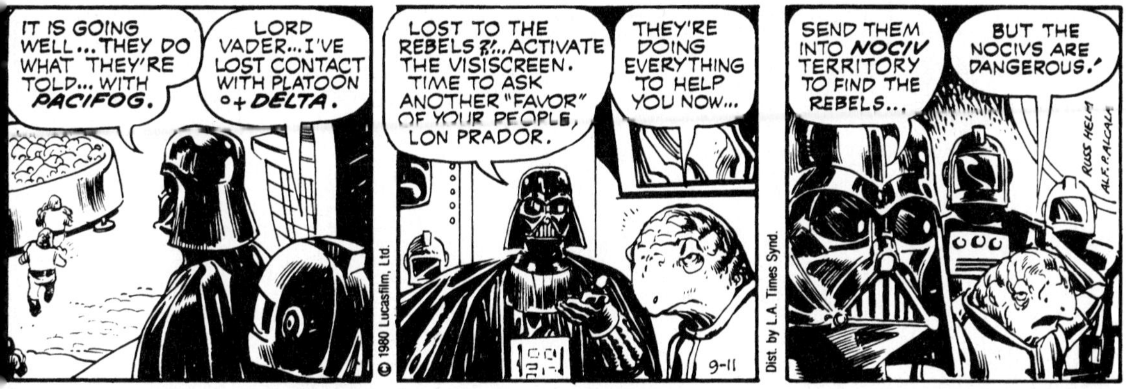
IT IS GOING WELL... THEY DO WHAT THEY'RE TOLD... WITH PACIFOG.
LORD VADER... I'VE LOST CONTACT WITH PLATOON ○+ DELTA.
LOST TO THE REBELS ?!... ACTIVATE THE VISISCREEN. TIME TO ASK ANOTHER "FAVOR" OF YOUR PEOPLE, LON PRADOR.
THEY'RE DOING EVERYTHING TO HELP YOU NOW...
© 1980 Lucasfilm, Ltd.
9-11
Dist. by L.A. Times Synd.
SEND THEM INTO NOCIV TERRITORY TO FIND THE REBELS...
BUT THE NOCIVS ARE DANGEROUS!
RUSS HELM
ALF. P. ALCALA

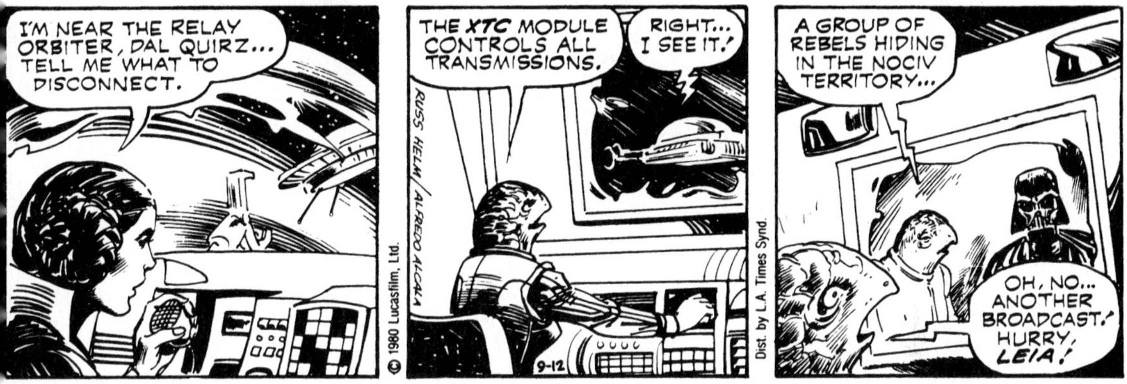
I'M NEAR THE RELAY ORBITER, DAL QUIRZ... TELL ME WHAT TO DISCONNECT.
© 1980 Lucasfilm, Ltd.
THE XTC MODULE CONTROLS ALL TRANSMISSIONS.
RIGHT... I SEE IT!
RUSS HELM / ALFREDO ALCALA
9-12
Dist. by L.A. Times Synd.
A GROUP OF REBELS HIDING IN THE NOCIV TERRITORY...
OH, NO... ANOTHER BROADCAST! HURRY, LEIA!

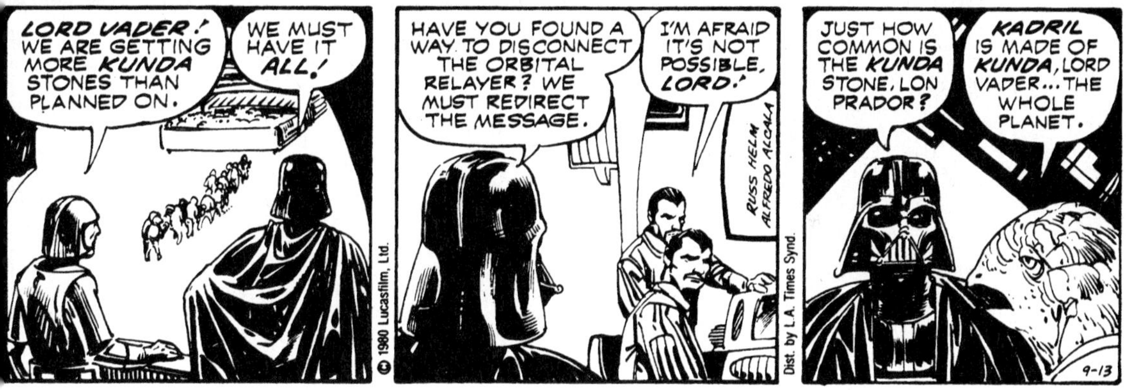
LORD VADER! WE ARE GETTING MORE KUNDA STONES THAN PLANNED ON.
WE MUST HAVE IT ALL!
© 1980 Lucasfilm, Ltd.
HAVE YOU FOUND A WAY TO DISCONNECT THE ORBITAL RELAYER? WE MUST REDIRECT THE MESSAGE.
I'M AFRAID IT'S NOT POSSIBLE, LORD!
RUSS HELM
ALFREDO ALCALA
Dist. by L.A. Times Synd.
JUST HOW COMMON IS THE KUNDA STONE, LON PRADOR?
KADRIL IS MADE OF KUNDA, LORD VADER... THE WHOLE PLANET.
9-13

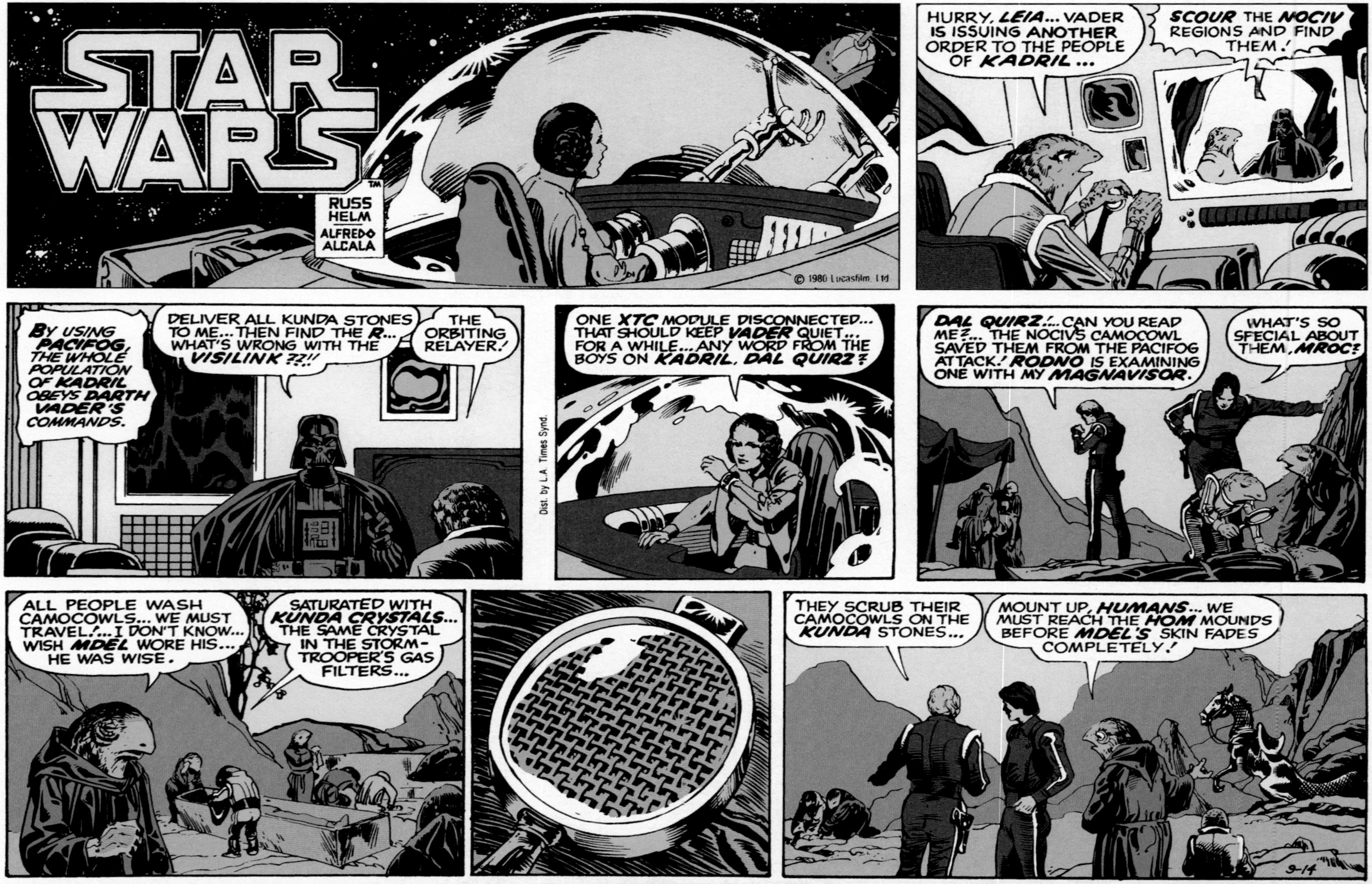
STAR WARS
RUSS HELM
ALFREDO ALCALA
© 1980 Lucasfilm, Ltd
HURRY, LEIA... VADER IS ISSUING ANOTHER ORDER TO THE PEOPLE OF KADRIL...
SCOUR THE NOCIV REGIONS AND FIND THEM.'
BY USING PACIFOG, THE WHOLE POPULATION OF KADRIL OBEYS DARTH VADER'S COMMANDS.
DELIVER ALL KUNDA STONES TO ME... THEN FIND THE R... WHAT'S WRONG WITH THE VISILINK ??!!
THE ORBITING RELAYER.'
Dist. by L.A. Times Synd.
ONE XTC MODULE DISCONNECTED... THAT SHOULD KEEP VADER QUIET... FOR A WHILE... ANY WORD FROM THE BOYS ON KADRIL, DAL QUIRZ?
DAL QUIRZ.'... CAN YOU READ ME?... THE NOCIV'S CAMOCOWL SAVED THEM FROM THE PACIFOG ATTACK.' RODNO IS EXAMINING ONE WITH MY MAGNAVISOR.
WHAT'S SO SPECIAL ABOUT THEM, MROC?
ALL PEOPLE WASH CAMOCOWLS... WE MUST TRAVEL.'... I DON'T KNOW... WISH MDEL WORE HIS... HE WAS WISE.
SATURATED WITH KUNDA CRYSTALS... THE SAME CRYSTAL IN THE STORM-TROOPER'S GAS FILTERS...
THEY SCRUB THEIR CAMOCOWLS ON THE KUNDA STONES...
MOUNT UP, HUMANS... WE MUST REACH THE HOM MOUNDS BEFORE MDEL'S SKIN FADES COMPLETELY.'
9-14

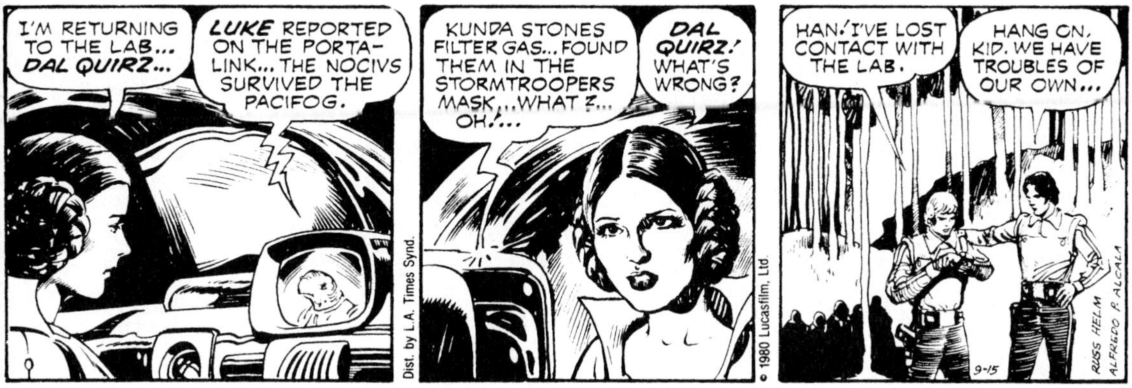
I'M RETURNING TO THE LAB... DAL QUIRZ...
LUKE REPORTED ON THE PORTA-LINK... THE NOCIVS SURVIVED THE PACIFOG.
Dist. by L.A. Times Synd.
KUNDA STONES FILTER GAS... FOUND THEM IN THE STORMTROOPERS MASK... WHAT ?... OH!...
DAL QUIRZ! WHAT'S WRONG?
© 1980 Lucasfilm, Ltd.
HAN! I'VE LOST CONTACT WITH THE LAB.
HANG ON, KID. WE HAVE TROUBLES OF OUR OWN...
9-15
RUSS HELM
ALFREDO P. ALCALA

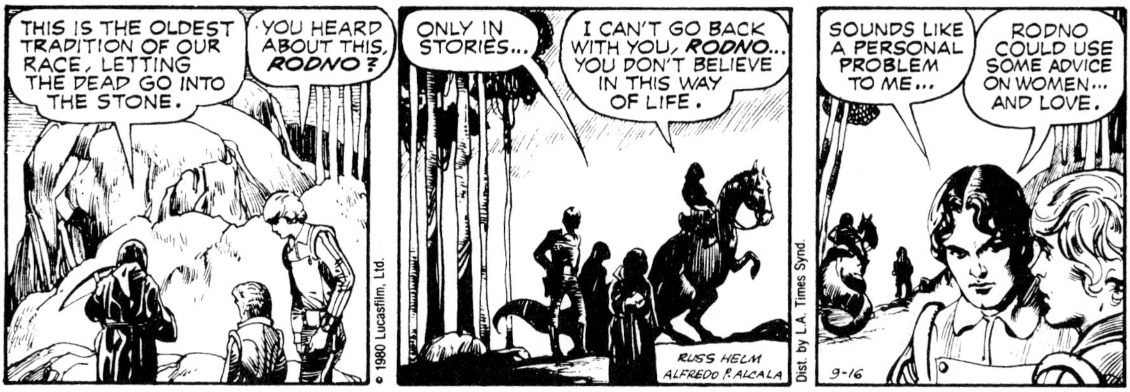
THIS IS THE OLDEST TRADITION OF OUR RACE, LETTING THE DEAD GO INTO THE STONE.
YOU HEARD ABOUT THIS, RODNO?
© 1980 Lucasfilm, Ltd.
ONLY IN STORIES...
I CAN'T GO BACK WITH YOU, RODNO... YOU DON'T BELIEVE IN THIS WAY OF LIFE.
RUSS HELM
ALFREDO P. ALCALA
Dist. by L.A. Times Synd.
SOUNDS LIKE A PERSONAL PROBLEM TO ME...
RODNO COULD USE SOME ADVICE ON WOMEN... AND LOVE.
9-16

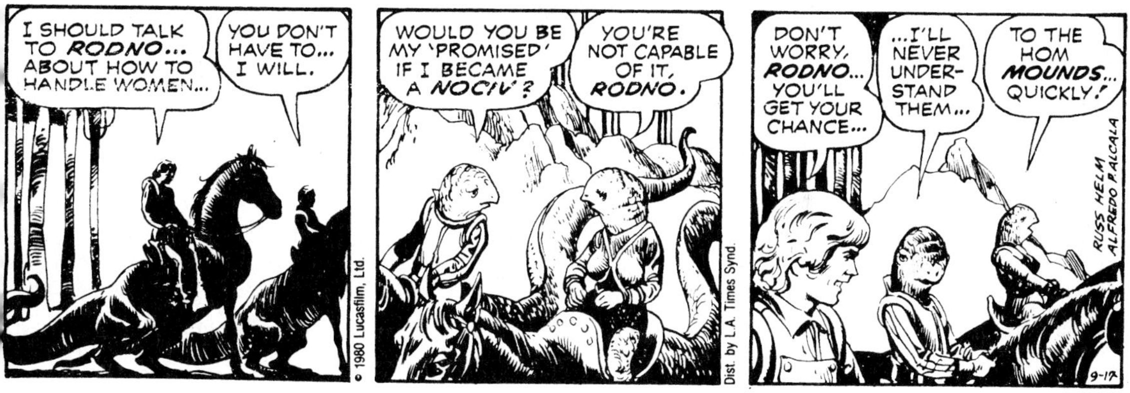
I SHOULD TALK TO RODNO... ABOUT HOW TO HANDLE WOMEN...
YOU DON'T HAVE TO... I WILL.
© 1980 Lucasfilm, Ltd.
WOULD YOU BE MY 'PROMISED' IF I BECAME A NOCIV?
YOU'RE NOT CAPABLE OF IT, RODNO.
Dist. by L.A. Times Synd.
DON'T WORRY, RODNO... YOU'LL GET YOUR CHANCE...
...I'LL NEVER UNDERSTAND THEM...
TO THE HOM MOUNDS... QUICKLY!
RUSS HELM
ALFREDO P. ALCALA
9-17

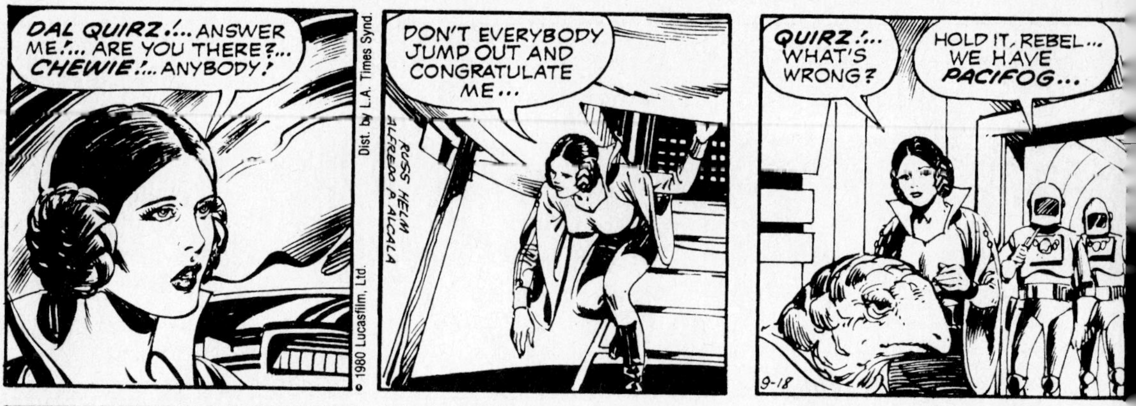
DAL QUIRZ!... ANSWER ME!... ARE YOU THERE?... CHEWIE!... ANYBODY!
Dist. by L.A. Times Synd.
© 1980 Lucasfilm, Ltd.
DON'T EVERYBODY JUMP OUT AND CONGRATULATE ME...
RUSS HELM
ALFREDO P. ALCALA
QUIRZ!... WHAT'S WRONG?
HOLD IT, REBEL... WE HAVE PACIFOG...
9-18

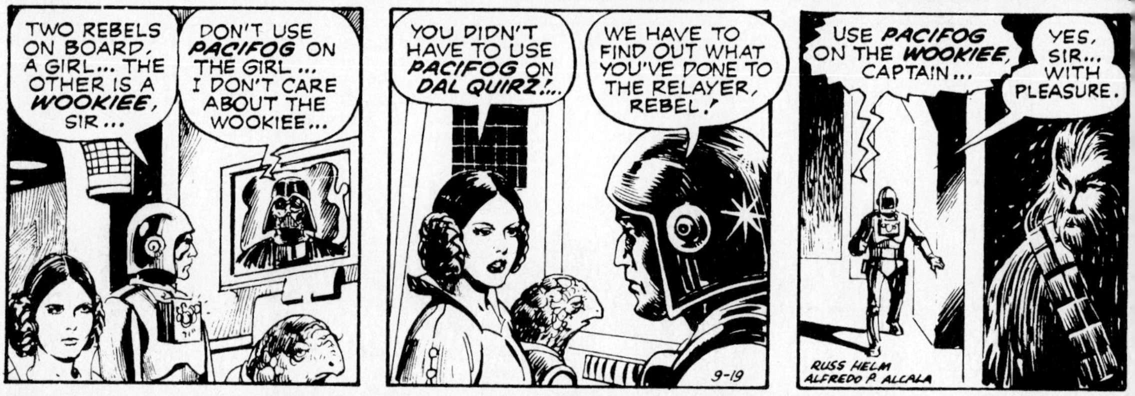
TWO REBELS ON BOARD, A GIRL... THE OTHER IS A WOOKIEE, SIR...
DON'T USE PACIFOG ON THE GIRL... I DON'T CARE ABOUT THE WOOKIEE...
YOU DIDN'T HAVE TO USE PACIFOG ON DAL QUIRZ!...
WE HAVE TO FIND OUT WHAT YOU'VE DONE TO THE RELAYER, REBEL!
9-19
USE PACIFOG ON THE WOOKIEE, CAPTAIN...
YES, SIR... WITH PLEASURE.
RUSS HELM
ALFREDO P. ALCALA

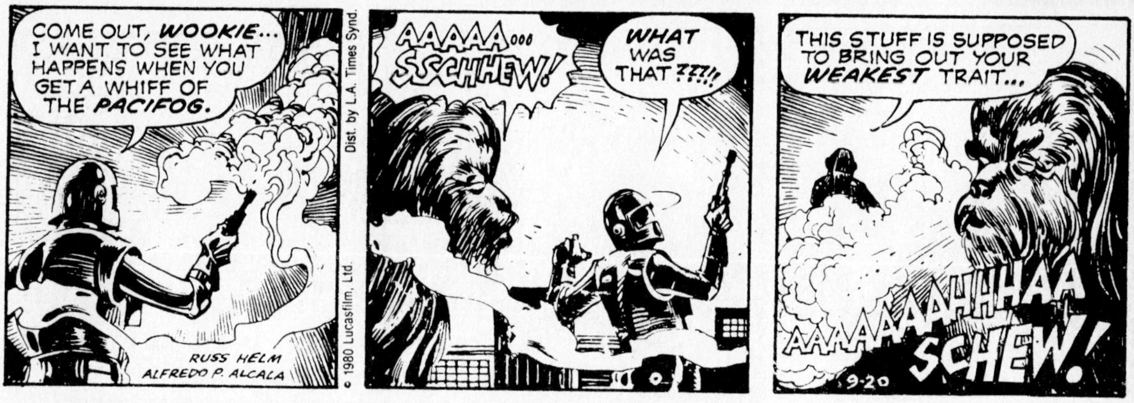
COME OUT, WOOKIE... I WANT TO SEE WHAT HAPPENS WHEN YOU GET A WHIFF OF THE PACIFOG.
RUSS HELM
ALFREDO P. ALCALA
Dist. by L.A. Times Synd.
© 1980 Lucasfilm, Ltd.
AAAAAooo SSCHHEW!
WHAT WAS THAT???!
THIS STUFF IS SUPPOSED TO BRING OUT YOUR WEAKEST TRAIT...
AAAAAAAHHHAA SCHEW!
9-20

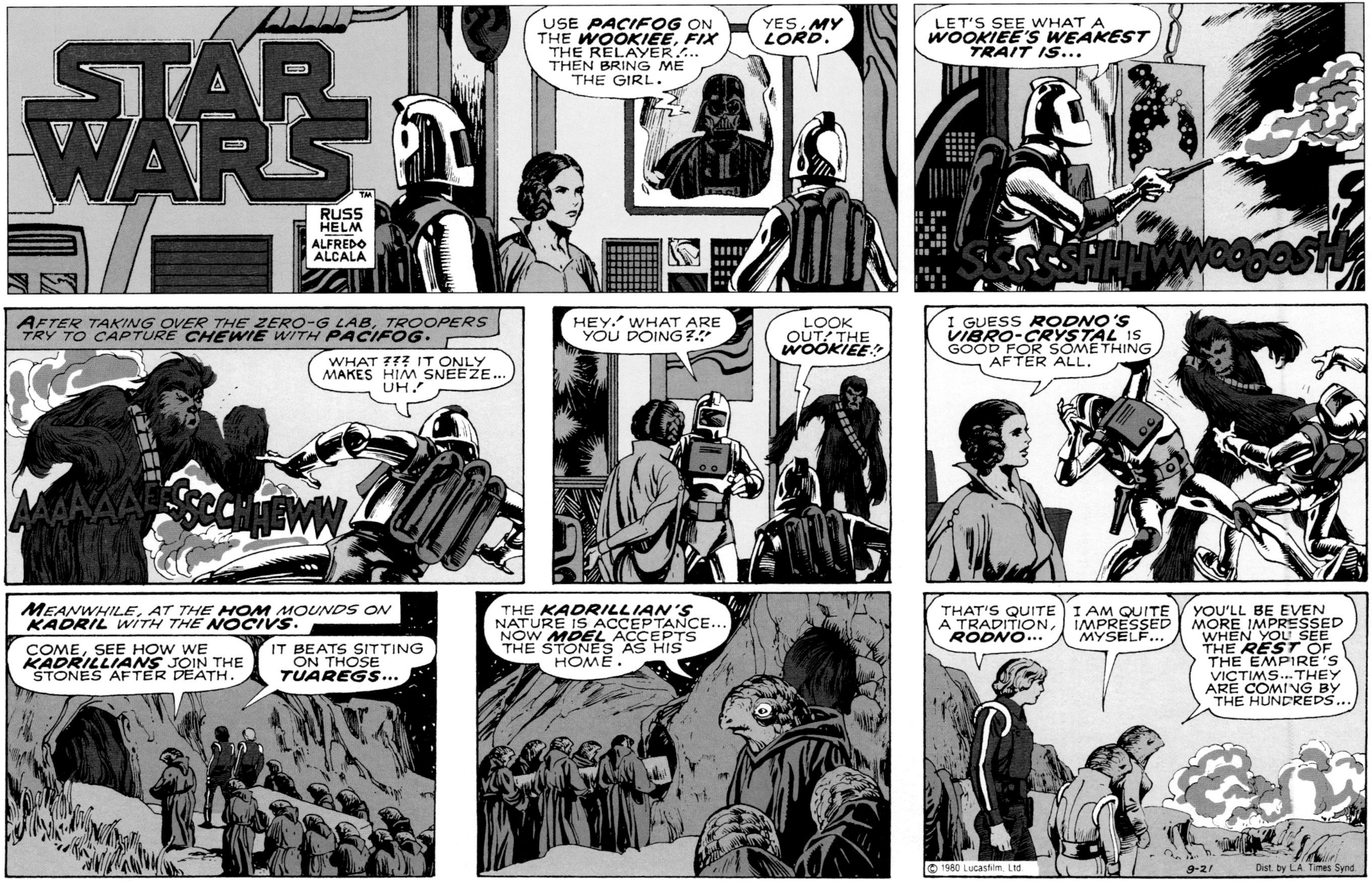
STAR WARS™
RUSS HELM
ALFREDO ALCALA
USE PACIFOG ON THE WOOKIEE, FIX THE RELAYER!... THEN BRING ME THE GIRL.
YES, MY LORD.
LET'S SEE WHAT A WOOKIEE'S WEAKEST TRAIT IS...
SSSSSHHHHWWOOOOOSH
AFTER TAKING OVER THE ZERO-G LAB, TROOPERS TRY TO CAPTURE CHEWIE WITH PACIFOG.
WHAT ??? IT ONLY MAKES HIM SNEEZE... UH!
AAAAAAEESSCCHHEWW
HEY! WHAT ARE YOU DOING?!!
LOOK OUT! THE WOOKIEE!!
I GUESS RODNO'S VIBRO-CRYSTAL IS GOOD FOR SOMETHING AFTER ALL.
MEANWHILE, AT THE HOM MOUNDS ON KADRIL WITH THE NOCIVS.
COME, SEE HOW WE KADRILLIANS JOIN THE STONES AFTER DEATH.
IT BEATS SITTING ON THOSE TUAREGS...
THE KADRILLIAN'S NATURE IS ACCEPTANCE... NOW MDEL ACCEPTS THE STONES AS HIS HOME.
THAT'S QUITE A TRADITION, RODNO...
I AM QUITE IMPRESSED MYSELF...
YOU'LL BE EVEN MORE IMPRESSED WHEN YOU SEE THE REST OF THE EMPIRE'S VICTIMS...THEY ARE COMING BY THE HUNDREDS...
© 1980 Lucasfilm, Ltd.
9-21
Dist. by L.A. Times Synd.

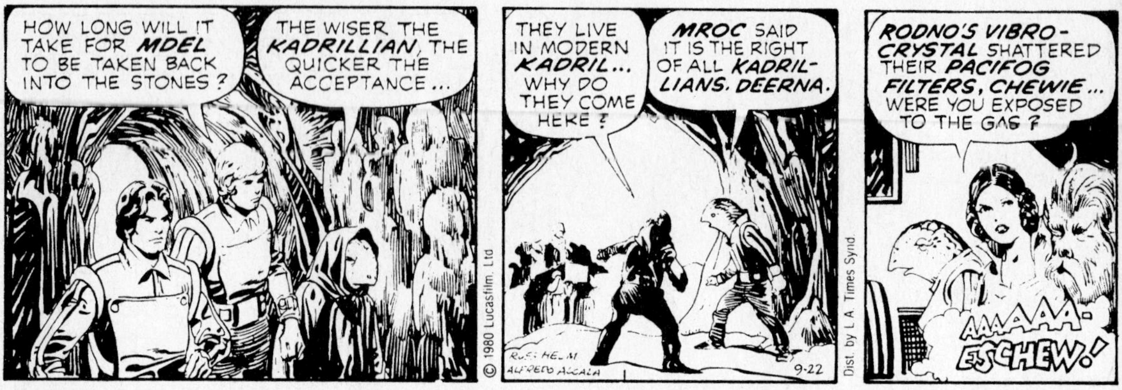
HOW LONG WILL IT TAKE FOR MDEL TO BE TAKEN BACK INTO THE STONES?
THE WISER THE KADRILLIAN, THE QUICKER THE ACCEPTANCE...
THEY LIVE IN MODERN KADRIL... WHY DO THEY COME HERE?
MROC SAID IT IS THE RIGHT OF ALL KADRILLIANS, DEERNA.
© 1980 Lucasfilm Ltd
RUSS HELM
ALFREDO ALCALA
9-22
Dist. by L.A. Times Synd.
RODNO'S VIBRO-CRYSTAL SHATTERED THEIR PACIFOG FILTERS, CHEWIE... WERE YOU EXPOSED TO THE GAS?
AAAAAA-ESCHEW!

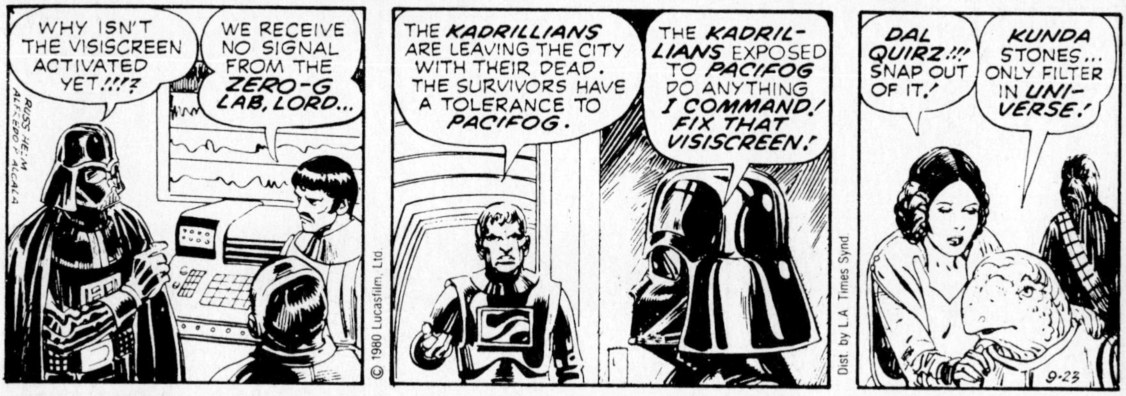
WHY ISN'T THE VISISCREEN ACTIVATED YET!!!?
WE RECEIVE NO SIGNAL FROM THE ZERO-G LAB, LORD...
RUSS HELM
ALFREDO ALCALA
© 1980 Lucasfilm, Ltd.
THE KADRILLIANS ARE LEAVING THE CITY WITH THEIR DEAD. THE SURVIVORS HAVE A TOLERANCE TO PACIFOG.
THE KADRILLIANS EXPOSED TO PACIFOG DO ANYTHING I COMMAND! FIX THAT VISISCREEN!
Dist. by L.A. Times Synd.
DAL QUIRZ!!! SNAP OUT OF IT!
KUNDA STONES... ONLY FILTER IN UNIVERSE!
9-23

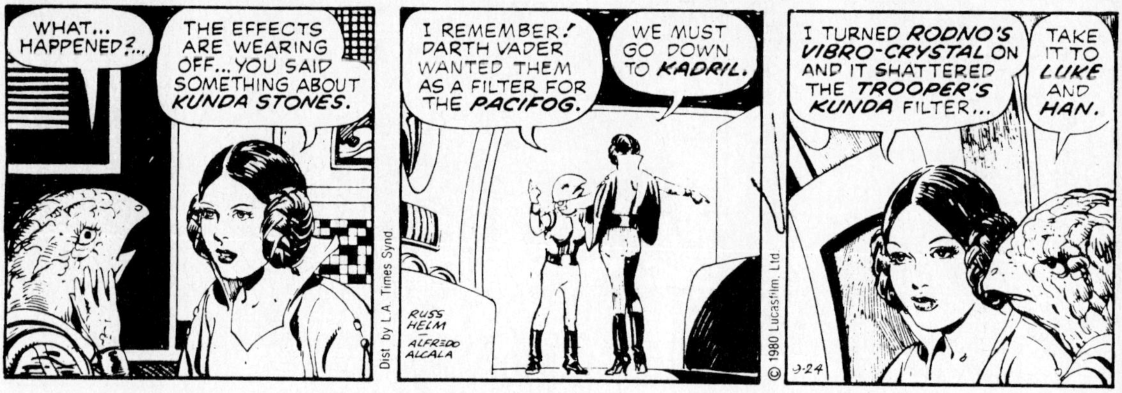
WHAT... HAPPENED?...
THE EFFECTS ARE WEARING OFF... YOU SAID SOMETHING ABOUT KUNDA STONES.
Dist. by L.A. Times Synd.
I REMEMBER! DARTH VADER WANTED THEM AS A FILTER FOR THE PACIFOG.
WE MUST GO DOWN TO KADRIL.
RUSS HELM
ALFREDO ALCALA
© 1980 Lucasfilm, Ltd.
I TURNED RODNO'S VIBRO-CRYSTAL ON AND IT SHATTERED THE TROOPER'S KUNDA FILTER...
TAKE IT TO LUKE AND HAN.
9-24

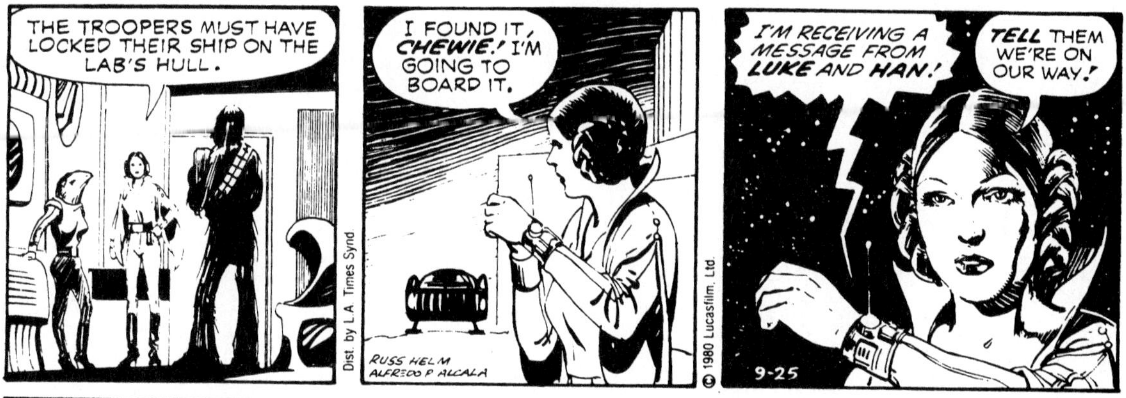
THE TROOPERS MUST HAVE LOCKED THEIR SHIP ON THE LAB'S HULL.
I FOUND IT, CHEWIE! I'M GOING TO BOARD IT.
RUSS HELM ALFREDO P. ALCALA
Dist. by L.A. Times Synd
© 1980 Lucasfilm, Ltd.
I'M RECEIVING A MESSAGE FROM LUKE AND HAN!
TELL THEM WE'RE ON OUR WAY!
9-25

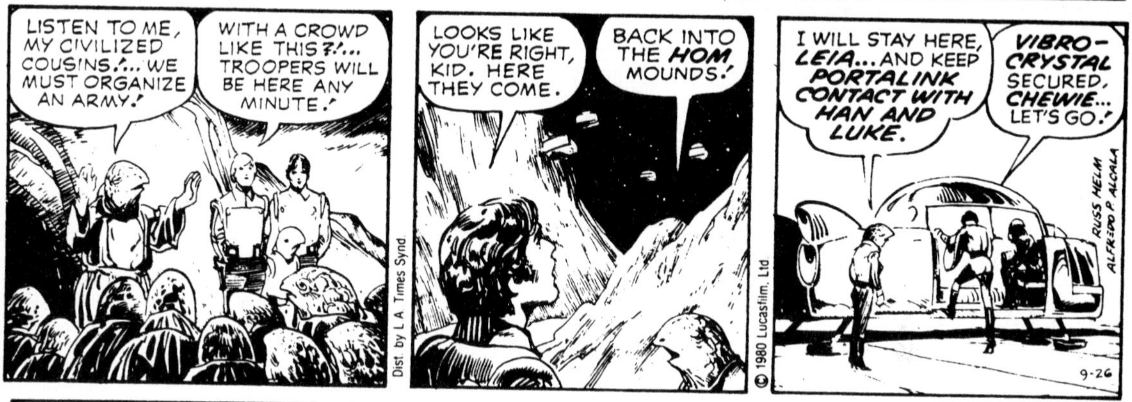
LISTEN TO ME, MY CIVILIZED COUSINS!... WE MUST ORGANIZE AN ARMY!
WITH A CROWD LIKE THIS?!... TROOPERS WILL BE HERE ANY MINUTE!
Dist. by L.A. Times Synd
LOOKS LIKE YOU'RE RIGHT, KID. HERE THEY COME.
BACK INTO THE HOM MOUNDS!
© 1980 Lucasfilm, Ltd.
I WILL STAY HERE, LEIA... AND KEEP PORTALINK CONTACT WITH HAN AND LUKE.
VIBRO-CRYSTAL SECURED, CHEWIE... LET'S GO!
RUSS HELM ALFREDO P. ALCALA
9-26

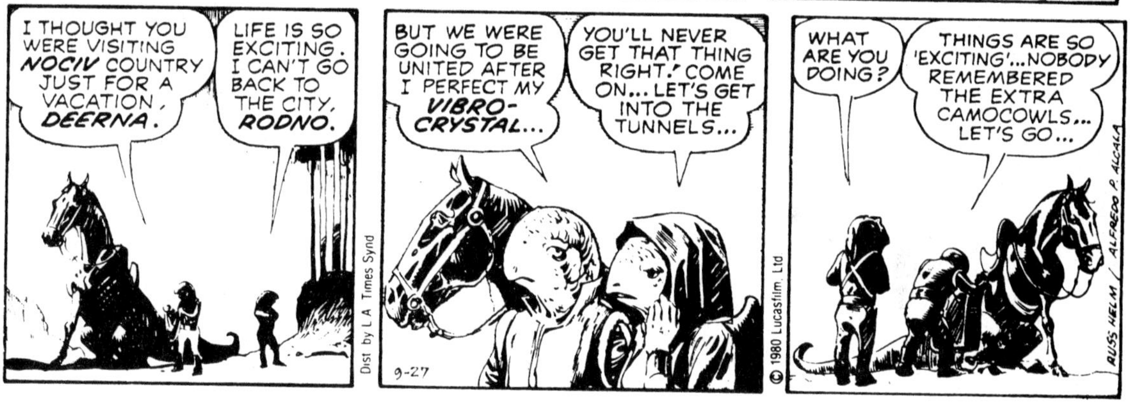
I THOUGHT YOU WERE VISITING NOCIV COUNTRY JUST FOR A VACATION, DEERNA.
LIFE IS SO EXCITING. I CAN'T GO BACK TO THE CITY, RODNO.
Dist. by L.A. Times Synd
BUT WE WERE GOING TO BE UNITED AFTER I PERFECT MY VIBRO-CRYSTAL...
YOU'LL NEVER GET THAT THING RIGHT! COME ON... LET'S GET INTO THE TUNNELS...
9-27
© 1980 Lucasfilm, Ltd.
WHAT ARE YOU DOING?
THINGS ARE SO 'EXCITING'... NOBODY REMEMBERED THE EXTRA CAMOCOWLS... LET'S GO...
RUSS HELM / ALFREDO P. ALCALA

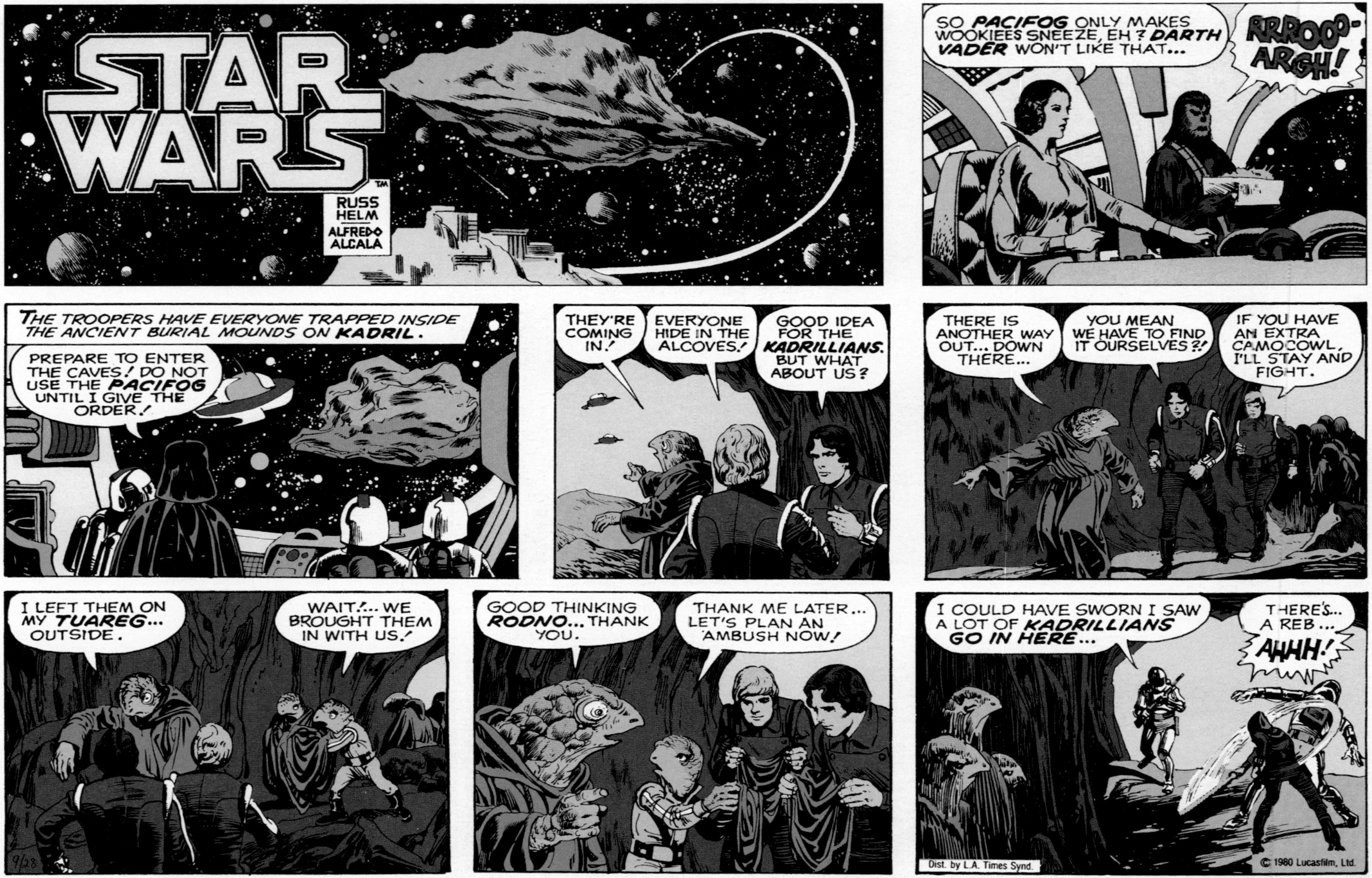
STAR WARS
RUSS HELM
ALFREDO ALCALA
SO PACIFOG ONLY MAKES WOOKIEES SNEEZE, EH ? DARTH VADER WON'T LIKE THAT...
RRROOO-ARGH!
THE TROOPERS HAVE EVERYONE TRAPPED INSIDE THE ANCIENT BURIAL MOUNDS ON KADRIL.
PREPARE TO ENTER THE CAVES! DO NOT USE THE PACIFOG UNTIL I GIVE THE ORDER!
THEY'RE COMING IN!
EVERYONE HIDE IN THE ALCOVES!
GOOD IDEA FOR THE KADRILLIANS. BUT WHAT ABOUT US?
THERE IS ANOTHER WAY OUT... DOWN THERE...
YOU MEAN WE HAVE TO FIND IT OURSELVES?!
IF YOU HAVE AN EXTRA CAMOCOWL, I'LL STAY AND FIGHT.
I LEFT THEM ON MY TUAREG... OUTSIDE.
WAIT!... WE BROUGHT THEM IN WITH US!
9/28
GOOD THINKING RODNO... THANK YOU.
THANK ME LATER... LET'S PLAN AN AMBUSH NOW!
I COULD HAVE SWORN I SAW A LOT OF KADRILLIANS GO IN HERE...
THERE'S... A REB...
AHHH!
Dist. by L.A. Times Synd.
© 1980 Lucasfilm, Ltd.

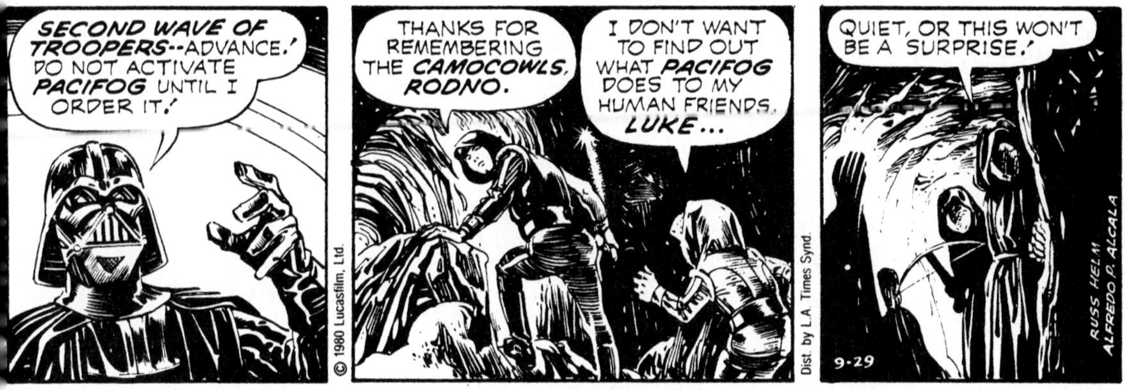
SECOND WAVE OF TROOPERS--ADVANCE! DO NOT ACTIVATE PACIFOG UNTIL I ORDER IT!
© 1980 Lucasfilm, Ltd.
THANKS FOR REMEMBERING THE CAMOCOWLS, RODNO.
I DON'T WANT TO FIND OUT WHAT PACIFOG DOES TO MY HUMAN FRIENDS, LUKE...
Dist. by L.A. Times Synd.
QUIET, OR THIS WON'T BE A SURPRISE!
9-29
RUSS HELM
ALFREDO P. ALCALA

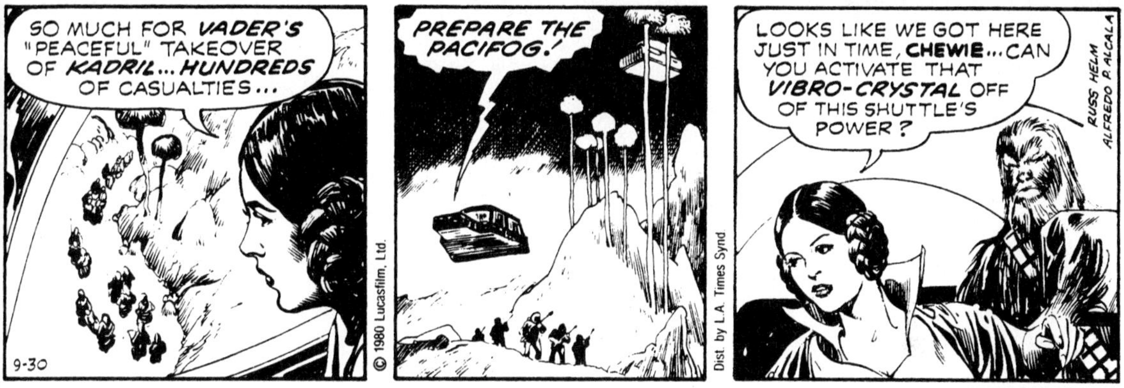
SO MUCH FOR VADER'S "PEACEFUL" TAKEOVER OF KADRIL... HUNDREDS OF CASUALTIES...
9-30
© 1980 Lucasfilm, Ltd.
PREPARE THE PACIFOG!
Dist. by L.A. Times Synd
LOOKS LIKE WE GOT HERE JUST IN TIME, CHEWIE... CAN YOU ACTIVATE THAT VIBRO-CRYSTAL OFF OF THIS SHUTTLE'S POWER?
RUSS HELM
ALFREDO P. ALCALA

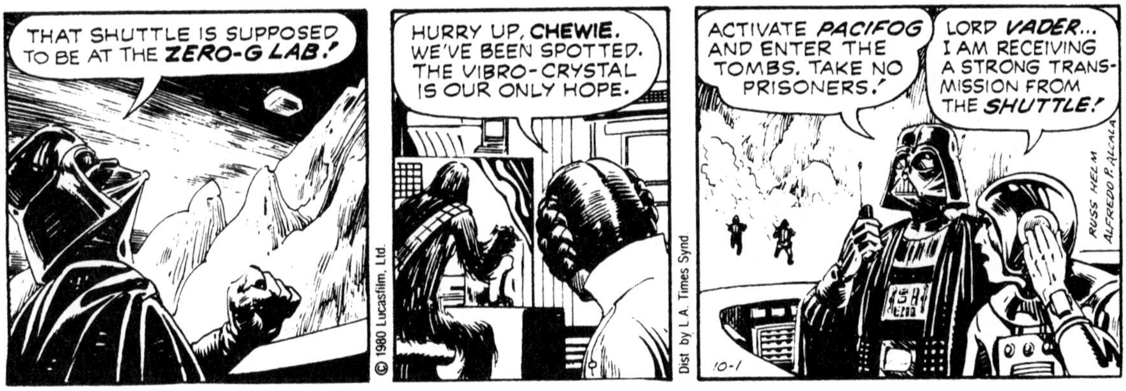
THAT SHUTTLE IS SUPPOSED TO BE AT THE ZERO-G LAB!
© 1980 Lucasfilm, Ltd.
HURRY UP, CHEWIE. WE'VE BEEN SPOTTED. THE VIBRO-CRYSTAL IS OUR ONLY HOPE.
Dist. by L.A. Times Synd
ACTIVATE PACIFOG AND ENTER THE TOMBS. TAKE NO PRISONERS!
LORD VADER... I AM RECEIVING A STRONG TRANSMISSION FROM THE SHUTTLE!
RUSS HELM
ALFREDO P. ALCALA
10-1

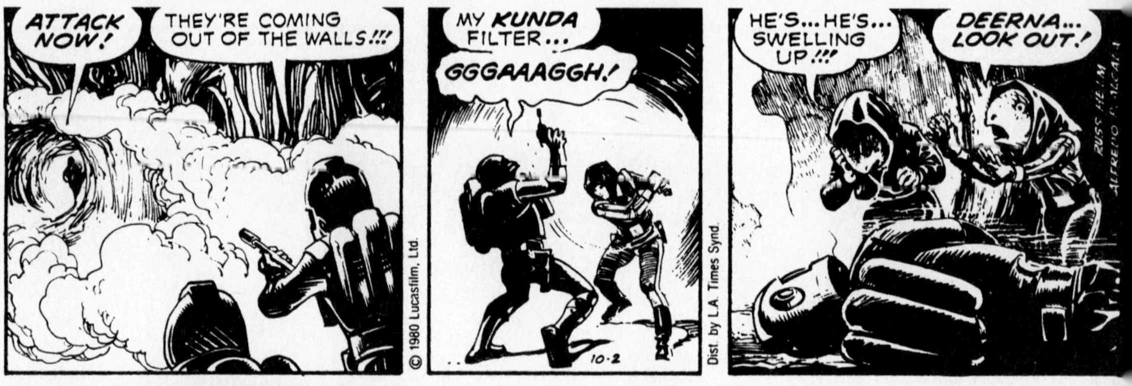
ATTACK NOW!
THEY'RE COMING OUT OF THE WALLS!!!
© 1980 Lucasfilm, Ltd.
MY KUNDA FILTER...
GGGAAAGGH!
10-2
Dist. by L.A. Times Synd.
HE'S... HE'S... SWELLING UP!!!
DEERNA... LOOK OUT!
RUSS HELM
ALFREDO P. ALCALA

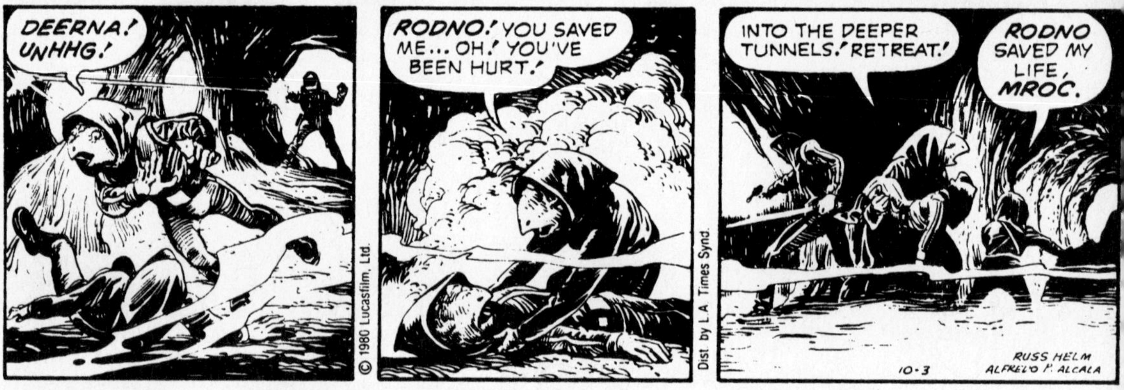
DEERNA! UNHHG!
© 1980 Lucasfilm, Ltd.
RODNO! YOU SAVED ME... OH! YOU'VE BEEN HURT!
Dist. by L.A. Times Synd.
INTO THE DEEPER TUNNELS! RETREAT!
RODNO SAVED MY LIFE, MROC.
10-3
RUSS HELM
ALFREDO P. ALCALA

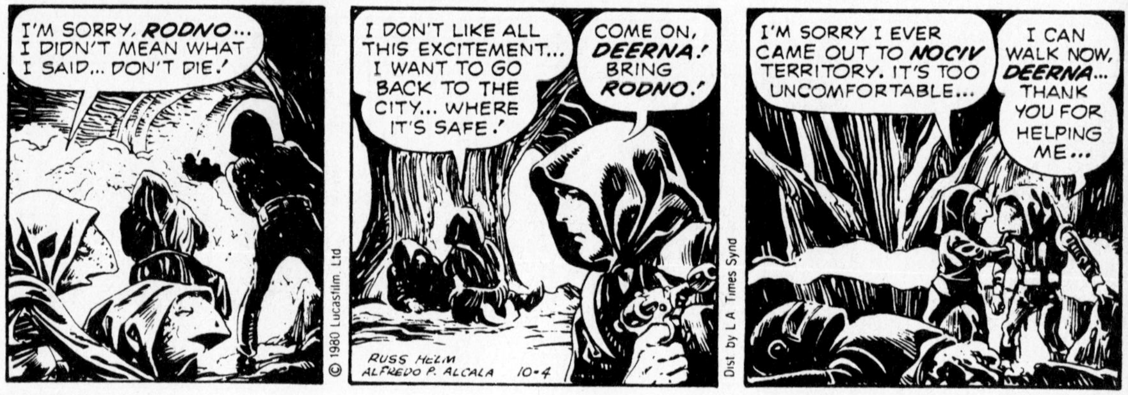
I'M SORRY, RODNO... I DIDN'T MEAN WHAT I SAID... DON'T DIE!
© 1980 Lucasfilm, Ltd
I DON'T LIKE ALL THIS EXCITEMENT... I WANT TO GO BACK TO THE CITY... WHERE IT'S SAFE!
COME ON, DEERNA! BRING RODNO!
RUSS HELM
ALFREDO P. ALCALA
10-4
Dist by L A Times Synd
I'M SORRY I EVER CAME OUT TO NOCIV TERRITORY. IT'S TOO UNCOMFORTABLE...
I CAN WALK NOW, DEERNA... THANK YOU FOR HELPING ME...

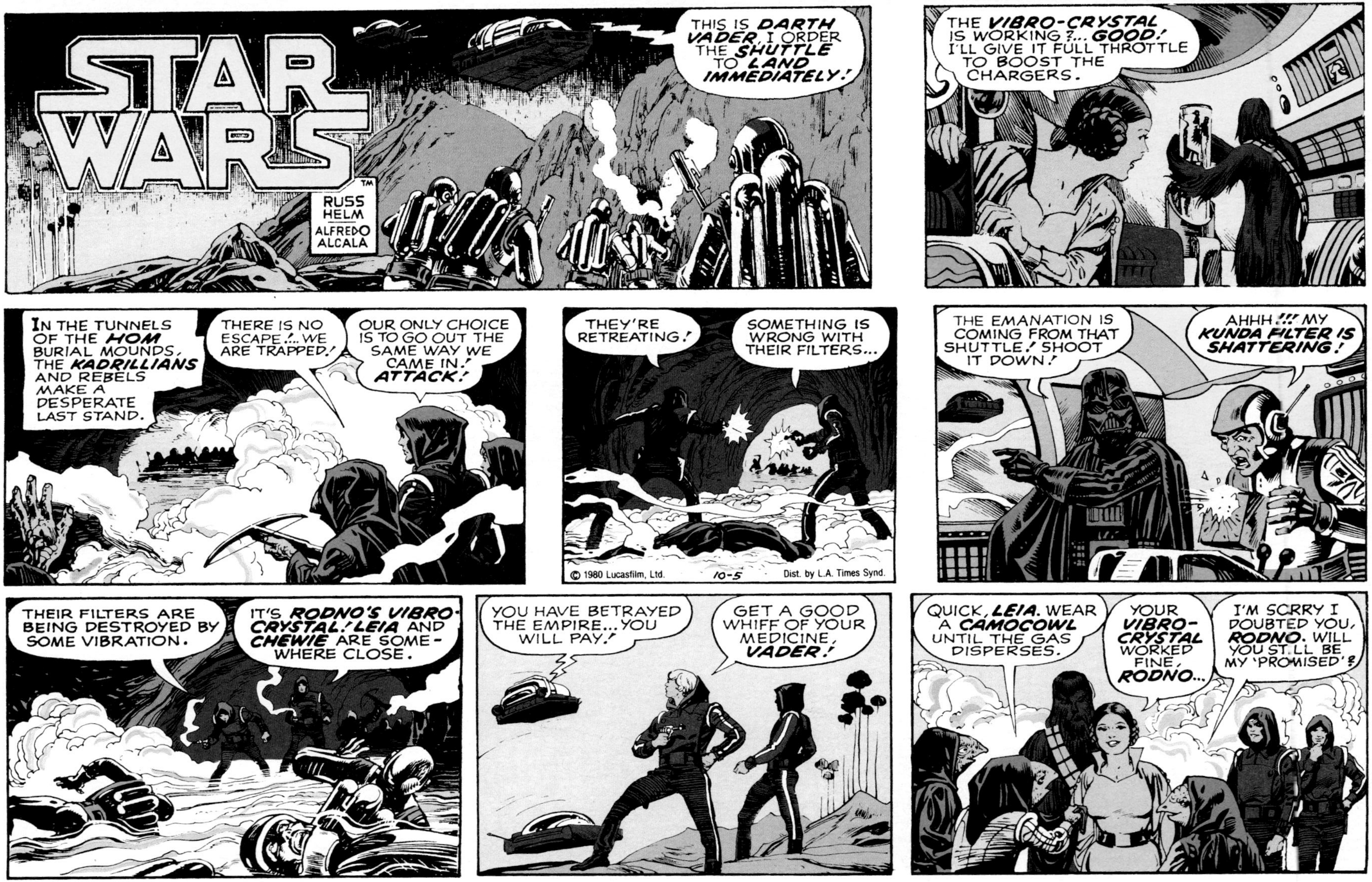
STAR WARS™
RUSS HELM
ALFREDO ALCALA
THIS IS DARTH VADER. I ORDER THE SHUTTLE TO LAND IMMEDIATELY!
THE VIBRO-CRYSTAL IS WORKING?... GOOD! I'LL GIVE IT FULL THROTTLE TO BOOST THE CHARGERS.
IN THE TUNNELS OF THE HOM BURIAL MOUNDS, THE KADRILLIANS AND REBELS MAKE A DESPERATE LAST STAND.
THERE IS NO ESCAPE!... WE ARE TRAPPED!
OUR ONLY CHOICE IS TO GO OUT THE SAME WAY WE CAME IN! ATTACK!
THEY'RE RETREATING!
SOMETHING IS WRONG WITH THEIR FILTERS...
© 1980 Lucasfilm, Ltd.
10-5
Dist. by L.A. Times Synd.
THE EMANATION IS COMING FROM THAT SHUTTLE! SHOOT IT DOWN!
AHHH!!! MY KUNDA FILTER IS SHATTERING!
THEIR FILTERS ARE BEING DESTROYED BY SOME VIBRATION.
IT'S RODNO'S VIBRO-CRYSTAL! LEIA AND CHEWIE ARE SOMEWHERE CLOSE.
YOU HAVE BETRAYED THE EMPIRE... YOU WILL PAY!
GET A GOOD WHIFF OF YOUR MEDICINE, VADER!
QUICK, LEIA. WEAR A CAMOCOWL UNTIL THE GAS DISPERSES.
YOUR VIBRO-CRYSTAL WORKED FINE, RODNO...
I'M SORRY I DOUBTED YOU, RODNO. WILL YOU STILL BE MY 'PROMISED'?

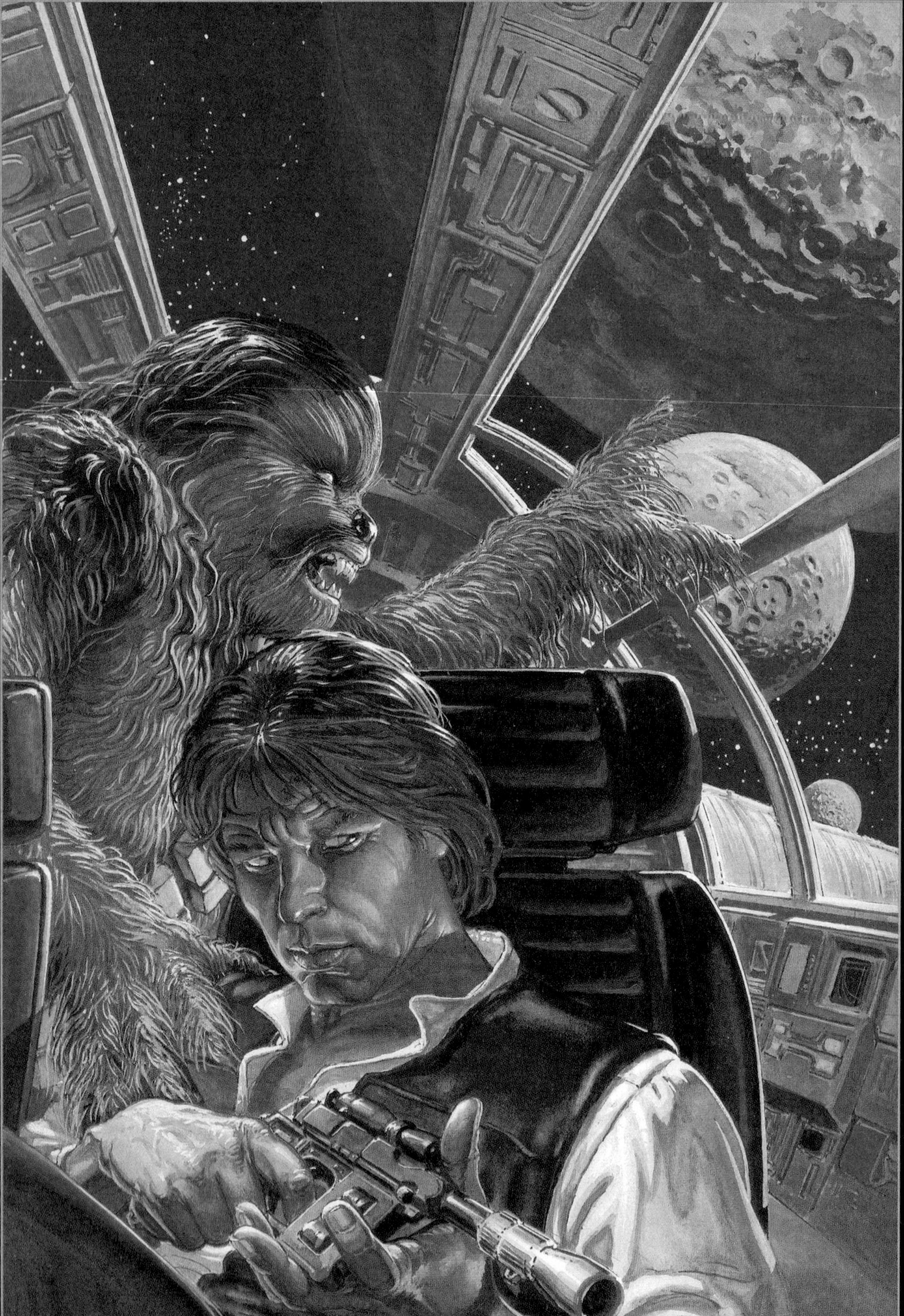

CLASSIC STAR WARS: HAN SOLO AT STARS' END #1
ORIGINALLY PUBLISHED FROM OCTOBER 6 TO NOVEMBER 17, 1980

BASED ON THE NOVEL BY BRIAN DALEY • SCRIPTER: ARCHIE GOODWIN • ARTIST & LETTERER: ALFREDO ALCALA • COLORIST: PERRY MCNAMEE
ASSISTANT EDITOR: IAN STUDE • EDITOR: PEET JANES • COVER ARTIST: IGOR KORDEY • SPECIAL THANKS: EVELYN HARRIS

NOTE: ADAPTED FROM THE NOVEL OF THE SAME NAME, THE "HAN SOLO AT STARS' END" STORYLINE TAKES PLACE PRIOR TO THE EVENTS OF *STAR WARS*: EPISODE IV *A NEW HOPE*.

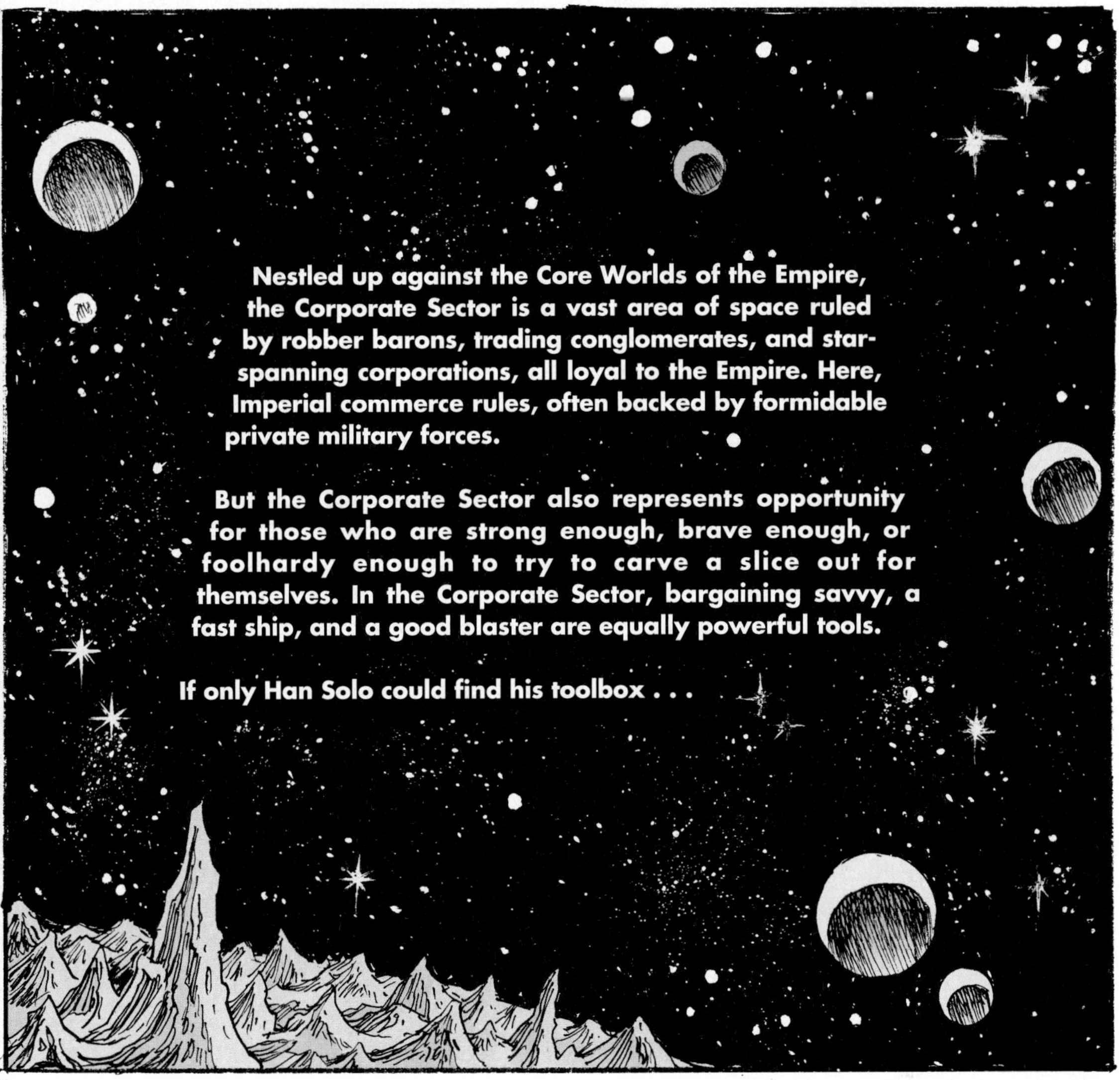
Nestled up against the Core Worlds of the Empire, the Corporate Sector is a vast area of space ruled by robber barons, trading conglomerates, and star-spanning corporations, all loyal to the Empire. Here, Imperial commerce rules, often backed by formidable private military forces.
But the Corporate Sector also represents opportunity for those who are strong enough, brave enough, or foolhardy enough to try to carve a slice out for themselves. In the Corporate Sector, bargaining savvy, a fast ship, and a good blaster are equally powerful tools.
If only Han Solo could find his toolbox . . .

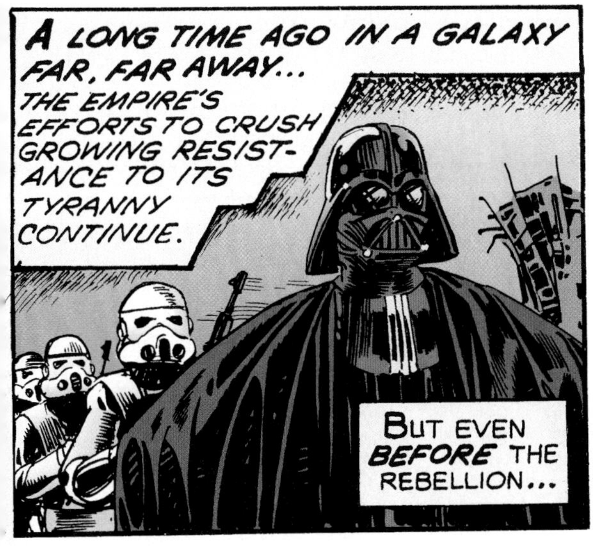
A LONG TIME AGO IN A GALAXY FAR, FAR AWAY...
THE EMPIRE'S EFFORTS TO CRUSH GROWING RESISTANCE TO ITS TYRANNY CONTINUE.
BUT EVEN BEFORE THE REBELLION...

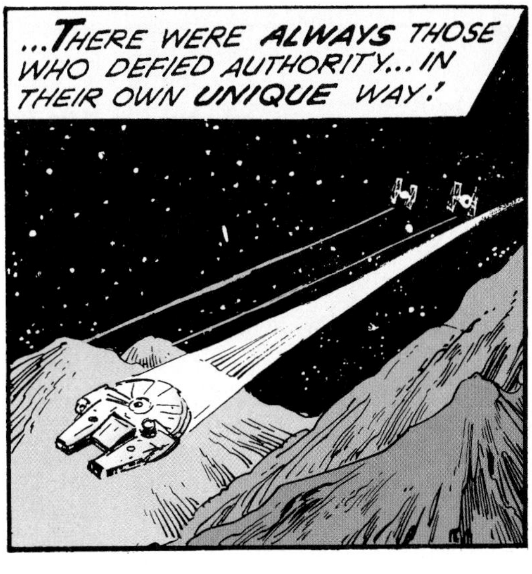
...THERE WERE ALWAYS THOSE WHO DEFIED AUTHORITY... IN THEIR OWN UNIQUE WAY!

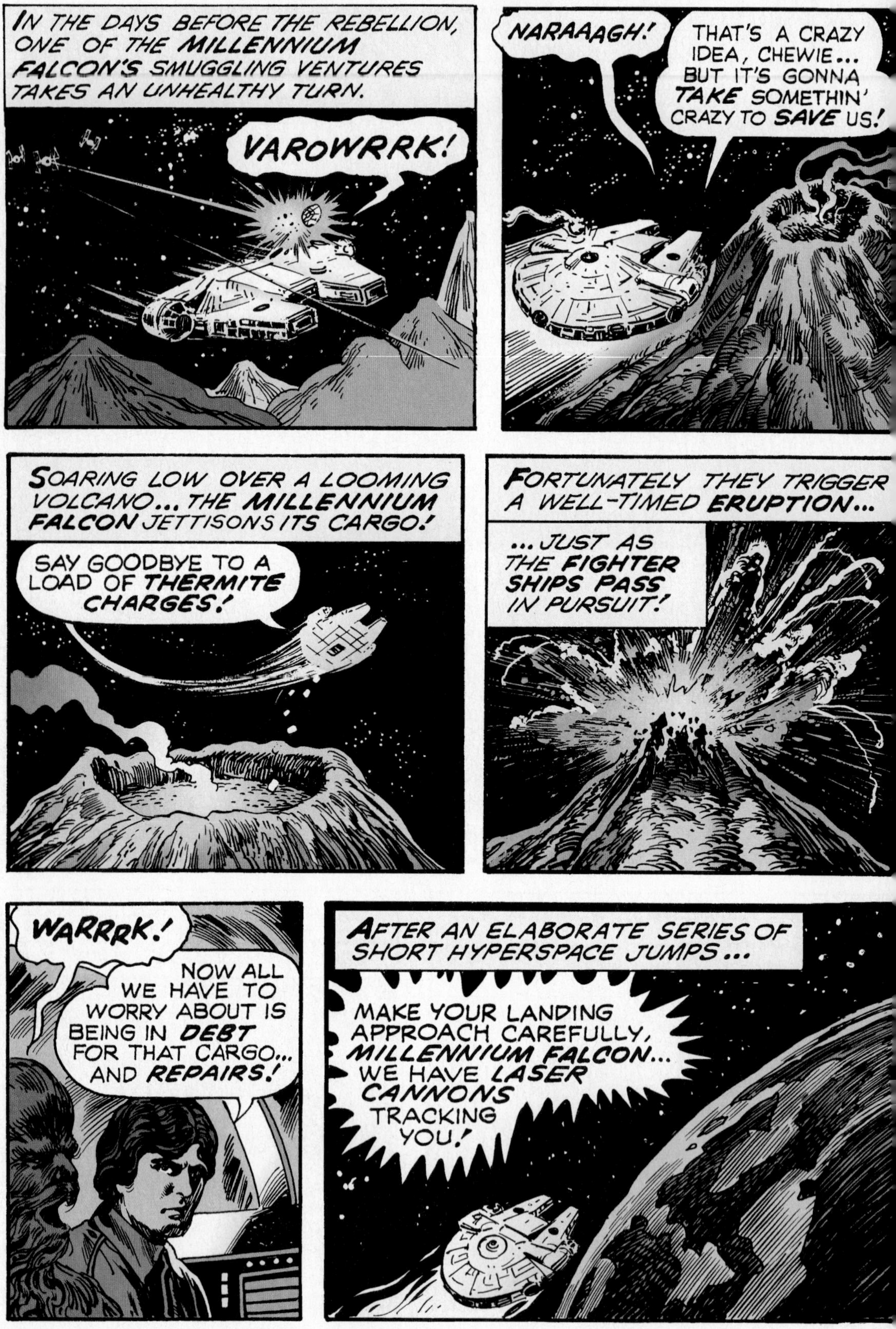
IN THE DAYS BEFORE THE REBELLION, ONE OF THE MILLENNIUM FALCON'S SMUGGLING VENTURES TAKES AN UNHEALTHY TURN.
VAROWRRK!
NARAAAAGH!
THAT'S A CRAZY IDEA, CHEWIE... BUT IT'S GONNA TAKE SOMETHIN' CRAZY TO SAVE US!
SOARING LOW OVER A LOOMING VOLCANO... THE MILLENNIUM FALCON JETTISONS ITS CARGO!
SAY GOODBYE TO A LOAD OF THERMITE CHARGES!
FORTUNATELY THEY TRIGGER A WELL-TIMED ERUPTION...
...JUST AS THE FIGHTER SHIPS PASS IN PURSUIT!
WARRRK!
NOW ALL WE HAVE TO WORRY ABOUT IS BEING IN DEBT FOR THAT CARGO... AND REPAIRS!
AFTER AN ELABORATE SERIES OF SHORT HYPERSPACE JUMPS...
MAKE YOUR LANDING APPROACH CAREFULLY, MILLENNIUM FALCON... WE HAVE LASER CANNONS TRACKING YOU!

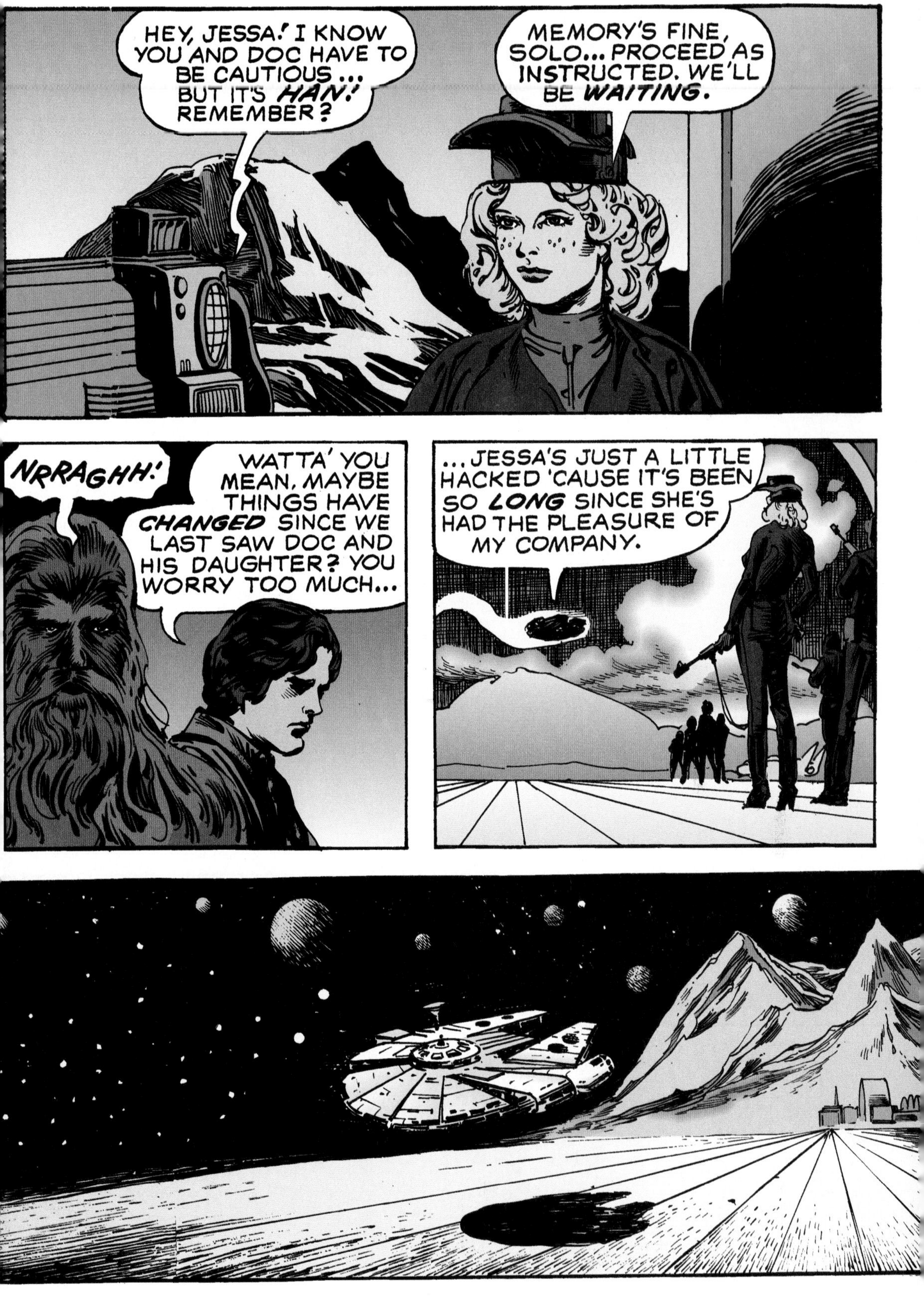
HEY, JESSA! I KNOW YOU AND DOC HAVE TO BE CAUTIOUS ... BUT IT'S HAN! REMEMBER?
MEMORY'S FINE, SOLO... PROCEED AS INSTRUCTED. WE'LL BE WAITING.
NRRAGHH!
WATTA' YOU MEAN, MAYBE THINGS HAVE CHANGED SINCE WE LAST SAW DOC AND HIS DAUGHTER? YOU WORRY TOO MUCH...
...JESSA'S JUST A LITTLE HACKED 'CAUSE IT'S BEEN SO LONG SINCE SHE'S HAD THE PLEASURE OF MY COMPANY.

HAN SOLO'S FREIGHTER! BEEN A LONG TIME SINCE WE'VE SEEN *THAT* SMUGGLER IN THESE PARTS.

THINK HE AN' THE WOOKIEE CAN STILL BE TRUSTED?

CONSIDERING WHAT'S HAPPENED LATELY... I'M NOT SURE *ANYONE* CAN BE.

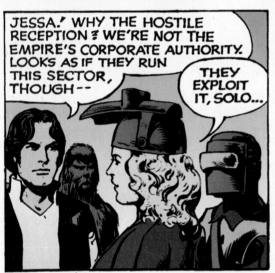

JESSA! WHY THE HOSTILE RECEPTION? WE'RE NOT THE EMPIRE'S CORPORATE AUTHORITY. LOOKS AS IF THEY RUN THIS SECTOR, THOUGH--

THEY EXPLOIT IT, SOLO...

...AND THEY'VE FINALLY GOTTEN THEIR PLANET-WRINGING CLAWS ON *DOC!*

YOUR *FATHER?!* UH, OH....! I WAS COUNTING ON HIM TO OVERHAUL THE *FALCON--*

YOUR GRIEF IS TOUCHING. DON'T FRET... I'LL SEE THE *FALCON* IS REFITTED. THE ONLY THING YOU WON'T LIKE...

...IS THE *PRICE!*

MEANWHILE, AT THE STAR SYSTEM'S EDGE... A SHIP DROPS OUT OF LIGHTSPEED FROM HYPERSPACE.

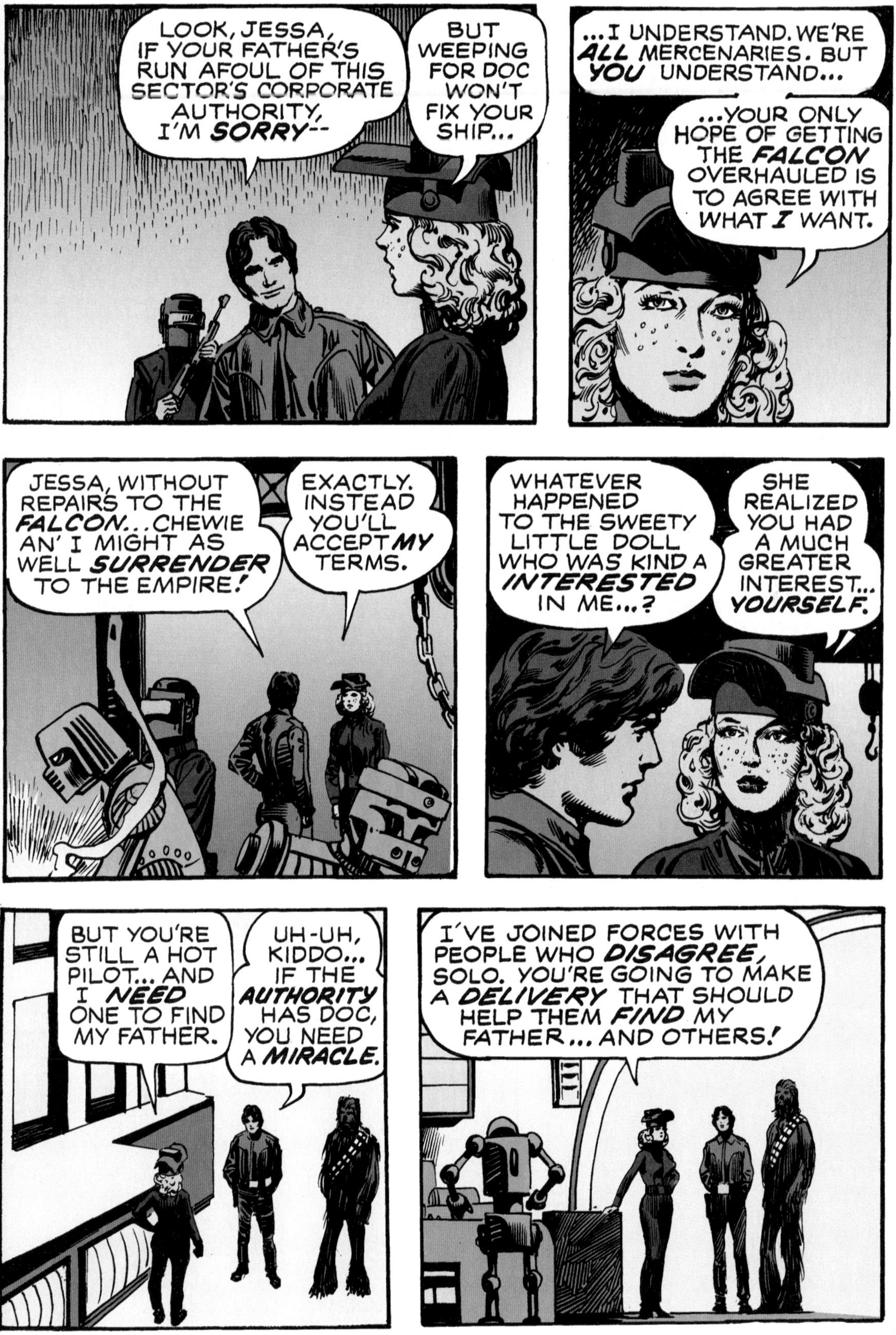
LOOK, JESSA, IF YOUR FATHER'S RUN AFOUL OF THIS SECTOR'S CORPORATE AUTHORITY, I'M SORRY--
BUT WEEPING FOR DOC WON'T FIX YOUR SHIP...
...I UNDERSTAND. WE'RE ALL MERCENARIES. BUT YOU UNDERSTAND...
...YOUR ONLY HOPE OF GETTING THE FALCON OVERHAULED IS TO AGREE WITH WHAT I WANT.
JESSA, WITHOUT REPAIRS TO THE FALCON... CHEWIE AN' I MIGHT AS WELL SURRENDER TO THE EMPIRE!
EXACTLY. INSTEAD YOU'LL ACCEPT MY TERMS.
WHATEVER HAPPENED TO THE SWEETY LITTLE DOLL WHO WAS KIND A INTERESTED IN ME...?
SHE REALIZED YOU HAD A MUCH GREATER INTEREST... YOURSELF.
BUT YOU'RE STILL A HOT PILOT... AND I NEED ONE TO FIND MY FATHER.
UH-UH, KIDDO... IF THE AUTHORITY HAS DOC, YOU NEED A MIRACLE.
I'VE JOINED FORCES WITH PEOPLE WHO DISAGREE, SOLO. YOU'RE GOING TO MAKE A DELIVERY THAT SHOULD HELP THEM FIND MY FATHER... AND OTHERS!

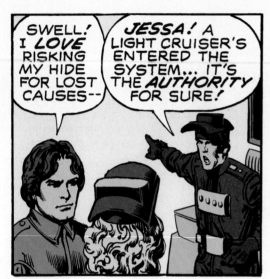

SWELL! I *LOVE* RISKING MY HIDE FOR LOST CAUSES--

JESSA! A LIGHT CRUISER'S ENTERED THE SYSTEM... IT'S THE *AUTHORITY* FOR SURE!

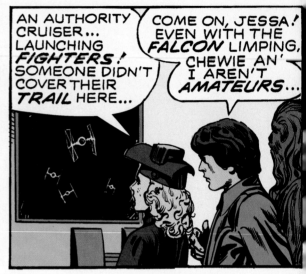

AN AUTHORITY CRUISER... LAUNCHING *FIGHTERS!* SOMEONE DIDN'T COVER THEIR *TRAIL* HERE...

COME ON, JESSA! EVEN WITH THE *FALCON* LIMPING, CHEWIE AN' I AREN'T *AMATEURS*...

...AND *SELLING OUT FRIENDS* ISN'T OUR STYLE!

GOOD! SINCE WE'RE SUCH FRIENDS YOU CAN JOIN ME IN *DEFENDING* THE PLACE... PICK YOUR SHIP!

YOU'VE ALREADY BLACK-MAILED ME INTO A *SMUGGLING JOB*... I HAVE TO FLY THIS *MUSEUM PIECE,* TOO?

MY PEOPLE ARE CRACK TECHNICIANS, HAN...

...NOT COMBAT ACES. ANY OTHER COMPLAINTS?

YEAH. THIS FLYING HELMET DOESN'T HAVE A *HOLE* IN IT TO MATCH THE ONE IN MY HEAD!

THEN THE TWO SHIPS ARE SCREAMING ALOFT TO MEET THE INCOMING ENEMY...

...AT TWO-TO-ONE ODDS!

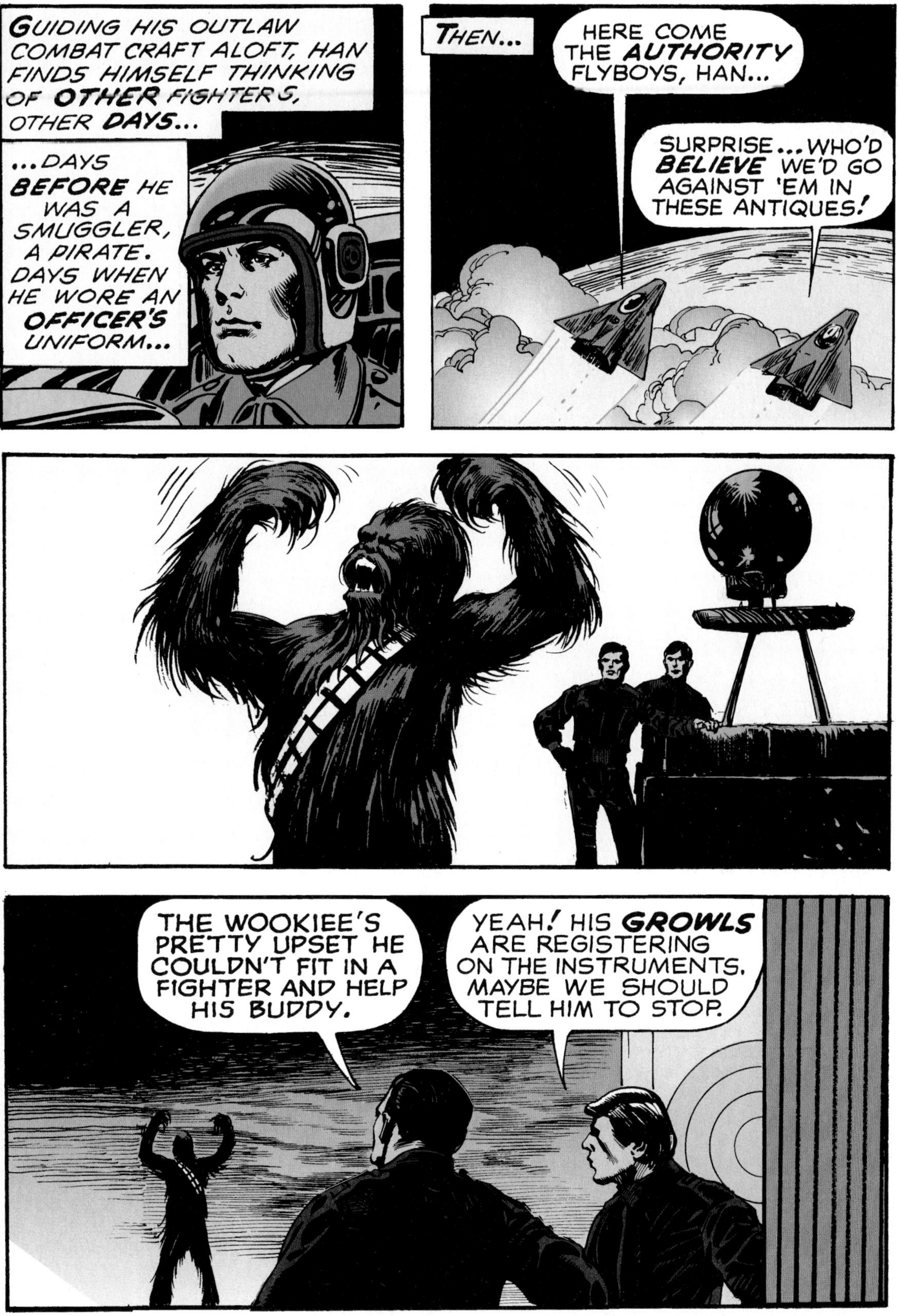
GUIDING HIS OUTLAW COMBAT CRAFT ALOFT, HAN FINDS HIMSELF THINKING OF OTHER FIGHTERS, OTHER DAYS...
...DAYS BEFORE HE WAS A SMUGGLER, A PIRATE. DAYS WHEN HE WORE AN OFFICER'S UNIFORM...
THEN...
HERE COME THE AUTHORITY FLYBOYS, HAN...
SURPRISE...WHO'D BELIEVE WE'D GO AGAINST 'EM IN THESE ANTIQUES!
THE WOOKIEE'S PRETTY UPSET HE COULDN'T FIT IN A FIGHTER AND HELP HIS BUDDY.
YEAH! HIS GROWLS ARE REGISTERING ON THE INSTRUMENTS. MAYBE WE SHOULD TELL HIM TO STOP.

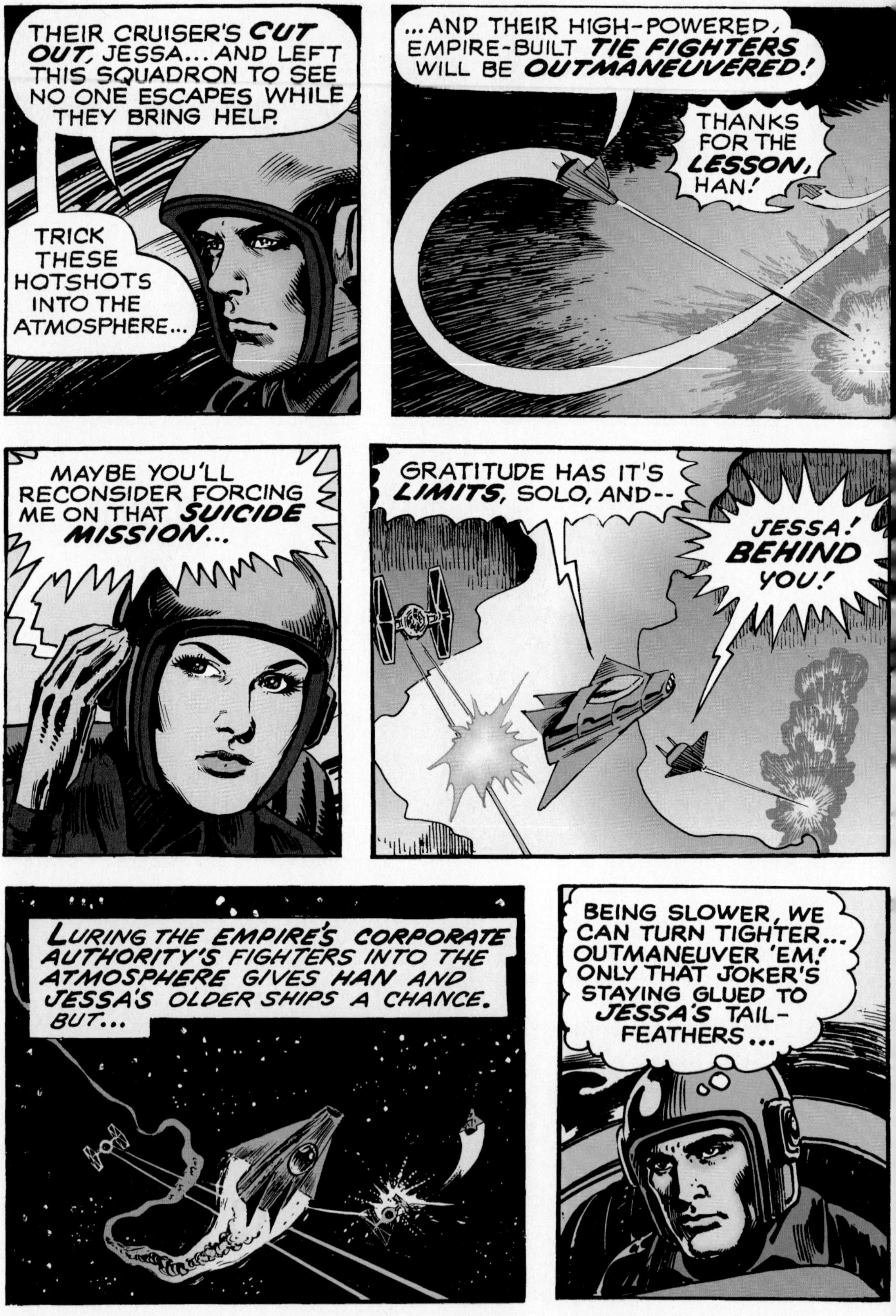
THEIR CRUISER'S CUT OUT, JESSA... AND LEFT THIS SQUADRON TO SEE NO ONE ESCAPES WHILE THEY BRING HELP.
TRICK THESE HOTSHOTS INTO THE ATMOSPHERE...
...AND THEIR HIGH-POWERED, EMPIRE-BUILT TIE FIGHTERS WILL BE OUTMANEUVERED!
THANKS FOR THE LESSON, HAN!
MAYBE YOU'LL RECONSIDER FORCING ME ON THAT SUICIDE MISSION...
GRATITUDE HAS IT'S LIMITS, SOLO, AND--
JESSA! BEHIND YOU!
LURING THE EMPIRE'S CORPORATE AUTHORITY'S FIGHTERS INTO THE ATMOSPHERE GIVES HAN AND JESSA'S OLDER SHIPS A CHANCE. BUT...
BEING SLOWER, WE CAN TURN TIGHTER... OUTMANEUVER 'EM! ONLY THAT JOKER'S STAYING GLUED TO JESSA'S TAIL-FEATHERS...

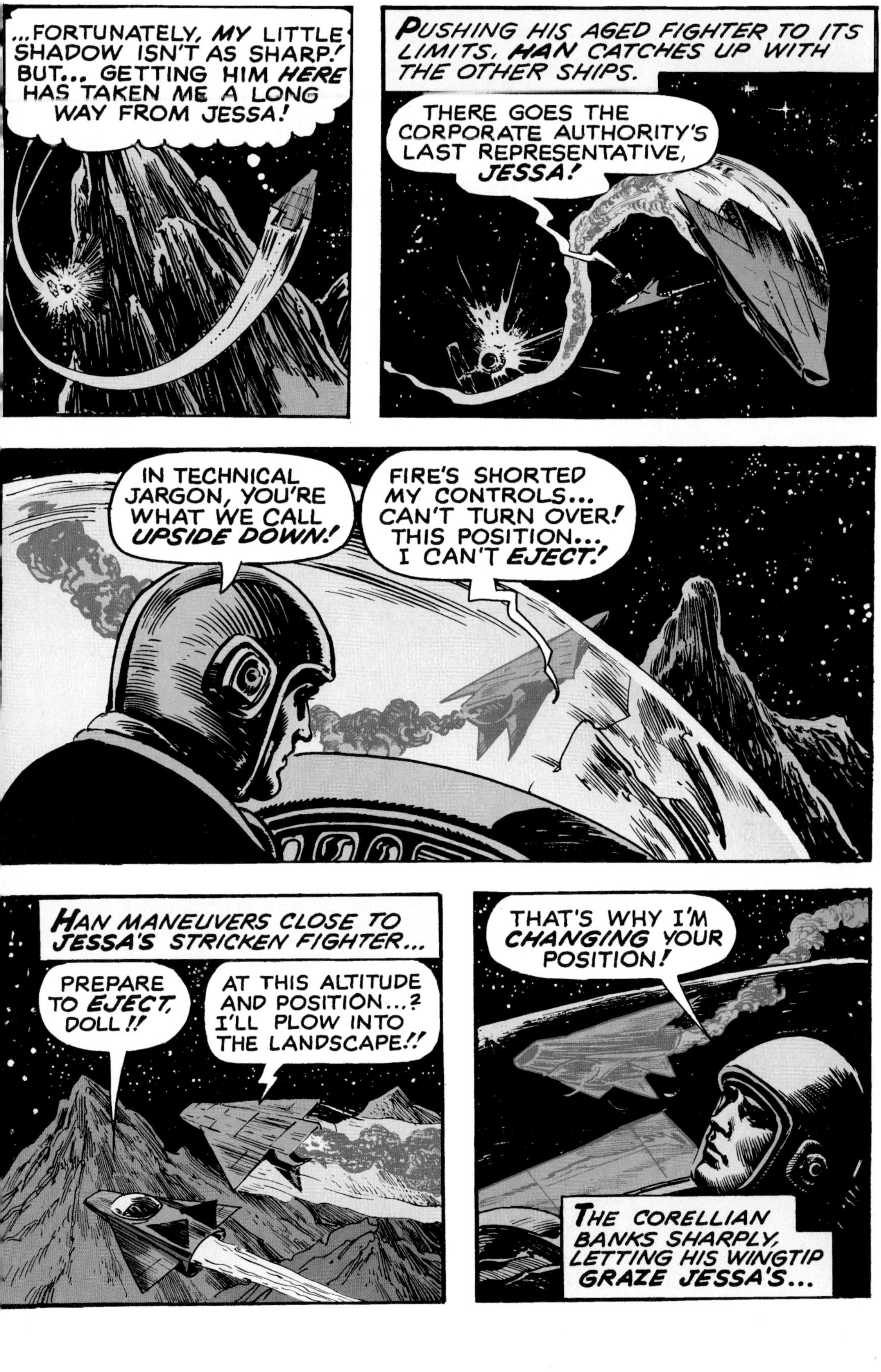
...FORTUNATELY, MY LITTLE SHADOW ISN'T AS SHARP! BUT... GETTING HIM HERE HAS TAKEN ME A LONG WAY FROM JESSA!
PUSHING HIS AGED FIGHTER TO ITS LIMITS, HAN CATCHES UP WITH THE OTHER SHIPS.
THERE GOES THE CORPORATE AUTHORITY'S LAST REPRESENTATIVE, JESSA!
IN TECHNICAL JARGON, YOU'RE WHAT WE CALL UPSIDE DOWN!
FIRE'S SHORTED MY CONTROLS... CAN'T TURN OVER! THIS POSITION... I CAN'T EJECT!
HAN MANEUVERS CLOSE TO JESSA'S STRICKEN FIGHTER...
PREPARE TO EJECT, DOLL!!
AT THIS ALTITUDE AND POSITION...? I'LL PLOW INTO THE LANDSCAPE!!
THAT'S WHY I'M CHANGING YOUR POSITION!
THE CORELLIAN BANKS SHARPLY, LETTING HIS WINGTIP GRAZE JESSA'S...

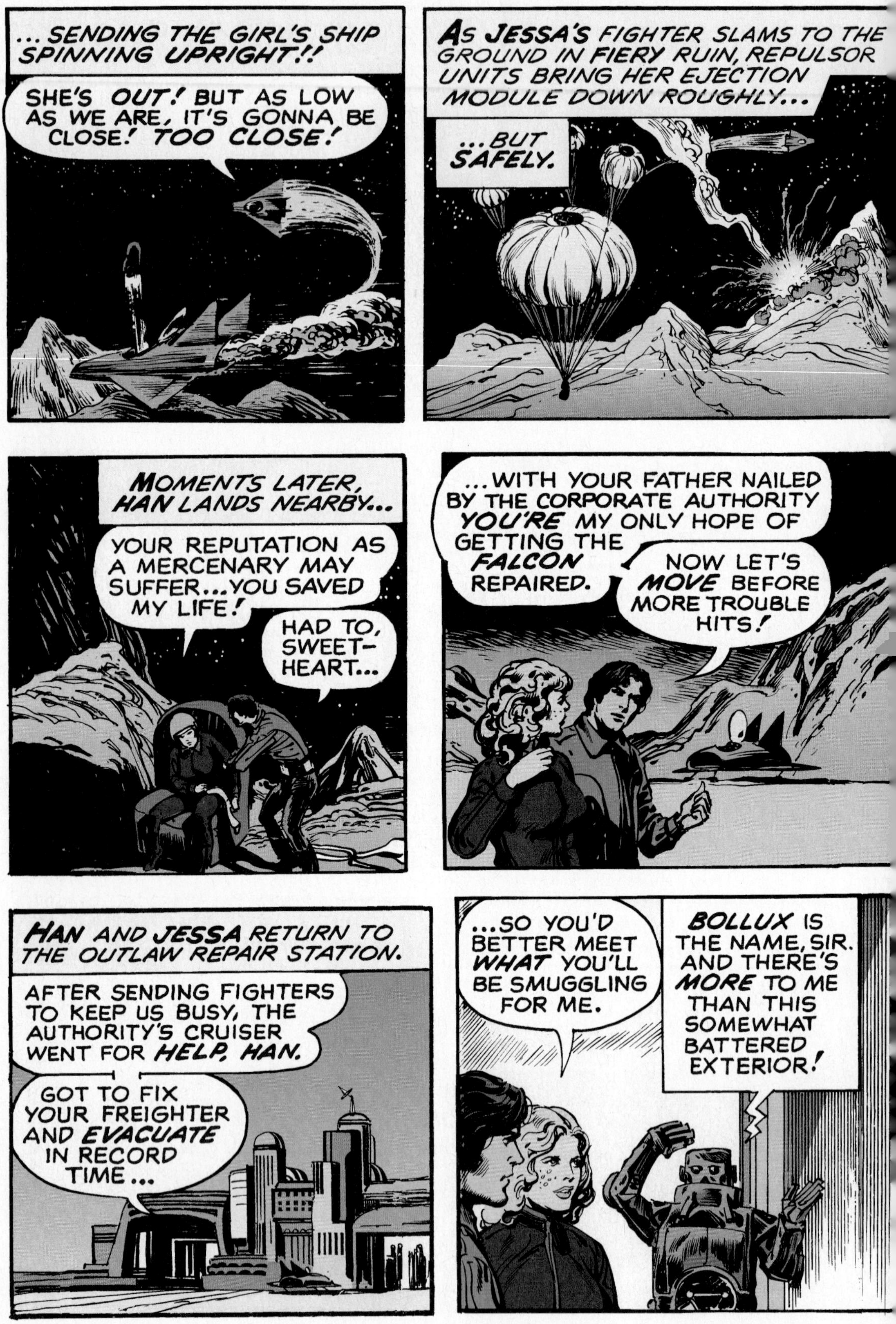

...SENDING THE GIRL'S SHIP SPINNING UPRIGHT!!
SHE'S OUT! BUT AS LOW AS WE ARE, IT'S GONNA BE CLOSE! TOO CLOSE!
AS JESSA'S FIGHTER SLAMS TO THE GROUND IN FIERY RUIN, REPULSOR UNITS BRING HER EJECTION MODULE DOWN ROUGHLY...
...BUT SAFELY.
MOMENTS LATER, HAN LANDS NEARBY...
YOUR REPUTATION AS A MERCENARY MAY SUFFER...YOU SAVED MY LIFE!
HAD TO, SWEET-HEART...
...WITH YOUR FATHER NAILED BY THE CORPORATE AUTHORITY YOU'RE MY ONLY HOPE OF GETTING THE FALCON REPAIRED.
NOW LET'S MOVE BEFORE MORE TROUBLE HITS!
HAN AND JESSA RETURN TO THE OUTLAW REPAIR STATION.
AFTER SENDING FIGHTERS TO KEEP US BUSY, THE AUTHORITY'S CRUISER WENT FOR HELP, HAN.
GOT TO FIX YOUR FREIGHTER AND EVACUATE IN RECORD TIME...
...SO YOU'D BETTER MEET WHAT YOU'LL BE SMUGGLING FOR ME.
BOLLUX IS THE NAME, SIR. AND THERE'S MORE TO ME THAN THIS SOMEWHAT BATTERED EXTERIOR!

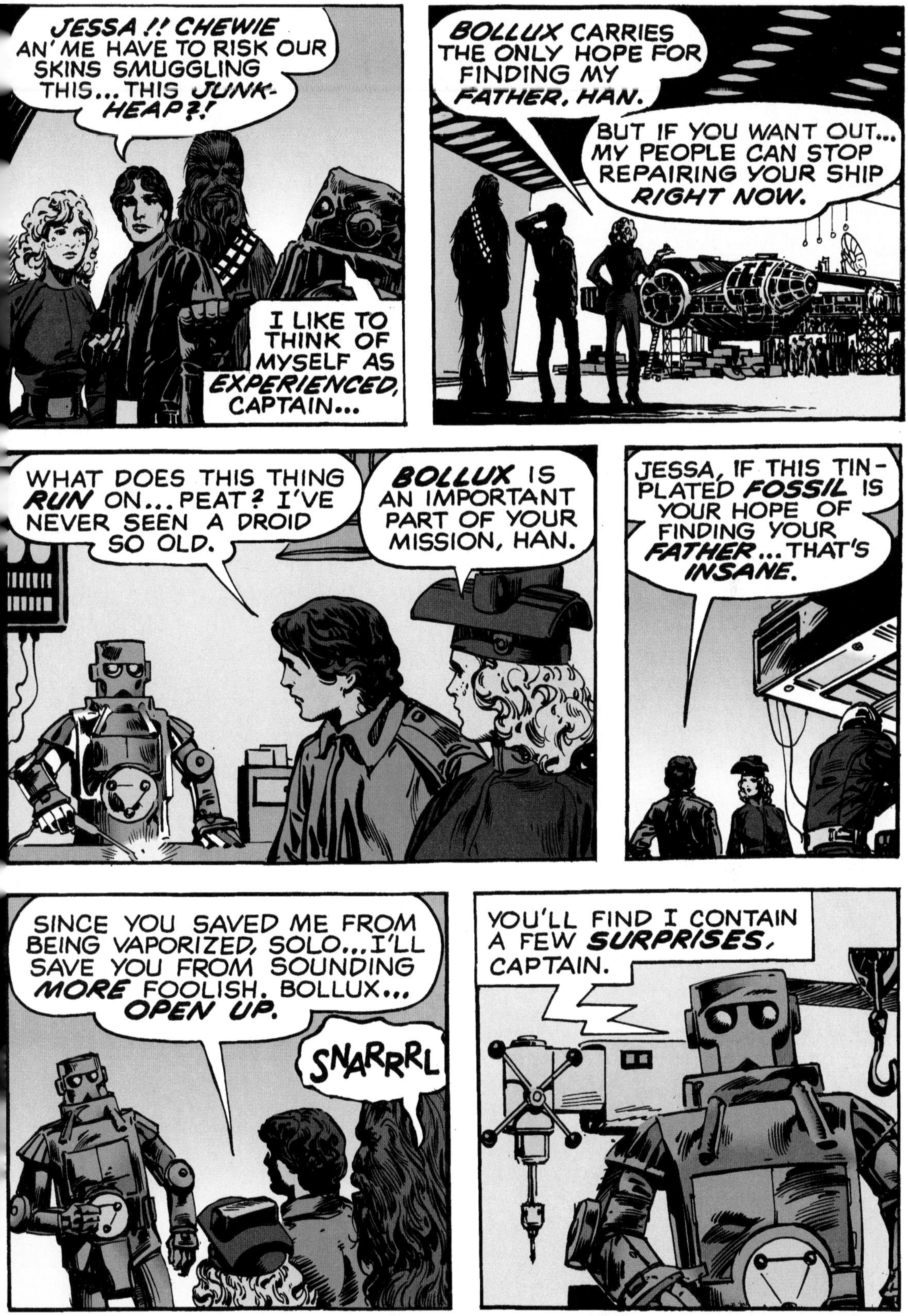
JESSA !! CHEWIE AN' ME HAVE TO RISK OUR SKINS SMUGGLING THIS... THIS JUNK-HEAP?!
I LIKE TO THINK OF MYSELF AS EXPERIENCED, CAPTAIN...
BOLLUX CARRIES THE ONLY HOPE FOR FINDING MY FATHER, HAN.
BUT IF YOU WANT OUT... MY PEOPLE CAN STOP REPAIRING YOUR SHIP RIGHT NOW.
WHAT DOES THIS THING RUN ON... PEAT? I'VE NEVER SEEN A DROID SO OLD.
BOLLUX IS AN IMPORTANT PART OF YOUR MISSION, HAN.
JESSA, IF THIS TIN-PLATED FOSSIL IS YOUR HOPE OF FINDING YOUR FATHER... THAT'S INSANE.
SINCE YOU SAVED ME FROM BEING VAPORIZED, SOLO... I'LL SAVE YOU FROM SOUNDING MORE FOOLISH. BOLLUX... OPEN UP.
SNARRRL
YOU'LL FIND I CONTAIN A FEW SURPRISES, CAPTAIN.

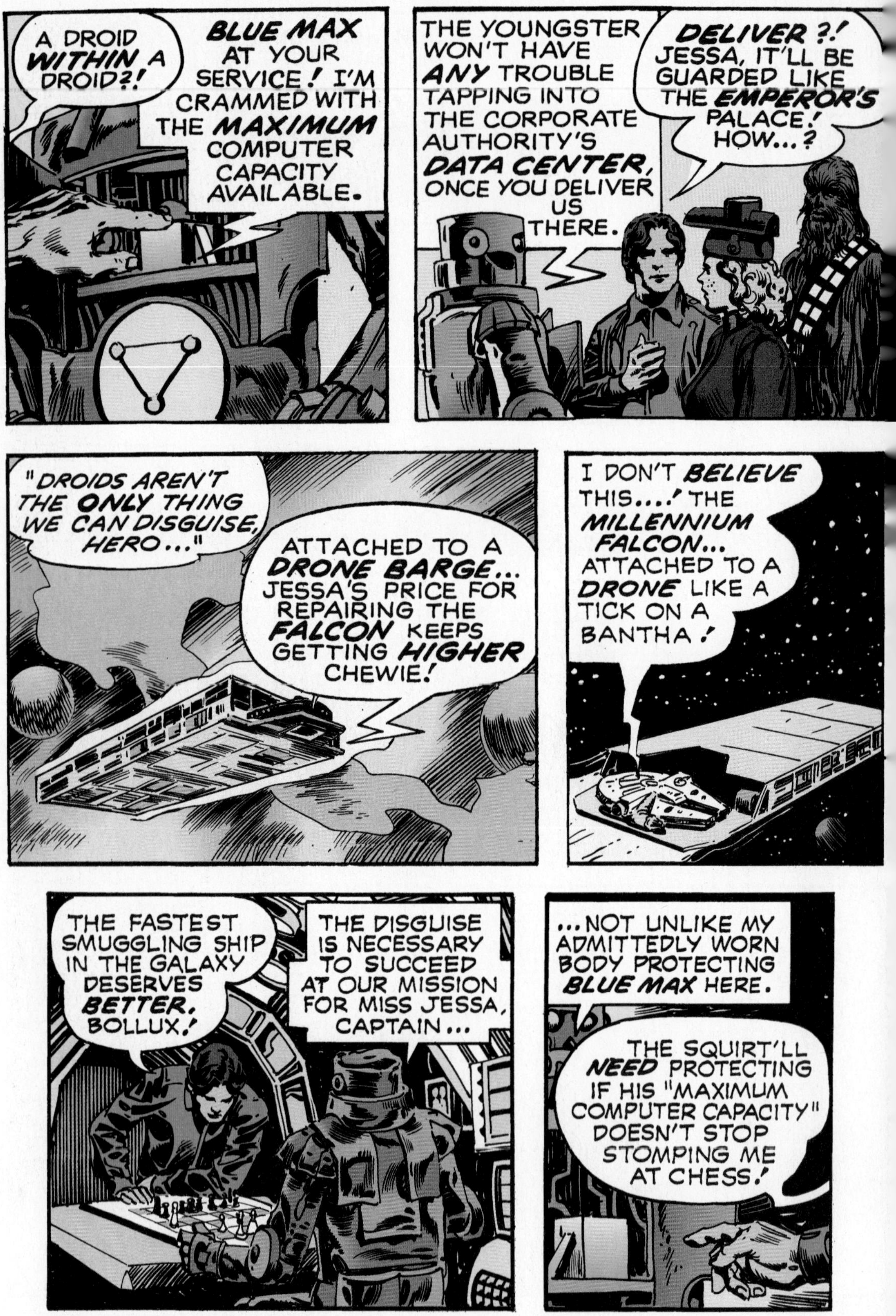
A DROID WITHIN A DROID?!
BLUE MAX AT YOUR SERVICE! I'M CRAMMED WITH THE MAXIMUM COMPUTER CAPACITY AVAILABLE.
THE YOUNGSTER WON'T HAVE ANY TROUBLE TAPPING INTO THE CORPORATE AUTHORITY'S DATA CENTER, ONCE YOU DELIVER US THERE.
DELIVER?! JESSA, IT'LL BE GUARDED LIKE THE EMPEROR'S PALACE! HOW...?
"DROIDS AREN'T THE ONLY THING WE CAN DISGUISE, HERO..."
ATTACHED TO A DRONE BARGE... JESSA'S PRICE FOR REPAIRING THE FALCON KEEPS GETTING HIGHER CHEWIE!
I DON'T BELIEVE THIS....! THE MILLENNIUM FALCON... ATTACHED TO A DRONE LIKE A TICK ON A BANTHA!
THE FASTEST SMUGGLING SHIP IN THE GALAXY DESERVES BETTER, BOLLUX!
THE DISGUISE IS NECESSARY TO SUCCEED AT OUR MISSION FOR MISS JESSA, CAPTAIN...
...NOT UNLIKE MY ADMITTEDLY WORN BODY PROTECTING BLUE MAX HERE.
THE SQUIRT'LL NEED PROTECTING IF HIS "MAXIMUM COMPUTER CAPACITY" DOESN'T STOP STOMPING ME AT CHESS!

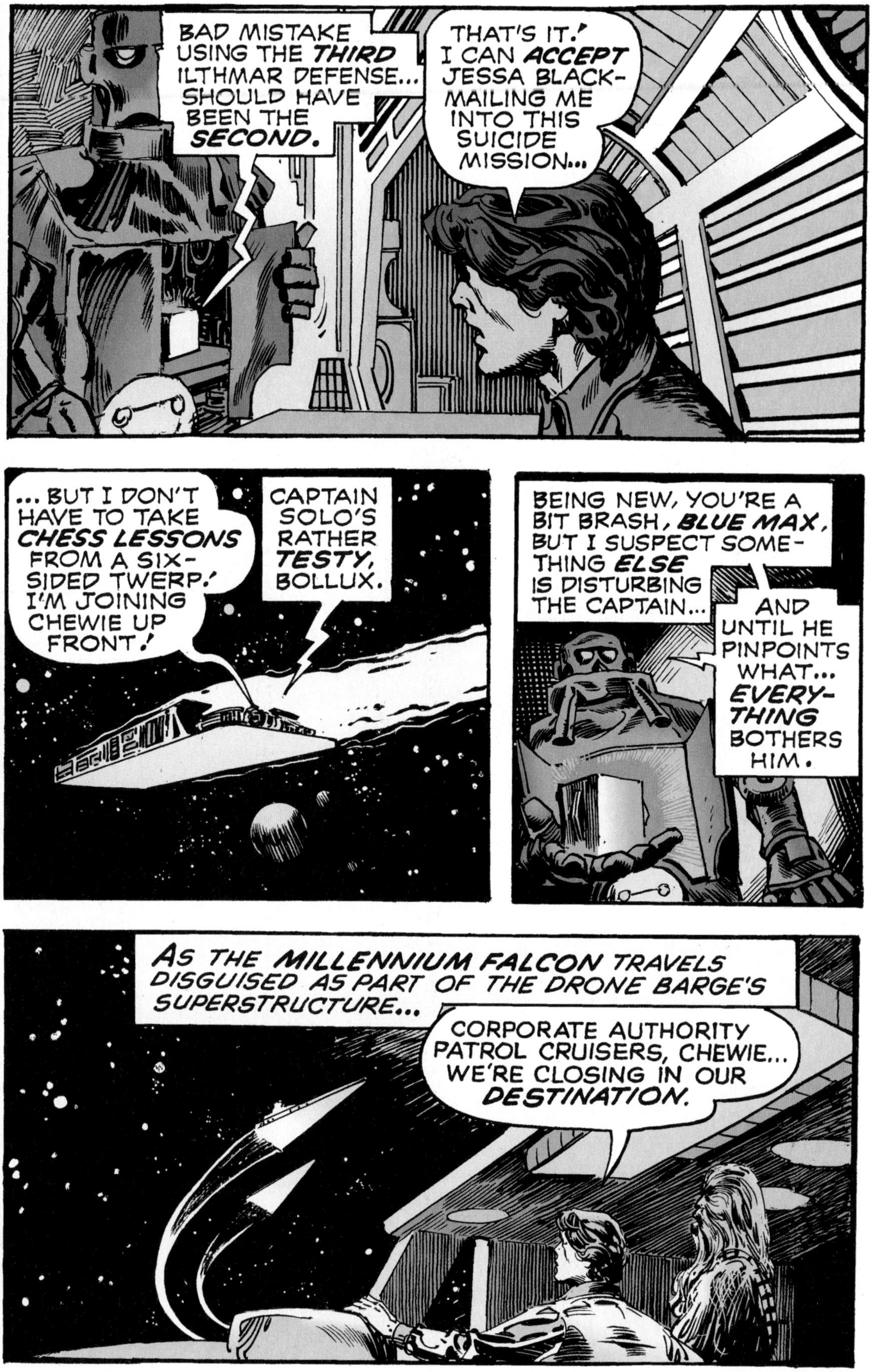
BAD MISTAKE USING THE THIRD ILTHMAR DEFENSE... SHOULD HAVE BEEN THE SECOND.
THAT'S IT! I CAN ACCEPT JESSA BLACK-MAILING ME INTO THIS SUICIDE MISSION...
...BUT I DON'T HAVE TO TAKE CHESS LESSONS FROM A SIX-SIDED TWERP! I'M JOINING CHEWIE UP FRONT!
CAPTAIN SOLO'S RATHER TESTY, BOLLUX.
BEING NEW, YOU'RE A BIT BRASH, BLUE MAX, BUT I SUSPECT SOME-THING ELSE IS DISTURBING THE CAPTAIN...
AND UNTIL HE PINPOINTS WHAT... EVERY-THING BOTHERS HIM.
AS THE MILLENNIUM FALCON TRAVELS DISGUISED AS PART OF THE DRONE BARGE'S SUPERSTRUCTURE...
CORPORATE AUTHORITY PATROL CRUISERS, CHEWIE... WE'RE CLOSING IN OUR DESTINATION.

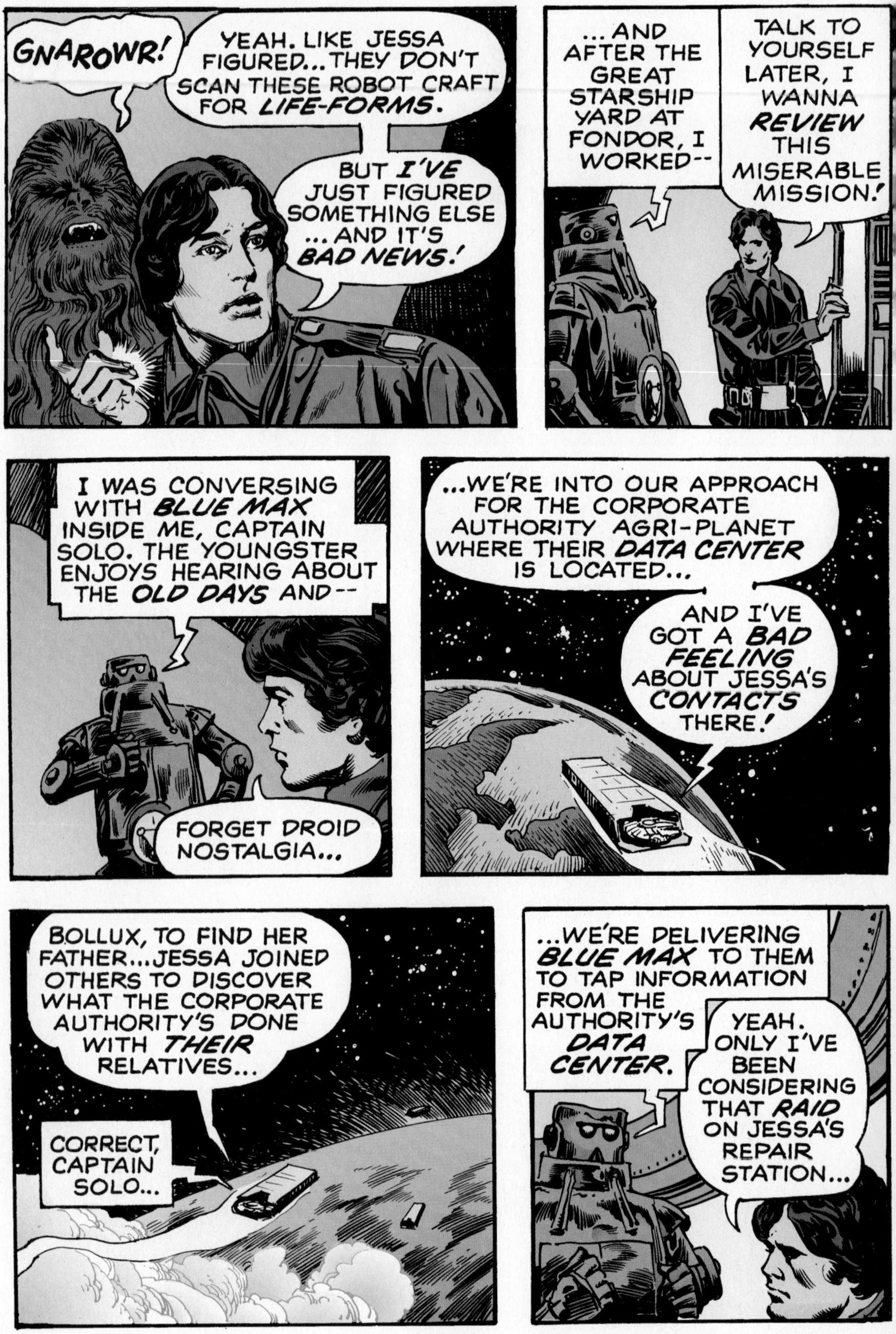
GNAROWR!
YEAH. LIKE JESSA FIGURED... THEY DON'T SCAN THESE ROBOT CRAFT FOR LIFE-FORMS.
BUT I'VE JUST FIGURED SOMETHING ELSE ...AND IT'S BAD NEWS!
...AND AFTER THE GREAT STARSHIP YARD AT FONDOR, I WORKED--
TALK TO YOURSELF LATER, I WANNA REVIEW THIS MISERABLE MISSION!
I WAS CONVERSING WITH BLUE MAX INSIDE ME, CAPTAIN SOLO. THE YOUNGSTER ENJOYS HEARING ABOUT THE OLD DAYS AND--
FORGET DROID NOSTALGIA...
...WE'RE INTO OUR APPROACH FOR THE CORPORATE AUTHORITY AGRI-PLANET WHERE THEIR DATA CENTER IS LOCATED...
AND I'VE GOT A BAD FEELING ABOUT JESSA'S CONTACTS THERE!
BOLLUX, TO FIND HER FATHER...JESSA JOINED OTHERS TO DISCOVER WHAT THE CORPORATE AUTHORITY'S DONE WITH THEIR RELATIVES...
CORRECT, CAPTAIN SOLO...
...WE'RE DELIVERING BLUE MAX TO THEM TO TAP INFORMATION FROM THE AUTHORITY'S DATA CENTER.
YEAH. ONLY I'VE BEEN CONSIDERING THAT RAID ON JESSA'S REPAIR STATION...

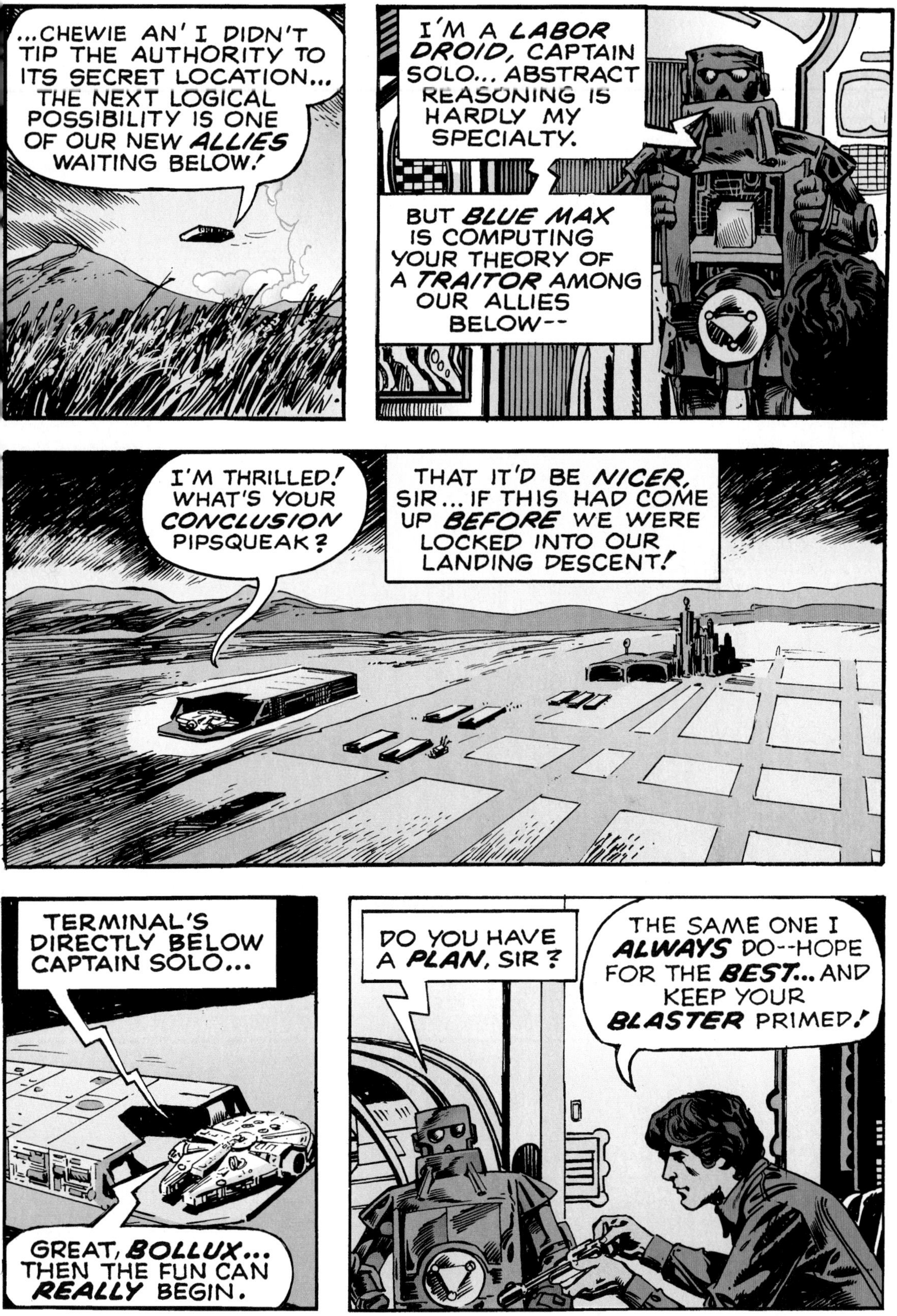
...CHEWIE AN' I DIDN'T TIP THE AUTHORITY TO ITS SECRET LOCATION... THE NEXT LOGICAL POSSIBILITY IS ONE OF OUR NEW ALLIES WAITING BELOW!
I'M A LABOR DROID, CAPTAIN SOLO... ABSTRACT REASONING IS HARDLY MY SPECIALTY.
BUT BLUE MAX IS COMPUTING YOUR THEORY OF A TRAITOR AMONG OUR ALLIES BELOW--
I'M THRILLED! WHAT'S YOUR CONCLUSION PIPSQUEAK?
THAT IT'D BE NICER, SIR... IF THIS HAD COME UP BEFORE WE WERE LOCKED INTO OUR LANDING DESCENT!
TERMINAL'S DIRECTLY BELOW CAPTAIN SOLO...
GREAT, BOLLUX... THEN THE FUN CAN REALLY BEGIN.
DO YOU HAVE A PLAN, SIR?
THE SAME ONE I ALWAYS DO--HOPE FOR THE BEST... AND KEEP YOUR BLASTER PRIMED!

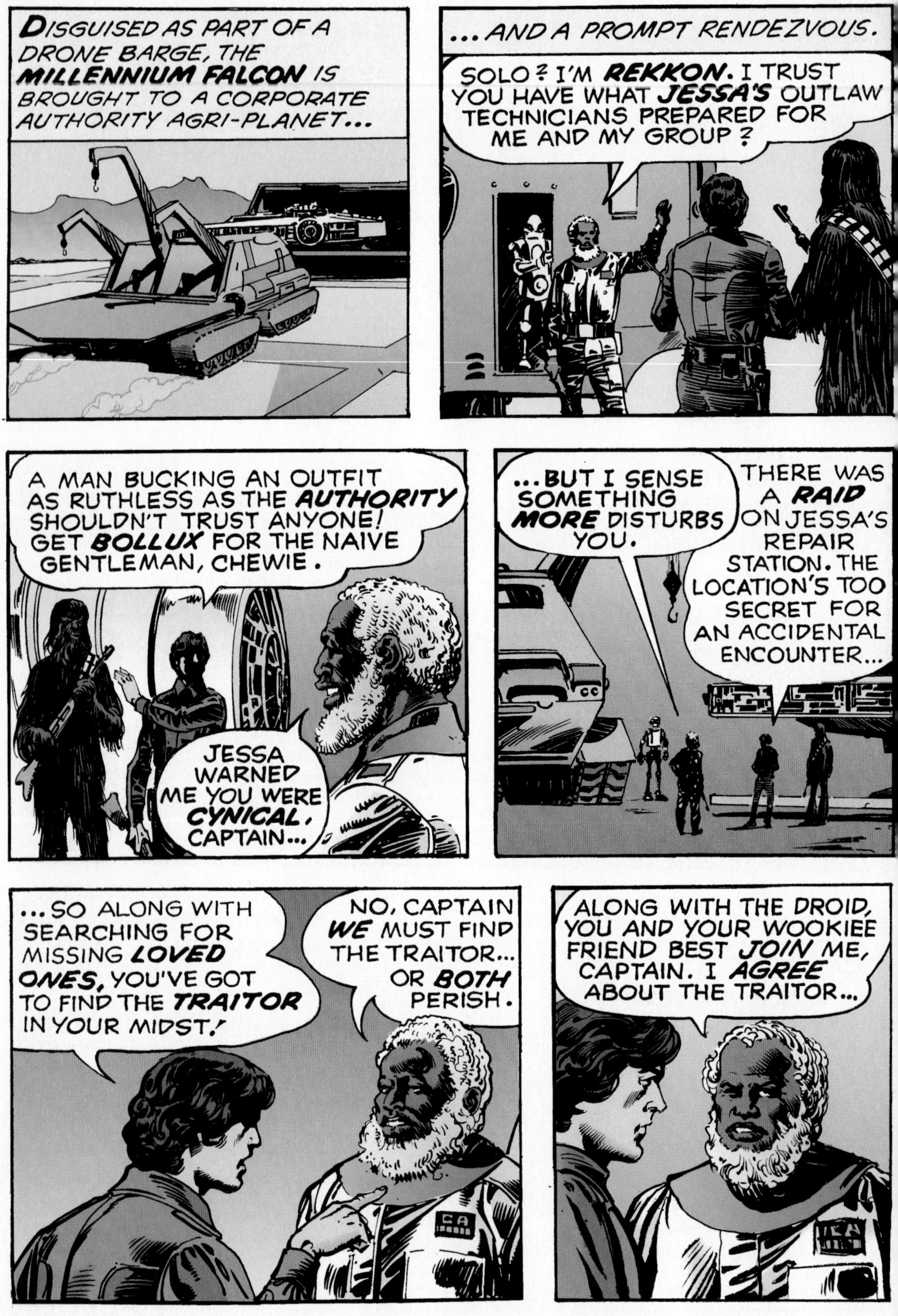

DISGUISED AS PART OF A DRONE BARGE, THE MILLENNIUM FALCON IS BROUGHT TO A CORPORATE AUTHORITY AGRI-PLANET...
...AND A PROMPT RENDEZVOUS.
SOLO? I'M REKKON. I TRUST YOU HAVE WHAT JESSA'S OUTLAW TECHNICIANS PREPARED FOR ME AND MY GROUP?
A MAN BUCKING AN OUTFIT AS RUTHLESS AS THE AUTHORITY SHOULDN'T TRUST ANYONE! GET BOLLUX FOR THE NAIVE GENTLEMAN, CHEWIE.
JESSA WARNED ME YOU WERE CYNICAL, CAPTAIN...
...BUT I SENSE SOMETHING MORE DISTURBS YOU.
THERE WAS A RAID ON JESSA'S REPAIR STATION. THE LOCATION'S TOO SECRET FOR AN ACCIDENTAL ENCOUNTER...
...SO ALONG WITH SEARCHING FOR MISSING LOVED ONES, YOU'VE GOT TO FIND THE TRAITOR IN YOUR MIDST!
NO, CAPTAIN WE MUST FIND THE TRAITOR... OR BOTH PERISH.
ALONG WITH THE DROID, YOU AND YOUR WOOKIEE FRIEND BEST JOIN ME, CAPTAIN. I AGREE ABOUT THE TRAITOR...

...UNTIL THE IDENTITY'S KNOWN... *NONE* OF US HAVE A PRAYER OF ESCAPING THE AUTHORITY.

NO ARGUMENT. I *KNEW* THIS WOULDN'T BE A SIMPLE DELIVERY!

ONCE IN THE SKIMMER'S CAB, HAN AND CHEWIE RECEIVE CORPORATE IDENTIFICATION...

YOU MUST HAVE A POSITION WITH SOME *PULL* AROUND HERE, *REKKON.*

TRUE, CAPTAIN SOLO... IN THE DATA CENTER, I'M ABLE TO PROGRAM ALMOST ANY CLEARANCE OR AUTHORIZATION NEEDED.

SOUNDS CUSHY.

IT'S NEVER MADE UP FOR THE AUTHORITY ROBBING ME OF MY *SON!*

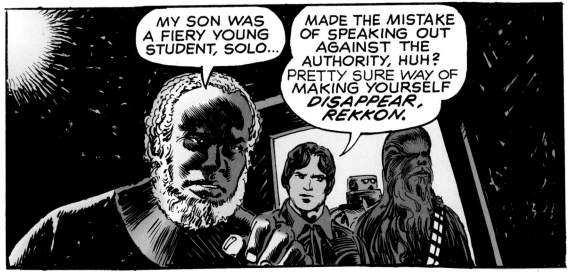

MY SON WAS A FIERY YOUNG STUDENT, SOLO...

MADE THE MISTAKE OF SPEAKING OUT AGAINST THE AUTHORITY, HUH? PRETTY SURE WAY OF MAKING YOURSELF *DISAPPEAR, REKKON.*

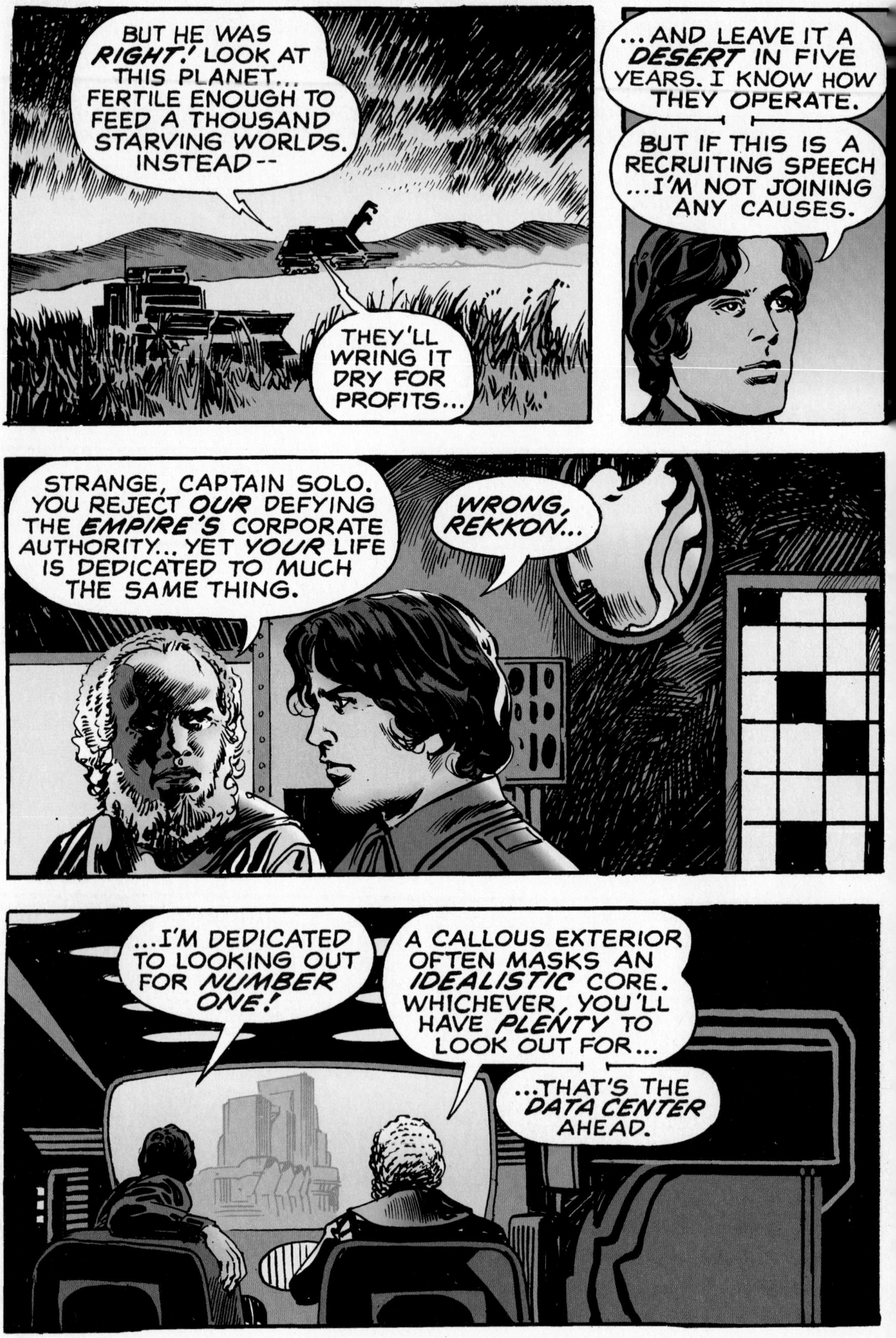

BUT HE WAS *RIGHT!* LOOK AT THIS PLANET... FERTILE ENOUGH TO FEED A THOUSAND STARVING WORLDS. INSTEAD--
THEY'LL WRING IT DRY FOR PROFITS...
...AND LEAVE IT A *DESERT* IN FIVE YEARS. I KNOW HOW THEY OPERATE.
BUT IF THIS IS A RECRUITING SPEECH ...I'M NOT JOINING ANY CAUSES.
STRANGE, CAPTAIN SOLO. YOU REJECT *OUR* DEFYING THE *EMPIRE'S* CORPORATE AUTHORITY... YET *YOUR* LIFE IS DEDICATED TO MUCH THE SAME THING.
WRONG, REKKON...
...I'M DEDICATED TO LOOKING OUT FOR *NUMBER ONE!*
A CALLOUS EXTERIOR OFTEN MASKS AN *IDEALISTIC* CORE. WHICHEVER, YOU'LL HAVE *PLENTY* TO LOOK OUT FOR...
...THAT'S THE *DATA CENTER* AHEAD.

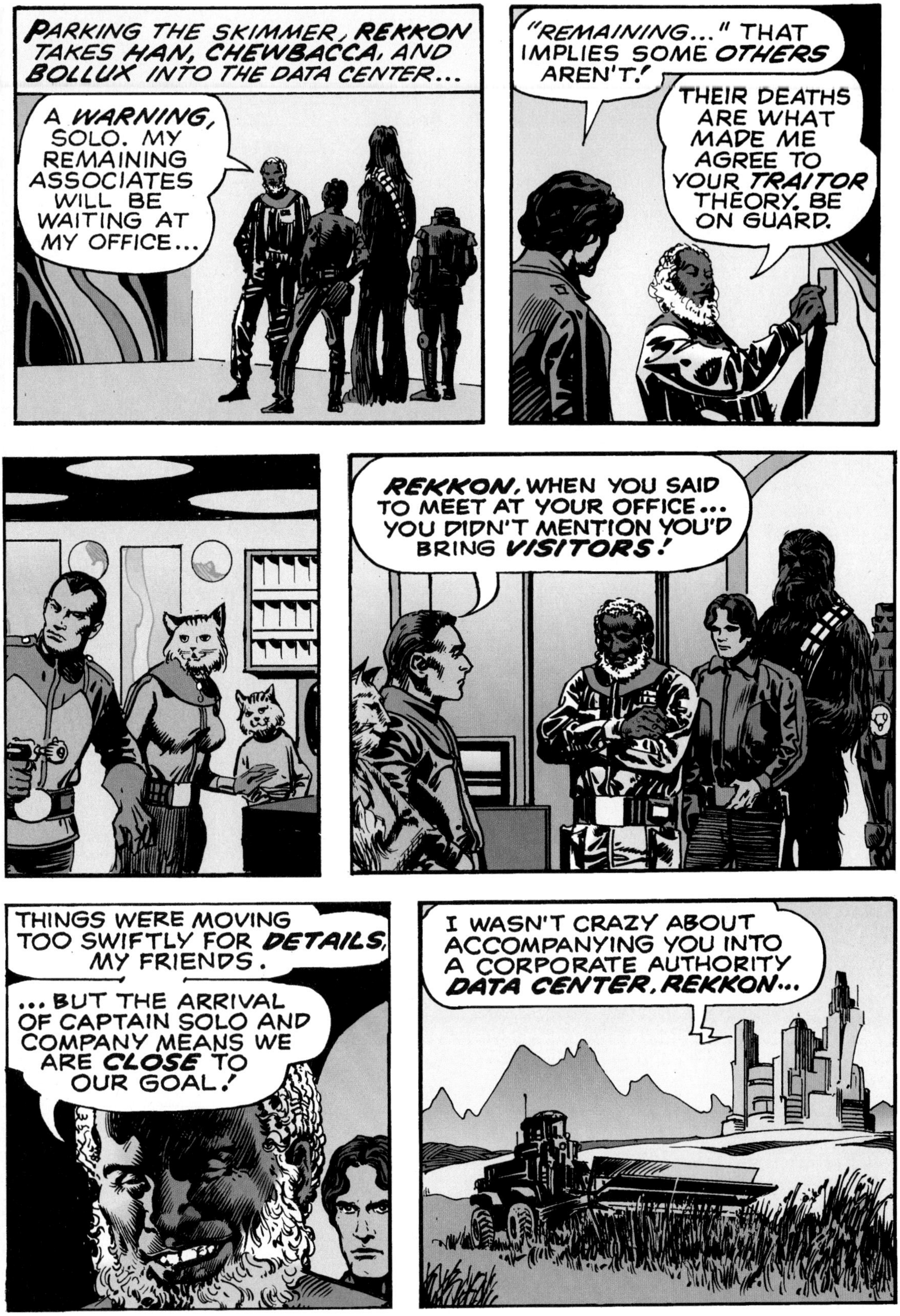
PARKING THE SKIMMER, REKKON TAKES HAN, CHEWBACCA, AND BOLLUX INTO THE DATA CENTER...
A WARNING, SOLO. MY REMAINING ASSOCIATES WILL BE WAITING AT MY OFFICE...
"REMAINING..." THAT IMPLIES SOME OTHERS AREN'T!
THEIR DEATHS ARE WHAT MADE ME AGREE TO YOUR TRAITOR THEORY. BE ON GUARD.
REKKON, WHEN YOU SAID TO MEET AT YOUR OFFICE... YOU DIDN'T MENTION YOU'D BRING VISITORS!
THINGS WERE MOVING TOO SWIFTLY FOR DETAILS, MY FRIENDS.
...BUT THE ARRIVAL OF CAPTAIN SOLO AND COMPANY MEANS WE ARE CLOSE TO OUR GOAL!
I WASN'T CRAZY ABOUT ACCOMPANYING YOU INTO A CORPORATE AUTHORITY DATA CENTER, REKKON...

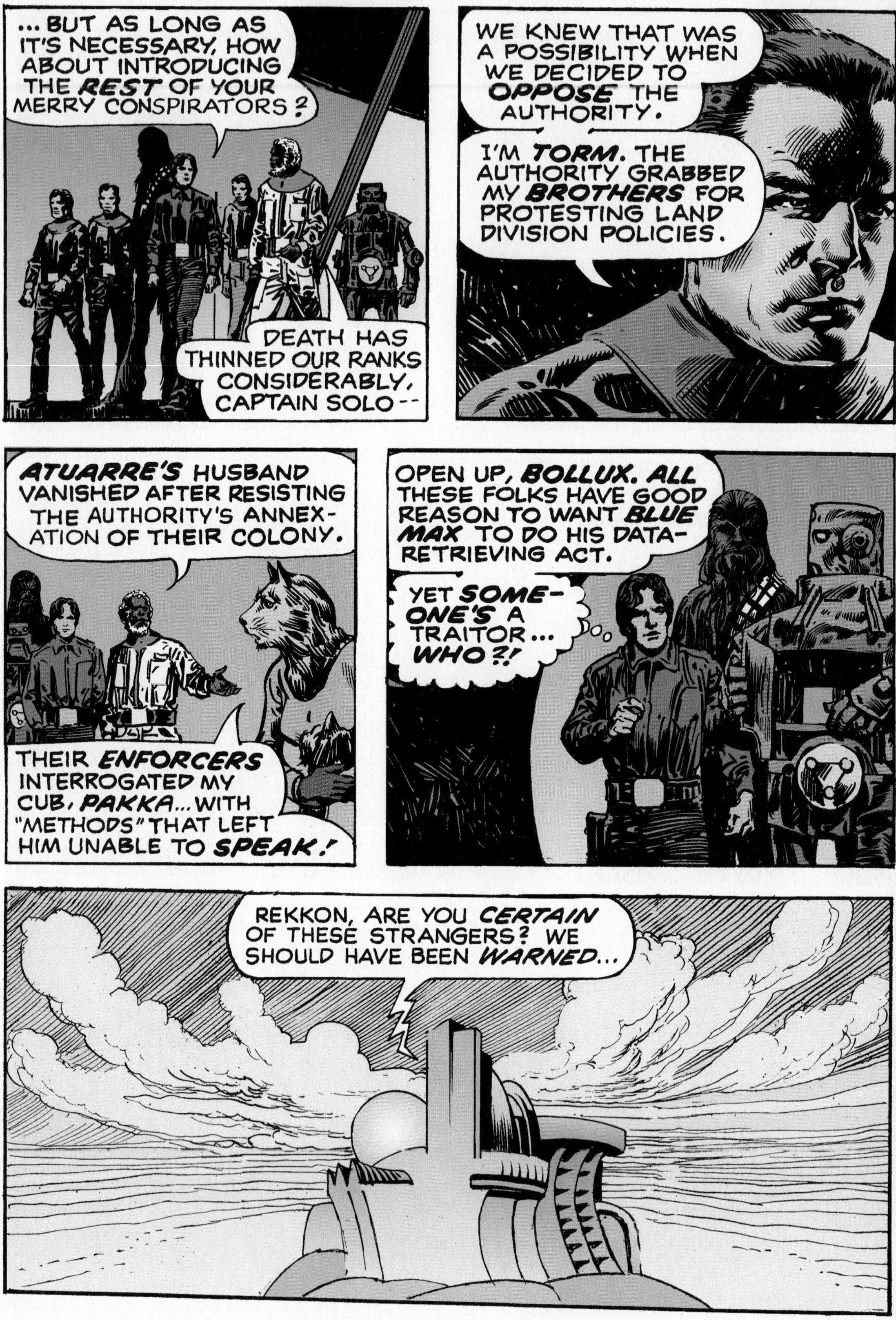
... BUT AS LONG AS IT'S NECESSARY, HOW ABOUT INTRODUCING THE REST OF YOUR MERRY CONSPIRATORS?
DEATH HAS THINNED OUR RANKS CONSIDERABLY, CAPTAIN SOLO--
WE KNEW THAT WAS A POSSIBILITY WHEN WE DECIDED TO OPPOSE THE AUTHORITY.
I'M TORM. THE AUTHORITY GRABBED MY BROTHERS FOR PROTESTING LAND DIVISION POLICIES.
ATUARRE'S HUSBAND VANISHED AFTER RESISTING THE AUTHORITY'S ANNEX-ATION OF THEIR COLONY.
THEIR ENFORCERS INTERROGATED MY CUB, PAKKA... WITH "METHODS" THAT LEFT HIM UNABLE TO SPEAK!
OPEN UP, BOLLUX. ALL THESE FOLKS HAVE GOOD REASON TO WANT BLUE MAX TO DO HIS DATA-RETRIEVING ACT.
YET SOME-ONE'S A TRAITOR... WHO?!
REKKON, ARE YOU CERTAIN OF THESE STRANGERS? WE SHOULD HAVE BEEN WARNED...

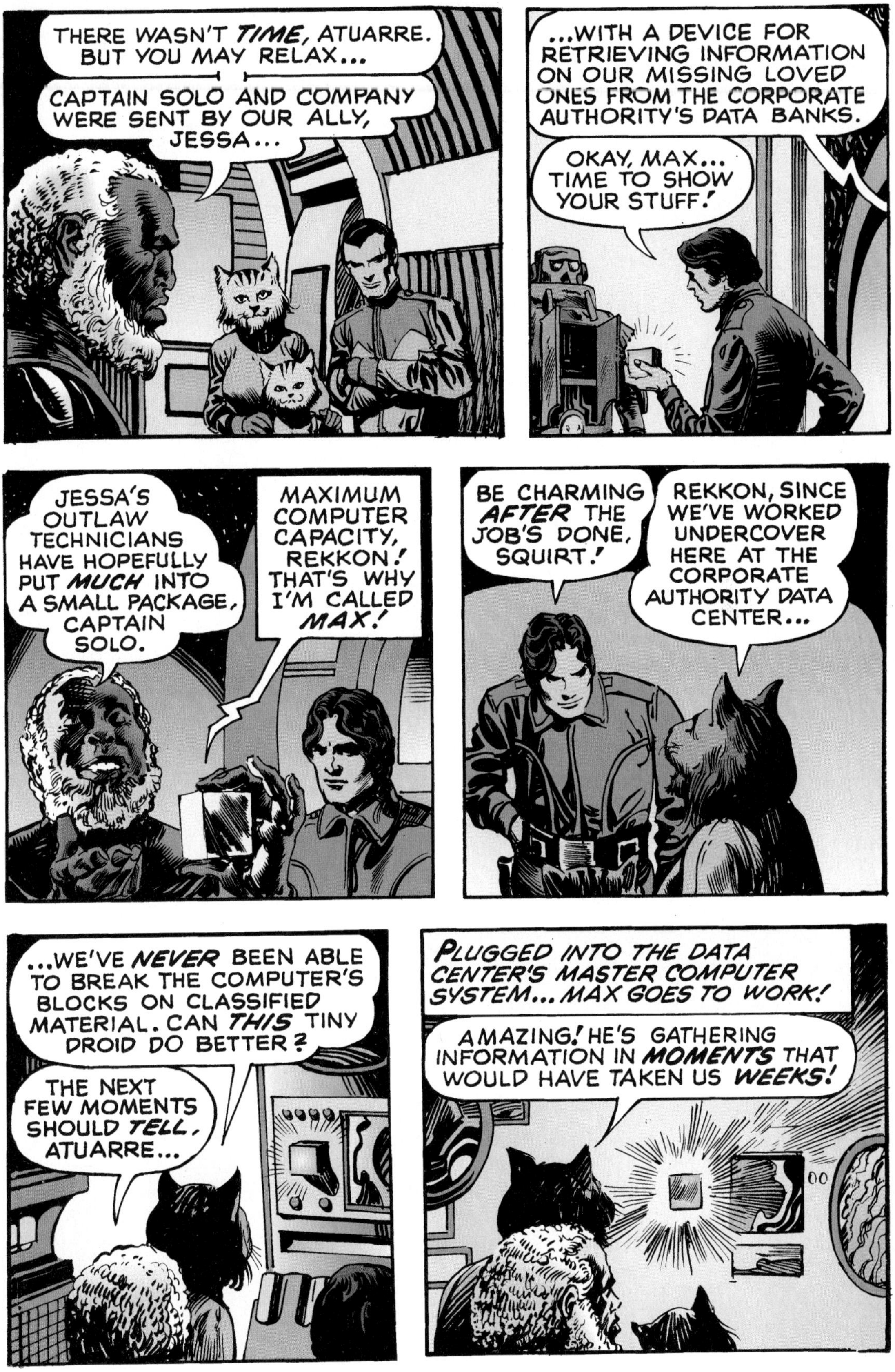
THERE WASN'T TIME, ATUARRE. BUT YOU MAY RELAX...
CAPTAIN SOLO AND COMPANY WERE SENT BY OUR ALLY, JESSA...
...WITH A DEVICE FOR RETRIEVING INFORMATION ON OUR MISSING LOVED ONES FROM THE CORPORATE AUTHORITY'S DATA BANKS.
OKAY, MAX... TIME TO SHOW YOUR STUFF!
JESSA'S OUTLAW TECHNICIANS HAVE HOPEFULLY PUT MUCH INTO A SMALL PACKAGE, CAPTAIN SOLO.
MAXIMUM COMPUTER CAPACITY, REKKON! THAT'S WHY I'M CALLED MAX!
BE CHARMING AFTER THE JOB'S DONE, SQUIRT!
REKKON, SINCE WE'VE WORKED UNDERCOVER HERE AT THE CORPORATE AUTHORITY DATA CENTER...
...WE'VE NEVER BEEN ABLE TO BREAK THE COMPUTER'S BLOCKS ON CLASSIFIED MATERIAL. CAN THIS TINY DROID DO BETTER?
THE NEXT FEW MOMENTS SHOULD TELL, ATUARRE...
PLUGGED INTO THE DATA CENTER'S MASTER COMPUTER SYSTEM... MAX GOES TO WORK!
AMAZING! HE'S GATHERING INFORMATION IN MOMENTS THAT WOULD HAVE TAKEN US WEEKS!

BUT AS EVERYONE ELSE WATCHES THE TINY DROID... HAN STUDIES REKKON'S COMPANIONS.

TORM... ATUARRE...HER CUB, PAKKA... ONE'S A TRAITOR!

YET ALL HAVE RELATIVES ABDUCTED BY THE CORPORATE AUTHORITY JUST LIKE JESSA! SO WHO--

ER...CAPTAIN SOLO? THERE MAY BE TROUBLE...

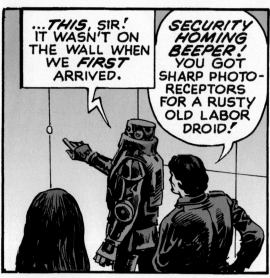

...THIS, SIR! IT WASN'T ON THE WALL WHEN WE FIRST ARRIVED.

SECURITY HOMING BEEPER! YOU GOT SHARP PHOTO-RECEPTORS FOR A RUSTY OLD LABOR DROID!

EVERYONE CAN STOP BEING FASCINATED WITH THE COMPUTER, REKKON!

UNPLUG MAX... IT'S CUT-AND-RUN TIME!

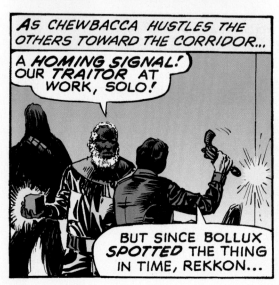

AS CHEWBACCA HUSTLES THE OTHERS TOWARD THE CORRIDOR...

A HOMING SIGNAL! OUR TRAITOR AT WORK, SOLO!

BUT SINCE BOLLUX SPOTTED THE THING IN TIME, REKKON...

"...WHOEVER PLANTED IT IS STUCK WITH FACING THE SECURITY GUARDS ZEROING IN ON ALL OF US!"

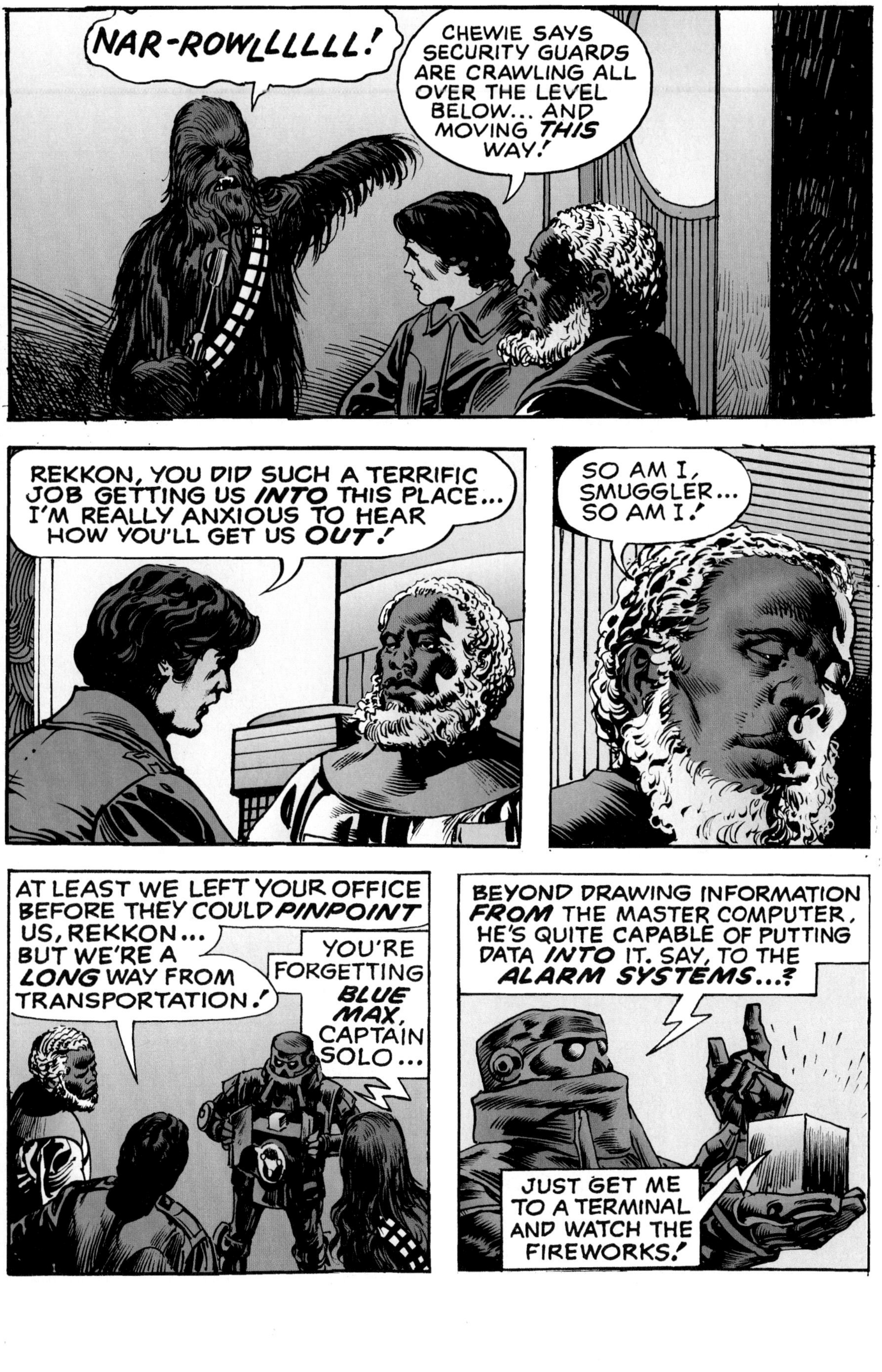
NAR-ROWLLLLLL!
CHEWIE SAYS SECURITY GUARDS ARE CRAWLING ALL OVER THE LEVEL BELOW... AND MOVING *THIS* WAY!
REKKON, YOU DID SUCH A TERRIFIC JOB GETTING US *INTO* THIS PLACE... I'M REALLY ANXIOUS TO HEAR HOW YOU'LL GET US *OUT*!
SO AM I, SMUGGLER... SO AM I!
AT LEAST WE LEFT YOUR OFFICE BEFORE THEY COULD *PINPOINT* US, REKKON... BUT WE'RE A *LONG* WAY FROM TRANSPORTATION!
YOU'RE FORGETTING *BLUE MAX*, CAPTAIN SOLO...
BEYOND DRAWING INFORMATION *FROM* THE MASTER COMPUTER, HE'S QUITE CAPABLE OF PUTTING DATA *INTO* IT. SAY, TO THE *ALARM SYSTEMS...?*
JUST GET ME TO A TERMINAL AND WATCH THE FIREWORKS!

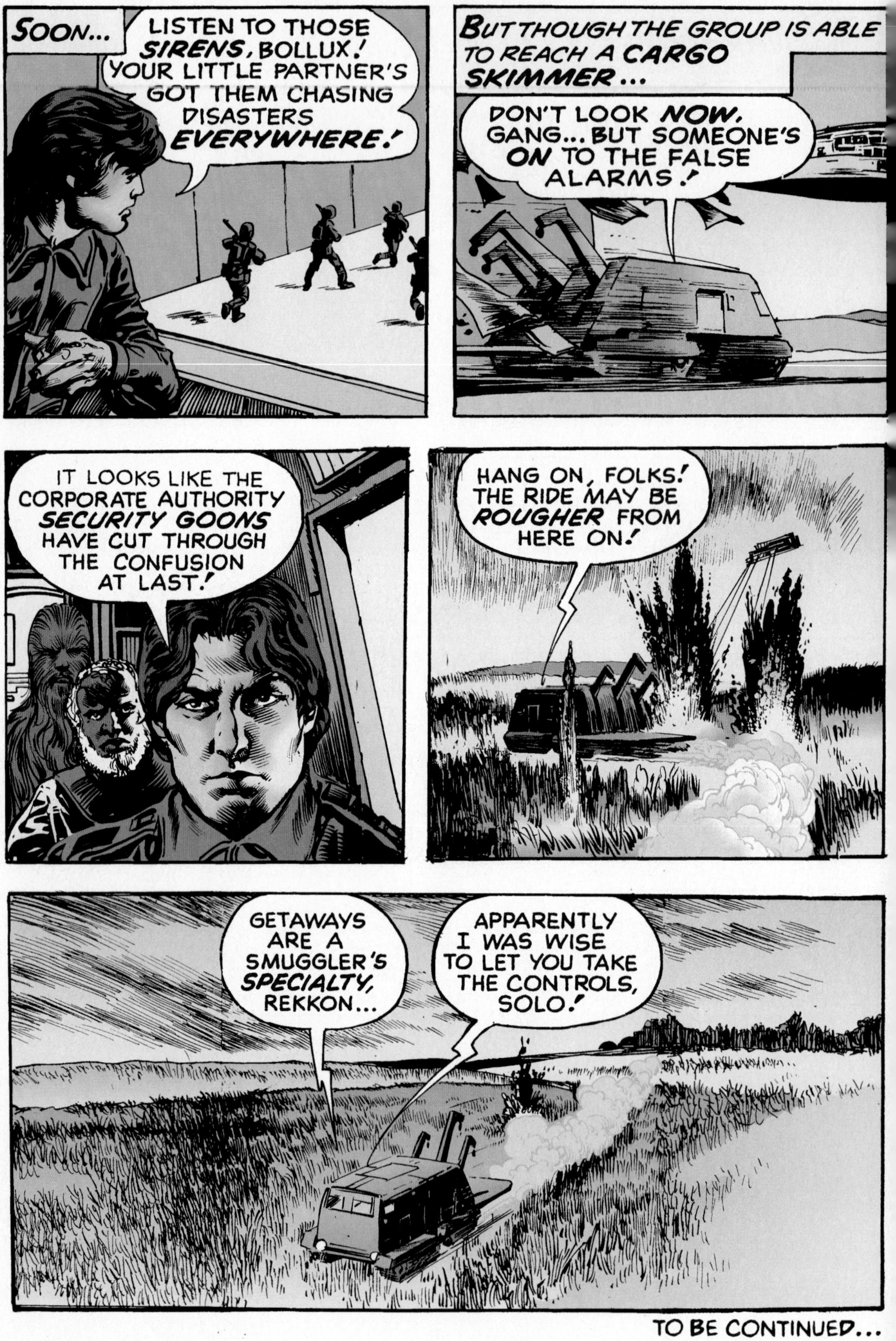
SOON...
LISTEN TO THOSE SIRENS, BOLLUX! YOUR LITTLE PARTNER'S GOT THEM CHASING DISASTERS EVERYWHERE!
BUT THOUGH THE GROUP IS ABLE TO REACH A CARGO SKIMMER...
DON'T LOOK NOW, GANG... BUT SOMEONE'S ON TO THE FALSE ALARMS!
IT LOOKS LIKE THE CORPORATE AUTHORITY SECURITY GOONS HAVE CUT THROUGH THE CONFUSION AT LAST!
HANG ON, FOLKS! THE RIDE MAY BE ROUGHER FROM HERE ON!
GETAWAYS ARE A SMUGGLER'S SPECIALTY, REKKON...
APPARENTLY I WAS WISE TO LET YOU TAKE THE CONTROLS, SOLO!
TO BE CONTINUED...

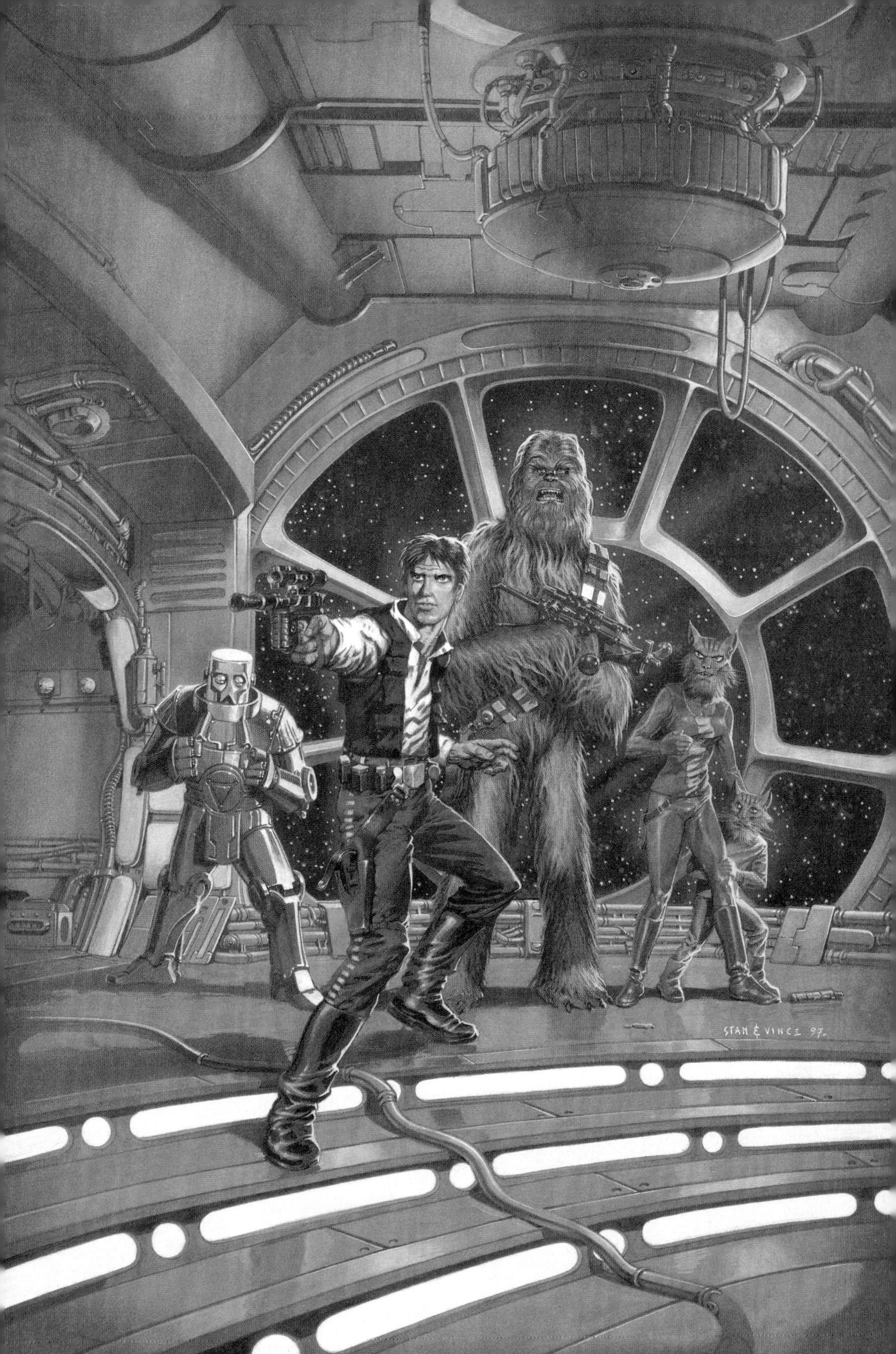
STAN & VINCE 97.

CLASSIC STAR WARS: HAN SOLO AT STARS' END #2
ORIGINALLY PUBLISHED FROM NOVEMBER 18 TO DECEMBER 28, 1980

BASED ON THE NOVEL BY BRIAN DALEY • SCRIPTER: ARCHIE GOODWIN • ARTIST & LETTERER: ALFREDO ALCALA
COLORIST: PERRY MCNAMEE • COLOR SEPARATIONS: BRIAN NEUBAUER & MICHELLE MADSEN • ASSISTANT EDITOR: IAN STUDE

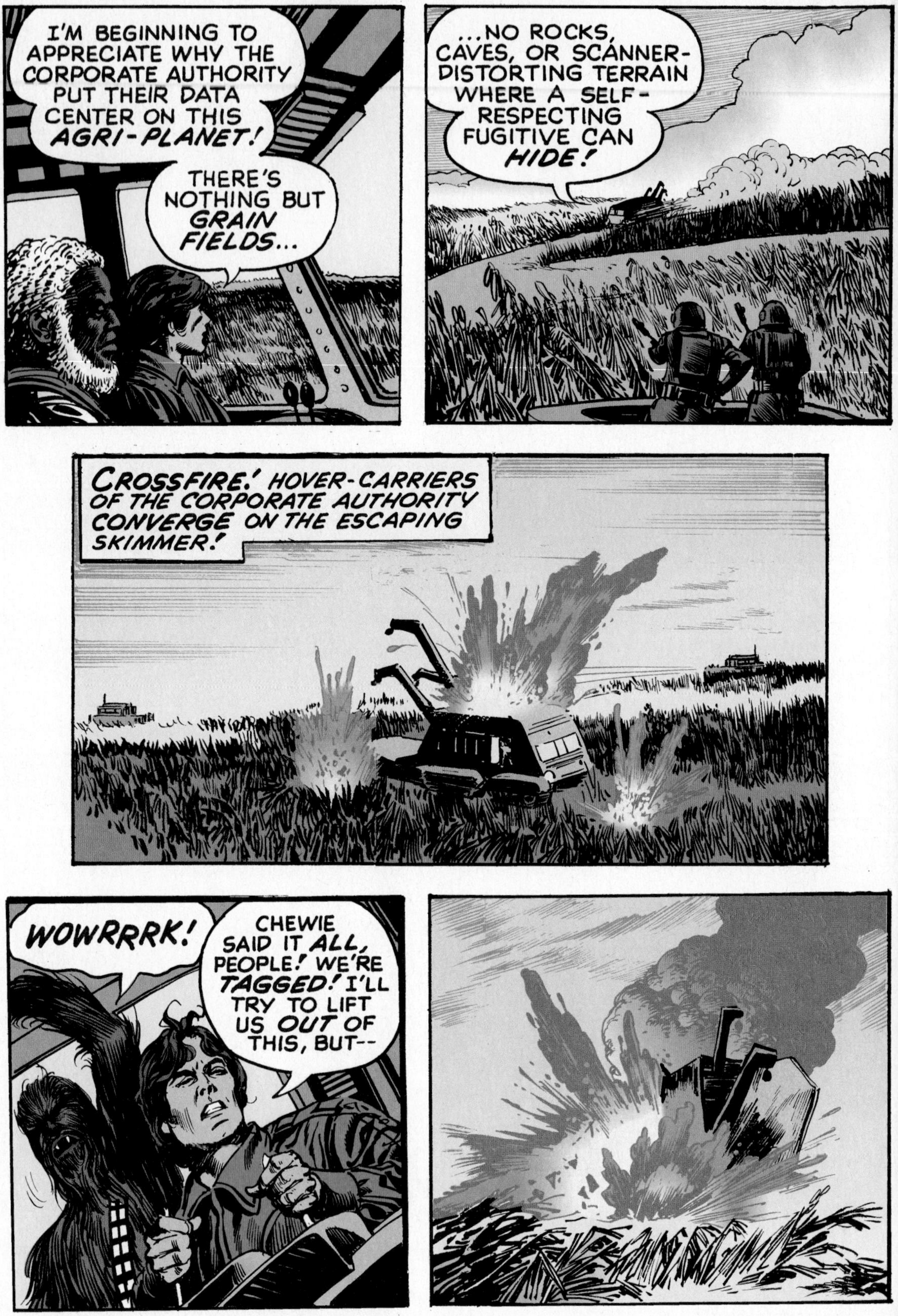

I'M BEGINNING TO APPRECIATE WHY THE CORPORATE AUTHORITY PUT THEIR DATA CENTER ON THIS AGRI-PLANET!
THERE'S NOTHING BUT GRAIN FIELDS...
...NO ROCKS, CAVES, OR SCANNER-DISTORTING TERRAIN WHERE A SELF-RESPECTING FUGITIVE CAN HIDE!
CROSSFIRE! HOVER-CARRIERS OF THE CORPORATE AUTHORITY CONVERGE ON THE ESCAPING SKIMMER!
WOWRRRK!
CHEWIE SAID IT ALL, PEOPLE! WE'RE TAGGED! I'LL TRY TO LIFT US OUT OF THIS, BUT--

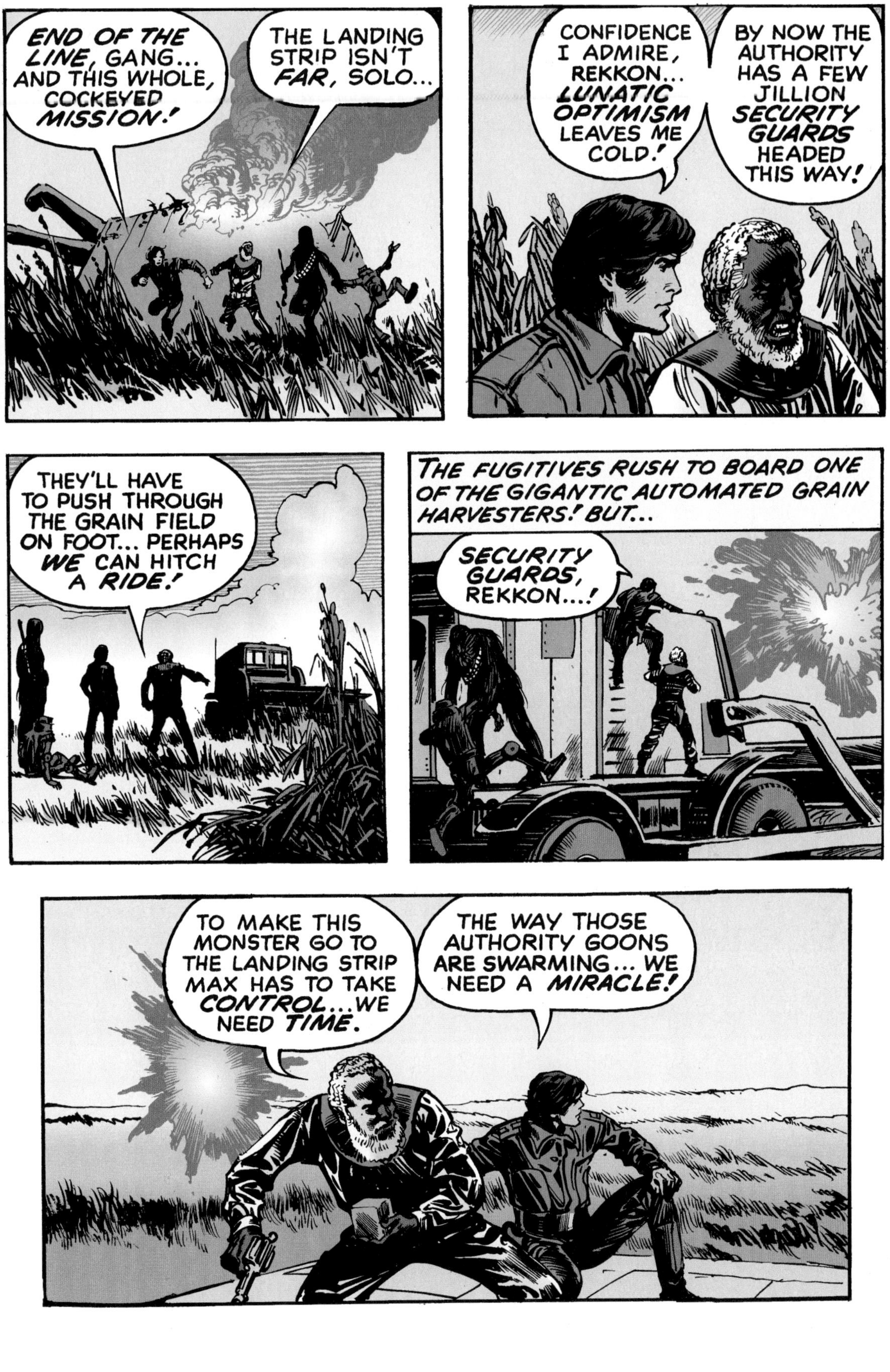
END OF THE LINE, GANG... AND THIS WHOLE, COCKEYED MISSION!
THE LANDING STRIP ISN'T FAR, SOLO...
CONFIDENCE I ADMIRE, REKKON... LUNATIC OPTIMISM LEAVES ME COLD!
BY NOW THE AUTHORITY HAS A FEW JILLION SECURITY GUARDS HEADED THIS WAY!
THEY'LL HAVE TO PUSH THROUGH THE GRAIN FIELD ON FOOT... PERHAPS WE CAN HITCH A RIDE!
THE FUGITIVES RUSH TO BOARD ONE OF THE GIGANTIC AUTOMATED GRAIN HARVESTERS! BUT...
SECURITY GUARDS, REKKON...!
TO MAKE THIS MONSTER GO TO THE LANDING STRIP MAX HAS TO TAKE CONTROL...WE NEED TIME.
THE WAY THOSE AUTHORITY GOONS ARE SWARMING... WE NEED A MIRACLE!

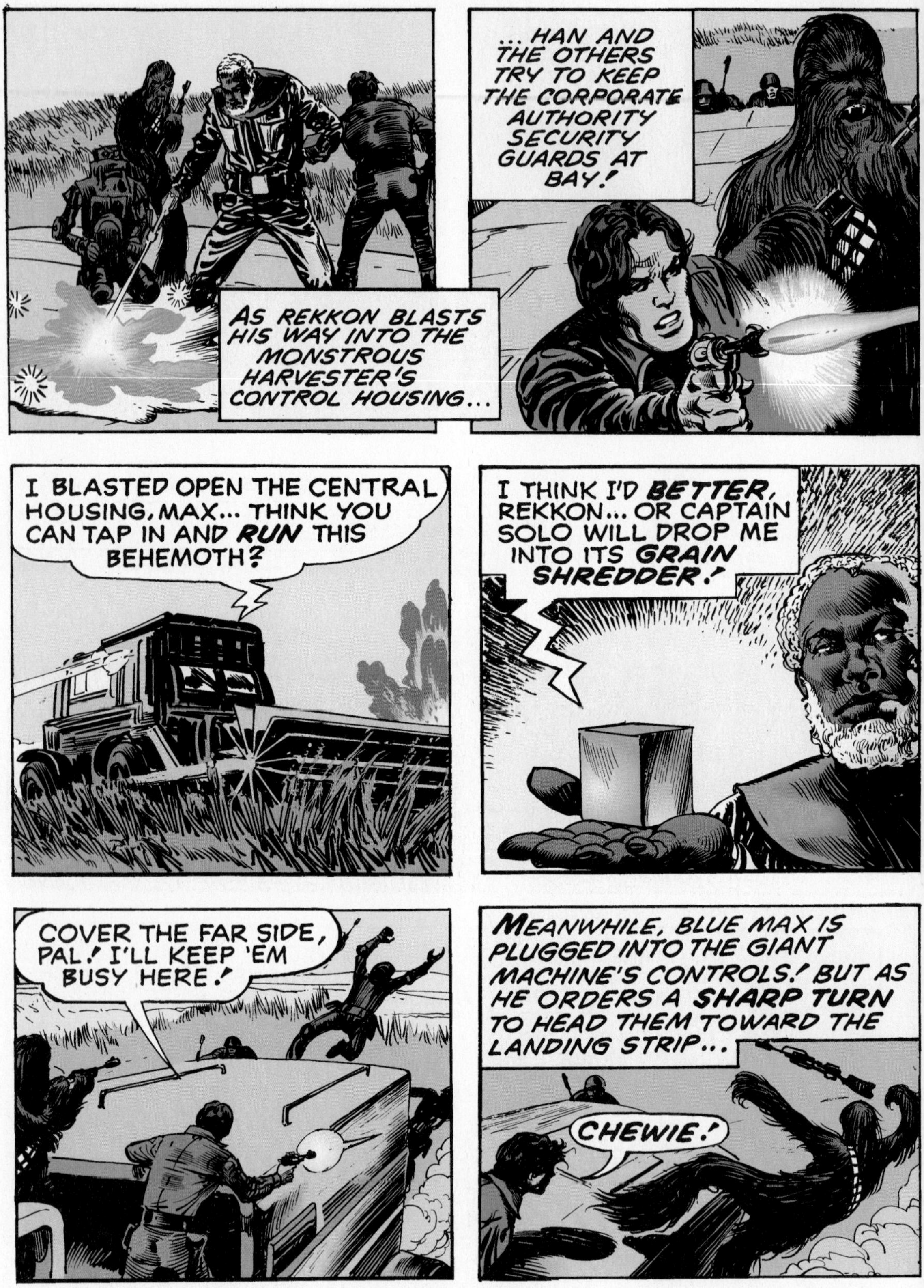
AS REKKON BLASTS HIS WAY INTO THE MONSTROUS HARVESTER'S CONTROL HOUSING...
...HAN AND THE OTHERS TRY TO KEEP THE CORPORATE AUTHORITY SECURITY GUARDS AT BAY!
I BLASTED OPEN THE CENTRAL HOUSING, MAX... THINK YOU CAN TAP IN AND RUN THIS BEHEMOTH?
I THINK I'D BETTER, REKKON... OR CAPTAIN SOLO WILL DROP ME INTO ITS GRAIN SHREDDER!
COVER THE FAR SIDE, PAL! I'LL KEEP 'EM BUSY HERE!
MEANWHILE, BLUE MAX IS PLUGGED INTO THE GIANT MACHINE'S CONTROLS! BUT AS HE ORDERS A SHARP TURN TO HEAD THEM TOWARD THE LANDING STRIP...
CHEWIE!

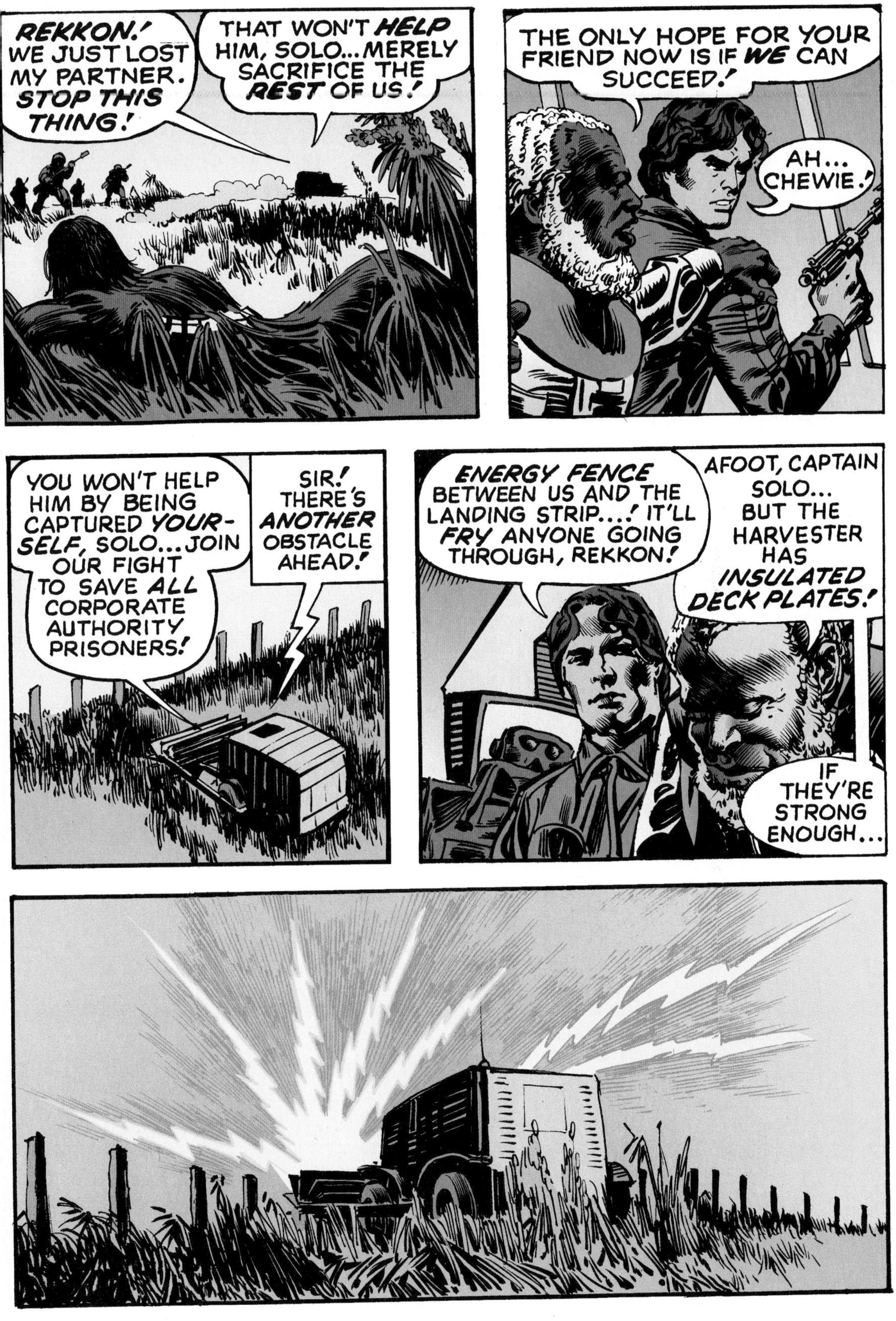
REKKON! WE JUST LOST MY PARTNER. STOP THIS THING!
THAT WON'T HELP HIM, SOLO...MERELY SACRIFICE THE REST OF US!
THE ONLY HOPE FOR YOUR FRIEND NOW IS IF WE CAN SUCCEED!
AH... CHEWIE!
YOU WON'T HELP HIM BY BEING CAPTURED YOURSELF, SOLO...JOIN OUR FIGHT TO SAVE ALL CORPORATE AUTHORITY PRISONERS!
SIR! THERE'S ANOTHER OBSTACLE AHEAD!
ENERGY FENCE BETWEEN US AND THE LANDING STRIP...! IT'LL FRY ANYONE GOING THROUGH, REKKON!
AFOOT, CAPTAIN SOLO... BUT THE HARVESTER HAS INSULATED DECK PLATES!
IF THEY'RE STRONG ENOUGH...

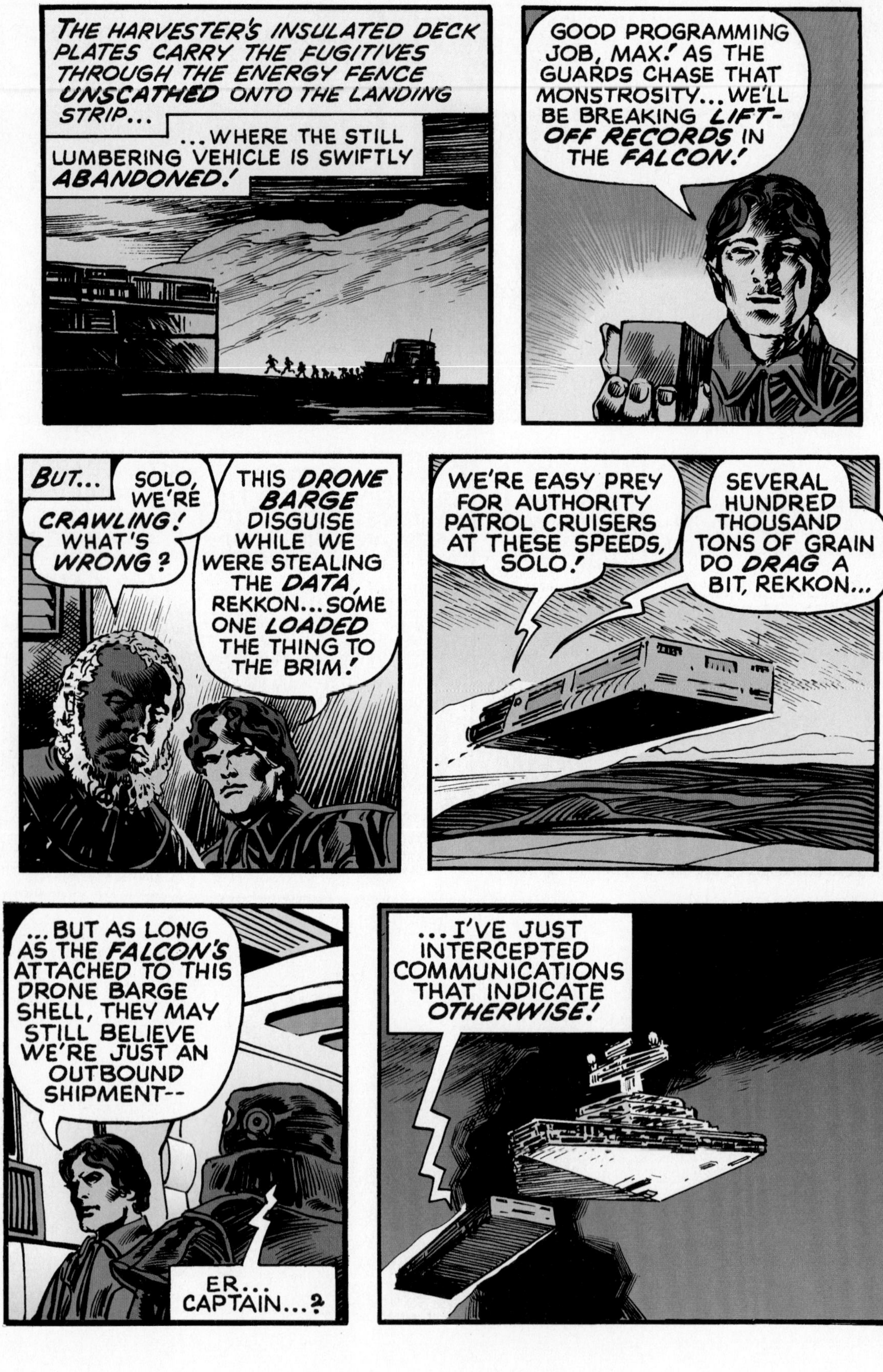
THE HARVESTER'S INSULATED DECK PLATES CARRY THE FUGITIVES THROUGH THE ENERGY FENCE UNSCATHED ONTO THE LANDING STRIP...
...WHERE THE STILL LUMBERING VEHICLE IS SWIFTLY ABANDONED!
GOOD PROGRAMMING JOB, MAX! AS THE GUARDS CHASE THAT MONSTROSITY...WE'LL BE BREAKING LIFT-OFF RECORDS IN THE FALCON!
BUT...
SOLO, WE'RE CRAWLING! WHAT'S WRONG?
THIS DRONE BARGE DISGUISE WHILE WE WERE STEALING THE DATA, REKKON...SOME ONE LOADED THE THING TO THE BRIM!
WE'RE EASY PREY FOR AUTHORITY PATROL CRUISERS AT THESE SPEEDS, SOLO!
SEVERAL HUNDRED THOUSAND TONS OF GRAIN DO DRAG A BIT, REKKON...
...BUT AS LONG AS THE FALCON'S ATTACHED TO THIS DRONE BARGE SHELL, THEY MAY STILL BELIEVE WE'RE JUST AN OUTBOUND SHIPMENT--
ER... CAPTAIN...?
...I'VE JUST INTERCEPTED COMMUNICATIONS THAT INDICATE OTHERWISE!

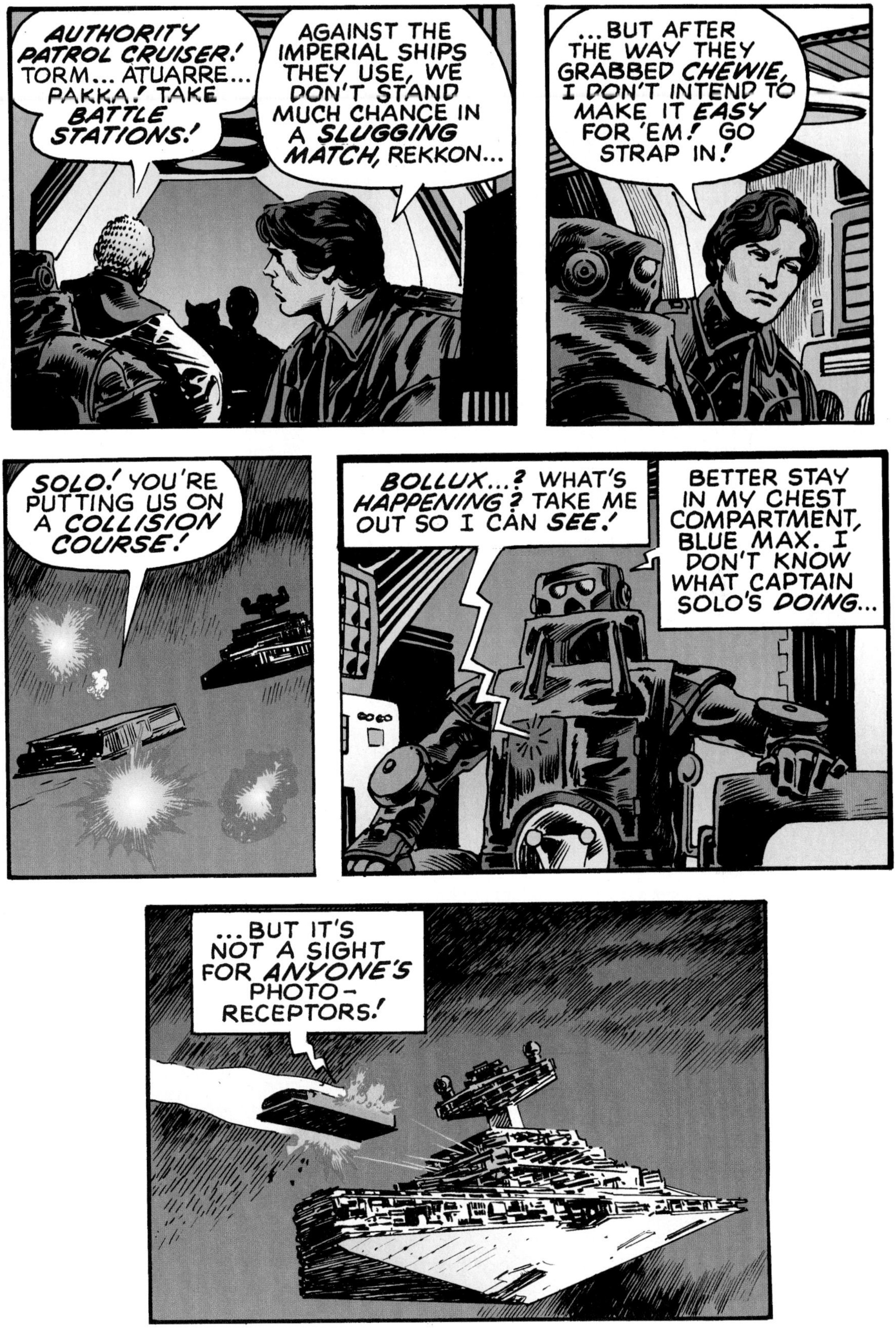
AUTHORITY PATROL CRUISER! TORM... ATUARRE... PAKKA! TAKE BATTLE STATIONS!
AGAINST THE IMPERIAL SHIPS THEY USE, WE DON'T STAND MUCH CHANCE IN A SLUGGING MATCH, REKKON...
...BUT AFTER THE WAY THEY GRABBED CHEWIE, I DON'T INTEND TO MAKE IT EASY FOR 'EM! GO STRAP IN!
SOLO! YOU'RE PUTTING US ON A COLLISION COURSE!
BOLLUX...? WHAT'S HAPPENING? TAKE ME OUT SO I CAN SEE!
BETTER STAY IN MY CHEST COMPARTMENT, BLUE MAX. I DON'T KNOW WHAT CAPTAIN SOLO'S DOING...
...BUT IT'S NOT A SIGHT FOR ANYONE'S PHOTO-RECEPTORS!

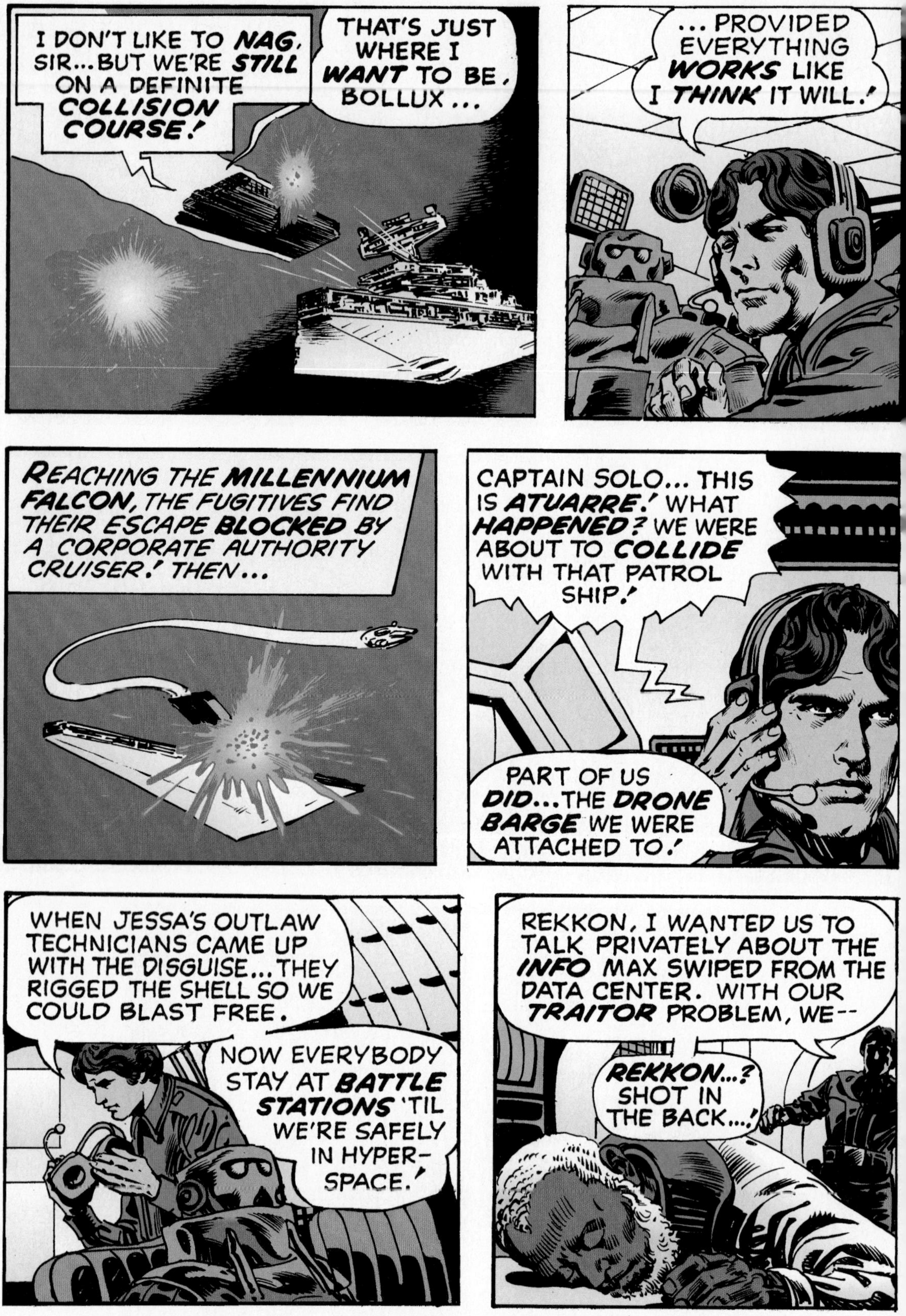
I DON'T LIKE TO NAG, SIR...BUT WE'RE STILL ON A DEFINITE COLLISION COURSE!
THAT'S JUST WHERE I WANT TO BE, BOLLUX...
...PROVIDED EVERYTHING WORKS LIKE I THINK IT WILL!
REACHING THE MILLENNIUM FALCON, THE FUGITIVES FIND THEIR ESCAPE BLOCKED BY A CORPORATE AUTHORITY CRUISER! THEN...
CAPTAIN SOLO... THIS IS ATUARRE! WHAT HAPPENED? WE WERE ABOUT TO COLLIDE WITH THAT PATROL SHIP!
PART OF US DID...THE DRONE BARGE WE WERE ATTACHED TO!
WHEN JESSA'S OUTLAW TECHNICIANS CAME UP WITH THE DISGUISE...THEY RIGGED THE SHELL SO WE COULD BLAST FREE.
NOW EVERYBODY STAY AT BATTLE STATIONS 'TIL WE'RE SAFELY IN HYPER-SPACE!
REKKON, I WANTED US TO TALK PRIVATELY ABOUT THE INFO MAX SWIPED FROM THE DATA CENTER. WITH OUR TRAITOR PROBLEM, WE--
REKKON...? SHOT IN THE BACK...!

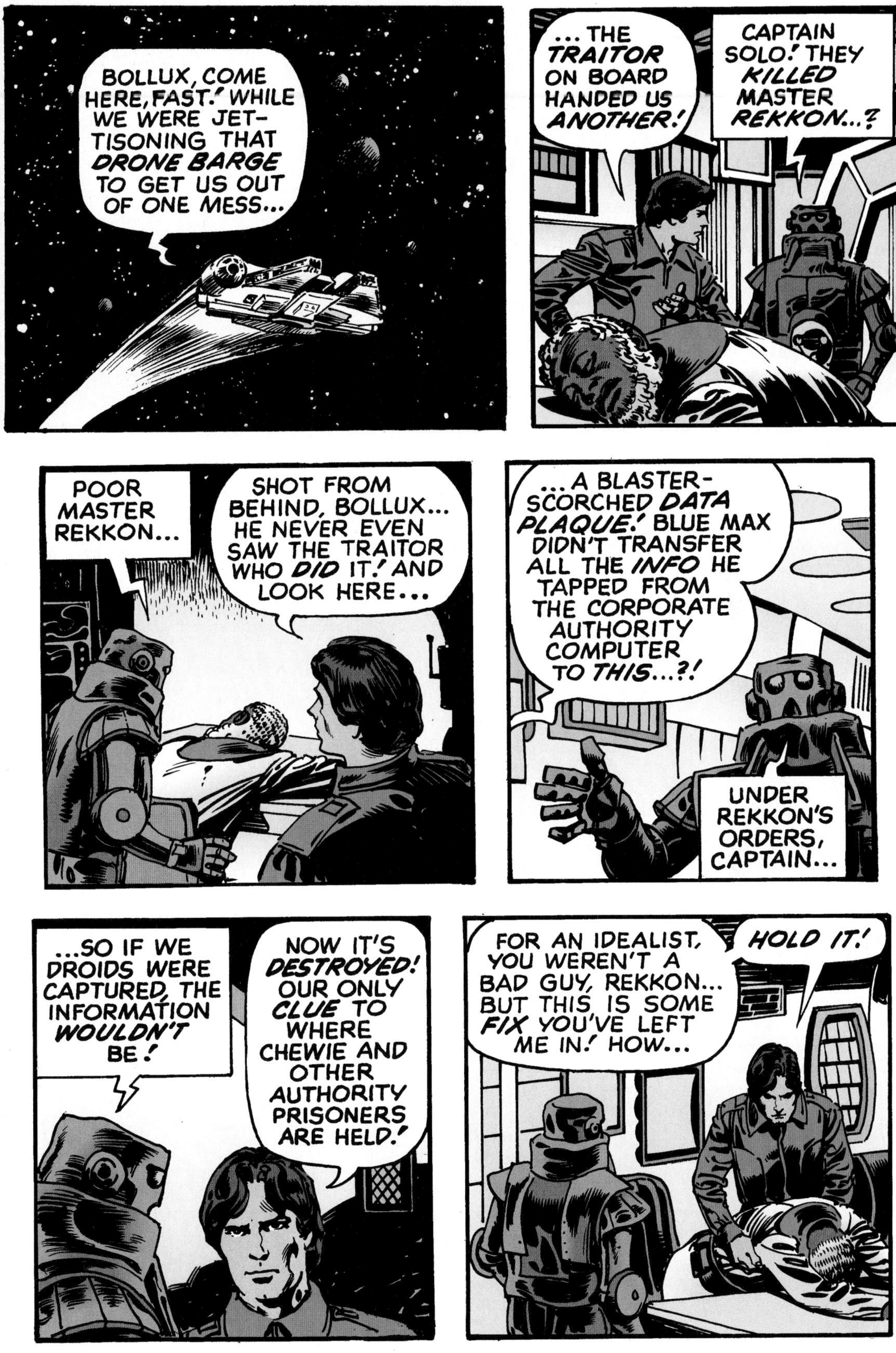
BOLLUX, COME HERE, FAST! WHILE WE WERE JETTISONING THAT DRONE BARGE TO GET US OUT OF ONE MESS...
...THE TRAITOR ON BOARD HANDED US ANOTHER!
CAPTAIN SOLO! THEY KILLED MASTER REKKON...?
POOR MASTER REKKON...
SHOT FROM BEHIND, BOLLUX... HE NEVER EVEN SAW THE TRAITOR WHO DID IT! AND LOOK HERE...
...A BLASTER-SCORCHED DATA PLAQUE! BLUE MAX DIDN'T TRANSFER ALL THE INFO HE TAPPED FROM THE CORPORATE AUTHORITY COMPUTER TO THIS...?!
UNDER REKKON'S ORDERS, CAPTAIN...
...SO IF WE DROIDS WERE CAPTURED, THE INFORMATION WOULDN'T BE!
NOW IT'S DESTROYED! OUR ONLY CLUE TO WHERE CHEWIE AND OTHER AUTHORITY PRISONERS ARE HELD!
FOR AN IDEALIST, YOU WEREN'T A BAD GUY, REKKON... BUT THIS IS SOME FIX YOU'VE LEFT ME IN! HOW...
HOLD IT!

HIS BODY COVERED *SCRATCHES* HE MADE ON THE GAMEBOARD, BOLLUX...LOOKS LIKE *COMPUTER CODE!*

BLUE MAX CAN *TRANSLATE* IT, CAPTAIN SOLO!

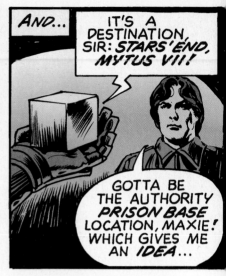

AND...

IT'S A DESTINATION, SIR: *STARS' END, MYTUS VII!*

GOTTA BE THE AUTHORITY *PRISON BASE* LOCATION, MAXIE! WHICH GIVES ME AN *IDEA...*

As THE *MILLENNIUM FALCON* LEAPS INTO HYPERSPACE, HAN SUMMONS HIS PASSENGERS FROM THEIR BATTLE STATIONS... AND *DISARMS* THEM!

WHAT DOES THIS *MEAN,* SOLO-CAPTAIN?!

THAT EITHER YOU, TORM, OR EVEN LITTLE PAKKA KILLED *REKKON,* ATUARRE! UNTIL I CAN PROVE *WHO...*

...I WANT YOU ALL HARMLESS AND ABLE TO WORK WITH *INFO* REKKON LEFT US!

MEETING *SEPARATELY* WITH EVERYONE, HAN DISTRIBUTES PORTABLE COMPUTER READOUTS...

...THEN GATHERS EVERYONE IN THE *MILLENNIUM FALCON'S* MAIN CABIN.

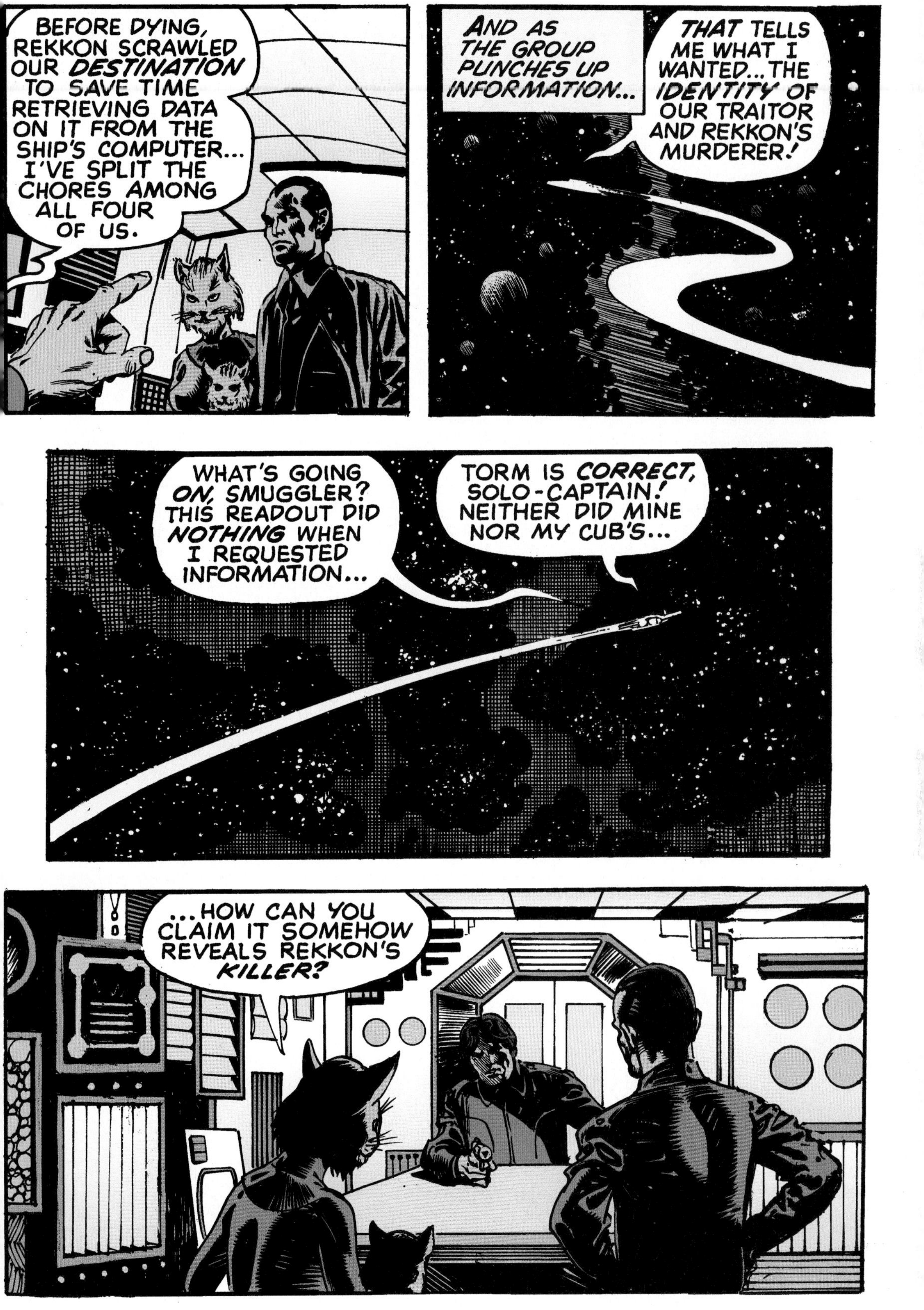
BEFORE DYING, REKKON SCRAWLED OUR DESTINATION TO SAVE TIME RETRIEVING DATA ON IT FROM THE SHIP'S COMPUTER... I'VE SPLIT THE CHORES AMONG ALL FOUR OF US.
AND AS THE GROUP PUNCHES UP INFORMATION...
THAT TELLS ME WHAT I WANTED... THE IDENTITY OF OUR TRAITOR AND REKKON'S MURDERER!
WHAT'S GOING ON, SMUGGLER? THIS READOUT DID NOTHING WHEN I REQUESTED INFORMATION...
TORM IS CORRECT, SOLO-CAPTAIN! NEITHER DID MINE NOR MY CUB'S...
...HOW CAN YOU CLAIM IT SOMEHOW REVEALS REKKON'S KILLER?

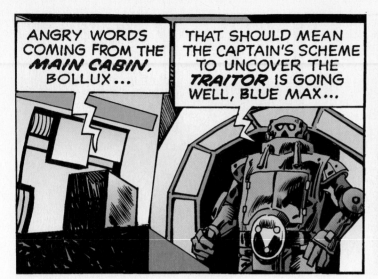

ANGRY WORDS COMING FROM THE *MAIN CABIN*, BOLLUX...

THAT SHOULD MEAN THE CAPTAIN'S SCHEME TO UNCOVER THE *TRAITOR* IS GOING WELL, BLUE MAX...

...OR ELSE TERRIBLY *BADLY*.

SOLO-CAPTAIN, WE DEMAND AN *EXPLANATION!* THESE COMPUTER PRINTOUTS DO NOT WORK... THEY *CAN'T* TELL YOU REKKON'S MURDERER!

WRONG, BEFORE DYING, REKKON SCRATCHED ON THIS GAMEBOARD THE INFORMATION HE WAS *KILLED* TO CONCEAL THE *LOCATION* OF THE CORPORATE AUTHORITY'S *PRISON BASE*.

AND YOU ASKED EACH OF US TO PUNCH UP DATA ON THAT LOCATION... *STARS' END MYTUS VIII!* BUT...

YOUR READOUTS DON'T WORK BECAUSE THEY'RE ONLY LINKED TO *MINE*... NOT THE SHIP'S COMPUTER.

MY READOUT REVEALED AN INTERESTING THING. I GAVE EACH OF YOU THE *WRONG DESIGNATION* FOR THE PLANET...

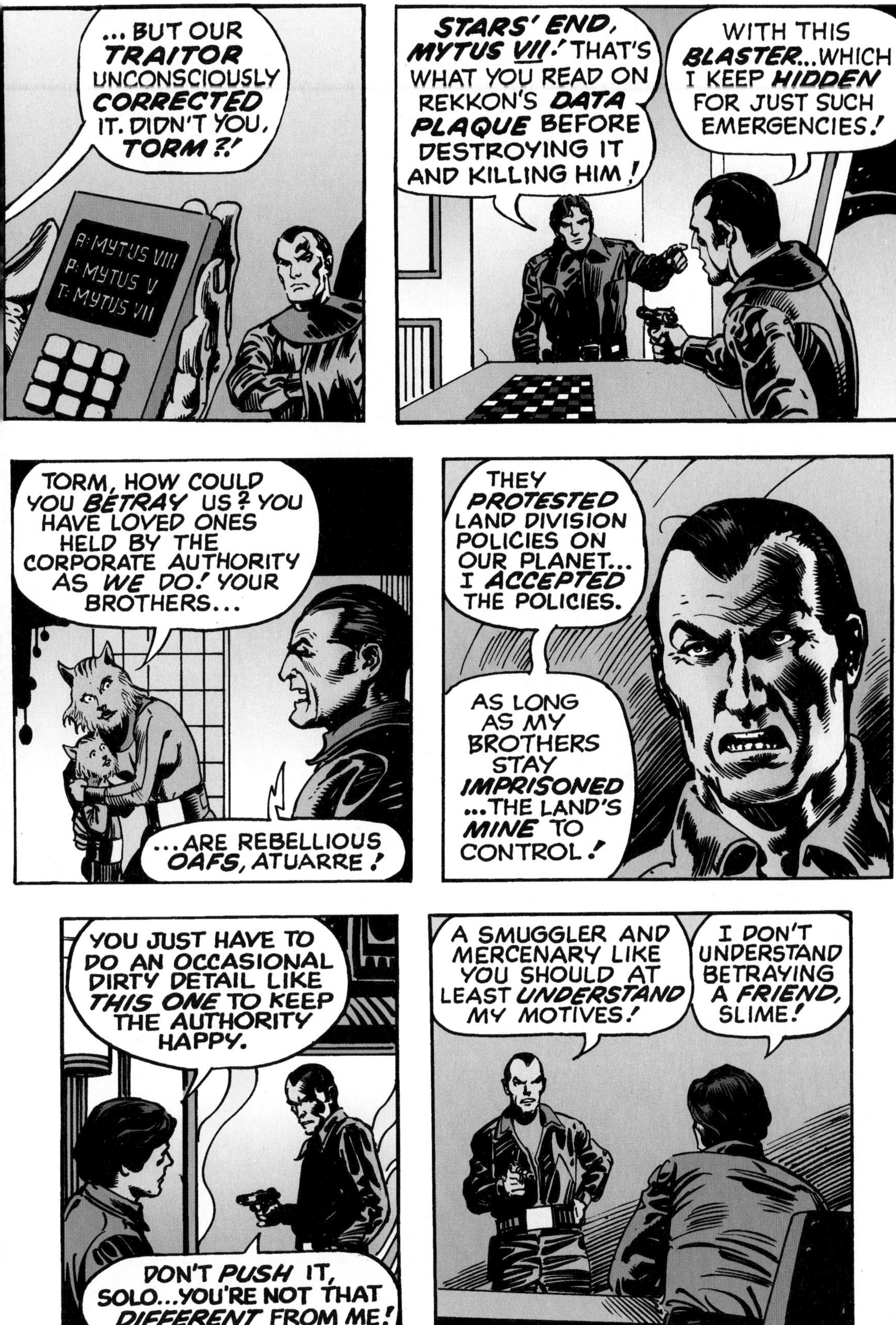
...BUT OUR TRAITOR UNCONSCIOUSLY CORRECTED IT. DIDN'T YOU, TORM?!
A: MYTUS VIII
P: MYTUS V
T: MYTUS VII
STARS' END, MYTUS VII! THAT'S WHAT YOU READ ON REKKON'S DATA PLAQUE BEFORE DESTROYING IT AND KILLING HIM!
WITH THIS BLASTER...WHICH I KEEP HIDDEN FOR JUST SUCH EMERGENCIES!
TORM, HOW COULD YOU BETRAY US? YOU HAVE LOVED ONES HELD BY THE CORPORATE AUTHORITY AS WE DO! YOUR BROTHERS...
...ARE REBELLIOUS OAFS, ATUARRE!
THEY PROTESTED LAND DIVISION POLICIES ON OUR PLANET... I ACCEPTED THE POLICIES.
AS LONG AS MY BROTHERS STAY IMPRISONED ...THE LAND'S MINE TO CONTROL!
YOU JUST HAVE TO DO AN OCCASIONAL DIRTY DETAIL LIKE THIS ONE TO KEEP THE AUTHORITY HAPPY.
DON'T PUSH IT, SOLO...YOU'RE NOT THAT DIFFERENT FROM ME!
A SMUGGLER AND MERCENARY LIKE YOU SHOULD AT LEAST UNDERSTAND MY MOTIVES!
I DON'T UNDERSTAND BETRAYING A FRIEND, SLIME!

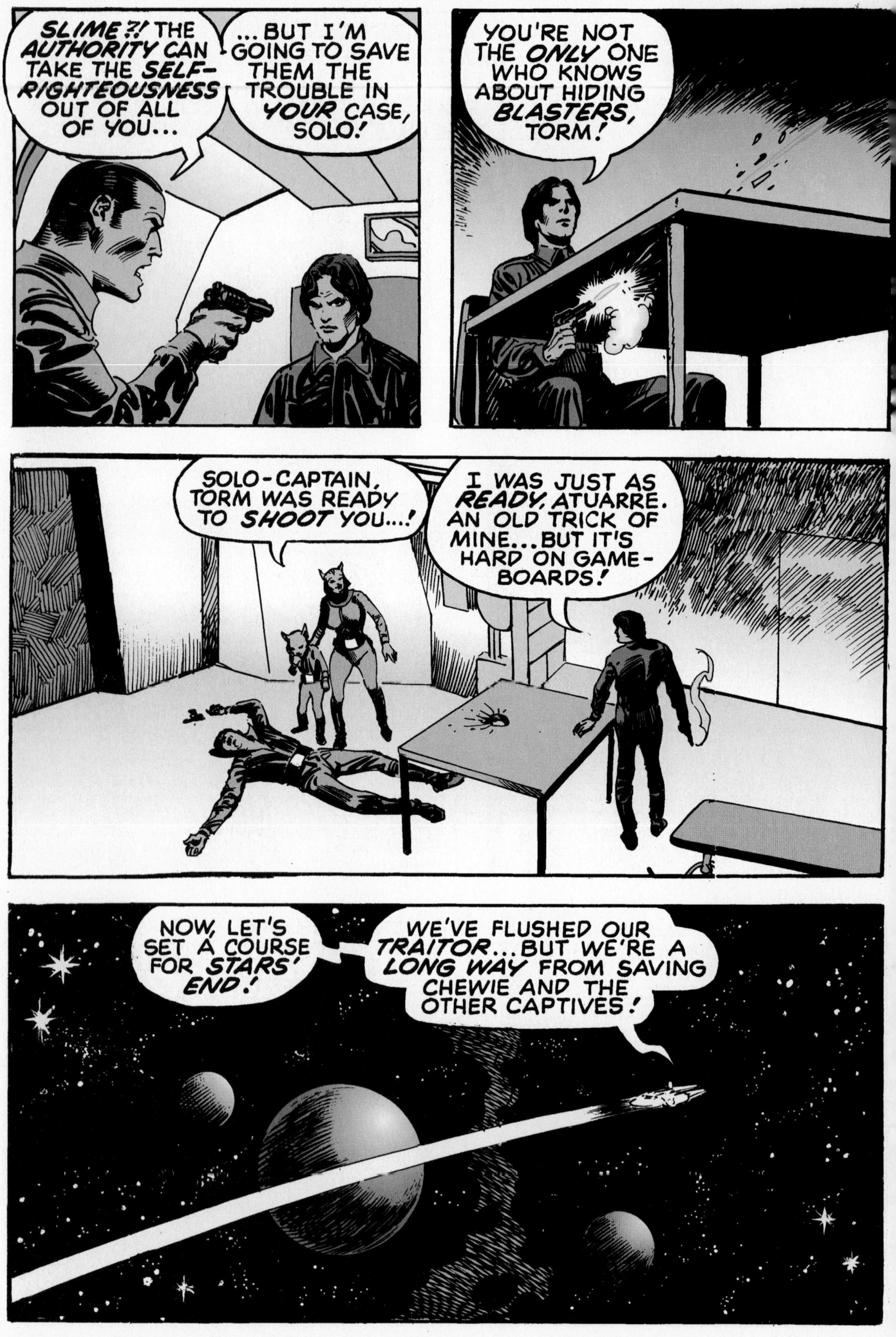
SLIME?! THE AUTHORITY CAN TAKE THE SELF-RIGHTEOUSNESS OUT OF ALL OF YOU...
...BUT I'M GOING TO SAVE THEM THE TROUBLE IN YOUR CASE, SOLO!
YOU'RE NOT THE ONLY ONE WHO KNOWS ABOUT HIDING BLASTERS, TORM!
SOLO-CAPTAIN, TORM WAS READY TO SHOOT YOU...!
I WAS JUST AS READY, ATUARRE. AN OLD TRICK OF MINE...BUT IT'S HARD ON GAME-BOARDS!
NOW, LET'S SET A COURSE FOR STARS' END!
WE'VE FLUSHED OUR TRAITOR...BUT WE'RE A LONG WAY FROM SAVING CHEWIE AND THE OTHER CAPTIVES!

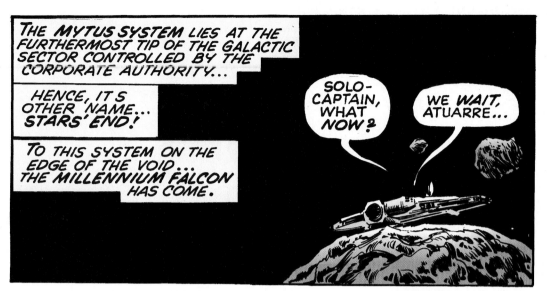

THE *MYTUS SYSTEM* LIES AT THE FURTHERMOST TIP OF THE GALACTIC SECTOR CONTROLLED BY THE CORPORATE AUTHORITY...

HENCE, ITS OTHER NAME... *STARS' END!*

TO THIS SYSTEM ON THE EDGE OF THE VOID... THE *MILLENNIUM FALCON* HAS COME.

SOLO-CAPTAIN, WHAT NOW?

WE *WAIT*, ATUARRE...

...AND MONITOR COMMUNICATIONS FOR *MYTUS VII*. WE NEED A BREAK-- OR A *MIRACLE*-- TO GET OUR FRIENDS OUT OF THE AUTHORITY'S PRISON THERE!

HIDDEN BY THE ASTEROID, WE ARE SAFE FROM SCANNERS ...YET YOU APPEAR UNEASY, SOLO-CAPTAIN. IS IT THE *WAITING?*

YEAH. IT'S NOT MY *SPECIALTY*, ATUARRE...

...ESPECIALLY WHEN I'M ALSO *WONDERING* WHAT THE CORPORATE AUTHORITY IS DOING TO CHEWIE AND ALL THE OTHER PRISONERS OVER THERE ON MYTUS *VII!*

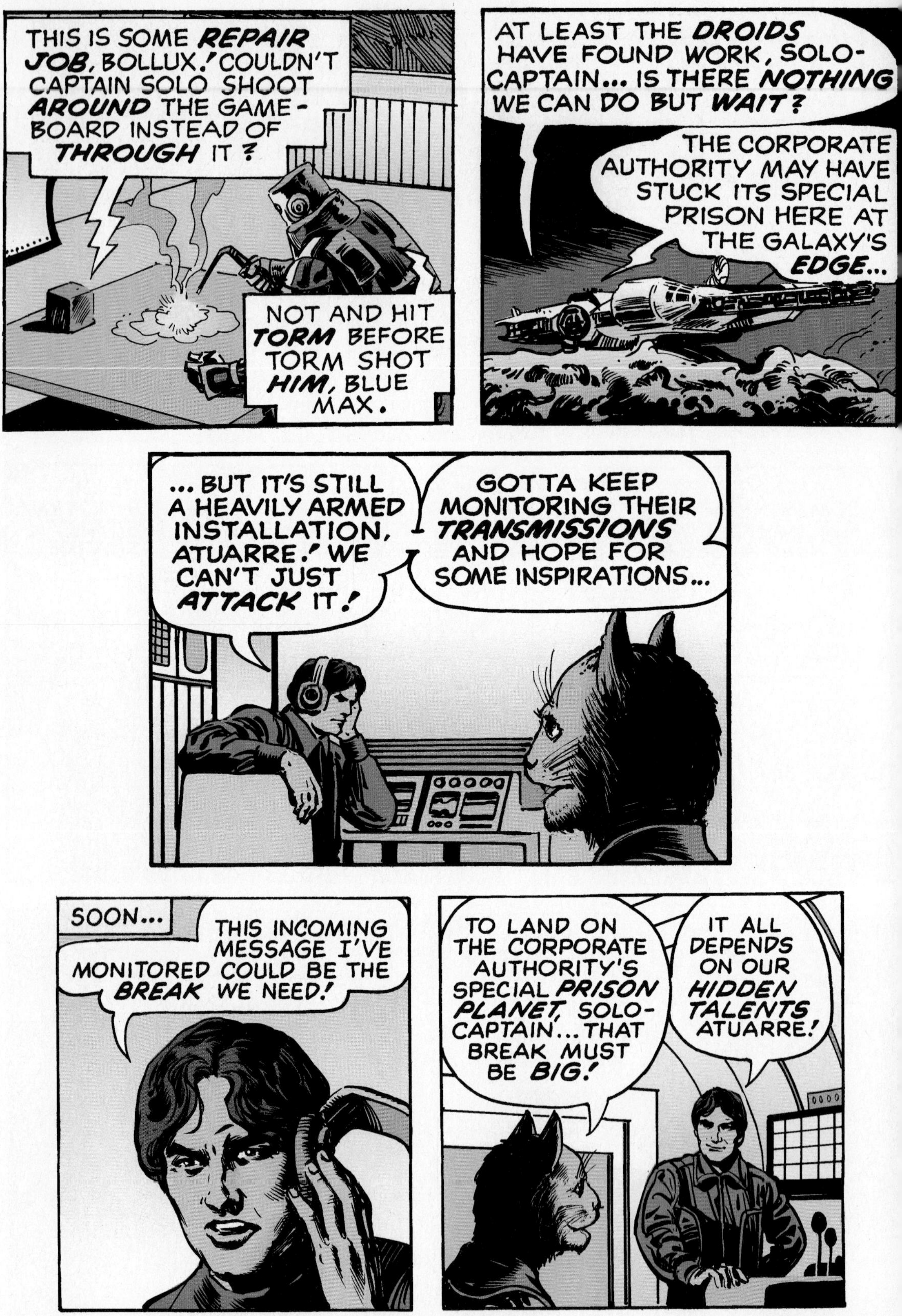
THIS IS SOME REPAIR JOB, BOLLUX! COULDN'T CAPTAIN SOLO SHOOT AROUND THE GAME-BOARD INSTEAD OF THROUGH IT?
NOT AND HIT TORM BEFORE TORM SHOT HIM, BLUE MAX.
AT LEAST THE DROIDS HAVE FOUND WORK, SOLO-CAPTAIN... IS THERE NOTHING WE CAN DO BUT WAIT?
THE CORPORATE AUTHORITY MAY HAVE STUCK ITS SPECIAL PRISON HERE AT THE GALAXY'S EDGE...
... BUT IT'S STILL A HEAVILY ARMED INSTALLATION, ATUARRE! WE CAN'T JUST ATTACK IT!
GOTTA KEEP MONITORING THEIR TRANSMISSIONS AND HOPE FOR SOME INSPIRATIONS...
SOON...
THIS INCOMING MESSAGE I'VE MONITORED COULD BE THE BREAK WE NEED!
TO LAND ON THE CORPORATE AUTHORITY'S SPECIAL PRISON PLANET, SOLO-CAPTAIN... THAT BREAK MUST BE BIG!
IT ALL DEPENDS ON OUR HIDDEN TALENTS, ATUARRE!

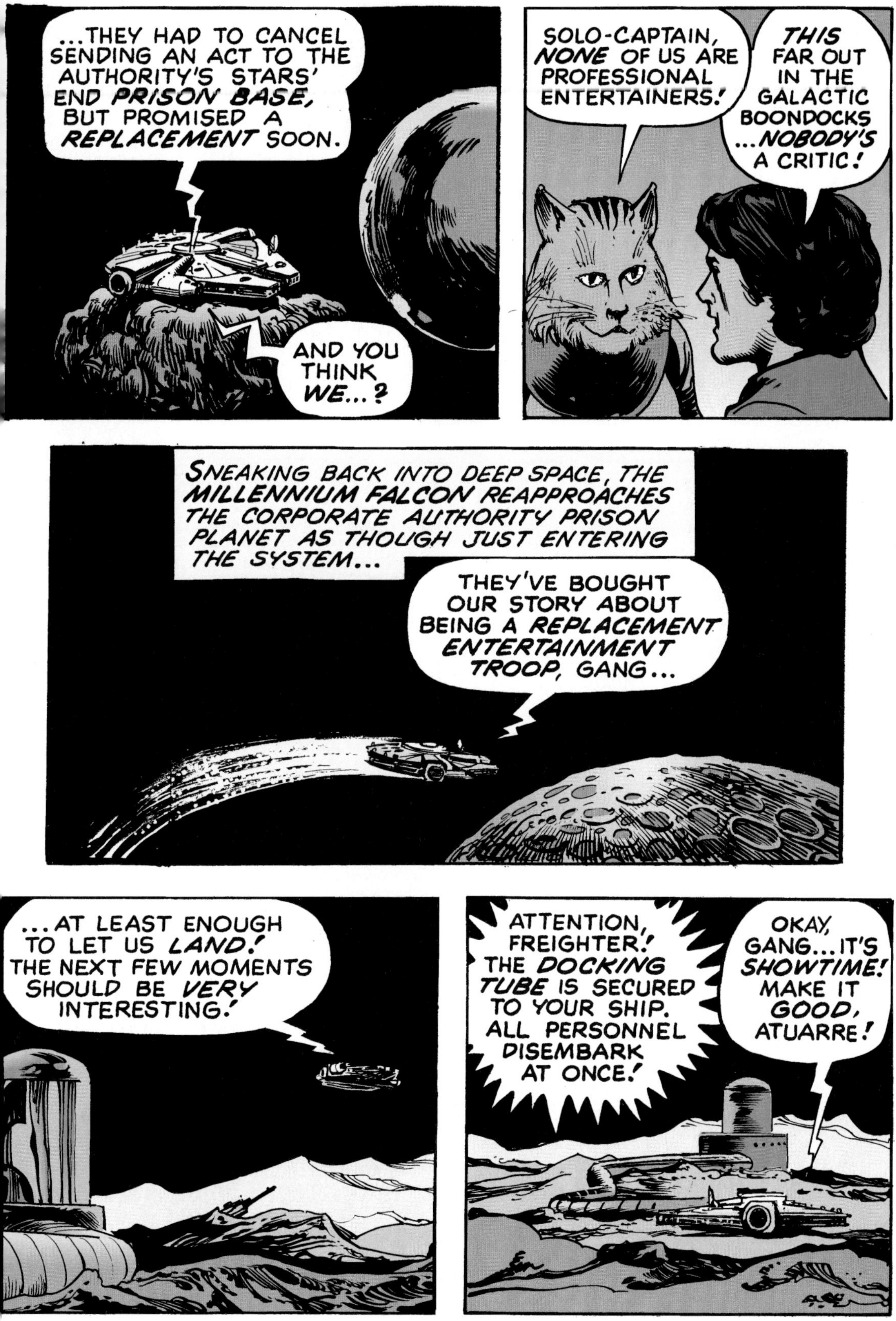

...THEY HAD TO CANCEL SENDING AN ACT TO THE AUTHORITY'S STARS' END *PRISON BASE,* BUT PROMISED A *REPLACEMENT* SOON.
AND YOU THINK *WE...?*
SOLO-CAPTAIN, *NONE* OF US ARE PROFESSIONAL ENTERTAINERS!
THIS FAR OUT IN THE GALACTIC BOONDOCKS ...*NOBODY'S* A CRITIC!
SNEAKING BACK INTO DEEP SPACE, THE MILLENNIUM FALCON REAPPROACHES THE CORPORATE AUTHORITY PRISON PLANET AS THOUGH JUST ENTERING THE SYSTEM...
THEY'VE BOUGHT OUR STORY ABOUT BEING A *REPLACEMENT ENTERTAINMENT TROOP,* GANG...
...AT LEAST ENOUGH TO LET US *LAND!* THE NEXT FEW MOMENTS SHOULD BE *VERY* INTERESTING!
ATTENTION, FREIGHTER! THE *DOCKING TUBE* IS SECURED TO YOUR SHIP. ALL PERSONNEL DISEMBARK AT ONCE!
OKAY, GANG...IT'S *SHOWTIME!* MAKE IT *GOOD,* ATUARRE!

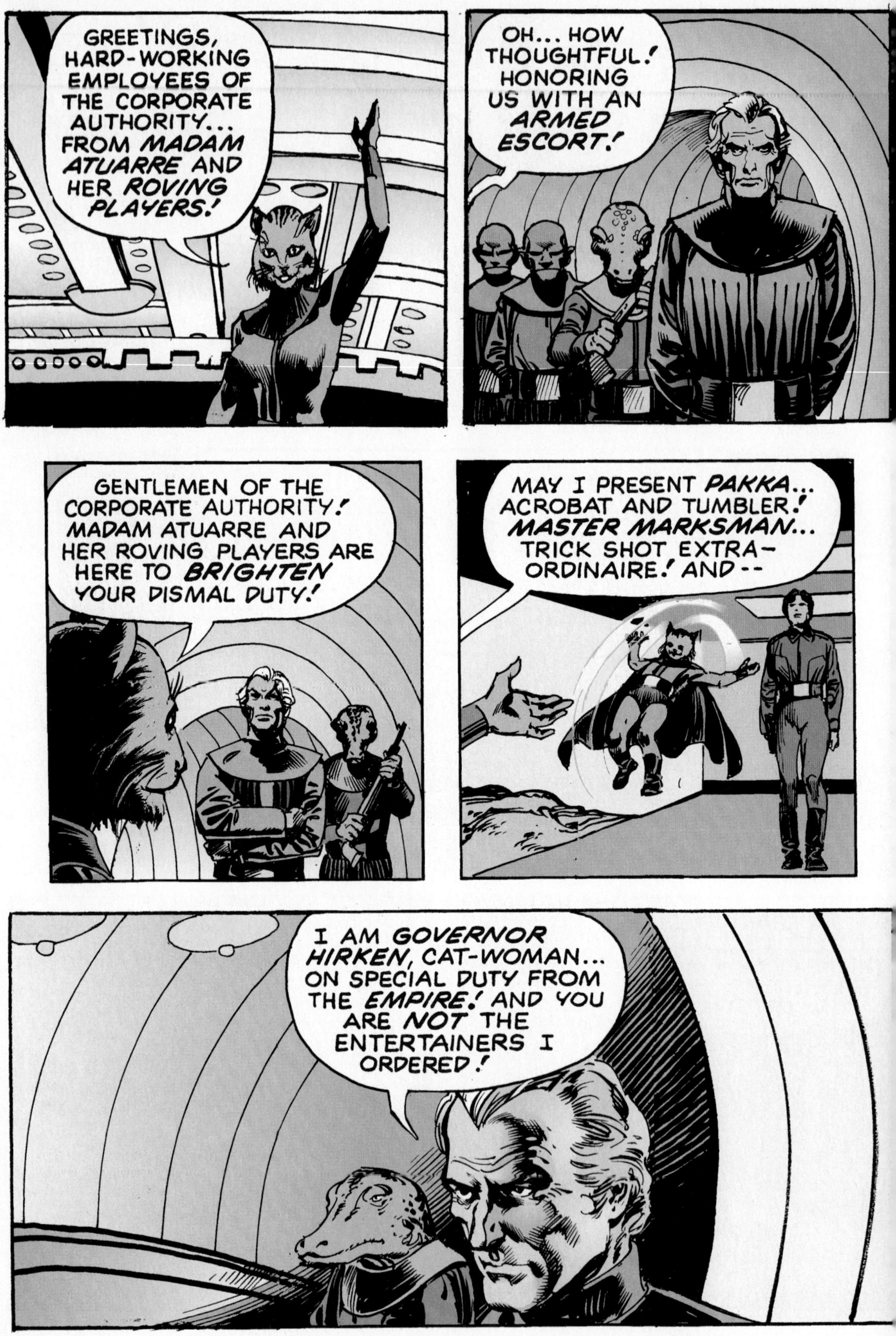
GREETINGS, HARD-WORKING EMPLOYEES OF THE CORPORATE AUTHORITY... FROM MADAM ATUARRE AND HER ROVING PLAYERS!
OH... HOW THOUGHTFUL! HONORING US WITH AN ARMED ESCORT!
GENTLEMEN OF THE CORPORATE AUTHORITY! MADAM ATUARRE AND HER ROVING PLAYERS ARE HERE TO BRIGHTEN YOUR DISMAL DUTY!
MAY I PRESENT PAKKA... ACROBAT AND TUMBLER! MASTER MARKSMAN... TRICK SHOT EXTRA-ORDINAIRE! AND --
I AM GOVERNOR HIRKEN, CAT-WOMAN... ON SPECIAL DUTY FROM THE EMPIRE! AND YOU ARE NOT THE ENTERTAINERS I ORDERED!

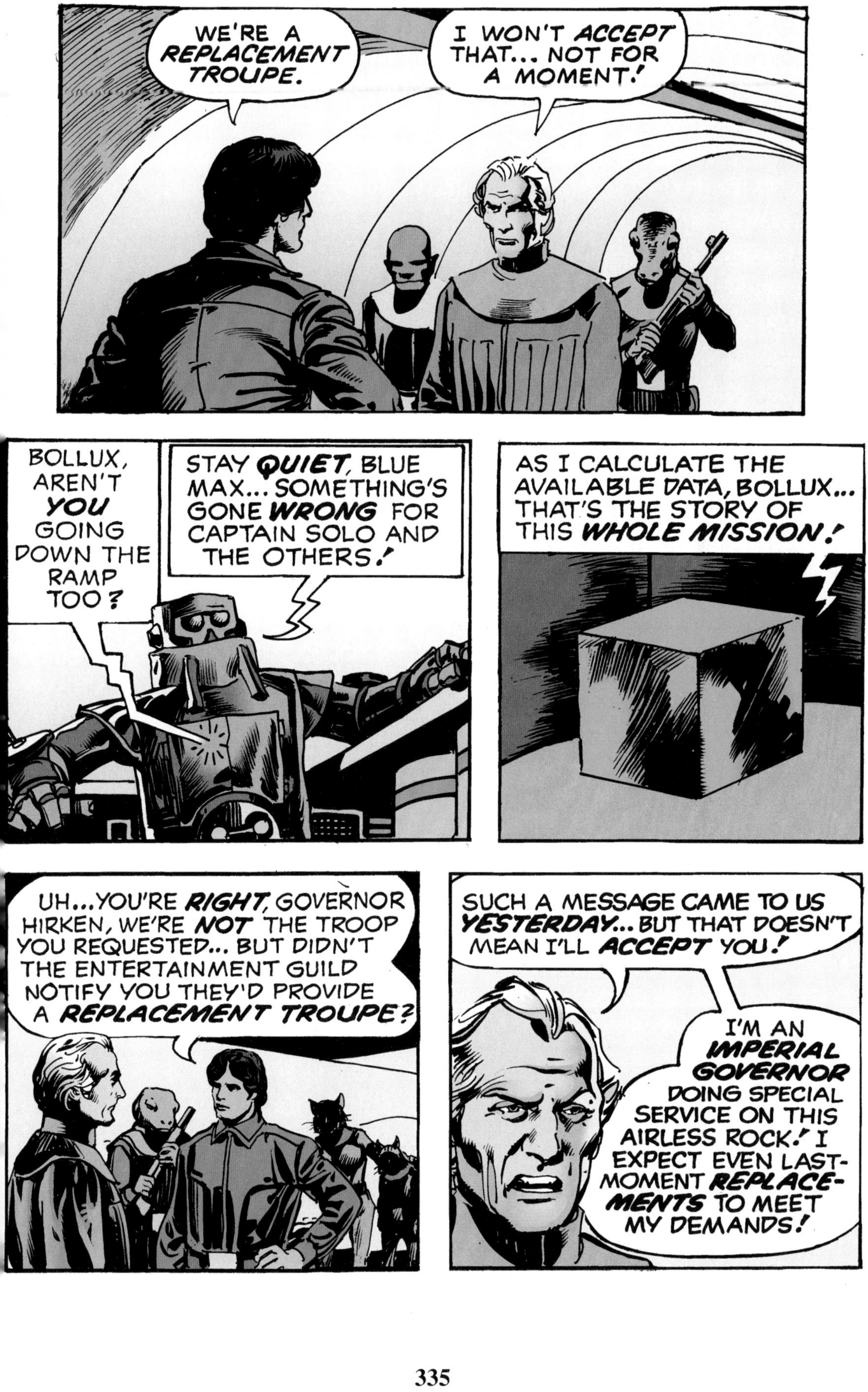
WE'RE A REPLACEMENT TROUPE.
I WON'T ACCEPT THAT... NOT FOR A MOMENT!
BOLLUX, AREN'T YOU GOING DOWN THE RAMP TOO?
STAY QUIET, BLUE MAX... SOMETHING'S GONE WRONG FOR CAPTAIN SOLO AND THE OTHERS!
AS I CALCULATE THE AVAILABLE DATA, BOLLUX... THAT'S THE STORY OF THIS WHOLE MISSION!
UH...YOU'RE RIGHT, GOVERNOR HIRKEN, WE'RE NOT THE TROOP YOU REQUESTED... BUT DIDN'T THE ENTERTAINMENT GUILD NOTIFY YOU THEY'D PROVIDE A REPLACEMENT TROUPE?
SUCH A MESSAGE CAME TO US YESTERDAY... BUT THAT DOESN'T MEAN I'LL ACCEPT YOU!
I'M AN IMPERIAL GOVERNOR DOING SPECIAL SERVICE ON THIS AIRLESS ROCK! I EXPECT EVEN LAST-MOMENT REPLACEMENTS TO MEET MY DEMANDS!

WHERE IS THE DROID I SPECIFICALLY DEMANDED?!
DROID...? YOU THOUGHT WE DIDN'T HAVE A DROID, YOUR HONOR...? BOLLUX! GET OUT HERE!
MADAM ATUARRE'S ROVING PLAYERS PROUDLY PRESENTS--
ENOUGH!
UUL-RHA-SHAN, GET THAT HUNK OF JUNK TO THE ARENA... READY TO FIGHT!
GOVERNOR HIRKEN! YOU WISH OUR DROID TO FIGHT...?
THAT'S THE ENTERTAINMENT I ORDERED, MADAM ATUARRE...
...AND THAT'S ALL I WILL ACCEPT! IF THAT UNLIKELY LOOKING JUNKPILE ISN'T A GLADIATOR DROID...
...THEN YOUR TROUPE'S COME TO STARS' END UNDER FALSE PRETENSES!
TIME TO TALK FAST, SOLO...!
LOOKS ARE DECEIVING, YOUR HONOR! WE DESIGNED THIS DROID OURSELVES. WE CALL HIM... UH... ANNIHILATOR!
SIR, THIS DROID HARDLY LOOKS LIKE AN... ANNIHILATOR!
MY BODYGUARD, UUL-RHA-SHAN IS OF A CYNICAL NATURE. BUT I ACCEPT YOUR WORD, CORELLIAN.

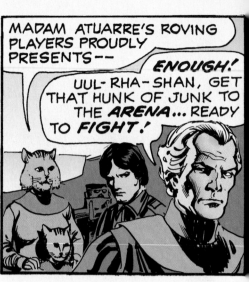

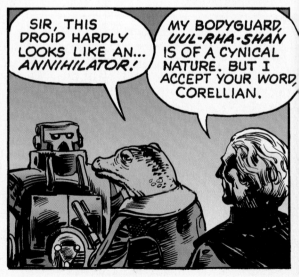

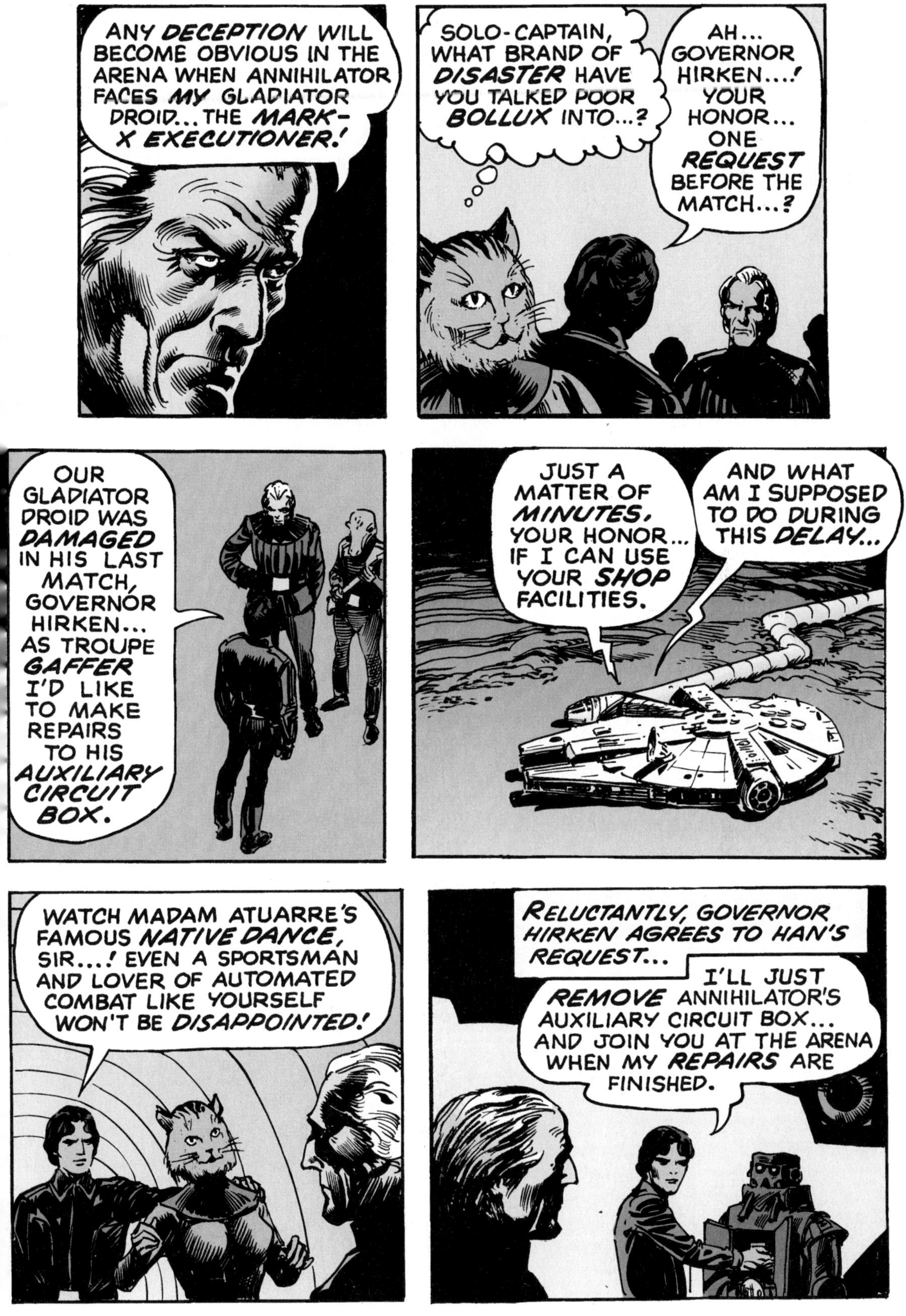
ANY DECEPTION WILL BECOME OBVIOUS IN THE ARENA WHEN ANNIHILATOR FACES MY GLADIATOR DROID... THE MARK-X EXECUTIONER!
SOLO-CAPTAIN, WHAT BRAND OF DISASTER HAVE YOU TALKED POOR BOLLUX INTO...?
AH... GOVERNOR HIRKEN...! YOUR HONOR... ONE REQUEST BEFORE THE MATCH...?
OUR GLADIATOR DROID WAS DAMAGED IN HIS LAST MATCH, GOVERNOR HIRKEN... AS TROUPE GAFFER I'D LIKE TO MAKE REPAIRS TO HIS AUXILIARY CIRCUIT BOX.
JUST A MATTER OF MINUTES, YOUR HONOR... IF I CAN USE YOUR SHOP FACILITIES.
AND WHAT AM I SUPPOSED TO DO DURING THIS DELAY...
WATCH MADAM ATUARRE'S FAMOUS NATIVE DANCE, SIR...! EVEN A SPORTSMAN AND LOVER OF AUTOMATED COMBAT LIKE YOURSELF WON'T BE DISAPPOINTED!
RELUCTANTLY, GOVERNOR HIRKEN AGREES TO HAN'S REQUEST...
I'LL JUST REMOVE ANNIHILATOR'S AUXILIARY CIRCUIT BOX... AND JOIN YOU AT THE ARENA WHEN MY REPAIRS ARE FINISHED.

HIS BACK TURNED, THE MILLENNIUM FALCON'S SKIPPER WHISPERS...

FOR THE SAKE OF BOLLUX AND THE REST OF US... ACT LIKE A SPARE PART, MAX!

HURRY, GAFFER! THE MOMENT I TIRE OF MADAM ATUARRE'S DANCE... THE DROIDS BATTLE! WITH OR WITHOUT YOU!

A CORPORATE AUTHORITY GUARD MARCHES HAN TOWARD THE STARS' END REPAIR SHOP...

HEY! THAT'S NOT WHAT WE WANT... IT'S THE COMPUTER CENTER.

YEAH...

MEANWHILE, ATOP THE AIRLESS PLANET'S LONE STRUCTURE...

GOVERNOR HIRKEN! THAT T-THING...

IT'S WHAT YOUR DROID WILL FIGHT, MY DEAR MADAM ATUARRE... MY MARK-X EXECUTIONER!

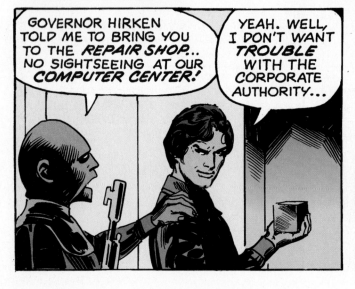

GOVERNOR HIRKEN TOLD ME TO BRING YOU TO THE REPAIR SHOP... NO SIGHTSEEING AT OUR COMPUTER CENTER!

YEAH. WELL, I DON'T WANT TROUBLE WITH THE CORPORATE AUTHORITY...

...BUT SINCE I'M ALREADY IN IT UP TO MY EYEBROWS, WHY STOP NOW?!

THAT CORELLIAN WHO REPRESENTED HIMSELF AS THE ENTERTAINMENT TROUPE'S *GAFFER* IS TAKING HIS *TIME*, YOUR EXCELLENCY!

I'VE NOTED THE *DELAY*, UUL-RHA-SHAN AND DECIDED THERE'S NO REASON TO *TOLERATE* IT ANY LONGER!

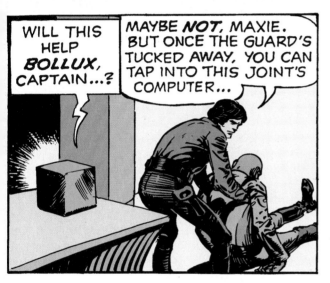

WILL THIS HELP *BOLLUX*, CAPTAIN...?

MAYBE *NOT*, MAXIE. BUT ONCE THE GUARD'S TUCKED AWAY, YOU CAN TAP INTO THIS JOINT'S COMPUTER...

... AND WE CAN FIND *WHERE* IN THIS KING-SIZE TOWER GOVERNOR HIRKEN AND COMPANY ARE HOLDING CHEWIE AND THE OTHERS

MEANWHILE, IN THE ARENA *ATOP THE TOWER*...

WE'VE DELAYED *ENOUGH*, MADAM ATUARRE! MY IDEA OF ENTERTAINMENT IS *NOT* YOUR NATIVE DANCES OR THE CUB'S ACROBATICS!

YOUR DROID CAN FIGHT *WITHOUT* THE CORELLIAN'S REPAIRS TO ITS AUXILIARY *CIRCUIT BOX*.

BRING ON MY *MARK-X EXECUTIONER!*

TO BE CONTINUED...

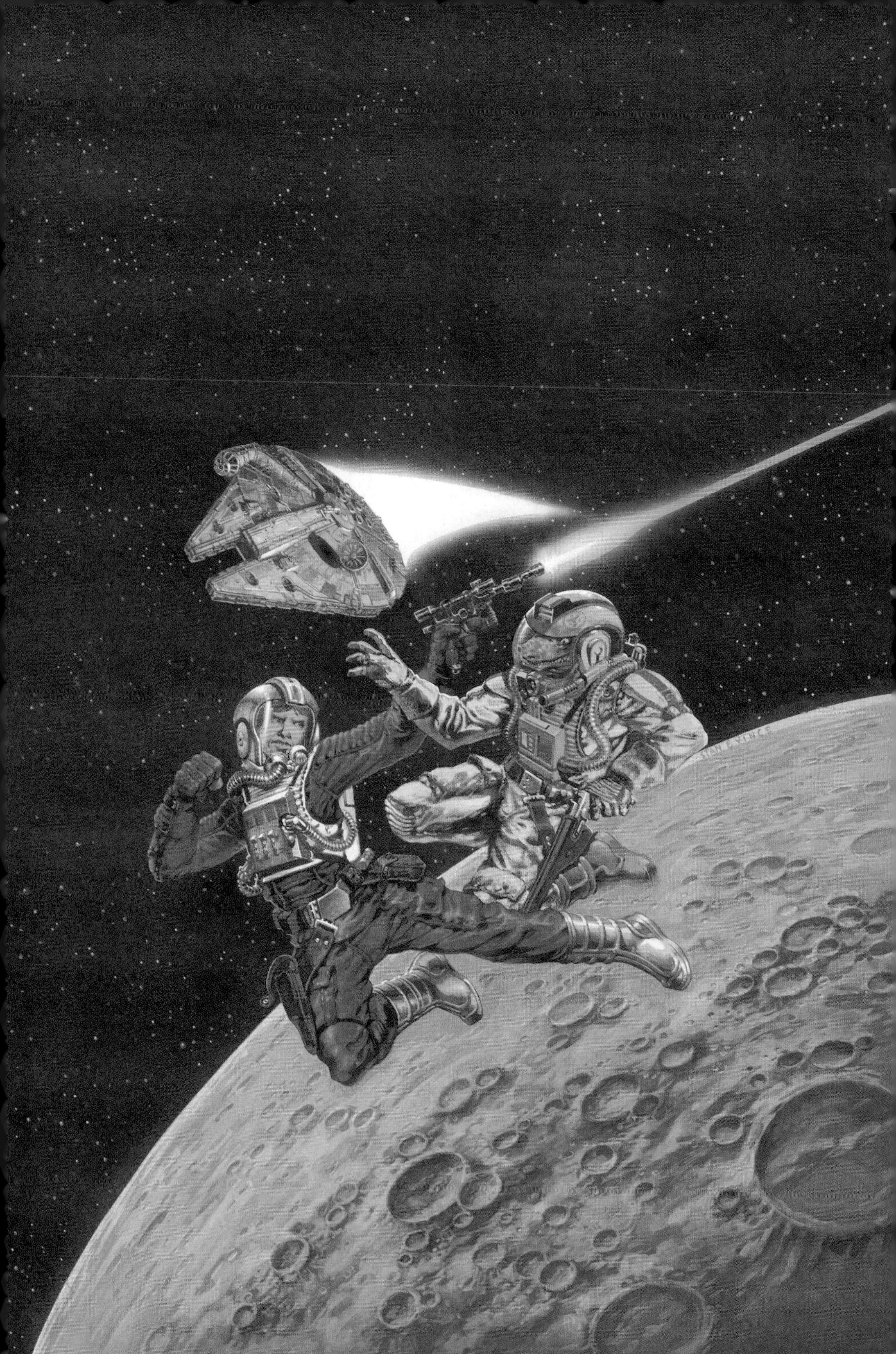

CLASSIC STAR WARS: HAN SOLO AT STARS' END #3
ORIGINALLY PUBLISHED FROM DECEMBER 29, 1980 TO FEBRUARY 8, 1981

BASED ON THE NOVEL BY BRIAN DALEY • SCRIPTER: ARCHIE GOODWIN • ARTIST & LETTERER: ALFREDO ALCALA
COLORIST: PERRY MCNAMEE • COLOR SEPARATIONS: BRIAN NEUBAUER & MICHELLE MADSEN • ASSISTANT EDITOR: IAN STUDE
EDITOR: PEET JANES • COVER ARTISTS: STAN MANOUKIAN & VINCE ROUCHER

THE GUARD'S KNOCKED OUT AND STOWED AWAY, MAXIE ...TIME TO DO YOUR *DATA TAPPING* ACT!

I'M CONCERNED ABOUT *BOLLUX* UP IN THE ARENA, CAPTAIN.

GOTTA FIND CHEWIE AND THE OTHER PRISONERS HERE *FIRST*, PIPSQUEAK... START TICKLING *INFO* FROM THIS COMPUTER!

MEANWHILE, GOVERNOR HIRKEN LOSES PATIENCE AND ORDERS THE DROIDS TO FIGHT...

PLEASE....! OUR GAFFER WILL BE BACK *SOON!*

YOUR *CHARADE* IS OVER, MADAM *ATUARRE!*

C-CHARADE...? I DON'T UNDERSTAND, GOVERNOR HIRKEN! BUT WITHOUT OUR GAFFER'S *REPAIRS* THIS FIGHT WON'T BE --

YOU'RE *STALLING,* MADAM ATUARRE!

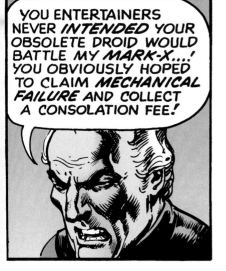

YOU ENTERTAINERS NEVER *INTENDED* YOUR OBSOLETE DROID WOULD BATTLE *MY MARK-X....!* YOU OBVIOUSLY HOPED TO CLAIM *MECHANICAL FAILURE* AND COLLECT A CONSOLATION FEE!

THEY SHOULD *DIE* FOR SUCH DECEIT, EXCELLENCY!

PERHAPS, UUL-RHA-SHAN... I'LL JUDGE BY HOW *AMUSING* A COMBAT THEIR ANTIQUE GLADIATOR PROVIDES!

HELPLESS TO DO ANYTHING ELSE, ATUARRE AND PAKKA STAND CLEAR... AND HIRKEN'S *MARK-X EXECUTIONER* ADVANCES ON BOLLUX!

THE GOVERNOR HASN'T GUESSED OUR *TRUE* PURPOSE HERE... BUT THINGS COULDN'T GO MUCH *WORSE* IF HE HAD! SOLO-CAPTAIN... WHERE *ARE* YOU?!

IN THE STARS' END COMPUTER CENTER...

I'VE FOUND THE *DETENTION LEVEL,* CAPTAIN!

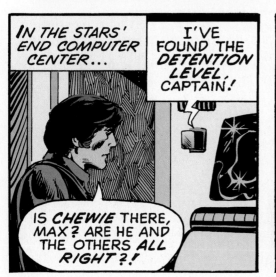

IS *CHEWIE* THERE, MAX? ARE HE AND THE OTHERS *ALL RIGHT*?!

GREAT, MAX! THIS READ-OUT SHOWS AN *AIR LOCK* ON THE DETENTION LEVEL! WE'LL CREATE A DIVERSION, BRING UP THE *FALCON,* AND--

NO, CAPTAIN! FIRST HELP *BOLLUX!*

AND IN GOVERNOR HIRKEN'S ARENA ATOP THE STARS' END TOWER...

...HELP IS *DEFINITELY* WHAT THE LABOR DROID NEEDS!

MAX, IF BOLLUX IS ALREADY BATTLING HIRKEN'S *GLADIATOR DROID*... IT'S *TOO LATE* TO HELP HIM! PRIORITY GOES TO CHEWIE AND THE OTHER PRISONERS!

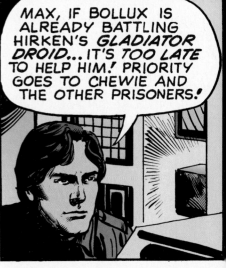

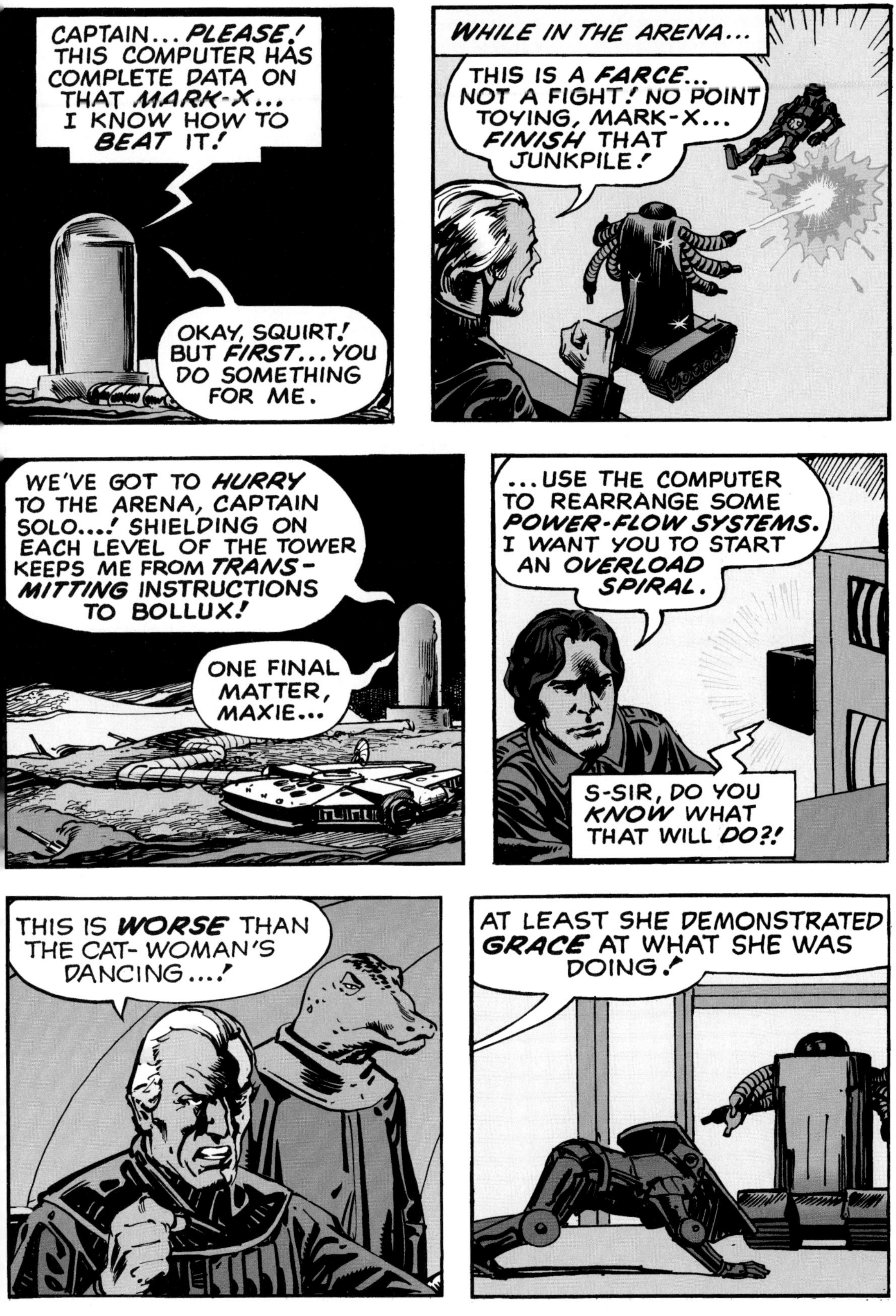
CAPTAIN... PLEASE! THIS COMPUTER HAS COMPLETE DATA ON THAT MARK-X... I KNOW HOW TO BEAT IT!
OKAY, SQUIRT! BUT FIRST... YOU DO SOMETHING FOR ME.
WHILE IN THE ARENA...
THIS IS A FARCE... NOT A FIGHT! NO POINT TOYING, MARK-X... FINISH THAT JUNKPILE!
WE'VE GOT TO HURRY TO THE ARENA, CAPTAIN SOLO...! SHIELDING ON EACH LEVEL OF THE TOWER KEEPS ME FROM TRANS-MITTING INSTRUCTIONS TO BOLLUX!
ONE FINAL MATTER, MAXIE...
...USE THE COMPUTER TO REARRANGE SOME POWER-FLOW SYSTEMS. I WANT YOU TO START AN OVERLOAD SPIRAL.
S-SIR, DO YOU KNOW WHAT THAT WILL DO?!
THIS IS WORSE THAN THE CAT-WOMAN'S DANCING...!
AT LEAST SHE DEMONSTRATED GRACE AT WHAT SHE WAS DOING!

THAT JUNK HEAP IS TOO INEPT TO EVEN BE *AMUSING,* GOVERNOR HIRKEN!

HIS OWNERS MUST *PAY* FOR THIS EFFRONTERY, UUL-RHA-SHAN... *AFTER* MARK-X DESTROYS

MEANWHILE, HAN RUSHES FROM STARS' END COMPUTER CENTER WITH BLUE MAX...

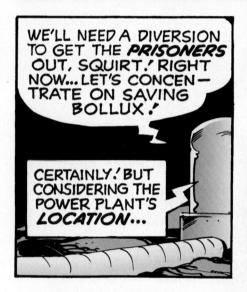

WE'LL NEED A DIVERSION TO GET THE *PRISONERS* OUT, SQUIRT! RIGHT NOW...LET'S CONCENTRATE ON SAVING BOLLUX!

CERTAINLY! BUT CONSIDERING THE POWER PLANT'S *LOCATION...*

LATER, MAXIE... ARENA'S JUST AHEAD!

SOLO-CAPTAIN... YOU'RE TOO LATE! *TOO LATE!*

WE TAPPED THE *MAIN COMPUTER* TO LOCATE THE *PRISONERS,* ATUARRE ...AND TO CREATE A *DIVERSION.*

ABOUT THAT *OVERLOAD SPIRAL* YOU HAD ME PROGRAM, SIR--

NOT *NOW,* BLUE MAX! NOT IF YOU WANT TO *SAVE* YOUR TIN-PLATED PAL!

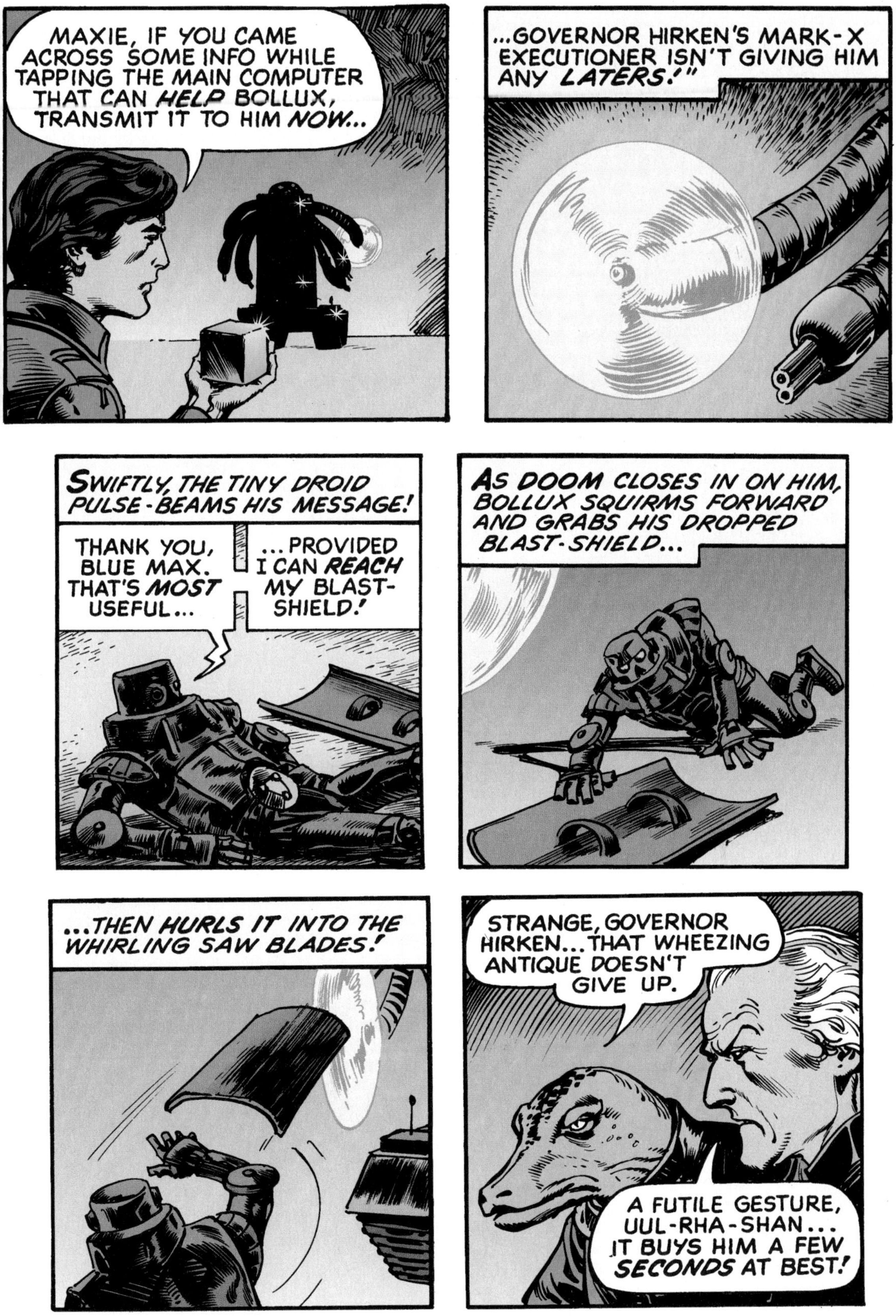
MAXIE, IF YOU CAME ACROSS SOME INFO WHILE TAPPING THE MAIN COMPUTER THAT CAN HELP BOLLUX, TRANSMIT IT TO HIM NOW...
...GOVERNOR HIRKEN'S MARK-X EXECUTIONER ISN'T GIVING HIM ANY LATERS!"
SWIFTLY, THE TINY DROID PULSE-BEAMS HIS MESSAGE!
THANK YOU, BLUE MAX. THAT'S MOST USEFUL...
...PROVIDED I CAN REACH MY BLAST-SHIELD!
AS DOOM CLOSES IN ON HIM, BOLLUX SQUIRMS FORWARD AND GRABS HIS DROPPED BLAST-SHIELD...
...THEN HURLS IT INTO THE WHIRLING SAW BLADES!
STRANGE, GOVERNOR HIRKEN... THAT WHEEZING ANTIQUE DOESN'T GIVE UP.
A FUTILE GESTURE, UUL-RHA-SHAN... IT BUYS HIM A FEW SECONDS AT BEST!

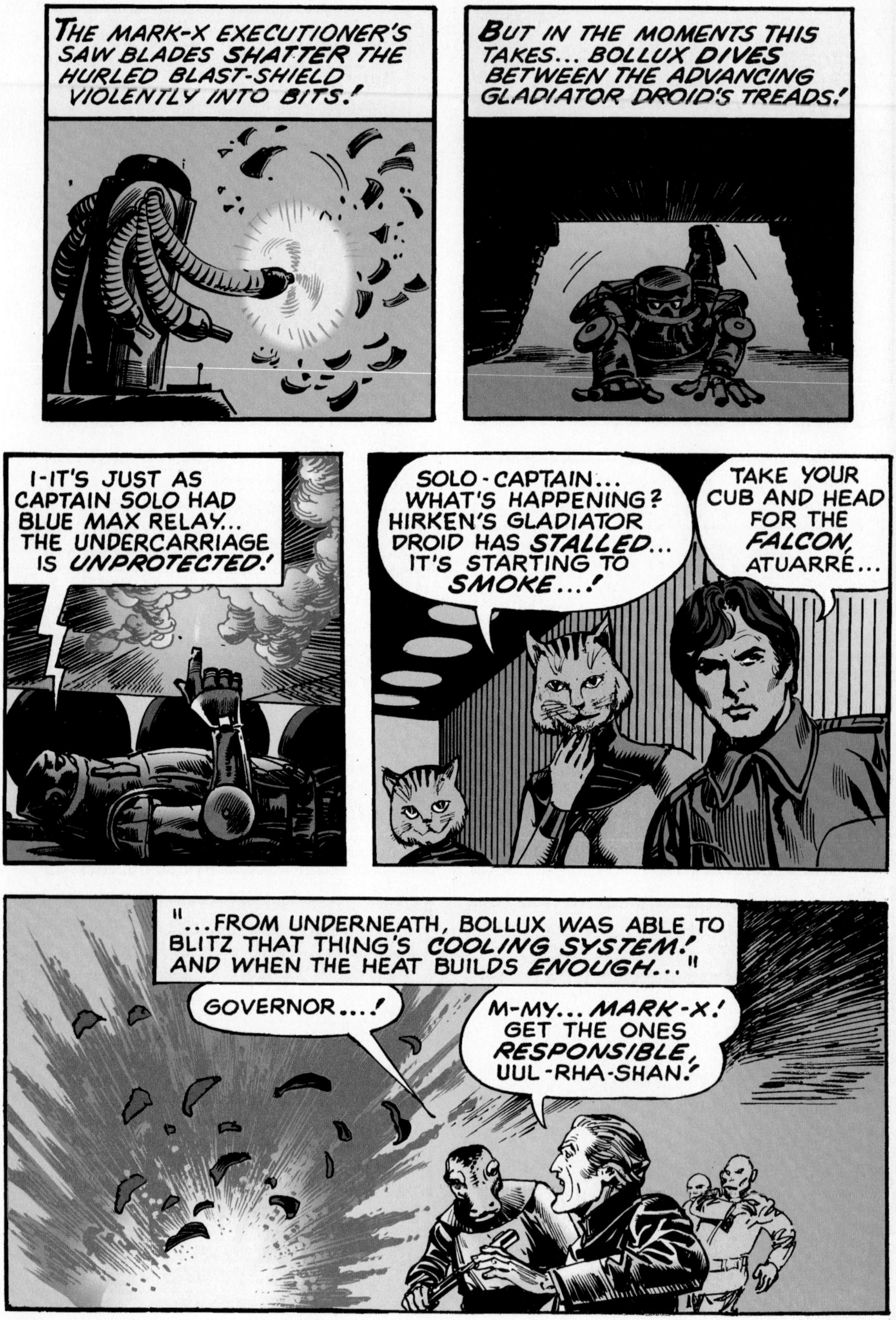
THE MARK-X EXECUTIONER'S SAW BLADES SHATTER THE HURLED BLAST-SHIELD VIOLENTLY INTO BITS!
BUT IN THE MOMENTS THIS TAKES... BOLLUX DIVES BETWEEN THE ADVANCING GLADIATOR DROID'S TREADS!
I-IT'S JUST AS CAPTAIN SOLO HAD BLUE MAX RELAY... THE UNDERCARRIAGE IS UNPROTECTED!
SOLO-CAPTAIN... WHAT'S HAPPENING? HIRKEN'S GLADIATOR DROID HAS STALLED... IT'S STARTING TO SMOKE...!
TAKE YOUR CUB AND HEAD FOR THE FALCON, ATUARRÉ...
"...FROM UNDERNEATH, BOLLUX WAS ABLE TO BLITZ THAT THING'S COOLING SYSTEM! AND WHEN THE HEAT BUILDS ENOUGH..."
GOVERNOR...!
M-MY... MARK-X! GET THE ONES RESPONSIBLE, UUL-RHA-SHAN!

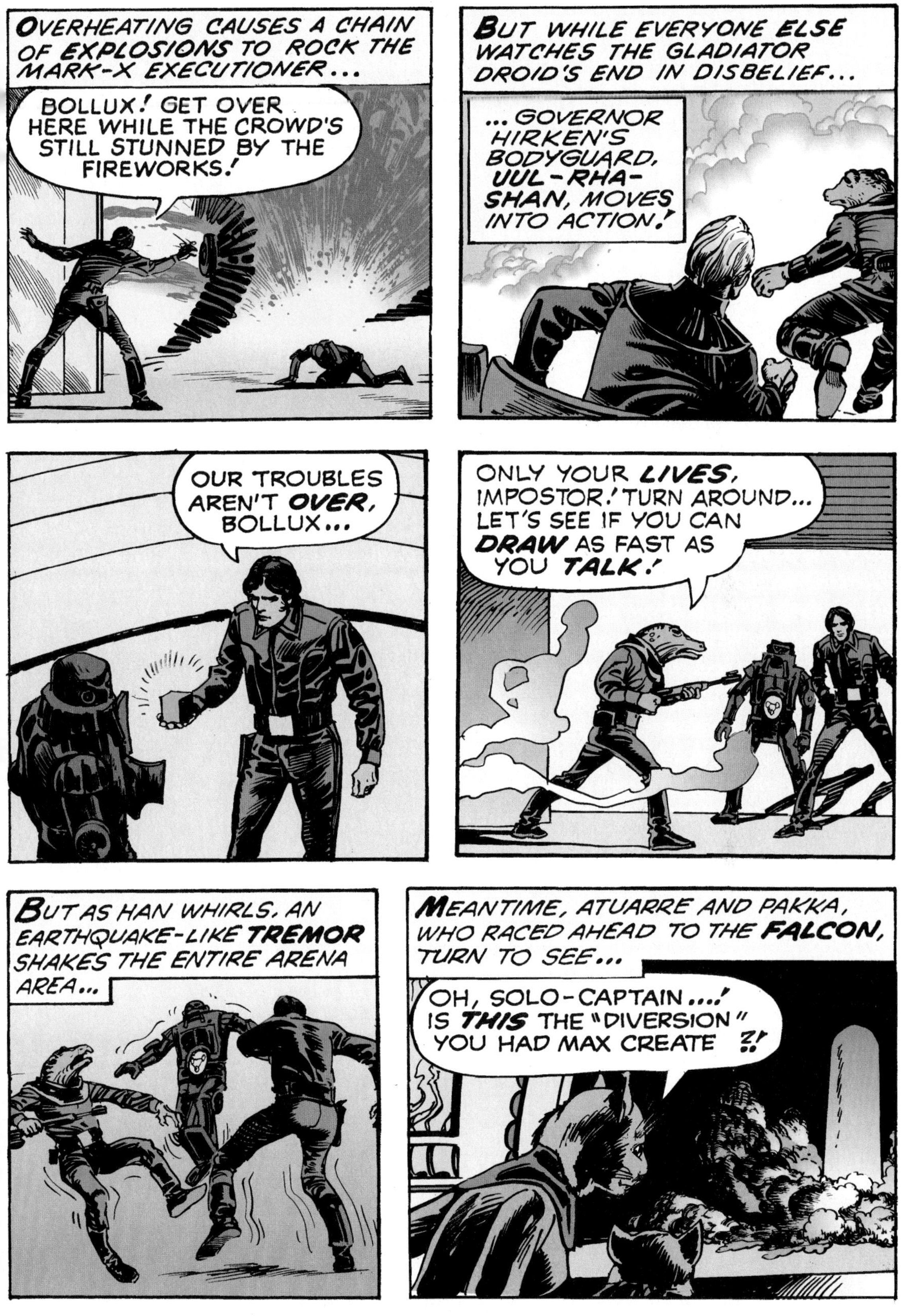

OVERHEATING CAUSES A CHAIN OF EXPLOSIONS TO ROCK THE MARK-X EXECUTIONER...
BOLLUX! GET OVER HERE WHILE THE CROWD'S STILL STUNNED BY THE FIREWORKS!
BUT WHILE EVERYONE ELSE WATCHES THE GLADIATOR DROID'S END IN DISBELIEF...
...GOVERNOR HIRKEN'S BODYGUARD, UUL-RHA-SHAN, MOVES INTO ACTION!
OUR TROUBLES AREN'T OVER, BOLLUX...
ONLY YOUR LIVES, IMPOSTOR! TURN AROUND... LET'S SEE IF YOU CAN DRAW AS FAST AS YOU TALK!
BUT AS HAN WHIRLS, AN EARTHQUAKE-LIKE TREMOR SHAKES THE ENTIRE ARENA AREA...
MEANTIME, ATUARRE AND PAKKA, WHO RACED AHEAD TO THE FALCON, TURN TO SEE...
OH, SOLO-CAPTAIN....! IS THIS THE "DIVERSION" YOU HAD MAX CREATE ?!

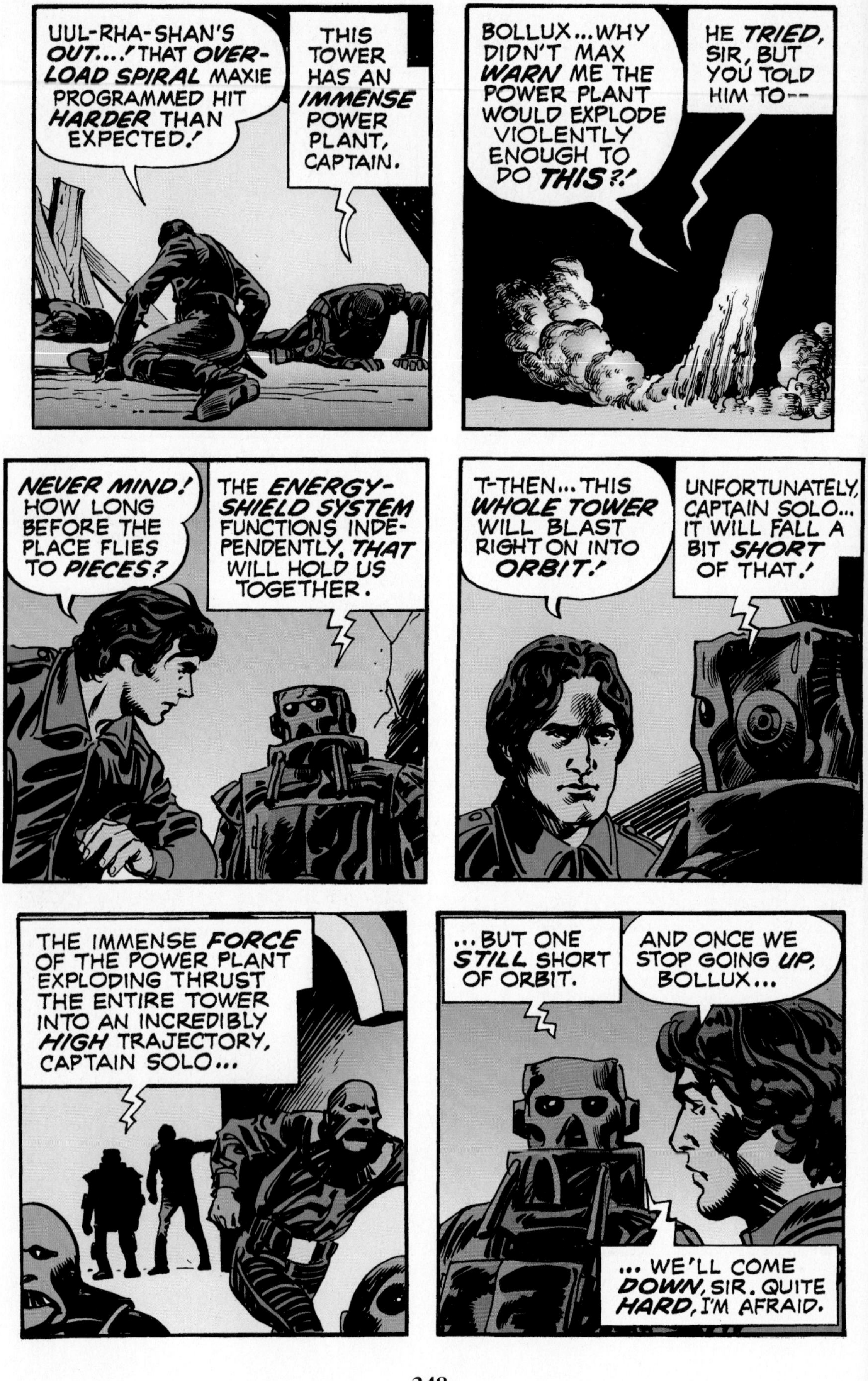
UUL-RHA-SHAN'S OUT....! THAT OVER-LOAD SPIRAL MAXIE PROGRAMMED HIT HARDER THAN EXPECTED.!
THIS TOWER HAS AN IMMENSE POWER PLANT, CAPTAIN.
BOLLUX...WHY DIDN'T MAX WARN ME THE POWER PLANT WOULD EXPLODE VIOLENTLY ENOUGH TO DO THIS?!
HE TRIED, SIR, BUT YOU TOLD HIM TO--
NEVER MIND! HOW LONG BEFORE THE PLACE FLIES TO PIECES?
THE ENERGY-SHIELD SYSTEM FUNCTIONS INDE-PENDENTLY. THAT WILL HOLD US TOGETHER.
T-THEN... THIS WHOLE TOWER WILL BLAST RIGHT ON INTO ORBIT.!
UNFORTUNATELY, CAPTAIN SOLO... IT WILL FALL A BIT SHORT OF THAT.!
THE IMMENSE FORCE OF THE POWER PLANT EXPLODING THRUST THE ENTIRE TOWER INTO AN INCREDIBLY HIGH TRAJECTORY, CAPTAIN SOLO...
...BUT ONE STILL SHORT OF ORBIT.
AND ONCE WE STOP GOING UP, BOLLUX...
... WE'LL COME DOWN, SIR. QUITE HARD, I'M AFRAID.

C'MON, BOLLUX! WE CAN'T *CHANGE* WHAT'S HAPPENED...

...BUT THE *TURMOIL* MAKES IT A CINCH TO GET TO WHERE *CHEWIE* AND THE OTHER PRISONERS ARE!

BUT EVEN IF WE *FREE* THEM, CAPTAIN SOLO... IN VIEW OF THE *PRESENT* PREDICAMENT... WHAT DO WE DO *THEN?*

IMPRO-VISE!

BUT AS HAN AND THE LABOR DROID FORCE THEIR WAY INTO THE CORPORATE AUTHORITY TOWER'S DETENTION LEVEL...

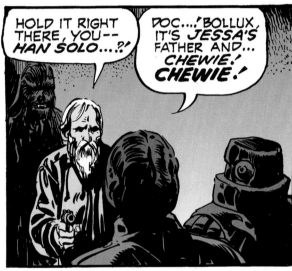

HOLD IT RIGHT THERE, YOU-- *HAN SOLO....?!*

DOC....! BOLLUX, IT'S *JESSA'S* FATHER AND... *CHEWIE! CHEWIE!*

ALL THE *POWER* SUDDENLY BLEW... FREED US FROM OUR *STASIS CELLS* AND WE OVERWHELMED THE GUARDS!

THAT WAS SORTA *MY* HANDIWORK, DOC...

...BUT THERE ARE SOME *DRAWBACKS* TO WHAT I ACCOMPLISHED!

AND MORE BEING ADDED, LAD... YOU'VE BEEN FOLLOWED BY WHAT SOUNDS LIKE AN *ARMY!*

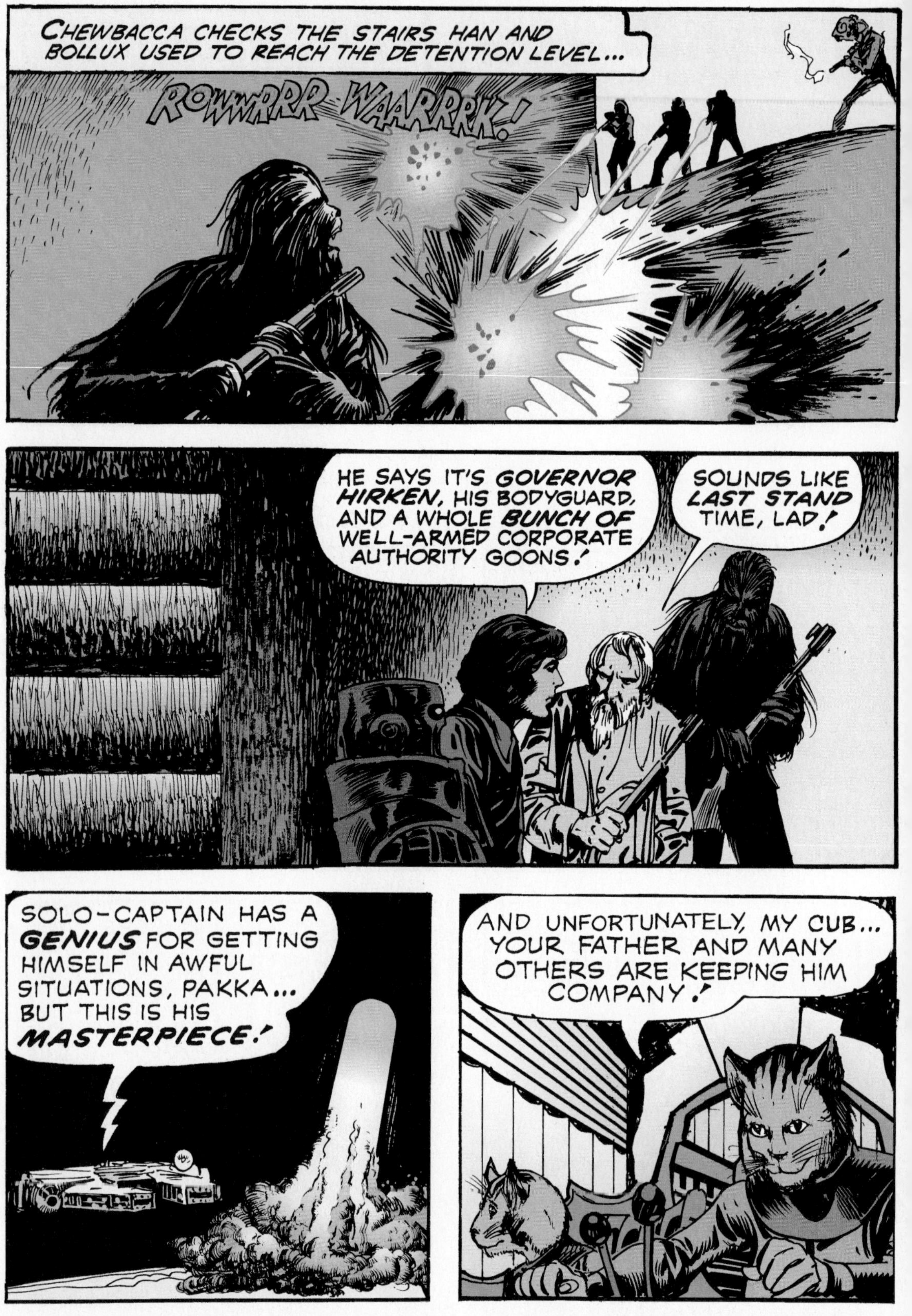
CHEWBACCA CHECKS THE STAIRS HAN AND BOLLUX USED TO REACH THE DETENTION LEVEL...
ROWWRRR WAARRRK!
HE SAYS IT'S GOVERNOR HIRKEN, HIS BODYGUARD, AND A WHOLE BUNCH OF WELL-ARMED CORPORATE AUTHORITY GOONS!
SOUNDS LIKE LAST STAND TIME, LAD!
SOLO-CAPTAIN HAS A GENIUS FOR GETTING HIMSELF IN AWFUL SITUATIONS, PAKKA... BUT THIS IS HIS MASTERPIECE!
AND UNFORTUNATELY, MY CUB... YOUR FATHER AND MANY OTHERS ARE KEEPING HIM COMPANY!

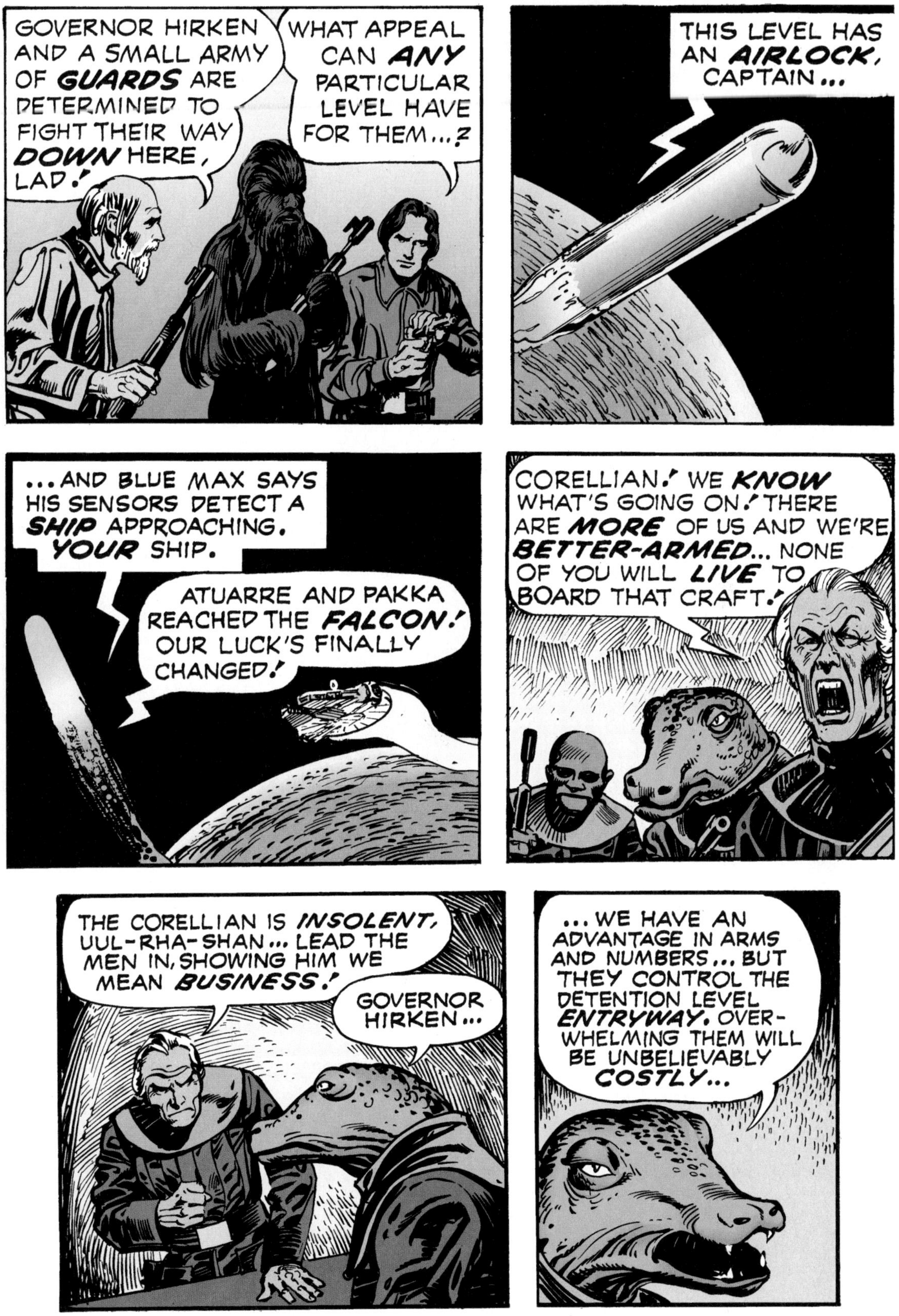
GOVERNOR HIRKEN AND A SMALL ARMY OF GUARDS ARE DETERMINED TO FIGHT THEIR WAY DOWN HERE, LAD!
WHAT APPEAL CAN ANY PARTICULAR LEVEL HAVE FOR THEM...?
THIS LEVEL HAS AN AIRLOCK, CAPTAIN...
...AND BLUE MAX SAYS HIS SENSORS DETECT A SHIP APPROACHING. YOUR SHIP.
ATUARRE AND PAKKA REACHED THE FALCON! OUR LUCK'S FINALLY CHANGED!
CORELLIAN! WE KNOW WHAT'S GOING ON! THERE ARE MORE OF US AND WE'RE BETTER-ARMED... NONE OF YOU WILL LIVE TO BOARD THAT CRAFT!
THE CORELLIAN IS INSOLENT, UUL-RHA-SHAN... LEAD THE MEN IN, SHOWING HIM WE MEAN BUSINESS!
GOVERNOR HIRKEN...
...WE HAVE AN ADVANTAGE IN ARMS AND NUMBERS... BUT THEY CONTROL THE DETENTION LEVEL ENTRYWAY. OVER-WHELMING THEM WILL BE UNBELIEVABLY COSTLY...

ARE YOU A *COWARD,* BODYGUARD?! THE THRUST FROM THE EXPLOSION IS RUNNING OUT... THIS TOWER WILL *FALL* IN MOMENTS!

I HAVE A *PLAN,* EXCELLENCY...

GOOD NEWS, HAN! ATUARRE IS RIGHT OUTSIDE WITH THE *FALCON*... PULLING IT UP TO THE *AIRLOCK!*

GLAD TO *HEAR* IT, DOC... 'CAUSE GOVERNOR HIRKEN AND COMPANY ARE MAKING THEIR *PLAY!*

ONLY... SOMETHING'S *FUNNY...!*

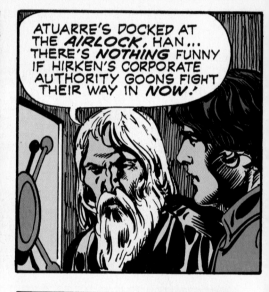

ATUARRE'S DOCKED AT THE *AIRLOCK,* HAN... THERE'S *NOTHING* FUNNY IF HIRKEN'S CORPORATE AUTHORITY GOONS FIGHT THEIR WAY IN *NOW!*

WE'LL ALL BE *EASY TARGETS* AS WE TRY TO RETREAT INTO THE *FALCON!*

THAT'S JUST *IT,* DOC! HIRKEN'S PEOPLE ARE LAYIN' DOWN LOTS OF *FIRE...*

...BUT IT'S ALL RICOCHETING OFF THE OPPOSITE WALL! INSTEAD OF *CHARGIN'* US... THEY'RE SHOOTIN' FROM THE *STAIRWELL. WHY?*

CAPTAIN... *BLUE MAX* MAY KNOW.

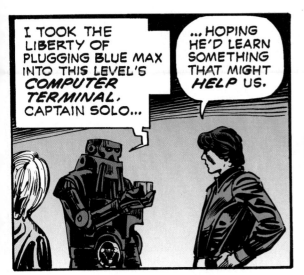

I TOOK THE LIBERTY OF PLUGGING BLUE MAX INTO THIS LEVEL'S *COMPUTER TERMINAL*, CAPTAIN SOLO...

...HOPING HE'D LEARN SOMETHING THAT MIGHT *HELP* US.

PLAYING GLADIATOR'S MADE YOU PRETTY INDEPENDENT, BOLLUX. WHAT'D THE TWERP *FIND*...?

THE LEVEL *ABOVE* US IS FOR EQUIPMENT STORAGE, SIR. NO WEAPONS OR EXPLOSIVES FORTUNATELY...

...BUT THERE ARE *SPACE SUITS*.

AND HIRKEN'S BUNCH HAS EASY ACCESS TO 'EM! THAT *EXPLAINS* WHY THEY'RE NOT *RUSHIN'* US!

DOC! GET SOMEONE UP FRONT TO HELP CHEWIE RETURN THE GUARDS' *FIRE* FROM THE STAIRWELL!

WHERE ARE *YOU* GOING, LAD?

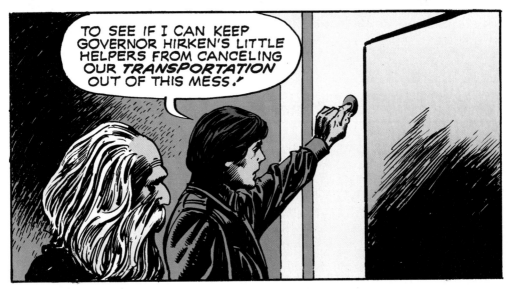

TO SEE IF I CAN KEEP GOVERNOR HIRKEN'S LITTLE HELPERS FROM CANCELING OUR *TRANSPORTATION* OUT OF THIS MESS!

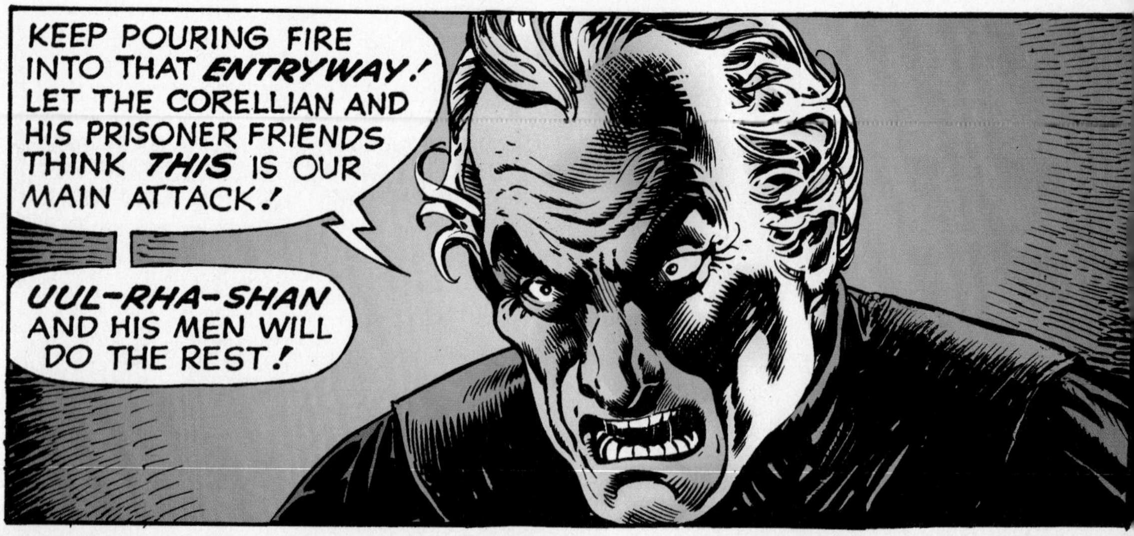
KEEP POURING FIRE INTO THAT ENTRYWAY! LET THE CORELLIAN AND HIS PRISONER FRIENDS THINK THIS IS OUR MAIN ATTACK!
UUL-RHA-SHAN AND HIS MEN WILL DO THE REST!

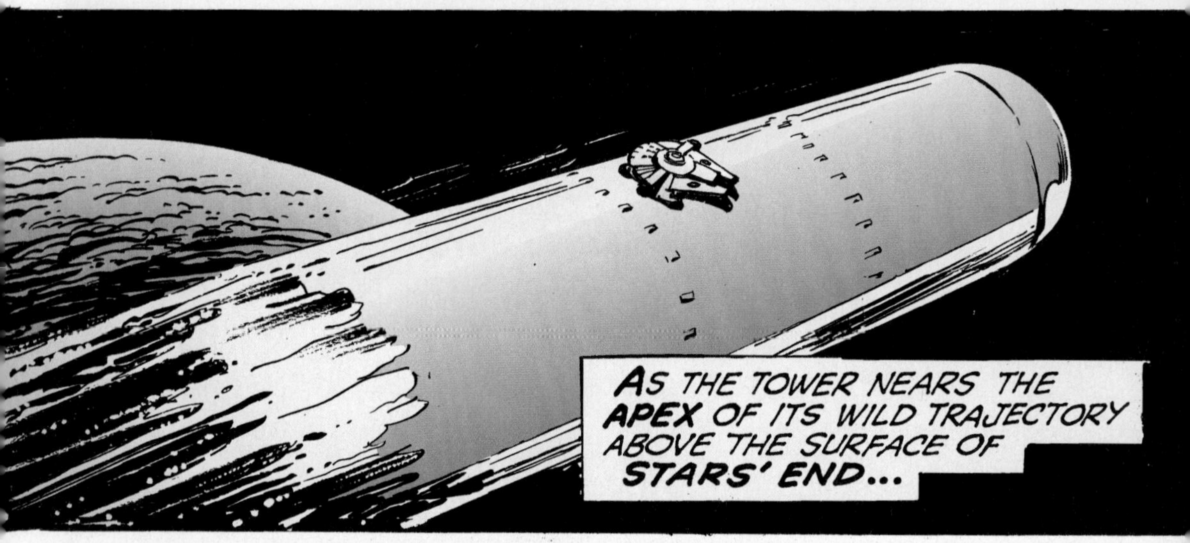
AS THE TOWER NEARS THE APEX OF ITS WILD TRAJECTORY ABOVE THE SURFACE OF STARS' END...

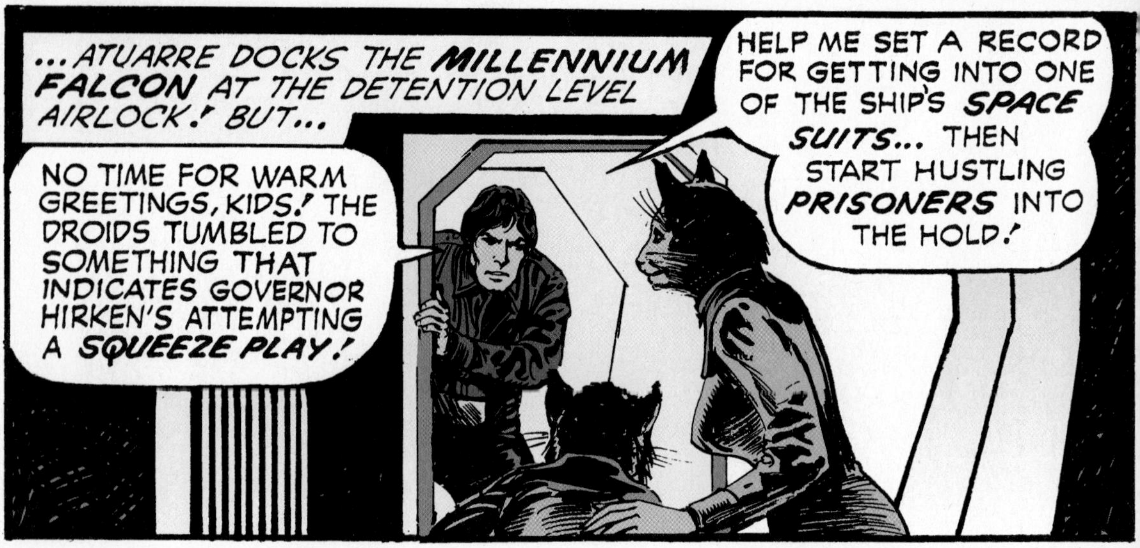
...ATUARRE DOCKS THE MILLENNIUM FALCON AT THE DETENTION LEVEL AIRLOCK! BUT...
NO TIME FOR WARM GREETINGS, KIDS! THE DROIDS TUMBLED TO SOMETHING THAT INDICATES GOVERNOR HIRKEN'S ATTEMPTING A SQUEEZE PLAY!
HELP ME SET A RECORD FOR GETTING INTO ONE OF THE SHIP'S SPACE SUITS... THEN START HUSTLING PRISONERS INTO THE HOLD!

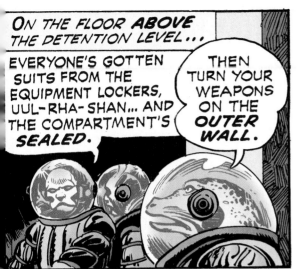

ON THE FLOOR *ABOVE* THE DETENTION LEVEL...

EVERYONE'S GOTTEN SUITS FROM THE EQUIPMENT LOCKERS, UUL-RHA-SHAN... AND THE COMPARTMENT'S *SEALED.*

THEN TURN YOUR WEAPONS ON THE *OUTER WALL.*

WHILE THE GOVERNOR KEEPS OUR REBELLIOUS PRISONERS WORRIED *WITHIN*... WE'LL STEAL THEIR SHIP... FROM *WITHOUT!*

ON THE FLOOR *ABOVE* THE DOOMED, SOARING TOWER'S DETENTION LEVEL, *LASER FIRE* SOUNDS...

...AS GOVERNOR HIRKEN'S BODYGUARD LEADS A PARTY IN BLASTING THROUGH THE *OUTER WALL* OF A SEALED-OFF COMPARTMENT!

NOW! OUTSIDE...TO CAPTURE OUR REBELLIOUS PRISONERS' SPACECRAFT!

BUT AS THE FIRST MAN FOLLOWS UUL-RHA-SHAN'S ORDER...HIS EYES GO WIDE IN SHOCK!

...*HAN SOLO!*

NICE *SQUEEZE PLAY* ATTEMPT, GUYS! BUT WE ANTICIPATED IT AFTER DISCOVERING THE *SPACE SUITS* STORED ON YOUR LEVEL!

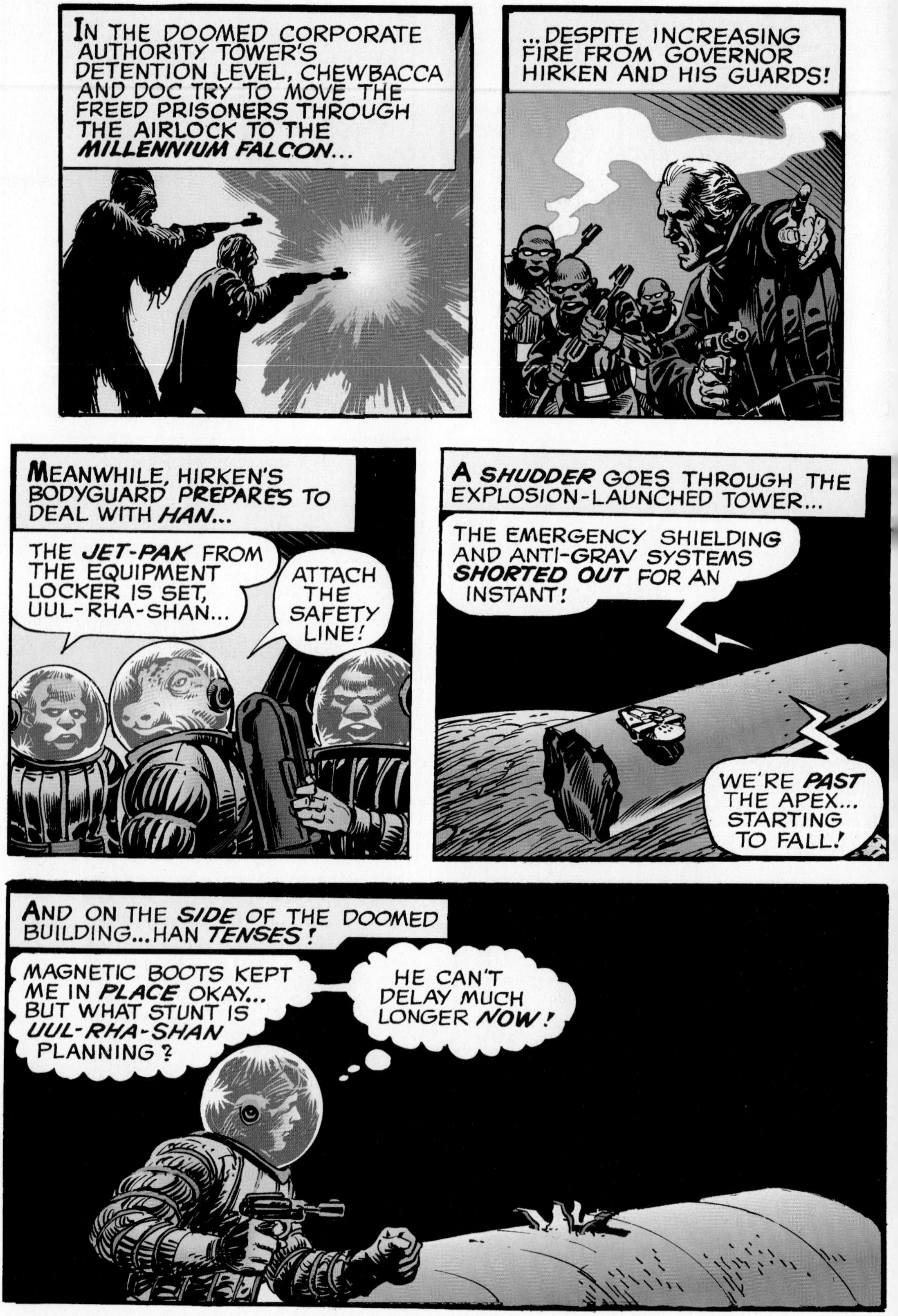
IN THE DOOMED CORPORATE AUTHORITY TOWER'S DETENTION LEVEL, CHEWBACCA AND DOC TRY TO MOVE THE FREED PRISONERS THROUGH THE AIRLOCK TO THE *MILLENNIUM FALCON*...
...DESPITE INCREASING FIRE FROM GOVERNOR HIRKEN AND HIS GUARDS!
MEANWHILE, HIRKEN'S BODYGUARD *PREPARES* TO DEAL WITH *HAN*...
THE *JET-PAK* FROM THE EQUIPMENT LOCKER IS SET, UUL-RHA-SHAN...
ATTACH THE SAFETY LINE!
A *SHUDDER* GOES THROUGH THE EXPLOSION-LAUNCHED TOWER...
THE EMERGENCY SHIELDING AND ANTI-GRAV SYSTEMS *SHORTED OUT* FOR AN INSTANT!
WE'RE *PAST* THE APEX... STARTING TO FALL!
AND ON THE *SIDE* OF THE DOOMED BUILDING...HAN *TENSES*!
MAGNETIC BOOTS KEPT ME IN *PLACE* OKAY... BUT WHAT STUNT IS *UUL-RHA-SHAN* PLANNING?
HE CAN'T DELAY MUCH LONGER *NOW*!

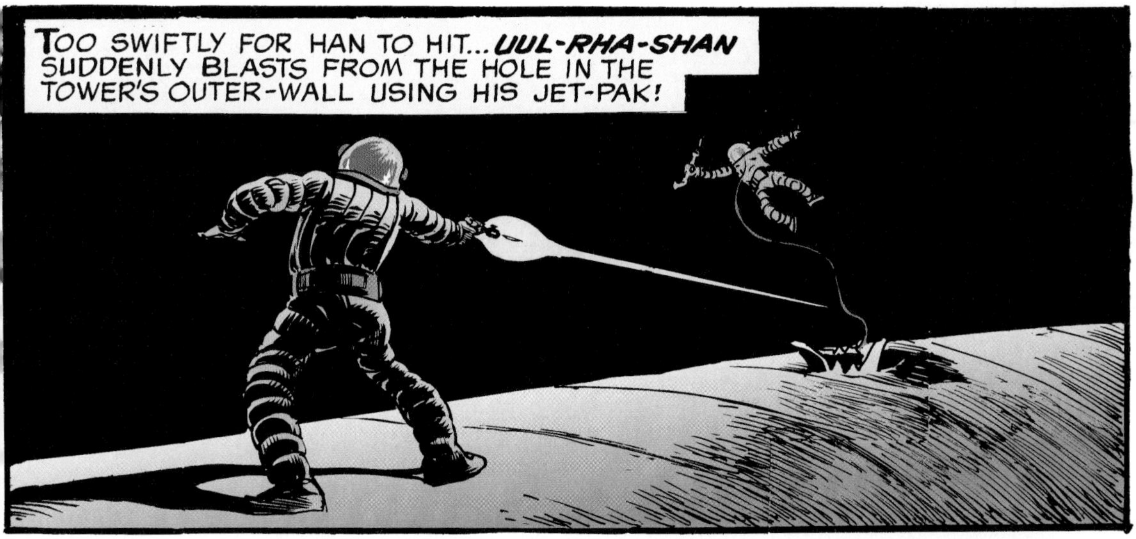
TOO SWIFTLY FOR HAN TO HIT... UUL-RHA-SHAN SUDDENLY BLASTS FROM THE HOLE IN THE TOWER'S OUTER-WALL USING HIS JET-PAK!

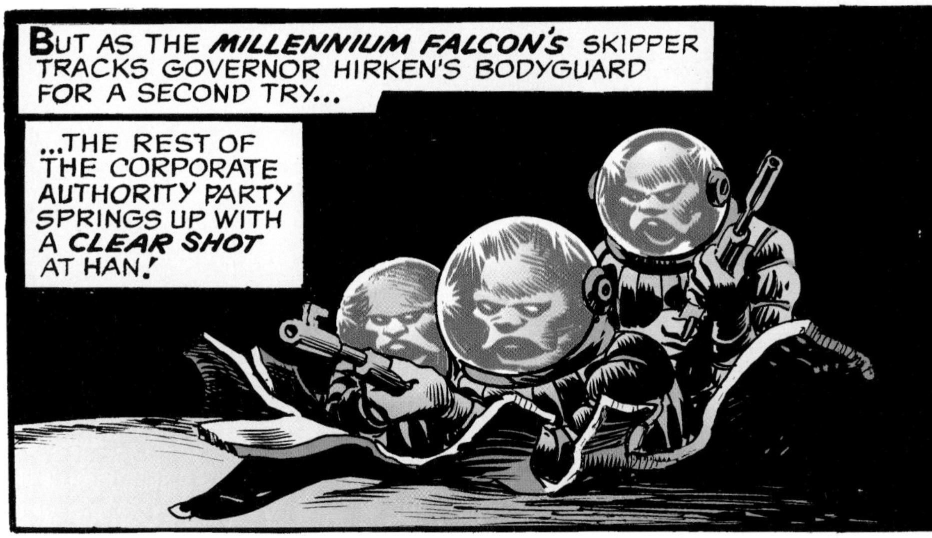
BUT AS THE MILLENNIUM FALCON'S SKIPPER TRACKS GOVERNOR HIRKEN'S BODYGUARD FOR A SECOND TRY...
...THE REST OF THE CORPORATE AUTHORITY PARTY SPRINGS UP WITH A CLEAR SHOT AT HAN!

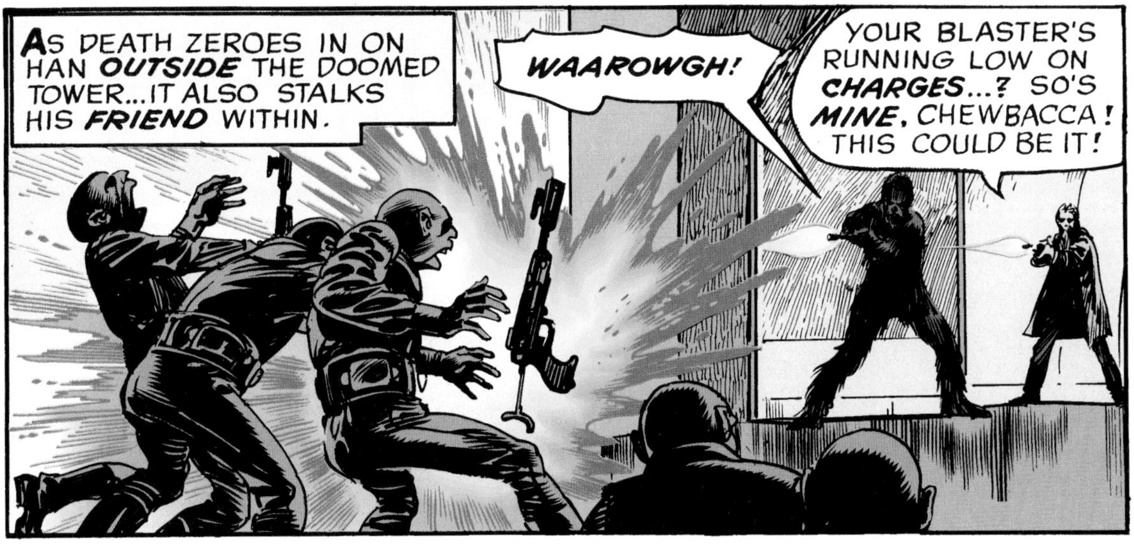
AS DEATH ZEROES IN ON HAN OUTSIDE THE DOOMED TOWER...IT ALSO STALKS HIS FRIEND WITHIN.
WAAROWGH!
YOUR BLASTER'S RUNNING LOW ON CHARGES...? SO'S MINE, CHEWBACCA! THIS COULD BE IT!

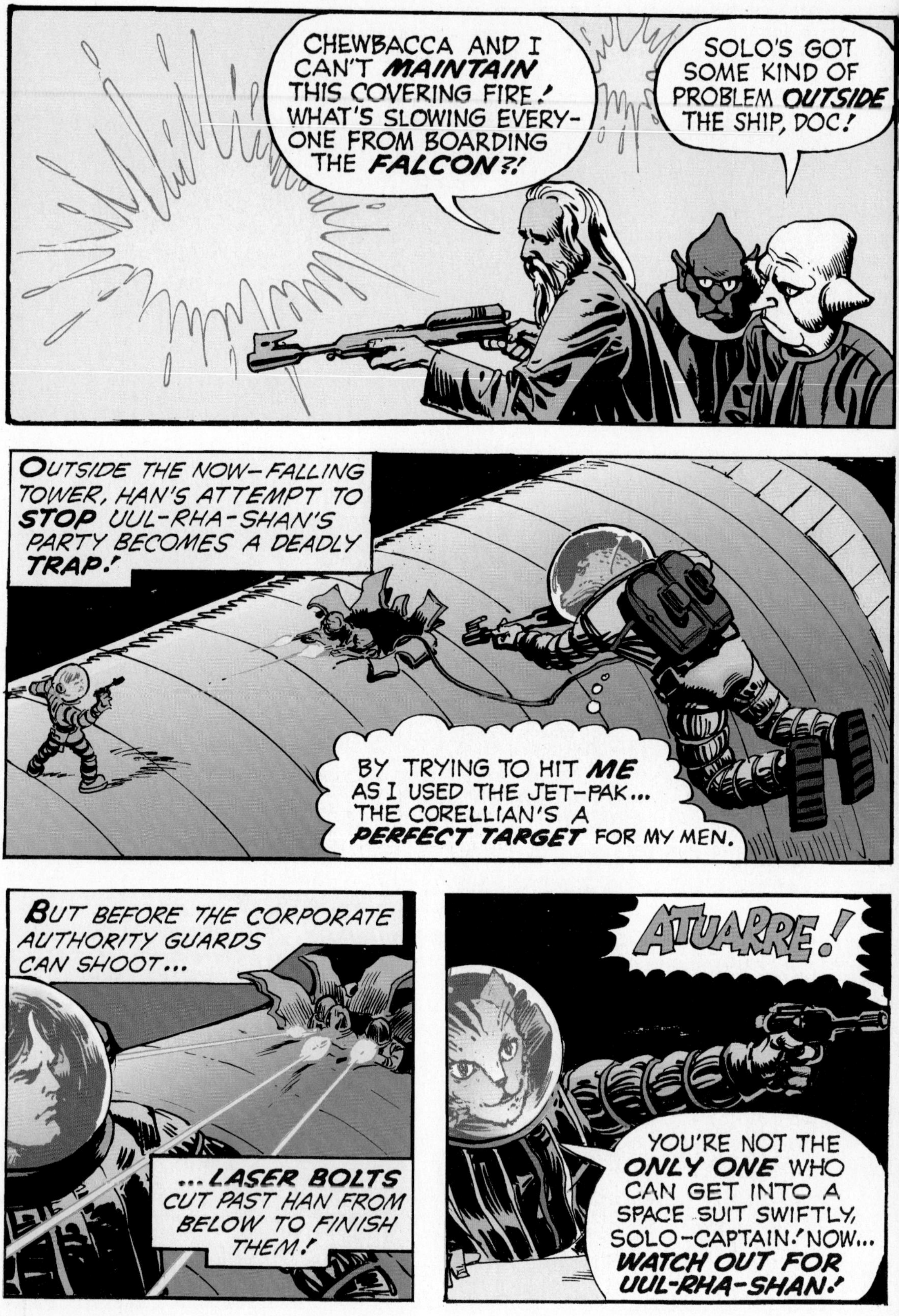
CHEWBACCA AND I CAN'T MAINTAIN THIS COVERING FIRE! WHAT'S SLOWING EVERY-ONE FROM BOARDING THE FALCON?!
SOLO'S GOT SOME KIND OF PROBLEM OUTSIDE THE SHIP, DOC!
OUTSIDE THE NOW-FALLING TOWER, HAN'S ATTEMPT TO STOP UUL-RHA-SHAN'S PARTY BECOMES A DEADLY TRAP!
BY TRYING TO HIT ME AS I USED THE JET-PAK... THE CORELLIAN'S A PERFECT TARGET FOR MY MEN.
BUT BEFORE THE CORPORATE AUTHORITY GUARDS CAN SHOOT...
...LASER BOLTS CUT PAST HAN FROM BELOW TO FINISH THEM!
ATUARRE!
YOU'RE NOT THE ONLY ONE WHO CAN GET INTO A SPACE SUIT SWIFTLY, SOLO-CAPTAIN! NOW... WATCH OUT FOR UUL-RHA-SHAN!

TWO BLASTERS FIRE SIMULTANEOUSLY...

...ONE WITH A HAIR MORE *ACCURACY* THAN THE OTHER!

BUT AT THE AIRLOCK WHERE THE *MILLENNIUM FALCON* IS DOCKED...

VARRWK!

MY BLASTER'S *EMPTY* TOO, CHEWIE... THERE'S *NOTHING* TO STOP GOVERNOR HIRKEN AND HIS GOONS FROM *CHARGING!*

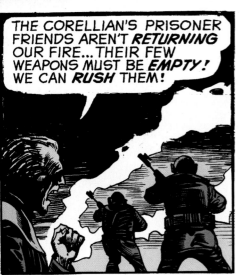

THE CORELLIAN'S PRISONER FRIENDS AREN'T *RETURNING* OUR FIRE... THEIR FEW WEAPONS MUST BE *EMPTY!* WE CAN *RUSH* THEM!

BOLDLY, GOVERNOR HIRKEN LEADS HIS CORPORATE AUTHORITY FORCES *CHARGING* INTO THE DETENTION WING...

FIGHT STRAIGHT TO THE *AIRLOCK*...THEY'VE *NO WAY* OF STOPPING US!

TRUE! EMPTY WEAPONS RAISED AS CLUBS, CHEWBACCA AND DOC PREPARE TO DIE DEFENDING THE WAY TO THE *MILLENNIUM FALCON!* THEN...

IT'S *PAKKA*...ATUARRE'S CUB! W-WHAT...?

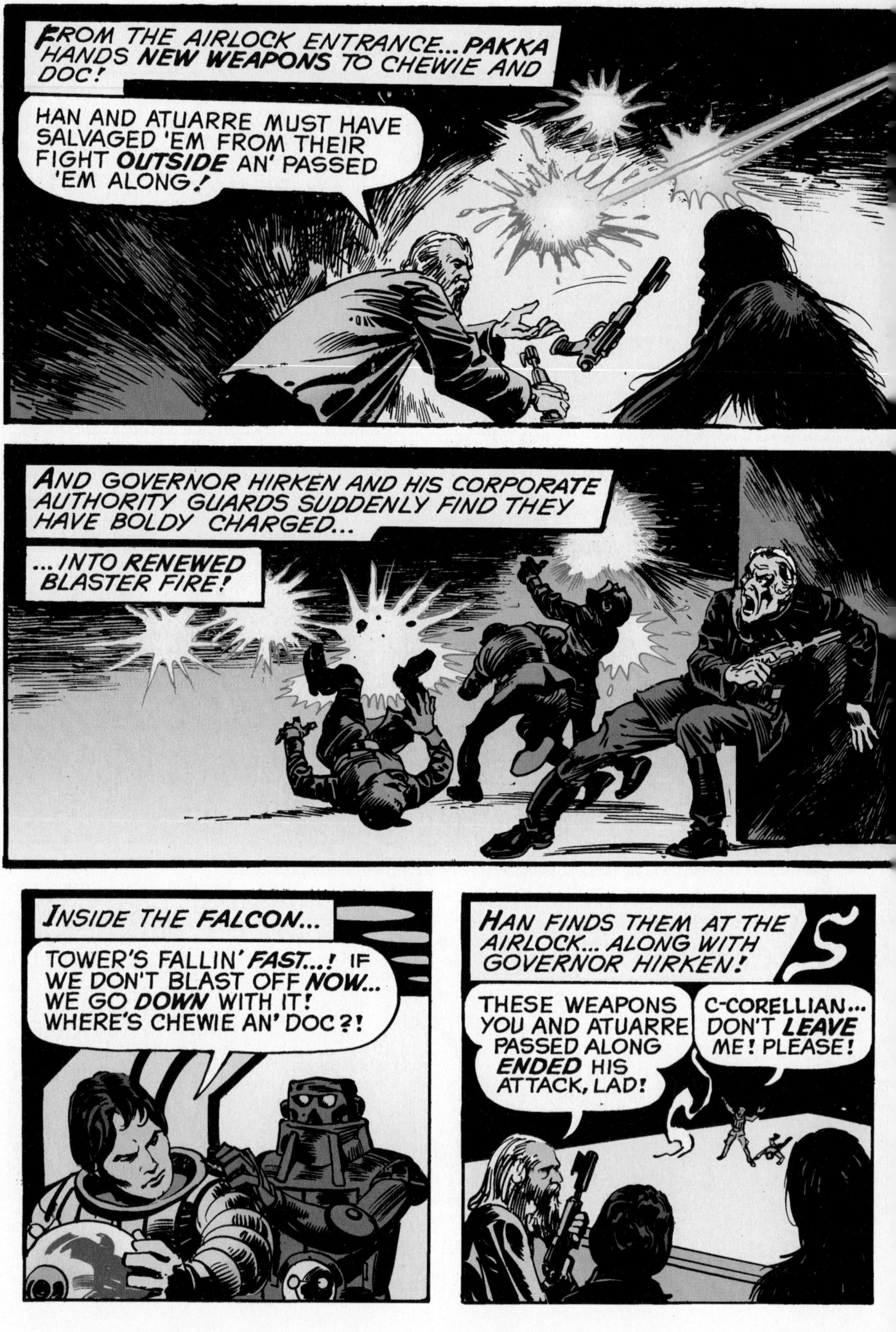
FROM THE AIRLOCK ENTRANCE... PAKKA HANDS NEW WEAPONS TO CHEWIE AND DOC!
HAN AND ATUARRE MUST HAVE SALVAGED 'EM FROM THEIR FIGHT OUTSIDE AN' PASSED 'EM ALONG!
AND GOVERNOR HIRKEN AND HIS CORPORATE AUTHORITY GUARDS SUDDENLY FIND THEY HAVE BOLDY CHARGED...
...INTO RENEWED BLASTER FIRE!
INSIDE THE FALCON...
TOWER'S FALLIN' FAST...! IF WE DON'T BLAST OFF NOW... WE GO DOWN WITH IT! WHERE'S CHEWIE AN' DOC?!
HAN FINDS THEM AT THE AIRLOCK... ALONG WITH GOVERNOR HIRKEN!
THESE WEAPONS YOU AND ATUARRE PASSED ALONG ENDED HIS ATTACK, LAD!
C-CORELLIAN... DON'T LEAVE ME! PLEASE!

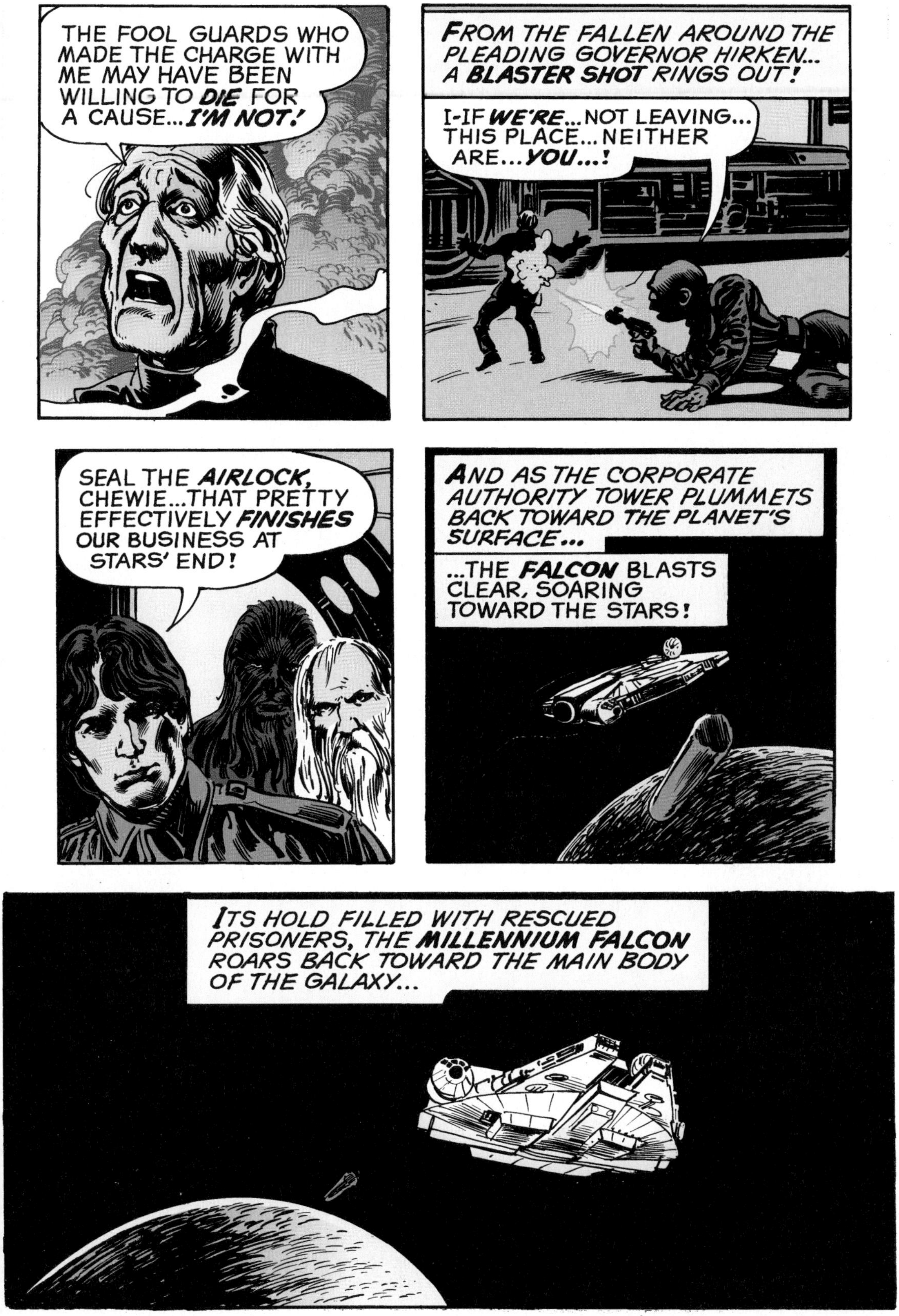
THE FOOL GUARDS WHO MADE THE CHARGE WITH ME MAY HAVE BEEN WILLING TO DIE FOR A CAUSE...I'M NOT!
FROM THE FALLEN AROUND THE PLEADING GOVERNOR HIRKEN... A BLASTER SHOT RINGS OUT!
I-IF WE'RE...NOT LEAVING... THIS PLACE...NEITHER ARE...YOU...!
SEAL THE AIRLOCK, CHEWIE...THAT PRETTY EFFECTIVELY FINISHES OUR BUSINESS AT STARS' END!
AND AS THE CORPORATE AUTHORITY TOWER PLUMMETS BACK TOWARD THE PLANET'S SURFACE...
...THE FALCON BLASTS CLEAR, SOARING TOWARD THE STARS!
ITS HOLD FILLED WITH RESCUED PRISONERS, THE MILLENNIUM FALCON ROARS BACK TOWARD THE MAIN BODY OF THE GALAXY...

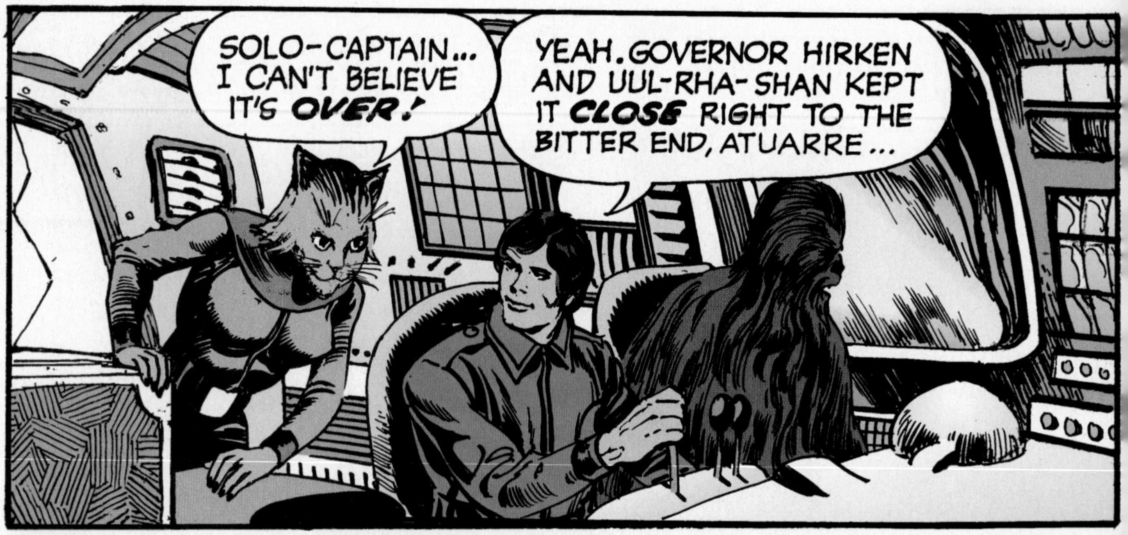
SOLO-CAPTAIN... I CAN'T BELIEVE IT'S OVER!
YEAH. GOVERNOR HIRKEN AND UUL-RHA-SHAN KEPT IT CLOSE RIGHT TO THE BITTER END, ATUARRE...

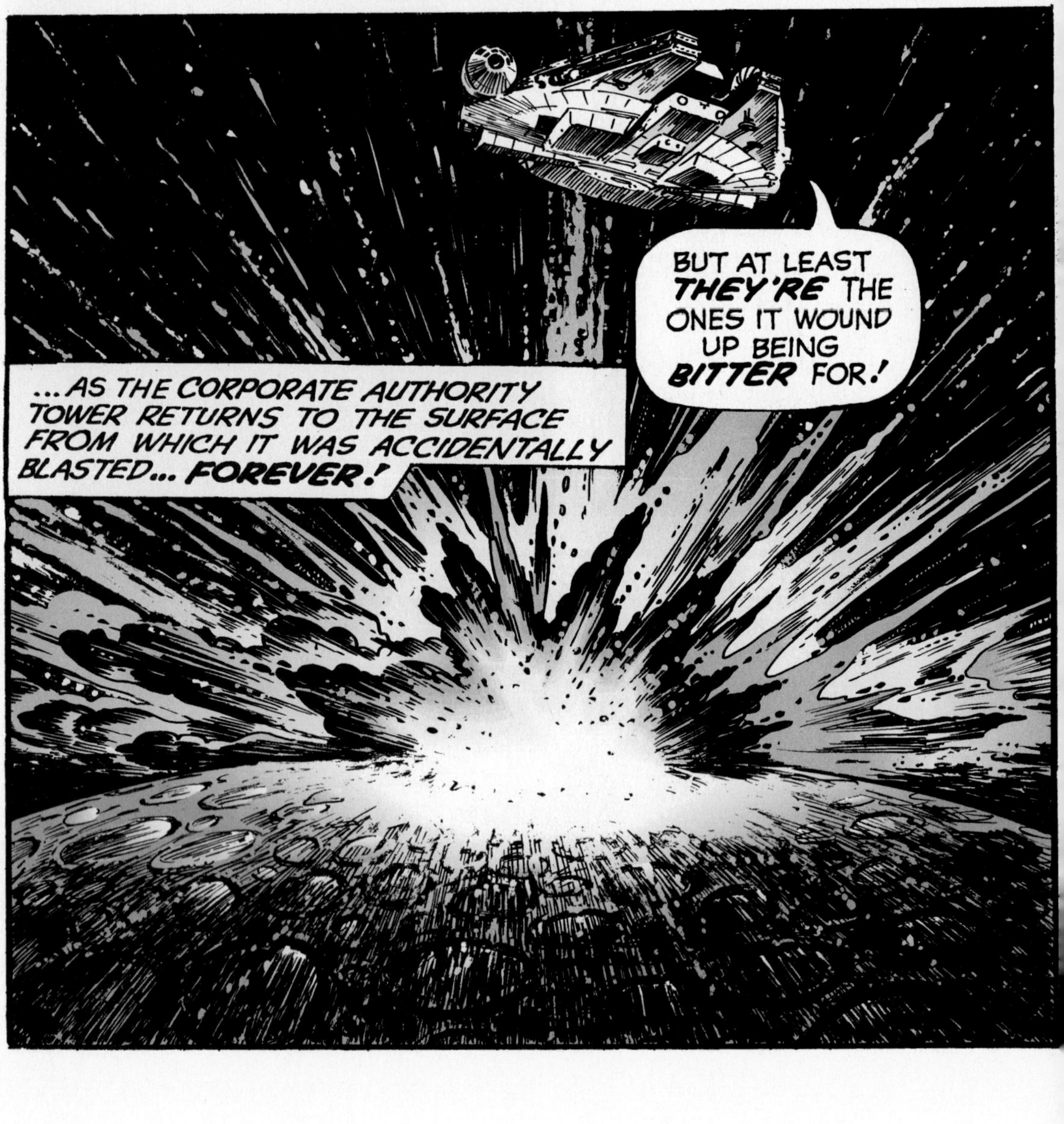
BUT AT LEAST THEY'RE THE ONES IT WOUND UP BEING BITTER FOR!
...AS THE CORPORATE AUTHORITY TOWER RETURNS TO THE SURFACE FROM WHICH IT WAS ACCIDENTALLY BLASTED... FOREVER!

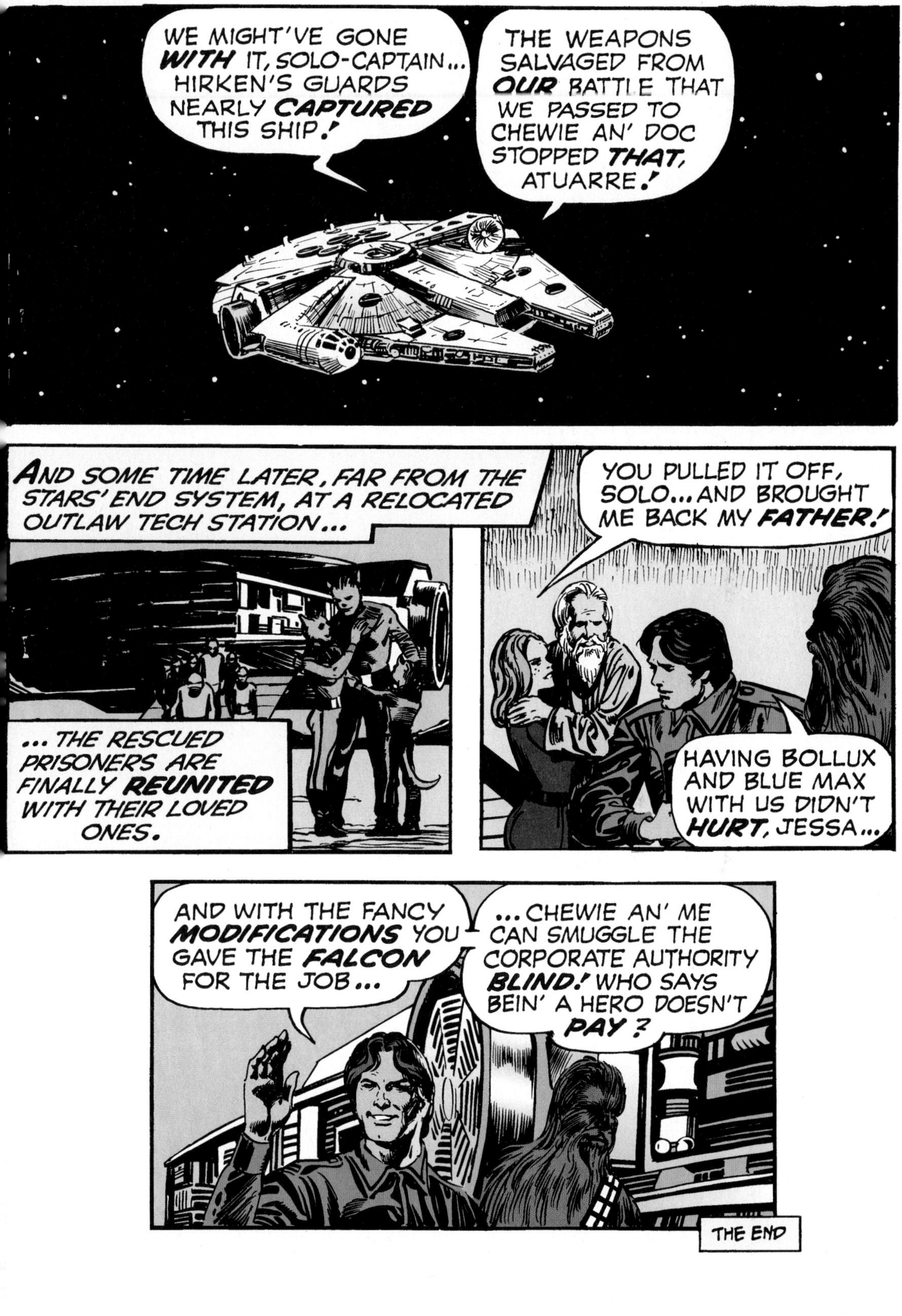
WE MIGHT'VE GONE WITH IT, SOLO-CAPTAIN... HIRKEN'S GUARDS NEARLY CAPTURED THIS SHIP!
THE WEAPONS SALVAGED FROM OUR BATTLE THAT WE PASSED TO CHEWIE AN' DOC STOPPED THAT, ATUARRE!
AND SOME TIME LATER, FAR FROM THE STARS' END SYSTEM, AT A RELOCATED OUTLAW TECH STATION...
...THE RESCUED PRISONERS ARE FINALLY REUNITED WITH THEIR LOVED ONES.
YOU PULLED IT OFF, SOLO...AND BROUGHT ME BACK MY FATHER!
HAVING BOLLUX AND BLUE MAX WITH US DIDN'T HURT, JESSA...
AND WITH THE FANCY MODIFICATIONS YOU GAVE THE FALCON FOR THE JOB...
...CHEWIE AN' ME CAN SMUGGLE THE CORPORATE AUTHORITY BLIND! WHO SAYS BEIN' A HERO DOESN'T PAY?
THE END

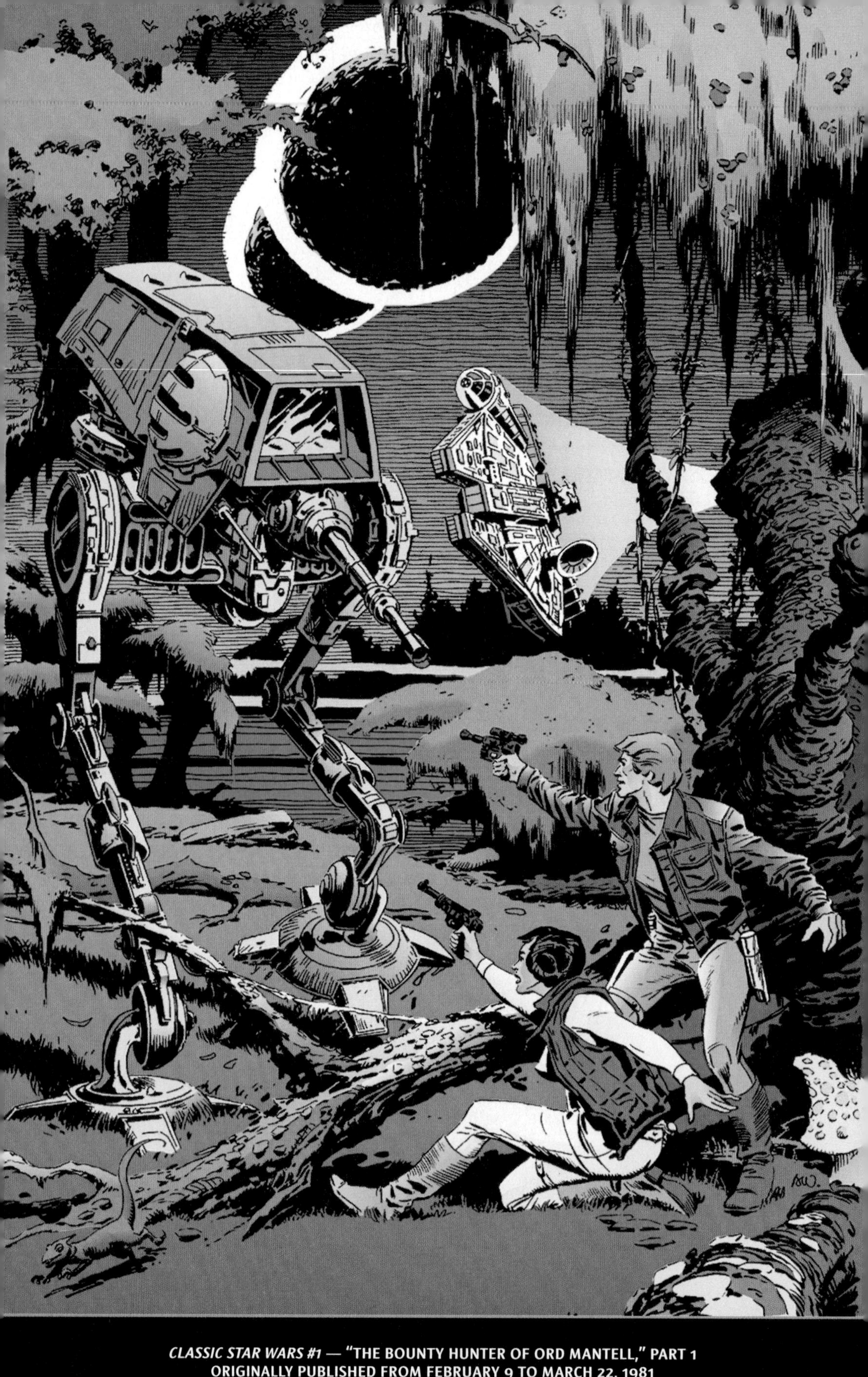

CLASSIC STAR WARS #1 — "THE BOUNTY HUNTER OF ORD MANTELL," PART 1
ORIGINALLY PUBLISHED FROM FEBRUARY 9 TO MARCH 22, 1981

WRITER: ARCHIE GOODWIN • ARTIST & LETTERER: AL WILLIAMSON • COLORIST: STEVE BUCCELLATO • PRODUCTION ARTIST: MARTY TODD
EDITOR: ANINA BENNETT • COVER ARTISTS: AL WILLIAMSON & GREGORY WRIGHT

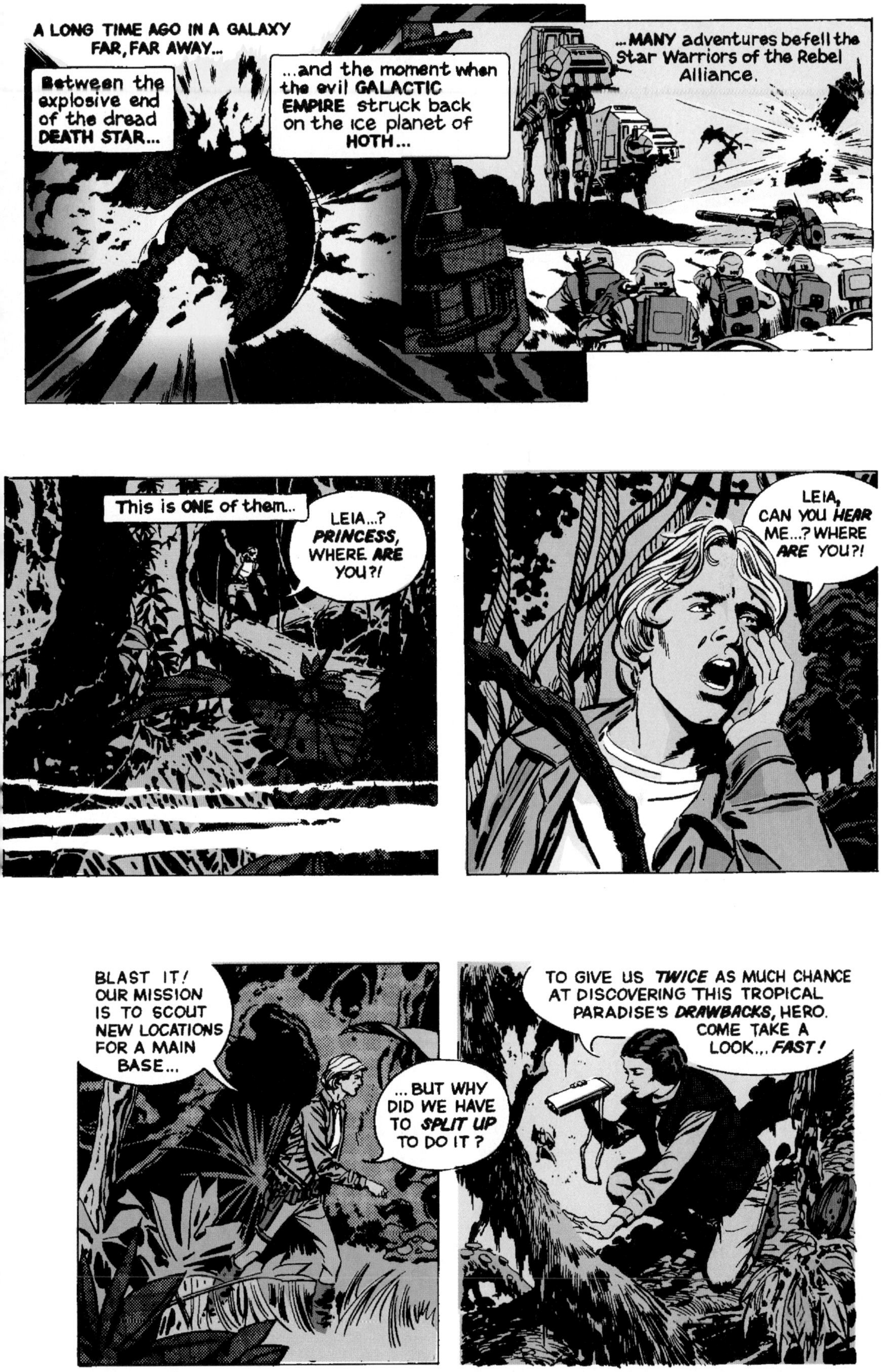
A LONG TIME AGO IN A GALAXY FAR, FAR AWAY...
Between the explosive end of the dread DEATH STAR...
...and the moment when the evil GALACTIC EMPIRE struck back on the ice planet of HOTH...
...MANY adventures befell the Star Warriors of the Rebel Alliance.
This is ONE of them...
LEIA...? PRINCESS, WHERE ARE YOU?!
LEIA, CAN YOU HEAR ME...? WHERE ARE YOU?!
BLAST IT! OUR MISSION IS TO SCOUT NEW LOCATIONS FOR A MAIN BASE...
...BUT WHY DID WE HAVE TO SPLIT UP TO DO IT?
TO GIVE US TWICE AS MUCH CHANCE AT DISCOVERING THIS TROPICAL PARADISE'S DRAWBACKS, HERO. COME TAKE A LOOK... FAST!

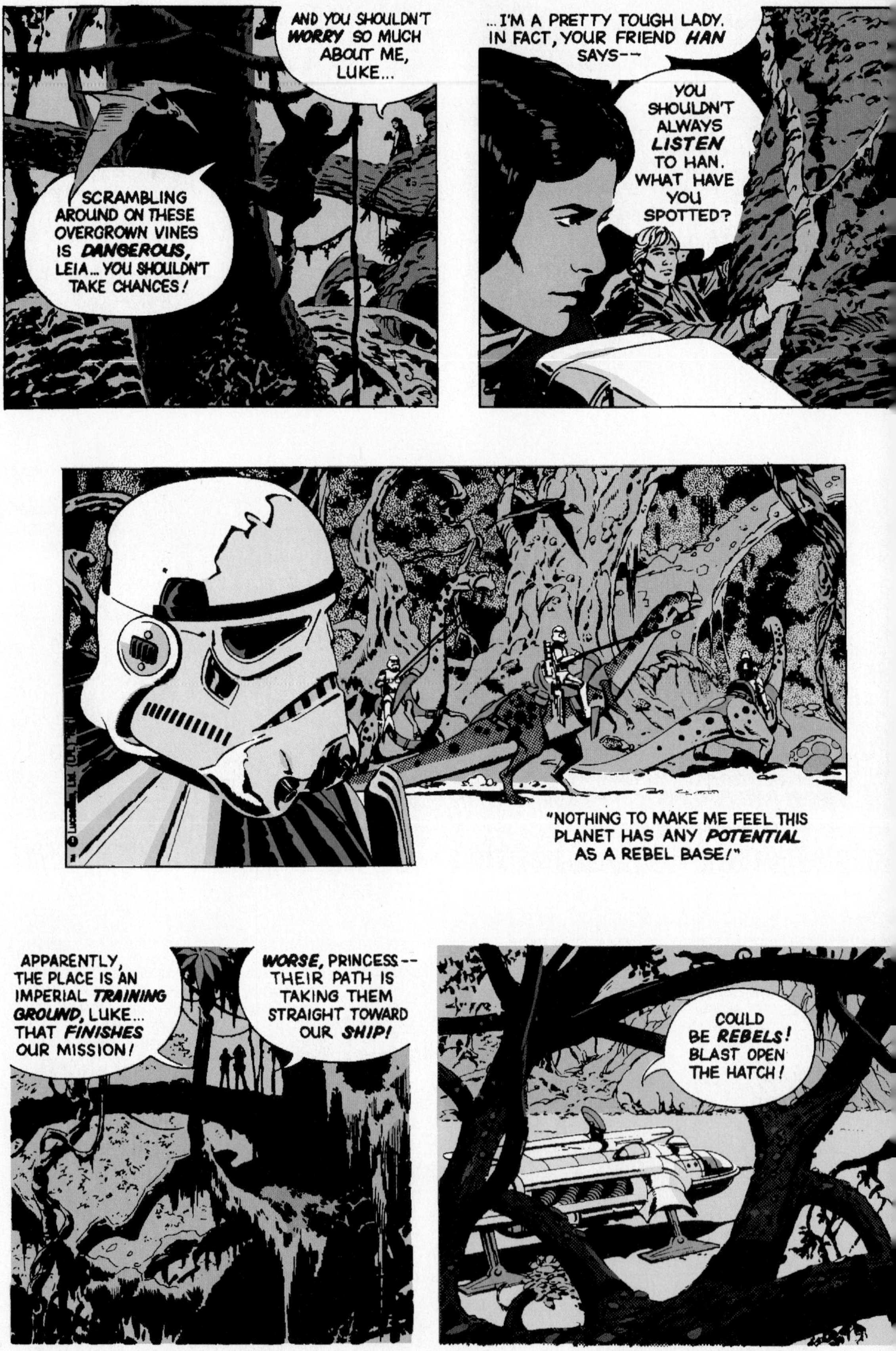
AND YOU SHOULDN'T WORRY SO MUCH ABOUT ME, LUKE...
SCRAMBLING AROUND ON THESE OVERGROWN VINES IS DANGEROUS, LEIA... YOU SHOULDN'T TAKE CHANCES!
...I'M A PRETTY TOUGH LADY. IN FACT, YOUR FRIEND HAN SAYS--
YOU SHOULDN'T ALWAYS LISTEN TO HAN. WHAT HAVE YOU SPOTTED?
"NOTHING TO MAKE ME FEEL THIS PLANET HAS ANY POTENTIAL AS A REBEL BASE!"
APPARENTLY, THE PLACE IS AN IMPERIAL TRAINING GROUND, LUKE... THAT FINISHES OUR MISSION!
WORSE, PRINCESS-- THEIR PATH IS TAKING THEM STRAIGHT TOWARD OUR SHIP!
COULD BE REBELS! BLAST OPEN THE HATCH!

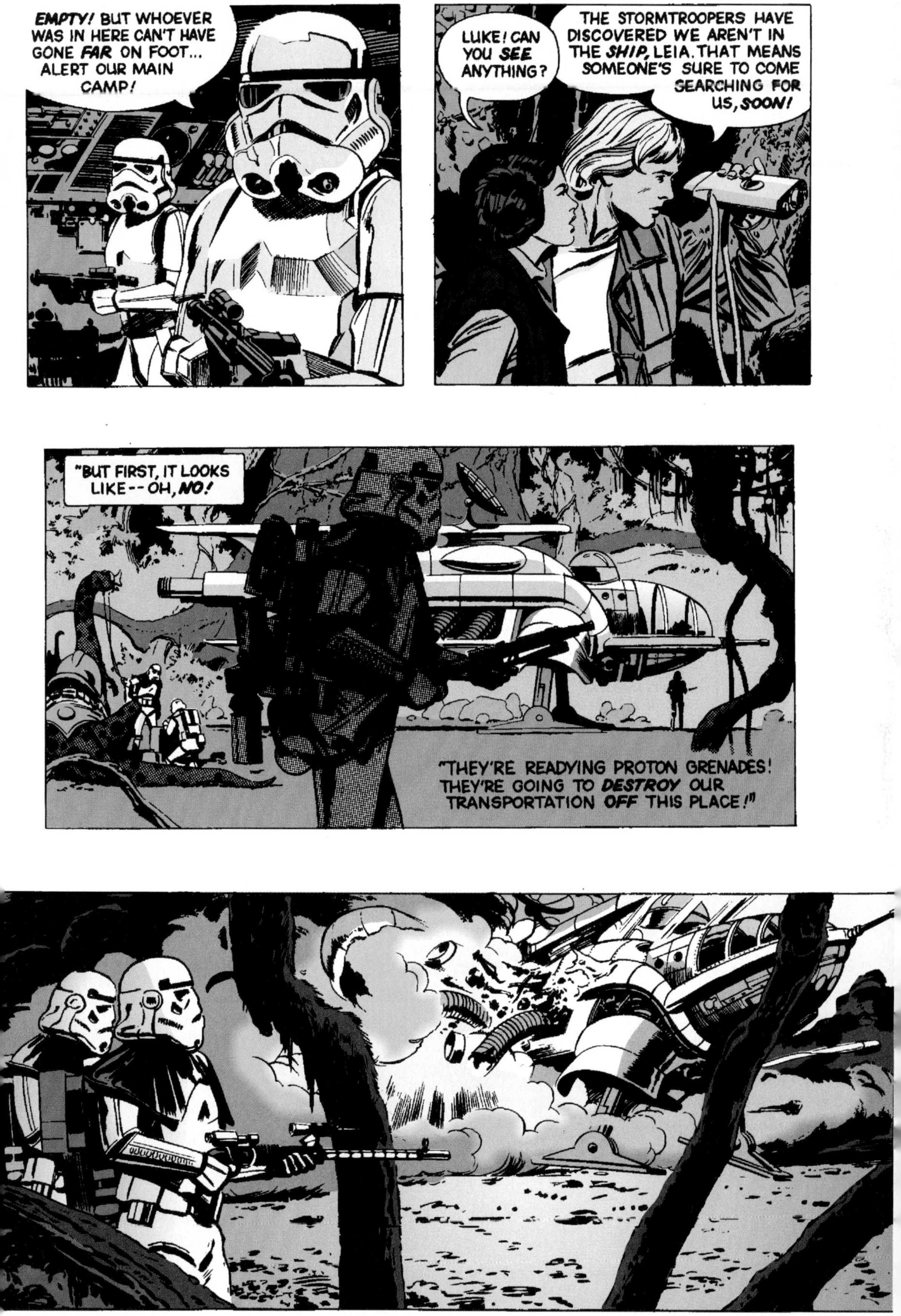
EMPTY! BUT WHOEVER WAS IN HERE CAN'T HAVE GONE FAR ON FOOT... ALERT OUR MAIN CAMP!
LUKE! CAN YOU SEE ANYTHING?
THE STORMTROOPERS HAVE DISCOVERED WE AREN'T IN THE SHIP, LEIA. THAT MEANS SOMEONE'S SURE TO COME SEARCHING FOR US, SOON!
"BUT FIRST, IT LOOKS LIKE--OH, NO!
"THEY'RE READYING PROTON GRENADES! THEY'RE GOING TO DESTROY OUR TRANSPORTATION OFF THIS PLACE!"

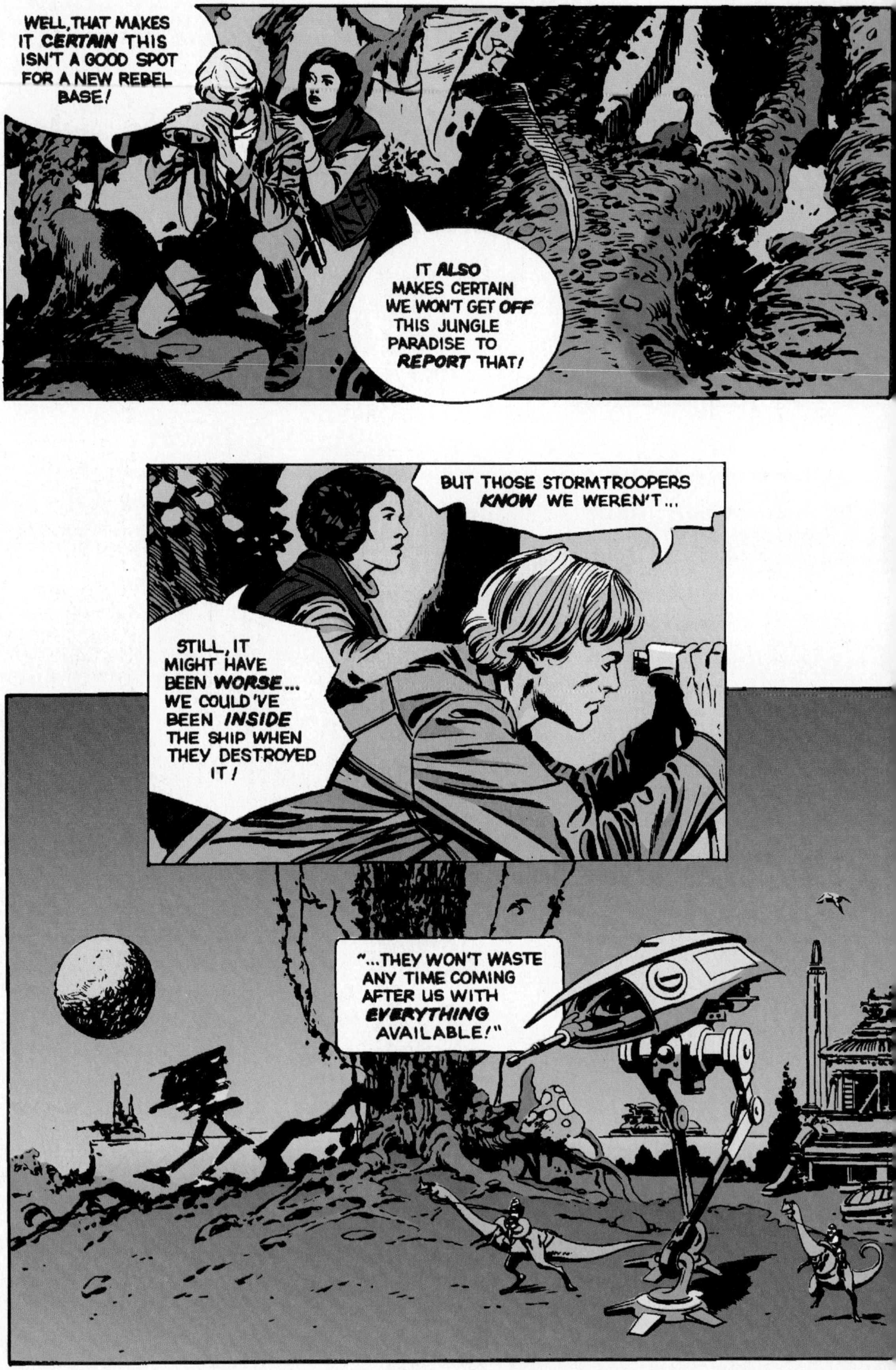

WELL, THAT MAKES IT CERTAIN THIS ISN'T A GOOD SPOT FOR A NEW REBEL BASE!
IT ALSO MAKES CERTAIN WE WON'T GET OFF THIS JUNGLE PARADISE TO REPORT THAT!
BUT THOSE STORMTROOPERS KNOW WE WEREN'T...
STILL, IT MIGHT HAVE BEEN WORSE... WE COULD'VE BEEN INSIDE THE SHIP WHEN THEY DESTROYED IT!
"...THEY WON'T WASTE ANY TIME COMING AFTER US WITH EVERYTHING AVAILABLE!"

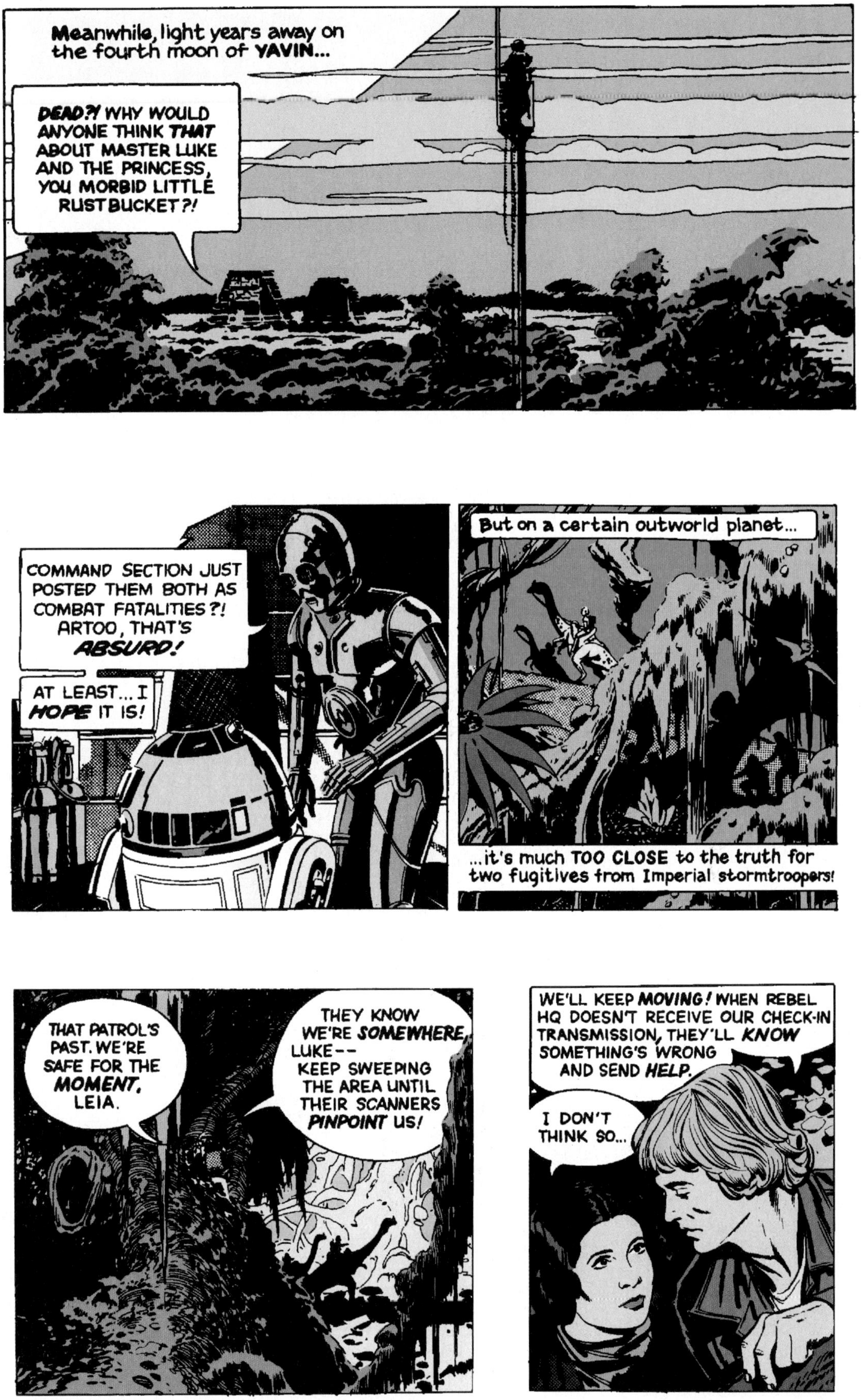
Meanwhile, light years away on the fourth moon of YAVIN...
DEAD?! WHY WOULD ANYONE THINK THAT ABOUT MASTER LUKE AND THE PRINCESS, YOU MORBID LITTLE RUSTBUCKET?!
COMMAND SECTION JUST POSTED THEM BOTH AS COMBAT FATALITIES?! ARTOO, THAT'S ABSURD!
AT LEAST... I HOPE IT IS!
But on a certain outworld planet...
...it's much TOO CLOSE to the truth for two fugitives from Imperial stormtroopers!
THAT PATROL'S PAST. WE'RE SAFE FOR THE MOMENT, LEIA.
THEY KNOW WE'RE SOMEWHERE, LUKE-- KEEP SWEEPING THE AREA UNTIL THEIR SCANNERS PINPOINT US!
WE'LL KEEP MOVING! WHEN REBEL HQ DOESN'T RECEIVE OUR CHECK-IN TRANSMISSION, THEY'LL KNOW SOMETHING'S WRONG AND SEND HELP.
I DON'T THINK SO...

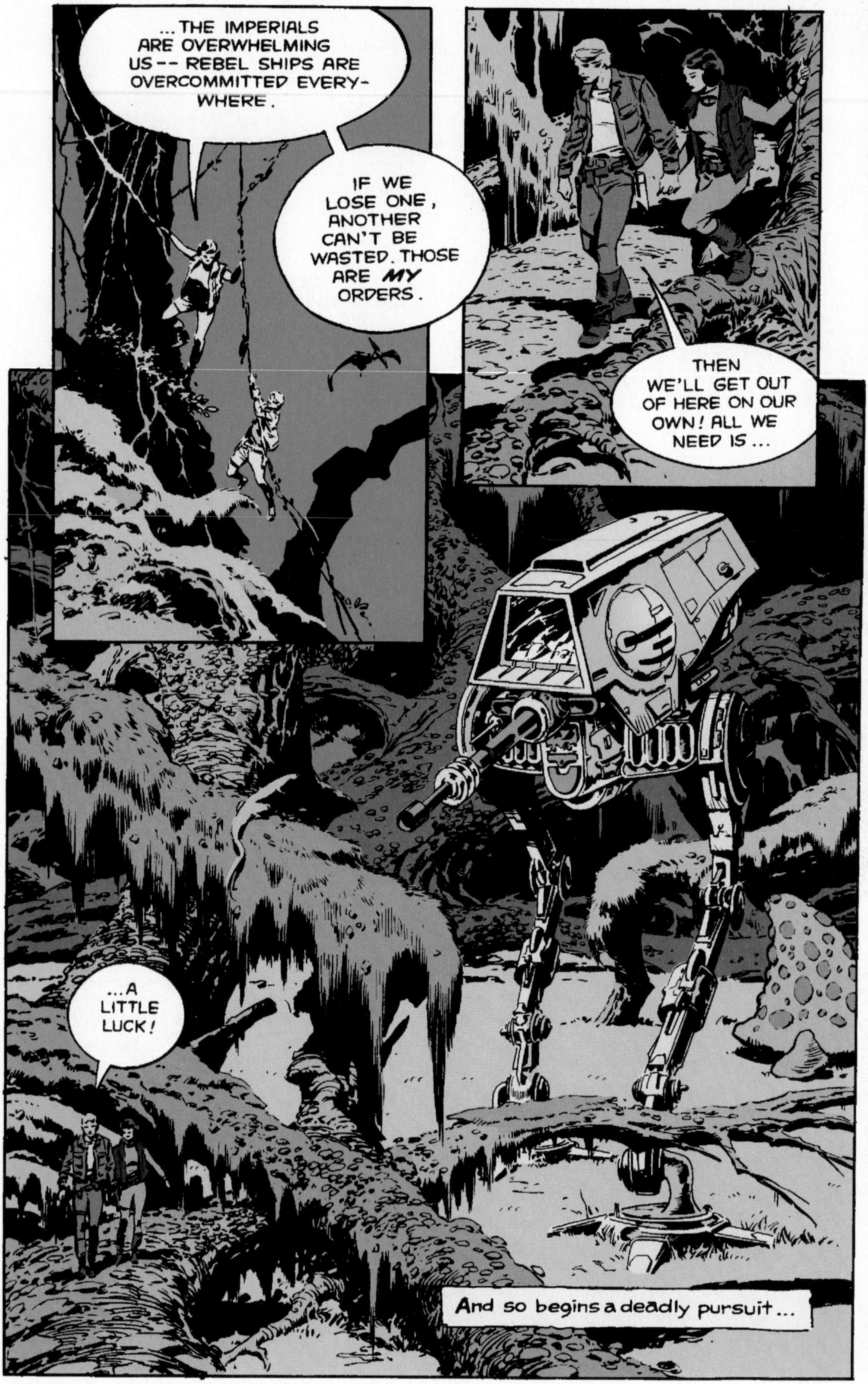
...THE IMPERIALS ARE OVERWHELMING US-- REBEL SHIPS ARE OVERCOMMITTED EVERY-WHERE.
IF WE LOSE ONE, ANOTHER CAN'T BE WASTED. THOSE ARE *MY* ORDERS.
THEN WE'LL GET OUT OF HERE ON OUR OWN! ALL WE NEED IS...
...A LITTLE LUCK!
And so begins a deadly pursuit...

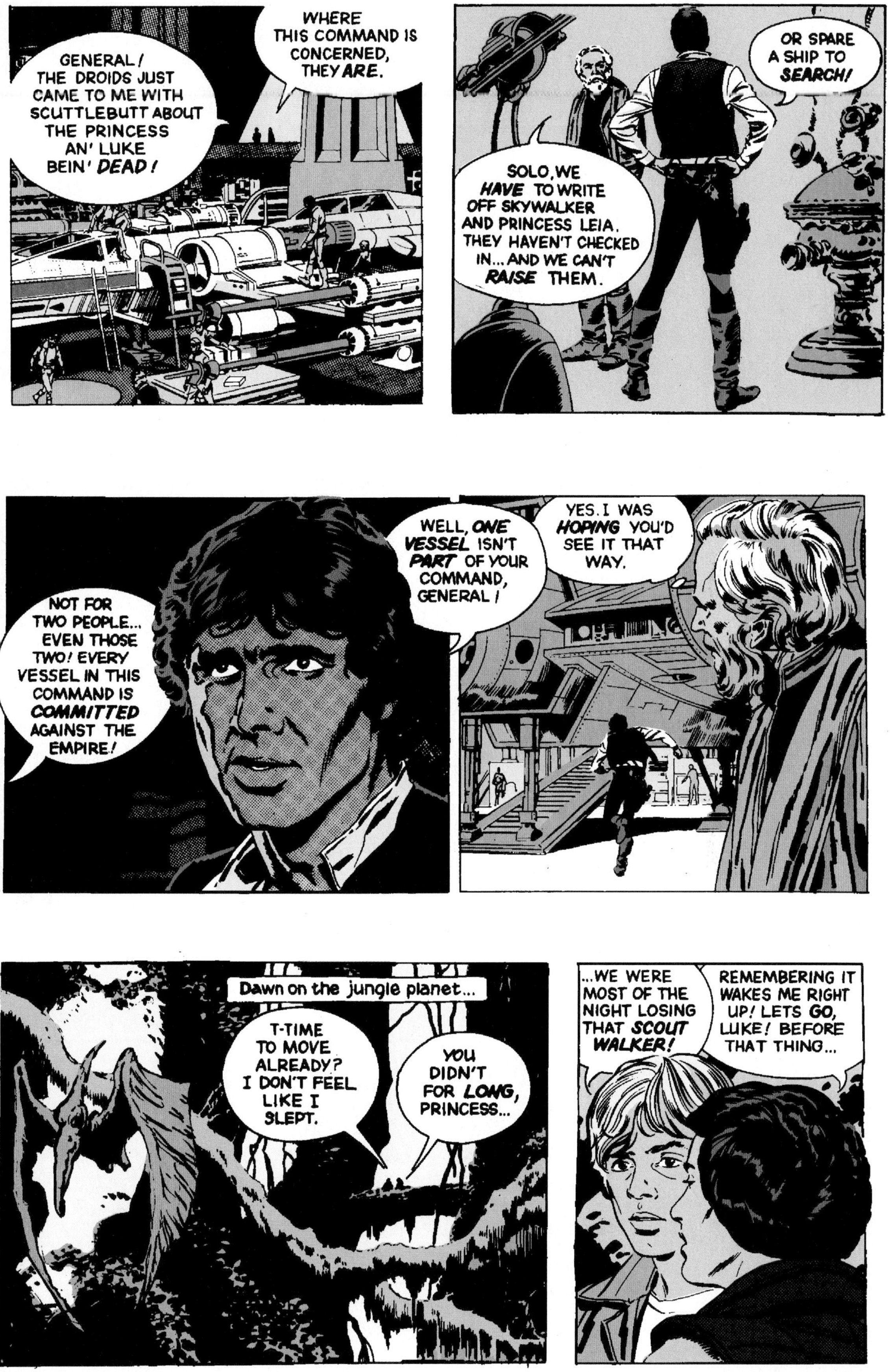

GENERAL! THE DROIDS JUST CAME TO ME WITH SCUTTLEBUTT ABOUT THE PRINCESS AN' LUKE BEIN' DEAD!
WHERE THIS COMMAND IS CONCERNED, THEY ARE.
SOLO, WE HAVE TO WRITE OFF SKYWALKER AND PRINCESS LEIA. THEY HAVEN'T CHECKED IN... AND WE CAN'T RAISE THEM.
OR SPARE A SHIP TO SEARCH!
NOT FOR TWO PEOPLE... EVEN THOSE TWO! EVERY VESSEL IN THIS COMMAND IS COMMITTED AGAINST THE EMPIRE!
WELL, ONE VESSEL ISN'T PART OF YOUR COMMAND, GENERAL!
YES. I WAS HOPING YOU'D SEE IT THAT WAY.
Dawn on the jungle planet...
T-TIME TO MOVE ALREADY? I DON'T FEEL LIKE I SLEPT.
YOU DIDN'T FOR LONG, PRINCESS...
...WE WERE MOST OF THE NIGHT LOSING THAT SCOUT WALKER!
REMEMBERING IT WAKES ME RIGHT UP! LETS GO, LUKE! BEFORE THAT THING...

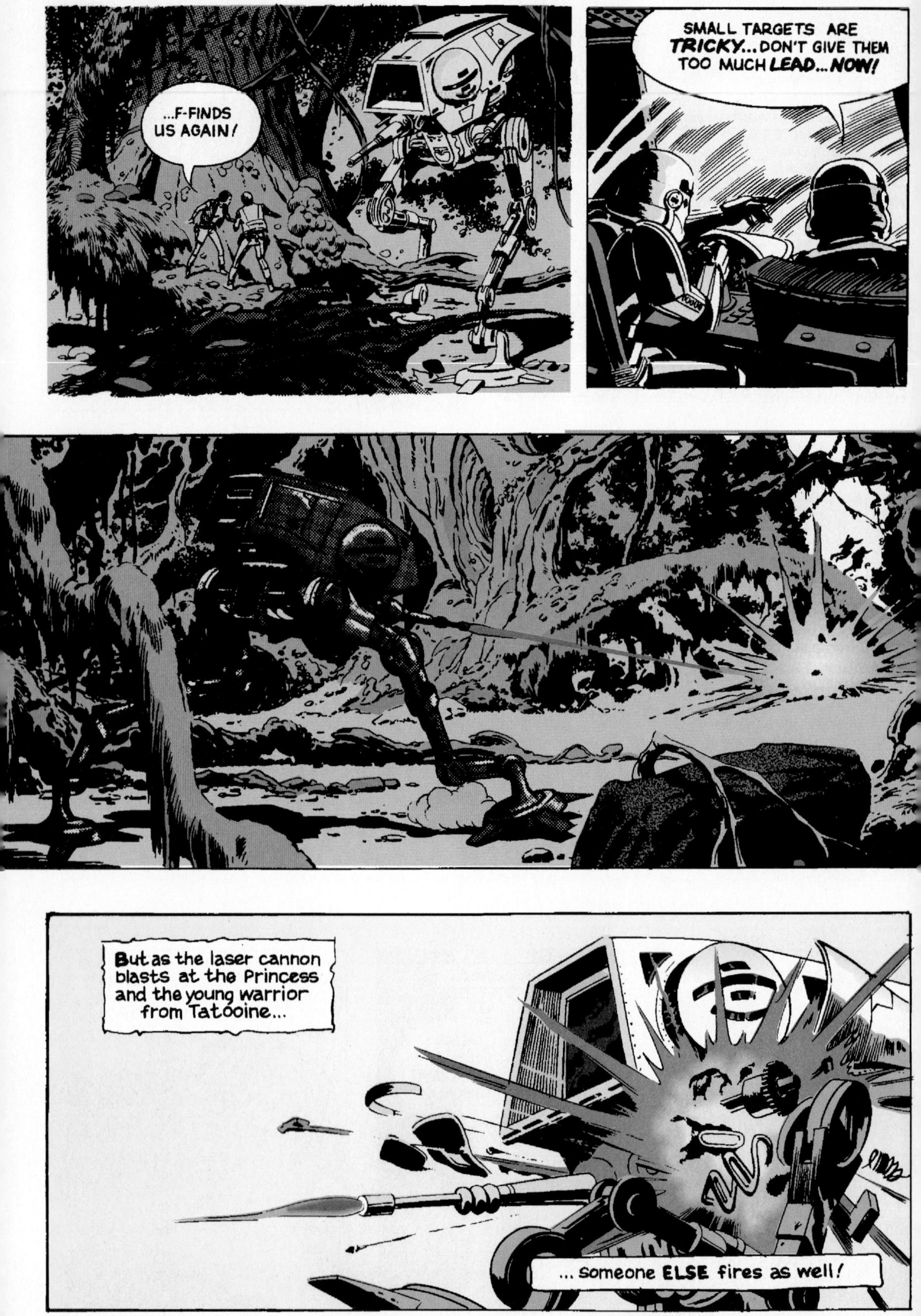
...F-FINDS US AGAIN!
SMALL TARGETS ARE TRICKY... DON'T GIVE THEM TOO MUCH LEAD... NOW!
But as the laser cannon blasts at the Princess and the young warrior from Tatooine...
... someone ELSE fires as well!

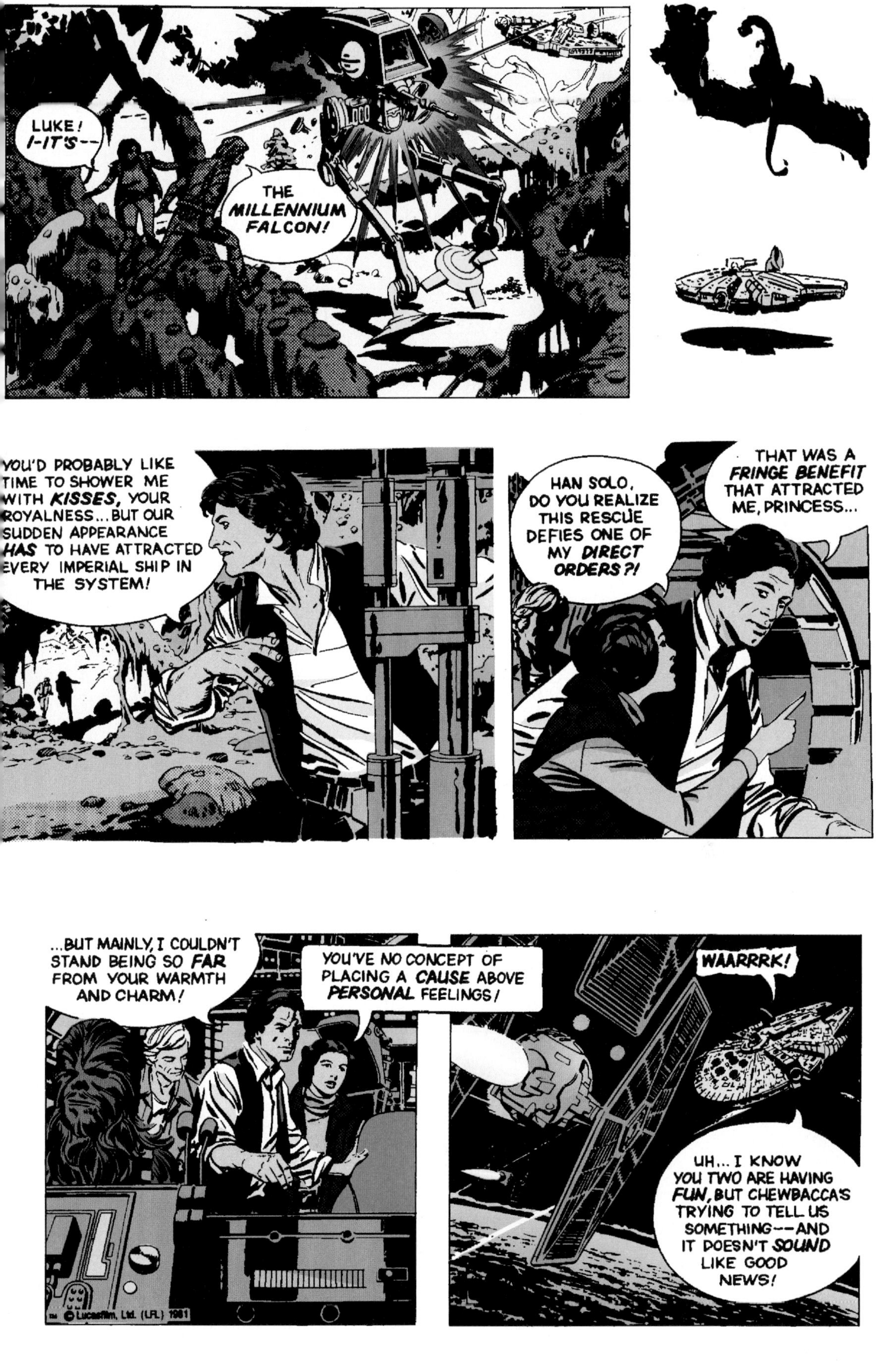
LUKE! I-IT'S--
THE MILLENNIUM FALCON!
YOU'D PROBABLY LIKE TIME TO SHOWER ME WITH KISSES, YOUR ROYALNESS... BUT OUR SUDDEN APPEARANCE HAS TO HAVE ATTRACTED EVERY IMPERIAL SHIP IN THE SYSTEM!
HAN SOLO, DO YOU REALIZE THIS RESCUE DEFIES ONE OF MY DIRECT ORDERS?!
THAT WAS A FRINGE BENEFIT THAT ATTRACTED ME, PRINCESS...
...BUT MAINLY, I COULDN'T STAND BEING SO FAR FROM YOUR WARMTH AND CHARM!
YOU'VE NO CONCEPT OF PLACING A CAUSE ABOVE PERSONAL FEELINGS!
™ © Lucasfilm, Ltd. (LFL) 1981
WAARRRK!
UH... I KNOW YOU TWO ARE HAVING FUN, BUT CHEWBACCA'S TRYING TO TELL US SOMETHING--AND IT DOESN'T SOUND LIKE GOOD NEWS!

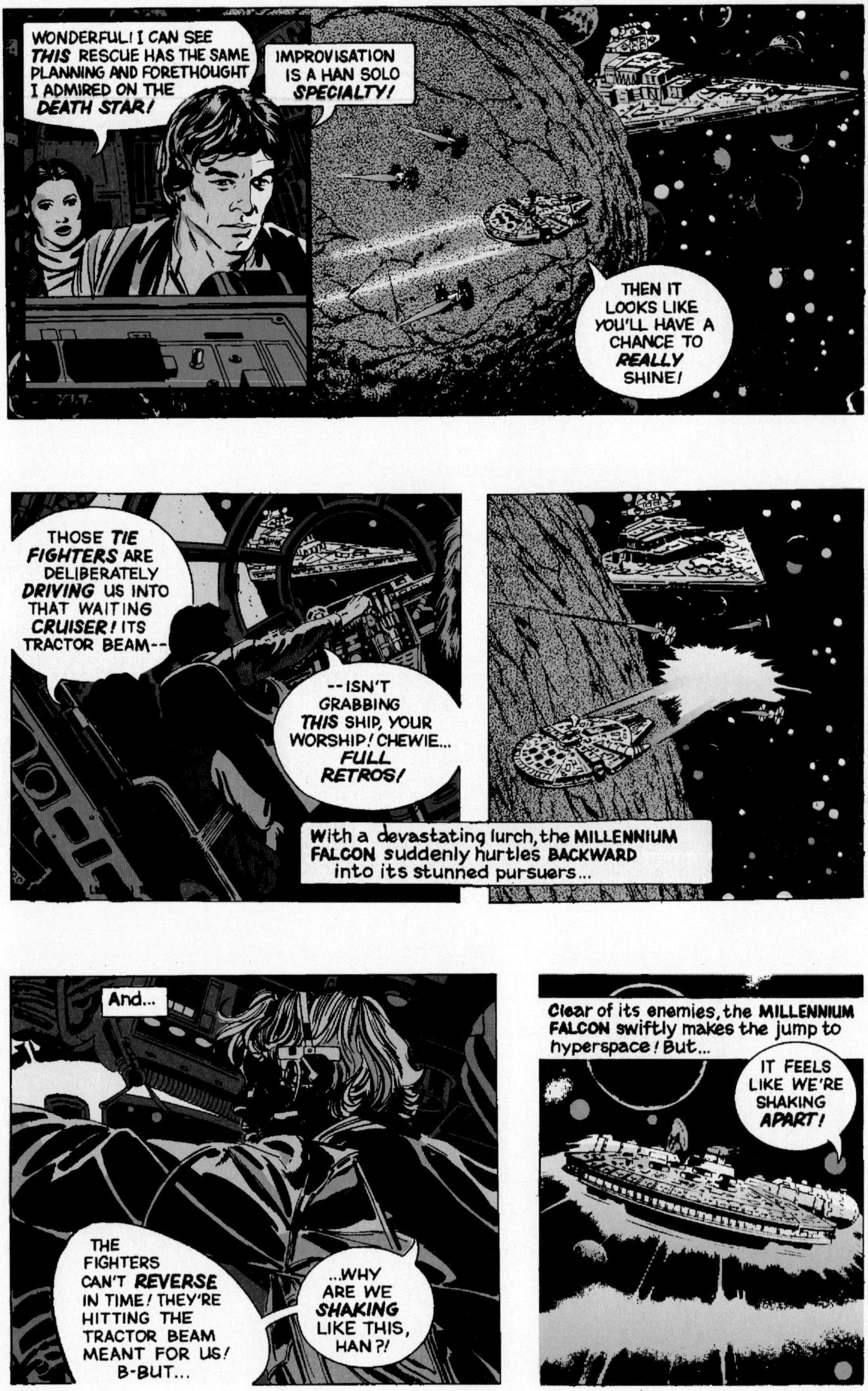
WONDERFUL! I CAN SEE THIS RESCUE HAS THE SAME PLANNING AND FORETHOUGHT I ADMIRED ON THE DEATH STAR!
IMPROVISATION IS A HAN SOLO SPECIALTY!
THEN IT LOOKS LIKE YOU'LL HAVE A CHANCE TO REALLY SHINE!
THOSE TIE FIGHTERS ARE DELIBERATELY DRIVING US INTO THAT WAITING CRUISER! ITS TRACTOR BEAM--
--ISN'T GRABBING THIS SHIP, YOUR WORSHIP! CHEWIE... FULL RETROS!
With a devastating lurch, the MILLENNIUM FALCON suddenly hurtles BACKWARD into its stunned pursuers...
And...
THE FIGHTERS CAN'T REVERSE IN TIME! THEY'RE HITTING THE TRACTOR BEAM MEANT FOR US! B-BUT...
...WHY ARE WE SHAKING LIKE THIS, HAN?!
Clear of its enemies, the MILLENNIUM FALCON swiftly makes the jump to hyperspace! But...
IT FEELS LIKE WE'RE SHAKING APART!

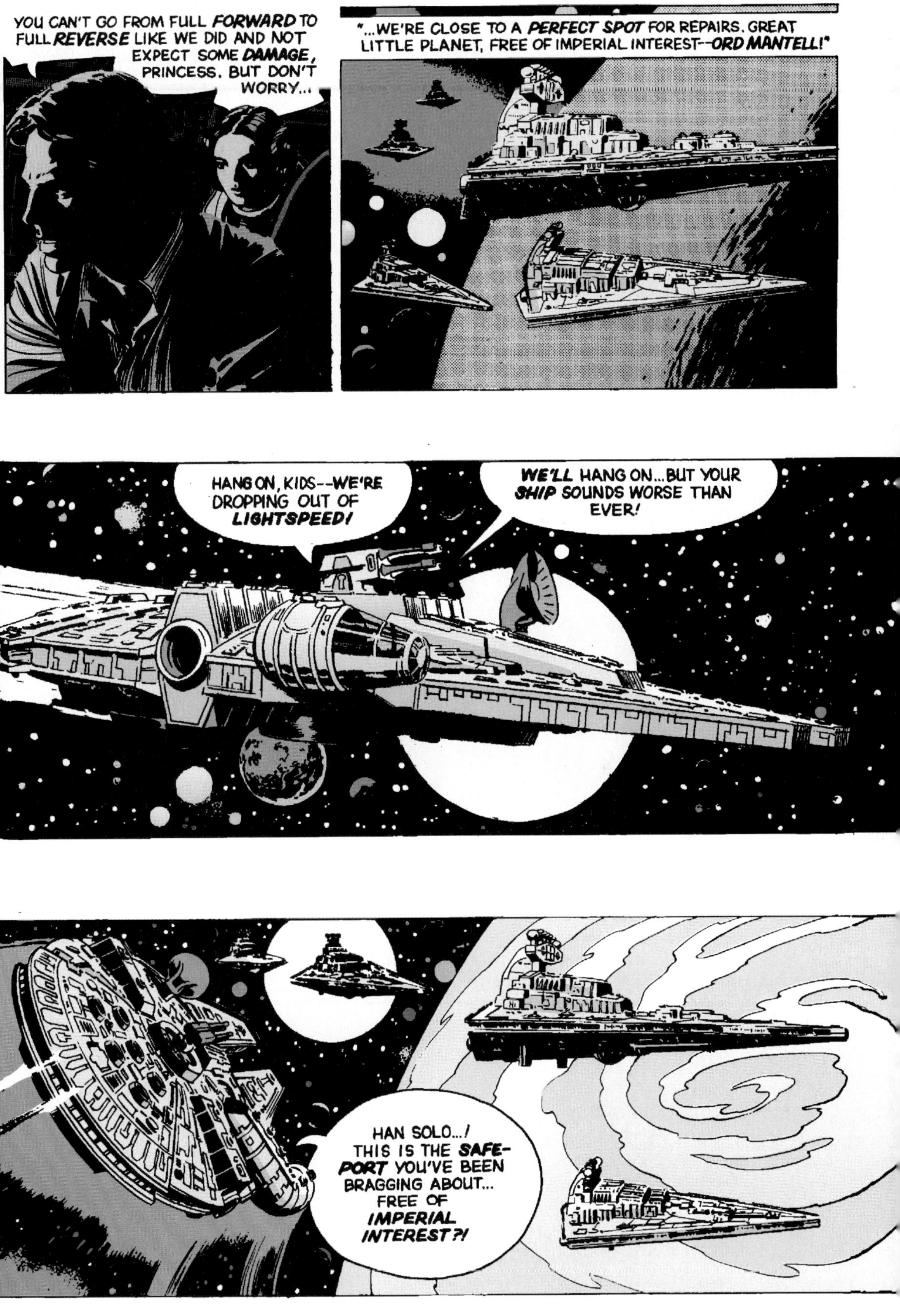
YOU CAN'T GO FROM FULL FORWARD TO FULL REVERSE LIKE WE DID AND NOT EXPECT SOME DAMAGE, PRINCESS. BUT DON'T WORRY...
"...WE'RE CLOSE TO A PERFECT SPOT FOR REPAIRS. GREAT LITTLE PLANET, FREE OF IMPERIAL INTEREST--ORD MANTELL!"
HANG ON, KIDS--WE'RE DROPPING OUT OF LIGHTSPEED!
WE'LL HANG ON...BUT YOUR SHIP SOUNDS WORSE THAN EVER!
HAN SOLO...! THIS IS THE SAFE-PORT YOU'VE BEEN BRAGGING ABOUT... FREE OF IMPERIAL INTEREST?!

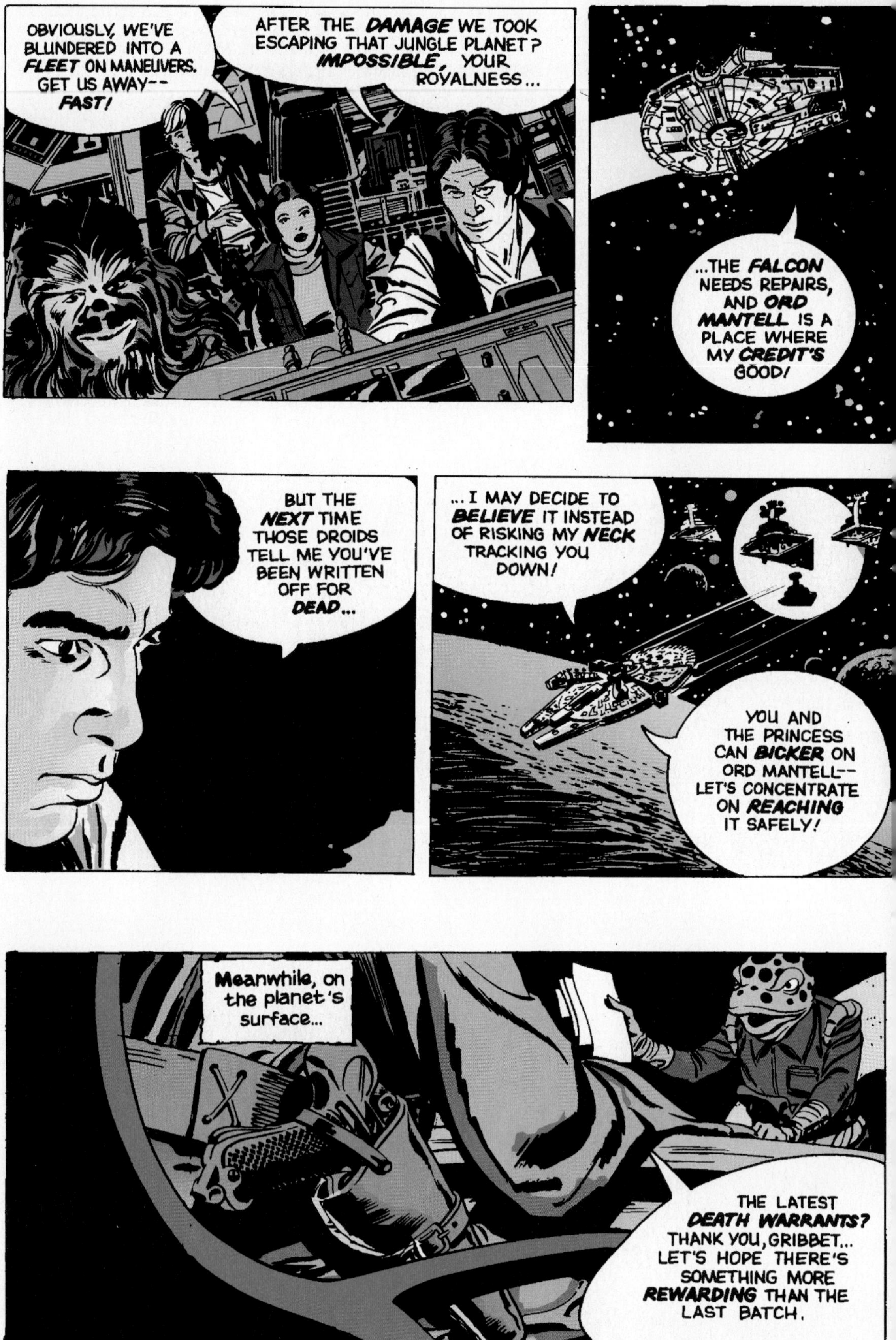
OBVIOUSLY, WE'VE BLUNDERED INTO A FLEET ON MANEUVERS. GET US AWAY-- FAST!
AFTER THE DAMAGE WE TOOK ESCAPING THAT JUNGLE PLANET? IMPOSSIBLE, YOUR ROYALNESS...
...THE FALCON NEEDS REPAIRS, AND ORD MANTELL IS A PLACE WHERE MY CREDIT'S GOOD!
BUT THE NEXT TIME THOSE DROIDS TELL ME YOU'VE BEEN WRITTEN OFF FOR DEAD...
...I MAY DECIDE TO BELIEVE IT INSTEAD OF RISKING MY NECK TRACKING YOU DOWN!
YOU AND THE PRINCESS CAN BICKER ON ORD MANTELL-- LET'S CONCENTRATE ON REACHING IT SAFELY!
Meanwhile, on the planet's surface...
THE LATEST DEATH WARRANTS? THANK YOU, GRIBBET... LET'S HOPE THERE'S SOMETHING MORE REWARDING THAN THE LAST BATCH.

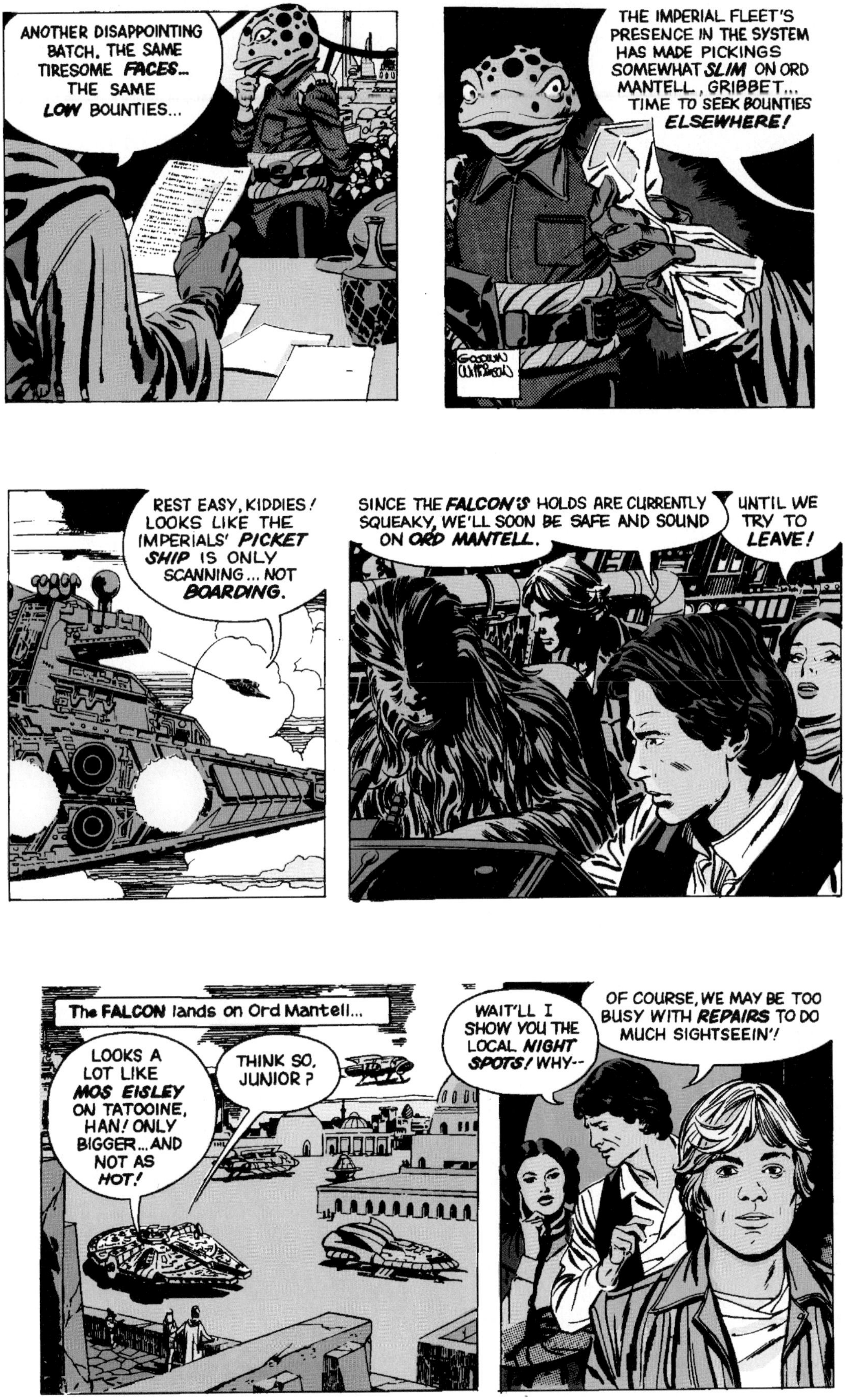
ANOTHER DISAPPOINTING BATCH. THE SAME TIRESOME FACES... THE SAME LOW BOUNTIES...
THE IMPERIAL FLEET'S PRESENCE IN THE SYSTEM HAS MADE PICKINGS SOMEWHAT SLIM ON ORD MANTELL, GRIBBET... TIME TO SEEK BOUNTIES ELSEWHERE!
REST EASY, KIDDIES! LOOKS LIKE THE IMPERIALS' PICKET SHIP IS ONLY SCANNING... NOT BOARDING.
SINCE THE FALCON'S HOLDS ARE CURRENTLY SQUEAKY, WE'LL SOON BE SAFE AND SOUND ON ORD MANTELL.
UNTIL WE TRY TO LEAVE!
The FALCON lands on Ord Mantell...
LOOKS A LOT LIKE MOS EISLEY ON TATOOINE, HAN! ONLY BIGGER... AND NOT AS HOT!
THINK SO, JUNIOR?
WAIT'LL I SHOW YOU THE LOCAL NIGHT SPOTS! WHY--
OF COURSE, WE MAY BE TOO BUSY WITH REPAIRS TO DO MUCH SIGHTSEEIN'!

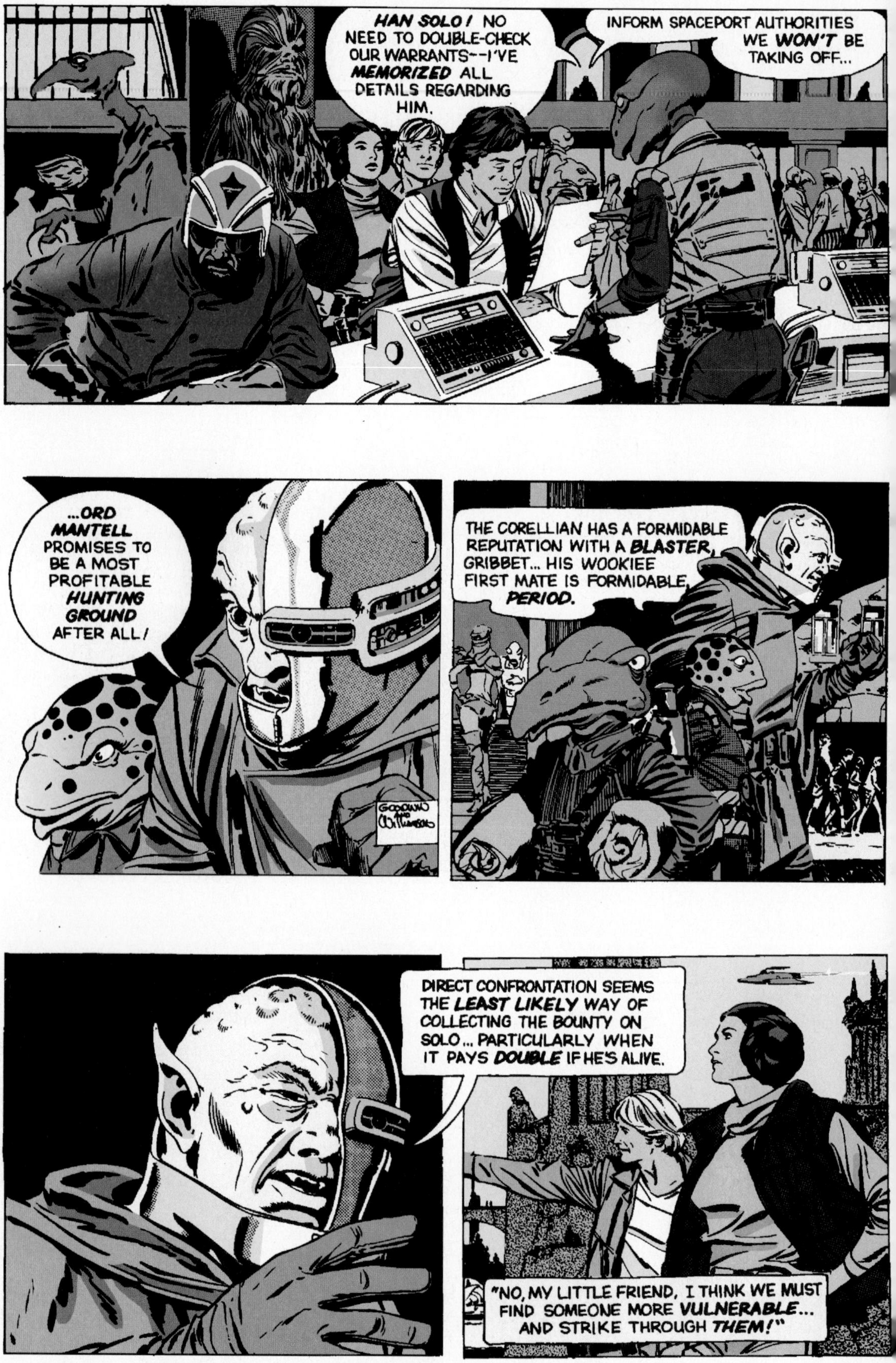
HAN SOLO! NO NEED TO DOUBLE-CHECK OUR WARRANTS--I'VE MEMORIZED ALL DETAILS REGARDING HIM.
INFORM SPACEPORT AUTHORITIES WE WON'T BE TAKING OFF...
...ORD MANTELL PROMISES TO BE A MOST PROFITABLE HUNTING GROUND AFTER ALL!
THE CORELLIAN HAS A FORMIDABLE REPUTATION WITH A BLASTER, GRIBBET... HIS WOOKIEE FIRST MATE IS FORMIDABLE, PERIOD.
DIRECT CONFRONTATION SEEMS THE LEAST LIKELY WAY OF COLLECTING THE BOUNTY ON SOLO... PARTICULARLY WHEN IT PAYS DOUBLE IF HE'S ALIVE.
"NO, MY LITTLE FRIEND, I THINK WE MUST FIND SOMEONE MORE VULNERABLE... AND STRIKE THROUGH THEM!"

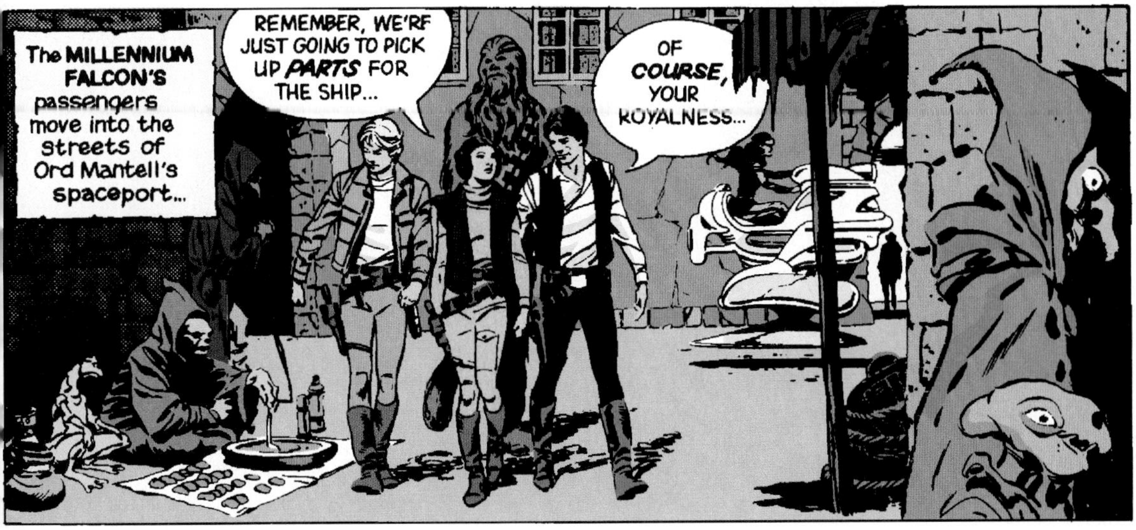
The MILLENNIUM FALCON'S passengers move into the streets of Ord Mantell's spaceport...
REMEMBER, WE'RF JUST GOING TO PICK UP PARTS FOR THE SHIP...
OF COURSE, YOUR ROYALNESS...

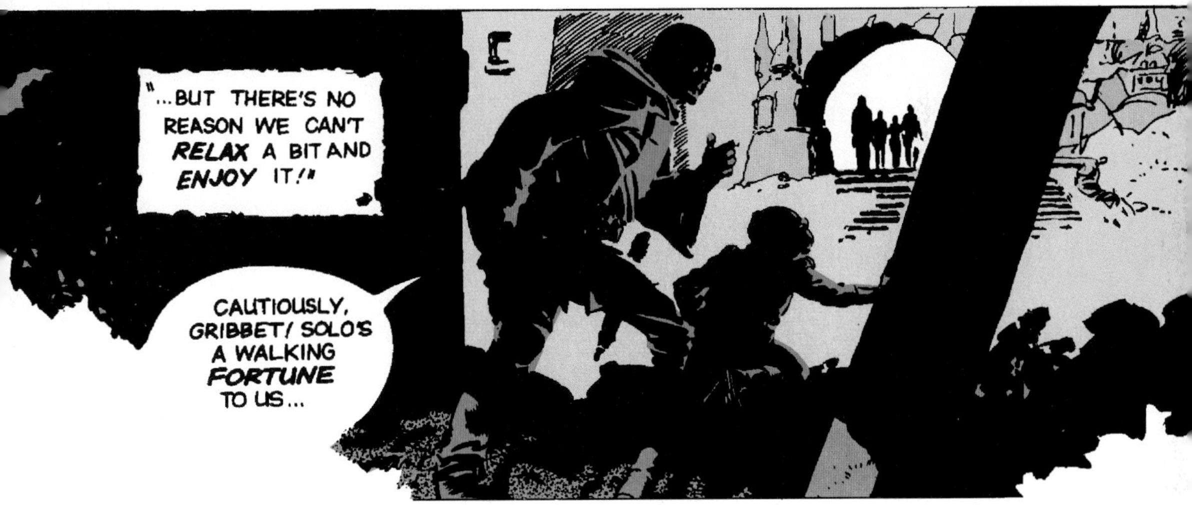
"...BUT THERE'S NO REASON WE CAN'T RELAX A BIT AND ENJOY IT!"
CAUTIOUSLY, GRIBBET! SOLO'S A WALKING FORTUNE TO US...

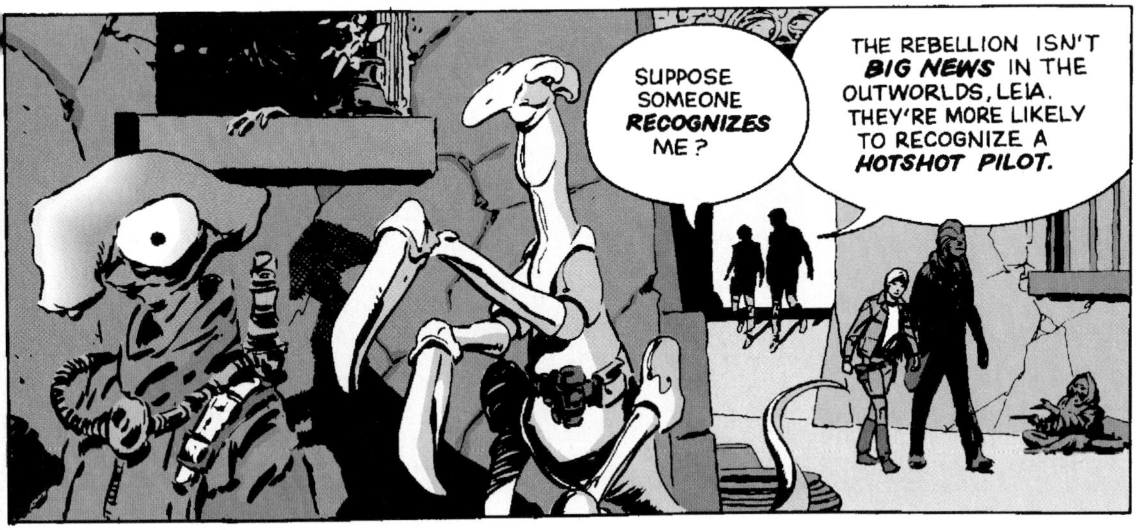
SUPPOSE SOMEONE RECOGNIZES ME?
THE REBELLION ISN'T BIG NEWS IN THE OUTWORLDS, LEIA. THEY'RE MORE LIKELY TO RECOGNIZE A HOTSHOT PILOT.

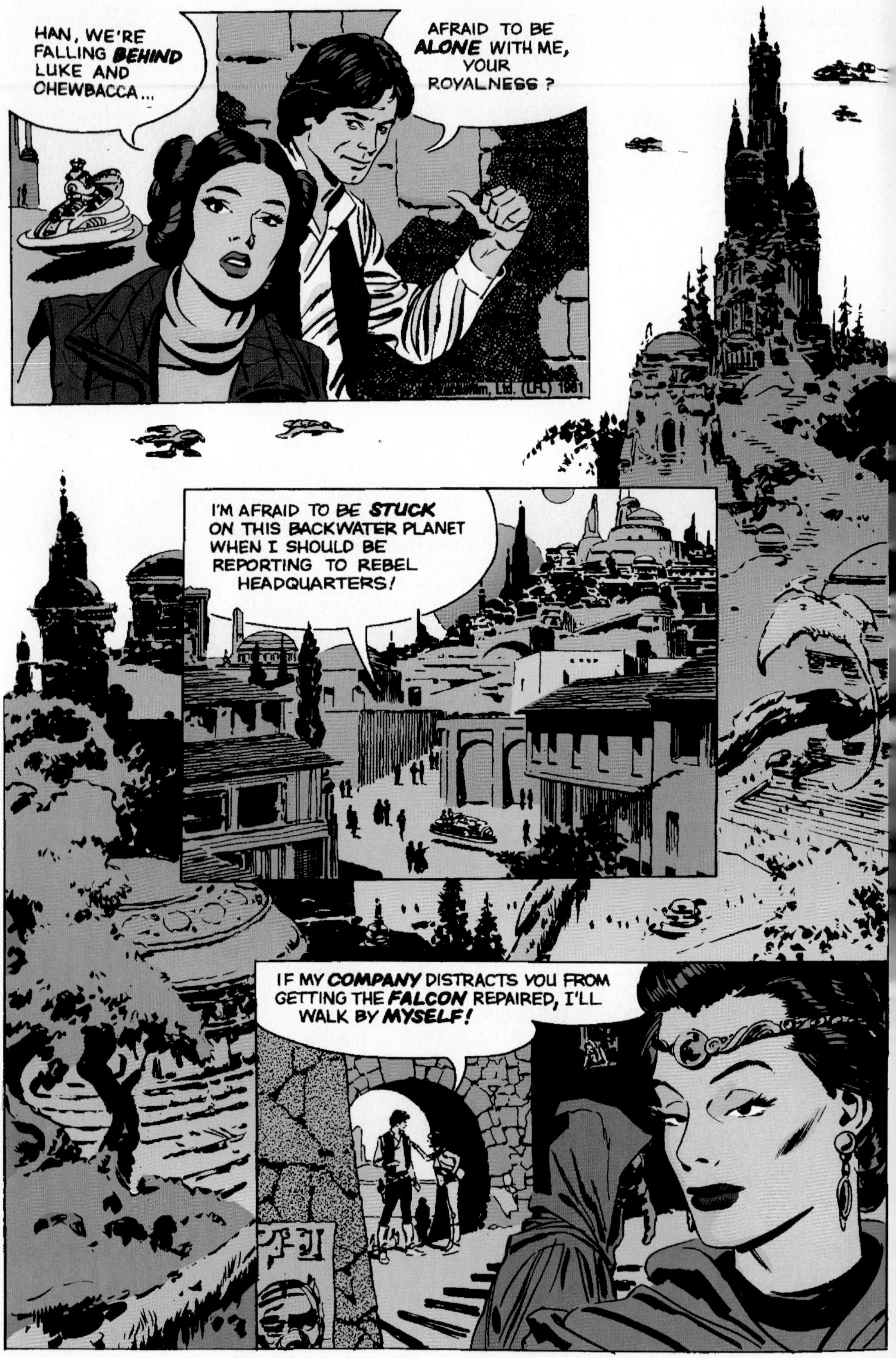
HAN, WE'RE FALLING BEHIND LUKE AND CHEWBACCA...
AFRAID TO BE ALONE WITH ME, YOUR ROYALNESS ?
I'M AFRAID TO BE STUCK ON THIS BACKWATER PLANET WHEN I SHOULD BE REPORTING TO REBEL HEADQUARTERS!
IF MY COMPANY DISTRACTS YOU FROM GETTING THE FALCON REPAIRED, I'LL WALK BY MYSELF!

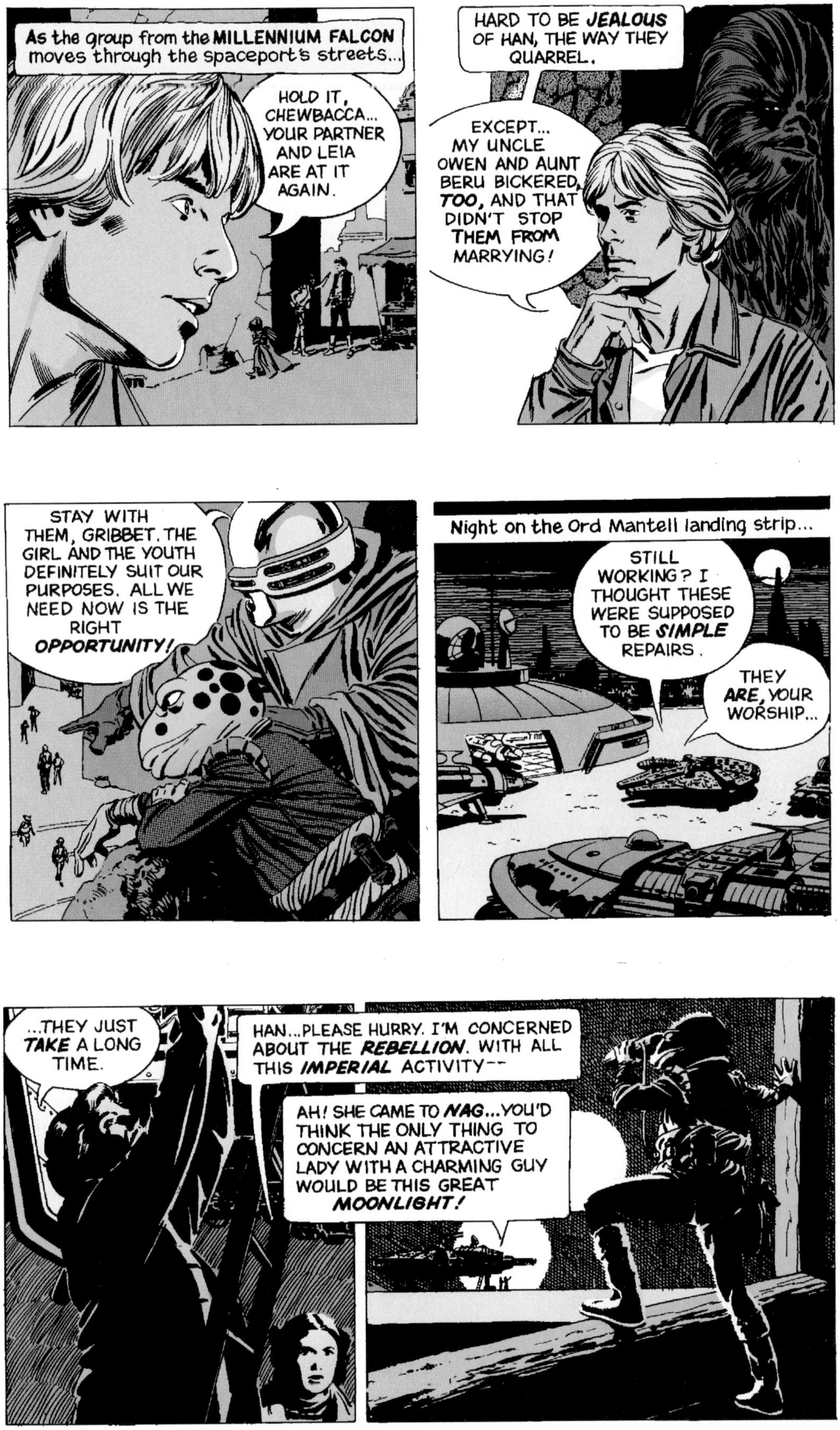

As the group from the MILLENNIUM FALCON moves through the spaceport's streets...
HOLD IT, CHEWBACCA... YOUR PARTNER AND LEIA ARE AT IT AGAIN.
HARD TO BE JEALOUS OF HAN, THE WAY THEY QUARREL.
EXCEPT... MY UNCLE OWEN AND AUNT BERU BICKERED, TOO, AND THAT DIDN'T STOP THEM FROM MARRYING!
STAY WITH THEM, GRIBBET. THE GIRL AND THE YOUTH DEFINITELY SUIT OUR PURPOSES. ALL WE NEED NOW IS THE RIGHT OPPORTUNITY!
Night on the Ord Mantell landing strip...
STILL WORKING? I THOUGHT THESE WERE SUPPOSED TO BE SIMPLE REPAIRS.
THEY ARE, YOUR WORSHIP...
...THEY JUST TAKE A LONG TIME.
HAN...PLEASE HURRY. I'M CONCERNED ABOUT THE REBELLION. WITH ALL THIS IMPERIAL ACTIVITY--
AH! SHE CAME TO NAG...YOU'D THINK THE ONLY THING TO CONCERN AN ATTRACTIVE LADY WITH A CHARMING GUY WOULD BE THIS GREAT MOONLIGHT!

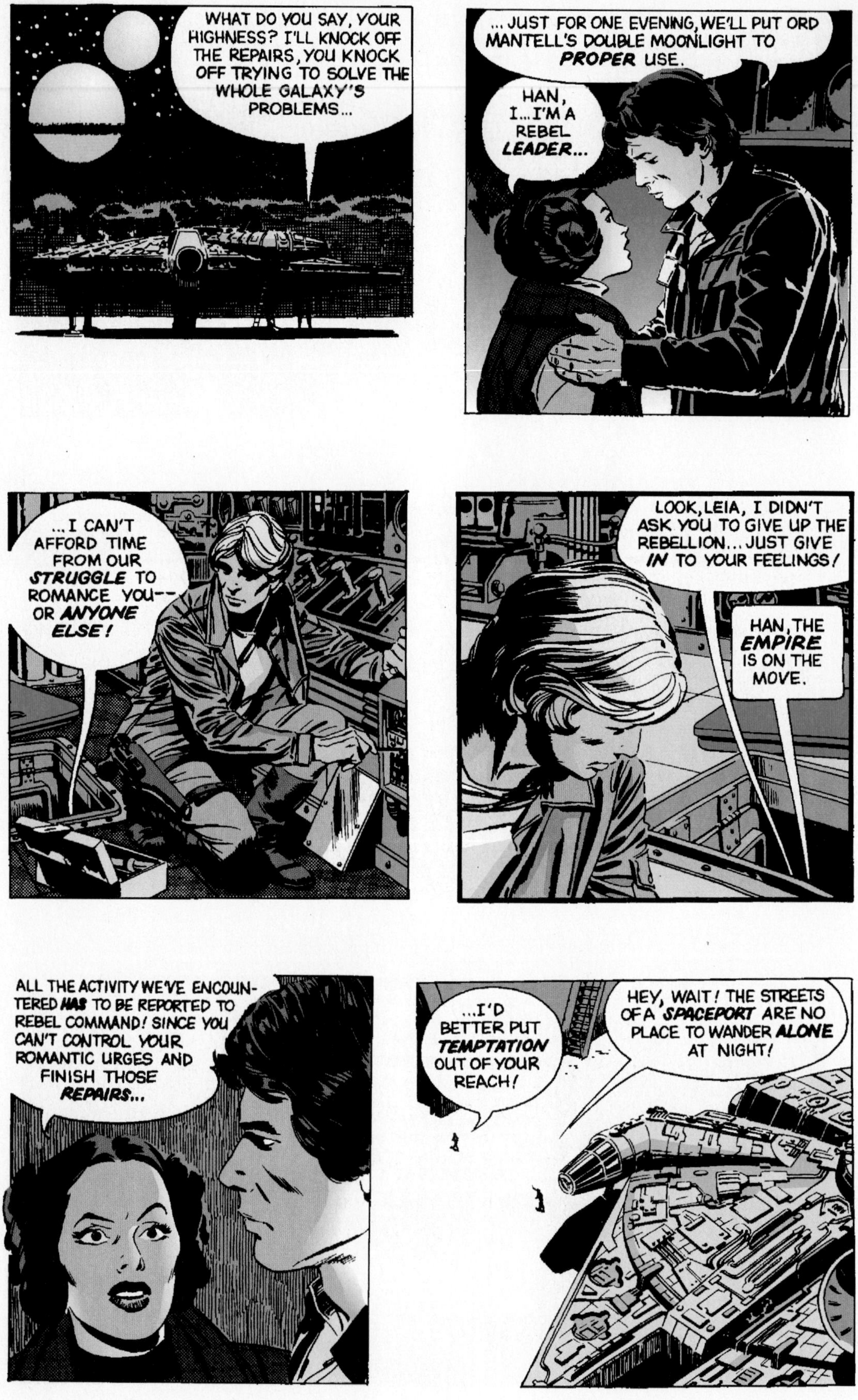
WHAT DO YOU SAY, YOUR HIGHNESS? I'LL KNOCK OFF THE REPAIRS, YOU KNOCK OFF TRYING TO SOLVE THE WHOLE GALAXY'S PROBLEMS...
...JUST FOR ONE EVENING, WE'LL PUT ORD MANTELL'S DOUBLE MOONLIGHT TO PROPER USE.
HAN, I...I'M A REBEL LEADER...
...I CAN'T AFFORD TIME FROM OUR STRUGGLE TO ROMANCE YOU-- OR ANYONE ELSE!
LOOK, LEIA, I DIDN'T ASK YOU TO GIVE UP THE REBELLION... JUST GIVE IN TO YOUR FEELINGS!
HAN, THE EMPIRE IS ON THE MOVE.
ALL THE ACTIVITY WE'VE ENCOUNTERED HAS TO BE REPORTED TO REBEL COMMAND! SINCE YOU CAN'T CONTROL YOUR ROMANTIC URGES AND FINISH THOSE REPAIRS...
...I'D BETTER PUT TEMPTATION OUT OF YOUR REACH!
HEY, WAIT! THE STREETS OF A SPACEPORT ARE NO PLACE TO WANDER ALONE AT NIGHT!

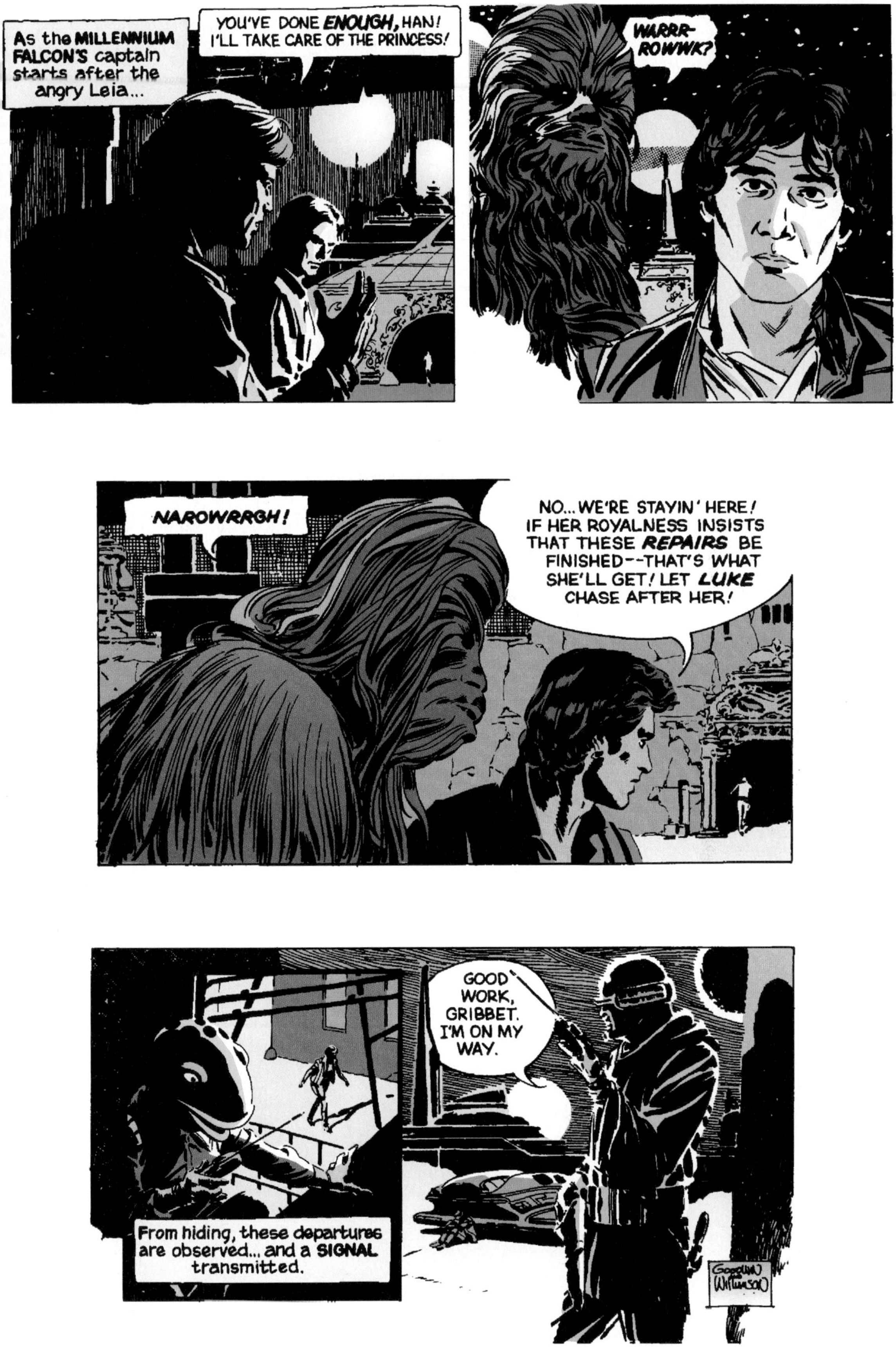
As the MILLENNIUM FALCON'S captain starts after the angry Leia...
YOU'VE DONE ENOUGH, HAN! I'LL TAKE CARE OF THE PRINCESS!
WARRR-ROWWK?
NAROWRRGH!
NO... WE'RE STAYIN' HERE! IF HER ROYALNESS INSISTS THAT THESE REPAIRS BE FINISHED--THAT'S WHAT SHE'LL GET! LET LUKE CHASE AFTER HER!
From hiding, these departures are observed... and a SIGNAL transmitted.
GOOD WORK, GRIBBET. I'M ON MY WAY.

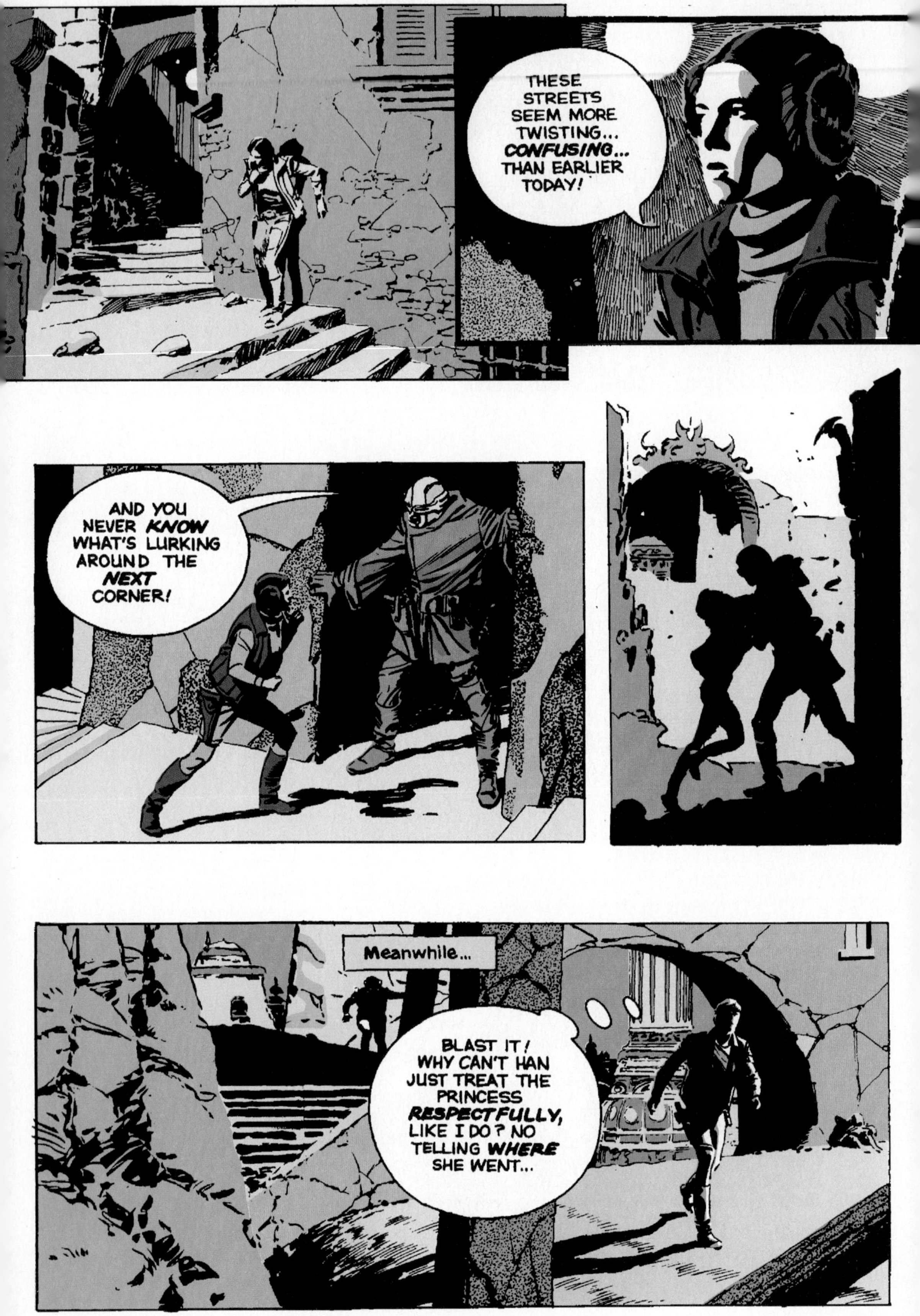
THESE STREETS SEEM MORE TWISTING... CONFUSING... THAN EARLIER TODAY!
AND YOU NEVER KNOW WHAT'S LURKING AROUND THE NEXT CORNER!
Meanwhile...
BLAST IT! WHY CAN'T HAN JUST TREAT THE PRINCESS RESPECTFULLY, LIKE I DO? NO TELLING WHERE SHE WENT...

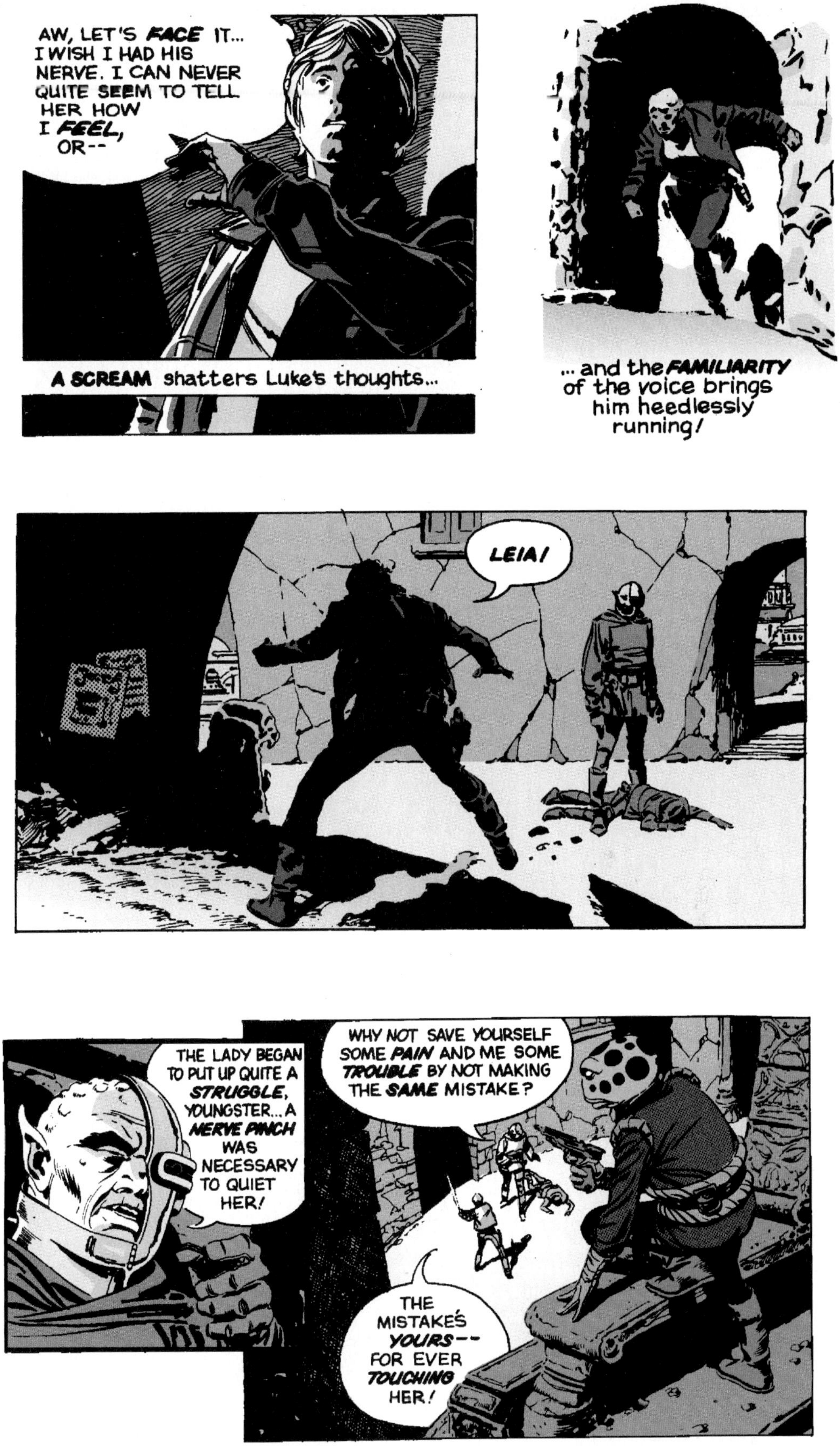
AW, LET'S FACE IT... I WISH I HAD HIS NERVE. I CAN NEVER QUITE SEEM TO TELL HER HOW I FEEL, OR--
A SCREAM shatters Luke's thoughts...
... and the FAMILIARITY of the voice brings him heedlessly running!
LEIA!
THE LADY BEGAN TO PUT UP QUITE A STRUGGLE, YOUNGSTER... A NERVE PINCH WAS NECESSARY TO QUIET HER!
WHY NOT SAVE YOURSELF SOME PAIN AND ME SOME TROUBLE BY NOT MAKING THE SAME MISTAKE?
THE MISTAKE'S YOURS-- FOR EVER TOUCHING HER!

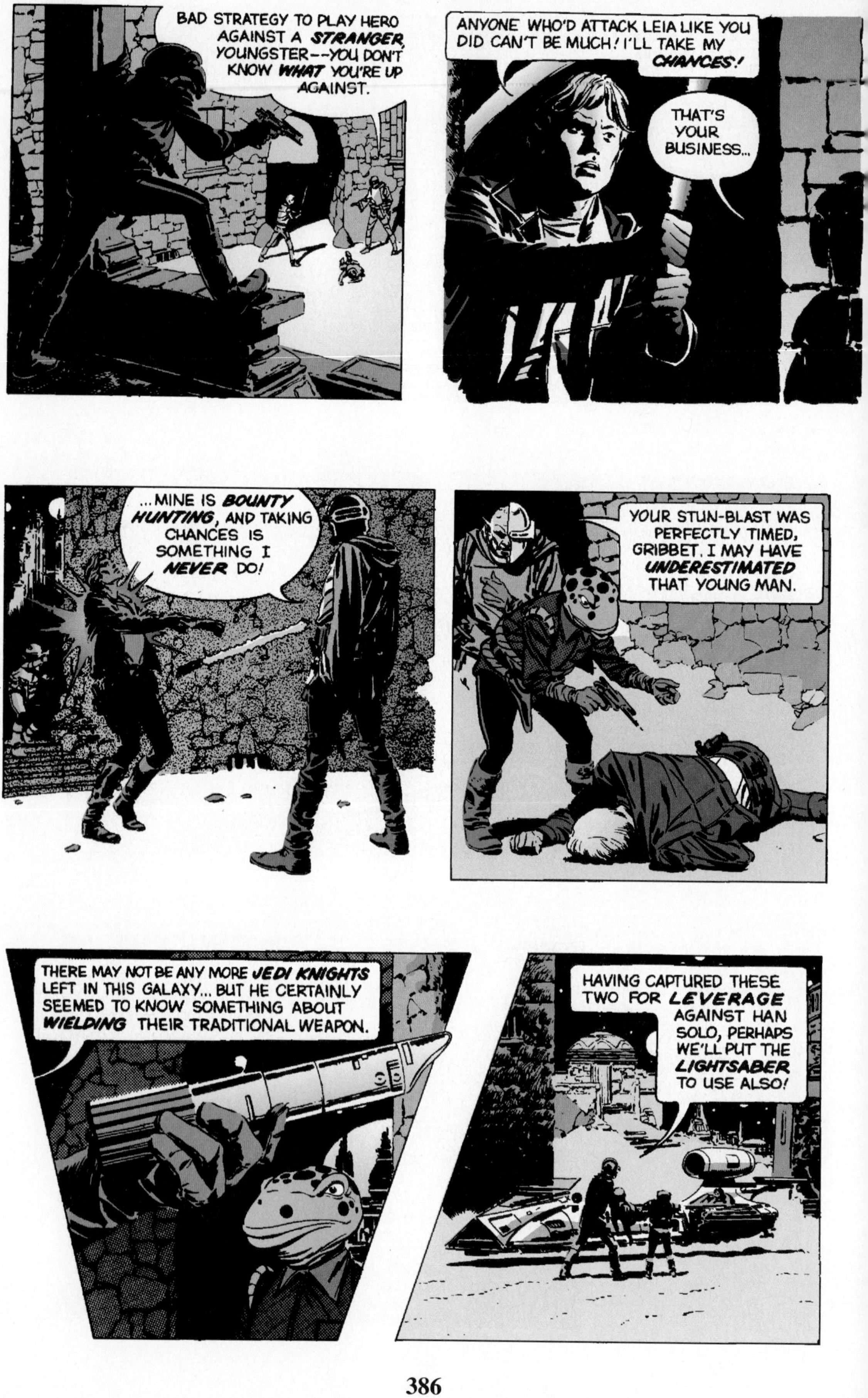
BAD STRATEGY TO PLAY HERO AGAINST A STRANGER, YOUNGSTER--YOU DON'T KNOW WHAT YOU'RE UP AGAINST.
ANYONE WHO'D ATTACK LEIA LIKE YOU DID CAN'T BE MUCH! I'LL TAKE MY CHANCES!
THAT'S YOUR BUSINESS...
...MINE IS BOUNTY HUNTING, AND TAKING CHANCES IS SOMETHING I NEVER DO!
YOUR STUN-BLAST WAS PERFECTLY TIMED, GRIBBET. I MAY HAVE UNDERESTIMATED THAT YOUNG MAN.
THERE MAY NOT BE ANY MORE JEDI KNIGHTS LEFT IN THIS GALAXY... BUT HE CERTAINLY SEEMED TO KNOW SOMETHING ABOUT WIELDING THEIR TRADITIONAL WEAPON.
HAVING CAPTURED THESE TWO FOR LEVERAGE AGAINST HAN SOLO, PERHAPS WE'LL PUT THE LIGHTSABER TO USE ALSO!

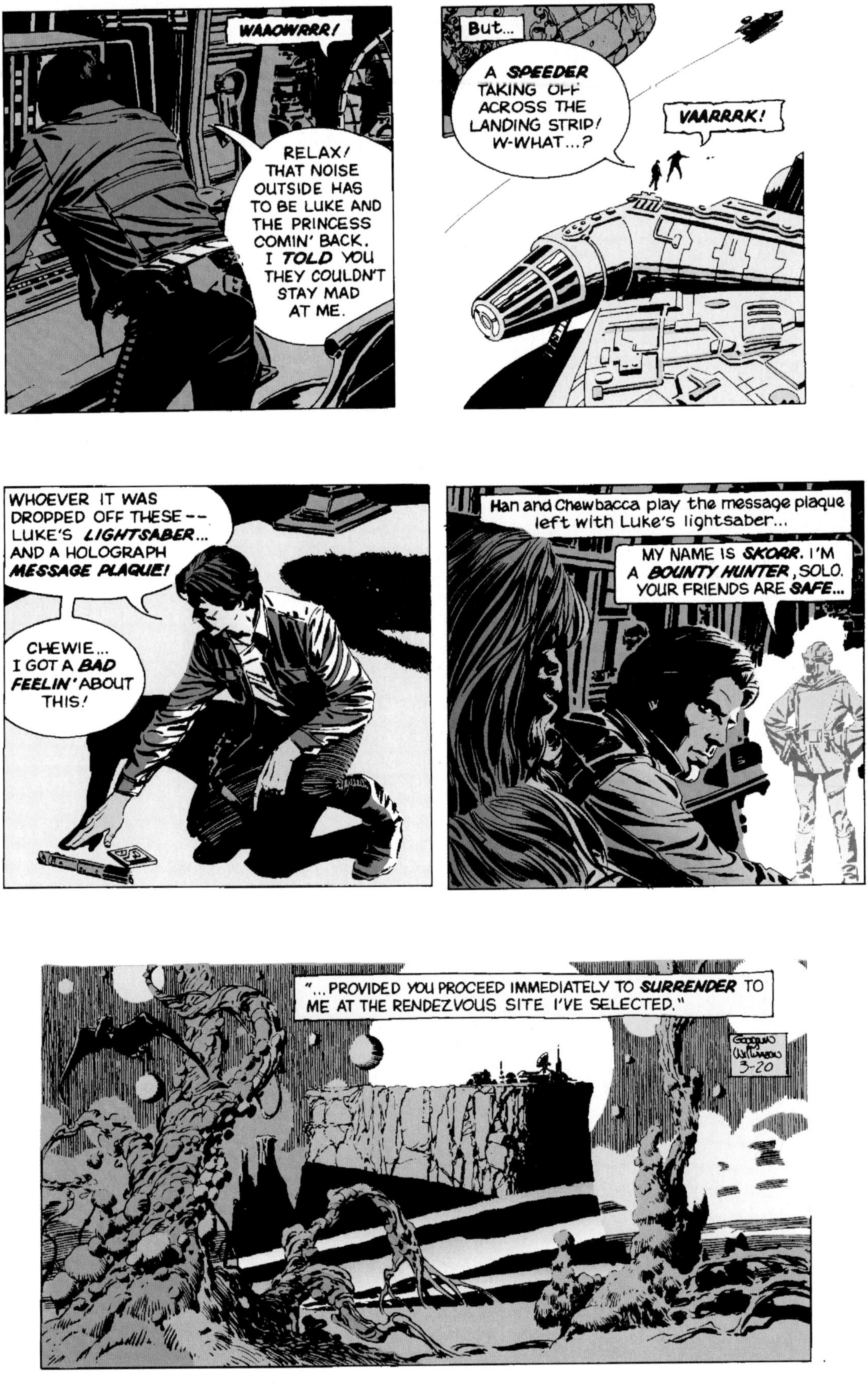
WAAOWRRR!
RELAX! THAT NOISE OUTSIDE HAS TO BE LUKE AND THE PRINCESS COMIN' BACK. I TOLD YOU THEY COULDN'T STAY MAD AT ME.
But...
A SPEEDER TAKING OFF ACROSS THE LANDING STRIP! W-WHAT...?
VAARRRK!
WHOEVER IT WAS DROPPED OFF THESE -- LUKE'S LIGHTSABER... AND A HOLOGRAPH MESSAGE PLAQUE!
CHEWIE... I GOT A BAD FEELIN' ABOUT THIS!
Han and Chewbacca play the message plaque left with Luke's lightsaber...
MY NAME IS SKORR. I'M A BOUNTY HUNTER, SOLO. YOUR FRIENDS ARE SAFE...
"...PROVIDED YOU PROCEED IMMEDIATELY TO SURRENDER TO ME AT THE RENDEZVOUS SITE I'VE SELECTED."

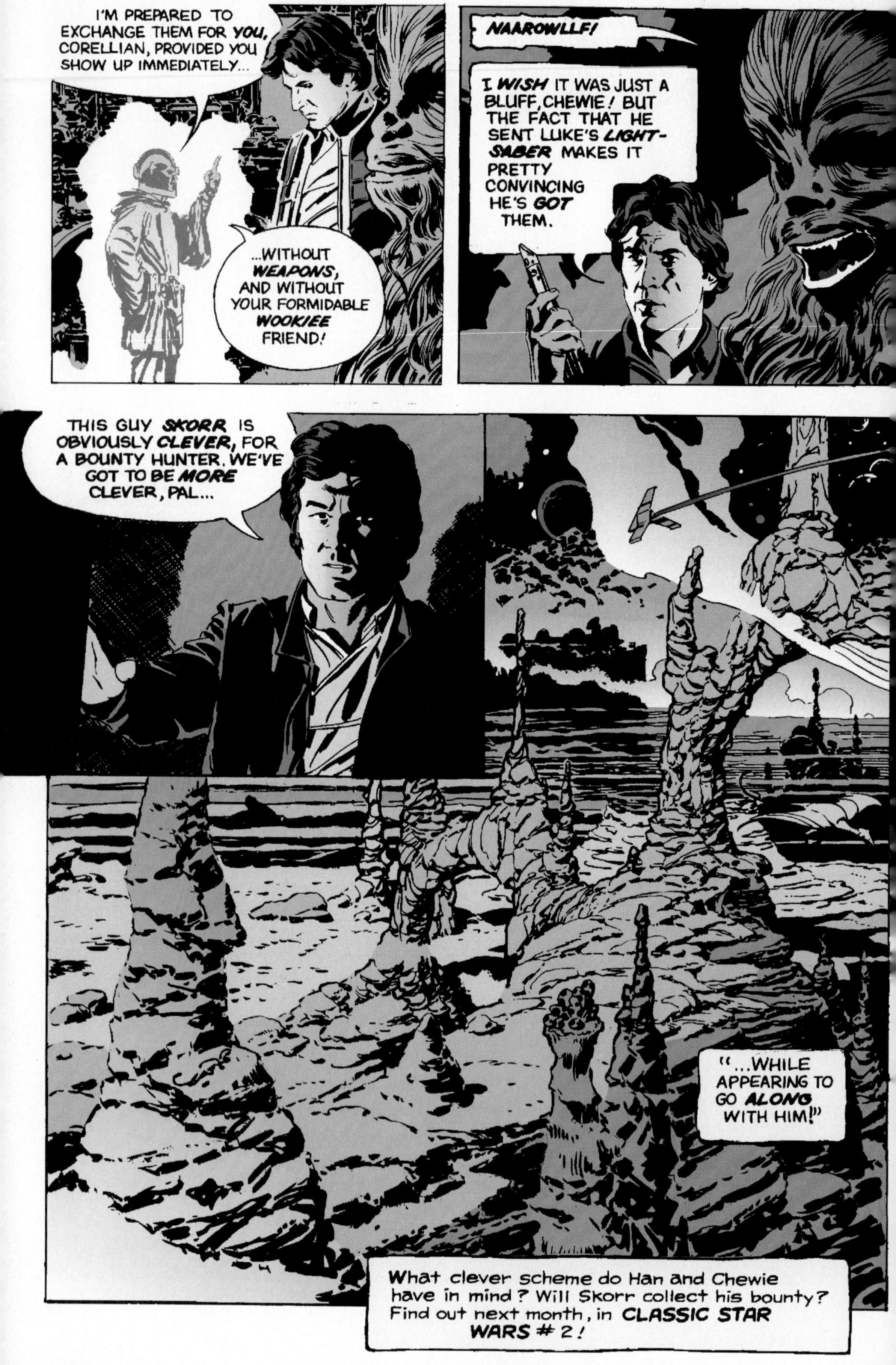
I'M PREPARED TO EXCHANGE THEM FOR YOU, CORELLIAN, PROVIDED YOU SHOW UP IMMEDIATELY...
...WITHOUT WEAPONS, AND WITHOUT YOUR FORMIDABLE WOOKIEE FRIEND!
NAAROWLLF!
I WISH IT WAS JUST A BLUFF, CHEWIE! BUT THE FACT THAT HE SENT LUKE'S LIGHT-SABER MAKES IT PRETTY CONVINCING HE'S GOT THEM.
THIS GUY SKORR IS OBVIOUSLY CLEVER, FOR A BOUNTY HUNTER. WE'VE GOT TO BE MORE CLEVER, PAL...
"...WHILE APPEARING TO GO ALONG WITH HIM!"
What clever scheme do Han and Chewie have in mind? Will Skorr collect his bounty? Find out next month, in CLASSIC STAR WARS # 2!

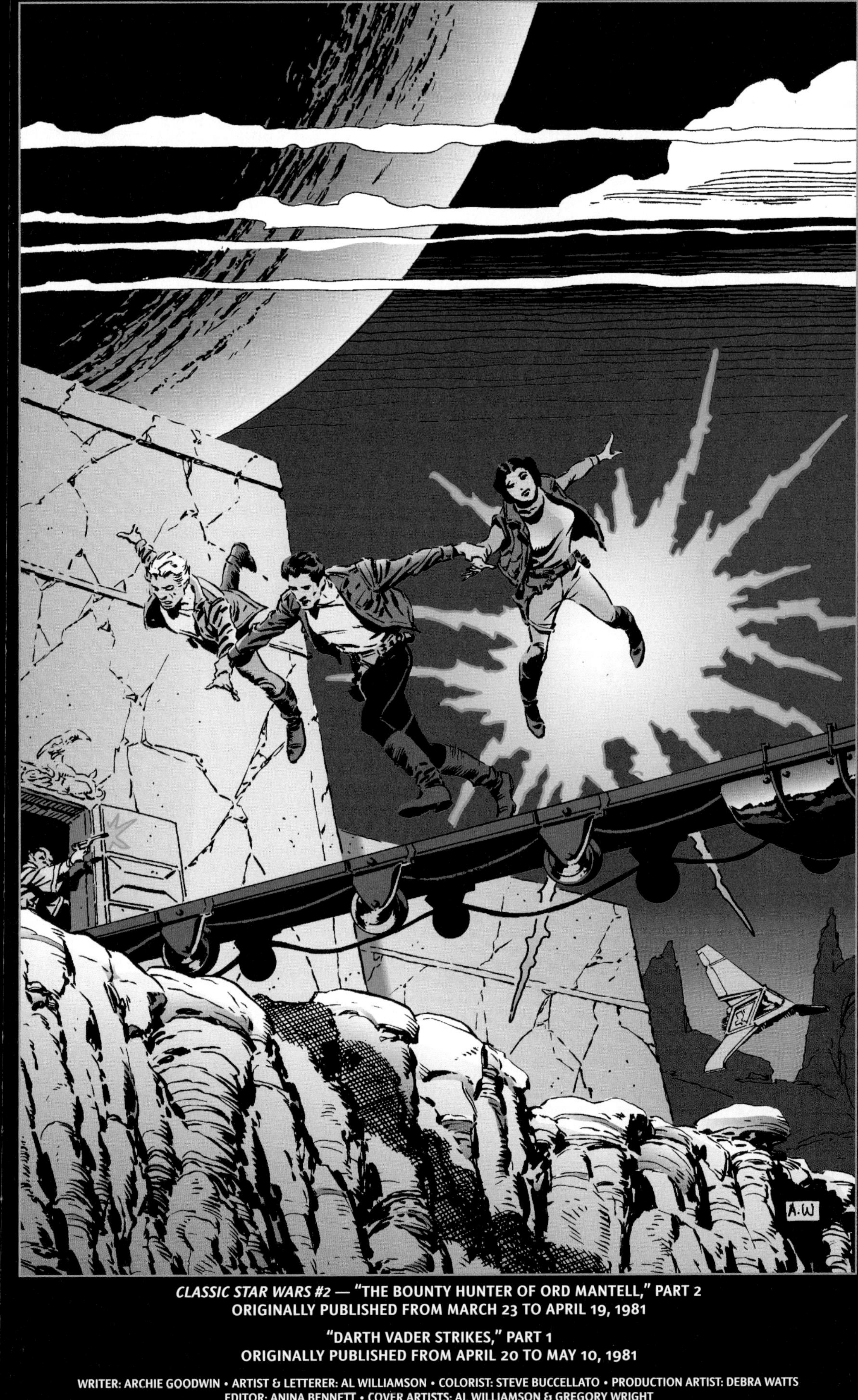
A.W

CLASSIC STAR WARS #2 — "THE BOUNTY HUNTER OF ORD MANTELL," PART 2
ORIGINALLY PUBLISHED FROM MARCH 23 TO APRIL 19, 1981

"DARTH VADER STRIKES," PART 1
ORIGINALLY PUBLISHED FROM APRIL 20 TO MAY 10, 1981

WRITER: ARCHIE GOODWIN • ARTIST & LETTERER: AL WILLIAMSON • COLORIST: STEVE BUCCELLATO • PRODUCTION ARTIST: DEBRA WATTS
EDITOR: ANINA BENNETT • COVER ARTISTS: AL WILLIAMSON & GREGORY WRIGHT

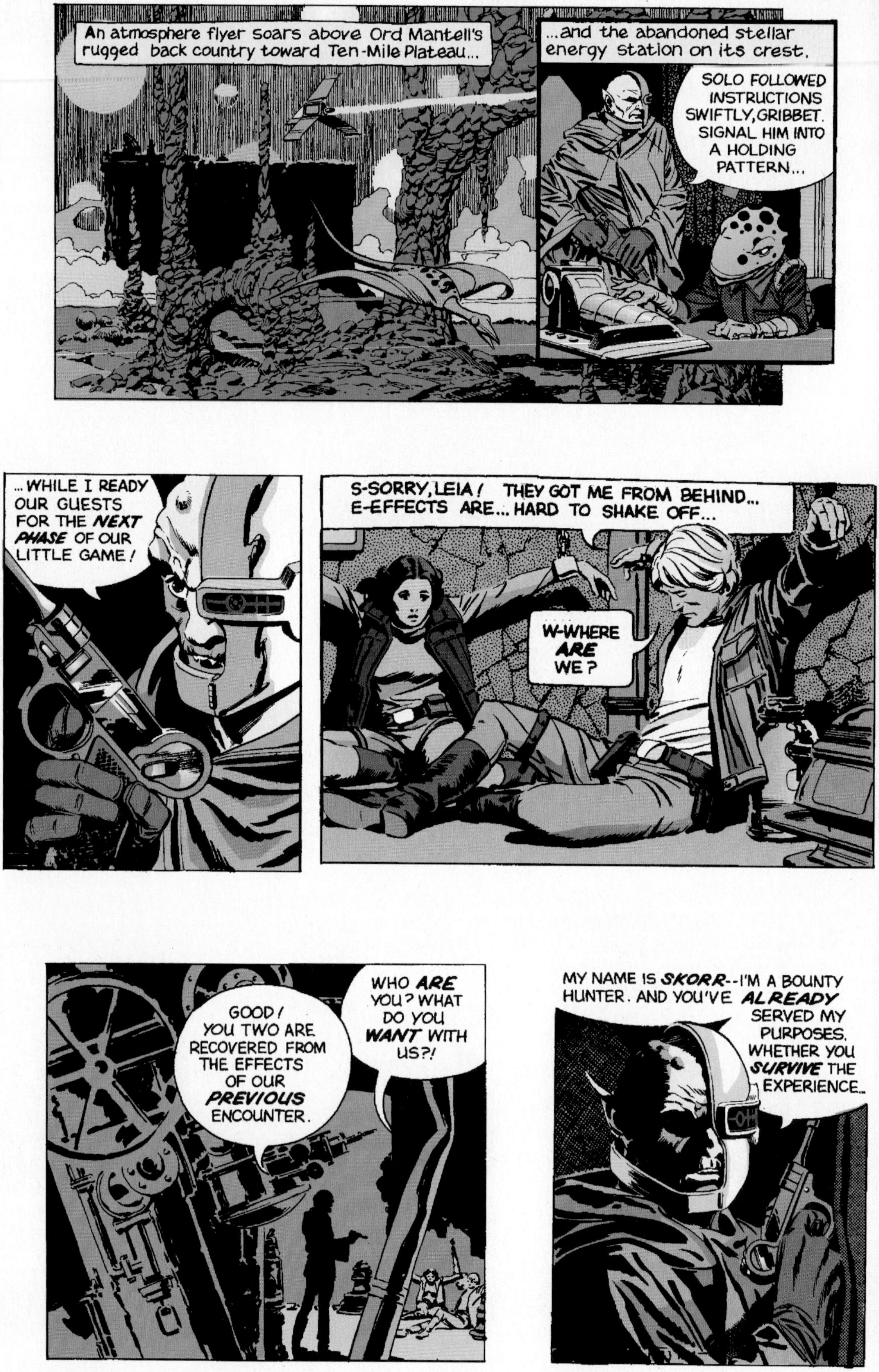

An atmosphere flyer soars above Ord Mantell's rugged back country toward Ten-Mile Plateau...
...and the abandoned stellar energy station on its crest.
SOLO FOLLOWED INSTRUCTIONS SWIFTLY, GRIBBET. SIGNAL HIM INTO A HOLDING PATTERN...
... WHILE I READY OUR GUESTS FOR THE NEXT PHASE OF OUR LITTLE GAME!
S-SORRY, LEIA! THEY GOT ME FROM BEHIND... E-EFFECTS ARE... HARD TO SHAKE OFF...
W-WHERE ARE WE?
GOOD! YOU TWO ARE RECOVERED FROM THE EFFECTS OF OUR PREVIOUS ENCOUNTER.
WHO ARE YOU? WHAT DO YOU WANT WITH US?!
MY NAME IS SKORR--I'M A BOUNTY HUNTER. AND YOU'VE ALREADY SERVED MY PURPOSES. WHETHER YOU SURVIVE THE EXPERIENCE...

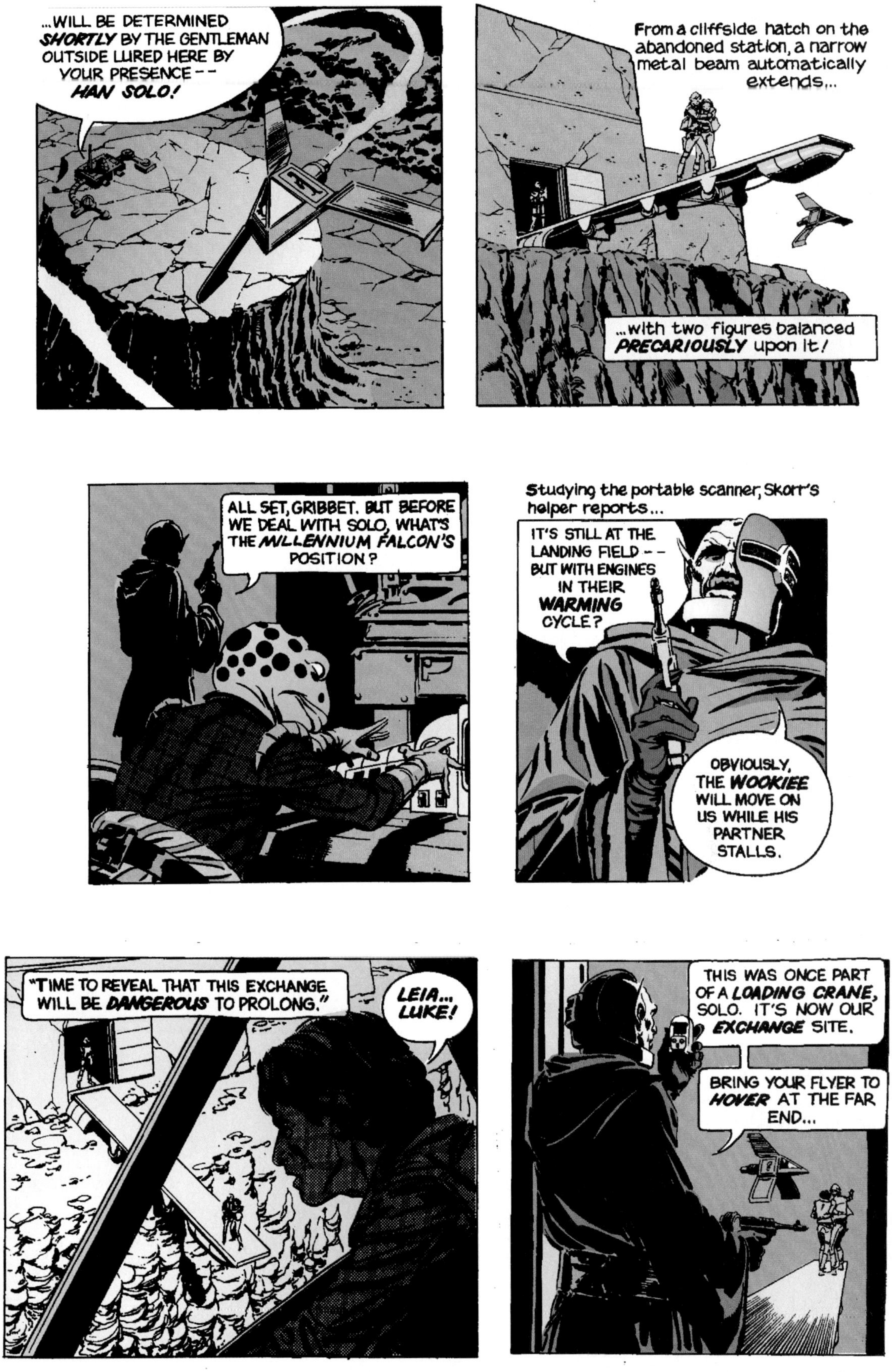

...WILL BE DETERMINED SHORTLY BY THE GENTLEMAN OUTSIDE LURED HERE BY YOUR PRESENCE -- HAN SOLO!
From a cliffside hatch on the abandoned station, a narrow metal beam automatically extends...
...with two figures balanced PRECARIOUSLY upon it!
ALL SET, GRIBBET. BUT BEFORE WE DEAL WITH SOLO, WHAT'S THE MILLENNIUM FALCON'S POSITION?
Studying the portable scanner, Skorr's helper reports...
IT'S STILL AT THE LANDING FIELD -- BUT WITH ENGINES IN THEIR WARMING CYCLE?
OBVIOUSLY, THE WOOKIEE WILL MOVE ON US WHILE HIS PARTNER STALLS.
"TIME TO REVEAL THAT THIS EXCHANGE WILL BE DANGEROUS TO PROLONG."
LEIA... LUKE!
THIS WAS ONCE PART OF A LOADING CRANE, SOLO. IT'S NOW OUR EXCHANGE SITE.
BRING YOUR FLYER TO HOVER AT THE FAR END...

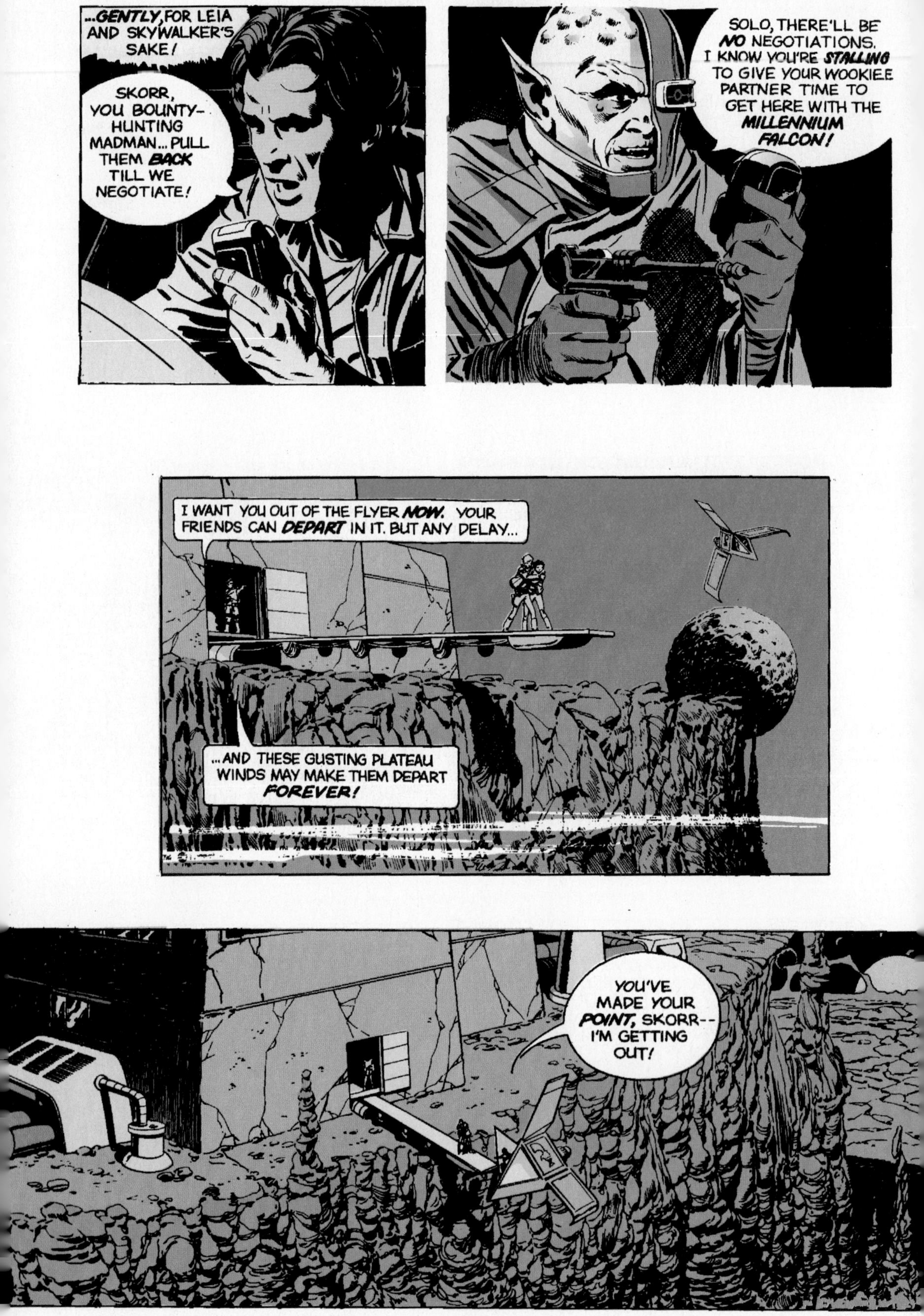
...GENTLY, FOR LEIA AND SKYWALKER'S SAKE!
SKORR, YOU BOUNTY-HUNTING MADMAN... PULL THEM BACK TILL WE NEGOTIATE!
SOLO, THERE'LL BE NO NEGOTIATIONS. I KNOW YOU'RE STALLING TO GIVE YOUR WOOKIEE PARTNER TIME TO GET HERE WITH THE MILLENNIUM FALCON!
I WANT YOU OUT OF THE FLYER NOW. YOUR FRIENDS CAN DEPART IN IT. BUT ANY DELAY...
...AND THESE GUSTING PLATEAU WINDS MAY MAKE THEM DEPART FOREVER!
YOU'VE MADE YOUR POINT, SKORR-- I'M GETTING OUT!

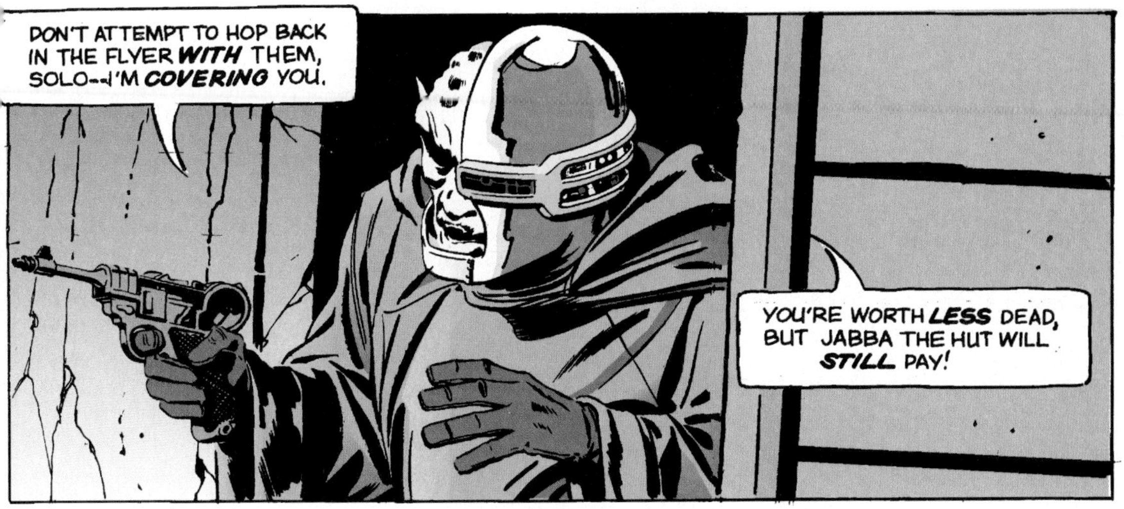
DON'T ATTEMPT TO HOP BACK IN THE FLYER WITH THEM, SOLO--I'M COVERING YOU.
YOU'RE WORTH LESS DEAD, BUT JABBA THE HUT WILL STILL PAY!

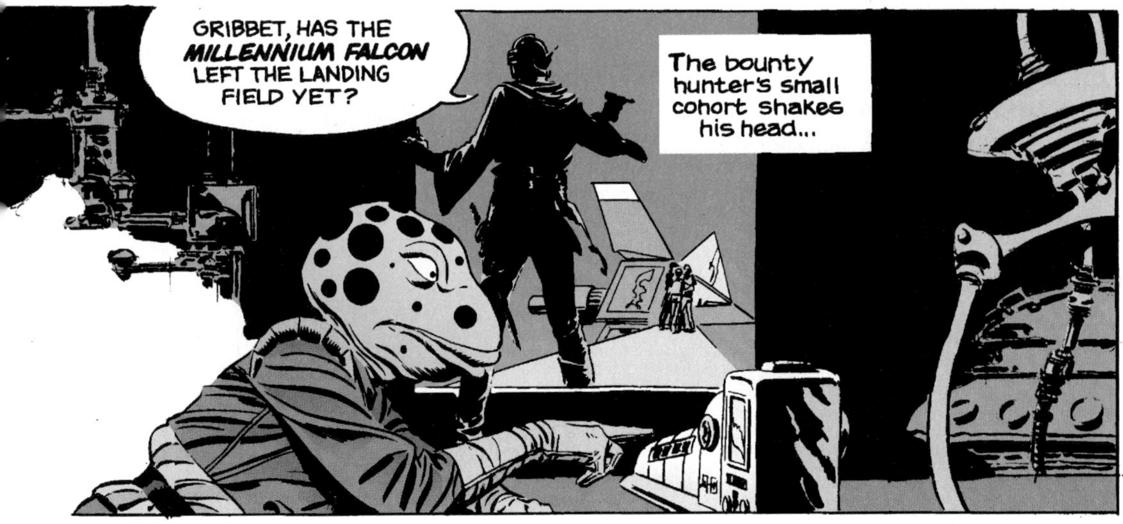
GRIBBET, HAS THE MILLENNIUM FALCON LEFT THE LANDING FIELD YET?
The bounty hunter's small cohort shakes his head...

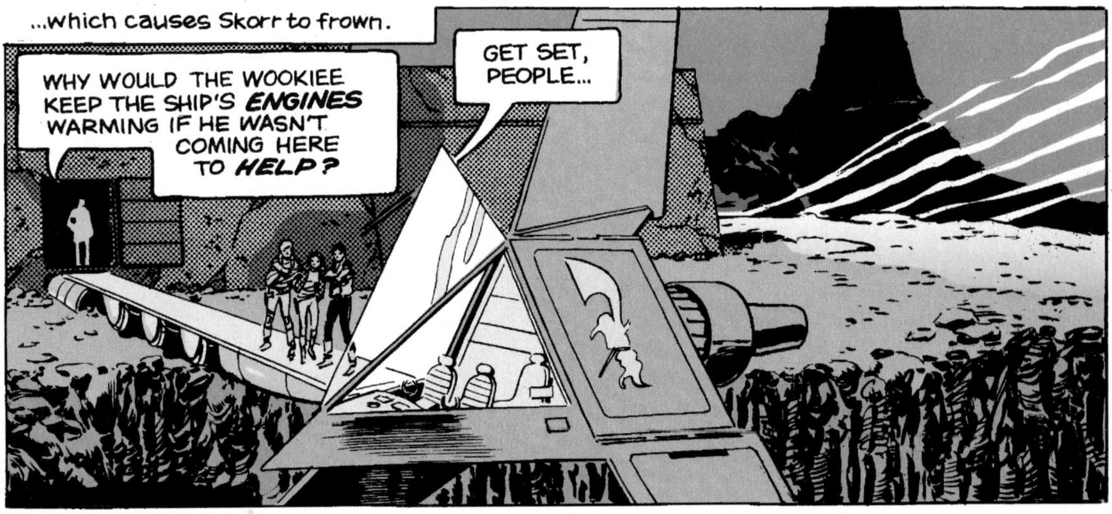
...which causes Skorr to frown.
WHY WOULD THE WOOKIEE KEEP THE SHIP'S ENGINES WARMING IF HE WASN'T COMING HERE TO HELP?
GET SET, PEOPLE...

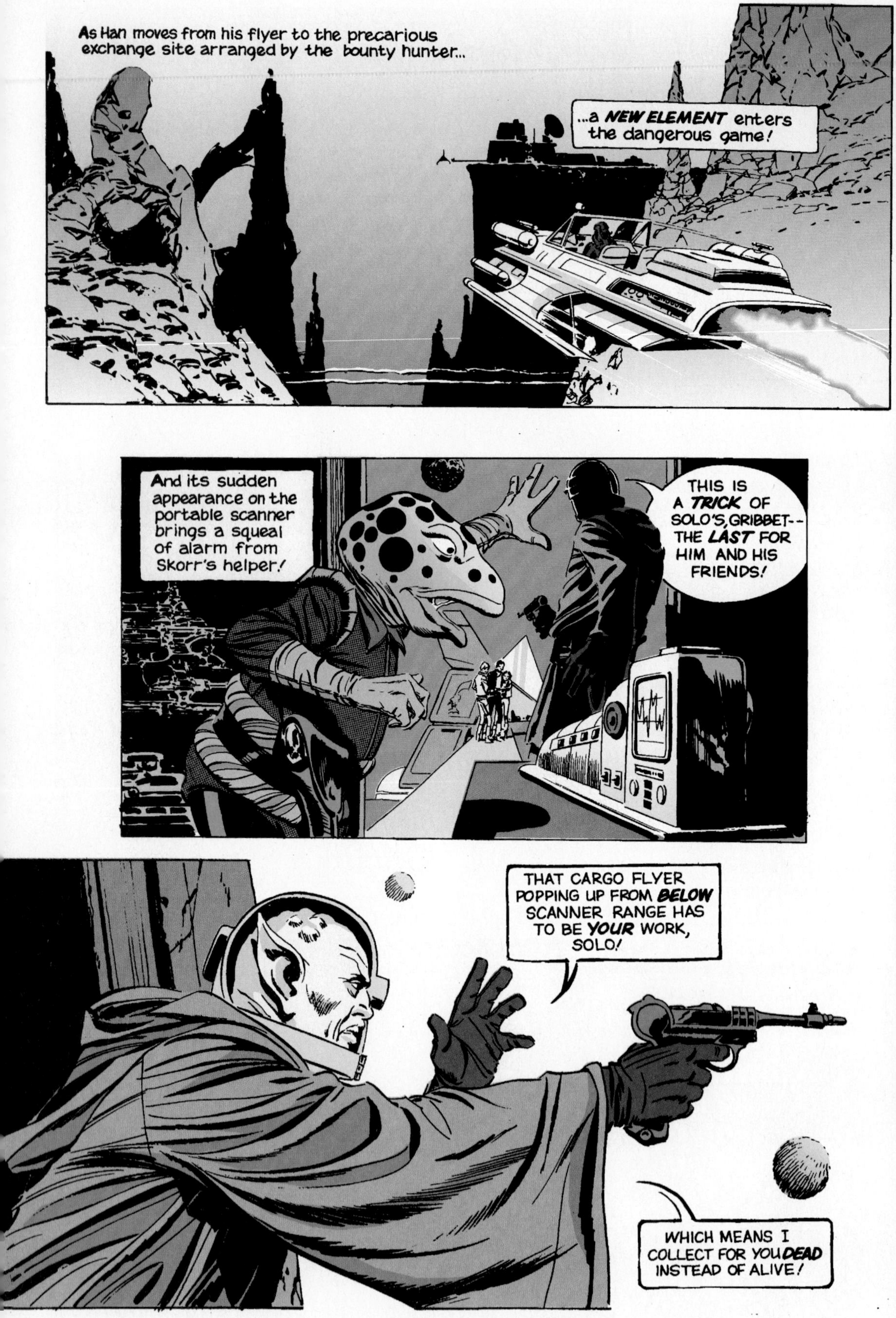
As Han moves from his flyer to the precarious exchange site arranged by the bounty hunter...
...a NEW ELEMENT enters the dangerous game!
And its sudden appearance on the portable scanner brings a squeal of alarm from Skorr's helper!
THIS IS A TRICK OF SOLO'S, GRIBBET--THE LAST FOR HIM AND HIS FRIENDS!
THAT CARGO FLYER POPPING UP FROM BELOW SCANNER RANGE HAS TO BE YOUR WORK, SOLO!
WHICH MEANS I COLLECT FOR YOU DEAD INSTEAD OF ALIVE!

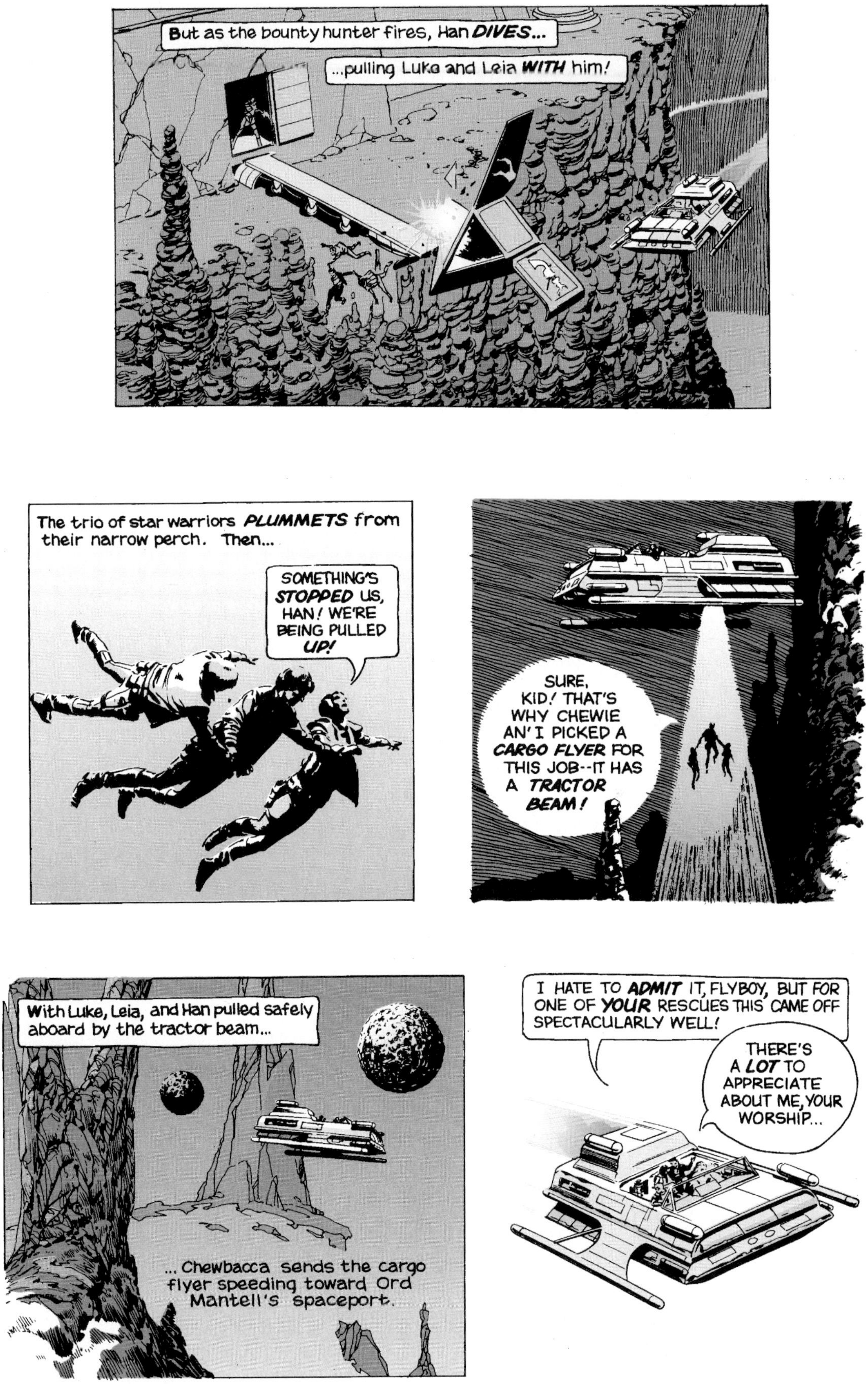
But as the bounty hunter fires, Han DIVES...
...pulling Luke and Leia WITH him!
The trio of star warriors PLUMMETS from their narrow perch. Then...
SOMETHING'S STOPPED US, HAN! WE'RE BEING PULLED UP!
SURE, KID! THAT'S WHY CHEWIE AN' I PICKED A CARGO FLYER FOR THIS JOB--IT HAS A TRACTOR BEAM!
With Luke, Leia, and Han pulled safely aboard by the tractor beam...
... Chewbacca sends the cargo flyer speeding toward Ord Mantell's spaceport.
I HATE TO ADMIT IT, FLYBOY, BUT FOR ONE OF YOUR RESCUES THIS CAME OFF SPECTACULARLY WELL!
THERE'S A LOT TO APPRECIATE ABOUT ME, YOUR WORSHIP...

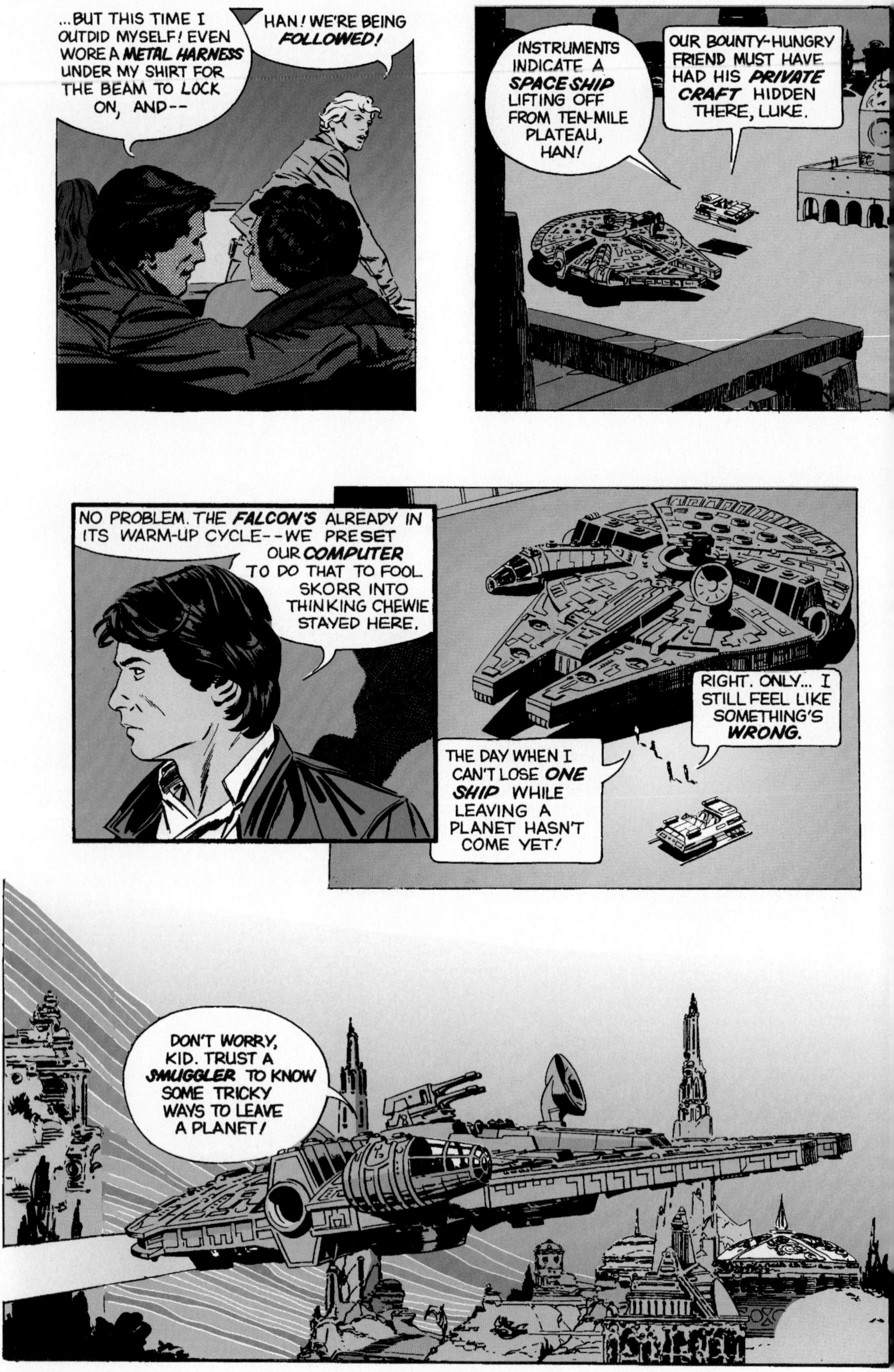
...BUT THIS TIME I OUTDID MYSELF! EVEN WORE A METAL HARNESS UNDER MY SHIRT FOR THE BEAM TO LOCK ON, AND--
HAN! WE'RE BEING FOLLOWED!
INSTRUMENTS INDICATE A SPACESHIP LIFTING OFF FROM TEN-MILE PLATEAU, HAN!
OUR BOUNTY-HUNGRY FRIEND MUST HAVE HAD HIS PRIVATE CRAFT HIDDEN THERE, LUKE.
NO PROBLEM. THE FALCON'S ALREADY IN ITS WARM-UP CYCLE--WE PRESET OUR COMPUTER TO DO THAT TO FOOL SKORR INTO THINKING CHEWIE STAYED HERE.
RIGHT. ONLY... I STILL FEEL LIKE SOMETHING'S WRONG.
THE DAY WHEN I CAN'T LOSE ONE SHIP WHILE LEAVING A PLANET HASN'T COME YET!
DON'T WORRY, KID. TRUST A SMUGGLER TO KNOW SOME TRICKY WAYS TO LEAVE A PLANET!

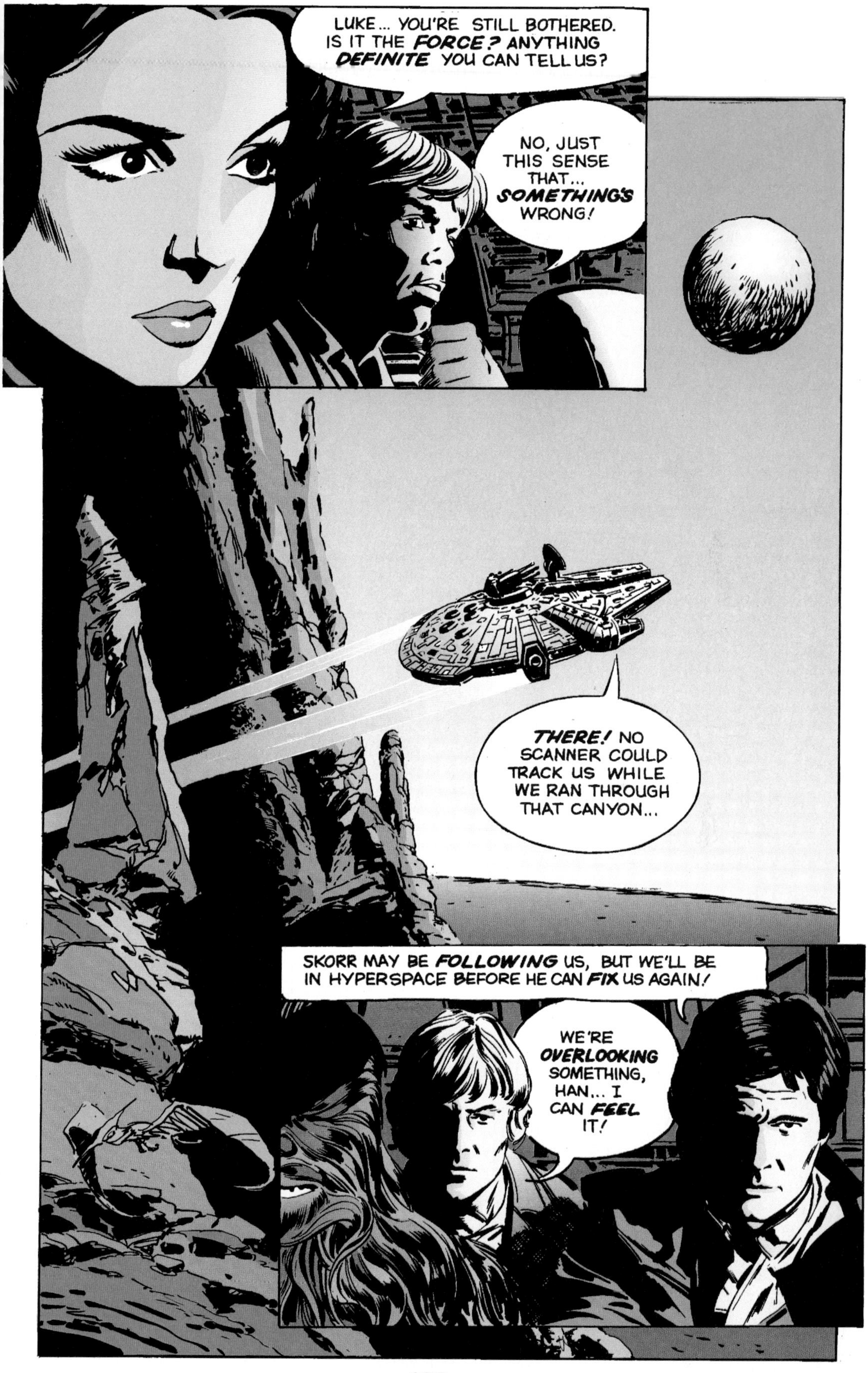
LUKE... YOU'RE STILL BOTHERED. IS IT THE FORCE? ANYTHING DEFINITE YOU CAN TELL US?
NO, JUST THIS SENSE THAT... SOMETHING'S WRONG!
THERE! NO SCANNER COULD TRACK US WHILE WE RAN THROUGH THAT CANYON...
SKORR MAY BE FOLLOWING US, BUT WE'LL BE IN HYPERSPACE BEFORE HE CAN FIX US AGAIN!
WE'RE OVERLOOKING SOMETHING, HAN... I CAN FEEL IT!

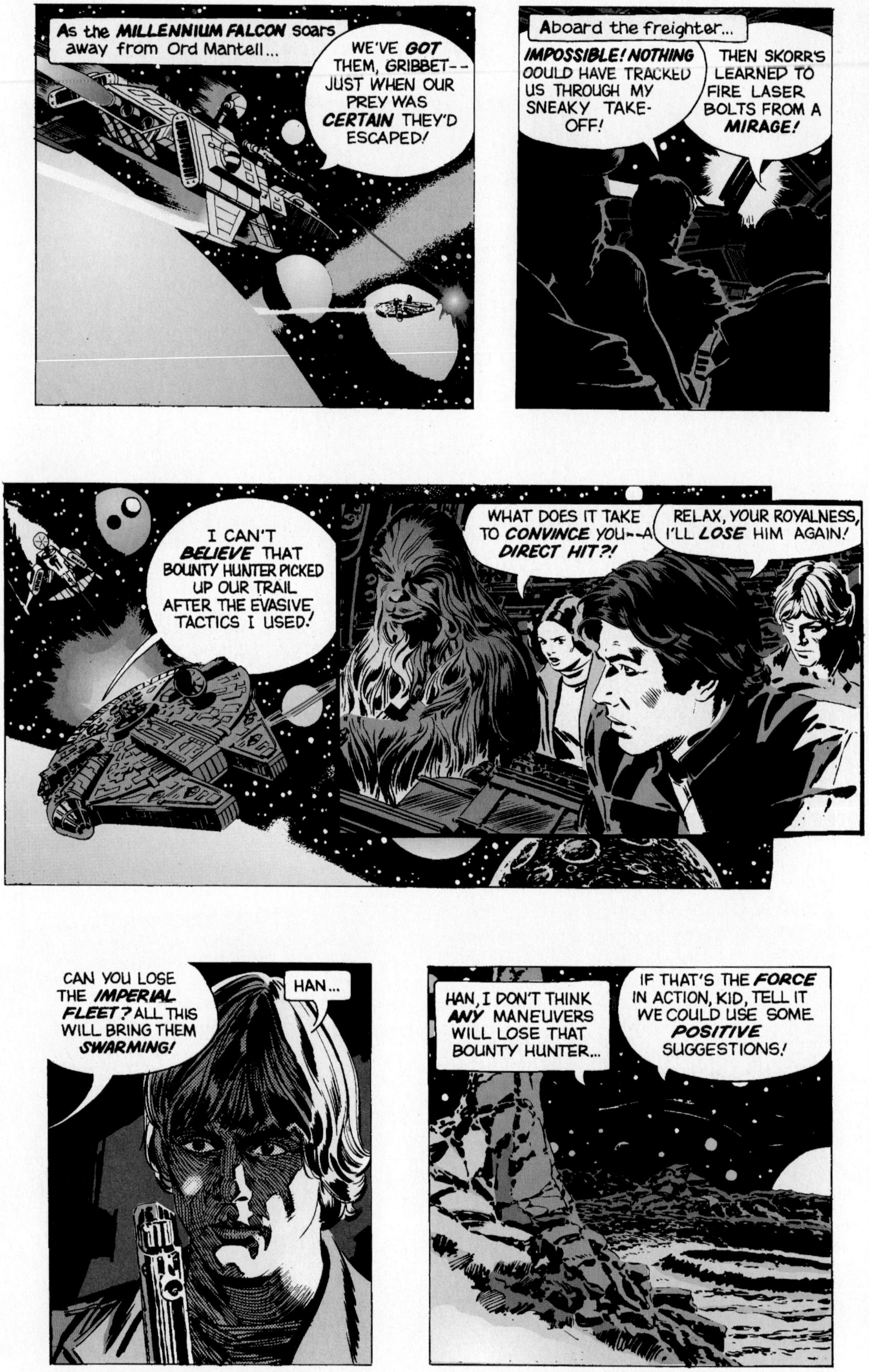
As the MILLENNIUM FALCON soars away from Ord Mantell...
WE'VE GOT THEM, GRIBBET--JUST WHEN OUR PREY WAS CERTAIN THEY'D ESCAPED!
Aboard the freighter...
IMPOSSIBLE! NOTHING OOULD HAVE TRACKED US THROUGH MY SNEAKY TAKE-OFF!
THEN SKORR'S LEARNED TO FIRE LASER BOLTS FROM A MIRAGE!
I CAN'T BELIEVE THAT BOUNTY HUNTER PICKED UP OUR TRAIL AFTER THE EVASIVE TACTICS I USED!
WHAT DOES IT TAKE TO CONVINCE YOU--A DIRECT HIT?!
RELAX, YOUR ROYALNESS, I'LL LOSE HIM AGAIN!
CAN YOU LOSE THE IMPERIAL FLEET? ALL THIS WILL BRING THEM SWARMING!
HAN...
HAN, I DON'T THINK ANY MANEUVERS WILL LOSE THAT BOUNTY HUNTER...
IF THAT'S THE FORCE IN ACTION, KID, TELL IT WE COULD USE SOME POSITIVE SUGGESTIONS!

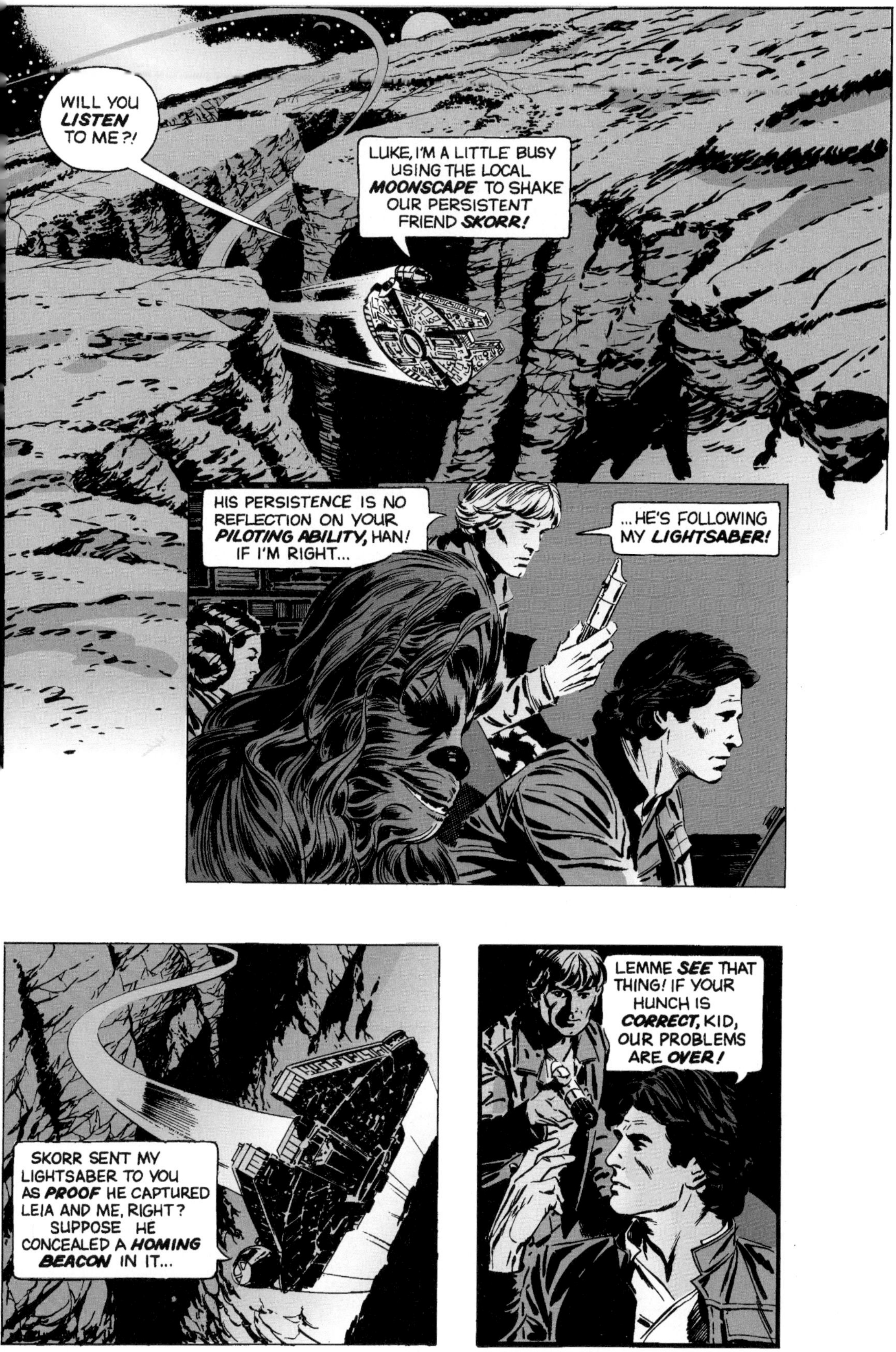
WILL YOU LISTEN TO ME?!
LUKE, I'M A LITTLE BUSY USING THE LOCAL MOONSCAPE TO SHAKE OUR PERSISTENT FRIEND SKORR!
HIS PERSISTENCE IS NO REFLECTION ON YOUR PILOTING ABILITY, HAN! IF I'M RIGHT...
...HE'S FOLLOWING MY LIGHTSABER!
SKORR SENT MY LIGHTSABER TO YOU AS PROOF HE CAPTURED LEIA AND ME, RIGHT? SUPPOSE HE CONCEALED A HOMING BEACON IN IT...
LEMME SEE THAT THING! IF YOUR HUNCH IS CORRECT, KID, OUR PROBLEMS ARE OVER!

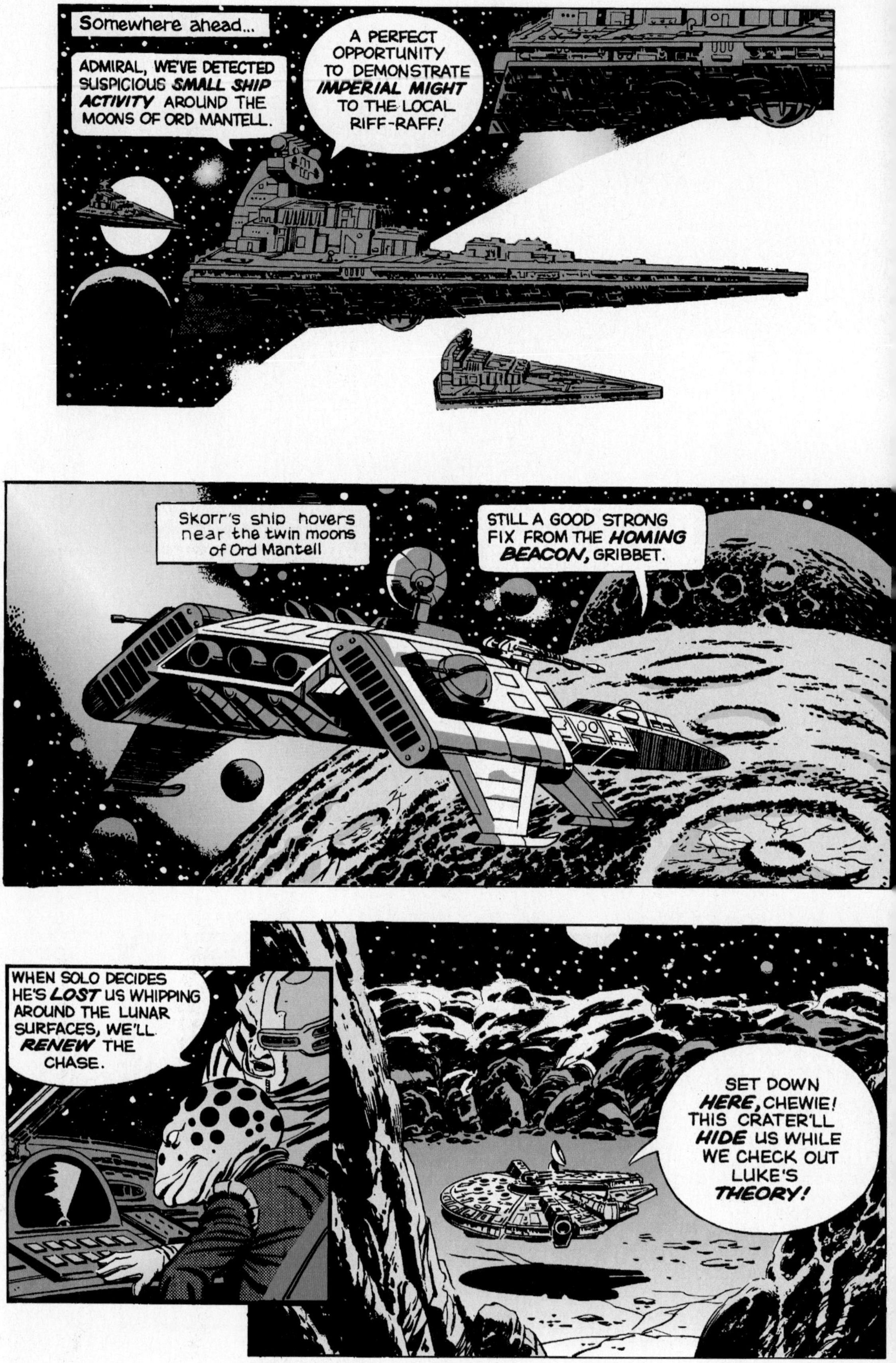
Somewhere ahead...
ADMIRAL, WE'VE DETECTED SUSPICIOUS SMALL SHIP ACTIVITY AROUND THE MOONS OF ORD MANTELL.
A PERFECT OPPORTUNITY TO DEMONSTRATE IMPERIAL MIGHT TO THE LOCAL RIFF-RAFF!
Skorr's ship hovers near the twin moons of Ord Mantell
STILL A GOOD STRONG FIX FROM THE HOMING BEACON, GRIBBET.
WHEN SOLO DECIDES HE'S LOST US WHIPPING AROUND THE LUNAR SURFACES, WE'LL RENEW THE CHASE.
SET DOWN HERE, CHEWIE! THIS CRATER'LL HIDE US WHILE WE CHECK OUT LUKE'S THEORY!

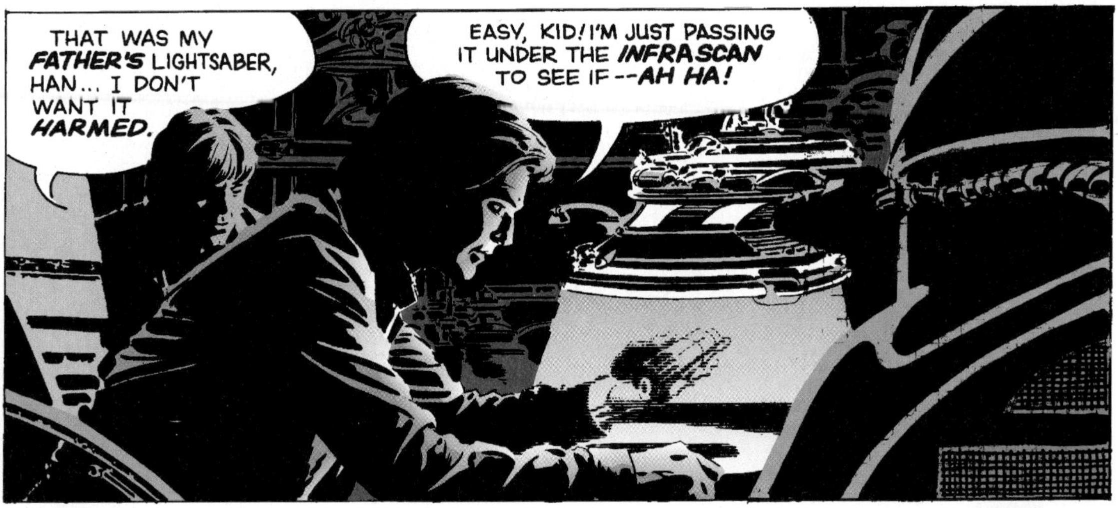
THAT WAS MY FATHER'S LIGHTSABER, HAN... I DON'T WANT IT HARMED.
EASY, KID! I'M JUST PASSING IT UNDER THE INFRASCAN TO SEE IF --AH HA!

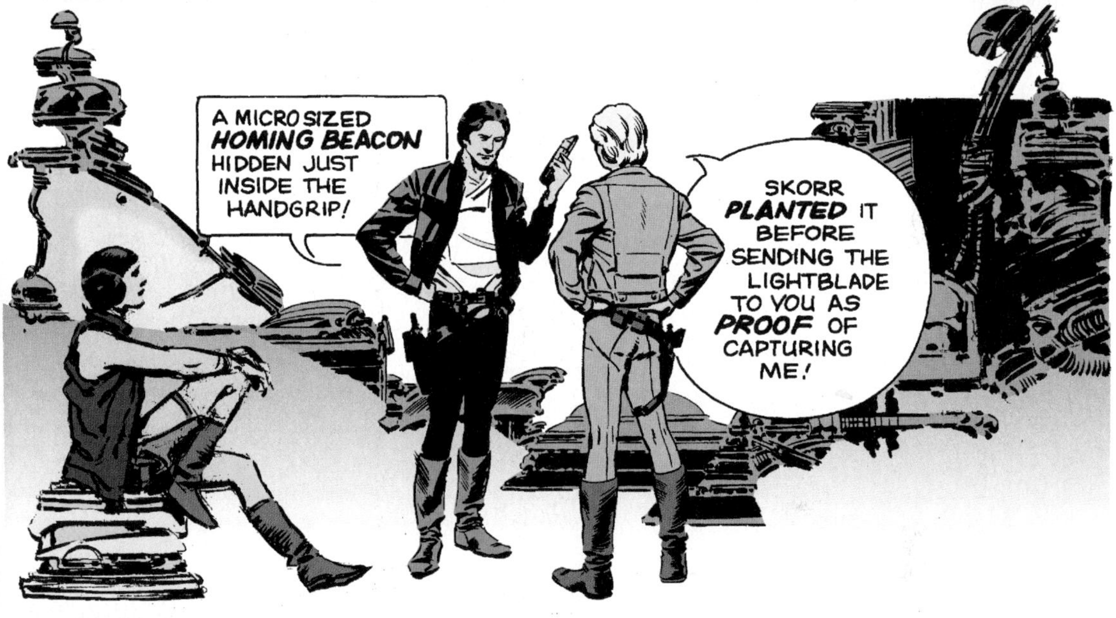
A MICROSIZED HOMING BEACON HIDDEN JUST INSIDE THE HANDGRIP!
SKORR PLANTED IT BEFORE SENDING THE LIGHTBLADE TO YOU AS PROOF OF CAPTURING ME!

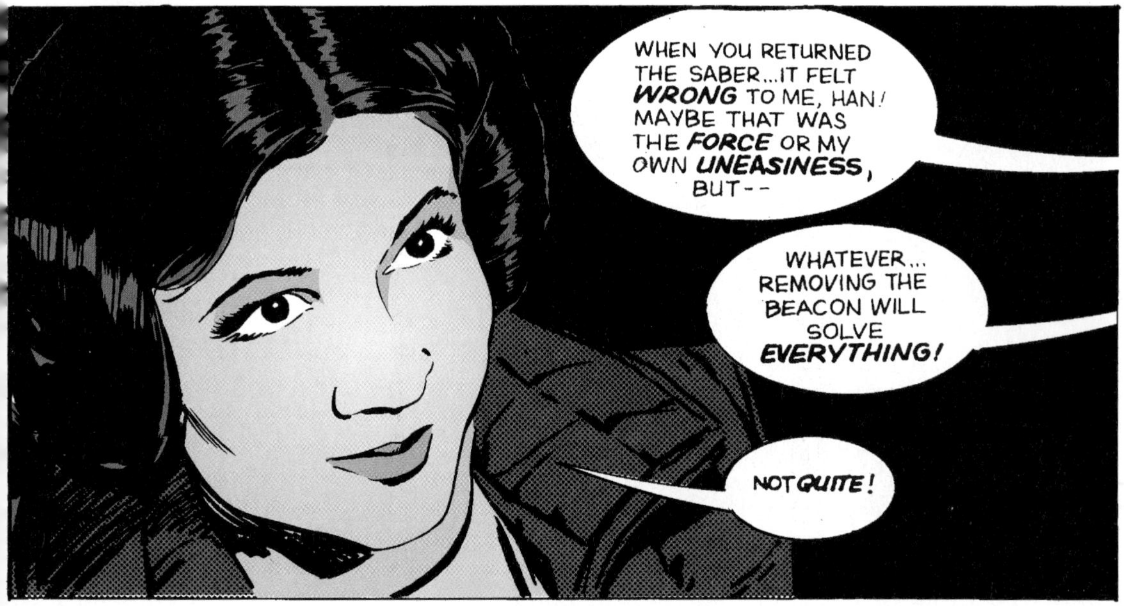
WHEN YOU RETURNED THE SABER...IT FELT WRONG TO ME, HAN! MAYBE THAT WAS THE FORCE OR MY OWN UNEASINESS, BUT--
WHATEVER... REMOVING THE BEACON WILL SOLVE EVERYTHING!
NOT QUITE!

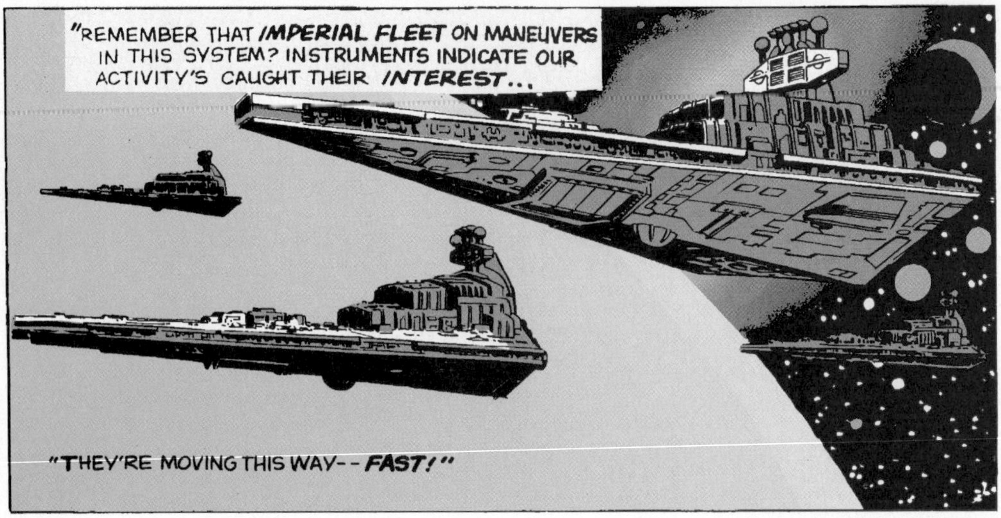
"REMEMBER THAT IMPERIAL FLEET ON MANEUVERS IN THIS SYSTEM? INSTRUMENTS INDICATE OUR ACTIVITY'S CAUGHT THEIR INTEREST...
"THEY'RE MOVING THIS WAY--FAST!"

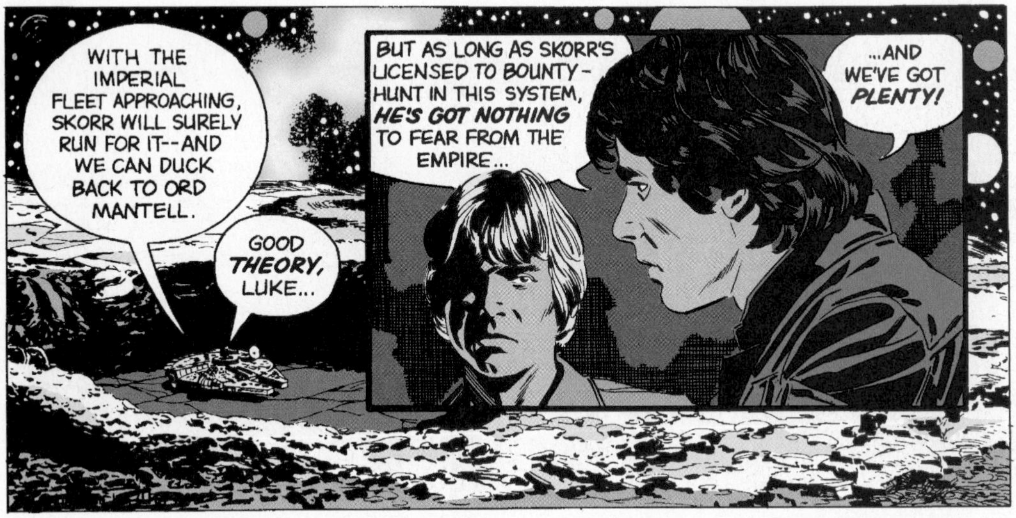
WITH THE IMPERIAL FLEET APPROACHING, SKORR WILL SURELY RUN FOR IT--AND WE CAN DUCK BACK TO ORD MANTELL.
GOOD THEORY, LUKE...
BUT AS LONG AS SKORR'S LICENSED TO BOUNTY-HUNT IN THIS SYSTEM, HE'S GOT NOTHING TO FEAR FROM THE EMPIRE...
...AND WE'VE GOT PLENTY!

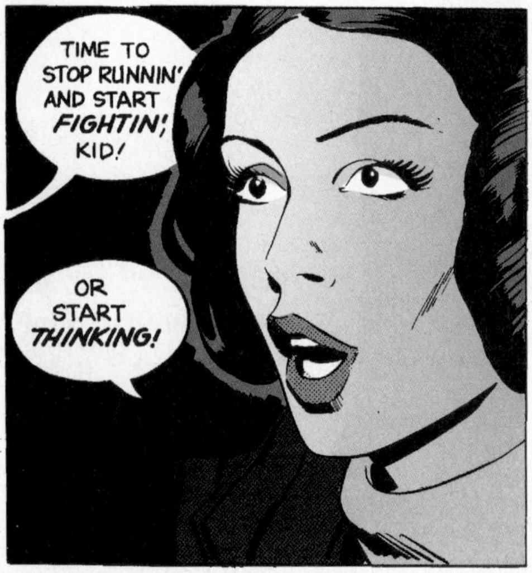
TIME TO STOP RUNNIN' AND START FIGHTIN', KID!
OR START THINKING!

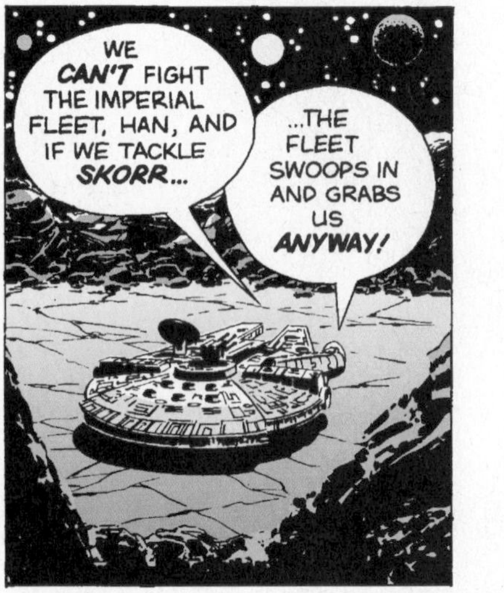
WE CAN'T FIGHT THE IMPERIAL FLEET, HAN, AND IF WE TACKLE SKORR...
...THE FLEET SWOOPS IN AND GRABS US ANYWAY!

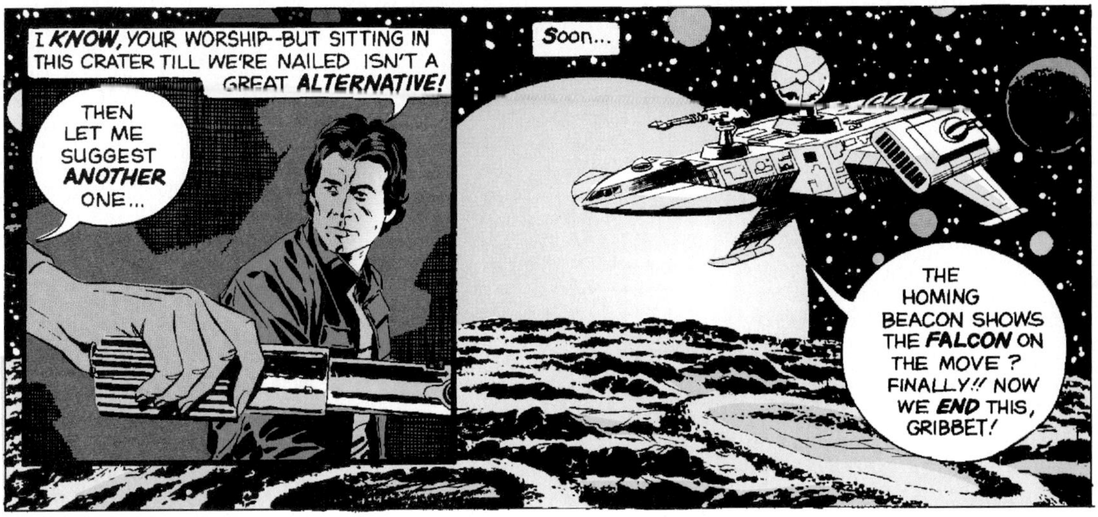
I KNOW, YOUR WORSHIP--BUT SITTING IN THIS CRATER TILL WE'RE NAILED ISN'T A GREAT ALTERNATIVE!
THEN LET ME SUGGEST ANOTHER ONE...
Soon...
THE HOMING BEACON SHOWS THE FALCON ON THE MOVE ? FINALLY!! NOW WE END THIS, GRIBBET!

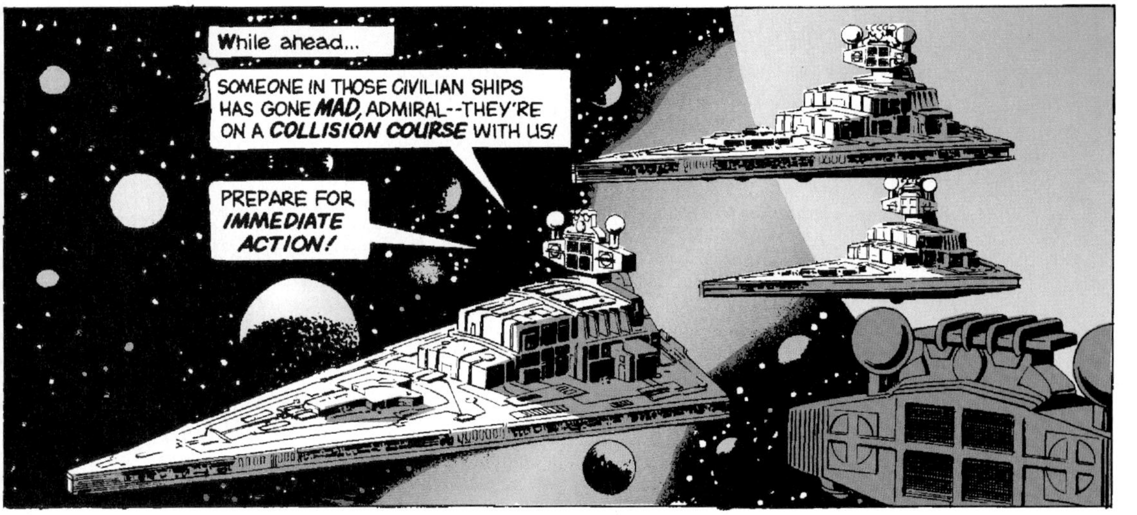
While ahead...
SOMEONE IN THOSE CIVILIAN SHIPS HAS GONE MAD, ADMIRAL--THEY'RE ON A COLLISION COURSE WITH US!
PREPARE FOR IMMEDIATE ACTION!

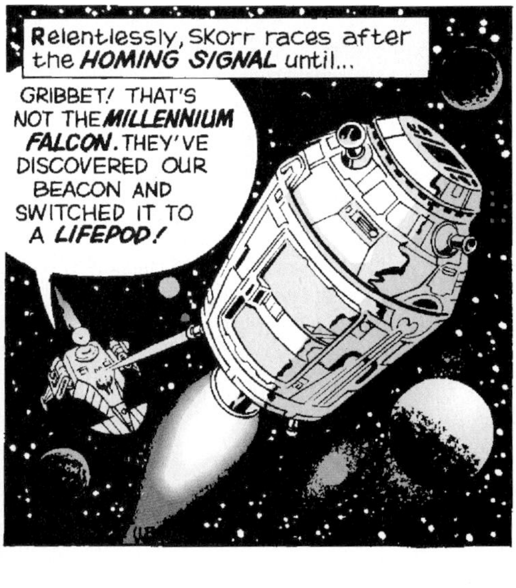
Relentlessly, Skorr races after the HOMING SIGNAL until...
GRIBBET! THAT'S NOT THE MILLENNIUM FALCON. THEY'VE DISCOVERED OUR BEACON AND SWITCHED IT TO A LIFEPOD!

A lifepod leading him into the **EMPIRE'S FLEET** -- and the **TRACTOR BEAM** OF ITS FLAGSHIP!

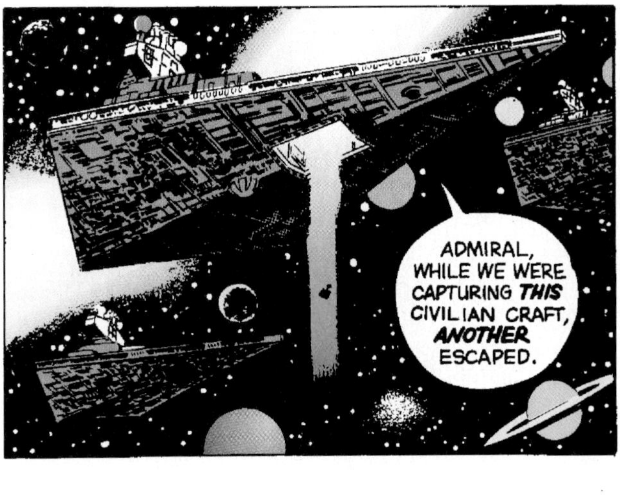
ADMIRAL, WHILE WE WERE CAPTURING THIS CIVILIAN CRAFT, ANOTHER ESCAPED.

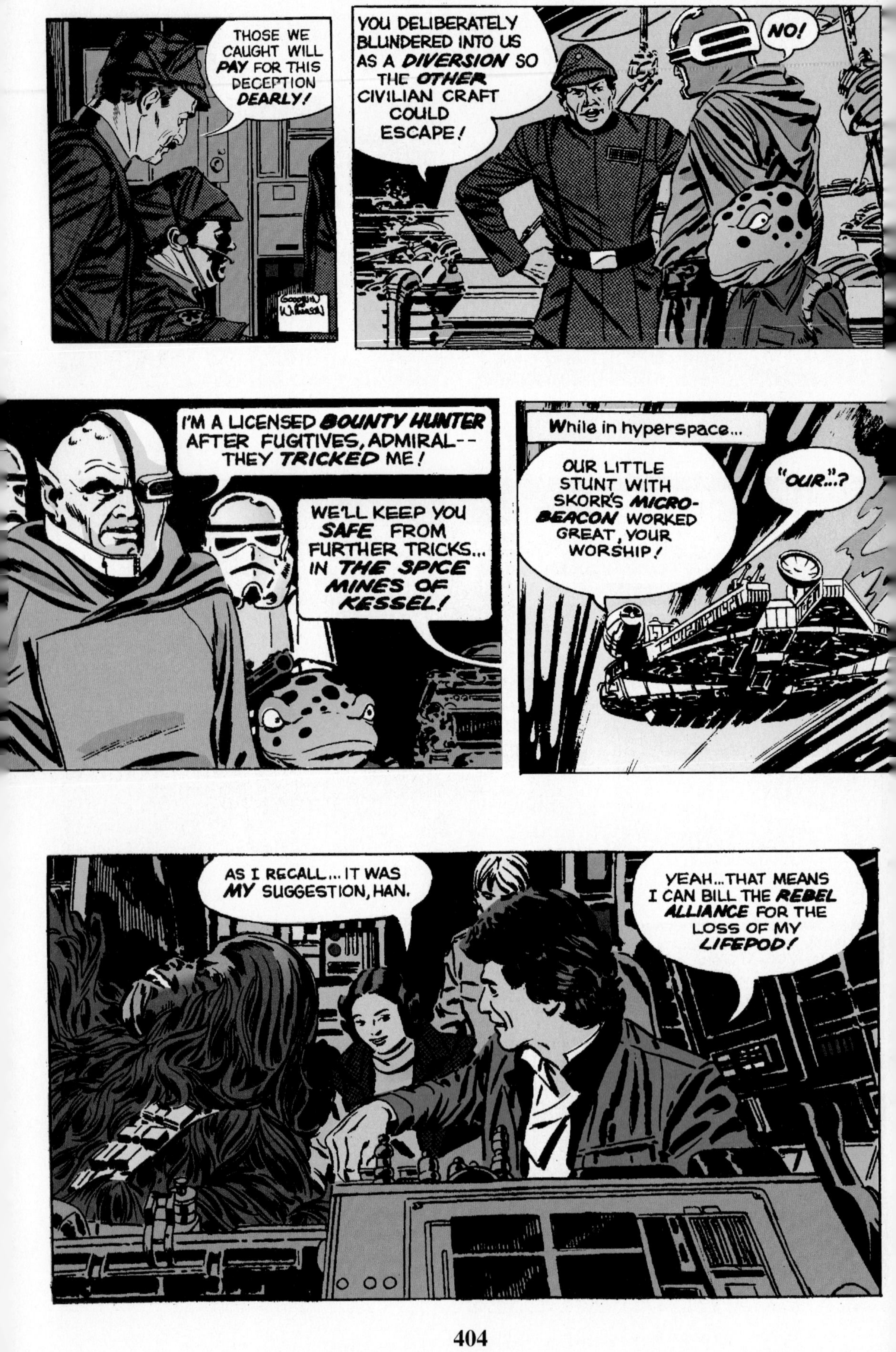
THOSE WE CAUGHT WILL PAY FOR THIS DECEPTION DEARLY!
YOU DELIBERATELY BLUNDERED INTO US AS A DIVERSION SO THE OTHER CIVILIAN CRAFT COULD ESCAPE!
NO!
I'M A LICENSED BOUNTY HUNTER AFTER FUGITIVES, ADMIRAL-- THEY TRICKED ME!
WE'LL KEEP YOU SAFE FROM FURTHER TRICKS... IN THE SPICE MINES OF KESSEL!
While in hyperspace...
OUR LITTLE STUNT WITH SKORR'S MICRO-BEACON WORKED GREAT, YOUR WORSHIP!
"OUR"...?
AS I RECALL... IT WAS MY SUGGESTION, HAN.
YEAH...THAT MEANS I CAN BILL THE REBEL ALLIANCE FOR THE LOSS OF MY LIFEPOD!

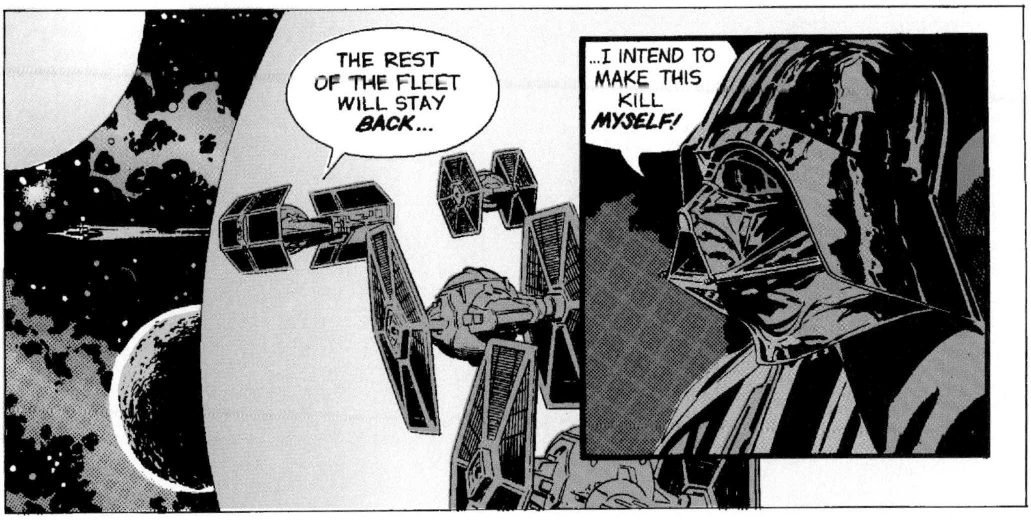
THE REST OF THE FLEET WILL STAY BACK...
...I INTEND TO MAKE THIS KILL MYSELF!

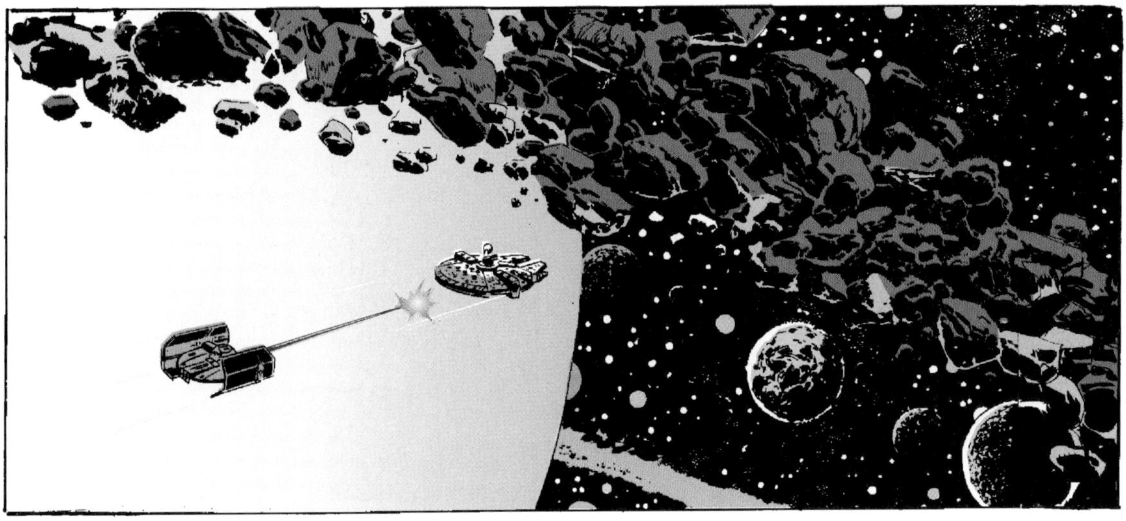

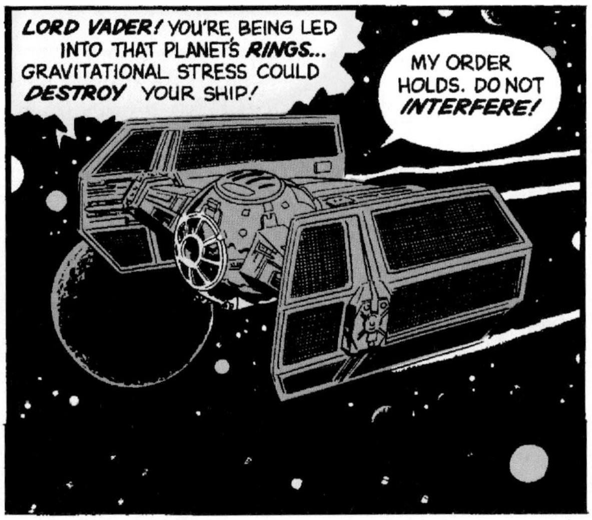
LORD VADER! YOU'RE BEING LED INTO THAT PLANET'S RINGS... GRAVITATIONAL STRESS COULD DESTROY YOUR SHIP!
MY ORDER HOLDS. DO NOT INTERFERE!

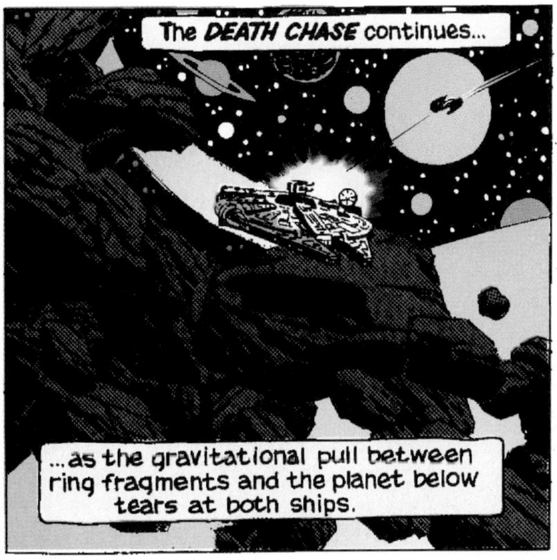
The DEATH CHASE continues...
...as the gravitational pull between ring fragments and the planet below tears at both ships.

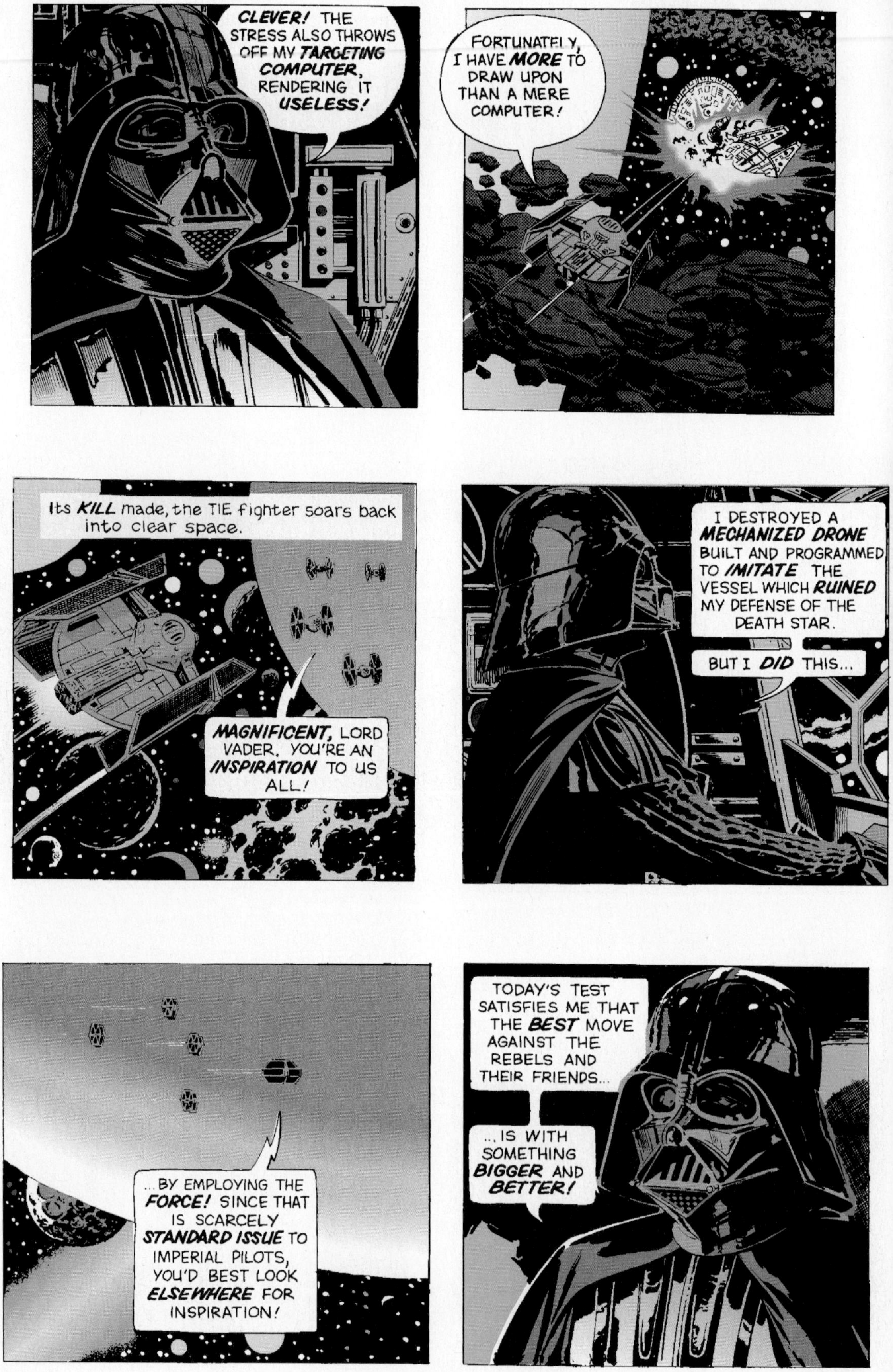
CLEVER! THE STRESS ALSO THROWS OFF MY TARGETING COMPUTER, RENDERING IT USELESS!
FORTUNATELY, I HAVE MORE TO DRAW UPON THAN A MERE COMPUTER!
Its KILL made, the TIE fighter soars back into clear space.
MAGNIFICENT, LORD VADER. YOU'RE AN INSPIRATION TO US ALL!
I DESTROYED A MECHANIZED DRONE BUILT AND PROGRAMMED TO IMITATE THE VESSEL WHICH RUINED MY DEFENSE OF THE DEATH STAR.
BUT I DID THIS...
...BY EMPLOYING THE FORCE! SINCE THAT IS SCARCELY STANDARD ISSUE TO IMPERIAL PILOTS, YOU'D BEST LOOK ELSEWHERE FOR INSPIRATION!
TODAY'S TEST SATISFIES ME THAT THE BEST MOVE AGAINST THE REBELS AND THEIR FRIENDS...
...IS WITH SOMETHING BIGGER AND BETTER!

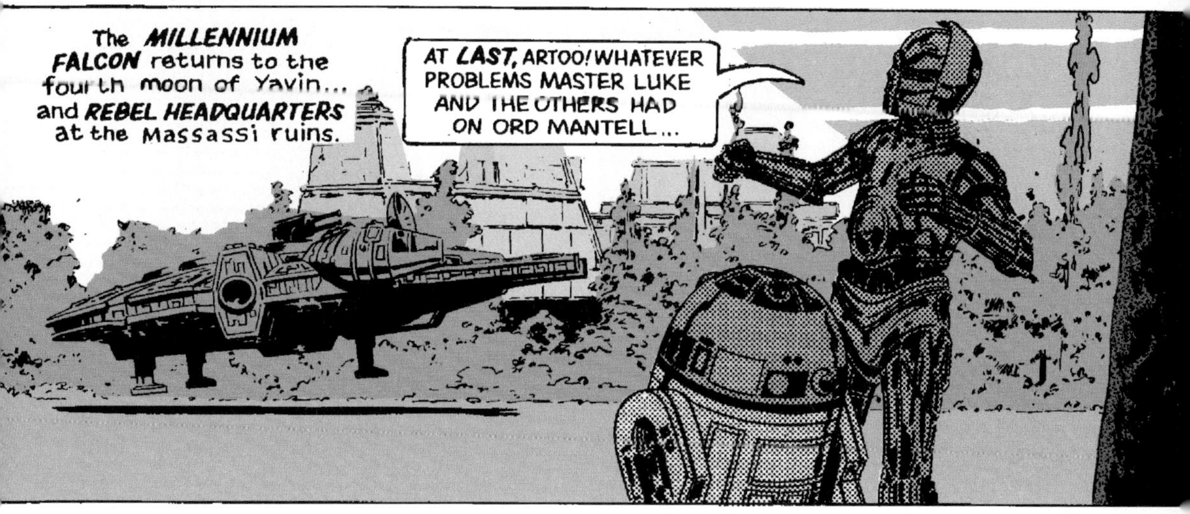
The MILLENNIUM FALCON returns to the fourth moon of Yavin... and REBEL HEADQUARTERS at the Massassi ruins.
AT LAST, ARTOO! WHATEVER PROBLEMS MASTER LUKE AND THE OTHERS HAD ON ORD MANTELL...

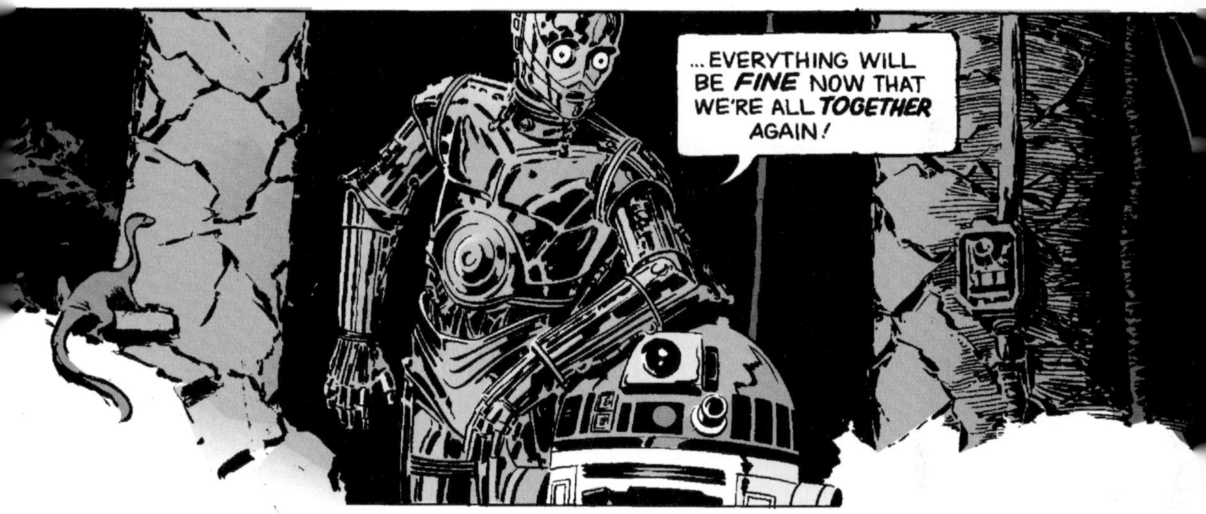
...EVERYTHING WILL BE FINE NOW THAT WE'RE ALL TOGETHER AGAIN!

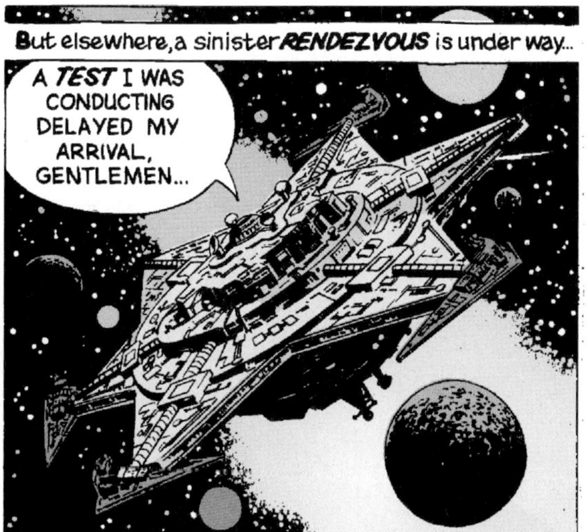
But elsewhere, a sinister RENDEZVOUS is under way...
A TEST I WAS CONDUCTING DELAYED MY ARRIVAL, GENTLEMEN...

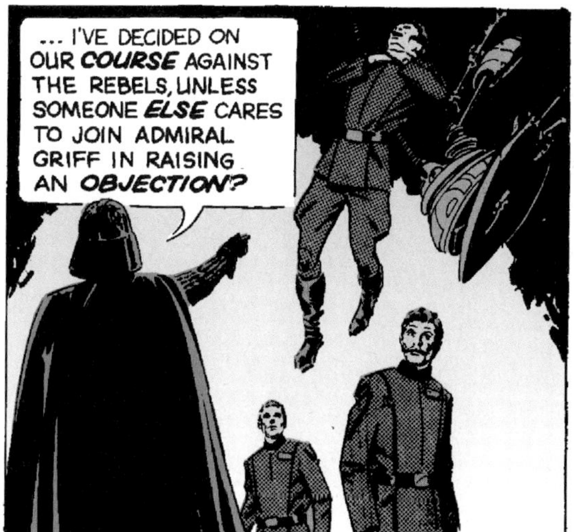
... I'VE DECIDED ON OUR COURSE AGAINST THE REBELS, UNLESS SOMEONE ELSE CARES TO JOIN ADMIRAL GRIFF IN RAISING AN OBJECTION?

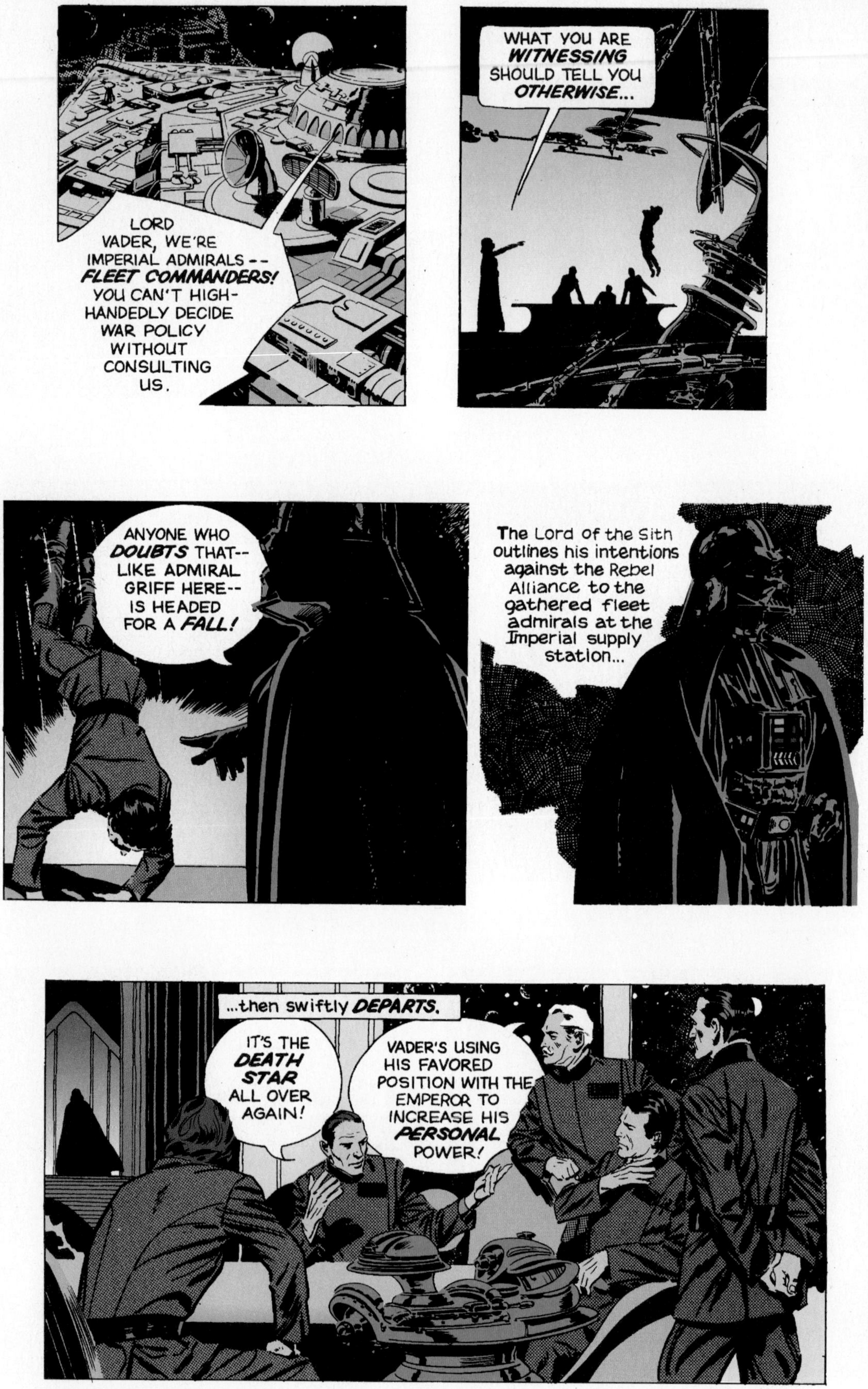
LORD VADER, WE'RE IMPERIAL ADMIRALS -- FLEET COMMANDERS! YOU CAN'T HIGH-HANDEDLY DECIDE WAR POLICY WITHOUT CONSULTING US.
WHAT YOU ARE WITNESSING SHOULD TELL YOU OTHERWISE...
ANYONE WHO DOUBTS THAT--LIKE ADMIRAL GRIFF HERE--IS HEADED FOR A FALL!
The Lord of the Sith outlines his intentions against the Rebel Alliance to the gathered fleet admirals at the Imperial supply station...
...then swiftly DEPARTS.
IT'S THE DEATH STAR ALL OVER AGAIN!
VADER'S USING HIS FAVORED POSITION WITH THE EMPEROR TO INCREASE HIS PERSONAL POWER!

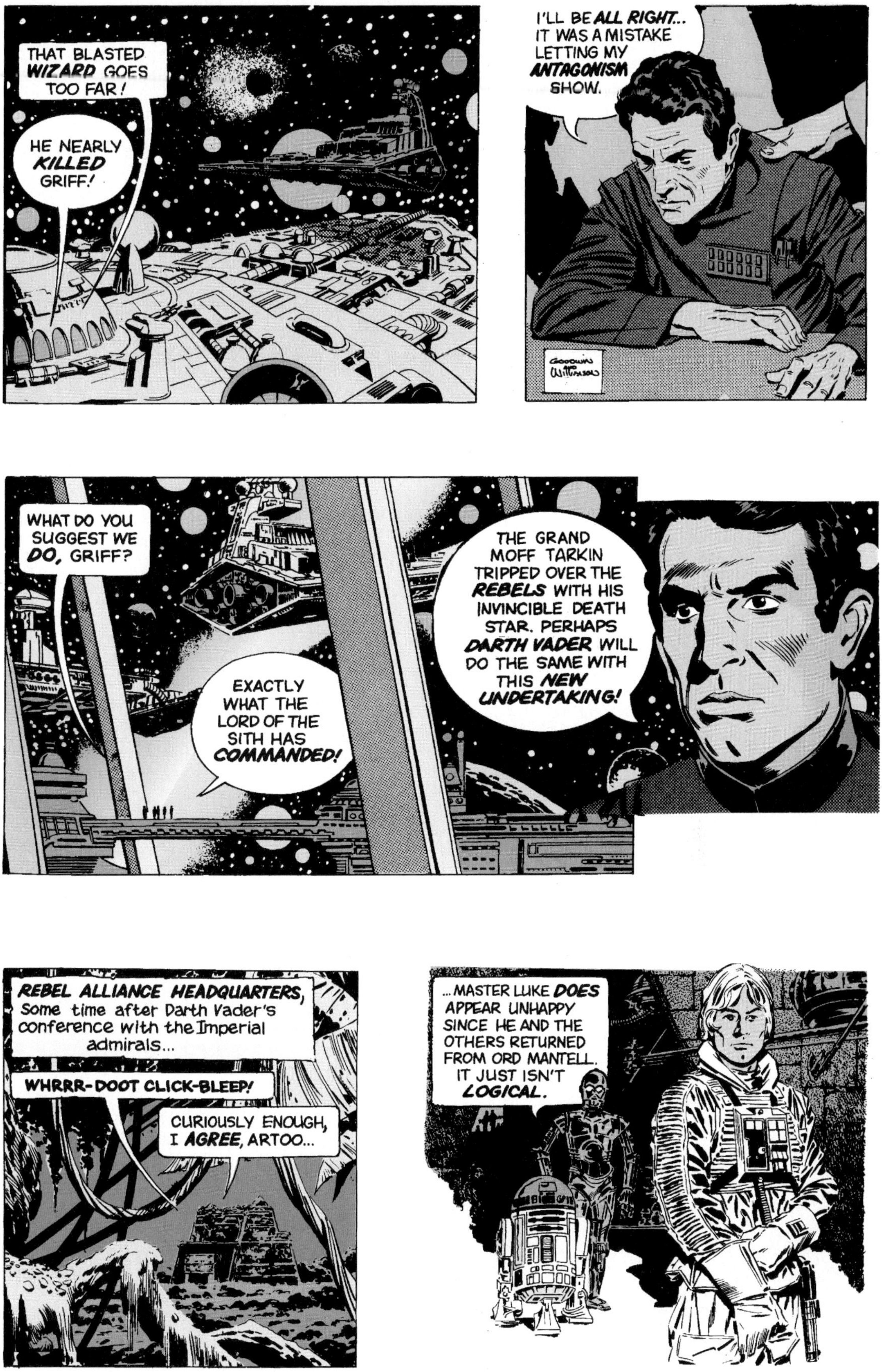
THAT BLASTED WIZARD GOES TOO FAR!
HE NEARLY KILLED GRIFF!
I'LL BE ALL RIGHT... IT WAS A MISTAKE LETTING MY ANTAGONISM SHOW.
WHAT DO YOU SUGGEST WE DO, GRIFF?
EXACTLY WHAT THE LORD OF THE SITH HAS COMMANDED!
THE GRAND MOFF TARKIN TRIPPED OVER THE REBELS WITH HIS INVINCIBLE DEATH STAR. PERHAPS DARTH VADER WILL DO THE SAME WITH THIS NEW UNDERTAKING!
REBEL ALLIANCE HEADQUARTERS, Some time after Darth Vader's conference with the Imperial admirals...
WHRRR-DOOT CLICK-BLEEP!
CURIOUSLY ENOUGH, I AGREE, ARTOO...
...MASTER LUKE DOES APPEAR UNHAPPY SINCE HE AND THE OTHERS RETURNED FROM ORD MANTELL. IT JUST ISN'T LOGICAL.

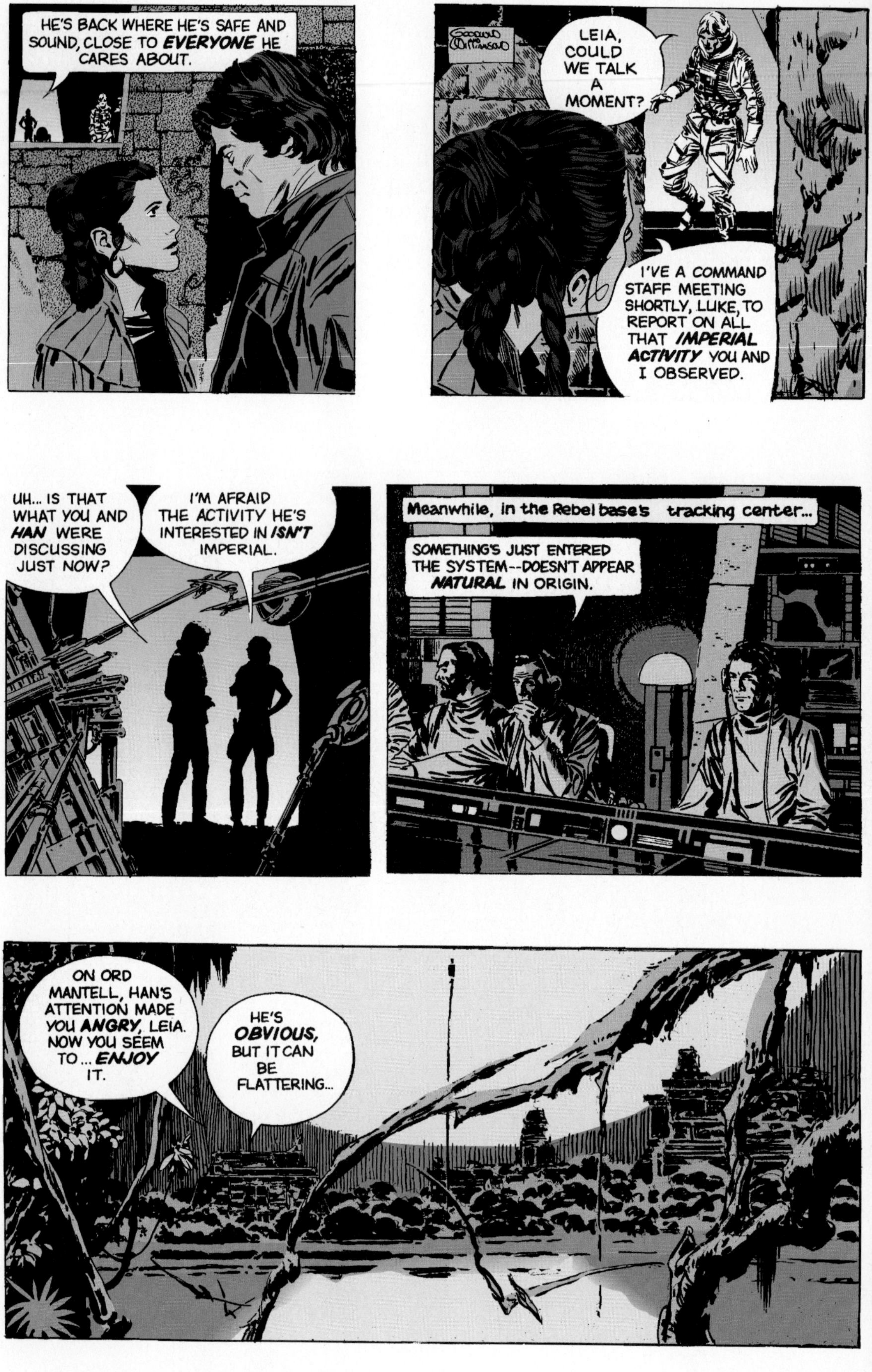
HE'S BACK WHERE HE'S SAFE AND SOUND, CLOSE TO EVERYONE HE CARES ABOUT.
LEIA, COULD WE TALK A MOMENT?
I'VE A COMMAND STAFF MEETING SHORTLY, LUKE, TO REPORT ON ALL THAT IMPERIAL ACTIVITY YOU AND I OBSERVED.
UH... IS THAT WHAT YOU AND HAN WERE DISCUSSING JUST NOW?
I'M AFRAID THE ACTIVITY HE'S INTERESTED IN ISN'T IMPERIAL.
Meanwhile, in the Rebel base's tracking center...
SOMETHING'S JUST ENTERED THE SYSTEM--DOESN'T APPEAR NATURAL IN ORIGIN.
ON ORD MANTELL, HAN'S ATTENTION MADE YOU ANGRY, LEIA. NOW YOU SEEM TO... ENJOY IT.
HE'S OBVIOUS, BUT IT CAN BE FLATTERING...

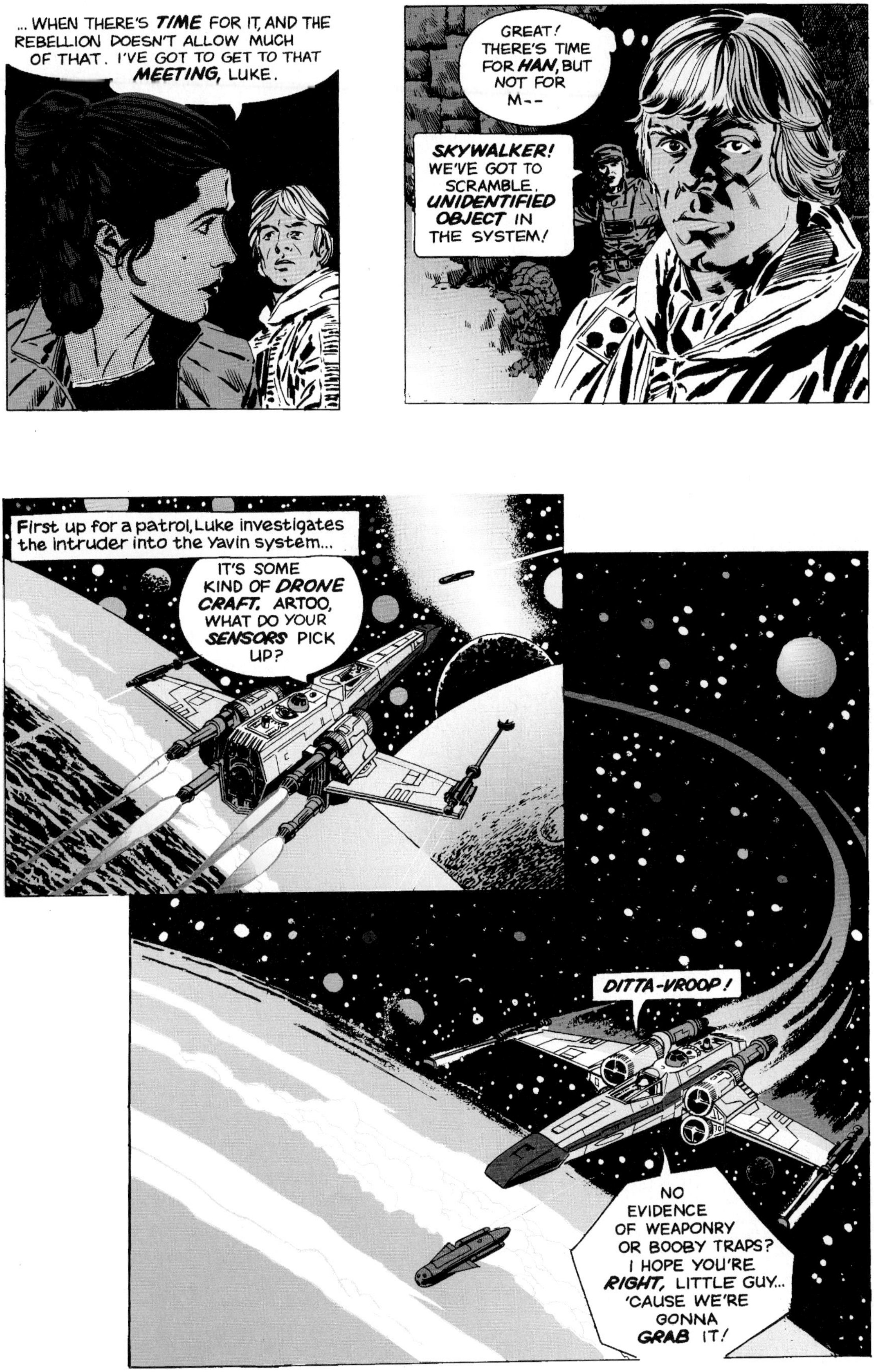

... WHEN THERE'S TIME FOR IT, AND THE REBELLION DOESN'T ALLOW MUCH OF THAT. I'VE GOT TO GET TO THAT MEETING, LUKE.
GREAT! THERE'S TIME FOR HAN, BUT NOT FOR M--
SKYWALKER! WE'VE GOT TO SCRAMBLE. UNIDENTIFIED OBJECT IN THE SYSTEM!
First up for a patrol, Luke investigates the intruder into the Yavin system...
IT'S SOME KIND OF DRONE CRAFT. ARTOO, WHAT DO YOUR SENSORS PICK UP?
DITTA-VROOP!
NO EVIDENCE OF WEAPONRY OR BOOBY TRAPS? I HOPE YOU'RE RIGHT, LITTLE GUY... 'CAUSE WE'RE GONNA GRAB IT!

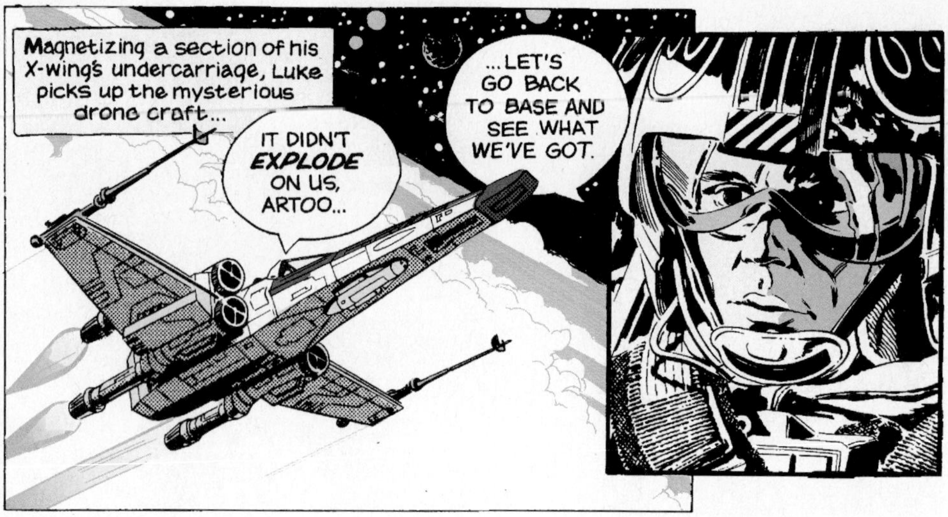
Magnetizing a section of his X-wing's undercarriage, Luke picks up the mysterious drone craft...
IT DIDN'T EXPLODE ON US, ARTOO...
...LET'S GO BACK TO BASE AND SEE WHAT WE'VE GOT.

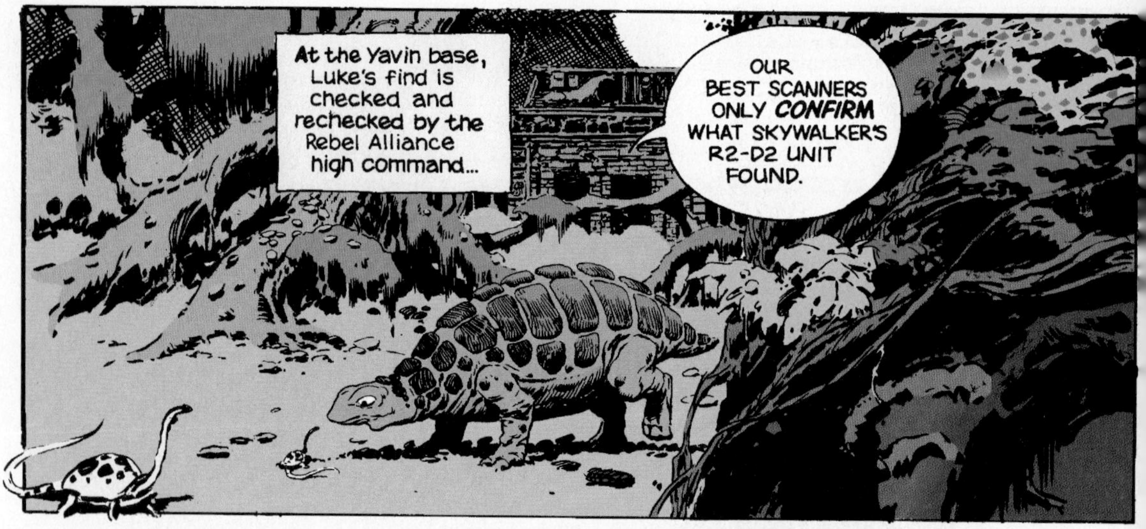
At the Yavin base, Luke's find is checked and rechecked by the Rebel Alliance high command...
OUR BEST SCANNERS ONLY CONFIRM WHAT SKYWALKER'S R2-D2 UNIT FOUND.

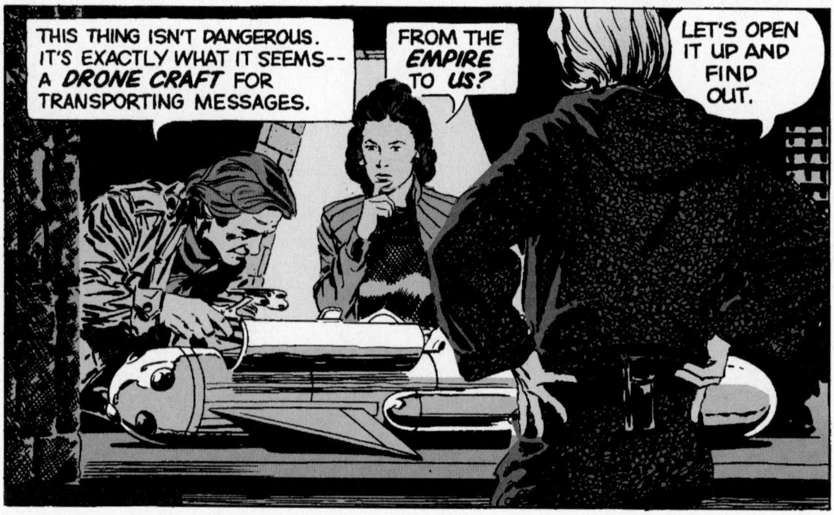
THIS THING ISN'T DANGEROUS. IT'S EXACTLY WHAT IT SEEMS-- A DRONE CRAFT FOR TRANSPORTING MESSAGES.
FROM THE EMPIRE TO US?
LET'S OPEN IT UP AND FIND OUT.

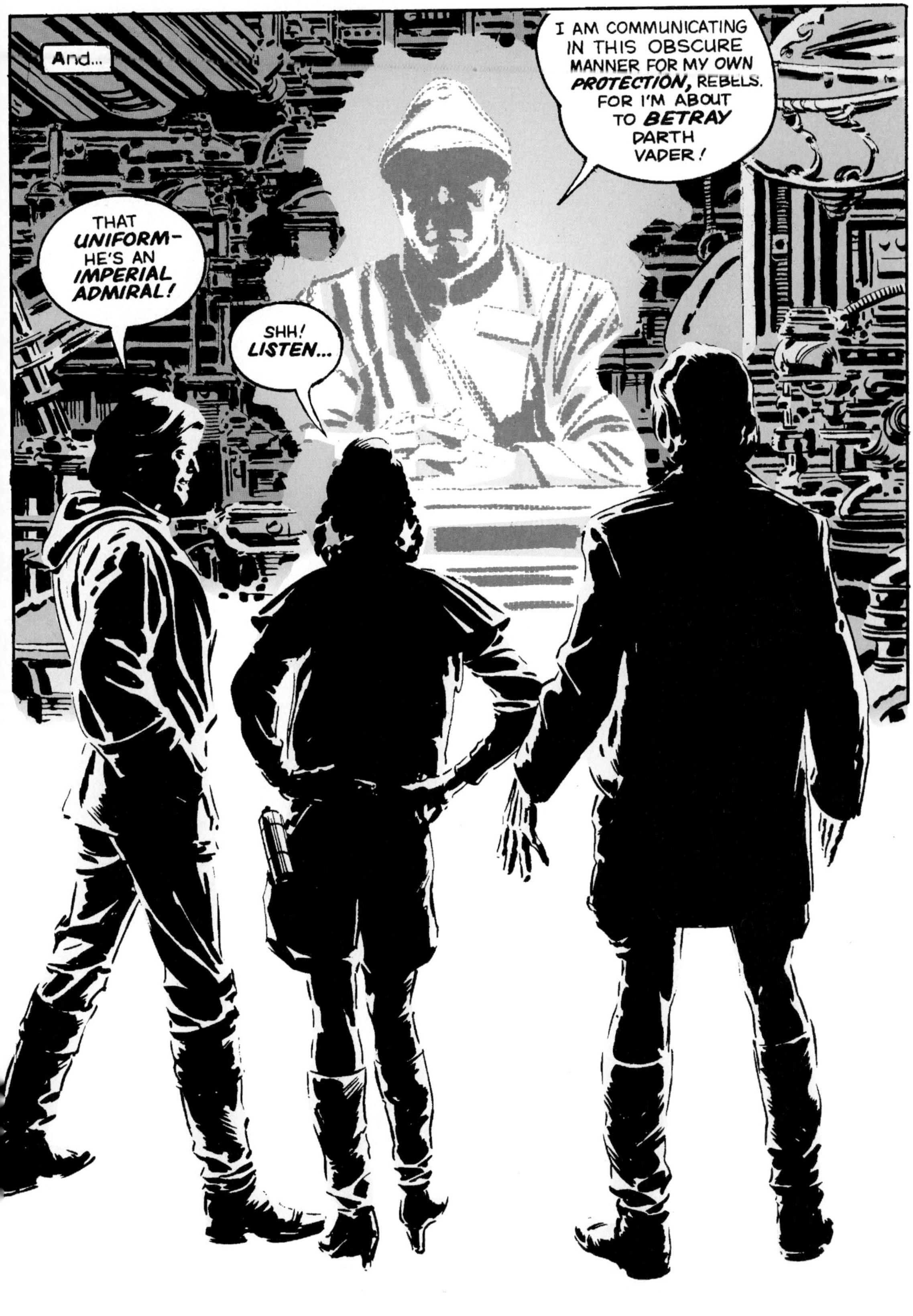
And...
I AM COMMUNICATING IN THIS OBSCURE MANNER FOR MY OWN PROTECTION, REBELS. FOR I'M ABOUT TO BETRAY DARTH VADER!
THAT UNIFORM-- HE'S AN IMPERIAL ADMIRAL!
SHH! LISTEN...

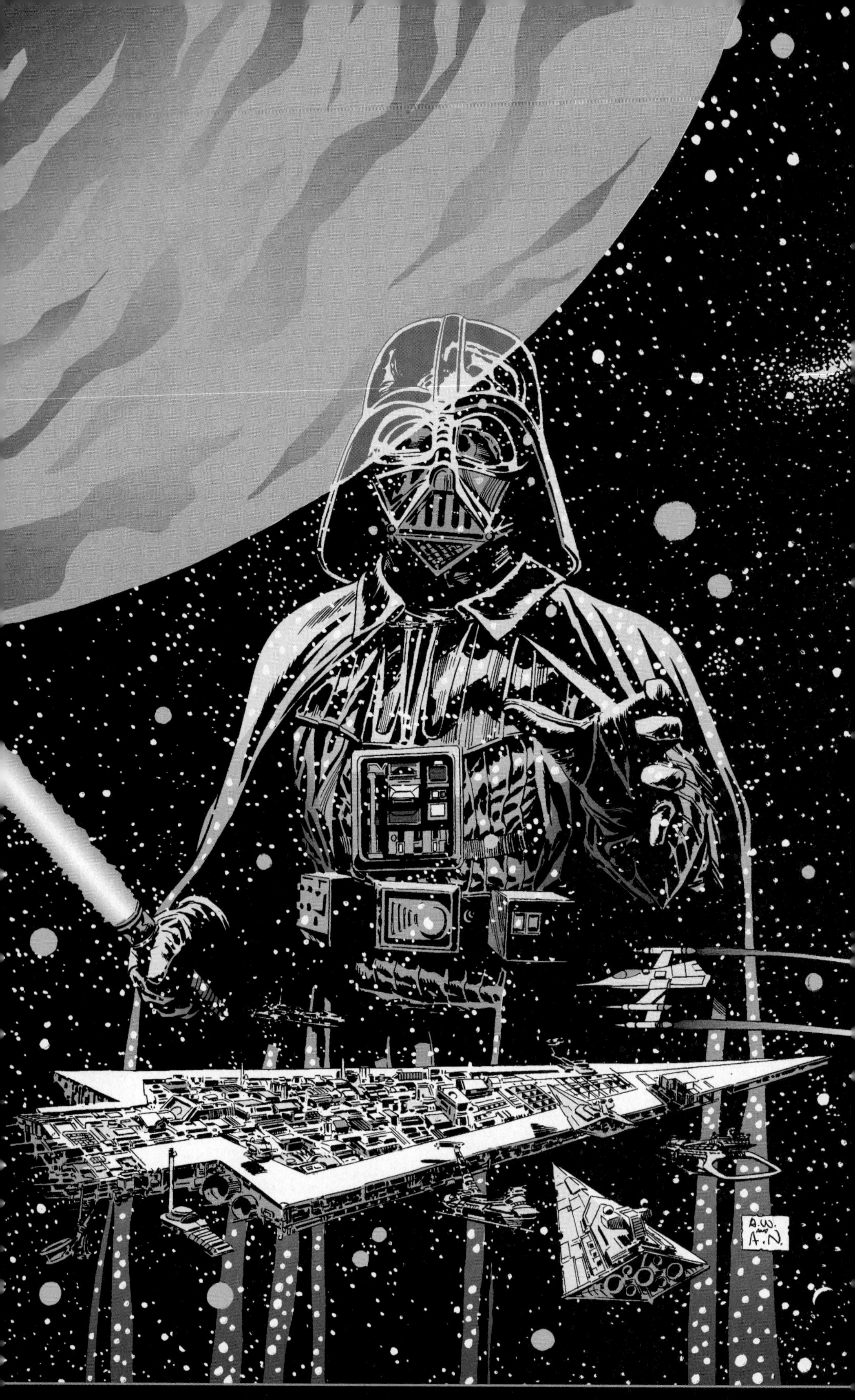
A.W. AND A.N.

CLASSIC STAR WARS #3 — "DARTH VADER STRIKES," PART 2
ORIGINALLY PUBLISHED FROM MAY 11 TO JULY 5, 1981

WRITER: ARCHIE GOODWIN • ARTIST & LETTERER: AL WILLIAMSON • COLORIST: STEVE BUCCELLATO • PRODUCTION ARTIST: DEBRA WATTS
EDITOR: ANINA BENNETT • COVER ARTISTS: AL WILLIAMSON, ALLEN NUNIS & GREGORY WRIGHT

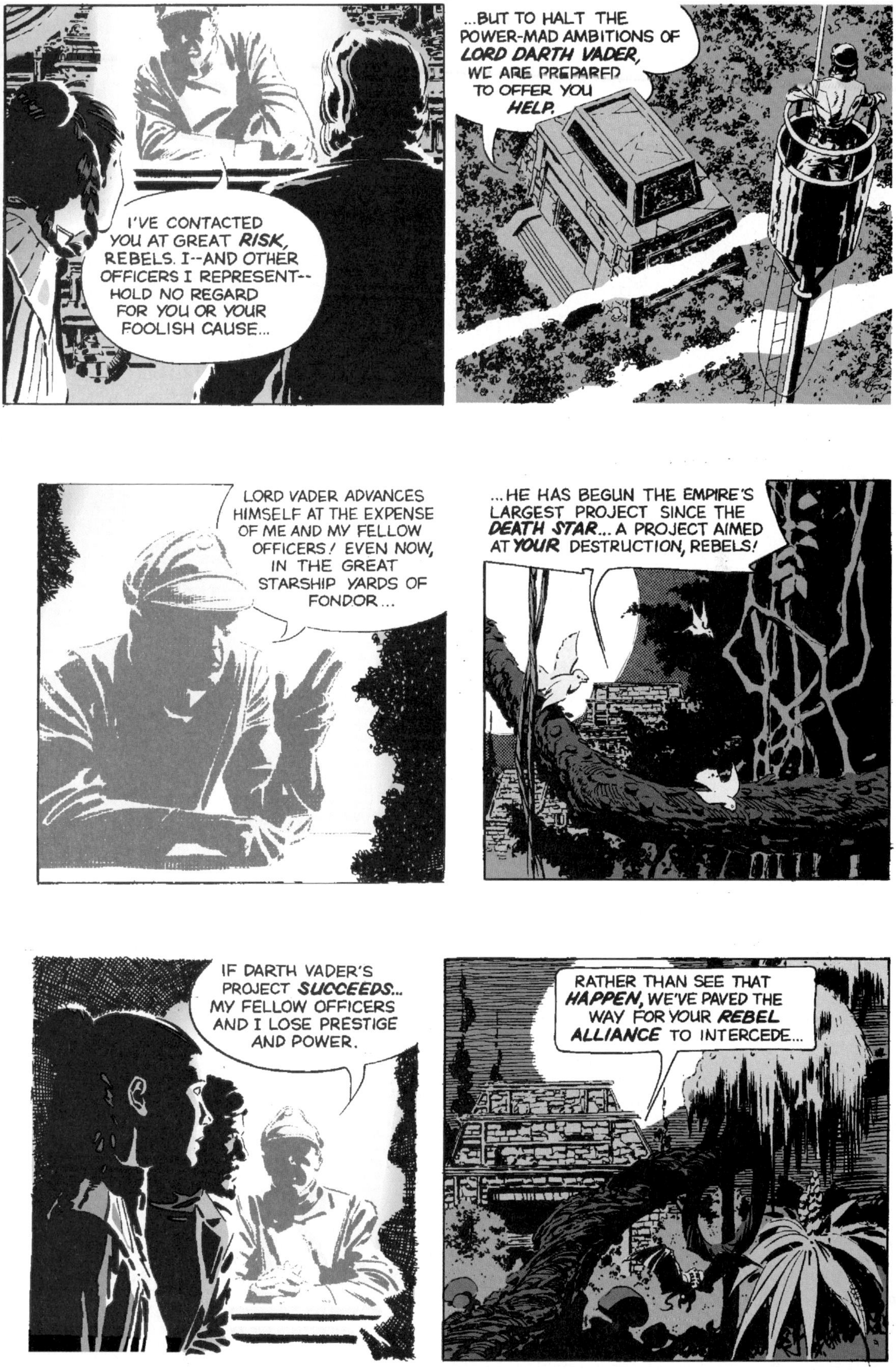
I'VE CONTACTED YOU AT GREAT RISK, REBELS. I--AND OTHER OFFICERS I REPRESENT--HOLD NO REGARD FOR YOU OR YOUR FOOLISH CAUSE...
...BUT TO HALT THE POWER-MAD AMBITIONS OF LORD DARTH VADER, WE ARE PREPARED TO OFFER YOU HELP.
LORD VADER ADVANCES HIMSELF AT THE EXPENSE OF ME AND MY FELLOW OFFICERS! EVEN NOW, IN THE GREAT STARSHIP YARDS OF FONDOR...
...HE HAS BEGUN THE EMPIRE'S LARGEST PROJECT SINCE THE DEATH STAR... A PROJECT AIMED AT YOUR DESTRUCTION, REBELS!
IF DARTH VADER'S PROJECT SUCCEEDS... MY FELLOW OFFICERS AND I LOSE PRESTIGE AND POWER.
RATHER THAN SEE THAT HAPPEN, WE'VE PAVED THE WAY FOR YOUR REBEL ALLIANCE TO INTERCEDE...

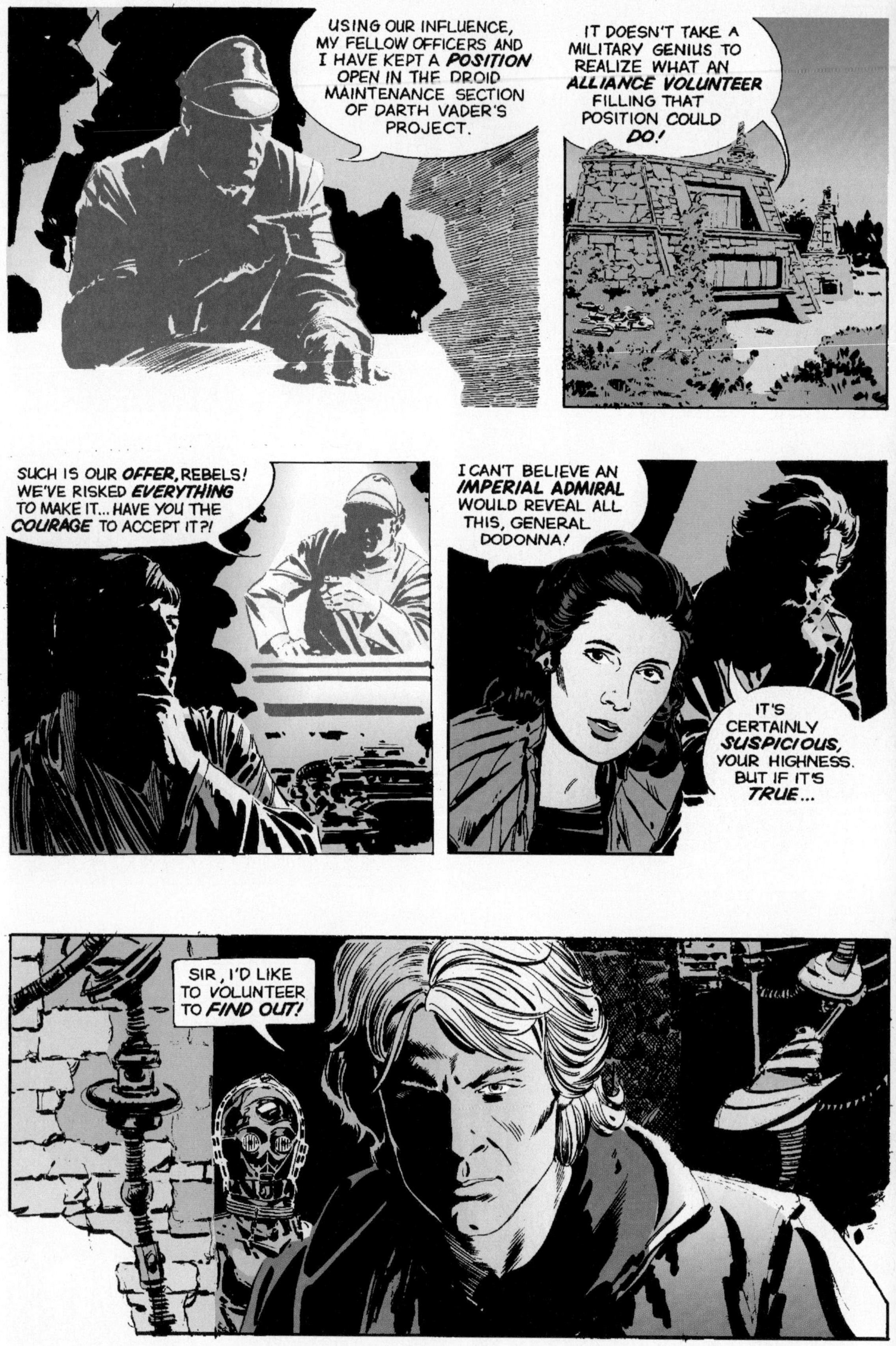
USING OUR INFLUENCE, MY FELLOW OFFICERS AND I HAVE KEPT A POSITION OPEN IN THE DROID MAINTENANCE SECTION OF DARTH VADER'S PROJECT.
IT DOESN'T TAKE A MILITARY GENIUS TO REALIZE WHAT AN ALLIANCE VOLUNTEER FILLING THAT POSITION COULD DO!
SUCH IS OUR OFFER, REBELS! WE'VE RISKED EVERYTHING TO MAKE IT... HAVE YOU THE COURAGE TO ACCEPT IT?!
I CAN'T BELIEVE AN IMPERIAL ADMIRAL WOULD REVEAL ALL THIS, GENERAL DODONNA!
IT'S CERTAINLY SUSPICIOUS, YOUR HIGHNESS. BUT IF IT'S TRUE...
SIR, I'D LIKE TO VOLUNTEER TO FIND OUT!

THE PRINCESS FEELS IT'S A *TRAP,* ARTOO...

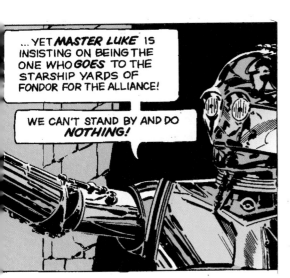

...YET *MASTER LUKE* IS INSISTING ON BEING THE ONE WHO *GOES* TO THE STARSHIP YARDS OF FONDOR FOR THE ALLIANCE!

WE CAN'T STAND BY AND DO *NOTHING!*

TA-DEEETA BLIP *WOOP!*

WE'LL VOLUNTEER TO *ACCOMPANY* HIM...? ARTOO-DETOO, THAT'S NOT *QUITE* WHAT I HAD IN MIND! *ARTOO!*

LUKE SKYWALKER, YOU'VE JUST COMPLETED *ONE* DANGEROUS MISSION... YOU CAN'T IMPETUOUSLY LEAP INTO *ANOTHER!*

OH? I'VE GOTTEN THE IMPRESSION YOU *ADMIRE* THE IMPETUOUS TYPE, YOUR HIGHNESS!

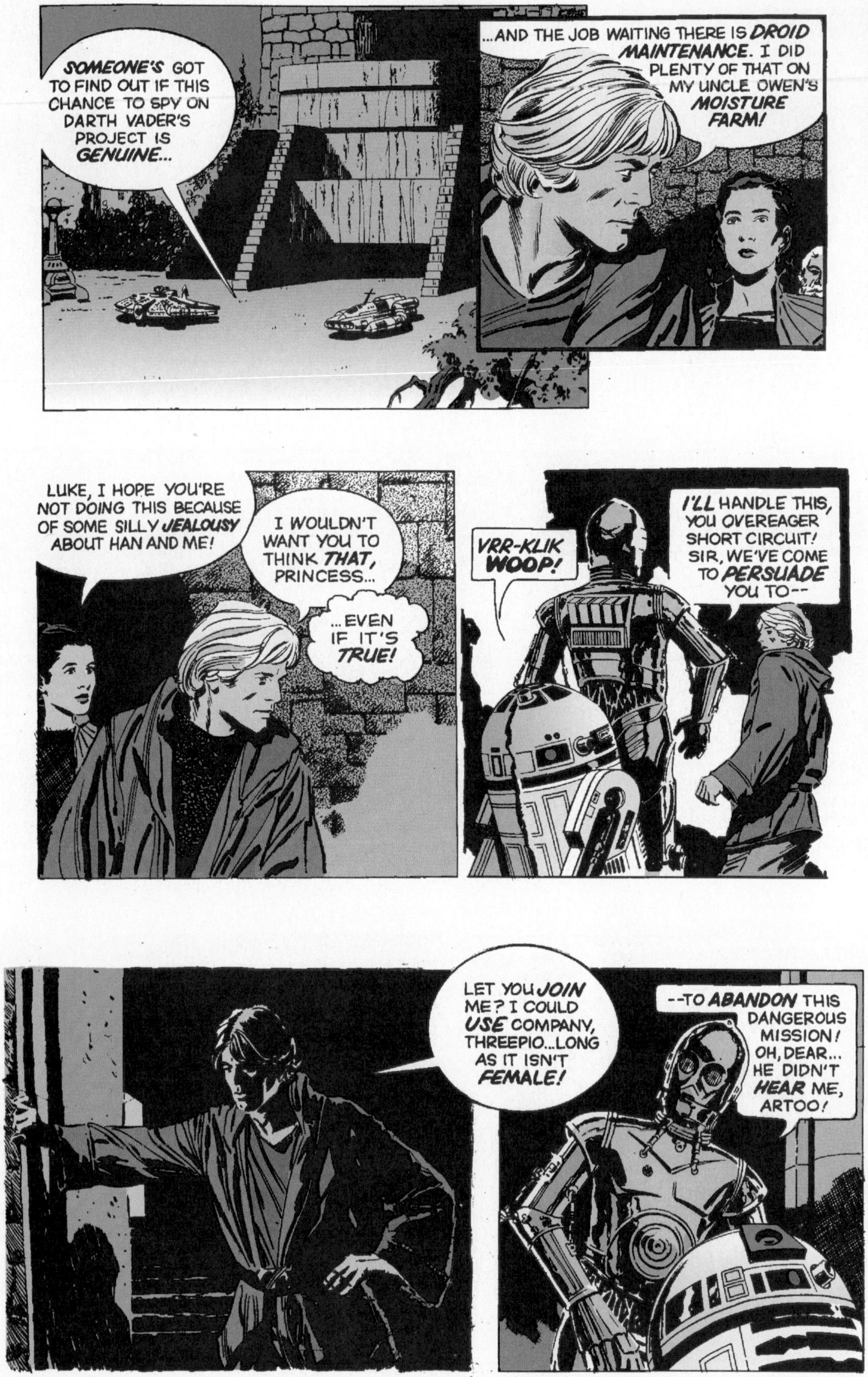
SOMEONE'S GOT TO FIND OUT IF THIS CHANCE TO SPY ON DARTH VADER'S PROJECT IS GENUINE...
...AND THE JOB WAITING THERE IS DROID MAINTENANCE. I DID PLENTY OF THAT ON MY UNCLE OWEN'S MOISTURE FARM!
LUKE, I HOPE YOU'RE NOT DOING THIS BECAUSE OF SOME SILLY JEALOUSY ABOUT HAN AND ME!
I WOULDN'T WANT YOU TO THINK THAT, PRINCESS...
...EVEN IF IT'S TRUE!
VRR-KLIK WOOP!
I'LL HANDLE THIS, YOU OVEREAGER SHORT CIRCUIT! SIR, WE'VE COME TO PERSUADE YOU TO--
LET YOU JOIN ME? I COULD USE COMPANY, THREEPIO...LONG AS IT ISN'T FEMALE!
--TO ABANDON THIS DANGEROUS MISSION! OH, DEAR... HE DIDN'T HEAR ME, ARTOO!

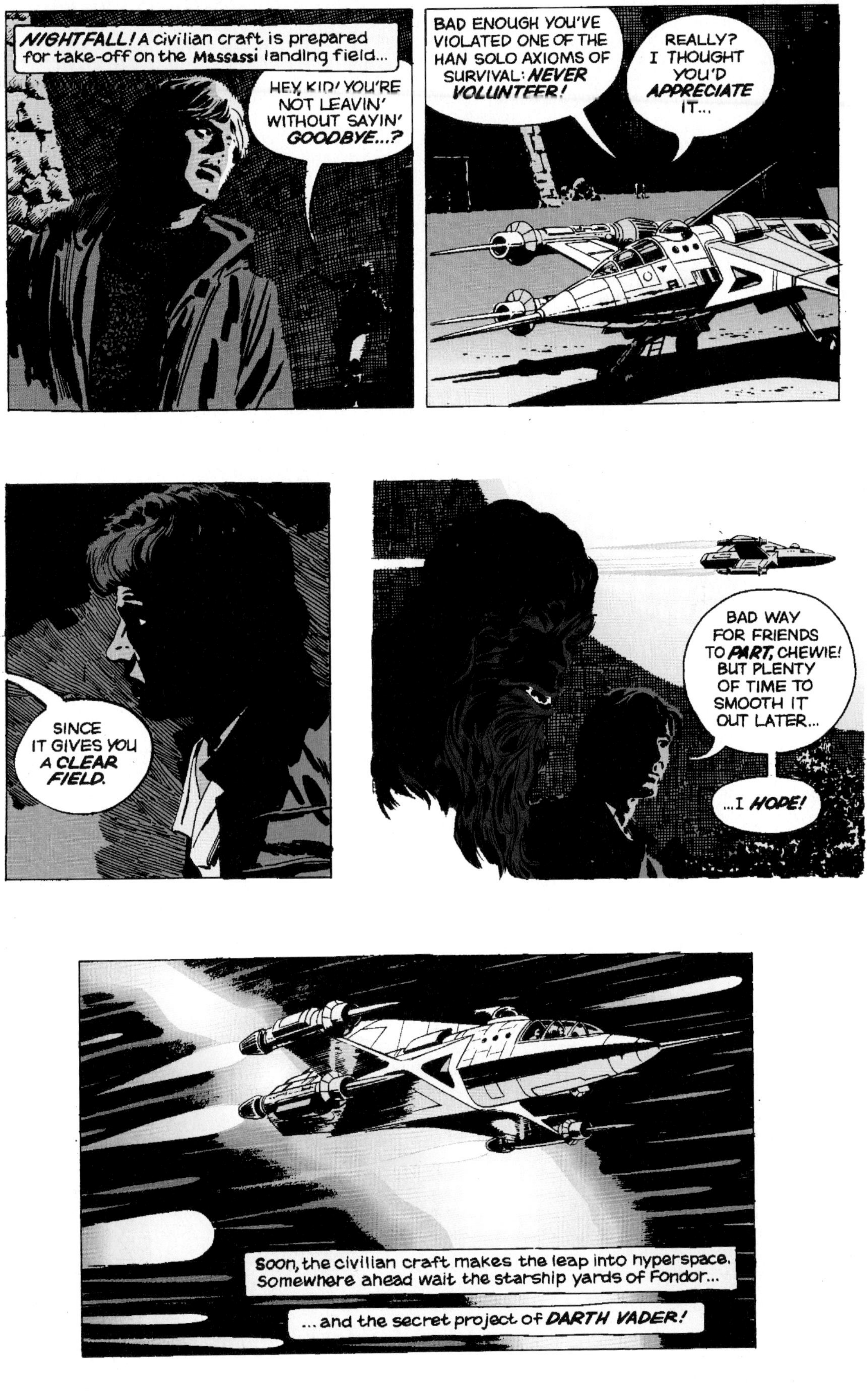
NIGHTFALL! A civilian craft is prepared for take-off on the Massassi landing field...
HEY, KID! YOU'RE NOT LEAVIN' WITHOUT SAYIN' GOODBYE...?
BAD ENOUGH YOU'VE VIOLATED ONE OF THE HAN SOLO AXIOMS OF SURVIVAL: NEVER VOLUNTEER!
REALLY? I THOUGHT YOU'D APPRECIATE IT...
SINCE IT GIVES YOU A CLEAR FIELD.
BAD WAY FOR FRIENDS TO PART, CHEWIE! BUT PLENTY OF TIME TO SMOOTH IT OUT LATER...
...I HOPE!
Soon, the civilian craft makes the leap into hyperspace. Somewhere ahead wait the starship yards of Fondor...
...and the secret project of DARTH VADER!

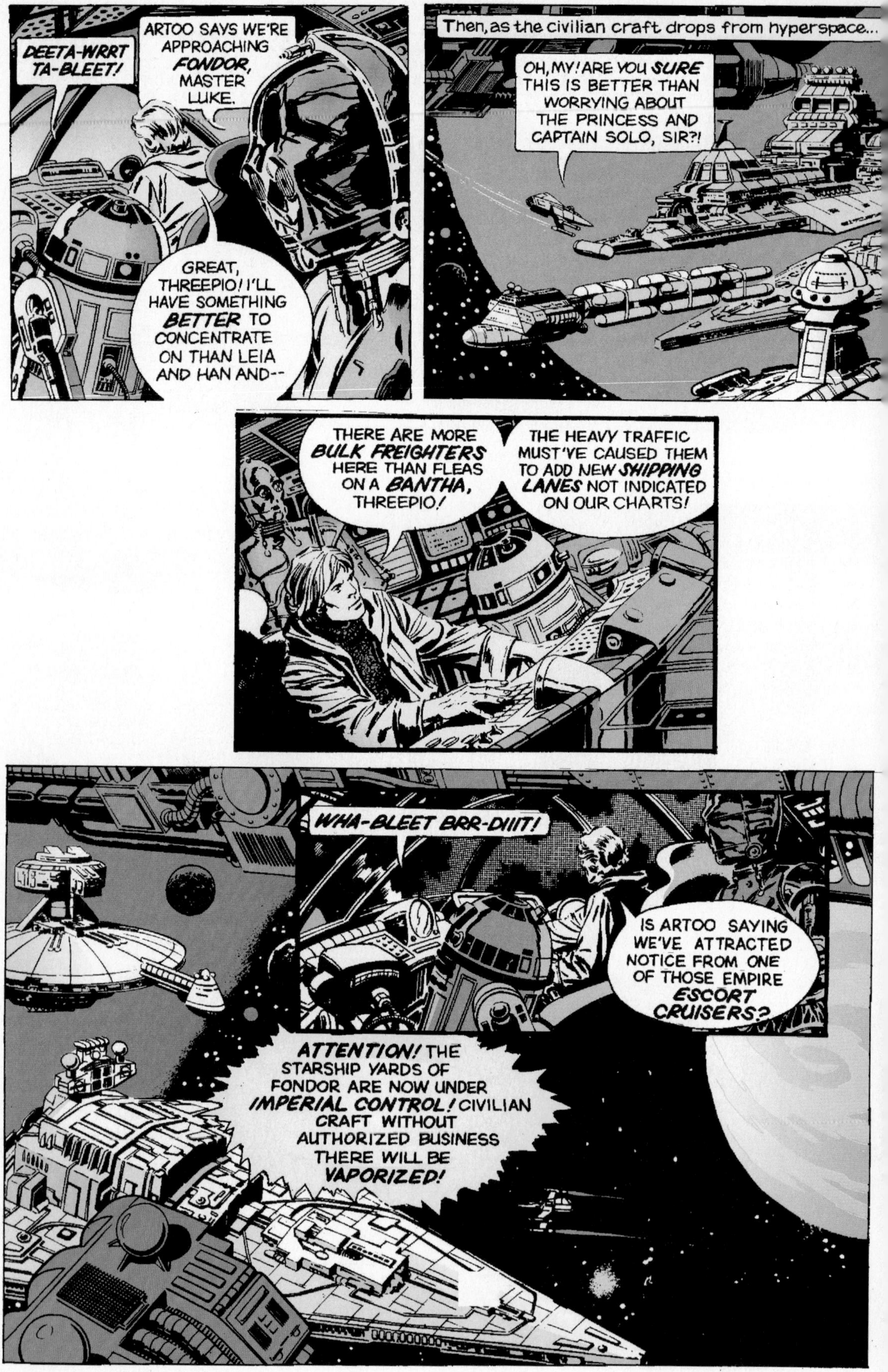
DEETA-WRRT TA-BLEET!
ARTOO SAYS WE'RE APPROACHING FONDOR, MASTER LUKE.
GREAT, THREEPIO! I'LL HAVE SOMETHING BETTER TO CONCENTRATE ON THAN LEIA AND HAN AND--
Then, as the civilian craft drops from hyperspace...
OH, MY! ARE YOU SURE THIS IS BETTER THAN WORRYING ABOUT THE PRINCESS AND CAPTAIN SOLO, SIR?!
THERE ARE MORE BULK FREIGHTERS HERE THAN FLEAS ON A BANTHA, THREEPIO!
THE HEAVY TRAFFIC MUST'VE CAUSED THEM TO ADD NEW SHIPPING LANES NOT INDICATED ON OUR CHARTS!
WHA-BLEET BRR-DIIIT!
IS ARTOO SAYING WE'VE ATTRACTED NOTICE FROM ONE OF THOSE EMPIRE ESCORT CRUISERS?
ATTENTION! THE STARSHIP YARDS OF FONDOR ARE NOW UNDER IMPERIAL CONTROL! CIVILIAN CRAFT WITHOUT AUTHORIZED BUSINESS THERE WILL BE VAPORIZED!

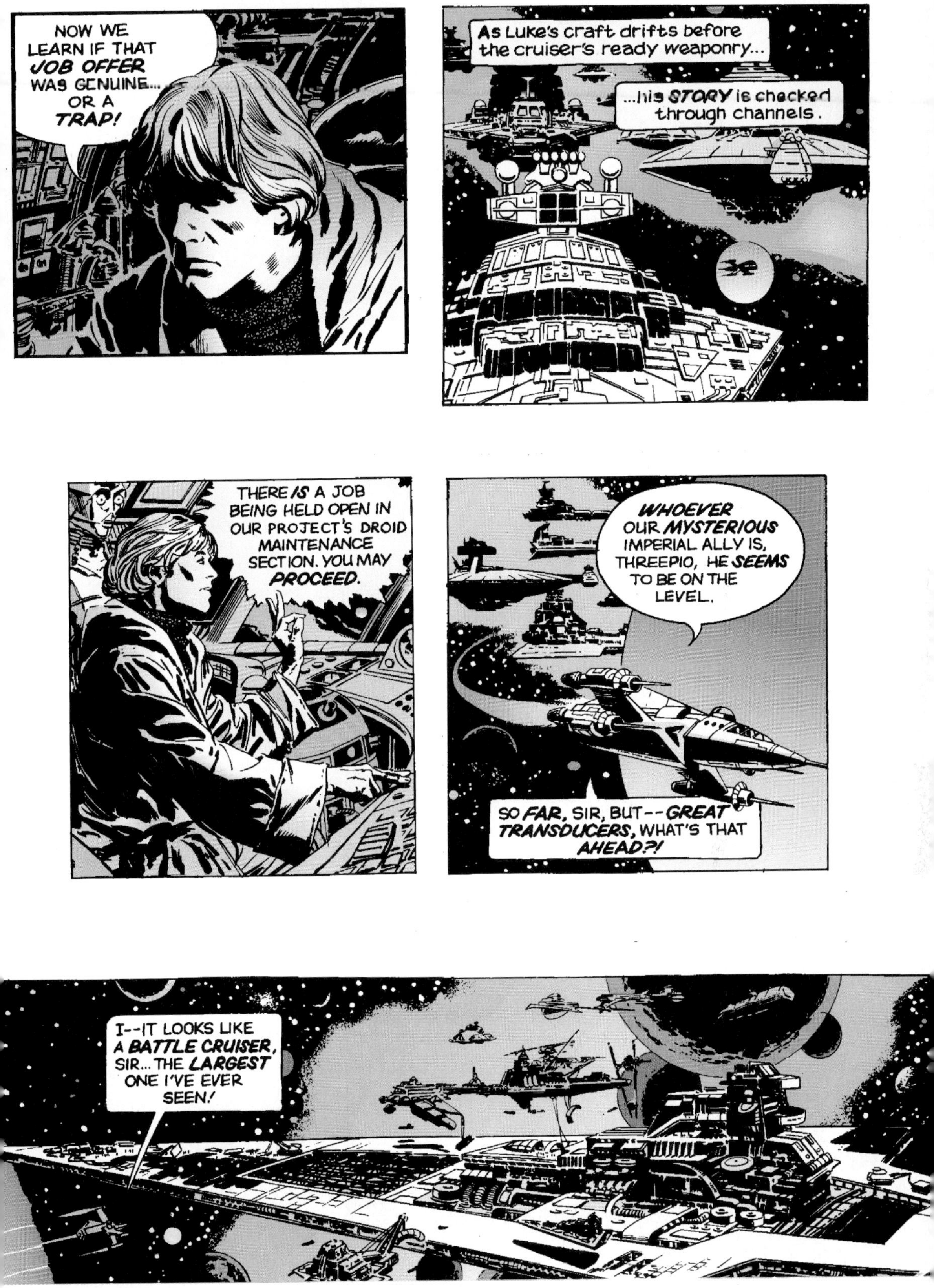
NOW WE LEARN IF THAT JOB OFFER WAS GENUINE... OR A TRAP!
As Luke's craft drifts before the cruiser's ready weaponry...
...his STORY is checked through channels.
THERE IS A JOB BEING HELD OPEN IN OUR PROJECT'S DROID MAINTENANCE SECTION. YOU MAY PROCEED.
WHOEVER OUR MYSTERIOUS IMPERIAL ALLY IS, THREEPIO, HE SEEMS TO BE ON THE LEVEL.
SO FAR, SIR, BUT--GREAT TRANSDUCERS, WHAT'S THAT AHEAD?!
I--IT LOOKS LIKE A BATTLE CRUISER, SIR... THE LARGEST ONE I'VE EVER SEEN!

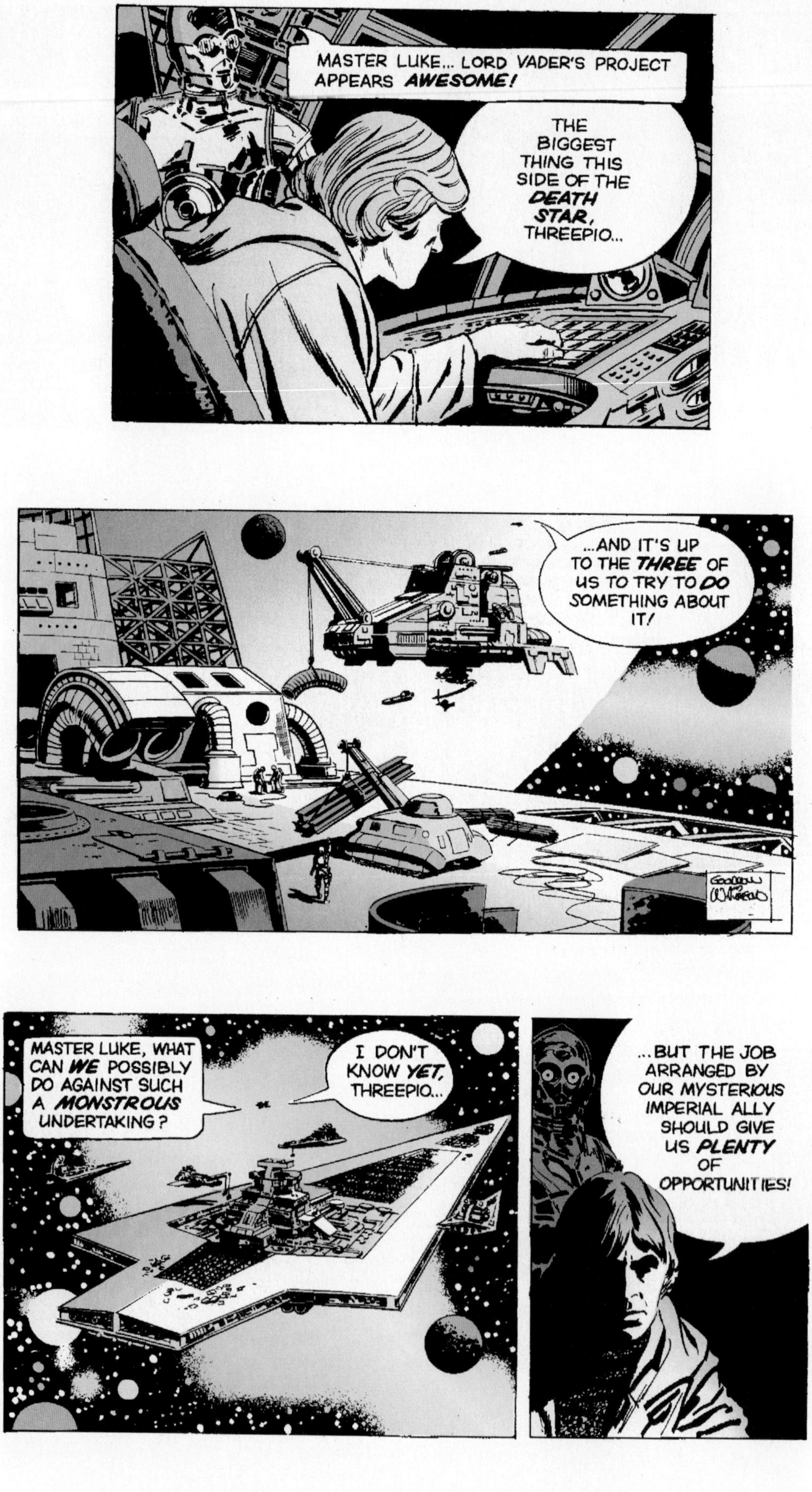
MASTER LUKE... LORD VADER'S PROJECT APPEARS AWESOME!
THE BIGGEST THING THIS SIDE OF THE DEATH STAR, THREEPIO...
...AND IT'S UP TO THE THREE OF US TO TRY TO DO SOMETHING ABOUT IT!
MASTER LUKE, WHAT CAN WE POSSIBLY DO AGAINST SUCH A MONSTROUS UNDERTAKING?
I DON'T KNOW YET, THREEPIO...
...BUT THE JOB ARRANGED BY OUR MYSTERIOUS IMPERIAL ALLY SHOULD GIVE US PLENTY OF OPPORTUNITIES!

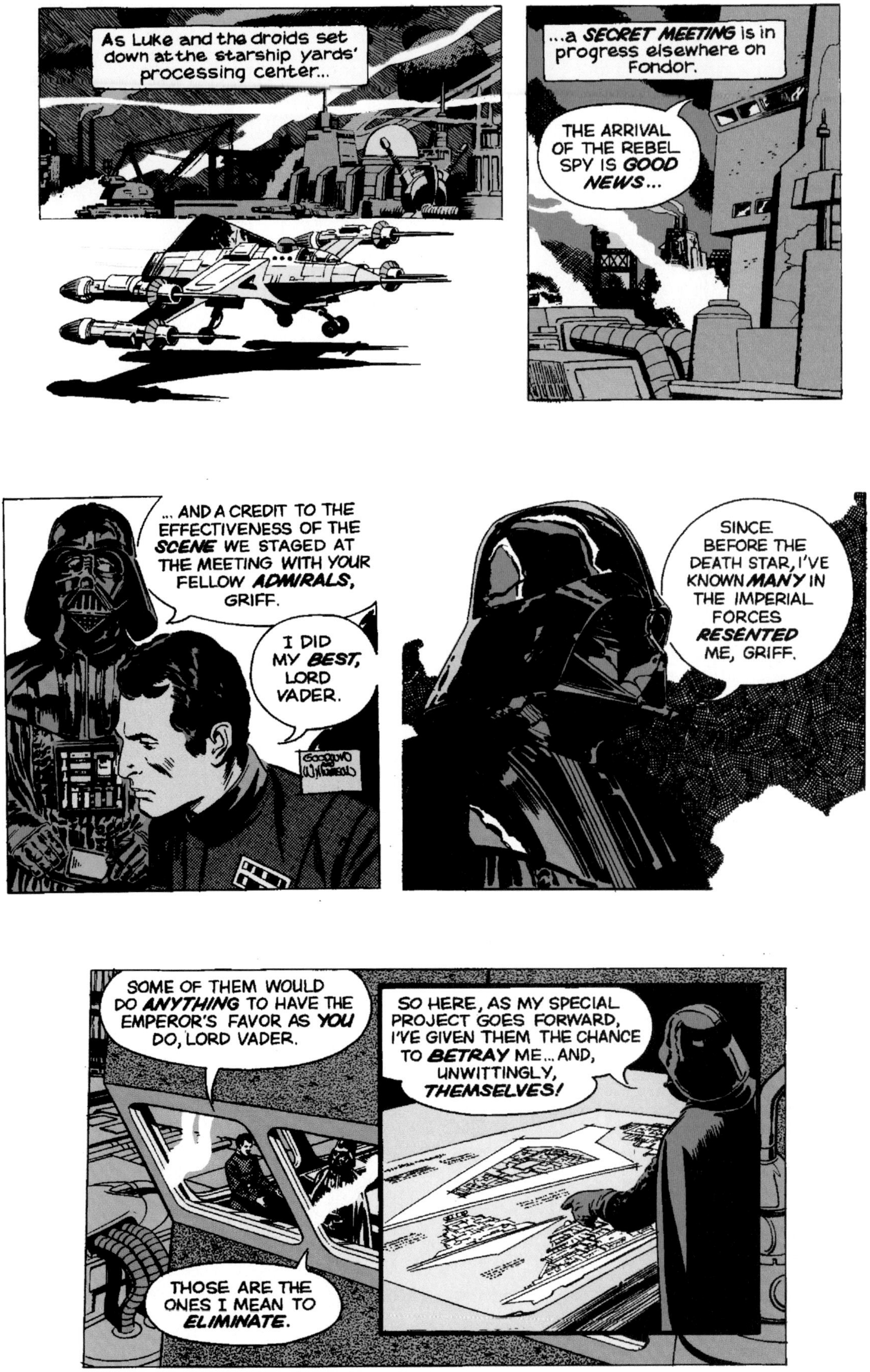
As Luke and the droids set down at the starship yards' processing center...
...a SECRET MEETING is in progress elsewhere on Fondor.
THE ARRIVAL OF THE REBEL SPY IS GOOD NEWS...
... AND A CREDIT TO THE EFFECTIVENESS OF THE SCENE WE STAGED AT THE MEETING WITH YOUR FELLOW ADMIRALS, GRIFF.
I DID MY BEST, LORD VADER.
SINCE BEFORE THE DEATH STAR, I'VE KNOWN MANY IN THE IMPERIAL FORCES RESENTED ME, GRIFF.
SOME OF THEM WOULD DO ANYTHING TO HAVE THE EMPEROR'S FAVOR AS YOU DO, LORD VADER.
SO HERE, AS MY SPECIAL PROJECT GOES FORWARD, I'VE GIVEN THEM THE CHANCE TO BETRAY ME... AND, UNWITTINGLY, THEMSELVES!
THOSE ARE THE ONES I MEAN TO ELIMINATE.

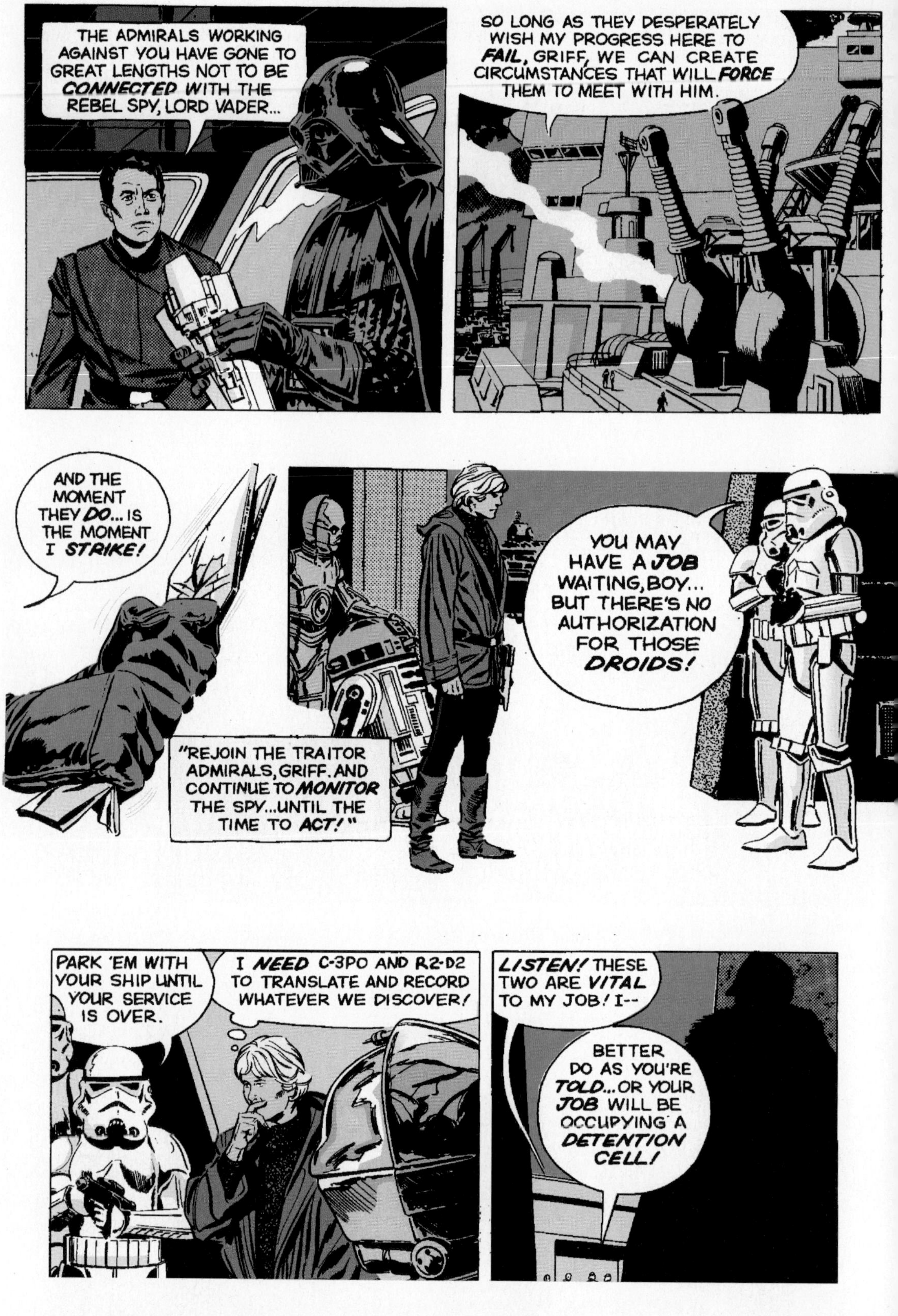

THE ADMIRALS WORKING AGAINST YOU HAVE GONE TO GREAT LENGTHS NOT TO BE CONNECTED WITH THE REBEL SPY, LORD VADER...
SO LONG AS THEY DESPERATELY WISH MY PROGRESS HERE TO FAIL, GRIFF, WE CAN CREATE CIRCUMSTANCES THAT WILL FORCE THEM TO MEET WITH HIM.
AND THE MOMENT THEY DO... IS THE MOMENT I STRIKE!
"REJOIN THE TRAITOR ADMIRALS, GRIFF. AND CONTINUE TO MONITOR THE SPY...UNTIL THE TIME TO ACT!"
YOU MAY HAVE A JOB WAITING, BOY... BUT THERE'S NO AUTHORIZATION FOR THOSE DROIDS!
PARK 'EM WITH YOUR SHIP UNTIL YOUR SERVICE IS OVER.
I NEED C-3PO AND R2-D2 TO TRANSLATE AND RECORD WHATEVER WE DISCOVER!
LISTEN! THESE TWO ARE VITAL TO MY JOB! I--
BETTER DO AS YOU'RE TOLD...OR YOUR JOB WILL BE OCCUPYING A DETENTION CELL!

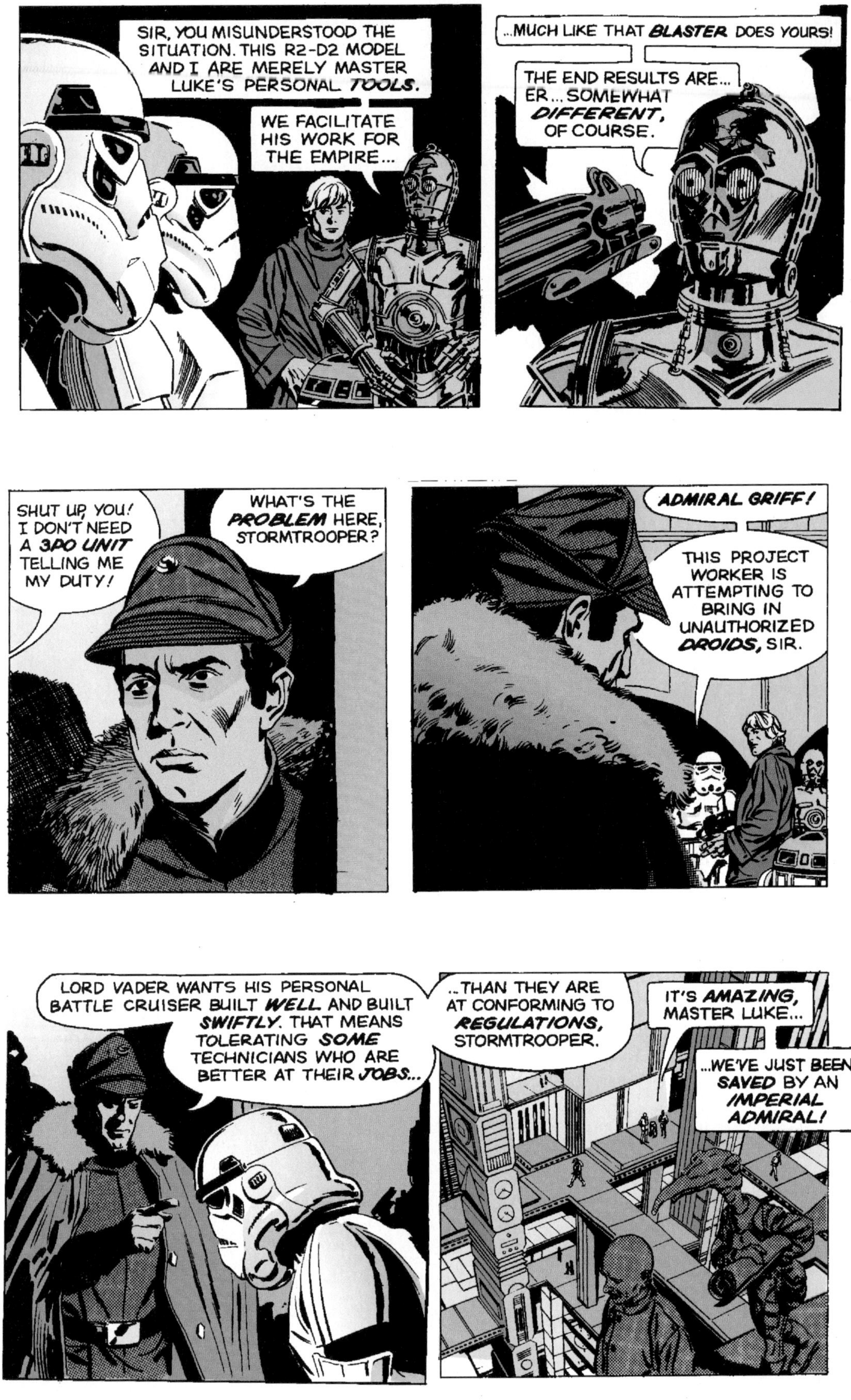
SIR, YOU MISUNDERSTOOD THE SITUATION. THIS R2-D2 MODEL AND I ARE MERELY MASTER LUKE'S PERSONAL TOOLS.
WE FACILITATE HIS WORK FOR THE EMPIRE...
...MUCH LIKE THAT BLASTER DOES YOURS!
THE END RESULTS ARE... ER... SOMEWHAT DIFFERENT, OF COURSE.
SHUT UP, YOU! I DON'T NEED A 3PO UNIT TELLING ME MY DUTY!
WHAT'S THE PROBLEM HERE, STORMTROOPER?
ADMIRAL GRIFF!
THIS PROJECT WORKER IS ATTEMPTING TO BRING IN UNAUTHORIZED DROIDS, SIR.
LORD VADER WANTS HIS PERSONAL BATTLE CRUISER BUILT WELL AND BUILT SWIFTLY. THAT MEANS TOLERATING SOME TECHNICIANS WHO ARE BETTER AT THEIR JOBS...
..THAN THEY ARE AT CONFORMING TO REGULATIONS, STORMTROOPER.
IT'S AMAZING, MASTER LUKE...
...WE'VE JUST BEEN SAVED BY AN IMPERIAL ADMIRAL!

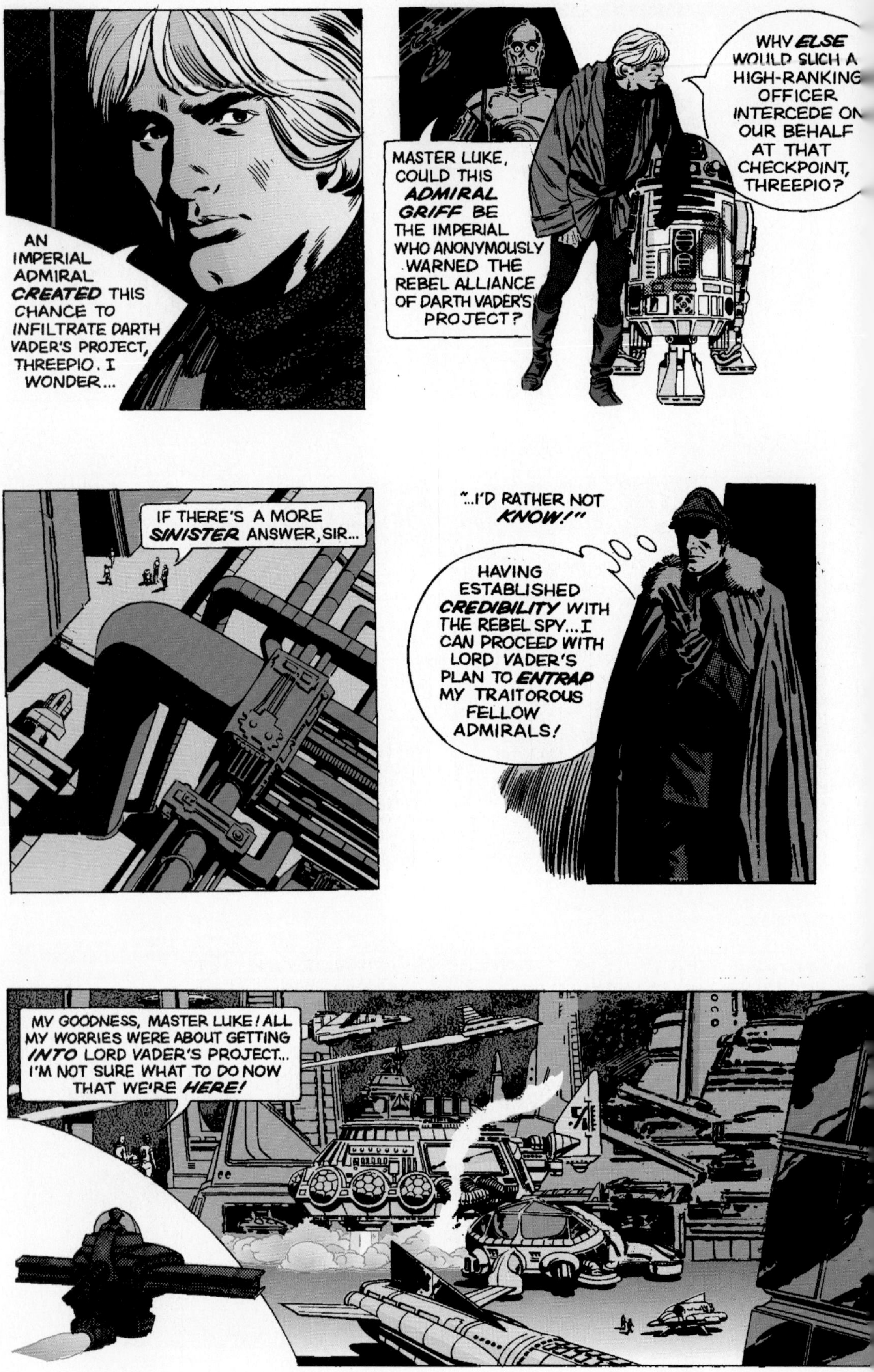
AN IMPERIAL ADMIRAL CREATED THIS CHANCE TO INFILTRATE DARTH VADER'S PROJECT, THREEPIO. I WONDER...
MASTER LUKE, COULD THIS ADMIRAL GRIFF BE THE IMPERIAL WHO ANONYMOUSLY WARNED THE REBEL ALLIANCE OF DARTH VADER'S PROJECT?
WHY ELSE WOULD SUCH A HIGH-RANKING OFFICER INTERCEDE ON OUR BEHALF AT THAT CHECKPOINT, THREEPIO?
IF THERE'S A MORE SINISTER ANSWER, SIR...
"...I'D RATHER NOT KNOW!"
HAVING ESTABLISHED CREDIBILITY WITH THE REBEL SPY...I CAN PROCEED WITH LORD VADER'S PLAN TO ENTRAP MY TRAITOROUS FELLOW ADMIRALS!
MY GOODNESS, MASTER LUKE! ALL MY WORRIES WERE ABOUT GETTING INTO LORD VADER'S PROJECT... I'M NOT SURE WHAT TO DO NOW THAT WE'RE HERE!

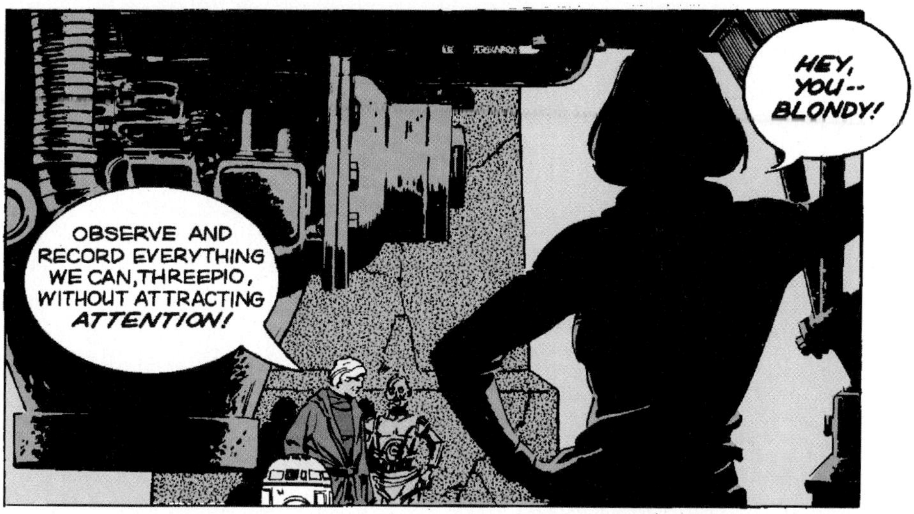
HEY, YOU-- BLONDY!
OBSERVE AND RECORD EVERYTHING WE CAN, THREEPIO, WITHOUT ATTRACTING ATTENTION!

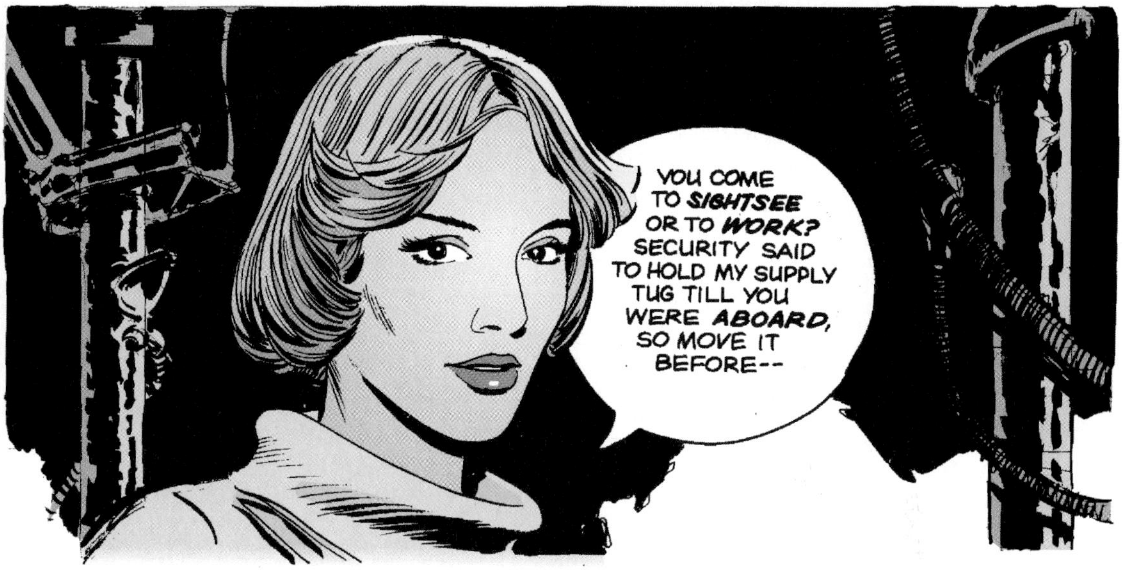
YOU COME TO SIGHTSEE OR TO WORK? SECURITY SAID TO HOLD MY SUPPLY TUG TILL YOU WERE ABOARD, SO MOVE IT BEFORE--

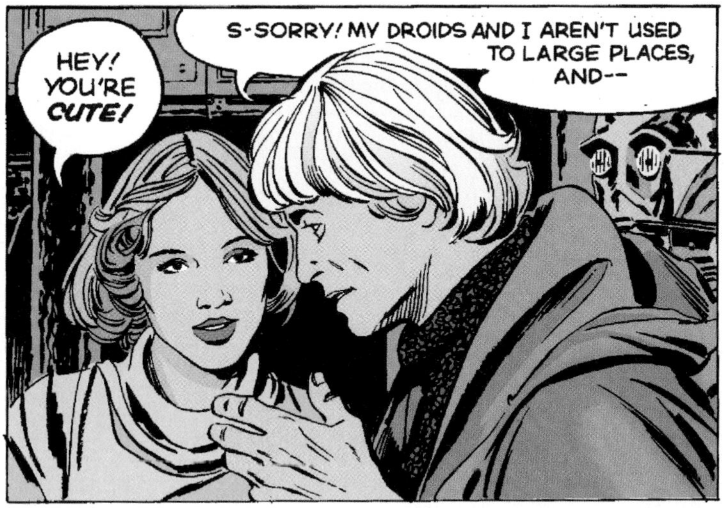
S-SORRY! MY DROIDS AND I AREN'T USED TO LARGE PLACES, AND--
HEY! YOU'RE CUTE!

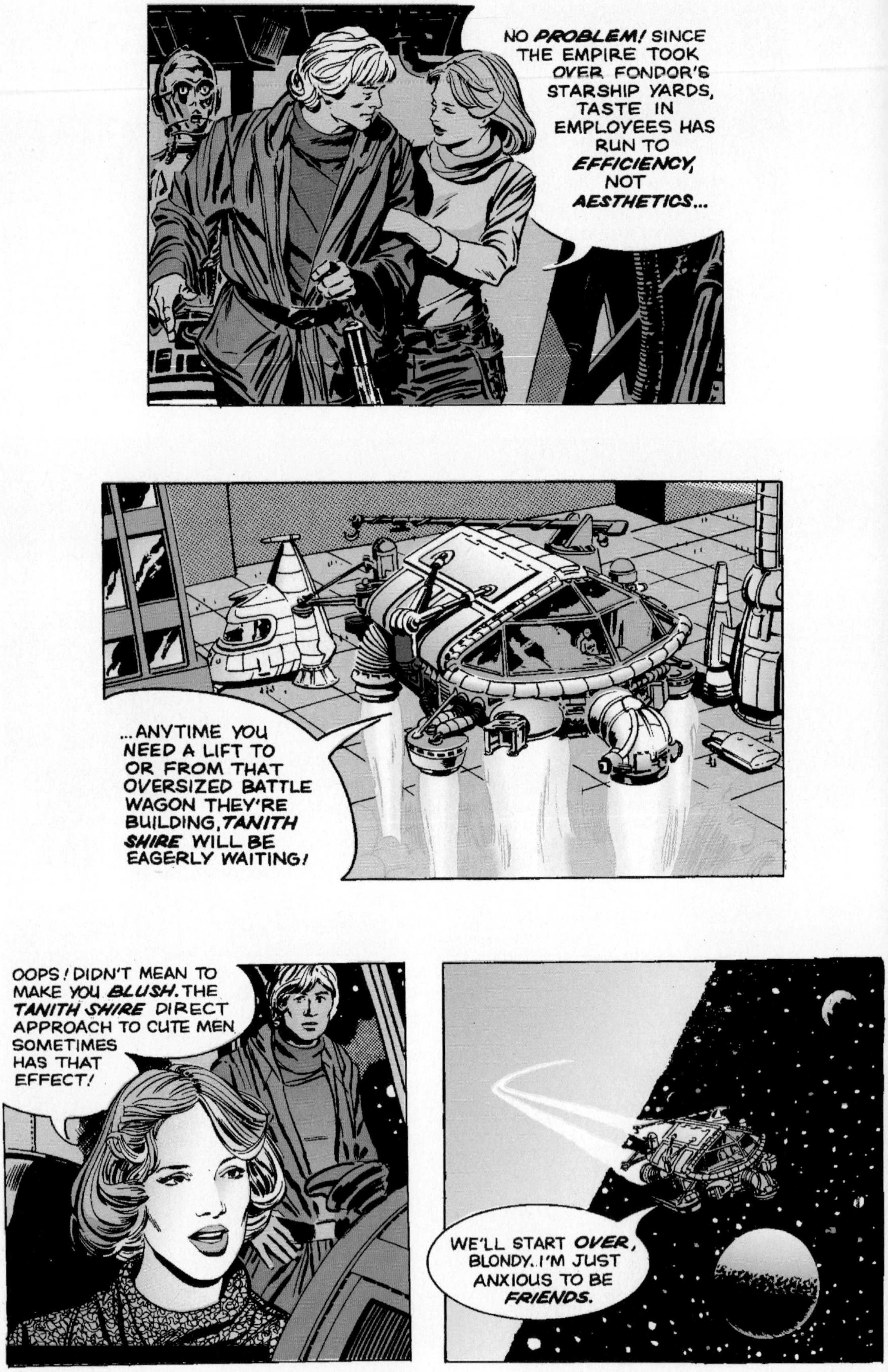
NO PROBLEM! SINCE THE EMPIRE TOOK OVER FONDOR'S STARSHIP YARDS, TASTE IN EMPLOYEES HAS RUN TO EFFICIENCY, NOT AESTHETICS...
...ANYTIME YOU NEED A LIFT TO OR FROM THAT OVERSIZED BATTLE WAGON THEY'RE BUILDING, TANITH SHIRE WILL BE EAGERLY WAITING!
OOPS! DIDN'T MEAN TO MAKE YOU BLUSH. THE TANITH SHIRE DIRECT APPROACH TO CUTE MEN SOMETIMES HAS THAT EFFECT!
WE'LL START OVER, BLONDY..I'M JUST ANXIOUS TO BE FRIENDS.

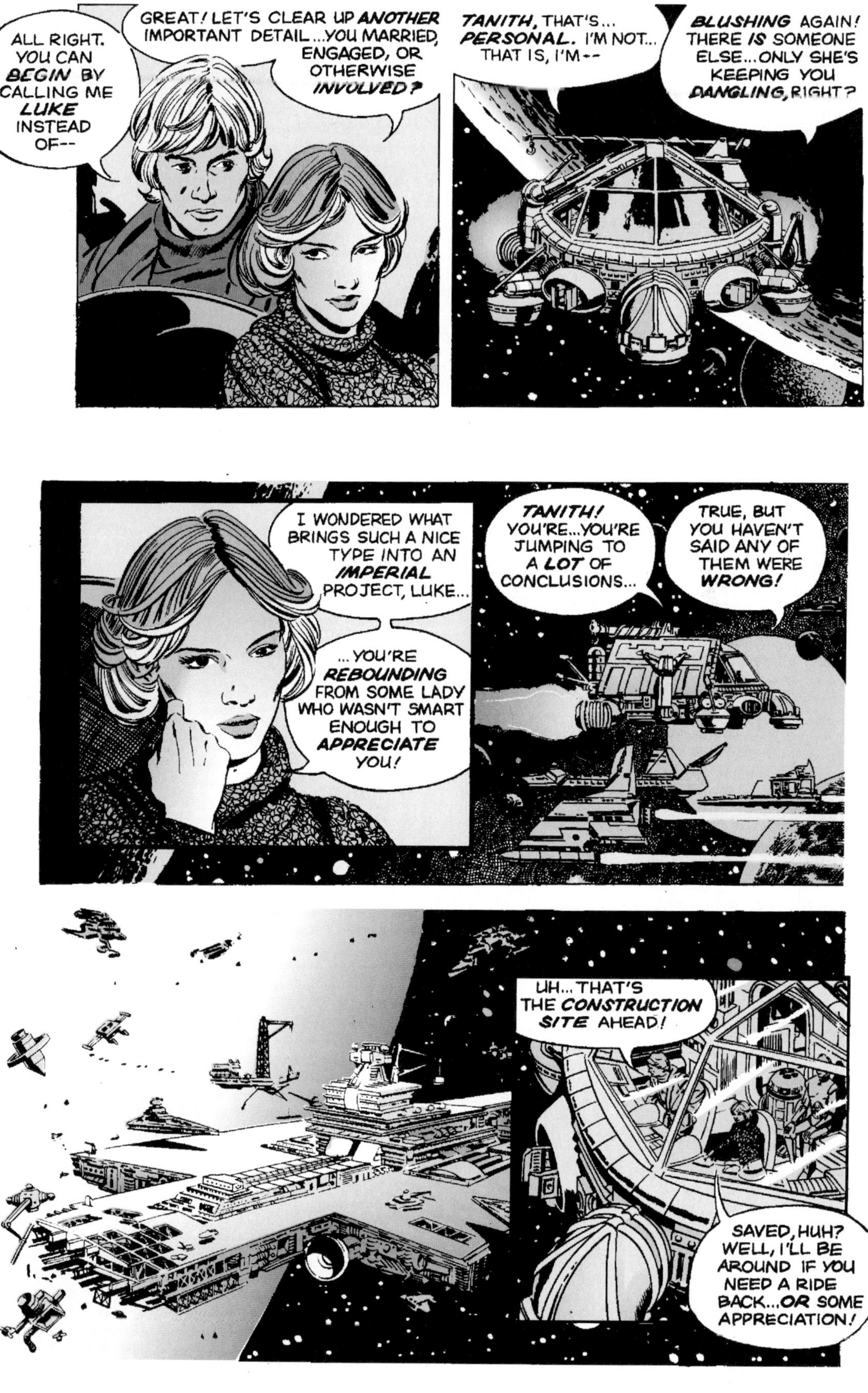
ALL RIGHT. YOU CAN BEGIN BY CALLING ME LUKE INSTEAD OF--
GREAT! LET'S CLEAR UP ANOTHER IMPORTANT DETAIL...YOU MARRIED, ENGAGED, OR OTHERWISE INVOLVED?
TANITH, THAT'S... PERSONAL. I'M NOT... THAT IS, I'M--
BLUSHING AGAIN! THERE IS SOMEONE ELSE...ONLY SHE'S KEEPING YOU DANGLING, RIGHT?
I WONDERED WHAT BRINGS SUCH A NICE TYPE INTO AN IMPERIAL PROJECT, LUKE...
...YOU'RE REBOUNDING FROM SOME LADY WHO WASN'T SMART ENOUGH TO APPRECIATE YOU!
TANITH! YOU'RE...YOU'RE JUMPING TO A LOT OF CONCLUSIONS...
TRUE, BUT YOU HAVEN'T SAID ANY OF THEM WERE WRONG!
UH... THAT'S THE CONSTRUCTION SITE AHEAD!
SAVED, HUH? WELL, I'LL BE AROUND IF YOU NEED A RIDE BACK...OR SOME APPRECIATION!

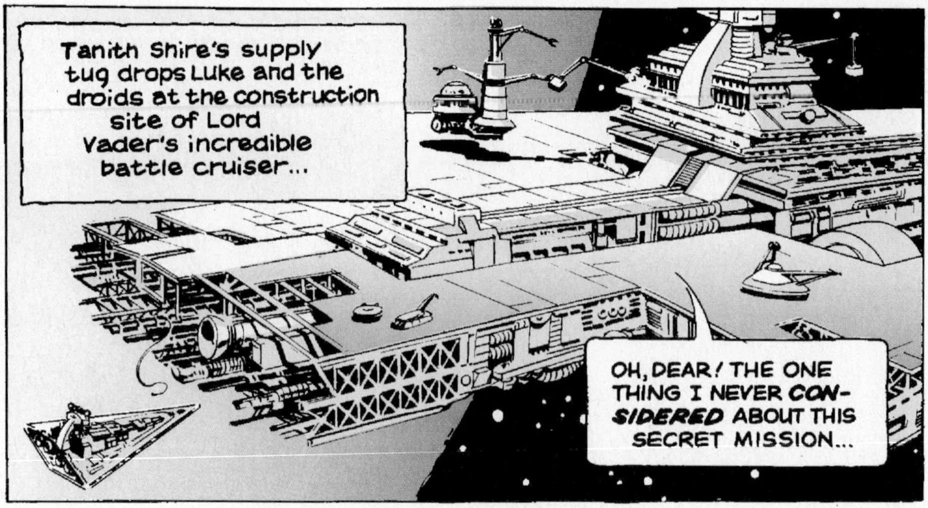
Tanith Shire's supply tug drops Luke and the droids at the construction site of Lord Vader's incredible battle cruiser...
OH, DEAR! THE ONE THING I NEVER CONSIDERED ABOUT THIS SECRET MISSION...

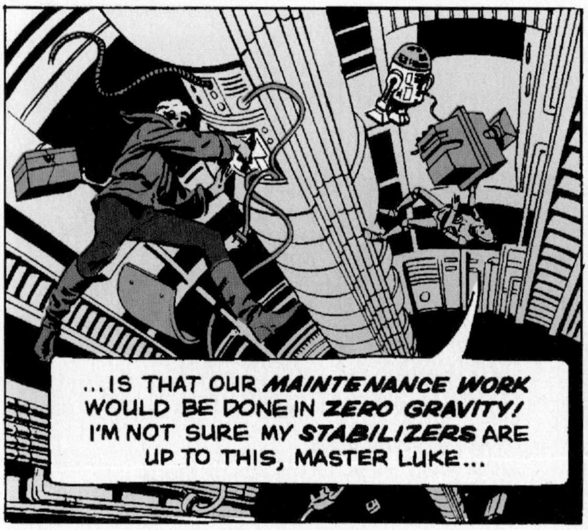
...IS THAT OUR MAINTENANCE WORK WOULD BE DONE IN ZERO GRAVITY! I'M NOT SURE MY STABILIZERS ARE UP TO THIS, MASTER LUKE...

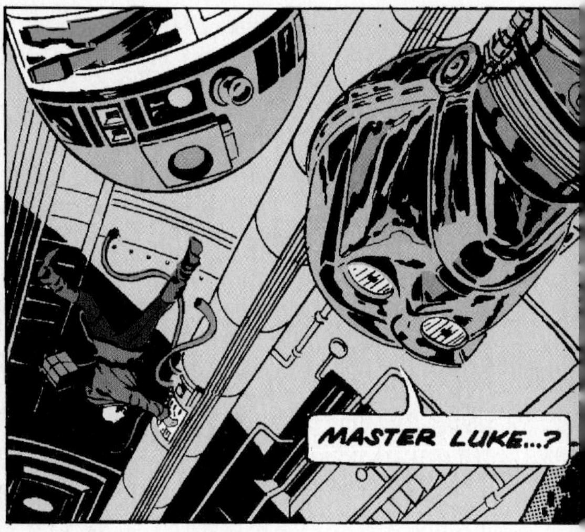
MASTER LUKE...?

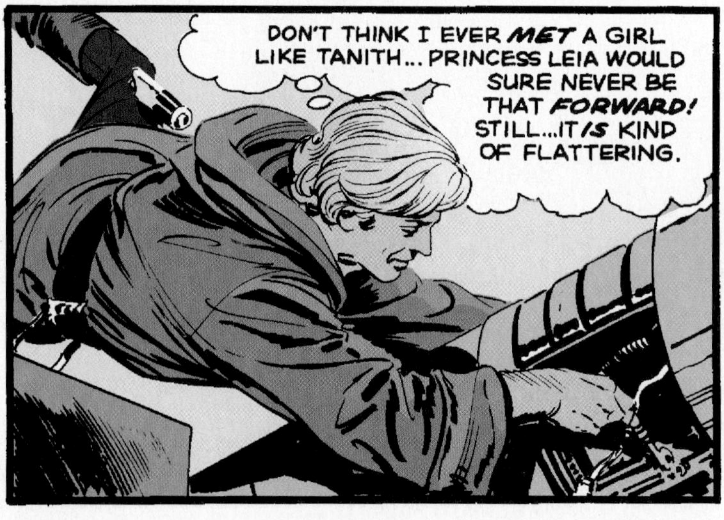
DON'T THINK I EVER MET A GIRL LIKE TANITH... PRINCESS LEIA WOULD SURE NEVER BE THAT FORWARD! STILL...IT IS KIND OF FLATTERING.

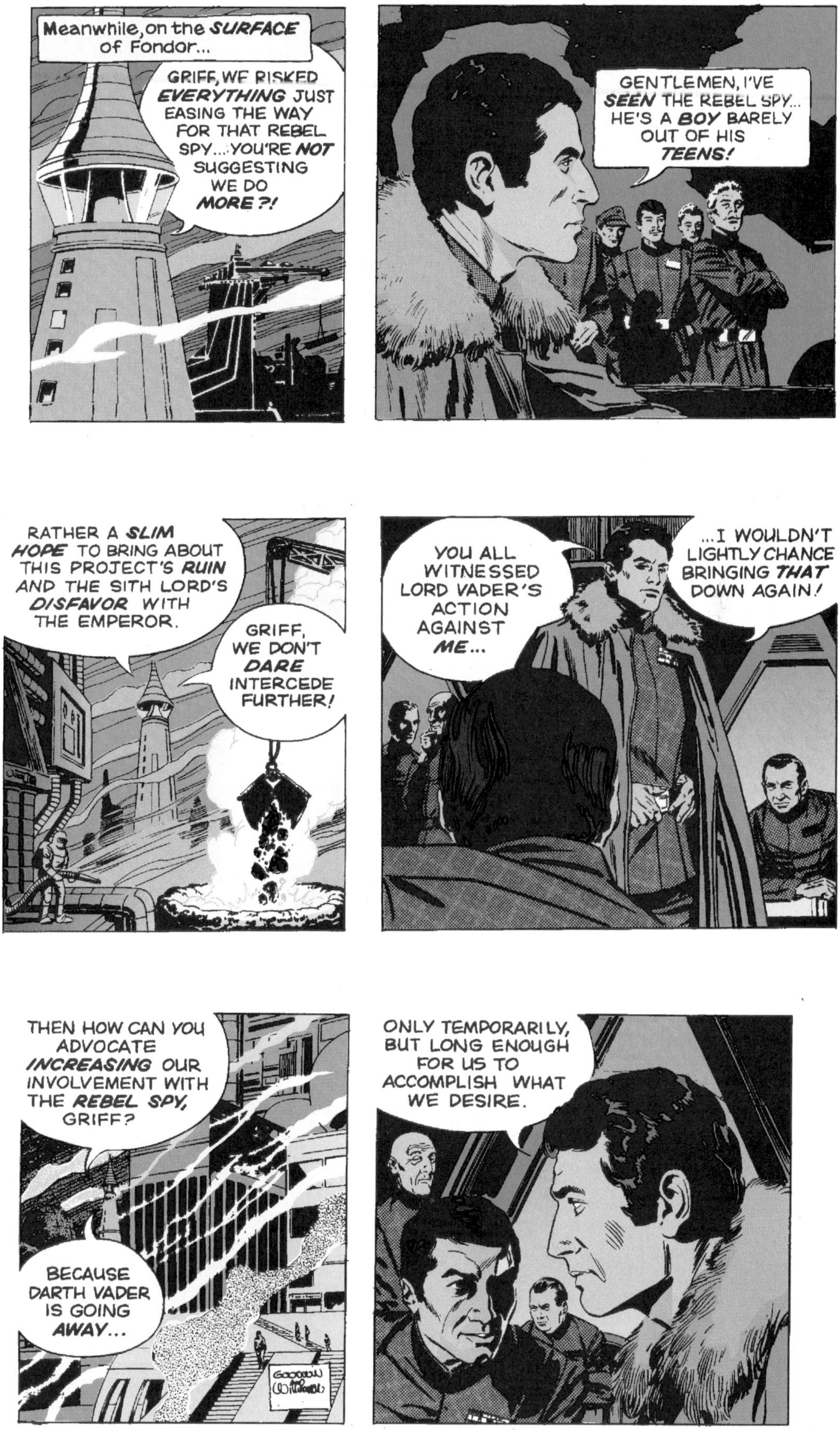
Meanwhile, on the SURFACE of Fondor...
GRIFF, WE RISKED EVERYTHING JUST EASING THE WAY FOR THAT REBEL SPY...YOU'RE NOT SUGGESTING WE DO MORE?!
GENTLEMEN, I'VE SEEN THE REBEL SPY... HE'S A BOY BARELY OUT OF HIS TEENS!
RATHER A SLIM HOPE TO BRING ABOUT THIS PROJECT'S RUIN AND THE SITH LORD'S DISFAVOR WITH THE EMPEROR.
GRIFF, WE DON'T DARE INTERCEDE FURTHER!
YOU ALL WITNESSED LORD VADER'S ACTION AGAINST ME...
...I WOULDN'T LIGHTLY CHANCE BRINGING THAT DOWN AGAIN!
THEN HOW CAN YOU ADVOCATE INCREASING OUR INVOLVEMENT WITH THE REBEL SPY, GRIFF?
BECAUSE DARTH VADER IS GOING AWAY...
ONLY TEMPORARILY, BUT LONG ENOUGH FOR US TO ACCOMPLISH WHAT WE DESIRE.

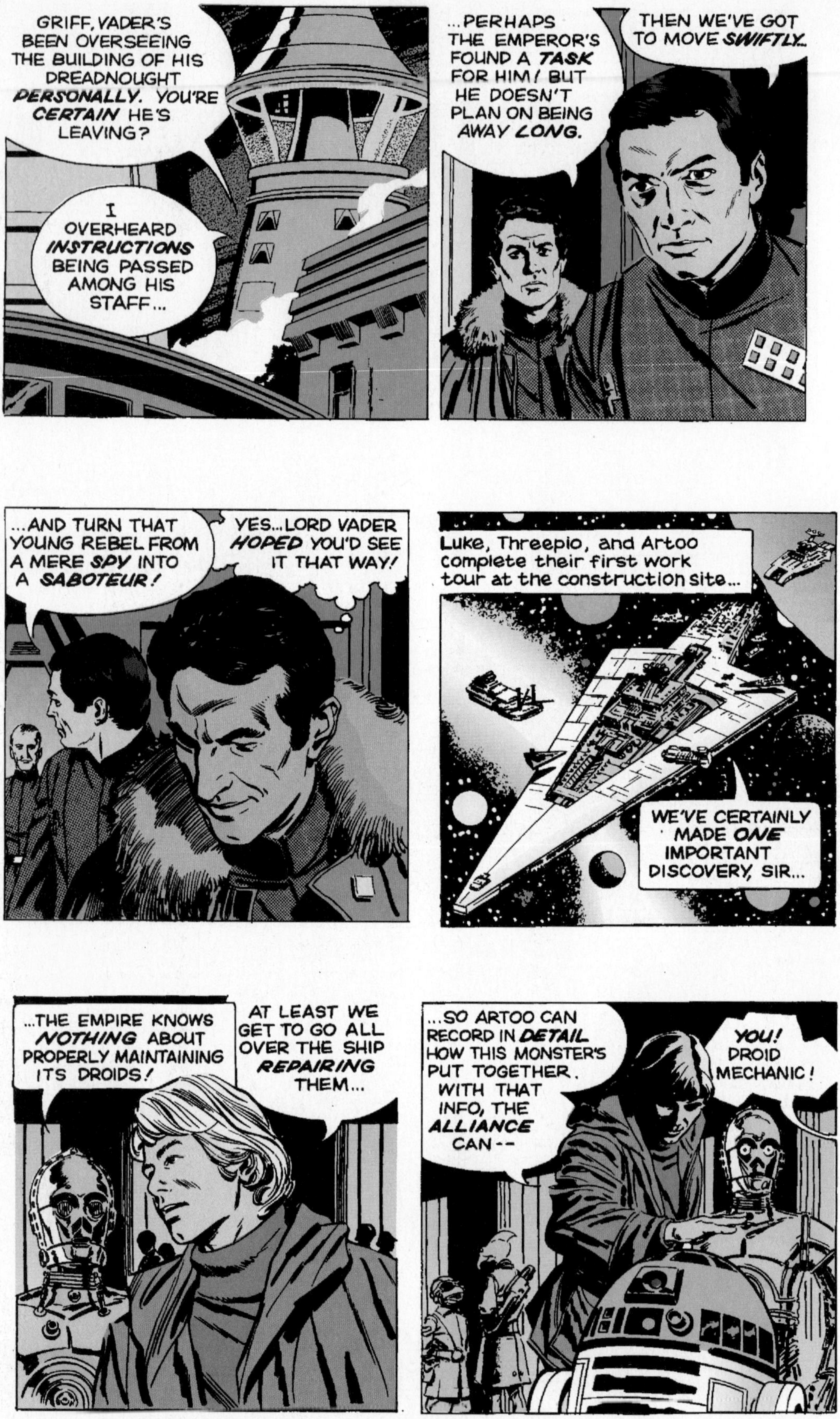
GRIFF, VADER'S BEEN OVERSEEING THE BUILDING OF HIS DREADNOUGHT PERSONALLY. YOU'RE CERTAIN HE'S LEAVING?
I OVERHEARD INSTRUCTIONS BEING PASSED AMONG HIS STAFF...
...PERHAPS THE EMPEROR'S FOUND A TASK FOR HIM! BUT HE DOESN'T PLAN ON BEING AWAY LONG.
THEN WE'VE GOT TO MOVE SWIFTLY...
...AND TURN THAT YOUNG REBEL FROM A MERE SPY INTO A SABOTEUR!
YES...LORD VADER HOPED YOU'D SEE IT THAT WAY!
Luke, Threepio, and Artoo complete their first work tour at the construction site...
WE'VE CERTAINLY MADE ONE IMPORTANT DISCOVERY, SIR...
...THE EMPIRE KNOWS NOTHING ABOUT PROPERLY MAINTAINING ITS DROIDS!
AT LEAST WE GET TO GO ALL OVER THE SHIP REPAIRING THEM...
...SO ARTOO CAN RECORD IN DETAIL HOW THIS MONSTER'S PUT TOGETHER. WITH THAT INFO, THE ALLIANCE CAN--
YOU! DROID MECHANIC!

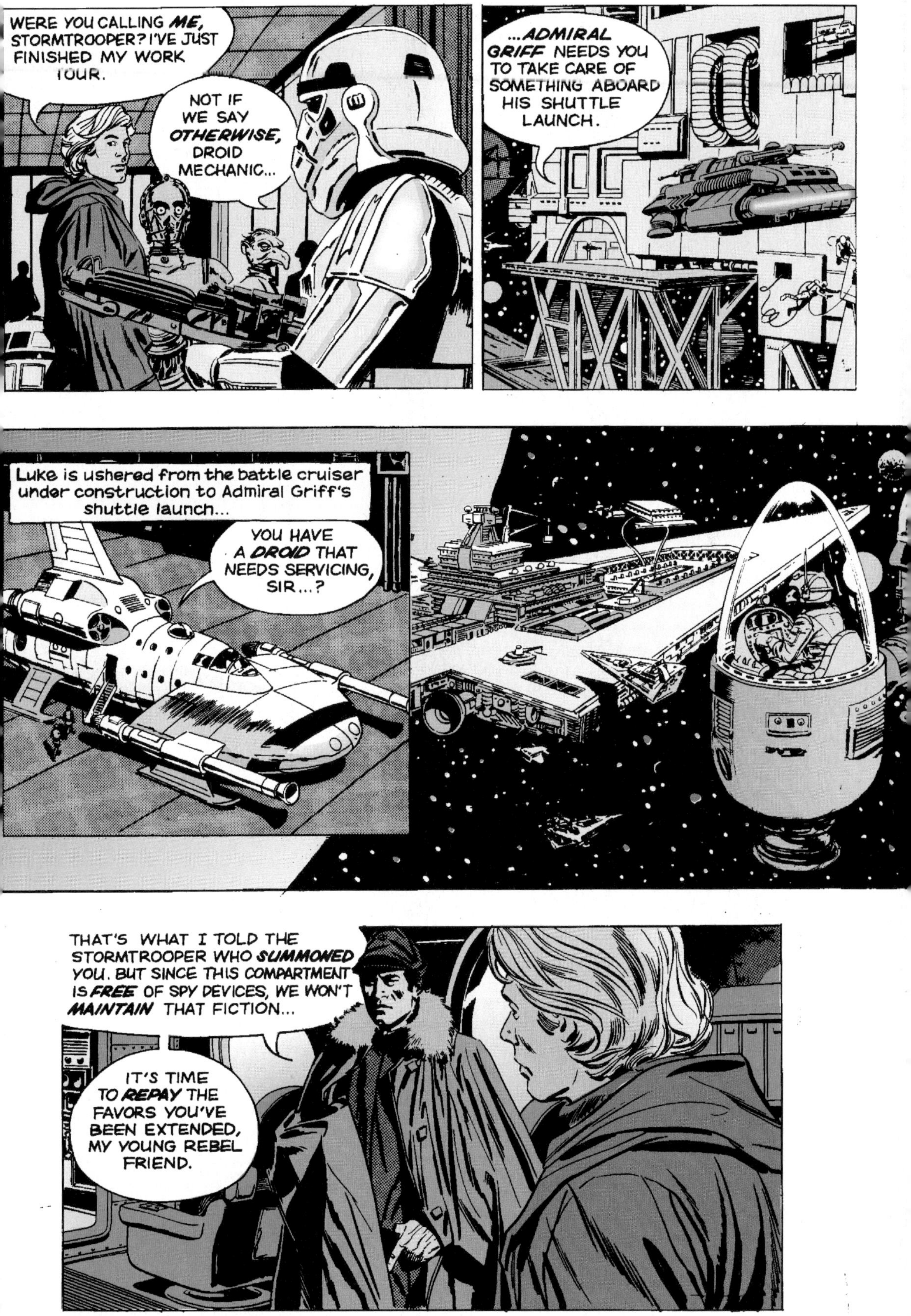

WERE YOU CALLING ME, STORMTROOPER? I'VE JUST FINISHED MY WORK TOUR.
NOT IF WE SAY OTHERWISE, DROID MECHANIC...
...ADMIRAL GRIFF NEEDS YOU TO TAKE CARE OF SOMETHING ABOARD HIS SHUTTLE LAUNCH.
Luke is ushered from the battle cruiser under construction to Admiral Griff's shuttle launch...
YOU HAVE A DROID THAT NEEDS SERVICING, SIR...?
THAT'S WHAT I TOLD THE STORMTROOPER WHO SUMMONED YOU. BUT SINCE THIS COMPARTMENT IS FREE OF SPY DEVICES, WE WON'T MAINTAIN THAT FICTION...
IT'S TIME TO REPAY THE FAVORS YOU'VE BEEN EXTENDED, MY YOUNG REBEL FRIEND.

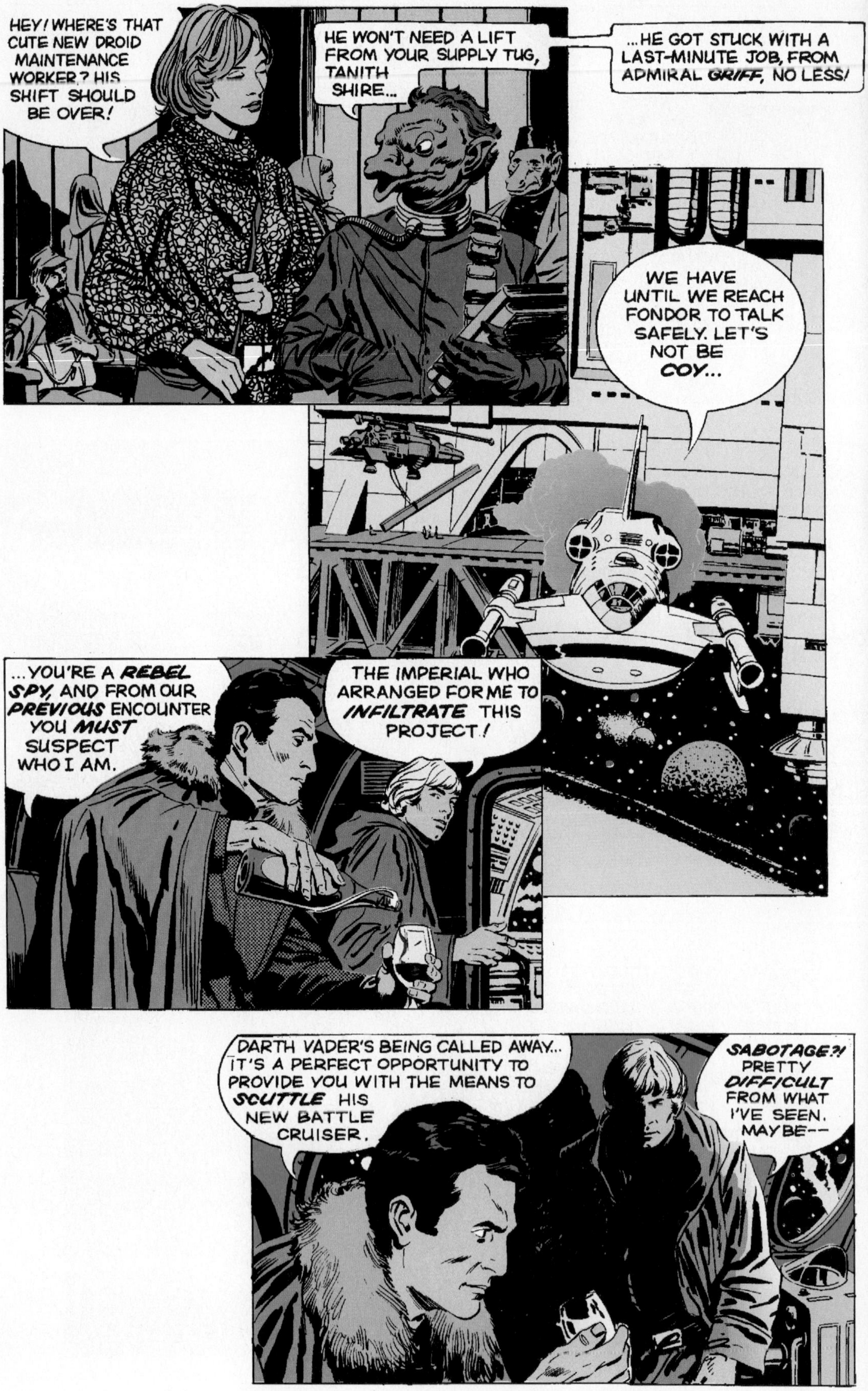
HEY! WHERE'S THAT CUTE NEW DROID MAINTENANCE WORKER? HIS SHIFT SHOULD BE OVER!
HE WON'T NEED A LIFT FROM YOUR SUPPLY TUG, TANITH SHIRE...
...HE GOT STUCK WITH A LAST-MINUTE JOB, FROM ADMIRAL GRIFF, NO LESS!
WE HAVE UNTIL WE REACH FONDOR TO TALK SAFELY. LET'S NOT BE COY...
...YOU'RE A REBEL SPY, AND FROM OUR PREVIOUS ENCOUNTER YOU MUST SUSPECT WHO I AM.
THE IMPERIAL WHO ARRANGED FOR ME TO INFILTRATE THIS PROJECT!
DARTH VADER'S BEING CALLED AWAY... IT'S A PERFECT OPPORTUNITY TO PROVIDE YOU WITH THE MEANS TO SCUTTLE HIS NEW BATTLE CRUISER.
SABOTAGE?! PRETTY DIFFICULT FROM WHAT I'VE SEEN. MAYBE--

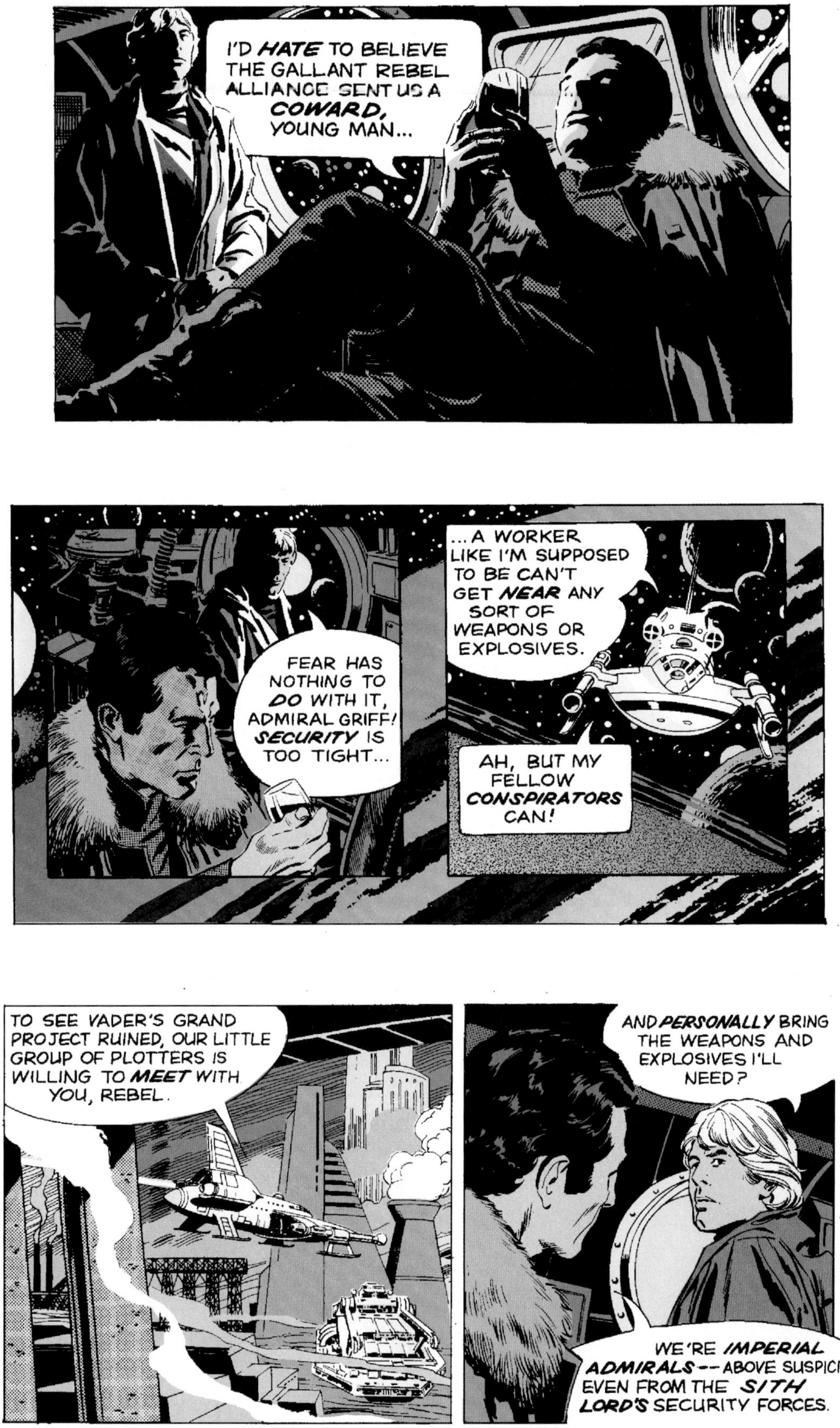
I'D HATE TO BELIEVE THE GALLANT REBEL ALLIANCE SENT US A COWARD, YOUNG MAN...
FEAR HAS NOTHING TO DO WITH IT, ADMIRAL GRIFF! SECURITY IS TOO TIGHT...
...A WORKER LIKE I'M SUPPOSED TO BE CAN'T GET NEAR ANY SORT OF WEAPONS OR EXPLOSIVES.
AH, BUT MY FELLOW CONSPIRATORS CAN!
TO SEE VADER'S GRAND PROJECT RUINED, OUR LITTLE GROUP OF PLOTTERS IS WILLING TO MEET WITH YOU, REBEL.
AND PERSONALLY BRING THE WEAPONS AND EXPLOSIVES I'LL NEED?
WE'RE IMPERIAL ADMIRALS -- ABOVE SUSPICION, EVEN FROM THE SITH LORD'S SECURITY FORCES.

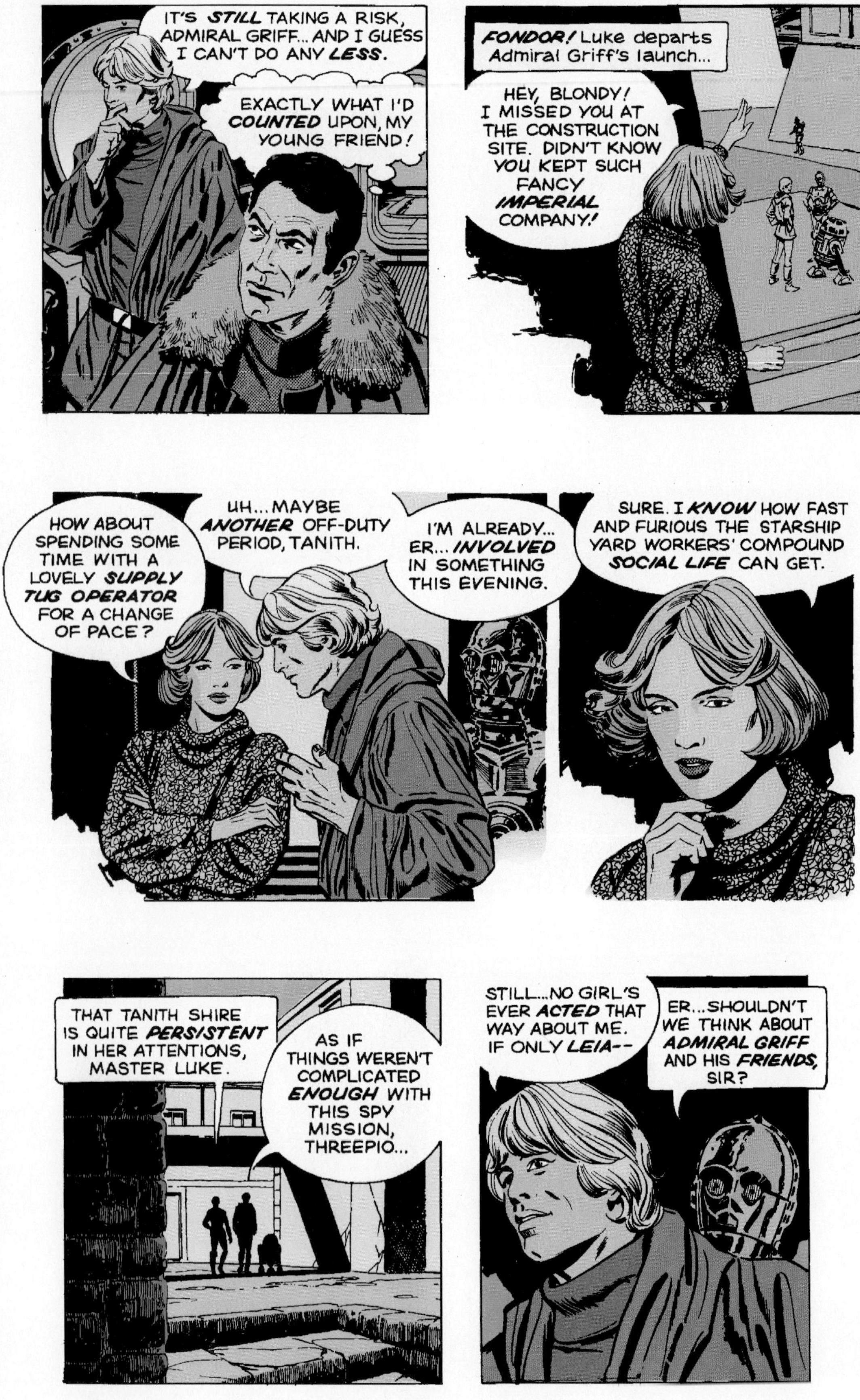
IT'S STILL TAKING A RISK, ADMIRAL GRIFF... AND I GUESS I CAN'T DO ANY LESS.
EXACTLY WHAT I'D COUNTED UPON, MY YOUNG FRIEND!
FONDOR! Luke departs Admiral Griff's launch...
HEY, BLONDY! I MISSED YOU AT THE CONSTRUCTION SITE. DIDN'T KNOW YOU KEPT SUCH FANCY IMPERIAL COMPANY!
HOW ABOUT SPENDING SOME TIME WITH A LOVELY SUPPLY TUG OPERATOR FOR A CHANGE OF PACE?
UH... MAYBE ANOTHER OFF-DUTY PERIOD, TANITH.
I'M ALREADY... ER... INVOLVED IN SOMETHING THIS EVENING.
SURE. I KNOW HOW FAST AND FURIOUS THE STARSHIP YARD WORKERS' COMPOUND SOCIAL LIFE CAN GET.
THAT TANITH SHIRE IS QUITE PERSISTENT IN HER ATTENTIONS, MASTER LUKE.
AS IF THINGS WEREN'T COMPLICATED ENOUGH WITH THIS SPY MISSION, THREEPIO...
STILL...NO GIRL'S EVER ACTED THAT WAY ABOUT ME. IF ONLY LEIA--
ER...SHOULDN'T WE THINK ABOUT ADMIRAL GRIFF AND HIS FRIENDS, SIR?

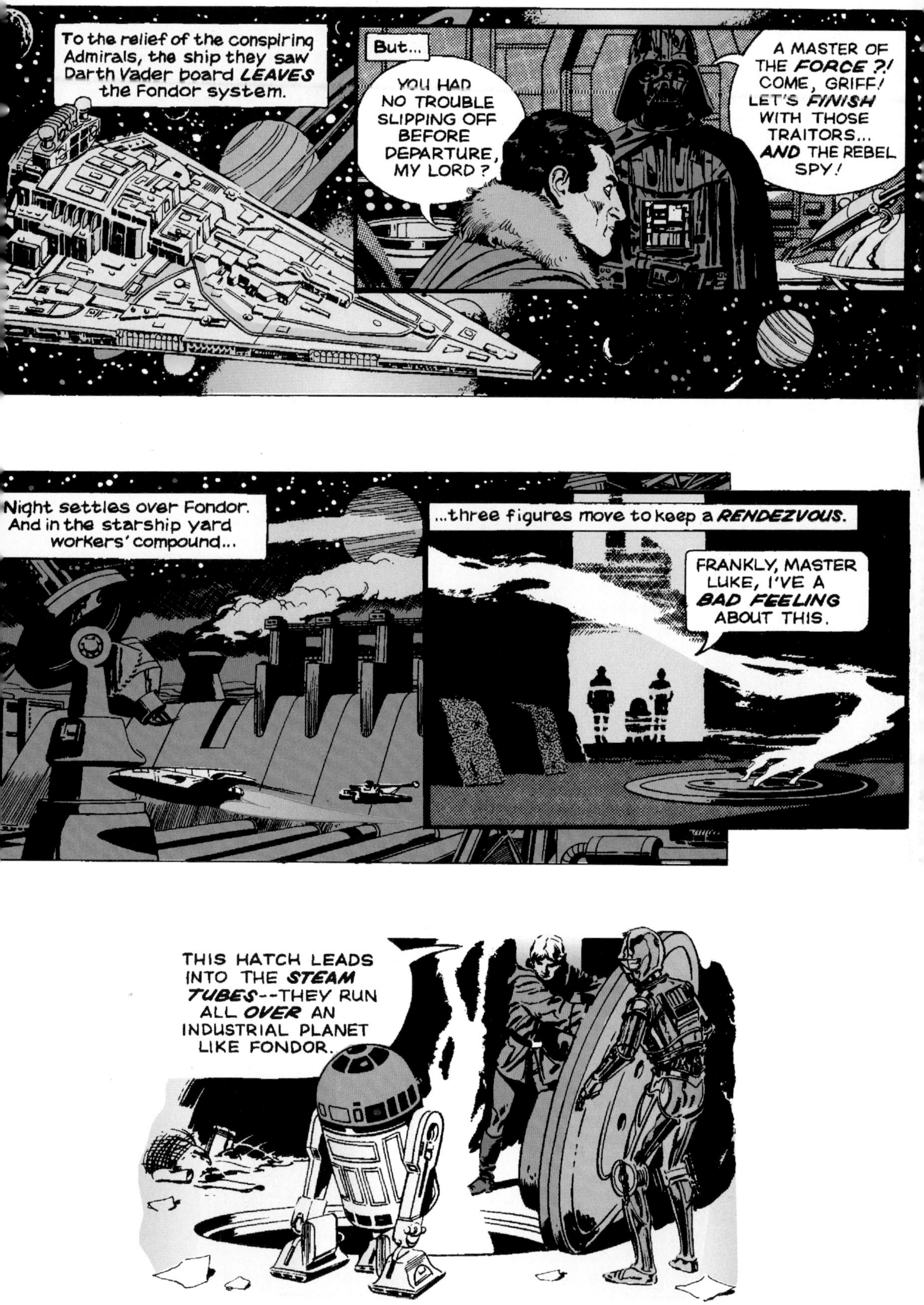

To the relief of the conspiring Admirals, the ship they saw Darth Vader board LEAVES the Fondor system.
But...
YOU HAD NO TROUBLE SLIPPING OFF BEFORE DEPARTURE, MY LORD?
A MASTER OF THE FORCE?! COME, GRIFF! LET'S FINISH WITH THOSE TRAITORS... AND THE REBEL SPY!
Night settles over Fondor. And in the starship yard workers' compound...
...three figures move to keep a RENDEZVOUS.
FRANKLY, MASTER LUKE, I'VE A BAD FEELING ABOUT THIS.
THIS HATCH LEADS INTO THE STEAM TUBES--THEY RUN ALL OVER AN INDUSTRIAL PLANET LIKE FONDOR.

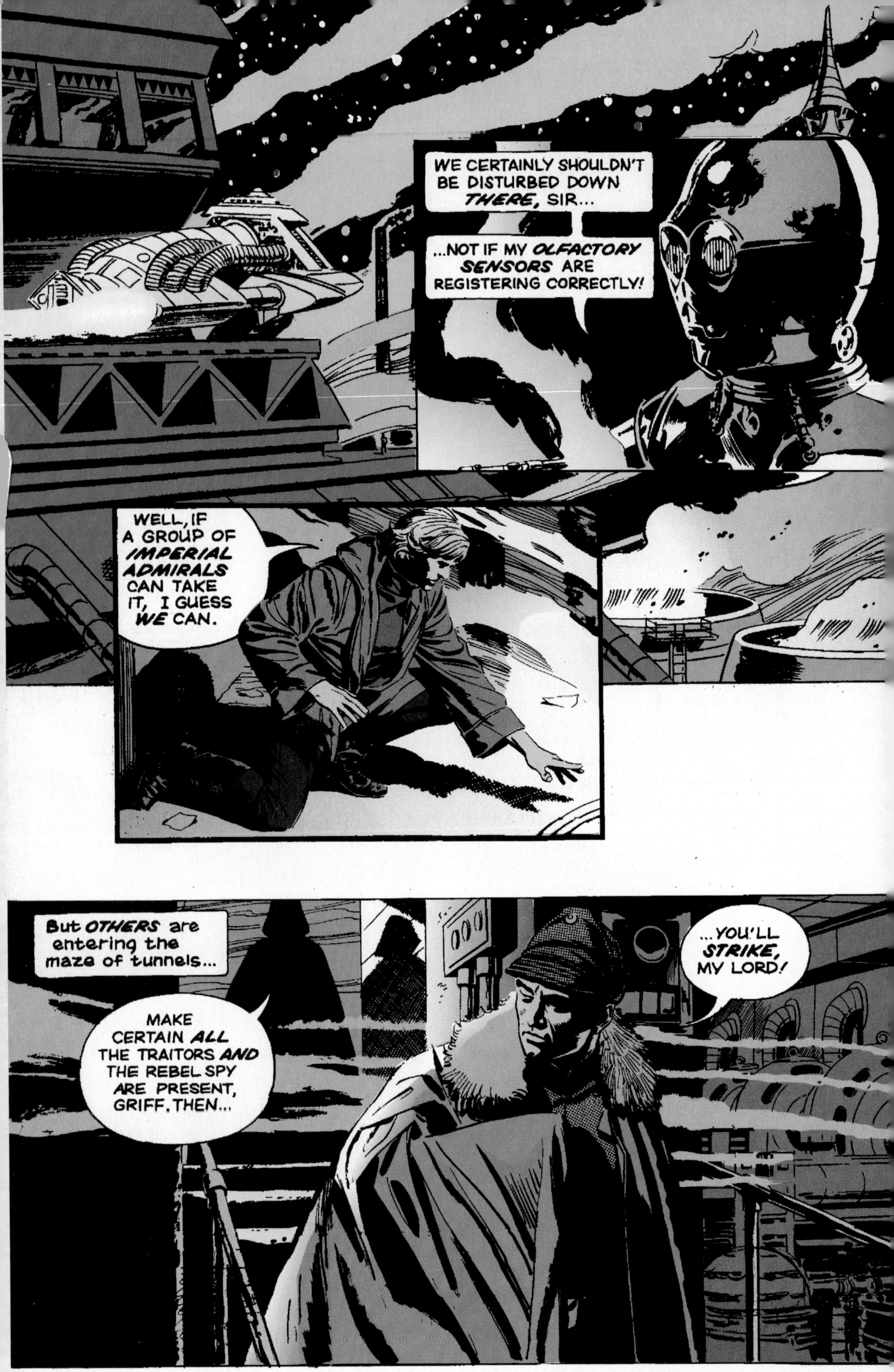
WE CERTAINLY SHOULDN'T BE DISTURBED DOWN *THERE*, SIR...
...NOT IF MY *OLFACTORY SENSORS* ARE REGISTERING CORRECTLY!
WELL, IF A GROUP OF *IMPERIAL ADMIRALS* CAN TAKE IT, I GUESS *WE* CAN.
But *OTHERS* are entering the maze of tunnels...
MAKE CERTAIN *ALL* THE TRAITORS *AND* THE REBEL SPY *ARE* PRESENT, GRIFF. THEN...
...YOU'LL *STRIKE*, MY LORD!

The adventure continues next month in *CLASSIC STAR WARS* #

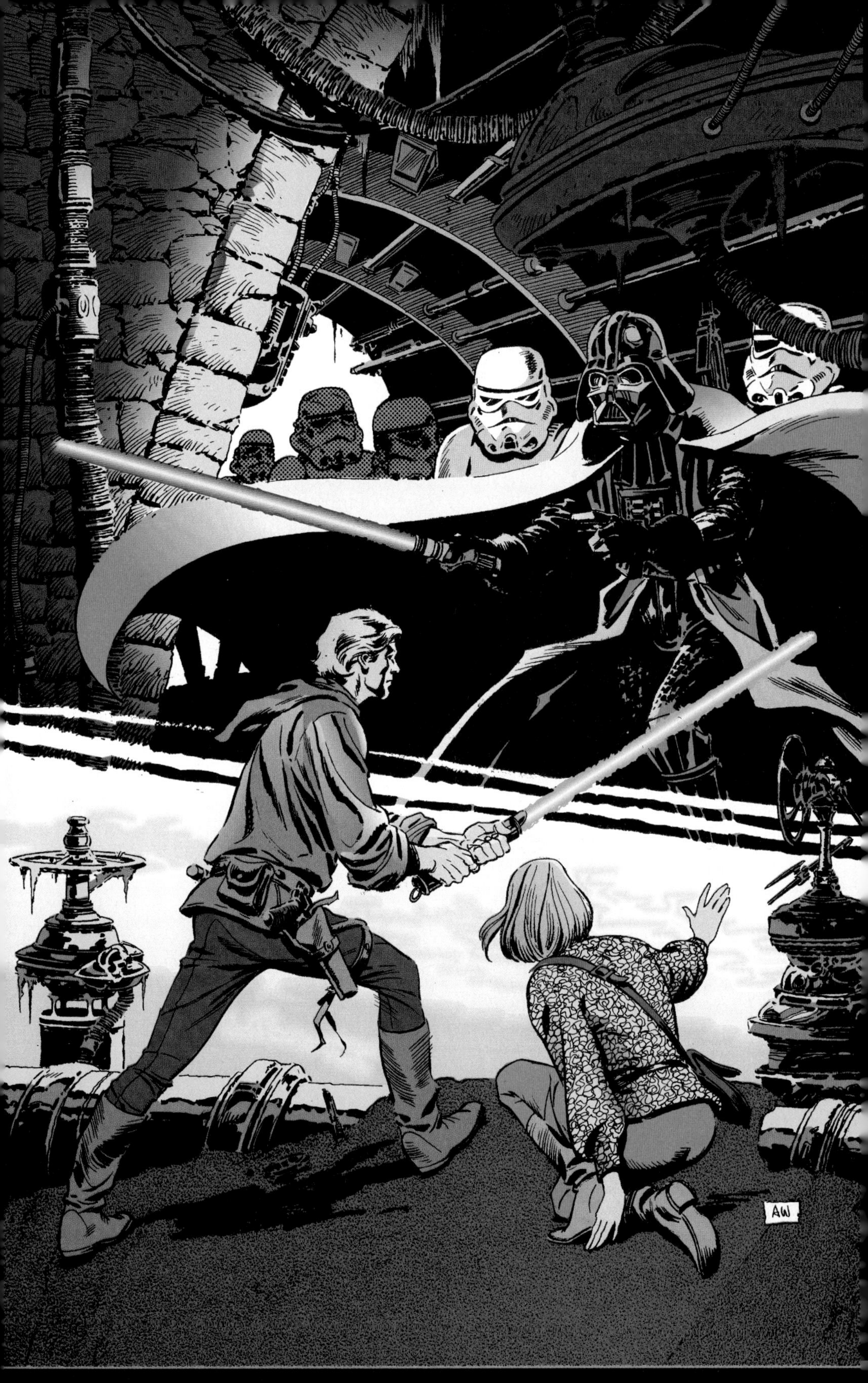
AW

CLASSIC STAR WARS #4 — "DARTH VADER STRIKES," PART 3
ORIGINALLY PUBLISHED FROM JULY 6 TO 26, 1981

WRITER: ARCHIE GOODWIN • ARTIST & LETTERER: AL WILLIAMSON • COLORIST: STEVE BUCCELLATO • EDITOR: ANINA BENNETT

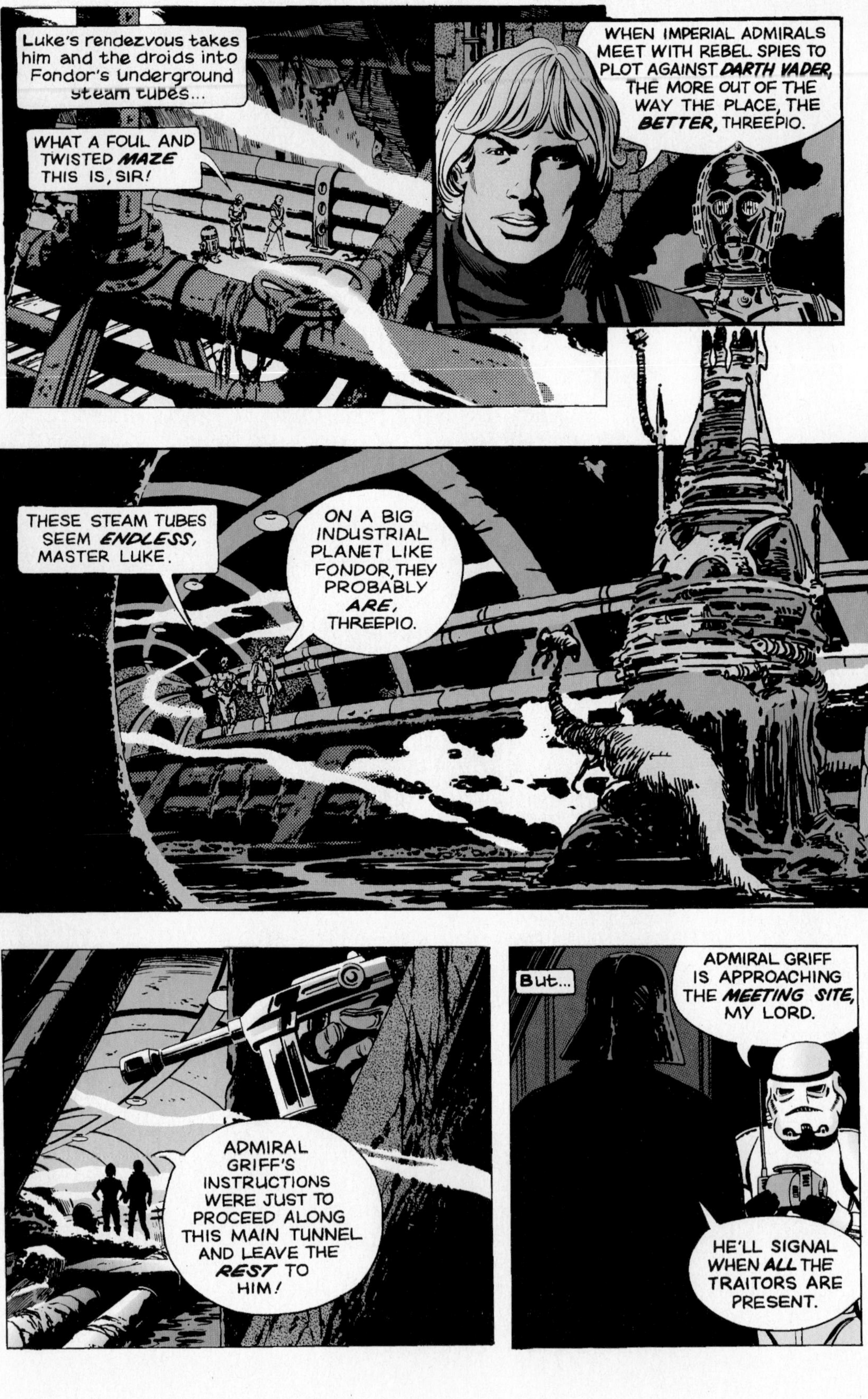

Luke's rendezvous takes him and the droids into Fondor's underground steam tubes...
WHAT A FOUL AND TWISTED MAZE THIS IS, SIR!
WHEN IMPERIAL ADMIRALS MEET WITH REBEL SPIES TO PLOT AGAINST DARTH VADER, THE MORE OUT OF THE WAY THE PLACE, THE BETTER, THREEPIO.
THESE STEAM TUBES SEEM ENDLESS, MASTER LUKE.
ON A BIG INDUSTRIAL PLANET LIKE FONDOR, THEY PROBABLY ARE, THREEPIO.
ADMIRAL GRIFF'S INSTRUCTIONS WERE JUST TO PROCEED ALONG THIS MAIN TUNNEL AND LEAVE THE REST TO HIM!
But...
ADMIRAL GRIFF IS APPROACHING THE MEETING SITE, MY LORD.
HE'LL SIGNAL WHEN ALL THE TRAITORS ARE PRESENT.

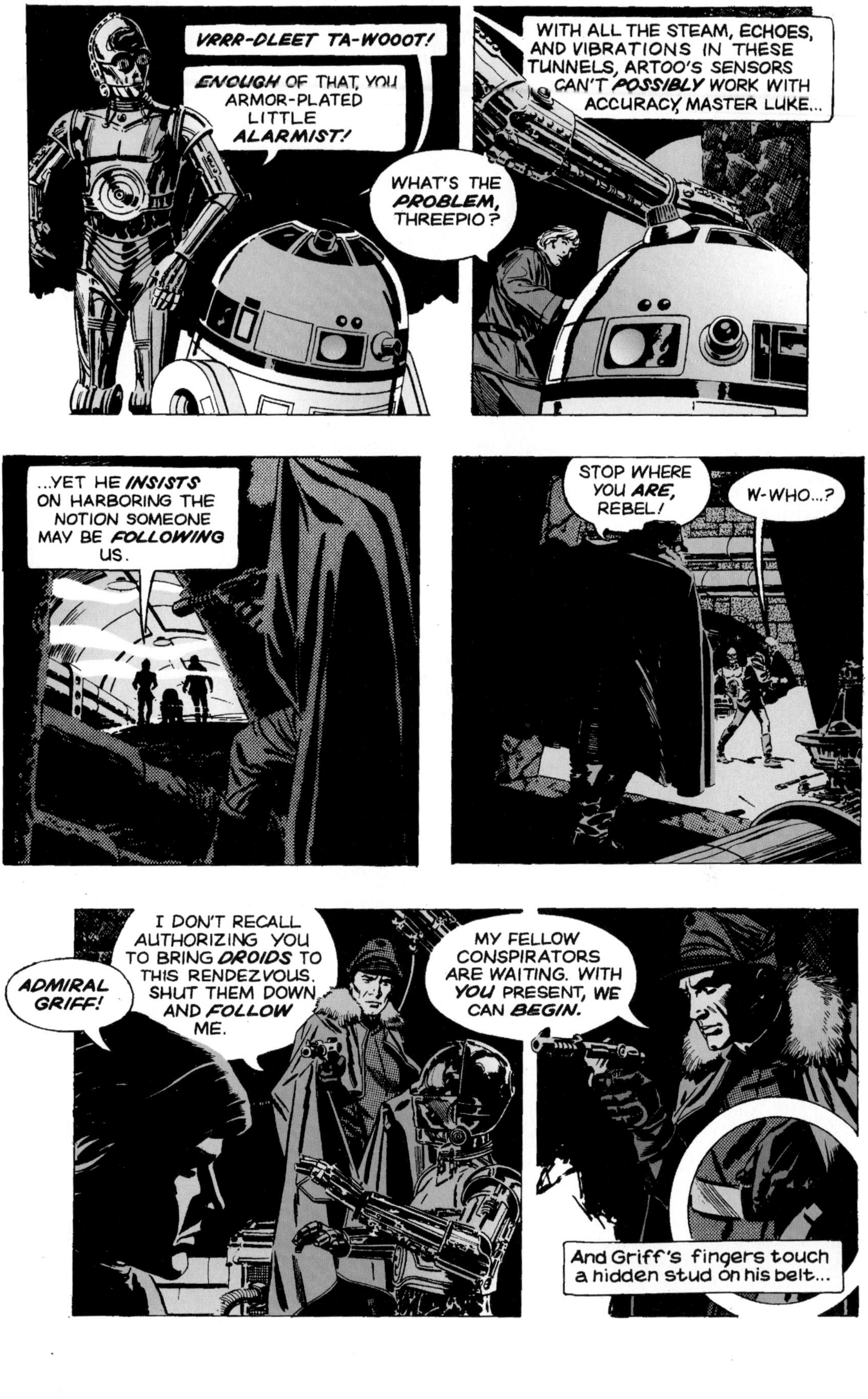
VRRR-DLEET TA-WOOOT!
ENOUGH OF THAT, YOU ARMOR-PLATED LITTLE ALARMIST!
WHAT'S THE PROBLEM, THREEPIO?
WITH ALL THE STEAM, ECHOES, AND VIBRATIONS IN THESE TUNNELS, ARTOO'S SENSORS CAN'T POSSIBLY WORK WITH ACCURACY, MASTER LUKE...
...YET HE INSISTS ON HARBORING THE NOTION SOMEONE MAY BE FOLLOWING US.
STOP WHERE YOU ARE, REBEL!
W-WHO...?
ADMIRAL GRIFF!
I DON'T RECALL AUTHORIZING YOU TO BRING DROIDS TO THIS RENDEZVOUS. SHUT THEM DOWN AND FOLLOW ME.
MY FELLOW CONSPIRATORS ARE WAITING. WITH YOU PRESENT, WE CAN BEGIN.
And Griff's fingers touch a hidden stud on his belt...

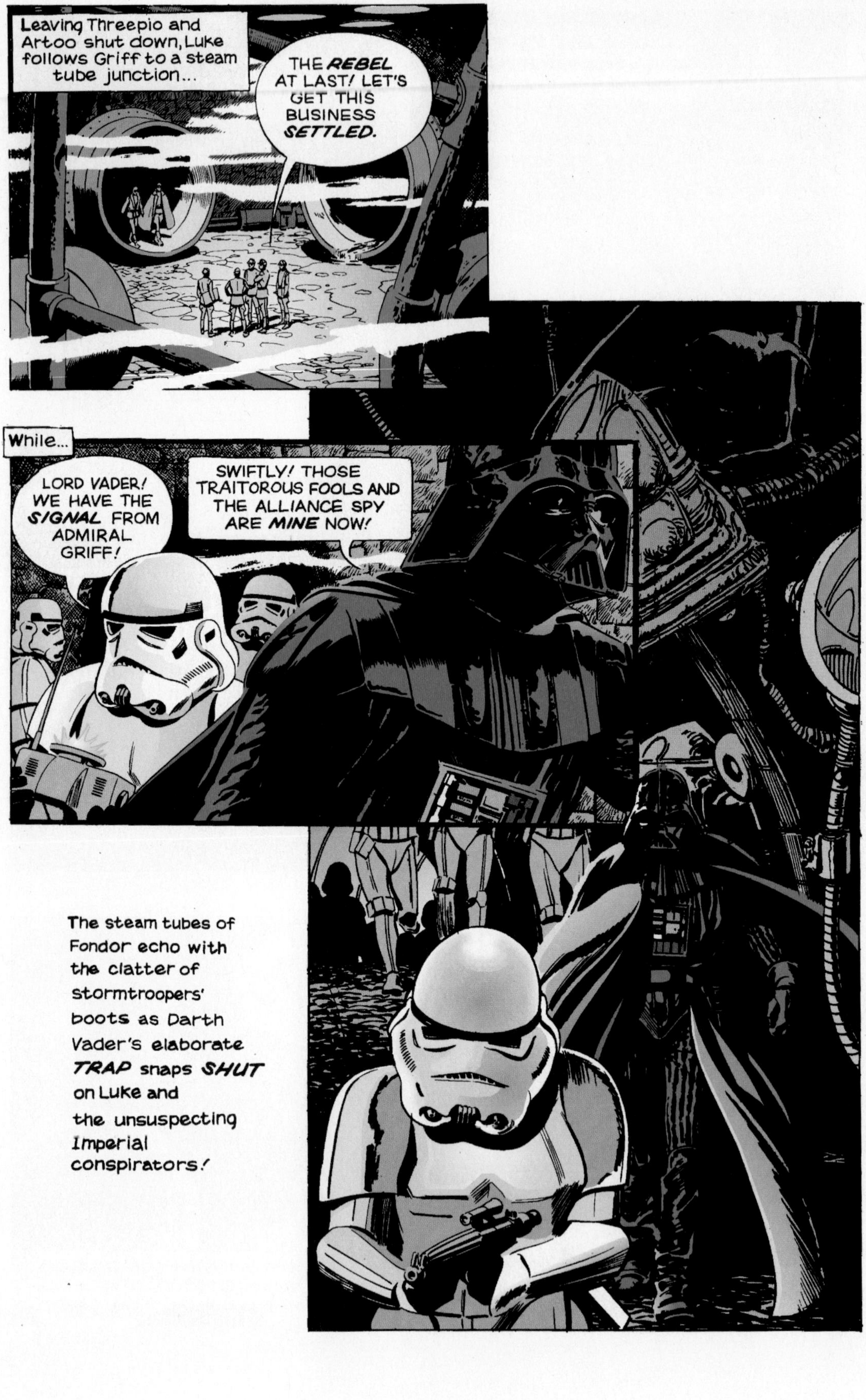
Leaving Threepio and Artoo shut down, Luke follows Griff to a steam tube junction...
THE REBEL AT LAST! LET'S GET THIS BUSINESS SETTLED.
While...
LORD VADER! WE HAVE THE SIGNAL FROM ADMIRAL GRIFF!
SWIFTLY! THOSE TRAITOROUS FOOLS AND THE ALLIANCE SPY ARE MINE NOW!
The steam tubes of Fondor echo with the clatter of stormtroopers' boots as Darth Vader's elaborate TRAP snaps SHUT on Luke and the unsuspecting Imperial conspirators!

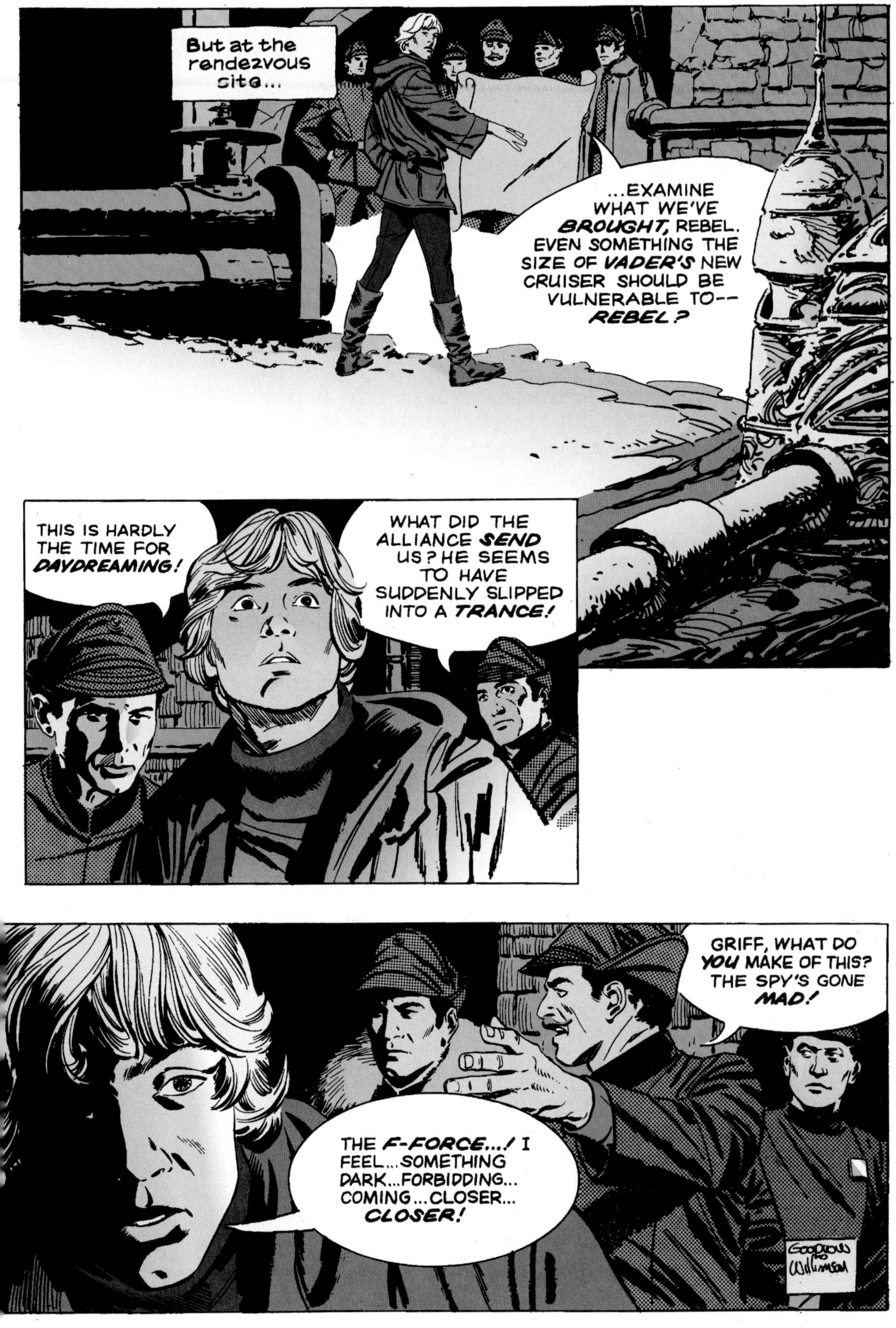

But at the rendezvous site...
...EXAMINE WHAT WE'VE BROUGHT, REBEL. EVEN SOMETHING THE SIZE OF VADER'S NEW CRUISER SHOULD BE VULNERABLE TO-- REBEL?
THIS IS HARDLY THE TIME FOR DAYDREAMING!
WHAT DID THE ALLIANCE SEND US? HE SEEMS TO HAVE SUDDENLY SLIPPED INTO A TRANCE!
GRIFF, WHAT DO YOU MAKE OF THIS? THE SPY'S GONE MAD!
THE F-FORCE...! I FEEL...SOMETHING DARK...FORBIDDING... COMING...CLOSER... CLOSER!

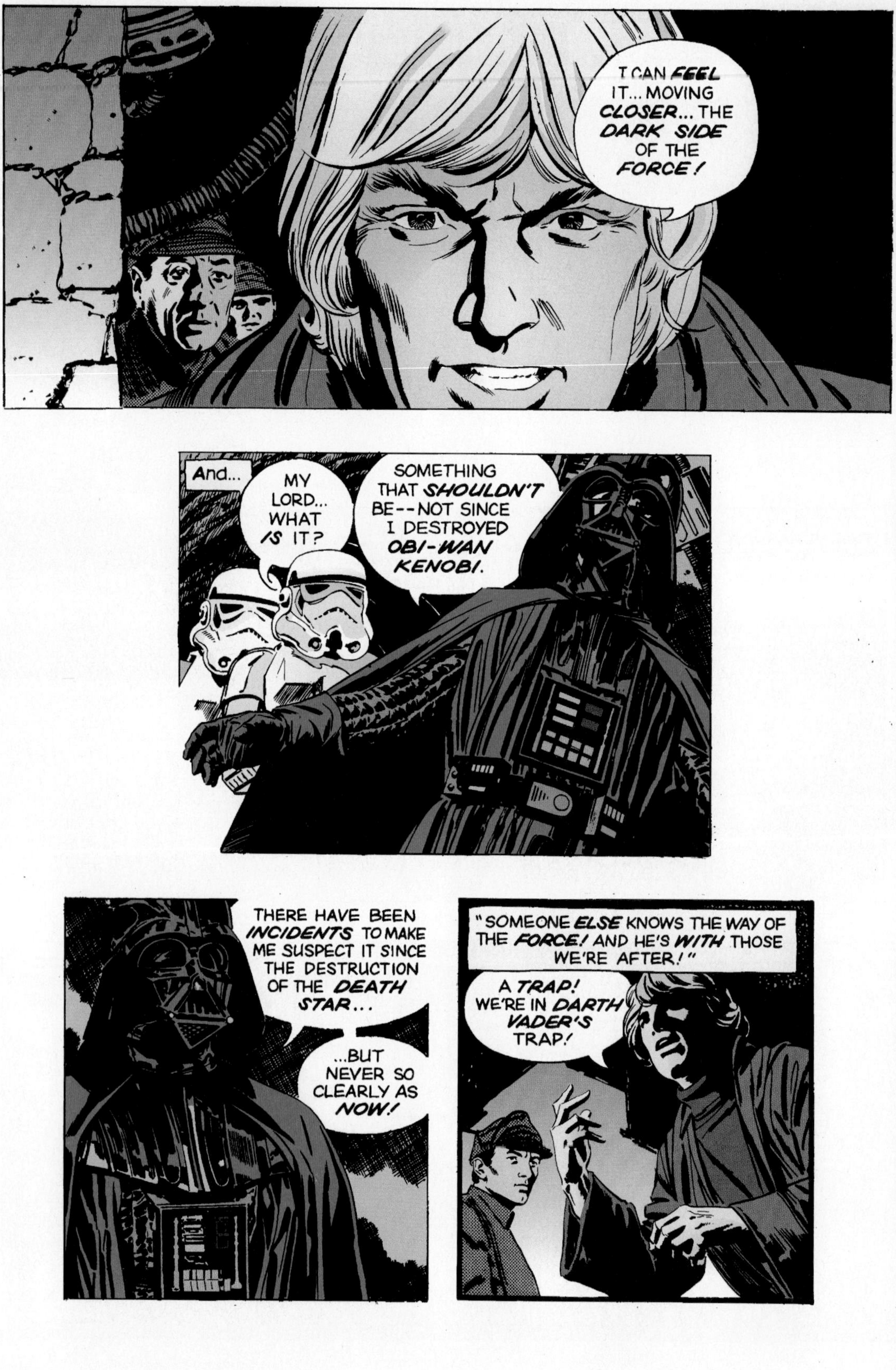
I CAN FEEL IT... MOVING CLOSER... THE DARK SIDE OF THE FORCE!
And...
MY LORD... WHAT IS IT?
SOMETHING THAT SHOULDN'T BE--NOT SINCE I DESTROYED OBI-WAN KENOBI.
THERE HAVE BEEN INCIDENTS TO MAKE ME SUSPECT IT SINCE THE DESTRUCTION OF THE DEATH STAR...
...BUT NEVER SO CLEARLY AS NOW!
"SOMEONE ELSE KNOWS THE WAY OF THE FORCE! AND HE'S WITH THOSE WE'RE AFTER!"
A TRAP! WE'RE IN DARTH VADER'S TRAP!

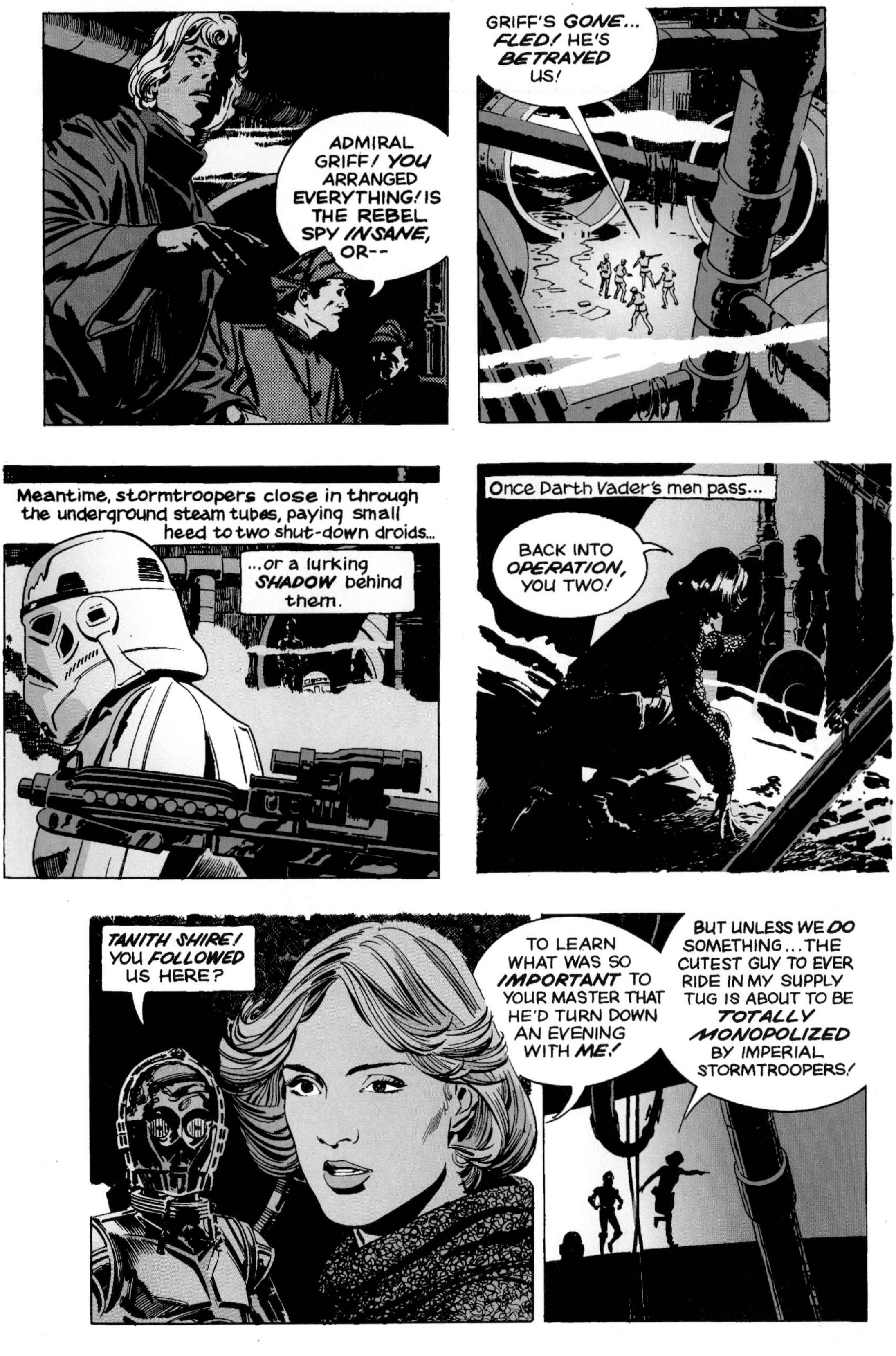
ADMIRAL GRIFF! YOU ARRANGED EVERYTHING! IS THE REBEL SPY INSANE, OR--
GRIFF'S GONE... FLED! HE'S BETRAYED US!
Meantime, stormtroopers close in through the underground steam tubes, paying small heed to two shut-down droids...
...or a lurking SHADOW behind them.
Once Darth Vader's men pass...
BACK INTO OPERATION, YOU TWO!
TANITH SHIRE! YOU FOLLOWED US HERE?
TO LEARN WHAT WAS SO IMPORTANT TO YOUR MASTER THAT HE'D TURN DOWN AN EVENING WITH ME!
BUT UNLESS WE DO SOMETHING... THE CUTEST GUY TO EVER RIDE IN MY SUPPLY TUG IS ABOUT TO BE TOTALLY MONOPOLIZED BY IMPERIAL STORMTROOPERS!

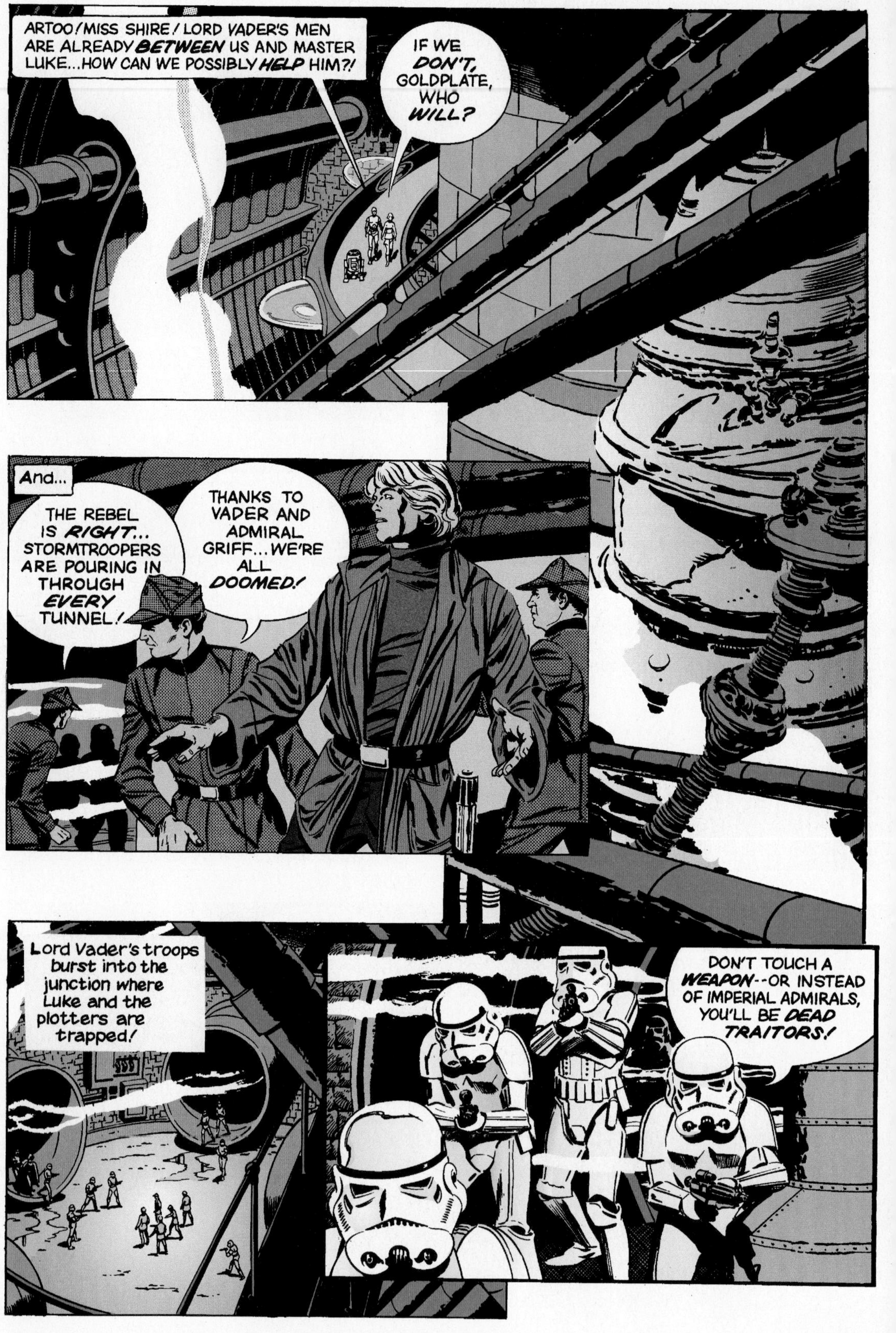
ARTOO! MISS SHIRE! LORD VADER'S MEN ARE ALREADY BETWEEN US AND MASTER LUKE...HOW CAN WE POSSIBLY HELP HIM?!
IF WE DON'T, GOLDPLATE, WHO WILL?
And...
THE REBEL IS RIGHT... STORMTROOPERS ARE POURING IN THROUGH EVERY TUNNEL!
THANKS TO VADER AND ADMIRAL GRIFF... WE'RE ALL DOOMED!
Lord Vader's troops burst into the junction where Luke and the plotters are trapped!
DON'T TOUCH A WEAPON--OR INSTEAD OF IMPERIAL ADMIRALS, YOU'LL BE DEAD TRAITORS!

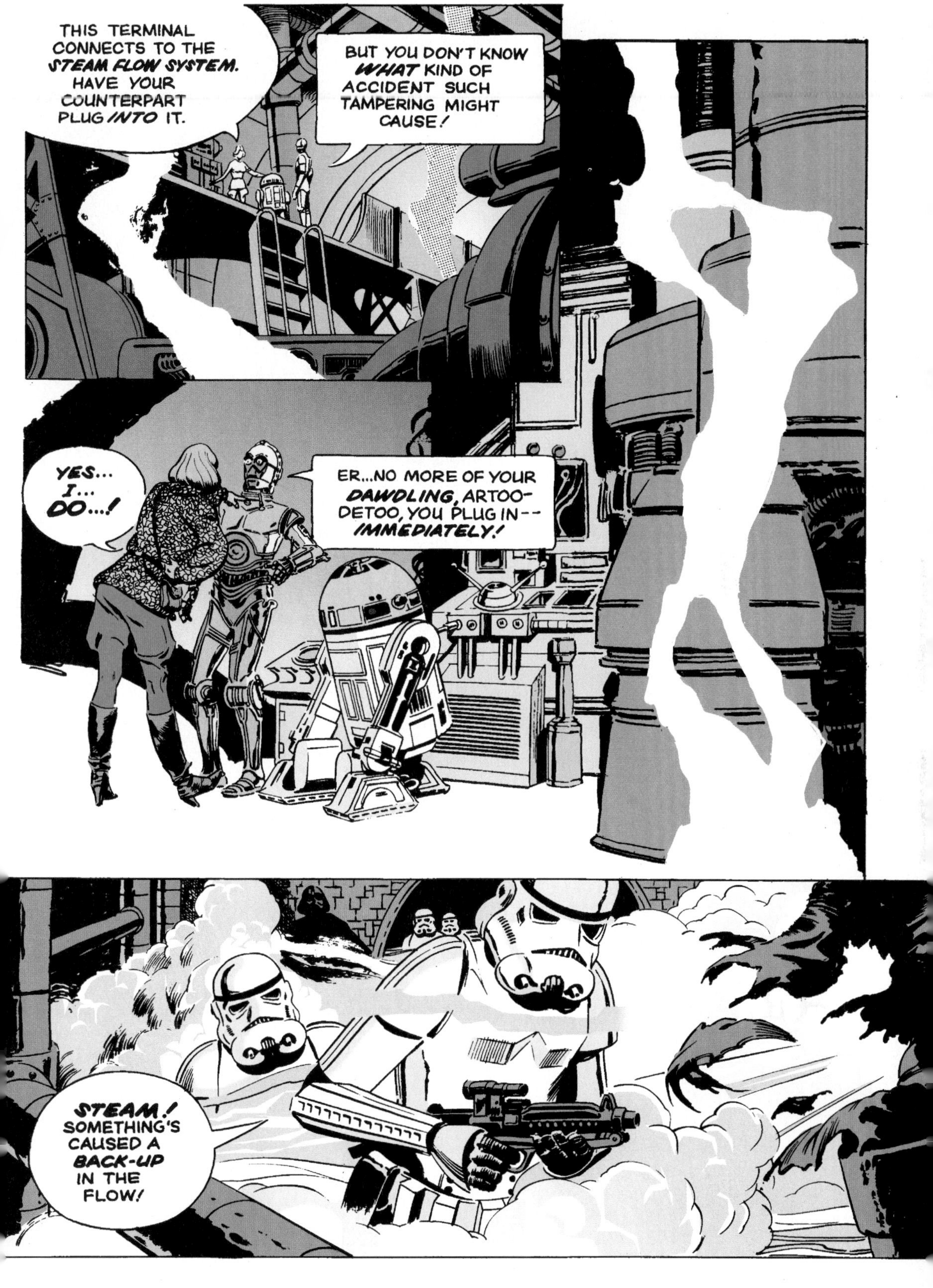
THIS TERMINAL CONNECTS TO THE STEAM FLOW SYSTEM. HAVE YOUR COUNTERPART PLUG INTO IT.
BUT YOU DON'T KNOW WHAT KIND OF ACCIDENT SUCH TAMPERING MIGHT CAUSE!
YES... I... DO...!
ER...NO MORE OF YOUR DAWDLING, ARTOO-DETOO, YOU PLUG IN-- IMMEDIATELY!
STEAM! SOMETHING'S CAUSED A BACK-UP IN THE FLOW!

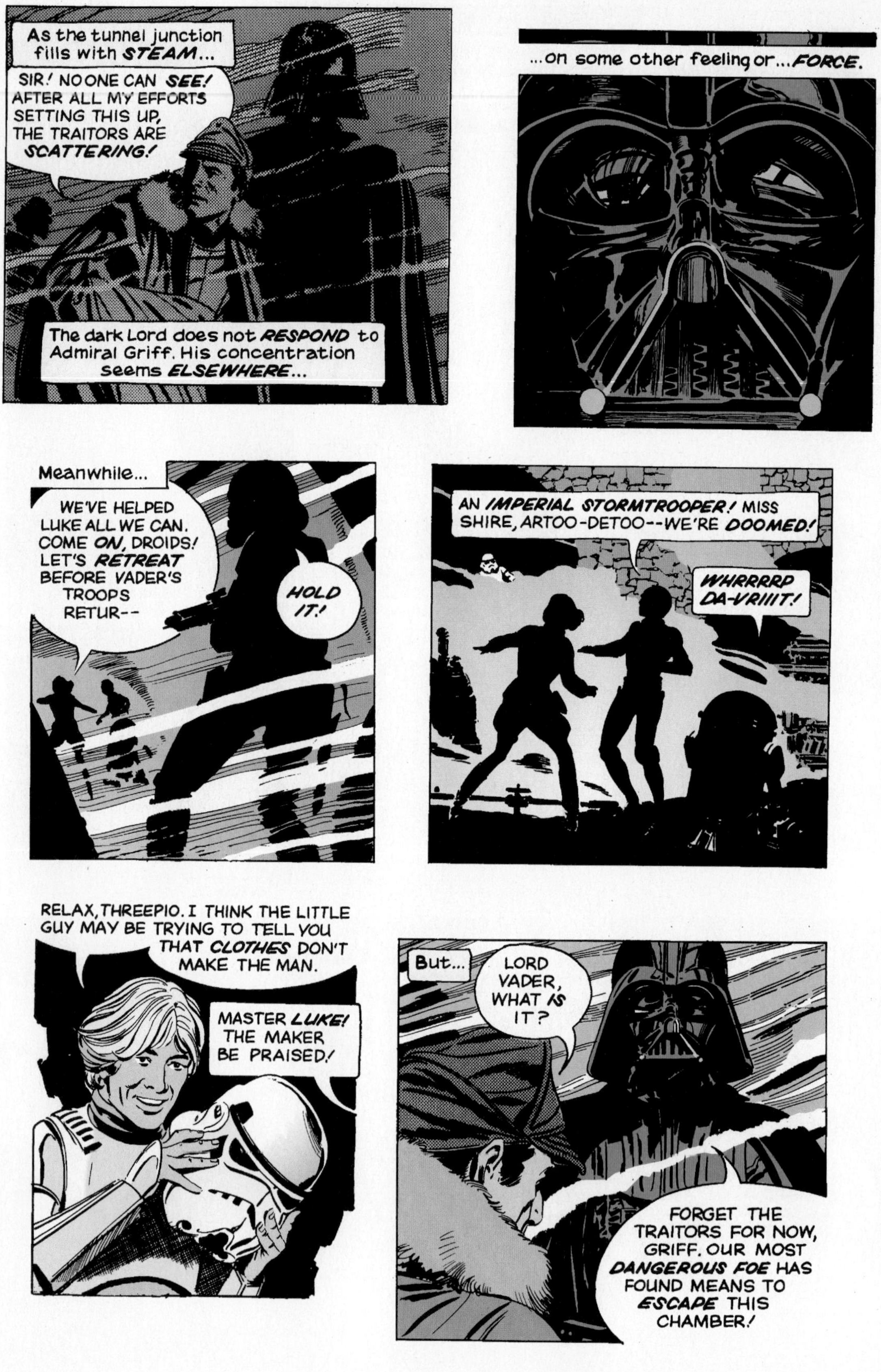

As the tunnel junction fills with STEAM...
SIR! NOONE CAN SEE! AFTER ALL MY EFFORTS SETTING THIS UP, THE TRAITORS ARE SCATTERING!
The dark Lord does not RESPOND to Admiral Griff. His concentration seems ELSEWHERE...
...on some other feeling or... FORCE.
Meanwhile...
WE'VE HELPED LUKE ALL WE CAN. COME ON, DROIDS! LET'S RETREAT BEFORE VADER'S TROOPS RETUR--
HOLD IT!
AN IMPERIAL STORMTROOPER! MISS SHIRE, ARTOO-DETOO--WE'RE DOOMED!
WHRRRRP DA-VRIIIT!
RELAX, THREEPIO. I THINK THE LITTLE GUY MAY BE TRYING TO TELL YOU THAT CLOTHES DON'T MAKE THE MAN.
MASTER LUKE! THE MAKER BE PRAISED!
But...
LORD VADER, WHAT IS IT?
FORGET THE TRAITORS FOR NOW, GRIFF. OUR MOST DANGEROUS FOE HAS FOUND MEANS TO ESCAPE THIS CHAMBER!

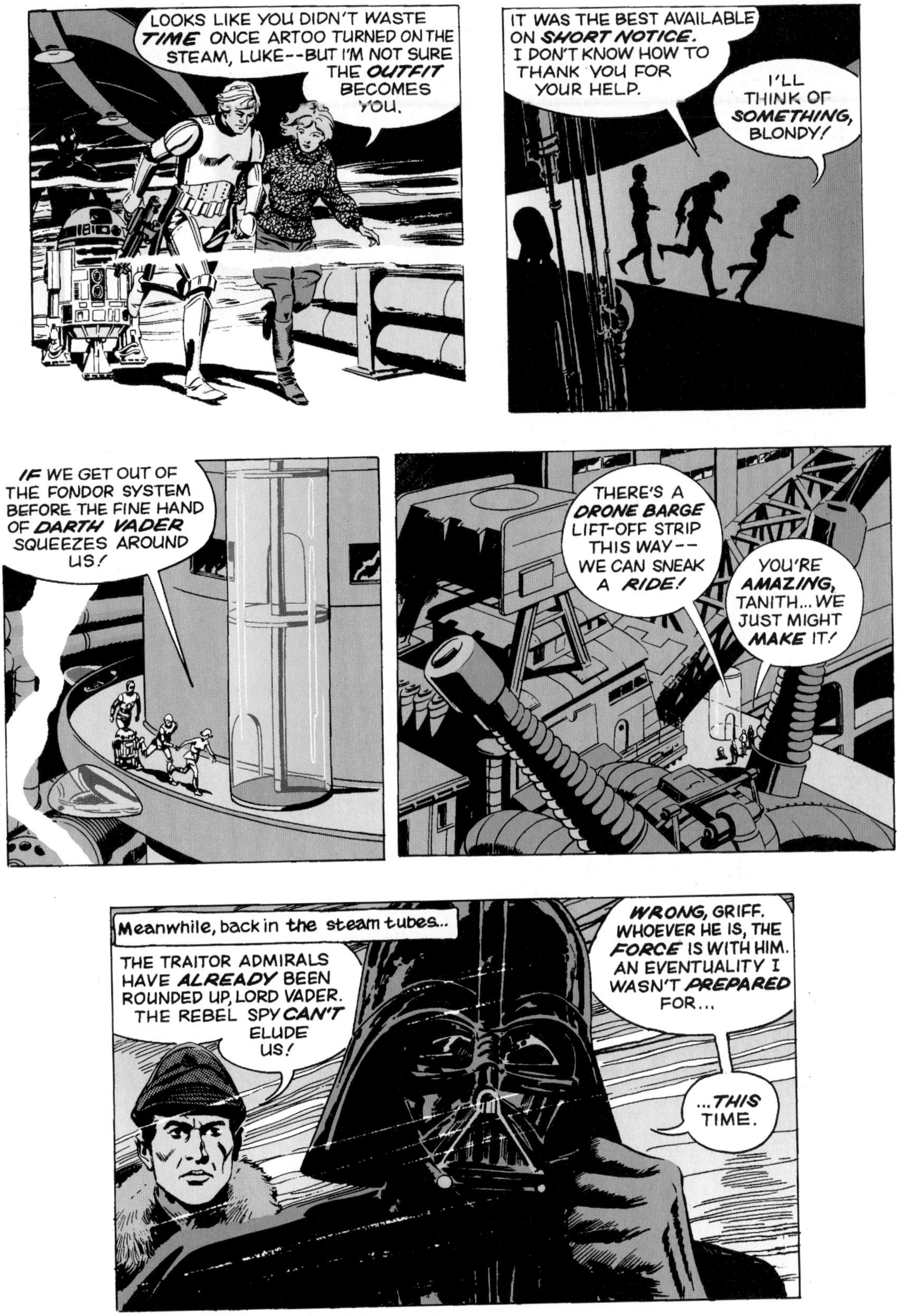
LOOKS LIKE YOU DIDN'T WASTE TIME ONCE ARTOO TURNED ON THE STEAM, LUKE--BUT I'M NOT SURE THE OUTFIT BECOMES YOU.
IT WAS THE BEST AVAILABLE ON SHORT NOTICE. I DON'T KNOW HOW TO THANK YOU FOR YOUR HELP.
I'LL THINK OF SOMETHING, BLONDY!
IF WE GET OUT OF THE FONDOR SYSTEM BEFORE THE FINE HAND OF DARTH VADER SQUEEZES AROUND US!
THERE'S A DRONE BARGE LIFT-OFF STRIP THIS WAY-- WE CAN SNEAK A RIDE!
YOU'RE AMAZING, TANITH... WE JUST MIGHT MAKE IT!
Meanwhile, back in the steam tubes...
THE TRAITOR ADMIRALS HAVE ALREADY BEEN ROUNDED UP, LORD VADER. THE REBEL SPY CAN'T ELUDE US!
WRONG, GRIFF. WHOEVER HE IS, THE FORCE IS WITH HIM. AN EVENTUALITY I WASN'T PREPARED FOR...
...THIS TIME.

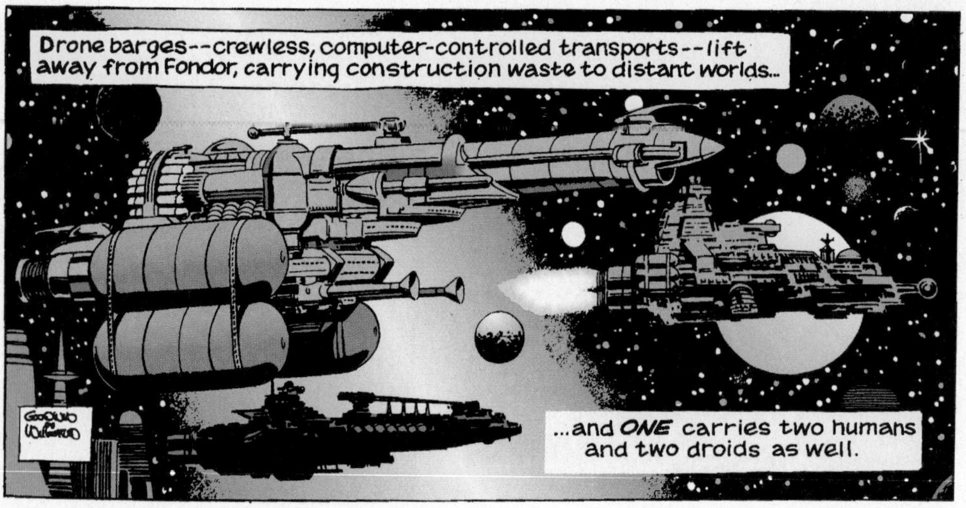
Drone barges--crewless, computer-controlled transports--lift away from Fondor, carrying construction waste to distant worlds...
...and ONE carries two humans and two droids as well.

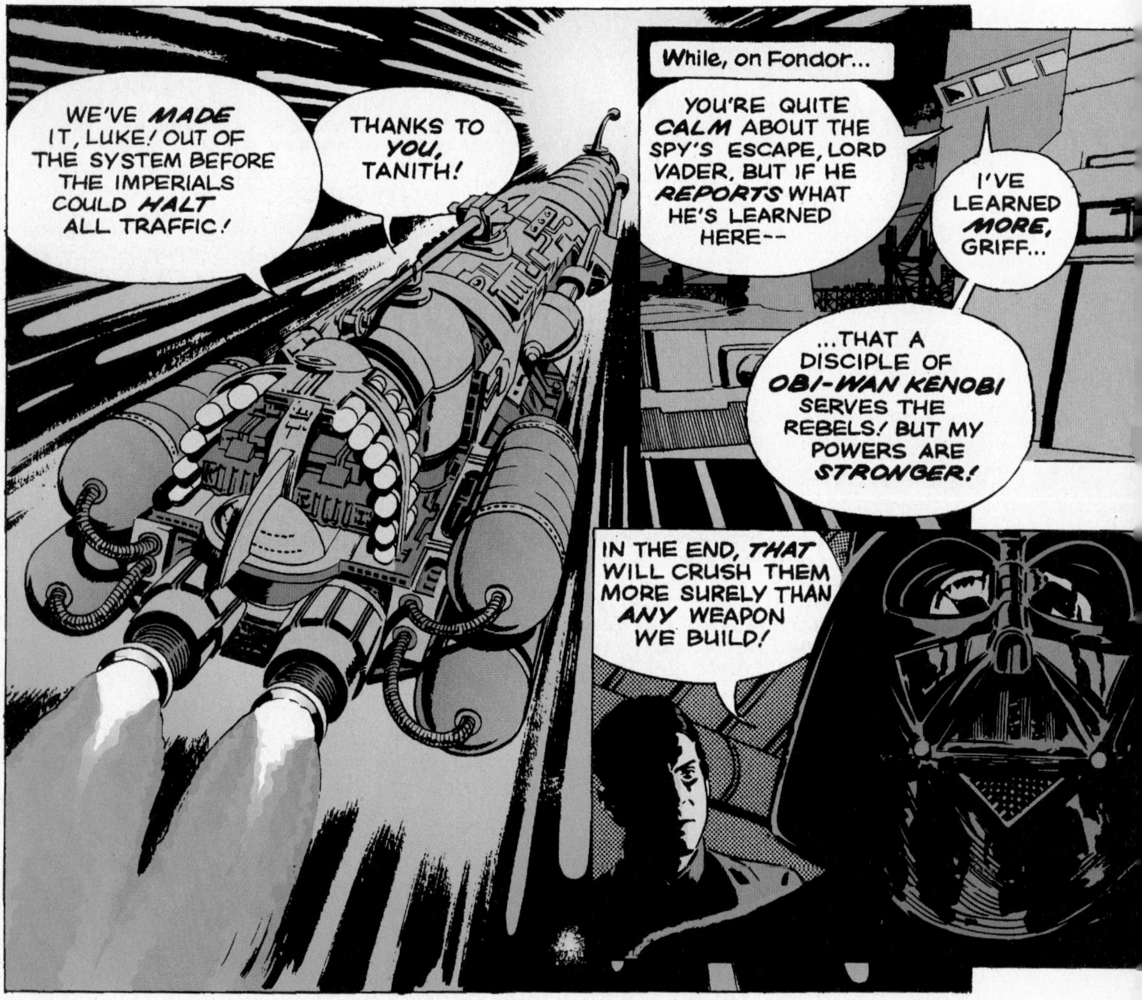
WE'VE MADE IT, LUKE! OUT OF THE SYSTEM BEFORE THE IMPERIALS COULD HALT ALL TRAFFIC!
THANKS TO YOU, TANITH!
While, on Fondor...
YOU'RE QUITE CALM ABOUT THE SPY'S ESCAPE, LORD VADER. BUT IF HE REPORTS WHAT HE'S LEARNED HERE--
I'VE LEARNED MORE, GRIFF...
...THAT A DISCIPLE OF OBI-WAN KENOBI SERVES THE REBELS! BUT MY POWERS ARE STRONGER!
IN THE END, THAT WILL CRUSH THEM MORE SURELY THAN ANY WEAPON WE BUILD!

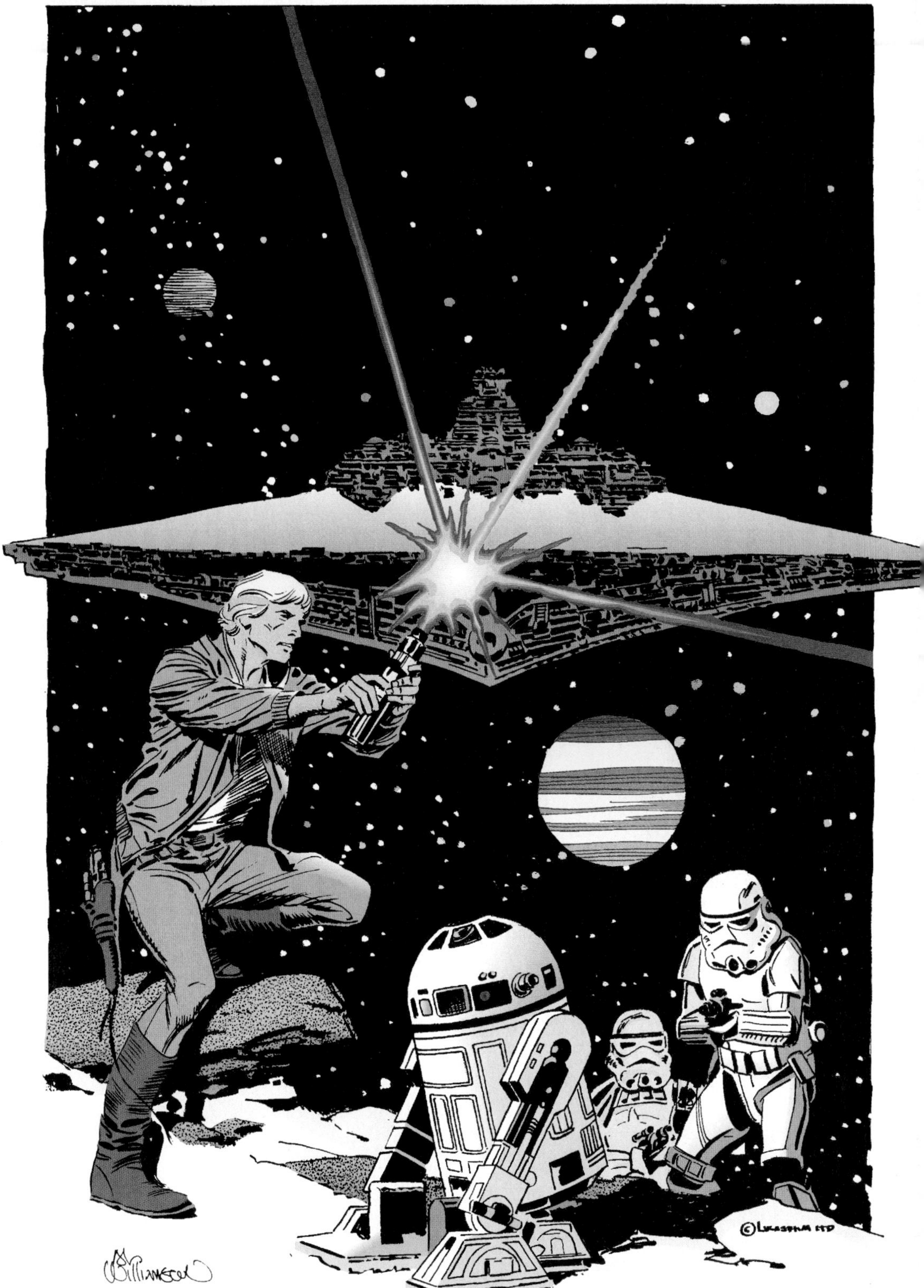

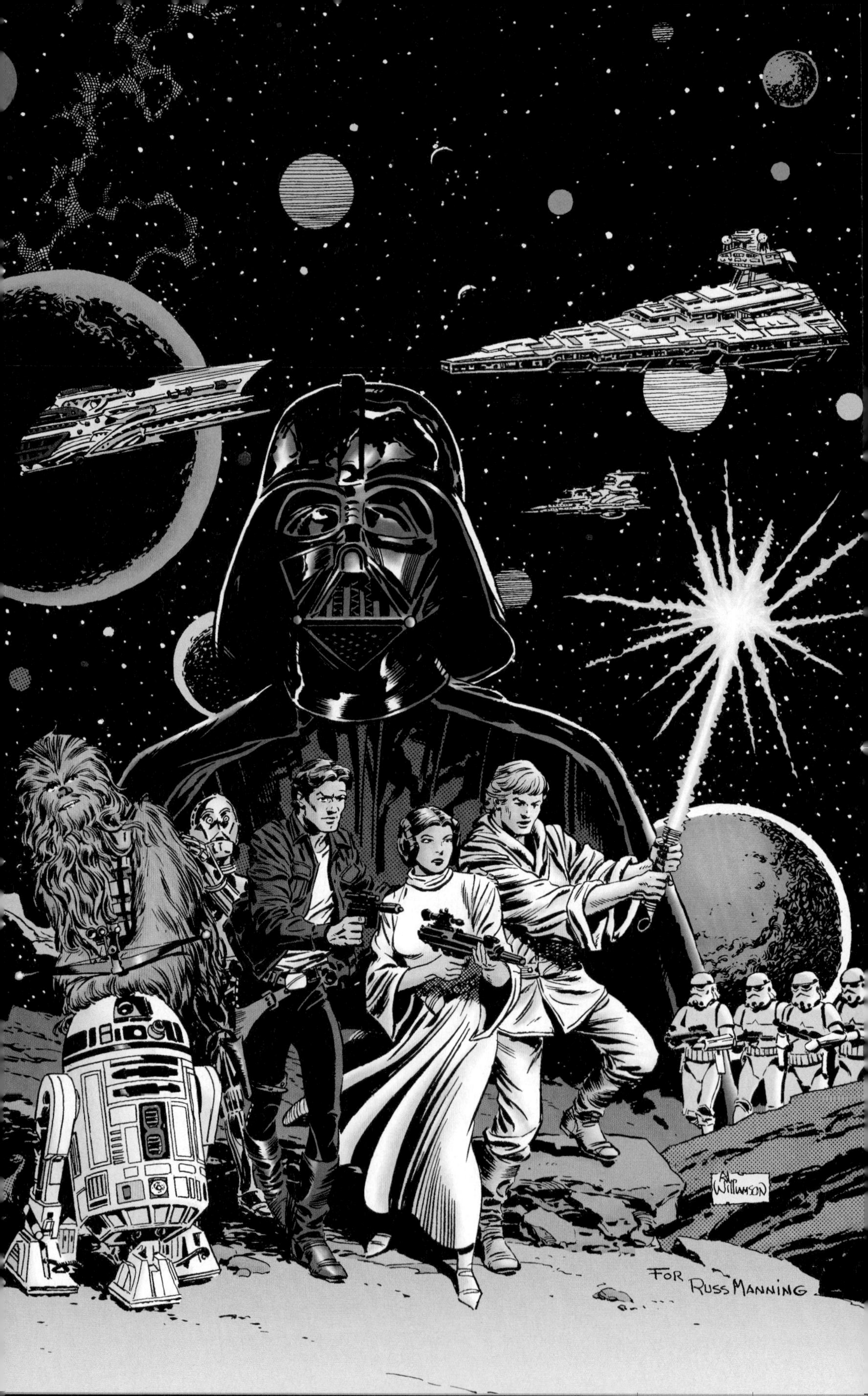
AL WILLIAMSON
FOR RUSS MANNING

A MASTER STORYTELLER

To say that Russ Manning was an influence on me and my career is an understatement. Simply put, I would not have spent the last 31 years doing what I love, supporting family, home, and hobbies with the product of my hand and mind if not for the encouragement and tutelage of Russ Manning, my mentor. I am a member of what I consider a select group of artists who worked with and were influenced by Russ Manning...such illustrious talents as Bill Stout, Dave Stevens, and Rick Hoberg.

I was born in 1941, and, as a youngster, I fell in love with comic strips...old, yellowed pages of Foster and Hogarth's *Tarzan*, Raymond's *Flash Gordon*, and Caniff's *Terry and the Pirates* discovered in my grandmother's attic as well as the contemporary Tufts's *Casey Ruggles and Lance*, Foster's *Prince Valiant*, Caniff's *Steve Canyon*, and Hamlin's *Alley Oop*. The comic books I bought were usually those reprinting the aforementioned titles. Most "new material" impressed me little, with the exception of Kirby (that's another story) and the artist doing back-up stories in *Tarzan*, and then full titles such as *Dale Evans*, *Sea Hunt*, etc. With the early '60s publication of *Magnus, Robot Fighter* I finally learned that artist's name: Russ Manning. I held in my hands the finest example of comic-strip art created exclusively for comic books. It was then that I decided the direction my life should take — the world of comic art.

Somehow, I discovered Russ's interest in Burroughs fandom, and I naively assumed he would attend the Dum-Dum at the upcoming World Science Fiction Convention. After securing permission from Hubert Burroughs, another Burroughs fan and I produced a 36-page *Wizard of Venus* comic book, which we took to Oakland for the '64 World Con. My goal was to meet Russ, show him my attempt at comic art, and see what would then transpire. However, he did not attend.

Undaunted, I returned home to Oregon. I drew up new sample pages and sent them to Russ's home outside Orange, California. In early '65, Russ responded saying that the samples showed some promise, and "If I ever needed any help, I don't see why you wouldn't be capable of it." That was all the encouragement I needed. Within three months, my family and I were residents of Southern California.

Russ Manning, perhaps remembering the help and encouragement given to him at the beginning of his career by Jesse Marsh, really didn't need help with his comic-book assignments, However, he found work for me to do, a kindness for which I will always be grateful. For about a year, my evenings and weekends were spent circling balloons, finishing rough pencils, completing partially inked figures, etc. I was "assisting" and learning from a master.

The second year, as a result of Russ's recommendation, I went from working days for Sherwin-Williams Paint to the limited animation *Marvel Super Heroes* television series and continued to assist and learn from Russ Manning's Gold Key comic-book assignments. As Russ's popularity grew with comic-book buyers, Gold Key wanted more work from him. Russ informed his editor that the only way he could produce more work would be if I worked with him more than I already was. The only way I could do that and give up the animation business would be by having full-time employment in comic books.

Thanks to Russ, I was now working full-time in the comics industry, assisting him and pulling assignments from Gold Key comics. It transpired that Russ's efforts on the *Tarzan* comic book (the "more" Gold Key wanted) resulted in Edgar Rice Burroughs, Inc. offering him the *Tarzan* syndicated comic strip. Russ left Gold Key/Western Publishing to do what he'd always wanted to do — a syndicated comics feature — and I now had my foot firmly planted in the door of the comic-book business.

In a few months, I was assisting on the *Tarzan* daily and Sunday strips, working with and learning from the most dynamic syndicated strip artist of the decade. Russ found new ways to do wonderful panel breakdowns within the mechanical restrictions of the Sunday strip that have never been equaled for sheer beauty and execution...it was an ability he would bring to his next assignment. As I began inking almost full-time for Jack Kirby, the talented Bill Stout joined Russ's team. Benefiting from Stout's color experience, Russ utilized the time saved in coloring the Sunday release to do even greater work on his *Tarzan* graphics.

One day in mid-1978, Russ telephoned to say he was going to be writing and drawing the *Star Wars* daily and Sunday strip and would be continuing to produce the Sunday *Tarzan*. He asked if I would be interested in doing all the inking and lettering. Russ would be trusting me with *all* the inking! Talk about intimidating! It turned out to be an exciting 17 weeks. Then Disney called, but that's yet another story.

Russ Manning was the consummate cartoonist/illustrator. He rightfully took great pride in his work, both the art and the written word. He was the kind of creator who, I believe, felt that the work should all come from his hand to be truly his. With the amount of work he had to produce, there was just no way he could do it all himself, and I feel very privileged, that, as a "necessary evil," Russ selected me.

I've spoken little of Russ's work on *Star Wars* because you hold in your hands a collection of some of the greatest daily comic-strip art and writing done in the last quarter of the 20th century. It speaks for itself. Within prescribed guidelines of continuity length, separate daily and Sunday adventures, and instructions to not involve the complete cast in both continuities, Russ drew on his love of science fiction, his admiration of the cinematic achievements of *Star Wars*, and his years of experience as a master of graphic storytelling and poured himself completely into his challenging new assignment.

It's all here...the great design sense, the masterful use of black, the "framing" of set-ups so we see just what the master storyteller wants us to see, and, above all, "The line defines the form."

Russ Manning was a unique talent. As an artist he believed one should strive to do what movies and television couldn't do... make the impossible "work." As a human being, he believed in putting family and community above all else. When a member of his family entered his studio, the work waited. Since most of the residents of his canyon community were away during the daytime, he became a volunteer fireman. Many a time his studio alarm would go off and he'd leap for the door with "It's a fire or rescue...see you later!" We worked many late hours because, in Russ Manning's world, real life took priority over "make believe." Fortunately for us, the product of his "make believe" remains to be enjoyed again, or to be discovered for the first time.

To me, Russ Manning is not really done. Occasionally, in my dreams, I'm driving up to Russ's studio in the canyon. He's sitting at this drawing board while an operatic aria is wafting through the room...a pile of strips are in his outstretched hand, and he smiles and says, "We've got lots to do."

Enjoy these adventures.

—Mike Royer
January 1997

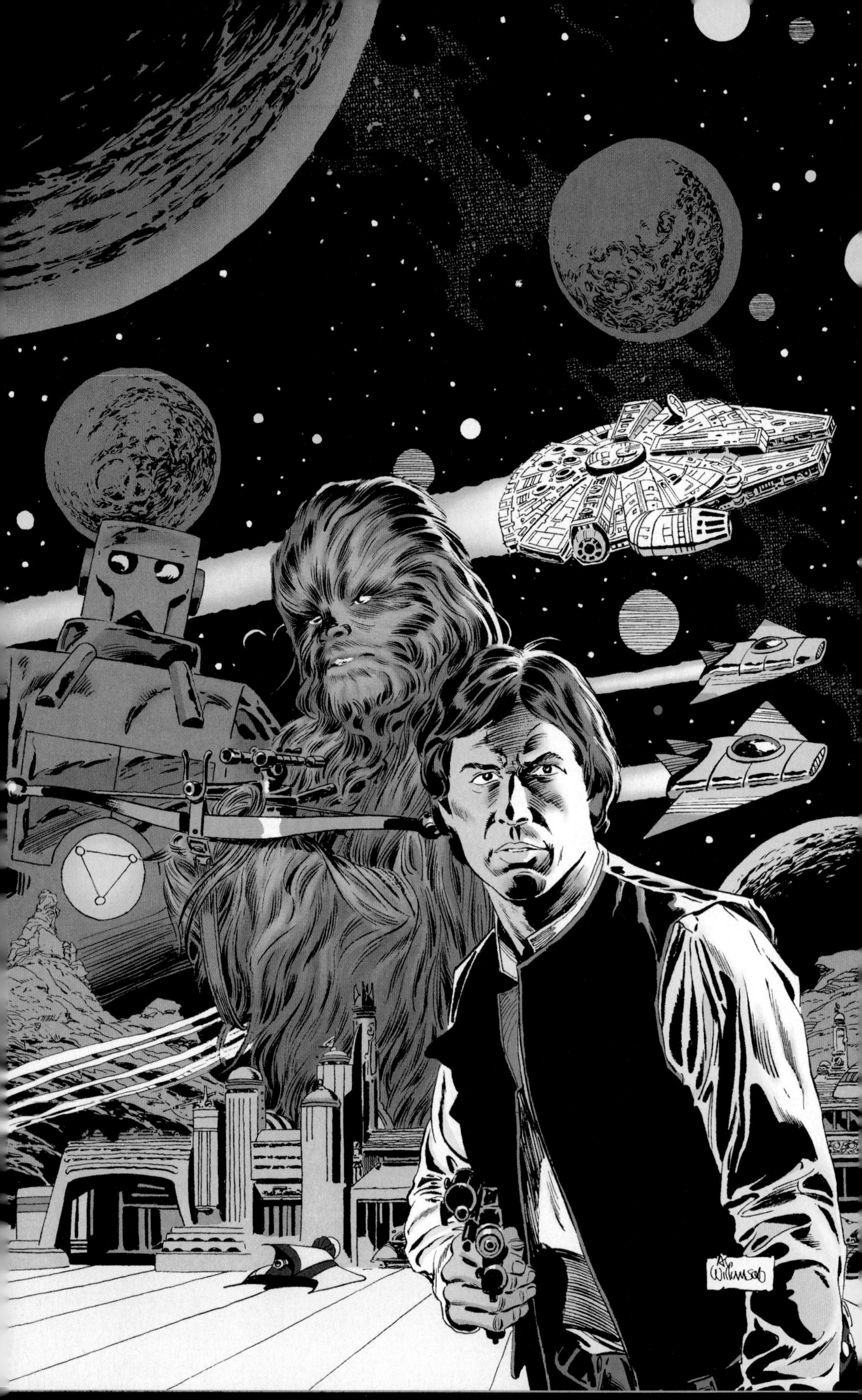

MY DINNER WITH ALFREDO

Tom yum gung is a kind of soup, an aromatic jumble of flavors: shrimp, mint, cilantro, tomato, but mostly lemon grass. A bad bowl will clear your head and scald your uvula in its acid wash. A good bowl leaves you shaken but suddenly and sharply aware of life's unexpected joys.

I think of Alfredo Alcala every time I eat tom yum gung. It was the very first time I'd ever eaten Thai food, and Alfredo told me to order tom yum gung -- well, he didn't tell, he insisted. (Alfredo insists on many things.) I did and was glad. Alfredo always seems to know what's best, whether it's about soup, or music, or comics.

But now I'm getting ahead of my story. Alfredo Alcala, the artist of Han Solo at Stars' End, is one of the two greatest figures in the history of Filipino comics. (The other is the late Nestor Redondo. The two were friends and rivals for over 30 years.) Since the history of comics in the Philippines ranks somewhere below the genetics of lemurs and above cheese on the scale of Obscure Topics, I'll fill you in a little.

When American G.I.s returned to the Philippines following the Japanese occupation back in World War II, they brought with them all things soldier-like, including comic books. Although Filipino comics had existed before this, the market suddenly took off.

For some reason, Filipino artists decided to make Alex Raymond and Hal Foster their gods (with a nod to pen-and-ink founding father Charles Dana Gibson). The visionary Lou Fine, with his expressive anatomy and linework, also left his mark. The result: a lush, highly illustrative style where real draftsmanship was king. The subject matter was historical pulp: Indian sagas, pirate tales, historical romances, monkey humor. The market was thriving.

Thither came young Alfredo. During the war, he'd been employed as a spy because of his photographic memory: the innocent-looking teen would wander by the Japanese encampments and, upon his return, draw astonishingly accurate maps from memory.

His reading included old issues of The Saturday Evening Post, which explains how he fell under the spell of Cornwell, Wyeth, and Leyendecker. Turning to comics, he soaked up the inspiration of Fine, Raymond, and Foster. Alfredo's first big hit was Ukala, an adaptation of the Hiawatha legend which combined great art with soaring melodrama. Soon, Alfredo had his own weekly magazine.

The culmination of Alfredo's style — and perhaps of the entire Filipino school of inky rendering — was Voltar, a barbarian saga that out-Conaned Conan long before Barry Windsor-Smith had ever touched a fur skirt. With its incredibly detailed linework and astonishing play of light and shade (all achieved with varying degrees of brushwork), Voltar was a sensation and won every award they were giving out. A common reaction on seeing Voltar is "flabbergasted." So many lines, so much detail. You've never seen so many lines before. It's a mythical landscape of barbarians, wizards, and fantastic creatures, delineated with such precision and complexity that it becomes strangely surreal.

So does all this have anything to do with American comics? Let me explain. In the 1980s we had our British invasion, but this wasn't the first time an influx of foreign artists had changed the face of the industry. Back in the early '70s, DC's then-publisher Carmine Infantino had gotten wind of all the amazing artists in the Philippines and set off on a scouting expedition. He brought back Alcala, Redondo, Alex Niño, Jesse Santos, and even Sonny Trinidad. Their intricate embellishing techniques quickly set new standards for inking, including Alfredo's distinctive work over John Buscema on Conan. (Alfredo was also on hand for the British invasion, by the way, when he inked early issues of Alan Moore's Swamp Thing.)

Somewhere in there, he collaborated with Archie Goodwin on the comics strips you are holding in your hands. Star Wars is a far cry from the barbarian fantasy of Voltar or Conan, but Alfredo meets the challenge with his usual aplomb. While there are touches here and there of his fantastic skill at rendering, this is more a showcase for Alfredo's storytelling skills. His bold, direct composition more than compensates for the small size of the original comics strips.

The Filipino inking style was highly influential back in its day, and I would hazard a guess that among those it touched are inker Terry Austin and artist Mike Golden, who in turn influenced Scott Williams, Art Adams, and thus just about every superhero comic book on the stands today. Of course, inspiration eventually becomes copying, which becomes misunderstanding. Today everywhere you look, you'll see pointlessly over-rendered inking that tries (and fails) to achieve what Alfredo and his contemporaries mastered. I think a little history lesson might be in order; people might be surprised to see where it started. Enjoy Han Solo at Stars' End, but if you have a mind, look for Voltar or Alfredo's adaptation of The Wizard of Oz, or works by Nestor Redondo and Alex Niño. You'll see comics as they were, and also as they should be again.

But now to go back to some Alfredo stories. We met through mutual friend Phil Yeh, publisher of Frank the Unicorn and founder of Cartoonists Across America. I had just moved to L.A. and Phil would often come to town for dinner with a changing band of cartoon-types, including Alfredo. Over the course of these dinners, I had Thai food for the first time, and discovered the joys of both tom yum gung and conversation. Over the years, and mostly in the course of working on the book about Alfredo that Phil and I co-wrote, there were many more dinners and much more conversation.

A dinner with Alfredo is a trip through a maze of passionate opinions. When Alfredo loves something, it's not just the best, it's the only thing. Listening to him describe what he saw in great illustrators like Dean Cornwell or Frank Brangwyn was amazing: I would see one of these artists through Alfredo's eyes, understand what he saw in their work, and begin to see where he had taken that inspiration. Once again, his photographic memory allowed him to analyze illustrations he hadn't seen in 20 years with unnerving accuracy.

I don't know what you call "photographic hearing," but Alfredo has that, too. I'm an expert on classical music, but Alfredo had me stumped one night, going on about his favorite conductor, one "Scherkin," with a particularly rhapsodic description of a certain passage for the triangle in a Tchaikovsky recording. I kept insisting this guy couldn't be so great, for the simple reason I've never heard of him, but Alfredo ran down all the things that set Scherkin apart with devastating clarity.

Alfredo has a theory about everything — some of them make perfect sense, others have yet to be proven, but all are entertaining. He's a character, certainly, but where would we be without those fascinating characters who challenge our perceptions and give us new perspectives? I've seen Alfredo argue the existence of god with Moebius, and discuss Filipino politics with the famous painter Manuel Ocampo. (It's no surprise that Alfredo is a hero to the current group of highly respected fine artists from the Philippines.) He's given me devastating, one-sentence critiques of comics artists most people think are the greatest thing since the bread knife (like pointing out how one very famous artist gets away with his inability to draw feet). With equal incision he's explained what makes an Alex Toth or a Gil Kane or a Lou Fine a great artist. He's shown me how to draw a hand, and how to draw a table. (Now I wish I'd asked him to show me how to draw the Millennium Falcon!) He's told me about being a child in the Philippines, carrying fried bananas in a bamboo basket, wars, and stacks of old magazines.

Like that bowl of soup, Alfredo is a blend of spices, some lovable, some exasperating. But like that perfect bowl of tom yum gung, a conversation with Alfredo leaves you shaken but suddenly and sharply aware of life's unexpected joys.

—Heidi MacDonald

Heidi MacDonald has been writing about comics for many years and is the co-author of Secret Teachings of a Comic Book Master: the Art of Alfredo Alcala, published by the International Humor Advisory Council.

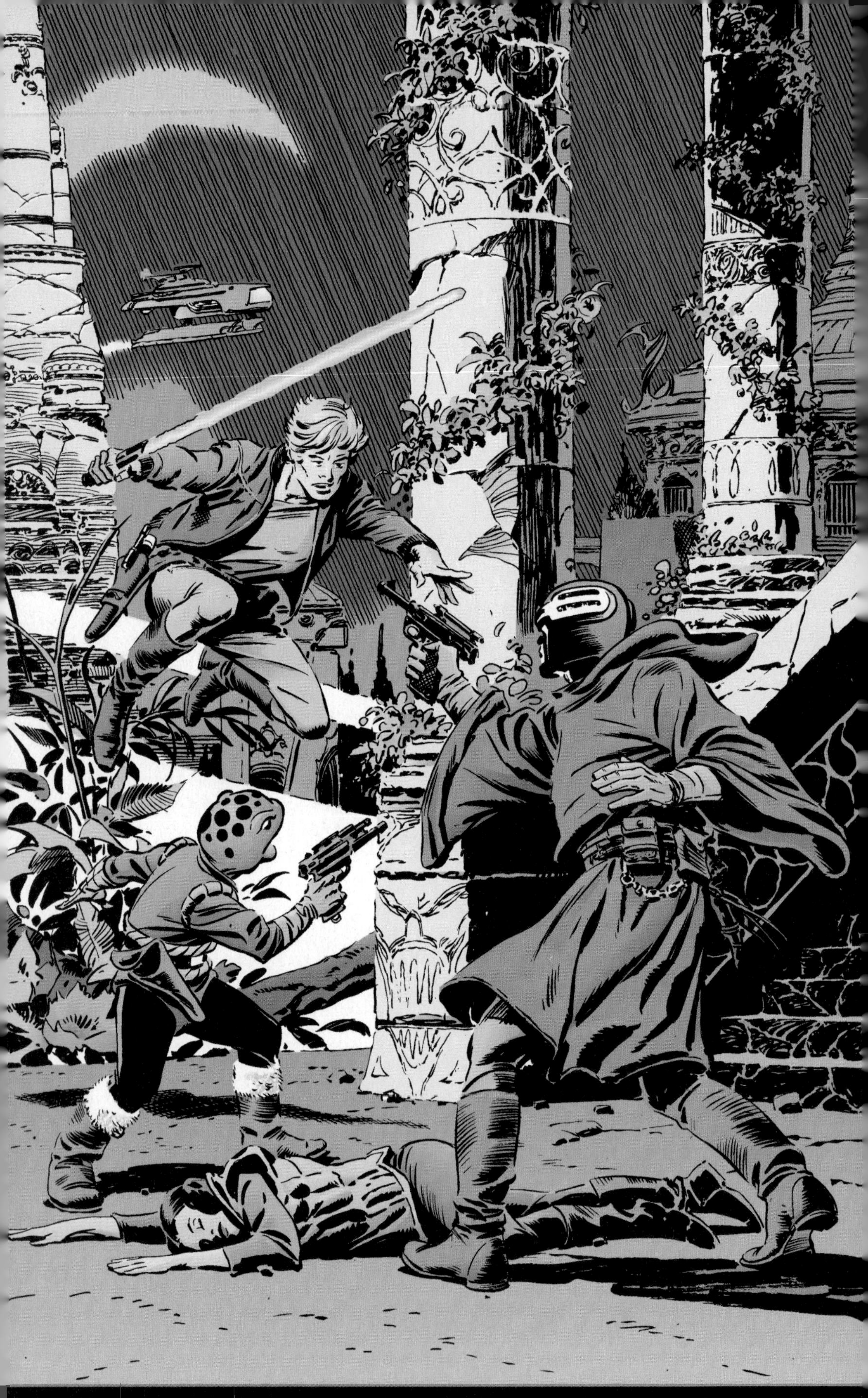

CLASSIC STAR WARS VO

eja vu. Well, not quite. That would be the *feeling* that I've written an introduction to this material before. The fact of the matter is, I *know* I have. I did it in the limited-edition book set published by Russ Cochran that originally collected the *Star Wars* newspaper strips drawn by Al Williamson and written by me that are currently being reprinted in Dark Horse's *Classic Star Wars* comic, the first seven issues of which are collected here.

o why slog over ground I've already covered before? That was my initial reaction when editor Kij Johnson asked me to write this introduction. A big part of the answer to my own question is that it's not really the same ground. The Russ Cochran book set was a collection of daily and Sunday comic strips that appeared in the newspapers in 1981-1984. Printed oversized in three hardcover volumes on heavy stock, complete with slipcase, it's one of the best strip collections ever done...for those who can afford the price of a limited edition. *Classic Star Wars* takes the same newspaper strip material and makes it work as a popularly priced monthly 32-page comic book reaching a much larger audience. In other words, it adapts material created for one medium into another. Kind of what Al Williamson and I (along with other talented folks like artist-writer Russ Manning before us) were doing with the strip in the first place.

Thinking about it, comic strips are a weird way to tell a story: in bursts of two or three panels every twenty-four hours or so, designed to be read in a minute or less (with slightly more lushness and leisure built in for Sunday, the day of rest). It may be why, as more and more alternative forms of entertainment appear, the adventure strip or story is becoming extinct. Yet a lot of brilliant things have been done by masters of the form like Milton Caniff and Leonard Starr. And, of course, Alex Raymond, creator of *Flash Gordon*, the strip that was an inspiration source to George Lucas for his *Star Wars* films, and we wouldn't be here without those, right?

Still strips are an odd beast. Not the least odd thing about them — particularly when you are dealing with something is dependent on visual sweep, mood, and scale as *Star Wars* — is that they are usually printed exceedingly small, about the size of an unfolded matchbook but without any of the production values. When the artwork involved is by Al Williamson, one of the few artists still working today who is able to combine draftsmanship, technical mastery, and the sense of wonder needed for the *Star Wars* kind of grand fantasy, it goes beyond odd to criminal. The limited-edition *Star Wars* collection, newly engraved in pristine black-and-white from Al's original art, corrects that injustice. The *Classic Star Wars* comic — adjusting and laying out the book set's material to work as comicbook-size pages (with Al, and occasionally his neighbor and fellow artist, Allen Nunis, doing the required retouching to make it seamless) — provides even more opportunities to see Al's amazing illustration at sizes and scales where it can be even more fully appreciated.

Adding another dimension to the whole thing is the color by Steve Buccellato (an old colleague, even though he's a young guy, from our days as about a third of the Epic Comics editorial staff), who is fast becoming recognized as one of the best color artists in the business. It's a tricky task. With the exception of the Sunday pages, Al's artwork was created to stand in black and white, which it does magnificently. But the general expectation is for a comic book to be in color. And with a *Star Wars* comic there is also the expectation that it will relate to the movie experience. Color, particularly with the range made available through computers today, makes that more of a reality. Done carelessly or incompetently, it could clog and obscure the rich Williamson artwork. Steve doesn't let that happen; he helps give our material new life for a new medium.

The same could be said for the editing done by Anina Bennett on the issues collected here. I mention earlier that comic strips are a weird way to tell a story, broken up into little daily chunks? Well, that has a killer impact on the way you pace and write. Each strip has to be designed to include a strong reminder to the reader of what happened the day before and should always end with a verbal or visual cliffhanger to bring 'em back the next day. That leads to repetition and inflated suspense. And that's not the end of it. Each week is also supposed to have its own pacing. Big recaps for Mondays because not everyone gets a Sunday paper, plus a strong climax to get readers hooked for the week. Another strong climax for Wednesday, so you're not losing them. Then on Friday, the strongest climax of all, because some papers don't carry the Sunday strips so you've got to hold interest for the entire weekend. Not every paper publishes on Saturday and circulation is often down that day anyway, so you're not supposed to have anything take place then that anyone might miss. Sunday has to be like a combination of the best Monday and Friday strips with hopefully striking visuals to take advantage of the bigger panels and greater space. Because some papers carry the strip only on Sundays, it also has to be designed so the story can be followed without reading the dailies. And, just to make it a little more fun, the Sunday strips have to be designed so certain panels can be dropped depending on what size, space, and arrangement each individual newspaper wants to give you based on what advertising they do or don't get on whatever particular Sunday this is. Put it all together and there are times when it feels more like you're doing a puzzle than doing the adventures of some of the greatest fictional characters of the twentieth century. Put it all together and it needs a great deal of help to read smoothly. If it does, then I don't deserve credit. The editor does.

So, being able to go on a bit about all of the above was part of what convinced me to go ahead and do this introduction in addition to the one I had previously done for the Cochran edition. Two other things also drew me to doing it.

One is that I miss the *Star Wars* universe, its large cast of characters and the even larger galactic tapestry on which their lives and adventures unfold. I'm grateful for what George Lucas created, brought to stunning realization, and then allowed so many more of us to play with. Having written *Star Wars* comics for three years along with three years' worth of the strips, I had plenty of time to get bored with the subject or sour on the experience. It didn't happen. Going over some of the comics prior to writing this reminded me that the *Star Wars* universe is still a great place to visit... even if I don't live there anymore.

Similarly, I was also reminded of the pleasures of collaborating with Al Williamson. We've been doing it for around thirty-five years. Al got me my first job in comics and a great many more ever since. When George Lucas was looking for Al to do the comic strip version of *Star Wars*, Al was right there pitching for me to write it. One of the toughest things about being a comics writer is that if the art doesn't look great, almost no one is going to read your story. Thanks to Al, a lot of my stuff always got read. Because I'm currently under contract to DC Comics, and Al is currently under contract to Marvel, our opportunities to work together are now much fewer and far between. So I'm particularly glad to have *Classic Star Wars* projects like this one around. It makes me feel like Al and I are still collaborating.

Hopefully, you'll enjoy the collection as much as we did the collaboration.

—Archie Goodwin
February 1994

How a Classic Newspaper Strip
Became a Comic-Book Series:
The Story Behind *Classic Star Wars*

by Bob Cooper, Editor
Dark Horse Comics

Virtually all of the fans of *Classic Star Wars* who wrote to us about the series mentioned their memories of the original newspaper strips from the late '70s and early '80s — how they fondly remember racing home from school each day to grab the comics section of the newspaper and hungrily devour the latest star-spanning adventures of Luke Skywalker, Princess Leia, Han Solo, and their faithful droid companions. Many of them carefully cut out each daily and Sunday installment and pasted them in sequence into a scrapbook — in a sense, constructing their very own home-grown precursors to *Classic Star Wars*.

In 1990, Russ Cochran did all *Star Wars* fans a great service by collecting each and every newspaper strip panel that appeared during the longest continuous run of *Star Wars* strips by a single creative team — the one that ran from 1981 through 1984, and was authored by Archie Goodwin and drawn by Al Williamson — in a beautifully produced three-volume collection of hardcover books. Even with this wonderful set of collectors' editions, however, some fans clamored for more.

The concept behind *Classic Star Wars* was to provide for the first time colored versions of the classic newspaper strips, reformatted in a manner so that the panels told a single, coherent story, with no redundant panels and smoothly flowing dialogue throughout, laid out so that the panels comfortably fit on a comic book page. Easier said than done. The standard dimensions of the original strip art produced by Al Williamson did not lend themselves all that easily to translation to the comicbook page. One of the goals in reproducing the art in this new format was to retain as much of the original art as possible.

As luck would have it, Al had retained *all* of the original art from the newspaper run! He was not only happy to allow us to use photostats of his original art for our reprint series, but was adamant about contributing original covers for the series, as well as helping to retouch the artwork or add new artwork where needed. Certainly the next best thing to an honest-to-goodness new Al Williamson *Star Wars* project!

The production of the *Classic Star Wars* comic books turned out to be a fairly unique process. Normally a new color comic book is created by the progressive application of the talents of a writer, penciller, letterer, inker, and color artist. A script is written, which the penciller then uses as a descriptive guide for adding the pencil art that completes the basic storytelling. The letterer, inker, and color artist then add embellishments to the basic pencil art: the letterer adds dialogue in balloons and captions, sound effects, display lettering, and inked panel borders; the inker darkens and embellishes the pencil art; and the color artist adds color notes to the black-and-white inked art. By the time the inked artboards and color guides make their way back to the editor, all but a very small portion of the creative and editorial effort that goes into the making of a comic book has been completed.

The *Classic Star Wars* series provided a bit more of an editorial challenge, however. It was a much more editorial-intensive process than a standard new color comic book — despite the fact that the finished black-and-white art already existed.

The first editor of the *Classic Star Wars* series, Anina Bennett, developed a method for laying out newly formatted comic-book pages that succeeded in making a potentially confusing procedure manageable. Following is a brief tour through the process we followed to make several weeks' worth of decade-old newspaper strips read like a brand-new comic book; the art used as an example throughout is what eventually became page 29 from issue #10 of the series:

The editor began by reviewing the individual daily and Sunday strips as presented in the Russ Cochran *Star Wars* reprint collections, reading through the story to determine where the redundant art and dialogue were, or where we might have wanted to add additional new art to help flesh out the story a bit. The Russ Cochran volumes were invaluable in providing a complete and beautifully reproduced record of the strips. The very nature of a daily newspaper comic strip requires that in order for the strip to be accessible to new readers, a certain

STAR WARS
Written by: ARCHIE GOODWIN
Drawn by: AL WILLIAMSON
Smoke curls over the ruin of an Imperial patrol speeder...
BEN, IF YOU AREN'T ALREADY A LEGEND AMONG THE CHUBBITS... THESE LITTLE GUYS WILL SEE YOU'RE ELECTED!
MAYBE WE SHOULD HAVE PUT OUR MISSION AHEAD OF JUMPING BACK INTO THE FIGHT... BUT THIS MAKES ME REALLY GLAD WE DIDN'T!
YES, LUKE... I-IT'S... MOST GRATIFYING...
"BUT NOW," the impersonator says, "WE HAVE BUSINESS TO COMPLETE... AT THE IRON TOWER!"
WHERE IS THAT FOOL?!
IF THE ACTOR HAS FALTERED WITH SKYWALKER WHEN WE'RE SO CLOSE TO SUCCESS...
NO! MOVEMENT ON THE SCOPE... THEY'RE APPROACHING AT LAST!
7-11

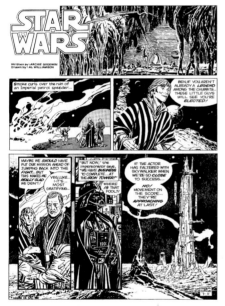

amount of the story be rehashed at the beginning of each week's run, as well as in each Sunday strip. Copies of pages from the Cochran volumes were used as reference layouts throughout the process of reformatting the pages for *Classic Star Wars* (Figure 1).

The panels were reconfigured into a preliminary new comic-book page layout by numbering them according to their intended *Classic Star Wars* page and panel locations ("1B" refers to the second panel on page 1, "3E" to the fifth panel on page 3, etc.). At the same time, instructions were added by the editor, noting sections of panels to be trimmed, cropped, deleted (especially the ubiquitous Lucasfilm copy-

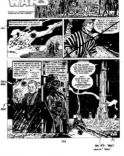

right notices, and Goodwin and Williamson credit boxes), and bled to the page borders, as well as indicating preliminary changes or corrections to be made to the art and dialogue (Figure 2).

In the case of some panels, the new comic-book layout turned out to be so radically different from the original newspaper strip panels, with bits of dialogue cobbled together from several different panels, for instance, that the editor needed to manually develop a mock-up of the in order for the Dark Horse paste-up artist to make sense of it.

"BUT NOW," the impersonator says, "WE HAVE BUSINESS TO COMPLETE... AT THE IRON TOWER!"
WHERE IS THAT FOOL?!
ADD NEW INSET PANEL
MOVE 1ST BALLOON IN PANEL 29B TO NEW INSET PANEL
IF THE ACTOR HAS FALTERED WITH SKYWALKER WHEN WE'RE SO CLOSE TO SUCCESS...
NO! MOVEMENT ON THE SCOPE... THEY'RE APPROACHING AT LAST!
ADD NEW ART
– NEW LAYOUT FOR PANELS 29A + 29B

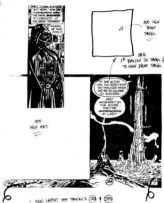

As the new page layout took shape, a simple thumbnail sketch of the panel configuration was made by the editor as well, showing the approximate size and position of each new panel on the comic-book page (Figure 4).

Whereas the original Goodwin and Williamson strips were presented as a series of individual stories — beginning with "The Bounty Hunter of Ord Mantell" (presented in *Classic Star Wars* #1-2) and running through "The Final Trap" (included in issue #20) — due to the 32-page format of a standard comic book, we had to extend some stories over multiple issues. It was something of a trick to find a good ending point for some of the

#10
P. 25
P. 26
P. 27
P. 28
P. 29
– BLEED –
– END –

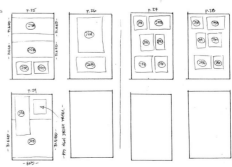

Classic Star Wars issues, but we were able to vary the actual story page count per issue from 24 to 32 to accommodate some of the story lines — without having to break off a story in midstream, or fabricate an unintentional cliffhanger ending.

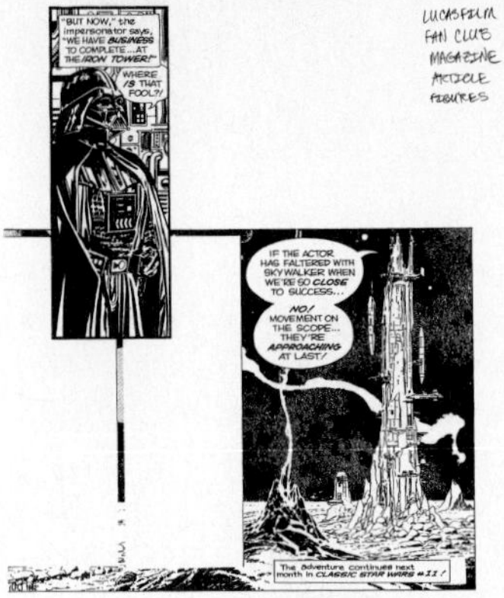

"BUT NOW," the impersonator says, "WE HAVE BUSINESS TO COMPLETE...AT THE IRON TOWER!"
WHERE IS THAT FOOL?!
IF THE ACTOR HAS FALTERED WITH SKYWALKER WHEN WE'RE SO CLOSE TO SUCCESS...
NO! MOVEMENT ON THE SCOPE... THEY'RE APPROACHING AT LAST!
The Adventure continues next month in CLASSIC STAR WARS #11!

Responsibility at this point shifted from the editor to the Dark Horse paste-up artist. The new page layout was pasted up on regular comic artboard, using full-size photostats of the original art provided by Al Williamson (Figure 5). The paste-up artist carefully followed the editorial instructions for moving dialogue balloons, trimming, cropping, deleting, bleeding, and doing minor touchups to the art and lettering.

Once the paste-up was completed by the paste-up artist, the artboards were returned to the editor for checking. After ensuring that the paste-ups were clean and correct, the editor annotated the artboard with instructions to the retouch artist — these being primarily to point out where to extend the existing art in certain directions, or where to fill in new art in blank areas that had been created from the paste-up process (Figure 6).

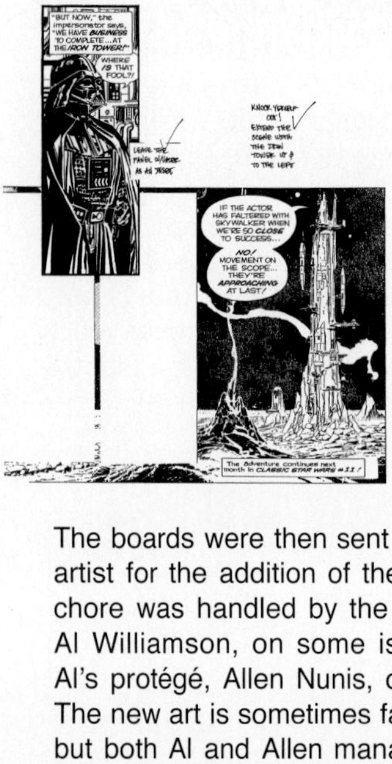

"BUT NOW," the impersonator says, "WE HAVE BUSINESS TO COMPLETE...AT THE IRON TOWER!"
WHERE IS THAT FOOL?!
IF THE ACTOR HAS FALTERED WITH SKYWALKER WHEN WE'RE SO CLOSE TO SUCCESS...
NO! MOVEMENT ON THE SCOPE... THEY'RE APPROACHING AT LAST!
The Adventure continues next month in CLASSIC STAR WARS #11!

The boards were then sent to the retouch artist for the addition of the new art (this chore was handled by the original artist, Al Williamson, on some issues, and by Al's protégé, Allen Nunis, on the others). The new art is sometimes fairly extensive, but both Al and Allen managed to create beautiful and seamless additions to Al's original strip art (Figure 7).

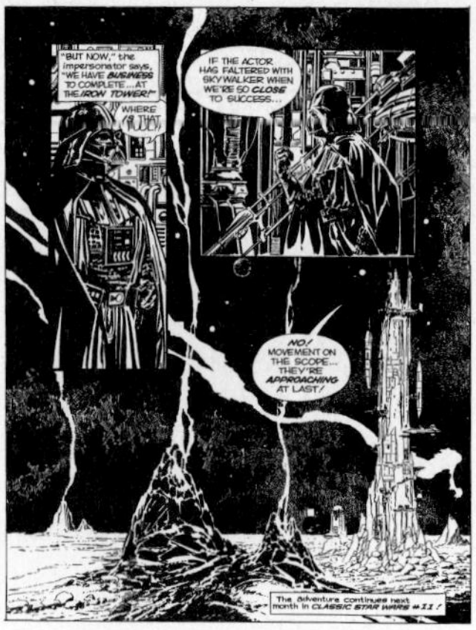

"BUT NOW," the impersonator says, "WE HAVE BUSINESS TO COMPLETE...AT THE IRON TOWER!"
IF THE ACTOR HAS FALTERED WITH SKYWALKER WHEN WE'RE SO CLOSE TO SUCCESS...
NO! MOVEMENT ON THE SCOPE... THEY'RE APPROACHING AT LAST!
The Adventure continues next month in CLASSIC STAR WARS #11!

Once the artboards were returned to Dark Horse, the final step in the re-creation of the newly formatted black-and-white art was for the editor to once again check for problems, inconsistencies, or mistakes, before sending the artboards off to be scanned into our computer system to begin the computer coloring process.

From this point on, the procedure was basically the same as for any other Dark Horse color comic book: the color guides (Figure 8) provided by the color artists (Steve Buccellato, Matthew Hollingsworth, and Ray Murtaugh) were used by the computer coloring crew at Dark Horse to create four-color separations of the colored pages. This detailed process involves the painstaking translation of the color indications and codes provided on the color guides into distinct colored shapes on the computer. From there, the computer software creates four-color separation files (red, yellow, blue, and black) for each comicbook page, in preparation for output to film, and eventually printing of the final comicbook pages (Figure 9).

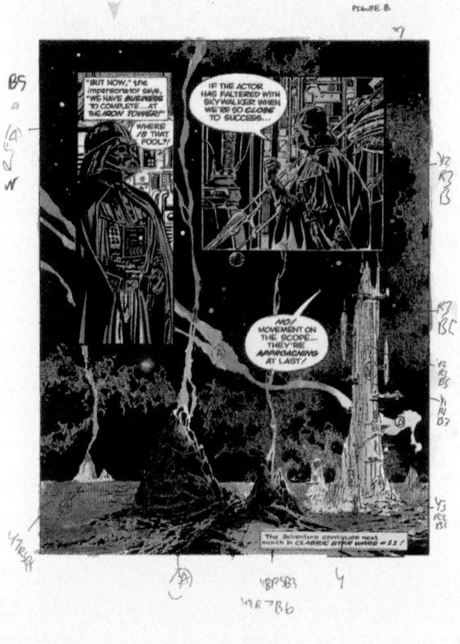

"BUT NOW," the impersonator says, "WE HAVE BUSINESS TO COMPLETE...AT THE IRON TOWER!"
WHERE IS THAT FOOL?!
IF THE ACTOR HAS FALTERED WITH SKYWALKER WHEN WE'RE SO CLOSE TO SUCCESS...
NO! MOVEMENT ON THE SCOPE... THEY'RE APPROACHING AT LAST!
The Adventure continues next month in CLASSIC STAR WARS #11!

The finished page

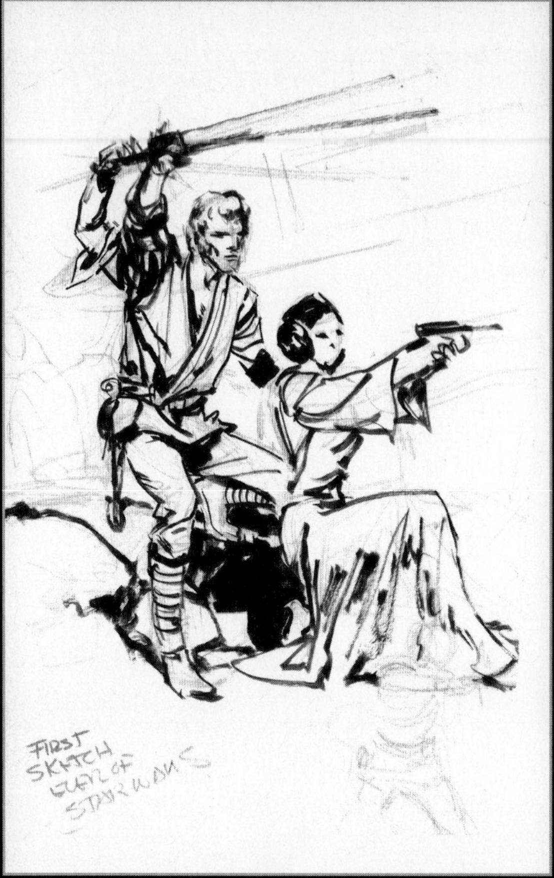
FIRST
SKETCH
EVER OF
STAR WARS

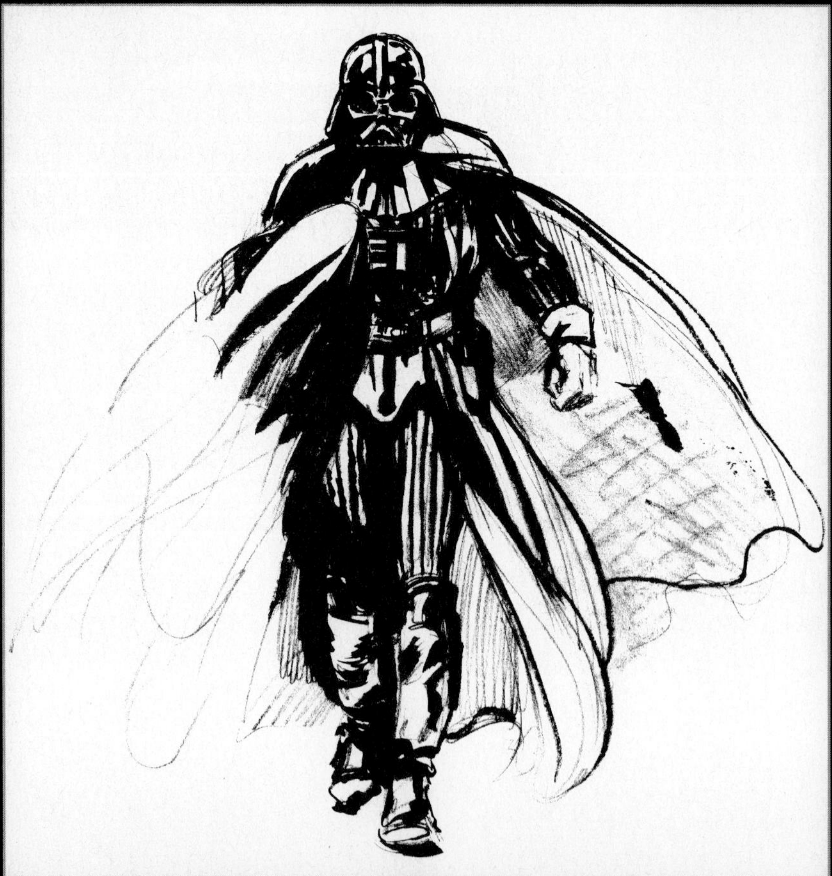

CHARACTER SKETCHES BY AL WILLIAMSON, FROM *CLASSIC STAR WARS VOL. 1: IN DEADLY PURSUIT TPB*

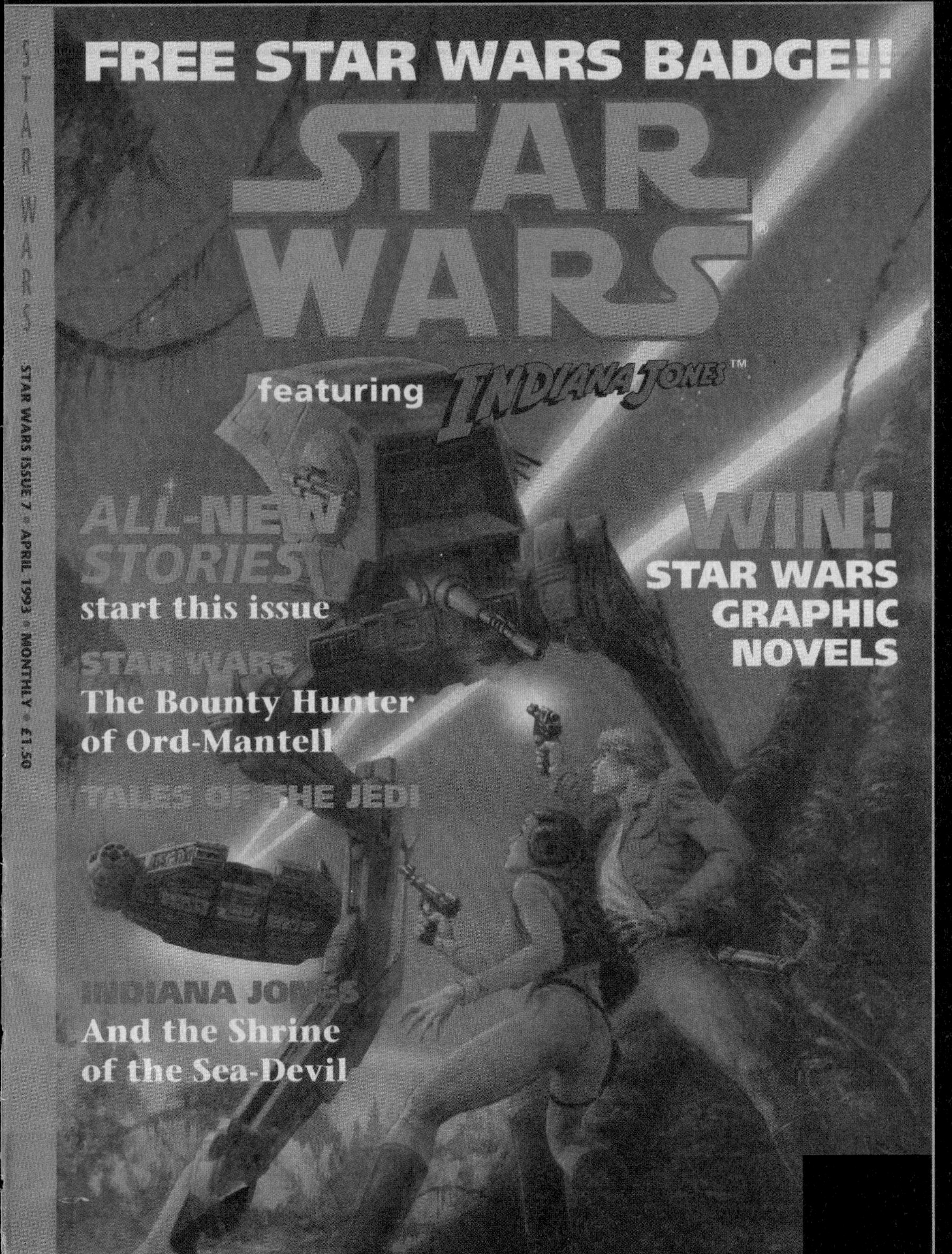
STAR WARS
STAR WARS ISSUE 7 • APRIL 1993 • MONTHLY • £1.50
FREE STAR WARS BADGE!!
STAR WARS®
featuring INDIANA JONES™
ALL-NEW STORIES start this issue
STAR WARS
The Bounty Hunter of Ord-Mantell
TALES OF THE JEDI
INDIANA JONES
And the Shrine of the Sea-Devil
WIN!
STAR WARS GRAPHIC NOVELS

PUBLISHED IN THE UK, DARK HORSE INTERNATIONAL'S *STAR WARS #7* REPRINTED THE FIRST HALF OF THE "BOUNTY HUNTER OF ORD MANTELL" STORYLINE. COVER ART BY ROBERT MENTOR.

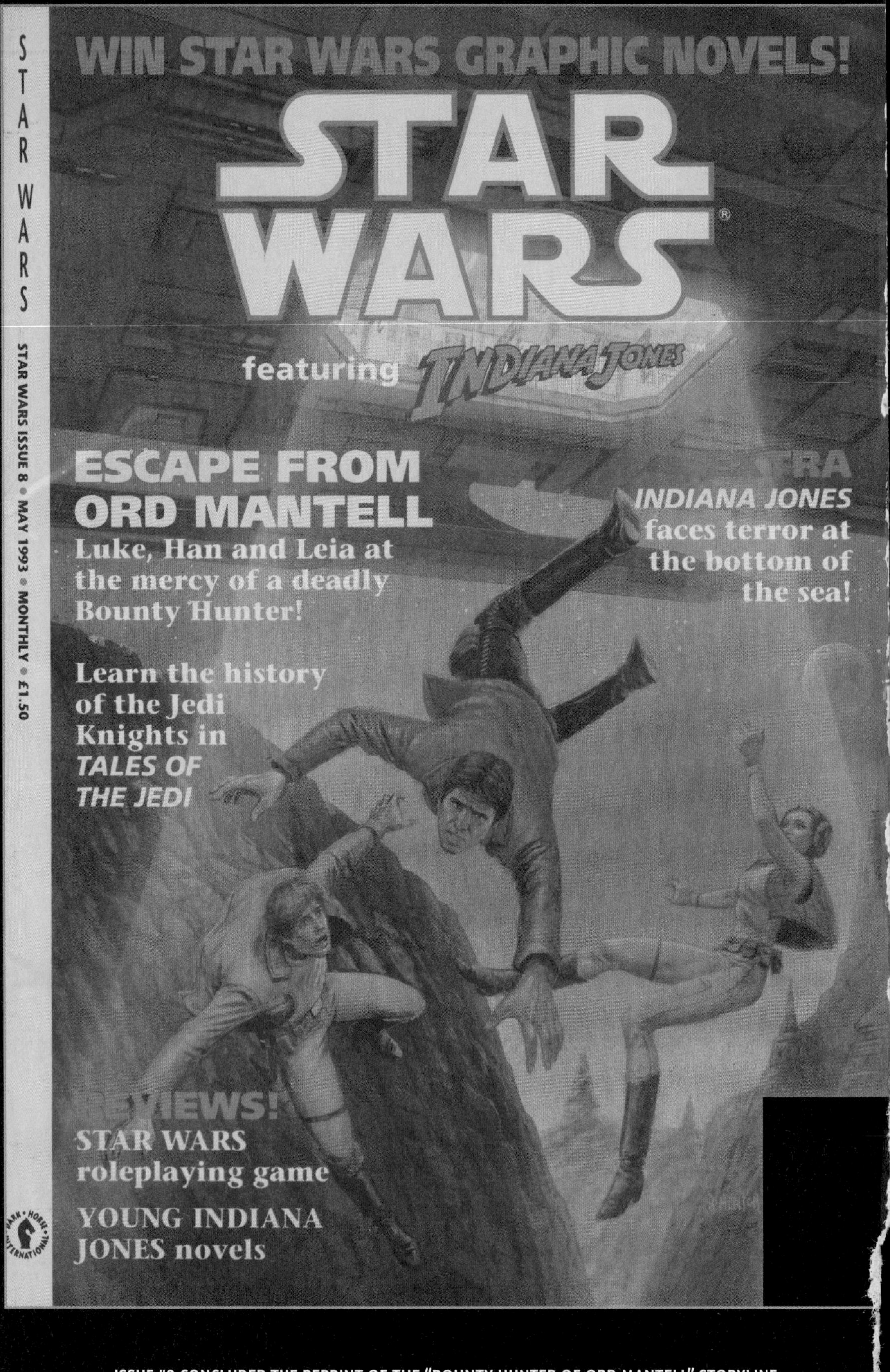
STAR WARS
STAR WARS ISSUE 8 • MAY 1993 • MONTHLY • £1.50
WIN STAR WARS GRAPHIC NOVELS!
STAR WARS®
featuring INDIANA JONES™
ESCAPE FROM ORD MANTELL
Luke, Han and Leia at the mercy of a deadly Bounty Hunter!
INDIANA JONES faces terror at the bottom of the sea!
Learn the history of the Jedi Knights in TALES OF THE JEDI
STAR WARS roleplaying game
YOUNG INDIANA JONES novels
DARK HORSE INTERNATIONAL

ISSUE #8 CONCLUDED THE REPRINT OF THE "BOUNTY HUNTER OF ORD MANTELL" STORYLINE.
COVER ART BY ROBERT MENTOR.